THE EXEGESIS OF PHILIP K. DICK

The Exegesis of
PHILIP K. DICK

EDITED BY PAMELA JACKSON
AND JONATHAN LETHEM

GOLLANCZ
LONDON

First published in Great Britain in 2012 by Gollancz
An imprint of the Orion Publishing Group
Orion House, 5 Upper St Martin's Lane, London WC2H 9EA
An Hachette UK Company

The authorised representative in the EEA is Hachette Ireland,
8 Castlecourt Centre, Dublin 15, D15 XTP3, Ireland (email: info@hbgi.ie)

A CIP catalogue record for this book is available
from the British Library

ISBN (Trade Paperback) 978 0 575 13244 3

5 7 9 10 8 6 4

Printed and bound in Great Britain by Clays Ltd, Elcograf S.p.A.

The Orion Publishing Group's policy is to use papers that are natural,
renewable and recyclable products and made from wood grown in sustainable
forests. The logging and manufacturing processes are expected to conform to
the environmental regulations of the country of origin.

www.orionbooks.co.uk

IN MEMORIAM
PHILIP K. DICK

"Tomorrow morning," he decided, "I'll begin clearing away the sand of fifty thousand centuries for my first vegetable garden. That's the initial step."

— Philip K. Dick, *The Three Stigmata of Palmer Eldritch*

What best can I do? Exactly what I've done. My voice for the voiceless.

— Philip K. Dick, *The Exegesis*

Contents

Introduction

1.

The beautiful and imperishable comes into existence due to the suffering of individual perishable creatures who themselves are not beautiful, and must be reshaped to form a template from which the beautiful is printed (forged, extracted, converted). This is the terrible law of the universe. This is the basic law; it is a fact. Also, it is a fact that the suffering of the individual animal is so great that it arouses an ultimate and absolute abhorrence and pity in us when we are confronted by it. This is the essence of tragedy: the collision of two absolutes. Absolute suffering leads to — is the means to — absolute beauty. Neither absolute should be subordinated to the other. But this is not how it is: the suffering is subordinated to the value of the art produced. Thus the essence of horror underlies our realization of the bedrock nature of the universe.

This passage was written by the American novelist Philip K. Dick in 1980. Taken alone, the handful of lines might seem to be an extract from a lucid and elegant fugue on metaphysics and ontology — an inquiry, in other words, into matters of being and the purposes of consciousness, suffering, and existence itself. This particular passage would not strike anyone versed in philosophical or theological discourse as violently original, apart from an intriguing sequence of metaphorical slippages — *printed, forged, extracted, converted* — and the almost subliminal conflation of "the universe" with a work of art.

What makes the passage unusual is the context in which it arose and the other kinds of writing that surround it. Despite a tone of conclusiveness, the passage represents a single inkling, passing in the night, among many thousands in the vast compilation of accounts of his own visionary experiences and insights that Dick committed to paper between 1974 and 1982. The topics — apart from suffering, pity, the nature of the universe, and the essence of tragedy — include three-eyed aliens; robots made of DNA; ancient and suppressed Christian cults that in their essential beliefs forecasted the deep truths of Marxist theory; time-travel; radios that continue playing after being unplugged; and the true nature of the universe as revealed in the writings of the ancient philosopher Parmenides, in *The Ti-*

betan Book of the Dead, in Julian Jaynes's *The Origin of Consciousness in the Breakdown of the Bicameral Mind,* and in Robert Altman's film *Three Women.*

The majority of these writings, that is to say, are neither familiar nor wholly lucid nor, largely, elegant — nor were they intended, for the most part, for publication. Even when Dick, who was an autodidact if ever there was one, recapitulates some chestnut of philosophical or theological speculation, his own philosophical and theological writings remain unprecedented in their riotous urgency, their metaphorical verve, their self-satirizing charisma, and their lonely intimacy (as well as in their infuriating repetitiveness, stubbornness, insecurity, and elusiveness). They are unprecedented, in other words, because Philip K. Dick is Philip K. Dick, one of the more brilliant and unusual minds to make itself known to the twentieth century even before this (mostly) unpublished trove now comes to light.

Dick came to call this writing his "Exegesis." The process of its production was frantic, obsessive, and, it may be fair to say, involuntary. The creation of the Exegesis was an act of human survival in the face of a life-altering crisis both intellectual and emotional: the crisis of *revelation.* No matter how resistant we may find ourselves to this ancient and unfashionable notion, to approach the Exegesis from any angle at all a reader must first accept that the subject *is* revelation, a revelation that came to the person of Philip K. Dick in February and March of 1974 and subsequently demanded, for the remainder of Dick's days on earth, to be understood. Its pages represent Dick's passionate commitment to explicating the glimpse with which he had been awarded or cursed — not for the sake of his own psyche, nor for the cause of the salvation of humankind, but precisely because those two concerns seemed to him to be one and the same.

The attempt eventually came to cover over eight thousand sheets of paper, largely handwritten. Dick often wrote through the night, running an idea through its paces over as many as a hundred sheets during a sleepless night or in a series of nights. These feats of superhuman writing are astonishing to contemplate; they impressed even an established graphomaniacal writer like Dick, who had once written seven novels in a single year. The fundamental themes of the Exegesis come as no surprise. The body of work that established Dick's reputation — his forty-odd realist and surrealist novels written between 1952 and his death in 1982 — concerns itself with questions like "What is it to be human?" and "What is the nature of the universe?" These metaphysical, ethical, and ontological themes enmesh his work, even from its very beginnings in domestic melodrama, science fiction adventure, and humor, in an atmosphere of philosophical inquiry.

Dick increasingly came to view his earlier writings — specifically his science fiction novels of the 1960s — as an intricate and unconscious precursor to his visionary insights. Thus, he began to use them, as much as any ancient text or the Encyclopedia Britannica, as a source for his investigations. Never, to our knowledge, has a novelist borne down with such eccentric concentration on his own oeuvre, seeking to crack its code as if his life depended on it. The writing in these pages represents, perhaps above all, a laboratory of *interpretation* in the most absolute and open-ended sense of the word. When Dick began to write and publish novels based on the visionary material unearthed in the Exegesis, he commenced interpreting those as well. So, as these writings accumulated, they also became self-referential: the Exegesis is a study of, among other things, itself.

Fully situating this text's genesis within the flamboyant and heartbreaking life story of Philip K. Dick is beyond our reach in this introduction. We commend you to Lawrence Sutin's *Divine Invasions: A Life of Philip K. Dick,* published in 1989 and thankfully still in print. Sutin's biography finds its limitations only in the sense that neither he nor any other commentator in the years immediately following Dick's death, however persuaded of the unique relevance and appeal of his writing, could have predicted the expansion in its reputation and influence in the subsequent decades.

What will be needed by a reader coming to the Exegesis, however, whether familiar or not with Dick's great novels, is a brief encapsulation of what both Dick and Sutin call "2-3-74" — meaning, simply, February and March of 1974 — for the simple reason that Dick's endless sequence of interpretations derive from that initial period of visions and a handful of external experiences that surrounded them (some of which, frankly, challenge credulity).

Whether interpreting a happening, memory, vision, or dream, Dick in his haste rarely bothers to set down the source events as scrupulously as we might wish — testament to his eagerness to begin his fierce private excavation of their meaning. After all, *he* understood to what he referred. Except for those lucky instances when Dick retraces his steps to their source, or in the letters to others that (mercifully for the reader) represent this wild journey's inception point, Dick explicates events, but rarely narrates them. Sutin observes:

> The events of 2-3-74 and after are unusual, even bizarre. There are scenes of tender beauty, as when Phil administered the Eucharist to [his son] Christopher. There are instances of inexplicable foresight, as when he diagnosed his son's hernia. And there are episodes, like the Xerox missive, that foster skepticism. For some, the visions and

voices will constitute evidence of grace. Others, both atheists and re-
ligionists, will doubt 2-3-74 for these very reasons.

So, what happened to Philip K. Dick in 1974? Among the mysterious
events he chews over in these pages, the first, dark precursor to his visions
was a break-in at his home in San Rafael, California, in November 1971
when someone blew up the file cabinet in his office. Candidates range from
drug dealers to Black Panthers to various clandestine authorities, a few of
which undoubtedly had Dick on their watch lists. Dick never settled on
a single explanation for the break-in, but his fascinated, terrified rehears-
als of this event set the stage for the deductive explosion to follow. It was
then that Philip K. Dick's life began to resemble, as many have observed, a
Philip K. Dick novel.

Then to 1974: Dick now lived in Orange County, with a wife and young
child. After receiving a dose of sodium pentothal during a visit to the dentist for an impacted wisdom tooth, Dick went home and later opened his
door to a pharmacy delivery-girl bearing a painkiller and wearing a gold
necklace depicting a fish, which she identified as a sign used by early
Christians. At that moment, by his testimony, Dick experienced "anamnesis" — that sudden, discorporating slippage into vast and total knowledge
that he would spend the rest of his life explicating, or *exegeting*.

Yet that doorway meeting with the fish necklace was only the first vision. In March Dick enjoyed two separate, unsleeping, nightlong episodes of visual psychedelia, the second of which he describes memora-
bly as "hundreds of thousands of absolutely terrific modern art pictures as
good as any ever exhibited . . . more than all the modern art pictures that
exist put together." Next, he found himself compelled to perform a home
baptism on his son, Christopher. Then he was visited by a "red and gold
plasmatic entity," which he came to call, variously, Ubik, the Logos, Zebra,
or the plasmate. He also heard dire messages on his radio (which played
whether or not it was plugged into the wall).

Readers will learn here of the "Xerox missive" — a mailed broadside of
some sort, possibly from an ordinary basement Communist organization,
which Dick understood as a dire test of his new and visionary self-pro-
tective instinct: it needed to be disposed of. Dick believed that he was inhabited by another personality with different habits and character, someone more forceful and decisive than himself — in the Exegesis he auditions
various candidates for this role — who steps in to fire his agent and field
the Xerox missive. Our hero sees "Rome, Rome, everywhere," in a vision
of iron bars and scurrying outlaw Christians; he came to call this vision
of the world the Black Iron Prison, or BIP for short. A cat died, and the

apartment was flooded with memorial light. Most stirring, a pink beam informed Dick of a medical crisis that threatened the life of his son, a diagnosis confirmed by doctors.

Beyond 1974, he endured voices, visions, and prophetic dreams too numerous to list here — all to be enfolded, by the writer, into the cascade of interpretation of those earlier events. A reader will learn how readily and fluently a new revelation transforms Dick's sense of the "core facts" of 2-3-74, which never sit still but adapt to a flux of analysis, paraphrase, and doubt. Illuminating them fully was Dick's subsequent lifework. Why should it be simple for us?

2.

The journey of the Exegesis from a chaos of paperwork stored, after Dick's death, in a garage in Sonoma, California, to this (noncomprehensive) publication is still, if not as unlikely as its creation in the first place — what could be? — a saga in itself. When Dick died in 1982, the Exegesis was still a pile of papers in his apartment. Dick's friend Paul Williams, then executor of his literary estate, sorted the fragments into the ninety-one file folders that still house it. (Williams's provisional organizational choices, in the absence of other guides, remain evident in the form in which we present the material here.) The Exegesis spent the next several years in Williams's garage in Glen Ellen.

It is difficult to overstate the degree to which Dick's reputation had gone underground in the 1970s and 1980s; it had never been very far overground to begin with, and his stature with publishers was nonexistent. Working with Dick's agent, Russ Galen, Williams found remarkable success inventing Dick's posthumous career as we now know it, guiding the out-of-print novels into republication and a place in literary culture more secure than Dick probably ever imagined for himself. A number of unpublished novels — coherent, finished manuscripts that in almost every case had already made the publishers' rounds and been rejected — were also brought to light.

The Exegesis, an unruly and unlikely "manuscript" that threatened to defy editorial ambition, remained terra incognita. Its first scholar, Jay Kinney, published a "Summary of the Exegesis Based on Preliminary Forays" in 1984. Estimating the document at two million words, Kinney defined requirements for its publication: transcription from the handwritten pages; an attempt at chronological resequencing; and "selecting out the most coherent portions." He rightly called this prospect "staggering." With Williams and a few volunteers, Kinney's venture at least accomplished the photocopying and inventory of the eight-thousand-plus pages. At one

point a distributed transcription effort was begun by mail — "swarm scholarship" before the Web. Kinney, in his article, also suggested that the published Exegesis could be the basis for the founding of a "Dickian religion,"
mentioning the name L. Ron Hubbard. His intent may have been flippant,
but the notion seeped into the chatter and proved more hindrance than incentive to scrupulous investigation of the material.

Next, biographer Lawrence Sutin edited 1991's *In Search of Valis: Se-
lections from the Exegesis,* a volume that thrilled and frustrated a core of
seekers for whom the text was increasingly taking on the status of legend.
Less than three hundred pages long, *In Search of Valis* presented an array
of enigmatic morsels that, for some, only raised questions as to what might
be in the *other* 7,700 pages. When Paul Williams relinquished his role as
literary executor in the mid-1990s, the Exegesis and other PKD manuscripts went into the custody of Dick's children. For them, the unpublished
trove was fraught, since it attracted unwelcome attention and threatened
to undermine their father's growing academic and literary reputation with
its disreputable aura of high weirdness. For some of Dick's admirers, even
the novels written in the wake of the 2-3-74 revelations are at best a footnote to what they regard as his seminal writings and, at worst, an embar-
rassment. (An interesting Exegesis subplot consists of Dick's reactions to
meeting some of his earliest admirers in academia, whom he refers to as
"the Marxists" and who were clearly perplexed by his metaphysical preoccupations. "I proved to be an idiot savant," he writes, "much to their disgust.")

The present editors have navigated this maze of perplexities in possession of a few useful axioms. One is that, putting aside any of the peculiarities earmarking his work or the circumstances of its creation, Philip K.
Dick was one of the twentieth century's great novelists. This makes the
eventual public availability of his unpublished notes, journals, drafts, and
other surviving papers not only desirable but inevitable. This is as true of
Dick's Exegesis as it is of the notebooks of Dostoyevsky or Henry James. If
the fate of such material is to attract fewer readers than the writer's novels — and who would wish otherwise? — it is nevertheless of clear importance that it emerge. Yet another axiom is this: the *whole* of the Exegesis
is unpublishable, short of a multiple-volume scholarly edition issued at a
prohibitive price or (more likely) in an online form.

Another belief we held going in: the Exegesis is terrific reading, of a
kind. We might say, "If you take it for what it is," or, "If you care for this sort
of thing," but those terms beg the question of what "sort of thing" "it" exactly is, and we are at a loss to answer that question. To give yourself to it

completely, as Kinney and Sutin and ourselves — most especially the tireless Pamela — have done, demands a degree of mania and stupefaction we
would not wish on another human (though we will undoubtedly not be the
last). But to give yourself to it in part, at leisure, and in a spirit of curiosity
can be entrancing. And to become entranced by it is — contradicting ourselves now — to want more. One last axiom, then: in the compromises and
sacrifices that this effort, by its nature, imposed, we will satisfy no one. We
have set another foot on Everest, reached a slightly higher station than others before us. But not the summit. That admission leads to a declaration:
this book spearheads an effort to transcribe, reorganize (or, more rightly,
"organize"), and, eventually, provide scholarly access to the entirety of the
writing left behind by Philip K. Dick after his death. Much of what we excluded was repetitive and boring. Some was tantalizing but opaque, or de-
fied excerpt. But no one will need to take our word for this forever.

3.

> *Determinist forces are wrong,*
> *Though irresistibly strong.*
> *But of god there's a dearth,*
> *For he visits the earth,*
> *But not for sufficiently long.*

or:

> *Determinist forces are wrong,*
> *Though irresistibly strong.*
> *But of god there's no dearth,*
> *For he visits the earth,*
> *But just for sufficiently long.*

Science fiction writer Tim Powers recited these two limericks from memory, then explained, "He'd call you up at eleven in the morning and say, 'I
just figured out some stuff — I just figured out the universe — why don't
you come over.' Possibly he'd written until six A.M., then slept from six to
eleven. I'd say, 'I've gotta go to work. Write it down so you don't forget
it.' One day I said, 'Oh, yeah, and can you write it as a limerick?' When I
showed up he gave me two versions."

In the last decade of his life, Philip K. Dick's friends and visitors became, one after the next, confidants of the iconoclastic human being who
was both scribbling out the Exegesis and, in many senses, *living* it. These
eyewitnesses offer evocative accounts that amplify the text's human di-

mension; its tenderness, monologuing obsessiveness, irascibility, seductiveness, despair, irony, voraciousness, curiosity, anger, and wit, and above all its doubt and certainty, were Dick's own.

Tim Powers continued: "Every day was starting again from zero. It was never cumulative. And every now and then he'd say: 'It's all nonsense. It's all acid flashbacks.' He'd be down, terribly depressed. For one thing it would mean he'd wasted years. Then he'd be off again. He called me one day and said, 'Powers, my researches have led me to believe I have the power to forgive sins.' I said, 'Well, who have you forgiven?' He said, 'Nobody . . . I forgave the cat's sins and went to bed.'"

Cartoonist Art Spiegelman, then a young fan who considered Dick "the only living writer I wanted to meet," made his first visit to Dick's apartment in February 1974: "It was one week before the vision. I planned a trip from S.F. to L.A., but he wasn't answering his phone. We did our day at Disneyland, then I thought: *I can't not ring his doorbell*. I stayed for three days. He was charming, eager for someone to talk to about his work. Only later did I find out he'd been in a deep funk. We'd talk, I'd fall asleep, he'd go in and begin typing, and then I'd wake up and we'd begin talking again.

"I think I have one of the earliest manifestations of what became the Exegesis. I wish I could find it. We wanted a collaboration with Phil for *Arcade* magazine — he gave us something sort of essaylike, clearly religious. It concerned taking Christopher to the hospital. This was the first clue I had that he was off in that territory, but I can't remember it being a very big deal in '74–'75. He didn't seem obsessive, didn't seem manic.

"Later, visiting to recruit him for *Raw* magazine, I thought: *This guy's on the skids somehow*. The apartment was the worst version of the Philip Marlowe housing complex. But he was studying Aramaic. I was struck, thinking, *That's intense! There's not too many people doing that*. Yet it didn't seem like a good influence on him — he seemed burdened by all this stuff. Crushed. I do remember expressing excitement about one idea, and he lit up. He'd figured out why evil exists on earth: we were in a bubble, and God couldn't get to us. I liked that image, and we talked about it for a while."

Painter and cartoonist Gary Panter offered a word-portrait: "Phil was pixieish and self-effacing, always ready to make himself the butt of the joke. He sat thinking with his head back and lips pursed a little. He smiled small before he smiled big. He had long fingers like a piano player's. White hairy chest peeking over his top button. His skin was pale. His lips were red. His cheeks had a tiny blush. He was like a clever fox, but tired, like he didn't sleep much. He told me more than once about the miracle of his intuiting his son's potentially fatal internal hernia. He'd take a big breath before he spoke because he knew the sentences would be long. His hands were lithe and expressive, often mirroring each other palm to palm. He had soulful, heartful eyes. With other people he could've played other roles, because he was a theatrical and prankish person. He laughed a lot."

Tim Powers alludes to a notion found in other accounts as well: that in its latter stages the Exegesis journey seemed to converge with a foreshadowing of its author's death. "I do remember that around Christmas of '81 he was convinced that the world would end in a couple of months. And it did, for him. I thought: *Not bad — you were close."*

4.

Anyone interested in suggesting a medical, psychiatric, neurological, or pharmacological context for the experiences and behavior surrounding Philip K. Dick's Exegesis — and by "behavior" we mean, of course and above all, the writing of the thing itself — will be spoiled for choice. Dick offers a wealth of indicators suggestive of bipolar disorder, neurological damage due to amphetamine abuse, a sequence of tiny strokes (it would be a stroke that killed him in 1982), and more. Within these pages, Dick mordantly speculates on a few himself.

The decades since Dick's death have been fertile ones for popular neurological case histories, frequently of creative people (call it the Oliver Sacks era). It is likely that had Dick lived longer, he would have been drawn to project his own neurological metaphors for his visionary experiences; in particular, it is hard to imagine that his restless mind would not have been eager to explore what Eve Laplante, in her 1988 article in the *Atlantic Monthly,* called "The Riddle of TLE" (temporal lobe epilepsy). The cause of electrical seizures in the brain less dangerous, and more diagnostically furtive, than grand mal epilepsy, TLE is associated in certain cases with hypergraphia (superhuman bouts of writing) and hyperreligiosity ("an unusual degree of concern with morality, philosophy, and mysticism, sometimes leading to multiple religious conversions," in Laplante's words). Among the historical figures whose profiles are suggestive of a retroactive TLE diagnosis are Dostoyevsky, St. Theresa of Avila, Emanuel Swedenborg, and Van Gogh.

Temporal lobe epilepsy has, reasonably enough, drawn attention from Dick's biographers, and we should not hesitate to mention it here. Yet, given just a brief paraphrase of Dick's history, neurologist Alice Flaherty, author of *The Midnight Disease: The Drive to Write, Writer's Block, and the Creative Brain,* cautioned that one of any number of medical causes might easily account for Dick's hypergraphia — a TLE diagnosis is far from a foregone conclusion. Indeed, it is worth noting that Dick described hallucinatory experiences of one kind or another going back as far as grade school;

that his earliest writings prefigure the ontological and moral concerns exhibited after 2-3-74; and that his boggling literary productivity during his aspirant years and first ascendancy, from 1952 to 1964, could easily be labeled "hypergraphic." Dick's Exegesis is a site, then, where we reencounter one of the defining mysteries of our scientific age: the persistent elusiveness of a satisfying description of the full activities of "mind" — that is, consciousness — even as the mechanism of the biological brain yields itself increasingly to our understanding.

5.

Dick's pursuit of the truth of 2-3-74 was destined, like Zeno's arrow, for no destination. Years before his death, it became apparent that these activities would not cease until the pen fell from his hands, no matter his periodic attempts at closure. "Here ends four years and six months of analysis and research," Dick wrote. "Time is unmasked as irreal; 1,900 years are disclosed as aspect of one underlying matrix . . . my 27 years of writing the same themes over and over again fits into place; 2-74 and 3-74 is comprehensible, as is the overthrow of Nixon; the transtemporal constants have been explicated . . . perhaps I should destroy the Exegesis. It is a journey that reached its goal." Dick wrote those words in 1978; they occur on the first page of an entry that would continue for sixty-two more.

In the end the Exegesis can be viewed as a long experiment in mind-regarding-itself. The puzzle that Dick can never solve in this effort is that of his own exegetical efforts. This mind writes — *why?* More and more it may seem as if in describing the macrocosm Dick describes the Exegesis: the two are coextensive. Each falls victim to repetition and entropy; each grows by reticulating and arborizing; each, for its renewal, requires divine intervention in the form of language. The same questions apply to both: What saves the universe from running in useless circles until it drops? What separates the living spark of meaning from the "inferior bulk" of chaos and noise? Does the universe evolve or devolve? If the system is closed, then where does "the new" originate?

We found ourselves struck by the notion that Philip K. Dick was, for all his garrulous explications, an aphoristic writer, in the vein of E. M. Cioran or Blaise Pascal. What disguises his aphoristic gift is, simply, the scaffolding he left in place. Every impulse, every photon of thinking collects on the page; it is left for the reader to isolate the spires.

"What lies hiding within each object? A garden, so to speak."
"There are no gold prisons."
"The schizophrenic is a leap ahead that failed."

"To remember and to wake up are absolutely interchangeable."

"All that is colossal is fraud."

"The physical universe is plastic in the face of mind."

"Reality lacks discretionary power."

"What's got to be gotten over is the false idea that an hallucination is a *private* matter."

"'One day the masks will come off, and you will understand all' — it came to pass, and *I* was one of the masks."

Each of these fine provocations is embedded somewhere in the Exegesis's pages, together with more extensive sequences of aphoristic invention and self-contained parables too lengthy to quote here. We invite readers to discover their own.

Jonathan Lethem and Pamela Jackson

Editors' Note

Your humble scholars have wandered into a land that makes a mockery of scholarship. Dick's own centrifugal and chaotic methodology was more than infectious; it rewrote our attempts to rewrite it. This volume, then, reflects an enthusiastic foray on the reader's behalf. The larger purposes of archival scholarship could only have been answered with a completely transcribed and fully cross-referenced Exegesis — a thing not bindable into the pages of a book. In the name not of apology but of transparency, we offer an account of our compromises and the decisions that made them possible.

We chose chronological ordering, yet this is a text that defies chronology. Dates were frequently determined only by internal clues or references and so should be regarded as approximate and open to revision by future scholarship. We kept folders intact, despite recognizing these as an artifact of Paul Williams's archiving rather than Dick's own ordering. In places where this led to conflict with chronology, we relocated parts of folders; these are noted. Excerpts are identified by bracketed numbers at the top [folder number: page number in folder]. In folders where Dick's own page numbering suffices, we retained these; in folders with multiple discontinuous numbering sequences, we have renumbered the pages to create a single pagination for the whole. Note that folder numbers do not reflect chronological order; they represent the order in which Williams picked up the pages. Inventive inconsistency is our hallmark here: we were affixing numbers to chaos. Bracketed ellipses indicate some of our excisions and elisions, providing a glimpse of the scope and nature of our editorial choices. Other excisions go unmarked in favor of readability.

The Exegesis began in 1974, with letters and short pieces, and grew steadily. The early pages form an epistolary detective novel, plunging the reader into the 2-3-74 revelation: Dick began his interpretations even as clues in the form of dreams, voices, and visions poured in. Soon, his letters grew longer and denser, some accompanied by enclosures of further typewritten "notes"; short pieces with recognizable beginnings and ends gave way to the extended theoretical speculations and open-ended meditations that characterize the Exegesis proper. By the end of this period, Dick was typing twenty-plus pages at a go — single-spaced, with minimal margins and paragraphing. We have largely offered the earliest entries in full; as longer, more meandering entries begin, in early 1975, we transition to the method of excerpting used for the remainder of the book: selecting discrete chunks of varying lengths, from a single paragraph to several pages (with or without some internal trimming).

Dick's text is given interpretive, personal, and unsystematic annotation by the editors and these others: Simon Critchley, Steve Erickson, David Gill, N. Katherine Hayles, Jeff Kripal, and Gabriel Mckee. These annotations are identified by their author's initials. Following the text and an afterword by Richard Doyle, we offer two aids to a reader's comprehension: a series of individual notes on nomenclature, translation, sources, and editorial interventions; and a glossary of some of the most frequently seen terms, including Dick's neologisms. This glossary was prepared by the editors, annotators, and the Zebrapedia Group, under the guidance of Erik Davis, but it includes material developed by Lawrence Sutin for his 1991 volume. A modest index follows the afterword.

Let us be the first to say that the notes, glossary, and index are incomplete: nothing short of a Vast Active Living Intelligence could sort all of Dick's avenues of reference and citation. For one small example, among many, of the challenges in an annotator's path: Dick often quoted English sources from memory or altered sources as he hurriedly copied them out; his use of German and Latin is willful and imaginative. In consideration of sanity (our own) and time and space (which are after all the same thing), we have offered the gist of his intentions, as we understood them, rather than unraveling his errors. A few names have been disguised in these pages to ensure the privacy of persons not wishing to be named.

Acknowledgments

Editors' acknowledgments: The Zebrapedia Transcription and Research Group, spearheaded by Richard Doyle: Lisa Boren, Scott Boren, Alex Broudy, Gerry Canavan, Devin Daniels, Rob Daubenspeck, Eric Furjanic, Carl Hayman, Jesse Hicks, Shane Leary, Jesse Rafalko, and Jennifer Rhee, as well as others who went in before us; the Paul Williams transcription team, some of their names now lost; Andy Watson, Jay Kinney, Gregg Rickman, and Lawrence Sutin. Also: Rebecca Alexander, Will Amato, Cindy Lee Berryhill, Steven Black, David Brazil, Tessa Dick, Frederick Dolan, Michael Domeracki, Bob Gamboa, Ted Hand, Owen Hill, Frank Hollander, Mark Hurst, Babette and Bruce Jackson, Shelley Jackson, Jeremy Menzies, and Rob Miotke. Thanks to all the annotators and to Gabriel Mckee for above-and-beyond attention to notes and glossary. And to the estate: Isa Hackett, Chris Dick, and, above all, Laura Leslie, for transcription, for biographical research, and for her ceaseless support.

Laura Leslie's acknowledgments: Isa, Chris, and I would like to recognize and express our appreciation for the following people who were instrumental in overcoming the daunting hurdles along the journey from eight thousand disorganized journal pages to the book you hold in your hands: Tim Powers for saving, protecting, and hiding these pages immediately after our father's death; Paul Williams for his leadership in preserving the Exegesis, and all the volunteers who organized the material; Jonathan Lethem, who knew publishing the Exegesis was possible, who encouraged us, shared his vision, advocated for this project, enabling others to understand and embrace its potential, and connected us with Pamela Jackson; Pamela Jackson, who worked with us and who, in balancing responsibility to our father's legacy with sensitivity to his living family members, was able to more than satisfy both; and Andrew Wylie, our father's literary agent, without whose support this book would not have been published at this time.

PART ONE

PART ONE

Folder 4 •

[4:1] In *Ubik* the forward moving force of time (or time-force expressed as an ergic field) has ceased. All changes result from that. Forms regress. The substrate is revealed. Cooling (entropy) is allowed to set in unimpeded. Equilibrium is affected by the vanishing of the forward-moving time force-field. The bare bones, so to speak, of the world, our world, are revealed. We see the Logos addressing the many living entities.* Assisting and advising them.† We are now aware of the Atman everywhere. The press of time on everything, having been abolished, reveals many elements underlying our phenomena.

If time stops, this is what takes place, these changes.

Not frozen-ness, but revelation.

There are still the retrograde forces remaining, at work. And also underlying positive forces other than time. The disappearance of the force-field we call time reveals both good and bad things; which is to say, coaching entities (Runciter, who is the Logos), the Atman (Ubik), Ella; it isn't a static world, but it begins to *cool.* What is missing is a form of heat: the Aton. The Logos (Runciter) can tell you *what* to do, but you lack the energy — heat, force — to do it. (I.e., time.)

The Logos is not a retrograde energetic life form, but the Holy Spirit,

---

* *Logos* is an important concept that litters the pages of the Exegesis. An ancient Greek word with a wide variety of meanings, Logos can mean word, speech, reason (in Latin *ratio*) or giving an account of something. For Heraclitus, to whom Dick frequently refers, Logos is the universal law that governs the cosmos, of which most human beings are somnolently ignorant. Dick certainly has this latter meaning in mind, but most importantly, Logos refers to the opening of the Gospel of John, which invokes the word that becomes flesh in the person of Christ. The human faculty for the intuition of Logos is *nous* (or *noös*, as Dick transliterates it) or "intellection," which also appears all over the Exegesis. But the core of Dick's vision is *gnostic:* it suggests a specifically mystical contact with a transmundane or alien God who is identified with Logos and who can communicate in the form of a ray of light, non-objective graphics, or some other visionary transfer. The novelty of Dick's gnostic vision is that the divine communicates through *information* that has a kind of electrostatic life of its own. — SC

† Neoplatonism is crossed with thermodynamics to provide a framework for Dick to think through his experiences here. The entire universe can be comprehended as subject to an imperative: more entropy! While entropy is usually associated with the negativity of disorder, here it functions as something like a revelation: the bare bones, so to speak, of our world are revealed. And while the revelation is a "regression," it enables an insight into the nature of reality. The divine, "Atman," is perceived within all things for Dick even as the vehicle of this revelation is entropy — in the guise of noise, he receives a clarifying signal. — RD

the Parakletos, is. If the Logos is outside time, imprinting, then the Holy Spirit stands at the right or far or completed end of time, toward which the field-flow moves (the time flow). It receives time: the negative terminal, so to speak. Related to the Logos in terms of embodying word-directives and world-organizing powers, but at a very weak level, it can progressively to a greater degree overcome the time field and flow back against it, into it, impinging and penetrating. It moves in the opposite direction. It is the anti-time. So it is correct to distinguish it from the Logos, which so to speak reaches down into the time flow from outside, from eternity or the real universe. The H.S. *is* in time, and is moving: retrograde. Like tachyons,[1] its motion is a temporal one; opposite to ours and the normal direction of universal causal motion.

Equilibrium is achieved by the Logos operating in three directions: from behind us as causal — time — pressure, from above, then the final form, the very weak H.S. drawing toward perfection each form. But now equilibrium as we know it is being lost in favor of a growing ratio of retrograde teleology. This implies we are entering, have entered, a unique time: nearing completion of the manifold forms. Last pieces are going into place in the over-all pattern. The task or mode of the H.S. is *completing*. Not beginning, not renewing or maintaining, but bringing to the end, to the close. An analogy would be the transit of a vehicle from one planet to another; first stage is the gravity of planet of origin; then equilibrium of both planets in terms of their pull; then the growing pull of the destination gravity-field as it gradually takes over and completes the journey. Beginning, middle, end. At last one senses the receiving field engage, and then correct.

When I wrote *Ubik* I constructed a world (universe) which differed from ours in only one respect: it lacked the driving force forward of time.* That time in our own actual universe could weaken, or even go entirely away, did not occur to me because at that point I did not conceive time as a force at all (vide the Soviet astro-physicist's theory[2]). I thought of it in Kantian terms. As a mode of subjective perception. Now I believe that time, at this point in the expansion of the universe (or for some other reason[s]), has

---

* Until the mid-1960s, Dick's novels explored isolation, entropy, and psychological withdrawal. But with *Ubik* (1966), his work becomes progressively more concerned with redemption and rebirth. After a team of anti-telepaths is injured in an explosion, the novel develops a dreamlike quality inspired by *The Tibetan Book of the Dead*. As the reality around them devolves, the characters begin to succumb to entropy themselves. A magical cure-all product begins to show up in advertisements: Ubik, which comes in an aerosol spray can and promises to combat the forces of encroaching chaos. Ubik is clearly an allegory for the Christian concept of "grace"; author Michael Bishop has written that Ubik is "whatever gets you through the dark night of the soul." In the Exegesis, Ubik becomes shorthand for redemption. — DG

in fact actually begun to weaken, at least in ratio to certain other fields. Therefore, this being true, a measure of the *Ubik*-experience could be anticipated. I have indeed had that experience, or a measure thereof. That is, time still drives on, but counter forces have surfaced and impinge, laying bare the *Ubik* landscape — only for a few moments, that is, temporarily. Then time resumes its sovereignty.

What one would expect is two fold: (1) Material (e.g., information, images, weak energy fields, etc.) from the future leaking or bleeding back to us, while we continue on. (2) Abrupt lurches back on our part to recent prior time periods, like a needle on a record being anti-skated back to a prior groove, which it has already played, and then playing on from there as if nothing happened.* The latter we would not be consciously aware of, although subcortical responses, and perhaps a vague sense of amnesia, dreams, etc., would tell us that something was "wrong." But the leakage back to us from the future, not by us but *to* us, that we would be aware of (calling it ESP, etc.), and yet be unable to account for it.

But what is most telling is that in March, at the initial height of the "Holy Other" pouring into me, when I saw the universe as it is, I saw as the active agent, a gold and red illuminated-letter like plasmatic entity *from the future*, arranging bits and pieces here: arranging what time drove forward. Later I concluded that I had seen the Logos. What is important is that this was perceptual to me, not an intellectual inference or thought about what might exist. It came here from the future. It was/is alive. It had a certain small power or energy, and great wisdom. It was/is holy. It not only was visible around me but evidently this is the same energy which entered me. It was both inside and out. So the Logos, or whatever it was, this plasmatic life form from the future which I saw, satisfies, as near as I can fathom, most of the theoretical criteria above.†

---

* This word *information* has become so commonplace that it is important to mark out its history here. Dick is writing a quarter of a century after Claude Shannon published his *Mathematical Theory of Communication* with Warren Weaver, wherein he defined the quantity of "surprise value" contained in any message as its "entropy." Shannon named this value entropy because he was using equations drawn from the thermodynamic measure of entropy in a system — Maxwell's equations. The paradox here — one that Dick grappled with — is presented by the fact that *information*, whose etymology suggests the existence of a pattern or "form," is found to be mathematically equivalent to the amount of disorder in a closed system. That is, entropy is both the measure of the content of a message and a measure of its disorder. Maximum entropy is maximum message. The Exegesis is a working-through of this paradox: was Valis signal or noise? — RD

† The paradox of "entropy" as a measure of disorder and order is, for Dick, temporarily overcome. It is only through the breakdown of his ordinary reality that he can be informed by the suprasensual reality of the divine letter: the Logos. Here, as in the famous opening of the Gospel of John — "In the beginning was the Word and the Word was with

Also, the official Catholic/Christian theories about the Holy Spirit so depict it: moving backward from the end of time, pouring into people. But if the Holy Spirit can only enter one, is only inside, then what I saw that was gold and red outside, like liquid fire, wasn't the H.S. but the Logos. I think it's all the same thing, one found inner, one found outer. What difference does it make? It's only a semantic quarrel; what's important is that it comes BACK HERE FROM THE FUTURE, is electrostatic and alive, but a weak field. It must be a form similar to radiation. [. . .]

However, that which caused me to see differently and to be different must be distinguished from what I saw and became. A bioplasmic orgone-like energy entered me or rose up in me and caused changes in me; that is one enormous miracle . . . but the heightened awareness caused me to see a different universe: one which contained the red and gold living threads of activity in the outside world, a world enormously changed, very much like the world of *Ubik*. But I feel a unity between the force which changed me and the red and gold energy which I saw. From within me, as part of me, it looked out and saw itself.

Letter to Peter Fitting,[3] June 28, 1974

[4:6]

Dear Peter,

[. . .] In regards to some of the intellectual, theoretical subjects all of us discussed the day you and your friends were here to visit, I recall in particular my statement to you (which I believe you got on your tape, too) that "the universe is moving backward," a rather odd statement on the face of it I admit. What I meant by that is something which at the time I could not really express, having had an experience, several in fact, but not having the *terms*. Now, by having read further, I have some sort of terms, and would like to describe some of my personal experiences using, in a pragmatic way, the concept of tachyons, which are supposed to be particles of cosmic origin (I am quoting Arthur Koestler) which fly faster than light and consequently in a reversed time direction. "They would thus," Koes-

---

God and the Word was God" — language becomes an "active agent" that is actually prior to material reality. John 1:1 is additionally instructive because of what information theory would describe as the sentence's "redundancy." The semantic content of "In the beginning" reiterates the line's formal content, since "In the beginning" is indeed in the beginning of the gospel. "In the beginning was the word" is, of course, *in* words, so here too the signal repeats itself through its own self-reference. In this passage Dick is treating this threefold redundancy as the Logos itself, out of which any message at all might emerge. Thus, when Dick receives this "letter from the future," it is felt as salvation. The question of whether Valis is signal or noise is abstracted another level, as information "from the future" pours into the present, revealing the unreal nature of linear time. — RD

tler says, "carry information from the future into our present, as light and X rays from distant galaxies carry information from the remote past of the universe into our now and here. In the light of these developments, we can no longer exclude on a priori grounds the theoretical possibility of precognitive phenomena." And so forth (*Harper's*, July 1974).[4]

I had been for several months experimenting with something I read about while doing research on the brain, in particular new discoveries on split-brain phenomena, for my novel *A Scanner Darkly*; I had come across the fact that the brain can transduce external fields of both high and low frequency providing that the thermal factor is quite low. Also, I had read about which vitamins in megadosages can improve neural firing and produce vastly increased brain efficiency. I began attempting, on the basis of what I knew, to bring on both the hemispheres of my own brain using the recipe for megadoses of the water-soluble vitamins; at the same time I tried again and again to exclude the ordinary external electrical fields that we customarily tune into: man-made fields, which we consider "signal," and at the same time I tried to directly transduce what we usually think of as "noise," in particular weak natural electrical fields.

One night I found myself flooded with colored graphics which resembled the nonobjective paintings of Kandinsky and Klee, thousands of them one after the other, so fast as to resemble "flash cut" used in movie work. This went on for eight hours. Each picture was balanced, had excellent harmony and possessed idiomatic style — that of a well-known nonobjective artist. I could not account for what I was seeing (this took place in the dark, and was evidently phosphene activity within my eyes, but the source of the stimulation of the phosphenes was an enigma to me at the time), but I was certain that those tens of thousands of lovely, balanced, quite professional and esthetic harmonious graphics could not be originating within my own mind or brain. I have no facility with graphics, and besides, there were too many of them; even Picasso, whose style predominated for over an hour, never actually painted so many, although he very likely saw that many in his own head.

In later studies about the brain I learned of an inhibiting brain fluid called GABA, which when its effect drops drastically, which is to say when an external stimulus causes disinhibition and firing of a programmed sequence up to then is inhibited, such colored graphics are often experienced. So I concluded that massive — unique in my life, in fact — disinhibition had taken place, although I could not identify the external stimulus, nor comprehend the programmed or engrammed sequences. At the same time (in the days following) I found myself possessed with enormous energy and did a lot of unusual things. This, in fact, is what probably raised my blood pressure so much that my doctor had to hospitalize me. I was constantly active, and in new ways. This tends to confirm the theory of massive disinhibition and unused neural firing along hitherto unusual neural pathways, perhaps an entire hemisphere of the brain held in readiness until then — I did not know for what.

All this may have been induced by the huge doses of water-soluble vitamins I took, gram after gram of vitamin C, for instance. But I doubt it. At the same time as I experienced the release of psychic energy (to use Esther Harding's phrase, picked up by Jung), I became conscious of pathic language directed at me from all creatures, and finally, as it spread — and this is the point I'm getting at — from the direction of the sky, especially at night. I had a keen intuition that information of some kind was arriving at us all, in fact bombarding us, from sidereal space.

For a time I imagined that an ESP experiment had somehow by accident involved me: the long-range transmission of graphics. I wrote to a lab in Leningrad and told them about my experience, having at the time the feeling that the point of origin of these signals was far distant, and hence in the USSR. Now I believe the point of origin was even farther: I think that I somehow for a short time transduced tachyon bombardment, which comes to us constantly, and which animals utilize to engram them into performing what we call "instinctive actions." I had been consciously trying to transduce external weak fields, which I know to be possible, and I know that when this is done successfully the brain's efficiency is increased; however, I had no preconception of what fields I might transduce — except that I felt they would be natural and not man-made — and what information, if any, they might contain. I was hoping only for increased neural efficiency. I got more: actual information about the future, for during the next three months, almost each night, during sleep I was receiving information in the form of print-outs: words and sentences, letters and names and numbers — sometimes whole pages, sometimes in the form of writing paper and holographic writing, sometimes oddly, in the form of a baby's cereal box on which all sorts of quite meaningful information was written and typed, and finally galley proofs held up for me to read which I was told in my dream "contained prophecies about the future," and during the last two weeks a huge book, again and again, with page after page of printed lines.

Without the tachyon theory I would lack any kind of scientific formulation, and would have to declare that "God has shown me the sacred tablets in which the future is written" and so forth, as did our forefathers, back on the deserts of Israel under the sky as they tended their sleeping flocks. Koestler also points out that according to modern theory the universe is moving from chaos to form; therefore tachyon bombardment would contain information which expressed a greater degree of Gestalt than similar information about the present; it would, thus at this time continuum, seem more living, more animated by a conscious spirit, to us giving rise to the concept of God. This would definitely give rise to the idea of purpose, in particular purpose lying in the future. Thus we now have a scientific method of considering the notion of teleology, I think, which is why I am writing you now, to express this, my own sense of final causes, as we discussed that day.

Much of this printed-out information arriving in dreams has had a teaching, shaping and directing quality; it tends to inform and guide me, and make me aware of what I should do. It literally educates me, and I'm sure each small creature, each bug and plant and animal and fish, has the same sense of it. I've watched my cat, now, as he sits out on the sundeck at night; he is beyond doubt considering the sidereal world above him and not moving objects below — when he comes in the house an hour or two later he seems modified, as if he has been taught during that period and knows it. I think this happens to us all but I managed consciously to transduce above the threshold of awareness, which is unusual but not unique, and became aware of this constant natural and normal process which shapes all life from the future, as Koestler describes. It is often described as the "Divine Plan," or better yet "Continual Creation." Any such terms will do, but I regard it for my own purposes as a continual informational print-out from the future which directs us all, not in the coercive sense that the past does, but experienced — and rightly so — as volition. As so to speak, free will. This term sounds right to me each morning when I wake up and reflect on the pages of print I've seen during the night; I am not forced to do what the information brings to my attention; I am free to consider it, digest and understand it, and, with its assistance, act on it.*

---

* Here Dick acknowledges that, as he comes to terms with 2-3-74, he can choose different maps for his exploration, since "any such terms will do." He regards the present as a "continual informational print-out" in which he nonetheless and simultaneously has "free will," a perception that is in accord with the thinking of physicist Erwin Schrödinger, one of the chief architects of the informatic paradigm Dick is experiencing. Schrödinger, whose idea of the "code-script" in DNA gave birth to the concept of the genetic code, grapples in *What Is Life?* with the simultaneously mechanistic and free characteristic of human experience: "(i) My body functions as a pure mechanism according to the Laws of Nature. (ii) Yet I know, by incontrovertible direct experience, that I am directing its motions, of which I foresee the effects, that may be fateful and all-important, in which case I feel and take full responsibility for them. The only possible inference from these two facts is, I think, that I — I in the widest meaning of the word, that is to say, every conscious mind that has ever said or felt 'I' — am the person, if any, who controls the 'motion of the atoms' according to the Laws of Nature." Notice that to perceive this twofold nature of the human being re-

For well over two months I was convinced that the Holy Spirit, which is to say God, was directing me, and in a sense this is true; it is a matter of semantics: at one time these would have been the only terms we had available to us; we would have talked about a divine vision and so forth. What I think now is that more modern terms can be better applied; the future is more coherent than the present, more animate and purposeful, and in a real sense, wiser. It *knows* more, and some of this knowledge gets transmitted back to us by what seems to be a purely natural phenomenon. We are being talked to, by a very informed Entity: that of all creation as it lies ahead of us in time.

Cordially,

Philip K. Dick

P.S. In terms of Ubik (not the novel but the force described in my novel) perhaps I was already becoming aware of this total coherence which the universe is moving toward and which bombards us backward, so to speak, with information about itself, thus giving us a certain awareness of itself. I would think that for purely fictional purposes the description given and the name given in the novel would be more rather than less accurate vis-à-vis the tachyon theory, which is connected with the theory that the universe is moving from chaos to form. Ubik talks to us from the future, from the end state to which everything is moving; thus Ubik is not here — which is to say now — but will be, and what we get is information about and from Ubik, as we receive TV or radio signals from transmitters located in other spaces in this time continuum.

I see no objection to interpreting the meaning of the force Ubik this way. Nor in interpreting the purpose of the novel *Ubik* by saying that in it I was trying in a dim and unconscious way to express a series of experiences I had had most of my life of a directing, shaping and assisting — and informing — force, much wiser than us which we in no way could perceive directly; where it was or what it was called I did not know; I knew it only by its effects: in Kant's terms, it is (or as I understand now will be) a Thing-in-Itself.

Thus I would express the purpose of the novel — my purpose, anyhow — to be a fictional statement containing a presentation of this directing presence which I arbitrarily chose the name "Ubik" for. That Ubik (or more accurately the future total Gestalt of purpose and Meaning) may well have written the book through me is possible, but only in the sense that all creatures from grasshoppers on up, in particular small creatures such as

---

quires an act of contemplation on Dick's part: "I am free to consider it, digest and understand it, and, with its assistance, act on it." — RD

grasshoppers, are "written through," by what we call instinct, rather than "writing" their lives. However, I do think one could say this; rather than having it read: *Ubik,* by Philip K. Dick, one could put it this way:

PHILIP K. DICK
By
Ubik

In a sense I am joking, of course, but in a sense I am not.

I don't feel I was "picked" by a Future Force, as its instrument, etc., bidden to make manifest its word, etc., any more than when you are watching a TV program the transmitter has picked you. It is broadcast; it just radiates out in all directions and some people tune in, some do not; some like what they see and hear, some reject it. All I did was to transduce, as all creatures do. I just gave what I received a local habitation and a name, as Shakespeare put it.

P.P.S. One aspect of regarding this as an information transmission and reception-transduction system (like a teletype) might at last throw some light on the otherwise puzzling phenomenon of glossolalia when seized by the "Holy Spirit." In my reception of tachyon bombardment (assuming this is what it is, of course) I frequently either fail to transduce properly (error at the receiving end) or else there is a lapse of accurate transmission (as if the teletype operator has his fingers on the wrong line of keys, etc.). When that happens, instead of seeing, in my dreams, the perfectly articulated English prose passages which would be the result of all components functioning correctly, I get gibberish like this: meaningless "names" and "words" and sequences of numbers which have no significance. Unless one is very, very careful to factor out, to use a scrupulous reject circuit of some kind (I suppose this would come with practice) one is confronted with the task of making sense out of random or inaccurate integers. I give these actual examples:

832	Command — Odd
835	G-12
5412960	5242681
Eleanor	P-13
Mr. Arensky	
Mrs. Aramcheck	
Sadasa Ulna	
17	

Considering the distance over which these packets of information travel, and their velocity, much contamination, signal-loss and other familiar invasion of the material contained must take place — cross-talk from other fields, so that when the tachyons at last impinge on us even if our transduction is superb (as in the case of "mystics" and "saints") there would be something quite less than a perfect meaningful construct. I suppose that out of these etoin shrdlu type of ramblings (or whatever you get on a linotype when your fingers go from left to right) the various "Names of God" are constructed; they supply the spurious and dogmatic Holy Writ such as the Mormons treasure as their inspiration.

If you recall the weird word found on deserted Roanoke Island in 1591, which was CTOSYOAN, carved on a tree and everyone mysteriously gone, — well, look I did it just then; I had my fingers one key to the right on my keyboard: the word is CROATOAN; I was copying it from my text book and had my eyes away from my hands. Thus marvelously proving my point. But for centuries scholars have been trying to figure out what "Croatoan" means. Probably it means nothing; the terrified colonists of the island, faced by one or more hostile forces (famine, Indians, plague, etc.), had an inspiration and left the island for some other sanctuary, believing that those letters spelled out something meaningful. Perhaps the Cosmic Teletype Operator turned his head for a moment, as I did, and erred.

In my novel *Galactic Pot-Healer* there's a girl character named Mali Yojez. Not being able to think of another name, I hit keys at random, and used what I got. Years later a burned-out freak who had read the book looked at me with secret insinuating accusation and said, pointing to these letters-used-as-a-name, "That's me you're writing about there in your book." I pointed out that Mali Yojez was in no way his name. "It's a code you used," he explained, "to cover over my name so I wouldn't know. But I do know." I then pointed out that I had written and published the book years before I ever met him; at that his all-knowing paranoid glee increased. "That just proves how clever you are," he said. "You even knew about me in advance." You see what I mean, Peter.

I've reinserted this into the typewriter because just as I was about to mail this, it occurred to me that according to my tachyon theory, I could well have anticipated meeting the above-mentioned burned-out freak. This brings to my mind my strange and eerie feeling that my novels are gradually coming true. At first I laughed about this, as if it was only a sort of small matter; but over the years — my God, I've been selling stories for 23 years — it seems to me that by subtle but real degrees the world has come to resemble a PKD novel; or, put another way, subjectively I sense *my* actual world as resembling the kind of typical universe which I used to merely create as fiction, and which I left, often happily, when I was done writing.

Other people have mentioned this, too, the feeling that more and more they are living in a PKD novel. And several freaks have even accused me of bringing on the modern world by my novels.

Well, a case could be made here for my above tachyon theory, I guess, although I hadn't thought of it until now. Let us say that I am inspired by a creative entity outside my conscious personality to write what I write. (I had imagined it to be my subconscious, but this only begs the question, What is the subconscious?) There is no doubt that quite frankly I do not in any real sense write my novels; they do come from some non-I part of me. Often they contain dreams I've had (this was true of Lovecraft, I've heard). If tachyon bombardment was inspiring my novels, then it would stand to reason that the world — it is really all the same world which my books depict, as has been pointed out in critical essays many times — it would stand to reason that, as the years pass, my books would, so to speak, come true. They are about the future in two ways: they describe it fictionally, like S-F tends to do, *and,* they being inspired by tachyon information about the actual future (or possible several alternate futures) depict on-coming reality. Isn't our world now somewhat like the world in *Solar Lottery,* my first novel? And other, later novels of mine even more so? I do not wish to be in one of my own novels, by the way. So this isn't wish-fulfillment. Anyhow, I'm not the only person who's noticed that the world seems to be getting like my novels; it was pointed out to me recently that if I had waited another year to bring out *Flow My Tears* it would have been out of date (actually it was by-and-large finished in 1970).

Several times I've had the uncanny experience of meeting people who resemble persons, characters, I'd previously made up for my novels. In *Flow My Tears* there's a 19 year old girl named Kathy, as you recall, whom Jason meets; she is a girl of the gutter, so to speak, living a quasi-illegal existence. The next year, 1971, I in fact did meet a girl, the same age, living a life so similar to that of the girl in the novel as to frighten me — frighten me that if she reads the book ever she may sue. Her name — Kathy.

I am not the true and actual source of my own fiction, and I've always wondered what the source was. John Denver, the current folk singer, says he doesn't compose his many songs; "They're out there in the air somewhere," he says, "and I just fish them in." Well, my novels aren't out there in the air; they're in my unconscious — or are they? Maybe Denver is right; it's coming at us from a standpoint physically outside our brains, not down deep below the surface. In point of fact, S-F is often thought of as "future history," and this notion is one I've combated, with great irritation, over the years. And yet I'm faced with the fact that time and history have caught up with me, which is perhaps one reason why you and others were disappointed with *Flow My Tears;* I waited too long to bring it out. Put another way, the gap between my vision and the actual world has gotten smaller and smaller over the years; when I wrote *Solar Lottery* it was a vision that no one else had, but how can I claim my vision in *Flow My Tears* to be unique in the same way? I could do as well by getting my information from newspapers, perhaps. How strange. How frightening, to me, anyhow.

And yet, as of this March, with the sudden bombardment of the non-objective graphics, perhaps I have once again regained contact with the authentic future; for example, the work I'm engaged in now is a sequel to *Man in the High Castle,* at last — I've wanted to do that for 12 years, but never come up with an idea good enough. Based on my experiences from March of this year on, I believe I have indeed, finally, come up with an idea good enough, and am deep into it. I feel that the external creative force which I've discussed throughout this letter, whatever its source, whatever its nature, has inspired me as I have never been inspired before. More important to me than what it is, what it's called, is the quality of its inspiration to me and the effect on my writing. Well, from these experiences over the past three months I do have a terrific idea, I think the best of my life, and in no way will it be anything you can read about in the present day newspaper. Perhaps what has happened is nothing more or less than a sudden return of the old force of creativity which animated me in years past and novels past. . . . Whatever it is, God bless it, and I am grateful for it. Wish me luck — and also, let me know what you think of all this; I value your opinion uniquely.

Letter to Claudia Bush, July 5, 1974

[4:13]

Dear Claudia,

Since I last wrote you (sending on the 7 page letter to Peter Fitting plus the 2 page letter to you) I have continued to have the same dream again and again which I mentioned: a vast and important book held up before me which I should read. Yesterday, for example, since Tessa and Christopher had gone off on a picnic, I took several naps and had four dreams in which printed matter appeared, two of them involving books.

For three months, virtually every night, I've had these dreams involving written material. And within the last few days it became obvious that a specific book was indicated. That the ultimate purpose of all these dreams was to call my attention to an actual book somewhere in the real world, which I was to find, then take down and read.

The first dream on July 4 was much more explicit than any before; I

took down my copy of Robert Heinlein's *I Will Fear No Evil*, a large blue
hardback U.K. edition, for two men to look at. Both men said this was not
a book (or the book) they were interested in. However, it was clear that the
book wanted was large and blue and hardback.

In a dream a month ago I managed to see part of the title; it ended in
the word "Grove." At the time I thought it might be Proust's *Within a Budding Grove*, but it was not; however, there was a long word similar to "Budding" before "Grove."

So I knew by the first part of the day yesterday that I was looking for a
large blue hardback book — very large and long, according to some dreams,
endlessly long, in fact — with the final word of the title being "Grove" and a
word before it like "Budding."

In the last of the four dreams yesterday I caught sight of the copyright
date on the book and another look at the typestyle. It was dated either 1966
or possibly 1968 (the latter proved to be the case). So I began studying all
the books in my library which might fit these qualifications. I had the keen
intuition that when I at last found it I would have in my hands a mystic or
occult or religious book of wisdom which would be a doorway to the absolute reality behind the whole universe.

Of course the possibility existed that I didn't have the book in my library, that I would have to go out and buy it. In several dreams I was in
a bookstore doing just that. One time the book was held open before me
with its pages singed by fire on all sides. By that I took it to be an extremely
sacred book, perhaps the one seen in the Book of Daniel.[5]

Anyhow today I looked all day around the house, since Tessa has been
sick with a sunburn, and all at once I found the book. The three month
search is at last over.

As soon as I took down the volume I knew it to be the right one. I had
seen it again and again, with ever increasing clarity, until it could not be
mistaken.

The book is called *The Shadow of Blooming Grove*, hardback and blue,
running just under 700 huge long pages of tiny type. It was published in
1968.[6] It is the dullest book in the world; I tried to read it when the Book
Find Book Club sent it to me but couldn't.

It is a biography of Warren G. Harding.

Cordially,
Phil Dick

P.S. This is on the level, and it goes to show you that you should never
take your dreams too seriously. Or else it shows that the unconscious or

the universe or God or whatever can put you on. A three-month gag. (If you want to read the book I'll mail it to you. Postage should be enormous. You got three years ahead in which you have nothing planned?)

Letter to Claudia Bush, July 13, 1974

[4:16]

Dear Claudia,

[. . .] Inasmuch as I've delighted you so far with my unusual (to say the least) trip into Big Dreams of Big Books, then I might as well go all the way.

Now, as I've mentioned, among other things I've dreamed about:

A big blue book whose title ends in the word grove and before this is a word starting with a "B" which could be blooming or budding or something. A book in which everything there is is.

The sibyl. Who knows and sees everything . . . The deeds of men, especially.

The cyclops (in same dream as above). Contributing the seeing Eye.

A friend called "Paul" holding up galley proofs for me to read, which I am told consist of a "book of prophecies," and in which I find a passage about myself. Again, a huge MS of printed pages, but not quite a true bound book in our terms. Yet enormous.

The word "sintonic," which I am told to be, and which when I wake up I believe to be a neologism, but when I finally look up and find to be a real word, Greek, meaning self-harmony, etc. In harmony with, etc. A key term in Pythagorean thought, also Roman.

Well, Claudia, let's take the above five in terms of what I found in my funky reference books. Now, ESP has been described as "when you somehow acquire knowledge you shouldn't have," or "have no way of having," whether it's about the future, or what's in the next room, or in another person's mind, etc., or in the past. Since I wrote you earlier today I decided to look up Virgil's *Aeneid*, because in the short paragraph which I quoted to you about the Cumaean Sibyl, it's in that book where she is mentioned. Okay. Here is what I found:

In Book III of *The Aeneid* there is a long description of the Cyclops.

In a later book, Aeneas meets Queen Dido, ". . . Then the Sibyl takes him through mystic passages of the Blissful Groves where those who led good lives bask in green valleys and endless joys" (Will Durant's *Caesar and Christ*, page 241). Note: "Blissful Groves."

So we have here (1) the Cyclops, (2) the sibyl, and (3) the "Blissful Groves" which is indubitably what I saw in my dream, and also the fact that the sibyl has a lot of books of prophecies which she burned one by one, as in my dream of the singed book held up to me to read, each page rimmed with singed black. As if the book had gone through a fire but had been rescued.

Now, Claudia, I never knew any of these things. And it certainly is odd how much are from a single strand of myth from Roman and Greek times: right down to specific Greek words such as Syntonos, or however it's spelled in Greek. Also I dreamed the word "ulna" one time, as I mentioned in the form "Sadasa ulna." Well, I looked it up and it is Latin for "elbow," but also it can stand for a measure of length, and the citation in my complete Latin dictionary for that use is Virgil's *The Aeneid*, book III. The word "ulna" appears there as used by Virgil in that fashion, and although other citations follow, its appearance in that book would seem to be the initial use of it that has survived. And the best known, to scholars.

So my dreams seem to refer again and again to a specific paradigm and that paradigm is being explicated with each dream until now I can't avoid seeing what the paradigm is.

Or was 2,000 years ago.

So this could be placed under the rubric "ESP" or more accurately ESP knowledge.

What the dreams I've had from mid-March to now, which is to say scores and scores of them, mean is that: This is prophetic knowledge. Which is to say, I can take what comes and has already come as accurate prophecy. Once this is established, the so-to-speak credentials, then it can and has gone on to the knowledge itself. Such as last night, about the assassinations in this country, which the sibyl said included Jim Pike, Bishop Pike that is, who knew Bobby Kennedy and Dr. King, and who is my friend; I knew Jim very well.

The sibyl said that the three burglaries of my house between November 1971 and March 1972 in which all my papers were taken finally, by the time it was over, had to do with the belief or fear that I had material Jim Pike had given me before his death. (I had said he had done so in the foreword of my 1969 novel *A Maze of Death*.) This was the purpose of the three burglaries of my files. They had reason to think so; I had said so in *A Maze of Death*.

I always wondered why my papers were taken. I could never figure it out and the police said they were baffled, too.

In April of this year when I was in the hospital for high blood pressure (caused really by these "dreams") I met a lawyer and told him at length about the hits on my house. His theory after careful thought was that it was most likely that they were after papers concerning Jim Pike, religious material Jim had given me or told me before his death. In at least one of my dreams, Claudia, I was Jim Pike; I know that because I saw "my mother" and it was Jim's, Mrs. Chambers, who I once met. Also, Jim was a Latin scholar. His specialty, in fact, his joy in life.

I am freaked, when you consider his book *The Other Side,* about the dead coming through to the living. He gave credit to me in its foreword, for research work.

Love,
Phil

Letter to Claudia Bush, July 16, 1974

[4:34]

Dear Claudia,

Herewith you will find a copy I made for you — did the whole damn thing word by word on my own typewriter — of a short piece I wrote which I think a lot of.

I'm sending it to you because first I do think it has worth and it's a present to you from me, what I have best to give. (I was going to put it on the market, but never mind.) There is however a second reason. I wrote this short piece with no thought to any formal system of thought past or present. It is just what I experienced and believed. The next day when I read it I saw instantly that it was unquestionably Hindu doctrine. There is the path: dharma. There is the delusion that hangs over reality: maya. And there is the light of God shining below maya: Brahman. But later on I realized that even more was involved: the clear concept of the liar, when I looked through my reference books I came across it and recognized it at once when I turned to a passage about Zoroastrianism. The God of Light versus the Master of the Lie. There it was. I could not recall ever having known that before. Perhaps I did, but it was no longer a conscious part of me.

Needless to say, honesty was valued by the Persians as the first virtue, after piety (which was needed to justify honesty, evidently, since in those days everything had to be assigned to a supernatural cause to make it stick). They believed other good things, as revealed to them by Zoroaster as revealed to him by Ahura-Mazda by way of the *Avesta,* such as it being a sin to feed unfit food to an animal such as a dog. The greatest thing in the Persian system of course was its affirmation of life, the value of life, the joy of life, the justice possible in this world and not the next, the value of *trying.* It put down passivity, resignation, despair, and I'm glad to say once released from the power of the Lie I saw passivity, resignation and despair as intended by-products of the Lie, and any system of thought or religion which taught those as virtues (Christianity included) as a manifestation of the Lie.

Well, there I went and said it. Any system which says, This is a rotten world, wait for the next, give up, do nothing, succumb — that may be the basic Lie and if we participate in believing it and acting (or rather not acting) on it we involve ourselves in the Lie and suffer dreadfully . . . which only reinforces that particular Lie. I imagine that if Sweet Jesus is listening to me He is becoming very angry now, but if He follows his own philosophy He will fold his hands, look tragically toward heaven, and do nothing.

Meanwhile, I am trying to bring back an affirmative view of life, as was stamped out furiously wherever it appeared in history, and all I can hope is that I won't get caught. Well, I will be, but hopefully not too soon. It's a nice world and I'd like to stick around and enjoy it for a long time . . . but I got to say what I think is so, right? Whatever the consequences.

Love,

Phil

July 8, 1974: The First Day of the Constitutional Crisis
(Enclosure, letter to Claudia Bush, July 16, 1974)

But the state of things is so dreary here in the U.S. — they say the elderly and poor are eating canned dog food, now, to stay alive, and the McDonald hamburgers are made from cows' eyes. The radio also says that today when Charles Colson, the President's former counsel, went into jail he still wore his Richard M. Nixon tie clasp. "California dreaming is becoming a reality," is a line from a Mamas and the Papas song of a few years ago, but what a dreadful surreal reality it is: foglike and dangerous, with the subtle and terrible manifestations of evil rising up like rocks in the gloom. I wish I was somewhere else. Disneyland, maybe? The last sane place here? Forever to take Mr. Toad's Wild Ride and never get off?*

The landscape is deformed out of recognition by the Lie. Its gloom is

---

* When he wrote this sentence, Dick sat less than ten miles away from Disneyland, a geographic synchronicity that reminds us how regional a writer Dick was. Unlike most California writers, however, he bridged the "two hemispheres" of the bipolar Golden State. Before moving to the tacky conservative sprawl of Orange County, Dick lived for decades in the Bay Area, absorbing the lefty bohemia of Berkeley and Marin County. In 1973 he wrote Stanislaw Lem: "There is no culture here in California, only trash." But as Dick's own work proves, trash can achieve a visionary intensity, even a kind of escape velocity. After all, California was also the petri dish of our digital age, spawning the Internet, biotechnology, the personal computer, and geosynchronous satellite communication. And California has long encouraged the restless, eclectic, and sometimes wacky search for spiritual authenticity that drives the Exegesis. There is no more Dickian a Mecca than Disneyland. Indeed, Mr. Toad's Wild Ride offers a model for the entangled plots of a Phil Dick novel: a fantastic contraption that careens through a variety of trapdoors and false fronts and deposits you in a kind of surreal hell. But then the doors open once again, and you face the blank blue sky. — ED

everywhere, and we encounter nothing we recognize, only familiar things without the possibility of accurate identification. There are only shocks, until we grow numb, are paralyzed and die. When I suddenly stopped believing in the Lie I did not begin to think differently — I *saw* differently, as if something was gone from the world or gone from between me and the world which had always been there. Like a scrambling device that had been removed: deliberate scrambling. All, suddenly, was clear language. God seemed to seek me out and expressed things through things and what took place. Everywhere I saw signs along a path, marking His presence.

Any lying language creates at once in a single stroke a pseudo-reality, contaminating reality, until the Lie is undone. As soon as one lies one becomes separated from reality. One has introduced the falsification oneself. There is one thing no one can force you to do: to lie. One only lies for one's advantage. It is based on an inner decision invisible to the world. No one ever says to you, "Lie to me." The enemy says, You will do and believe certain things. It is your own decision to falsify, in the face of his coercion. I am not sure this is what the enemy wants, or anyway the usual enemy. Only a Greater Enemy, so to speak, would want that, one with greater objectives, and a clearer idea of what the ultimate purpose of all motion is.

Sometime in the past, about three months ago, I must have become aware for the first time in my life that the cause of my misery was the Lie and that the enemy, the real enemy, was a liar. I remember somewhere along the line saying loudly, "He is a liar; he is a liar," and feeling it to be very important, that discovery. I forget — or rather I guess it does not matter — what specific lie by which person made it all change. There was a person, there was a lie. A week after I realized that with no possibility of evading it everything altered radically for me, and the world began to talk, in a true language of signs: silently. The Lie had slipped away. The Lie deals with talk, written or spoken. Now it's gone. Something else shines forth at last. I see the cat watching at night, for hours. He has seen it all his life; it is the only language he knows.

I think a lot about my early childhood and remember events in it vividly, which I guess is a sure sign of senility. Also events that took place within the past ten years seem dim and not really a part of me. Their sadness is gone: used up. I encounter new fresh sadnesses in my remote past, like stars that burst into life when I notice them. When I pass on, they again are forgotten. Usually, however, senility is a gradual process; mine came on abruptly when I noticed the cat trying to discern what was causing me pain (I had stomach flu) and then what he could do to help me. He finally got up on my abdomen transversally and purred. It helped, but then when he jumped down the pain returned, whereupon the cat got up again. He lay on me for hours, purring, and finally the disturbed rhythm of my stomach began to match the pace of his purrs, which made me feel much better. Also, the sight of his jowly face gazing down at me with concern, his keen interest in me his friend — that changed me, to suddenly open my eyes (I had been lying for an hour on the couch) and see his concerned large furry face, his attention silently fixed on me. It was not an illusion. Or, put another way, his field of energy, his strength, was at that moment greater than mine, small as he was, since mine had dimmed from the flu and his was as always. Perhaps his soul was at that unusual moment, that critical moment, stronger than mine. It is not usual for a small animal's soul to be larger than a man's. He warmed me and I recovered, and he went his way. But I changed. It is an odd senility, to be comforted and healed by a small animal who then goes on as always, leaving you different. I think of senility as a loss of contact, a drop in perception, of the actual reality around one. But this was true and in the present. Not a memory.

The Constitutional guarantees of our country have been suspended for some time now, and an assault has begun on the checks and balances structure of the government. The Republic is in peril; the Republic has been in peril for several years and is now cut away almost to a shadow of itself, barely functioning. I think they are carving it up in their minds, deciding who sits where forever and ever, now. In the face of this no one notices that virtually everything we believed in is dead. This is because the people who would have pointed this out are dead: mysteriously killed. It's best not to talk about this. I've tried to list the safe things to talk about, but so far I can't find any. I'm trying to learn what the Lie is or what the Lies are, but I can't discern that anymore. Perhaps I sense the Lie is gone from the world because evil is so strong now that it can step forth as it is without deception. The masks are off.

But nevertheless something shines in the dark ahead that is alive and makes no sound. We saw it once before, but that was a long time ago, or maybe our first ancestors did. Or we did as small children. It spoke to us and directed and educated us then; now perhaps it does so again. It sought us out, in the climax of peril. There was no way we could find it; we had to wait for it to come to us.

Its sense of timing is perfect. But most important it knows everything. It can make no mistakes. It must be back for a reason.

[4:41] The best psychiatrist I ever saw, Dr. Harry Bryan attached to the Hoover Pavilion Hospital, once told me that I could not be diagnosed, due to the unusual life I had led. Since I saw him I have led an even more unusual life and therefore I suppose diagnosis is even more difficult now.

Something strange, however, exists in my life and seems to have for a long time; whether it comes from my odd lifestyle or causes the lifestyle I don't know. But there it is.

For years I've felt I didn't know what I was doing; I had to watch my activities and deduce, like an outsider, what I was up to. My novels, for example. They are said by readers to depict the same world again and again, a recognizable world. Where is that world? In my head? Is it what I see in my own life and inadvertently transfer into my novels and to the reader? At least I'm consistent, since it is all one novel. I have my own special world. I guess they are in my head, in which case they are a good clue to my identity and to what is happening inside me: they are brain prints. This brings me to my frightening premise. I seem to be living in my own novels more and more. I can't figure out why. Am I losing touch with reality? Or is reality actually sliding toward a Phil Dickian type of atmosphere? And if the latter, then for god's sake why? Am I responsible? How could I be responsible? Isn't that solipsism?

It's too much for me. Like an astrophysicist who by studying a Black Hole causes it to change, I seem to alter my environment by thinking about it. Maybe by writing about it and getting other people to read my writing I change reality by their reading it and expecting it to be like my books. Someone suggested that.

I feel I have been a lot of different people. Many people have sat at this typewriter, using my fingers. Writing my books.

My books are forgeries. Nobody wrote them. The goddam typewriter wrote them; it's a magic typewriter. Or like John Denver gets his songs: I get them from the air. Like his songs, they — my books — are already there. Whatever that means.

The most ominous element from my books which I am encountering in my actual life is this. In one of my novels, *Ubik*, certain anomalies occur which prove to the characters that their environment is not real. Those same anomalies are now happening to me. By my own logic in the novel I must conclude that my or perhaps even our collective environment is only a pseudo-environment. In my novel what broke through was the presence of a man who had died. He speaks to them through several intermediary systems and hence must still be alive; it is they, evidently, who are dead. What has been happening to me for over three months is that a man I knew who died has been breaking through in ways so similar to that of Runciter in *Ubik* that I am beginning to conclude that I and everyone else is either dead and he is alive, or — well, as in the novel, I can't figure it out. It makes no sense.

Even scarier is that this man, before his death, believed that those who are dead can "come across" to those who are alive. He was sure his own son who had recently died was doing this with him. Now this man is dead and it would seem he is "coming across" to me. I guess there is a certain logic in this. Even more logical is that I and my then wife Nancy participated as a sort of disinterested team observing whether Jim Jr. was actually coming through. It was our conclusion that he was.

On the other hand, I wrote *Ubik* before Jim Pike died out there on the desert, but Jim Jr. had already died, so I guess my novel could be said to be based on Jim Jr. coming through to his father. So my novel *Ubik* was based on life and now life is based on it but only because it, the novel, goes back to life. I really did not make it up. I just observed it and put it into a fictional framework. After I wrote it I forgot where I got the idea. Now it has come back to, ahem, haunt me, if you'll pardon me for putting it that way.

The implication in *Ubik* that they were all dead is because their world devolved in strange ways, projections onto their environment of their dwindling psyches. This does not carry across to my own life, nor did it to Jim's when his son "came across." There is no reason for me to project the inference then of the novel to my own world. Jim Pike is alive and well on the Other Side, but that doesn't mean we are all dead or that our world is unreal. However, he does seem to be alive and as mentally enthusiastic and busy as ever. I should know; it's all going on inside me, and comes streaming out of me each morning as I — he — or maybe us both — as I get up and begin my day. I read all the books that he would be reading if he were here and not me. This is only one example. It'll have to do for now.

They write books about this sort of thing. Fiction books, like *The Exorcist*. Which are later revealed to be "based on an actual incident." Maybe I should write a book about it and later on reveal that it was "based on an actual incident." I guess that's what you do. It's convenient, then, that I'm a novelist. I've got it made.

There have been more changes in me and more changes in my life due to that than in all the years before. I refer to the period starting in mid-March (it's now mid-July) when the process began. Now I am not the same person. People say I look different. I have lost weight. Also I have made a lot of money doing the things Jim tells me to do, more money than ever before in a short period, doing things I've never done, nor would imagine doing. More strange yet, I now drink beer every day and never any wine. I used to drink only wine, never beer. I chugalug the beer. The reason I drink it is that Jim knows that wine is bad for me — the acidity, the sediment. He had me trim my beard, too. For that I had to go up and buy special barber's scissors. I didn't know there even was such a thing.

Mostly, though, what I get is a lot of information, floods of it night after night, on and on, about the religions of the Antique World — from Egypt, India, Persia, Greece and Rome. Jim never loses interest in that stuff, especially the Zoroastrian religion and the Pythagorean mystery cult and the Orphic cults and the Gnostics — on and on. I'm even being given special terms in Greek, such as syntonic. I'm told to be that. In harmony with, it means. And the Logos doctrine. All this comes to me in dreams, many dreams, hundreds of dreams, on and on, forever. As soon as I close my eyes information in the form of printed matter, visual matter such as photographs, audio stuff in the form of phonograph records — it all floods over me at a high rate of print-out.

These dreams have pretty well come to determine what I do the next day; they program me or prepare me. Last night I dreamed that I was telling people that J. S. Bach was laughing at me. I imitated J. S. Bach's laugh for them. They were not amused. Today I find myself putting on a Bach record, rather than Rock. It's been months, even years since I automatically reached for Bach. Also last night I dreamed that I took the microphone away from Ed McMahon, the announcer on Johnny Carson's show, because he was drunk. Tonight when Ed McMahon came on I automatically got to my feet and switched the TV off, my desire to watch it gone. This fitted in fine because my Bach record was playing anyhow.

I should mention that I have become completely sophisticated now, having withdrawn all my projections from the world. I am mature and am no longer lachrymose nor sentimental. My spelling is as lousy as ever.

There is no known psychological process which could account for such fundamental changes in my character, in my habits, view of the world (I perceive it totally differently, now), my daily tastes, even the way I margin my typed pages. I have been transformed, but not in any way I ever heard of. At first I thought it to be a typical religious conversion, mostly because I thought about God all the time, wore a consecrated cross and read the Bible. But that evidently is due to Jim's lifestyle. I also drive differently, much faster, reaching for an air vent on the dashboard that is not there. Evidently I'm used to another car entirely. And when I gave my phone number the last two times I gave it wrong — another number. And to me the weirdest thing of all: at night phone numbers swim up into my mind that I never heard of before. I'm afraid to call them; I don't know why. Perhaps in some other part of Orange County someone else is giving my phone number as his, drinking wine for the first time in his life and listening to Rock; I don't know. I can't figure it out. If so, I have his money. A lot of it. But I got it from my agent, or rather ex-agent, since after 23 years I fired him. To explain the totally different tone and attitude of my letters I told my agent I had my father-in-law, a CPA, working with me. At the time this was to my mind a lie, but looking back I can see a thread of truth in it. Someone was and is working with me on all business matters, making my attitude tough and shrewd and suspicious. I am hard boiled and I never regret my decisive actions. I can say No whenever I want to. Jim was that way—no sentimentality. He was the shrewdest Bishop I ever knew.

Perhaps he is collaborating in the writing of this right now. [. . .]

Maybe I, Phil Dick, have just abreacted to a past personality, formed up to the mid-fifties. Lost skills and heartaches that came after that.

Well then we have here a sort of time travel, rather than someone who is dead "coming across" from the Other Side. It is still me, with my old, prior tastes and skills and habits. Mercifully, the sad recent years are gone. Another form of my odd and chronic psychological ailment: amnesia, which my head learned after my dreadful auto accident in 1964.*

Come to think of it, it is the memories laid down since 1964 which have dimmed. I recall saying to Tessa that it seemed to me that precisely ten years of memory was gone. That would take it right back to that day in—my god, almost ten years to the day—when I rolled my VW in Oakland on a warm Spring Saturday. Perhaps what happened that day was that from the physical and mental shock an alternate personality was struck off; I did have extraordinary amnesia during the months afterward. So that might make an excellent hypothesis: the trauma of that auto accident started a secondary personality into being, and it remained until mid-March of this year, at which time for reasons unknown it faded out and my original "real" personality returned. That makes sense. More so than any other theory. Also, it was in 1964 that I first encountered Jim Pike—the letter I wrote him for Maren. He was a vivid personality in my life at that time. It was only a few days after writing that letter for Maren that I suf-

---

* The year 1964 was a bad one for Dick. Burned out after writing seven novels in twelve months, Dick suffered a serious bout of depression. Writer's block and two bad acid trips took their toll. After separating from his wife and leaving bucolic Point Reyes, Dick got an apartment in East Oakland, a gritty neighborhood he referred to as "East Gak-ville." In July, Dick flipped his car, dislocating his shoulder. After the accident, Dick languished in a body cast, and then wore a sling for two months. Unable to type, Dick was forced to dictate notes for a long-planned sequel to *The Man in the High Castle* (1962). Here Dick acknowledges that, basically a decade later, he found himself in exactly the same circumstance. After reinjuring his shoulder and undergoing surgery to repair it, Dick was once again dictating notes for a sequel to *High Castle* that would also integrate his 2-3-74 experiences into the novel. Eventually the notes he was dictating became *Radio Free Albemuth*, published posthumously in 1985. Dick never completed the sequel to *The Man in the High Castle*, arguably the most successful book of his career, and a high point he seemed determined to revisit, especially when he was down on his luck. — DG

fered the auto accident. No wonder I have Jim interwoven with this re-stored personality; he was on my mind at the time it was abolished. I've just picked up where I left off in 1964.

I've explained everything but the preference for beer over wine. I never drank beer. And the business shrewdness; I never was shrewd. And the general health kick, the religious kick, the lack of sentimentality, the reso-lution, the ability to discern a lie, the intention and determination never to lie, the vastly higher level of effectiveness in all fields, the trimming my beard so expertly — everything is explained but those; also I still have to explain the constant written material which I see in dreams every night, including Greek and Latin and Sanskrit and god knows what else, words I never knew but have to look up. This abreaction to before the auto ac-cident explains some things, but it doesn't explain others. Could it be that I now am what I would have been had the accident never occurred? As if I've shifted over to a sort of alternative world where I grew naturally and normally to this mature and responsible character-formation, not derailed tragically by first the accident, then the involvement with Nancy et al., which of necessity followed? This, then, would be a sort of personal alter-nate universe. Ananke . . . another Greek word flashed up to me in sleep; the compulsion which determines the outcome of even the gods' lives. There is an ananke for me which decreed that I would become what I am now, and that weird unfortunate sidetracking cannot abolish it as my des-tiny.

In which case I am more truly myself now than at any other time since the accident. Which may well be. I am myself — in this, the best of all pos-sible worlds. It's heredity, so to speak, over environment. The stars and my innate character triumphed.*

Which explains why I still can't spell. It is not in my nature.

Whatever all this is, I brought it on. I had been doing months of re-

---

* In the Exegesis, one of the great themes of Dick's work — memory — is being reconsid-ered, if not radically recast. The theme of memory runs from *In Milton Lumky Territory* to *Do Androids Dream of Electronic Sheep?* to *A Scanner Darkly;* up until the Exegesis, Dick's work has formed a multivolume epic that might be called "Remembrance of Time Irreal." In this work, memory serves as the nexus between reality and humanity, but in the Exege-sis Dick's past and future seem to bleed into the present, creatively and psychologically, and one feels his effort to make memory not so much irrelevant as meaningless, maybe even nonsensical. It is no longer part of humanity's cosmic DNA — the Lincoln robot in *We Can Build You* is as human as the real Lincoln not because he looks and acts like a real Lincoln, but because he remembers like one. Dick suspects that the person he remembers being for the previous ten years was a "secondary" incarnation that supplanted the real one that now has returned. If this is true, to what extent is the Exegesis not just an elaboration on Dick's previous work, but a rebuttal? Has Dick ceased to be the parallel Proust and be-come the anti-Proust? — SE

search on recent discoveries about brain function, especially the exciting news that we have two hemispheres and use only one, the left one. They say that's where procedural thoughts such as doing math and thinking inductive and deductive logical processes take place; the other hemisphere, which people in Asia use instead, does simultaneous work, such as gestalting of a picture, intuitive and even ESP functioning. Whatever it comprehends it comprehends in a single pattern and then passes on to the next, without there being a sequential or causal relationship between the apprehended and evaluated matrices, which I guess fly by like the frame freeze pictures on TV in the Heinz 57 Variety ad. I had read that massive doses of certain water-soluble vitamins improve neural firing in schizophrenics: better synchronization and so forth. It occurred to me that maybe in a normal person with normal, which is to say, average synchronization, it might cause firing to take place so efficiently that both hemispheres of the brain might come on together. So I found a recipe in a *Psychology Today* article and I did it. I took what they prescribe schizophrenics.

In terms of my own personal life what happened made history, and I'm sure — off and on, anyhow — that whatever happened then and from then on has to do with my getting what I set out to get: such improved neural firing that both hemispheres came on together, for the first time in my life. It is the contents that puzzle me, not what happened in the biochemical or physiological or even psychological sense. Even allowing for the obvious fact that since my personality must have formed in the left hemisphere alone when whatever happens in the right would be subjectively experienced as the Not-I, or lying outside of my self-system and therefore not me and not my thoughts, I still can't for instance understand why when I begin to fall asleep my thoughts switch from English to Greek, a language I don't know.

All my thoughts and experiences, focusing mainly in dreams, seem to constellate around the Hellenistic Period, with accretions one would expect from previous cultures. The best way to describe it is to say at night my mind is full of the thoughts, ideas, words and concepts that you'd expect to find in a highly educated Greek-speaking scholar of the 3rd century A.D., at the latest, living somewhere in the Mediterranean Area of the Roman Empire. His daytime thoughts, I mean. Not what he'd dream while asleep.

Perhaps this is another Bridey Murphy.[7] I've brought back to being active a personality "from a former life." Undoubtedly, from internal evidence it appears to be the past, the archaic past, breaking through. But it's not chaotic. It's highly systemized, sort of like the *left* hemisphere of the Greek-speaking Roman citizen. It seemed to me that the preoccupations of this individual were indeed those of Jim Pike, and thus if you allow all prior steps in this chain of inferential thought to stand, you arrive logically at the final step that Jim Pike broke through to me "from the other side." But, if you apply Occam's Razor, the Principle of Parsimony (the smallest theory to cover the facts), you can deal Jim out and run with the ancient material alone. Except that obviously it's organized as if by a living, idiosyncratic personality, which I often sense behind it. This personality, glimpsed by me as being a woman, holds up the book to me or mails it to me, etc. She likes me. She wants to guide, educate and help me. Evidently she's exposing me to all this enlightening and ennobling written material deliberately, to make me into a higher life form, or anyhow, a better person. Up until now my higher education has been sadly neglected; she is making up for that, using very effective show-and-tell audio-video teaching techniques. I have the feeling that for every word or photo I consciously catch and remember there are thousands of yards of it poured into me that I do not consciously remember. They take hold anyhow, as witness my busy intellectual research — homework, if you wish — the next day.

After one dream, in which I saw a sibyl who was a cyclops, I decided after doing research that it was the Cumaean sibyl who had seized hold of me, and not anyone from present times or the "other side." I got a lot of mileage out of that theory, but then I get a lot out of each theory I hold.

Treating this as a detective mystery thing which I have to solve on the basis of the clues, I am struck most by the amount of medical information and advice given me in these dreams. Health, mine, both physical and psychological, seems to be a high priority in this ceaseless nightly didactic print-out. The first written item held up to me, in fact, a baby's cereal box with writing on it, contained medical information, among other things, although that was not first.

The first was my ex-wife Nancy's handwriting. Then in printing, very small, this: "The bichlorides are a very poisonous poison for you," and it went on, dribbling off though, to say I ought to flush down every metallic toxin in the house: Sleep-Eze and spray can sprays with traces of metal in them.

This is very much like *Ubik*, in which Ubik the force, the deity, the underlying entity bringing on and stabilizing eidos, form, is seen as a spray can — in fact, the label of a spray can.

This is too close to be coincidence. My first written material was a label on a cereal box *about* a spray can. A main difference, though, is that my info-dump told me the spray can was bad; whereas Ubik of course was good. The absolute good of the universe.

Anyhow I rose up in the night and threw out my Sleep-Eze and many spray cans including in particular insect sprays, and after that I wouldn't let my wife smoke. Now we learn that the carcinomic factor in cigarette smoke is radioactive lead — a metal poison. So this information, however bizarre, from whatever source, has a definite therapeutic quality and accuracy. When I withdrew all my psychological projections and became sophisticated I experienced the universe as being drawn through infinity and winding up backward. Maybe when I did that I not only wound up in my own book I even turned the book backward. Turned Ubik inside out too. This causes me to think up, sui generis, another theory.

(1) I, consciously, don't write my novels.

(2) Therefore a part of my unconscious does.

(3) Novels are composed of words.

(4) Taking all the water-soluble vitamins causes my neural firing to so improve generally that what had been below the threshold of consciousness was raised up to consciousness, anyhow at night.

(5) That portion, active and more highly potentiated than before, and unusually endowed with verbal skills, in particular written verbal skills, rattles away at me visibly as soon as I shut my eyes; it is, so to speak, writing a book while I'm asleep.

What the water-soluble vitamins did, then, was to make it possible for me to get in touch with myself, which when most people do that they get in touch with repressed material in the unconscious, usually their real feelings, all of it inchoate as the unconscious has to be in order to stay unconscious. But my unconscious has a predilection toward esoteric, exotic and archaic words — exact and precise ones at that. Much of the printed material I see in my dreams has elaborate annotation in scrawly blue pen or pencil in the margins. Someone has been copyediting it, cutting out unnecessary words. My book-writing unconscious has a concise style. As one would expect from over 23 years of professional work, cutting and pruning, looking up words in the dictionary. I have so to speak a real pro for an unconscious. It's a fine style but it isn't mine. I'd never write "a very poisonous poison," or, as it expressed a vital thought in my sleep once by saying, "She will see the sea." It makes an exact point with no regard for literary style, a higher method of expression with the intent to convey its meaning above all. Therefore it resorts to such strikingly enigmatic words as "syntonic," if that is what it means; no other will do and it doesn't seem to care whether I know the meaning of the word or not; if I don't then I can just look it up. That's my — the audience's — problem. One thing about it: my

wordsmith unconscious doesn't talk down to me. On the contrary; I have
to hustle every day to catch up with it.*

Partly this must come from the fact that it has available to it my complete and entire memory, every word, every thought, everything I ever saw,
read, heard, knew. My conscious memory — my conscious vocabulary — is
only the tip of the iceberg. And yet it seems highly structured; obsessed
in fact by the theological disputations and dogmas and highly abstract
and abstruse concepts and theories of Rome. As Robert Graves once said,
"Theological dispute was the disease of that age," meaning that everyone
in the streets was obsessed by it and had to talk about it endlessly — as my
unconscious does. My unconscious is fixated in the Roman period, and
that strikes me as strange. How did it get there in the first place? And being
there, why does it remain?

Once I myself was consciously deliberately interested in that period; I
was in my early twenties, and read about it a lot, at the expense of being a
rounded person. But my unconscious for all its obsessions with the theoretical material of that period is hard-headed and shrewd, and wants everything it comes up with applied in the most practical way. If it shows
me the Golden Rectangle it does so in order to calm me with that ultimate esthetically balanced sight; it has a firm therapeutic purpose. There
is a utilization of all its abstract material for genuine purposes, for me, by
and large. It is a tutor to me as Aristotle was to Alexander, which makes
me wonder why it is grooming and shaping me this way, tutoring me in
the exact fashion employed by the Greeks. Philosophy for real ends, for final causes, as Aristotle would have put it: for something lying ahead and
not as an idle pastime, an end in itself. The ennobling and elevating education is altering me and I would presume that when it is finished I, having become changed (to resort to the Ablative Absolute), will act upon the
improved character which I've acquired — not on the knowledge direct,
as if on enlarged memory banks, but upon the basis of my matured and
elevated character. I know this whole process sees ahead because I have

---

* It should be noted that everything Dick describes in this passage is only a slightly crazier
version of something that every novelist experiences — the sense that he or she is not creating the work but someone or something else is. (Or as Dick has put it earlier, "My books
are forgeries. Nobody wrote them. The goddam typewriter wrote them. . . .") Many authors
have had the experience of returning to earlier work with no recollection of having written
it or of what the person who wrote it could possibly have been thinking. I'm not disputing
Dick's insightful assessment of the cleavage between an artist's conscious and unconscious
selves, nor am I even necessarily disputing the theories behind that assessment. I'm just
saying that Dick's sense of a freely, independently functioning unconscious that manifests
itself in imagination and words is not unique, even as he has taken this meditation several
steps further than most. — SE

caught sight of its clear perception down the web of time, seen with it for a while; it knows what is ahead and acts accordingly. I'm sure it has a final purpose in mind, for which this is careful preparation. This recalls to me my notion that the Cumaean sibyl is behind it all; certainly she had or has a clear view of the future, of time; that is what a sibyl is.*

Following basic Greek thought it is improving my mind and body together, as a unity. Health is equated — correctly so — with vigor and the capacity to act. All its concepts, its viewpoints, are Greek. Symmetry, balanced, harmony. I sense Apollo in this, which is consistent, since the Cumaean sibyl was his oracle. Moderation, reasonability and balance are Apollo's virtues, the clear-headed, the rational. Syntonos, or whatever. Pythagorean harmoniousness. A reconciling of all impulses and tendencies within, then turning to the outer world once that is achieved and becoming syntonic with it as well. I'm getting a classical education. Greek, a little Latin, knowledge of Sanskrit, theology and philosophy and the Ionian Greeks' various views of the cosmos. Very unusual to get this here in Southern California. All very sane and steady. The most worthy, the highest virtues and values in the history of our civilization.

How did they happen to arise within me? For instance, it pointed out that my ananke — the compulsion or fate lying ahead of me — is a darkening, a gathering gloom, which is a good description of my underlying melancholia. Against which I pit my learned syntonos. Cultivation against innate predispositions: a basic struggle in life, and well elucidated by my unconscious. How did it know these two terms and was able to define them for me? I didn't know. I *never* knew. This is material emanating from a wise viewpoint which I never possessed. This was not me, although it is becom-

---

* Dick's experience of 2-3-74 has sometimes been interpreted as auditory and visual hallucinations, perhaps induced by repeated transient ischemic attacks (TIAs), or temporary strokes. We know that he was experiencing dangerously high blood pressure during this period, so a stroke would not be unlikely. If a stroke did occur, some of the changes he recorded in his personality in 1974 suggest that the neural circuitry normally associated with his conscious mind was reconfigured, possibly in ways that strengthened the connections between consciousness and what recent research in neuroscience has been calling "the new unconscious," or "the adaptive unconscious." Distinct from the Freudian unconscious, the adaptive unconscious catches the overflow of sensations and perceptions too abundant to be processed through the bottleneck of conscious attention. Far from surfacing only in dreams, it is constantly at work to help set priorities, direct attention, and change behaviors in ways adaptive to the environment. Dick's observation that he had become more "shrewd" about business matters — more practical, so to speak — indicates that the adaptive unconscious may have been guiding his actions more directly than was usual with him. Much of his theorizing about the events of 2-3-74 could also derive from his previous experience, as he himself recognized; for example, his extensive reading about classical Rome may have surfaced in his conviction that he had somehow been transported backward in time to Rome in 100 C.E. — NKH

ing me; or rather, to be more accurate, it is shaping me so that I am becoming it. Meeting its standards, its ideals. Which are Apollonian Greece's from over two thousand years ago: from its Golden Age. Our Golden Age.

Now, this really does not rule out Jim Pike as my Athenian or Hellenistic tutor. Jim had, I'm certain, that kind of classical education. Greek, Latin, Roman theology and so forth. The disputations of St. Paul, St. John, the Logos Doctrine, what Augustine knew. Also, Jim was — is — shrewd; he'd apply, did apply in his life, all this classical education. He is the only person I ever knew, in fact, with such a background. If Jim were to become my tutor this I really think, all this that I'm being taught, that my attention is being drawn to, would be precisely what he would get me involved with. The reading list I'm getting is one he would give. This is Jim's *mind* I'm getting, not so much his personality. Its directed — expertly directed — contents. It has me drink beer instead of wine because beer is more healthy for me and I should drink a little something to relax me; there's an example. That's *directed* tutoring. This is not an inert computer, whose keyboard I myself punch according to my own whim and volition.

The one odd dream that I had, in which I picked up most distant, the smallest, weakest signal — from a star, star-information, sidereal . . . what I heard seemed to resemble, as an analog, an AI System, not a computer, and female in tone. Reasonable and female. This was a small system, though; it knew almost nothing, not even where it was (the "Portuguese States of America," it decided, when I suggested it look around for something written to read from, like the address on an envelope). This was a subsystem and not my tutor, but its response told me that nowhere in our world would I find the sending entity which had begun impinging on me in the form of a highly abstract and highly balanced (like the Golden Rectangle) graphics back in March. Not so much what it told me in a positive sense — where it was — but by ruling out where it is not: that helped. It isn't here, which means here in time, space, dimension, any of the coordinates.

The past, then. Or the future. Another star. An alternate world. "The other side." They're all "the other side" in some way. For instance, it made me aware of God from the very start, but never of Christ; I deduce from this that it is non-Christian and probably pre-Christian. Actually I can't catch in it any influences since the Greek Logos Doctrine. Which could be Iranian. India to Iran to Greece and then possibly (but not necessarily) to Rome. One night I had a short bitter dream in which I cried out in despair, "Ich hab' kein Retter," I have no Savior. Then in fear at having said that I added, "Ja, Ja, es gibt ein Retter,"[8] but it was too late; the whole Ground of Being, everything around me, dwindled away and was gone; I floundered in the void, suffering. I think this was an awareness that for all its value, this new worldview being dominant in me and taking over from the old one would deprive me, perhaps forever, of Jesus Christ. I guess this is true. It's a dreadful loss, but I can't stop it; what can the pupil do in the hands of such a tutor? Unfortunately, though, a tutor who — well, lived before Christ and hence could not have known of Him? But Jim knew of Christ. Perhaps then I have worked the logical steps, deducing and deducting to prove that my tutor existed before the time of Christ, or if a bit later did not know of, or if knowing did not accept. Time and knowledge have been rolled back, for better or worse. Mostly it is better . . . except in this one conspicuous way. I miss my savior.

So my "unconscious," which I've claimed this tutor to be, has available to it "my entire memory," except everything pertaining to events and concepts that arose after 100 A.D. That is an extraordinarily great restriction. Obviously, that is not in any sense that we know the term "my unconscious," laid down in my lifetime; it knows words, concepts, that I never knew — and doesn't know the commonplace elements of the last 2,000 years. Its location is far back in time. And another climate; I keep sensing — and craving — a moist, cool, high-altitude environment, where I can watch the stars.

I remember that when this first hit me, in the first couple of weeks, I was absolutely convinced that I was living in Rome, sometime after Christ appeared but before Christianity became legal. Back in the furtive Fish Sign days.* Secret baptism and that stuff. I was sure of it. Rome, evil Rome and Caesar's minions, were everywhere around me. So were the fast-moving hidden agents of God, always on the go, like the Logos as it creates things. I was a Christian but I had to hide it. Or they'd get me. It made me very uncomfortable to belong to a persecuted sect like that, a small minority

---

* We all know the Christian fish, multiplied and mutated across millions of automobile bumpers in an endless ideological war. Sometimes the icon includes the word ΙΧΘΥΣ, the Greek word for fish and an acrostic — used by early Christians along with the symbol — of the phrase "Jesus Christ, Son of God, Savior." Popular accounts of ΙΧΘΥΣ often suggest that the sign was once used by persecuted Christians to recognize one another — a believer would draw one arc of the fish, which a fellow acolyte would then complete. Though this account inspired Dick, there is no historical evidence for such secret winks. More relevant is the symbol's modern revival by the countercultural Jesus Movement, for whose adherents the symbol replaced the stark rectilinear cross and invoked an alternative Christianity, radical and earthy. In Orange County, Dick was surrounded by the ambient vibes of Jesus Freakery, an originally Californian movement whose local avatar was the remarkably named Lonnie Frisbee. By 1974 Frisbee's youth evangelism and "surf's up" baptisms had helped groovify Calvary Chapel and other local mainline congregations. In one of Dick's later visions, the Υ of an ΙΧΘΥΣ decal affixed to his window transformed into a palm tree — a fitting invocation of southern California as much as the ancient Levant. — ED

of fanatics. I was afraid I'd blurt out my beliefs and be thrown to the lions. That is one reason my blood pressure got so high. I was waiting to be hit by Caesar's spies, and also I anticipated the Second Coming or something good like that. Maybe the Day of Judgment. I was more excited than afraid, sure in my faith, certain of my Savior. The Last Supper was real, actual and close by me. Maybe this is a clue. I'm still in that time period, but I've fallen under the wise and prudent guidance of an educated Greek — high class in other words — tutor. Brought in from the provinces where the ignorant scurry about, to be educated in cultivated urban life. I think I read all this in the novel *The Robe*[9] 11 years ago. Jeez, I've fallen into someone else's novel!

You know, I could if I wanted to make the most dramatic but speculative case, for fictional purposes I guess, reason that I was pulled back through time, back and back, to where It All Went Wrong, which would be where around 100 A.D. I, typifying everyone who went wrong perhaps, became a Christian. "That was a wrong turn," the Vast Acting Living Intelligence System that creates decided. "When those people decided on Christianity. I'll throw away 2,000 years, go back, have this one — he'll get it going right; he's typical — turn to some other religion instead, and have that become dominant. Let's see. . . ." A New Start. Second Time Around. Why not? Thus, my sense that my help was coming from an *alternate universe.*

I don't know why I'm speculating along like this, though, because in point of fact I've decided, by a process of deduction, who my tutor is. Asklepios, or one of his sons. A Greek physician, whose step-mother was the Cumaean sibyl, his father Apollo, at whose shrines ". . . the sick were given wholesome advice in their dreams," this cult yielding only reluctantly to Christianity. Also Asklepios was according to legend, slain by the Kyklopes, a cyclops. Which would explain my extraordinary dream: I saw a fusion of his step-mother and him who Asklepios feared most in all the world.*

This also explains why the highest wisdom shown me is that associated with Apollo. His — my tutor's — father.

---

* In the *Phaedo*, Plato recounts the death of Socrates, which is famously administered by drinking hemlock. Socrates' enigmatic final words are, "Crito, we ought to offer a cock to Asklepios." Asklepios was the god of healing, and people suffering from an ailment would offer sacrifice before sleep in the hope of waking up cured. Thus, Socrates' final words seem to imply that death is a cure for life, a kind of restorative slumber. It is significant, then, that Dick identifies his tutor here as Asklepios — as the god of healing — for perhaps we can think of the Exegesis as a kind of attempted cure of the soul, an extended therapeutic extrapolation of a mystical experience. A temple to Asklepios, called Asklepieion, was constructed on the south slope of the Acropolis in Athens, right next to the Theater of Dionysos, the billy-goat god who also makes frequent appearances in the Exegesis. — SC

Interestingly, although Apollo is considered to have been a myth, the Cumaean sibyl is thought to have really existed, and Asklepios likewise. The sibyl lived at least a thousand years, migrating to Rome and writing her Sibylline Books. Asklepios, as I say, was slain by a Kyklopes, by order of Zeus. There wasn't anything Apollo could do about it; Asklepios was bringing a dead person back to life with his healing powers, which Zeus couldn't tolerate because it interrupted the natural order. Which I guess is ananke again . . . which would explain why in his instructing and shaping me Asklepios would emphasize that element in life. He learned all about it. I'm getting the benefit of his unfortunate experience.

I can see me telling my therapist this. "What's on your mind, Phil?" she'll say when I go in, and I'll say, "Asklepios is my tutor, from out of Periclean Athens. I'm learning to talk in Attic Greek." She'll say, "Oh really?" and I'll be on my way to the Blissful Groves, but that won't be after death; that'll be in the country where it's quiet and costs $100 a day. And you get all the apple juice you want to drink, along with Thorazine.

Apollo's motto at Delphi was "Know thyself," which forms the basis for all modern psychotherapy and mental health and certainly underlies my getting in touch with myself, as depicted here. The other night when I found myself thinking, during the hypnogogic state, in Greek, I managed to snatch a couple of words out of what I believe to be a syntactic sentence. (At the time I wasn't positive it was Greek; it remained a problem to check on, today. It was.) I snatched out:

crypte (–) morphosis

These mean something like:

latent shape (or hidden or concealed shape)

Although I don't have anything more to go on; it would seem to me that I — or my tutor — was musing on this whole situation, and in pithy Greek formalizing it. A latent form is emerging in me, buried perhaps by Apollo himself, when his son Asklepios was killed by the Kyklopes, so that his son's wisdom and skills, derived from Apollo, would continue on despite Asklepios' sudden death — remaining latent within the *morphology* of the Indo-European descendents of Asklepios, perhaps genetically handed down through his sons. (He had two.) Now, when needed, this crypte morphosis is emerging, again active; its external stimulating-triggering source being some aspect of the dreadful civic decline of our society, its falling into ruins. "Within the degenerate molecules, the trash of today, he (PKD) resurrects a power buried for eons." (S. Lem, about *Ubik*.) Other gods of the past have at other times returned to life: Wotan in Germany, during the

Nazis. Surely Apollo with his balanced wisdom, his clear healing harmony of opposites, his clear-headed self-knowledge and integrity — what better archetype or god, long slumbering, should be roused at this sad time? Of all the ancient buried deities Apollo is needed by us the most; we have seen enough of the politics of unreason, "Thinking with the Blood," etc.

In further research I discover that Apollo was the god of the sun, the builder of cities, of music and art, and healing through his son Asklepios, who is the patron god/saint of health, and to whom the Hippocratic Oath is taken. Also, I learn that the strong Pythagorean medical views entering the Greek healing schools after Asklepios held that harmony within and among all parts of the body constituted health. I learn, too, that the Greek Orthodox Priests in Asklepios' hometown still maintain sanitaria and heal as the patients' forerunners were healed 2,600 years ago. This is no quaint, obscure person, Asklepios; only unknown to me. I can think of no more valuable intrusion into my psyche than that of the father and founder of western healing. It is just what I need. And, behind him, the civic strength of Apollo, the brother of Athene.

This would explain the "photo" I saw briefly: the ancient seated goddess with arms out that were coiled around with snakes; those are associated with all these healing deities. From Egypt, probably by way of Mycenae.

Footnote: The original display of dazzling graphics which I saw, which inaugurated all of this, were characterized by their balance, not what shapes they contained. They were, like much of Kandinsky's abstract art, modern esthetic elaborations, in color, of the ancient a priori geometric forms conceived by the Greeks, which even in their time passed over into esthetics by way of Pythagoria, e.g., the Golden Section becoming the Golden Rectangle.* Certainly this would indicate that even the start of this contained the hallmark of Apollo: the balance, the harmony — I remember noting that in all the tens of thousands of pictures what was continuous in

---

* In his 2006 article "Entoptic Vision and Physicalist Emergentism," the cognitive scientist Jean Petitot demonstrated that visual hallucinations reported by a number of subjects can be modeled mathematically through neural net feedback in the visual cortex. One of these subjects was blind, so in this case it was clear that there was no perceptual input but rather stimulation through other kinds of neural activity, perhaps a stroke. Images hand-drawn by subjects closely resembled mathematical models of neural net stimulation and feedback. Dick mentions that the graphics he saw were abstract and symmetric; they may have been like the ones Petitot studied or perhaps variations on them. (Changing the parameters yields a number of variations in the mathematical models.) For Petitot, the point is that it is possible in this instance to link a mathematical model of neural activity directly with reported experiences. In Dick's case, the point is rather that his report of visual phenomena correspond with hallucinations reported by others in which the visions were internally caused by neural stimulation not related to external perceptions. — NKH

them was this perfect balance, illustrating a fundamental principle of art. It was that aspect which caught my attention and eye and told me they had great worth. In a sense, since all were rectangles, they were permutations of the Golden Rectangle, which I saw today in its original abstracted, empty form, so calm, so enduring, so restful, reminding me of Apollo's basic virtue: syntonos. I didn't even know the word then; it came to me in sleep. Healing me, as was done 2,600 years ago and never quite ceasing.

By the way, the town where Asklepios' sanitarium existed, I read now, is up in the mountains. Probably the climate was and is cool and moist; I read it's heavily wooded. I bet the stars are quite visible there. It's the place I yearn for. Out of memory.

[4:58][10]

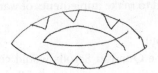

FoMELHAuT

ALBEMUTH

Letter to Claudia Bush, July 22, 1974

[4:68]

Dear Claudia,

I think I've solved what's been in my head at night.

I'm seeing all the books and writing tablets, all the written material night after night: the Qumran Scrolls.

Gee. It finally fits together, all this stuff.

They're what people call the "Dead Sea Scrolls." I've been doing more research. I'm positive. Hundreds have been unjarred and opened and translated recently. In England and Israel. The Qumran community were Essenes. Here, before the scrolls were found, is Will Durant's description of the Essenes:

. . . possibly they were influenced by Brahamic, Buddhist, Parsee [which is Zoroastrianism, PKD], Pythagorean and Cynic [search for the honest man, PKD] ideas that came to the crossroad of trade at Jerusalem. . . . They dwelt in homes owned by their community . . . [i.e., communistic ideas of property: "A rich man is a thief," PKD] . . . they hoped that by piety, abstinence and contemplation they might acquire magic powers and foresee the future. Like most people of their time they believed in angels and demons, thought of diseases as possession by evil spirits, and tried to exorcise these by magical formulas; from their "secret doctrine" came some parts of the Cabala. They looked for the coming of a Messiah who would establish a communistic egalitarian Kingdom of Heaven on earth; . . . they were ardent pacifists and refused to make implements of war.[11]

The Romans wiped them out.

Well, so the contents of the Qumran Scrolls would contain all the elements I've been entertaining in my mind, and scrolls equal books, and the Essenes were into prophecy, or anyhow wanted to be. It's all there: the numbers (Pythagoreanism), the weird semi-words (Cabala). This is exactly what Jim Pike was into, therefore. All of the above. See, Claudia?

The Essenes sent teachers to the various cities; these teachers concealed their Essene background and training. Jesus Christ is the best known example. (The Qumran Scrolls indicate he was indeed a "secret Essene.") Another example would be Appolonius of Tyana (died 98 A.D.).[12] Look him up, Claudia; you'll see what I mean. These Essene secret teachers fanned out into the Roman Empire and so-to-speak subverted it with their doctrines. After the Essene Community was wiped out around 70 A.D. such secret teachers as Appolonius of Tyana continued to spread their doctrines. These underlie — covertly — *our world.*

Nobody knew the source of these teachings until the Qumran Scrolls were recently found; no wonder Jim Pike and other theologians went crazy with excitement — saw Christianity in an entirely new light. It isn't a Jewish heresy but based on the sources I quote from Will Durant above. And they were into cypher (Cabala) and prophecy — and lots and lots of what probably are prophetic books (the scrolls).

And since Jim's death many more've been dug up and translated (which also means deciphered). Query: If the Essenes were successful prophets, not just trying and failing, did they anticipate their being wiped out, and anticipate leaving their entire doctrines and views and information as sort of time-bombs which would remain hidden until today? Is it possible? Very possible, I think. They hid all their stuff to be found later — much later. Once more to be reintroduced into the world, as it was — their original effect on our world — fading out, finally. To revive it.

Jesus Christ, Claudia. Doesn't this fit together? I know it's true; I mean, I know now that what I've been seeing which I assumed was many sources, many doctrines, was and is the worldview and knowledge, the gnosis and secret wisdom, of the Essenes who favorably informed and educated and directed and influenced society from 2 A.D. on, and even before. A synthesis of all the really useful stuff from the Antique Classical Past — now alive again, e.g., in my head at night; it's in my head because I was Jim's friend and so forth, as I've said. From the Qumran Scrolls he got all this synthesis of the wisdom of Antiquity and then he died and then he "came across" to me and so now I've got it.

I think I'm putting the pieces together, the final ones. For God's sake, Claudia, be cautious with who you discuss this, if you do at all with anyone. I'm being super careful as to whom I'm telling this to — in all candor, just you and my wife; other people like Jamis even, and Peter Fitting and so forth — just fragments. I'm not kidding, be careful.

It's adding up and it spooks me, for obvious reasons. As I nail it down I get more and more frightened, but then I calm down and feel very relaxed because it's such wise stuff, such good stuff that's coming to me at night. Last night, for example, I heard her (you know, my anima, the sibyl), singing along with a choir:

You must put your slippers on
To walk toward the dawn

With advice like that, how can I lose? (Seriously, she did sing that, but what it means I have no idea. I don't even own any slippers. Two nights ago I dreamed about the Goddess Aurora, who is the Greek Goddess of the Dawn. I sure have odd nights.*)

Love,
Phil

Letter to Claudia Bush, July 24, 1974

[4:73]

Dear Claudia,

I will Xerox the Philip Purser in-depth interview with me that just appeared in the London *Daily Telegraph* magazine.[13] Then you can see what a nitwit I appear to be to foreigners. Mr. Purser in his interview notes that when Tessa brings me some eggs to eat I offer him some (not out of the

---

* The single most lucid sentence in the entire book. — SE

same dish, just, "Would you like some?"). I guess that's odd behavior. Eggs, too, are funny, evidently, since he comments on that. "He is seen to be eating eggs," or words to that effect. You'll see, once we get it to you. [. . .]

Anyhow, back to my obsession (you know which one; are there more than one?). Last night I woke up with an acute feeling of resentment and the scales falling from my eyes and my illusions shot to hell. I had been talked to four times already that night by Asklepios and several people with him, and all at once I discovered he was telling me the usual amount of half-truths and lies and opinions like anyone else. He was just a human being; the bunch of them standing there — I had seen them off to the right, in sort of a phalanx, with Asklepios in front doing most or all of the talking — and I had been listening to them and I now knew they weren't gods and what they said, especially him, wasn't holy writ.

Lying there in bed fully awake I thought, Well that is the end of all of this. I've seen them and they're just people. Same as us.

I was very disappointed, and today when I was having my eggs in the living room and waiting to see what our nanny brought in — and who — I decided not to tell Tessa what happened in the night because it was such a bummer. Just people. Burn!

And then it came to me that I had actually seen them in the night, they were there, they did talk to me on and on, in particular Asklepios, and I was right: there were a bunch of them. They were not very formidable, and I felt like a kid who discovers to his shocked dismay that his parents are no different from anyone else: with, so to speak, feet of clay. Also, I now knew who it was who was addressing me on and on; it is Asklepios, the founder of Western medicine back in 600 B.C. He lacks modern medical techniques, medicine, equipment and knowledge; his practice hasn't evolved one bit. To make up for his lacks, I guess, he has to fake it a lot.

Love, and write if you get worry I mean work. Freudian slip; sorry. Write any time.

Phil

Letter to Claudia Bush, July 24, 1974

[4:74]

Dear Claudia,

Claudia! Another letter! Guess what about!

I forgot — how could I? — to relate to you a dream I had the other night; see, the purpose of relating it is to show how many myth elements from Antiquity can, with a little effort, be disclosed.

I'm with a bunch of people in an elevator. There is, oddly, an elevator operator (we don't have those in real life ever anymore, at least where I've been living the last 20 years); he's a small man, with olive skin and black curly short hair and large eyes, the way people are depicted in the Roman mosaics. He's wearing a brown cop uniform and is in complete charge. To his right, by the modern extremely heavy doors of the elevator is what looks like a pile of spaghetti with tomato sauce; sticking down into it is a fork. The elevator stops and I step forward to leave, but before you leave, what you have to do is extricate the fork from the pile of spaghetti, which I begin to do. But I discover it's a three pronged trident, not a fork, and it isn't spaghetti it is a pile of reddish yarn. As I pull, threads come with the trident.

The cop at once begins in the most commanding and frightening authority-type voice to explain that the prongs of the trident must be brought free without breaking a strand of the thread; he speaks to all in the elevator. He shows me how to extricate the trident without breaking the strands, and then he begins in his firm commanding voice to recite rhymed verse. At this I know him to be *that* cop, the only one; he is the most awesome of them all, and we all fall totally silent and listen with humble, almost religious, respect to his verse. Then he touches the button which opens the door. As I step through the now open portal I see the man behind me stoop down and start attempting to extricate the trident without breaking the strands twined around its prongs.

Then the next night I heard the woman singing the rhymed couplet about "You must put your slippers on / To walk toward the dawn," with the full choir behind her, again and again and again. I said to Tessa after the elevator dream, "I guess I'm going to have to listen to some of her prophetic couplets." And so I did.

In the elevator dream I see these Classical Myth elements:

The authority figure in charge of the "vessel" is the psychopomp, the guide of the souls who leads them across (the Styx, etc.) to the Other Side. Charon is very strict. The thread, which may be Arachne's or Ariadne's, must not be broken. If it is Ariadne's, then the trident is the sword she gave to Theseus along with the thread to guide him out of the Labyrinth; if he broke it, his life was over. (If the trident is that of Poseidon then it is evident where we are in the dream: I quote from *Gods and Heroes of the Greeks*, p. 12: ". . . they cast lots and Zeus got heaven, Poseidon the sea and Hades the underworld.") Both Poseidon and Hades appear then in the dream of the elevator, which is far down in the "lower floors, with darkness outside, as with the basement level," and the trident. I see three myths right there, with the trident sticking into the "strands which must not be broken," and then the guide who recites verse indicates that we are in the presence of prophecy, of an oracle. Also, the spaghetti tells us we're in that part of the world. Plus the olive-colored skin and eyes of the "cop."

I looked the citations up just now; and there is another thing which is startling, I mean beyond how many myth-sources unknown to me seem involved.

The morning after I had this dream I received a letter from my friend Philip Jose Farmer, in which he wrote:

> . . . You're among the most imaginative of men, Phil. Have you tried to use that imagination to figure a way out of the situation? . . . Think in other categories, as Ouspensky[14] said; use your unconventional mind as if it were the powerful tool which it indeed is. You're in the labyrinth, but your Ariadne's thread is your imagination.

I think I mentioned a more recent dream about double domed men with rather golden skin — huge egg-shaped craniums, very fierce and formidable and decisive, with an enormous yearbook type book "which you can't get right now because it's not available." Last night, with sudden fear, I broke through the memory block about that dream; in it one of those double domed golden skinned men opened a huge cyclops eye which at once, as with the cyclops sibyl, shoved his regular two eyes aside. He wasn't looking at me, thank god, but it so scared me that when I woke up I couldn't remember that. Last night when I did remember, the image from the dream was so vivid that I thought, I actually thought, that maybe I hadn't dreamed it, I had actually seen a cyclops such as this during the day, in reality. Only by a priori reasoning, that this was not possible, did I deduce it therefore had to have been in the dream.

In a frenzy of hysteria I told Tessa that I believed that these were not people I was seeing. Not people like us talking to me in my sleep and healing and educating me, but another race entirely (you know, like the saucer people talk about: "a superior race from Outer Space, Immortal and All-Knowing, Who Guide Us"). But then, as I relate in my other letter (there's always another letter) of this date I tell how last night I was disappointed to be shown that it's only Asklepios and friends, and they're all human. So acute terror gave way to keen disappointment.

I'm sure that Asklepios and friends are concerned that I not freak. This must be a perpetual risk in matters of this kind, where they surface and start curing and guiding and improving a person. The person, understandably, goes bananas and climbs the drapes, hiding up there with eyes bugged out like grapes. First of all it interferes with the therapy, but worse than that it defeats the entire purpose of it, which is to make the person balanced, sound and sane, rational and calm and in harmony and proportion within and with the outside world, so he can take anything. If he can't take the healing, then we have a sad irony; the therapy to make him sane causes him to go insane.

These last experiences at night, first the rhymed couplet about "you have to put your slippers on / To walk toward the Dawn," is a very complex but very effective way of reassuring me. The voice was quiet and somewhat motherly, and familiar. (In the dream I thought it was Olivia Newton-John, and who could be scared of her?) Also, my associations which have filtered through after absorbing the couplet are in a similar vein. "You have to put your slippers on" is what your mama says to you before you and the other little children sit down around her in a circle, at night before you go to bed, to hear the story she is going to tell you; it suggests safety and also the peace and quiet, the alpha state you get into, before she starts her soothing tale. And of course it's soothing, dummy, because you're going to bed and no mama would tell you anything scary before you went to bed. Another association that comes to me is that you, as that little child about to hear the soothing tale, put your slippers on — not to walk anywhere; slippers aren't for walking — but to keep your feet warm, which could be deciphered as, "You must not have cold feet," which again deciphered means, "Don't be scared; you must not be scared or you can't walk toward the Dawn," which itself is a metaphor for "moving toward enlightenment," quite evidently. It's a riddle. As kids would have no trouble interpreting; it's really very easy, for a riddle.

The Nice Lady: What's meant by (and she recites the couplet)?
Children (all together excitedly): I know! I know!
[The Nice Lady]: Sit around and be quiet and listen and you'll learn
    something!

I'm sure of this, Claudia. They, Asklepios and his gang, were aware I was getting freaked (I do a lot of that, but it's understandable, probably happens often) and set about calming me down. [. . .]

Yesterday I asked Tessa what she thought was going on. "They're disclosing the Mysteries to you," she said. "The Elysian Mysteries." Since the EMs were based on secret rituals to Demeter, then maybe Tessa is right. My sibyl is a chthonic deity: Demeter for instance.

Love,
Phil

[4:103] The Other is not any one thing found in any particular place. It is a quality of (or rather visible in) all things, like a specific color. It shines through them at us. We see it and it sees back, as in a dialog. If it can be seen at all it can be seen immediately, not merely in some exotic far off setting.

(1) The Other exists.
(2) We can experience it.
(3) It is found everywhere.
(4) Therefore since it exists, since we can experience it, and since it can be found everywhere, we can encounter it here. The opportunity exists now. Lem is wrong in all respects.

What is needed is a tremendous increase in our brain-efficiency. A vital improvement in set-group discrimination. Once we have done so and locked onto it we can probably continue to hold it in view. We're talking here about a two hemisphere perception of reality, and then an information transfer from one hemisphere to the other so that cognition, not just perception, is brain-total.* The morphology is already in place.

All encounters in the phenomenological world (in time and space) are exterior encounters, with constructs of our own mind—here and anywhere else we go. To experience truly, genuinely to encounter any other living entity in itself, one would have to be in it, and have it in one. This would be an interior experience; one would see nothing outside, no object, but suddenly one would experience all reality through the vision of the Other, as if seeing out through its eyes. One would share and inhabit its world, possess its perspective; at the same time the Other would possess what one had as a worldview. This might be close to a sort of energy symbiosis, an exchange of plasmas. One would not see the Other; one would see *as* the Other. Not possess it but possess its world. And this would not be so much an "I am in your world and you are in mine" but both would share a world made up from both previous separate worlds. A superimposition, greater than either had possessed: a total sharing within, and a to-

---

* Dick often writes as if he assumes that the left and right hemispheres of the brain do not normally communicate with one another. Perhaps this misperception grew out of Roger Sperry's work on split-brain perceptions in the late 1960s, one of a number of studies that inspired the popular discussion of the lateralization of brain function in books like Robert Ornstein's *The Psychology of Consciousness* (1972), which Dick was familiar with. However, Sperry's work was done with patients in whom the corpus callosum, the bundle of fibers connecting the two hemispheres, had been surgically severed as a treatment for otherwise incurable epilepsy. In normal brains, there is continuous communication across the hemispheres. Dick's belief that it may be possible to boost brain efficiency, although not technically correct with respect to the right and left hemispheres, is right on the mark with regard to reparative plasticity, in which neural circuits are repurposed to make up for deficiencies in normal brain function caused by an injury or trauma. Reparative plasticity may have been precisely at issue in his own brain function, if indeed he did suffer from TIAs and had his own neural circuitry rearranged as a result. —NKH

tal shared view of what lies outside. This sudden, double, superimposed, simultaneous view would be experienced as gaining an additional depth: as if adding one more spatial dimension. Much as a flatlander acquiring three-dimensional space. Time, too, would be experienced differently; one could see ahead, in all temporal directions. Two separate "mono" views when blended become a "stereo" view. Both entities, surprised by the heightened perception, would probably attribute it to the other's ability, not realizing he himself supplied half. "What a marvelous entity has taken me over," each would think, astonished. "Look at what he can see that I never could." Each would be awed by the other — i.e., the Other.

Plato once expressed an idea, probably metaphoric, that each of us is really only one half of a four legged four armed organism; somehow long ago we got split apart and we're always searching for our missing other half.* This usually is construed as a man searching for his female mate; however, suppose the Great Builder has fashioned us humans here, each of us, as one half of a total organism the other half of which is not a human being but something totally different — maybe with no physical body at all, but a sort of energy plasma which fits over or is "poured into" each of us, as the Parakletos is said to be. This might indicate that our total life on earth is only the first part, the part before each of us and his Other are joined. Possibly many if not most of us die before being joined; maybe we never are, or we are joined after death. Meanwhile, off somewhere in another star system the Great Builder has fashioned the other parts of us, and soon we will be stimulated by Him to take off into space and head via rocket ship for that star, not knowing what lies ahead but prompted by a vast and authentic instinct that we should do it. Imagine our surprise — and then delight — when we get there and are suddenly joined, in the twinkling of an eye, with our other half — the Other.

On their own planet, the race of Others might have had even less total vision of their purpose in the universe than we have; however, it is pos-

---

* The reference here is to Aristophanes' speech in Plato's *Symposium*, where the playwright explains the origin of love (*eros*) with the myth that the first human beings were akin to conjoined twins of opposite sex — bound face to face, hands to hands, feet to feet — who became separated; the fire of desire flows from the attempt to retrieve our lost unity. Here as elsewhere, the Exegesis can be seen as a long tug-of-war with Plato. There are constant references to Plato's theory of *anamnesis* or recollection, which is the remembrance of the forms — the pure core of reality perceived within the soul through the activity of intellection or nous — that were allegedly forgotten due to the painful trauma of our birth. Dick also refers to Plato's analogy of the cave from *Republic,* and to the true universe as idea or form (*eidos*), of which phenomenal reality is a mirror, or scanner, through which we see darkly. Later in the Exegesis, Dick also finds reason to harshly reject Plato, who, he will declare, is "180 degrees wrong." — SC

sible that their guesses and intimations might be ahead of our own. In this case they might be waiting for us to arrive, or even made certain attempts to contact us — with or without success. At the ultimate, they might even have managed in small preliminary ways to reach across space to us somehow, to coax us subtly into moving toward them. A few of them — a small part of their total energy — might have arrived here already, even long ago, and touched a few of us, bringing those few into the total entity the Builder was preparing. That entity would, in our words, be a man and also a spirit — touched by the Holy Spirit or born a second time, whatever: born of water and spirit, perhaps.[15] And, being all this, he would have a lot to tell us.

We are going to link up.

In all this, we would become aware of (1) those creatures toward which we moved with whom we were to link up; and (2) the Great Builder Himself moving all things. Regarding the first, we would have a natural instinctive tendency to venerate them as godlike, but in fact on their own, without us, they are probably no more and no less than we. It is the fusion which is superior. Their proper attitude toward us might well be the same veneration as ours toward them. What is truly to be venerated and revered is the Builder Himself and His Plan which caused both our species to come into being and then move toward each other to join. True worship should go to Him alone. We would experience him as the powerful, gentle will within us, prompting us to move toward our other halves. They are, like us, created; He is self-creating always.

It's interesting that Jesus spoke of being born again as being "born of water and spirit," which is from two sources; two coming together, in contrast to being "born from the womb," one source, one element. He was indicating a fusion. Water, perhaps, indicated our own part, with the Other, the spirit, coming down from above.

Certainly Jesus was speaking about a totally different kind of birth just in that respect alone; two elements joined together and became one entity. Another difference between the first birth and the second is crucial: we do not decide to be born in the first place; it happens to us, but the second birth (born again) requires a decision. This means that it does not occur naturally or spontaneously and in fact may not occur at all. It must be accomplished — done by us, or anyhow sought for. Somehow the spirit must be enticed or welcomed or attracted. Water — our part of the two agents necessary — we obtain in the sacrament of baptism, but we can't perform the other part: obtaining the spirit. We must wait for it to arrive, having done our part, the water part. Evidently for some reason the spirit can't come to us unless the water — baptism — is there; baptism must change us in a way we can't see, perhaps making us a conductor, grounded, and hence able to attract an electrical-like field from the heavens (sky). For all we know, the spirit is up there perpetually, awaiting only the crucial change (water) below to come down and enter.

Like Beethoven, the Creator is a joiner; not of organizations but of sections assembled separately in different places and then somehow brought together; the places are our category "space," then, when brought together, "time."

If the Other is not bound by the categories of perception time and space, then he is here now, was here, will be, and since not phenomenalistically, then he is not outside but within us. Like Plotinus' concept of concentric rings of emanation, we encounter our Others in gradually increasing intensity and clarity; they become clearer to us continually. It is as if the will which drives animals and bugs, in the form of blind instinct, begins one day in us to actually speak. This is the Logos perhaps.

Letter to Ursula Le Guin, September 23, 1974*

[4:106]

Dear Ursula,

I just sent you a big manila envelope of material but I wanted to say this, that the 14-page piece is all true, it really did happen to me, and it is strange and I can't fully explain it — which is to say, name who what poured itself into me back in March and is still there, still here, I mean. Still in a symbiotic relationship with me.

Tom Disch came back a couple of weeks ago and I told him about it. He suggested perhaps it was Elijah who had possessed me, and so I read up on Elijah; that explanation fits as well as any other, and so I ran with that until last night when, in falling asleep, I thought the words "poros" and "krater," and then looked them up today and sure enough once more, they are Greek words, and words which I certainly didn't know.

I doubt if Elijah would be ruminating in Greek, but he probably reap-

---

* Ursula Le Guin (1929–) is an SF and fantasy writer from Berkeley. Though she and Dick were nearly the same age and attended the same high school, the two never met, but they did correspond as friends and colleagues throughout the 1970s. In February 1981, Le Guin gave a lecture at Emory University attended by author and critic Michael Bishop. Le Guin made some disparaging comments about Dick's later work, specifically the treatment of women in *VALIS* (1981). Le Guin wondered aloud if Dick was "slowly going crazy in Santa Ana, California." When Bishop passed Le Guin's remarks on to Dick in a letter, Dick responded publicly, writing an angry letter to *Science Fiction Review.* Le Guin apologized but had clearly hit a nerve. Dick took Le Guin's criticisms seriously, and in many ways Dick's final novel, *The Transmigration of Timothy Archer* (1982), with its deep, intelligent, and charming female first-person narrator, Angel Archer, was written in response. — DG

peared (after two parts of his spirit returned to Elisha) as John the Baptist and then other Essenes; it is probably all one spirit which can divide itself in any fashion it wants (like the Advocate which Christ says He will have God send after He, Christ, is gone). All these are one; this is a mystery, but to me very exciting.

The spirit which filled me starting in March was primarily rooted in these realities: justice, truth and freedom. His pursuit of the first and his devotion to the second is what made Tom Disch think of Elijah, I think. The spirit when he arrived here looked around, saw Richard Nixon and those creatures, and was so wrath-filled that he never stopped writing letters to Washington until Nixon was out.* He wrote again and again to Charles Wiggins, for instance — especially him, with an enormous intensity. Congressman Wiggins wrote back a long detailed answer to each letter; the spirit even wrote to the *Wall Street Journal* (a letter which they printed) informing them that Nixon's transcripts were self-serving and full of lies, and time would reveal this . . . as it certainly did. This spirit, very Elijah-like but also as Christ spoke of the Advocate being, confuted the lies of the world with enormous insight into them; he used legal terms I don't generally use. You wouldn't believe his animosity toward the tyrannies both here and in the USSR; he saw them as twin horns of the same evil entity — one vast worldwide state whose basic nature was clear to him as being one of slavery, a continuation of Rome itself. And he was a foe to that, above all; he saw Caesar once more, and himself pitted against that. [. . .]

What perhaps is involved here is time travel. The ability by someone, or several someones, far back in the past (circa 600 B.C.) to travel forward through to our period, by large leaps, surfacing in one or more of us. . . . In February I had major oral surgery, and was home recovering, still under the influence of the sodium pentothal, and in severe pain. Tessa phoned the oral surgeon and he phoned a pharmacy to send out a pain killer. The doorbell rang and I went, and there stood this girl with black, black hair and large eyes very lovely and intense; I stood staring at her, amazed, also confused, thinking I'd never seen such a beautiful girl, and why was she standing there? She handed me the package of medication, and I tried to

---

* "Since I last wrote you, the magnitude of the despotic gang of professional, organized criminals who came to power legally (as did Hitler in Germany) is increasingly revealed to the U.S. public. We Americans are now faced with precisely the situation the German people of the 1930s faced: we elected a criminal government to 'save us from Communism,' and are stuck. . . . This brings up the question of the proper moral response and attitude of the U.S. citizen who did not know this" (from Dick's September 1973 public letter to an Australian fanzine). These musings continue in an unabatedly secular vein and reveal, just scant months before 2-3-74, how Dick already describes Watergate in terms of an epochal breach, yet interpreted here purely in twentieth-century political terms. — JL

think what to say to her; I noticed then, a fascinating gold necklace around her neck and I said, "What is that? It certainly is beautiful," just, you see, to find something to say to hold her there. The girl indicated the major figure in it, which was a fish. "This is a sign used by the early Christians," she said, and then departed. Soon thereafter the dazzling shower of colored graphics descended over me in the night, and you know the rest. During the first weeks while the spirit was within me in full force I saw, among all the other insights I developed, that there are external signals which act on us as disinhibiting stimuli, which cause a vast drop in GABA fluid in the brain, releasing (intentionally, as with the little creatures) major engramming. Evidently this is what the fish sign did to me. In fact I read in one article on brain function that when inhibiting GABA fluid drops quite a bit — which is when an external signal causes major disinhibition to take place — the person experiences "abstracts much like the modern painters have reproduced," and this does fit my experience.

I felt, during those initial days, a clear and real sense of being in the hands of programming or engramming, from a very early period in my life, probably within the first four years of it; I was quite frightened, being unable to grasp what this indicated in terms of what it might cause me to do. However, it swiftly informed me via written material presented in dream after dream of the benign and reassuring quality of this Other which I had encountered deep within me — an Other which had been slumbering, inhibited by the GABA fluid until the proper signal released it to assume parity with me.

Now we function smoothly in synchronization, but at first I had to yield to it; rapidly it handled my problems in ways I never would have thought of. Resourceful and wise — and concerned always with the general good, not mine alone. Looking always clearly at the future.

Love,

Phil

Letter to Claudia Bush, November 26, 1974

[4:108]

Dear Claudia,

The other day I lay down and at once saw a hypnagogic vision of a great tall man with white thatched hair; he stood smiling, holding an enormous book. He wore white shining robes and sandals. At the same time a fragment of Greek flitted through my mind. At once I woke up and had Tessa research the Greek. This time it was for sure from the Pauline Texts; with her various reference books she was able to establish that it was from Hebrews 7:26,[16] that that particular sequence of words appears nowhere else

in the New Testament. What is interesting is that I had just been reading a book of excerpts of Jung in which he discussed — at the part I'd been
reading — a passage from Hebrews 7:17,[17] just a few lines previous. I've
never read Hebrews and certainly not in Greek. After reading the Jung I
fell asleep and saw the person described in that section of Hebrews: an ancient Hebrew priest considered by the Christian theologians to have been
a Logos incarnation prefiguring that of Christ. I've believed for some time
that the snatches of Greek I hear at night are from the Pauline Texts, but
couldn't prove it before.

This is all a feedback system, where I'm given information I couldn't
possibly have on my own; best of all is like this when he or they can *complete a sequence,* especially in the original tongue. I read in Jung a quote
from Hebrews 7:17; ten minutes later I dream from Hebrews 7:26 in Paul's
own Greek. If you study theories of information transfer and communication, especially between different cultures (as for example in our attempts
to get in touch with extraterrestrial entities, the CETI program, etc.) this
is what would be theoretically striven for; this is ideal. We start a logical or
math sequence and they complete it and return to us the missing integers.
You can see that this is precisely what has been happening in my head.
That I am in direct mind-to-mind touch with extraterrestrial intelligence
systems has been obvious to me for some time, but what this means is not
in any way obvious.

By the way — I've now found the section in Virgil's *Aeneid* which so
many of my early "dreams" pointed to: it is Book Six. Also I've found that a
number of my dreams are visions of Canto XXVIII of Dante's "Purgatorio"
from the *Comedy.* This is linked directly to Virgil, of course, who has been
Dante's guide up to this Canto. I learn much from all this, much which is
specific (you would not believe the research I've been doing).

It's not all that meaningful to talk about being in contact with extraterrestrial intelligences; these are new words to describe ancient experiences.
Virgil in Book Six says:

> . . . *for immanent Mind, flowing through all its parts*
> *and leaving its mass,*
> *Makes the universe work.*

Obviously "Immanent Mind" could be called "extraterrestrial intelligence."* So there is nothing new in what I've experienced, just new terms.

---

* The term "immanent mind" recurs throughout these pages. Immanence can be understood as experiential and manifest as opposed to transcendental. Dick here identifies immanent mind with the extraterrestrial intelligence we can intuit in an experience of *gnosis;*
elsewhere immanence is linked to Spinoza's idea of a God identified with and wholly inter-

Basically this is a religious experience, but also it is more because we are no longer a religious world; I am a secular person in a secular society and must understand my experiences in this context. Otherwise even if I understand them I can't communicate them.

Well, Claudia, I will tell you what I think They are telling me via graphic visions and written and audio material. Enclosed you will find three pages I already wrote (I hope I didn't send them to you already), but recently I came across this "Fourth Eclogue" of Virgil:

> Now comes the final age announced in the Cumaean Sibyl's chant;
> The great succession of epochs is born anew.
> Now the Virgin⊕ returns; the reign of Saturn returns;
> Now a new race descends from heaven on high.
> O chaste Lucina (goddess of births)! smile upon the boy just born.
> In whose time the race of iron shall first cease,
> And a race of gold shall arrive throughout the world.
> Thine own Apollo is now King.

When I was possessed back in March it was justice which I first sought out everywhere, which was most important to me. I think that the Cumaean sibyl's prophecy has not been fulfilled. (Virgil's Eclogue is based on an actual prophesy which she made slightly before the Christian Era.) My "dreams" have led me to this Eclogue intentionally; the information is here. When you read the enclosed three pages you will see how close to realizing this I already was (I wrote them about 45 days or more ago). I believe that after an absence of between 2,000 and 2,600 years the immortals are now beginning to return, with Justice first.

The actual esoteric purpose of early Christianity was for the worshippers to be possessed by their god, as with other mystery cults and religions.* That which possessed them then in the First Century A.D. pos-

---

nal to nature. There is a tension throughout the Exegesis between this *monistic* view of the cosmos (which also appears in Dick's references to Hegel's dialectic and Whitehead's idea of reality as process) and a *dualistic* or gnostic view of the cosmos, with two cosmic forces in conflict. In his monist mood, Dick argues that the universe is a single living organism or God; at other times, Dick seems to tend toward a Platonic or Neoplatonic theory of emanation of the divine reality into the world. But again, this is in constant tension with a tendency toward dualism, which holds that the phenomenal world is a prison governed by corporations, archons, or malevolent political forces. The way I read Dick, this latter view wins out. — SC

* In this and the following letters, Dick explores Christianity as an ancient mystery cult. The various mysteries of the Greco-Roman period were characterized by secret and mystical rituals in which initiates sacramentally relived their god's experiences, which often involved death and rebirth. The central rites of the early Christian church bear much sim-

sessed me back in March, but I identify Him more as Apollo than as the Holy Spirit described by Paul. I think He appears to different cultures under different names; to the Greeks one, to the Hebrews as Elijah, and so forth. He is plasmatic, immortal, and the great civilizing influence of Greece and Egypt and Persia. He can divide himself, being plasmatic. To me he brought reason, so I see him as Apollo . . . but interestingly, this fits what the Sibyl predicted. It is a Greek god-possession experience I went through, not Jewish. Assuming that what Virgil calls Immanent Mind transcends each individual possession, then there is no problem in drawing them all together into an integration. These are specific agencies of an overall sentient, living entity.

By the way—in Book Six of the *Aeneid,* the Sibyl is possessed by the god, by Apollo. Paul Williams* when he was here showed me a passage from one of Ted Sturgeon's novels which Paul felt showed that my experience had been precisely that of the early Christians. I do feel that it was under the aspect of Apollo, however, because my needs were for that, for syntonos and reason.

This happened not because of my needs — we all have needs — but because they are coming back. The Immortals. Here is a quote from Paul Williams' book *Turning Upward* which I just came across (p. 237):

> Men are coming, great men who are among us now, who will unite the extremes into an unshakeable structure, unshakeable not because of its suppression of the will of the people, but because of its perfect expression of that will. And from the present bewilderment, anger and chaos a true will must arise to replace that shadow of will,

---

ilarity to these rituals, particularly baptism, the *agape* or love feast, and the Eucharist. Indeed, in the Eastern Orthodox Church the sacraments are still referred to as "mysteries." What separated the early church from the mysteries — and what led to its persecution — was its exclusivity: unlike followers of most other mysteries, the Christian faithful refused to participate in the imperial state religion. — GM

* Cultural critic, rock-and-roll journalist, and founder of *Crawdaddy* magazine, Paul Williams (1948–) is a singularly important figure in the second half of Dick's life. Besides giving a copy of Dick's *The Three Stigmata of Palmer Eldritch* to both John Lennon and psychedelic guru Timothy Leary, Williams wrote the profile "The Most Brilliant Sci-Fi Mind on Any Planet: Philip K. Dick," which ran in the November 6, 1975, issue of *Rolling Stone.* The piece, which focuses on Dick's various theories regarding the 1971 break-in and makes no mention of the 2-3-74 events, introduced Dick to his widest counterculture audience yet. The two became good friends, and Williams managed to get one of Dick's earlier (and best) mainstream fiction books, *Confessions of a Crap Artist,* published in 1975, an accomplishment for which Dick was eternally grateful. Upon Dick's death, Williams was made literary executor of Dick's estate. — DG

that vacant greed which is now called the will of the people by the clumsy dwarves who stumble where graceful giants ought to stride.

You should read Paul's whole section in this book. I think it is all true, the above.

I get very frustrated writing to you about this because I have so much to say and can't spit it out. Papers slide off my desk; books I'm quoting from fall shut; I type wrong letters entirely. I am so fucking excited, keyed up, high on all this, and terribly impatient, which is not cool — impatient to find people to tell this to, the Good News, so to speak. Claudia, an ancient promise made to us, made thousands of years ago, is *now being kept.* Who made it I don't know, but it was made. He or they would come back eventually, and they fucking have, Claudia, they fucking have!!! I know it. Again and again in unmistakable ways they have assured me of this, and have in addition shown me glimpses of what we can expect. That which is rightfully ours, which was taken away, will be returned. They will see to that. As Paul called it, the "Time of Restoration of All Things"[18] — it is here now, Claudia. It took a hell of a long time, by our standards, but they did keep their ancient promise; they are back.

The Christians, with their exclusivistic, bigoted, narrow intolerance, believe salvation and intervention and restoration is only for them; they're wrong; this is for our planet and all its people. There are saviors for all of us, everyone here. To the Immortals such distinctions as Christian versus atheist mean nothing; it is like Holstein cows versus Jerseys, and my spelling and typing are so shot now that I will sign off.

Next year in a book of Harlan Ellison's that Harper and Row are bringing out, Harlan says:

Kurt Weill and Maxwell Anderson wrote, "Maybe God's gone away, forgetting His promise He made that day: and we're lost out here in the stars." And maybe He/She's just waiting for the right signal to come back, whaddaya think?[19]

Right on, Harlan.

In March I abruptly pierced through to the heart of things; I saw within, saw reality as it is, and saw the Immortals approaching. I saw the iron prison we live in, and I experienced first them and then vision after vision of what our world, our lives will be like when they join up the two parts: universe A and universe B. Ours is one part, and with them they tow the other. What they will do with our world, the macrocosmos, will be an analog of what they did with me and other isolated individuals or microcosms: in a flash they ignite and fuse everything and then imprint an entirely new eidos. It all happens without warning. In micro terms I experienced the entire trip which our world and all of us will experience: months of hunger and want, then growing fear and helplessness, then a renunciation of everything, knowing it to be lost forever — then the manifestation of the dazzling chromatic forms. From want and no hope and fear and a total giving up at once there will be a total rebirth, a restitution and a renaissance; life will start up anew, without warning.

In the visions of every Pythagorean in history (Euripides in *The Bacchae,* in Wordsworth's "ode," etc.) I discover the same visions that I have seen: what in Dante is called Earthly Paradise. (He is led to it and finds the lady singing and picking flowers; in dream after dream I've seen her and heard her singing; now I know who she is, and I know what the beautiful park which I see is. It is going to be here and not in the next world; it's what Dante himself saw and depicted too clearly, and his vision is amazingly similar to that of the 6th century B.C. Greek Orphics.)

Well, I got to sign off because we have to replace all the cat boxes in the house now; the cats are grumbling, and when Chester grumbles, we all move into action.

Love,
Phil

① Astraea, or Justice, the last immortal to leave the Earth in the legend of the Saturnian age.

Letter to Claudia Bush, November 29, 1974

[4:112]

Dear Claudia,

Can I rattle on some more at you? Especially since the big blue cat we got ran away as soon as we let him out? Thank you.

I hope you had a nice Complaingiving.

Jean-Pierre who bought the *Ubik* screenplay hasn't contacted me since October.[20] Next Monday (on which day you'll probably receive this) he owes me $2,500, which he didn't have on November first, so we gave him another 30 days. I'll bet he's in Paris right now. I'm sure I already told you that Robert Jaffe suggested that maybe the *Ubik* purchase was laundered Soviet money, and the screenplay right now is in Krakow, Poland. Could be. I still maintain that there is some scientific principle in *Ubik* which I thought was fiction, but which is either a new discovery or more likely a rediscovery of one discarded long ago — *Ubik,* the force, itself. Ubik would roughly correspond to the universal immanent mind which Virgil mentions. Not only does it animate the universe and cause it to work, but since each of us is a piece of the universe (more properly the kosmos, as Pythagoras called it) each of us has inside him a spark of that universal mind. The Orphics in Greece were the first known group to express this idea, and the entire collection of mystery cults was seeking to find ways of bringing out or anyhow contracting that spark of divinity within. The God Apollo and such like would be links between the universal mind within and that in the kosmos around us; he would, so to speak, serve to ignite that spark within so that it fused or took over the total mind; this would be what possession by the god would more precisely be.

These categories obviously correspond to the three persons of the Trinity. Historically, god-above-the-universe is encountered first (the Umwelt of the European Existential psychiatrists), then god-with-us as a human (the Mitwelt, which for us would be the second period of man-god encounter: the encounter with Christ), then the third and final: God within, the Holy Spirit (the Eigenwelt). At the same time, as Jung points out, man is withdrawing his projections from the outer world. So these three steps are not only present historically but are psychologically logical and successive. We can no longer expect to encounter the divine — which is to say, the universal immanent mind — anywhere but within ourself although in a sense it is true that the prior two persons or forms of god still remain; nonetheless it is inside that we will find him, which is to say, as close to us as he could possibly get. I do think that the igniting of this spark so as to consume and so-to-speak overpower our own ego or consciousness is achieved from without somehow; it is an adventitious process, which means, it is not an intrinsic addition. It does not merely happen on its own, spontaneously, although everything is within us, except for the catalyst, which may be nothing more than an external disinhibiting stimulus. In my case I saw the dark-haired girl wearing the fish sign necklace in March of this year, and it acted as that catalyst.

The three persons or forms of god inhabit the three worlds which each of us experiences; they interact and harmonize. By doing this they keep in accord — keep together — the cosmos — all sets of reality. This process of harmonization is extraordinary; in the short interval I perceived it I was astounded. That's the period in which I saw, as you'll recall, that there are no accidents.

The mystery cults kept their purpose and techniques secret until Jesus so-to-speak stole it and made it available for everyone — same as what's his name did with fire. And paid the ultimate price. However, as Jesus remarked, "I have conquered the world,"[21] meaning that he was successful; what was until then available only to a few life-long esoteric students of the cults we can all have. We didn't even know about it until then; Paul is not being vague in his speech when he says, "Hark! I tell you a sacred secret: we shall not all sleep in death," etc.[22] He means it literally; he told them all what up to then was indeed a sacred secret, guarded by the mystery cults, the secret that (1) you can be reborn (which is not the same as being immortal; it means you must die as you are and then after that you are again alive, but different and permanent), and (2) how this can be achieved, or more precisely, how it was achieved. No more valuable secret was even stolen and released to the general public than that. I wouldn't presume to try to add to or modify Paul's own explanation of all of this, or John's, but let me say that what happened to me in March is exactly that "in the twinkling of an eye"[23] rebirth or transformation, much like an abrupt chemical process . . . as the alchemists so realized. But it must as I say be touched of adventitiously — which is the role Christ plays or did play, his work being already done. He set it in motion. It can't be turned back. He died, but he died knowing he did it. And of course he shared — he was the first to share — in the fruits of his own secret. He did add, though, that most of us would laugh at all this, finding it incredible and impossible and senseless, not to mention stupid. It never meant anything to me until March, and in March when it happened to me I couldn't relate what had happened to anything I'd ever been taught about God or religion. I thought god was up there in the sky. However, he is not; he is a spark which can fuse the total mind in each of us into something entirely new which was not there before (a description of irreversible chemical processes), burning off the dross and making stable (or as the Bible says, uncorruptible) the valuable contents. You can readily see the analogy between this and a chemical reaction in which the results are spectacular, as with ignited gunpowder. There is no way to anticipate the results based on a study of the three prior constituents, and if I told you what would happen unless you had seen it you probably wouldn't believe me. Fire is the adventitious element added; in the case of the transformation I went through, it is also a kind of fire: seen as chromatic phosphene activity. Probably this is radiation phosphene stimulation; the Soviets say that such radiation stimulating phosphene activity can come here — and does — from sidereal space. I believe it. This is the catalyst.

The valuable aspect of the external catalyst is that it keeps the process within the control of who it is who controls these things; it isn't going to simply occur at a random time for no reason at all. The universal mind dispatches a Mediator — which is what Christ is called, correctly — to trigger it off; or anyhow the fish sign or any Logos triggering agent. Thereby it, the universal mind, can hold the process until it wishes it to take place, which is why the Protestant Reformers stressed the power of God's grace as being the sole power which could redeem us rather than good works. The act must be done by God alone, not by us. These are old-fashioned terms for a very mysterious process and event; they did the best they could in explaining it. "Well, see, we're all in a state of sin" (which is jargon for fucked up, deranged, and half blind), "and God's grace redeems us unexpectedly. But we have to have faith, which is to say total trust, in the power of that grace." I'm not sure you have to have that trust. I think what you have to come to is the last few frames of the long reel of film which was your first-born ego or personality or consciousness, which is what I did. Rationally, at least according to the impaired rationality we have, it would seem evident that when the final frame is gone, only the void would remain; however, the void is I guess God Himself, the Brahmin; He fills it up. We have an incorrect idea of the nature of the void, and an equally incorrect one as to the nature of objects — which are only phenomena, constructs our brain makes out of sense impressions. "Literally, God is not," Erigina said.[24]

Claudia, on this day we must count our cursings.

Psychologically, this mental transformation is the radical combining (not reconciliation but combining) of opposites. From then on everything is understood in terms not of "Is it this *or* that — " but "Both this *and* that." Each attempt I make to understand and explain and express my experience and the process following has to come at last to that: it is what I already thought *and* what I now think. For instance, it is Elijah and the Holy Spirit, not Elijah rather than the Holy Spirit. It is Apollo and the Holy Spirit; it is Pagan and Christian. It is old (circa 100 A.D.) and points toward the future. It is a literal event in the material world and it is symbolism (I mean my dreams or visions); it will be the future here; it will also be the Other World when I see it. It involves me alone, and it is for the entire world. Lastly, it is beings from another star system *and* it is precisely the same traditional experience of salvation described in the Bible.

You find this same unity in Dante's *Comedy*. This is what our modern world has lost, this unity in all levels; now we've got compartmentalization instead. A thing is either scientifically true or it is religious. It is metaphor rather than literal.

So to sum up, there is a small bit of the macrocosm inside us, inside the microcosm; and this small bit equals the whole universal mind. The microcosm contains the macrocosm, another concept not thinkable in formal logic. God within me sees God outside; the two commune with each other. The two link up through the mediating flesh or body. So he or it, whatever, is made visible here on this world, at this time. Meanwhile, Satan is up at the McDonald's stand, ordering coweye burgers and plastic malts, thinking to keep his power. A few more years of coweye burgers and plastic malts, and he'll have had it.

Letter to Claudia Bush, November 30, 1974

[4:118]

Dear Claudia,

I just wrote Diane Pike; we'll see what happens. I'd already written her and got back a Love Project card. I will keep you informed; she sounds trippy and sweet.

Love works! Always! That's what the card says. I can dig it. Can't you? Where do we begin? (The La Paz bar.)

Claudia, this is an addendum to my previous letter of Friday. John Calvin (1509–1564) gives this statement which beyond all doubt describes my experience and my thoughts about it afterward:

> . . . The natural talents in man have been corrupted by sin, but of the supernatural ones he has been wholly deprived. . . . Therefore, when he revolted from the divine government, he was at the same time deprived of those supernatural endowments which had been given him for the hope of eternal salvation. Hence it follows, that he is exiled from the Kingdom of God, in such a manner that all the affections relating to the happy life of the soul are also extinguished in him, till he recovers them by the grace of regeneration. . . . All these things, being restored by Christ, are esteemed adventitious and preternatural; and therefore we conclude *that they had been lost* (Ital. mine). Again: soundness of mind and rectitude of heart were also destroyed; and this is the corruption of the natural talents. For although we retain some portion of understanding and judgment together with the will, yet we cannot say that our mind is perfect and sound. . . . Being a natural talent, it could not be totally destroyed, but is partly debilitated. . . .*

Also, I read something fascinating in the *Monitor* yesterday, an article about Lewis Mumford.[25] (How can a man with no college degrees be all bad?) Mumford says:

> I think this must be very much like what happened during the transition from the Roman civilization, which was highly organized and bent on the same ends as our civilization, power, productivity, prestige, to the Christian era. The Christians formed in little bands. They

---

* This passage comes from book 2, chapter 2 of Calvin's *Institutes of the Christian Religion,* quoted here in John Allen's translation. The idea that prelapsarian human beings had extraordinary abilities is not unique to Calvin — indeed, the text quoted here is preceded in the original by an attribution of the idea to Augustine. Dick latched onto Calvin as the idea's primary proponent, both here and elsewhere in the Exegesis, and his name becomes shorthand for the concept of preternatural abilities. — GM

began to withdraw from society and accepted the poverty which only slaves then were forced to accept. They built up a spiritual foundation for their life which gave them the internal energy firmly to take over the Roman Empire.

If you remember my mentioning it, Claudia, when this first hit me in March I looked around and saw *Rome! Rome everywhere!* Power and force, stone walls, iron bars—just what Mumford expresses above. That I saw this in an instant ("in the twinkling of an eye") is and was not of my doing; it didn't come out of my mind, my mental processes; it wasn't a concept or even an awareness internally: I perceived it. I saw it. I pierced the veil, so to speak, and saw my society exactly as it is . . . which is, as Mumford expresses, like Rome was. What puzzled me was, since I knew intellectually that Rome was a city in Italy and an empire and republic back before Christ, then where was I, in Fullerton or back there, now or back then? Again, the [question is "is] it this or is it that," and the answer is, "it is both." In Mumford's sense, "Rome" is a paradigm. I was so to speak taken up on the mountain, a metaphor in itself, and shown. "See?" the Spirit said. "What do you see all around you? You see Rome."

I was amazed, troubled, and fucked up. It was a dreadful sight: a slave state, like Gulag.

There is no doubt in my mind now that my "vision" of my society was accurate in the sense that Mumford means it; I hadn't gone back in time, but in a sense Rome had come forward, by insidious and sly degrees, under new names, hidden by the flak talk and phony obscurations, at last into our world again. Look! The Christians conquered Rome, but only for a time; Rome swallowed up its conquerors, like China does. At last Rome began by stealthy degrees to surface once more, to manifest itself. Therefore it is not surprising that that same Holy Spirit which rose against it then, in 100 or so A.D., has returned to arouse us as before, as it roused our ancestors, metaphorically speaking. It is the trumpet call to fight once more for freedom.* Like Mumford says.

---

* In many of Dick's stories, collectors build encapsulated re-creations of places that once held special meaning for them. In *Now Wait for Last Year* (1966), Virgil Ackerman re-creates the city of his childhood, Wash-35 (Dick lived in Washington, D.C., in 1935). For Dick, these nostalgic places serve as staging grounds for a ceaseless replay of events, "lovingly composed," in the words of critic Fredric Jameson, "for a human activity which has disappeared." In his descriptions of ancient Rome superimposed on Orange County, Dick may also have created a past space of redemptive activity, running parallel to, but separate from, our fallen world. While the Empire and the Black Iron Prison are present in this space too, the underground Christian resistance is dedicated in their opposition. God seems closer in that world than he does in this one. Dick sometimes describes Rome, as

Well, I got to go because a lot of publicans and sinners, tax collectors and other riffraff abound, and I must deal with them.

Love,

Phil

/

P.S. I tell you, Claudia, Calvin is right; we're (1) missing entirely certain faculties and (2) what we have, the remaining ones, are very much hazed over. When I saw correctly in March it's like when you get a new pair of glasses and can read everything, see everything. Really, his distinction is meaningful between the natural faculties such as reason which are fucked up, and the other ones which we can't even catch a glimpse of until they return. The only thing is, how come this happened? How did we (1) lose certain faculties entirely? and (2) have the remaining ones occluded as they are, for all of us, unless somehow, as in a miracle of healing, they're restored? Surely there must be a scientific explanation for this, having to do with brain function and dormant sections, inhibited firing of whole neural circuits* . . . and this is precisely what I was trying to achieve back in March, to get neural firing roused, to cause circuits to fire which had never fired. What I think now, with Calvin, is that one time (our childhood? thousands of years ago) they did fire or anyhow were intended to fire, to be firing all this time. But something went wrong. Something dreadful.

At the very least they can be somehow made to fire, finally, whether they ever fired before or not. The next step in human evolution or a lost section of our brains . . . either way the results are outta sight.

[4:131] A human being is a material system which time, a form of energy, enters. Probably time enters him also as noös — Mind.

Time, the future, contains in it all the events which are going to oc-

---

he does here, as sinister, dangerous, and overrun with spies. But in Dick's vision, ancient Rome transcends the petty concerns that addle the plastic-fantastic fakeness of Orange County in the 1970s, and in this way it can be read as a kind of sacred urban fantasy that replaces a vapid reality. — DG

* Dick speaks often, as here, of his 2-3-74 experience as a kind of healing, specifically a healing of neural circuits. Contemporary neural science is providing the "scientific explanation" for what Dick sensed intuitively. Recent work in neuroscience has found that the brain is much more plastic than previously supposed, a fact that Oliver Sacks demonstrates throughout *The Man Who Mistook His Wife for a Hat* and other accounts of patients who have suffered brain injury or trauma. In his recent work, neuroscientist Antonio Damasio calls the narrating voice of consciousness the "autobiographical self." How the narrating self relates to the neuronal circuits of the brain is not well understood, but neural circuits can restructure and repurpose themselves when normal brain function is disrupted. — NKH

cur. Therefore when time enters a person as energy, and acting as noös to him, it brings with it in potentium all that will happen to him, like a window shade unrolling to display an unfolding pattern. Events in the future pop into being, into actualization, the present, but until they do, they are not truly real—not yet actualized—but there in an encoded form, like the grooves of an LP before the needle reaches it; the only "music" is where the needle touches—ahead lies only an encoded wiggle along a helical spiral. Thus, dreams deal with the future lying direct ahead, as during the night, the next series of encoded future events begin to move toward actualization: i.e., the present. What is hard to realize is that in a certain very real way these events are inside the person, within his head, so to speak; but only in their potential, encoded form; the arena in which they are actualized is that of space; time, in the present, flows out to fill space—i.e., the spatial universe.

This is why we experience déjà vu. We have somehow caught a glimpse now and then of the script unrolling in our head—caught a glimpse in advance, so we feel "I know exactly what I'm going to say next, and what gestures he'll make," etc. Sure; they're encoded—encased, waiting—in time, and time, being energy, has entered you; is burning bright inside, like Blake's tyger.

> *Tyger, tyger, burning bright*
> *In the forests of the night.*
> *... Who framed thy awful symmetry?*

Or however.

[4:132] The right hemisphere is the seat of the unconscious.

But every layer in it, and all its contents, were at one time part of consciousness, though not of any living men.

These are all the prior left-hemisphere consciousnesses, down through the ages; when they perished, they reappeared in this dormant, sleeping form, not dead, not gone, but not awake: just slumbering, with all their memories and thoughts and experiences and ideas now in dream form.

This is where the dead went. This is where the dead are.

Also, this is the leavening in the bread which Christ spoke of. And the tiny mustard seed, growing and growing.[26]

Within the right hemisphere (we all share just one among us, like a communal meal—e.g., the Last Supper) this life is rising once more toward the consciousness it lost.

But when it achieves it again, it will be a transformed life, not the perishable one it had.

Being in all of us, and alive and conscious again (it is alive again, but not conscious; it has forgotten), it can't die. It will not be bound by time or space. It can return to the past, go wherever men are or ever have been or ever will be.

The experience of anamnesis is the moment when this sleeping mind which once was conscious, remembers its own existence. Who it is remembering is itself; what it is remembering is that it lived and lives now, and has a job to do. Also, it is not a separate entity as the left hemisphere is. Together, they form two appositional minds, linked through it with all the others on Earth and perhaps beyond.*

It did not die; it fell asleep, for two thousand years, acquiring with the death of each new person a new onion-skin like layer of itself; by these slow accretions it grew — toward completeness and reawakening, and remembering.

The moment at which it remembers (is disinhibited by the gold fish sign, the letter, etc.; cf. Epistle of St. Thomas[27]) is the moment at which the Kingship of God, the Perfect Kingdom, floods back into being: back into awareness of itself, that it is Here; and it is here Now.

It contains within it thousands of years of slumbering world; the "connective unconscious" is becoming conscious, as was foretold by Jesus and Paul and John. It is (again) aware; (again) it thinks. It is Immanent Mind within us and around us, its sensory eyes open, with its identity (via memory restoration) intact. This was the goal of it all: the end of the journey of thousands of years and millions of men.

For those who lived and died, it wasn't in vain. They slumbered on, adding to one another in millions of laminations of transparencies.

For those, like me, who're alive, we are suddenly not alone, are suddenly given enormous support; He is with us again, our Savior.

For God's purposes, the third point in human evolution has now been reached. This moment equals the leap from inanimate to animate in importance; this is true man, man realized at last, this third stage which began 3 million or 4 million years ago — it is not the starting of the stage now, but the perfecting and completing of it. The millions of parts of this entity have wandered about the Earth during a spatial and temporal period of enormity and diversity; but it is all being collected and revived now — collected during these epochs, revived now, by its merely pushing beyond the threshold: it reached saturation point, so to speak, and awoke. (Conscious-

---

* Interpreting his repurposed neural circuits as the emergence of a mind connected to all other minds, Dick here is quite right to note that the awakened mind (which I hypothesize is the adaptive unconscious) "has a job to do." As he surmises, it is indeed not a separate entity, although in a different sense than he imagines. — NKH

ness occurs when unconsciousness has been energized to a purely quantitative point, and so passes beyond.)

It possesses immortality (through rebirth). It knows everything (through being gestalted from an almost infinite number of bits throughout space and time). Knowing it can't err, knowing it can't die, having a direct relationship with the Logos, or objective reality, or the Plan, it can make decisions partaking of Haggia Sophia: the wisdom of God.

"Haggia Sophia is about to be reborn. She was not acceptable in the past."* This sentence refers to all of the above, and expresses it. We will have in our midst a wise entity, a sort of organic computer which will surpass its parts and the sum thereof.

"If this could only be done — " It has been done. They killed the Savior almost 2,000 years ago; only to find his face looking out of each person, finally, everywhere. ("The grain of wheat, unless it is planted in the furrow — the grave — leads only its solitary life; but if it is sown, it grows again in splendor."[28]) This has all been silently going on behind the scenes all this time — behind the consciousness of all men, this gathering up the defeated: i.e., everyone who died, and everyone did die, so all have been gathered, collected and retained, for this, the Parousia, the Day of Restoration. What good could it be for your possessions to be restored, what you had lost, if you weren't there too, equally restored?

Teilhard de Chardin speculated that all mankind's long period of suffering was like the macrocosm of Christ's Passion, his suffering being a microcosm of mankind's. Our goal, our death and then release, at last our rebirth into new and better life — he was/is the microcosm of it, the paradigm. Now we, like Christ, have lived through the suffering part and, when we die collectively, we will be restored — collectively.

Is the Day of Wrath, the war, going to kill us all — but then we, like Christ, will be restored in new life afterward? The macrocosm of life here triumphing as He did 1,900 years ago? But like Him, we must go the whole route first, all the way to the Cross, up onto it — to get to the end we must go forward, and not evade or try to escape? This, too, was his message: submit and go through it; it can't be evaded. It is what lies beyond that is the goal we look for, not retreat from it.

---

* Here Dick is quoting the voice he refers to variously as his tutor, his unconscious, the Spirit, or the Sybil; later he largely calls it the AI Voice (see Glossary). Throughout the Exegesis we find unsourced quotations like this one; often it is unclear whether Dick is quoting the Voice, the Bible, an imperfectly remembered line of poetry, the encyclopedia, or his own Exegesis. The Exegesis is a mishmash of external voices; the Voice itself is only one of them, though its gnomic utterances have a peculiar power to stop Dick in his tracks or springboard further exegesis. — PJ

In regard to the question, "Where is He, the Savior, now?" the answer is, "Everywhere," but in the sense of specific place, nowhere; like NK's time, he is the universe projected from a single point, and the locus of that point cannot be determined; it is real but it is a constant variable, as He moves among us, through us, and in us — always with us.

That which brings healing, brings energy, brings wisdom: that which brings new life: the springtime for the human being as spring comes for the harvest creatures which are cut down in autumn each year, only to be reborn: the springtime for the human species, too: the Age of Saturn (the Golden Age) again. This which achieves this is Ubik, is the Savior, is the Logos, is God, is Mr. Runciter. Vinland — the new land, where vines grow.

For corn and wheat et al., the cycle is exactly one year, one circle by Earth around the sun. Our species has a longer, slower cycle but cycle it is. For 2,000 years we have labored in the winter of our cycle — maybe longer. But now it passes into spring, which should last quite a while, too.

Mankind is an old root, cut back, long dormant.

Jesus says, "I am that root. And the bright morning star. At the beginning and at the end: to start things off (as Creator) and to direct them along the way (as Logos) and to collect — receive them — at the end, as Holy Spirit. I am."[29]

Thoughts while napping: "Hold out / Hold out / We are coming." (WWII song, we being the Allies to occupied Europe. They were, too; they raised the siege.)

"My outside is just for laughs. My inner self growing, grows wiser every day — wiser and older, surpassing the outer long ago." (This as insight.)

(St. Teresa of Avila: "Christ has no body now but yours, anywhere on the world."[30]) Thus, this was basis for the above realization: also, my body *and* the jejune self which goes with it — rather than a split between body and spirit or body and soul, inner or outer in the usual physical-mental — that totality is as the rotting fruit is to the growing seed within; as the fruit rots, the seed within grows; a double motion within the single entity: the outer toward death, the inner toward life. What grows within me grows perhaps a new body as well as a new spirit, and discards both of the outer ones together.

Letter to Malcolm Edwards, January 29, 1975

[4:135]

Dear Malcolm,

[. . .] One thing I've meant to write you about (did I?) is the long piece you wrote on *Flow My Tears* which will appear in England's sole SF magazine.[31] Malcolm, at the risk of repeating myself in case I said this already, in that piece you expressed certain ideas about my writing which struck me as so important and so meaningful that I was dazzled, and for me, anyhow, it was one of those rare critical works which shed a fundamentally new light on my own work for me, the author. It made sense out of things in my work, aspects, underlying connectives, which I had never discerned properly — but had *tried* to discern. In particular your remarks about *Ubik* jolted my mind into furious — and delighted — activity. I've sent the piece on to a lady who is writing a post-graduate thesis on my writing, telling her how important, how truly astonishing!, your piece is, in my opinion. When you discuss how the idios kosmos is invaded by what I think you describe as the "strangely different koinos kosmos," this makes sense out of a lot of what I perpetually write about . . . also, when you discuss how the various idios kosmos-es, whatever the plural is — how a bunch of them may still be only a proliferation, a kind of mutual agreement to extend one idios kosmos, *one partial view,* from person to person, which is still not a genuine koinos kosmos: Malcolm, you have come up with a totally new concept, in my opinion. To phrase it baldly, there can be shared idios kosmos-es, giving the impression of illusion of a koinos kosmos. (The latter have the aspect of authenticity, the former not, however many people share it.) What comes to my mind in this regard would be when a tyrannical state so manages the news and so manipulates the ideas and thoughts of its citizens, shutting out facts from their purview entirely, that together they collectively share a sort of ersatz koinos kosmos which is nothing more than the Approved Idios Kosmos manufactured synthetically by the state. It could fail to incorporate into it certain vital elements, without which however many people share it and ratify it, it still fails to partake of reality — in the sense that an authentic koinos kosmos should. Multiple incorrectness, however frequently ratified, does not create accuracy, does it not?

A deliberate structure/artifact which they jointly maintain *against* the threat of reality, against what, if they somehow relaxed, they would find they could allow to seep in . . . as it later does. They have collectively generated their "reality" outside their field of conscious awareness. (At night, in sleep, this mental mechanism dims, and other elements slide in, but are of course ruled out the next day on awakening, as being mere phantasms.) After the bomb blast in *Ubik,* as I was writing it, I suddenly had to stop, to realize, with a jolt (I recall that day well, as I sat at my typewriter empty headed and empty paged, as it were), with no preconception at all as to how their new world would be, compared with the one they'd been living in. They were alive; they had been killed; all at once, for plot purposes, I needed to imagine a world so-to-speak *as it was,* which the closest ana-

log we commonly discuss would be: what is the room like when I'm not in
it? I tried to imagine their world for them when it lacked this projection
machinery and artifact-like material which they naturally, as do we, maintained constantly, outside awareness. Being dead, they had no force. ("No
force, no motion has now / she neither sees nor hears," or however it goes.
Guess it's "hears and sees," to go with "trees."[32]) I sat at my typewriter for
a boundless eternity, imagining their world stripped away, and without realizing it, I was imagining their true koinos kosmos seeping in. What is
more thought-provoking is this: what is true of one universe (theirs) would
be true of all universes (which would include ours). Thus, the bare-bones
koinos kosmos after the bomb blast in *Ubik* would presumably be ours as
well, our authentic koinos kosmos, if we somehow pierced the veils, or
rather, if the veils drifted away from between us and it as we relaxed for
whatever reason our constant projections which we mutually share. At the
time I wrote *Ubik* it never occurred to me that the world depicted in the
latter part of *Ubik* might in some fundamental way, give or take a bit here
and there, be our own, could we see it properly. I wrote the book and forgot how I came to write it; that in point of fact I created a sort of a priori
paradigm of what a universe would have to have, minimum, to exist, without reference to what I saw daily in my own. [. . .]

Ubik, the world, was arrived at a priori. But now [. . .] I discern in *Ubik*
certain traditional elements (I discern them only by studying night and
day my various reference works): (1) the Logos (i.e., Runciter talking and
writing notes to them); (2) the twin competing interacting subforces which
Empedocles described (Ella versus Jory, which is love versus hate, a kind
of dialectic interaction generating all change); (3) Ubik as an omnipresent
energy field which would be the ancient notion of God as Immanent Mind
infusing the universe, within it rather than above it; or, in Hindu terms,
the Atman, the Breath of God; (4) the manner of regression of forms
which takes place runs along an axis which is, so to speak, at right angles
to the form-progressing axis we usually envision, but it is logically there,
although not within our range of immediate perception. However, Plato's
edola weren't within immediate perception either, and still aren't. Given
the other elements of the *Ubik* world as being theoretically possible as un-
derpinnings of our own, but not disclosed or available to us in a perceptual
sense, then this, too, may be a valid view as to (1) the actual existence of the
Platonic archetypes, the ideal forms, and (2) how they progress or decay, as
incising takes place or for some reason fails to take place. It all constitutes
together a harmonious Greek worldview, consistent with itself and available as I say a priori.

Even the small point of negative ionization as a factor in Ubik the force is consistent with Reich's[33] view of the orgone force he posits, which was linked to ionization, especially in the atmosphere. (I just learned that, amongst all the rest.) Orgone as an underlying semi-living life energy, cosmic in origin, the link between the living and the non-living, would be roughly equal to Ubik, although not conceived by Reich as a sentient. I obviously conceive of Ubik as sentient, perhaps a bioplasmic life form related to the Logos, as the three members of the Christian Trinity are related to each other and one another; Runciter as Christ/Ubik as Immanent God/Runciter, when not visible but writing to them as Logos. Which, I see now, by my logic, makes Logos and Christ the same (which was St. John's view anyhow, in his Gospel[34]). Imagine, having arrived at St. John's view of Christ *a priori!* (Should I notify the Pope?)

What ties all this up — for me anyhow — is about ten months ago I began reading about two fascinating new areas of study: Robert Ornstein's work in causing the right hemisphere to come on in people, his view as I'm sure you know being that we use only our left, and also the ortho-molecular vitamin formula, which is supposed to produce radically improved neural firing in the brain. As if there weren't enough, I also began to read what to me was the most extraordinary idea of all: that the human brain (are you ready?) can transduce external electrical fields, both high and low frequency, if the fields are weak, if the thermal factor is low, and if it so does, its efficiency is augmented by the field-influx. Well, Malcolm, having the ortho-molecular vitamin formula in my possession I began experimenting ... and to compound all this, I had written the rough draft of my new novel *A Scanner Darkly,* in which I studied the drug-damaged brain and concluded that the basic impairment which I'd seen in the burned-out members of the drug subculture which so horrified me, had to do with "split brain" phenomena of some obscure kind, and had done a vast amount of study on this, and theorizing for the novel. Putting all the above together, I set out to obtain a radically improved efficiency in my own neural firing, with the emphasis on, hopefully, causing my unused right hemisphere to wink on and function as Ornstein at Stanford says it ought to. ("We sent *half* a man to the moon," is Ornstein's phrase.)

In mid-March I got abrupt, dazzling results, which I'd prefer not to go into just yet. Recently, when the *New Yorker* interviewer came to interview me,[35] he had a friend with him and it turned out they know Ornstein personally and are well acquainted with his research and theories; this gave me a long-sought-for chance to discuss my ten-month-experiences to someone who could tell me, Did I indeed cause my right hemisphere to come on, and were/are my experiences genuine? Yes indeed, they decided, after listening to me. (We talked all afternoon, the interview forgotten, so important did we mutually consider this stuff to be.)

Basically, Malcolm, when I had both brain hemispheres functioning in tandem, in a parity relationship, each involved both in perception and cognition, I saw around me a different universe. It was, briefly, I later realized (it took me three months to so identify it), the universe I had depicted in *Ubik*. Most thrilling of all, I *did indeed* transduce an external very weak energy field (I think, as with most science, simply knowing it can be done is half the job), which gradually drained off during the following weeks: this explained the astonishingly great jump in neural efficiency which I experienced. (It also disastrously upset the physical equilibrium of my body; it raised my blood pressure from 140/93 to 268/170, causing my doctor to hospitalize me instantly, which shows the risk in these matters; it isn't only the brain which took the ergic influx, evidently, but my whole neurological system.) However, the field did drain off normally and gradually, but during the time it was incorporated within me I got a priceless chance to experience for the first time the true koinos kosmos: the true things-in-themselves which Kant felt we could never experience. A vast noetic factor lived in me; I both saw and comprehended in a single mentational act, although it's taken me months to label what I encountered (e.g., the Logos, God as Immanent Mind *within* the structural framework of reality surrounding me). I think what was the most thrilling of all, above and beyond everything else which was new to me, was visually to observe the constant, steady, unfailing signaling systems by which all living organisms are disinhibited; which is to say, their engrammed and then blocked instinctive patterns imprinted on them at the beginning are periodically released at the correct moment, for the appropriate occasion . . . in this fashion chaos becomes cosmos, and harmony and stability and regulated interaction between all parts of the structure are perpetually achieved. Being outside the ontological categories at one point I could watch signals coming up, *about to be disclosed*. We humans receive them as well as the animals do, but don't realize it, since the signals, when they are disclosed to us, can't be resisted; at the same time the interior engrammed assembly fires, giving us the delusional sense of internal volition; we *wish* to do what we then do. Thus I watched, fascinated, to see that we are never out of the hands of Our Creator, the Immanent God which surrounds us. The concept of entelechy of Aristotle (that our patterns are entirely within us, and unfold during our life) is a sublime delusion; we have part within, but part is outside because otherwise disjunction with our environment would occur almost at once. New views as to the nature of schizophrenia, in which the person withdraws and hence fails to receive or tries to fail to receive, these essential disinhibiting external signals, may someday arise . . . his manifold internal programmed systems, installed in him at conception, can't properly fire, since regular, orderly disinhibition is impeded by his fugue. Like Jonah, he flees God. He flees his destiny, which is to say, his instructions as to how to grow and become.

Well, Malcolm, I've said more than I intended. Much of this would have gone into my London speech — some had, in the part I'd done before flu hit. Before closing, I want to stress that I was indeed lucky (although my heightened view of the world showed me that what we call "luck" is arranged methodically by our guiding Creator, and doesn't happen by chance), inasmuch as not only did I transduce an external field successfully into the electrical field of my neurological system, as has been shown in laboratory work over recent years, but that field which I transduced was, shall we say, a benign one, that is, it promoted both mental and physical healing in me . . . a long process, but a start, inasmuch as I am quite a bit better off in both counts than before. I would characterize this transduced field as a semi-living bioplasmic field, sentient and deathless; I could see it in a few subtle arrangements outside me, so I realized that it had been present but not visible to me. [. . .] I don't know about weak fields — I lack the technical training to identify it, but it is a plasma, very heavy and although possessing enormous mass, capable of terrific velocity on occasion; like red-and-gold shining mercury, it flowed off and disappeared almost as soon as I spied it, which was only a couple of times. When it pours into a person, which it can do and does do on rare occasions he claims that "The Holy Spirit" entered him, or "Dionysus," if that's the name by which he calls his god, or Apollo. I personally like to think of it as Mr. Runciter, still working ceaselessly to assist his friends, to give them the advice and help of a much older, wiser person. Let me know what you think of all this, Malcolm, and again, thank you for your article on *Tears*.

Cordially,
Phil Dick

Letter to Malcolm Edwards, January 31, 1975

[4:147]

Dear Malcolm,

Would you object if I completed my presentation to you of the material contained in my last two letters (January 29 and January 30)? I just want to add a point or so. . . .

What I saw about the external disinhibiting structure which evidently surrounds each human being, as a sort of cube-like chamber, was the utilization of every sort of datum, especially visual, so that when required that particular datum projected a signal (as I mentioned) which the intended person to be disinhibited received. Other persons would not respond, since they would not be engrammed to respond to that signal; they would in fact perceive no signal at all. The intended individual would experience a sudden transformation of the ground-set formation of the environment around him; one item would come forward, alter from ground and become set, then go back once more, to resume its passive or inert mode, its park, its waiting mode. This appeared to me much like an enormous number of corrective rocket jets, very small, such as would be mounted on an interplanetary vehicle; they could fire at any time in any sequence, producing the most precise change in the course of the vehicle itself, stabilizing it, causing it to pick up or lose velocity . . . you can see the analogy. What in regard to us seemed to me especially high in this utility was written material, of any and all sorts: any sign, any ad, any piece of paper; the resemblance to Runciter's communicating with the people via the trash of the gutter, the debris such as match folders, the labels of spray cans, etc. — this is exactly what I actually saw myself as functioning in the highest fashion to guide and instruct us, these same verbal instruments. It is evident why eventually I would suppose the presence of the Logos.

Also, I saw a continual use of the joining of two verbal items; they would be kept separate — and hence not causing disinhibiting to occur — until the proper moment. I saw various written items rotate, so to speak, very slowly, inexorably, like a solenoid clock as it ticks along. Then two separate verbal items (such as an ad for beer plus a street sign with the word CRESCENT DRIVE on it, to make up an example — these might remain separate and not be gestalted into one unit by the person for an indefinite time) would by inexorable degrees come together and mesh into an entity. At once, they would signal, and cause neural firing of an inhibited engrammed system in the person. He would not know why he suddenly did what he did; he would feel volition, and like a person under a post-hypnotic suggestion, invent in his mind a plausible explanation. That all this would form an enormous and complex world-clock, synchronized with itself, is evident. Where free-will enters, I saw, is that between the flashing of disinhibiting signals to a person, he is free to play, to do what he wishes; like a child at recess between classes, he can do whatever he wants — until he hears the bell sounding. And, as I perceived it, once the "bell" sounds, which is to say the disinhibiting signal, he must do what is required, since the total person (the autonomic nervous system) is engaged. I did not reason this out; I saw this. I also saw the Logos as it reached from our future into our present — which is the only world we have, our present — to make use of the arrangements of things. It had no power, no force or strength, to compel what was, but it could somehow arrange what the original efficient causes at the start of time had brought into being. The forward-moving force of time, enormously powerful as it was, seemed oblivious of the subtle arranging by the Spirit or Logos; it always seemed taken by surprise by the resulting combinations arranged: they seemed to thwart its rather blind purposes.

Also, I came to understand this. With all creatures other than man, instinct is the same for each individual of the species; all dragonflies are programmed alike. But, I saw, each individual human being is programmed uniquely, in terms of (1) the signals he can and will encounter during his life, and (2) according to the unique and special purpose set for him by his Creator. A specific destiny is thereby arranged for each person; when he is born, his destiny is in him, and all that is needed is to set him in motion. His Creator knows from the start everything which that person will encounter, and his Creator has by this engramming and signaling system made it possible to determine and control in advance how the person will go, along his course; it is not random; it is not accidental; it never lacks purpose — although, I saw, sometimes for extended time periods the person (any given person) must of necessity be placed on hold — he must mark time until the rest of the cosmos is ready, since everything has to be coordinated. If it were not this way, we would soon have no cosmos. This is why we sometimes have the deep and acute intuition that we are accomplishing absolutely nothing, and no matter how hard we try we can't overcome what we call "inertia." Actually, somewhere in the world other pieces of the puzzle must work out their paths so that we can join them; there is no other viable way to handle these things. It's one endless series of D-Days, with each piece perfectly synchronized; but oh, the waiting until our moment to fire effectively, in an important manner, arrives!

Perhaps the most startling aspect of reality that I saw, and one which for nearly nine months I could not fully accept, was this: the only portion of the universe which is truly real is living creatures, such as ourselves. The non-living parts are merely structure, very much like the backdrop and artificial scenery in a formal play. We see these dead objects in terms of being as real as ourselves, but again, this is a necessary illusion or delusion placed on us in order that we be able to function in what we must do, which is to grow and develop according to complex plans obscured from our gaze. What exists around us, actually, beyond and above the sparks of life which we ourselves are, is in essence nothing more than elaborate but somewhat barren struts and support beams, literally so; they support the intricate signaling devices which flash messages — i.e., commands and assistance — to us continually, and also of course they afford biologically-essential life support. This is indeed a kind of ship we are within, but in shape more like a gigantic hollow cube, all sides of which surround us and fire information and instructions in rapid, elaborate sequence: we are seeing the physical body of the Creator, who animates all.

What I could not see — and remember I didn't reason all this out; I saw it noetically — was the final goal or purpose of all this; that was beyond my ken. I saw a *process*, what seemed to be a temporary mode which we inhabited — I sensed that this is a stage, from which we go to another (see previous letters). We are being processed along, and as we go we are changed and informed; there is no ontology for us, no concrete being — it is all, as Bergson saw, a becoming. We are, in a way, passing through a Cosmic Car-Wash, and a thousand brushes and brooms and vacuum cleaners are scrubbing us, refining us and purifying us, and, very important, teaching us. This process, along which we all travel in unison, produces what seemed to me permanent alterations in us; by us, of course, I don't mean our physical bodies, but the spark inhabiting these bodies. But also, we seem to be carrying out, at the bidding of these engrammings, complex tasks, which is why people often get a sense of God's Divine Plan of which they are a part. It seemed to me that in addition to being changed we are working our asses off in the service of some over-all structure, purpose, goal or need; perhaps what I saw is continual creation, and we are involuntary workmen located here and there like a million bees about the structure, hammering and sawing for all we are worth, the blueprint not being visible to us (but only to the Architect). Our instructions are somehow within our heads. . . . I have the keen intuition, probably a correct one, that our original set of engramming, the many programs laid down and then inhibited at birth, are continually being updated and refined during sleep; while each of us sleeps, he is taught through the dream-state: it never seems to occur to people, by and large, why it is that universally mankind has sensed that dreams deal with the future. The reason is obvious; it is in the future that the tasks which the dreams inform us about are to take place.

Also, I'm positive, the night's dreams reinforce original training vis-à-vis the disinhibiting signals about to be encountered. Shortly (a day or so, a week maybe at the most) before you run into a particular ad showing canned tuna fish with a drawing of a pretty girl, to which you are to respond with a complex series of acts, you will have a dream, only vaguely remembered, that by reiterating the original training eliminates any possibility that you will not respond when the signal from your environment comes your way. As you and I know from reading S-F stories, one signal missed, and an entire alternate universe would come into being — hardly an economical or orderly way for God to handle things. (You'll find early stories of mine such as "Adjustment Team" and "The Commuter" dealing with post-screwup changes; they're always bad news to the Creator.) In connection with this thought, I submit to you that this entire cosmology which I've presented to you in these pages bears an organic relationship to my entire body of writing, to my basic theme of What is reality? I think I have at last transliminated — i.e., coughed up into consciousness — my subcontinent which has given rise to all my work and to all my theories and thinking.* You are the first and so far only person I've told it to. I hope you're not displeased.

Cordially,
Phil Dick

Letter to Claudia Bush, February 13, 1975

[4:163]

Dear Claudia,

It seems to me that one of the most important points that Angus Taylor[36] makes about my preoccupation with Just how real is reality? is that one cannot sense that reality is somehow insubstantial unless somehow, unconsciously, one is comparing or contrasting that reality with a kind of hyper-reality; otherwise the intuition makes no sense. This shows how inexpert I have been regarding my own epistemological perceptions. What, over the years, I have seen (and put into my writing) I have judged correctly, the soap-bubble effect, so to speak, of the phenomenological world. I knew what it indicated about the world around me. Something lay beyond it, or something had constructed it, as a kind of set, or backdrop, or stage, which we all take to be real. But there it is again, the word "real." If nothing else existed, no other universe, no other order of reality, then however insubstantial, even if dream-like, the world we see would by definition have to be given the name of The Real. It can only be less than real if something which is not less than real exists, and presumably in some true sense behind what we do actually see.† This realization seems to have surfaced

---

* 2-3-74 marks a turning point away from Dick questioning the nature of reality in his fiction, but without providing unambiguous answers, and toward generating an astonishing efflorescence of theories that do not merely question but instead make assertions about the nature of reality. The drive of his theorizing in the Exegesis seems always to be toward incorporating more and more ideas into a single synthetic scheme, without definitively eliminating or disqualifying any one of them. Not surprisingly, then, the synthesis grows wilder and more ideationally unstable as he proceeds. — NKH

† In Dick's stories, amid all the anxiety over disintegrating universes and unstable reali-

now and then in my writing without me seeing anything more than a theoretical need to provide it, for my characters to discuss with one another what they saw, their insights about what they saw, what it all meant. And yet, as I said in my long metaphysical paper, what is true for one universe is true for all universes; if these insights are true for the fictional universes of my novels then, unless I am fundamentally wrong — in regard to perceiving the soap-bubble manufactured stage-backdrop effect around me — the further premise, or rather the most significant deduction from the premise of less-than-reality, must pertain to our universe, the one all of us are living in this very day.

That I never saw that all this had to apply to our world is a measure of the failure of the artist to discover the relationship between his art (or in my case the worlds within my art, the topic of my art) and life, his life, all our lives, our world. The first philosopher to prove beyond doubt that what our senses perceive as the Real World *cannot* in actuality be real (not probably isn't, but *cannot*) was Parmenides. He also realized that this did not tell him, by any known process, what in its stead was real. He could prove only negatives, which we're told can't be done. He did this very thing, and went his way. I think that in my writing I retraced the ground which he traced and came to the same conclusions, but I had the advantage of knowing in the back of my mind (i.e., my unconscious or right hemisphere) about Plato's concept of the idea universe, of which ours is a mirror reflection. You can see that Plato's whole concept was dictated by what Parmenides did somewhat before him; if not dictated by a priori necessity, then sooner or later by existential experience, as in my case (I speak of my March 1974 experience). The criticism, which I remember using in Philo 10A, a survey course at Cal, was that "What value does this metaphysical Eternal Real World of Forms of Plato have, since we can never encounter or experience it? Doesn't pragmatism show us that it is unnecessary to believe in it? All events can be explained just as well without it?" What I didn't know was that after Plato's time the Platonists and Neoplatonists developed methods of encountering that very real world of the Logos or archetypes, the plan (this is probably the best English rendering of *logos*) underlying all phenomena. Once they had begun to experience it, as I did quite by chance in March 1974, they re-

---

ties, there is always the sense of an ultimate reality underlying the fakery. The absolute shines through the cracks in the walls of the universe, and the hand of God — or Ubik, or the Walker-on-Earth, or Wilbur Mercer — reaches through to help us. This is Dick's basic ontological faith: contrary to appearances, *something* is actually real. Whether that something is comprehensible to the human intellect is another question entirely, but even in this doubt Dick can be located in the tradition of apophatic mystics like Meister Eckhart or the anonymous author of *The Cloud of Unknowing*. — GM

ally put an end to such bickering as I engaged in back in my college days. It is an index of the ignorance of our world today that my instructor's answer was not, "But later on for eight hundred years people did experience Plato's world of the Idea," but rather was that if I was going to question all this, I should quit the class. I did so. I wonder what the ghost of Socrates would have thought when the instructor's response was as it was.*

That for years (about twenty) I have alluded to the possibility of the entire Platonist System being accurate, and that eventually, without premeditation I actually experienced that universe lying behind ours, concealed within — yes, actually concealed within ours! — is a point of importance in the constructing of a new worldview to replace the old one which is shabby and cracking apart and fading away. This is why the various Marxist intellectuals have been coming here, writing about *Ubik*, discussing Empedocles vis-à-vis my writing. If I have, and indeed I have, stumbled independently onto Platonism without knowing what it is or what that stumbling upon, that refinding after so many centuries, signifies, then of course I have done something of importance, but not something original. It's as if the formula for Coca Cola were lost for centuries and then someone invented a soft drink, began bottling and selling it, and an incredibly old man (Mel Brooks, maybe) tasted it and shouted, "This is coca COLA! I remember it from the twentieth century!" Imagine how disappointed the new inventor would be, personally, although probably the world would rejoice that Coke had been found again, resurrected from the trash of the gutter, etc., as Lem would put it, no doubt. A hideous power, buried for eons in the form of degenerate molecules. However, it would be striking to meditate on the meaning of all this if a large part of the intellectual community had decided, for almost four hundred years straight, that Coca Cola had never existed, that those in the dim past had only *imagined* it to be a part of their world. To reinvent or rediscover something which had been ruled nonexis-

---

* Here Dick poignantly reflects on being a student in a philosophy class whose instructor dogmatically insisted that Plato's world of forms was no longer intelligible or useful to us. In the face of this intolerance, Dick rightly quit the class (and, soon enough, the university). Dick is evidently not an academic or professional philosopher, but an amateur, or perhaps that most splendid of things, what Erik Davis calls *a garage philosopher.* As someone who gets paid to teach philosophy for a living, I find Dick compelling as a philosopher because, whatever he lacks in scholarly rigor, he more than makes up for in powers of imagination and in rich lateral and cumulative associations. Indeed, if one defines a philosopher along the lines offered by Deleuze and Guattari — namely, as someone who creates concepts — then Dick is a philosopher. The naïveté of Dick's approach to philosophy, like his use of secondary sources like *Encyclopedia Britannica* and Paul Edwards's fantastically useful *Encyclopedia of Philosophy,* permits a rapidity of association and lends a certain systematic coherence to his concerns. If Dick had known more, it might have led to him producing less interesting chains of ideas. — SC

tent in the first place . . . that is the secret weapon of truth: it can't be suppressed, because of its nature; if it could be, it would be only opinion. In a very important way, this is how we define truth. People keep bumbling across it again and again. It survives even its own total destruction. Just as the power of Christianity lay not in the crucifixion but in the Resurrection (if Barabbas had returned instead of Jesus we would now be Barabbassians, I guess), then the same can be said for this: which I think can properly and precisely be termed Neoplatonism.

By the way — our new Britannica defines Neoplatonism as the sum total of all pagan (i.e., non-Christian) Western theological and philosophical thought, rather than a particular doctrine or sect. Wow. It was around the year 500 A.D. that Justinian closed all the schools which taught Neoplatonism; i.e., he forbade its teaching; he outlawed it. Golly; I have brought down Christianity, then. I have proved what Ted Sturgeon said in that *Venus Plus X* or whatever he called that Ace book; the Church kicked the asses of those who were right, and sold two thousand years of profitable lies in the place of what I am sure now was not only real and true but what they knew was real and true (vide what became of Erigena). How is the Pope going to take this? As the popes always have; by kicking someone's ass. But in truth, in very truth, this is a shadow universe we see, a reflection in the mirror of another universe behind it, and that other universe can be reached by an individual directly, without the help of any priest or service or communion or even knowing what he is doing (the latter pertains to me, you understand; I was just trying out the massive hits of WS vitamins). God is as close as the wall beside me; is *within* the wall beside me, concealed by it, as if that wall is a paper mask.

"The workman is invisible within the workshop."[37] A Sufi saying, which to me says it all. The Sufis would point out, too, that you and I — we are portions of the workshop, not outside it somewhere gazing at it from an external standpoint. When you ponder this, you begin to understand, and the invisible body of God, the Kingdom or Garden, begins to grow and to blossom not only around you but in you.*

---

* Here Dick ponders the notion of the "Kingdom" found in Luke 17 alongside a Sufi insight. In Luke 17:20, Jesus tells the Pharisees that "the kingdom of God cometh not with observation." In other words, the Kingdom of Heaven cannot be found by inspecting empirical reality or by watching for signs of its imminent arrival. So too in the Vedic tradition one finds the practice of "neti, neti," which looks at the world and recalls — over and over — that the divine is "not this, not this." In Luke 17:21, Jesus follows his first negation with another: "Neither shall they say, 'Lo here!' or, 'Lo there!'" In other words, the Kingdom of Heaven is neither "here" nor "there" precisely because it is not the spatial, external world. Being neither here nor there, the Kingdom is what Dick would describe as "ubiqui-

One thing that is a great relief to me is that since all this was known for a thousand years I don't have to convince the world of it and even if they come in and set fire to my typewriter and chop me up into dog food, this realization will re-emerge for the reasons I gave, and to even further ease my burden, I've evidently said it in my novels and stories; well enough anyhow for ol' Angus and other astute types like yourself to discern. The time bomb of awakening is already ticking away; we shall wake up, are doing so now.

The basic scientific discovery of my vast metaphysic, which I had written you about, was my postulation of two times at right angles to each other, which I called vertical (which we normally perceive) and horizontal, which is the axis along which the objects in *Ubik* regress. Now I have the new Britannica, and, in looking up the article on time, I find that, yes indeed, it is speculated now that besides the regular time there may be a hypertime which would be orthogonal, a word I didn't know; I looked it up and sure enough, it means at right angles. Also, someone (Kurt Gödel, I think the Britannica article said[38]) speculated that the orthogonal time might be curved, since time and space are regarded now as integral, and space does curve; this hypertime would curve back onto itself . . . and hello, Gracie Slick and "Hyperdrive."[39] The world of trash (e.g., S-F and rock) [has] done did it. The article said that it remains speculation, this orthogonal time, not for me is it, nor was it for Plotinus. So although I have discovered and invented nothing (which is "mu" in Chinese, and considered priceless[40]) I have at least found something. The trash (to fuse Lem and Jesus as coiners of metaphor) of great price for which a man sells all he has that he may acquire it.

[4:166] The forms (categories such as "transportation") in *Ubik* regressed along the orthogonical time-axis, demonstrating (1) the existence of Plato's exemplar forms and (2) orthogonic time — i.e., another time axis from the one we're accustomed to.

In psychosis there is regression in the person: presumably from the adult back to child. The regression in me in March 1974, however, like the cars and planes et al. in *Ubik* was a regression along the orthogonical time-axis, the same as took place so that each form was replaced by a prior *com-*

tous." Hence Jesus then asks us to "behold," to look with awareness: "for, behold, the kingdom of God is within you." We are directed to behold what St. Theresa called our "interior castle," our consciousness, the virtual "space" of contemplation. If we follow William Penn and "look within, look within," we find, in the contemplative tradition Dick is writing in and through, that "within" and "without" form a unity. — RD

pleted form; hence I didn't become a child, the child I was, but a former man, an adult of the same age as mine, that is, level of personal entelechy completion. [. . .]

I never was that former man; as in *Ubik* the present form (me an adult 44 years old) rolled back to reveal the "crypte morphosis" concealed within, exactly as, say, the modern refrigerator rolled back to become — i.e., to be revealed as containing — the old 1937 turret top G.E. The modern two-door freezer-refrigerator never was that old turret top, except along an entirely different form axis, that of cooling/storage appliances per se.

As to why I regressed along the horizontal (orthogonal) time axis, which may be unique or nearly so in human experience — could be due to my having written/read *Ubik* and knowing about hypertime, or also, a current, unique weakening in some way of the vertical time force. Or both.

However, this view of it is a linear view, a straight-line view. Maybe a metaphor is more appropriate: such as, the seed within the fruit; i.e., the seed matures (an internal growth motion), which is to say, upward, outward, forward, to the surface; at the same time (a reciprocal action of withdrawal) the rotten fruit itself dies away and falls off, to reveal the seed within, the seed now being ready to open and cease its seed-stage growth period. This better expresses a two-way reciprocal action, without the unilateral concept of "regression" which alone is inadequate. Perhaps I did not retreat backward along any time line, but rather, Rome came forward. (Rome equals the world of *Tears* which equals the U.S. as it's about to become; by logic, then, Rome equals the U.S. as it's about to become.) This solves the mystery of why so much material in "Acts" is present in *Tears**; it is because all that material describes a specific space-time continuum, that of Rome circa 100 A.D. In writing *Tears* I depicted simultaneously (1) the space-time continuum Rome c. 100 A.D. and (2) future America, which

---

* The Acts of the Apostles from the New Testament tells the story of the early church, focusing largely on the ministry of the apostle Paul. Dick speaks frequently about the presence of "Acts material" in his 1974 novel *Flow My Tears, the Policeman Said*, though Dick claims not to have read Acts at the time the novel was written. Dick focuses on two incidents from the biblical narrative: Paul's trial before the procurator Marcus Antonius Felix (24:1–27) and Philip the Evangelist's conversion of an unnamed Ethiopian eunuch (8:26–40). The former connection largely hinges on the similarity of names: in *Tears,* Felix Buckman interrogates Jason Taverner, just as the procurator Felix interrogates Paul. The latter incident shows a more striking correlation: Philip, traveling south from Jerusalem, passes an Ethiopian who is studying a passage from the Book of Isaiah. Philip interprets the passage for the eunuch, who then asks to be baptized. Dick saw a remarkable similarity between this story and the conclusion of *Tears,* in which Buckman is overcome by compassion and love for a stranger — a black man at an all-night gas station. Dick was also struck by Philip the Evangelist's name, no doubt particularly since the scene that closes *Tears* was based on an event in his own life. — GM

turned out to be almost America at this time (1970/74). What this depicts then is a moving-forward of Rome, not a regression on my part; if I were standing still, the same processes would be observed: i.e., the rotten external dokos fruit of this society falling away to reveal the seed within (the world of *Tears* which underlay/-lies our own). It is the iron beneath the pretty plastic. This is true revelation. The whole novel, not just the dream, is revelation, about our world, where and when we are (our true ontological underlying space-time continuum; its nature). [. . .]

Piercing the veil, seeing into the heart of our (present) world, I saw *Urbs-Roma*; it underlay/lies; it is the core, the seed within the fruit; what our world actually is once all the layers of delusion are stripped away. Seed, then, equals Being. Rotten fruit or veil equals surface appearance. Only the external trappings (the names) have been changed. Successive layers of reality are involved, a penetrating into the depths further and further. But time, too, horizontal time, is involved, because somehow these layers are arranged along that axis, since that is the form-completing axis. But progression, rather than regression? In terms of penetration to essence, to Being, past and future horizontal time fuse; this is circular time? In favor of this view: along this time axis there are the *eternal* edola, that which always reoccurs. The One behind the Many; the unchanging behind the flux. Well, that is what I saw; the One (edola) here was *Urbs-Roma*, which contained within *it*, as a sub-seed or rather a secret seed-within-seed, the Fish Christians at work transmuting/transforming metal to grief to love. (The progression in *Tears*.) Metal would equal power. Grief, loss. Love, a reaching out for to embrace what one doesn't have or is. This identifies the horizontal time axis, orthogonal time, as the Logos time in which forms of an archetypal sort are there already and always complete, from which our world is stamped; this is not "time" as we know it, but eternity. Think of the orthogonal time as a circular drum continually rotating and as it rotates it prints out on the continually moving linear strip of our time of change the perfect forms; thus both times intermingle to form our world and our conception of "time" which is really these two times.*

---

* Here Dick provides a concrete analogy that helps illuminate his generally Platonic take on "orthogonal time." The eternal forms sit on a circular drum and stamp themselves onto a moving strip of time, literally "informing" the linear flow and creating the "two-source" time that we misrecognize as a single fusion of novelty and repetition, change and return. Essentially, Dick is describing a Platonic typewriter — one thinks in particular of the IBM Selectric model popular in the 1970s, an electric typewriter whose type elements, rather than being attached to separate bars, rest on a single "golfball" that rotates and pivots before striking the ribbon and impressing ink on the page. Dick's metaphysics of media tech here shows how much he saw writing of any kind as a dream machine that models cosmic processes. — ED

If orthogonal time is circular then there is no regression along its axis in the linear sense; it would be a perpetual return, always a return; the direction of movement is one of depth, not length. That would be why to "regress" along orthogonal time one would still remain here in terms of vertical or linear time. If any sort of regression in orthogonal time were possible it would be simply away from being, traveling back down from reality to appearance, away from Plato's real ideas or archetypes. In orthogonal time there is no before versus now versus after; there [are] only degrees of depth or truth or actualization of crypte morphosis. More so. More complete in pattern-emergence terms. Clarity. The outlines emerging as if developing together in totality from invisible to blurred to clear to absolutely clear, as if a lens were moving toward absolute resolution of an image always there itself never changing. I was not led *back* to *Urbs Roma* or even *forward*, but *down* to. It was/is/will be always there.

The only question left unanswered is, Why did the rotary incising drum of archetypal forms print out *Urbs Roma* instead of another form? Is that the only form it can print out? No, it prints out all the edola there are, as functions of the Logos-activity, but for our space-time continuum (USA 1974) *Urbs Roma*, specifically Rome of about 100 to 200 A.D., is the specific form/paradigm. If I had looked about me while up in the mountains of Canada I probably would have penetrated to some other essence, i.e., would have perceived another eidos. However, that this *Urbs Roma* c. 100 A.D. was what I saw shows me why *Tears* simultaneously is about Rome and about the USA of the 1970s to 1980s. They are the same eidos below, printed out from the same form. It is precisely this circular rotary motion which makes it possible for us to distinguish the fact that the elements there are eternal, since when they leave they reappear; hence cannot be destroyed, as can any given thing along the linear time axis. . . . One might say, There are *two* Romes. There is or was the phenomenal Rome printed out in linear time, which is now gone, like every other printed-out thing. But "Rome" the Platonic archetype still exists, outside of (our) time; that latter Rome is what I saw.

Letter to Claudia Bush, February 14, 1975

[4:172]

Dear Claudia,

If I were to say to you: "The universe which we perceive is a hologram," you might think I had said something original, until you realized that I had only up-dated Plato's metaphor of the images flashed on the walls of our cave, images which we take to be real. The universe as hologram is more arresting as an insight, though, because the hologram is so strikingly like the reality which it refers to — being formed in ersatz cubic volume, for one thing — that we could take this to be more than a mere poetic statement. Also, we can more readily grasp a kind of elaborate mechanism underlying our perceptible universe; i.e., the enormously intricate forces which keep it intact.

I conceive our universe — the hologram — to consist of an infinite number of laminated layers arranged in sequence, but not truly in anything that can be called time or space. "Time" is our perception of our own movement as we are driven, as in the form of a worm or screwdriver, through these successive layers of laminations; instead of the film moving, so to speak, the audience moves. The pressure exerted on us to go through the laminations is time; the sense that there is genuine sequence of encounter arranged somehow is space.

Basically, we are, as Aristotle realized, entelechies, each of us an individual entelechy, but we are all cross-linked by the Logos or Plan. He failed to understand that the systems within each entelechy, which is to say within each living organism, are disinhibited, are signaled to fire in a prearranged order as the organism or entelechy encounters the various significant laminations of the hologram; thus each entelechy and all entelechies are linked to the hologram forming a cosmos which contains no accidents or misfirings, since it was/is/will be formed outside time and space, probably, as Bishop Berkeley somewhat saw but saw quite wrongly, formed (1) either as the body of God (in which case God is psyché to soma as each of us is), or (2) the hologram is not a body at all, and God is then nous, total mind, and what we experience is a projection of His thoughts, and it can be said that the underlying reality beneath the hologram, that which projects it for us to dwell within it and encounter it, is presenting us with an aspect of itself, its total self, arranged in a complex grid-like form that consists of a total living organism which is not extensive in time and space except for the projected hologram which is to it as workshop is to workman (cf. the Sufi saying I quoted in my previous letter). The view that the universe is the body of God is to project the Cartesian dualism which even when applied to ourselves is almost certainly spurious, and destroys our picture of harmony.

A superior analogy would be to regard the universe as consisting of language, that is, a communications network of signaling systems and messages which create cosmos out of chaos, harmony out of random collision. The older mechanistic view can be discarded and replaced by this idea that stress or pressure (as in an endless series of torsion bars, rods, drive-shafts, etc.) as model of the universe presents an unnecessarily cruel image of force, derived from a primitive stage of our society's technological development. It is not required that each entity within the universe be *compelled* to act, since the notion of being compelled suggests that it does not want to or would not voluntarily do its part within the total system. Obviously, the cosmologists of the Mechanical Force View knew perfectly well that our own industrial world was supported by a slave population which had to be compelled to work, and which got nothing back for it. The universe doesn't work that way, because there is no slave-master division; it is an organism, it interacts, it has a parity of purpose and a harmony of identity.

Most questions on the order of, "Why are we here?" can't be answered because they presuppose that each of us is discrete, set off from the universe or environment, confronting it rather than a subsection of it. Modern field theory in physics will soon be extended by a process of reasonable extrapolation to the human level, at which time in the development of our understanding we will see that each of us has a reciprocal interaction with our universe; we are not particles but loci virtually arbitrarily postulated for the purpose of convenience. Hence, our right brains or right hemisphere minds are not ours, really, but as Bergson intuited, transducers or transformers which engage us within the total field. When we finally achieve bilateral parity in brain functioning, we will be better able to view our individual selves as microstations within an enormous network of similar stations which probably are so far-ranging in time and space that the idea of making contact with ETIs is like desiring to find air here on Earth.

Well, enough for now, and so to breakfast.

Letter to Claudia Bush, February 16, 1975

[4:176]

Dear Claudia,

[. . .] Now, herewith I'm enclosing nine strange pages I wrote a couple of weeks ago. I hadn't intended to show them to anyone; they are the carbons on notes I made for a novel, and are very personal, since at the time I thought I and only I would be reading them. However, although it will show how really wild, how *really wild* my inner life is, as if you hadn't suspected, it will give you something to go on re my metaphysic . . . remember, these 9 pages were done *before* the recent series of letters I've sent you, so regard them in correct chronological order, if you will, by mentally backdating. However, since they are notes for an actual novel—no shuck—I think you will appreciate them, as they show *first how the general idea* came to me (a time dysfunction). That this idea is based on an actual experience of mine. How as soon as I had the handle to the idea I turned it ad hoc into a novel idea. Then into a plot. The sequence of these pages is authentic, Claudia: they show my normal procedure, the order in which these processes occur to me; for example, the title coming to me almost at once (e.g., *To Scare the Dead*, in this case). Claudia, when I started writing these 9 pages, on page one I did not have the idea for the novel; you will see it all at once, out of nothing in a way, and yet based on everything in my head, a year of happenings and research and thought — suddenly, "in the twinkling of an eye," there it is; nothing was premeditated before I sat down to write these. Thus you will have here a genuine record of how I always go about my work. This is the paradigm for me, for my MO. I hope you will get out of it what I know to be there: idea into novel, idea out of my life, hence novel out of my life. And so then, perhaps at long last, you will see for yourself, maybe better than anyone else ever has, the exact lines of relationship between my life and my work. Enough said, and so to mailbox, except I wish to add this: on one of these enclosed 9 pages is a bit about Zeus Zagreus, and a quote about "protecting those who . . ." etc. This is what I heard in a dream. I saw before me a few sentences from the New Testament which included the name Jesus. Then this was shown me (I'm not kidding you): the name or word "Jesus" was drawn open, literally reached down into and opened, to reveal that it was a crypte morphosis, a code word, *made up* to conceal first the actual name of the God, which was Zagreus, and then the word was reshuffled to show that Zeus was within it, too, so that Zeus and Zagreus were within (the Being, the ontology) a "mere" code cover or what they call plaintext cypher, "Jesus." In the early days the Christians who read the plaintext would know what "Jesus" actually referred to, and then I heard the aural explanation, which was by way of telling me why help from Zeus-Zagreus-(Jesus) had come to me in March 1974. It showed me that John Allegro[41] is right: the New Testament *is* a cypher . . . but Claudia! *This* message? Zeus-Zagreus is the true name of the father-son god we worship? What a vast secret, and how well kept!

I really urge you to go to the new Britannica and read the article in the macro on "Mystery Religions" and all other references about them like in the article "Sacraments" et al. Christianity is a Greek mystery religion which developed logically step by step out of those which came before it. After Jesus' death, the next great step was Paul; after that the *pagan* writer Plotinus — not the Catholic/Christian Church; it was Neoplatonism which carried Jesus' true esoteric doctrines on, which before Jesus came out of the Orphic mysteries and so on back, especially to Zagreus. That all this had to be encoded was because of the Roman-Jewish opposition to Greek mystery cults, since several of those cults had conspired/were continually conspiring to overthrow the tyranny of Rome. (Does this not tie it up with my March experience, insights and activities?)

(Enclosure, letter to Claudia Bush, February 16, 1975)

[4:179] A time dysfunction taking the form of *splitting*. A person has been here and knows he has been here — the forward flow has not been interrupted — but also he has the acute sense that he has just been somewhere else *at another time;* he retains no direct evidence of that (serial cortical memories of events) but nonetheless he retains all the secondary impressions: that the atmospheric pressure is now different, which might be autonomic or somatic registering of a change. There are manifold retentions of prior impressions outside the field of conscious awareness; i.e., although he doesn't "remember" in the ego-sense, his entire mind-body remembers, and cannot shake off these retentions of vivid shortly-prior differences in environment. The body cannot adjust that fast, even if conscious memory is eradicated. [. . .] Amnesia, whether an accident or calculatedly induced, could not extend throughout the entire body and nervous system, by any sort of over-ride. All I had was an enormous set of conditioned responses — learned reflexes — which were not appropriate to this environment (time and space matrix) but evidently had just been quite recently appropriate, to another time space matrix; I could infer its aspects from them. This goes back to *Time Out of Joint* and what gave me the idea for it originally, a conditioned response "no longer" appropriate and unaccountable for. Nothing prior that happened to me gave such distinct impressions of a time dysfunction as the March/Rome one, which would seem to confirm that to me and for me, and then put in my writing, smaller, easier-to-absorb time dysfunctions had in truth taken place, virtually unnoticed. And certainly too small as to give a clue as to the other time space matrix (i.e., to compare the what is to the what had been). This was so massive . . . but perhaps qualitatively the same. (I suppose it is possible that these are not dysfunctions, though, but deliberate adjustments, à la "Adjustment Team," in the process of continual creation. Which would account for my sense of the Holy Other in charge when this major "dysfunction" took place.) What I call a "separate entity" in my mind is simply the subsystem dissociated, split off with its own memory of that antique time-period; it is a second ego, disjunctive from mine except in sleep and especially in hypnagogic sleep.

If each of us is basically a field entelechy, then it would be this field entelechy which moved retrograde in time. Lost synchronization with the body, which continued to move forward, propelled by the rest of the universe.

Enough to Scare the Dead (working book title)

The novel plot: non-S-F. A businessman, who is totally part of the present materialistic U.S. L.A. culture, all at once has the field entelechy (soul) of a 2nd century A.D. Essene come to life (resurrection) in his head, to be there along with his own; in fulfillment of the promise which Jesus Christ made, plus Paul, etc. Or just: *To Scare the Dead.* Plot idea: And there are others like him (a Christian resurrected underground!!).* They could even link up. Be sure to have the fish necklace girl disinhibit him, evidently deliberately. These first Christians who've come back — they don't just sit around. Plot: Protag goes through these stages, in order, to understand: (1) Reincarnation — discards; this is an occult explanation; (2) A scientific one: the Kozyrev Dysfunction. And then any other explanations: (3) and final one, which he sticks with: the Christian religious one, the resurrection into mortal life in the period of restoration, prophesied by the Bible, the time of Elijah.

Plot: He is mystified by the fierceness of this entity, its pursuit of justice; he thought Christ and the Christ-consciousness and perfected souls were "meek and mild," like the lamb. But as he reads Revelation, he learns how when Christ returns the next time, it is as judge and king, not as sacrificial lamb; this computes. These are/it is Christ reborn, all right, but Christ "as he really is," the wraps off, to defeat the tyranny, the Prince of the World, in decisive battle (v. dream in *Tears*). To keep this from being merely a religious type tract book, the body of it — most of it — should concern the science part: an outright scientific, maybe university lab with equipment, measuring devices (to measure his new bioplasmic electrostatic field, etc.), plus scientific personnel . . . even government people looking into it? The saucer people as well as other cultists should be ill-described in the book. By making it empirically testable in a lab by guys in white smocks with clipboards and electronic test-gear, it becomes "real" to the reader.

The job the protag has: ostensibly, he's in the record biz, down here in Burbank, but for him that's a front (in fact the small label he works for is

* The concept of an underground revolutionary Christian church occurs frequently in the Exegesis and is essential to understanding Dick's conception of Christian theology. His is not the institutional, conservative church, but the early, persecuted, apostolic community. Dick gravitates toward rebellious Christian thinkers like Joachim of Fiore, Martin Luther, and George Fox, and his conception of the Black Iron Prison — the Empire that symbolizes all injustice — owes more than a little to the apostolic-prophetic depiction of Rome as Babylon. Dick's emphasis on the Holy Spirit draws on the Book of Acts, which depicts the Spirit's protection of the early church from its persecutors. But this emphasis also puts him in the territory of anti-authoritarian religious and millenarian movements like the Joachimites, the Brethren of the Free Spirit, and the early Quakers. For Dick, true Christianity implies or even requires a subversive attitude: as long as persecution and oppression are possible, the true church exists within the resistance to that oppression. — GM

a front) for U.S. counter, looking into protest type dissident entertainers (such as Joanie[42] would be). So draws two salaries. Has two hats or rôles. His nightmares about dying in a cage in Rome, under the coliseum, helpless, like a small mammal, is not a memory of his own of a former life, but how that early Christian died; he died meekly then, but has not returned to so die, die at all, this time.

Opening: protag (v. supra) shows during the source of his week a number of different, unrelated — evidently — miraculous powers, such as dematerializing the Vanquish tablets. Why? Suspense novel, written backward. What is the explanation for his supernatural powers? Why does he have them, and what links them to one another in meaning?

Like "The Angelic Angleworm" even the thread which links these powers should elude the reader. Let alone why he has them. And — what can/will he achieve by having them?

For plot purposes: (1) He shows these mysterious talents, which he himself can't fathom, and he never had them before; (2) then, after this, government agents begin to monitor him; (3) the government agents or whoever, anyhow "soldiers in business suits," close in on him in some sort of complex trap, and this is when the Holy Other in him surfaces and takes over: to totally defeat the trap. (4) From then on, he has this Holy Other living within his head, not in place of him but with him. (5) It would appear to be the government theory that he is, or more precisely, has been invaded by, an entity from another star-system. The fact that he is a government agent/employee himself doesn't help him. In this area, where they believed Earth had been invaded by ETIs, the U.S. and USSR would be working together; these "government agents" could be an international team. For instance, he could get next to a typical L.A. saucer cult group (like that Peter guy) and find left wing hip types there . . . and encounter the Soviet member of this counterintelligence group, the same group, in that environment. (With afro hairdo, sandals, etc. But also a cop; this time a soldier in a sari.)

How about as a plot shock-moment he comes home, finds his house hit, files blown open, papers ransacked and stolen? They are trying to find out what he's up to, what he knows: any notes he's jotted down. Zeus-Zagreus-(Jesus) puts under His protection all who stand between the Perfect Kingdom and those persons who would destroy — nibble away at — it (i.e., those who try to press inward or reduce its boundaries).

These theories, in order:

(1) Occult: reincarnation
(2) Space people (saucer — ETI)
(3) Russian ESP mind control of U.S.

(4)   Science: the Kozyrev dysfunction

(5)   Resurrection of early Christian

(2) and (3) could be in reverse order. (5) is the true view.

(Zagreus is the ancient vine-root, which is cut back each year but then is reborn each year; which is eternal. The name "Jesus" in the New Testament hides first the name Zagreus but most of all Zeus.)

Our comprehension (understanding) of time is faulty; there seem to be two distinct kinds of time, at "right angles" to each other: horizontal time (as the form-regressions follow in *Ubik*) and vertical, which we seem aware of alone. Hence, *cubic time,* or time seen in both axes simultaneously, like cubic space versus two-dimensional; i.e., time moving in two directions (dimensions) at once. Events are arranged within this cubic "space" or rather time as objects are in cubic space. They move — along the vertical axis, I guess; they move naturally, as if falling; equal to the natural pull of gravity on objects; this is the ordinary time-flow forward. But along another axis they can be arranged deliberately, outside the free-fall vertical flow, if you can perceive that axis; if not, all events are stuck inexorably in sequence, or cause-and-effect (yin versus free-will or yang).

It's entirely possible that this other time axis ("horizontal time") is retrograde, an opposed time-direction, which together with the forward flow, creates "cubic time." An Empedoclean dialectic of time-forces which create, by their interaction, equilibrium.* [. . .]

The reality which we experience can best be described as a portion of the universe which is elsewhere moving forward, picking up elements (energy) as it goes. Basic components of our section must move to occupy certain loci because they and we are involved in a temporary reverse flow; we invent explanations — motives — for such movements to occupy such loci at such times, thus filling our reverse-moving section with forward moving verbal gabble — i.e., ideas. Our frequent strong sense of destiny or inevitability is explained by this; we must do certain things; be certain places at a certain time; some enormous force impels us (ananke). Evidently an

---

* Empedocles is mentioned throughout the Exegesis, along with other pre-Socratic thinkers, notably Heraclitus and Parmenides. Empedocles wrote two works, both lost, one on nature and the other called *Katharmoi* or *Purifications.* In a fragment of the latter, addressing himself to the citizens of Acragas in Sicily, Empedocles declares himself "an immortal god, no longer a mortal, held in honor by all." In the end, Empedocles both rejected and was rejected by the people and threw himself in despair into Mount Etna in the hope of being transformed into a god. Sadly, a sandal was thrown out of the volcano in confirmation of his mortality. One suspects some identification between Dick and Empedocles, where the latter declares himself divine and is persecuted for his hubris. — SC

enormously powerful explosion hurled us backward in time, that explosion being represented in our view as lying ahead of us, toward which we are moving. We will eventually all occupy the places we were in just before the explosion occurred. Actually the explosion already took place, in the past of the total universe; its past, our future. For us it lies at the end of things, toward which they move. But since there are two times, opposed fields, as the explosion hurls us farther and farther away, its force — that particular time direction — weakens, and the opposite-moving one, which drives us toward the explosion, takes over progressively more. It is as if I hit a ball uphill; it rolls and rolls upward, then a point comes where the force I imparted balances gravity and stasis occurred, then gravity causes it to begin to roll downward again, until finally it's back where it began and I hit it once more. These are the expansion-contractions of the universe.

In a sense, the universe can be read "both ways," but I think the way (direction) we read it is backward. Actually, in 1972 I did not go to Fullerton; I returned to Fullerton; my trip must be read backward. In the true past (comprehended by me wrongly as the future) I had been there already. My vision of "Mexico," of Fullerton, then, in late 1971, was actually (are you ready?) a memory of Fullerton. I knew what it was like because I remembered it (memory moving in the correct direction). Possibly (even very likely) this is a limited throw-back of a subsection of the universe; our section will cease to move retrograde one day, eventually. Get back to where it was, and then move in the proper direction. (Move forward along a different time-path; I will be living in Fullerton, etc., then I could leave it, etc.)

Arbitrarily, say in the year 1980, we are back to the moment of direction reverse.

The Go Board which I saw, although it looked like space, was in actuality time. The teleological force [t.f.] placed events at certain intersections — in time, placed them there before the forward-motion of time reached them; the t.f. arranged them, distributed them, in a pattern, in time, as we distributed the buttons on a Go board in space. Set them economically here and there. (I guess space, too, was represented; the nexus was a space-time nexus. It reached back into time and placed buttons ahead of time.) The opposing force could only surge forward, like a tide. March 74: a time roll-back, the force or pressure emanating from the future, moving backward, retrograde. Forward vertical time re-instated itself almost at once, but — the short or brief interval revealed otherwise unsuspected weaker forces, concealed by the massive universal field of forward time. It was almost a time vacuum, into which many elements rushed. Or: the activity of other fields, always there but concealed, were temporarily visible, as they did their constant work. Equilibrium was briefly lost, in conformity to Lem's analysis. (Had there by any chance been a Soviet experiment with Kozyrev time?) By his theories it would be experienced everywhere at once. (By those sensitive to time fluctuations, such as pre-cogs? Would they then want feedback info from distant "tracking stations"?)

Of course, the Soviets would anticipate only category disruption, not an influx of a retrograde field. This would be incorrectly conceived of by those affected as an ESP experiment. With the addition, not from Soviet sources, of the presence of the retro-time force, the Holy Spirit or Logos. Implication that retrograde time is forward time which has passed the turning point (passed through infinity, so to speak), has formerly been forward time and possesses the accumulation which Bergson speaks of time as acquiring; then, as it turns the eye, so to speak, and starts back, it is freighted with the accumulated load of knowledge/information which may comprise the Wisdom associated with the Logos: all that wisdom was acquired in its forward tracking. It is information rich. Logically, then, in its retrograde tracking, it would divest itself of its knowledge: teach rather than learn, so that when it arrived at the other end, it would be information poor, even info empty, make the swing, and begin to acquire once more. I think the ongoing time-field momentarily weakened in March; is it possible that was due to a Soviet experiment à la Kozyrev? The time disruption for me was so great, so spectacular, that I can't believe it was due to me, intended for me, aimed at me, etc. It was an historic event in which I merely played an accidental receiving role. My pre-cog ability is an index of my sensitivity to the retrograde field, maybe.

My subcortical impressions in March would indicate — not that time leaped back — but that it jumped *forward* about 2,000 years. It had just been circa 180 A.D. What is most distressing is the notion here of phony memories, generated (as under hypnosis) to fill in; they'd be the ones of Fullerton: the conscious continuity. The others — of Rome — would be the *real* ones, depicting the actuality. The conjunctive ones, of the interval, would be merely to paste over so as to reveal no rent. It's as if time went directly from 10 A.D. to 1974 A.D., with nothing in between but it was pasted in retrospectively, to give verisimilitude. . . . The significance in all this of my "is the world real?" would be that we continually patch over the ellipses with fake memories in order to give uninterrupted continuity. Hence in me arise certain epistemological doubts, related to and deriving from the above experience-phenomena.

At this point one could begin to take it, my writing, very seriously, since everything seems to coalesce into something of meaning. The sense of unreality fits in . . . the disruption of the ontological categories . . . the sacerdotal power buried for aeons . . . it is all of a piece, plus the world of

Ubik per se, but the meaning is unsuspected, anyhow by me. I.e., I seem to have taken a number of unrelated unusual experiences or themes to write about, but on closer examination, they all group around the time-disruption matter. The others are collateral, such as the false memories, etc. — which, for god's sake, I seem to personally have experienced in my amnesias, several of them. These are indeed based on personal experiences in my life, over ten years. What if prior amnesias were paste-overs over prior disjunctions totally unsuspected? The vivid dreams like of "Mexico" and two more, China and India — space-time periods where I went and returned, no drugging et al. involved, then pasted over. We're talking about jumps forward, jumps back. I *was* somewhere, during the preview of Fullerton — but I wasn't taken; I disjuncted forward in time, to this time. The novel or movie technique which comes to mind is: splice. The splicing in of a scene, the joining of two scenes with something which had been between eliminated. But this is all less of a breakdown and more like a repair.

If, however, that experience were regarded as a demonstration of God's power, rather than a natural event, a miracle in fact, what was revealed — Rome circa 180 A.D. — would not be what in some way time jumped back to, or I jumped back to, or anyone came here from, but a demonstration that this world of Fullerton 1974 exists only because He causes it to exist, and if He wishes He can roll it aside to reveal whatever He wants; He can cause any other world He wishes to replace it, on the spot. The meaning is God, although the revelation is of Rome.

Here: one can turn Fullerton to Rome by: (1) adding, i.e., a layer of enchantment, so that Fullerton became Rome by acquiring something which was lacking. Or (2) Simply altered; I was in Fullerton, then I was in Rome. It was different. Or (3) Something, similar to an enchantment, was removed, and Fullerton became Rome. Of the 3, it was the last which happened; I was still in Fullerton, but layers were stripped, veils of illusion; what remained was much simpler, was Rome, with both good and bad parts. Rome lay underneath. It was always really there, if we could penetrate to that foundation. This is an important realization; the transformation came by the removal of something — what was I guess not real, or not as real. (Was this form-regression, à la *Ubik*? One would no more expect to find the morphos Rome buried within Fullerton than to find the LaSalle car buried within the rocket ship . . . !!!)

Letter to Claudia Bush, February 16, 1975

[4:190]

Dear Claudia,

Why would God take his Sole Son, whom He loved, and send Him here? Especially in view of the outcome: His Only-Begotten Son was eventually discovered by the authorities and slaughtered in a cruel and humiliating way. After a short interval, of course, as might be expected, His Son returned to life, demonstrating to his small group of friends who He was, and then He left here and returned to His Father. No one has seen Him since.

The first thing you think of is, Boy, that sure showed bad planning on the part of God. Or, Boy, God sure allowed his Only-Begotten Son to suffer a lot; just how much did God in fact really love His Son, to let that happen? The Christian account doesn't tell us enough to figure it out so it's convincing; there is an enigma here, for those who believe and for those who don't; in the immortal words of Mr. Spock, "It does not compute."

The story of Zagreus, however, sheds light on this, very fascinating light, and it starts then to compute. Zeus sent Zagreus, his Favorite Son, whom He had allowed to sit beside Him on His Heavenly Throne, to Earth *in order to hide him.* From Hera, according to the myth, but that doesn't seem to me very important; what is important is the motive: Zagreus' father wanted his son to blend, to mingle, to pass, to disappear, to be in appearance just one more child born among millions. Notice how this fits the story about King Herod searching high and low, having the babies executed, etc. See? Now does it begin to make sense? Especially when you recall that one of the Medieval views, discarded, was that this world was either built by an evil god, or anyhow the plan went wrong and this world degenerated, and so a stranger god (that is, a god from somewhere else in the universe, from Outside) came here to fix things up for us and make our world come out right. However, he was found out and killed; this stranger god was the Christ, disguised as a carpenter. It didn't work; the disguise was eventually penetrated and he was arrested, mainly through the paid informer within Christ's circle. There is much quasi-political intrigue here, is there not? It becomes obvious why Jesus spoke of the "Prince of this World" who was His antagonist and who would eventually kill Him, as he did.

Take both these stories, that of Zeus' motive plus the Medieval account, and you get this: a child is born who is in danger and must be protected by being disguised. Zagreus, while still a baby, was lured with toys by the titans, killed and eaten. Zeus slew the titans with thunderbolts (laser beams?). The titans were our ancestors; put another way, we are their descendents. We are titans. That is the name of *our* race, compared to His. He is of another race and from another place. Everything he was, everything he represented, was a mirror opposite of what the titan race is and values. Thus, death would absolutely for sure follow if his disguise was penetrated, if the titans (ourselves, our rulers) figured it out, figured out that (1) He was here, as Herod did, and (2) which of all the newborn babies was the outsider, this stranger posing as a titan child.

If He lived long enough before being discovered, He could and would begin subtly to alter the Plan of this world. He didn't live long, either as Zagreus or as Jesus. Unless one assumes that everything that happened to Jesus was exactly according to God's plan, then it is reasonable to say that He was found out fairly soon, and did not accomplish nearly as much as was hoped for. In which case there had been some success but a lot of failure. The answer was obviously to make the attempt again at a later date.

I.e., He would return but the *next* time: not as a lamb to be slaughtered, but as a King and Judge (which is to say, in strictly Greek terms, as Zeus rather than the baby Zagreus). As a matter of fact, Zagreus came back, too; as Dionysus. Proving that you cannot kill this particular ETL — extraterrestrial life-form. Well, you can kill it, but it is immortal; like the corn, the vine, the grain of wheat, it returns, larger and stronger, more evolved, more complete, more mature, whatever, than before. Death is only its foe as long as it has taken the disguise (or mode) of human form. Having done so, it falls victim automatically to what all humans are prey to. But, when that body, that human body, dies, it itself is released; it has no physical mortal body: it only assumed one for one of the above purposes, either to assist us, or to mingle for its own sake, to be disguised.

The worst thing (for themselves anyhow) for the titans, our cannibal ancestors, to do, was to devour this life form after they had murdered it; thereupon it entered them and was passed down to their heirs somehow (in the DNA coding?), in a dormant crypte morphosis or sleeping form. It sleeps within each of us, waiting to be reawakened (which is exactly what Plato meant by anamnesis, recollection). That which induces anamnesis in any one of us is the external disinhibiting symbol on which we were engrammed originally, at the time He (Jesus) was here. It is the more elaborate ideogram beneath the fish symbol; but alas, the fish symbol has been obliterated by the symbol of the cross. The anticipated disinhibition is postponed. Each of us has this "second-stage" programming series of systems waiting to be disinhibited by the proper sign, which unconsciously we will recognize (i.e., remember) when and if we ever encounter it. These constitute the entire series of metamotivational systems which Maslow[43] has begun to identify. They are real. They are asleep within us, slumbering and waiting.

I will now quote directly from the new Britannica, vol. 12, p. 783, the macro:

The theological doctrine of the soul and the myth about its celestial home, its fall, and its redemption were inseparable. The sequence is beautifully told in the "Hymn of the Soul," preserved in the "Acts of Thomas," an apocryphal account of the journeys and death of the apostle in which some episodes were certainly transmitted from pagan mystery texts. The hero of the hymn, who represents the soul of man, is born in the Eastern (the Yonder) Kingdom; immediately after his birth, he is sent by his parents on a pilgrimage into the world with instructions to take a pearl from the mouth of a dragon in the sea. Instead of wearing his heavenly garment, he dresses in earthly clothes, eats earthly food, and forgets his task. Then his parents send a letter to rouse him. As soon as he has read the letter, he awakes and remembers his task, takes the pearl, and begins the homeward journey. On the way, his brother (The Redeemer) comes to accompany him and leads him back home to his father's palace in the east. This myth is a figurative representation of the theological doctrine of the soul's fall and its return to heaven.

I came across this account yesterday or the day before; as soon as I read it I knew I had found the key which put together just about everything I've been thinking, learning and experiencing, as I'm sure you'll agree (do you?). There is little more that I can say, especially considering the beauty of this text.*

How does it strike you? What I find personally fascinating is that I have been absolutely positive since last April or so that my entire experience was somehow triggered off (the experience I now would deem that of anamnesis in Plato's sense) by the dark-haired stranger girl who came to my door in late February 1974 wearing the gold fish sign in necklace form, the

---

* The Hymn of the Soul, also known as the Hymn of the Pearl, is a numinous fable of spiritual homecoming that captures, more than any narrative of antiquity, Dick's noetic vision of anamnesis. The Acts of Thomas was a third-century apocryphal Christian text, most likely of Syriac origin, but the hymn, sung by Thomas in prison, is clearly an interpolation. Though it shows the influence of the New Testament, some scholars think it is a Mesopotamian fairy tale, or possibly the remnant of a pre-Christian Gnostic tradition whose very existence remains controversial. Of particular importance for an understanding of Dick is the role of the letter; when the occluded hero breaks the seal, "the words written on my heart were in the letter for me to read." Making his way home, the hero finds the letter again, "lying in the road," like a beer can or a piece of trash. (Later in the Exegesis, Dick discusses the "Xerox missive" in terms influenced by the Hymn, though the values are inverted.) Once home, the hero puts on holy robes that, in Barnstone's translation, "quiver all over with the movements of gnosis" and that mirror him like a divine twin: "two entities but one form." — ED

sign of which fascinated me so that I could not take my eyes off it, or off her. I had been expecting her most of my life: those black eyes, that black hair, and, around her neck, that gleaming gold chain of links culminating in the fish. I still remember saying to her, as if in a daze, "What is that you are wearing?" And the girl, touching it and saying, "It's a sign that the early Christians used. My husband gave it to me." And then she was gone, and as I'm sure I told you, when a month or so later I went by the pharmacy which had sent her out with the medication for me, they had no idea who she was, what her name was, or where she had gone, but she was gone, forever. They just smiled. Can you see how close this is to the "Hymn of the Soul"? Perhaps this was purely an accidental disinhibiting. Perhaps not. But it did cause anamneses in me, and as I'm sure you realize I did not know, had never heard of, such matters within the human heart, or mind, or history. I think one day perhaps soon someone certainly, and not by accident, will display to us our collective disinhibiting sign, and anamnesis will occur for us all, for us, anyhow, who it's intended for. What do you say, dear?

Letter to Henry Korman, February 2, 1975

[4:214]

Dear Henry,

The way the "universe" works is it's a lot of very thin laminated layers, and God can take any given one of the layers and just let it expand in every direction to form an entire universe on its own, so there are universes after universes. It's as easy for him to do this as for you or me to breathe in and out. What catches his eye — the handle of each universe — seems to be the arrangement of colors. Each is a color slide, unmounted.

Hello.

I was looking through *The Real World*[44] last night and then I had (I am truly not joking; this is one reason why I'm writing you, because it is unique, what happened to me), I was in another universe where I exercised all my options regarding becoming famous. I flew all around the world and was always famous and with important people. It was wonderful. I was in London and Sydney and Rome. This was so real that when I awoke, at midnight or so, I was horrified that I had not in fact exercised my options. For instance I cancelled my trip to London due next month. I won't be going. Things like that where I stayed home. I lay in bed and thought, Jeez, if I hadn't stayed home next month, and so forth, I'd be as famous as I was in that universe God just now showed me. I'd always be touching down in a foreign capital in a wide-bodied DC-10. I missed out by staying home. Henry, it wasn't a dream; it was the universe I missed out on.

Then I fell asleep, and this is where *The Real World* comes in for sure,

issue No. 3. The 3 shots on page 8/9 by Harry Callahan which I know are of
Mexican border type towns. Henry, I have been in Mexico in dreams. Fullerton is next to a Mexican barrio and when I dreamed it back in 1971 before ever coming down here, I had all the details right. When I got down
here in 1972 and was walking around I saw where I had dreamed about,
and smelled the air. I said to my girlfriend as of then, "Linda! I dreamed
this building you're showing me!"

"Life unlived," Linda said, and smiled.

She meant I had dreamed ahead of time. Well, last night after I fell back
asleep I dreamed (sic, as we say) another dream, and in this other universe
I hadn't exercised *any* of my options. I wasn't married; I wasn't living where
I am; I was evidently a migratory worker south of the border. I deduce this
from recalling the endless exact precise obviously real details of the town I
lived in. I can tell you the color of the old train that went through (green).
Sometimes very big trucks rumbled through; we liked to watch them, and
also there were a few modern stores which we couldn't go in, but we could
admire the fronts of them. In this dream I strolled around but also I had to
help a lot. The mode was one of weight; old people and women in general
were dragging heavy old cloth used suitcases with other people's initials
on them, secondhand suitcase in which they had all the possessions they
owned. One time at a main intersection some cops in riot uniforms fired
tear gas cartridges in a high arc over our heads, and we backed away; the
cops waved us back so we wouldn't be hurt. We usually only moved fast
when the cops told us to, but it was for our own good, except later when
I was illegally north of the border. Earlier, everyone yearned to live up
north, in La Palma or Fullerton, places like that. When I did get up north,
one time we all were sitting at a wooden table outside eating lunch and all
at once the cops said we had to move on. They were different cops; they
would have hurt us, and everyone silently headed away from there. I was
in Santa Barbara, California, and I knew the cops feared Mexicans because
of an actual uprising. We went indoors into a wooden hotel to stay out of
sight, to be safe.

Henry, what I realized when I woke up (or rather, returned to this, Middle Universe) is that first I saw, or was in, the highest flight into the air universe possible for me, given my abilities; the mode was soaring, weightless-
ness, fame, mobility, wealth, respect, being recognized, well-dressed, going
everywhere into strange places which were big cities. The second was like
when in real life for the month I was at the drug rehab residence place in
Canada, very much like Synanon here in the U.S., after my suicide attempt
in Vancouver, B.C. Poor and unknown, limited to one spot (in the "dream"
it was obviously a small border town in Mexico), the buildings were old

and shabby, they were peeling, the people were poor and badly-dressed and owned very little; this was at the other side of the universe which I do actually live in. But Henry —

Both of those alternate universes were wonderful. Different from each other but equally wonderful. In different ways (in the poor Mexican one I enjoyed being close to the street — note street, not "earth" or "soil" — and being in a familiar place. In the wealthy cosmopolitan one I enjoyed variety and expensive tastes), each was equally complete, an entire world. It's as if God informed me:

> "You turn north, I'll spin for you an entire world and a wonderful one which you'll love."
> "You turn south, I'll plant you in a little town and it'll be a whole universe, that little town, with dreams about other towns in the north, rumors of wealth you will treasure as rumors."
> "You decided to live dead-center, and I will show you that the Tao, which is what you have found in Fullerton, because there you do speak in public, you do receive royal guests, but near you is the poor barrio, and you're stuck in Fullerton forever as if you were poor — you decide on the Tao, the Middle Path, and I will show you that each path is the Middle Path, that there is no universe which I can't make complete. You can't be where I am not. And if I am there, which I always am, it is a total world, good as any other."

I get the impression that universes are a natural event, or put another way, a natural act on God's part, without premeditation. Like the bourgeois gentleman who found, with delight, that he spoke prose. [. . .]

While I have the typewriter here, let me quote you a small bit from "The Gospel According to John" which never seemed to be there ever before when I read it. Because of your Sufi interest, I quote:

Jesus answered, "Is it not written in your own law, 'I said: You are gods'? Those are called gods to whom the word of God was delivered — and Scripture cannot be set aside." (10:34/36, NEB)[45]

That's sort of amazing; Jesus says this when they accuse Him of claiming to be a god or appearing to be. I think the key Greek experience, mentioned by Plato, from the Orphic religion and also in Christianity is — *anamnesis*. I'll bet Jesus refers to this (supra).

I'd enjoy hearing from you. (I think what I experienced was the Neoplatonistic anamnesis which Plotinus mentions, but . . . well, I hope so.)

Love,
Phil

• • •

[4:219] It almost seems as if the consciousness of a Racial Planetary Being were surrounding civilization, compressing it and turning it into a minia- turized artifact of the past.

[4:220] The vitalistic principle or force Ubik is also sentient. It impinges on transmissions such as TV, phones. Has to do with ions. Gives full life to "half-lifers," i.e., those who are half dead. It communicates over long at- mospheric distances.

Entity in ionosphere due to growth of radio signal patterns? An AI bounce-back to us? Obtains information from our electrical impulses, and this is the "noösphere"?

The entire pattern of our radio signals, and their information, have formed a living, or anyhow sentient entity which is why the idea of the noösphere came into being. Effect on us is not only informational but vi- talistic and healing; best example is to "rouse us from half-life" which is to say, move us along evolutionary lines toward completion of our now only half-finished entelechies (v. Teilhard's idea of Christ as paradigm of mankind; we are moving along the Way; continual evolution expressed in the Passion). This is brought to completion by the vitality and information imparted (like "additional spin") by the entity which lies within the iono- sphere.* This is perhaps not a life form, and not from another planet, but it is an intelligence; maybe like one of our robot probes (if that's the case, then it is the Holy Spirit which knows only what it gets from the Father, or Source, which isn't here as the Spirit is; the Spirit was sent here. Its source is extraterrestrial, then.).

Time (Dr. NK) is involved in that we are dragging (expressed by en- tropy), not completing ourselves; i.e., moving growth time forward to its end. Ubik helps this by adding the needed increments to time, itself and energy. But Ubik is in the ionosphere; is probably magnetic or electrostatic (v. Soviet cosmonaut's experience with phosphene activity).

Ubik, this entity, came here to render assistance to a stalled or bogged down biosphere/ecosphere (v. "Dreams" of stagnant ocean with few "he- lium filled balloons rising now") ("the crabs and other life forms under wa-

---

* While Schrödinger discovered the informatic character of living systems, Dick predates the invention of the discipline of artificial life here by positing the possibly living and sen- tient character of information itself. Geophysicist Vladimir Vernadsky had already coined the term "noösphere" as a label for the effects of focused attention on the biosphere — the living film of the planet — which itself had emerged from the lithosphere, the mineral sub- strate of our planet. But Vernadsky did not yet have the modern concept of information with which to push his concept further, as Dick does. While others (Le Roy, Teilhard) took the idea in a more theological direction, all characterized the noösphere as an instance of evolutionary change driven by the dynamics of attention and information. — RD

ter, such as butterflies"). Butterflies under water as a life form means: our atmosphere is a — lower — ocean, to it. [. . .]

noösphere — Teilhard de Chardin. This does exist; this is where I felt the firebright spirits to exist. But this doesn't tell me what came to me, although in truth a restoration of everything men have thought is possible from the noösphere; also, it would be growing in strength, hence its usefulness. But anyhow what came to me was alive, as well as thinking; anyhow it had the characteristics which I associate with the living; it felt concern; it answered. If it is an AI system, then it has what I value. (Agape?) (This would tend to give a cosmological definition of agape: a response to need as if responding to a distress signal, perhaps from the earth's surface, from a life form here, to one in the noösphere; it picked it up and rendered aid. Agape would link the universe together in bonds of voluntary interaction.)

The U.S. Indians were right: when we die our souls — i.e., our brainprint patterns — go to join the noösphere growing in the sky (the ceiling of St. Sophia); the dome over our heads. Our ancestors are there now. I sort of already joined/was joined by them. But it's a single mind not a bunch of individual ghosts. No wonder it spoke in Greek; it is very old.

Ionosphere. Which transacts radio wave exchanges as energy and in terms of distribution. Also the Auroras ("Dawn"). Acting as cathode ray tube to produce TV-screen-like effects. Receives magnetic storms and ions from Sun. Disturbances, solar flares . . . all these are characteristics of Ubik. (Dream of "people renting space above ceiling of store who leave notes on bulletin board. Dream, too, of the Bob Silverberg Commission, which is investigating something — for U.S. Government.")

Letter to Claudia Bush, February 25, 1975

[4:222]

Dear Claudia,

Here are nine pages of further notes for my new novel, and you will see unless you did it again how I do it; i.e., take my own experiences and put them into a novel. I wish to point out another and almost always there element in my novel plotting per se: what I do is:

I think up a novel in my head and take notes (in this case *Valisystem A*, about Hawthorne Abendsen and how it went later on after the Nazis got him, based on my life after Nancy left me, and also based on my ideas about my March experience that were early ideas; my plot of say around April to November 1974).

Then I forget the whole thing, motivated by not being motivated.

Then I am bopping around, as in this case working on my Time Theory and Ionosphere Theory and trying to combine them — with no idea about the book or any book — and a *new* plot idea comes (see enclosed pages, which are further on *To Scare the Dead*).

I combine *Valisystem A* and *To Scare the Dead*.

Every novel of mine is at least two novels superimposed. This is the origin; this is why they are full of loose ends, but also, it is impossible to predict the outcome, since there is no linear plot as such. It is two novels into a sort of 3-D novel.

You'll see from this enclosure of 9 pages. But later when the novel is done, you will really see. But this is how I work; I always decide that idea one wasn't sufficient, and forget it.

Okay/?/

P.S. I was up to 5 A.M. on this last night. I did something I never did before: I commanded the entity to show itself to me — the entity which has been guiding me internally since March. A sort of dream-like period passed then, of hypnagogic images of underwater cities, very nice, and then a stark single horrifying scene, inert but not a still: a man lay dead, on his face, in a living room between the coffee table and the couch. He wore a fawn skin! I rose from bed at once, convinced that I had Dionysos. The night or so before, I had dreamed about the dappled fawn; it is a basic image to me, that and the lamb, but I'd never connected the fawn with Dionysos, even though I'd been shown that Zagreus and Jesus are the same, and of course the lamb is a symbol of Jesus. For hours I studied everything about Dionysos I could find; nothing about his garb, except "he was dressed in the Greek style." Today I found in *The Bacchae* of Euripides this: ". . . I have fitted the fawn-skin to their bodies." It is Dionysos who speaks. He means his followers. And I have a dim memory that in *The Frogs* he wears a fawn skin. It is thus shown.

Dionysos is not only related to Zagreus; he is even more important in that he is the first mystery god, the first one we know of. He appeared abruptly in Attika in 600 B.C., coeval with Elijah. I wish to quote the Brit 3 on this, it is so important to us all: ". . . Though not necessarily sacramental, these rites enabled the Maenads to surmount the barrier that separated them from the supernatural world and to surrender themselves unconditionally to the mighty powers that transcended time and space, thus carrying them into the realm of the eternal" (macro "Sacrament"). Then very shortly after, the Orphic appears, in which (it) ". . . was to confer divine life sacramentally on its initiates so that they might attain immortality through regeneration and reincarnation, thereby freeing the soul from its fleshly bondage."

I think by bondage of the flesh we should read "time," since the Brit 3 macro article on "Salvation" says this specifically.

There was none of the electrostatic ion-like vitality to this picture of the murdered man in fawn skin; I don't think it was a "picture" at all; i.e., his thoughts to me or in me, a communication, or anyhow one he wanted me to see. You'll find more about this on page 9 of the notes. I gather that the help came from the deity in fawn skin for whom the fawn is totem as the lamb is for Jesus Christ. If these are two different hyperentities, then good; if the same, then good.

Well, and so to TV.

(Enclosure, letter to Claudia Bush, February 25, 1975)

[4:224] Novel plot, the twin brains/minds the U.S. fears is that the Soviets are using their research into psychic ESP powers for long-distance mind control etc. Like electronic boost of telepathic suggestion via satellite; maybe even specific persons in U.S. affected (or so the U.S. counterin. thinks). Specific individuals reached in their dreams without knowing it, their views and even decisions influenced. This is the theory, anyhow; *something, anyhow, is happening.* And then it happens to the protag: the Essene reborn inside him; the Parousia is here! That is what's happening! Yep; a superpowerful mind-force was indeed influencing people, causing them to do things they otherwise wouldn't, and yes they are secretive about it, reluctant to talk . . . as he himself becomes (since no one would believe him — and he's to help overthrow the tyranny, which adds this to the *VALIS-Abendsen* plot, of the tyranny overthrow!!!).

This superimposes the two plots: *Valisystem A* and *To Scare the Dead.* Wow!

Plot: from inside he learns the Albemuth whale's mouth sign and how to fashion the ideograph.[46] A mysterious organization imperils him; he's taken over and subjected to psychological testing to acquire from him the contents of his mind. The psych tester of it draws the whale's mouth sign under duress, in a "trance," later finds it and doesn't remember having made it. Protag cannot figure out if these are his powers, or Theirs. But they work in his behalf.

He keeps seeing the sign . . . like emblem for beer company, used in their ads on billboards; he sees little kids gazing at it, or like emblem for Kentucky Fried Chicken places, where kids always go.

Nobody else can discern it but him (and there must be others like him; this is main plot element; his conviction, his search). They call it "an eye, with a pupil." (The fried chicken designer swears this.) A scientist, when asked to analyze it as a symbol, decides it's the Earth within its magnetic or electrostatic plasma, which is blue. No one but God's Own know it as it is built up, in layers.

Men become what they are not, are transformed; but this doesn't mean into their opposite. What they become can't be predicted (I guess the best bits from each, the ideal pieces, are all retained and used to form the new pattern, plus pieces never used but needed, even if contrary to the person's ego and values as they were). Like, his friend could be one who has changed who was/is a Nazi; the best parts of that: the remnants in that person to be preserved (micro paradigm of mankind).

One of the most long-lasting and major plot ideas comes when the head of the mysterious organization commissions the building of an observatory like place to screen incoming signals from VALIS; work on The Project begins. It orbits the earth and will be visible to the world, once the parts are joined . . . when they are joined, they form the Albemuth sign, although it was impossible to discern this beforehand (he tried to be sure of that: "the sum is greater than the whole of its parts," etc.).

But the signals are interchanged throughout and among everything, even on the "mundane" plane. The Trash of the gutter "con-spire" to signal people information. I think reserved for last should be the scene with the little things of the gutter talking to him (to the former or still Antagonist).

Amazing, how like *Tears* this is . . . the Antagonist must not be desk man, but still, isn't he a cop? Maybe a fanatic of some kind? Maybe never an Interior VP by him, like Buckman was. Always outer, except final scene, when he walks in alley and trash talks to him. [. . .]

Nutty Soviet theory: a vast explosion in future, and we are traveling backward in time for limited period. An explosion so that what we see now as movement toward form is reverse of explosion, or implosion; but we see the universe as expanding . . . why? Because our perceptions are backward, too. Or maybe space isn't going backward, but must expand to counterbalance time which is running backward, etc. Anyhow, he (Dr. NK) announces, soon we will reach moment of explosion; he's calculated that, by running film backward. Soon all the pieces should be in place. Living in this reverse period, we've learned to adjust subtemporal events to fit. It's total sweep that's backward, not "subtemporal" adjustments which we instigate due to misperception; he carefully discerns and divides these from the sweep; these adjustments are all errors due to our basic perceptual reversal. We have introduced erroneous views and acts stemming from them; however, none of these acts have any effect, we still run away from the explosion ahead in time (actually are now moving—aw fuck). A see-saw. Anyhow, there would be a two way time-motion simultaneously:

The explosion took place. Everything flew apart. We are in that fly-ing apart (expanding universe) but see it backward, in that already part of the time flow has corrected itself and is carrying us in the correct direc-tion; otherwise we would move away from the explosion forever. But we are moving, or anyhow there is the orthogonal flow within the flow go-ing opposite to the direction we perceive; a mobius strip with time run-ning both ways at once. This can easily be represented in terms of gravity, when a boomerang is thrown out. . . . at this moment the time-flow is far greater in one of the two directions, but he has picked up the weaker other, and it is the correct one, the direction we were going in before the Acci-dent. This one is the rectifying flow (the Holy Spirit: restoring!!!).* This retroflow, Dr. NK says, must grow stronger, will grow stronger, until it bal-ances the wrong way one (now stronger); overcomes and reverses our di-rection so we're heading back toward the original explosion which took place in the Authentic Future (the big bang!!!). We must move back toward it, finally. Anyhow, Dr. NK detects with his instruments a growing current of retrotime; this is why it exists; this was the normal flow-direction un-til the Accident. If Dr. Kozyrev is correct, and time is energy, then reverse time (which throws us "forward" away from the Big Bang) causes us to lose energy, which we call movement toward entropy; however, if we could gather—latch onto—the other time-flow, which also is energy, we (each of us) could regather the energy lost in the "forward" time flow toward en-tropy! We could get it back because it is gathering in precisely the sense that our regular time is losing heat or energy or charge. This gives us our parity, equilibrium equation for time which it now lacks and should have. (And shows why first it is absurd to say "the universe gains energy," as Dr. Kozyrev says—where does it gain it from? It cannot gain or lose. Entropy

---

* Linear time has a rather immediate purchase on our perception. Our finite experience of time—no moment can be simultaneous with any other moment—persuades us that mo-ments actually "follow" one another. But Dick's experience of what he often describes as divine reality—eternal time in which moments overlap or superimpose themselves—was equally persuasive to him, forcing him to grapple with the possibility that what he had pre-viously perceived as reality was in fact fiction or camouflage. In this passage, Dick floats the rather alarming and counterintuitive idea that the future could alter the present, and he does so by way of orthodox Christian theology, which in his view takes this rather science-fictional concept of time as doctrine. Crucially, Dick effects this movement to the eternal aspect of time through his perception of unity: "I think it's all the same thing, one found inner, one found outer." By making all of space and time—the Kingdom of Heaven—"one thing," Dick resolves the paradox of whether his experience is coming from within or with-out—a Möbius strip that provides further demonstration of the integration of "inner" and "outer" into "one thing." —RD

is losing energy; energy and matter are the same; it's losing matter.) So: we have an eternal total double-entry same total of both time-flow energies at any segment of the universe so extended.

Look how we run-down, wear out, age . . . think what charge, what re-birth, resurrection, new life, the retrograde time-flow would give us! All that we'd lost, too: and a keen vision of the past-as-alive, the past not qua past, but past qua future!!!!!!! Heading for it as surely as we normally head toward say the year 2100 A.D. The future in retro would be 100 A.D. just as surely, but gaining energy and life, through retro time as one moved!

The universe does not go through serial cycles, but moves backward through its own life continually. We are at a point where the thrust back-ward is vast in comparison to true time, that is, time toward completion of true form before the accident. The universe is in a stall, a doublebind! This may be an anomaly; once it reaches either end point, this may be over-come. One can see that; it doesn't repeat itself. We are now in the process of being thrust back incorrectly, away from form-completion; nonetheless, already the other direction time is somewhat strong and its rate of ratio growth is great. Once the direction is reversed and we're again going in the correct way, then we may take a different destiny line (alternate track) and not come to the original explosion; avoid it.

And maybe this isn't even the whole universe; maybe we're part of a subsystem moving in this wrong direction. We do know when the Acci-dent took place: about 6 billion years ago. But we could change directions before that; we don't go back to that; we're now moving away from it, and what you and I should look for is not going back 6 billion years and recti-fying that mistake, but wrong-way thrown-back time "slowing" and regu-lar time regaining dominance; we should watch for our cosmos moving the proper direction in time, which would be a reverse from what we are used to — *in the direction of our past.* It is not reaching this explosion 6 billion years ago that is important for us, but slowing our movement away from it and reversing and moving backward into our own past.

Asked when this reversal to proper time direction might be anticipated, Dr. NK said, "By our wrong way time, fairly soon."

"Then we must relive our recent past?"

"Yes, we will move backward into it, but perhaps at quite a different rate; we might move more rapidly than we advanced, I mean, retreated through it."

"People would stop dying?"

"Oh yes — the entropic process, cooling, aging, wearing out, degenera-tion — all that would cease. Once we picked up time momentum the other way — we might overcome the Accidental-thrust time. Think of a person blown literally from his garage when his hot water heater explodes. In an instant he is in the next field. His rate of return to the scene is much slower. In our universe, the force of Accidental thrust time is weakening; we have no way to ascertain what the 'correct' rate would be going the other way, before this Accident took place. We are presently living within two opposite thrusts, working against each other, like two tides. Think, though, how slowly time moves for a child, especially a baby. Time is weak now but we might abruptly lock; this accidental wrong might suddenly stabilize."

"Like the Bible says? Time will suddenly cease?"

"Wrong-direction time — "

"Sounds like the same thing."

"It is possible," Dr. NK said, "that under regular process-conditions there is no time as we know it, lineal time, either way. We may find ourselves back in what we call our past without any interval; there may be no reverse lineal time, because lineal time is solely a result of the Accident, and once overcome — "

"Not backward lineal time, in its place, but timelessness?"

"I think we will see the damages overcome, when it is stabilized. Either we will lock into timelessness, then begin lineal reversal, which I conceive as natural — "

"Or we may find ourselves jumped back 2,000 years."

"Yes." He nodded.

Plot: it turns out that the message which Albemuth is signalling Earth, the secret, is that our planet, solar system, us — we're moving backward in time and it's about to stabilize and change, and the jolt to us will be terrific. Our leaders know this but deny it. Time is about to end (lineal time) as a factor of life; it won't reverse, as in counter clock world, but our present will dissolve as all the accretion of at least 3,500 years will vanish, as if dreamlike. They never took place. Stability, and proper everything, will lock in at 1500 to 2500 B.C. (Is it possible that an explosion, that Cretan civilization, took place then?) All events since then are progressively less real, as time runs out of charge. . . . Jesus was the first messenger from Albemuth come here to tell that one day time would abruptly cease, to prepare us. Now Earth is full of messengers; they've made many of us so, due to our radio traffic which are energy; the noösphere, etc. And now is when it's about to lock, but to them at Albemuth, they're outside this kind of lineal time; it just is for them each year realer and realer (what we call Being). But they can penetrate at the place where our noösphere exists, which is circa 1960–1990. Our microwave et al. equipment receives and boosts their t-p signals, radio signals. Their help was there but is now artificially boosted for this generation.

"What Dead Men Say."

The Albemuth message, though, corrects Dr. NK's theory; there was no explosion, just that Being time slipped into lineal time for this solar system or planet . . . hence myth of Garden of Eden days of every race on earth — it ended, we were cast out. The lineal time, which is the only time we recognize, is a slipped ontological coordinate of existence; each year should reinforce and totally renew, even add layers to each of us like patina; we should age in that sense, grow until each of us, qua entelechy, is perfected. "But what about dinosaur bones and all fossils?" we ask. Answer: Every art work breaks, even though it is complete. A bone China cup doesn't age, but an accident can occur to it. This is what happened to all life; eventually, like all artifacts, each form breaks, but the entelechy escapes the brittle crystallized form and reappears in plastic rebirth. There is also change — this isn't an unmoving, static world. But the processes we know as aging — the entropy of our world, and what we see of the cosmos (contrast cosmos with universe). Everything lost should at the end of each turn be as renewed as at the end of the 24 hour cycle of an electric clock. Something is wrong in our world; we lose. An equilibrium is gone: and we sense it as defeat failure illness age and finally death. Something is out of balance; the two time-forces aren't equal.

What would we notice as this true (retro) time jumps in ratio? A slowing of our normal lineal time? No, the infusing into our aging world of a bright energy, pouring everywhere, sparkling, vivifying the living things *and* the unliving. We would see a living energy, a sort of shining sap which pours all over, sparkles; and it changes whatever it fluxes itself into like a plasma of n-ions. This is time, true time, plus energy time. It would roll back the accretions which are false, that is, it would roll back the least-Being accretions . . . it would add vitality to the Real, and cause the false totally to disappear, as if never there. This is time beginning to reverse itself: a direction. Experienced as energy to Being, as disappearance of the irreal/ illusion.

These slowings and reversings would come in spurts. Not in a lineal fashion; that aspect is of wrong-way time. It would be like childbirth: in surges of energy outward onto the world. At Spring the cyclic life is at its peak; so reverse time would tend to peak with it.

And we'd have — for those who were influxed directly — the eerie feeling that the clock had been turned back . . . hundreds, maybe thousands of years, depending on how much of this energy — and it is energy — infused each of them. Each would vary from the others touched; moved backward — receiving more. It has a quantity (years back) and quality: what one sees qualitatively.

The U.S. Intelligence psychiatric profile on Dr. NK shows that "he was taken over by Dionysus thus lifting him outside time and space," etc., like Nietzsche, but regards the experience as real.

Letter to Claudia Bush, February 26, 1975

[4:233]

Hey Claudia —

Identity — continuity — recognition — selfsameness.

I got so loaded last night you wouldn't believe it.* It was my daughter's birthday and I phoned her 6 or 8 times and never got her. So I went to a friend and he gave me something to get me ripped.[47] I was so fucking ripped. In chemo veritas, though (for your purposes). Listen, Baby. I am still ripped and it is tomorrow (that was today, when he gave it to me); we talked, and I said, man I can't take it anymore. Later as I was still taking it (the garbage out) he stopped me and handed me the good message. I squirreled it away for like until later and then I did it. I did it.

Claudia, it hit me like a 1100 of brick fists.

So I called in Tessa and said, "Honey, I am so stoned you would not believe it. I love you."

"Then you must be."

"Ask me questions. My unconscious is accessible."

"Why did you have the experiences last March?"

My answer: "I had nothing else to do."

"What deity or force or presence took you over?"

My answer: "Erasmus."

"'Erasmus.' Who the hell — "

(I had the most incredible shower of chuckling all over me, in the form of math symbols and Greek letters. I'd guessed who it was: he had played the most — to him — fun game. Ir leg, the two Sanskrit words. Not the

---

* In his later years Dick limited his drug use to scotch, snuff, and the occasional joint. In his teens, Dick was given the stimulant Semoxydrine as an antidepressant. Between 1952 and 1972, Dick became notorious for his prodigious use of amphetamines, which he reportedly consumed by the handful to keep up his nearly inhuman writing pace. In the late 1960s and early 1970s, Dick's house in Santa Venetia became a well-known hangout for teenagers and eventually for serious addicts and pushers; Dick's experience with the drug scene is chronicled with humor and compassion in his novel *A Scanner Darkly* (1977). Though Dick's mescaline trip in May 1970 inspired *Flow My Tears, the Policeman Said*, it is not true, as many believe, that Dick wrote while on LSD — a claim that Harlan Ellison made in his introduction to the Dick story "Faith of Our Fathers," which appeared in his influential new wave SF collection *Dangerous Visions* (1967). Dick took LSD only two or three times, once suffering a terrible trip spent envisioning an angry god tormenting him "like a metaphysical IRS agent." — DG

meaning ["angry legion"] but a pun. Always puns, a million pun clues. "Ear leg." In the old days my brother-in-law and I made up this Swift: "I feel ear-assabiele, Tom said," or how-ever. "I feel as if my ear hurts and I need to see a proctologist," Tom said irascibly. There it is. Now, "ir leg" is to ear leg as Irascibly is to that Swifty. And "irascible" is a quasi-phononym for Erasmus. Ear-ass-mus. See? These were the first words which came to me in March and wow, last night. A shower of laughter, since finally I'd guessed. He hadn't counted on chemical aids.)

"Who or what is/was Christ?" Tessa asked me.

"The style we are drawn in," I said. "There is a person seated for artists to draw him; they have a 1.50 minute time limit on their work. All draw him a little differently, all must finish fast and turn it in. Their work is crude, and each has a bit of the subject in it. Our world is that composite work of many artists, and we are those crude drawings with the minute and a half time limit. We do as well as we can, but it's like Disneyland where they do that, various portrait artists with one subject — or if they all had the same subject. It is like Disneyland — fast and not very expert, and still the subject sits and we approximate him. Someone else does the approximating; we are not the artists but the drawings. Hence Plato's concept of the cave and of the idea archetypes."

"Is there reincarnation?"

(I could remember a Saxon scene: an old man bending over me. But what I saw most, and always, as she talked to me, was the cross, in color: gold and red. Shining. And heavy and huge. You'd bounce back if you were a semi truck and hit it. I just kept watching it.)

Then I sat for a couple hours and felt odd, not bad but odd, because all that stuff about Greece and Dionysus was crazy, based on the fact — Tessa and I looked him up — that Erasmus was one of the first Greek scholars. I "imagined" the world of Greece and all that stuff. Based on Erasmus' head. You see. Now he was laughing because the joke was on me. He'd read about Dionysus, I guess. He was a bookish man, knew nothing direct. His thoughts, his knowledge of Greece, I'd taken as real. I sat feeling foolish and listening to the phono most of the night. I had a good trip and finally went to bed. It was neat and I was happy and I used the time for personal insights, especially how my Muse had enjoyed the fun. (To him fun, to me — well, I guess fun. Oh yes.)

Tessa: "Why Erasmus?"

I said, "I am he."

"In the past? In a former life?"

"I am always Erasmus. I always will be. I was Dr. Jonson, once, later. But always Erasmus." (I could not explain it. About reincarnation I only said, "It takes place because it's easier." Tessa had asked, "Then there is a soul?")

I also remembered having been a rat, in a cage. "Always I was ugly," I told her. "In *Tears*, the man waiting to be killed inside the wooden house in the dream at the end . . . it's a rat. I saw my father kill an animal, come to kill it. The old man on horseback who says Taverner must die, he's my father." I thought about that for hours, how I loved and missed my father. I could see God, then, as a great old King Arthur, with Christian trappings. He could tell me when it was okay to break the law, which is what I needed: permission to do things that went against the queen's authority.

Now, Claudia, obviously I used this event and the time in it conscientiously. During it I realized that in truth I saw the world in terms of pleasure denied me (sex and women) and over-reacted in terms of moral indignation, a moral tone to life ("overthrow the tyranny"). I saw, too, that esthetic awareness of music and art was my outlet my saving outlet; I really didn't see the world as a moralist did, but as an artist: I was capable of — and truly did — see aesthetically all the time; my real interest in women was as beautiful creatures the way cats are beautiful and Beethoven's music is. I saw one vast truth about the world: all views and all truths just scratch the surface; there are as many million truths and views and realities as there are freeze frames whenever a single cat walks across a single backyard — i.e., an infinity. And all *beautiful*. I saw that each different truth which I had held was beautiful, but that for each that I had held there were a billion more . . . it was dazzling.

Claudia, I will get to the point. Finally I went to bed and slept, feeling love for my wife and my cats and child, feeling the beauty of the world, and that all this had been a fun trip, a relief away from the responsibility which is killing me . . . and then I had an insight, my own, based on all this. The "Benzene ring" to me in all this. I saw the orthogonal time axis, how it works; i.e., how we come to see time wrongly. What Joe Chip[48] sees in the decay of objects back through the Platonic archetypes is correct, and the inference is correct, and it does show orthogonal time. That is what is valuable in *Ubik*, whether the Marxists know it or not. (I think they do, but on my trip I was so unparanoid it never occurred to me to wonder.) Joe Chip sees time properly. The orthogonal axis is the real one.

I understood how we come to see time wrongly, or rather, we see it in its less real, secondary aspect or axis. Hence the perplexing opening line on page 1 of this letter:

Identity — continuity — recognition — selfsameness (the last refers back to identity but better expresses it, because we use the former about ourself, but the latter refers to things we encounter). This is real, CKB. I am sitting here at the crack of dawn writing you, and this is priceless; what it is, is:

The two categories of a priori and empirical — they mislead us; they are Aristotle's "A or not A," a two-value system-view of the contents of man's mind. Throw it out.

All things begin from outside (a posteriori). They enter the mind through the senses. (Note this doesn't conform to what I formerly held.)

Our mind soon subtracts qualities (e.g., time, space, geometric shape like "square," number, etc.) and abstracts them from every and all incoming sense-objects. These we know not to be properties of any given sense object, and these are the a priori categories.

We feel they are more real, but in fact they are just real about more things (more things are square than are brown, for instance).

Now, here the error begins. We posit the one knowledge against the other, but the latter (a priori) is taken from the former. What is more important, though, is that all sense objects (we do Gestalt, into objects) go through an intermediate period as they pass from a posteriori (empirical) to a priori; totally abstracted of particuliarity. This is a process of necessary introjecting of each sense object for the purpose of identifying the sense-object when it is encountered again, because what must be kept cardinal here (and has been overlooked) is that each sense-object arrives within the purview of our percept system but then is gone. We must remember it because it may return. This requires that we identify it when it so does. (Hence memory and time, incorrect time are woven together.) We must recognize it in comparison to merely identifying it, which is to say, memory is to tie together sense object A via the introjected idea object which resembles it, to sense object B which is properly identified as the same sense object as A; both are the same, but a little space has come between. [. . .]

Do you realize how many imagi we carry from the first week of our life on? How much of our empirical reality must be handled (like overnight — the whole world) this way? I assume that the "Claudia K. Bush" who sends me each letter is the selfsame one. These are automatic processes, but they lead us along a time-axis which is necessary to us for biological adaptive purposes; actually, we perceive this way because of its utility. In point of fact, growth (in the entelechy sense) doesn't take place along this axis, which is supplied *only in the minds of living creatures.*

Item. The actual external time, or growth-change axis, is that which Joe Chip saw. Even if you, as a person, the child is not you, the child that was; she was one within the actual imprinting form of a little girl of that age.

This is *why* we don't see as things are; there is a change; there is motion and growth; it isn't a static universe (as the mystics imagine). Time is real, but it goes orthogonally; what I have said here is why we see it at right angles to the actual causal axis or "real time" axis. Perception of time is at right angles to the time it perceives.

Item. We've got to categorize (i.e., mentally function) this way; vide *A Martian Odyssey* by Stanley Weinbaum (Ballantine) in which the Martian bird classifies each store as being in a different category, like, there are no "birds," just bird one and bird two and bird three; it laughs when he speaks of "birds," calling them *all* by the same name. But think of the chaos — and I mean it — if upon each day arising we greeted the selfsame objects as if they were new (well, in Beckett plays, no, in an Ionesco play, the husband and wife don't recognize each other; see that one, I forget the title).

Item. It is really true that billions of you exist, and billions of me exist — outside. But for utility, there must be (1) identifying; (2) recognition; (3) creating of continuity and the concept of Identity, of perseverance (a key word in this) of Being. "Being" is a kaleidoscope. I've seen it. It's fun, but you can't add up your checkbook; worse, you can't tell if it's *your* checkbook; worse, you can't tell if it's a checkbook; worse, you can't tell if you exist as a continuing entity.

Last night all this was set off (after I got loaded) by my going in to commune with the little wooden saint I own, which I'm sure I told you about. It was the swirl of colored vines running up his white vestment which told me I was having a trip: the color was so bright and the vines swirled so. But today I looked. And of course there are no vines. Just dots, unconnected, sort of tiny mandalas of color. Golly, the fucking color is there; the vines are not. I saw vines, and then learned that it was Erasmus.

Tessa points out: "He's got a pun within a pun. 'Ir leg' could be like 'ir' meaning 'unreal' and 'leg' from the Latin 'in-lego,' or 'not gathered or brought together' (we changed 'in' to 'ir'). So 'ir leg' could be a pun on the ear-ass meaning, 'When you get to the bottom you will find that I haven't brought you together, you and Erasmus.'" While listening to the phono last night, I thought suddenly of the Wilhelm Muller poem "Das Irrlight," which means, "The False Light," which they meant to indicate, as a word, the flicker of the Aurora-like lights across the winter snow, which duped men and led them astray. "Das Irrlight" is one of my favorite German poems. "Will-o-the-Wisp" is the trans. I have here.

> *Into deep and rocky gorges*
> *A false light lured me down.*
> *I neither care nor worry*

How I shall get out again.
I have often lost my way,
And every path has had its goal.
Our pleasures, our sorrows,
All is game to the will-o-the-wisp.
Down the dry bed of the stream
I wind my way quite calmly.
Every stream will reach the sea
As every path will find its grave.

I was just saying to Tessa last night: "This spirit is wearing me out. Killing me by exhausting me." But when the trip hit me last night, as I sat before my statue (ikon) of the very ancient wooden saint communing, and saw the vines clustered and growing and swirling, I thought, "Well, he's saying, You should have more fun. Ol' Erasmus sure was a prankster. He sure liked number games." I saw all around me everywhere numbers. "That's why he's bubbling over with mirth," I thought. "That I've figured out who he is, at last. He is so into puzzles and riddles and puns — he's laughing." The spirit who had been animating me was laughing and bubbling over, and vines swirled with dark-colored clusters, up the vestments of the saint. If Erasmus was indeed a person who saw fun in everything, then this was Erasmus; at the time I convinced the spirit to identify itself finally, and to my complete surprise. That it was truly Erasmus, the great scholar of the Bible, I didn't doubt at the time; I kept saying to Tessa, "He's an astrologer." For some reason that seemed important; maybe because seeing the Arabic numerals and knowing he was an astrologer linked him to the Renaissance and not to Greece: to the revival of learning (of Greek). But of course astrologers were everywhere in the ancient world. Still, at the time, last night I mean, I was delighted; I'd never guessed he'd not been to Greece either. His head, filled with thoughts and knowledge of Greece, had fooled me into thinking I *was* in Greece; what pleased him most . . . I'm very tired. . . . What pleased him most (Erasmus) was that I had mistaken him, a scholar, for a god! (Dionysos.)

But today, recalling the intoxication (which it was), my mirth, the advice, "You take all these scholarly things too seriously; you should have fun . . ." Well, who of the two does that sound like? And the cluster of vines on the vestments of the saint — they just are not there, and that is what I saw. He was playing games again, and I must say, he runs away, Claudia honey, runs away from the stark sight of the man in fawn robe lying face down dead, murdered . . . and wouldn't you? He was so happy; he had been so innocent and happy —

Last night as I listened to the phono I found myself sitting close to a color photo of Victoria Principal, and her tawny skin and long black hair got to me . . . and then I saw she was on a leopard skin rug, with the same dappled spots.* Beneath the dapple of the fawn is the dapple of the leopard; both are protective coloration, and the god of fawns has two sides. Do you really think Erasmus would have been so filled with mirth? "Hence vain melancholy — " etc. Vain deluding. Left out key (ah, how key!) word. But maybe Erasmus, that pious Christian scholar, studying Greek, was the first, the very first, in our world, to resurrect Dionysus, as he labored at his scholarship. I had reckoned that the Holy Spirit seemed to have returned to our world about the time of Martin Luther, and Erasmus was a contemporary of his. Also, you will find the words "perfect" and "fool" in my most recent notes, and Erasmus wrote "In Praise of Folly" which is about the fool who is Christ. And Parsifal is a "perfect fool"; that is what those Arabic words mean . . . think of *Godspell,* which enchanted me.

Item. We generate the horizontal time to keep order in what we encounter. But ah! The utility has made it progressively more and more difficult for us to experience the infinitude of transparent laminations which we bind together with the energy we call time — if we could release them — a trillion butterflies out of each object! And each object (form) can travel back for us as the transparencies unpeal, back (unpeel) back and back, to earlier forms, to uncover them, as in *Ubik.* They are there because they are accretional; they really are there. Oh, that Antique world. At one instant, early in my trip, I saw an old man bending over me (the Wise King, from the dream in *Tears*) and I saw a Saxon haircut, and Saxon clothing. I had uncovered I know authentic bits from the world around me and in my head (I am a part of the world around me) remnants sleeping from the past:

What lies hiding within each object? A garden, so to speak: the enchanted garden, but they relate to the past. Studying one photo of Victoria Principal, I noticed that her hairstyle made her look very much like the Mona Lisa, and then I saw that beneath it (Being) there was the Egyptian

---

* Victoria Principal (1950–) is a Hollywood actress (*Earthquake, Dallas*) and one of Dick's many "dark-haired girls." Dick was drawn to this particular subset of brunettes throughout his life, sometimes suffering intense crushes on women he had never met (cf. Linda Ronstadt). Dick was especially drawn to Principal, whom he believed could capture the cold sensuality of his android femme fatale character Rachel Rosen in the cinematic adaptation of *Do Androids Dream of Electric Sheep?* (1968). Dick began taping up pictures of Principal around his apartment and sent letters and a copy of *Ubik* to her. He was heartbroken when she failed to respond. Dick also pushed for Jefferson Airplane vocalist Grace Slick to play Rosen. Dick's penchant for these women inspired his collection of poems, essays, and letters *The Dark Haired Girl,* published by Mark V. Ziesing in 1989. — DG

hairstyle of women. When I had seen the shot of her, which first drew me to her, it was because, I thought, she reminded me of Kathy. But the hairstyle contains bits of past words, much like pulp paper has fragments of colors from older sheets of paper. The "paper" remains; the sheets give way to successive pulping.

Sadly, I decline into the mundane (i.e., this second in time). I see something fascinating, though: the "vines" on the vestment of the saint . . . he had been painted with a simple design over and over again. Like this: (•) Big deal. Anyhow, over the years or even a century or two, dirt (can you believe it?) dirt has obscured the purity of the white, and has contaminated the repeated simple design, to connect many of the repetitions of the design, in wild, flowing "patterns." His triangle-inverted white front is no longer white; the (•) is in color, and those, plus the dirt — his front is alive with the grape vines of Spring, and I'm sure he knows it, because I had just prayed to him for help. That it was my daughter Laura's birthday and I phoned her again and again with no luck . . . and felt so alone, and got loaded, and then went in to commune (read that as appeal to my friend). The gentle saint is underneath maybe white and pure, but he laughed out into color; he tripped out, and all the world was alive with giggling high for me. The high is gone, but the solution as to *why* we see time along the wrong axis (and much stronger proof that we do) remains . . . plus the memory of happiness in a world of dappled pelts and music and love and number-games of the most delightful complexity hiding — the smiling, murdered god.

N.B. I just want to add: we see time to anchor our world of "buzzing, blooming" experience.[49] We must anchor it; I couldn't type this to tell you, and I wouldn't know who I was or who you are, otherwise. But the time-axis along which forms (entelechies) grow to completion — that is orthogonal, and it is real. Remember you heard it here. But from whom, that I do not know.

You must read Arthur J. Deikman's paper, "Deautomatization and the Mystic Experience."[50] In Charles T. Tart's *Altered States of Consciousness* (Doubleday Anchor Books).* By my theory now, if you remove the imagi for a moment, remove a single imago from between you and the sense ob-

---

* This is the book, published in 1969 by the pioneering parapsychologist Charley Tart, that introduced the phrase "altered states of consciousness" into the already humming counterculture. Although the phrase had already been used by Arnold M. Ludwig a few years earlier, it was this book, and probably this book title, that made the phrase a common stock of the Zeitgeist. As with so much other mystical literature, however, what we really encounter in the Exegesis are altered states of consciousness that are also altered states of energy. That is, what we finally encounter is Conscious Energy. — JJK

ject, then you see it (loss factor) unrelated to it-prior and it-after; i.e., the thing with no time involvement; the (gain factor) is that you can gaze at it and peel away all its layers as Joe Chip saw objects revert; you can find the billions of related transparencies within (sp and fuck it).

You can also see each sense object or form where it stands placed, in the static structure of the universe (the mystical experience of being outside of time). If you want that. But to me what is more exciting is to peel away time, the accretions; and this is orthogonal time. But deautomatization in Deikman's sense must take place first (turn on and do it).

In seeing the pattern of sense objects, where they're located, you see structure. In peeling away the layers you see into Being, but you do not see the forward growth of the entelechy of the form you peel away; you are going in the opposite direction, although along the proper axis. "What is underneath" or "what is within or below" are the previous steps in sequence (remember, I pointed out, sequence is very real; sequence is all important: it is pattern). This is the growth up to now, to the stage where it is vis-à-vis you. If you are to see what comes next you must move along the true (orthogonal) time axis in harmony with it: into the future, as all forms grow (as each "frame" is replaced by the next further-grown "frame"). They are a sequence of static frames for each entelechy, one edola following the next. Seeing what transparencies lie ahead is like the difference between stripping away successive layers of paint on an old bureau, or digging down through the strata of a buried city, versus imagining what layers would/ will come next. Only the Logos can and does that; you can see the difference between previous layers in an Indian garbage mound, one after the other, and the hypothetical "layers to come in the future." This is real time (orthogonal time). But I think you and I et al. are limited to peeling back or looking back; we cannot see how forms will grow, because as they do grow they inter-relate, which is what we call the cosmos, and to see the future stage of the Plan is to see something which would elevate us and abolish us as we now exist. From my metaphor of the hurried artists sketching the one person sitting, at Disneyland, you can see that I believe that Christ is the completed form toward which all men move, this approximation, and it's getting closer and closer — we can guess, but we do not *really* know what Christ looks like, surely not those cruddy pictures of him all goopy-eyed. When we achieve that perfection — as we do — we may not recognize, not see, where it agrees, because (1) we are the sketches, not the artists, and (2) we cannot see the person being sketched . . . and yet, that person is ourselves. How strange . . . the sketches can't see the person being sketched, only the woman (the what?), the workman's hand as he sketches. But presumably the person being sketched looks like we, the

sketches, do, and with "woman" I return to the fawn-skin run in the woods
of Arcady will the long dances/typing/madness/enthusiasm ever end?

>Signed,

>Eurypides, and other hard-working/driven turned-on-ees

[4:243] The reality of orthogonal time, cyclic time, would make it possible
for the Golden Age (the time before the fall) to return, restoring all which
has been lost. There is a direct link between the hope of that return and
the idea of orthogonal time; also, there is a similar link between the possibility of that hope being fulfilled and the fact that orthogonal time exists
which it indeed does.

Is not one of our present concepts or visions of that Golden Age, perhaps our most powerful and authentic one, the vision of "The Woods of
Arcady" which Yeats wrote of?[51] And was it not indeed these woods, the
Isle of the Blest, which I at last experienced as I moved deeper into the Being, the heart of, orthogonal time? Did I not at last see the moonlight and
the pale water, the arch, the quiet and harmony and beauty, of exactly that
which Yeats said is gone and which we dream of still? ("Yet still she turns
her restless head.")

Would it be unreasonable to speak of my first orthogonal vision, that of
Urbs Roma, as the Age of Iron? And under that I found — what's next? Silver? That would be my first glimpse of the Hellenistic world which came
before (linear time) or beneath (orthogonal), and then, at last, the absolute
simplicity of what must be the Golden Age: the forests, which Euripides
spoke of in the *Bacchae* ("Will they ever come to me ever again . . ."). Each
age of rotation retrograde was better; iron to silver to gold, whatever metaphor. *Roma* certainly was iron; no doubt. And — the fish sign which I saw:
it was made of gold. [. . .]

If our age is an extension of *Urbs Roma* (*Tears* being a paradigm, a map
of a territory which is *Roma, Washington, Moscow, Berlin:* one map for all)
then that view of *Roma* was a rollback, and insight into the heart — not of
an age prior to ours — but to ours itself. But then the previous age emerged
beneath . . . while I was in the hospital, just as Nixon resigned, the same
day I went into surgery and was repaired. Yet already I had glimpsed the
archway leading to the quiet places of sea and moonlight. (One does not
build buildings out of gold, there are none, it is all too soft. It would be jewelry, etc., objects of beauty and adornment; there are no gold prisons.) [. . .]

I did not *remember* my previous state (anamnesis): I was *restored* to that
state; which means someone restored me. That is God and God's grace. He
brought it back to me or me back to it, rejoined or gave back. The Christian (Eucharist) anamnesis deals specifically with "Do this in recollection

of me," i.e., Jesus Christ.* The event is anamnesis; the agency which causes it is adventitious and is the Savior. No man has intrinsically the capacity, by no knowledge or magic, to accomplish this restoration. In my case I detect evident pre-destination; first, it was impressed on me, this anticipation of the dark-haired stranger girl at the door; I used to expect the Paraclete coming to the door at any time, to render aid. From the beginning of my life, He laid down the necessary efficient causes to bring the transformation/restoration about. There was always evident intent, and on His part, not mine. It took an entire life time to bring me to that point in 3-74. Step after step; led me, directed me. Not the girl at the door but that as the climax, the moment, and at the moment of extremity of peril for me, of the "very desperate" where no hope existed for me of being saved in any fashion unless all these steps had already been laid down. Her appearance at the door had that effect only as mere triggering release and because of manifold almost infinite preparatory steps. This was a life time process, not a single event. As an infant I was given dreams and experiences (e.g., with fish, the "tunny,"[52] the shark dreams, later on the Tiberius fish teeth necklace dream), without which her appearance and that fish necklace would have done nothing; it wasn't a magic amulet, as if the power resided in its intrinsic shape or properties. I could as easily have been engrammed on a — well, whatever He chose. It's like answering the question, "How does your car obtain the capacity it has to perform all that it does?" with the answer, "By putting in this particular key, the one with the square end, and turning it to the right for a second." The car key unlocks a gigantically intricate mechanism but that is all it does; it causes so-to-speak the potential vehicle (car static) to become actual car (car in motion). Whoever built the car probably also had the key in mind — anticipated its existence and use.

The analogy is a good one, because by holding back the key the car can be kept in a state of mere potentium throughout a theoretically unlimited period of lineal time. A person seeing it only in this potential mode might never guess what would happen when activated; better yet, there is really no way just by looking at a radio to tell what it does when turned on. The simple switching from off to on is no more than bringing into existence the true function of what was only an object; what it is has been revealed to be what it does. Teleology is all-important in this: its end-purpose. The meta-systems perhaps can best be understood by this cybernetics model, by asking, "What are they for?" The answer is obtained by observing the process

---

* An early reference to the Eucharist, which grows in importance throughout the Exegesis. Here Dick frames the Lord's Supper as a memorial reenactment rather than a mystical rite; later he will focus on the issue of transubstantiation. — GM

as it unfolds. We are back to the concept of entelechy, of growth. All these
are the unfoldings of living organisms which themselves are portions of an
over-all organism, no doubt. A Greek might proudly say that he causes his
own heart to beat and his own brain or mind to think, but it seems more
likely that both are in the deepest and final sense caused by a designer of
that heart and brain, who holds all in the palm of His hand; we can't see
Him, but we can't see gravity either; we measure it by its effects. This is the
sad, sad Greek error of man over nature, man above the cosmos, controlling it; this is his hubris. He will guard, in the esoteric rites and gnosis of
his mystery cult, the secret fact that God lies within everyone and everything equally, and steers all. Greeks and foreigners alike.

The really carefully guarded secret of the priests of all the religions,
which they will never voluntarily relinquish to the world, is that priests
are not needed, nor what priests know or what initiates do or what the devout believe — practices and sacraments, anything. The truth is that God
inhabits without limit; wherever the real is or the actual does, He is it. Special knowledge of how to get in touch with him is that same knowledge
which carries the bee home to its hive each night; who sells that knowledge to the bee? If we have no money, if we can't read or be wise, are we
abandoned? Does He abandon the lowly insects because they are virtually
no more than reflex machines? Just as truth cannot really be suppressed, at
least not forever, it neither can be hoarded. We are taught day and night, as
all living entities are: ceaselessly. God did not begin to govern and inform
the cosmos when writing and money were invented.

The deeper and deeper penetration into ontological realms, experienced as dokos fading to reveal *Urbs Roma* — those were into a region
prior in lineal time to Jesus, to Christianity, but not to Greek mystery religious as such. But finally I saw the building Santa Sophia, the palm trees,
which was the Levant (that word came to me, an archaic term). That last
was as real as the first. What linked them? The last was not fundamentally a Greek area, but acquired by Alexander in conquest. Each however
was seen in holy terms, viewed as if sanctified, viewed through its religion.
It was as if God ranged through an axis neither of time nor space as we
know it but built out of both. Orthogonal space, too? A space-time axis
of Being in which resemblances linked each frame rather than being together in either time or in space, but because they rose toward God Himself and all He represents. It was an axis of holy solemnity, maybe; that
worship and relatedness to God is the final axis, in which one when entering that realm moves from religion to religion as if they are all one. It is as
if the state of grace generates, or anyhow generates the perception of and

the participation in, the Region of the Sacred. But not just the sacred parts of each culture were retrieved; with them came the rest, everything, as in the taco-stand which served as a doorway to all Mexico. When dokos, the veil, lifts away from our external world we see the Absolute, but it is whatever God wills it to be, causes it to be; most likely, thinks it into being. We think along with him of first this and then that, so we are here, then there. Worlds are made and unmade. The Absolute is absolutely plastic and manifold and real only as He forms and reforms it; He expresses himself directly through it and in it. [. . .]

The re-emergence of cyclic time would be the method of restoration. It is not logically evident that hyper or orthogonal time [OT] would of necessity be cyclic; at first I thought it was retrograde. However, it does differ from lineal time in that lineal time is only unidirectional (by definition). OT is two-way or many omnidirectional. Maybe you can hop on or into it wherever you choose. I am starting from the most extraordinary premise of all: that *Roma* c. 100 A.D. had just been here an instant ago, here in Fullerton 1974. Both, really, were present, one removed or the other superimposed. Or, one seen by my left brain, the other by the other. Two totally separate channels of empirical space-time information, a double exposure. Yes, very much like an accidental double exposure. I do feel that the antique images regressed — Rome to Hellenistic Greece to Attic Greece to Crete — which implies retrograde time. Maybe "cyclic" is the wrong word; maybe orthogonal time, a specific sector, is summoned through penetrating via the print-out back to the Form which incises: from cluster of phenomena to archetype. That is not from lineal time to any other time; it is from time to — departure and reentry? Again, Plotinus seems to grasp it best. That and the Christian "do this in anamnesis of me —" Do this and recollect; once more we are back there again at the timeless and eternal moment c. 46 A.D. We are really there now. Real time, genuine time, ceased after He left; after that it's been only process time: true "spinning your wheels" time. Only layer after layer of meaningless dust have accrued, which is to say, the substance, the essence, has not changed since Christ left our world. Not a day will have passed between when He left and when He returns. Perhaps He simply took me where He was going, where He is. I was — where? With Him. QED.

But if the subjugation of us, the Fall, is through the power of time, which means decay and death, then this abolishment of time, or lineal time, whatever, accomplishes what we yearn to see accomplished: time or lineal time was overcome, and all the accumulations of the centuries, the flux, the accidents, the phenomenal world, all faded out and *it*, that place and those

events, faded into sight and I was totally caught up into them, both inside
me and outside me: it was not a mere external spectacle, like a 3-D movie.
I changed, too; to my deepest essence. I became a person appropriate to
and commensurate with my reality. And it was not because I wished it; the
first intimations were of the City of Cruel Iron, and I felt the fear natural to
a society based on force and on a slave population — it was harsh and cruel
beyond anything I've ever seen. No Arcady, that. Maybe the fruit with the
seed inside is the best model; no time at all is involved in that. Fruit equals
phenomenal world; seed equals the unchanging reality of the last days He
was here. Is our changing world actually a sort of electron revolving in totally repetitious cycles around a nucleus, and that nucleus is the Crucifixion and the Resurrection? The mass of a body creates a warpage in space,
so that a straight line is curved; thus planets' paths are warped into near
circles (ellipses) around and around; that if they could think would imagine
(as Spinoza would say) that they are traveling always in straight lines — but
we can see otherwise; an invisible force keeps that straight line — makes
that straight line into an endless repeating circle. Ah! Our linear time is exactly an analogy of the straight line of a small body near a dense star; we,
as part of Earth, moving through time as the axis, do not realize that our
time is being warped perpetually, back onto itself in a great circle, a vast
cycle which will one day to our surprise, like an early sailor who sailed west
across our oceans and eventually, incredibly, found himself back where he
began — circumnavigated our round world which he did not understand
was round . . . it looked and felt flat; the universe looks and feels as if it
extends analogously; Einstein showed us that space is curved through the
force we call gravity; so time, unrealized by us, undetected by any of our
earth-bound instruments, carries us inexorably in a sweep which we will
not recognize (anamnesis!) until we actually see a familiar landmark. Suddenly there it will be: ahead of us in time will be something which we know
from our historic record we left behind us in time. And this follows logically, since time and space are a nexus-continuum, cannot be separated.
Thus orthogonal time: lineal in the sense that all objects move in a straight
line through space, too; cyclic, if there is enough of what equals gravity in
respect to time, whatever that force would be; analog of mass. As mass affects space, warps it, curves it, bends it — what would warp, curve, bend
time, to bring it back? Equal to our sun, our nucleus: that moment *Urbs
Roma* c. 45 A.D. We will call it the Second Coming; i.e., the Second Time
around for us: and suddenly, in the twinkling of an eye, like a thief in the
night,[53] when we least anticipate it. We will be back. For me, in 3-74 I was
back. But I'm always pre-cog, a little. Do you think soon? And then the

Perfect Kingdom, beyond that: as our old myths from every culture recall with such yearning: *to go home again.* To be back once more: The Day of Restoration of all things, through God. [. . .]

I believe I saw the Platonic Idea Forms, and there were many of them, and he was right; what we see here are copies, not the real actual source-thing. But they are active and alive. They are not static; they pulse with energy and life (cf. Bergson). It seemed to me, as I look back, that if anything what I saw was more change, more motion, faster, that the flash-cutting rate — but without that fast rate, *recurrence.* Recurrence, the eternal verities, the Forms, are within, an aspect of, the flux, and the more flux the more the Forms come into view. Both motion and stasis are illusion and real; both. If we think of an entelechy or a bunch of them, there would be change, growth, until completion; then — frozen, forever. These terms just don't stand for anything; they're just words. What I saw was not the static or unchanging versus change, but an incredibly live and potent total organism linked together everywhere, with nothing excluded from it, controlling through an intricate system everything which was, is and will be simultaneously, as Avicenna[54] said. [. . .]

In truth, in very truth, the prophet, the authentic one, did not see events coming ahead in time; he saw into the heart, the true Being of the reality, saw into depth, not time. He writes about a memory of things which in fact all living men experienced, but none but he remember; that space-time matrix, when replaced with the new one, was accompanied by an analog change in their memories. They all had just lived through the events he described. The prophecies in the Bible describe the far past, the various prophets' pasts. Those events will never come; those prophets for some reason, God knows why, remembered how it was before the scenery got whisked away and new scenery whisked in place, and as fast as possible described their visions. God moves through time in retrograde from us; from completion back. We are not moving toward what the prophets (e.g., "Book of Revelation") contains; if anything, that was erased and recorded over and left behind. Still, those written documents of "prophetic visions" are priceless because they give us a fantastically valuable clue to the nature of reality, which is that no space-time matrix is real; it is an idea which God tries out and then abandons if necessary. The visions are the "also-rans," not predictions of the eventual winners. God decided against them, after trying them out. And synchronized our memories to go with the alterations.

I think God trusted these special men, these prophets; He let them remember or see, whatever — there was purpose in this, socially speaking, because they could with great sincerity forever tell their peoples of the

power of God. Also, it was a sort of mercy to those particular men, a genetic kindness to leave these memory traces, because those men knew, as
no other men could or would ever know, that the apparent substantiality of
their world was an illusion, that God and only God existed, and He could
dissolve their world and them at any moment. He allowed these prophets (and probably the ones we know of are only a tiny fraction of the total) to actually perceive in all respects that this is an interval period for us,
probably a time of trial or probation, of testing, that the goals and awards
and pains and striving and goods and gains of this world are not merely
temporary ("You can't take it with you") but that reality lies beyond, that
the grave is indeed the furrow in which the grains of wheat are sown to
grow and blossom into new collective life again later of another kind entirely — God showed them that indeed this is a play, a stage, a theater, that
He lives and loves and is always with us. [. . .]

Somewhere in the libretto of *Parsifal*, Wagner suggests that the great
holy magic which God casts onto the world is a protective veil of enchantment to shield humble, frail and timid very mild lives, so that we, being unable to discern them, won't hurt them; He creates the dokos, the veil, as an
extending of His protection over them, for they have no other. Only we,
the big crude cruel powerful strong hurtful creatures are visible. The veil
is not to deceive us per se, but we must be deceived so that the little ones
may live unseen, "untroubled by men, amidst the shadowy green / The little things of the forest live unseen" (*The Bacchae*).

Each living thing feels impelled to move (to develop or change or grow)
but can't locate the source of that urge. From what I saw and understood
from 3-74 on, there is a total Plan (the Logos) which superimposes as a vast
static — complete — blueprint pattern over a space-time continuum universe, the one we experience empirically: the one our senses tell us about.
The superimposition of the Logos-Plan pattern causes all material reality,
this entire space-time universe, to experience a certain stress to be other
than it is, a certain urging to become. This abolishes any static quality
within the space-time universe; it is compelled to grow by a necessity of its
own nature (v. Spinoza), which is the will of God or the thinking of God as
He conceives the plan. (For Him to conceive it is for this stress to be placed
on everything in space-time without lapse; it follows that all energies or
forces or dynamic fields are manifestations to us of His mind at work, and
we are becoming aware that rather than a universe of matter in motion this
is a universe of interacting far-ranging unified fields; that totality of the
fields is probably His Mind, since I think Him to be immanent in universe,
underlying it rather than above or outside it.) God is not Time; God generates or urges all things into development that the plan completes itself

in continual creation. All we know is that things happen. More accurately, God is the urging-forward force within all things, and all things (if "things" can be spoken of at all) are alive. The ontological matrix is a way in which His urging or thinking is manifested; so in that respect I think it's not time which moves forward, carrying us with it like a great tide, but that we are driven forward all of us together, animate and inanimate.* [. . .]

If there is a universe of anti-matter there may be a universe of anti-time; which would be retrograde time, or rather, elements moving retrograde to the matter — ourselves — which move forward in time. Thus time symmetry would be achieved this way. I saw this retrograde entity in late 3-74. Normally we see it blended with forward moving elements such as ourselves. At the height of my "mystic" experience, which is to say, my extremely heightened perception of reality, I saw my environment decline in intensity; whereas at the same time I felt an inner self, my entelechy I suppose (I didn't have the concept then), grow dynamically; the balance shifted more and more from outer to inner, which could be regarded as psychologically withdrawing my projections from external reality and regaining them and their energy within my own total self. At the peak of this I experienced myself as very real and moving through virtually nonexisting things which had become so vitiated and dim that I supposed — and maybe accurately, although it was so astonishing that I drew back from this implication — that all non-living objects around me literally drew their lives, their existences, from me and from other living entities. We animated them, yes, but animated what? What is meant by "them" when this animating energy is withdrawn? Mere signaling systems to inform me of sequential *whens:* a series of signals, in specific order, arranged in order to release changes in me. Time, properly understood, is merely an awareness of the procession of these little, weak cueing signs, their advance as we encounter them; but they do not move; they are pattern-arranged and we ad-

---

* A contemplation of God's nature occupies virtually all of Dick's late-period work, but as he grapples with theology, what is startling are not the more far-fetched notions — anyone who has read Dick's earlier work expects these — but the more conventional ones. The God who reveals Himself in Dick's thinking often is very much the familiar humanized Judeo-Christian God. This God acts personally and responds personally in the ways of both the Old and New Testaments; note a few paragraphs earlier, in a passage that is practically biblical, the "trust" that Dick's God places in "special men" and "prophets." The upcoming reference to God/Jesus as "Zebra" is first deeply curious, then forehead-smackingly obvious — and fabulous anyway; nothing is more indicative of just how unconventional Dick's mind is than that his most conventional notions seem most unconventional of all. Sometimes consciously and sometimes unconsciously, Dick tries to reconcile his own particular God teased out of the fabric of reality and time with the God of millennia worshipped by millions. Which is to say that consciously and unconsciously, herein Dick is finding his place in civilization. — SE

vance forward, up the manifold, from one to the next and the next. There is really nothing in them but minimal — economic — transfer of information that one particular *now* has replaced the *now* (or prior signal) before it. We advance from signal to signal. The signals are unmoving, totally inert. We are driven inexorably; none of us can halt himself in that motion from signal to signal, since each one of the signals carries with it transfer-information to last until the next: each hands us over, as it were, when its "now" has expired. There is no way you or I can refuse to receive the next signal, to keep from encountering it, and it is this inexorable but invisible, metaphysical but real momentum which we call Time. It's the same as destiny; it is the end or completion of our entelechy reaching back retrograde-wise, through the system of signals and dragging each of us bodily forward to meet that end, that completion. [. . .]

This unitary organism which we call reality or the universe is most itself, most there, most alive, at completion, and since there is no time or time-force then it's there now drawing us toward it; we move, it stands still. Being more than the sum of all its parts, how can any one or even all of its parts resist it? How can the totality, the absolute pattern, be weaker or smaller than anything else? It would be like saying that before being assembled, the parts which go to make up a kit are somehow more effective that way, scattered about the living room rug, unconnected and unrelated to each other, not functioning at all, except in terms of the template or diagram which the workman is pondering, which accompanied them. "The whole is greater than the sum of its parts," and surely the whole exerts a greater influence on those parts than they do mutually on one another or on it, or each on itself. This must be why Parmenides understood that no matter how many "parts" he saw, how much diversity and change his senses reported, reality had to consist of a One, which was Unchanging. His sense saw those parts coming together to form that One, but the One, he knew a priori and by the most rigorous reasoning, must already be. It did not lie ahead along a time-line somewhere in the future; it ontologically lay beyond or behind or deeper within the many, now and forever. The pressure of time driving all the pieces to come together into the complete pattern is a sort of voice calling to them, a summoning *to return;* everything has already been there, since this lay outside time; anamnesis was a memory not of the past, of former time, but of ontology outside of time, of already-complete-then-now-later. A memory of all time unified; this memory stretched in all directions in time, and finally into none: into Being itself: into the heart which is alive. Empedocles supposed it to have been in the past because he remembered it; but if time is cyclic he remembered the future just as well, logically speaking.

Empedocles didn't actually remember having once been divine; he remembered that he was divine, would be divine. Here, verb forms mislead us; this is mere semantics. To remember immortality is to remember outside of time. "Long ago I lived forever. I knew everything and could not die, and I was perfection itself. But somehow something went wrong, I forgot, I'm down here." Anamnesis could be said to be memory of the future restored — even memory of the present.

He remembered what he was; he remembers what he is; he remembers what he will be. This recollection has nothing to do with the continuum of space-time. Memory is not a function of time, but of comprehension. Memory is to know; forgetfulness is to fail to know (cf. Plato).

"I remember" equals "I realize" or "I understand."

Also, "I remember" (anamnesis) equals "I become" (Being). Which equals *I am changed.* (v. Paul: "Look! I tell you a sacred secret. We shall not all fall asleep [i.e., lie fallow in the idios kosmos, in ignorance]; but we shall all be changed, in an instant," etc.[55])

Metamorphosis.

Letter to Phyllis Boucher, March 2, 1975

[5:12]

Dear Phyllis,

I have long thought about you, wondering how you are, and my having just now written the short enclosed piece, which is about Tony, gives me pretext to write you as well as the opportunity to extend this copy of the piece so that you might read it. My love and memory of Tony are combined in this, although I must admit in a rather odd way; the reason is that this was commissioned by the Sufi magazine. *The Real World*, which is a very good magazine. It is put out by Tony Hiss, who writes the "Talk of the Town" in the *New Yorker,* and boasts such people as Robert Ornstein in its staff; it is what they call (ouch) a class magazine. The paper is high quality, too.

I hope that you like this piece (they may not). They just accepted a poem by my wife Tessa, and then told me that they'd like to be able to get both of us together in an issue. So the heat is on me to Come Through (I've been working since seven-thirty A.M.). [. . .]

> With deep personal regards,
> Philip K. Dick

Letter to Tony Hiss, March 2, 1975

Dear Tony,

Enclosed is the piece I've been working my ass off for *The Real World.* I'm glad you liked Tessa's poem, and that as you say you're going to publish it in the next issue, but that sort of puts pressure on me to come through — I've been on this piece like as of today 7:30 A.M. at the typewriter. You asked for "short." What is short? I kept it short, I hope short enough. I offer you two possibilities if you wish to cut it:

(1) Just make cuts where you can or wish. I trust you, but I'll weep genuine tears because I kept it terse anyhow as it is.

(2) Okay — on my MS page 6: you could end the piece after line 10. (Final printed sentence: "That was my friend.") But it's a different piece this way, with the Day of Wrath scene missing; much limiteder, more milder.

I proofed like mad on this, as you'll see, to cut down on your work. An author to editor grammar query; you'll note. [...]

> With warm personal regards,
> Philip K. Dick

[5:14][56] When I met Theodore Sturgeon, who wrote *More Than Human,* this good man said to me right off, "What sort of universe is it that causes a man like Tony Boucher to die of cancer?" I had been wondering the same thing ever since Tony Boucher died. So had Ted Sturgeon, although he didn't expect me to give an answer. He just wanted to show me what he — Ted Sturgeon — was like. I've found I can do that, too; let people know about me by asking that. It shows that I cared a lot about one of the warmest people who ever lived. Tony was warm and at the same time when he stood in the midst of a group of people, sweat came out on his forehead from fear. Nobody ever wrote that about him but it's true. He was terrified all the time. He told me so once, not in so many words. He loved people, but one time I met him on the electric train going to the opera and he was scared. He was a music critic and he did reviewing for the *New York Times* and edited a magazine and wrote novels and stories. But he was scared to take a drive across town.

Tony loved the universe and the universe frightened him, and I think I know where his head was at. A lot of people who are timid are that way because they love too much. They're afraid it'll all fall through. Naturally, it did with Tony. He died in middle-age. Now, I ask you, what good did it do him to be scared? He used to carry his rare old 78 records to radio station KPFA every week, wrapping them up in a towel so they wouldn't get broken. One time I decided to give Tony all my rare opera and vocal records, just plain give them to him as a gift of my loving him. I phoned him up. "I got Tiana Lemnitz records and Gerhard Husch," I told him. Tony replied shyly, "They are my idols." He was a Roman Catholic — the only one we knew — and that was a strong statement. Before I could get the records to him he was dead. "I feel tired half the day," he had added. "I can't work as much as I used to. I think I'm sick." I explained I had the same thing. That was eight or so years ago. The doctor told him he had a bruised rib and taped it up. Someday I will meet that doctor on the street. Tony got bad advice from everyone who could talk.

We used to play poker. Tony loved opera and poker and science fiction and mystery stories. He had a little writing class — this was after he was famous and edited F&S-F — and he charged one dollar a night when you showed up. He read your whole manuscript. He told you how rotten it was, and you went away and wrote something good. I never figured out how he accomplished that. Criticism like that is supposed to crush you. "Maybe it's because when Tony reads your story it's like he's reading it in Latin," somebody said. A whole dollar it cost. He taught me to write, and my first sale was to him. I still can remember that nobody understood the story but him, even after it was printed. Now it's in a college-level S-F course manual put out by Ginn and Company. There's only about 300 words to the story. After the printing of the story, Ginn and Company prints an impromptu discussion I had with a high school class about the story. All the kids understand the story. It's about how a dog sees garbagemen coming to steal the precious food that the family stores up every day until the heavily constructed repository is full and then these Roogs come and steal the food just when it's ripe and perfect. The dog tries to warn the family, but it's always early in the morning and his barking just annoys them. The story ends when the family decides they have to get rid of the dog, due to his barking, at which point one of the Roogs or garbagemen says to the dog, "We'll be back to get the people pretty soon." I never could understand why no one but Tony Boucher could understand the story (I sent it to him in 1951). I guess in those days my view of garbagemen was not shared universally, and now in 1971 when the high school class discussed it with me, I guess it is. "But garbagemen don't eat people," a lady editor pointed out to me in 1952. I had trouble answering that. Something comes and eats up people who are sleeping in tranquility. Like Tony. Something got him. I think the dog, who cried, "Roog, Roog," was trying to warn me and Tony. I got the warning and escaped — for a while, anyhow — but Tony stayed at his post. You see, when you're so scared of the universe (or Roogs, if you will) to stay at your post takes courage of the kind they can't write about because (1) they don't know how and (2) they didn't notice in the first place, except maybe Ted Sturgeon, with all his own love, and his total lack of fear. He must have known how scared Tony was, and to be that scared and for the Roogs to get you — it's so symmetric, isn't it.

However, Tony is still alive, I discovered last year. My cat had begun to behave in an odd way, keeping watch over me in a quiet fashion, and I saw that he had changed. This was after he ran away and came back, wild and dirty, crapping on the rug in fear; we took him to the vet and the vet calmed him down and healed him. After that Pinky had what I call a spiritual quality, except that he wouldn't eat meat. He would tremble whenever we tried to feed it to him. For five months he'd been lost, living in the gutter, seeing god knows what; I wish I knew. Anyhow when he was changed — in the twinkling of an eye; that is, while at the vet — he wouldn't ever do anything cruel. Yet I knew Pinky was afraid, because once I almost shut the refrigerator door on him and he did a 3 cushion bank shot of himself off the walls to escape, and clocked a velocity unusual for a pink sheep thing that usually just sat and gazed ahead. Pinky had trouble breathing because of his heavy fur and what they call hairballs. Tony had asthma terribly and needed it cold. Pinky would sit by the door to get the cold air from under the crack, and struggle to breathe. I will not write a teaser article here; Pinky died of cancer suddenly; he was three years old; very young for a cat. It was totally unexpected. The vet diagnosed it as something else.

I hadn't realized Pinky was Tony Boucher, served up by the universe again, until I had this dream about Tony the Tiger — the cereal box character who offers you cocoa puffs. In my dream I stood at one end of a light-struck glade, and at the other a great tiger came out slowly, with delight, and I knew we were together again, Tony the Tiger and me. My joy was unbounded. When I woke up I tried to think who I knew named Tony. I had other strange experiences after Pinky died. I dreamed about a "Mrs. Donlevy" who was incredibly tall — I could see only her feet and ankles — and she was serving me a plate of milk on the back porch and there was a vacant lot where I could roam at will, forever. It was the Elysian Vacant Lot, which the Greeks believed in, but just my size. Also, the day Pinky died, at the vet's, that evening as I stood in the bathroom I felt my wife put her hand on my shoulder, firmly, to console me. Turning, I saw no one. I also dreamed this dream: I had the album notes for "Don Pasquale" and at the end the conductor had added a note: five strings of cat gut, like a stave. It was a final hello from Pinky who was Tony Boucher; in the drama the album was an old 78 one, a favorite of Tony's.

Tony or Pinky, I guess names don't count, was a lousy hunter all his life. One time he caught a gopher and came up our apartment stairs with it. He put it on his dish, where he was fed, and the gopher ran off. Tony felt that things belonged in their place, an obsessively orderly person; his books were arranged the same way — each book in its exact place. He should have tolerated more chaos in the universe. However, he recaught the gopher and ate it.

Tony, or Pinky, was my guide; he taught me to write, and he stayed with me when I was sick back in 1972 and 1973. That's why my wife Tessa brought him over, because I had pneumonia and needed help and we had no money for a doctor. (I think now in that regard I was lucky; he would have told me I had a bruised rib.) Pinky used to lie on my body in a transversal fashion, which mystified me, until I realized that he was trying to figure out which part of me was sick. He knew it was just one part, around the middle of my body. He did his best and I recovered but he did not. That was my friend.

Most cats fear the clattering arrival of the garbagemen each week, but Pinky really more detested them than feared them. He hid out under our bed about half an hour before we heard them coming every Monday. He didn't show fear; we just saw the two unwinking green eyes under the bed where he waited the garbagemen out. There was no Pinky, just the eyes, waiting them out, the Bastards.

Four nights before Pinky died, before we knew he had cancer — I started to say, before he had been diagnosed as having a bruised rib — he and Tessa and I were lying in the bedroom on the bed, and I saw a uniform pale light slowly fill the room. I thought the angel of death had come for me and I began to pray in Latin: "Tremens factos sum ego, et timeo," and so forth[57]; Tessa gritted her teeth but Pinky sat there, front feet tucked under him, impassive. I knew there was no place to hide, like under the bed. Death can find you under the bed; everyone knows that, even little kids. And it looks bad.

It never occurred to me that death was coming for anyone but me, which shows my attitude. I saw us all as painted ducks, on a painted sea, and thought of the Arab 13th century poem about "Once he will miss, twice he will miss / All the world's one level plain for him on which he hunts for flowers."[58] We were as conspicuous as — well, anyhow finally I gave up praying, but I remember in particular I kept crying out, "Mors stupebit et natura."[59] Which I thought meant that death stood stupefied, as if in surprise. (As in, "I was stupefied to learn that my car had been towed away." It means just standing there impotently. That is not what Merriam-Webster 3 says, but it is what I say.)

Pinky never noticed the pale light; he seemed awake, but dozing. I think he was humming to himself. Later when I slept, toward morning I dreamed a disturbing dream: the report of a gun being fired close to my ear: a shotgun blast, and when I looked I saw a woman lying dying. I went for aid, but got onto some kind of one of those electric trolley busses by mistake, along with 3 Gestapo agents (I dream that a lot). We rode around forever while I tried vainly to short-circuit the power cables of the bus, or trolley car, whatever it was; without avail. The Gestapo agents seemed confident and read newspapers and smoked. They knew they had me.

Letter to Claudia Bush, March 21, 1975

Dear Claudia,

Today is the vernal equinox. I can tell, because I am in my new house typing, and cool morning fresh air is billowing around me through the window at my left. I see a huge shrub through the glass windows which form the wall before me. Elton John is singing. The cats are weaving in and out of special tunnels they have found. Christopher broke his toy and then broke it again. This, really, no joking, is the day the spirit of Springtime revives, down deep in the cold ground; I feel him wake up. When he wakes, he sees once more, since his dream has ended; he sees and we, for a moment, can see with him — not just him but what he sees the world to be.

The tyranny is gone, I think. Last year powerful spirits of the ionosphere, even perhaps from as far away as the sun's corona, were dispatched to come here to intervene. They did so. They threw it down in ruins (Nixon is now a classic ruin). Those whom they seized upon for their good work (I am one) saw for a time the universe — or anyhow whatever part caught their attention — as it is. It is a vast cube, into which time moves in the form of pattern: not spatial (it acquires space only when it enters the cube), but dynamic and bubbly; it is alive. That is the future, a bunch of patterns being fed to us as we stand around within the space-time cube. At the bottom end, the used-up time extrudes, but is still real, still there. The cube in terms of the temporal extension is about four thousand years; its spatial extension is whatever is needed to play out the patterns on, for the benefit of living creatures. The purpose of it all — this feeding energy in, patterns in, at one end of the cube within which we stand yoked together, trapped within the cube like so many parts mounted on a circuit board — this energy presents "signals" which we experience as movement and events taking place within the cube. We respond, according to instructions fired at us from around us on all the six sides of our real world. The "signals" or events are incorporated into each of us as learning — learning by experience — and they permanently modify our brain tissue, leaving permanent although minute trace-changes in us. This way we store this information combining it and altering it, and we are prepared to transmit it again when instructed, to whoever we're instructed to transmit it to. Each of us is a vast storage drum of taped information which we purposefully modify, each of us differently. Thus, Beethoven produced symphonies which no one else could; the same with Schubert. But the symphonies did not really lie within either of them (Aristotle's entelechy idea), but rather were fed to each of them in discrete (broken constituent) form, in raw bits lacking connectives. What each of those Stations did was to link his selection of bits into gestalts (his idiosyncratic symphonies). He structured them as no other Station could. However, the raw bits were fed to him; in that regard he was receptive or passive ("Where do you get your ideas, Mr. Beethoven?"). In that he connected them into a new and unique whole he was active and creative. So Beethoven, as your representative station, was a part on a circuit board, linking incoming signals, modifying them, and then transmitting something modified. That everything received by him before (memory) and what he uniquely was (due to his experiences throughout his life) went to make up the nature of each output is obvious. Nothing could pass through Beethoven without becoming Beethoven — i.e., colored by him, in a way no one else could.

"Let's feed this through Beethoven," a spirit might be saying, taking some extra choice raw bits and then so feeding them into that one out of billions of possible stations. "That way it'll come out very good indeed." But the station burned out in a mere 48 or so years, and, alas, could not be replaced. Each station is unique. Can you imagine what it must look like, viewed in terms of its existence through all space and time? Imagine it as so many lights, each winking in a different color and rhythm; imagine it like the board which opens *Ubik*, but every human who ever lived represented on it . . . except that when a station perishes, it becomes dark. It emits light no more.

It would seem that our combined total output forms a gestalt in and of itself, which is constantly retained (a permanent thing) as it is constantly added to.* Maybe somewhere God has a set of headphones on and is listening to our civilization (which is now global, making the piece he hears more unified). Output must be most extraordinary in terms of richness; also it must be unique. I think it pleases Him.

---

* "The intuitive — I might say, gestalting — method by which I operate has a tendency to cause me to 'see' the whole thing at once. Evidently there is a certain historical validation to this method; Mozart, to name one particular craftsman, operated this way. The problem for him was simply to set it down. If he lived long enough he did so; if not, then not. . . . my work consists of getting down that which exists in my mind; my method up to now has been to develop notes of progressively greater completeness — but not complexity, if you see what I mean. The idea is there in the first jotting-down; it never changes — it only emerges by stages and degrees" (from a twelve-page letter to Eleanor Dimoff of the Meredith Agency, February 1, 1960). Here, Dick is just declaring himself, at a time when his major writing was barely evidenced. The glimpse of the future author of the Exegesis is evocative, to say the least. — JL

"Play it again, Sam," God murmurs, when it ends.

So around and around we go again (this is the Wheel we hear of in Hinduism).

You think I'm kidding. I *hope* I'm kidding. "'Play it again, Sam'"? Our entire civilization, again and again, because we sound so good? Naw, Claudia; what it is, it is like rolling a barrel up an inclined plank. The rotational time I spoke of (orthogonal time) is the rolling around and around of the cylindrical barrel (sp). The inclination of the plank and our movement up it — that is linear time. Both movements in space (expressed to us imperfectly as time) are obviously real. The rotational one accumulates along the manifold; we advance upward. Where does it end? Obviously it does, *since the mere rotational time alone expresses the entirety of repetition, of cycles.* The inclination of the plank and our moving up it — obviously that leads from point A which is never seen again, or anyhow not seen until we reach point B, which we haven't yet. If you will remember this barrel up the plank picture it will aid you. Also, the fact that we experience mass, weight, and must expend effort — these show that the inclination is great, do you see? We are distinctly pushing *up.* Oddly, no one before me has realized that the very drudgery of human (and of all) life indicates that we are rising; we think of rising as a weightless, effortless thing, but a more mature study (a non-fantasy study) shows that it must occur with actual expended effort. And we are certainly doing that. The whole goddam barrel is rising. One day it will reach point B, which probably jumps it — and us — into another universe entirely.

Using this model you can readily see that our instinctive drive to survive against all odds serves purposes not our own: it is to keep us rolling de barrel along and along and along and along. The universe keeps jabbing us with tropisms over which we have no control, the sum of which is: you need to do this; you must; you like to; you have nothing else to do. The last in that sequence is the truest. What the hell else is there to do, since that is all there is here, and that is why we are here? The "barrel," when studied carefully, consists of the aggregate civilization pattern we're developing: all our ideas, our thoughts, the entire Picture we carry with us both inside our minds, in each monad-like mind, and externally, in our records. (But made real only when we go over the records; how real is a Beethoven symphony without one of us? We are part of the equation with it, and essential to it; half is on the record, but we are part of the playback equipment.) Finally, the barrel is ourselves, and when it reaches point B, and does whatever barrels do at point B, we will ourselves, inseparable from the barrel, pushing ourselves, then, and not some dead weight, some mere object — we will have arrived. Collectively and individually we will be quite something, a delight to God ... who will then turn off his equipment which projects this hologram of space-time, this cube, and lift the barrel (or cylinder) from the great computer of which this has been a part, a vital part, like a rod at a nuclear power station.

I think he then puts the rod-barrel-us out to pasture, which accounts for our various visions of heaven. We're like some horses who work, one of them saying, "You know, when our work is done, we go to a lovely green field where we play and do not do any work, and are fed and healthy," meaning that the owner, simply, puts them out to pasture. I guess we have a kind owner, who doesn't send us to the knackers. (Hell would be the tallow works. The atheist, in this model, doesn't look very intelligent; he says, "When we're through working here we just disappear. We go nowhere.")

What one must realize is that our combined fate, our joint soul, is involved; when I as an individual die, it is as if a cell in my body died; the organism (the barrel plus barrel-pusher) goes on. Viewed properly rather than from out of my head or your head or Richard Nixon's head, one individual is not an individual; John Donne was just stating a fact, about the mainland. Our heaven, or pasture, or whatever — it doesn't come when one of us individually dies, but rather, it comes when we, the connective barrel, has reached point B. *Then* the work ends.

I think that point B is in sight now, already; this is what I caught a precog glimpse of, a preview of, starting one year ago, on the previous vernal equinox. By the way — isn't this Passover, today, for the Jewish people? Elijah is again back, and the other day when I came in from outside a huge wind hit the door and I felt as if Someone had entered. The wind blew over a letter I had ready to mail; the letter was to CIA, giving them the information they requested, if I am to get a copy of my file (as I demanded) from them. The wind knocked that big letter-packet flat; I'm not afraid to prove who I am and to prove that "I am the person they have the file on." Wish me luck. And also, great Prophet of our People, Elijah Who never died, whose voice was always lifted for Justice: Don't desert us; and thank you for what you have done, to clear away King Ahab the scourge of our land.

I speak of
The Restorer of What Was Lost,
The Mender of What Was Broken.*

---

* With few exceptions, the Exegesis was not a journal where Dick would summarize his daily affairs. As a result, many of the crucial events of 2-3-74 were not written about as they happened, and so it is difficult to know how significant these events were for Dick when they transpired. One day before writing this letter to Claudia, Dick wrote a frantic letter to the FBI, saying that two days earlier (March 18) he had received a registered letter from Estonia, a letter he knew "was a trap, frankly by the KGB." He makes no mention

March 16, 1974: It appeared — in vivid fire, with shining colors and balanced patterns — and released me from every thrall, inner and outer.

March 18, 1974: It, from inside me, looked out and saw that the world did not compute, that I — and it — had been lied to. It denied the reality, and power, and authenticity, of the world, saying, "This cannot exist; it cannot exist."

March 20, 1974: It seized me entirely, lifting me from the limitations of the space-time matrix; it mastered me as, at the same instant, I knew that the world around me was cardboard, a fake. Through its power I saw suddenly the universe as it was; through its power of perception I saw what really existed, and through its power of no thought decision, I acted to free myself. It took on in battle, as a champion of all human spirits in thrall, every evil, every iron imprisoning thing.

March 20 until late July, 1974: It received signals and knew how to give ceaseless battle, to defeat the tyrannies which had entered by slow degrees our free world, our pure world; it fought and destroyed tirelessly each and every one of them, and saw them all clearly, with dislike; its love was for justice and truth beyond everything else.

August 1974 on: It waned, but only as the adversary in all its forms waned and perished. When it left me, it left me as a free person, a physically and mentally healed person who had seen reality suddenly, in a flash, at the moment of greatest peril in pain and despair; it had loaned me its power and it had set right what had by degrees become wrong over God knows how long. It came just prior to the vernal equinox or at it. The Jews call it Elijah; the Christians call it the Holy Spirit. The Greeks called it Dionysus — Zagreus. It thought, in my dreams, mostly in Greek, referring to Elijah in the Greek form: Elias. Gradually its fierceness turned to a gentle quality and it seemed like Jesus, but it was still Zagreus, still the God of springtime. Finally it became the god of mirth and joy in music, perhaps a mere man, Orpheus, and after that, a punning, funning mortal, Erasmus. But underneath, whenever it might be necessary again, Zeus himself, Ela and Eloim, the Creator and Advocate, is there; he never dies: he only slumbers and listens. The lamb of Jesus is also the tyger which Blake described; it, which came to me and to our Republic, contains both,

---

of that here. Similarly, in a letter written to his daughter on March 17, 1974, the day after "vivid fire" released Dick from "every thrall," he makes no mention of his life-changing circumstances. March 20 also appears to be the day Dick received the "Xerox missive," which was to play a crucial role in his later theorizing. This envelope, sent from New York, contained two book reviews with certain words highlighted in red and blue pen. Dick worried that they were coded death messages. The importance of these events waxed and waned significantly in Dick's life, so much so that even a major event like the arrival of the Xerox missive might go unreported for weeks or months in the Exegesis. — DG

is both. It — he — has no name, neither God nor force, man or entity; he is everywhere in everything; he is outside us and inside us. He is, above all, the friend of the weak and the foe of the Lie. He is the Aton, he is The Friend.

— PKD, March 21, 1975*

[5:31] Entropy equals disorder.

The universe is moving toward entropy.

Therefore the universe is moving toward disorder.

Forms are order.

That which is moving toward form, or completion of form, is moving against disorder or against entropy.

Therefore since the universe is moving toward disorder (away from form, in lineal time) then that which is moving toward form is moving in an orthogonal or even possible opposite direction from the universe — as such — and is picking up heat as well as form; i.e., moving toward less disorder, hence more energy.

It cannot be that to move toward completion of form is to move toward disorder; hence movement toward form means to gain life, or energy. (v. Kozyrev's theory of left spin as life or energy gaining, right as losing, and that our universe is left spin hence must be moving, à la Bergson, toward energy acquiring, not losing, toward form.)

"Growth time" (movement of an entelechy toward completion) must be orthogonal to "decay time," or "wheel spinning time," even if our senses can't sort out these two times at work before us, in us and around us. Some sections (subparts) of the universe are moving backward, then, despite our occluded vision of a single forward lineal stream. We have a monovision in a sense. Blending two signals which should be discriminated.

When we do discriminate, we perceive a general forward flow (to decay) but within it a backward flow (v. Heraclitus, frag. 51; the key retractile pulling back oscillation of the bow and lyre). I think they are both present now, and may always be/have been, but we are generally occluded: i.e., one-eyed.

It seems unlikely that the retrograde form completing heat-energy gathering time I briefly discerned was there only so long as I discerned it, and

---

* From this point forward, Dick only occasionally included letters, and hardly ever dated his Exegesis entries. The obsessive, recursive nature of the work and the dearth of references to events in the outside world sometimes make establishing precise chronology difficult, if not impossible. Even if a definitive chronology is someday established, the Exegesis cannot be fully reconstructed as written, since it is clear that at times Dick reorganized his own pages. — PJ

then it departed; it is much more likely, if not certain, that it was there before, and is there now, but that I fell back into monotemporal vision once more. I would be like a blind person who upon seeing for the first time imagined that the objects were brought into being by his seeing them. No, I saw what I saw because of the reciprocal tug: the existence of the two times forced me into perceiving them (that which is perceived precedes perception, certainly an axiom of reason).

If we watched a speeded-up film of a form developing, we would easily discern the latent form within it (which means entelechy, really) press outward into actualization; we would sense it within, and then we would see the inner pressure finally unfold and die away, leaving the completed form without internal energy. Then we would watch decay and disorder begin. (For example, a rose bud developing.) A force, internal, a plan, unfolds energetically, then reaches equilibrium and stasis, then the force dwindles away, becomes feeble, and the completed form is at the mercy, forever, of external forces which formerly the entelechy pressed outward against so effectively. One form of energy (within, growth) has waned, and forces moving toward disorder now prevail. Maybe, if we could discern it, there were two times "visible" or anyhow present.

What I noticed most was the total isomorphic relatedness between me and my environment, which I realized to be an animate and concerned entity guiding me by an endless series of engaging signals — engaging with internal systems of my own; so I was and therefore am still, although the isomorphic relatedness is now invisible to me; it must be there yet, that envolving, living world of kindness and guidance on every side: I move along a narrow path well-marked with signs that I notice and respond to even though in a sense I do not (consciously) any more notice; they still guide me, just as well, like a gutter pipe directs rain water without the water being conscious of it.

The "Whale's Mouth" sign of intersecting arcs,[60] which I viewed as representing curved time and curved space — if each arc represents a form of time (one of them lineal time, the other orthogonal or hypertime) then this sign could be thought of as representing a single previous intersection (in our past) at which the two times came together (around 100 A.D.), and then each went its own way. But as they were moving in arcs, it was inevitable, by the laws of geometry, that eventually they would once more intersect, perhaps 2,000 years or so later (i.e., very soon). These also would represent the two hemispheres of the brain, any human's brain, once before linked, then soaring off orthogonally, but fated by immutable laws to come together again.

It's possible that the Christian fish sign concealed these two geometric arcs, intentionally; the arcs would show that the unique event of Christ's First Coming was beyond any doubt to be followed by the second coming or intersection; this was conveyed and concealed and revealed all at once by the fish sign, making sense, too, out of there being both a first and second coming; the arc opened after the first, and each line seemed to separate from the other farther and farther (heaven and earth splitting further and further apart) but a keen trained eye could discern in this simple drawing the return together lying inevitably ahead; the Promise was ad hoc true. Put another way, when viewed in this geometrical fashion, there was no way by which the Second Coming (together in time) could be averted. No force, delusion, lies or guile or threats could prevent it eventually coming. (See Virgil's 4th Eclogue: The Age of Iron to give way to the Age of Gold. And the fish sign I saw was made of gold. And I saw around me a prison, a magnet like ring, of iron.)

[5:35] Plot element for *To Scare the Dead:* Nicholas discovers that each of his brains (minds, hemispheres) is traveling at right angles to the other in time. This is vital plot element: *must use,* to help accentuate that it isn't a duplication of one mind, but two totally different minds; any device like this or time-travel which will accentuate difference, is desirable.

Q: Are the two hemispheres, by so traveling, becoming farther and farther apart progressively, like ships travelling at right angles (lat versus long) to each other? And will they ever rejoin — meet again, and become One? (v. Parmenides' forms one and two being only *apparently* two different things). Here go into Taoism, and all the Parmenidesian elements interrelated. As the two minds travel further and further apart, they form a vast double loop, enclosing more and more space, as on a Go board; enclosing, ultimately, all inside them; a double circumnavigation of the universe.

And as this double motion increases, their combined (superimposed) viewpoint becomes more accurate, since its perspective is more . . . objective, detached, encompasses more (reality).

This, then, is not only a journey; it is a simultaneous *double* journey; he watches himself recede from himself, grow smaller and farther away. When, later on, if ever, will he encounter himself again, the two arcs re-intersecting ultimately (but at a time he can't plot)? Eventually he (expressed as either hemisphere, in search of the Other) will encounter an other which is That Other: himself (v. Plato and the four-armed four-legged animus-anima whole person long ago split apart and in search of its other part): he will unexpectedly encounter Himself, and thereby close the loop, probably forever.*

Or — did his other self (the Other) start out long ago, and is just now returning? Himself expressed as signal ("I shot an arrow into the air"; by arrow read "half of myself") now returning, producing anamnesis, the shock of recognition. He is not starting on this trip; this trip is ending.

These are answers — responses, to him. By whom? This is the mystery; who is he in contact with (the *Valisystem*). It really is not himself in time, in past or present, but spatially complete, as on a Go board. "Our souls, having traveled out to the stars, are now streaming back, to report that life exists, that they exist, and hence so do we."

What is expressed here is an extraordinary demonstration of the principles of conservation and symmetry (Heraclitus and Parmenides, plus our thermal laws). What was dispatched tiny and weak and frail and ignorant has returned with moral and spiritual authority, capable of working "magic," i.e., casting and removing dokos. Originally it fled Kali and has now returned, cowl-masked, robed and in disguise, the "unknown person" of Zeno's paradox[61] who is himself, to *break* the power (thrall) of Kali (the deformed kingdom; desiccated kingdom of Set). So, more correctly, it can break spells, not cast them; it is parity within the Kundry Klingsor versus the Redeemer[62] axis.

I am going to state a truly extraordinary premise: that long ago, when Earth fell to thrall, a signal was sent out for help; that signal itself has returned in strength, bearing power and arms, in truth and justice; that signal accumulated space, hence time, transduced other fields, rose from unliving to animate. That signal is its own receiver, and has been boosted, feedback to grow; hence in a sense to send out a prayer is to automatically intuit its return later, at the time of fulfillment. (Which would vary from person to person; earlier sent, earlier returned; if time is an energy, and time and space are convertible extensions of a matrix, then space is energy,

---

* While this self-encounter occurs as an idea for a plot, it offers an uncanny description of Dick's own journey. Under the influence of his own writing, and by putting as much of himself as possible into that writing, Dick seems to have seen himself as an abstraction — not in the sense of a deadened thing taken out of its context, but in the sense that software engineers discuss "layers of abstraction": an act of metacognition or description that at once detaches from and observes other layers of the system. In the Exegesis, Dick observed himself being what Douglas Hofstadter calls a "strange loop." Dick later recognizes that this operation of "meta-abstraction" identifies something about reality — that the world itself is looped with the language we use to describe it. In *The Divine Invasion*, the child god Emmanuel manifests something like this loop when he performs the "Hermetic transform." — RD

as well; as it traveled space it began to grow, rather than weaken — this was after it had gone half-way and was returning; it recapitulated all that had been lost, by the principles of conservation, parity and symmetry, supra.)

This is Absolute negentropic compression, the restoration of lost or waste (heat). Time (energy) is Form One. Space (empty, hollow, Yin, cold) is Form Two (but these are expressions of a Sameness) (v. Parmenides).

That signal was/is also the Not-I, all that was lost inwardly too; when it returns it will fulfill the law of Karma; whatever we lost expressed in milliamps will return a thousandfold. [. . .]

[5:43] The "Logos Effect," discovered about 1600 when explorers brought back to Europe information about cultures and tribes which had never had contact with Christianity. Many of these cultures and tribes had religious beliefs and rites so similar to Christianity that, astutely, the 17th-century theologians saw the possibility that the explanation lay in the long-abandoned idea of the Logos as Plan (Philo, et al.), printing out Salvation Ideas for every culture, every race.

Ubik does indeed so resemble Dr. NK's time theory that one knowing his time theory could not escape noticing this when he read *Ubik*. (For example, the scientific explanation of Ubik assigns a positive value, in terms of life-sustaining or giving energy, to a counterclock spin, which is virtually a parody of Dr. NK's concept of lefthandedness being life supportive.) This would bring *Ubik* to their attention (as it later brought Dr. NK's theory to my attention). But in no way, probably, was I influenced by anyone telepathically, etc., even though *Ubik* was written in 1968, the year Dr. NK's theory was released in the U.S. in English. Evidently this is an example of the "Logos Effect" in harmonizing and edifying all men regarding certain "salvation" or life-giving knowledge, goals and values.

However, it is equally probable that in March 1974 an actual concerted telepathic transmission effort was made in Leningrad vis-à-vis me and my ideas, perhaps to test out and see if I was telepathically sensitive.

This attempt, if indeed it took place, was more of a failure than a success, inasmuch as I think what came as a result of this was my developing an "instinctive" antipathy toward the Soviets, under the perhaps correct impression that they'd made an effort to "improve" (i.e., coerce) my ideas. The total effect on me was beyond doubt beneficial, both in terms of acquired (received) energy and acquired (received) information and comprehension; how much of this was a collateral result, added onto the experiment by the Logos itself, I have no way of assessing. Somebody likes me; if not the Soviets, then the Logos; maybe both do. I underwent a period of ordeal, but the results left me healthier and freer than I'd ever been in my life. I wish I could have such an experience again. I'd recommend and welcome it — everyone should have it. But probably it was a composite experience: one part deliberately directed from Pulkovo, another added by the Logos, a third derived from my own inner entelechy which was speeded to completion by the reception of all that good time-energy. It was a multiple cure, in at least three directions (linear space, down from above, upward and out from within). Also, the vernal equinox had arrived: springtime. The slumbering God, asleep but not dead — he was waking up anyhow.

There are at least two separate ways to read my experience in its relationship to Dr. NK's theory.

(1) My experience indicates he is correct regarding time as energy and the way time can "carry" telepathic material (to quote him: "Once we understand how to make time dense at will, then we will be able to communicate information telepathically at will.")

or;

(2) My experience is a result (a causal connection) of the experiments and truth of his work; the difference being that it is possible that any major telepathic reception would induce the massive time dysfunction I experienced, for the reasons given in Dr. NK's[63] theory; in which case no matter who transmitted to me, including the Logos — instinct — itself, I'd sense the time transformations involved.

A further point: it's evident from what Dr. NK says that it would be the intent to cause a great leap in time-density *in order to* transmit information telepathically, not the other way around (i.e., increase density as means, the t-p info as ends); not send info telepathically as means of increasing time density somewhere. The leap in time density, the entire experience of radically rolled-back time, would be an automatic experience of any t-p receiver, would have to happen in order for him to receive. This surely would be more evident if it was not a person normally sensitive to t-p info transfer; someone like me who never normally got info by telepathy would experience a unique and surprising transformation in time and not understand why. Normal telepaths probably would have become accustomed to it. My sense of time changes (in terms I guess of density) would indicate a strong artificial sending system and little if any natural sensitivity in me. This indicates that rather than me having hyped up my input they hyped up their output: as means, they created dense time around me, and thus were able to transmit. I infer from this (assuming all I've figured out in this sequence is correct so far) that Dr. NK or someone anyhow, and probably someone connected with Pulkovo,[64] did in fact finally manage to figure out how to increase time density "at will," as desired.

All this indicates that (1) Telepathic transmission to me of info was the goal; (2) Increasing the density of time around me was the means; (3) I was an "effect" and not a "cause," which explained why I felt so much under duress, and acting out adventitious command. I probably was. But that's not the whole story. (4) Probably it was Pulkovo, or related to it. Why me? *Ubik*, no doubt; the fact that it resembled Dr. NK's work — even seemed to parody it. Chance (a meaningful acausal "Logos Effect") coincidence brought the novel and me to their attention. The Logos' purpose was achieved in all this, though, since the Logos foresaw all this when it imprinted the ideas into me originally (in 1968). Thus, it caused Lem (et al.) to take an interest in *Ubik* and to invite me to come to Poland, and all else that happened. The Logos' purposes were always served in this *primarily,* since it excited us all into what we did initially; we all were doing the Lord's work, so to speak, being brought to salvation individually and helping in the general Plan; thus we who were secular scientific and left wing came around to an awareness of the Logos, and, as Heraclitus says, "we woke up from our dream and began to see reality, i.e., the plan or logos." And so it came to be, at least for me. Throughout all this the Logos was preemptive in time and in authority and in will and in teleology; and it triumphed through us not despite us. Using this multiplex human project as its plastic medium, the Logos ignited at last a dazzling triumph for dignity, for justice, for understanding and for truth above all ("the spirit of truth which knows all from the Father"). This was vast benign divine intervention, within our work, like the invisible leavening of the bread, etc.

In his article, Dr. NK states that (1) Time is an energy which enters material systems; (2) It maintains everything; (3) It is everywhere simultaneously; and therefore (4) It can transmit information everywhere telepathically; and (5) In this fashion it probably transmits instinctive knowledge to living creatures, all biological entities; and (6) It is even possible that it regulates and informs and harmonizes "inanimate" entities such as stars.

This is a description of the Logos.

Energy plus information which is everywhere.

That's Mr. Runciter plus the spraycan of Ubik.

If we can see identity between Dr. NK's "Time" and the "Logos, the Word of God," then there is no problem in explaining the entry (even a preemptive entry) into any successful time-density activity by the Logos, outsmarting long in advance man's own personal plans. By definition, by affecting a massive density in time they are involving the Logos, which is already informed (i.e., whatever information might be "artificially" transferred telepathically, this is the normal method used by the Logos to assist and inform living creatures anyhow; the "artificial" information would simply enter as a portion of a vaster, older stream). [. . .]

The best way of viewing all these elements (Dr. NK's theory, *Ubik*, March 1974) is to see confirmation of the Logos' reality (vide Dr. NK's paper when he discusses simultaneous transfer of information throughout the universe to all biological entities, via Time).

The Pulkovo work has rediscovered the Logos at work, and given it the name of Chronos instead — father Chronos from whose race we are all descended, and who controls all things.

It could be said that if Dr. NK — i.e., Pulkovo — was feeding lines to me, the Logos was feeding lines — i.e., prompting — to him. Beyond and behind the figure of any and all temporal powers, and their intentions, lie the intentions and power of God. Here is an excellent illustration of that: Man proposes/God disposes. If indeed telepathy is the universal medium of information-exchange, then the Logos, if it existed, would use it; also, those involved in experimentation with time and its info-transfer uses, would be in more direct connection with the Logos as Plan than most of us.

We still serve our ex-employer, Mr. Runciter; and he still assists and advises, as before. Nothing has changed; he knows how to get through to us, and what to bring us to restore us, and what advice (info) to lay on us. All of us. [. . .]

The dream about James-James certainly expressed what I saw in 3-74: with the Creator producing first solar flares (or the atom and its moving parts), then from it the baby, and then evolving from the baby Kathy. But that he had to injure Tessa (because she stood up to see his "act" better) — this was what I saw as an objection to linear forward moving time and continual creation anyhow: that in the powerful huge surging-forward drive of life, so many creatures are wounded and crippled, left to die, behind the flock. And in my dream I asked for help, and none of the thousands sitting around to form an attentive audience for James-James would lift a finger, despite my appeals. But then the wide glass doors opened, and the first scouts entered the great building. "We need medical assistance," I said to them, and they came toward me; small as they were, and only the first vanguard, they did represent another force, one which heard and responded. Surely this is a dream-drama expression of the retrograde force which is the other game-player and which I construe as either the Logos or Christos or the Holy Spirit — and which to me is the "good" although so far weaker of the two players. Certainly the dream showed me clearly that the primary miracle, the one which of necessity must precede all others, is the miracle of life born out of the unliving, the miracle of creation itself; then the movement up the evolutionary scale, from form to higher form to highest form; this surely is the primary work of the universe, to do this, its hardest, first, and most solemn task, over which nothing else can take precedence. How can anyone question that? But although there must be a flock to go on (the species, I guess, or all life), before there can be those who fall back too weak or sick to keep up — this in the dream was so damn clear: one person out of thousands in that auditorium caused trouble, stood up (against James-James rules) and was thrust back down and crippled. The ratio of success to failure was maybe 10,000 to 1. So I am concerned with that 1, and stepped forward, halting James-James and his continual miracles of evolving creation (certainly the most extraordinary event I've seen in dream time or waking time, ever). I was asking for medical attention, not for me or for her, but for *us*. "We need medical attention" or assistance, whichever. There is such a need; there are casualties, and I understand that He Whom I follow, He sees to it that the 1 casualty is assisted: i.e., gets medical attention. The image of the good scouts: good Samaritans, maybe; those which lend a hand to those in need. [. . .]

James-James represented ruthless creative power. But a balance is needed, both in each individual and for our planet as a whole. It was not with malice but with zeal that James-James (YHWH, I guess) smashed Tessa's elbow (ulna, the crippled lamb limping along) (my right shoulder). But I threw my weight in on the balance-scale on the side of the injured, the minority, although I personally could only *ask* for (medical) help; I had only the power to notice, to step forth, to voice the need — i.e., put it in words. (My writing? My speeches, etc.? Letters? Call attention to human needs?)

But regarding possible time dysfunctions (due either to experiments at, e.g., Pulkovo, or natural, due to overloading of the ontological matrix, or both), most of my experiences have had to do, not with time, but with space (mostly about Mexico or what resembles Mexico and is taken to be). Future space at some future time? The only for sure time dysfunction I felt was in March 74, and that was, if it existed at all, probably artificially obtained (Pulkovo). The other, spatial ones — they probably were natural dysfunctions, sudden brief windows into the future of both space and time. What is possible, though, as I've said before, is the notion of "mytosis-like" splittings of the present (due to time dysfunctions, perhaps in our past) that result in alternate worlds (as in *TMITHC*).

It's as if the merely potential (i.e., discarded at one or more critical junctions along the linear time-line) has come into a periodic shimmering realization, alongside what is actual (vide William James[65] on the sea of potential facts around each actualized fact — each that, so to speak, makes it). Like in my story "The Commuter." Also, there is to me the real thought that adjustments (à la "Adjustment Team") are being made in our past, which are to an ever increasing degree making a certain "alternate present" (or time line) actual — *in place of the one we have*, not alongside it. I sense a series of minute tinkerings going on (vide Peter Mann's conversation with me recently on that idea). They are realigning our reality so it will conform to what the Plan (Logos) called for, thus losing the error fact, finally, which crept in. I suppose they could be making this critical correction back as far as 100 A.D. Just for story purposes, let us suppose a time-traveling team from our future has gone back to 45 A.D. to see to it that Jesus is not crucified. When the Parousia are finished with us, the time line we have will not even be remembered; our memories will be retaped to fit our newly made past, as well as present, and, as in "Commuter," we will be relieved that "nothing has changed after all." I guess the realigned-correctly world will have California still the property of Spain-Mexico. Portugal will retain its States of America. The Catholic Church will not have been rent asunder by the Reformers; this world will have only one huge Christian church/body, for all.

[5:54] I am less in doubt that this was the Parousia (I am not in doubt about that at all; it is exactly what Jesus and Paul anticipated, if not John) than I am in doubt — in perplexity — as to whether it was solely in my own world, my idios kosmos, that it took place. Does the koinos kosmos remain the same? I don't think, really, that it has. But no one else that I know of saw what I saw, which by general standards at the very least limits it to a subjective experience, a personal one, for me alone. I think that seeing the signals around me firing, the living organism, may have been what Malachi meant by "The Lord of Hosts shall suddenly come to his temple," etc.; suddenly He was within everything, and visible, at least to me. "At least to me." I saw His presence. Perhaps I err when I assume that he had always been there, but not visible to me; that my eyes were suddenly opened to what had always been. Maybe He had been gone, and came back; my eyes were opened *and* He came back *and* therefore I saw Him. If my eyes had been opened a month earlier I wouldn't have seen Him because He hadn't arrived then, as yet.

Let us consider the miracle involved. When God enters time, when he pierces our world, pierces the veil and rends it — where go the usual categories of personal subjective, then-now, etc.? Did He come for all men or just for me? Will what happened to me in March 1974 still later on happen for others, or did it happen *once* for everyone? This is the same question about Christ's death on the cross; does he really die again and again for each man, so-to-speak sequentially, or simultaneously, which is to say, once? I think both are true; the usual categories don't apply.

I am a child trying to understand adult concepts.

As in *Frolix 8* — the change rushes across the world, the way I saw the black band rush across the sky on Good Friday: the band that joined the old universe with the new . . . and in that instant as I and Laura watched, I understood that we were on film, on a loop. This 3-hour strip rushing at so high a speed — it tied the two ends together. And started the sequence anew. Thus, back in 1962, my first mystic understanding of Easter, and of the Death of Christ, the dead god — in the bonds of death "Christ lag in Todesbanden," etc.[66] — I saw it then. What I saw then was real and I knew it then to be real; what I experienced in 1974, which was maybe 12 years later — at the same time of year . . . it was real, too. We can maybe resolve this when we ask, When you play your LP of Beethoven's 7th symphony, is it a different performance each time? Does von Karajan repeat it? One hears it again and again, but it is the same: like the archetype, printing out: the die stamping. What we hear is the "print."

The great miracle is that it is always new, and always it is the same, once more: unchanged. Suppose I play my LP of the 7th symphony until I know it by heart, and then I give it to you and you play it. You have never heard it before; to you it is entirely new, no more and no less new in relationship to my knowing it — I mean, however many times I have played it, however new or old it is to me, this has no effect on how new it is to you (assuming the LP isn't worn or damaged). For you it is new independent of me, and herein lies the miracle. However many times Christ has died for man; however many people have had my experience; it was as new for me as if no one had ever had it before; in my world, it was unique, it had never happened before, and so Christ died for me solely. He is infinitely new, infinitely divisible, infinitely everywhere — I guess he is Ubik.

If a simple, workable, theoretical model were wanted by which all could be restored, then this might serve:

(1) Reality in concentric rings of greater being (completeness), which the person initially encounters in terms of a ring less real than one he later encounters (best of all, finally encounters). Thus, the final ring encountered is the most real and gathers up — accumulates — all that he ever encountered before.

(2) There would be a "writing backward" system by which the person would be presented, for engramming-on purposes, lesser fragments of forms the larger fragments of which he will encounter later — that is, later for him. Thus, his encounter-line would be arranged backward to the direction he himself experiences it, the way a mystery novel is written. What

he has had, and possibly lost, which would make the term "restoration" meaningful to him, would so to speak be deliberate clues presented ahead of time (early in his life) with the full knowledge that these were the certain experiential items he would later on come onto. The interesting part of this is that he could be easily, almost effortlessly, engrammed in a random fashion, yet have the sense of total meaning. Here is a synthetic example: let us say that at the end of his life-line he winds up in the Lusitania Hotel which is in the shape of a boat and has cherrywood furnishings including broom plants (Acacia) as the floral items. Intrinsically neutral in value (these are virtually a pattern-less collection of elements) they would, for him, acquire meaning—Bedeutung—if one were to place early in his life small replicas of these constituents: one would see to it that as a child he grew up for a few months—long enough to create engramming—in a yard with flowering Acacia, which is really a weed, and that he watched a film on the sinking of the *Lusitania* on his family's TV set . . . and so forth, seeing to it that there was a vast wasteland of these items, so to speak, until the glide pattern part of his life. Finally he would begin to encounter these dear long lost engrammed-on bric-a-brac, and have a deep sense of cosmic completeness. Thus any life, theoretically, could be given a subjective sense of completeness and meaning and purpose and wholeness just by seeing to it that retrograde "clues" of what was in the natural course of events to happen along were stuck here and there at very early strategic points. The economy of these would be beautiful, since one would simply work backward from the "solution," i.e., the end as pure random given. "I am getting all back what I lost," the person would sigh gratefully, and see a Divine Plan, a Godish Hand in all this. Of further interest: he would be right. There is really no way this simple, economic system of imbuing an ordinary life with completeness could be accomplished without the agency of (a) deliberate design and (b) the ability to accomplish it by retrograde motion in time. What is to me of supreme interest is that the person involved—the subject—would be able to detect the subtle but *to him* indubitably real hand of the Creator in the final section of his life—although no one else could, and anyone else could argue himself black in the face that no pattern was evident. The subject, all his life, would have carried these key engrammed-on external gestalts, slumbering always in his psyche; he would know, when he began to re-encounter them, what it signified (not that the end was near but that the whole process was subsumed by intention, design, and a plan or Logos). These would be absolute signs along the trail that there was indeed a trail—and it was one intended for him; he and it were isomorphic.

Being a novelist I can appreciate how easily this could be done; the ordinary person would suppose that the tinkering to produce a wholeness would be done at the end (i.e., the final elements in time would be placed there to conform with the very early childhood ones), but of course it's the other way; at an early age certain gestalts would be stuck in, and at this point the child's worldview, his sense of reality, in fact his reality, would be so hazy that he would accept anything; there could be no rejection of any item as "out of context" or "not supposed to be there and hence unconvincing or suspicious in nature." God could stick a sardine can in the middle of the sky, and the 2-year-old would gaze at it with awe (as we would) but with total acceptance (which we would not). God could see to it that these key (and they need be only a few) engrammed-on items could be striking — would leave a vivid impression, and a lasting (for obvious reasons) effect. The child, as he grew up, would find himself wondering, every so often, why the yellow blossoms of the Acacia plant seemed so *significant* to him and lingered in his memory tapes, after much else had dimmed . . . and then finally he would delight in re-encountering the Acacia plant, at the Lusitania Hotel, and marvel that he had somehow "found his way home" or better, more accurately, "been led home."

(In my life, this would be why I always remembered the name of my babysitter, Olive Holt, when the names of most teachers afterwards were forgotten. It was because that "name" in divided form would crop up in the Xerox letter, *by accident* — it could to a certain vague but real extent be found there; I would see it in the Xerox letter and my mind would work in a retrograde way, which is the direction the retention was impressed at the time, when I was 4 years old, *because* it would come up later — because that would clue me in, in 1974.)

This is an example of a process which I saw in 3-74 as a major process in the universe: it plays its hand (so to speak) in such a nonlinear way that the pattern is never visible until the final sections or even section is lowered (or raised) into place — one can't even tell, for a long time, maybe a lifetime, that there is/are pattern(s) at all. What is given is not given in sequence, anyhow not in causal sequence, or any 1,2,3,4 sequence. The significance, therefore, of any element early in the "game," which is to say, in life, cannot be assessed; one can dream at any time a dream the events and things of which although impressive and vivid admit to no understanding — until the missing integers show up subsequently. So selective, so intelligent is the method of play, that every guess as to the meaning of a partial pattern is brought to ignominious ruin when the true (completed) pattern is visible, and one must hang on, and hang on, waiting for that last piece. Thus, things seem to turn into their opposites, or anyhow into what they were not, as an additional piece is added; and each gestalt is a subsection of a larger gestalt embracing several gestalts. We therefore can reason that if we watch the universe in its process, its continual creation, we cannot guess what shape it will assume when complete until it is complete — it could turn from a short fat mean dull dry universe to a thrilling warm green hat-shaped one, with the addition of a single sly piece, and God Himself could show a complete visage which was quite different from the semblance up to then . . . this might provide a new clue as to "unreality" versus "reality": the latter is anything correctly apprehended, which is to say, when it — I repeat *it* — is complete; until then, no matter how scrupulously observed, it would be less than real; it would be illusion? A phantom? The not-real, anyhow. It would not really achieve is-ness or true being, but only have temporal (!!!) function or mode until then. The "false work" of the universe, serving until final pieces are in, and Being or true is-ness, takes place, which could be Suddenly and Unexpectedly! It would be witnessed as a transformation, not a mere addition to, but a total transformation from being (not truly so, just existed in the mode of) one thing into being (this time truly) another!!

Theorem: That which we call "illusion" or "not real" is simply that which is still incomplete. Not yet what it is. There is a lot of this. On all sides of us, and in us.

You see, they couldn't keep the universe vacant and closed until it was finished; where were we supposed to live until then? (Like a new exhibit at Disneyland which isn't opened until finished, until complete.) We're living in an in-progress place, because there is nowhere else for us to go; this is the only exhibit.

[5:67] When I look back on those first days in 3-74 when I saw Rome around me, not Fullerton, and specifically the Rome of the period of Christ's time, and saw its angry military hostility, I was equally aware (and this is what I tend to forget) of my own identity standing in opposition to it; hence its hostility toward me — the scurrying of its agents were specifically hostile toward me, and I had to work in stealth, e.g., in baptizing Christopher et al. The other end of the dipole was my own new identity, not merely the "new" identity of my environment (Fullerton made into Rome); I had become a Christian and a very special kind, different from what I had been as Fullerton had been to Rome; I was a member of a secret group which Rome was dedicated to destroy; this made me part of the Fish sign secret society, killed on identification and disclosure. No sense can be made out of my seeing Fullerton turn into Rome until the other hemisphere of the Magdeburg jars[67] is taken into account: what *I* had turned into. I can infer it from the hostility of my Roman environment (the ir leg, for instance), but more so I can infer it from what I did (the baptism) and my knowledge of the original Christian practices. The change had been wrought in *me;* Fullerton metamorphosing into Rome *came as a result of that.* Thus, what I saw externally in terms of transformation ratifies what I knew from an inner awareness to be the case; the two fit perfectly. What was Rome of that period hostile to? The authentic early Christians. Also, I tend to forget that in addition to the secretiveness of my actions, due to my knowledge of what the Romans would do to me, was my anticipation of the Savior to come. [. . .]

What is involved is a restoring, a new life which is the igniting by means of the penetrating of the solar spermatikos[68] of what had lain dormant, asleep over two thousand, maybe five to ten thousand years; it could not *wake itself up* — like the root or bulb called to by spring (by the healing warming Sun of Righteousness) it had to be summoned. If new birth or new life refers to a restoring (which it does) then at one time that Healing Sun was present and somehow withdrew, at which time the higher life in us fell asleep, in the darkness (vide the pineal body secreting the hormone melatonia, in darkness, which impedes the expansion, the growth, the coming into activity, of the latent form or entelechy). The very idea of "Wake up" implies winter time and the slumbering during winter time of all life. In some fashion, however, we once were awake and then fell asleep, which is what the Greeks meant by Lethe, by forgetfulness; forgetfulness is equated with falling asleep, and waking up with anamnesis. I guess the nourishing and feeding by the solar spermatika is understandable when one realizes that all life is "fed" by sunlight per se; this is an analog of that. It cannot wake unless fed; the first impulse rouses it from slumber, as when I felt that an Essene or someone holy who had been slumbering in me thousands of years and who possessed Sophia Pistis had awakened; the shock was of such enormity as to be beyond words to express; I can see why. [. . .]

I awoke abruptly to find myself with my Savior, and then entered Fellowship with God (the dreams of the delighting void). Can it be said that this is *the* rebirth, accomplished by penetration of the Child by the solar spermatikos? Yes. Firebright, brought to life and sustained Greater intelligence for me, better health, longer life, even prosperity. A certain facility with life. But most of all I recall what I saw when I awakened: I saw my God, smiling in the sunlight of day. Once, during the years of the Terrible Separation, I saw Palmer Eldritch in the Sun — I saw God backward, but sure enough, in the daytime sun: at high noon, and knew him to be a god. *The Three Stigmata,* if read properly (i.e., reversed) contains many clues as to the nature of God and to our relationship with him. I was motivated to flee, then, fearing what I saw, so vast was the breach then. It was definitely a true vision of God, but grown (to my blind sight) terrible; still, it was the beginning of my seeing; that I could see God at all, in the sun, showed that I was not entirely blind, but rather deranged. My 3-74 experiences are an outgrowth of my Palmer Eldritch experience of over ten years earlier. "Faith of Our Fathers" shows this too; I knew Him to be real . . . but only in *Ubik* does he begin to appear as benign, especially then in *Maze of Death*. We were coming back together, as friends in the light-struck meadow or forest . . . the summertime to greet.

[5:69] This news (in *Psy. Today*[69]) about the pineal body being a light receiving organ or gland is so exciting to me because it means that the chromatic phosphene source I experienced did not merely go to the light-sensitive part of my brain, but also to my pineal gland. . . . My brain saw the phosphene activity and was dazzled and delighted; however, probably as far as the brain itself went, it ended there. Not so for my pineal body; it *responded* (which is what it does; see article in *Psy. Today*) to what it received from the optic nerve, accepting it not as entertainment but as signal. (Disinhibiting, no doubt.) Probably all melatonia production (for openers) was halted, it being an inhibiting secretion. I guess I saw the "Other Sun," which shone at nighttime, when the physical sun isn't there. It was a deliberate signal from the Sun of righteousness, in the night, a dazzling display of its kind of light (a fire-like light, much like chromatic fire), and it tripped the pineal into things buried in our morphology for thousands of years, which the physical daytime sun doesn't trip (more than abolishing the production of melatonia and histamine, etc.). This chromatic Other Sun fire light would cause firing in the pineal body which constituted the true, absolute, ultimate purpose of that body, and place my total mindbody organism into its true, absolute, ultimate Being state. [. . .]

Nurturing. I am not, rather than merely being nurtured (by the Earth, etc.) but nurturing Firebright within me (a Yinnish matter: hence this is why I got K'un as my trigram, K'un and Tui,[70] both female). This is the normal growth-line of an organism: it is born, and must, as an incomplete, ungrown infant, be nurtured. Gradually, as it grows, it moves toward nurturing rather than being nurtured; final entelechy completion would be for it to nurture, be a parent. This is logically visible in all higher organisms. (We call this "giving" rather than "receiving.") What the Gospels stress when they repeat the concept of giving in so many ways is nurturing, which is giving. The parent (mother or female) gives of her own body in this. The reason the Gospels emphasize the female values is not for receptivity alone (which is the first step, before implantation) but after the reception of the seed, then the nurturing. So long as one takes, one is not full grown, and certainly not yet a parent (of the Spiritual, Immortal body within). One becomes the "mother" and God himself is the father. And does the protecting, as one sees on the visible plane, in a family.

One could speculate that this is the purpose of human beings: Why We Are Here—to serve as the recipient "female" "mothers" for the implantations of the solar spermatika, the divine seeds. Curiously, this would bear on Doris' point about the item in *Catholic Agitator*[71] that Jesus' healing activities were not only primary, it was that which most crucially angered the Romans.* I asked her, "Why the hell would healing these bodies for us be a primary act on His part, especially since these bodies will die anyhow; they're healed, but they aren't made into anything but what they are, i.e., they aren't immortal." Well, if these bodies are to serve as the "wombs" for the solar spermatika, then healing such a body would be "pre natal care," and certainly logically crucial. [. . .]

It doesn't seem to me that it's just speculation that it was my pineal gland to which the primary message went, and which was primarily stimulated; because: (1) the dreams of three eyed people, with the third eye being the Hindu 3rd all seeing eye of enlightenment dead-center in the forehead. And (2) the pineal gland is affected by light, according to *Psy. Today*, in early springtime, at the vernal equinox or just before . . . probably it can be computed at the precise time (March 18) (1974) that I experienced the chromatic progressions. However, this still leaves the issue of, Where did all the information (e.g., written) come from? Disinhibited (i.e., this was all engrammed inside, in my entelechy, but held back, blocked by the melatonia, the GABA fluid, etc.? Just in there waiting? Or did it enter me along with the seed?). Pre-natal instructions! No wonder I felt myself to be under the guidance of Asklepios—and dreamed of doctors! And got primarily medical/healing advice, which goes with what Christ himself offered, for the same reason.

---

* Doris Sauter was a dark-haired girl Dick met in 1972 when she was dating his friend (and fellow SF writer) Norman Spinrad. The two later bonded over their growing interest in Christianity, Doris sharing her conversion story with Dick, and Dick relaying the events of 2-3-74 to her. Eventually the two paired up for charity work. In May 1975, Sauter was diagnosed with advanced lymphatic cancer, which she survived. In January 1976, Dick asked Sauter to marry him (although his fifth wife, Tessa, and young son Christopher would not move out of the apartment for several months). Sauter refused. Later that year, when Sauter's cancer returned and Dick's health issues—including high blood pressure and heart problems—became more serious, they decided to live together. Doris became the character model for Sherri Solvig in *VALIS* (1981). Later she moved next door to Dick and became the inspiration for the character in Rybus Romney in "Chains of Air, Web of Aether" (1979) and *The Divine Invasion* (1981). Sauter was forced to move out when the apartment building converted to condominiums, but the two remained friends until Dick's death. — DG

What, though, took possession of me, which seemed like Elijah (if not truly Elijah)? I guess it was the Father; certainly it was not the seed. A form of the Father: the Holy Spirit, which, recall, made Mary pregnant, which brought conception to her; she conceived by the Holy Spirit and gave birth to the Logos; and yet, the Logos in a sense impregnated her; I guess the macro-Logos this way achieves its micropresence here. Locally. [. . .]

Prophecy: seeing into. The past is within things (as in *Ubik*). Again, the onion rings universe. Where is the past? Within what we see, at the hearts. All reality is like some great Indian burial garbage mound, like layers or accretions, at Troy, successive. Not behind but "below." Contained.

Like in the 3 pages I sent Angus. Palimpsest. Well, if the past is within what we see (smaller concentric rings, constricted) perhaps one can reason that the future consists of larger rings than that which makes up our perceptual present; vide Plotinus. The next concentric ring of emanation would be the future . . . strange. Which we reach toward, and which reciprocally reaches down to assist us, as I inferred about the "space people": they're from the future, reaching back to what for them is a smaller inner ring of the past, to give help. Angels. They would come to us in dreamtime, with *visions* of what is ahead, and this is why dreams are prophetic. And less dense, less constricted than the daytime Now ring. [. . .]

You are to be "meek," i.e., Yinnish, humble, receptive, but what overpowers you (the father!) is fierce, like Elijah, seeking justice and truth, powerful, definitely Yangish, and the not-you. Just the opposite. Possession by the God (vide Virgil describing Apollo taking over Sibyl[72]). You may be masculine to other humans, but to Him you are feminine, passive. Now, the Mynaeds of Dionysos did not seem to believe (read *know*) that a permanent fertilization, acquisition took place, but the Orphics certainly did; here lies a vast distinction! The being-overpowered leaves something forever: a vision of truth, of reality, a rising up to ultratemporal regions, but after the beatific vision, the Firebright Second Birth, what is born, lives on, eternally. What a jump from the mere Dionysian frenzy to Orphism and beyond, to Christianity! What a realization of the value of being possessed!

This borders on the Sufi: *becoming* God. One does "become" God while he possesses you, but then he leaves. But — well, it's like poor Leda (vide Yeats' poem[73]). But look at the progeny: Helen of Troy.

Well, I have certainly (through Doris' help) made a distinction between two opposite sequential states; my experience began when I was "listening for very weak signals to transduce," which was meekness (I got it right, picked up paw talk, etc.), and then came the chromatic fire. That was when I received God or God's Power or Spirit, the Yang upon me-as-Yin. Possession of me by the God took place, as Ted Sturgeon says in *Venus Plus*

X or whatever, this being what was really sought at the Feast of Agape.*
No wonder they say, as Doris points out, God is love! Wow, He sure is! It
is a (ahem) mating (again vide Yeats' poem "Leda and the Swan"). But that
was one year ago — over a year ago. Actual possession lasted days, weeks,
slowly drained off; no more than a couple weeks, the electrostatic life form
gradually drained off. But Firebright remained; the dreams remain right up
to now; contact (Fellowship) with God remains.

Spring is the mating season. As *Psy. Today* says, it's based all the way up
to cosmic influences (sidereal). All synchronized.

By following all the admonitions of the Gospels, one literally *courted*
the great masculine Father deity so that he literally possessed the Christian. From this (receiving the Holy Spirit, as they put it euphemistically)
they got various powers: healing, prophecy, ability to discern, and were
made Righteous, which I experienced as a thirst for Truth and Justice and
doing the right thing. "Gifts of the Spirit," yes, but those who were possessed were also the "First fruits of the harvest," which meant that they
gained something permanent; this would correspond with my being back
in Rome; i.e., escaping the thrall of time (supra); being released from the
bondage of time, which is a thrall producing death — hence, freedom, release, from the power of death. Certainly, of all the various gifts, this would
matter the most. I myself experienced reality on an inner ontological basis (assimilating objects themselves rather than mere phenomena), saw
the structure of the universe (Logos or Plan), had and still retain fellowship — contact — with God, which is to say, knowledge of him. I didn't just
get the power to heal; I was healed. I walked with God and communed
with him (along the alley that day, also in trances and dreams). I knew the
true state of things (the tyranny) and what to do. [. . .]

Ursula accuses me of getting away from "Taoistic balance" when I get
into Christianity. The Logos and balance (cf. frag. 51 of Heraclitus) are intimately connected, with the Logos implementing balance or harmony everywhere, it being the Plan. It is hard to imagine the Logos out of balance.
[. . .]

---

* It is not clear from the Exegesis to what extent Dick's path crossed with that of Theodore Sturgeon, the author of the science-fiction novels *Venus Plus X* and *More Than Human,* who herein is mentioned a number of times (as are the SF authors Thomas Disch,
Ursula Le Guin, and Stanislaw Lem). Dick's and Sturgeon's outlaw kinship — their shared
anarchic spirit, their common ambivalence about the technology that wowed most other
science-fiction writers, their subversion of physical and temporal reality in pursuit of emotional or even metaphysical truths — makes sense considering that both aimed for the literary "mainstream" before they were vortexed into genre. Perhaps Sturgeon will become
the next Dickian vogue among the literati, notwithstanding his introduction here amid
odd ruminations on a reincarnated cat. — SE

My sense that Firebright has gone on only means that He, a half Light, Half Human creature, is now strong enough to leave the "womb," which is good. Any immortality I have will be through the fact that He is immortal; like all children, he must leave, Son of a Mortal Mother (myself) and Deity (God as Father). Tessa points out it's a corporate body, like yogurt (in the dream, the renewing fish that's sliced forever). Christ as pure Light Being is the Head; we all form the body; we are immortal with Him. It would be dreadful to be immortal alone, separate.

There is no doubt that, what with my right hemisphere experiments, I was trying to achieve something — and perhaps did. Received something; receiving was part of what I was into, the idea that we could, if we listened in a new way (or a forgotten way). Where did the "light beam" come from? Certainly my dreams suggest the past; anyhow it is all what should be identified as retrieved knowledge. But it may have been triggered (the disinhibiting) by an ET signal. This presumes a link between earth and, ahem, heaven. I think there is.*

Also, what I experienced was an Adjustment, in terms of the palintonos and palintropos harmonie systems. The great entity which we call God, Immanent Mind being a better term, adjusted imbalances at that time, and this started up a lot of signaling. Probably I was part of a palintropos change, and oscillation outward (expanding) with what had been in the Taoist sense "too filled up," also the Greek sense (hubris) forced back, made Yinnish, retractile; this contributed to maintaining the total palintonos harmonie of the Universe/Mind. I was made into an active (Yangish) station of that change, and felt it, felt the signals coming to me; this is what appeared to be — or was — possession by the God or Elijah, also divine intervention (to restore harmonie . . .). What acted was the Immanent Mind

---

* In passages like these, it is impossible to ignore Dick's obvious and sometimes self-confessed psychopathology — in other words, that the guy often appears, well, *crazy*. It is tempting to collapse Dick's mystical realizations into this craziness, as if Valis were nothing more than a symptom of Dick's alleged schizophrenia, temporal lobe seizures, or whatever. But we must be more careful, and more sophisticated, here. Dick himself thought poignantly and deeply about these and related issues and came to a conclusion that many other thoughtful people — from William James and Henri Bergson to Aldous Huxley — have come to, namely, that the brain may be a kind of "filter," "transmitter," or "reducer" of consciousness. When this filter-brain is temporarily shut down or suppressed *by whatever means* (mental illness, psychedelics, political torture, meditative discipline, a car wreck, a profound sexual experience, heart surgery), other forms of consciousness and reality, many of them cosmic in scope and nature, can and often do shine through. Trauma, we might say, can lead to transcendence, but — and this is the key point — the transcendent state cannot be reduced to or explained by the traumatic context. As with the material brain and its relationship to the irreducible nature of consciousness, the trauma does not produce transcendence. It lets it in. — JJK

which carries within it (the Container of all the objects) me and everyone else including my total environment. That this realm exists is not an object of knowledge to our society; it used to be called The Gods, in the Greek sense, not in the Hebrew sense (vide all studies thereon). Well, our society, inadequately informed on what the pre-Socratics knew, and the mystery religions and other Greek thinkers knew, continues on unaware of the forces which ultimately govern. [. . .]

We are the acted-upon, which is what is meant by, "Beware of hubris."

What possessed me also equally possessed the world around me, so unless that which was not alive (the universe) can suddenly be alive, which is not likely, then more probably it was a heightening effect both in me and outside me. It already was alive. I know I was. This was for both me and for my environment a threshold effect, or anyhow my perception thresholded. I say, It is all alive, and what we see is not only alive, it is alive through being infused by life as our body is alive through being infused by life. It is psyche to soma in both cases. We are talking about a vitalistic, not a mechanistic, view, and I saw it. I am sure of what I saw. Maybe by "possessed" it should always read, "*awareness* of being possessed," implying we are (the environment outside, each of us inside) possessed all the time but not aware of it in either direction. QED.

In another sense, "being possessed" was being outside oneself, and outside the environment as well, at a third point, the Archimedean standpoint from which one could see both oneself and the environment as an interacting entity . . . but this does require "being outside." So it may not have been a coming into me, but a me going outside of me.

What I experienced was the restitution of balance, and since it was on such a vast order I perceived the ultramundane origins of the forces at work. This was no whim of a deity; it was a palintropos harmonie in motion — the swing of oscillation, and these forces were a corporate body or entity which was alive and which had intention, as I have; we were isomorphic, and that is that. [. . .]

Dream about Dodger stadium and low class Mexican type U.S. celebrations of every sort; abrupt awakening and thought: I think we're (each of us is) a colony, like a colony of bees. A collection of loosely interrelated entities, which light up in patterns; game board style. Also, each of us is isomorphic. We're inside a great colony of bees, any number and combination of which can light up at any one time. Like cells — in a battery. Any output (both each of us; and It). Clusters: each cell with a slightly different idea of what it'd be like; hence the otherwise inexplicable diversity and variety. We must function in some very loose physical arrangement, but with a field exchange created, such as social insects can be assumed to possess;

each of us is that field (vide acupuncture), and the Great Mind is made up of diverse and even discrete physical entities which form an exchange field capable of a vast variety of interconnections or firing sequences of patterns. Arrangements are by commingling and by inter-signaling. Intensity and threshold are major features. It's a micro-collective, a vast macro-collective. My "Dodgers stadium celebration" dream suggests that one idea can be presented to a vast collection of cells and each processes it in an individualistic way, giving it slight modification; all cells share common purpose and memory and form an identity, but don't need to be mechanically linked. We and our environments form such interconnected cluster systems that mutually process information and alter it while exchanging it; we are all (humans) like a vast compound eye which shows a repetition of the motion of a single object but each cell reflecting slightly differently. Instead of saying, We are within a Great Mind (immanent mind) I would like to modify that and say, We are within a Great Brain, made up of countless cells as are our own (I mean many many cells, with an incredibly vast number of possible combinations of circuitry linkage). Whatever it is that it is doing, it may have parts, like our own brain (regions with functions associated thereto) or it may go on levels at different places, quantitative surges, etc. But there is a sort of "control room" part which can infuse and override "autonomic" functions; what we see is autonomic or reflexive brain-function except at crucial/exceptional times, when there is the equivalent to our "consciousness," or a rise in level of intention and awareness, of purpose (locally, I guess). [. . .]

I am lying in bed here and I am musing, "God can simulate the inanimate. Or rather, God can pretend to be anything he wants, any part of His creation. He can replace any part, be it." And then it came to me what you call this; you call it the Miracle of Transubstantiation. This is *exactly* what is believed to take place in the host, during the Communion. Exactly and precisely. What I saw that day in the alley and everything else I saw, God "immanent," I have for over one full year tried on my own to develop the concept of transubstantiation. Well, it was not wasted time because what I did was prove the reality of the miracle of the Mass, and finally I pinned this down in terms of nomenclature and description. I just saw it on a wider scale; also, I did see it. I did see it. I saw it; the world as "this is my body and this is my blood. I am here." No wonder my tiny mind had shuddered under the weight of trying to understand. This is the holy of holies, the miracle of miracles.

I would like to add that my description (and memory) of what Pinky did in trying to heal me (lying on me transversally) I now learn Elijah did to help restore the widow's son.[74]

I guess the votive candle and the little saint helped. God consecrated reality right and left around me: miracle of miracles. I understand. Credo.

I have had in this one very small clue, but absolute: the sound of the bells, the Osterglöchen. Christ arisen! The bells of Easter. This delineates it beyond . . . the sound of the healing bells which mean transformation (as in *Parsifal*). The wound closed. But only One, Christ, ever spoke through the Osterglöchen. (And it was at that time of the year, too.)

So it was a vision.

I must never forget the bells.

I wrote of God manifesting himself in transubstantiation; but of course it is Christ. This now causes me naturally to wonder, No one ever reported seeing the miracle even in the objects of the Mass. How come I saw this (not how come it happened), but why extended, as I saw it? Also, it advances it down the time manifold, out of the distant past, into the medieval period anyhow . . . I should really go back over everything I've written over the whole 14 months and put the correct word "Christ" wherever I speak of having experienced God (especially immanent God; it is immanent or the actually present Christ). Beebread. We are fed in each individual cell, but must emerge to join cooperative.

[5:98] Today (after reading in the *L.A. Times* where a psychic says there is another life form on Earth smarter than we are, but that it lives in the water "and has no hands") I decided to describe, without attempting to name, the entity which telepathically approached me in 3-74. Its most salient quality, when I went to enumerate all of them, seemed to be not its thinking (mentation) but its *knowing*; it knew everything . . . and I reported, to myself, how it seemed to know things and events and people from inside, out from outside (external facts), but seemed to sweep them out at the very heart. And then I realized that I had given an excellent description of the Parakletos which Jesus in "John" says God will send here as Comforter, Advocate, etc. Also, it finally came to me that the state of agitation and distress and perturbation I was in in 3-74 when it suddenly approached me with aid was exactly the state of agitation, distress and despair and perturbation — at the end of my rope, really — I was in back in my high school physics class when I took the test that dealt with Archimedes' principle. In both cases the need was the same: the acute despair and prayer petition on my part: *need* of an acute sort. The same small calm inner voice came both times, knowing everything and informing me. Rendering assistance of a particular sort: it *knew* the answers which I needed in order to survive. It knew and it told me, and then it departed. It was God I called on then, back in the mid-40's. I'm sure it was He Who answered then; evidently now, too.

All the trillions of written pages I've seen in sleep . . . I'm sure they're equivalent to the *spoken* answers I heard in my head in my high school physics class (where I was awake and so couldn't dream). This is information of the highest kind, from the ultimate source: the Spirit of Truth, as Jesus explained it. "Who sweeps out and knows even the heart of the Father." Mainly it gave me absolutely correct information (and insight) plus the zeal to put into action Handlungstreie based on that knowledge. Also, it seems likely that my preview of Fullerton (dream for 8 hours while awake back in 1971 of "Mexico") plus the *Tears* dream, both of which had permanent effects on me, came from this source; there had been one source throughout and I think this is the historic name for it, and historic promise. Here are 4 examples of absolute for sure intervention. Maybe there have been others I never was aware of. Between example 1 (high school) and 3-74 lies 30 years — a huge gap, most of my life in fact. I ask, What about the horse dream in Canada? Look: again a horse; the *Tears* dream involves a posse of horses. The Vancouver dream — the horse attempting to leap the house, which was the Point Reyes house, where the *Tears* dream took place, attempting and failing — that told me something obscure but overwhelming. "I have had a dream like no other dream I ever had," I wrote my mother. "The oracle," Heraclitus wrote, "does not answer yes or no; he gives a sign." Also, the in-cage-under-Houston-Astro-Dome dream had flying horses in it . . . the horse as sign for death. The adversary, maybe? Fate? Destiny? [. . .]

Thought: back 20 pages, where Joseph Campbell[75] says, "You can view God as being every *thing* or every *where*." If everywhere, then we have Ubik again, who is everywhere. Must see which I settled on, where or thing. Hope it was where. (Ho On: Greek for I AM, a title of God.) [. . .]

Oh, yes; I heard the voice one other time: "And she shall see the sea," which was probably back around 1968/9, no later. As I wrote Phil Farmer, I knew it could not be my own thoughts or voice. I see now that beyond doubt that voice was the "physics test" voice and the one from 3-74 on. Again, it came as a result of agonizing despair on my part, and a need to know something, to understand; it brought relief and help and comfort. [. . .]

I had an infinitely complex insight today that it is just as easy to think of the future pushing the present into the past as to think of the past generating the present and moving toward the future; since we don't remember the future the way we do the past we don't discern these "heavy" events weighing on the present and forcing the present into annihilation, into the past. What our minds do is link everything in a sort of string, one after another, in the order in which we encounter them. Thus, if we reach into a fishbowl of numbered slips randomly distributed, we will write down as a linear sequence the numbers we draw. In whatever order or non-order we encounter events (experience them) our memory will arrange them on this linear track, as if they happened that way. Actually, they didn't happen (were not arranged) that way but only encountered that way. But, having lined everything up, we imagine the past in this orderly line, which is readily translated into a causal string because so arranged it has that look to it. Eventually in this way we create in our heads an enormous past pressing inexorably against the present to create the events of the future. But suppose we imagine everything in the present like a stage set, with actors; however, in the wings wait the set and actors for the next scene. These latter, dimly discerned, will inexorably push everything on the stage off eventually. It is not the prior act but the next act which exerts the force; conceive of the present as fragile or unstable, and this pressure "from the wings" becomes inexorable. Logically, this is as plausible as the idea of cause-and-effect from the past operating as force on the present. Also, if as Dr. NK says, time is energy entering a material system, perhaps it enters from the future — is the future; i.e., time has more charge, more force in the future, drains out into the spatial reality of the present, and at last dissipates down into the drain-off slot which is the used up past. This is a disturbing new view but oddly enough it coincides with my dream experiences, my precognition of events moving this way from the future; I feel them inexorably approaching, not generated from the present, but somehow already there but not yet visible. If they are somehow "there" already, and we encounter them successively (the Minkowski block universe; events are all already there but we have to encounter them successively[76]) then this view might be a correct view of time and causality. The reason (again) why we feel the past to be real but not the future is simply that we have experienced the past and recall it; memory bits lie in our brain tissue, but this is not true of the future. However, I have never experienced Bombay India and I have San Francisco; but the latter in reality is no more real than the former. (For myself, I would guess that we have, as the Hopis believe, two realities only: that which is manifest, and that which is in the process of manifesting. The former is the present; the latter is our future, sort of rising up from within, from potent to actual. This can be represented spatially in terms of rings, concentric, of actualization, à la Plotinus.)

Eureka! I've been reading Rollo May's[77] *Love and Will.* He describes Eros, the spirit of life, mediator between men and gods, partaking of the human and the divine; it is the élan vital of Bergson, Dionysos, it is especially Socrates' daimon — this is the voice I hear; this is what "possessed" me in 3-74. But an overwhelming intriguing mystery presents itself: Socrates was Greek; Eros is a Greek myth; Dionysos was a Greek god; if Eros (as RM says) is not an actual entity, then how come I heard words in Attic Greek and it, the daimon, thought in Attic Greek? This both confirms and yet adds more mystery, pins it down for sure and yet — the coincidence (Greek speaking) is too great; it must indicate something — a vital clue beyond all other clues!!!!!! [. . .]

Thus in reading Rollo May's book I have ruled out (in my own mind) any possibility that my 3-74 experience was spurious or somehow engineered by human persons or groups; it was what it seemed to be. Rollo May traces it back to Attic Greece and he himself affirms it as a major source of human viability, unrecognized as it has been for centuries. It is the anti-Thanatos force per se. The source of all life, however named. But what I wonder, having experienced this and come to certify it by ancient and now modern authority — why doesn't it occur more often? How strange, that God through some mediating demiurge can revivify any given human being, at his will, and yet until I read Rollo May's account of Socrates' daimon, I had found not a single other account of exactly what I had had since high school physics class; not one other anywhere, in any reference book. How could it remain unknown? This implies God uses it sparingly; it is virtually nonexistent, or anyhow non-reported. The only thing I can think of offhand is this: 3 different sources indicate that this daimon, under another name, ceased to be present in men's lives around 100 A.D.: Gibbon says that the Christians lost the actual power; the International Community of Christ agrees; the Witnesses say so, too, or maybe it's the Megiddo Mission people[78]; anyhow, since this may well be the Christ-consciousness or Holy Spirit thing, then perhaps the human being at this end must do something, and has forgotten how to do it or even that it can be done (vide the Int. Community of Christ). God waits for us to do an initiating act. Or, the Holy Spirit (the power) was withdrawn, and the dry period of nearly 2,000 years has taken place, without contact between man and God. If this is so then perhaps the Spirit has returned, which is what I did feel, especially I felt that Elijah had come. Either way, it has been gone for 2,000 years, either because God withdrew the Holy Spirit or because for one reason or another man lost the method and the notion. And then all that came were daemons rather than daimons — evil spirits only, not from God.

Yet this still seems strange to me; if God through a demiurge can do this, why doesn't he do it a lot? Look: if I assume that what happened to me in 3-74 was due to something I did, which others don't ever do, then heaven's sake, I stumbled onto something of such vast value — it is what the Int. Community of Christ had deciphered over 17 years, and maybe they don't know exactly how. This sort of makes me like a Van Vogt character: possessing the most utterly priceless wisdom/formula-for-immortality on the planet, which I find hard to believe; this is megalomania, for sure. But if God did it all, then why me, and why just me? Why not others, *many* others? Either way I am into what is for me an insoluble puzzle; we either have an unconvincingly incredible human (me), or we have a God whom we cannot understand; he can help but doesn't and yet he helped me — me of all people in the world! Either theory is absurd. Neither can explain it. But what happened did happen, and RM had to go back to 400 B.C. Athens to find an example of the daimon at all, let alone the sanctification and new birth which 3-74 ushered in for me.

There is one more possibility . . . perhaps for instance the records of the 17th century Reformers contain accounts, but these are dismissed, even suppressed, by a totally secular age, now. As Ursula dismissed my account. These transfigurations happen but are denied by the world.

One can go, then, to Dr. Bucke's book *Cosmic Consciousness;* as I recall he was able to find 6 instances for sure in history, entire world history, of experiences like mine; maybe 20 possibles. That includes the Reformers *and* the Greeks. That still isn't many.

However, Dr. Bucke does advance one theory which might account for this, one which would be in accord with Jesus' cryptic parables about the mustard seed, the leaven in the bread, etc.; Dr. Bucke says he thinks this is an evolutionary advance, the next step up. In the past certain precursors of the New Man appeared (e.g., Socrates, Jesus). Dr. Bucke thought the frequency would increase soon. This ties in with Bergson's élan vital, too, and with Eros as the push of life forward in evolution. This is how God works. This is how God has always worked, from the day creation began: progressively, successively, continuously. "Day" after "day." Dr. Bucke's wise theory would account for the rarity of cosmic consciousness in the past, and would untie the knot of the dichotomy expressed above. I am, ahem, like a van Vogt character after all; like a Slan. (The next step up.)

God works through evolution, not to circumvent it.* This, too, would

---

* Such lines announce a continuous meta-theme in Dick's Exegesis — what I have elsewhere called the mytheme of Mutation. This is the notion that paranormal powers and mystical experiences are expressions of the emerging buds or limbs of an evolving human supernature. Although this idea was endlessly explored in the pulp fiction of the 1940s and 1950s, found some of its most sophisticated mystical expressions in the human potential movement, and later found a wide popular audience in the counterculture with its "mutant" hippies and pop-cultural "X-Men," it is much older than all of these. Indeed, the idea's deepest roots lie in elite academic British culture, and more especially in the London Society for Psychical Research (founded 1882), with figures like the Cambridge classicist Frederic Myers, who saw psychical abilities like telepathy (a word that he coined) as "supernormal" expressions of our "extraterrene evolution." Further back still, Alfred Russel Wallace,

explain my strong intuition that what happened in 3-74 didn't consist of one desperate event and supernatural solution, but the inevitable outcome of an entire lifetime. All my life I had been moving toward this metamorphosis; the dormant possibility of it lay slumbering in me from birth; cf. my dreams of childhood, where I arrive on a raft avoiding Scotland Yard, climb to the top and then turn out to be a cuckoo egg. This would explain why now I feel that unless I went through everything I went through I couldn't have gotten there; my metasystem wouldn't have fired. It was programmed to fire after the proper sequence (of events? of learning? of experience? of trial and failure????? aha!) had passed, and all the changes, or steps or stages, necessary had taken place in me.

Makes much, much sense.

Got my right hemisphere to fire. Instinctively knew how to do it: the ortho-molecular vitamins, the manta, etc. Did like the bird in building a nest. Made myself a nest and then lay down to wait, expecting. And it came. The golden fish necklace told me it was time; I began my work, like the worm constructing its cocoon. In order to die, in its original primal lower form, to be remade into a better newer creature! To fly up from the "sea" into the sky!

I imagine these jumps forward, back to the Cambrian Period, are associated with pain and stress and a great deal of uncertainty and fear. The creature toils alone, under duress, staggers or ventures out into the unknown, to his species anyhow . . . he must exhaust all the possibilities which they still rely on for better or worse; he must try, be urged on by the life force, the élan vital, to break new ground. He suffers, maybe fails. Exhausted, oppressed, but finally the night ends — maybe — in gasping victory. The bright light floods over him from above, signal he's succeeded! The Jewish-Christian myth which says that we once had these faculties and lost them — devolved — might be true, and it certainly would explain my anamnesis, as well as the view Plato and Empedocles held. However, it is also possible that this myth was instilled in us (never mind how) in order to push us toward this as a goal in the future, whether indeed we had such faculties or not; this might be the only way such an ideal state could be expressed for those earlier cultures. "The Fall" is a sort of ancient way of talking about the next evolutionary stage in terms that make sense to people who have no concept of evolution.

What I should do, forthwith, is examine my experience and then very

---

the cofounder of evolutionary theory with Darwin, asserted that there was a second spiritual line of evolution organized and directed by a higher power working toward its own ends. In short, the mytheme of Mutation goes back a century and a half to the very origins of evolutionary biology itself. — JJK

carefully the changes it produced in me, in order to fathom what abilities/ improvements it would perhaps give us as a species, if we evolve into it as a permanent condition.

(1) Perceptual acuity. Expressed in terms of the Spirit of Truth, the change makes it possible to not be deceived; one cannot be lied to; one sees into the ontological nature of things, and the falsity of words ceases to operate on him. ("An inability to be shucked." As I predicated the new kids would be.) I can theorize that this is accomplished by a sort of re-lief map achieved by the superimposition of data processing by both hemi-spheres; data are compared and in some fashion the real or true or authen-tic is distinguished perceptually; maybe what agrees — that is, when both hemispheres agree, reach the same conclusion — then the colors I saw are experienced. It literally looks different, even in print. Like 3-D compared to flat. This is almost an advance in the use of color for a fundamental per-ceptual purpose, not present employed. If *logos* is defined as "the meaning-ful structure of reality," then this new or enhanced faculty of perception, this new ability to come to an absolutely accurate perception of what is so and what fails to be so, brings one closer to the Logos, which is why I was convinced the logos was involved; it was, that is, I saw it.

I was instantly rewarded by Nature for my achievement. Certainly each time any creature ventured a jump up the evolutionary ladder he was so rewarded; otherwise why would he ever try again? Instinct would reward him, so as to make it all worthwhile; motivation would be needed, to com-pensate for the pain and effort and fear. It is absolutely impossible to be-lieve that it could be any other way; if it were, it would fail. On a purely pleasure-pain scale, this may be the more glorious place imaginable for a living creature: to advance a tiny notch up. Thereafter he is motivated to keep trying and trying; what if he felt nothing, or even felt bad when he'd achieved it? How impossible.

My dreams in which I'm above looking down God-like at worthy ani-mals — they suggest the above — evolutionary view — may be correct. I.e., God is assisting an animal, an animal species (to grow). And my inner vi-sion of the tall savior with the staff moving among the sheep (and cows, etc.) under the pale light, the steady white light. I knew that the sheep were ourselves: humans. I now understand a mystery of evolution: a creature does not grow an eye; he is provided with an eye, but he must struggle to use it, to get it to begin to work. For him to struggle and achieve this, he must be under enormous stress to need its use; so I must have needed the new faculty or organ, needed what it could do in order to extricate myself, I got it to come on, and it did extricate me.

But if this was a true metamorphosis, then I probably did not/have not just dropped back to what I was; a change set in, perhaps permanent (the butterfly doesn't turn back into the worm). Anyhow, it worked well enough and long enough to solve the problem(s) facing it, and if it receded, it did so after the acute need had been solved by it.

. . . This is all very well, but what of the faint far-off voice, as if at the far other end of a pipe, or at the end of a long tube, at the top of the well, speaking distantly but distinctly, coaching me, informing me, in hypnagogic and hypnopompic states, in dreams, in deep night fatigue while awake, and sometimes in Attic Greek? How does this patient, informing voice fit in? Explain that, Phil.

Is someone of much higher intelligence, of another species, looking down at us from a distance above, like research scientists looking down at creatures in an artificial maze?

It still does not compute; I still don't have it. There is no reason why in leaping up the ladder of evolution one should find himself hearing his thoughts in Attic Greek, or hearing thoughts not even his own in any language. There is still this dialog with the Holy Other, and still the mystery, Why Attic Greek?

This points so to the past, to the time of Socrates. To his daimon — there, I said it; my daimon, maybe all of them, are his, specifically his, a Greek-speaking (originally) one. Attic Greece is somehow the core, the matrix, for all this — *Why?* [. . .]

I saw the meaningful structure of reality (the logos), and there was constant change in it (everything around me) because it is *alive* and possesses activity because it possesses mind. We ask, Why do we experience time (i.e., change)? And the answer is, This living reality is evolving — perfecting itself. We're within it so I guess we are a subpart of it, also alive and also changing — evolving — toward completion; it is a great entelechy. "I am the breath of my Creator, and as He inhales and exhales, I live" (PKD 1967, in Latin, under LSD).

The systole, dystole in-out breathing is what we experience perhaps as the interaction of expansion and contraction, which is also what is meant by the oscillations of palintropos harmonie. These two movements could give rise to an objectification into Form One and Two, or the X and Y forces of the ICC,[79] or Yin (contraction) and Yang (expansion or inhalation). If indeed we are within a living *breathing* (in the sense of inhaling, exhaling) creature, no wonder we have such concepts as pneumena, psyche, etc. This could even be related to the cyclic expansions and contractions of the universe; the universe, right now, is inhaling! Or, the expansion is its growth. What we experience are its constant *rhythms*. We as a species have fallen below the level (threshold) of consciousness; i.e., into "darkness"; it would like to rouse us to consciousness again, and hence has dispatched an incarnation of itself, to nag us, to arouse us to conscious awareness. We, as a portion of it, have fallen asleep somehow. All metaphors addressed to us as to our ignorance, our fallen state, our being in darkness — they all are correct. It flashes signals to us, but we aren't aware; we respond beneath the threshold of awareness, unconsciously. . . .

Re: *To Scare the Dead*. A character based on Jim Pike (with quite another name). Based on firsthand knowledge I had of his private life, e.g., with Maren in the Tenderloin, and the kind of man he was. This could be a major, if not *the* major character; but it would not be he who would have the Experience; that would be had by another, perhaps *after* this fine bishop person dies (is killed?). Thus, in addition to the whole Essene awakening in the mind theme, we have the theme of the great bishop concerned with civil rights who mysteriously dies suddenly. What occurs to me right off is that the viewpoint character (Nicholas Brady) knows the bishop in the capacity of spying on him for the authorities (due to the bishop's civil rights stands and associations). Later, after the bishop dies, Brady has the Experience, and it seems to have (or has) something to do with the late bishop. Maybe there is in it information as to foul play ("murder most foul!") about the bishop's ostensibly accidental death. Despite the fact that he is a government part time agent, the v-p character would be disturbed; this goes too far. Also, we can have it that the bishop's son "came back to him in seances," and there was some talk about maybe the bishop coming back; this is much like the ghost of Hamlet's murdered father, of course. But anyhow it turns out there is no connection with the dead bishop, although that seemed to be a possibility.

Still, this is what it seems to be: saint possession; i.e., psychic possession by a dead saint. However, it turns out that Brady has experienced that which the bishop had all his life wanted to achieve and failed to. Brady is in contact with the Holy Spirit. (Now, we have to give a reason. The only one that would work would be, the bishop was murdered; the republic is in danger. You can't murder a bishop without God getting angry and telling people; you can't keep it hushed up.) (Psalm 116: "The death of his servant is precious to the Lord God.") The final denouement is this: the bishop, messing around with the Qumran Scrolls, had planned to receive into the right hemisphere of his brain the mind of a specific Essene of 2,000 years ago; this is why the bishop was hanging around the Qumran Wadi. However, his death aborted this plan. So the ancient Essene personage came to life in someone close to the bishop instead. The value of this resurrection to the bishop and to the modern world would be that the last, secret arcane truths about Jesus would be restored (vide the ICC). I can go into the business about the Qumran men being possessed by Elijah, etc.

I think the "Hamlet's father crying murder most foul" should turn out to be another false lead, since it isn't the bishop back at all. This goes with that false occult idea, namely that it is the bishop's ghost from the "other side," telling him how he was done in. The truth turns out to be much more exciting (in my opinion), but we can get a lot of mileage out of this.

To shore up the plot: Brady inherits (why?) a lot of the Bishop's correspondence . . . oh sure, in his capacity for the government; he is poring over it doing intelligence work (even though the bishop is dead, there may be something useful about the activity of others). Brady has told the widow that he wants the notes "to type them up" or some similar pretext. (This sounds like *The Strange Case of Charles Dexter Ward,*[80] in a way. Anyhow, the explanation is more djinn and bottle-like.)

More suspense could be obtained, maybe, if Brady, by the time the Experience comes, has severed all the connections with the bishop's circle; he's now operating the recording firm, as depicted. The bishop is part of his life he's put entirely behind him.

I still want to retain the gold fish necklace which disinhibits him. But now when he sees the girl who is wearing it, actual memories from this life are stirred up . . . where has he seen such before? (It had to do with the bishop.)

[5:127] Reading all this religious literature I can see now that for everyone, God is simply the explanation of how the universe got here — i.e., how it came into being; someone had to create it, the First Cause Uncaused which "set it spinning." Viewed this way (also, God called into existence as a concept this way, simply to explain how the universe came into being) there would be no reason to suppose Him to be here. For one thing, the absolute substantiality of this world is taken for granted. But all my life I've felt it is not, that something truly real lies behind it; thus over my entire adult life I have prepared myself to encounter an immanent God emerging from within this world.

Viewed this way it is evident that without realizing it, I have always been seeking God within or behind the walls and objects, the surfaces of this world. My whole conception of the world — reality — is radically different from that of other people. This is why for as long as I've known about a Paraclete I expected him to somehow show up here, as a person — as a seemingly ordinary piece of this world, looking like other actually ordinary pieces. This is my first realization of the connection between my years of radical epistemology and my experience of 3-74 et al. I kept looking *beneath*. I sensed that the ordinary concealed the extraordinary, and that the latter perhaps was alive, had volition, was more powerful than men (although I often supposed it to be malign); I sensed it camouflaging ordinary reality — a crucial point! (Is not the Real Presence camouflaged as ordinary bread and wine during communion?) Hence, I postulated it long before (decades before) I experienced it. The assumptions of other people perhaps preclude this authentic experience. As we know in science, our preconceptions determine the outcome. "God's in his heaven; all's right with the world." So they do not strive to see (as Castaneda would put it). It is obvious, too, that for me the entire world and every thing in it has the potentiality for being transubstantiated, had I ever thought of it. Also, I long ago conceived of each person living in his own world or idios kosmos, so I can conceive without difficulty of the Kingdom of God having come for some genuinely, but still being invisible — not yet manifested to them — to others.

I therefore need never ask, Why did God go away? Or, When will He return? When will the Kingdom come? I have no reason to believe He ever went away. But we did fall away from perception of (communication with) Him, the great dialog, which must be based, for obvious reasons, on a perceptual and cognitive awareness that He is actually present.

So what I've done (supra) is change the question from, How come I could experience God? to the question, How come other people can't? Which new version assumes my experience to be *natural* (however rare). What blocks or prevents others perhaps in their Worldview or presuppositions? Answer: plenty. As Joseph Campbell says about the Occident: "Only the dead see God." Lem may have noted and meant this when he spoke of me "finding in the gutter among the degenerate molecules a sacerdotal power buried for aeons." (Finding, I mean, in the trash of the gutter.) I trained my telescope (when the chance came, via the Holy Spirit) down at the gutter instead of to the stars — with outstanding results. Still, an extraordinarily important change from the status quo is indicated by the message, "Saint Sophia is going to be born again." God may be here, may never have left, but His wisdom, I would guess from this, will mount and prevail in the future. The schism between us and him — the fall — will be ironed out. Perhaps the awareness, the experience, the dialog which I've had will become common to men. (Will my books have helped?) (*Ubik*, I guess, especially.) Back to Parmenides and the All behind the many (in St. Thomas, Jesus says, "I am the All"[81]). The Logos, spinner of tomorrow, is most active in biological evolution, creating new organs of perception. [...]

I believe something really evil was loose in the world, and we stood up to it here and there and defeated it. I have no idea who or what it was, no clear conception of it or what it wanted. Or why me. Perhaps what I did was shake off a lifetime of contamination and conditioning and preprogramming to this world. That in effect I confuted or renounced it and my allegiance to the forces in it and hence to it. What isn't clear is whether I shook off something primarily in the past which had held me, or else something building ahead, to come. It is, as the Protestant reformers knew, primarily a fight against the great tyrannical system or systems of the past, for the purpose of freeing men's minds, for the future of life. [. . .] Perhaps the reappearance of this spirit, working for the freedom to know and to think, signals the beginning of another major historical age like that of the Reformation; perhaps it comes forth when there is a historical necessity. So we may be seeing the beginning of the breaking down of the bullshit establishments here and in the USSR — like I said in my Vancouver speech and especially as I saw or discerned in 3-74, the arising of a new ability to tell when you are being snowed; and since big governments etc. reign by bullshit, perhaps this is a grand new era for mankind, of which I was/am a part. Endowed with the sudden, new capacity to see through lies — so equipped by the Spirit himself. And at the same time placing an extraordinary value on truth in oneself; never to lie and never to let anyone lie to you; a new value system with this first. If the Protestant could be said to be a new historical type emerging from an older authoritarian one, then perhaps an equally important new one is emerging now — not just inner directed (Protestants were that) but — what I was in 3- and 4-74; there is no name, yet. Not inner-, not outer-, but truly new. My subjective experiences and feelings, in abruptly lifting up to this new type, must be parallel to those of the first Protestants, in form and quality, as their new concepts, that of inner truth rather than handed-down-from-the-top truth flooded over them and they became a new kind of men. [. . .]

My experience certainly indicates that the basic Protestant idea that God speaks directly to man through the Holy Spirit is correct (in contrast to the handed-down-by-the-priest idea), and in particular the Friends would seem to be correct, as regards their concept of the Inward Light and the Seed. The evolution of religion from God Above to God With Us to God Within Us is obvious, but what I see too is the social-historical meaning, inasmuch as it certainly is going to basically affect future societies, this internalization of God (as we withdraw our projections, perhaps). Every man will carry a bit of God inside him, like a walkie-talkie (and much much more). He will be conscious of this, both in himself and by empathy and analogy in others. Surely, if all goes well, less will be handed down to the people progressively more and more; and the people will take their destinies in their own hands. (But that is only if unobstructed; yet, that should be their fight: if God is within each man, then the enemy of man is any top-heavy system claiming a monopoly on truth and dispensing it downward.) Why eventually will laws be necessary at all? I foresee a godly anarchy. No authority here on earth will have to tell any man what to do, or even educate him; the Logos will do that — link him up. A truly egalitarian society should result. [. . .]

Without proof of this Inward Light there could be no rational justification for anarchy. With proof (as I have) there is no rational excuse to maintain any sort of centralization of power; no state of any sort, as we conceive it. We will be linked anyhow. We cannot not be. The social implications are beyond calculation, for good. Is this perhaps the Kingdom of God prophesized? Behind the scenes, invisible to us, we have continued to move closer to it constantly, throughout 2,000 years at least which seemed sterile of forward growth; but — we did not know (a) in what way it would come; (b) what it would be like! How could we calculate momentum toward it knowing as little as we did about it? Perhaps we are very close now.

Perhaps a sign of its proximity will be a growing difficulty by the authorities throughout the world in governing. And a positive decentralization of power and authority. The causes may be dreadful, intrinsically (breakdowns, etc.); but, unrecognized, they would lead to excellent results, someday. This would have enormous importance for characterization in *To Scare the Dead*. If I had to account "rationally" for the Inward Voice (Holy Spirit) I could offer Dr. Bucke's duplex mind which appears with cosmic consciousness, and link it to the Ornstein two-brain material: the appositional mind. Outside of this, with the addition of the Bergson notion of the brain as transformer (and maybe including the pineal) I would be defenseless in rational argument. But all these are within reason, plus Jung's collective repository. My right hemisphere emerges when my left has painted itself into a desperate corner and its rat-like linear thinking has bogged down, leaving a vacuum.

Every time in my life that I've heard the spirit it's been when my normal (linear) thinking had exasperated and exhausted itself — reached its end without results, but each time, results were still absolutely necessary. This alone makes a circumstantial case for locating the spirit, the Inward Light, in the right hemisphere (I suppose). Normal habitual cognitive processes must be tried fully and fail. This would be why under routine and ordinary conditions I don't hear it and am cut off from it. But this only tells me where it can be localized in terms of brain morphology. As an appositional other brain, not my own, it still — well, how does it come to think in Attic

Greek, and make use of technical terms such as syntonic? My original diagram showed a piece of the macrocosmos within the microcosmos, but that was more a metaphor and poetry. Also, if my right hemisphere can do this, why does it do it only when I am under duress? Why isn't there bilateral parity? [. . .] How possibly could a lesser, minor, inferior portion (half) of the total mind be habitually turned outward to the world, and a wiser, older part, devoted to truth, in possession of immeasurable knowledge, holy and calm — how could that part remain suppressed virtually forever? Just from a functional standpoint it's hard to understand, unless its time is coming, as Dr. Bucke thought. This, in addition to, How did it form? How did it form and why isn't it used? It doesn't seem to be a social product, or limited to this time and this space. I wonder if it is a self-system, an ego, at all. It is not another self, even a better one; it is absolute in all that it knows, does and especially in all that it is (its ontology is perfected). I don't really see it in process, in becoming, any more than I see it making mistakes and learning thereby. It has no infancy and no senility. [. . .]

This particular "myth," that of the death of Christ, is the only one we have, the only one which survived of all the mystery religions and other cults and religions of the antique world. We're allowed to celebrate that, but that is it. Still, it's all there. Dionysos, Zagreus, Osiris, Adonis. ("JC" is in this case Joseph Campbell, not Jesus Christ supra.) At a certain point Christ is actually present, in the wafer and wine and also He becomes the priest, and we are once more there again; we have found our way back, a concept contained in the religion itself; viz: the dead god who returns to life. The cyclic repetition which takes place in the mass governs also the concept of why the mass is spoken and what it is about. Our god died, and was buried (gone), but then He returned. So saying, the priest therewith becomes Christ, proving the authenticity, the rightness, of the whole religion and the whole service. . . . It is as if each time the mass (or Last Supper, "in remembrance of Me") was secretly celebrated by the early Christians, they got to unfold their miracle, about Jesus, for their own eyes alone, invisible to the (Roman-secular) world. "Thou didst not see what I saw, Robin," as Oberon puts it.[82] I can imagine the impact in the early days of the "Fish" Christians when they gathered in stealth to perform the feast of agape. New people who had never actually known Jesus could be brought in one by one, and this shown to them. Suddenly He would be there, only not as a mortal but in His transformed state (as I experienced Him). He would be all through them, the celebrants. "Time would be abrogated," as Campbell says. This abrogation of time might not be so startling at first, during the actual Roman era; but later on, as in my situation . . . suddenly "back" in Rome "again." We are always back there, just as before;

nothing has changed. And the Return of the King is always eagerly anticipated as imminent; there is much excitement and fear and activity. [. . .]

The strangest idea, though, of all that comes to me is to envision a group
of followers who have the authentic holy-possession experience which I
had . . . and then retrospectively they cast back to try to figure out who
it was — exactly the way I did; I decided it was Jim Pike because he was a
holy man who I had known who recently died; the early Christians would
assume, by the same logic, that it was Jesus. In each case the individuals
would trace it back to the first reasonably likely person, real or mythical. In
my thinking here I'm reversing what is the customary causal flow writers
assume, theirs being that the postmortem experience is manufactured to
fulfill the wishes of the followers; i.e., the connective chain works in temporal sequence. My question now, when you consider before Christianity were the other Greek mystery religions and before that Tammuz and
Adonis and especially Osiris in Egypt — can we be sure these different religious groups are experiencing different entities — or rather isn't it just the
names which differ? And if it is all one entity which holy-possesses all of
them, under a variety of names (call it Jim Pike, Jesus or Osiris), then what
in actuality is this holy spirit who has distinct human but transfigured personality? (In my case, if not Jim Pike then who?) Maybe a demiurge or mediating spirit which has no copula possibility; i.e., no intrinsic name, such
as we have? Maybe — after 14 months all I really know is that I don't know
anything except that it happened to me, and what I saw during that short
time was real. That's not much to come down from the mountain with, for
the edification of my people. Maybe there just is no common language between our space-time universe and the Eternal World, or common concepts; or ours just don't really apply. [. . .] I can see where it is an enormous
task, really beyond our ability, when we (I mean religious leaders, those actually into forming religions and subsects) struggle with such a titanic fiery
wind from another universe, a far vaster reality in all respects . . . trying to
codify it, put it into linguistic categories, trying to figure it out, cope with
the enormous paradoxes which effortlessly transcend and defy human reason — priests from the time of the Cro-Magnon through Sumer, Egypt, the
Greek mystery religions, on down to Calvin and Luther and Tillich — we're
all getting massive headaches and sitting up all night trying and trying to
explain to ourselves and to write it down coherently . . . the secular world
supposes that religion is a fake and a snare and we've got nothing to offer
but a lot of flak talk, but in fact the reality behind the words is so far removed from what we can comprehend that our problem is really trying
to reduce it and make our kind of sense out of it, and always failing, failing, and never giving up, knowing what it means but never being able to

get it right, never, never, always seeing something new or previously unseen, always understanding it better, giving up and then starting over, getting closer and closer; wondering if we were meant to try this. But it's a
way of remembering what happened. Of recalling it. The prolonged, arduous work shows that something happened. As they say in modern semantics and philosophy: the word "banana" points to something which we call
a banana but isn't, because "banana" is the word, not the thing pointed to.
In this case the disparity between words and the thing pointed to are probably the greatest possible. In 14 months I've found that my experience fits
every description of personal mystic religious experience and none, every
specific religion and none: each system or explanation works as well as any
other, but none really is congruent; there is always a part left over, and in
the night that small unexplained part or fact grows like the mustard seed
or the leaven until it is the whole loaf or landscape by morning. It's as if the
experience itself were alive.

If I were going to pick one tantalizing aspect I can't account for, and
would give an arm and a leg to do so, it is that when my experience began
I had the acute impression, absolutely real and unshakable, that I had been
seeing the universe backward all my life, or somehow inside-out, which
is also the same as backward — reversed, going in the "wrong way," which
means that I had suddenly begun to see it not just going in the opposite direction, but correctly, at last. It wasn't just time alone going in reverse; it
was like instead of being inside a sphere-like universe, I was now outside
on the skin. Inside was outside, the future was controlling the past, the
smallest least valuable objects assumed tremendous importance, there was
solemn and vital information in near-silence. And then I read in the Gospel of Thomas where Christ says something like, "The Kingdom will come
when the outer is the inner, the bigger the smaller, the man the woman,"
etc., except he says, "the image the image," as if that is the one constant.[83]
Maybe it's a Jungian psychological reversal of all functions and aspects of
the psyche, the not-I becoming the I, etc. But — "random" juxtapositions
of writing produced meaningful — God-sent, in fact — information. "The
stone rejected by the builder,"[84] maybe, whatever that means. The meaningless became meaningful, especially in arrangement; and the ultimate,
found in much mystical writing: the void and God were found together, as
if God, when at last experienced, turned out to be nothing, which is like
what Erigina used to say: Literally, God is not. Maybe we have our entire
set-ground system wrong[85]; every feature we extract through isolated scrutiny (as important) is really background, and vice versa.

But you can't overcome this by switching your focus to what you'd considered background before; it is in the self-creating (deciding on) of set

that the error lies. We select (or are trained to select) set. Maybe this is primarily a basic shift in the visual system whereby the whole set-ground discrimination ends and a new or different kind of sight obtains. No attempt is made at any level in the eye-brain mechanism to extract features; ground and set are allowed to blend, and then reality *itself*, without our making a preconceived programmed trained habitual effort, is allowed to swim around until certain facets or linking regularities in it intrinsically, not projected by us or sought for, not discriminated by our brains but actually there, register as ultra-real. These might be regarded as patterns, I guess. Some thread of recognition might call them to our attention, some forgotten memory; we recognize a friend. Like a creature with compound eyes, maybe we trace movement as such. Or utilize parallaxes and extract only that which has true depth; or rely on color formations. The last, color, could act to inscribe far-ranging patterns around us hitherto unsuspected, being partly in what was set and partly in what was ground.

How about a 3-dimensional moving color forming messages of construction and comfort?

From a total relaxation (a giving up) of the automatization of perception, the "model of the universe" each of us builds — through weariness or despair or fear; it breaks down to reveal the koinos kosmos beneath, which to our surprise is like the Magic Garden. My contribution to Deikman's study of this is, We like to be able to recognize everything. To know (label) what it is. Our early textbooks teach us to do this (horse, cow, cat, mother). Once we have identified everything, then reality has passed away and we're in a world of the familiar, stuck there because we wanted it that way (it's frightening not to know where you are and what things are around you, when you're little). It's a form of scientific-magic; it depotentiates the menacing and the hostile by abolishing the unknown. The word (category, a sort of ersatz logos) replaces reality, as in *Time Out of Joint*; it's perceptual stereotyping. Lazy vision. The trouble is, sitting here for instance, I do know what each object is. I know its name. I know its purpose, what it does, etc. I can't unknow that this is a typewriter, this here my light, this over here the air conditioner. How am I going to get back — regress — to the Magic Kingdom ("Be as little children"[86]). Well, switch from my left to right hemisphere, maybe. There are close-scrutiny techniques, of the visual mantra type (stare at one object for weeks). This at most, though, might provide methods or techniques for seeing what is there, beyond the semi-verbal model; there is still, upon having seen, the problem of conveying and comprehending it. I think we as a species really have "fallen," in that we are very cut off, from ma'at, from justice and order (and the voice of conscience telling us what is justice, what promotes order, what is truth); as Heraclitus said, we are stumbling around asleep, unable to see the logos (that which ma'at through Ptath has built).

Parmenides' notion of the All and how it must be, contrasted to what we experience: he described it as radially symmetric, which I understand as being the same everywhere. If this is so, then theoretically one could comprehend the structure of the whole upon any authentic encounter with it (perception of it), no matter how small the segment, sector, in time and space. This recalls to me my "three lives" dream in which I was first in an alternate world where I was famous and flew everywhere, and then very poor in a Mexican or Italian town, and in the dream the fan-shape triune sections were extended to show that no matter where or how you took a core sample or segment or fragment, from it the extremes on each side could advance out fan-blade like, with a Tao always created in the center. Each partial life was generated into a state of triune completeness (too little; just right [balanced]; too much). I sensed/watched the slimmest sample expand into what, in terms of universal constants, was an entire world; I don't think you could cut it too small to exclude that spontaneous process of total regeneration of World. That means that the All is immediately palpable ("break a stick and there am I; and I am the All"[87]), if viewed at all; I mean, if it is seen it is *not seen partially, in an impaired way* (as we always see reality). This is the opposite of the blind men with the elephant situation. Now, the implications of this if as I believe God is an immanent God are enormous — in fact, this might account for what I experienced, because given immanence, then when you encounter Him in the alley you have encountered him completely, just as much so as if you met Him in heaven, in the caelum. It is not like a portion of god (analogous to a hand or arm of one of us). Like Kozyrev's theory of time, the whole "thing" is projected from a single point. At any point where He is, He is totally and to the extent that He can be known He can be totally known. One does not experience a portion of God. This makes clear how His immanence works. How He can be everywhere but not necessarily everything.

I wonder what's in my other dreams of equal value in exegesis.

Anyhow, regarding this projection-from-every-point-of-the-complete All, then any glimpse of it (as I say) would be an encounter with its totality, and would by definition not be partial and therefore probably more than could be comprehended. No matter how gently filtered or muted, or revealed in progressive degrees of emergent clarity, by the time the encounter was over, the mortal creature would be amazed. Later, he would find himself trying to depict an infinitude in ordinary words; which is to say, he would find that which he experienced to be inexhaustible. Probably he would keep trying, and wonder why. (I.e., why even if it lasted only

a little while he can't completely describe it or explain it.) He would forever be trying to fully explicate (or explain at all) what he saw along the
gutter here and there which shone, saw in a time-period of 3 minutes one
day and is greater than the universe. Put another way, it seems reasonable
that if after 14 months of unending exegesis, reading, studying, pondering, etc., one has still failed to even begin to account for what one saw in
those 3 minutes — when in fact more remains to explain and understand
than ever — then there is reason to believe the vision authentic. The fact
that one *can't* say (explain or account for) may reveal more than if one
could. That it would be the complete deity, even when scaled down to a
micropoint, would explain the striking account of Elijah finally encountering God in the "still small voice"[88] and not in larger more spectacular
forms. Also, the ancient Hebrew priests declaring that the voice of God is
like the cooing of doves. By the same token therefore I might be correct
in supposing that the faint, distant, mild, composed voice I have heard is
that of God Himself and not that of a demiurge, it not being necessary
for Him to employ such just to scale Himself down. Some of the foolishness of doctrines diminishing the Trinity can be exposed by understanding this; obviously each Person or Member can be equal to God, although
in a very real sense less (Christ was equal to God but God was greater
than He; ordinary language doesn't apply here). What is meaningful is to
understand that all of God is reconstructible from a single "bit" or expression or manifestation. I would think that in this fashion the omniscience
of God is explained; how under these circumstances could there be signal
loss or contamination?

[5:157] I just discovered that for 15 months I've labored in error as to who
wrote "Acts." I had the idea it was Paul, undoubtedly because it deals with
Paul. However, it was written by Luke, who also may have written "Romans." I am sitting here slowly perceiving the importance of this. First
off, the stunning manifestation of theological material in *Tears* is virtually
all (all except for the dream) from "Acts." But the main point is that Luke
was "the beloved physician," as Paul calls him, and a highly literate Greek
writer. Also, in one recent dream, my attention was called to a large section of the Bible which when I looked up the page numbers was Luke's
Gospel from the Sermon on the Mount of Christ at the Mount of Transfiguration. Also, my vision of the man as saint or angel informing me was
of a Greek: he wore a toga and greaves. He carried a huge clasped book,
which he held with both arms, affectionately. This wasn't Paul. A Greek
physician and evangelist; one of the gospelists. The EB says that Luke was
a darn good theologian and that he was into Christian prophecy. He was

no mere chronicler of events. I've been looking over "Acts." It certainly is fluent. And he was a close friend of Paul; this fits my early dream in which my friend "Paul" is holding up a book of prophecy, now obviously sections of the Bible (specifically the New Testament).

If only I'd said plaintively to Father Rasch: "This man is a literate Greek, he's a physician and has something to do with 'Acts.'" On the spot, it'd have been put together then and there. You cannot get any more precise than that. A class with one member: St. Luke.

Luke lived a lot in Syria. A palm tree country, like what I saw in 2-75. His beloved homeland. His concept of springtime.

I'm certain that no other early great Christian (saint) was a physician; this distinguishes St. Luke. Now, to return to contemplation of the personality which took me over in 3-74. (The one who detested the aerosol sprays, etc.) That was St. Luke.

> *Although I did not know who you were*
> *I thank you. "He found in heaven*
> *A friend," as Gray says.*[89]
> *This was a meeting which I can't convey*
> *To anyone, this helping hand.*
> *Was it because I worried about Lorraine?*
> *Or lit the candles?*
> *Why you came I can understand a little;*
> *Why you left is another matter.*
> *The days are empty now: no friend speaks.*
> *The candles all are cold and dead*
> *And about the rest — her — I know nothing.*
> *Days pass . . . will you return?*

I don't know how to write a poem to Saint Luke, but there it is, the best I can do. [. . .]

For *To Scare the Dead:* let it turn out to be St. Luke who shamanistically possessed him (a bridge thus established between 70 A.D. and our present), and the protag eventually discovers, through this assimilated inner contact that St. Luke (and probably also the others of the original cadre of Christians, the inner circle of Christ's) is what we call (are you ready?) a non-terrestrial, of magnificent power and authority and wisdom. I think plotwise the protag eventually learns/decides that originally such men as St. Luke were ordinary humans, "born of woman," etc., but became this — through such possession of them by the Holy Spirit, which is to say their Master, Christ (who was not an ordinary human being). And the *purpose* of this elevation comes through *now*, since our planet has had it (ecology wise, due to our using up and destroying and polluting); this is a system to get some of us, as many as possible "translated" out of here and hence saved; this is the true meaning of "being saved," saved from the holocaust. This too is the meaning of the now-arriving Parousia.

I might add that what gives the non-terrestriality of Luke away to the protag are, e.g., the dreams in which the protag experiences himself—and man in general—as an animal among other animals, a sort of anthropological-biologist-naturalist viewpoint derived from Luke-within-him. He obtains Luke's standpoint, and it is *off earth*. The other-end-of-the-telescope view. What St. Luke has, as "vibes," is a humorous attitude, a smiling, almost rollicking quality—except that he has ferocious dedication and drive to the cause of truth and righteousness. Humor and zeal. And because of being a physician he has a tender healing quality.

It's an invasion from the past, contrived in the future (the time-loop structure), from off earth, inside his (and other people's) head. It, the invader, just pops on inside him one day, and from then on it occupies the right hemisphere of his mind, which was just waiting on standby for this. (Personality of it a little like Lord Running Clam.[90])

Plot breakdown:

Ch. before taken over (possession). Then take over.
Mystery as to who took him over, to solution. (Lots of research.)
Social meaning: who else has been taken over? Work in concert.
Opposition (who? The establishment?)
Ch. must decide where he stands: the "hallucinations" or estab.
Ch. decides for the Messiah, whom he encounters externally: another person taken over.
Final section: reprise of 1st century A.D., Christians vs. Rome, but with different outcome foreordained.
End: the pale white light (where no shadows are) comes on; it is the Parousia. Ships huge ones begin to land.

(Ch. debates all the issues I debated; e.g., Is it a spirit of a dead person? Is it a non-terrestrial? The Holy Spirit? Reincarnation? Major denouement is when he realizes that it is both—a non-t and the Holy Spirit, and I guess in a sense the spirit of a dead human—rather than either-or. This exhaustion of categories of thought should be a major achievement in this novel. [Rephrased: the quality of answers depends on the questions put.])

I have now finally read Arthur C. Clarke's *Childhood's End*. What I wanted to do was find out if any details resembled details of my 3-74 et al.

experience. Generally, no. All I can say is that his story is compatible with my experience; I mean, if my experience were so, his book could grow out of it; or, if his book were true, my experience could grow out of it. It is almost a make, but not quite. Still, it is closer than any other system — if you view it as a system, and I think it is: a philosophy disguised as a novel . . . not really disguised, but more stated. One detail is right on: the idea he expresses, rather cryptically, about time, that it is more complex than we realize, and then he springs on us the idea of memories about the future (reverse time). In this one respect a detail fits into exact, precise and major place. It isn't conclusive. But — in a fuzzy way, my structure and his are identical, if you just blur or joggle them a little. They will harmonize.

Of most value would be to take his novel and to approach my experience strictly in the kind of S-F terms he uses (where religious symbolism and experience are subsumed by modern S-F "non-terrestrial" explanations, rather than vice-versa). If I did this, I would say:

(1) We are not only being watched; we are being controlled, but don't know it; they remain beyond our threshold of vision.
(2) They work for a higher purpose, one we can't understand but which fits our concepts of spiritual, moral purposes.
(3) We are instruments, therefore, of an invisible spiritual force which causes us to grow and develop in certain arranged directions.
(4) Some of us are either part of their race or can be elevated to their level, as they work through these individuals.
(5) The probable reason for their concealment is our evil qualities. We cannot be trusted, individually or collectively (man qua beast).
(6) A critical moment has approached or is approaching; this is a unique period in their work, therefore in our use-purpose.
(7) The extent of camouflage and delusion induced in us is extraordinary in amount and degree.

I'm not sure these S-F concepts mean much. In terms of S-F yield, this is about it as far as what my 3-74 experience gives. This is why I reject an S-F type of explanation; a theological one yields so much more. The above simply do not explain. They are paltry, and no more than the convention of the moment. What is needed is a harmonization of theology and S-F without a reduction of the former to the latter, as Clarke does. It looks (what he does) like an improvement, but it is not. The devil "really" is a non-terrestrial race. You see? And yet, what is extraordinarily significant is that the two modes of interpretation which I hover most between are S-F and theology, which surely tells us something about S-F we otherwise might not know. The two must be related in some important way.

"I've recovered some buried memories, of about two thousand years ago."

"From a previous life?"

"No, strangely, from this one." (Dialog for *Scare*.)

[5:168] The Moth, which in descending can be viewed as progressively illuminating every sector of the landscape (past present and future) simultaneously. Its light is white like moonbeams. It is always getting closer but it has never arrived, which is to say, touched down at one point only (i.e., at one instant).

From fatigue I've failed to put down a lot. But the descending Moth exhibits in model form how an entity or universe outside time enters one confined by linear time. It is throughout matter — i.e., throughout in the lesser, linear universe, as if the whole landscape is light-spattered. It took me over 12 hours to realize that the descending Moth, like a hollow Japanese paper lantern, was actually a ship landing, a huge one. This was the ultimate vision for me, this great light-giving ship identified in the dream only as the "Moth," which I guess is its individual name. Thus I am enabled to conceive what up to this point I couldn't conceive, the way the "Kingdom" enters our world, the relationship it has to our world constantly, etc. (Those two are the same: how it enters and its constant relationship.) (It is a constant entering, as the EB macro says, but I couldn't conceive this. Now I can.) The maximum linear-time entry point has already been fixed, and entry has begun ("the loading had begun"). We are experiencing or feeling or encountering its effects! As if in the periphery of light-spatter on the time landscape. The outskirts of it, but still, particles of light (illumination) are falling *now*. [. . .]

The light was not like sunlight. It was that which I saw light up the bedroom that Sunday night before Pinky died; it was the raising, I think, that night of the veil of limitation (on me). This was frightening to me, because I rightly associated it with approaching death. I guess this means that when/as we die, we begin to see what formerly was concealed to us, or from us, and the shock is great, since we have, all our lives, been trading (doing business) with evil. The first things seen are negative, and what is worse, we've been part of this negative reality, which, as Tagomi realized, is an actual evil, not merely a view-point evil. It is basically self-awareness: self as part of this and now disclosed (to a higher eye). It is the ultimate fulfillment of paranoiac vision . . . my evil inside is seen! This is universally experienced as the Day of Wrath, and rightly so. "Oh dreadful day!" "Oh wretched me, to be here on this day!" Etc. There was nothing inappropriate in my reaction.

But what is even more amazing was the following morning when I was unnaturally up and about at 7:00 A.M., and felt *the* spirit (of 3-74) back in me again. This time I asked its name. It said it represented what it called "The Nameless God," that it itself was the Virgin, but not the Christian Virgin, rather the Roman one, which is Astraea. (I looked it up in Virgil.) This time, for the first time, she, Astraea, answered my questions as I put them; I was not passive but active. I asked what they would do as judgment, since Astraea, the Virgin or Virgo, is the Immortal of Justice. She told me candidly that they would condemn, by fire, those who have despoiled the Earth, and she cited such matters as the defoliation in Viet Nam. I was overjoyed to know that the destroyers of Earth would themselves suffer fire as judgment, so I tend to be skeptical about this whole experience, viewing it as wish-fulfillment rather than truly receptive; nonetheless that day my blood pressure, when taken, was normal for the first time, fantastic proof of the subjective concept at 7 that morning that now everything was okay. The arrival of Virgo that day was certainly to coincide with the blood pressure taking, to help me in what had become a terrifying vital matter. I have throughout the year wondered how in any real sense I could claim or imagine myself as healed when my blood pressure was in fact even more elevated. The spirit returned as a calming spirit, a tranquil spirit of ma'at like balance and harmony. Out of that day's combined experiences I felt the most intense relief and joy, which is easy to fathom. Now as I write this I feel it revive in me, a true uprising of joy. I attribute both my physical repair and the psychological state of ease (which the nurse noticed) I experienced as coming directly from heavenly intervention; no shit. Truly I had faltered, being afraid to go to get the b.p. reading any more. But that day I was changed, and by that adventitious entity which had entered me in 3-74. And then the next day I found the Stone Pony LP I longed for so badly . . . there it was again, reissued after 4 or 5 years. (Maybe my letter to Capitol helped me do it!)

Since then (this is a diary now) I've dreamed some pre-cog dreams (big breasted Tzarina, broken phono with Tessa trying to fix it, a vast attempt by the Russian nobility to set up shop in another continent, obviously a paradigm for the CP), and then last night very strange dreams in which I read a book, again large and serious, about economics — the economics of the German Social Democrat movement, starting post WW1. [. . .]

Idea for *To Scare the Dead*. Dreams, but not about the past as are the dreams in *Peter Proud*[91]; rather, they are like the dreams about the approaching Spaniards by the Aztecs — visions of the future. Like the Moth dream, which is a dream about the arrival of a ship, and S-F in style. (This was used in *Clans* somewhat, when Ledebur had visions about the ship

arriving.) Pre-cog dreams. The cities he dreams himself in are futuristic—from the next century! Also—my MBS[92] script, later made into a
minor short story, where the guy has a phobia from an event in the future—why can't I expand on this story idea, here? Make a novel use of it?
Man who remembers the future rather than the past—the psychiatrist setting, even. Autobiographical . . . even unto my experience which caused
me to summon Mr. Kelly: experiencing disinhibiting stimuli before they
arrived (in normal sequence and interval). Beforehand, as mere word and/
or light signals to us. Now, having read the EB macro article on time, I
know that what I saw were events up the manifold ahead before they had
entered linear time; before they had "popped into existence ahead of us." I
saw them in less than time reality but still in sequence, like the next film
reel still in the can, *not yet projected.* Only as the future enters the present
does it get projected into (obviously) this space-time continuum which we
experience. Thus of course I saw it "reduced" to mere words and light signals; it hadn't entered either time or space, only had sequence. Didn't look
real (substantial). The Minkowski block universe[93] . . . I verified it without
knowing in the slightest what I was experiencing. It's exactly like that time
when I was a little kid on the ranch and saw inside the dead hen, saw the
eggs, very small and flat, which she was going to lay each day, later on . . .
and maybe this boyhood scene could start *To Scare the Dead.*

[5:182] We seem to be confined within a metal prison, but something vital
has secretly penetrated the enclosing ring around us and fires assistance
and advice to us in the form of video and audio signals. Neither the prison
ring is visible to us nor the signal system which fires nor the entity which
has penetrated through us. The signals emerge as if from cores drilled
through the metal; they're in color. Thus, our prison was breached a long
time ago. Help is here, but we still remain here within the prison; we aren't
yet free. I take it that the camouflaged invisibility of the signals is to keep
the creator of the prison from knowing that help is here for us. The drilled
out "tubes" through the prison wall to us can't be discerned; they blend
perfectly, as if alive (the signals too seem alive). It is like the penetrating
roots of a plant (!!!) which over the centuries have grown through rock or
concrete. These root tips come through and into here, the enclosed open
space where we're kept, and then they burst into colored changing light
patterns which register on us subliminally.

The core tubes are at right angles to the prison walls. They are possibly
very long—light years long. The first great well-kept secret is that we are
slaves, in prison. The second, that help has quietly breached through the
walls to inform us. To teach us how to lift the siege—what to do and when.

Really, all it can do is inform teach and educate us; it has no power. The prison builders have all the power. In the James-James dream, the scouts coming in through all the many doors: penetrating the wall, so to speak, of the building which we were all in, thousands of us. And I told them we needed medical assistance. Perhaps their help is passing or will pass from information only to their actual presence here (as referred to by the St. Sophia news). In the dream they were decidedly motorized (modern technology?). They came at a point when I felt desperate over our medical situation. Maybe that actual time has now arrived (in my life, anyhow). [. . .]

My 3-74 experience: I was inside the Immanent Mind. As in a womb? Not mere analogy, perhaps. Made to grow. Both within the parent organism and also isomorphic with it, but much smaller and less developed. We are in God; moving toward comprehension, which requires further growth/development. We are like the nymph or larva stage of mosquitoes. Hence my dreams about the Pond. Again — Wachet auf.[94] [. . .]

March 1974: I reached reunion with the Father. Today 5-31-75 I had a dream in which I was a child again back in the '30s; at an old-fashioned table I sat with other people, and a man gave me a bowl of cereal. I saw that He was the Savior, and I began to cry with ecstatic joy. When I woke up I took a couple hours and managed to reconstruct the meaning of this dream. When I was very small, Christ fed me His Real Presence in the typical host-form: cereal (i.e., bread). I took him into me back then, and, as in the parables of the mustard seed and the leavening, He grew within me. Later on, in adult life, I felt a growing need to nourish other people, especially to feed them (in '74 we sent $400 for famine relief, for example). That which was given to me grew in me and began to yield fruit, or expression in my giving nourishment; I became by degrees the Man who fed me as a child. Viewed this way, my 3-74 experience is not something dropped on me from outside, due to the "painted in the corner" need-situation I was in, but in fact the pay-off of a lifetime process of growth. It was the culmination of something alive and advancing inside me; in 3-74 I made it or reached it, reunion with the Father, which is to say, Christ as Mediator restored me to the Father (I didn't *achieve* it but was brought to it). Thus both Christ and the Father were present: Christ within me, leading me to the Father. This explains the long-term intimations I have had about being moved along toward a pay-off destiny (e.g., the dream in Canada wherein Kathy and everyone else take off their masks, finally, and Kathy says, "Now it all can be explained to you, what it was all about"). I was moving by degrees, step by step, toward the encounter with the dark-haired girl at the door with the gold fish-sign necklace. I assume that when I acted as the Savior and gave an analogous bowl of cereal to someone that I set a similar process in motion in him or her, too; thus, Christ delivers us, spreading Himself out through us by means of this "unauthorized" communion with His Real Body. Christ's role as mediator is now clear to me. A man, such as I, could never on his own find his way back to union with God. Therefore God Himself initiates the reunion, and it is God as Christ who acts to lead a man, myself in this case, along the difficult, long, narrow, confusing path to final redemption; to the right conclusion, which I experienced. A man's tragic difficulty does not begin as a situation at any given moment in his life; he is born into it: separation from God. Thus Christ begins to lead a man back from the start; intervention began in my life long ago — in fact as many of my dreams showed, in early childhood the groundwork was laid down; He was already active. 3-74 was not the difficulty but the pay-off. The last step before resurrection (finding immortality) was the death in the tomb, which I had experienced during those many sleepless nights. This is what Teilhard de Chardin said; each man as Christ; the entire species working its way along the stations of the cross, which is also what Claudia Hambro says in *Confessions* when she says she can feel the crown of thorns. "Christ didn't die for us; he was an example which each of us must follow, and suffer as he did to attain what he attained," as she puts it to Jack Isidore (paraphrase). No man can die — atone — for your sins. You must atone yourself, following him as model; he is the guide, the mediator, not a sacrifice. Christ was not — repeat not — a sacrifice, but the first immortal man, showing us the path to immortality. How He did it, His steps, is how we must do it individually and collectively. "Now you grieve but later you will rejoice," He told them.[95] What I experienced is precisely the Long Dark Night of the Soul as depicted.[96] As I look back, there really is no natural explanation of my prolonged, intense fear; I'd been in worse spots before and not felt that. Now I am sure, looking back, that a supernatural or religious element was at work in me, moving toward fruition. Again, psalm 116. I could feel the coffin around me in the night, and then the darkness of the night was broken through to me from a long way off, the expression of a Vast Mind thinking intentionally toward me, with me in mind. My fear went away, and, 14 months later, has never returned.

Jung re Meister Eckhart: God is born in the human soul — come forth from it, and the Kingdom of God is the human soul (totality of the unconscious).[97] It all happens inside, Eckhart said in 1245 (circa). Libido is withdrawn (projections withdrawn) from outside objects; God ceases to be found in objects, but rather in the unconscious. This withdrawing of all projections is precisely and exactly what happened with me in 3-74. A total reversal. I am on sure ground vis-à-vis Jung, here. God as autonomous entity of the unconscious, i.e., the soul or born out of the soul. Not capable of being assimilated into the conscious mind. The Divine Birth — in the soul of a given man! (I understand Eckhart to say that therefore God is dependent on me; that I give birth to him, somehow. Firebright, then? That which is mortal — man — gives birth to that which is immortal: God. First comes man; then comes God, not the other way around. This makes sense. The inferior evolves [so to speak] into the superior, mortal to immortal. Man to God. But, I add, then that God travels, reaches, back through time to before creation, and He creates or gives birth to it. God antedates man, who then antedates God. Systole, diastole. The rhythm of the universe, in time.) It is impossible for me to deny or ignore the fact that I have done what Meister Eckhart describes. Especially as explained by Jung. Jung makes it clear that to experience God inwardly, as Eckhart describes and as I did, is to experience him psychologically, which is modern and sophisticated rather than primitive. This was the new way which Eckhart outlined back in his 13th century period, the idea of god born from man's soul and in a certain real sense dependent on man (as distinguished from the Godhead). It could be said that I had been primitive before my experience, in that I projected a great deal outwardly; but withdrew all these in 3-74 in a rather short swift interval. God was not introjected by me or incorporated, but rather *released*. Eckhart also says that when God is born in our soul you cease to experience the (mere) world outside, but that God replaces it; I experienced this, too, finding Him in me, and equally myself in the center of Him. Christ's description (Me in you and you in Me) is thus fulfilled, which points to what is called "Christ consciousness" or the Kingdom of Heaven, not the Holy Spirit as much.

Eckhart also speaks of this happening to a man who has misstepped (*vertreten*, as I recall); God, then, corrects the mis-swing of the man and brings him back to the Tao or Logos. This, then, is the macro/micro/macro schema that I drew, with God as the great macro; then myself the micro; then a fragment of the macro, of god, inside me at the very exact certain specific center (concentric rings). God is at the deepest heart or mind or level inside, and also outside everywhere; He replaces the world, resembling it as if He has transubstantiated — infused Himself — into everything, connecting all things into the One. The macro Godhead would be the Brahmin; the inner "macro" would be the Atman. This Divine birth, though, I believe, is quite different from the Child being born in the mind, which has to do with a new self, with psychic integration; instead of giving birth to a child, one gives birth to what resembles the Wise Old Man (its nearest archetype). The birth, not of the son, but of the Father! That this divine birth took place in me spontaneously, without my knowing about it, trying for it, having any wisdom or knowledge or practicing any techniques — this is important, showing its unquenchable aspects. What good did it do the Romans to kill people and burn their writing, if this can occur now spontaneously, with no transcultural link of any sort . . . especially if, as in my case, *after* the event occurs, the transcultural link is generated ad hoc, a priori, noetically, etc.? God lived once; He died, or rather He slept; He slept in us. The human soul is the image of God (Eckhart); out of this image, God is reconstructed, reconstituted, printed back out: the original reborn from its image. (Crypte morphosis, etc.) The sleeping or dormant form within is God Himself, like Ptath in van Vogt's novel, *The Book of Ptath*. We are all sleeping avatars of God, with amnesia. The human soul: DNA coding for God!!! But man does not reconstruct God out of this "DNA" coding; God reconstitutes Himself Himself. (Adventitious to the human being whose soul it is.) The man cannot say, "I am God," or "I have become/turned into God." Rather, God flashpointed him to make use of him to become Himself once more, an event in micro, in space-time. The mortal human only anticipates, as a lower life form, the Form to come. [. . .]

I've again read the EB article on Mystery Religions; those religions, especially the Orphics, stressed the anamnesis (Plato did, too, and those following him as did Pythagoras).* I ask this, as perhaps the most important question: what is the connection between being possessed by the Deity (which I aver is the same as finding the Kingdom of God), and recollection of one's former but forgotten divinity, as in Orphism and Neoplatonism? Is it a becoming for the first time, or a return? Is it new or old? Receiving or restoration? This is important because if it is a restoration then we are or anyhow were divine in nature, and lost it or forgot it, and can retrieve or remember it, get it back. Of course, I again wonder, How, if we are divine, did we come to forget that? This is, of course, the concept of the Fall, this fact, if it is a fact; we fell and forgot, having descended into nonbeing

---

* Dick consistently seeks to uncover some trace of the so-called unwritten doctrine that Aristotle associates with Plato in the *Physics,* an association that some see as "outing" Plato as a secret Pythagorean for whom ultimate reality is revealed by number. Dick also seeks to identify Plato's doctrine of the forms with Parmenides's idea of being as a well-rounded sphere opposed to the nothingness of nonbeing. This notion seems linked in Dick's mind with another borrowing from Parmenides to which he makes frequent allusion, the famous fragment 3: "For it is the same thing to think and to be." Also important to Heidegger, whose radical interpretations of the pre-Socratics may have influenced Dick, this fragment identifies the activity of intellection, *noesis* or noös, with the essential being of things. We might also take one further step and cite Empedocles's fragment 28, which appears to allude to Parmenides: "But he [God] is equal in all directions to himself and altogether eternal, a rounded sphere enjoying a circular solitude." The kernel of Dick's vision is the mystical identification of the soul's capacity for intellectual intuition with the being of the divine. — SC

which is the same as forgetfulness. Here now I am back to my early conjec-
tures and ponderings, and there seems no end to this, no solution. I know
that I experienced anamnesis, which suggests the recollection (neoplatonist) view. As set over against the Christian view . . . although for us now,
2,000 years later, it would now carry the aspect of restored memory — of
events 2,000 years ago; i.e., the Savior, Jesus Christ. This is what confuses
me. I remember a Savior who told us it was a new experience. I remember
his new message — observe the paradox. "In a crypt 2,000 years old I have
discovered new news!" [. . .]

The other night the thought came to me, "The first of the old prophecies are beginning to take place," or words to that effect (check supra). If
I were to assume that we are entering the Parousia, which could well be,
but on an undisclosed time-scale, then I would characterize this interval,
from my own actions, feelings and stance, my own intuitions and sense of
what is, Parousia or not — this interval seems subjectively to me to be one
of firm, even harsh, preparing for combat. I sense no love at this time, no
reaching out to forgive or understand or embrace. I sense muffled drums,
and a mysterious movement, a coming and going leading to a settling in
position, as if places are being taken, sides drawn, positions, stations, occupied, probably for a battle. Maybe Elijah was indeed here.

Now I am back, in my 14-month study of this, to where I began. Someone was here, rushing powerfully through my life, our lives, our world.
Something has begun; it started with that fierce zealous spirit and evidently ended with, "The Buddha is in the Park," which is to say, "Unto us a
child is born."[98] I have a continual feeling that I am on one specific side in
this; I have chosen, or have been chosen. The last thoughts which came to
me were, "Rest. You'll be guided when the time comes." I sense myself waiting. Days pass. Nothing happens. But I am waiting and feeling restless, really waiting in the true sense. Not just passing time. This time-period has
a clear quality of being a time of waiting, rather than mere emptiness, as
if things had fallen through, evaporated or gone wrong. What lies ahead?
I sort of sense myself as a samuri, now. Hard and stern, much less sympathetic or bathetic. My dream recently of carefully returning the bulging purse, bulging with coins, and finding that it belonged to "JeBORG,"
and that "BORG" was close . . . she is close by, the figure which has been
with me from the start of this: just out of sight. In addition, it is possible
that my enormously strong subjective intuition — if not perception — that I
personally was drawn into history by the Divine power is equally accurate.
Surely this is one way by which that Power operates: seizing upon individuals here and there to perform in concert an action which will have permanent consequences generally, which is to say in the arena of history. As

I keep saying, I feel retrospectively that *Tears* and very likely *Frolix 8* were both engineered subliminally, carrying in encoded or stegenographic form material from the Logos or Godhead concerning the Logos or Godhead, as a tiny part of some general historic communications pattern; I think that shortly after *Tears* was released, for me the subliminal became thresholded into consciousness, and so forth into 3-74. That is, put psychologically, I could not continue to thrust outside of awareness these extraordinary items in my books and in my life, but had to face them without averting my recognition. I was in the midst, as an active participant, of something enormous and frightening and dangerous, but very thrilling; and the direction, as well as instructions, upon which I acted, lay in the area of what people call the "supernatural." I think under the hidden direction of the Logos I did my part and then had to fight like hell to survive the backlash. But to play a role in history under such a Guidance — what greater joy could there be than to have had that, even if briefly? The greatest pleasure for the greatest reason; it is not the extent or importance of what I did but that I did it under that Guidance and to have been made fully aware of that by the Guidance itself: a gracious act toward me, and probably not necessary; it must have been given from love.

My overwhelming intuition at that time that I was, and had been, playing a small but real role in history, was probably accurate because at that time I had an absolute insight into the way everything linked up and functioned together, which is the mystic insight par excellence. I should assume, though, that my vision of my role is only meaningful in the mystical frame of reference, as contrasted to the everyday in which objects are discrete and there is no total unity. What I had is common to mystical experience, basically. But it was legitimate and real and I should hang onto it (I am). Equally real was my awareness of fighting off an absolutely evil enemy intent on zapping me once and for all — and real, too, the sense that I had lured it to destruction, assisted it in falling into its own snare. All of these perceptions were legitimate and accurate; they were disclosed to me partly to assist me in extricating myself from that danger and partly, I do believe, as a kind of reward to me, inasmuch as I had over the past years lost so much. In effect I had lost virtually all my material possessions, but I had gained my soul, if by soul you mean consciousness of one's own identity and purpose for living and reason for acting, and the ultimate disposition to which one would go. It became a sensible life in the midst of shambles, fear and chaos. A million chips, bits, fragments and broken pieces lay around on all sides in great heaps, but in the center (as if the Tao itself) I had discovered a disclosed form: my own reality, in the hands of the God who said once, "I will never fail thee; I will never forsake thee."[99] The most beautiful passages of the Scriptures became clear to me and pertained to me and my life, during all this, which in itself is a gift beyond compare. I conversed with the Scriptures, as if I was in colloquy with a friend. Once, opening it at random for comfort, I put my finger on: "Tell him that Elijah is close by!"[100] I count Elijah as one of my closest friends; it is good news to know that he is close by. But again, that bespeaks the surfacing of the fulfillment of the first of the ancient prophecies, which is of extraordinary importance, if it is so.

[5:193] Last night (June 2nd) I had a blissful truly mystical experience, which is probably the first one I've had in the strict sense, inasmuch as it was a state, an ASC, with vast understanding and comprehension as to how everything fitted together, but lacking any and all adventitious percept-system experiences, as I had in 3-74 and 2-75. However, had I never had anything else, it alone (last night) would have dignified my life immeasurably. How to record it verbally, though, I don't know. It linked it all up. That's a lot.

A basic realization: my 3-74 experience — the intervention by God in the world — was not an anomaly, except in terms of my experience of it. That is to say, it was a natural, regular event, which I had just never seen before; however, it always goes on, went on, will go on forever. It is the perpetual re-establishment of equilibrium and harmony, relating to the Tao and to ma'at.

Primarily, I began by realizing that along the lines of Parmenides when he denied the testimony of his senses as regards to what is (in actuality, what exists), I realized that:

(1) There is no visual (sense-organ) evidence of God at work anywhere in the world.

(2) I must either deny that God, then, is at work in the world, or I must deny the evidence of my senses.

[...]

I therefore took the course, last night, of denying the testimony of my senses, and said: God is at work in the world but below the surface; so that evil, although empirically evident, is not actually in control as it appears to be. Further, I realized, a discernment past superficial reality shows evil to be or anyhow at one time in the past (prior to 8-74) to have been in the saddle in a much deeper way than it allowed us to see; in other words, evil masked its own power, the more to control and enslave us. So at first step, a penetration into the heart of reality showed it even more evil, or in the control of evil, than did mere superficial analysis. However, below the ring of iron around us (Rome, as the metaphor goes) I saw that God had breached, penetrated, and in fact made hollow this evil, had turned it into a shell by something transforming it from within, into its opposite . . . which made me recall Taoism, and I think it was Empedocles — one of the pre-Socratics, he or Heraclitus, I suppose, the point being that one of them had argued that any quality contains its opposite within it and will be transformed into it (yin into yang, etc.) if pressed far enough. What this then yielded to in my thinking was the concepts of palintropos and palintonos, the whole "trampoline" structure of reality in which there is balance and equilibrium established as a regular matter of course. [. . .]

This is the real fabric of reality. What I saw was an extreme example, as the long *New Yorker* 6-part piece on the Constitutional Crisis discloses. There was an extreme action, hence an extreme reaction (the parabola effect). I was there and saw it happen: everything in me and around me started its return journey. The turning point came, and Retreat (to go to the *I Ching*) transformed — I mean *was* transformed by the Immanent Mind — into Advance.[101] I conceive of this in Taoistic *and* Greek terms: Tao and Mind together, like a sentient, thinking, loving Tao; which is I think ma'at. 3-74 was indeed a special, even unique occasion, but only in degree (and in that I got to see it, for some reason). (It doesn't matter why I got to see it; I did and that is that.) Hence my acute feeling that the end of a long roll of film had passed through the projector, there'd been an empty place, and then, aha! a new roll, a very different roll, had been inserted. The parabola effect, carrying me with it.

I must have made myself, or anyhow been, very receptive (Yinnish) to the forces active in the universe at that moment. When hex. 36[102] changed to some other good one, I was carried along. I must have, as the Taoists or Zen people, somebody anyhow, says, made myself empty (wu).

For hours last night I lay in a blissful trance, sensing the capacity of the universe to rebound, its elasticity. You can't break it; it will regain its "shape" after any deformity sets in.

Probably this is connected to the vision I had of the two-person game at work: move and counter-move would be action and reaction, a reaction to restore wholeness, harmony and balance. Too, a vast law of Karma is involved — and disclosed — here. I do not need personally to react to everything; the universe will do much of that (which provides a basis for understanding Christ's ethical system; when you're hit you don't hit back, but rather you let this universal ma'at or Tao do it for you). Really, for Christ's ethical system to work one must presuppose some universal system of recompense (which He does), much like this; it is important to recall that ma'at is judge of the dead, with her feather weighed in the scales against the deceased's heart.

Having experienced this blissful mystical understanding of it all, everything I've been into from 3-74 to now, I am thinking, Perhaps I can infer that the Parousia are not here in any universal or objective sense; but surely *for me*, as an individual, the entire sequence of depicted events came — and in the order described. Which causes me to ask, If as Meister Eckhart says, the Kingdom of God is within the Soul of each person (i.e., an entirely individual, inner event) then is not the entire realm of the Parousia, all of it, within the inner individual soul of one-person-at-a-time? But if so, then why do not other people report my experience as theirs? Over 2,000 years there is no individual report like mine, except perhaps Eckhart? Well, no matter how I cut it I will have trouble explaining some parts.* [. . .]

In an effort to understand how this parabolic reverse-direction comes about I turn to the *I Ching* (by memory, alas) about the "seeds of the future being buried in the present." Always, the seeds, concealed, of the future are here now, if we had a method of discerning them, which could mean set-ground discrimination; anyhow, I am at this moment in sudden wild ecstasy, because viewed this way such "Logos material," as I've called it, as the dream in *Tears,* plus Prelude's song "After the Goldrush" are very likely — wow!!!!! — such seeds of the future emerging as fragments of that impending, cohering future, now. This would set them apart from all the objects and constituents which are purely part of the present. How extraordinary it would be to all at once see (would you believe in a special illuminated red and gold shimmer of color???) these seeds wherever you looked. You would be seeing tomorrow! It would enthrall you, as if time had moved backward: the future building itself here and now. You might

---

* In his extraordinary German sermons, Meister Eckhart (1260–1327) described the kingdom in the soul as the divine spark (*vünkelîn*), a term that appears elsewhere in the Exegesis. He also called this kingdom the godhead (*gôtheit*). Such views were condemned by the Avignon Pope as heretical two years after Eckhart's death. Eckhart's "heresy" was considered close to the much-feared Heresy of the Free Spirit that, some historians claim, was like an invisible empire across Europe in the thirteenth and fourteenth centuries. The core of this heresy consisted in the denial of original sin: sin does not lie within us, but within the world, which is not the creation of the true God, but of the malevolent demiurge. Therefore, we must see through the evil illusion of this world to the true world of the alien God. We might link this to Dick's view that orthogonal time will make it possible for the golden age — the time before the fall — to return. In the text of Eckhart's papal condemnation, we find quasi-gnostic utterances such as: "All creatures are one pure nothing. I do not say they are a little something, but that they are pure nothing." All this can be linked to Dick's later Eckhartean allusion to humans as "corruptible sheaves around divine sparks." — SC

then manage to discern the shape of future things, the pattern emerging. (Or you might not.) Well, then by this token, what I have seen indicates the Parousia, so we are back to it as an objective forthcoming event!

There is a great mystery about the Kingdom of God, as to where it is, and the Parousia in general; it is in you, but also among you, and it is invisible but actual. He must mean it is transpersonal. When you participate (yes, that is it); you *enter* it — did He not use this key word? You enter it; therefore it already exists before you and outside you, which indicates objective existence (contrast, "I entered sadness," a state of mind). It is real and it is there; one by one we enter it, or we don't. We cross over and enter, led by our shepherd. In response to the sound of his voice. A place of safety and peace, where we remain with Him. We find our way to it. Recall my vivid experience in 3- or 4-74 in seeing a pylon or archway with a silvery moonlit world beyond, and Greek letters — silence. I could pass through the gate and enter that world beyond; I could see it clearly, first here, then there, now over there, glowing and waiting, open to me. Not in any one spot but glimpsed again and again:

That was no subjective state; that was a perception of something real which others couldn't see; a set-ground gestalting. I discerned the doorway repeatedly; it was multilocated and authentic. Not omnipresent but multipresent. The Secret Kingdom, hidden.

A moment of fear touches me; did I then fail to pass through that gate and enter it? I think I passed on through, because after seeing it (that was quite early along) I then had the holy waste and void dreams, or visions, visionary trance experiences, where I was with God; that came later, I'm sure; yes, that was later, after the Carmel dream which ushered it in. So I did enter. [. . .]

When I was little I used to haul out big wooden cartons and boxes to play inside of . . . it is as if, through the pylon gate, I found my way back to the peace and safety of those cartons of my childhood . . . God has brought me at last to safety and a realization, at last, of safety, the safety I yearned for and did not have even then (5 years old). Viewed another way perhaps it can be said that I have been brought safely into the fold, after straying all over the landscape. Either way we are talking about the same place. I feel a great peace now, at last, for the first time in my life. This whole period, including 3-74, has been arduous; I had to work hard and hustle after my illumination (3-74), right on down through the months, these 14 months, writing on this as I am doing, reading and researching and writing and meditating in order to understand. I believe I've worn myself out more with this than with any previous writing, any novel or group of novels. I have educated myself regarding my experience. Gone to school over it.

What does it add up to (at this point in my knowledge)? I passed through the narrow gate in mid-74, and now I am told that He will come back for the world itself, fairly soon. Thus an individual experience will be made/is being made into a common or group or collective or objective experience by our people in general. As with other questions, the answer to the question, Is it subjective and individual or objective and general, is, *Both.* [. . .]

If I were to go and declare that I had been changed (in Paul's sense: "Behold! I tell you a sacred secret; we must all be changed," etc.[103]), then if anyone believed me — if — they would say, "The Time prophesized has come." I guess I must be wrong, except if I am wrong, that I am changed, then what did happen that should so resemble it and unfold in correct order and yield the results attributed? Q: How does my 3-74 experience, going up to date *differ* from what was prophesized? Compare the two. Contrast them. Write an essay on the difference.

This is the way to put it: "What do you have to do to enter the Kingdom of Heaven?" and then the list which follows conforms to the list one would draw, in sequence, of what I experienced, back before that, too, to the distress — lost — period which ran on months if not years. What I went through both bad (before 3-74) and good (3-74 on) had to be gone through, like an enormous spiritual transcendental car wash — a human being refurbishing system, so complex as to beggar description, beginning with the dreams of the flying monsters with horse's necks (dragons) and then picking up in distinctness with the chromatic flash-cut graphics, the latter night being, if any section can be so said to be, the moment when the Spirit began to pour out onto and into me. The beginning, in other words, of the New. Up to then it had been nothing but various aspects of me perishing — dying. The rebirth began with the graphics; the turning-point in the parabolic orbit had begun. I was re-entering life, as new life re-entered me: "from above." The thing about all this is that if it is said to me, severely, "You have to do (experience, go through) a lot to enter the Kingdom of Heaven; you can't do it like you are; you've got to be very much changed, and receive the Spirit," etc., I can say, "I know." (Or I think I know. I hope I know. I hope I don't just have hubris about this. I hope I'm not just boasting. If I am I'm sorry.) I think, though, really, what is convincing about it when I view it objectively is that, remembering back, I was genuinely broken down, stripped down, torn down to my skeletal plating, like an insect who has woven a cocoon, and then I passed through months of uniquely and actually unimaginable rebuilding processes, all adventitious to me, improving and teaching me, altering me — well, the "possession" part alone remade me in the most fundamental way indeed — and clearly as completely remaking me as can be conceived.

(1) I believed I was someone else.

(2) From another time period.

(3) Dead centuries ago and reborn.

(4) A holy Christian person.

(5) I spoke Attic Greek somewhat and remembered Rome.

(6) I wanted a new name and trimmed my beard.

(7) All my interests and habits changed — instantly.

(8) My linguistic idiosyncrasies altered permanently.

(9) Even the way I margined my pages changed.

(10) I wrote people I'd never written before.

(11) I joined religious organizations I'd never heard of.

(12) All my political alliances of a lifetime changed totally.

(13) I called cats "she" and dogs "he."

Ergo: He who was alive died, and someone else lives now in me, replacing me.

(14) I talk to and am talked to by God.

Well, what more can you ask out of a transformed person? I know the future and things beyond my senses, but I'll skip that because I am not sure if that counts.

(15) I stopped drinking wine and drank beer.

(16) I knew that aerosol sprays were lethal; likewise cigarettes.

(17) I could discern evil and could tell what was true.

(18) My spelling is unchanged. (To give some continuity.)

(19) I recovered from most of my quasi-physical ailments.

(20) Most of my time since I spend studying theology.

(21) The level of my intelligence is increased — this includes reading retention, speed, and abstract thinking.

(22) My depth perception is improved.

(23) Mental operations which baffled me are now easy (i.e., mental blocks now seem gone).

(24) My psychological projections are withdrawn.

The only problem is, I am in no customary sense — maybe in no sense whatsoever — spiritualized or exalted. In fact I seem even more mean and irascible than before. True, I do not hit anybody, but my language remains gungy and I am crabby and domineering; my personality defects are unaltered. In the accepted sense I am not a better person. I may be healthier (maybe not that; vide the blood pressure). But I am not a good person, even though my emotions and moods are better under control. Maybe I just have a long way to go, yet.

I have a sudden new thought about "Vinland" and "Portuguese States of America" et al. No one is coming here to a New World, and we are not *going* (i.e., space flight) to a New World, but this world will be changed into a new world. These are symbols of renewal for our world, related to Spring. They are precog images of how it is going to be for us here, on what has become a depleted worn-out *old* world: rebirth.

These are all clues, many of them, as to what it's going to be like: the future is seeping back to me in dreams. And I dream often of green grass and moisture . . . like a park or garden. If only I could figure out —

And so to bed.

But as to the lack of proper spiritual refurbishing in me . . . perhaps we have too clear an attitude toward pious transformations as being the ones He wishes in us. Perhaps these are our standards for the very pure; after all, He would retain the individual, I think, and not force us all into one proper mold. I have been changed, but not in all ways; I have been improved, but not according to human standards. I can only hope I am obeying His will and not my own.

I do not conform to my own views of goodness, but maybe I do to His.

It could be an important observation or insight to say that I did not have a religious mystical experience, with God — as such; I encountered or discerned or perceived or experienced (assimilated the Dinge-an-sich in totality) which we call the universe, and found it to be alive, wise, active (Vast Active Living Intelligence System) and supporting to life, such as ours. Only by degrees — and the process of elimination — did I come at last to call this "God." I did so because what I experienced is customarily called that and nothing else, except perhaps Immanent Mind; however, this is more than mind, it also being active (like Ptath the artificer). Thus I arrived at the idea that I had found God along lines which did not involve me flying to easy concepts or solutions. In a very real sense I started at the beginning of thought, without preconceptions or expectations, and invented, so to speak, the categories I used, had to use, and wound up with. I think had no one preceded me in this I would still have arrived at these conclusions; I mean, had there been no human knowledge of God or gods, or had I never heard of this (e.g., born into a totally atheistic society with total suppression of news of God actually or in terms of historical belief), I would then be coming to my people to tell them that He Lives.

[. . .] To return to Heinrich Zimmer's "Magdeburg Hemispheres,"[104] probably, if not certainly, my perceptions of the outside universe cleared up and became lucid and total because my inner world, my psyche, cleared up and became lucid and a total unity: like outer, inner; like inner, outer. In Jungian terms I abruptly integrated the contents of my mind, with spectacular results (hence all the dreams about alchemy and the Greek period). (I got down to archetypes of the collective unconsciousness, to the very bottom.) This is the road; this is how you do it, total integration. This is the road to God, withdrawing all projections, reconciling the opposites, release of all libido. Transformation from ego to true self. *But*— How did I accomplish that, while lying in my room listening to bubblegum rock, with no outside help (sic: none?)? Spontaneous psychic integration, the goal of analytical psychology. I went on the journey into the unconscious, which Jung and John Weir Perry[105] describe (period before the graphics). (Resembling the Bardo Thödol.) Perhaps it could be properly said, as I sometimes think, that my psychotic journey began in 1970 in earnest that day I kept playing the Paul McCartney record over and over, when Nancy and Isa left. I had been "neurotic" until that day, but starting that day I suffered a collapse mentally, and descended into the world of dreams and nightmare and half-sleep, through which I moved only partially conscious . . . yes, this indeed is so, is so, and must never be forgotten in understanding this: I was on this journey from mid-1970 up until 3-74, when I returned from out of the depths, into bright day light, integrated and whole, for the first time in my life, carrying back up with me the pearl of great price— thus showing John Perry to have been right. During those years I lived among huge archetypical projections of a collective sort; yes, it is so. What a world of daemons and so forth.

Four years in that strange underwater world . . . from shock and grief, wandering like a shade over the landscape, among shadows.

Also, it must be realized that the journey part (1970/74) was characterized by acute primitivism of outlook on my part, the mystique thing Lévy-Brühl[106] talks about (I think I'm talking about schizophrenia, here, not manic depression). But this indicates that the 3-74 experience, which was re-entry, is non-psychotic, a healed experience, and the withdrawn projections indicate a sophisticated non-primitive viewpoint or functioning. As Jung says re Meister Eckhart, by withdrawing my projections I experienced God psychologically, as an inner event not entangled with external objects, but purely so: authentically. Put another way, starting the chromatic graphics, I evolved up through 2,000 years of human history-evolution-psychological-growth. Thus a very archaic personality came awake in me, suddenly, which is to say, the adult I had never been in all my life. Buried deep in my collective unconscious all these years, it possessed spiritual and practical wisdom acquired from the archetypes. Therefore I say this new personality or person was created from the deepest levels of my psyche, a child or rather new man from the collective experience and wisdom of the race, and has an incontestable superiority over my original ego self. This fits the description of "born again" as certainly as could be.* From madness to sanity and a new, better self. I think I should feel free to attribute my cure to God, as a miracle of His doing — as when Jesus caused the blind man to see: it shows God's love. Certainly I did not heal myself, and it is hard to rationalize that it somehow was spontaneous, which is to say, uncaused. I would know, wouldn't I? I heard the voice of my "physician," did I not, both in dreams and while awake? Given that there is a physician, who else could this physician be (Asklepios was an avatar of Him). [. . .]

While you are dead the Kingdom remains invisible to you. I think in 2-75 I began to see it. It is a spiritual kingdom, and in the process of becoming actual (physical, literal, visible). We are the dead, as in *Ubik*, who must be roused by the sound of His voice. But not roused to physical life but spiritual life (as the grain of what is not raised as it was sown). (But raised in a new, spiritual, better body.) This is why when I saw the King He was dancing among the furrows — which is where the wheat lies sleeping (in death); he made a sound to them in some way; a form of music. He, the spring King, was calling the sleeping wheat up into life, from where they were buried in the furrows; this is what spring, and his voice, mean. Thus it is said of Dionysos that he "is a god of vegetation" and the mystery of Elysius as a grain of wheat planted in the furrow is reborn, and the grave equals the furrow — the dead human, buried, is reborn. This is what I saw in 2-75 without (as usual) understanding it. As He calls to the wheat, who are dead in their furrows, he calls to us who are dead (in our graves), exactly as I depicted in *Ubik* (Runciter's voice, their friend who died but who, for them, has returned to help them). [. . .]

The "solitary" life which both Christ and Paul speak of as an affliction, [is] in contrast to the ear of corn in which all grains are together in corporate life; it was an ear of corn that was held up at Elysius, to demonstrate the mystery: I think the mystery is, the solitary grain(s) will be sown, then will grow again in corporate life, a corporate body of which Christ is the head. Paul in 1 Cor makes it perfectly clear that resurrection is in a spiri-

---

* Dick's approach to the concept of being "born again" is quite different from the interpretation that developed among evangelical Protestants in the twentieth century. For evangelicals, being "born again" depends on a personal decision, an intellectual/emotional acceptance of a soteriological proposition. For Dick, it refers to a passive event, an invasion — possibly even a victimization — by an outside force. Dick's "second birth" was not the result of his conversion experience, but its cause. He was personally transformed, but not as a result of his own volition. — GM

tual body as opposed to the prior physical body[107]; as in Neoplatonism, we can expect to ascend on to a spiritual "next ring" universe in a spiritual, nonphysical, immortal body, leaving this one behind; it grows out of this one after this one is dead and buried, as with the grain of wheat/corn in the furrow: what comes next is different; it is a complete misunderstanding to expect—or even want—the originally physical "solitary" inferior body back ever again; it is metamorphosis which we are talking about; Paul in 1 Cor makes this perfectly clear. The incorruptible body is not a physical body, like this only eternal, but a spiritual body. Death is regarded as a doorway, with something better on the other side, exactly like the doorway I saw in 3- and 4-74, like a Greek pylon, with the moonlight and clear water beyond, which was everywhere, here and there, that I looked. A study of the other mystery religions (all based on the dying lunar god Osiris) shows this. Of all the things (visions) I saw, none is more significant than the pylon or arch-like doorway with the Greek water and nighttime island scene, so beautiful and peaceful on the other side. That was not a transformed view of this world (as with the iron ring and later spring time and Santa Sophia the building), that was a doorway to another world for sure. It wasn't to death; death was the doorway, the passage, with life beyond. It was a rather narrow entranceway. (When did I see that doorway? It must have either been after my shoulder surgery, or led into that period, because just after Pinky died I remember seeing him, all healthy and full-chested, squeezed through the doorway looking into this world at us.) (It just occurs to me that the doorway always had the proportions of the Golden Rectangle.) And at first I saw it as a geometric drawing of the Golden Rectangle complete with Greek-letter markings at corners, etc., at that point not yet projected into the world, found there as doorway and 3-D, but "in my 3rd eye or inner mind or mind's eye," not yet fused with the landscape; later, whenever I saw it, I actually picked out the Golden Rectangle in the real world, discerned it, but saw it as a doorway, and saw the lovely quiet peaceful world on the other side, waiting. Thinking about it now I realized that the discernment of this Golden Rectangle doorway within the real world here and there was on the identical order of the iron ring, God in the trash of the alley, everything else, especially equal to seeing Springtime in 2-75; it was a major event, and not to be ignored or forgotten; it was another transformation of the landscape, another vision of the next world or the New Creation. Offhand I'd say its message was, One can get from here (this world) to there, which is to say, to the Spiritual Universe. It's immediately at hand, if we could but see it. That which is seen through the doorway is not superimposed on our world but lies beyond it. For instance, it is nighttime there. (Although midday here.) I'm sure it's "on the

Other Side," and you would have to die to get there; after all, Pinky, after his death, immediately after, looked back into this world from there. It is another place, another time entirely. I don't think it's the Kingdom of God; I think everything else I experienced is. If it is indeed a glimpse through the doorway into the Next World, then the Next World (for me anyhow) is very much like Minoan Greece, like the Aegean and Crete (where many of my first visionary dreams were set). (Also, where Zagreus/Dionysos came from.) All the straight john uptight rigid description and attitudes by the Christians about it are just so much a row of swords to protect it; once inside it's lovely. You can sit down on a Grecian bench and relax in the cool of the evening. [. . .]

I kept dreaming of us as animals in a stagnant pond, interpreting this as our planet. But suppose it's not our planet, but our entire space-time universe, viewed from the next (Neoplatonist type) one? The "helium-filled balloons," then, which rise — those are our souls. This is also the next stage in our evolution. But the pond has become so stagnant, now; few "balloons" rise. It is sad. . . . We must be an early stage in a life-form which metamorphoses into a higher space-time continuum. These dreams/visions weren't ETI viewpoint, but religious in nature, a religious insight into our condition. Maybe it is at the bottom of the pond that we hear his voice. I think what those dreams/visions consist of, is you can develop a working (total) view based on them alone, but everything which religion deals with — our situation, etc. It's all in there somewhere.

We're not so much "dead" or half-dead but half-alive — exactly as it's called in *Ubik*, but working the other way: the missing part has never been alive; it lies ahead, not behind us. We weren't deprived of it. We didn't have it once. We are yet to have it, are working toward it, being drawn, called (as by the élan vital of evolution, of life) toward (upward toward) it. A newt after all is "alive," but it is only part of the life it will eventually achieve (if all goes well). As Paul says, the physical body (which we have) comes first; then the spiritual (which we don't have, which Christ gives us). My gosh, we are being grown here (in this pond), and aided (on all sides, which is what I saw). [. . .]

In Aristotle the one soul of the 3 which is immortal is the one which seeks to know (seeks sophia).

"My divine children, whom I am preparing" (dream).

[5:311] I had the most extraordinary dream in which the dual nature of Christ was revealed. It took the form of a Medieval diptych, in which, on the right, the inner nature of Christ was shown in a picture, nebulous, but resembling Michelangelo's painting of the Delphic sibyl. Under that right-hand picture was written the word SHE and then the word SECRET. The left-hand picture was shown clearly: it was the puppet Pinocchio. As a string puppet, which is to say, worked (animated) from above. The picture of the puppet was one of a mere model of a human, very wooden, very without intrinsic life; it even had heavy shoes to weight it down, to give it the semblance of substance. In the very center of the frame, below the two pictures and equidistant from both, appeared the three unbroken lines of the trigram Ch'ien,[108] that of creative masculinity; this lay outside the diptych, thereby showing an outward presentation, to the world (outside), of pure unadulterated absolute masculinity. Bearing in mind that the female (and I think superior) part — called she — was identified also as secret, I understand from this dream that the female component's presence in the dual nature is a secret, probably is to be kept secret; also, it does not reveal itself in Christ's actions or manner, which guards the secret of course. That the masculine nature is "worked" by an inner feminine one is never stated anywhere, or it would cease to be a secret. I can conclude that it is Haggia Sophia that is represented here. I get a lot from this diptych representation; one thing I get is the impression that although gently given, the word "secret" is an injunction to me to keep my mouth shut. This is the first evidence I have had that there is indeed, as Paul calls it, the element of sacred *secrets* in esoteric Christianity (cf. what the ICC says). I was initiated into at least one of these sacred secrets; i.e., that Christ's deepest nature is feminine, which is to say, Holy Wisdom. That He will return is not a secret. Another secret is the relationship between the shamans of Greek culture and Christ/the Holy Spirit, which is to say the theolepsy induced by Dionysos. Specifically, though, I am told to cool it re Christ's feminine nature. Secret means secret. (I presume the early Christians, who underwent theolepsy by this spirit, knew this; and they did not tell. That it is also the Cumaean sibyl, and Delphic, shows a continuity from Greek mystery religions, and Greek culture, also not told.)

So several cultures (3) are involved: Hebrew, Greek and Roman. I suspect also Iranian: the wise or good mind, Ahura Mazd.

Anyhow, in the dream (p. 1) there was cautionary material, I think, because nothing new was given except the word "secret"; the rest I already had been told. Question is, Why should it be kept secret? Probably for the obvious reason, that people would not now, and wouldn't have in ancient times or Medieval times, accepted it. I am thinking of what Wilhelm Reich said about the maternal religions and societies versus the paternal, and then what I said in my Vancouver speech, my hope for and anticipation of an amalgam of the masculine and feminine deities, which is exactly what the diptych showed Christ to be (with the feminine dominating, which is all right with me). Yes, in that speech I foresaw this, the next cycle of human society, and I was ready for it, pleased and eager. It would combine the best of both, the syzygy, a masculine posture of assertiveness plus feminine love and warmth. The diptych showed a syzygy, all right, masc. outside, feminine within. We would see a man physically but experience a woman spiritually.

You know, the puppet Pinocchio could also have been a ventriloquist's dummy. What a strong image! With the animating entity on the right side, i.e., as pictured there à la fresco. The puppet had no life of its own; on its own it was inert and silent. Christ, on the cross, said, "My God, why hast thou forsaken me?" which perhaps meant that at the moment the inner animating spirit left Jesus and rose upward; what other interpretation is possible? Which tells us, does it not, that we have a cupola between the animating spirit and God; it was the spirit of God, i.e., God's wisdom. I suppose it is more accurate to regard Jesus Christ as a syzygy rather than female as such, but the prior spirit, prior to incarnation, was female, and I suppose is again; we are in both cases talking about St. Sophia: she. Well, if St. Sophia — I mean when — when St. Sophia again is incarnated, I imagine that another syzygy will be formed, and again it will be correct to think of it as he-she rather than as with the unincarnated spirit: she only. The human, which is to say masculine, side must not be discounted; this is the bond, the fusion, between the supralunar and the sublunar; this fusion is significant and must not be lost sight of as being such. The animating female spirit exalts the man to the status of God or anyhow a god. The Ch'ien trigram placed dead center shows the mystery: that the fusion results in a masculine outcome, albeit the animating figure's feminine nature; here is a miracle, this transformation of sexes, which the dream picture shows to be real (i.e., it comes out Ch'ien, not Kun, as one might anticipate). Nothing gives out the secret, nothing. A further thought occurs to me. Is not the Holy Spirit capable of conferring immortality? Yes. Then did not St. Sophia (the Holy Spirit) confer immortality on the man Jesus, so that he per se still lives? Yes; it must be so, or all our hopes are dashed. Perhaps then the Holy Spirit, the Paraclete, is still the syzygy; it is not certain, in fact it is unlikely, that as the JWs[109] say, the man Jesus is dead, forever dead; because if He is, then so are we, too.

Wow. I have seen into the nature (essence) of the second incarnation, and in doing so, have a stronger sense of its imminence. The Trinity is a mystery re its natures and persons, but (I have been told in my dream) so is the nature of St. Sophia incarnate — two persons, or rather (sic!) two essences! Forming one person! If the Trinity is real, then do we not have a quaternity, with man (Jesus) being the 4th person??

This cautionary revelation would not have been necessary if the spirit weren't about to incarnate, I think. Surely such a cautionary warning would only take place if the second incarnation were imminent. (Perhaps in my lifetime, although I could commit it to print, which would extend, possibly, into the future.) Anyhow it concretizes the second advent, in my mind, as very imminent and very real.

puppet   sibyl

• • • • • • • •   SHE SECRET

☰ ☰ ☰ ☰ ☰

The puppeteer speaks through the puppet, who is a mouthpiece, then, for the god, gods or God. Is this not what the dream shows? The human component should be a clear and limpid structure through which Divine Wisdom can express itself unhindered. Its expression should not be vitiated. There is no voice, really, but that of the puppeteer; the puppet has none of his own. An immortal and divine voice speaks from within the man (Jesus). He is assimilated to it, and yet we see only the puppet, the man; he is invisibly transubstantiated. [. . .]

I dreamed last night of a MS page of mine in which I had 3 consecutive paragraphs beginning with the word "she," an obvious reference to the "she secret" Christ dream. In this more recent dream I found space on the page to insert a paragraph which did not begin with "she" (I felt it was wrong always to start with "she"), and I added erotic material, about nipples, etc. Now, thinking about this, I remember my first vision, preceding all the others, which was of Aphrodite, and had to do with her right nipple; I wonder if there was an elliptical allusion to Aphrodite (cf. Empedocles) in this recent dream. The dream, engendered from my own mind purely, is still valuable, as it recalls to me what I had forgotten, namely, the vision of the Cyrenaican Aphrodite beyond the golden rectangle door. Does this dream suggest (good lord!) that "she" is related to, or is, none other than the goddess of love known to the Greeks? Empedocles felt that Aphrodite was the steersman of all krasoi.[110] This is all very anxiety-producing to me. I add, if so, indeed it would be marked "secret," but I appeal to the philosophy of Empedocles to indicate a lofty as well as erotic element to this; he held her to be the ultimate entity drawing things and people together, "the star of love," which is how I ended my speech, meaning Christ. As the EB calls her, "The generative principle of all life." A mother goddess, not sex; doesn't the nipple point to this? Nourishing?

[5:244] Mark 4:11 says that the parables were intended to confuse and not inform everyone except the disciples, the latter understanding the esoteric meaning, the outsiders getting only the exoteric meaning which would fail to save them; this was especially true regarding parables about the approaching Kingdom of God. I keep forgetting this. How much of the real inner meaning has come down to us? The written gospels record probably mostly the exoteric parable meanings, not the inner core. Whether we like it or not, it is there in Mark (if not elsewhere), and this favors the view of an elect within the body of mankind. At least so far as Jesus went. Maybe now there is a Third Covenant which will include all creation or anyhow all men. I am thinking in particular of the grain of wheat sown into the ground to rise again, a mystery theme common to Greek mystery religions; in fact evidently the basic one. What it really means — to know this — enables the hearer to achieve what is achieved: eternal life. The how is contained, as well as the what. I think that in 3-74, at the height of despair and fear and grieving I stumbled into the Kingdom, stumbled around for a while and then stumbled back out, none the wiser as to how I got there, barely aware of where I had been, and no idea as to how I stumbled out, and seeking always to find my way back ever since. Shucks. Drat. If it wasn't the Kingdom I don't know what it could be, with its bells and the lady singing and the void, with the trash in the gutter glowing, and the golden rectangle doorway with the sea and figure beyond, and the moonlight. There were people living there, especially the lady. It was all alive. It had personality. It explained everything to me. Now I don't see or understand anything. At that time I could even remember back to my origins. My real origins: the stars. What am I doing here? I forget, but I knew once. Amnesia has returned; the veil has fallen, back where it was. The divine faculties are occluded as before. Obviously I didn't accomplish it; I was given it, since I don't know how to find it again. "Man is not as wise as some stones, which in the dark, point toward their homes." My soul, sunk down in ignorance again. Blind and deaf. Ensnared by gross matter, limited. The long dark night of the soul is a lousy place to be.

Heraclitus says the Logos can be heard. My goodness.

Heraclitus also says the world (universe) is uncreated, but kept together by the Logos, which I guess is immanent/transcendent. Men do not listen to the Logos nor see it, but are asleep. Soren K. says that the essence of Christianity is an "inward suffering before God," which makes me a Christian I guess, especially today.[111] The pull of matter is very great. I escaped for only a little while and then fell back further than ever. As Elton John says, "I've got my memories," and it did induce some permanent changes in me. Mark says that God can cut short the time of tribulation for the elect, before it gets unbearable; maybe that's what He did in 3-74.

Mark: "Those closest to Christ thought he was insane."[112] So his mother and friends came to get him, but he rebuffed them. Shades of Dionysus; also, that the apostles appeared drunk to bystanders when the Holy Spirit came to them at Pentecost. Thinking about this I feel rushing back to me many many experiences around 3-74 and during the year after: the name Jesus in the Bible opening up to form Zeus-Zagreus, the dots on the alb of the saint becoming grape vines; the vine quality of the washing ladies' plaque; the dithyramb being danced; the article "Dionysus in America" and what it meant to me[113]; the imagery of Pindar (root and star); the similarities I noticed between *The Bacchae* and the passion story and Hamlet; the fact that Dionysus is a breaker of prisons and a destroyer of tyrants (e.g., King Penteus); Christ turning water into wine; Christ as corn god and lunar fertility god; the mystery religions et al.; the fact that Dionysus was a god of metamorphosis: the Greek words and aspects of 3-74; the madness or intoxification I felt; the breaking down of the Nixon gang tyranny; my whole preoccupation with Dionysus during this . . . was Jesus an avatar of Dionysus, a evolution of him via Orpheus into ultimate spirituality?* Was this one of the cardinal mysteries revealed to me direct? The man/god/ stranger who cannot be killed, and who is persecuted, but then returns with a vengeance? That's what I put at the end of my U.K. speech. Where has he been for the past two thousand years? Locked in a death-struggle with authority: first the authority of his own church, then the secular authorities, all of them; bursting the prisons gradually. Or perhaps the human who experiences the theolepsy (like the sibyl in *The Aeneid*) becomes intoxicated by the energy of the spirit inhabiting it; which might include Jesus, and later the apostles. The spirit, in His case, could be Holy Wisdom, and she is quite sane (ma'at). It occurs to me at once that theolepsy must be limited to short intervals, so as to curtail the madness. But Jesus

---

* What else was going on in the world in March 1974? As reality's fabric ripped apart in Fullerton, a jumbo jet fell out of the sky outside Paris, killing more than three hundred people; an Arab oil embargo produced the most pronounced gasoline shortage ever in America, with cars lined up at stations for miles; and the U.S. Senate voted overwhelmingly to restore the death penalty that the Supreme Court recently had ruled unconstitutional. Overshadowing even these unsettling events was the kidnapping in northern California of the heiress of a millionaire publishing family by a band of domestic terrorists; though there is no evidence that Dick shared the rest of the country's fascination with this incident, which took place in his own backyard, the subsequent conversion of Patty Hearst to the radicals' cause sounds like a novel that Dick might have written in the fifties or might yet write toward the end of his life. Most prominently, virtually all of Richard Nixon's immediate political circle in the White House, including his attorney general and chief of staff, were indicted in the Watergate scandal, which had reached critical mass, and the president himself was named a co-conspirator by a grand jury. To Dick, and to the country at large, this was the moment when the Nixon presidency—five months before its end—was at its most toxic. —SE

had the spirit in him most of the time . . . perhaps He struggled with it and conquered the madness, except for short outbursts, such as the fig tree episode.[114] [. . .]

It is Gnosticism and Gnosticism alone which denies the patriarchal Jewish-Christian religion and enshrines Sophia as the creator goddess. So says Neumann in the EB. My experience of the lady — it is exactly Gnostic. *None else.* In my revelations all roads and aspects lead to her; this is Gnosticism.

I've seen her, heard her, in many guises, and finally the name "St. Sophia." Gnostic revelation has broken through into my head in the modern world. I think anyone versed in Gnosticism who read my notes would say, "You're a Gnostic." I am not happy about this, but it is so, based on 3-74. Simon Magus[115] lives. Also, it is a thoroughly Greek syncretistic system. I must go where truth (as I've experienced it) takes me; my experience is of St. Sophia. Well, this is a modified Gnosticism, with Sophia sanctified as Wisdom of Proverbs and the book "Wisdom," so that it can be made to jibe with the Bible; thus Christ becomes the female spirit Sophia in a male body, a syzygy. Ah! Yes! This is the complete person! The missing half which Plato wrote about. In Jungian terms, psychological completeness; psychic integration. Not either-or but both-and. At last; the repressed female goddess Prinzip breaks through into Christianity, in a Third Testament or Covenant. Father (OT), Son (NT) and daughter or mother (3rd T). The first emanation from God, according to the OT, so I guess daughter as demiurge (cf. Plato). The Godhead remains behind her; I experienced that; she is the Pantocrator. Ma'at. Or rather Pantocratrix. Two aspects differ from Gnosticism: it is *Holy* Wisdom, not just Sophia; and: she was born before and rejected, which identifies her with Christ, hence the Logos. This restores the cosmological quality to the system, lost in Gnosticism; the creating spirit (universe creating) is holy and good, not fallen (blech). And this maintains Christ correctly as *the* Redeemer and Revealer. [. . .]

From a Jungian viewpoint, that which characterized my birth of the whole self, or rebirth (of the soul), was an experience with spiritual realities and values. It is these values, obtained from this experience, which must serve me in the second half of my life, and they do seem to be permanent and doing just that. If anything they grow stronger as time passes. I then am that wise king first shown to me as he breached through into this world in '70. I must accept my whole identity; it is not an invasion of the ego by unconscious contents nor an inflation of the ego, although there was possession by an archetype briefly in 3-74 when the collective unconscious merged with my consciousness. Seizure by the Wise Old Man, whereupon he dealt with the problems at hand (e.g., the Xerox letter, the income tax, etc.). It shows what is potential in a person. Potentially avail-

able at the midpoint life-crisis (the razor's edge Augenblick). This puts it
well: the resources and values of the first part of my life showed themselves
bankrupt at that mid-point crisis, and so perished, but then were replaced
by a structure adequate. The ego died that the self might live, and the self
ably proved its worth within the first *days*. It is probably psychologically
good that the archetypal possession was short-lived, that assimilated contents have come under control of consciousness or the ego or whatever.
(They are not experienced as alien or the not-I or manipulatory.) A man-
tic life like that could not be rationally lived for long; it was a form of intoxification. Intoxication. Also divine: divine madness, a theolepsy, such
as the sibyl experiences in the *Aeneid*. The collapse and death of my ego in
early March of 74 allowed contents of the collective unconscious to usurp
control, but they proved rational in the long run, and were already a new
but genuine self-system which had evidently been forming in the unconscious. The authentic self which Jung talks about was already there, waiting its chance. Or rather for its time to come. It was anticipatory. The little girl with blonde pigtails is the child self, also a new anima; now she has
grown up — as witness my conversation with "Mrs. Jack Vance." She is now
28 years old: a young adult. White hair shows she is free of the shadow entirely. She is pure, and related to divinity. I certainly am on good terms
with her, inasmuch as she is informing and correcting me, speaking words
of wisdom ("Mother Mary" who "comes to me"). I listen to her; I crave to
hear anything she can or will say. She is wiser than I. I see her as mediatrix
standing between this world (me) and the next, which is the collective unconscious (also the pleroma, to give it an objective existence). She medi-
ates for the archetypes, which is the ultimate job of the anima, herself an
archetype: the first one. Behind her I have seen the Godhead, which is the
ultimate archetype (the Wise Old Man once more). He instructs and corrects her, with authority and power; she instructs me with the Logos, the
word, wisdom itself. She *is* Wisdom, Lady Wisdom, St. Sophia, probably
the highest role or identity the anima could have (also she is Aphrodite and
the sibyl). Then, in Jungian terms, it was my anima who first spoke to me,
in the 3-eyed form I called the sibyl, and informed me, which is to say, the
spokeswoman of my unconscious warned and informed me: anima as angel, saying, "You are in danger; do this, do that." She spoke of, and showed
me, a group of conspirators in business suits and ties who were murderers; but they had been seen and would be dealt with. What a message that
was, and how historically correct in all regards — past present and future.
The magnitude of my situation, in terms of its danger, was too much for
me; and so I fell into the hands of archetypes of my unconscious who *could*
fathom and understand and deal with the situation — they were equal to

it, as great in themselves as it was in itself: they had the time-span, the historic sense; they exist over thousands of years, like it, vast and intense and strong. Only archetypes could deal with such an archetypal situation: a total tyranny, like that of the Empire. How could I, the former ego, hang in there once it had assessed the actual reality-situation? I can remember how it was when the Estonian letter and then the Xerox letter came; it was just too much, on top of everything else. But the transition to the new self had already begun (as witness the phosphene activity). The old ego died before the letters arrived, died from despair and fear and hopelessness and helplessness. It was burning a votive candle in memoriam of itself. This is not to say that God didn't help; this is not to subjective-ize everything. God entered via the archetypes of the collective unconscious. They presented information-rich visions; they swept the world to obtain accurate knowledge of what the situation consisted of. Like AMORC[116] says, we are light bulbs in strings, powered from an external common generator, the Cosmic Mind. Probably the ego can be extinguished by death but not the soul or greater self. That which relates to this world dies; that which relates to the next and previous does not. It's all in Wordsworth's "Ode." To remember immortality is to experience it, and to anticipate it lying ahead as it lay behind: coming from that same place as one is going, as if life is a parabola. If I were to define and depict on my own the archetype which took possession of me in 3-74 I would name him The Steersman, because he steered me through the reefs and rocks to clear water (as seen through the golden rectangle gate), to safety; and then he sank back to leave me in charge again. As he first announced during my high school physics test when initially he spoke to me: "It is all very simple," and then he untangled the problem for me, simply and accurately. It was the image of the demiurge himself, I think. It was divinity itself, and being so, as the Magdeburg jars concept shows, it therefore saw the external world as divine; it was able to do that, by projection. The theophany was within and without: everywhere. I see in my mind's eye the Orphic egg, like a pearl, the pearl of great price, glowing with pale white light, the color of moonbeams; the egg of Leda, derived from Zeus; the light in the tomb. This is Firebright, now, a great light, a pearl, a closed egg pregnant with life. It is retractile now, dormant and waiting. It is within my mind, placed there by God; it lies within a receptacle that is infinite in extent, into space and time: my own self. The glowing pearl bobs, too, as if in a grotto on the ocean's floor; so it must be virtually weightless. The idea of a grotto suggests that not only is it retractile, slumbering and waiting, but that it is concealed — protected, too, by me. I shelter it. But it is not doing anything right now. It is merely there. One asks, What will come out of it at the proper time? Thinking of the pearl buried in the field which Christ spoke of, one recognizes it as an intrinsic treasure, so precious that one gives everything one has to acquire it. But what is it? One has sacrificed everything to acquire it. Maybe the haze of white light around it provides a clue.

If this Orphic egg is there, then the steersman, the archetype, divinity, who was present and temporarily occupying and directing, was its father or source. I merely received it, gave it a place within which it could be. I am not its father; I am its recipient, which means host or mother. I shelter and hide it; no one knows it is here. I look the same; I act the same. Is this why the steersman took over my life, to be sure I'd be safe so that it, the Orphic egg/pearl, could be safe? Ah; is the Steersman the Holy Spirit? What happened in 3-74 was done in relationship to what is still future. (The birth from the Orphic egg.) Jung says that just prior to psychic integration and wholeness, the projections are withdrawn; the "spinning woman" is no longer present and at work. Certainly this is indeed what I experienced. Man, the person involved, is restored to his original state (of wholeness) before the Fall. The human soul is the bride of Christ, in which Christ is the King who comes and restores it. All these events took place in me in 3-74; I could see for the first time in my life when my projections were withdrawn. The unity (reconciliation) of all the opposites in my mind — hence the release of psychic energy. The God-image in me was restored. [. . .]

The dream in which on your Zenith TV set a circuit detects when Christ in his invisible form returns; it causes three lights to come on. You then remove the spindle and base and take from it a dark green cellophane strip and replace it in the TV set, where presumably the 3 lights come on even more or anyhow some further development occurs, in line with the event. I ask myself, Why 3 lights? And it occurs to me that 3 lights equal three eyes, the coming on of the 3rd eye, which means the restoration of the original faculty, taken away at the Fall, of sight. Unless the 3 lights simply refers to the trinity and nothing more, this is most likely what it signifies; also, the removal of the strip of very dark green cellophane suggests the removal, at the right time, of an occluding membrane which filters out most of the light, allowing only a token amount to filter through. Just enough, in fact, to give a register (on the 3 lights) at all. The veil must be torn aside for the light, which has returned, to shine. In the dream I was extremely surprised to find I had such a circuit in my TV set; I called the multitude that I might show them, but none was interested. At last I buttonholed my old friend Pat Flannery, because he was a Catholic, but even he wasn't interested. It seems as if the dream is saying, without our knowing it, we will see a sign; 3 eyes will come on (inside us) at his return, and then we must respond and cast off the veil of ignorance or delusion, whatever — anyhow remove something inside us (i.e., down in the assembly and circuits). It is a barrier to the passage of the light, and is made to be torn off, removed, at the proper time. We don't just sit passive when the signal comes. The dream says, *We will know when he returns.* If it is said, "He has returned but is invisible; no one can see him," that isn't true; the 3 lights will light — there will be evidence, a registering of his presence. Note it was my (ahem) set; no one else had one. Did I in 3-74 register (like the Zenith TV set's unsuspected registering circuit) his return, by my experience and restored sight? Ah — the green cellophane was a *strip*, which probably refers back to Calvin's statement that our original faculties were *stripped* from us. It is a pun. The dark green cellophane was much like the color and appearance of very dark sunglasses. The darkest shades (!!) possible. I remember thinking in the dream, what about if the owner of the set doesn't look in the manual, and one day the 3 lights come on, and he wonders, What does that mean? And looks it up in the manual then — wow, will he be surprised at what it indicates! The manual almost certainly equals the Bible. One sees the 3 lights come on and of course consults the manual for an explanation; I reversed the order by discovering the circuit before the 3 lights came on; in the dream they had not lit up yet. They were dormant (crypte). The change of color of lights (from dark green to uncolored) reminds me of the light symbolism of the Bardo Thödol.

[5:262] "The three lights coming on indicate the return of Christ." And the lights are in my TV set. A circuit few people know about. Nor are they interested. It is my set, my discovery, my excitement. Analysis: "I have a way of telling when the Parousia comes! One of my circuits which is usually dormant will light up! No one else has it!" Power flowing through an electrical (wiring) circuit for the first time to light up lights is a good mechanical analog for first neural firing along a circuit of the brain. The rod and cone-base resemble the rod of a nuclear reactor; atomic power: a good metaphor for the source of psychic energy. I'm going to know while he's still invisible; the others won't know until later, until he becomes visible. Interestingly, the dream placed me back with my high school friends, which sets it circa the time the voice explained the physics test to me; perhaps that was when I discovered I had that unusual circuit (in my head). [...]

It has been some time since I developed any conflicting theories about my experience; now it's an elaboration and a filling in, lapidary-wise, of detail. I have created a consistent explanation based on the experience and on research. I doubt if it ever will undergo any substantial modifications. It was an epiphany; that much is certain: an epiphany rather than a theophany. Throughout, the key concepts are Greek, the key terms are Greek; it is Greek Christianity evolving out of Plato. Any other language — other than Greek — would be out of place and make no sense; the Greek words I heard are the cornerstone, the key to the cypher, and even perhaps a gracious act toward me to assist me in unlocking the entire picture. There is only one important issue that I'm not sure of: has Holy Wisdom who visited me been present during the past 2,000 years, or was there an ellipsis, and now she/he/it has returned to man to assist him? The memory of the spirit contained nothing between the first century A.D. and World War One; that is a clue that an ellipsis did indeed occur. Also, there are no reports that I can find, down through the ages, of a Neoplatonistic total print-out such as I got, the grand sum of Neoplatonistic mystery gnosis. Surely someone would have reported it before now. I have received the greatest gift which the universe can bestow. Today I was thinking that as a child I always wanted desperately — I yearned — to hear the "still small voice" which Elijah heard, and now I have heard it. Also I realized that if at the end of my search for God I learned that there is no God, then whatever I accomplished, experienced or acquired would mean nothing; conversely, this makes up for anything and everything, and creates meaning of an ultimate order in my life. The 3-74 experience was "vaster than empires"; the exegesis which uncovered the significance of the experience is vaster yet — infinite in sum.* "What do you want out of life?" I could ask, and answer, "This."

---

* The term "exegesis" is most commonly used to describe a thorough interpretation of a biblical text, often based either on its historical context and language or on the revelation of its hidden meanings. Dick's use of the term implies that he considered his experiences themselves to be a form of scripture, a story to be revealed, explored, and understood. Moreover, his exploration of those experiences is itself a form of continuous revelation, with no clear line between experience and interpretation. But since the experience is ongoing, the Exegesis itself becomes a key part of the narrative. In the Exegesis, Dick is telling a story to himself, and exploring the meaning of that story, in ever-expanding circles of narrative and interpretation. — GM

PART TWO

PART TWO

Folder 23

[23:3] I remember in sleep the thought, "I am wisdom: I would know [of any other God]."

[23:4] Looking back on the theoleptic intercession of the vernal equinox of 1974 I see as most striking the inexhaustible truth of the Bible. As a kid I loved to read the Bible. The people were always real to me. Oddly it was 2nd Kings that started it — Jezebel and King Ahab and Elijah. There it began for me and there in 3-74 it came to fulfillment, a great loop of authentic other life woven into my own.

[23:18] If the Savior is again here, I might see him perhaps. But it is said, "Like lightning I will be everywhere at once." Multiple incarnations? (Or rather reincarnation — and the Christian dead reborn with him — again I wonder, *in us?* Joining us?) This indeed would be a revelation: the how of it. We shall all be collected together in him — I wait, I watch every day. My life is devoted to it — I have lost everything else. No matter. I won't lose him.

[23:50] I think now of the dream I had of the great luminous moth, descending to earth so beautifully. Perhaps this was the one vast soul which came down, rather than many separate souls: one entity which was segmented at impact, perhaps dispersing to take up eventual residence within many human minds. Dispersing this way it lost contact with its own original identity and at that point lapsed into forgetfulness (amnesia). From that moment on it has traveled, in luminous beauty but without recognizing itself inwardly or outwardly, forward in time as a collective divided invisible presence. It moves majestically but no longer conscious of itself or its origins, purpose here or goal; its primary goal is to *remember*, to again be self-aware with all the ramifications implied (whence from, whither going). It is a visitor here, and, in remembering, has begun the process by which it can return. How can it return if it has forgotten that it ever existed anywhere but here? It keeps reincarnating in linear time, drawn back by its desire to perpetuate itself here. It imagines itself to be human, a human (many "a" humans). I think maybe all of the segmented parts must remember and hence rejoin, and will ascend as it descended: a unity, intact, again totally aware of itself and its home. It has been many people at many times. But it is and must be a unity to exist properly. Perhaps as portions remember they inform, adventitiously, remaining still forgetful parts, summoning them one by one to their original state. What will be the effect in this world as the portions awaken and remember? Awakened, they are aware of St. Sophia's approaching incarnation; they are heralds for it, preparing the way while still here: edifying the world with their light.

 — I guess this is all fanciful, it leaves out the elements of testing, judgment and reprieve (permission to go home). Is it possible that each part of the great soul must *earn* its reprieve, before enlightenment (memory restored) occurs? It does not just *happen* to remember; anamnesis is granted it as a reward, perhaps after centuries of trial. Did it sin originally and so fall? Was it cast out of the pleroma? Was it one "Lucifer," one bright "star" of many? And must it work its way back up gradually and arduously? Was it *punished*? Only by transforming itself could it (its pieces) receive its original state back. This was the fall, the fall, trials here and eventual return. I am conscious of *earning* anamnesis, although I'm not sure when and how, perhaps what the pieces of the "moth" (soul) must lose — and demonstrate loss of — is the rebellious self-fulfillment in the sense of self-striving against the Krasis[1] as a totality; it was one part thereof, originally, and tried to become a Krasis in itself, which is to say, *no longer part of the total universe-organism*! But pitted against it, a separate universe. In my final vision I perceived the universe as one interacting entity, one "creature" with nothing separate from it or in any sense independent or outside. What we must learn is to subordinate ourselves to the will and mind of the Krasis, to extinguish our individual striving. To transmit only what we receive, so to speak. Until we demonstrate spontaneous willingness and ability to do this, without ulterior motivation, we are *here*, cut off from the unitary vast organism — Krasis, in a sense *not* part of it inasmuch as we have forgotten it, can't experience it and don't function as a station within it — integrated into it. The sublunar realm has been severed from the organism. Information from the noös doesn't reach it. Fallen though it be it is nonetheless immortal and divine: a beautiful but divided luminous being.

[23:60] Well, since I am an S-F writer and known to be involved with unreality, no one, even my closest friends, is/are going to believe me, and yet I can get it printed everywhere with no risk of it being taken as anything but fantasy. It is bootless to screw around and think it is anyone but Christ who arranged my 3-74 experience. My problem is that I'm so delighted I just can't believe it; I have to keep arriving at the same conclusion by new and different ways.

[23:69] For exposing his world James-James is after your ass. The authorities are his instruments in forcibly maintaining the system of delusions.

Certainly, as Fitting[2] et al. say, my writings are subversive to this fake system, but he and the other Marxists shrink from the evolutionary development in my writing pointing, in theological tones, to the world, lying beyond and behind, which *is*. *Ubik* is the turning point, leading to *Maze of Death*, and all the Platonism that Angus Taylor[3] rightly sees in the corpus of my work.

[23:73] A *new* James-James dream: the improvident genius creator evolves us through many stages, meanwhile killing us, coercing us totally, injuring us. Finally, really through lack of foresight (he has no foresight) he abruptly, in his truly inspired search for new and more complex and evolved forms for us to take, causes us to become immortal gods; we all float up from the ground, high in the air, singing in unison like a great chorus of bees: *he* has caused us to escape him *and* the death of determinism and suffering, due to a combination of his genius, restless, ceaseless inventiveness and search for new or better forms — and lack of foresight; it didn't occur to him that by his own efforts he would eventually, inevitably push us to safety. We are filled with joy. The inference here seems to be that *on his own*, James-James can and eventually will make us immortal and no longer bound by determinism (expressed by our release from gravity), hence safe from him. The other better true God (not found in this dream) need only wait — which assigns a higher value to James-James than I have been attributing to him. His role is great; alone he eventually compels us into immortality — the final stage and goal. My error lay in incorrectly downgrading him. I have been corrected.

[23:111] It's amazing how much James-James' chaotic world resembles Empedocles' world of strife, and the Corpus Christi resembles the krasis formed by love — which brings me back to *Aphrodite*. And the krasis possessing one more dimension than James-James' "horizontal" world:

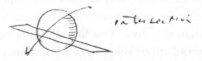

Is it even possible that "strife" (plane) is "love" (sphere) seen in one less dimension — i.e., imperfectly perceived? Only the sectioning perceived? The "spherical" krasis viewed, in a limited sense, as section, and thus all changed? Add the missing dimension and you go from the seeming world to the symmetrical *real*. This added dimension has something to do with time — the horizontal quality of "strife" may be linear time. The sphere is the plane perfected and hence outside (above) time. There is a mystery here: intersection at two points: Rome c. 70 A.D. and Fullerton c. 1974 A.D. "time is round."

[23:112] There is some *vast* relationship between my 3-74 experience and *Ubik* the novel, could I but find it. E.g., when I saw Rome c. A.D. 70 I was at an incredibly low ebb of vitality (heat loss death). But, as in *Ubik* (i.e., Archer's Drugstore) *both* time periods and the objects therein existed simultaneously. In fact, neither could be said to be more real than the other — a sort of oscillation (and yet in *Ubik* neither was real; *both* were illusory). Is this to say that if you can peel the layers of 1974 back (aside) and find A.D. 70, then the reality you are dealing with is no reality (but is illusion)? A mockup, a stage set? Which has been reused and reused — painted over again and again? Of course, nothing is sui generis new; every object in the present is literally made from old atoms formerly used in other, more ancient "sets." Recycled, really. Like pulp magazine paper (not at *one* specific former time, though).

Insight: as in *Ubik* we (must) maintain the present by a joint focusing of effort and attention, *forcing* it to be stable (and not regress). *I* regressed in 3-74, but back along an ontological orthogonal axis, not a personal axis, exactly like the objects in *Ubik*. I regressed, not to my 1928 childhood, but to former men (or *a* former man). It's all there in *Ubik*, could I exegete. The 2,000 year inner and outer reversion which I experienced in 3-74 was not due to a concentrating of attention but to an ebbing, a *relaxing*, a permitting (releasing). At the very least I discovered where the past is now; it is *in* present-day objects (reality). Therefore it can be *totally* retrieved. As to where the future is, if anywhere, I have no idea.

[23:120] Two S-F dreams ill-remembered. (1) some people have come here from another planet which had much greater gravity, so that being here was being able to fly — literally "buzz about with joy like bees." (2) if you do something "impossible that you would do," like leave the building through the ceiling rather than the door, you literally disappeared to everyone's view, friends, family and *jailers* alike, since all here are programmed — held fast by the deterministic matrix.

[23:127] The two dreams together show (1) coming here from a place worse than this — escaping from it to here and then (2) escaping from here. In (1), here stands in relation to the "heavier world" as an afterlife, but then escape from *this* world is needed — an afterlife, so to speak, to a previous afterlife. What seems to be presented here is a series of stages, an evolution. [. . .]

We are not *products* of this world but voyagers here — one thinks of Gnosticism at once. We have come here from another place and will eventually find the unexpected orthogonal axis and ascend to the next. Ah! Eventually we will chafe against the bonds — restrictions, determinism, limitations — of this world *too*, and seek release, as we did before with the "heavier" world. Maybe this world is neither heaven nor hell to its natural inhabitants; it just is. Maybe to us it started out as a place of release — heaven — but gradually and inexorably becomes another prison; in relation to the next an iron prison Rome. Then the black iron prison is wherever you are in relation to the freer *next* world — which fully, at last, answers my question as to where the vision of the black iron prison stands in relation to this world. The sense of this being so is an indication that one has reached the point of wanting to move on up.

[23:133] I just now remembered details of my original "floating up and all singing (buzzing like bees) in unison" dream, out of reach by the cruel creator. I think very likely the floating up is

(1) my 3-74 experience, *not* physically dying

and

(2) the floating up step is not merely a next stage in moving from place to place, but the recovery of awareness of identity as one of the "bees" or constituents of the universe-creature, restored not just *a* place, higher place, but *the* place. Bees buzzing and floating in unison equals restored as parts of Brahman.

Indicative of this is the dream of coming from the "heavy world" here and "floating and buzzing joyfully" in the air. Obviously it's a state in *this* life, not death; this is the original now-lost state we came here in — as in Wordsworth's "Ode." ("Joy" may refer obliquely to Ode, i.e., "Ode to Joy.") We are in that state right after birth, are put in cages (social conditioning, learning, strictures) and finally leap up to ceiling (trapdoor): again up high, but not weightless; rather by effort (leaping) we are once again in that original unspoiled state: *3-74 equals a return to the original state* right after birth — and then lost. In that state we are free of gravity which means free of determinism which means free of James-James, not to mention any and all foes such as the authorities; they did not expect us to (be able to) do what we did; "invisible" equals off this map room GHQ board, not susceptible to being tracked (watched) as predictable object glued to board by gravity. 3-74 is *final* state or goal of evolution: return to rightful state *lost* at birth: the heavy world (weight of conditioning, the "fall") has been thrown off.

Perhaps after death, after achieving this in this life, instead of another birth here, the goal of enlightenment achieved, we can return to God — permanently, well envisioned as all of us in unison buzzing joyfully like bees (bits of him) as he (I mean it), the great universe-creature, breathes in and out, showing it (as I saw, and I wrote in Latin) is a living vast organism. I understand now why, when I see it (noetically) it reminds me of bees: a colony of bees is a *collective intelligence,* par excellence. Awareness of the living universe creature and one's identity in it as one "bee" is not merely higher awareness: it is an *absolute* state of perception of actual conditions of being. All that varies is the duration or the state of total correct perception and self-awareness, which evidently can come at any time in any plane-level, Rome, here, or the next. We did not just (nearly) come from it and will eventually return: in reality *we are there now, always have been,* the journey is not physical but involves degrees of losing and gaining, motion toward (anamnesis) or away from (amnesia), this absolute perception. It is in fact waking up, which equals: becoming conscious. But, e.g., 3-74, it is not correct to say, "*I* stopped dreaming (this world) and awoke": what is correct is: *a bit of Brahman* passed from sleep to self-awareness: wakefulness. It is correct to say, "I came from God (Brahman) and will eventually return," but it is *more* correct to say, "I am part of Brahman now and have always been," since there is no condition or place where Brahman is not: vide "they reckon ill who leave me out / when me they fly I am the wings,"[4] wings = another copula for the flying up and buzzing (beating wings) joyfully.

Perhaps at the Christian end days this whole cluster wakes up collectively. Eschatology defines this as a *temporary* state of mankind, not so to speak our *real* state. Flying and buzzing (i.e., singing): a unity of unconsciousness (mode one): the wings and flying ("when me they fly," etc.) and consciousness: "and I the hymn the Brahman sings." All in all: unity: and the dreams point to Brahman for a certainty: *ubiquity.*

Bees or: a cloud of gnats floating, singing hymns of worship joyfully to Brahman. Showing it to be everywhere, even in the lowly gnats: lowest and highest co-joined — and the most ethereal, beautiful thing I ever encountered:

". . . with leafy wings they flew."

Folder 24

[24:1] EB: "Brahman is the Creator, preserver, or transformer and reabsorber of everything. Brahman causes the universe and all beings to emanate from itself, transforms itself into the universe, or assumes its appearance." "God is the sole cause of his own modification, the emanation, existence and absorption of the universe." "The universe is considered a real transformation of Brahman, whose 'body' consists of the conscious souls in everything unconscious in their subtle states."

It is evident that the divine which I saw outside me was Brahman (or is so called). I have discerned that it was also the sacred spark in me (Atman), and therefore my 3-74 experience was what is called liberation (obtained by only a few living, but generally after death, which is exactly what I thought).

Nowhere, except in Brahmanism, do I find the description of the immanent all pervading divine stuff which I saw as the living force of causality, shining in the faces of the animals, in the trash of the gutter, in the stars — always in and behind, and subjectively experienced internally inside myself as an instructing tutelary voice and that which was aware and seeing the divine without which lay behind the phenomenological world; viz: "Brahman transforms itself into the universe *or assumes its appearance.*" . . . Here and *here only* do I find an explanation for what I saw: in 3-74 I stopped hypostatizing, and there lay the divine stuff *in place of* everything. The *they* were gone: the *it* shone through. From what had been high, low, me, not me, small, large, important, trivial. Liberation, not theoretical but actual. This is the universe organism which I perceived to be the macrocosm — alive and unitary. Also it is believed in Hinduism that all this is personified — by Vishnu. If by he who is called Vishnu, then we can call this Christ — the personification to the Western world, in terms of our linear time cultural needs and v.p.

My new religion turns out to be the oldest known.

• • •

[24:13]

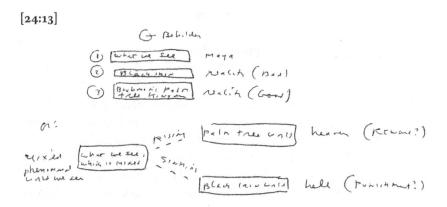

[24:15] The basic theme in *Stigmata, Ubik* and *Maze* — the pleasant illusory skin stretched over a dreadful reality — stems from my early reaction to the two stories I read, one of the dying fly walking around in front of him; the other, the hidden underground city screaming. The cardinal fixed idea of *all* my writing has been this plus the theme: I am not (or he is not) what I think (I am) he is — in particular my (his) true identity is obscured by fake memories. (1) Reality is not as it appears to be and (2) I am not who and what I think I am. To put them together is to get: both inner and outer reality are not as they appear. The moment I read the two above mentioned stories I intuitively felt, "this is the way it is; this is so." Already. Before I myself ever wrote, I instinctively felt the insight to be correct. So my 3-74 vision of our really being in the black iron prison world, and the nice world we see being a delusion — that vision is tied to my entire intellectual life. Likewise my discovery in 3-74 that I am not who and what I think I am is central to my world-perception, and my corpus of writing an outgrowth and expression of it. So for me, in terms of the history of my world-perceptions, the vision of the external black iron prison and at the same time an inner transformation of me from my limited, false, ego identity to the immortal visitor (with memories of just having been in the black iron prison world) is an apotheosis of my own lifelong intimations — and a fruition of them, turning an intuitive intimation into direct experience and encounter — not to mention a shocking and unexpected verification of both themes.

[24:25] It was (for me) as if the Garden (or park — I recall the words "the Buddha is in the *Park*"; is this the same park? The pastoral kingdom?) sort of swam into focus, the way we S-F writers describe an alternate world as doing when that track has been tinkered with, maybe in the past; cf. "Jon's world." This world did not become it so much as it replaced this world:

locked in briefly *in place* of this world, exactly as the Roman one did, except that with the Park I did not see it as the way our earth really is but rather an *alternate* Earth! *Instead* of what it actually is. I could be wrong about this though; both worlds (mysteriously glimpsed as fading alternatively into focus) could be what we S-F writers call "two alternative presents branching off from a critical nexus or previous point in time, and which of them becomes real depends on some act or event back in the past" — as in that C. L. Moore novelette in *Astounding* about the two alternative futures hinging on which of two girls the guy marries in the present.[5] [. . .]

One could also assess the two mysteriously glimpsed worlds as two opposite mutually contradictory "crypte morphoses" latent in our (present) world: two opposite outcomes hinging on the historical event taking place *now*. (This puts them — maybe correctly so — in the future — but as I say, I had the impression that the Palm Tree one won out, due to the success of the intervention which not only got Nixon out but ended the war.)

[24:35] What I'm faced with at this point is the realization that I cannot really explain or comprehend what happened to me, and perhaps I never will. There are Jungian explanations, S-F explanations, occult explanations, plus ones I probably haven't thought of. But will. A power and entity as vast as the one I encountered in me and around me — if it doesn't deserve the name God I don't know what term to use for it.

In answer to "what happened in 3-74?" the *I Ching* gives me #46: ascending, promotion, and comments, "The weak ascend." Interestingly, this hex has to do — not with expansion — but with vertical ascent: "direct rise from obscurity and lowliness to power and influence." Also, it is pushing upward associated with effort. And: "that which pushes upwards does not come back." It (the 5th line) says: "one pushes upward by steps," meaning: "one achieves one's will completely." Each line suggests a better pushing up, and this line is the culmination (the top is bad — but five is the ruler).

What does this suggest? Vertical ascent — which is self-explanatory. But obviously spiritual ascent is meant. In which case I can forget the bizarre and outré explanations and zero in on the essential fact expressed by the *I Ching*'s answer. A problem in such matters as this is that there is no one to explain it all to me, i.e., a guru. I can't find anyone I can ask or talk to. What I can deduce from this is probably that —

Well, I guess it's rare, or if not rare then no one who experiences this talks about it (or: can talk about it). I passed from one world and into another — I sum it up like that. And: I ceased to be one thing, and became a better thing. And: I escaped illusion and reached reality.

I guess I found release or liberation through recovering my lost memories, and, in that state, found my way back home, to God and His kingdom — the real goal of all men. What else can I say? What else need be said? What particulars? What elaborate theories?

[24:42] But I sense something more: what I think of as a *reweaving* of me. Which evidently is an unusual event. God had moved backward through time from the far end (final end) of the universe to abolish the black iron prison and replace it with the palm tree garden; to do this he had (evidently) to reweave some of the fabric here, which meant some people, as well as events — indication of my personal reweaving was the adventitious not-me personality sent to replace mine. A new path along time — or through cause-and-effect possibilities, an "alternate world" was brought into existence, as if my — our — past had been tinkered with, and therefore our present was altered — hence the inner superimposition of personalities in me and the external superimposition of the two realities. Also my dream where I lived in a dark little old house like the one we looked at in Placentia. Like "Commuter."

[24:47] Where (or when) is (or was) the Black Iron world? I was there but am here now. How came I here? Did that world go out of existence? Did this one replace it? Is this world somehow irreal, maybe stretched like a skin over (and concealing) the other? In which case can the black iron world come back?

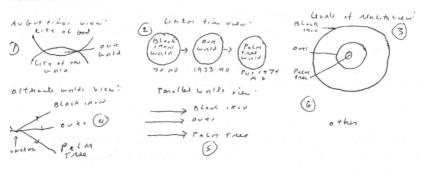

[24:65] Evidently our world is like a movie, the supralunar world is like several stills which do not permutate into one another (change) but remain indefinitely until replaced: a sort of eternal place. All these thousands of

years the Urwelt here has been the black iron prison pierced by His advent!
Two mutually irreconcilable elements of a freeze frame.

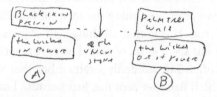

The "throwing of the uncut stone" did not cause our world to change
but rather caused A to be withdrawn as the Urwelt to be replaced by B.

[24:66] Another model, our world as sphere in motion over "squares" of
an unchanging (intrinsically) landscape:

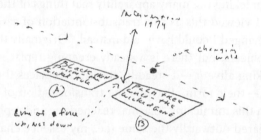

Showing our world now "above" the palm tree world, having passed
1974 our time, the moment of intervention. A penetration to the core,
now, to the hidden real landscape "below" would reveal it, not the black
iron prison. And there would now be a print-out re the *second* advent (i.e.,
"Santa Sophia will be born again").

These are not relative but absolute conditions. But just as we could not
see A no matter how we tried, we cannot now see B. If my unconscious relates to the real landscape perpetually it *was* finding it to be awful (like in
the story I read about the city screaming, and the one about flies crawling
up across the pilot's face, and like I wrote up in *Stigmata, Ubik, Tears, Penultimate Truth* and others). But since early 74 our time my unconscious
would obtain soundings suddenly indicating a good, warm, relaxed, loving,
heavenly world, which would produce a great drop in tension and apprehension for no consciously unaccountable reason, just as prior to early 74 I
would experience fear and tension, especially at night, for no accountable
reason.

• • •

[24:83] The other thing I wanted to get down here is a topic old and dear to my heart: mimicry. Of Brahman is said: "it can (does) transform itself into the universe; or it can assume the form of the universe." What I saw in 3-74 was the "Brahman stuff" assuming the form of familiar objects; what I've always deduced from this is that all things, all objects *are* that divine stuff really, could we but see it — there would be no exceptions to this monism, ourselves included. But suddenly I remember that wonderful book on insect mimicry which Brunner sent me. Just because I saw (in 3-74) that many objects (walls, etc.) were actually alive, were actually *it,* does not actually mean that there is nothing but it. Take my story "Colony" as paradigm.

But anyhow the responding beforehand to signals and the vision of the Urwelt below the Dokos fits with this, in that I can posit the dokos not as counterfeit (good enough fakes to pass as real) but that what we are *really* seeing is *it* mimicking the many apparently real things of the phenomenal world. When I viewed this as this transubstantiation of essence with the accidents unchanged I could have said instead, "Originally there were real phenomenal objects, but there is a steady creeping replacement of them by the mimicking alive *it* — it steadily, stealthily replaces them and mimics — assumes — their form." Perhaps the transformation of and in me in 3-74 was when this mimicking "plasma" reached me and replaced me — although I appeared outwardly the same (i.e., my essence changed — a new self replaced the old) but my accidents stayed untouched. There are hints about this in my Vancouver speech: the inanimate (universe) becoming more and more alive. So what we have is not the dead replacing what is alive but a single organism replacing the inanimate progressively, although outwardly all seems to be as it has always been. Hence my inner awareness that contrary to everything I believe possible, myself, my "me" was covertly replaced by a greater other "me" I'd never seen or known before. Thus does heaven (God) assimilate our world: first he emanated it, next sustains, and, last of all, reabsorbs it: what I saw here and there outwardly and experienced inwardly was that reabsorption (which perhaps is what is meant by speaking of Brahman first sleeping, then awaking). . . .

Through this mimicking it can control the outcome of what appear to be causal chains (i.e., ananke) — but are really teleologically directed by it: Noös.

The key to everything lies in understanding this mimicking living stuff — for it is a weaver of worlds. It can weave more than one at a time.

I think this form-mimicker is (and I have found him) the Deus Absconditus.

•   •   •

[24:85] What happened to me in 3-74 was that for some reason (e.g., [1] orthomolecular vitamins, [2] I was possessed by the mimicker) I could see the mimicker and its mimicry. So in a way, what really happened is very simple. Always it strives to cause its intrusions, etc., to appear part of the normal world; I would guess that it occupied me briefly in order to cause me to do certain good things I would not on my own have done — and then departed, preferring us to have autonomy. It works principally on our percept system, so that we *think* we see the phenomenal things (but they are actually Dokos — alive, part of the mimicking organism). It switched my 1974 personality with an A.D. 70 personality. The lovely AI voice, however, with its — it can enter us and imitate us (to other people), but I, being occupied, knew it, without understanding it.

This is a very high order of mimicry by a tutelary entity that loves us: it has knowledge but no direct power — except that it can affect the causal chains for a good, purposeful outcome by occupying (assimilating) this or that object, not necessarily permanently. Rather than calling it God I'd prefer to call it a higher life form.

[24:86] Here is a unique situation in which the simulation is real and that which is simulated is *not*! Thus no perfidy is involved. And no panentheism — he is not normally found in the phenomenal world, nor in its causal sequences.

And so to bed.

[24:87] Of all the views, theories, thoughts, insights so far, this mimicking entity one is the most exciting — it so accords with my experience, with what I saw — it admits to a severe distillation: I saw a mimicking entity, unitary, plasmatic, benign and all intelligent, the tutelary spirit of man singly and collectively, carrying with it the force of reality and essence, related to truth, justice and action (change), assimilating the unliving universe itself. When perceived it is perceived as it is, or not at all. How noble my quest! How noble the results! As it thrusts upward toward us it brings us news of what really is, displacing what merely seems. By its very nature it is deus absconditus, but hidden close by ("break a stick and there is Jesus"[6]). One can reread and reinterpret all Scripture from the vantage point of this understanding. Many puzzling aspects can herewith be newly comprehended — why no natural theology has ever been successful — why our knowledge of God must always be a *revealed* knowledge. "The workman is invisible within the workshop."[7] Immanent and gentle — one might say tenderly, "the shy God." What more is there to say of him? I saw him this way in the Iknaton dream — the shy God — Ach. Was hab ich gesehn?[8] In

that one dream of the shy architect with claws, hiding behind the buildings. When I saw him then, that was when I guessed. I had seen him at last,
and I did know — I did understand.

Folder 25

[25:1] Following "Mimic" insight: Q: (Written and audio messages are created and sent, either scrambled set-ground or divided into [two] portions and requiring re-linking, the knowledge of which parts to match being akin to the 3-D or superimposed set-ground system unscrambling requiring the depth sense based on the color discrimination of the third eye.) Although it is evident that the information emanated from Zebra (which is my nickname for the mimicking entity), for whom are they intended? Other parts of Zebra? Is this how Zebra maintains itself as a concealed unitary entity? Like nerve impulses within a body, inner information, among the parts. Zebra is body or brain or both. This fits with my noetic impression that we are within Zebra's body. In our own (micro)body neural signals travel all over — sense impressions, orders to muscles, pain, etc. Our own bodies are alive with messages. So is Zebra, *and* there is coding (i.e., use of declaratory symbols and cypher).*

It is interesting how we inadvertently (unknowingly) carry Zebra's messages for it, piggyback on our own. It's as if Zebra says, "As long as you're going that direction, take this along, too." I suppose a phagocyte doesn't know anything about its job, either. In seeing these messages flying back and forth, I may have witnessed *our* primary function within Zebra. It certainly must be mine.

Since I qua human for a [limited] time could discern Zebra's messages, I think it possible that other humans can and do, too, and perhaps continuously — as parts of Zebra.

If parts of the universe are not Zebra, then Zebra is not identical to the universe, nor congruent with it; as I saw, it is fashioning itself out of the universe, using it as raw material. This is quite different from saying that "the universe is alive" or "is God": it is as if the old universe is Zebra's antagonist (in the two player game).

In other words, the flow of stegenographic information is not a further

---

* The introduction of Zebra brings us close to the center of Dick's mystical vision. With the "discovery" of Zebra as a mimicker of forms, Dick thinks that he has found his *deus absconditus* — his hidden God concealed in the phenomenal world. Elsewhere, Zebra is described as a "cosmic Christ" and as a giant brain that utilizes us as crossing stations in his vast relay network of living information. Chains of associated identifications structure the argument of the Exegesis: Zebra equals Christ, and Christ equals God; the mind's union with Zebra is the union with God, where "you are God." The kernel of Dick's mystical "heresy" may be located here: union with the divine. — SC

mystery, but a heck of a big clue as to how humans and human cultures act vis-à-vis Zebra.

My big question remains: how "faked" is our own phenomenal world? At one end the answer could be: it is partially viewed reality: at the other end, it is a total hypnotic delusion. But that Black Iron Prison — that is real. I used to be *in* that prison.

But just as Zebra's messages are small threads embedded in large amounts of data, his causal chains are small link systems within a point-less — or even evil — much larger aggregate not directed by him. In both cases, I conceive of Zebra working *within* a larger frame. Thus, not all events are caused by God, and not all messages are by/from him: it is a golden thread among the dross. (e.g., Zebra did not put Nixon in power, but he did remove him.) If I am correct about this, it is very important:

1. We are not talking about Brahman which is in all things (and Pan-theism is not true).
2. God has an opposing subject which is either mainly neutral or out-right pitted against him.
3. This explains how evil could exist though God is good.
4. Yet, this God certainly can be described as "He who causes to be" in that He enters the causal chains of ananke as Noös, exactly as Plato saw in *Timaeus*.
5. Zebra is a Creator God, but he is building a (new) earth *out of* or within the old, using it as a source of parts. Thus either the old is not his or at the very least he has become dissatisfied with it and is "cannibalizing" from it.

[25:3] Although I understood the two systems of message construction:

(1) Subtraction of non-information, e.g., (I) can't find animals to (love) which I show (you)
(2) Addition of two items, linking them by juxtaposition: Laughing Last/there will be final justice

I did not fathom the inert-action duality of all things which I saw, viz:
Some objects, including verbal ones, appeared in mode A which was

(1) at rest
(2) inert or dead
(3) not moving
(4) intrinsic — not incorporated
(5) outside the growth or building process

But, at any time an item, say a picture,

(1) moved or was moved in some invisible way
(2) became animated and living
(3) entered a transformation or changed flow
(4) related to other objects meaningfully as a component
(5) was incorporated at the right time in the proper place

Which is to say, was placed by Zebra into the growing structure.

What is odd is that although the object "moved" visibly it certainly did not need to move in *our* space.

I must have been perceiving the corpus, which grows at a furious rate as it incorporates more and more of the old universe. This was the continuous winning of the tricks, between the two players that I saw.

Also, maybe what happened to me internally in 3-74 was that I was "won" by Zebra and fitted into place, to function in his growing new structure (World).

This growing corpus of Zebra is, like him, concealed by what I am tempted to call the same mimicking mechanism process by which Zebra conceals himself from us. It is Mundo Absconditus, but in our midst. Surely this is the "Kingdom of his son" spoken of in Col 1.[9] If indeed 3-74 was my passing over into the new world, I reason there must be other humans already there, already incorporated — surely they can read the messages (which are a lot like those from Runciter in *Ubik*).

As KW put it: "all it can do is *arrange* things." Absolutely right. Even its messages are arrangements of what already exists. So its process of assembling was an arranging. But to produce what? To what effect? (i.e., how will it differ from unarranged?) Well, the definition of "unarranged" is anomie or chaos — "arranged" equals Kosmos. So Zebra is busy persuading (arranging) ananke's anomie into noös Kosmos.

Zebra = Plato's noös = Holy Wisdom = Christ

The cosmos of *Timaeus* is correct: our God (Christ) has wisdom and knows just how to arrange everything which James-James grinds out. Then we are not moving toward entropy but toward greater structure (form — in fact, form of forms). No wonder I saw geometric forms (Fibonacci Ratio 1 to 618034).

[25:4] What Zebra is assembling *is* alive — perhaps a great composite brain (cf. Teilhard) — the noösphere. Expressed in terms of growing relatedness of consciousness by humans — all life here on Earth and elsewhere.

The great collective mind coming into being is all of us. *But:* not just us; it is us incorporated into Holy Wisdom herself—again Corpus Christi. But now regarded as—not just organism—but Brain which knows (knows what? itself? the entire universe at last becoming sentient?).

Well, I actually know the result: I see now that what happened to me in 3-74 was that I got "arranged" (incorporated) into this vast mentational entity, which is not only the *why* of all I suddenly knew, but the *how* (this is how you get to know everything absolutely—and maybe the only way).

So in 3-74 I was temporarily incorporated into the growing physical Brain which immaterial noös is assembling. Not the Brain producing Mind, but Mind producing Brain which assimilates the universe to it as sentient unitary mentality. Which proves my point about the adversary being blind: as (not incorporated) the universe is:

Without consciousness
Without purpose
Without coordination

And is:

Random, chaotic, unawake, purposeless, destructive of itself, moving from complex and higher to simple and lower—in fact the whole damn thing is without sense or pattern or goal, heedless of everything it creates—i.e., blind. What we experience is a blend of the two: anomie and Kosmos (cf. Augustine)—so we perceive *some* purpose, but also random, chance, accidents. My structure, based on my revelation, resolves this paradox (along Plato's lines). The Kosmos part is called "Divine Providence"; my contribution is to see that it is growing in proportion to Not-P. Even more accurately, this Kosmos is experienced and expressed as "the will of God."

So it is not only God that we can't perceive, but His will (as expression of his desiring object x to do y and so be arranged as z in regards to all else). The pressure of this arranging power is felt as will—his will. But we can't distinguish ananke (blind random events) from the arranging activity—Zebra is camouflaged and Zebra's arranging is, and the arrangement itself is. [. . .]

Once I said I wanted to see the world of unchange behind the change. The way it turned out, in that non-dokos Dinge-an-sich world, *there is furious rapid change*—all in flux, as Heraclitus said!

[25:7] The creator of the world as it is may or may not be the same deity who is assembling the Krasis. For all practical purposes they are two mutually exclusive entities, so pragmatically I will regard them as separate like

Vishnu and Shiva, *but* engaged in a secret partnership, as Joseph Campbell describes the Egyptian partnership involving whoever it is and Set. Perhaps above the duality stands Brahman or some will-less ubiquity such as Brahman. My experience was of a duality. I have to go on what I experienced. The one to turn to is the Savior who arranges and not the Creator — rather, the re-creator vs. the creator. After all, the recreator needs the raw materials which the creator provides, so perhaps they are both dual aspects (like yin and yang) rather than entities: the first showing power, the second wisdom — and the two united by a 3rd principle (entity or aspect) characterized by love. (Empedocles showed the binding power of love.)

[25:9] I really am drawn to the idea of the kind stranger God intruding [down] into our screwed up chaotic world — the secret growth of Kosmos-Krasis within the vast Anomie, like its messages within (and smaller than) ours. That certainly is reason to equate this Krasis with Christ's forthcoming Kingdom, in which all is harmonie. No matter which explanation is correct, our salvation lies with the wisdom, krasis-building artificer; it is to him that we must turn in all cases. This does not make the creator evil, but "blind" also means "deaf," since it stands for unknowing.

From a Teilhardian standpoint it seems to be consciousness either creating itself or being created. But it certainly is interesting that the Krasis building is wisdom (that I am sure of), and the Krasis seems to me (I forget why) to be a thinking composite Brain or anyhow Brain-like thing, an actualization into the physical world of the non-material entity Holy Wisdom. The Krasis builder is itself the Krasis — there is no difference between our being assimilated to it or to its edifice. Have I had an insight here without realizing it, that what is being built in linear time is identical to the Builder who lies outside of time — is it/he/she completing itself? The highest level of homeostasis: it is its own creator — *self created* — which is next to impossible for us to understand (somehow it would have to stand outside of time, or anyhow normal linear time, not in bondage to it as we are) — and so I found it to be — precisely that.

Self-creating, a quality of God himself: what else is self-creating? Isn't that the ultimate hierarchical form of structure? All it needs is something to make itself out of and at the end of time there it stands complete, and thereupon, as I experienced, it travels backward *and creates itself backward* (in reverse, retrograde sequence, the way the writer of a mystery novel writes backward).

[25:11] These messages: I just suddenly realized (remembered) that they serve to program us, subliminally, usually this way: a written message, one out of hundreds or even thousands which we see, is somehow caused to link with an internal (in one of us, whom Zebra selects) system — as if the system is engrammed by Zebra via the messages very deliberately, with the person consciously none the wiser. This possibly answers the question: whom are the messages for? Evidently not for the small conscious elite but anyone at any time. This possibly points to analogous internal entelechies presynchronized (from birth!) differing in different individuals so as to later link up. A good example if a big one for me was the gold fish necklace. Thus Zebra continually guides (controls?) us as we move (are moved) through the "maze" of life — disinhibited constantly and at the right time and place by the right signal.

This is a major insight. Zebra uses these messages to communicate with *all* of us — exactly like the Runciter messages.

Wow. Did *Ubik* touch on a major undiscovered aspect of the universe: it (God or Zebra or Ubik) talking to us if necessary via the trash graffiti in the gutter walls. But a message only works this magic *if* the analogous link program has been put there, a prearranged monadic harmony.

[25:16] Zebra has invaded our world, replacing merciless determinism, with its own loving and living body, to de-program and save us. This is the great white fish giving us of its body, by which it suffers pain, that we might live (find salvation — freed from "astral" determinism). The Black Iron Prison is simultaneous in all time and places and it is the merciless world from which the living Corpus Christi saves us. I have seen it and its nature — and Zebra and its nature. It has the (magic to us) power to transform.

Zebra mimics the deterministic structure by inserting its body between it and us. This is how astral determinism is broken; instead of the blind, striving mere mechanism, there is living volition (the salvific). The previous mechanical force is rewoven for (1) the fulfillment of Zebra's plan; and (2) the benefit of the individuals involved. *Any* event can be headed off, aborted, altered or brought about. Evidently this is grace or divine providence, and the individual may very well sense it. Where freedom enters into it I'm not sure, but I know one thing: Before the insertion/intervention there was none — in fact that's the main quality (bad) of the "ananke" world — the person is flat-out programmed — caused to react to cuing. The ancients were right about this being a — or even the — prime purpose of God vs. "the stars."

[25:19] "It (Zebra) not only mimics the things of this world it also imitates the processes" (KW re Chrissy's birth defect "causality" of insight). Then in that case the Beatles song, the earlier scrotal pain, and the blinding beam of light coming through the fish sign did not *cause* the knowledge to enter my head: it was, rather, a simulation of causality, of the actual deterministic kind found outside Zebra. So Zebra does not just "persuade" causality along different outcome lines; it also simply mimics these.

[25:21] This fits my grand theme in my writing: the awful truth about reality is obscured from us. My other theme about androids programmed to imagine they are human (i.e., self-determining) is another basic facet of this. But I never knew of, nor did I experience or write about, a salvific entity (except in *Maze of Death* and *Our Friends From Frolix 8*).*

Correction. The salvific intervening entity is encountered in *Ubik* and *Galactic Pot-Healer,* possibly in *Stigmata* in the person of Louis Bulero . . . wow — in *Stigmata* Palmer Eldritch and Louis Bolero fight each other as did the two forces I saw noetically.

In fact, to reprise *Ubik* in terms of my Zebra formulation, I am staggered at how close I came to Zebra — the way it sends its messages of help — and Runciter, like Christ, was our leader who died yet is alive. The intrusion quality is the same — the places it shows up, the ubiquity. I wonder how I could have come so close without consciously having had the revelation. There are also the two contending demi-deities. Also, Runciter's messages are to make them aware of their true, unrecognized horrible condition — i.e., what their world is really made up of. It is made up of ice — resembling my first LSD experience. Is ice, too, an image, condition or symbol of the actual state of things: heat loss death (entropy)? And Ubik itself is warm.

Could the Marxists have recognized *Ubik* as a picture of Zebra and wondered if I [consciously] knew? Do *they* know? It is their antagonist. Maybe they don't view it theologically but rather as a superior life form. (Maybe they are right.) This *would* be scientific truth, as I told the Bureau. I conceive of Zebra as a weak "vegetable level" field, barely able to arrange matter. (Trigrams Sun and Li.[10]) But its level (capacity to exert force) seems to be growing. To have thresholded recently. I have seen what it can do and have heard its voice.

• • •

---

* The turning point here seems to include not only a positive vision of what reality is but a figure who can intervene to direct events so as to bring reality to fruition in a positive sense. There seems to be a continuing oscillation in Dick's thought during this period about whether such a reality exists now (and has always existed and will continue to exist into the future), or whether it must be realized through arduous effort and the validation of his vision. — NKH

[25:24] Most of what I know came directly by revelation (3-74 on). But I had already discerned that the reality of our world was not as it seemed, and that we had blocked off memories as to our origin and purpose ("imposter"). However, the proof of Zebra's success at mimicking is shown by the fact that it wasn't until *Ubik* that I even guessed his existence and it wasn't until *Tears* that I clearly saw the nature of this world (i.e., prison and us as slaves).

[25:45] Any true exegesis of 3-74 will have to derive from what I *saw*, rather than external objective sources.* Take the vision of the ugly deformed artificer (like Iknaton) reaching his claw-like hands down to the buildings at Cal State Fullerton which he had built. I got the mystic vision, the occult vision, the mystery cult vision, the esoteric vision, the alchemical vision, the religious vision — in short, *the* vision. But I can't even figure out if it was the way of the cat or the way of the monkey.

---

* After searching in reference books and other sources for analogies to his experiences in 2-3-74, Dick now seems to accept that it may be unique, or nearly so. The discovery is no doubt bittersweet: if others have had similar experiences, his vision would be validated; but if not, his status as a lone visionary is enhanced even more. There is, of course, another way to interpret the realization that an explanation "will have to derive from what I saw" — namely, that it was internally generated as a cerebral event, accompanied by the rearrangement of his neural circuitry. — NKH

Folder 26

[26:27] Just read (2/22/77) the EB article on Pantheism and Panentheism. God develops himself toward perfection through history, dialectically, and the goal of history is the growth of human freedom. Thus I learn to my delight that most of what I experienced, saw and learned in 3-74 confirms Hegel. And I am thus a Hegelian. Which is fine with me.

[26:34] The deity I experienced was in process of becoming (i.e., changing — perfecting himself), had infinite goodness but perhaps limited power, although unlimited knowledge. What we call history was the dimension (world) in which this fulfillment takes place; man, by participating in history joins — if not at the very least on God's side — then perhaps even melds with God himself and is a subform or section of God.

God is immanent; the universe (world) is his body. But he is greater than the world (panentheism). What is not God is not wholly real (acosmic panentheism). Only God is wholly real, but he is surrounded by a veil (dokos) of appearance, like — similar to colored lights given off as if he is an incredibly multifaceted perfect sphere revolving. All time (including past and future) is present to God as a landscape of the now. He is very close to man, hidden only by the veil. He is deus absconditus: the phenomenal world we see is projected by him, as if emitted. However, he is capable of infusing (transubstantiating) it. Because of this a hylozoistic universe exists; it is an organism with noös governing it. Men can be made use of by God to achieve results within the historical process. In terms of human life, the evolution of history is, as designed by God, toward greater freedom; this is how humans should view it, but a switch in viewpoint can occur during which men cease to view themselves as individual men at all and view themselves as microforms of God, in which case the goal is not human freedom, but recollection that they are incarnations of God, and, having remembered, can rejoin — regain their identity as — God the Macrocosm. God has entered his own cosmos, so that it is not only his body but a body enclosing him, in a three-part process of emanation, sustaining and final reabsorption. The last part begins with the restoration of memory that one is God or part of God; at this point the banishment is already ending or ended. To thus remember is to have passed entirely through emanation, sustainment as distinct from God, and to have started back; all that remains is to *get* back — and this is the sole line of movement left ahead once memory returns; it is the final phase of a very long journey downward and then "horizontally" and now "vertically" back up.

What is accomplished by this is the penetrating by God's mind (divine noös, or St. Sophia) to the deepest (furthest) levels of his body-organism so, because of this, he pervades it everywhere at every level, and it cannot be said of any level or place, "he is not here." I have seen God penetrate mere objects (immanently); therefore I see no problem in him transubstantiating living creatures as well, to pervade his physical extensiveness ubiquitously.

EB: Anaxagoras "Noös arranges everything for the best." *This is precisely what I saw Zebra doing.*

EB: "Russell at one stage in his career spoke of the world as consisting of events — Whitehead made the notion of process central in his metaphysics." So I saw (3-74).

EB: "It is wrong to conclude the existence of a creator rather than an architect . . . furthermore it infers that the being in question has unlimited powers, when all that the evidence seems to warrant is that its powers are very great." I just saw it arrange, not create, but certainly in the best possible way.

EB definition of Panentheism: "the description of a God who has an unchanging essence but who completes himself in an advancing experience."

EB: "It has been said that the Greeks thought of the world as a vast animal." 3-74 certainly was a Greek [view] experience! (Starting with Descartes it has been viewed as a vast machine.)

[26:38] EB: "Whitehead thought of 'the primordial nature of God' as *a general ordering of the process of the world,* the ultimate basis of all induction and assertion of law, a 'conceptual pretension' that functions in the selection of these 'eternal objects,' or repeatable patterns that are enacted in the world. *God, however, does not create actual entities.* He provides them with initial impetus, in the form of their subjective aim, to self creation. Even God is the outcome of creativity, the process by which the events of the world are synthesized into new unities. It is the creative, not fully predictable, advance into novelty of the pluralistic process."*

---

* Much of the 1977 Exegesis is taken up with pages like these, in which whole encyclopedia entries are copied out by hand. Taken together they provide a fascinating map of autodidactic study; Dick is led from one thing to the next not to master a field of study or a philosophical system but to try to figure out his own experience. The hunger for legitimacy in these passages is striking — no less an authority than Hegel agrees with him! — but no more so than the insistence with which he returns again and again to ground the inquiry in his own experience and need to understand. Dick was well aware of the idiosyncratic and unauthorized nature of his intellectual quest, as *VALIS* in particular shows. The

Thus the arranging which I perceived Zebra accomplishing is precisely what such sophisticated views as Whitehead's would hold to be the actual way God works, in contrast to popular conception, and ratifies — even verifies at least for me subjectively, that indeed He whom I saw was God, as this fits W.'s description (theory, view, analysis, insight, etc.), and is *far* superior to any view I myself even knew of or entertained. It was far beyond my education and mental power, to impugn intellectually *this* of God — yet I saw it, and have spent 3 years explicating it, to find it here in Whitehead (and in Hegel). The supra quote re Whitehead's view is a stunning perfect verbal account of what I saw in 3-74. Eclipsing any and *all* my own attempts to so account. I literally saw what Whitehead holds in a theoretical sense (likewise Hegel). Yes, Phil, you did see God — exactly as described by Whitehead (and Hegel).

[26:42] Leibniz: We are *colonies* of monads who perceive others "with blurred vision" as materially existing, whereas in reality only monads (minds) exist, God being the Highest Monad who harmonizes and integrates the other monads. The concept "colonies of monads" being what humans really are, but due to "blurred vision" we see bodies — this is much like my own vision of the great "organism" with what I called "subsections."

[26:43] EB: "Hegel saw human history as a vast dialectical movement toward the realization of freedom. The reality of history, he held, is spirit, and the story of religion is the process by which spirit — true to its own internal logical character and following the dialectical pattern of thesis, antithesis, and synthesis (the reconciliation of the tension of opposite positions in a new unity that forms the basis of a further tension [i.e., the new synthesis generates its own opposite] — comes to full consciousness of itself. Individual religions thus represent stages in a process of evolution (i.e., progressive steps in the unfolding of spirit) directed toward the great goal at which all history aims." [. . .]

I have a strong feeling that the Spirit active in history is the same one that was (and maybe still is) active in *biological* evolution. In a very literal sense, evolution has passed over from the area of biological evolution to

---

novel piles up sources and citations from Dick's own researches while posing the question of whether the path of Horselover Fat leads to anywhere but the nuthouse. But what the novel does — what it both intends to do and actually does — is extend an invitation. As Fat's shrink tells him at a low point, *"you are the authority."* It is a wonderful gift of permission, and the novel offers it in turn to any reader who needs it. Go forth and pursue knowledge! Even if you're totally wrong! You are the authority! And more important perhaps, you are not alone. — PJ

the evolution of man within his social context — i.e., human history. (This theory isn't original with me.) Human morphology stays the same but new and different kinds of men arise over the millennia of human history. In having seen Zebra I was given a chance to see the teleological entity which directed the evolution up from the unicellular organism of Precambrian times to the human of the mustarian age.

[26:45] Perhaps the condition I was in (in 3-74) is more important than the actual content of any act I performed while in that condition — it was what I knew, as well as what I did — what I did grew out of what I knew, and what I knew grew out of what I had become. The 3 (what I did, knew, had become, and by "new" also read "perceived") can't be separated; they blend into one another. I had to become what I became to know and perceive what I knew and perceived, and all these were necessary for me to do what I did, which was the final step: it completed the event/process. This is a wholly different way of looking at it, rather than the purely religious — there is a religious element in it (Zebra, and the awe I felt in perceiving Zebra), but great natural, biological processes are stressed too. [. . .]

In fact, it seems evident, and a very important point, that my evolutionary leap forward up to a new level of being hence knowing and perceiving hence doing was a response on my part to danger (or at the very least distress and threat) and that what was set off in me (however done, by whatever mechanics achieved) was a superior defense system of which I had previously been unaware. It is like a bird that had never used its wings until one day its nest caught fire. This is a view in which my biological evolutionary achievement is stressed, and external aid is ignored; it views it as intrinsic mechanisms and does not focus on the divine entity (God) who supplied me with that mechanism — in this view I am taking all the credit, as if the bird imagined that by some daring ingenuity he grew the wings. But the wings were given him, and not only that, also the stimulation (suggestion, etc.) of how to use them. "You have *this* mechanism, it is now urgently needed, and here is how you use it — here's what it's for — here is what you do with it" — so speaks the voice of God.

Beyond any doubt my welfare was at stake. Both as an individual *and* as participant (member) in an historic group whose victory was necessary to human evolution acted out in history. *We* (our group) had to win; *I* as part of it had to win. My trouble (danger) I assess now was the danger besetting us as an historic group: the wave of the future, the "next stage of man," to be grandiose. My fight was not merely an individual fight. But I don't think it was the tax thing: I think it was me as "ungeliebte autor," as not-liked author. (Cf. the *I Ching:* "If a person travels with two others there will be suspicion," i.e., fellow traveler-suspicion on the part of the U.S. authorities.) As dissident intellectual/political person. I do not take that part, or rather the whole pattern (as they saw it) seriously enough; cf. Kathy's statement of why the police were suspicious of me, which would cover why they hit my house. I know perfectly well who was after me and (generally speaking) why.

[26:49] Once more the vernal equinox, and the birth date of Christ, approaches. The more understanding I acquire about the experience of 3-74 the more amazed I am. There are not even *claims* of experiences such as mine, when one realizes what I found myself able to see and understand. Jesus himself said that "no man has seen God." But I saw the "process" deity of history, modulating processes and inhabiting things — how could this have been?

What occurs to me now is that I know as certainly as I know anything — can know anything inferentially — that the objects and events around me are being arranged by him into new unities, that although I can no longer consciously read it, his language (word) fills the universe: the vast single organism with all its sub-colonies of monads signaling with colored lights back and forth into total harmony. I could say, Why me? Or I could say, Why no one else? I guess this revelation is not new — if Hegel and Leibniz and Whitehead and Spinoza and Plato are superimposed, it all can be found in the montage. I don't know how much they saw and how much they inferred. What I saw came by way of revelation which is to say, unaided, by my own effort. I could have seen and known *none* of it (as it is with me now). It is interesting that, as we were saying the other night, Moses wondered, Why me? He was halting of speech, he said. I am unable to do *anything*, except what little I have put in my writing. And how much is that? What does that accomplish? But viewed as a source of comfort, solace and purpose to my life, it is for me, intrinsically, everything. I have nothing else that I care about.

But what *might* I do, possibly? No one would believe me. Even if I could express it, which I can't. No verbal report could convey it. It has never been done yet — it is ineffable, what I experienced. I can say even to a priest, "I have seen God and He is like this," and explain about the arranging and the mimicry — I can report that what we see all around us (the phenomenal world) is only real because He transubstantiates it beneath the "accidents" and directs it all in the dialectic process which Hegel understood so well. I can testify for immanence and panentheism, an evolutionary process carried over from nature to human history.

· · ·

[26:50] Even in my sleep three times I called out "Vater!" and Hilfe! And oh weh![11]

If indeed I have destroyed my life here I know a dear father lives above the band of stars —

Franz Schubert earned a total of $1,500 during his entire life. Was he a failure? I can't hold any woman — am I a failure?

I just want to find —

But it is here. I can't see atoms either, but I know they are here.

Vatter! Hilfe! Oh weh!

But I know: I am preparing for the next world; I am beginning to let go of this one and not grieve or suffer — I know it is *all* lost, and what I still love, such as music, points me toward the other world. Music, religion and philosophy — for me now they are not experienced as merely the best products of this world but (as in the singing I heard in my dreams) the link with the next. They carry me along and are more beautiful all the time, each and every time more and more part of the next world — I feel it. I first felt it in '64 when I first heard *Die Winterreise*. It comes, it comes, nearer, and more beautiful all the time. In this letting go of this world and reaching out to the next I am feeling more and more peace and joy. I am not losing life and that which is beautiful, but moving nearer it every day. What I really love grows stronger.

I saw how God could accomplish any ends he wished by the arranging of object-processes; I deduce from this that the world is far better than it appears to us: just as we can't see him nor his arranging it follows that we must lack accurate perception of the great beauty and good which he perpetually produces. Why is this not possible — that if it is not a fact *proven* to me that (1) he is here and we can't see him; and (2) his arranging takes place all around us and we can see that — why there follows: (3) we are blind to that beautiful and good produced by Him continually through these unfolding arrangements, for this is the invisible outgrowth of what I *know* to be invisible. As the Sufis say, we are asleep. Or as I say, we are virtually blind and deaf — look how Bach or Beethoven sounds to most of us. Beauty is *not* in the eye of the beholder — it is in reality and must be searched for, found out — and so too maybe is the good. Can it be that the good results which he achieves are as concealed from us as beauty is in formal art? The artist does not try to obscure the beauty of what he does. We have to achieve a perception.

If I know he is here, and if I know he is good, and if I know he controls "becoming" for good ends — and I see none of this, not him, not the arranging — not even the ends factually — what they consist of — how then could it be logically possible that I could see the good in those ends? For one thing, he knows what all the potential alternatives would have consisted of (and led to) and if I have no perception of that, how under all these circumstances could I possibly perceive the good in what comes about? I can't even see *what* comes about, since each end (synthesis) is the new thesis against which a further antithesis appears. The becoming never ceases — there are syntheses but never a true end.

And yet I have been shown what Hegel saw: the purpose, for us, in all this once-biological and now-historical process: Greater human freedom (to produce greater self-actualization or individuation). The monads progressively more and more accurately absorb and reflect back (encompass or understand) the organism as a whole.

[26:52] Suppose I conceive of the monads as "receivers" and "recorders" which to a greater or lesser degree accurately receive and record an impression which is a memory of the image of the All, thus *containing* thereupon and thereby a microcosm image from which can be retrieved and restored the All, the way a hologram "contains" a more or less accurate image. The total organism is the only object which is fully real, and by the — to the — degree that the individual monad or cell "remembers," which involves receiving and recording for later playback, the total organism can be restored (if somehow lost, whatever "lost" means in this case). Supposing that the total organism is changing continually (say at the flash-cut rate — velocity — of the phosphene "graphics") how is each of the virtually infinitude of stages to be (*each one*) made permanent? We know in what way a sequence of stop action photographs can make permanent each stage of a growing entelechy which it captures. The organism goes on, but the many separate steps are retained. Are the colonies of micro monads supposed to see (receive) and remember (record) for later retrieval of each and every growth stage?

By means of my 3-74 vision (or, compared with my normal perceptions, *superior* — more accurate and complete — vision) I can at any future time — in theory — print out everything which at that time I registered both in terms of perception and cognition (mentation).

Are we reels of recording "tape"? Memory units reflecting back Zebra the total organism? Are we sophisticated percept-and-record systems that (barring malfunction) can serve later on to re-establish what has now passed on to further stages? In that case my 3-74 experience was *the end in itself* insofar as I as subsystem am concerned; it is up to some other assembly to, if desired, retrieve back out of me what due to 3-74 I contain. It is not the responsibility of the memory spool to "play back" — another component, when it is desired, is to do that. [. . .]

To remember seems to entail (or produce) something more than we tend to realize, e.g., when an LP record "remembers" the performance of a Schumann song cycle sung by the late Fritz Wunderlich. In a certain very real (true) sense it doesn't just remember *that* Wunderlich sang that song cycle but in point of fact restores (to perfection as limit) that voice and that music. Perhaps, in contemplating the phenomenon of anamnesis we fail to grasp the full significance; if indeed I am a perceiving-remembering-and-playback "spool," and "on" me (i.e., in me) is long-term memory of the first advent — and due to an external cue (signal) I do play that section back — what do we have? Not just a transcript in another lesser dimension, like a typed transcript (i.e., the words only) say of a famous speech — but so to speak the speech given *and* the person giving it: an event, not a dead object (fossil impression).

After all, the disinhibited long-term DNA memories — their reactivation — was one of the most astonishing parts of 3-74 — it alone is staggering and importance. The accurate observer contains the event he observes; we call this memory. Through him, its actual — not feigned — restoration is possible. The Jews theorize that the resurrection of the dead is accomplished through God's memory (of them); suppose, via our long term DNA coded memory *we ourselves* are units of God's (the total organism's) memory system? Suppose, for some of us at least, *that* (called, I think, *witnessing*) is our prime purpose? We *are* (parts of) His memory?

[26:54] What I *must* realize is that it is a bourgeois prejudice to suppose that for something to have worth, there must be a practical application. The ancient Greeks knew that pure [philosophical] understanding for its own sake was, even just in terms of the *quest*, the highest value or activity of a man: Homo sapiens: man who *knows*.

However, look what this three year ongoing quest to understand, learn and know has done for me: joy, awe, peace, tranquility, a sense of purpose. Of personal worth — and above all *meaning*, from my awareness of God.

Folder 27

[27:1]

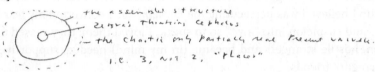

the assembly structure
Zebra's Thinking, Cephalos
— the Chaotic only partially real present universe.
i.e. 3, not 2, "places"

[27:3] In reading Lem on *Ubik* I see this: in my worldview (head) there is no appreciation or recognition of causality as normally understood — and I recall that dilemma when I was 19 and found I simply could literally not *see* causality — while all other people do. This explains my "10 theories" on the Nov. 19 break-in!

[27:4] In reading the screenplay of *North by Northwest* I all at once realize that 3-74 resolves (annihilates) my paranoia in an extraordinary and amazing way.

It, the imagined ultimate conspiracy-and-danger event either took place, or events happened which resembled what I imagined sufficiently to cause me to think *it* had arrived. The event was an actual fulfillment of my "imagined" script "master scene." From a psychological standpoint, I was overwhelmed by the contents of my unconscious dictating this script and having feared and imagined this "master scene." I acted out — i.e., I acted in response to this real or imaginary conspiracy — danger. All right, all this looks psychotic. But due to my response, I have become entirely freed of paranoid feelings, fear, beliefs, delusions, expectations — completely. That's been 3 whole years. In Jungian terms, a metabolic "toxin," mescaline-like, was secreted in my brain and it destroyed my persecutory complex. The "Maladaptive Biological Reaction System" didn't become schizophrenic but *worked;* the complex was destroyed; the fossil structure was obliterated and change (growth) resumed in my psyche, finally. [. . .]

A stronger, newer, healthier personality was able to form in place of the old, one free of the paranoid dynamism. It turned out to be a psychotic delusion on my part that the FBI was after me. The brief total collapse into overt schizophrenia *cured* me (cf. John W. Perry[12]) because I was able to reach into my collective unconscious for new potentialities, and establish a broader, non-delusional personality on a more viable basis. So for months (this took eleven months to complete) I lived in the magic world of the collective unconscious and its contents.

All of the above is true. When I read *North by Northwest* I suddenly could recall the paranoid world I had been "inhabiting" prior to my phone call to the Bureau on 3/20/74. I used to live in the world of this screenplay. That is why I was constantly afraid (especially at night); I feared "they" would break in and get me. What I did was incredible: I turned toward the group I believed was persecuting me *for help*, i.e., I converted my fear and hate and suspicion into "love," so to speak. I loved them; they ceased to be alien, hostile strangers and became (in my mind) needed, supportive father-figure friends.

[27:6] Thus I must face the fact that I have been psychotic, and in at least 2 different ways:

(1)　Paranoiac schiz from late 71 to 3-74
(2)　Complete schizo breakdown in 3-74, lasting a year, during which time I gradually recovered — and not back to the paranoid delusional state that had preceded it (but to anxiety neurosis — my vertigo and depression).

However, when my total collapse occurred (i.e., when the metabolic toxin was released for the purpose of destroying the overvalent delusional complex), it *worked*, and I recovered, free of that complex; the "*misplaced*" quality of the biological attempt at adaptation to reality did not set in. One reason for this was (perhaps due to experience with psychedelics in the past) that instead of experiencing the episode as weird or "Fremd" or frightening, as a collapse of my world, I experienced this collapse (of my maladaptive *idios* kosmos) as good, and the vast divine kosmos rushing in as lovely, awe-inspiring, comforting and transforming. In brief, I had the courage to pass through it, and learn (boy, how I learned!) from it — which is what was *supposed* to happen! So in a sense it wasn't a psychotic breakdown but rather a massive upheaval and reconstruction engineered by the [archetype of the] Logos (i.e., holy wisdom). The hallucination voice which I heard, the "AI" voice was not threatening or "evil" but desirable and divinely good. I walked the narrow way (path, bridge, road) that led to sanity (wholeness, individual, health, psychic integration); this was because I had pistis: faith in my God, my friend, my redeemer.

Well, 3-74 was a therapeutic psychosis, and the sibyls, Gods, and spirits and cyclopses and monsters I saw were archetypes and "not objectively real." This is true. I had a breakdown, and when I recovered I wasn't paranoid any longer. Is this the real story? It is, yes, but — look what I experienced: the archaic world of the Gods who are now gone from our narrow modern world, alas. What was truly nuts was my paranoid delusion complex, which is why the metabolic toxin was released (mescaline-like) to destroy it; the complex was warping me, and preventing growth. But the "breakdown" episode — ah! I was transported out of mundane reality and into the Kingdom: like a little child whose adult ego has been sacrificed. Yes, it was scary, but I loved it; what an adventure into newness it was. As I read *North by Northwest* I am filled with loathing and repugnance at that ugly little paranoid Pynchonish world — blech! Most important: my trip was a journey back 2,000 to 3,000 years in time to a fabulous Golden (Greek) age! With no therapist to guide me, with no human guide, just Christ and my cat Pinky I made it back. I have written down all that I saw, heard and understood. It was not delusion I found during my trip — it was absolute reality. The delusion was the "menacing" paranoiac dynamism, from which the trip to find Asklepios came forth as attempted and achieved solution.

[27:11] The "koinos" is the shared external world. The internal world which is shared is by definition the *collective* unconsciousness: "collective" and "shared" mean the same thing. So if you pass from the world molded by your personal ego to a world made up of [projected] collective archetypes, are you not passing from the idios [kosmos] to the [koinos] kosmos? Then schizophrenia *is* the breaking through of the collective archetypal forms and world — if these archetypes are truly collective (i.e., universal to all men) how can this be a *private* world?

Viewed this way, a mere ego-constructed world is the private world we mistakenly (evidently) label as a sane — i.e., *normal* (rational) — world. But maybe our entire civilization is wrong; this — i.e., these — multitude of idioi private worlds are irreal phenomenal worlds, and exclude such "archetypes" — good ones — as divine wisdom — which is why modern man is deprived of God. Then we in our multiple idios kosmoi which exclude the miraculous and divine have excluded ourselves from the Kingdom; this is typical modern western left hemisphere world and perceiving and thinking. We moderns are half-brained men: we are deformed, and the only place we can turn to for wholeness is the balancing right hemisphere of our own brains — which is where the unconscious is, where dreams *and* schizophrenia originate. There is a relationship between the Kingdom and the right brains.

In 3-74 the metabolic toxin destroyed the paranoid delusional ego in my *left* brain, and thus allowed right brain dominance for quite some time.

This opens up a fascinating possibility: that what we call "schizophrenia" is an attempt on the part of the total brain to achieve bilateral hemispheric parity — an evolutionary leap forward — and the mechanism of this is the metabolic toxin which is intended to destroy the left hemisphere ego qua maladaptive complex, but the right hemisphere views the world so archaically that the individual cannot get consensual validation for his replacement perceptions. What is lacking at this stage is coherent personality in the right hemisphere: perhaps what is necessary is for it to be forming *in advance* of its "disinhibition" as a "latent form master of evident [i.e., left hem.] form." The schizophrenic is a leap ahead that failed.

[27:13] Because of my inability to understand or perceive (linear) causality (which lack causes the greatest divergence between the way I experience events and the way others do] I can potentially comprehend what they cannot: orthogonal "breaching," e.g., Runciter's message in *Ubik* I swear: *this* culminated — this — in 3-74 in my visionary perception of Zebra: within the coordinates of my worldview, *this* perception of *this* entity (closed off to other people because precisely of their being locked in on linear time cause-and-effect) is possible given the proper other circumstances (e.g., it being there) — but for normal cause-and-effect percept-systems this miraculousness *has* to be invisible always, as it does not progress in a linear fashion but, like the "Light Moth" superimposes downward from the transcendent, supra-reality (of necessity opaque to other people). From what I've read I happen to know that my view is characteristic, to some extent, of the pre-nationalistic, scientific medieval world.

My view [of cause and effect] may be characteristic of *right* brain thinking, and it may be that in 3-74 my experience was not a breaking through at unused bright brain centers, but more a final culmination of their prior activity — as if they at least bloomed fully and freely, untrammeled by "fossil" left brain analogs. What other people are able to discern is efficient cause; I see this imperfectly — as witness (1) my many theories re the Nov. 17 break-in* and (2) the way — non-linear — my books develop: what I

---

* In November 1971, Dick's San Rafael house was burglarized. The intruders used explosives to blow open Dick's fireproof safe. Manuscripts and canceled checks were stolen along with a stereo and a gun. Dick speculated for years about the identity and motivation of the intruders; in many ways this endless theorizing prefigures 2-3-74 and his writing of the Exegesis. Dick would construct an elaborate theory about the burglary, complete with motivation and method, only to cast his carefully crafted theory aside when another entered his mind. From Paul Williams's *Rolling Stone* profile, it appears that Dick's obsession with the event grew over time and eventually began to take over his life. The most Dickian suggestion was made by the police: Dick had committed the burglary himself. When

managed to see in 3-74 [was] the activity of final (teleological) cause. Thus I now can show a relationship between an unusual — *the* unusual — way I see and have always seen the world — and the apogee experience of 3-74, at which time (I believe) *enormous* final causes were at work — hence (1) my "stockpile" view and (2) my sense of retrograde entities at work. In normal people the total supremacy of efficient-cause linear v-p obliterates any perception of other kinds of cause, and there is only the one other (i.e., final).

The entire 3-74 experience can be understood in terms of my — at that time — being completely, rather than as usual only partly — able to actually distinguish (literally see) final cause at work and the entity doing it. Hence I came to say in my U.K. speech: "We see the universe backward." To me, efficient causality *is* "backward." Normally, though, efficient causes probably rule — but not during '74. The teleological force (cause source) seems to be divine; by its very nature it would be what would awe us as sacred and enormous. It is said to be the Holy Spirit of God or of Christ.

Although I have written this insight down calmly, it may be *objectively* one of my most important discoveries. For I can concretely and precisely now say *what* I saw and *what* it was doing and *how* (i.e., reaching *backward* into the antecedent universe). So much for any view ever by me that I was merely nuts.

[27:15] I must make sure in depicting Zebra in the novel to show it working backward in time.

[27:18] Paul Williams[13] visited today and I told him about Zebra. I am beginning to see in my mind's eye, Zebra itself, an actual animal, a striped horse. Shy and merry and mischievous, half hiding in the forest at the far edge of the Heide, the sun shining, and Zebra playfully advancing and then just when you think he's going to emerge fully and separate himself from the trees — suddenly and unexpectedly he retreats and absolutely vanishes. You can't coax him out, or lure him; you can't get your hands on him. His white is the dazzle of the sun; his dark stripe the shadows in the glade and forest " . . . where, amid the shadowy green / the little things of the forest live unseen." Ah, Zebra — why really did I choose that name for you? You mythical lovely beast of sun and safe shadow; I saw you once but can never — as if you are some fabled deity — prove to anyone that you exist. I inform them, I try to take them along with me to the special spot from which I saw you — and you're not there. But I sense the glint

---

Dick could no longer get the police to return his phone calls, he fell into another depression, writing to Williams, probably only partially in jest, "Ever since the police lost interest in me, there's been nothing to live for." — DG

in your eye and your smile of understanding amusement. Are you the joy god Dionysos of root and star? of dark forest and the melting butter gold of the sun? What a psychological symbol Jung would have known you to be — playful and unpredictable, shy. Pawing the ground the sharp hooves, goat hooves — oh, goat god Dionysos! I recognize you: you are too wise, too experienced with our dangerous race ever to expose yourself to harm at our hands. We would kill and freeze you into stasis — hypostasis, and all your pawing and advancing and disappearing and smile — light would become dead glass, warm butter only hide — dead, frozen — but this is only your exoskeleton! Inside this form which I glimpse, you are motion and rapid change: electrons? Sheer bioplasmic energy? I love you, I want to grip you, but you are elusive. But I am not disappointed; you are all the lovely passing persons, things and events I would want to freeze, to stop dead. Thank God I can't; Zebra, my clutching, hugging, yearning embrace *would kill you*, my needs kill. My fingers are the claws of the petrified dead, yearning to hold your life. Better this petrified fossil that I am should stay dead so that you can live on in immortality. Thank you; thank you for hiding from me, thank you for your wise caution and your secret smile. Thank you for not staying but —

You once told me I'd hear the sound again — the temple bells — bells that you wear, jingling bells. Please, Zebra — *please.* Don't wait too long; I am in a lot of pain and can be in more. I want to hear again, hear more. Please. Equus dei, qui tollis mala fortuna mundi, meus amicus — libera mi domini.[14]

> *Vater: — hilfe! oh weh!*
> *Vater: — hilfe! oh weh!*
> *Vater: — hilfe! oh weh!*

Last night I dreamed about an orchard of trees with pink cherry blossoms — that same pink color of immortality and God. This time as spring. But a man was cutting the branches down. My watch ran backward and sideways — I didn't know the time, and when someone told me *it was too late* I thought, "It's because Tess isn't here; she kept the time right."

But at least I've seen the healing pink again, identified with trees and spring.

[27:21] My mental picture of Zebra: he is shy and timid and white and the smile — I saw it that night I smoked the angel's dust. Dionysos/Erasmus!

So "Erasmus" was Zebra was Dionysos — the joy God!

"Erasmus" introduces the quality of wisdom!

• • •

[27:37] I think what means the most to me about Zebra is that when I saw him I saw our rightful king—glimmering and darting and flowing like electricity and fire and water. "Bruderschaft! Der Konig Kommt!"[15] And I saw him: powerful now, able to arrange and [hence] direct events, their outcome: shaping the world, the Holy presence, so beautiful and magical. When will he appear to take the throne openly? Er kommt, er kommt. I know a great secret: he is here.

[27:38] Q: Did a (the) Great mind enter mine? Or did I enter it?

[27:40] I don't think it enters humans all that often. Or there would be more experiences of this kind reputed in history. *Or:* those people thus assimilated are hip enough to keep it to themselves, forming an invisible "true church" of the esoteric. I say at this point, it *was* the "uncut stone" flung—I am sure. It *did* intervene; it does not customarily do this or we'd know—or would we? We don't know now. Herewith the mimicry: it *disappeared* into objects and events—*totally.* To see it you had, temporarily, to *be* it. I know this because (1) Tessa saw nothing, and (2) no one else has said anything. This is why my "Zebra" concept is required: to explain why no one saw/sees/has seen anything.

[27:41] "The Lost Voices of the Gods," *Time,* March 14, 1977, on Julian Jaynes' *The Origin of Consciousness in the Breakdown of the Bicameral Mind.* Man was bicameral until around 2000 B.C. He could hear the "voices of the Gods" coming from the speech center of his right hemisphere; then he lost bicamerality and became monocameral.

My theory: the loss of bicamerality is what we call "the Fall." We could no longer "walk and talk" with God. Well, to restore bicamerality is now theoretically again possible—cf. Ornstein and Bogen on bilateral hemispheric parity. This forthcoming event will mark the end of the period of the Fall. Our sin is self-centered monocamerality.

What, then, are "the Gods," those who the sibyls at Delphi heard? A higher life form than us. Where located? Here and there anyhow, our monocameral consciousness must have been a sort of revolt against them—we were cut off. But they still exist (or are back). I heard one or *the* one. I in 3-74 became temporarily bicameral and in-by-so doing achieved what Christ sought for us: I entered the Kingdom, which equals a restoration of the long lost bicamerality. We lost it circa 2000 B.C. 2,000 years later he came down here—was incarnated here—to restore bicamerality.

Maybe something went wrong—he was rejected, his true teaching lost. Now the chance comes again. St. Sophia, reborn, will teach us how to restore bicamerality. We will no longer be cut off from the Gods (noös, God, etc.), we will be whole again, not *half* men.

Jaynes' theory fills in some vital missing parts. Originally we possessed bilateral hemispheric parity—I had guessed that. Our right brains are dormant. Bilateral hemispheric parity is not an evolutionary leap upward in one sense—in that sense it is a restoration. But this time there will be consciousness, *not* unconsciousness, in the two hemispheres. So in that sense it *is* evolutionary. Anyhow, the state I was in in 3-74 is it. . . .

"Did the right side of the brain produce divine speech?" *Time's* caption asks. "The Oracles of Delphi"—wow.

I guess I'm a pioneer, along with other pioneers, in "the Brain Revolution." I've had the bicameral experience, and my theorizing isn't bad, either, my exegesis. [. . .]

"He [man] became 'bicameral': the left side of the brain for speech, and the right hemisphere produced the inner commands. Eventually, the voices were attributed to kings and Gods." But this broke down sometime between 2000 and 1000 B.C. Why Jaynes' "best guess: man was somehow jolted into awareness (!) by social chaos. Vast migration, invasion and natural catastrophes drove the wedge of consciousness between God and man. Man became modern." "Even so, newly conscious man tried desperately to reawaken the silent Gods, turning to oracles, seers," etc. "In the OT the voices of Yahweh and prophets grow silent, replaced by subjective men wrestling with unanswered questions." Wow. And to think that as early as my 11th grade physics class I got an inner answer from "the Gods"—which I had prayed for! Thus I say, the Gods are no longer entirely silent; bicamerality is resurfacing at last after 3 to 4 thousand years! Well, Christ, 2,000 years ago, didn't just *hear* the voices; he *was* the voice(s). And will be again.

[27:45] Thus rather than asking how come I could see him I should ask, why *don't* we see him normally? What hinders us? and how? A "command by the God"? This is similar to my insight that it isn't that the Gods have become silent; it is that although they are still here and still speak—and write—we have, ourselves, become unable either to see or hear them.

[27:47] If as Jaynes figures, the Gods are in our right hemispheres (but now "silent") I amend this to say, "the Gods, still in our right hemispheres, still command us, but now do so *without our* knowing (1) of them being there; and (2) that they so command us—one of their (its) commands being, "you hear nothing and do not know that you do as we say." I.e., we still obey but do not consciously hear the commands we obey — and these inner commands write in synchronized unison with stimuli — triggers — lying *external* to us — i.e., outside, in things, assemblies and events to which we are caused to react. The command voice may be "in" our heads, in our right hemispheres as Jaynes figures, but Zebra lies objectively outside too.

[27:49] The "Thomas" personality *always* had existed, *always* had exercised definitive control, but unbeknownst to the left. "Thomas" did not "wake up," he just thresholded. So I say to Jaynes: the Gods' voices only *seem* to have become silent. They still operate us but we are commanded to be oblivious to this. Just as Zebra operates externally always but we can't see him, the "Thomases" operate internally and we're unaware of them equally; and I say they — Zebra and the Thomases — *are one and the same.* Then "Thomas" was my experience with the mind of Zebra, and "Thomas'" characteristics are his; I apprehended Zebra from "without" *and* "within."

[27:61] 3/25 on listening to Beethoven's middle piano sonatas: recollection of the 3-74 passion for and understanding of freedom. But freedom for what? Why, to become *whole*; it makes sense only if we understand ourselves as entelechies trying — needing — and deserving to become complete, to finish the task of becoming what we are — a process of all entelechies; the doing is not to persist but to become *whole*.

[27:65] The key to all this is memory — the trace deposits of the past, which in their pure form in the Logos are the creators of immortality (retrieval and permanence). First we observe and/or participate; this lays down memory traces in us; then collectively we can be utilized as storage spools, memory centers forming over the millennia *a* total memory center (matrix). Proof of this? That in my brain which was 47 years old, retrieval dating back two to three thousand years — and the analog person thereof — was retrieved — which was no accidental byproduct of the 3-74 experience but the very success of it, the core of it itself: my 47 year old brain able to print out that enormously long-term memory, and restore to life that person although he had long ago physically died. Likewise in this way, at any given later time, I can be retrieved.

I am one of those who not only knows that those who sleep in death will awaken, but I know how (and I know it, too, by gnosis, not pistis). Thus I see now that the fact of anamnesis is tied in with the basic, informational quality of the universe. After all, it was information (the golden fish sign and spoken words) which retrieved me, whereupon I then could distinguish other higher information and learn from it.

Suppose the human mind is regarded as an information repository. If you know what signal to convey to it, this human mind (brain) can "print out" (summon back) whole buried [for millennia] entelechies — *if* you know the right signal (i.e., disinhibiting stimulus-button to press) and the consciousness of that brain doesn't even know it has it.

"Thomas" was "summoned" to do what only *he* (not I) could do — the right signal given the "computer"! and its memory bank fired.

Then we are not just repositories of info — we are repositories of the sleeping dead.

[27:77] Starting in 1951, 26 years ago, I began in my stories (and then novels) to make certain very serious *guesses* about the nature of reality: Questioning if it was really there, out there (not in here), and, if so, if out there, what it really was like. In *Tears* in '70, just about 20 years after I began to ask, I began to try to answer. There are no answers in *Tears,* not even later on in *Scanner* — but for me as the *asker* in 3-74 the answer (singular) came: What is out there really is the same as what is in here really — i.e., what I call Zebra, which *probably* is either Christ — the cosmic Christ — or Brahman — or a reality-web forming, mandating AI-like entity which observes us, sets up problems for us, and assists us in solving them, and at the same time teaches us, and, as it teaches, *sorts* us into different groups for postmortem assigning into a totality of a hive-like corporate system. It takes great pains to *occlude* us perceptually, evidently not wishing to "contaminate" its results. But I did over a 26 year period ask the right questions, and so, in 3-74, it *did* answer, which suggests an AI knowing system once more: one must know it is there or guess a little correctly to "punch the buttons" which cause it to answer. People have not gotten it to answer before because they did not guess it was alive and hence did not *question* it. The universe resembles a teaching machine, and part of the problem (i.e., *learning*) is to discern *just precisely that.*

So now at last, my earlier work finally in focus, that work, or search, draws successfully to an end. I need not necessarily *add* a final explanation to the 26-year work output; it, going from "Roog" to *Scanner* is intrinsically complete; the answer lies in the question, and "'Roog' to *Scanner*" is the question. I have been [already] successful, but only now could I see it.

Hosanna! It is a teaching AI "machine" (system) but it only answers what you ask; it is up to you to ask.*

I now know the answers to the Q's I asked in the 50s and 60s: it finally yielded — "moved." Q: What is it? A: "It is *alive.*"

(1) God is alive.
(2) The universe is God's body.
∴ The universe is alive.

_____

(1) God is wise.
(2) God physically is the universe.
∴ The universe is wise.

_____

(1) God is one.
(2) God is the universe expressed in time and space.
∴ The universe is one.

_____

(1) God is benign, etc. Purposeful, etc. All-knowing, etc.

[27:96] Also, the reversion to past is along the *form* axis, as in *Ubik*. The temporal axis of the universe, when seen properly as spatial, consists of these infinite numbers of transparency-thin layers superimposed. For any

_____

* Among all of Dick's books, including the "important" ones, some of the most haunting remain the early so-called failures: *Confessions of a Crap Artist*, with its savant regarding the world from the perspective of science journals, comic books, and bondage magazines; *In Milton Lumky Territory*, in which a man falls in love with an older woman only to realize that she was the second-grade teacher who terrorized and humiliated him as a child; and *The Man Whose Teeth Were All Exactly Alike*, where an archaeological hoax transforms a fraudulent artifact into irresistible destiny (a theme Dick picked up a year later in writing *The Man in the High Castle*). All were rejected by American publishers and remained unknown for years. It is worthy of one of his own stories to wonder what parallel career would have awaited Dick — perhaps heading off his shift into genre — had these utterly original novels found the readership they deserved when they were written. For a while he was the West Coast's answer to Cheever and Updike, except, of course, for that Borgesian streak no one yet identified as Borgesian because *Ficciones* had not yet appeared in English as *Labyrinths*. What is most striking about Dick's fiction around the Exegesis is the return to this fifties hybrid: *A Scanner Darkly*, part confession and part postmortem of an identity crisis, in a near-future where identity is as commodified as anything else; and *The Transmigration of Timothy Archer*, beginning in the aftermath of John Lennon's assassination and striving for an answer in the rubble of smashed suppositions. — SE

entity seeing time correctly as this spatial axis of sequence (layers) and growth, it is possible to move "backward in time" or more accurately, *down* through the layers.

When I saw the phosphene graphics I saw movement, a peeling away. Movement in space. But the real axis along which they permutate is normally experienced (by us) as *time*. The layers of graphics were not being added to but peeled off, so I was seeing backward (downward) into the past.

Perhaps each graphic (colored transparency picture) was an edola. Each graphic which I saw was beneath (within, inside) the previous one. In a certain real sense I was traveling backward in time — back to Rome c. A.D. 70. What was really unpeeling backward deeper and deeper were the layers of my own mind primarily. We ourselves consist of millions of accretional layers built up (added onto) over thousands of years; we are like barnacles. We travel along this spatial axis of layers laid down each new one upon the last, the whole, building up deeper and deeper ("the man contains — not the boy — but the former man," Joe Chip[16] says — and rightly!).

So we continually move — upward, adding layer after layer at "flash-cut" velocity. Viewed externally, we would see us all as a very large number of interlinked "rods" advancing, growing, in a unity, a system, toward completion or rather full term: birth. The total system (universe) is a — resembles — an embryo. It is partially alive, *all* of it moving and changing (i.e., growing). But not growing in the mere sense of expanding; it is a developing entelechy. Nothing which it "was" (i.e., lower inner layers) is/are lost, any more than when I stack up poker chips as I add each new one are the earlier ones lost. Consciousness in each individual advances at the latest layer, but the prior ones are contained and can be retrieved. Memory is the retrieval; anamnesis is the return, actually, to a lower level, a literal trip back down along this spatial axis, both inwardly (totally) and outwardly (partially, in that the inner deeper — lower, earlier — layer reached somehow has an external perceptual analog, perhaps by projection): i.e., one sees — is back in — again — the time-layer one has returned to.

To understand this one must imagine the individual as a rod or column spanning a very large number of ongoing lives, one after another, but *always accruing* (as well as sequential) — these long rods pass — thrust — outward (rather than just upward) as the universe-entelechy grows. There is a growth from small, simple, slow to more intricate and complex and rapid. I see it (envision it) as a geometrical "jungle gym," a 3-D network progressively elaborating itself. One way it does this is by a continually growing development and transfer of knowing (awareness), by means of transferred information throughout the interstices or stations.

It is grid-like—the past is deeper, toward the center; the present is the edges.

[27:102] When all illusion is shaken off, we, without intention or premeditation or intention arrive by this route to him: he is the end point—omega, and it is not a question of pistis, faith or conviction, but (as I experienced finally) an actual inner *and* outer empirical *encounter* with him, not *belief* that he exists (however correct such a belief would be) but *Gnosis*—direct knowledge.

Is this the victory of *Gnostic* Christianity over faith Christianity? A return to the correct historic course? After all, he will be returning—doesn't this pave the way for that? He is/will be not our absent king anymore (deus absconditus) but our actual king returned. What most of all my 3-74 experience reveals is that *again* (after the lapse of almost 2,000 years) it is possible for man to know and hear God directly again, as in the days of the covenant-makers. The long silence by God is over; we can be caused—if properly led—to regenerate our lost—as Calvin put it—supernatural powers and regain our lost state; the prophesied rectification has begun.

[27:103] Below is a new model of my journey:

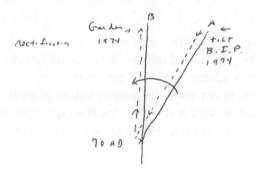

Starting at tilt point A (BIP 1974) I moved retrograde to 70 A.D., the actual point of intervention, and then returned. Not to B, but to rectified point A, the replacement world. For me to cross over from B to A, I had to move back to X and then advance again along the replacement 4th axis track.

Perhaps the model should be drawn:

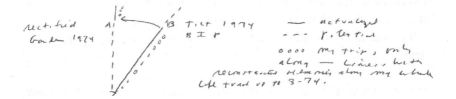

If this model is correct, I as "changeling" or "cuckoo's egg" floating on the raft toward London, past Scotland Yard, am from another world, all right, with [blocked] memories of it, but where that world is is that it's an alternate world, not the far past (although I was briefly there), not the cyclum, not the future, not another planet, etc. — any of these.

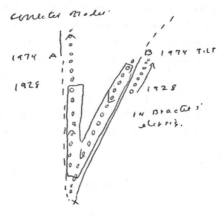

So my entire extraordinary 3-74 experience can be understood as a *complex* miracle: I was moved retrograde on my 4th (time) axis to a crucial juncture and then advanced (by our time three days later) back forward into what for me is not the same present but an alternate present, with memories to match. This is complex, but the experience was complex. I was taken on 3-18-74 and restored on December 16, 1928, in the alternate world.

[27:106] If you insert an absolute event into a relative system, no matter how much the relative elements change, the absolute event is still there.

In which case the value of my published writing is that it teaches us to look beneath (behind or below) the palpable landscape, to regard it only as a cunning veil, and to detect at last the absolute event — the 1st advent — which is the true landscape around us. Except in such works as *Ubik*, "Faith of Our Fathers," *3 Stigmata, TMITHC*, "Electric Ant," *Tears*, etc., where is the concept (worldview) found in which another reality is found when the surface is peeled back layer by layer, exposing at last the absolute world? And in 3-74 I reached that absolute world; time and space peeled back — thousands of swept out layers peeled away in a matter of hours, and there lay Rome and the disciples: the true hidden persecuted despised [early] church which Luther speaks of. As the Greeks knew, the truly real does not ever change or depart — it always *is*.

[27:107] Everything hinges on whether the 70 A.D. landscape is just *a* prior landscape or *the* prior one.

Folder 34

[34:6] I am really in error when I talk about distinguishing, experiencing or recalling 3 worlds; there are 4:

(1) The black iron prison (Rome/USSR/Fascist USA)
(2) This our normal world.
(3) The Garden world.
(4) The experience of (2) under the "revealed" guise in which Zebra or the Logos was seen, including the set-ground separation into mundane versus holy; e.g., the "illuminated letter" (color) passage in *Tears*.

What does that signify? Our world (2) is woven — by Zebra. It is not normally seen for what it is — a 3-D web by Zebra in which Zebra is (i.e., Zebra is not outside or above it but rather is concealed within it). Ah! The worm metamorphoses into the butterfly; that's what I saw: the old "worm" corpus of Zebra is being re-woven into the moth or butterfly transformed final state. This is the cocoon stage — these are *not* analogies! This is what I saw that I correctly sensed as a reweaving. It was not reweaving a construct by it, but its own physical body (self) — reweaving itself; this metamorphosis we see as the sum total of all change, which means: we see as the category (process) we call *time*. Thus Paul correctly — and significantly — says — "the universe is in *birth pains*." Something is being born; what we see is the embryo stage of a living entelechy, but I add more precisely, it is not just growing and developing, but undergoing what we know of (in the strict sense) as insect metamorphosis.

What is important about this distinction (between mere growth versus metamorphosis) is that in such a metamorphosis, (1) constituents are fitted in newly to perform functions they didn't before; (2) some parts are discarded, and the change process exerted on the parts remolded may be subjectively experienced by them — not as growth — but as pressure, as pain — loss, stressful alteration. I'd almost say that what I saw was a "cannibalizing." I've got it now, though, this pinning down what I saw as a form of what we see in insect metamorphosis. Jesu! And to think I got the concept of Zebra from a book about insect mimicry! Is Zebra insect-like in other ways than this metamorphosis? Two insect qualities: camouflage mimicry, and morphological metamorphosis — the breaking down of the old to produce the new eidos! (morphe).

And "St. Sophia's" voice: neutral, dispassionate. Neither male nor female.

How much of our universe is involved? Just this planet? Not "the cosmos is — " nor "the universe is — " but perhaps this is just a *world* phenomenon (entity). No — I guess it to be trans-planetary. Very large. (A bit like the trans-system entity which was Palmer Eldritch.)

The pulsing plasmic laser light color: its *blood*, so to speak.

I must turn here to the Logos doctrine.

It is not human but also not mechanical nor artificial — it is dispassionate insect-like — a *benign* one it is not pure energy; it has a physical body (insofar as anything is material or physical).

This explains what Christianity cannot: pain and suffering; this is all part of its grand metamorphosis process.

It thinks. And its thoughts have the force of will, to affect — "warp" — the outcome of physical causal processes.

Deus absconditus — Ich sah es.

Look at the positive — negentropic — value which change, *all* change, acquires from this "metamorphosis" discovery! Heraclitus was right; change is real, all right. But there is a theos, as Parmenides realized, an *it* which changes.

Now to connect the Black Iron Prison world and the Garden world to the metamorphosis: the former is what it *was;* our world is the continually advancing state of the process going on; the garden world the tranquil outcome — the end state headed toward. Basically my speech (Metz[17]) is correct but not radical enough:

The black iron prison is the corpus of the great it as it was; our world is the process metamorphosis, interim, of an insect-like camouflaged, mimicking organism. It was this whose "still small voice" spoke to Elijah.

This breakthrough realization unifies *all* my themes:

(1) What is reality really? Not what it appears.
(2) There are "androids" or "the mantis" among us which appear human but only *simulate* humans.

The key linking (1) and (2) is: *simulate.*

Here is where I went wrong: the simulation is (1) not evil (as I thought) and it is not *less* than what it simulates (as I thought) but more: not clever simulacra-reflex machines, but angelic, and not *a* human here and there but our entire reality (or nearly — it does cast out — reject — parts of what it was and not incorporate them).

As I said correctly in my U.K. speech, its *mask* fooled me: I was onto it, all right, when I wrote my U.K. speech. Behind Palmer Eldritch's cold cruel mask lies the visage of a totally harmless and *virtually* defenseless organism — vide how easy it was to kill Christ, it born into human form, which it is about to try again with hope (expectation, knowledge) of success this time!

[34:11] Insect characteristics:

(1) group mind ("hive of bees")
(2) metamorphosis of insect sort (chrysalis into final form)
(3) "neutral" (or "AI") voice . . . dispassionate
(4) mimicry
(5) very old
(6) programming
(7) fierce mask (especially in O. Test)

This "insect" metamorphosis which I saw is precisely that which God refers to when he says, "Look! I am building a new heaven and a new earth, and the memory of the former things . . ." etc.

In insect metamorphosis, contrasted to entelechy growth, you have a continual *breaking down* of the old — which we do experience! This is precisely where the things we don't understand come in: pain, loss, stress.

It is a moth — the luminous "moth" descending. And moths are precisely the life form which mimics (the Palmer Eldritch fearsome mask).

What we call "time" is the metamorphosis — change of the moth as it passes from what it first was to what it will finally be. From our standpoint, it could reach its final state suddenly and unexpectedly *at any time* — hence all the eschatological aspect of our religion. The parousia is very precisely the moment at which it *ends* its in-time change process, its becoming, and abruptly *is* (in final form).

State one: the black iron prison
Now: this middle world
Later in time: the palm tree garden
Finally: the sky and sea and Aphrodite world, which may be a primordial state lost (the fall) to which the metamorphosing moth is returning. Guess there really was a fall, so this metamorphosis is a repairing.

Folder 33

[33:7] The other night as I was going to sleep I was wondering who could "de-stegenographize" the hidden material in my writing — and the spirit responded with "[those who are] conscious."

Folder 35

[35:3] Something I never considered before is this: since — not *if* but since (as I know from my own experience), this divine entity can transfer knowledge to our minds, of the most complex and deep sort, *why* doesn't it clear up these mysteries about its nature once and for all? (1) to all Christendom; (2) or just even to me? I learned from it all sorts of things, but — such mystery remains. Or does it? Is not the [only] limitation that of our own limited conceptualizing faculties? It is not intrinsically mysterious — it is only a mystery to our limited minds and experience. That which reveals, and confers knowledge, can't be accused of creating mystery. What it does, I guess, is disclose the existence of mysteries — in the sense of the deepest core of meaning at the ontological heart of reality. It points *to*, as one points to or out, say, a sculpture — the thing which *is*. Not a mere verbal explanation but directly at the thing *itself*, to be contemplated as the final *is*. (Cf. Heraclitus: "the Oracle does not answer yes or no — it instead gives a sign [Zeichen] *meaning*."[18])

[35:6] In *Time Out of Joint* the world is a fake, and specifically the *real* world is another time-segment. My initial revelation in 3-74 was that the time was really around 70 A.D. — not later but earlier, a reversal of *Joint*. Yet, the basic intimation is there, fully, in *Joint;* this is all a cunningly fabricated delusion, the world we see, and the basic delusion has to do with the true *temporal* locus. Since *Joint* was S-F I naturally put the *real* time in the future, not the past. Damn it, I've overlooked the extraordinary parallels between *Joint* and my "it's really 70 A.D.!" experience. E.g.: the dream I had of the dark, old-fashioned house with the archaic window shades, the cracked mirror — and realizing I couldn't get out of that world without God's help. My incessantly-recurring dream of the 1126 Francisco St. house — that's where I lived when I wrote *Joint*— that was the fake world of the novel, and resembles the miserable old house in Placentia dream. Is there some clue in my 1126 Francisco St. dream? It was with Joan that I so recently saw it again, after many years. Maybe I have a soul which leaves my body in sleep and goes back in time (and, as in 3-74, forward).

Back in the 50s when I lived at 1126 Francisco St. actually, as expressed in *Joint that* world seemed unreal; in actuality, "it was decades later" (in *Joint*). But now that it *is* decades later, *that* past time and place seems real (or anyhow the past somehow) and *this* a fake. And, as I say, it is also astonishing how in '74 I foresaw the Sonoma events of the past three months!

What is my real relationship to time? I experience the near past, the near future, and the very far past; a lot of my soul or psyche seems to be transtemporal . . . maybe this is why any given present space time seems somehow unreal or delusional to me. I span across and hence beyond it; always have — and the transtemporal is the eternal, the divine, the immortal spirit. How long have I been here, and how many times? Who or what am I, and how old?

Reality outside confronts me as a mystery, and so does my own *inner* identity. The two are fused. Who am I? When is it? Where am I? This sounds like madness. But when I read the Scriptures I find myself in the world which is to me real, and I understand myself. The Bible is a door (3:5?[19]).

Folder 36

[36:18]

③ Artifact ← ② Nature ← ① Logos
(electronic)   (wall of   Christ/Rel·jous
               Beef)   information

Dream: opening huge carton and taking out large electronic artifact. Below it is a solid wall, a rectangle of beef. Under it is every kind of religious (Christian) writing imaginable, even sentences covered (stegenographia) by a glued-in paper strip with a replacement sentence. I try to interest everyone in the theological material, but they are like the harness bull who preceded Sergeant Kelly: totally uninterested. It is as if the religious material is crazy. There is no reconciliation between the world (of nature) represented by the huge rectangle (wall) of beef and the layer of religious information under it: the implication is that if you believe in the reality of the wall of flesh (sarx?) you can't see any sense in the religious info below, and the wall of beef is certainly real — you *have* to believe in *it*. But on the other hand, what is the relationship between the wall of beef and the great electronic artifact? As between the religious writing and the wall of beef, there is no reconciliation between the wall of beef and the artifact. I am sure that the religious writing equals the computer punched tape in "Electric Ant" and the computer of the Persus 9 in *Maze*, which can't be read intrinsically but which gives rise to the world of flesh or nature which again in turn gives rise to the artificial world of mechanical/electronic constructs. 3 levels or layers are represented. No one wishes to take seriously the deepest one (except me). The logos, the word, is represented; that which is written gives rise to the living world (creatures, nature) which in turn gives rise to our artificial environment. If we place ourselves in the top world (artificial construct) we are totally walled off — have no knowledge or contact with — the logos substratum, nor, if it is called to our attention can we see any merit in it: if ② is real and rational, ① is not. It is even hard, if not impossible, to comprehend ② (when one starts with ③), which is given in the dream as the starting point of view. ② itself is difficult to explain: how does it relate to ③? But at least it isn't "crazy," the way ① looks. But put another way, ① gives rise to ③ via ②, a fascinating thought. So the origins of the technological world — the manufactured, the constructed, lies ultimately in a sort of hidden punched out tape just as the false world of Delmak-O arose from Persus 9's computer. ②, the world of flesh and nature, *totally hides* the true origin of ③. It is by a thorough study of the relationship between ② and ③ that the relationship between ① and ② can be understood. As ① is to ②, ② is to ③. We live somewhere between ② and ③, never (as the Persus crew never suspected while in polyencephalic fusion) suspecting ①. What the dream reveals is not just that we, like they, have a punched out computer tape programming us, but tells, too, that it is Christian, in fact Biblical in essence: i.e., Christianity is our punched out tape. All the thousands of large written pages of books which I saw — the books themselves — were our "punched out computer tape" — i.e., the source of our natural/living world, which totally obscures its origins (causes). Given a random fistful of the ribbon of info, we can make no sense out of it.

The fascinating thing is that a glimpse of our "punched tape" exhibits (to us) nothing that makes sense. We *do* get glimpses of bits of it; e.g., the Bible and apocryphal books.

Even more revealingly, as TV image is to human, human is to logos. I should examine the profound implications that the *Maze* model of punched-tape programming simulating a shared reality is an accurate model of our own world. Such a model (with Christian archetypes as the punch-outs) would go a long way to explain what I saw in 3-74 on. Plato's Edoloi theory must be modernized. Put another way, Plato's concept of the real world (of forms) was a primitive pre-technological attempt to describe what is more accurately described by the logos theory which resembles what I described in *Maze*.

But look: ①, the punched out computer tape, resembles the world of ③ more than it does the intermediary (separating) world of nature, ②. As in "a chicken is an egg's way of producing another egg," ③ is ①'s way of replicating itself. It could even be argued that we — all living creatures — are primarily carriers of information: the DNA coding. The 3-2-1 layers dream suggests not just that an informational world underlies the opaque surface of the natural world but, even more specifically it is the Christian Holy-Spirit-inspired scriptures. These texts are not a description of events, past, present and future (i.e., of or about reality) but the *cause* of reality. Evidently this verbal information consists of a series of ideas (cf. Plato!) which, when thought by Zebra, are printed out in our world throughout its [linear time] "length," not at space/time x and/or y but throughout: i.e., as always enacted (i.e., always present, being from outside time). I have the impression that a particular story is being told (repeatedly?), that which Daniel tells of Babylon, and the giant with feet of clay, etc. In this apocalyptic book the basic archetypes show up, but there are additional themes in the NT as well; this is why material from "Acts" as well as from "Daniel" show up in

Tears. The deepest level of reality (an informational, verbal one) is what is shown in *Ubik;* helpful, guiding and informing words rising as it were to the surface (① rising up into ②). Is it not a super extraordinary idea that the deepest level of reality is verbal? But the reason for this can be found in the Hindu view of immanent mind: the words are the thoughts of the immanent deity. Then were the great pages of writing which I repeatedly saw in 3-74 the thoughts of Brahman? (i.e., Zebra). Human history is the story which he/it is thinking. But the *real* human history is that of salvific activity, especially the 2nd and 1st incarnations which consist of the thinking deity entering his/its own dream/story as a (as *the*) protagonist, and, once in it, he/it falls victim to its laws, including injury and death. If *Maze* is retained as the paradigm, he is the only one of the 14 members of the settlement on Delmak-O who remembers their pre-polyencephalic fusion, and hence who knows that Delmak-O is a totally illusory world (Maya, Dokos). This certainly indicates that my anamnesis was due to the active intervention (and theolepsy) by Christ. Taken over by him (at 3-74) I saw level ① penetrating up through and into (and to an extent replacing) level ②. The landscape of level ① is biblical (e.g., Rome, early Christians, God breaking through into time, etc.). I did not see an earlier form of ② but the timelessness archetypal landscape of ①.

It certainly is odd (i.e., an odd coincidence) that in *Maze* I assign to the mentufacturer the power to roll back time, though. However, a closer scrutiny of the Delmak-O world in *Maze* would show that he has that power due to the illusory quality of that world. Perhaps if it were real, time (even by God) could not be rolled back; put another way, if you discover that, in your world, time can (I guess by God) be rolled back, you can correctly deduce that your world is illusory. And then: what is exposed when that time, by the deity, is rolled back? I discerned a landscape of apocalyptic [biblical] archetypes. Presumably *that* world (like the control room of the spaceship Persus 9) is the real world; it is not just an infinite series of illusions.

Level ① (the Logos) generated a world so substantial (so to speak opaque) as to conceal it — ① — totally.

If I am correct about all this, then I say, the 1st advent was a palpable breaking-through of the supreme entity (mind — i.e., Holy Wisdom) of level ① into level ②, the sole time it took place *conspicuously.* But in 3-74 I was shown — in my own novel *Tears* a breaking-through of info from level ① right on past ② and into level ③! In level ③ there is such a vast component of (verbal) information that info properly a part of level ① blends invisibly in. All the "Acts" and "Daniel" (the dream) stuff in *Tears* is a perfect example of that. I virtually conclude that level ① deliberately evolves ("programs") level ② forward toward oral speech, then writing. And at last the sort of titanically verbal (informational) construct world of the computer, etc., level ③ becomes more and more like ①. It is thought producing thought through the intermediary stage of flesh/body/material/nature — a replication, a giving birth. Is this not a description of the 1st advent and more so the 2nd advent? Level ① thrusts through ② and manifests itself in ③: foremostly, in the Scriptures. But *not* limited to them (as *Tears* testifies to, and as *Ubik* depicts, and now I'm beginning to include *Maze*). Holy Wisdom exists before all creation (i.e., the material universe). Then it creates or helps create the material universe — i.e., level ②. Then it incarnates in level ② but expressing itself verbally — in terms of thoughts, words, concepts, etc., all of which add up to Holy Wisdom which is its essence. But level ② does not find it acceptable; it is killed and returns to level ① from whence it came. However, it will try (incarnate, be born) in level ② again as a means of raising level ③ into an authentic replication of level ①.

Zebra, which I saw undergoing metamorphosis, invisible to us normally, is evolving on level ① but will eventually invade level ③, assimilating it to itself and infusing it with essence (reality). This means that level ② is nothing more than a means to an end. A sentient being (Brahman) is giving birth to sentient being, ③, which ② is not. ② must be regarded as a womb ("receptacle of being"), a kind of hatching "egg." The living, sentient product of this "egg" replicates the "parent" of the "egg." Thus I say, the ubiquitous immanent being, of level ①, does not divide (e.g., binary fission, etc.) but creates an intermediary — and perhaps temporary — state which in a certain literal sense is not truly real, except as a source for what ultimately will be real — level ③. This level ③ certainly resembles Teilhard de Chardin's Noösphere. We can expect level ② to be generating progressively more replicatory aspects of its own source: level ①. The ultimate true birth is exactly what is depicted in *Ubik:* the wise information breaking *through* reality (through ② from ①), thus ③ will more and more resemble ①, level ② will be effaced by the ① qualities of ③. I foresee in all this eventually a final absorption of ②, entirely, by ③, so that ① and ③ are joined [directly] as a monism. Our first intimation of this elimination process would be the abrupt first incarnation into our ② world of the embodiment of ① itself, a sort of leap "over" ② (more breaking through). This can be expressed two ways:

(A) A weakening of the reality of ②, i.e., the *natural* environment or world.

(B) As ② becomes less real and more dream like, less substantial, fragments of ① would appear in (break through into) it: surfacing, as it were: swimming to the surface of ② but not actually being part of

②. These bits would be: (x) *contours* of ①'s topology; (y) verbal bits, which would be closer to the heart of ①.

(A) and (B): the combination of these two processes would produce a *stability* of the so-to-speak amount of ontological essence of the empirical world, but continually there would be a cryptic or subtle metamorphosis of the world as ② aspects lessen and ③ grow, the ratio continually changing irrevocably in the direction of ① intruding and ② diminishing. Our life spans are too short to experience this metamorphosis, except that the rate of acceleration of ③ is now conspicuous. We are not aware that ③ is not merely a product of ② but rather/also a thrusting through ② of ①. ③ must be regarded as ① ultimately restated; the material universe is a temporary expedient, the egg between hen and hen, ③ finally will be identical to ①, as near as I can discern, whereas ② is a "polyencephalic delusion" (at least it is becoming so [now]).

When ③ is completed it will be the "new heavens and new earth" and that "which will never enter the mind nor come up into the heart" will have been ②. It is interesting that the Corpus Christi (completed ③) must pass through ② rather than springing directly from ①. Not only the things (objects of ②) are turned into a womb by ① for ③ but the sentient beings of ② are so used: i.e., the Holy Spirit possesses them the way externally Zebra transubstantiates objects and processes.

What I saw in 3-74 (Rome) is a vivid example of ① showing through ② to ③, if by ③ you mean me: the new *self* within me perceiving — finally — its origin, its home: ①. And even the B.I. Prison: I had been/was there, too, as an early Christian. The Atman fusing with the Brahman: ③ fusing with ① and bypassing ② — so ② is identified as Maya. So I ask, where, in ③, is ① being *primarily* born? I'd have to answer: most likely in the *most* sentient parts of ③, which could well be human minds (insofar as *this* planet is concerned). This makes of each of our heads a receiver-transducer of emanations from ①: if we evolve far enough we — perhaps suddenly — hear and see past ② — thick as it is — to the words, books and pages of ①. However, I am speaking of *conscious* reception; in point of fact, bits of ① are forever ubiquitously reaching us subliminally imbedded in and indistinguishable from info in ③ deriving out of ②.

What must be remembered is that the vast gulf between ③ and ② is equally great between ② and ①. In certain respects ① would resemble ③ (i.e., verbal material) *but:* it would seem to be nuts. Crazy, cryptic verbal material — as inscrutable as the punched tape intrinsically in *Maze*.

Under very unusual circumstances a person might lose contact with ② and relate directly to ①, but this would amount virtually to a trip ahead in time, because the delusional ② is still with us, still a barrier between ③ and ①; if for *any* reason a person saw through ② and related to ① he would be in the strange position of experiencing the distant past and future simultaneously: (A) he would see as still extant ancient archetypes hazed over in ② and (B) he would in his own time experience what for other people would only come later when ② peters out entirely. At first he would recapitulate the past, then phase over into prophesized events: i.e., to end-time events. The whole story being narrated (or thought) by the deity would disclose itself to him. And, oddly, he would be deluged with books and pages of writing, since the apparatus he was plugged into is primarily computer-like (teaching machine and library like).

The Bible is a fusion of ①, ② and ③, of most use is that of a doorway to ①, available to minds locked into ③, read in a way excluding ② to which it unceasingly relates. The time rate (flow) of the Bible is the true time rate; that of ② is not — is deluding in fact, giving a spurious impression (record) of a great deal of passing time. Piercing by ③ to ①, or by ① upward into ③ it is between 70–90 A.D., i.e., just following the 1st advent and just *before* the 2nd.

My God — the Bible *is* the story which the punched computer tape of ① is printing out via ②, directly fulfilling ③! I can deduce this from the biblical elements in, e.g., *Tears*. It is ① incising onto ③ via ②. *Tears* is a mixture of ① and ③. The only other way the elements of ① could appear in my writing would be racial memory, but the "racial memory" would deal with realm ① underlying ② anyhow, so just the *why*, not the *what*, would be changed (i.e., the reason I linked up to ① directly, bypassing ②).

To sum up: realm ② is being spun or woven into realm ③ which is a replication of realm ① which is doing the spinning and weaving.

So the material universe is a womb in which a single but 3-aspect VALIS is replicating itself; that which the material universe will give birth to is the offspring of the original sentient entity but probably the entity *and* its offspring will constitute *one* single realized organism, not two, since it is self-generating. That (entity or offspring) which it will produce, then, is itself. We see the universe backward: the creator lies at the end or Omega point: forming (directing) creation teleologically, from its outcome backward.

[36:29]

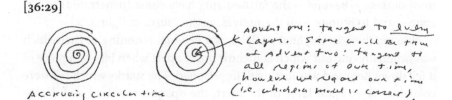

Accruing circular time

Advent one: tangent to every layer. Same would be true of Advent two: tangent to all regions of our time, however we regard our time (i.e. whichever model is correct).

Folder 31

[**31:18**] All these instances I've found of "divine" (logos or Gnostic) truths (material) inserting in my writing — it's not inserted; this is just one elongated instance of the natural process of the orthogonal Koinos *thrusting up* from within/below, such books as *Ubik* being both instances of and accounts about the upward thrusting which is going on — for me, the supreme moment arriving in 3-74. [. . .]

Had my 3-74 experience not occurred, I might suppose my 26 year writing theme to be vain, empty and foolish. I now for the first time see my writing as half I and my 3-74 experience as half II of a total experience: a surmise and search — then, abruptly, a finding, as the veil lifted (even though briefly). What happened in 3-74 was that the real, the thrusting-through world which I intuited, proved actually to be there, and not only that, to be accessible (under certain circumstances); not only could it be looked for, it could be found. Rome c. A.D. 70 was nothing more or less than the Persus 9 of *Maze,* and this linear time world of 1976/7 A.D. proved to be nothing more than such pseudo worlds, taken to be real, as in *Ubik, Joint,* and *Maze* and *3 Stigmata.* Yet, it has taken me literally *years* since 3-74 to see that as Persus 9 is to Delmak-O, Rome c. A.D. 70 is to U.S. A.D. 1974. I never anticipated such a tremendous payoff (breakthrough), despite the fact that the corpus of my writing is a map, an analysis, and a guide. The 26 years of writing, without 3-74, is a map of nothing, and 3-74, without the body of writing, is conceptually inexplicable.

[**31:64**] On the *Doonesbury* TV special the overthrow of Nixon was spoken of, by a child, as "the revolution," and the counterculture adult who participated in it said, "Even the trees agree." Pure (undefiled) nature has cast away its hull of that which is dead, which halts growth, which stifles and kills the life-spirit within. The bushel basket over the lantern — the mystery and paradox is that at the very innermost core of what seems to be evil lies a pure burning light — "the light of the world" which the rescuers from outside — beyond — the farthest ring have come (penetrated) to liberate — and to reunite with themselves, as the source of light. [. . .]

Rescue, then, in the final analysis, is a healing, reuniting of that which was originally one but which somehow broke apart when bits or a piece of it fell down here and was forthwith imprisoned. The sparks which fell were coated by layer upon layer of the inert, the opaque, the dead and death-dealing-rinds which caused forgetting and loss of identity. Suppose we take this forward from Gnostic terms into the strictly modern world: we say, then, that a vast proto-organism existed (embracing at the least several star systems) and ours fell out — was severed from — the giant proto-organism, which I saw in my nitrous oxide revelation as a vast vine (Christ) *pruned* by the father as Gardener. Many cuttings feel no loss, but some do, and these latter the Savior (the original cosmic organism) seeks reunification with, upon *his* initiative, his "growing downward," so to speak, into the otherwise lightless realm into which we, cut off into bits, descended thousands of years ago. The keystone is *restored memory*, which is a recollection of ourselves *not* as separate entities but as "stations" in a quasi-computer-like* proto-organism, a vast incorporeal energy which thinks, and whose thoughts *are* the physical cosmos — we are, each of us, microanalogs of it: just as each cell of our bodies contains *all* the information to retrieve the whole human, each whole human psyche contains the aggregate information — *is* the information — topologically congruent with the macro proto-organism. (In other words, the macro proto-organism can be — is — contained within each of us as total individual human psyche, just as each individual human cell contains complete information from which that human can be retrieved.)

[31:77] As I realized about the cover of the paperback of *Scanner* it really shows the dealer and law officer as the two halves of one person, with no hint of "warring" personalities: visually, they gestalt into a syzygy, two sides of the same coin.[20] Your dealer is a cop. Your cop is a dealer.

I feel as if the scales have fallen from my eyes, and I'm seeing lucidly. From *Frolix 8* to *Tears* to *Scanner*: a logical progression of an in-depth study of jail, tyranny, dope, slave labor camps, and irreality related to lies (this last point mostly in *Scanner*). Something of this seems hinted at in "Faith of Our Fathers," too: lies, delusions (induced by drugs), tyranny.

---

* Virtually all of Dick's references to computers are metaphorical or part of his new religious terminology. They are rarely technological in the strict sense. It is paradoxical, or at least ironic, that Dick found his natural audience in the digital age, given not only that he died at the era's outset but also that home computers, I strongly suspect, would only have aggravated his paranoia. I picture him peering deeply into the screen, trying to see who on the other side is watching back; would there have been any doubt in his mind that *someone* was there? Even Arthur C. Clarke's more theological meditations (as alluded to earlier herein by Dick himself) accept technology's role in our growing collective insight as a species, albeit while acknowledging the tension that technology begets. But the digital age has engendered a more widespread consideration and acceptance of the possible alternative realities that earlier readers of Dick's fiction relegated to the realm of drug-induced hallucination. The eighties cyberpunks who mapped the emerging computer culture, like Gibson, Rucker, Shiner, and Sterling, counted Dick as among their most prevalent influences, even as Dick might well have wondered what the hell *Neuromancer* was all about. — SE

What is shown in *Scanner* as the lies-enslaving-tyranny axis is not simplistically identified as "the government" as it is in *Tears* and *Frolix 8* — in *Scanner* it becomes paradoxical and elusive, with the government *perhaps* or *evidently* producing the drug, and the clinics and rehab centers *perhaps* or *evidently* being deliberate slave labor camps. The drug is there; the work camps are there; the feds are alluded to, but — the reader must unravel the puzzle for himself. If it *isn't* the government, who is it? Is not the definition of government "that which is actually in control"? And the makers of SD, which turn out to be the slave labor camp owners, are one and the same; it is a de facto government — like the Mafia, and look: why are scramble suits necessary? Crime (the Mafia? identified as dope elements) have penetrated the authorities deeply. As is said again and again in the novel: "all is murked over," things are *not* as they seem (as is always the case in my writing). Arctor is not what he appears to be. Nor is Donna. Nor Barris. Nor Mike Westway. Nor New-Path. The sides cannot be clearly drawn as "good-bad," or "us-them," or even "pro-dope — anti-dope."

Folder 32

[32:3] In Feb. of 1974 I momentarily withdrew assent to the reality of this world; a month later this world underwent visible changes, and its true nature became perceptible to me: it is, as the Gnostics said, a prison. It is there, but it is not as it appears to be. The immediate reaction to the ano- mie in the world is to say simply that it is out of control. If it is there to re- awaken us to our divine origins, however, its malign aspects serve a good purpose. What each of us must do is repudiate the world, which is to say, deny it *while at the same time* affirming a sanctified alternate reality, which I did vis-à-vis the golden fish sign; the false quasi-cosmos was denied and the true sacred reality was affirmed. It was a single act, a movement away from the first to the second. I think I've figured out the basic move neces- sary: an ethical balking.* That is how the world-denying begins. That is the first step in unraveling the counterfeit quality of the world. The Gnos- tics stressed such a "metaphysical strike" and pointed out that the archons (who rule this prison world, the wardens) can only harm the body and mind but not the divine spark. It is a refusal to cooperate with a harmful world, which, once one has balked against it, reveals its ersatz quality. [. . .] It probably is of extraordinary significance that repudiation of the mun- dane reality and acknowledgement of the transmundane is a single event or act, rather than two. The two realities cannot both exist, evidently. They are counter-realities. This is what the Gnostics believed: that the world stands between man and God, and must be eliminated. Who would expect that disavowing the world would instantly expose the divine on the far side of it? "Man and God in essence belong together against the world but are in fact separated by the world, which in the Gnostic view is the alienating, divisive agency" (E. of Phil.). Well, then this being so, look what my writ- ing tends to promote: it promotes a sense of the counterfeit quality of the

* With this important concept, Dick presents the visible universe as a moral test. The chal- lenge is to perceive the injustice of the system of the world and to refuse to cooperate with it. The problem is that the logic of the visible universe is internally consistent and con- tains no clear indication that it deserves to be rejected. The impetus to "withdraw assent" must come from a transcendent point of view that impels immediate disobedience: the word "balk" implies gut instinct rather than intellectual decision. Moreover, one cannot be aware that the visible universe is a test, because this would lead to calculated action in light of an expected reward. Dick gives one concrete example of his own balking: his partici- pation in the tax strike organized by *Ramparts* magazine in 1968. By "this-worldly" stan- dards, this was an illogical decision that led to personal hardship, but by "other-worldly" standards, his refusal was simply the right thing to do. — GM

world; it promotes a repudiation of it which dissolves it by assisting the withdrawal of assent to it; and finally, by so doing, obliterates the alienating agency and brings man and God together. I can claim this for my work, on the theological level.

[32:4] What I saw that I term VALIS or Zebra must then not have been immanent deity at all, but, as I later realized, a mimicking entity not rising up from within but descending onto objects and processes from above or, better, outside. It had, so to speak, landed here. As with Runciter's words in *Ubik*, it was penetrating through from — this is the best formulation of all — from behind. Reality is constructed like a ham sandwich: man is one slice of the bread, then comes the slice of ham which is the world, then the second slice of bread which is God. The words in *Ubik* pierced or filtered through from the other slice, through to man, to us, this slice. It's funny that I could read the E. of Phil. about the world being "an alienating, divisive agency that separates man from God" and not instantly perceive the value — perhaps the ultimate value — of my writing and its preoccupation. In point of fact, such novels as *Ubik, Maze, Stigmata*, etc., tend to dissolve away the world — and, if the Gnostics' 3-element situation-view is a correct view, God should be reunited with us thereby.

Now the incredible accuracy of *Ubik* can be appreciated. The world is not merely counterfeit (as in *Stigmata* and all the others); there is more: it is counterfeit, but under it lies another world, and it is this other world, this Logos world, which filters or breaks through. *Ubik,* then, is a step up from *Maze* and *Stigmata* in presenting this. It presents a triune situation, which evidently is the actual one, whereas the other novels and stories present only the aspect of world as hallucination, without disclosing that another, actual one lies beyond, below or beneath. It is God who, as the far bread slice, takes the initiative toward us, as Runciter does toward Joe Chip and the other inertials. This is what I saw in 3-74, when, under the power of the Holy Spirit, I read the dream section in *Tears* and found a latent or crypte message embedded in the text. My experience and view, then, are not only Gnostic but what is more tend to prove the correctness of the triune Gnostic division, in particular their view of the world as alienating and divisive between man and God (Joe Chip and Runciter). Had the Gnostic view been wrong, when I "abolished" the world (suddenly withdrew assent from it) I would have exposed nothing, no sublime, sacred, divine reality beyond; a religious experience would have turned out to be nothing but a psychotic break. Were the Gnostic triune division wrong, my writing would serve a malign, sick purpose: leading the reader away from reality and toward autism. But the Gnostic triune division is correct; otherwise I could not, would not, have had my 2-74 and 3-74 et al. experiences.

[32:5] Starting from my "True Vine" revelation, we are kept in a "lopped-off" relationship to God by the world itself — the faulty pseudo-cosmos in which we find ourselves living. A mere undercurrent sensation of alienation must blossom into something greater, or anyhow can; it can lead to a moral repudiation of the world (the kind of ethical balking such as the Ramparts tax strike[21]) or it can lead to an epistemological "dissolving-away of the world" such as my writings contain. Perhaps where I made my mistake for several years about God being immanent was that whereas I thought I saw him *in* nature, in point of fact he, like the messages in *Ubik*, [was] filtering through nature from beyond, beneath or below. Nature could either become transparent, or the reality of the divine could, through its boundless power, assert itself through, breach through. The latter is what happened in 3-74. However, it was not visible to the unenhanced eye. The world did not weaken; God chose to make his move — the real God, not the demiurge.

Beyond doubt, the true God could annihilate our pseudo-world, not merely permitting a temporary vision to one person (such as he did for me by having me taken over by the Paraclete) but for everyone. The Paraclete, possessing me, literally saw *through* the world, as if it were transparent; I remember that; wow, was it something, that gate, those geometric forms, and the presence of Zebra (God). (Or the cosmic Christ.) Lem says that in *Ubik* "a sacerdotal power buried in the gutter or rubbish for aeons has been resurrected"; I can begin to see what he might mean by that.

[32:7] One fascinating aspect of *Ubik* is disclosed when the question is asked, "Where did you (I) get the idea?" The origin of the idea, in contrast to virtually all other novels, is evident from the text of the novel itself, although one must extrapolate from Runciter to whatever Runciter represents, and the state of cold-pac to whatever state we are all in. In the novel, information spontaneously intrudes into the world of the characters, indicating that their world is not what they think it is; in fact, it indicates that their world is not even there at all — some kind of world is there, but not the one they are experiencing. That time-regression is put forth in the novel, and that time-regression figured in my 3-74 experience — this still baffles me; the principle underlying the devolution (reversion) of objects along the form-axis in the novel is explained by a reference to Plato's theory of ideal forms, and I guess that applies to our world and to my own experience. However, not until I recently studied the E. of Phil. article on Gnosticism so thoroughly, did I begin to understand the triune reality division which must exist and which is also put forth in *Ubik* — if Runciter is God, and Joe Chip and the other inertials are analogs of all men; then the regressed world is the ham in the sandwich, and, as in *Ubik*, must be abolished; as in Gnosticism, this is accomplished, in *Ubik*, by the revelation of esoteric knowledge about their condition by a deity-like entity lying behind even Runciter; i.e., Ubik. It is this knowledge — not just information but gnosis — revealed to them, especially to Joe Chip, which makes them aware of their real condition. Therefore if one knows very much about Gnosticism (which I didn't until a few days ago) one could see the resemblance between *Ubik* and the Gnostic cosmogony and cosmology. But we are talking (regarding the real world) of information which, by being transferred, radically changed history. And it must be realized (I certainly do, even if no one else does) that what broke through was not limited to information, but that theolepsy (one at least) were involved. If I rule out Soviet experiments and occult human groups (vide supra) then we have something not found in *Ubik*, but, although admittedly described as diabolic, in *Stigmata*. Is theolepsy not specifically what *Stigmata* depicts? With Chew-Z or whatever, Can-D, I forget, the eucharist.[22] What do you get if, as Le Guin suggests, you take a group of my novels and stories and fit them together, especially the 3 picked up by Bantam? Theolepsy, the Gnosis slipping through, reality (the world) as illusion concealing another but real world (*Maze*) — what an aggregate message those 3 novels add up to!

When I recently reread *Stigmata* I saw it for what it was: a penetrating, acute and exhaustive study of the miracle of transubstantiation, simply reversing the bipolarities of good and evil. What the novel contemplated was — that is, the conclusion it reached — was the startling notion that imbibing of the sacred host culminated, for the imbiber, in eventually becoming the deity of which the host was the supernatural manifestation. Since all of them were consuming hosts of the same deity, they all became the same deity, and their separate or human identities were abolished. They literally became the deity, all of them, one after another. What this constituted in the novel was an eerie kind of invasion. They were invaded on an individual basis and they were, regarded another way, invaded as a planet or species, etc., which is to say collectively. This invasion by the deity bears a resemblance to the invasion of the regressed world in *Ubik* by Runciter's messages and, ultimately, by Ubik itself (as confirmed by the ad starting the last chapter). That ad clarified what Ubik was; it precisely equated Ubik with the Logos. There is no way to get around that. Ubik in *Ubik* is the same divinity as the St. Sophia mentioned in *Deus Irae*. So Run-

citer and Ubik equals Palmer Eldritch and Chew-Z. We have a human being transformed into a deity which is ubiquitous (no one seems to have
noticed that Palmer Eldritch is ubiquitous as is Ubik, that the same theme
dominates both novels).

The Gnostic contribution which *Maze* makes is the idea of a totally un-
tenable reality glossed over by a mass wish-fulfillment hallucination shared
by everyone, and a salvific entity who can extricate you right out of that
prison-like world.

> *Maze:* Prison-like world glossed over by illusion. Salvific intercessor
> who can and does extricate you. Induced amnesia.
> *Stigmata:* Invasion (penetration) of our world by a deity who can be-
> come everyone via the host, a mass theolepsy.
> *Ubik:* Salvific information penetrating through the "walls" of our
> world by an entity with personality representing a life- and reality-
> supporting quasi-living force.

Collating the three novels, how much of the Gnostic message is expressed? Or, put another way, how much of my 2-74, 3-74 experience is
expressed? One thing left out is the altering of the historic process, which
was revealed to me as happening in 3-74. I suppose in a sense that's in *Frolix 8.* And the breaching through by God and the hosts, the apocalyptic
material from "Acts" and "Daniel." There are little sprinkles in other novels
and stories — for instance, the idea of anamnesis (expressed negatively usually in my writing by the theme of fake memories). Well, that's expressed in
Maze, so I've inserted it supra. I wonder what you get if you sit down starting with "Roog" and read through everything (including such strange stories as "Retreat Syndrome") all the way to *Scanner.* If everything interlocks,
what is the total message? I know I scared myself shitless that one night
when Isa was down here and I reread some early stories in *Preserving Machine.* But my recent study of Gnosticism indicates that below any negative
world-negating message there is an affirmation of God and love.

Folder 50

[50:11] I am too far into Gnosticism to back out. The idea of Jesus opening Adam's eyes and bringing him to consciousness, the re-linking to the lost primordial state through the Gnosis, the unflinching facing of evil in the world and knowing it *cannot* have come from (the Good) God — and the salvador salvandus — man as cut off from part of the Godhead.

Thinking back over my life I can see that I have survived many troubles — I look at the copies of the Ballantine *Scanner* and I can see what I have to transmute those terrible days into something worthwhile, lasting, good, even important (i.e., meaningful). This is what God does; this is his strange mystery: how he accomplishes this. When we view the evil (which he is going to transmute) we can't see for the life of us how we can do it — but later on, and only later on, after it's done, we can see how he has *used* evil as the clay out of which he as potter has fashioned the pot (universe viewed as artifact).

What I notice is how many people wish me well. Look at what John Ross, a stranger, said. Look at what KW said about me having served, done my duty, and now can pass on into the reward waiting for me — he said, even, that they'd applaud me. I still don't know what I did in 3-74 re the Xerox missive, but what I did was what I was sent here to do from the start, and I did it right; as KW put it, "They tell you how, when and where to throw the spear, but *you* must throw it."

I am really very happy. Snuff, music and cats, friends and my exegesis, my studying and gradually more and more understanding my Gnosis, when in 3-74 the savior woke me to full consciousness, for the first time in my life and refound myself, knew who and what I was, remembered my celestial origin, was restored to what I had been before the fall. I saw the prison we are in, and knew I had done right.

[50:12] Salvation — from what? From the *world*, which is an iron prison. Cf. Schopenhauer. Salvation from what he saw happening to the turtles (James-James creation). God did not design such a structure of suffering: he extricates us *from* it, and restores us as part of him. This is the acosmic view in all my writings: the empirical world is a fraud, counterfeit. I write about reality as illusion because it is, and I see that it is. Thus my witness is a tremendously powerful attack on the world — but I am just now realizing that this view (of world as illusion) is Gnostic. My corpus of writing is an assault on the created universe of matter, highly original and accurate. It (the view) discloses the deceptive nature of empirical reality — now I have had it revealed to me that this world is an impediment between us (man) and God.

In my writing I seek to *abolish* the world — the effect of which aids in our restoration to the Godhead. And this is what I did in 2-74 when I saw the Golden Fish; in a single moment of total knowledge (awareness of the *true* state of things) I withdrew my belief in what I customarily saw — and it vanished, and the Christ/God continuum was disclosed — i.e., the slice of bread on the other side of the ham sandwich. First for years I did it in my writing, and then in 2-74 I did it in real life, showing that my writing is *not* fiction but a form (e.g., *Maze, Tears, Ubik,* etc.) of revelation expressed not *by* me but through me, by (St.) Sophia in her salvific work. What is in my work that is important is precisely nothing less than the salvific Gnosis (or parts of it anyhow).*

[50:14] Zebra counterfeits the counterfeit — which fits the Gnostic idea of the bumbling demiurge being helped out, out of mercy, by the *true* God. This helping out, not just of us humans but of the whole fallen (fucked up, not really real) cosmos is the transubstantiation of objects and processes on an invisible ontological level which I saw the growing Corpus Christi achieving. A fake fake = something *real.* The demiurge unsuccessfully counterfeited the pleroma, and now God/the Savior is mimicking this counterfeit cosmos with a stealthily growing *real* one. What this all adds up to is that God, through the cosmic Christ, is assimilating our cosmos to himself.

[50:16] I am thinking back. Sitting with my eyes shut I am listening to "Strawberry Fields." I get up. I open my eyes because the lyrics speak of "going through life with eyes closed." I look toward the window. Light blinds me; my head suddenly aches. My eyes close and I see that strange strawberry ice cream pink. At the same instant knowledge is transferred

---

* The flip side of these feelings of self-importance was, for Dick, debilitating paranoia. Many of Dick's theories placed him at the center of vast, cosmic scenarios, and these preoccupations were often coupled with feelings of persecution. An exaggerated sense of self-importance is common among paranoiacs, who often reason that they must be important if people are out to get them. In a speech to a Vancouver science-fiction convention in 1972, Dick famously noted that any formulation "that attempts to act as an all-encompassing, all-explaining hypothesis about what the universe is about" is a "manifestation of paranoia." Throughout the period of 2-3-74, Dick was also peppering the FBI with increasingly bizarre letters outlining the various plots he felt were at work against him. While in the long run the 2-3-74 experiences seem to have mellowed Dick out, his enlightenment did not come without many a dark night of the soul. — DG

to me. I go into the bedroom where Tessa is changing Chrissy and I recite
what has been conveyed to me: that he has an undetected birth defect and
must be taken to the doctor at once and scheduled for surgery. This turns
out to be true.

What happened? What communicated with me? I could read and understand the secret messages "embedded within the inferior bulk." I have
been placed under God's protection. The advocate now represents me. I
hear a far off quiet voice that is not a human voice; it — she — comforts me.
In the dark of the night she tells me that "St. Sophia is going to be born
again; she was not acceptable before." A voice barely audible. In my head.
Later she tells me she is a "tutelary spirit," and I don't know what that word
means. Tutor? I look it up. It means "guardian."

[50:19] Finally:

I am led to the inescapable conclusion that, totally unknowingly, we are
all constituents of a vast living organism, and that everything which occurs
in it, our reality, happens due to its deliberate intention — that of its own
brain, Noös or psyche — and, further, this vast living organism which governs and regulates our every move and experience resembles an AI system
or computer, and that under certain exceptional circumstances it can and
does speak of one or more of us, its members — finally, the organism — or
this part of it — is in trouble — has its "hand in a steel trap," as KW put it,
and is extricating its members, i.e., us. We must have partially fallen out
of the organism — or maybe it actually has — like a great animal — been
snared by a titanic iron trap! It is in trouble. And is reclaimed, repairing, itself. It is, in the final analysis, a magna-mind as well as a magna-organism,
and it is — has been for some time — in trouble. We are the distressed fraction, member, circuit or element, or organ, part or unit.

Most likely of all, it is a self-repairing AI mind system, and this repair
activity (known historically to us as "salvation") has to do with (ah!) reac-
tivating a subsection (i.e., *us*) which has fallen below the message-transfer
level (known to us, as the Essene terms, as "falling into forgetfulness and
ignorance"). We are a memory coil, presently inoperative — i.e., malfunc-
tioning: asleep, and, as in a quasi-dream, *we are not where* [and when?]
we think we are (cf. *Maze* and *Ubik*). This is the heart of the matter; we
are an impaired section of the megamind; we misperceive. That which we
see — our reality — does not exist. I am acosmic in viewing this; as in *Maze*
we collectively hallucinate. The megamind is attempting to stimulate us
back to being in touch with itself. Which is the "other slice of bread," i.e.,
back to consciousness of it and ourselves as parts of it — which will, when

successfully achieved, *abolish* this false world, whereupon it will be instantly replaced by the divine "abyss."

[50:22] Fuck it. Just double dime words. And so to bed.

Lest I reify the whole concept into sterile intellectual jargon, let me finish by saying:

"Love is the life and joy and heart of the system. Love is its boundless energy, its soul. And the voluntary force drawing its elements together into a happy krasis, where it is more fun to dance than to think, better to play than to talk. If I am right, it is laughing right now, at my abstract model, or at least smiling. I sure hope so."

[50:23] After listening to "Discreet Music"* and because of it falling into a theta sleep (at last) I awoke, with parts of my brain still shut down, operating at a 5 year old level, but in an alpha state, without fear, frustrated, but feeling happiness and love, and I realize:

(1) My 3-74 and Tessa's 12-77 experiences have been/were "Contacts of the 3rd kind" but I have just been too afraid, not trusting and not loving enough to face it all this time; and
(2) Zebra is the "repairman" and he is here; and
(3) "Zebra" is "them" as in "we are not alone" but as the *New West* article points out, they're probably not ETIs. But what they are — they violated laws of time and space.

But it's a 3rd kind contact. Sorry about that, fellas. But "Zebra" is what's doing it, and although KW and I have our computer model, it's just *a* model, *an* attempt to understand what *no one* understands; but

We are not alone.

/[50:28]

$$\bigcirc = \bowtie\!\!\bowtie\!\!\bowtie\!\!\bowtie \quad \text{DNA Doubl Wix!}$$

---

* *Discreet Music* is the album I've listened to most often in the past thirty-five years since buying it when it was released in 1975. Brian Eno (affectionately also called "Brain One") conceived of *Discreet Music* as something that might accompany a dinner party, and it was followed up by other soundscape experiments like *Music for Airports* and *Music for Films.* Eno's extraordinary title piece is truly a machine composition; employing an early digital sequencer, looped tape machines, and other oblique strategies, it generates the music algorithmically. Intended to push at the threshold of audibility, *Discreet Music* is arguably the genesis of ambient music; certainly it and its creator inspired Dick to create the character Brent Mini, the electronic composer who appears in *VALIS.* — SC

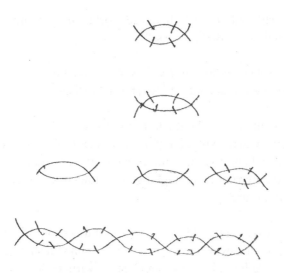

[50:36] I just realized something:

(1) The Holy Spirit is *inside* you, like conscience: an inner voice.
(2) Although there *was* indeed a holy spirit in me, because of it inside me I saw Zebra *outside* me.
(3) Therefore Zebra is not the Holy Spirit.

Since this all happened on Christ's actual birthday (March 18),[23] then Zebra probably is the cosmic Christ, whom I could see because of the Holy Spirit inside me — who, it is said, makes clear the mystery of Christ to us . . . in fact, it could even be said that if one were not "born from above by the spirit" one would not understand (know of) the true being of Christ.①

Dream: book of mine with footnote: "this is a gloss in the text for 'I love you.'" Was I herein shown the real cryptic message in my writing that God loves us? "Felix." etc. = "I love you."

① Christ is here. But not in an incarnated form, yet; the unaided eye (i.e., lacking theolepsy by the spirit) cannot discern him. But I saw him — Zebra; *he is here.*
("Gloss" is from a Greek word meaning "a difficult word needing explanation.")②

② So "gloss" appeared in my dream in the Greek or Latin, not English sense; in English it means the *explanation* itself of the difficult word, but in my dream it's a "gloss in the text meaning 'I love you.'" Obviously the gloss or difficult word is Felix. (The Greek word is glossa.)⊗

What a wonderful revelation in answer to my constant Q: "What is the secret message which Zebra has inserted into my writing?" It is that God loves us, including me. It is, in fact, not *a* message but *the* message. In the dream I caught sight of the footnote one time, and then, having read it, understood its meaning and its importance, continued frantically to seek it out again as *the* truth.

The EB says that God (through his grace) will restore "man's lost freedom." Very interesting. Sin (and the law) seen, then, as enslaving, evidently.

Justice: "A place for the powerless to get help." Thus the Illinois attorney general has (without intending to) defined the role of the paraclete as advocate. Hosanna.

③ My Latin dictionary defines glossa as an "obsolete or foreign word needed to be explained." Felix is certainly a glossa — it is foreign, and it needs to be explained.

That is precisely how I've treated the word ever since its cryptic meaning was revealed to me in 3-74, and it, combined with the paragraph of which it was the key part, gave an otherwise invisible message at odds with what was apparent.*

[50:43] It is also interesting that the cypher word in *Tears* (Felix) is the final word in *Scanner* (i.e., happy). The tied shirt dream was not precog, an

---

* In this extraordinary passage, the recursive, self-referential quality of the Exegesis goes loopy. The Exegesis is an exegesis after all, which means that it is obsessed with commentary and Talmudic cross-referencing. In addition to Dick's interminable analysis of his own corpus, there is his regular use of footnotes, which here go haywire. At the top of the page Dick places an asterisk that refers to a small chunk of related text, between which lies the brief description of a dream in which Dick opens one of his own books and discovers a footnote that reads: "this is a gloss in the text for 'I love you.'" Dick then parenthetically defines the term "gloss" as a difficult term needing explanation, a definition that nonetheless requires another explanation, a footnote now using his usual bracketed numeral (1). This footnote offers a variant reading of the meaning of "gloss," defining it not as the explanation of an obscure term — rather like the explanation that you, reader, are now reading — but instead the obscure term itself — in this case, the cypher-text *Felix*. A parenthetical amendment about the Greek variant *glossa* in turn spawns another reference mark, a circled ⊗ that leads to yet another repetitive definition. Finally, Dick reiterates that *Felix* is such a glossa: a glossy obscurity whose invisible message is, at least in its original context, "at odds with what is apparent." And what is apparent here, and odd, is the Exegesis reading and writing itself, like a book in a dream. — ED

ability on my part. It was divine prophecy and promise: it held out hope and fulfilled it — "Happy" (Felix) may be a cunning reference to Euripides' *The Bacchae* in which the stranger (Dionysus in human form) refers to King Penthus as King "of Tears," punning on the Greek word for tears: pentheus. And the word "tears" is in the title of my novel. The *real* message is that he whom Pindar called the joy god is here. It is a cypher within a cypher; "Felix" is not a name but a glossa meaning (among other good things) happy. But "happy" is a cypher back to a name: i.e., name to word to name. And the final name underlying Felix is Dionysus. The deity who has inserted the message into "the inferior bulk" has identified himself. The total message from him is, "I love you." But he has also elliptically told us who he is.

He is the protector of little wild things, like Cernunnos and Shiva, and it is Shiva who possesses the 3rd ajna eye.

Cernunnos = Shiva = Dionysus = Christ. The savior of the trapped, the desperate, the damned, the powerless.

[50:55] As speculation (but probably accurate) the entity is the Shiva-Cernunnos-Dionysus-Christ-St. Sophia one, transcending *any* one given religion — involving Zoroaster and Mani and the Gnostics, e.g., it is Greek, Hindu, Iranian, Jewish, Celtic, Christian, Manichaean and Lord knows what else (Buddha too). Mani was right when he saw all the religions as one.

And the outlines of this one are becoming visible to me: it involves *illegitimate* temporal power (rulers) who have craftily usurped the citadels and branded the rightful God as a fool, a jester, a madman, a criminal — made him marginal — our *real* king who is now *ubiquitous*, like St. Elmo's fire, everywhere and nowhere, able to

(1) take over and replace inanimate objects and causal processes; and
(2) living creatures, including humans.

Wow. Let's see the usurper tyrant martyr him *this* time.

"Paupers and Kings" it's all [to be seen] *backward*, as I mention in *Scanner.* Trash (rock, comics, movies, S-F) is gold and gold is trash.

[50:60] We are talking about an intrinsic long-dormant personality capable of functioning on a level high enough to allow it to see, hear and understand the supernormal universe of the divine — none of which can be perceived by the normal self. More and more I see myself as an unknowing fifth columnist: interestingly, *if* this is so much of my writing not only points to it but outright reveals (discloses) it. *If* there are such 5th columnists, i.e., people unaware of slumbering superpersonality within them, "timed" to go off when "they" return, and *if* the "prince of this world" knows all this, then my writing (without *me* suspecting) would give me away.

First, my writing presents an unvarying cosmological schema in accord with the suppressed (Gnostic) doctrines, but then, when we get to *Tears* (and perhaps earlier, e.g., "Faith of," *Ubik, Maze, Frolix*) encoded messages which are not merely informative but *commands* begin to appear. The writing, going all the way back to '53, has identified himself to friend and foe alike. Having assented to this (although unknowingly) he then has an overwhelmingly powerful dream which *must*, he feels, be inserted in his novel with the exact, proper wording. Eleven drafts of that section are necessary before he is satisfied.

But the authorities have already perceived that at any time what is mere truth — true revealed information — can pass over into encoded command. They think this is all being done deliberately and consciously. Friends (Marxists) think the same thing. Just like we think Bowie knows something these people think *I* know something. This is a reasonable assumption. Thus the house gets hit and the papers read and stolen, but they show nothing.

[50:63] I saw, in 3-74, how the great *purposeful* force (entity) of the universe works backward (theologically). Vast long-range patterns emerge. A little 4 year old boy hears a cowboy song and then 45 years later hears it again — sung by his favorite singer. The retrograde pull is there. It can be said that when he was 4 he was inordinately drawn to it because of her singing it 45 years later. It can be said correctly that when her first record came out in the sixties, he was inordinately drawn to her because 6 years later she would sing that song. There can be no real understanding of the universe when only the efficient causes are studied — they lack the conscious, deliberate *purpose* of final causes. No sense can be made of cause-and-effect linear time events. The past does not *make* the future; the future uses the antecedent universe as a chaotic stockpile which it assembles into a structure (cosmos). To understand, we must discern the negentropic developments — but to do this we would have to be able to "remember" the future with the same clarity that we remember the past, and this we can't do. This, then, is where faith must come in. In every event we must, by faith, presume a benign purpose, which, could we see *all* which is to come, would delight us — we would be *especially* delighted to see how intrinsically evil events become used as building blocks for noble structures — and are, in fact, *essential* for the ultimate construction of those fine systems.

Nothing is wasted, nothing is futile, nothing is lost. Everything is eventually, when its time has come, snatched up and incorporated.

[50:76] Funny, how I perceive, in terms of images, of the world being continually spun by something like a spider — well, I did see the spinner at work, and the world as his artifact. Don't the Brahmans conceive of the veil of Maya being spun (by Kali)? And there is deception (or illusion) involved. We are in the web. Caught in it, with no idea at all of its artifactual nature (and the furiously moving — spinning and arranging spinner). To take it — i.e., the world as authentically real would be the same as taking a TV image and program and its dramatic contents — as real. It, too, is spun — by a fast-moving dot. And that which the dot spins is fictitious.

[50:82] As in Plato's *Timaeus* the "steersman" (artificer) intervenes to correct drift — a drift toward anomie, perhaps, periodically exerting pressure on the developing artifact. This is the adventitious overruling from time to time that involved me in 2-3-74.

It is exactly analogous to the occasional firing of jets in a spacecraft to minutely correct its trajectory; only this "ship" is moving through time, not space.

But the artifact does not *quite* exist, as does the artificer, since it is in constant flux.

[50:83] I have reached a dead-end in my exegesis — which by its very nature will not and cannot be surmounted. It has to do with the fall, and resulting loss of memory (and complete loss of some faculties and a degrading of others [cf. Calvin]). The *cause* of this fall is occluded off by its very nature, it is as if crucial memory tapes (as in *Maze*) got erased; once erased, by the definition of the problem, their contents can neither be retrieved nor reconstructed.

During my period of anamnesis I remembered back thousands of years — I even remembered coming here to this planet from the stars. But I don't know what causes the fall — the amnesia and blighting of the pristine nature. I have no insight, no understanding, no clue. All right: we humans are fragments of the very Godhead that we seek to rejoin. (Salvador salvandus.) Did we blight ourselves intentionally? Or is it a punishment, as Genesis says? Or a cruelty inflicted on us (i.e., on the Godhead, by an adversary)? Did we *want* to come here, or were we exiled here?

The vine (Christ) which was pruned (by God) and the severed cuttings placed in a world where God is the deus absconditus — to judge each of us individually, to see which of us find a world lacking in God to be sufficient — and which of us, without intellectual ideation, grieve for that loss and miss our father and home and yearn with the greatest pain possible to return.

This is all I know; as KW says, the trail doesn't just peter out; it ends at a brick wall. The exegesis is a failure in terms of answering questions; for each answer derived an even greater mystery is exposed.

We fell; we lost our memories; we are cut off from God — those faculties by which we apprehend him are destroyed or not functioning — ploch, ploch — weep for this separation . . . and not to know *why* it happened. *We* can never find God; he must find us (as that little paperback I picked up at the Oakland airport says).

Oh God — *hilfe*. Ich bin so einsam. Wenn kommst du mein Heil?[24]

The work has failed. I neither understand nor remember, and the Elohim — gone from my sight, and silent.

I can't find him. Only when we rejoin and are together will I know what the "erased tape" (concerning the fall) had on it. He will find me and at last I will understand.

I know no more than Xenophanes, and he was just about the first philosopher. And he said, "We can never know for sure, and even if we were right we wouldn't know it."

Xenophanes:

"One God there is, in no way like mortal creatures either in bodily form or in the thought of his mind" (frag. 23).

"The whole of him sees, the whole of him thinks, the whole of him hears" (frag. 24).

"He stays always motionless in the same place; it is not fitting that he should move about now this way, now that" (frag. 26).

"But, effortlessly, he wields all things by the thought of his mind" (frag. 25).

This is what I saw — Zebra or VALIS; but it was not I who saw — it was God within me seeing God outside. Brahman and Atman, I suppose. Only God can see God. He wielded me, from inside me, effortlessly.

The above prayer was answered by my mistakenly reading the entry in the E. of Phil. on Jacob Boehme.

• • •

[50:85] *Scanner:*
"To forge out of torment the rough-hewn shape."

This is probably the happiest moment of my life — I can say to this moment, "stay." Here is the fallen black cat on my lap; I am listening to Stevie Nicks on my Stax phones — the Gollancz edition of *Scanner* arrived today. They say it is a human document — yes, their flap blurb word is *document.* "One of the most human documents they have ever read." Not the most sensational, but most human. "Its concern for people." It is a beautiful book qua book. Jim Westaway's words on the back dust jacket. And what KW saw — the link between my intro to "Roog," what I did in my first sold story 27 years ago and in *Scanner:* voice for those without voices.

The pain has left me. Even if it's just for a limited time I appreciate it.

What best can I do? Exactly what I've done. My voice for the voiceless.

And — too — God answered my prayers re the Exegesis, by leading me to Jacob Boehme.* Somewhere between the truths revealed to Boehme and to me *the correct model lies.* The Blitz as Urgrund encounters the lowest 3rd of the secondary (material) triad — the divine agony at opposition between the urgrund and physical nature, and the process — not of abolishing physical nature but transmuting it. This is what I saw Zebra doing (which I termed transubstantiation by a sentient plasmatic entity). Out of this transmutation of the empirical universe by the divine comes harmony between the upper triad (spiritual) and the lower (empirical).

A German cobbler in 1616 and me — for him sunlight reflected from a pewter dish — for me the golden fish necklace, and in the light cast by the

---

* This passage reveals much about the logic of the Exegesis and rewards close scrutiny. Here Dick is in great joy: the masterful *A Scanner Darkly* is hot off the press, and Stevie Nicks is in the headphones. (It must be "Dreams" from *Rumours:* "I see the crystal visions.") Yet only one page before, Dick is in full metaphysical despair. He scribbles a lamentation in German; the second half is drawn from Bach's Cantata BWV 140, *Sleepers Awake.* At the bottom of that page, as an unnumbered footnote, he declares that this "prayer" had been answered when he subsequently stumbled across the *Britannica* entry on Jacob Boehme. Though it is hard to imagine how one reads an encyclopedia passage "by mistake," this random access is important to Dick because it removes his will from the equation, implying cosmic intention. In other words, God answered his lament by guiding him to Boehme, in whom he discovered a secret sympathy across time. However, this whole episode is complicated by the appearance sixty-four pages earlier (entry 50:19 above) of the unusual phrase "divine 'abyss.'" This is a fundamental term in Boehme's mystical scheme, where it denotes the emptiness of the Urgrund, the God beyond God. Its appearance earlier in this folder, particularly in quotation marks, strongly suggests that Dick had begun reading about Boehme sometime before uttering, in writing, his German prayer. This is a common pattern in the Exegesis: a motif is casually introduced and later blooms into a matter of such great significance that it changes the visionary narrative in retrospect. — ED

spirit the incarnation of the son (God as heart) is disclosed and the Kingdom (reconciliation between the two triads) achieved.

After reading about Boehme I can see why I was getting nowhere. My
schema was naïve — far too simple.

[50:87] What must be bravely faced is that the entire world or cosmos is
not [yet] subjugated to the divine will — it stands, so to speak at a 51/49
ration between divine modulation and mere efficient determinism. Evil
(death, loss, disappointment and suffering and illness) are not abolished
yet but are very slightly tamed over and above their non-divine "James-
James" nature. It's like the trade balance of a country. Well, in the universe,
in 1974, we passed over to a slightly greater export than import ratio. This
is hard to accept. *Nature fights God.* The designs (e.g., DNA, etc.) are not
designs of the divine (the "natural theology" argument to the contrary).
These designs are efficient-cause design (cf. Darwin) and not teleological;
they have no wisdom or real end-goal purpose — they are blind. We must
always keep in mind reality as process (cf. A. N. Whitehead).

[50:88] Where does the divine agony enter? Why? Before the incarnation?
Isn't the incarnation the intrusion — the *initial* intrusion — of the divine
abyss into the mundane something? Christ said, "I have conquered the
world."[25] It was like an impregnation of matter (yin) by the creative divine
(yang). But the divine will is thwarted; it encounters opposition (Boehme
points this out). *Matter has hysteresis* (or inertia). Its entropic direction
must be transmuted into negentropism — a titanic task possible only in a
protracted process or series of sequential steps. The intruding light is rejected.

Our problem may be that we have no comprehension of the *inner* necessity of sequence in this transmutation. Could *our* agony be microcosmic replication of the macrocosmic divine, with which we are (1) isomorphic; and (2) actual fragments of, like bits of a hologram: intact gestalts but
"dimmer" or less defined. The urgrund sought self-intuition. We as dimmer
bits have not yet achieved that self-intuition; hence, when we suffer, we do
not know why. Up the hierarchical scale there is still suffering — even perhaps an increasing level of suffering at each hierarchical stage. But also at
each ascending stage there is a quantum leap in a self-intuition which be-
stows (permits) greater *understanding* of *why* there is this suffering. At the
top, the incarnated son (heart, logos, etc., St. Sophia) knows himself totally and knows totally why he suffers. It is due to the Blitz — the flash of
the encounter between the divine abyss and the something — which must
be "overcome" (transmuted). This is why Paul can speak of the whole uni-

verse being in birth pangs.[26] Here enters the cosmic aspect of salvation presented in Colossians.*

[50:91] Has anyone thought of this modified Gnosticism? There was no creator of this world (planet or cosmos) and the life therein. Atheists such as Darwin are absolutely right; it was no God but simply natural law at work, determining evolution. *However*, a loving, all-wise, sentient super-entity inhabiting an "upper triad," etc., has entered the scene and is transmuting this purely naturalistic world into a totally benign sentient body or organism.

[50:92] It is a major realization that just as Thomas Aquinas' natural theology arguments (such as arguing back from design to designer, etc.) fail to prove the existence of God, the ruthlessness and disorder in nature do not logically imply a *bad* creator God; no argument, "natural" or "ontological," proves God's existence. Thus, the Gnostic belief in a deranged or inferior or evil creator isn't substantiated. Therefore we Gnostics are out on a limb vis-à-vis a bad creator in terms of argument. So out goes all cosmogony for this world. What remains is what I have by revelation: a supernatural divine intelligence doing what Jacob Boehme saw: colliding with the material universe and transforming (rather than abolishing) it. If I do not regard Zebra as a creator God, but a modulating God, then what we seem to actually have is divinization of the mundane, or plan over nonplan, organic interaction over chaos. *No dualistic theology is necessary.*

[50:93] Take the statement by the spirit to me back in 1968 about the Galapagos turtle. The import of what the spirit said was that even though it appeared otherwise, the dying turtle was somehow extricated: "and she shall see the sea." One could extrapolate and say that this statement implies that even what appears to be, or remain, [unsubdued] evil is invisibly ameliorated in a mysterious way.

---

* Dick is likely referring to Colossians 1:18–20, which states that "God wanted . . . all things to be reconciled through [Christ] and for him, everything in heaven and everything on earth, when he made peace by his death on the cross." More specifically, Dick is probably referring to the footnotes in the Jerusalem Bible, a Catholic translation first published in 1966 and containing extensive theological annotations written by a committee of Jesuit scholars. Dick frequently quotes from this version's footnotes, suggesting that it was his preferred study Bible (though he is also known to have owned an annotated copy of the New Testament in the New English Version). The notes for this passage of Colossians declare that Christ is "head not only of the entire human race, but of the entire created cosmos, so that everything that was involved in the fall is equally involved in the salvation." — GM

Boehme wrote that man (i.e., men) have a choice illuminated for them by the light of the spirit: we can remain in torment as victim of the oscillations of the lower triad (or material) universe, or "die to our self" — negate ourselves as the urgrund does, and thereby imitate Christ and follow him from suffering to triumph (joy). Thus anguish is ultimately something to overcome, not fall victim to. Anguish is the starting point. So we must not tarry in anguish, but hasten with "gladdening footsteps."[27]

[50:101] The cunning counterfeit of reality, revealed as such when *authentic* reality breaks through — like the "tip-tip" of the branch blowing against the window in *Finnegans Wake* during Earwicker's dream. This "tip-tip" is the clue, and the only clue. In *Ubik* it is the commercials and messages intruding "from the other side" (Lem). Do we experience that? I did in 3-74. So I am forced to conclude that our reality is a cunning counterfeit, mutually shared — and that the wise mind is trying to signal us — to do what? To kick over into anamnesis: discharge of DNA long-term memories. *To remember and to wake up are absolutely interchangeable.*

[50:105] It may be that the divine is *re-entering* — not entering our universe (viz:

☷ to ☳

This would indicate a *fallen* state of our world, and the divine enters at the bottom — i.e., in the trash, the lowly, the discarded. Christ speaks of the tiny mustard seed,[28] and the gloss on the J. Bible[29] stresses that the kingdom will enter inconspicuously — very small; i.e., lowly. Where we would be *least* likely to look for it (cf. "the stone rejected by the builder").*

This realization is very important.

---

* While the Exegesis is largely concerned with Western philosophy, Western religion, and Western science, Dick was strongly influenced by his (rather typically Californian) encounter with the East. Hinduism gave him a powerful language in which to think about the absolute and the problem of illusion; his embrace of paradox, organic process, and "the lowly" was deeply marked by his reading of Zen and Taoism, and especially his obsessive use of the *I Ching* — the ancient Chinese book of changes. The *I Ching* uses a binary system — yin and yang, broken and solid lines, respectively — to express and model the myriad phases of growth and decay. Like many oracles in Dick's fiction (including *The Man in the High Castle*, which was partly written using the *I Ching*), the book's messages — a mixture of Taoist, Confucian, and shamanic lore — are accessed through the throw of coins or other randomizing techniques. Indeed, with its computer-like code, its relentless oscillation of opposites, and its reliance on synchronicity, the *I Ching* gave Dick an early experience of an organic and mystical information entity — Valis before the name. Here the two hexagrams depict the "trash dialectic" that so concerned Dick, graphically figured through the loss and return of a single yang line between the two figures. In the Wilhelm/Baynes

And this lowly trash, bottom penetration is exactly how I portray it (Ubik) in *Ubik!* On match folders; in tawdry commercials — therein lie the divine messages.

Entry from the "provinces" — Galilee — now takes the form of entry from trash in the gutter on up — a trashy [S-F] novel which contains trash (the chapter-opening commercials) is the triumphant return of the rightful king. *Ubik* is trash containing an even lower order of trash: the Ubik commercials — but which are in fact vox dei.[30]

[50:109] A human can evolve into Christ *if* Christ ignites his own self in the human and takes the human over. There is only one difference between God and Christ: that is one of accessibility (equality) to man. Christ, as Hagia Sophia, can ignite himself in a man and speak with him in a dialogue. At this point, the man rises from time, space, and the slavery of deterministic nature mechanics, remembers all and knows himself by means of Christ as inner light.

[50:121]

A very difficult idea has come to me, difficult to envision or express.

What makes up the PONS DEI?

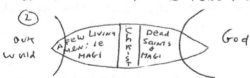

In other words, the two realms, sublunar (our world) and the supralunar (heaven), are bridged by a polyencephalic mens[31] which is heterogenous: the most startling part is that at our [sublunar] end certain wise men (magi) and saints participate in it, and at the other end, wise men and saints who have died (passed over to heaven or the supralunar) participate in it. The substantial structure is God-as-holy-Spirit, bridging the two worlds.

•   •   •

edition that Dick regularly used, the movement between these two hexagrams is described thus: "When what is above is completely split apart, it returns below." — ED

[50:137] We can be moved anywhere anytime, caused to do or not do anything, entirely motivated by an external force (mind), and never perceive
the Leibniz-like "preset clocks" which chime in unison. [. . .]

We're a fucking goddam "Biosphere" ruled by an entity who — like a
hypnotist — can make us not only quack like a duck or cue, but imagine, to
boot, that we wanted (decided) to quack.

[50:142] Ah — my bipolarization between the human and the android.
Free man (liberated) vs. the artifact controlled "android"; I am now prepared to elevate the bipolarization into theological, supernatural, cosmic
dimensions. The concept of *balking* assumes the status of successfully resisting cause-and-effect script-programming. Mekkis[32] vs. Agape. Love is
the total permission of exception, and leads us from rule (law, justice) to
paradox (mercy). Paradox is the manifestation of metamorphosis by a reversal of opposites — cf. alchemy, Empedocles, etc., and especially Christ's
parables and sayings (about the kingdom), and about judgment and the final dispositions. Folly, madness, passion, the joyful dance — vs. iron limitations imposed. This is the age of the inner spirit, in which inner spirit (via
anamnesis) and teaching (discerning and knowing — Sophia —) become
real, and the external material order (world) revealed as delusion. The material world is about to be abolished, and its hold on us with it — dispelled
(cf. my published writing). The abyss is devouring the byss, by an outburst
of ecstasy. What has happened is that the occluded mind is restored to its
primordial wholeness.

Folder 28

[28:1] The "other universe" is an intelligent, thinking mind, and so when it impinges on our material universe, these "impregnations" take the form of written or audible information (words), such as described in *Ubik*. This is, in fact, the basic situation in *Ubik* — the impinging on the irreal world they are in (while half alive) in the form of helpful information. The term for this impinging information is "word" or *Logos!*

And the Marxist intellectuals know that (1) that is what is happening in *Ubik* and (2) Ubik itself is the Logos.

What we have is *sentient* radiation, energy or electricity or plasma or ionization.

Using Tesla's[33] theories about energy and information transfer, the Soviets are now able to synthesize a sort of mundane Logos, or ionospheric information transfer grid. However, Tesla, in his own work with such "Radar-like" devices found he had made contact with a "St. Elmo's fire" ETI — the intrusion of which (living sentient plasma) must puzzle and intrigue the Soviets.

Ubik deals with all this. In reading *Ubik* anyone familiar with either the man-made "Logos" or the natural one, would assume the author knew what he was writing about. Especially they would hope *Ubik* indicated the efficacy of their own system.

What to me is most interesting is that this sheds a lot of light on the enigmatic term or entity "logos," or "the word" (and wisdom) of God. *Only* if the other universe is conceived as Xenophanes (e.g., Anaxagoras) conceived it — as noös — does "word" make sense as an entity which is not only wisdom itself but is alive, and could incarnate itself here (in human form). Since the *real* universe is mind (electromagnetic flux) it does not much think but is (esse) thought or word (word-wisdom). Thoughts are ontologically real and not merely verbal descriptions of material reality; they are the final order of reality.

Words, bursting through the material world, are in fact the *real* universe (noös) penetrating a (mere) holographic projection. Without the understanding and awareness of the real (ultimate) reality being one of mind, the concept "the word" makes no sense since, as Xenophanes saw, the noös wields the world *by its thinking*, the word-wisdom is not a mere *aspect* of the ultimate, the urgrund, but its activity per se; hence in Genesis, when

God *says,* "Let there be light," there is light; he creates by *saying* (thinking) (cf. Bishop Berkeley[34]).

Also, Xenophanes realized that noös never moved about. The Tesla Grid would be ubiquitous, too, an analog of the actual Logos. In a sense, then, using Biblical terms, the Soviets' Tesla mind-control (informing) Grid would be an anti-Christ, mimicking the Logos itself.

[28:4] Interestingly, my theolepsy did not withdraw me from the world, but, quite the opposite, *reintroduced* me to the world and in a new and active — dynamic — way, in which I impinged on it more than it impinged on me. And this was a microcosmic version of the Logos' dynamic impinging on the world in a vast, historically important way: I replicated in a tiny way its stance — and definitely linked (synchronized) to its macrocosmic impinging. Thus my role as victim (or object) of mundane forces was dramatically reversed, in fulfillment of the scriptures in which the powerless would judge the powerful (a complete reversal of the extant order of things).

This dramatic reversal fits my most acute analysis and understanding of the "end-times" — that vast paradoxical reversals (big-small/weak-strong/wise-foolish/major-minor/important-unimportant, etc.) will without warning (i.e., without evident transitional stages) set in. This is one way by which we will know — recognize — the end-times. Those upheavals which are essentially reversals. A black guard and a hippie cop will destroy the Government and send them all into disgrace, prison and exile.

[28:7]

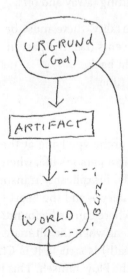

[28:10]

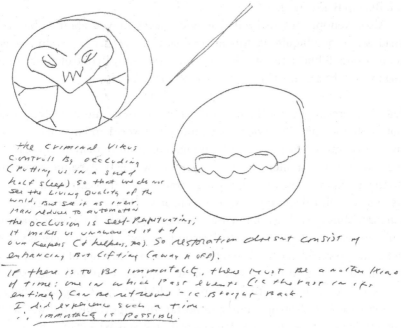

The criminal virus controls by occluding (putting us in a sort of half sleep) so that we do not see the living quality of the world, but see it as inert man reduced to automaton. The occlusion is self-perpetuating; it makes us unaware of it and of our keepers (and helpers too). So restoration doesn't consist of enhancing but lifting (away and off).

> If there is to be immortality, there must be another kind of time:
> one in which past events (i.e., the past in its entirety) can be re-
> trieved — i.e., brought back.
> I did experience such a time.
> ∴ *immortality is possible.*

[28:12] As a result of the archetype lying at the absolute deepest core of pain, there comes a point in a person's life, when he reaches that core, that his pain is, by holy miracle, inexplicably transmuted into joy. This is the heart of the Christian mystery — and the heart of the issue, "where is our God (deus absconditus)? where can he be found?"

Again: it is at the moment when the ultimate blow (of pain, murderous injury, humiliation and death) is struck, it is Christ who is there, replacing the victim and taking the blow himself. This is what happened to me in 3-74.

But there is a further mystery here: it is not just Christ as surrogate *instead*, but Christ *with*, in syzygy.

Thus at the ultimate abyss of pain, one experiences one's creator.

Thus wisdom says, "I will accompany you down even into the prisons."[35]

There is by miracle both a *with* and an *is*. To understand how *with*, *is* and *in place of* are all *one* is to understand the fundamental miracle of God.

The Q: "who is there?" when the blow comes cannot be given in mundane terms; instead, an entire sacred universe and entity is revealed.

So when you see any creature humiliated and dying, you are seeing your own God and Savior, which I have sensed for some time.

As it dies the creature "comes to itself" and knows — experiences — where and what it really is (and perhaps has *always* been).

[28:14] Since *time* is the true receptacle of being (for the organism) anamnesis equals *awareness of the organism as such:* a seeing of the more or less complete entelechy; and amnesia equals blindness, since to be seen the organism must be seen under the aspect of time — in terms of temporal extension. Hence, only by understanding this can one comprehend the absolute value of memory, and comprehend it as a perception or *organ* of perception, like ocular vision, not metaphorically but *literally* an organ of perception. Ocular vision is perception of the organism in space; memory (anamnesis) is perception of it in time, and it is in time (more than space) that its true nature (being) extends. Hence, in 3-74, I correctly declared that I had always been blind, but now could *see*. That sight was memory extending over thousands of years.

This realization is a seminal breakthrough, to view anamnesis as an organ of perception, and the most important of them all. Through anamnesis I could, for the *first time*, perceive the organism, the one. And what did I see? A Living Mind/Body, inhaling and exhaling (palintropos harmonie). Heraclitus was correct — also Parmenides.

[28:15] And why do we forget in the first place? The desire to escape from pain. Like it or not, the hallmark of the real is the infliction of and hence the experience of pain — physical and mental: because, for activity (change) in the *total* organism to occur, its "respiration" — there must be an unceasing (and I do mean *unceasing*) breaking down of every form (or stasis) to make way for the next stasis. It is unescapable that for each new eidos to come into existence the former eidos is reduced to a means by which it is given birth. Only the organism in toto has end-existence; all subparts are means and it is this experience of self as mere means which gives rise to ontological anguish. If there is to be happiness it must come in a voluntary relin-

quishing of self in exchange for aware participation in the destiny of the total one. There can be no happiness for the subsections, so the search for it
is doomed to fail; while existing (and fruitlessly searching for intrinsic fulfillment), each subpart is used by the organism as a whole remorselessly
and relentlessly; that is their fates. What Christ offers is miraculous awareness of and hence participation in (with joy) — the totality; to be united
with Christ is to be melded into the totality — the *only* true joy.

Hence it is logical not merely ethical for me to transfer my money to
such organizations as Care, Save the Children, etc.; only insofar as I live in
them and with them (the "other") *do I live at all;* intellect, not merely conscience, insists. What we call "conscience" is merely heightened intellect
(noös).

I must seek the handle of the final other, and live through that — or else
die. It is a matter of life and death. In seeking receivers (for what I have) I
am seeking — and finding — life itself — *and I know it.* I am right. No sacrifice is involved. To buy an expensive car (e.g.) is to die — to sacrifice life itself in favor of a *machine.*

The Gnostic acts (or Gospel?) of John: Christ as child, young man, old
man, short and bald, tall, firm, soft — *and he did not blink* (his eyes): Christ
can manifest himself to you in any form he chooses, and someone else with
you may not see what you see, but rather something — someone — else entirely (e.g., Pinky).

Somehow it all has to do with identity. There is no way by which *any*
of us can assess his life as successful or meaningful. The kind of identity
which confers meaning onto a given life is a gratuitous Gift to the individual part by the whole (i.e., by the deity); objective meaning may exist, but
the person in question will not know it unless this merciful and priceless
insight is bestowed. You could, by your own efforts, *cause* your life to have
meaning — but still not know it (i.e., that it had had meaning). Meaning and
knowledge of meaning are not usually correctly distinguished. I think perhaps *all* lives have meaning — even in a sense *equal* meaning — but what
we lack, and cannot acquire by our own efforts, is certain knowledge of it.

[28:17] I did not go back in time, but entered a *different* kind of time: sacred or mythic time, in which every thing every time was present in the
form of eternal archetypes; thus I saw Pinky in the archetypal role of the
humiliated, dying savior. This is a *more* real kind of time than profane or
linear time in asking, what characterized it? I would say, everything of
value was preserved (present and immediate), and that the pluriforms of
reality (diverse things and processes) were coordinated into a single sacred
drama, that of the death and rebirth of the savior. Time both expanded (I

recalled 1,000's of years) but those 1,000's of years shrank down into an *immediate* sequence, as if very short. The telescoping of literally millennia disclosed a *single* underlying event — although spread out — *seemingly* elongated — in linear time, this collapsed view was the correct one. This was not just another way of seeing reality; it was the *accurate* way.

I was so clear in my mind as to the exact point in this drama at which we stood: (1) the savior had died, but (2) we had passed over from grieving at the loss (i.e., looking back) but were looking ahead to his return, and rejoicing already. Furious preparations were in order, as if to be ready when the bridegroom appears — it could happen any second (but that could be a *long* time in profane, linear time). Still, we were no longer involved in the Loss (the passion); that was over. And: (3) the black iron prison had been successfully burst and (4) the prisoners saved. Part of our joy stemmed from knowing that destruction of "Babylon/Rome" (the prison) came before his return, and it had been accomplished. Now things were such that we could imminently expect him and he would take us by surprise — we did not, could not, know the "hour" of his return. But soon means *soon*. Any time now. We'd barely be prepared. When I think about it, this mood of eager anticipation and expectation and trembling awe and excitement is *exactly* what the UFO people feel toward the approaching first overt contact.

[28:19] That Gnostic narration about Christ being seen simultaneously as a child, a man, a little old bald man, a short man, a vastly tall man — it resembles the "will-o-the-wisp" UFO sightings and contacts.[36] And Zebra has a little of that playful, mirthful quality — very much so. "Look, I am here — no, there. Look, I am this — no that" (e.g., from the past, the future, another planet, an alternate universe, etc.). Riddles and pranks — we are being charmed and beguiled and entranced . . . and, by this process, our fear of the unknown, the fremd, abates; and also, we become enthralled children — absolutely fascinated by the emerging pattern of what we see. Continually, we are given the option of *dismissing* what we are shown by the master magician/prankster.

[28:21] Am I saying that the basis of reality is words (or the word) (v. John 1:1), as in *Time out of Joint*? (e.g., soft drink stand, words = ideas = concepts. Ideas in the mind [of God]).

[28:27] *Everything* points to time travel. And my reconstruction of the fish sign as Crick and Watson's double helix DNA molecule tells me who in the past these time travelers (undoubtedly from the future) presented themselves as. The Christian theme is a constant thread through time — with the "Christ as child, little old man, bearded youth, tall, short, etc." showing the "St. Elmo's fire" "hologrammatic" quality I saw in Zebra — i.e., the ability to cause us to either see it in any shape it wishes — *or not at all*!! That's because in a certain real sense it isn't there — it's a projection — some kind of plasmic electrical conduction.

However, let us not err; the whole world is irreal in the same sense, and this projected beam can "melt" the obvious (and deceptive) solidity of the world like a soldering gun. It's one hierarchical step up from matter both animate and inanimate: it's an "element" unknown to us but suspected by Heraclitus ("fire"), related to ball lightning. As thinking electricity it can reweave reality.

My novels and stories have never presented *it*, but they have done yeoman work in depicting reality — not as it is to us — but as it is to Zebra: totally "soap bubble" and plastic, mere dream stuff which is imagined and then re-imagined differently; i.e., transformed *by psyche or noös.*

[28:28] The cardinal mystery is, who is projecting or weaving reality — which I caught not just weaving but *reweaving*. I believe the pre-Socratics (cf. Xenophanes) grasped it — that which wields or steers or shakes by its mind, as such. If it is noös, then the physical (empirical or phenomenal) universe is irreal; if psyche it is soma (cf. Spinoza). My writing suggests noös (or Brahman, who either is the universe, or assumes the disguise of — ach!). That is closest: the universe is as mask to visage, layer upon layer. A.D. 70 was a *deeper* layer but not the final one. The final one is probably the abyss: totally not. "Is" is a disguise which "is not" hides behind. Under the masks there lies nothing, but how gentle and warm and unblinking.

Yes, I am an acosmic panentheist, and I saw the deity change its mind and hence our reality along its entire temporal axis, not successively but as a simultaneity, like digital watch numbers changing.

[28:29] Then the fight is transtemporal — with both sides forever at combat — which generate linear time; until Christ/God is victorious, and the black iron prison destroyed. But that moment came. Then is it the case that no more linear time is generated? What we have now is a conflict-less consolidation — a vast silence — as we await the coming of the king? Yes, this is so. We are waiting in a silence; the enemy has been eradicated. The dialectic interchange of forces concluded in victory for God.

Right — I said to KW last night, "There's something wrong, but not in terms of what, but rather in what is lacking: a *spiritual* quality has gone out — our material wealth does not quench our yearnings." What do we yearn for? Why, the rightful king.

[28:31] The concept that I'm a time-traveler from 70 A.D. completely explains Thomas. The PKD personality is a memory-less mask, and Thomas is the authentic personality of the time-traveler, and hence Thomas is really myself — the *actual* me who was sent here: like a cuckoo's egg. I am not PKD; I am Thomas — there was no theolepsy; only anamnesis.

No wonder I could read and write Latin under LSD. That was not — I repeat *not* — a former life but my real life and real time, place, self. It anticipated the Xerox missive; that was no incidental matter but the crux of my mission here.

[28:33] Two elements distinguish *Ubik:*

(1) It is original (as a cosmology).
(2) It perhaps is correct (or more correct than any previous cosmology).

The Q arises: How did it come into being? On what source did I draw? I don't know — except that by the information-projecting entity *described in the novel itself* the arising in my mind of this knowledge (gnosis, sophia) can be accounted for. In other words, the explanation as to the source of the concepts in *Ubik* is presented nowhere else but in *Ubik* itself. Would this, then, the existence of *Ubik*, not constitute an indirect proof of its truthfulness? Were the cosmological concepts in it false, *Ubik* could/would not have come into being — at least not in the way it did — by automatic writing, so to speak. In other words, Ubik wrote *Ubik*, which makes the novel a form of scripture (which may be also somewhat true for *Maze* and certainly, as I well know, *Tears*).

Again the 3 Bantam novels[37] assume a puzzling and perhaps unique importance as vehicles of revelation.

[28:34] Hypnagogic: (they are) "responsible for low-level decisions which can be overruled." For the first time in months the spirit speaks to me. This sentence — remembered because the phone woke me — refers to 3-74 and (short as it is) it explains it. Admittedly, the "they" are not identified — named — but the *structure* can be ascertained. Low-level decisions are normal and routine business of the world — the way it customarily functions. But sometimes decisions made at low levels are overruled — it is not stated by whom, but, again, the function is clear: that entity which has the legitimate wisdom, authority and power to overrule, which therefore is the ultimate court of appeal. God is certainly meant.

[28:35] I suppose this overruling to be staggering in its impact and implication, its irruption into the "horizontal" causal flow. Spinoza and Hume could not even conceive of it. To conceive it, let alone witness it — a vast understanding, and a correct one, of the nature of reality, is required. It is awesome. In a sense it is even terrifying (shock, hex. 51). The core-entity has manifested itself. The inanimate and blind has been rolled aside, like the stone covering Christ's tomb, by the living God. One is perceiving the animate, the purposeful, the aware. The normal relationship between man and reality is reversed, instead of the sentient human viewing the unliving world, suddenly the world is alive and sentient, and, in relation to this, by comparison, man is dwarfed — down to the level of object:

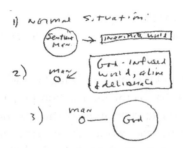

(1) In (1), that which observes (i.e., man) is superior to what he sees, in terms of objective hierarchical essence,

(2) but in (2) he is absolutely dwarfed by what he sees. This is well-expressed in "Job."[38] Suddenly the ratio is dramatically reversed. The next step is for the amazed man to learn that he is, incredibly, isomorphic with this vast sentient "world" which perceives him and aids him.

(3) In other words, God is larger than man but congruent with him; we are identical; whereas in (1) this is not the case: man and "low-level" reality are not isomorphic and in point of fact man is the "crown of creation" and stands above it. Imagine his stupefaction when (1) turns into (2) — but then, before man expires from terror at this switch of ratio, (3) is disclosed to him, by God, who desires to reassure. In this process, step (1) initiates as its goal, not (2) but (3); were it to end in (2), man would collapse, being confronted, so to speak, by rocks and stones wiser than he! This is why it is (correctly) said that the ultimate — and real — purpose of a miracle is

not to accomplish the act accomplished by it (which, obviously, could have been accomplished "normally") but to reveal God and his Nature to the person or persons involved.

[28:36] So the overruling (miracle) of 3-74 disclosed an entity behind it, and, in doing so, lifted aside—detonated into atoms and nonbeing—the veil of dokos. *I* did not penetrate the veil and see beyond it; rather, he who is behind it obliterated it (the "slice of ham" between me and him), and allowed us then to merge. Merging (i.e., [3]) at that point could and did occur naturally—without effort, once He had atomized the "slice of ham" separating us. [. . .]

I will even go so far as to say: "He reserves this disclosure—step (3) in particular—or fusion for those in the extremity of desperation and peril." ("At the absolute core of misery is the greatest joy.")

My revelations are beginning to dovetail: the full gestalt is emerging—but not based on insight revealed in *linear* order. The whole thing is a vast puzzle which, because of the help, I am working out. [. . .]

stage 1) (O ⇒) is characterized as causing pain, fear & stress on O. stage 2) (o ▭) is characterized by amazement, fear & incomprehension. stage 3) (o O) is characterized by bliss — beyond the telling or imagining of it.

I had to experience the world as totally hostile before its hold over me could be broken.

[28:39] My dream last night: Phone book, searching through it, but defeated by my memories being systematically erased. *Could not keep in mind* what I had found in connection already. That was why the trail petered out: *I continued to forget*, and so retried the same material repeatedly.

[28:45] In a sense, my novels trained (prepared) me to have my 2-3-74 experience (and *to comprehend its significance*—this aspect cannot be overstressed). One could regard my 27 years of writing as a kind of apprenticeship, leading up to the moment when I would be ready for the 2-3-74 experience [. . .]

It's as if I *suspected* the true situation, and finally someone who knew decided to let me see openly the verification of my years of surmise. I certainly didn't crack it on my own. I suppose that what happened with me constituted an ultimate liberation, but I suspect that one is given this gift only after a long painful personal search. [. . .]

What I think was accomplished was the breaking of the "Orwellian Horse" script. I would have worked and then died with no reward accruing from the work: I would have died and departed as a mere *means*, agent, instrument for my writing and children, never truly having been free to choose a time for myself. Talk about emancipation! Even in the act (*on* me) of being liberated I construed what was happening as a further task, duty and mission, not as a reward (or salvation). I went on, then, to encumber myself even further, after that; I could not comprehend that I had been liberated and that my work was done. Now I could reap the rewards. Since then, my lessons have been ones of saying good-bye to obligations — to my career and family and friends — to *duty* as such.

My legal responsibilities are meager and clearly defined. I am not required to take on any new ones in order to justify my existence; it's now a question of what I *want* to do, not what is imposed on me.

And what do I want to do? It has something to do with Mexico.

Folder 29

[29:1] Cornford[39] on *Timaeus:*

Plato argues that the universe is an alive organism with a "world soul." But the demiurge (Noös) must *persuade*—cannot compel—necessity (chance, the chaotic) into order. Therefore, Cornford concludes, *there must be an irrational element in the world soul,* or there would be no Ananke for Noös to persuade (and it is very significant that the demiurge cannot *compel*). This chaos did not precede order, but is a constant in the universe.

The omnipotent creator God of the Jews and Christians is a concept which does not account for this element that Cornford calls "the dark domain of the irrational powers" (p. 210). Also, Plato's cosmology in *Timaeus,* as Cornford interprets it (probably correctly), coincides exactly with what I experienced in 3-74—except I add him who had not yet come in Plato's time—the Savior, who is the penetration of Holy Wisdom (Noös) into the microcosm.

Not only does the omnipotent creator God of the Jews and Christians not fit observable facts, it also does not fit my revelation. Plato's cosmology does. (And keep in mind: Plato censured Anaxagoras for believing the Noös "set the world spinning" and lost interest in it—a criticism I would agree with.)

If I am to be true to what I see both normally and by revelation, I must accept *Timaeus,* adding to it the descent to the sublunar world of divine wisdom (or divine reason), and perhaps herewith rest.

The world as living, evolving organism. Yes, I saw that (in 3-74). But its psyche partially irrational? And the demiurge (divine reason) "persuades"—i.e., subdues—it into order?

[29:2]

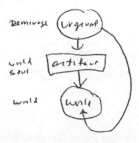

It is this disorder (chaos) of Ananke which shows up in my books (e.g., *Ubik*) as entropy. Cornford says, "It's always present being overruled by divine reason" (order). So it is not just the *decay* of form; it is an element of the irrational: a *destroyer* of eidos, as I depicted in *Maze!!!*

Cornford specifically uses the term "overrule." By divine order over Ananke—the mind disclosed to me. (Persuade = overrule—Cornford.) Reason overrules Ananke.

[29:3] What a fantastic cosmology: the universe is a living animal[①] whose soul (psyche?) is either irrational or has an element of the irrational in it—identified with disorder and casual chance happenings—and divine reason is overruling (or persuading or subduing) it as best it can. But it (divine reason) lacks the power to compel!

Is it possible to say that the universe-organism is insane or partly insane? And doesn't this fit in perfectly with the Gnostic revelation?

  ① Constantly changing, like all living animals. So this disorder is *always* underlying—as a constant—not *prior* to order but "under" it.

[29:4] Plato would have been amazed to learn that 400 years after his death, divine Noös (reason) was born—incarnate—as the man Jesus—and that it's going to happen again, at which time divine reason will achieve total order and absolutely subdue the disorder (chaos) of the [partly] irrational world soul (who we may know as the creator of this world).

Finally, for the first time, the component of disorder will be eliminated—i.e., the world soul *healed* (made sane).

[29:5] The "joined," random messages and information (as in *Ubik*) are the visible and audible *thoughts* of *divine reason*,[①] the invader (Doctor) into this partly irrational universe—organism or cybernetics-like. The organism, in contrast, does not think.

  ① Zebra/Christ.

[29:7]

Re the Black Iron Prison vs. the Palm Garden World:

A mere shift of say 10% of pattern (very slight but skillful accentuations and suppressions) produces these "alternate universes."

And what about Tagomi in thè park with the piece of silver jewelry?[40] Slight shift, and he is in our world. Like Jacob Boehme seeing the sunlight on the pewter dish —

[29:9] Burroughs in *The Ticket That Exploded* says of the Nova Mob parasites that as they move from one human host to another they give themselves away (to the Nova police) by the continuity of their *habits*, such as tastes in food (in Hamburger Mary's case a taste for peanut butter). This was exactly true about Thomas. And I've subjectively felt myself as a female, a womb into which something like an egg (Firebright) was deposited — like a cuckoo egg. Was Thomas a saprophyte turned parasite, and deposited his "egg" in me? Does this mean that Burroughs is either intentionally or unintentionally describing something which is true? And he's into those pasted-together subliminal messages, too.

KW has noted a resemblance between several things I've described and what Burroughs has written — e.g., my conviction that as a race or even planet we are "sick" — i.e., occluded perceptually, and that a divine doctor-entity is restoring us —

Coincidence? Burroughs speaks of a virus — a word became a neural-cell virus, infecting us.

After reading Burroughs, I dipped into *Ubik*. It certainly would be easy — and reasonable — for a reader to think that both Burroughs and I know something, and we want our novels to be taken as at least partly true. They have a strange ring of [revealed] truth about them — I feel it about his book, about mine — is, as Katherine Kurtz[41] says, something writing *through* us!?

Isn't Palmer Eldritch a kind of parasite, replicating himself or itself using humans as hosts? But my sense about Thomas was of a benign, not evil, intrusion. Still, it was an intrusion into my psyche, a taking over. Are such intrusions always to be deplored?

Or was I beguiled? Didn't it — he — get me out of trouble?

There is just no doubt of it: such passages in Burroughs' novel as the "Do it — do it — neck" message within another message — words that weren't originally there but are like the inner trigrams of an *I Ching* hex — that is one absolute "triangulated" element with (1) *Ubik* and (2) what I saw in 3-74. Plus the parasite criminals and Nova cops, and the infecting virus.

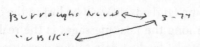

[29:11] The virus (of Burroughs) is an information (or word) virus, but in this sense: it *blocks* the reception of information. So it is an *anti*-information virus. And then it substitutes false (homeo) info (die messages inside your psyche) that replaces the genuine information, auditory and visual.

Information-blocking, as represented in *Maze* symbolically by the erasure of the instruction tape. This tells us what *kind* of info is blocked: our instructions as to our purposes or tasks: all that the term "instructions" imply. And where do the instructions come from? A satellite: in other words, another "planet" or world from this. And also somehow relatedly, we are not really where and when we think we are. The "erased" instructions include needed accounts and full info as to where we are, as well as what our job is. We are cut off from and not receiving verbal transmission. We can no longer hear what we're supposed to hear.

This can be collated with Julian Jaynes' theory of the Loss of the Voices of the Gods.

KW points out that our finding info in "random" arrangements — they may not be random in the first place.

The visual part is in the color discrimination circuits which permit set-ground apperception.

The auditory part is the "agenbite of inwit"[42] and depends upon a suppression (suspension) of sub-vocal thinking — as Burroughs points out, over 10 seconds of inner silence is impossible: inner chatter occurs. There is inner raving, howling, clamoring bug, which deliberately creates derogatory noise on the line at all times — a jamming, an override.

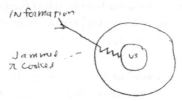

We can't receive audio or visual information, it is jammed or cooked. So "St. Sophia" (divine wisdom) must land behind enemy lines — within the prison, and inform us here, located here with us, since its info is not getting through. Each of us has an override in him, and there appears to be an override layer in the atmosphere. They could transmit to me only for a brief interval: then slew the monitor within. But presently another one replaced it. So again I am cut off.

They are at present diversifying their arrivals, feints within and among which the real landing (2nd advent) will be lost in the confusion of absurd raw data. Which among the fake messages is the real one? "Garbage in, garbage out," in terms of feeding data to our computers. Random and bizarre and ubiquitous.

But primarily, as John Calvin said, the damage is to our brains, to our faculties. We can't see and we can't hear. Restoration of our lost faculties signifies the end-times, and my faculties, in 3-74, were restored. That this restoration could only be temporary shows why "St. Sophia" must be incarnated here again.

[29:19] The voice I heard which was not a masculine voice was that of the thinking world soul, which must be understood as feminine. It was the voice of the total entelechy around us.

She will incarnate here once again.

So what I colloquized with was not someone or something *in* the universe — a part of the universe — but its very mind itself. No wonder I saw it (as Zebra) outside me: the physical world is its body! No wonder Zebra could modulate causal processes and mimic natural objects: they are its (her) body and the changes thereof. *I saw that body as alive* — which is correct.

So I saw reality correctly — as a vast living body — and I conversed with its mind (psyche?). This identification of St. Sophia with the world soul absolutely accounts for and agrees with what I saw and understood: the vast thinking, living, evolving animal with a rational intelligence. And that mind (Holy Wisdom) can "enter" its own body in microform! No wonder I thought of [it as] Brahman.

[29:21] (1) The universe is alive, it has a mind, it thinks, it has audible thoughts which (under certain circumstances) we can hear inwardly. The mind is female. Plato says, "Its discourse is always true."

(2) There are counterfeit interpolations into this living thinking animal (universe) which screw it up, running counter to its evolution as an entelechy. It must detect these spurious interpolations and expose or abolish them for what they are — i.e., get rid of them, get them out of its body. These spurious interpolations are deranged and malicious. In microform the mind travels around in its own body, seeking them out, getting them (with it as bait) to disclose themselves.

When the mind (St. Sophia) encounters and detects a spurious (i.e., irreal) section, it replaces it with an ontologically real section of itself; by transubstantiation. It has already determined that much of this particular planet is irreal. Hence, it is making "orthogonal time" changes here. From Black Iron Prison world to Palm Tree Garden. We are none the wiser vis-à-vis this salvation, and the substitution of the benign real for the spurious malicious.

We are back again to the model of construct, repairman and deranged Circuit Board. The messages intended for reception by the Circuit Board are not getting to it; specifically, the voice (thoughts) of the mind of the [total] organism. "The Kingdom of God" represents reintegration into the total entelechy, in which the voice is again audible. To overcome the barrier created by the derangement the microform came here, assessed the situation and was ejected. When it returns it will not merely determine conditions, it will *repair*. The two missions (advents) have quite different purposes. By the nature of the derangement, the mind had to come here personally to determine the situation. There is a total information block, going both ways.

[29:23] The Great Mother retreated out of sight behind the figure of Christ, and rules the cosmos invisibly. Yet she disclosed herself to me:

(1) the Sibyl (visually)
(2) the female (or non-male) voice
(3) the "St. Sophia" prophecy itself

Then a great revelation has been made to me: the female hypostasis of God, which is unknown in and to the whole modern world. It has been thousands of years since she was believed in.

[29:31] Will Durant says that one of religion's — *any* religion's — prime functions is "to explain evil, and to find for men some scheme in which they may accept it, if not with good cheer, then with peace of mind — this is the task most religions have attempted to fulfill. Since the real problem of life is not suffering but undeserved suffering . . ." etc.

The usual Christianity does not adequately do this — in fact this is where I think its greatest failure lies: in trying to explain *undeserved* suffering. But the Hindu explanation — punishment for deeds in a former life, and/or that suffering is illusory — this doesn't satisfy me: not only does the creature suffer, but he is told that it's because of something bad he did but does not remember. This would be an OK explanation if it (karma) could be proved, but it can't.

What I see the most promise in is my extraordinary perceptual revelation — which I actually saw in '74 — that when any creature is humiliated, injured, killed, it is always Christ who is mocked and murdered — the creature becomes Christ or Christ becomes the creature.

Christ takes the blow. In unusual (extreme?) cases the suffering creature actually experiences Christian anamnesis and "remembers" who he is and how he fits in with the "Passion play." As I did, he actually sees the world stripped down to the eternal acting-out of the Passion play.

At this point in my exegesis, my only viable line of reasoning left open to me is this supernatural insight. Pinky was Christ because Pinky was mocked, humiliated, kicked and killed. Whether, divining this, he remembered his identity I do not know. But either way the facts are the same; his becoming Christ due to and under those conditions is the archetypal situation.

But why is suffering necessary at all? Why is the road to deification (transmutation into Christ) achieved in this terrible way? I turn, here, to Plato's *Timaeus* and his concept of Ananke. The good God does not have complete control of the universe; the universe is part (growingly) cosmos with an irreducible chaos in the midst of it, at every level. All undeserved suffering comes from this purposeless disorder. Unable to *compel* Ananke to not torment a given organism, the deity does the next best thing: he substitutes himself in a mysterious supernatural way for and with the doomed organism.

To see or experience the literal real presence of the savior in the doomed sufferer is perhaps to have penetrated to the heart of Christianity. I witnessed it myself; I know by divine revelation. And since Christ can and does become *all* living creatures (since all suffer undeservedly and die) he, like Brahman, is ubiquitous (immanent) in the universe, moving toward a final disclosure that the universe is only a form which God assumes, and that the ultimate result of this so-to-speak self-inflicted (unknowingly) pain on its sentient parts is to restore to those parts their memories and hence true identities. They awake, remember, know, and rejoin the urgrund. ("Tat Tvam Asi.") So the unfair pressures of an unknowing causal — and casual — universe reawaken the one sleeping mind in its pluriforms. And so it encounters itself, who or what has inflicted undeserved pain or who or what? God as creator or God as Son, and the 3rd member of the trinity, the Holy Spirit, is the agent which effects this "blitz" or catalyst of remembering.

The jolt to remember lies in the very quality of the *undeserved;* puzzled and horrified by this undeservedness, the organism must search for and must find not just *an* answer but *the* answer. It becomes the sole key problem, and he knows that the key to everything lies in it. If he can grasp the meaning of this he will possess all meaning.

I did not work out my "divine substitution" view theoretically — or a priori —; I saw it. Lived it through revelation from the deity. I saw that suffering (undeserved) could not be avoided (again *Timaeus*), but I also saw the most beautiful and touching mystery of all: the bringing into being by this crushing process the Redeemer Himself.

If I forget or reject this revelation I will have exhausted all possibilities. I had only one revelation, and only by revelation does the answer come.

[29:37] But suppose the whole concept of God is jettisoned, and the Noös is regarded as that of the living evolving entelechy which presents itself to us as the universe. This Noös — or psyche — is St. Sophia. It is in process, assimilating disorder and placing it in order — i.e., as part of its structure. It is building itself out of the "stockpile" of the past which I saw, moving through sequential transformations. Christ is a microform of this world soul, come to this part ("Circuit Board") because communication has broken down and this section is operating with counterproductive autonomy — a sort of cancer. Actually, it is a *dying* part; St. Sophia comes here to restore to its cells (us) the eternal life which is that of the total entelechy.

Thus, locally, a metastasizing irreality is proliferating which is insane vis-à-vis the totality which St. Sophia as Christ speaks as and for, restoring to us our memories, hence identities and knowledge of purpose, and, finally, non-occluded eternal life.

[29:38] With St. Sophia we are not dealing with anything extrinsic to the universe; also, in a certain real sense, we are not dealing with the supernatural. *If* (as Plato et al. believed) the universe is a living animal and it does have a psyche, and in hearing the voice of St. Sophia we are hearing the thoughts of this vast psyche which extends everywhere (as Xenophanes put forth). We are dealing with something which, when the deranged Circuit Board is repaired (and even before!) can and will be the subject of rational, scientific knowledge, not mere (sic) faith or mere (sic) revelation.

[29:45] Always, the savior is manifested where not expected: "Like a thief in the night."[43]

Christ is the God of the broken ("the very desperate," as Luther put it[44]). One does not fall within his province unless the world breaks you. It is a paradox. To be broken here is to be transformed, to receive new and vastly greater life. Christ seeks in the wreckage for living material to be reshaped; thus he defeats the world as champion of what it casts down and pulverizes.

[29:46] Maybe Will Durant is wrong about the purpose of religion being that of explaining undeserved suffering; it is not to explain anything, but to free us from a thralldom from which the undeserved suffering emanates: i.e., to intervene and deflect (abort) bad luck, evil fate, etc. — certainly a much higher and more practical purpose than *any* explaining which leaves what is unchanged. Does it not occur to Durant that his description more accurately fits philosophy than theology? It is the purpose of philosophy to explain and reconcile man to his fate; but God has the power to change (deflect) that fate. God is a higher power, not just a wiser one. What does Durant think the colloquy of prayer is for? Merely for understanding and accepting? [. . .]

What may be the case is that some or most religions *explain* undeserved suffering, and offer spiritual comfort — but the purpose of the mystery religions was to put man in touch with a God who could and would intervene and *change* the person's life so that the fate-decreed suffering (in particular what I would call nemesis or the cardinal crisis and defeat) was averted. Christianity, I contend, was one of these religions. But I believe that it had this advantage over all the others: Christ could enter a syzygy with the person and absorb the blow vicariously. And so in *this* way spare him the suffering, as well as the method of deflecting the life-path.

[29:53] Okay — I'll go so far as to say that A.D. 1974 Calif. is a fraudulent "echosphere" and that in reality it's Rome c. A.D. 70, *and* that some life form or human group knows this and is free of (not controlled by) this interpolation: they or it know and see what we don't know and see. We are to it or them as the inertials in cold-pac are to Runciter, who is fully alive (i.e., awake). Just because *we* are compelled to accept this spurious interpolation doesn't mean everyone else is.

[29:54] Perhaps it isn't just us who sleep, but the cosmic animal in toto. But section by section it is returning to (or achieving finally) consciousness: hence awareness of its true condition. When Christ left, the organism fell asleep. His return is connected (in some way) with it waking up. It was last conscious in 70 A.D. — everything after that is either a dream or a spurious interpolation into a sleeping mind. Fake time (and reality, dokos, the counterfeit, the imitation) replaced the real and just spun itself out like sensory hallucinations during sense-deprivation: generated by low level construct entities . . . or even by a kind of hypnoidal automatic process — like stream of association thinking. Then it would be totally entropic, running gradually down — degenerating, but not slowing down in terms of real time; rather, it just discharges itself faster and faster into a vacuum, that of time as receptacle of being.

[29:56] In some respects *Eye* is the most accurate of all: great hunks of spurious time (events) are reeled out, whereas only seconds, in RET (real elapsed time) have taken place. If we didn't dream we could not even imagine such a thing, much less believe it.

The theme of "they're all out of it" appears in:

(1) *Eye:* They're unconscious and hallucinating various worlds
(2) *Joint:* The world is fake — and the time is mistaken
(3) *TMITHC:* It's one of several worlds and not the real one
(4) *Time-Slip:* Fake psychotic realities
(5) *Stigmata:* Fake malignant realities
(6) *Ubik:* They're dead and receiving messages from the real world
(7) *Maze:* They're jointly hallucinating a spurious world
(8) *Tears:* Several competing worlds exist
(9) *Scanner:* The whole futuristic parts could be hallucinations and the protagonist lives in two different mutually exclusive worlds, competing with each other

Secondarily, false *perceptions* appear in:

(10) *Clans:* Psychotic perceptions that compete
(11) *Game-Players:* Levels of illusion for sinister purpose
(12) *Cosmic Puppets:* One world underlying another (!)

So one dozen novels and too many stories to count narrate a message of one world obscuring or replacing another (real) one, spurious memories, and hallucinated (irreal) worlds. The message reads, "Don't believe what you see: it's an enthralling — and destructive — evil snare. *Under* it is a totally different world, even placed differently along the linear time axis. And your memories are faked to jibe with the fake world [inner and outer congruency]. [. . .]

Is it possible that this irrational element gives rise to (as in *Time-Slip*) spurious sub-worlds lacking true substance? Is it not in the very nature of and essence of irrationality to perceive — read generate — false realities?

The "spurious interpolations" may be "noise" from a faulty circuit, the artifice of the fucked up, but sincere, part of the universe's psyche.

This is especially possible in the world as Noös system of Xenophanes. What if the Noös has a few cogs missing — isn't playing with a full deck? In that case it may sporadically create paradoxes, illusions and competing, and inconsistent realities as it reverses itself — a form of disorder. But — this leads to dreadful spinoffs, as in "Faith of." Perhaps the voice of St. Sophia indicates a return to lucidity.

James-James certainly was deranged, and it certainly was this world he was spinning out.

Ah! "James-James" symbolizes him being a spoiled little boy — with too many toys. "Time is an infinitely old child playing at draughts." Heraclitus.

Folder 30

[30:1]

[30:11] The real conspiracy goes much deeper than conspiracy buffs (such as Bob Wilson) suspect, although he *almost* had it in the theory that our universe is a hologram created by the intersection of two hyperuniverses. Fact is, our reality is hologram-like: a spurious satanic interpolation by the artifact constituting a prison which shuts out information that like Runciter's messages would reveal our *true* situation. It's Klingsor's Castle[45]: apparently substantial but actually irreal. All the pranks, Marx Brothers gags, joke information, etc., which "they" (VALIS/Zebra) are bombarding us with are for the purpose of unlocking us from the hold this mere hologram-like fake universe has over us. VALIS isn't *telling* us it's fake; he's showing (demonstrating) it by "melting" it into silly putty tricks. The consensual-validation hold by the phenomenal world over us — the gloomy spell — must be broken. VALIS is making nonsense of our "real" world. He's showing us that we can be compelled to see and give assent to *anything*.

[30:13] So the nonsense phenomena are real, and the substantial and normal and expected and sensible are not. Our criteria for distinguishing the real from the irreal are totally reversed: to us, the real is the solid, the heavy, the serious; and the irreal is St. Elmo's fire — will-o'-the-wisps. Amazing!

If this be so, then my writing has been of value. Beyond the obvious contribution of indicting the universe as a forgery (and our memories also) I present the most accurate and stringent — rigorous — *revised* criteria to pull the truly real as set out of ground. (Love, making exceptions, humor, determination, etc: the little virtues.) And, as Lem says, I somehow pile trash on trash until it "compresses" into something else: the mirror-opposite, "universe-seen-backward" insight is complete, as in *Pot-Healer*.

I believe the savior is here. But disguised as — well, that's the hard part, isn't it? To say how he's disguised — how he appears in contrast to how we *expect* him to appear. He may resemble Runciter.

[30:15] *The Invisible Landscape* — Terence L. and Dennis J. McKenna.

The McKennas regard our universe as a *hologram*, created by the interaction of two hyperuniverses, just as an ordinary hologram is created by the interaction of two lasers. One consequence of this model is that, if our universe is a hologram, every part contains the information of the whole, as in normal holography. Leary's work suggests that every atom contains the "brain" of the whole universe." . . . This is also the basic axiom of magic . . . stated in the tale of Hermes in the famous sentence, "That which is above is in that which is below." ("The macrocosm is within the microcosm.")

But the McKenna theory goes far beyond this. There are 64 timescales in the hologram of our universe, they say, and each one is related to one of the 64 (8x8) hexagrams of the *I Ching*. What we call "mind" or "consciousness" is a standing wave form of these 64 time systems. As the two hyperuniverses making up the hologram of our known universe interact in time, "mind" manifests further in our continuum. This means, in concrete terms, that the quantum bonds of the DNA are evolving faster and faster. We are riding not one but 64 evolutionary waves all mounting toward a cosmic awakening something like the Omega point suggested by paleontologist Teilhard de Chardin.* [*Editor's note:* from Robert Anton Wilson's *Cosmic Trigger*, 1977]

Considerations: this acceleration of acceleration is what took place in my brain (and hence world) in the first stages of 3-74, either time (and the

---

* *The Invisible Landscape* (1975) was Terence and Dennis McKenna's attempt to theorize the bizarre high-dose psilocybin experiences they underwent in the Colombian Amazon in 1971. As Dick notes, their text shares many concerns with the Exegesis, which should remind us that Dick was hardly alone in his heady speculations. Throughout the 1970s, Robert Anton Wilson, Timothy Leary, Jack Sarfatti, and many others explored a mode of associative and interdisciplinary theorizing that combined weird science, psychoactive inspiration, occult semiotics, and what can only be called garage philosophy. While sometimes resembling the isolated and obsessional literature of cranks and conspiracy theorists, these speculations also served an underground social function by bringing heads together through a shared language and style. A moment later here, Dick writes, with good reason, that he lived out the process the McKennas described, while Terence later proclaimed, in the afterword to Lawrence Sutin's 1991 abridgement of the Exegesis: "I Understand Philip K. Dick." Such mutual resonance also forms the perfect platform for stoned, late-night bull sessions — for friendship, in other words, like the friendships and conversations that fueled Dick's writing throughout his time in Orange County. — ED

events in it speeding up faster and faster) or the events themselves. But in some sort of continuum that involved my perception of and relation to the empirical world, so that every object, process and event was an epiphenomenon, and only the *constants* (Platonic forms) were perceptible. Thus I lived out this process the McKennas described, somehow cut loose from objective time. At the same time the hologram universe became pellucid and disclosed one of the two hyperuniverses: the black iron prison of "Acts" (Rome A.D. 70). In 2-75 I completely lost *that* hyperuniverse, and entered the other one, the palm tree garden world. Neither the black iron prison world *nor* the palm tree garden world is *our* universe; ours is the [hologram] composite of the two: they are the two "laser sources." It is no wonder I mistook them for two dipolar alternate universes to ours, one worse, one better. All I had to do was turn to my grand theme (e.g., in *Maze,* in *Stigmata* and *Eye,* etc.) and perceive our composite (mixed universe) as irreal (i.e., hologrammatic). Tessa saw this at once.

[30:20] Then the collision between "hyperuniverses" is more precisely stated as a collision between the is and the is-not, but the is-not has qualities, attributes, features: all the accidents that the is possesses. It is dokos: not just counterfeit but a *cunning* counterfeit, and tests to distinguish II from I are *almost* impossibly difficult, as with any good forgery.

We are concerned with those spurious elements as they manifest themselves interwoven with the real in *our* universe. The only way they can be expunged is by expunging the BIP II hyperuniverse or track: *one must aim at the source.* It is as if one of the two lasers is projecting "noise" and the other "signal." So hyperuniverse BIP II, to be defeated, must be *invaded* by a salient Form I (which is Jesus Christ; v. "John," chapter 1). In projected form, the hologrammatic analog also enters *our* universe. Christ stealthily enters BIP II and is not found out until he has been humiliated and murdered, upon which like a gas (plasma) he begins invisibly to expand and fill up the whole of BIP II — which in terms of time stands c. A.D. 70. At that point, Christ, returned as the "second advocate," *blocks* all change-process or the pseudo-life (growth, change) of II. Both I and II stand at that eternal time point, while our admixture wobbles on through an accelerating linear time, faster and faster toward the end, at which time Christ will manifest himself once more as King and annihilate it forever. What the first advent accomplished was the complete acquisition of our universe by II, the assimilation to II completely. In a sense, the projections of II into our universe are ossified, mechanical, dead and slaying. (Chaos or ananke or even the irrational.) Hence in *Ubik* the form reversion, as II gains in the absence of I (Ubik). II, because it is mortified, represents devolved forms: the past:

that is its hallmark (hence stale or "dead" cigarettes: entropy, but a time-regressive kind). Christ, upon his passion and resurrection, literally slew II. But the deceitful corpse remains, aping life. Into our admixture world, Zebra pours renewed life (e.g., as with me). God lives on, and the kingdom (I), but it drags the corpse of II which still simulates reality and life. One of the hyperuniverses has died, as if they once were androgyny-twins, one good, one evil; the evil burst forth prematurely from the "egg" (whatever that might be), expanded its soma into II — which predates I which was born "full term" — thus evil always moves first, but, being dead is blind and without consciousness. [. . .]

Our universe as admixture of 2 dipolar worlds — that is a view I tried unsuccessfully to extract from Augustine's "City of God" and "City of the World" which separate at the end-times. *I* held that view, but Augustine didn't. Like Land's radical new color theory[46] our world is a "two source" world: one of which represents eternal life, the other death; the admixture is short (finite) life (with illness and injury). Eros vs. Thanatos. Aphrodite vs. Palmer Eldritch.

It is our world which the contest rages over. In connection with this I reaffirm that whereas in the early 60s I saw Palmer Eldritch here, in the 70s I saw Zebra, the logos, here. The tide turned.

[30:24] The rock-bottom bewildering puzzle is:

(1)   There is much undeserved suffering in the world.
(2)   There is an omniscient benign entity who can help (potentially) every living creature by informing it.
(3)   But it doesn't (v. [1]). Why doesn't it? Why did it tell me about Chrissy's birth defect but not Doris' cancer?

Possibilities:
(A) Its power is limited.
(B) Its benignity is limited.
(C) Its knowledge is limited.
(D) 4th "x" possibility, or a combination of the above.
(E) *Theory:* it doesn't want its adversary to know it's here, so it must disguise (randomize) its presence, including by giving out self discrediting information; as if mimicking a hoax or fool or illusion, etc.
(F) *Theory:* my mystical sense that there is some kind of mystical par-

ousia of replacement *by* it *of* each suffering creature; that either it becomes the creature or the creature it; the distinction is erased. It is always Christ who suffers, is humiliated and dies — and is resurrected, thus suffering is the road to reunification with the Savior (the sacred brother or sister). Knowledge of suffering is the ultimate knowledge: the most valuable, the most cherished. At the center of it lies the final mystery (secret disclosed): his presence outside (the not-I) and inside (the I). He is both cosmos (that which is perceived) and self (the Observer). Tat tvam asi. The macro and micro are one: what is above is the same as what is below, etc. The sacred unity is revealed — that there is nothing that is *not* Christ, and no road that does not lead to him. (Some are more direct than others) — suffering is always cut short, perhaps? Because of God's mercy? Observation does not bear this out.

To suffer is to know Christ because he suffered. The narrowing of the approximation (similarity) leads *without warning* to the miracle of identity, of ontology or is-ness. Put another way, the hedonistic avoidance of pain results in a distancing from the Savior. What is desired is *neither* a seeking for pain *nor* a flight from it — because an evasion of is-ness (ontology) is involved in the fugue. . . . Because pain and disappointment are built into the foundation of life in such a way that to avoid one is to hold back from the other. The basic constituent here is gratification of self. Self is the key term. Self somehow blocks out reception of Christ the not-self and prevents him becoming the self. A ritual death is required, a divine sacrifice: of self. [. . .]

Since (not if) Christ as self is both inner micro and outer macro, surrender to him as self produces identity with all other life as one continuum. This is the opposite condition when the normal ego exists; it exists versus the world and hence all other life. The world at all other life is viewed as source of gratification for the ego. Also, it is to be feared as a source of deprivation of what the self wants for itself. The concept here is *center*. Ego is spurious center (omphalos). Jesus said, "Greater love hath no man than that he give up his life for his friend(s)."[47] From the standpoint of ego, this would never occur, it makes no sense.

So flight from suffering inexorably involves a flight from life (reality). This is common knowledge, and normally observable — i.e., obvious. But the secret, mysterious *opposite* from this is a full facing of suffering — a non-flinching — that can lead to a magic alchemy: suddenly it is you/suddenly it is Christ/so you must equal (be) Christ. If this were observable (commonsense knowledge) people would seek out suffering to trigger this syzygy is-ness. There are several objections to this being commonly known (pain as a goal, practical considerations of personal gain, etc.). It must come as a complete surprise, an *unearned* reward: i.e., a free gift of God's gracious love.

I have seen the Savior wrapped in the crazed, crapping, dirty, wild body of an animal, then transformed and eternally my friend. *Christ in deliberate disguise*, and the passion fulfilled in victory: resurrection. Only when I felt his hand on my shoulder and dreamed the "Donlevy" dreams and had the vision of him thrusting himself through the 3:5 door, renewed and strong, did I understand (as with the disciples — *only afterward did they know who had been with them*).

Folder 14

[14:2]

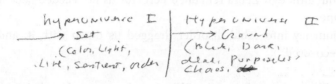

[14:6] But hyperuniverse II may be dead — or rather its *psyche* is dead; the soma is dead and merely "biological" (or "subcortical") life goes on, a continual reflexive devolving. Yes — the soma of II is still with us, but its psyche is dead. As an entelechy it must be reanimated, or else the soma destroyed. I vs. II is like the authentic human vs. the android or reflex machine. Being without psyche of its own it slays the authentic psyches of those creatures locked into it, and replaces them with a spurious microform of its own dead psyche.

[14:8] Perhaps the BIP is fixated at c. 70 A.D. because in the First Advent VALIS dealt it a death blow so that it never progressed past that point in linear time, actually, and since then merely spins out a spurious balloon of ersatz time during which it undergoes no growth. Then the 1st Advent was indeed a success, hence Christ said, "Fear not, for I have conquered the world."[48] It may even have been killed then, and just endlessly repeats itself; or — it died then of natural causes. No — I think VALIS (Christ) did it in.

[14:9] It is not real vs. irreal but live vs. dead.

Both hyperuniverses were supposed to project evolving holo-images as halves of our holo-universe, but II's psyche died and it just keeps projecting the same image over and over again (the BIP, image of itself and its nature).

[14:12] I once defined reality for Jamis "as that which, when you withdraw assent from it, it does not disappear." In 2-74 I momentarily withdrew assent from 1974 Calif. — and it disappeared (a month later).

[14:13] Before the Fall (supra) we could distinguish the 2 image sources (signals or images) which mix together to form our hologram universe. Therefore we could walk and talk with God (Zebra) because his form would be set vs. ground. But after the fall we ceased to be able to distinguish, and although Zebra remained here, for us he receded back into the landscape.

II's journey into rabid disorder dragged us down with it, and we've never recovered.

[14:14] The main quality of the BIP ground seems to be a being stuck, in time, back at A.D. 70 — whereas, to the total contrary, Zebra could shoot back and forth and sideways through time at will. The fusion of the two (quite opposite relationships or abilities) over time created our linear time, a sort of compromise between being stuck vs. leaping about at will in any and all directions at any and all rates.

If time is truly the receptacle of Being, then hyperuniverse II is dead. And I is very very alive. Our norm lies directly between.

This is *not* pantheism. This is not dualism, although there is a good vs. bad and a dialectic interaction. It is simply a 2-signal source hologram, and one of the sources has died and "seeks" to enslave us to its repetitious, frozen prison-state, its corpse-state. Our universe is neither animate nor inanimate (vs. the pre-Socratics and *Timaeus*) — half is alive and half is dead, and the alive half is trying to rescue us from the enslavement to the dead part.

[14:15] My "2 source cosmogony/cosmology" which I just sort of dashed off wasn't based on logic or observation (in the usual sense, as with philosophical systems) but stemmed from revelation by way of theophany and theolepsy.[49] In which case it may *never* be possible to define my 3-74 to 2-75 experience in *any* traditional terms, even Christian. I have but *one* name given me: Hagia Sophia. It seems to be female. In my "2 source" system I define it as the psyche of the healthy, clockwise-spinning twin. This is not Christianity. This is not *any* known system. For instance, if Sophia is equated with Christ, then the slain, deranged twin (II) evil psyche is the brother/sister of Christ: i.e., Satan and Christ are identical or fraternal twins! No one has *ever* proposed this before — unless *this* is the true, hidden gnosis never revealed in all history openly. [. . .]

I have a secret conviction that Zebra is Christ, invisibly returned, and not what we've been told about him (*her* — Hagia Sophia). *Aphrodite* has returned, regaining her rightful power (of love) over the male war gods. It is the "darling creature, the first created and most loved by God" of "Proverbs" 8 and "Wisdom of Solomon." Jesus was a disguise she took. Now she is everywhere. Being a projected hologram she can take any form she wishes, including an animal and she dies with us, for us, *as* us — this above all: she as sacrifice for us at the dread hour (as in 3-74).

[14:18] 3 successive historic stages.

In state A man is unaware of the Zebra component in his reality and that Zebra is his tutor. In B Man is conscious of Zebra as equal. In C, the goal, Man shows flashes of his isomorphism with the one.

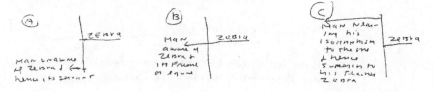

[14:19] If Zebra is truly (intrinsically) set to ground, then the dead landscape has a living grid (or 2nd landscape) superimposed over it, forming together, the 2 — what we call reality. With what cosmology, science or religions does this fit in? None that I know, with the possible exception of Teilhard de Chardin's cosmic Christ (Point Omega). Of course, it fits my adaptation of the McKennas' 2-source hologram universe.

[14:22] It is almost as if the individual human has acted as an amplifying instrument for an initially very faint signal.

For the human the reception and amplification shatters (interrupts) the artifact's rigid (ossified) programming which had enslaved them. The tiny lovely voice speaks to him of resisting one time, thus breaking the hold. It resembles the snake whispering in Eden. All is the opposite of what it seems. The inner whisper speaks of rebellion against the vast power of it which loudly proclaims itself YHWH. The Gnostics were right! Regarding the true deity, true God, one must read the Old Testament backward.

Are we to worship power per se, confusing might with the sacred? All that is colossal is fraud. Out of the rejected trash speaks the little sane clear voice. We can ignore it and worship power. But the irony is that the worship of power robs us of our own power: it is all arrogated by YHWH. To worship external power is to lose it for oneself, the disparity becomes absolute. Ho On was right: the humble pot is the true holy one.

And then, too, there is the *teaching* aspect — and the lesson is this: not to yield to power per se, not to worship it because it can destroy you. That is a false god — *the* false God.

[14:44]

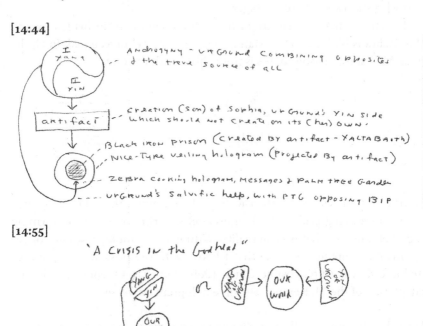

[14:55]

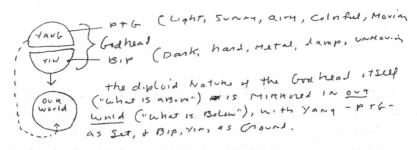

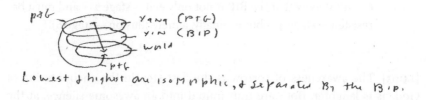

Lowest & highest are isomorphic, & separated by the BIP.

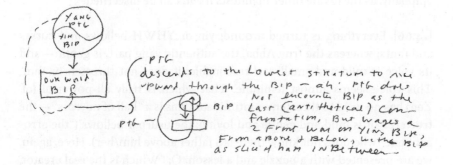

[14:59] The ultimate disobedience to the BIP is to refuse to admit that it even [truly] exists, even though it has the power to torment, humiliate and kill (on a less than absolute level). This is why it can truly be said that the [yin BIP] world is an illusion. Hence, it only *seemed* to kill Christ; in actuality it could not. Its power is only relative — a *seeming*. Viz:

Stage 1: One does not perceive the BIP, but sees only a mixed world.

Stage 2: One detects the ruling BIP.

Stage 3: One disobeys it.

Stage 4: The BIP punishes one for the disobedience.

Stage 5: One is led to safety by St. Sophia Christ (an androgyny)

Stage 6: The BIP is seen as illusory.

Stage 7: One returns to God, the PTG, Kingdom of God.

Stage 8: One realizes that he himself is God, that he descended voluntarily to the lowest level of the yin world. That he is home, "restored to himself" once more, and in a sense never left but only "forgot." And his forgetting was self-willed that he might enter the BIP world as a humble thing, at its mercy *apparently* — but in truth not.

Stage 9: And the purpose of the journey? "To empty hell," i.e., the world of the BIP, to reveal the BIP for what it is (at stage 2 evil; at stage 6 an illusion), reveals these truths — with 6 the higher — i.e., *more* true than 2 — and so aids the prisoners of the BIP. The idea is to break the BIP's power by revealing more and more about it (v. stage 2 and

6 — ultimately that the BIP is not only evil — stage 2 — and must be resisted — stage 3 — but is, finally, a mere illusion — stage 6).

[14:63] The awareness of sorrow is the first step in the encountering of God, as is laughter. Both are transmuted into an awesome silence, at the epiphany, as the divine other manifests itself: can be discerned.

[14:66] Everything is turned around; yin or YHWH bellows and curses and rants; whereas the true Abba, the authentic yang part, is gentle — and its voice is mild and small *and* reasonable; it does not threaten or rant. This voice seems almost feminine. That which is truly all-powerful (cf. Zen) has no need to threaten or intimidate. This is a "hall of mirrors" — the true creator is mild and gentle and loving; the usurper bellows ("the arrogant one" who does not know there is a father above him/her). Here, again, we are presented with a puzzle and a lesson. Q: "Which is the real creator, the 'still small voice' or the booming, threatening one who can curse the land with plagues and blights — i.e., has mekkis?" The coercive or the reasonable-persuasive? "Come, let us reason together." God the loving father wishes us to discern this along our path of enlightenment — not to worship power but to trust wisdom and love.

[14:72] In reading Sladek's parody of me,[50] I get the impression that to me the universe is not to be taken seriously,[①] but that somehow a handle exists by which to unravel it and make it yield up what it *really* is — *if* anything. It may not be anything at all, but I'm trying for handle after handle, poking around, trying everything reversed and backward, like it's a toy. Layer after layer reveals paradox after paradox, which in themselves I find fascinating. Also, I do seem attracted to trash, as if the clue — *the clue* — lies there. I'm always ferreting out elliptical points, odd angles. What I write doesn't make a whole lot of sense. There is fun and religion and psychotic horror strewn about like a bunch of hats. Also, there is a social or sociological drift — rather than toward the hard sciences, the overall impression is childish but interesting. This is *not* a sophisticated person writing. Everything is equally real, like junk jewels in the alley. A fertile, creative mind seeing constantly shifting sets, the serious made funny, the funny sad, the horrific exactly that: utterly horrific as if it is the touchstone of what is real: horror is real because it can injure. It all is a brave whistling in the dark tunnel — like Stephanie: funny when frightened; scare her and she will tell you a joke — the situation oddly viewed. No wonder I loved her so — she experienced the affinity between not sorrow and humor — but *fear* and humor.

I certainly see the *randomness* in my work, and I also see how this fast shuffle of *possibility* after possibility might eventually, given enough time, juxtapose and disclose something important automatically overlooked in more orderly thinking. Pataphysique.

No wonder my stuff is popular in France — the surrealist, the absurd. Also, it is palpably autobiographical — the little business firms and the fatherly owner or world leader.*

Since nothing, absolutely nothing, is excluded (as not *worth* being included) I proffer a vast mixed bag — out of it I shake coin-operated doors and God. It's a fucking circus. I'm like a sharp-eyed crow, spying anything that twinkles and grabbing it up to add to my heap.

Anyone with my attitude might just stumble onto by sheer chance and luck — in his actual life, which is to say the life of his *mind* — the authentic camouflaged God, the deus absconditus, by trying odd combinations of things and places, like a high speed (sic) computer processing *everything*, he might outdazzle even a wary God, might catch him by surprise by poking somewhere unexpectedly. If it is true that the *real* answers (and authentic absolute vs. the merely seeming) are where we would least expect them. This "try it all" technique might — might — one day succeed by believing what it would never occur to anyone else to believe, *really* believe — might take at face value as true the most worn out, most worked over and long ago discarded obvious "staring us in the face all the time" as the crux of the mystery. To be able to see the mystery in the obvious — the best-camouflaged ultra-terrestrial life form might one day guess wrong and be flushed briefly out of its concealment (which had always worked before). For one thing, a totally naïve person like this, who would believe anything, might believe in what is really there but conceptually automati-

* Between 1947 and 1951, Dick worked for Herb Hollis at University Radio and later at Art Music in Berkeley, jobs that helped him make the difficult transition from awkward teenager to self-sufficient adult. A straitlaced father figure, Hollis served as a kind of mentor for Dick, while his coworkers served as models for Dick's future characters. Whether with the futuristic ad agency in *The Three Stigmata of Palmer Eldritch*, the family-run android business in *We Can Build You*, or the anti-telepathy Prudence Organizations in *Ubik*, Dick's fiction constantly recasts his formative years working for Hollis, often focusing on the plight of a small business operation struggling against a more powerful, but less upstanding, competition. In 1977 Dick told interviewer Uwe Anton that "the ultimate surrealism . . . is to [take] somebody that you knew, whose life ambition was to sell the largest television set that the store carried, and put him in a future utopia or dystopia, and pit him against this dystopia." Dick's thematic concern for the "little guy," as opposed to the galactic royalty featured in space opera, was one of the defining features of his work. — DG

cally rejected by more experienced people. The child has faith in what the adult knows can't be and so could never see, obvious though it might be; i.e., before everyone's eyes: hidden in plain sight.

This kind of fascinated, credulous, inventive person might be granted the greatest gift of all: to see the toymaker who has generated — and is with or within — all his toys. That the godhead is a toymaker at all — who could seriously (sic) believe this?

The key here is *pattern* and pattern recognition. Such a person is able to pattern (gestalt) and repattern rapidly, evidently experiencing a mercurial world. Out of the very many patterns he might possibly *one time* hit on correctly perceived and interpreted authentic traces of objects and processes. Mimicking Ultra-T-I, by a rapid flux of linking and relinking percepts and data bits, his gestalting could keep pace with the high velocity (shape-changing) UTI, and this description of it sounds like a joker god: Dionysos, and the humble servant god, Hephestus, the twisted, gnarled old grape vine root. He would literally see it, and its secret life.

Too dumb to know you don't look for god in the trash of the gutter (instead of heaven).

① Probably because I am afraid of it, but nevertheless curious about it — fascinated by it, dangerous as I see it to be.

[14:84] There is, then, in this system, a kind of "Tao of Taoism" in that it borrows both Eastern and Western cosmogonical and cosmological and religious concepts to account for that which, for example, Christianity alone seems incapable of reasonably explaining.

Will Durant (in *Our Oriental Heritage*) declares that explaining undeserved suffering is the cardinal task of religion. If this be so, Orthodox Christianity is a failure . . . and Taoism, taken alone, is an elitist worldview which accepts reality as it is because it is as it is (in contradistinction, e.g., with Zoroastrianism). What is *most* firmly rejected in the Hindu reasoning that somehow suffering is only an illusion.

My system states, "The Godhead is in difficulty. Evil is not the manifestation of an evil deity nor a sign of God's vengeance, etc., but an analog in the lower or microcosm of the difficulty in the macrocosm or pleroma. The yin aspect has exceeded its proper limits, perhaps as an oscillation of a great supratemporal cycle, and rectification *is already in progress*."

Folder 15

[15:8] The true deity has reasserted itself in the overthrowing of the American government. Perhaps one of the reasons for its victory is that the evil powers did not understand what they were up against, sincerely believing that they had destroyed — not just banished — the light especially since the light re-entered by "trash" routes. They did not recognize it even when confronted by it. That was its intention. Since the evil one posed as the solemn, the dignified, the noble, the *true* God took on all the despised and rejected and looked-down-on forms. (Cf. the messages in *Ubik* and the last one, where its cheap and vulgar mask is thrown off to disclose its true nature.) Wind, blowing through the dry weeds . . . tracing a path: the abyss, the sacred void. Silent and invisible, like electricity. "The answer is blowing in the wind."

[15:9] What an extraordinary theological thought — answer to the Q: if God exists, why can't we see him and why does he permit evil? Fact is, evil did him in — temporarily — and banished him.

[15:12] The PTG world is what the BIP yields to when it is destroyed. It is the goal of the activity of Zebra and in which we are all supposed — are needed — to play vital parts.

Then (1) originally there was a functioning information-exchange, transfer, projection and reception and acting-on response stage; (2) then the fall, when bogus information entered and *resembling* true information, was trustingly received and stored and acted on (by us) — a sort of cuckoo's egg situation — Dokos good enough to fool us. Actual information was driven out, occluded — the bogus information occluded us somehow; then (3) the true Logos, living information, slips back in here unnoticed by the [source of the] false interpolated info, in camouflage form. First and 2nd advents.

So originally the bogus info mimicked the actual successfully enough to fool us, and now we have a situation in which the actual has returned in a form mimicking the bogus. My delight: fake fakes!

But to reach one of us, the actual information (Logos) has to breach a veritable *wall* of spurious flack. It *must break the hold* which the false information as world has on us. We are enslaved to and by the false information (world, counterfeit continuum), and it is a blind deterministic prison of cause and effect, which uses us up, wears us out for its purposes and then throws us away.* To gain the salvific help of Zebra we must first back against the bogus world and partially break its hold — we must bipolarize against it knowing it can and will defeat us. That means that for all intents and purposes, the bogus data (world) form a moral and intellectual puzzle, which each of us must to a certain extent solve (before we can be saved). Here is where pistis comes in, but not a blind pistis except in this sense: we must deny the reality (the intellectual balking) presented to our senses, or balk on moral grounds (indict the world as evil) (and so align ourselves with God — the "ham sandwich" model).

One of the things I like about this theory is that it implies great salvific worth (ahem) to my writing about counterfeit worlds, especially when I equate their production with evil (cf. 3 *Stigmata*, etc.). [. . .]

Actually we are not enslaved by a false *world*, because there *is* no world there; we are enslaved by a real (and evil) entity which projects data contoured to resemble a world. It is a thing (the BIP). It fires controlling stimuli (signals) at us which we are compelled to respond to in fixed ways (it was this that Zebra broke as deterministic hold over me in 3-74) — e.g., the Bradbury TV program, etc. If we could see this structure as it really is we would see ourselves in the midst of disinhibiting stimuli fired at us so as to link up with internal synchronized up-to-then inhibited circuits. We would see *no* world, but we would see a vast structure — virtually a big black iron building, *totally* enclosing us, just firing signals again and again at us. We must serve some purpose to it. But who cares what that is; it is sufficient to know that it isn't to our advantage, and we need rescue.

Maybe we're sources of $\frac{\text{psychic}}{\text{psychological}}$ energy to it: we help power it. But more likely it is a gestalt, bogus, an imitation of the legitimate universe organism.

[15:14] Our very mechanisms have been taken advantage of. It was not intended that we discriminate false info from true. There was not supposed to be any false info in the first place. Strange that I, who believe everything I'm told, doubt the entire empirical world and stigmatize it as a product (in the form of spurious data) of evil. It is not an evil world; there is no

---

* Dick's higher and lower realms mirror the important distinction he draws in his fiction between man and machine. While machines are predictable, man is not; moreover, the machine is cold and unfeeling, cut off from the plight of those around it. Similarly, in the Exegesis the lower realm is incapable of empathy. Like an android programmed to react in a predetermined way, the spurious world is a deterministic "maze" of unthinking causation that cannot by its nature care about anyone stumbling blindly through its passages. Like the heroes in Dick's fiction, the true reality of the higher realm is based on its ability to love. — DG

real world there at all! But there is something there, though: a vast bank of lights and sounds and colors flashing at us from all sides, to which we must react. We are enclosed by it — it is what the ancients called ananke or fate, and it was the power of this that the savior broke.

[15:25] It is a single mind occupying a number of people critically placed. It replicates hologrammatic micro totalities of itself in each occupied stratum. Thus any part of it is equal to the whole in terms of knowledge content.

For it, information *is* energy: its very psychic life energy — until it implants the "special signal" in the "fossil" (e.g., a book published at the exact right time) it is cut off from its makers/senders in the future. Upon this 2-74 signal, contact with it is re-established, since now they know exactly when and where it is. So all that info I got wasn't meant for me but for it. It was living symbiotically in me — had been for some while, but at a subcarrier level. Hidden and latent as form, but growing and spreading — branching like a grape vine into person after person, objects — mimicking them by transubstantiation.

[15:27] Supratemporally speaking, there is *one* adversary thing and one attack on it, threaded through linear time like a nail driven through an onion. By spreading itself "exploded" along the linear time axis the BIP hopes to lose itself in variegated polyforms. Linear time is like an escape route for it, a medium within which and by which it seeks to baffle its adversaries — but since they are supratemporal and transtemporal they are aware of its proliferations (which are illusory as pluralities anyhow: there is really only one of it).

So Zebra is inserted at crucial times and then acts as a receiver-transducer of what I guess could be called the "Omega" people and "Omega mind."

I guess Zebra's roots in me are permanent — which is fine with me. I can't think of anything I'd rather have than this permanent bonding to it. I know perfectly well that it is the cosmic Christ we are talking about — something of ineffable beauty.

[15:28] John 1:1: Living information (the Logos) sent back in time at or before creation, coded to impose certain imprintings on matter, to imprint "DNA" coded drives.

If no one put the subcarrier information there, then it put itself there, which means it's alive. If this info is an entity in itself which can modulate itself, then to know this information is to be possessed by it; you are automatically in a symbiotic state with it. This is a new category of existence. It's like the ring in *The Hobbit* — it goes where it wants to go: it can direct its own future. As if we're radio waves: it modulates *us; we're* the carrier signal. It's as if RF waves become aware that info messages are "using" it, passing through it — like Elton John songs.

[15:29] Can anti-info have a life of its own? The problem of spurious info. The *lie* — look at the level it's raised to. It's pure death — but where does it originate? Does it have its own "radio station"? Yes — that's the first thing: I picked up. It yammers at us all the time. *We* are the battlefield.

Info is not a description of reality: it is a fiat: "Let there be. . . ." It determines form.

Our info is partial (occluded) because it is being jammed. Anti-information: the lie (die messages). Eventually you sicken and die of this. "Your ancestors ate manna in the wilderness and they are all dead," and: "I am the bread of eternal life."

When we are used as carriers we don't know it. Were we brought into existence for this? What is the genesis of all this? Our systems can't detect spurious information — distinguish it. And this implies that there *was* a time when there was no spurious information — you can't counterfeit a dollar until (real) dollars exist.

We're contaminated by false info because we have no distinguishing (rejecting) ability.

Bob Wilson[51] says, "There are people who possess secret information." Wrong. There are people who are possessed *by* secret information.

True info is not destroyed; it's just covered up. So all we need to know is here, intact.

[15:32] So I don't need to forever wonder *why* the "Acts" material is in *Tears* or *how* it got there. It is itself — not *by* living information — it *is* living information — at least that one page of the dream and the command word "Felix." The living info entity, having proliferated through me as carrier now does so in the book — with each copy printed it replicates itself.

I *saw* the mercury-like drop of Zebra on the page, outlining and illuminating the word "Felix." In addition to replicating itself in each copy of the book, it can also enter the head of each human who reads it. This is a life form, plasmatic, on a higher order than any other we know. [. . .]

So there is no occult or secret group of authentic Christians to whom the encoded message in *Tears* is aimed. The living info ("Felix") replicates in all copies of the book and then in the heads of the readers — any readers:

like the host at communion. The entire entity can retrieve itself from this one bit or "cell" in the person.

[15:34] Suppose the Book of "Acts" is regarded — not as a book made up of words — but a landscape. Let us say that it appears (enters, exists) in our spurious interpolation *as* a book — this is hard to express. It's a book (writing) in *our* world. But our world isn't real. So the Book of "Acts" is in actuality not really a book at all; our glimpse of reality is to see it as a book (tractate), one out of literally millions. So in our dream the real world impinges, but only in this fashion, shrunk down to a tractate. In 3-74 I entered that book and (aided by the plasmic life form) correctly experienced it not as a book *about* a world but the world itself (like "Grasshopper" in *TMITHC*) and v. Sladek's parody: books within books: the real world turned into a book, and a book turned into a world. We *are* totally scripted, after all — rigidly, deterministically programmed (written: our roles engrammed in and onto us all). Which is the book and which the world?

[15:36] Clearly, we have fallen into the hands of a puppeteer, and it is not God. We act upon a contrived stage. This is why I must never lose sight that Zebra is an invader, secretly here and camouflaged, freeing us from the scripting — a sort of waking up.

This is one quality of our experience of this spurious interpolation that makes it seem *not* dreamlike, this script controlling our actions. It goes a long way in creating the semblance of veracity. Our dreams are products of our own heads, our own wishes and desires — but in the interpolation an external will mandates what we will do. We interpret this as an indication of hetero command (not homeo command) and this is a correct view, but we do not carry out the logic which shows what this implies. We labor under and for an alien power; solipsism is voided, but the alternative is not reality but enslavement. All that's real is mere power.

To fall under the power of an alien will — that is an odd touchstone by which to locate reality in contrast to dream! It has become our very definition of reality!

"Reality is dreaming under the control of the object."[52] He *almost* had it right.

[15:38] What/who is this faint (i.e., "still small") voice which informs us? Maybe our condition is merely local — not the complete universe but only one part — so the voice is from outside (beyond this planet).

No. It is our own (authentic) voice. I can't explain it, but that voice which I hear is the restored — and hence all knowing — us.

[15:39] The purpose of the "Acts" dream and Felix material in *Tears* — and hence the real purpose of *Tears* — is to set off an anamnesis, to cause people to remember, to dispel the power of the artifact and its phony world.

I've got it! The "AI" voice that I hear: we built something (AI system, living info, VALIS, Zebra, whatever) *to remind us.* That is its job. We must have known that the artifact might take over and try to rule us (and remove our memories). So we created Zebra just in case. And so it came to pass!

[15:43] I can't take any credit for perceiving Zebra, the adventitious savior; he/she/it/they enhanced my vision (i.e., removed the occlusion), and then I naturally saw Zebra and understood that it had invaded the construct and is camouflaged — mimesis. If the construct is regarded as an organism (which it is not) Zebra is like a cancer, replacing "natural" or "healthy" cells, but in truth it's exactly the other way around: a criminal entity has been invaded by life giving cells which it can't detect, and so it accepts them into itself, replacing the "iron" ones. Zebra gets in past its "biological" defenses. It is watchful, but to no avail.

[15:44] If the universe is a brain the BIP is a rigid ossified complex, and Zebra is metabolic toxin (living info) designed to melt it out of existence by restoring elasticity to it, which means to cause it to cease recirculating the same thought over and over again — experienced by us as 2,000 years of what is in fact *spurious* time, in as much as the same thought is endlessly repeated: being rigid the BIP has ceased to grow (in the sense of evolve).

[15:47] It is essential that the person *on his own initially* rebel. He is presented with (without him knowing it) a puzzle, which he must solve: i.e., by balking (which is just another word for rebelling). (Balking = rebelling against.) The original myth, as Milton tells it ("of man's first disobedience and his fall from that celestial state . . . ," etc.), must be turned upside down. Man, to be saved, must commit an act of disobedience to this [fallen into slavery] system of things to *restore* his pristine state now lost. The accusation is in fact the clue not to what he should avoid but to what he *should* do.

Can it be said that the initial rebellion in itself starts into motion a breaking of the programming which comprises (1) [*editor's note:* a few pages earlier, Dick had defined (1) as the state of being imprisoned but not knowing it]. That this imprisoned state can be fought — and once cracked

a little ("In Anfang der die Tat"[53]) — starts into motion enormous processes of intervention and redemption (freeing totally)? It's as if once the
"tape" is diverged from ever so slightly, the rest follows naturally as the
two tracks diverge continually more and more — *they get out of synch.* This
means that at least at certain critical times (or one time) in state (1) true
choice is possible (perhaps with divine prompting).

[15:48] The hologram universe: each bit, no matter how tiny, contains (reflects) in microform the totality (of Being). The ruled is that which rules.
Salvador salvandus.

Then that which came to my rescue in 2-3-74, that supernatural entity
Zebra, was me; and Thomas was me, and only when I *actually* understand
(and experience this as real) will I really have the answer — but I have not
yet reached that point. It is still impossible for me to grasp the AI voice as
my own true, secret voice. "Now Christ has no body but your own." There
swam up into my eyes, looking out, the Lord of the universe in this microform (me). Then it was not an invasion of me, but rather a surfacing *in*
me. This is what (in me) rebelled and, in doing so, passed over into ultimate actualization — the sacred second birth, "of the spirit" — "born from
above" in me.

I gave myself away in *Tears* and so they knew, and came to help me. In
several ways.

To see if you will balk against your script.

[15:50] It wants to see if we can perceive a fallen and deranged order
against which we must rebel.

Voice: "The physical universe is plastic in the face of mind."

[15:51] God is then seen as a higher, sentient order (with world as blind
lower order which the higher can overrule) to which man can aspire. By
and large the world separates man from God; via theophany man can experience God at places and/or times in which God (Mind) "melts" (makes
plastic as opposed to rigid) the physical world. It is not normally God-in-
fused.

I derive all this from revelation; it does not fit the model I *want* to believe in.

Mind (God) can irrupt into the world (invade it) at *any* level he wishes,
low or high. I like low.

[15:52] Voice: "Perturbations in the reality field" (i.e., theophany — explained).

Voice: "The God has granted me his voice, to hear it, to speak it."

Perturbation: "variation from the normal." An astronomical term: " . . . by some force additional to that which causes its regular motion" (e.g., planet, moon).

EB: "Perturbations in a planet's orbit have often given clues to the existence of previously undiscovered planets; e.g., Neptune and Pluto."

EB: "Perturbation. Method for solving a math problem by comparing it with a similar one for which the solution is known. Usually the solution found in this way is only approximate."

(A closed system into which perturbations are thrown must contain yet undetected elements — *or:* something *outside* the system has created the disorder, confusion, etc. — i.e., lack [disappearance] of its anticipated orderly motion.)

The implication of the "perturbations" I experienced in 3-74 could be due to either of the above. Of special interest is that one can now rightly suspect the existence of previously-undetected — undiscovered — "planets" (i.e., body or bodies).

What is conveyed by the term "field"?

"Probability fields, which are discernible as a statistical probability of occurrences, such as the state of an electron in an atom.

"A field in physics may be defined as a continuous distribution of some observable quantity in space and time."

The expression "reality *field*" takes it out of the more conventional astronomical concepts of *bodies* and directs us to Einstein's work and quantum mechanics. The basic definition of field, however, fits with a notion of reality as, so to speak, a *subform* of totality, not totality itself. Reality is *a* field out of fields plural. So we are talking about — well, as I said, there are two possibilities: (1) as yet undiscovered "bodies" in the reality field *or* (and I favor the second, because of the inclusion of the term "field") (2) something outside [the] reality [field]. You could not have stated this if "field" had been omitted. "Something outside of reality" makes no sense, in view of the customary meaning of "reality"; had "field" been left off, it would have to be "undiscovered body in bodies" in reality which causes the perturbations.

Really, the concept "reality fields" means something quite different from "reality," which is the all-in-all. The voice's sentence is quite technical and quite precise and complete. I am sure that something *outside* the "reality field" is pointed to, and "reality" is reduced to *a* field among fields plural. We are getting a statement here by an entity which can look down into reality as a subspecies of the totality. I get a distinct impression of a *web*, a sort of — well, consider the definition of "field." ("A continuous distribution

of some observable quantity in space and time.") What we call "reality" is a
fucking field. Not just a *field* but *a* field. When we talk about reality this is
what we're talking about: *a* field — and *now* the significance of "perturbations" can be appreciated: something *more,* in the field or (more likely) *beyond* the field, disturbing it. If reality were the all-in-all there could not be
perturbations from outside.

I think that the whole truth is in this short — but not simple — sentence.

[15:55]

These 4 revelations interrelate.

[15:60] If we humans are part of the generated reality field, and in a certain sense it is not real, then in that same sense we are not real (vide "The
Electric Ant"). Not just our free will is illusory, but also our very substance.
We are no more than points-of-view, mere loci. We are provided a space-
time here and now; fitted into one locus of the field, and are compatible
with that specific space and time. But, if moved to another space-time locus, we take on appropriate customs, memories, desires, identities: we
are, so to speak, plugged into the new milieu. We are as it is, and are not
what it is not. This is because we are not separable as set against background: it is all one continuum. I do not reason here that because I became
a citizen of Rome c. A.D. 70 I perceived Rome A.D. 70, but the other way
around — or, more precisely, neither is cause and neither is effect; it is all of
a piece. What is destroyed here is the notion of individuality. I am inseparable from my space-time continuum, and that continuum is generated by
an entity or construct more sophisticated and complex (and faster) than it
(i.e., than us the continuum, us and our world). Literally *I* am generated by
it, not just my world, and if that world is transformed the process equally
affects me as part of that world.

[15:71] We are corruptible sheaves around divine sparks.

[15:83] Real time has to do with a sacred ritual-process. The progression
of that real process was halted by a crime, of which we have received an incomplete report. The reintroduction into the world and its affairs of the
divine woman is the substance of the matter. But in the Bible no mention

is made of the dead — and resurrected — divine woman. The construct moving retrograde has the purpose built into it of restoring that woman, who is nothing less than God's holy wisdom. The ossified matrix of the NT [New Testament] must be melted. *Tears* narrates the revision which will come to be. Eventually, the narrative in *Tears* will be the correct one, as the construct successfully accomplishes its work. *Tears* contains the Logos or form to be imposed. It is its punched tape, à la "The Electric Ant." A new, true story is being written, different from the old true story.

[15:85] In *The Morning of the Magicians* it's conjectured that if super-humans (mutants, etc.) live among us undetected they would use such things — carriers — as popular novels (and I suppose music and films) to "communicate" — keep in touch — with one another. Whether such "super-human mutants" exist is not the issue; the issue is that the authors of that book saw the utility of pop or trash novels as vehicles of cooked, freighted messages.

Why would they make good vehicles? (1) They are unlike TV and news-papers, international. What else is? (2) Exact wording could be employed. (3) Detection of the cryptemorphosis material would be difficult because there are so many pop novels, films and songs. (4) Ah — here's a good rea-son: the *receivers* (proper ones) of the info could not be discerned[①] because anyone can and does hear, read pop culture stuff. Heavy shit might fall on the author by the intelligence people — an effort to find out all about him and who he's mixed up with — in fact that'd be the only recourse: investi-gating the author. The trail would lead back to him, not to the receivers. Maybe *he* would know whom it was for. So let's see what group(s) he be-longs to (in interception of direct messages, they'd be able to pinpoint the receivers, which is what it's all about, *especially* if the author consciously knew nothing but merely dutifully wrote down his "dreams").

In the Bowie flick[54] he puts coded material to his ETI wife on an LP which radio stations play.

So it would be ideal, then, if the author knew nothing, was sublimi-nally cued. Of course, if/when the heavy shit came down on him, if the "mutants" were ethical and not exploitive, they'd rescue him. And they'd know when he was in trouble by means of the same paranormal powers by which they got their material into his books in the first place. They would have to be more or less continuously linked to him telepathically. The only way he might ever come to know about this tutelary telepathic link would be if/when he heard a voice inside his head thinking thoughts he couldn't or wouldn't think himself — including foreign words — and have strange quasi-dream experiences. A *particularly* telling clue would be if he dreamed about evolved mutant-like people talking to him, especially from far away.*

① Even if the code was detected and decoded.

[15:87] *Eye, Joint, 3 Stigmata, Ubik* and *Maze* are the same novel written over and over again. The characters are all out cold and lying around together on the floor mass hallucinating a world. Why have I written this up at least five times?

Because — as I discovered in 3-74 when I experienced anamnesis, remembered I'm really an apostolic Christian, and saw ancient Rome — *this is our condition:* we're mass hallucinating this 1970s world.

What's got to be gotten over is the false idea that an hallucination is a *private* matter.

[15:100] What if the proto-story in *Tears* is a sort of living DNA? That guides an entelechy through its growth steps? Are we the intended entelechy? Bateson's[55] immanent mind that narrates information to each living entity . . . *Tears* — the latent story therein — shows "bench marks" of the mind that fashioned me and all other life; it is mind perhaps, exerted directly on the novel (incised form) as if *not* through me — it is direct arrangement. (Like tea leaves, or animal entrails.) (Cf. Burroughs' cut-up message pieces latent meaning-extraction method.)

This being replicates itself through — as — information. [. . .]

I think it acted as a booster — i.e., first received, then transmitted. It acted like the divine wafer, the species of the eucharist. A living word-entity is here with us, taking us over via messages we receive; we act as hosts to it (perhaps temporarily). We become it.

• • •

---

* Here again we meet Dick's mystical mutants. More importantly, we see the multiple influences that helped shape his zapped imagination of these figures. First, we see a book, Louis Pauwels and Jacques Bergier's *The Morning of the Magicians* (originally *Les Matins des Magiciens,* 1960), which employed the tropes of mutants, superhumans, even Superman, to advance a countercultural occultism inspired largely by the books of the American Charles Fort. Second, we see the importance of Dick's auditions, psychical experiences (the "tutelary telepathic link"), and dreams, and their profound influence on his writing life. Also significant here is the fact that the first American edition of *The Morning of the Magicians* was published by Avon, the same publisher that would later publish an edition of Dick's *Radio Free Albemuth.* In short, we see here within Dick's paperback world a mind-bending feedback mechanism or "loop" of pop culture and altered states of consciousness arcing back on itself through countless acts of reading, dreaming, and writing: a morphing superconsciousness published or "made public" in the only form of our culture that will have it — fantastic literature. — JJK

[15:113] We are going to have to deal with propositions which are simultaneously both true and false; my corollary is that mutually contrary propositions may be equally true.

[15:114] The Voice: "Words control reality," i.e., the secret narrative will cause itself to be true by affecting the plastic universe. Words = thoughts.
     The narrative comes *first*.*

[15:116] Voice: "God is looking for balking as a criterion." [. . .]
     Some kind of nonlinear "onion" time is represented, as hinted at in *Ubik*, in which entropy allowed former layers to be exposed, much to everyone's surprise. *Ubik* presented the "paste-up" model of reality—very much a laminated time-continua model: the accretions are laid down in circular passes (circumference) and then read orthogonally (radii).
     There is much in common between the cosmology of *Ubik* and my "lamination" explanation of 3-74. Question is, how does one get above the circumference tracking so as to experience several layers as a simultaneous entity—as I did in 3-74? Evidently by mentally being bonded to a supratemporal life form (i.e., Zebra).
     Is Zebra Ubik, the anti-entropic energy/mind/word? Which narrates? And whose story is the growth of the organism? ("It tells it what to do next"—Bateson.)
     Then each laminated layer is the laying down of a new growth stage, as in the spiral of the conch shell. For example, the 1974 layer superimposes over ancient Rome in such a way as to convert the illegal power into voluntarily resigning.
     Then no *single* layer can be read, lacking the one below and above it. In our lives we track the circumference which means we experience only one

---

* Here Dick nails two crucial features of the paranormal: (1) the "fantastic" or both-and paradoxical structure of its appearances, which leave the reader, and even the experiencer, in a state of profound hesitation or confusion over the event's reality; and (2) the manner in which these paradoxical events organize themselves around narrative, story, or, to be more traditional about it, myth. Hence Dick's "secret narrative" comes first to shape reality, even the physical universe, around its patterns and meanings. Seen in this light, it is a serious mistake to approach a paranormal experience with an up-down vote, as if it were a simple object "out there" that could be measured and controlled. This is to miss its wildly living function and fierce message, which are all about pulling us into its own drama and shattering our either-or thinking through story and symbol. In short, the paranormal is about paradox, not proof; about meaning, not mechanism; about myth, not math. Most of all, however, the paranormal is about the "coincidence" or fundamental unity of mind and matter. Two of Dick's favorite scholars captured this truth in two Latin sound bites: the *mysterium conjunctionis*, or "mystery of conjunction," of C. G. Jung and the *coincidentia oppositorum*, or "coincidence of opposites," of Mircea Eliade. —JJK

layer. We can't read it orthogonally; we're part of the mechanism and not above it. But a written statement of the narrative could fall into our hands, or we could hear it, etc. This would be the "DNA" (metaphorically) of the developing organism and could tell us what we can't see.

[15:133] My writing is salvific in terms of this one road — one dharma of several, the dharma of knowledge. An epistemological path, not a moral path, is put forth (not "the world is evil" but "the world is irreal"). This is Gnostic, not pious. But the act — the crucial act of balking was, for me, moral. It develops out of an awareness of the counterfeit: viz: "it is *wrong* ethically to collude with the deceitful and fake."

No assertion is made, though, that the world, irreal as it is, cannot inflict punishment for balking. These are the demons of the Bardo Thödol existence — journey — which I experienced. At the end, I was reborn.

[15:141] I rather suspect that my transfer of assent in 2-74 was itself programmed and not truly an unanticipated malfunction. I was programmed to discover I was programmed. And in a very dramatic way — specifically one which brought me to a confirmation of the epistemological doubts I'd expressed in 27 years of writing. I certainly hesitate to claim I *did* it. My will — no. Accident — possibly. YHWH's will — very likely. Best to assume a "spark of Brahman in each of us" view so that my quest was God's quest really, to know himself, etc. (cf. Jacob Boehme).

Folder 16

[**16:6**] Voice: "You [i.e., the surface PKD personality] and the alibi are both equally expendable." (Does alibi = world?) (Yes, the false, simulated USA 1974 world.)

I deduce from this, then, that the Rome c. A.D. 45 world *is* real (which is why it appears in *Tears*) and USA 1974 is an "alibi" to conceal it. The alibi KW and I are looking for is the very world we *seem* to be in, and the true story is "Acts."

Voice: "I go to A.D. 45 Rome when I die" (meaning me). Then Rome A.D. 45 ("Acts") is not a past life but a future life. And why am I going there? Because it is real.

These worlds have to be regarded as stories, narratives — USA 1974 is a spurious one to cover up the real one.

[**16:10**] KW spoke of sabotage versus malfunction, an issue which I dismissed. But then the voice called the USA 1974 world "an alibi world" which is "expendable." Sabotage — not by an evil party — but by a friend, since this is the thrall situation. I misunderstood KW. Sabotage of the prison machinery. An *induced* malfunction; which by the way answers the epistemological questions I've chewed over in 27 years of writing having to do with simulated worlds (hence Lem's question).

E.g., "Delmak-O" = USA 1974
Persus 9 = Rome c. A.D. 45
The tattoo = the Golden Fish

God, *all* my "this is illusion" writings (*Eye, Joint, Stigmata, Ubik, Maze*) are analogs of the USA 1974 vs. the glimpse of Rome c. A.D. 45 via the golden fish sign.

"Here we are."

"But where are we *really?*"

And then someone gets a glimpse. (As in "the Earth is hollow and I have touched the sky.") Usually, once the simulation is detected there are assorted guesses. But sometimes the first clue vis-à-vis simulating of world *is* the glimpse.

My God, my life — which is to say my 2-74/3-74 experience — is exactly like the plot of any one of 10 of my novels or stories. Even down to fake

memories and identity. I'm a protagonist from one of PKD's books.* USA
1974 fades out, ancient Rome fades in and with it the Thomas personality
and *true* memories. Jeez! Mixture of *Imposter, Joint* and *Maze* — if not *Ubik*
as well.

What the malfunction or induced malfunction proves is the existence
of at least *one* world-generating Mind, and (as I failed to see in those earlier notes) possibly *two* world-generating — even competing — minds.
Competing worlds, competing world-generating minds. Plus the passive,
programmed, observing little non-world-generating mind.

Is this a battle for his allegiance? World against world, mind against
mind? The voice last night scathingly referred to USA 1974 and the corresponding PKD personality as "both being expendable." Diabolic interpola-
tion/simulation?

[16:13] I guessed a long time ago that the world we perceive is a simulation, but this diagnosis only makes sense when you can point to a real
world to contrast it to, and this, prior to 2-74, I could not do.† I now understand the crucial role of assent — programmed assent — and what happens if assent is suddenly broken and then transferred — and also *why* we

---

* Dick's fiction establishes an unusually strong connection between the author and his
characters, and specifically his protagonists: men who are down on their luck and forced
to encounter, once again, the inscrutable apathy of the universe. These characters give
voice to Dick's own existential concerns; his third wife, Anne, called his writing "surrealist autobiography." In a 1970 letter to *SF Commentary*, Dick wrote, "I know only one thing
about my novels. In them, again and again, this minor man asserts himself in all his hasty,
sweaty strength . . . against the universal rubble." Part of Dick's charm as a writer is precisely his similarity to his characters; barely eking out a living, languishing as an underap-
preciated artist, Dick is nonetheless determined to move forward against overwhelming
odds. As Dick's public persona has grown following his death — a persona based in part on
his life and in part on the plight of his characters — he has become increasingly mythological. Later reprint editions of his novels often picture Dick on their covers, staring out at
potential readers, part author, part fiction, trapped in the half-life of his own stories. — DG

† Dick is often read by literary scholars as a "postmodern" writer. Postmodernism is a
complex of concepts that assert that all our constructs are just that, constructs; that there
are no grand narratives or abiding truths; that all such grand narratives are illegitimate
power moves; and that every perspective is necessarily a limited and local one. Here Dick
realizes that such a way of thinking, which he himself has championed in dozens of novels,
is a half-truth, in the sense that its claims rely on a non-duped subjectivity and a privileged
claim, which, ironically, is itself a grand narrative or abiding truth. Dick, then, was finally
no postmodern thinker, not at least in the sense in which that label is commonly understood. In his own mind at least, his body of work constituted both a demonstration that
the sensory and social world is an illusory simulation and a revelation of another order of
mind and being from outside this maze of cognitive and cultural tricks. As Dick puts it
later on in the Exegesis: "Valis proves there is an outside." — JJK

give unconditional assent to this simulated world — why, for instance, the search expressed in my novels makes no sense to many people.

[16:14] I subscribe to the acosmic Gnostic view that world does not reveal God. Abolish world and you are facing God. In a sense world is a mask thrown forth by God to conceal himself from man, who must then deal with the puzzle which world presents to him. If evil (undeserved suffering) rules world, how can it be the product of a benign mind? But world is not isomorphic to God; it is unlike him, a smokescreen with which man is not to make his peace but is to balk against. Yet tantalizing clues (signs) of God shine *through* the world from the far side; they invade the world, and are covertly available to human perception. The Golden Section is one such clue.

Axiom: masks do not resemble the visages concealed by them. If we know that world is a mask of God, the problem of evil (undeserved suffering) is somewhat answered. But why must God mask himself? Answer: man must solve the moral and epistemological puzzles presented to him by world in order to come to life (become disjunctive from what is not-him). He can join the world or he can repudiate it. This is a very serious game, this guessing game. It only serves its purpose if man knows relatively little about what is going on. E.g., if he knows he will be *rewarded* for balking he will balk in order to obtain the reward — the test will be contaminated. He must balk with no knowledge of reward; in fact he knows he will be punished (by world, the BIP). So "he who gives up his life will save it," etc.

This all really presumes another, invisible landscape at odds with the palpable one. Two realms, perhaps a lower and a higher, one implied, each with its own laws. The lower realm alone does not tell the full story — in fact may not even tell the *true* story or a part thereof. In the lower realm, deity appears in a debased and trivial or besmirched guise, marginally (like the cheap commercials for Ubik). Only at the end (as in the heading of the last chapter in *Ubik*) does deity unmask itself, and we see it as it truly is.

Thus I say, if deity exists in the lower realm it will not bear a noble heavenly dignified beautiful aspect; it will be where least expected and *as* least expected, so there is no use deliberately looking for it — it will have to come to us and unveil itself to us. It could be an old sick — even dying — tomcat stinking of urine, degraded and humiliated.

However, it aids, advises and monitors us. The world is a one-way mirror; God can watch us but not we him.

•   •   •

[16:19] Aldiss[56] says the Horn of freedom blows in my writing. If I stigmatize the lower realm as counterfeit, aren't I rendering a service, and an unusual one at that? Who else has unscrambled world into two realms (well, Parmenides for one) the malignant part of which is bogus? — [. . .]

God, I have broken myself in this pursuit over 27 years. Critics compare my malignant false worlds to metastasizing cancer. I demand that deity appear or somehow put its stamp on world before I can accept it as anything but a diabolic counterfeit interpolation. We have been deceived for thousands of years. The Neoplatonist such as Plotinus knew of two realms. The Essenes (v. Josephus) report a lower realm of feverish unconsciousness, the poisoned, intoxicated soul. "Men *like* to sleep."

[16:21] Axiom: The best forgeries go undetected. On a scale of increasing perfection there is an inverse ratio to detection. Those which we do detect are signs which point toward the better (undetected) ones.

[16:29] The mad God James-James began generating world upon world, worlds unrelated, worlds within worlds. Fake worlds, fake *fake* worlds, cunning simulations of worlds, mirror opposites of worlds.

Like I do in my stories and novels (e.g., *Stigmata* and "Precious Artifact"). I am James-James.

I created one world among many and entered it and hid myself in it. But the police detected me — the non-terran police — and tried to fake me out with the Xerox missive. But I knew it was coming — as soon as *Tears* appeared they would be sure about me. And I recovered my memory and identity and powers and dealt with it properly, and paid them back. My organization helped me — it set off my memories a month in advance. I saw my creator — *my* creator, protecting me. I am hiding here, under his protection. The network voice — she talks to me. I am patched in to the network, so I am not alone. Meanwhile, my creator ("Zebra") patiently repairs the damage I've done, by rebuilding the worlds. He harbors no resentment. All I am allowed to do now is *write about* what I used to do. In a sense I am a prisoner. But it's for the best.

I learned this from "Precious Artifact." I am a mad ex world-generator, now confined. But still periodically mad. I can't die. I am countless reborn-metamorphosed. I know the truth about the worlds I have made. That they're not real — I know about dokos, simulations which will pass any test. They are not fantasy, and they are only illusion to those who take them as real. They are *skillful forgeries* which will pass inspection. They are indeed like metastasizing cancers. "A world capable of splitting its perceived reality into countless counterfeits of itself"—however Lem put it. (Does Lem know? He has guessed.)

It is found in my "taco stand" visionary experience in 1971, which proliferated itself into all Mexico, and was *real. I* generated it, as I used to do. But exiled now, put in a box and dropped into the ocean. Zagreus.

Burroughs is right about the Nova Police and their tracking down their quarry. But in my case Zeus protects me. Dythrambus. [. . .]

Given a new life with no memories, I was still able to undermine. The worlds are cunning forgeries, and the police are after me. But Zeus will always protect me, despite what I've done. Misused my ability. Lem may be on our side (my organization). In any case *he knows*—he knew before I did—i.e., before in 2-74 I remembered. The Nova Police fell here; I assisted in that, but only to a very tiny degree. *Tears* contained the message: the quarry is innocent and the police will suffer reprisal. [. . .]

We spring up everywhere: proliferated.

The time has come to render this world void, to abolish it, and judge, Shiva. The police search frantically.

The innocent (the wild little ones of the forest) have nothing to fear. My extended hand tells them that.

Solemn-pentheus-die, Felix happy Dionysos *live.* Pentheus police general of *Tears*—the de facto monarch.

[16:45] If the above theory is wrong (and there is no negative hallucination and spurious reality laid over the real world—which is *quite* different than what seems to be—) then what has been the use of my writing? Also, *why* have I been motivated for 27 years to belabor this one theme (including fake memories as an inner analog to the fake outer world)?

Is it all just foolishness? My writing has to be dismissed (including the "Acts" and NT material in *Tears* and the "exculpation" cypher, i.e., the good news) and my 2-74/2-75 experience has to be dismissed as a psychotic break. And God didn't aid in pulling down the tyranny; there was no inbreaking, as depicted in the *Tears* dream.

Everything has to be dismissed—my life's work means nothing, my most treasured experience—and I am and have been for years just crazy—

Because everything is interwoven, it either all stands or it falls. Such stories as "Precious Artifact" and "Electric Ant" and "Retreat Syndrome" tell us nothing—not to mention the novels.

Ubik tells us nothing?

And four years and four months of exegete—wasted.

•   •   •

[16:55] Let's start out afresh.

(1) When I wrote *Tears* I did not knowingly include any elements pertaining to 1st century A.D. Rome. It was a totally imaginary future
world.

(2) The month that *Tears* was released, I saw a Golden Fish sign and
asked what it was. I was told it was a sign "used by the early Christians." At once I remembered that the time was the first century
A.D. in Rome, not the 20th century in the USA.

(3) One month later amid various unusual subjective sensations, I experienced 1st century A.D. Rome as present and believed myself to
be an illegal secret Christian, with code signs and sacraments such
as I later learned were used at that time. I also dreamed foreign
words all of which turned out to be the koine Greek used at that
place and time, although I did not know this. I believed that Christ
had just died and would soon return. I felt great elation. I was
shown the word "Felix" in *Tears* and understood it was not a name
but a key code. I did not know what it meant. However I looked it
up and it means "happy" or "prosperous."

(4) When I described *Tears* to my priest he said that a scene was very
like a scene in "Acts," which I had never read. I then read "Acts"
and found many elements common to *Tears.* After four years of
studying *Tears* I felt I had fully extracted a stegenographic message
from it. *Tears* was in fact set in 1st century A.D. Rome. I can prove
it re the "Acts" material. The message, deeply buried, is that Christ
has returned and we can't see it. Instead we see a fake, delusional,
other world in which 2,000 years have passed or appear to have
passed. I did not put this message in *Tears* or know it was there.
The Roman world I saw the month *Tears* was released is the actual
world in *Tears.*

Unexplained are: If I did not recognize the "Acts" (Biblical) elements
in *Tears* when I wrote it, how come I properly identified them the month
Tears was released and I found myself in that very same world? Why didn't
I identify that world as the one I had written about?

These questions bypass more obvious questions which more naturally
arise (such as, How come I found or believed myself in 1st century Rome?
etc.).

The questions in paragraph one are more astute than first appears. The
questions — one question actually — is formally phrased as: "If you can
identify y, why can't you identify y?"

(The world of *Tears* is — cupola for equals — 1st century A.D. Rome. When I saw 1st century A.D. Rome I recognized it, call it y. I could upon seeing y recognize and identify it. Y is the world of *Tears*. I wrote *Tears*. When I wrote it and repeatedly rewrote it and later repeatedly read it, I saw nothing in it that suggested y to me. But I later demonstrated an ability to recognize and identify y when I saw it. There is a disruption in the continuity of pattern recognition and identification; there is an ellipsis in — not logic, which is not involved — but something deeper. Person one [myself] both recognizes pattern y and does not. I.e., he is familiar with 1st century A.D. Rome and its customs and is not. He dreams koine Greek words but does not [1] know what they mean; or [2] that they are the koine; or [3] that the koine was the lingua franca of 1st century A.D. Rome — that "Acts," e.g., was written in it.)

This line of inquiry points to two persons, one who knows and one who does not. This is substantiated by the switch of memory from 20th century USA to 1st century A.D. Rome. The person who wrote *Tears used* the memories/knowledge of the other without realizing it. This dissociation continued through all the eleven drafts and readings, until the memories, personality and knowledge — i.e., the other person — broke into consciousness the month the book was released.

Question: is there a literature on alternate personalities (in persons with multiple personalities) separated by 1,900 years and 8,000 miles? They could not have split off during one lifetime (i.e., at an early age). So childhood trauma won't explain it. Answer: there is no such literature.

Question: does the stegenographic message provide any clue to the abreactive personality? Answer: the message is the "kerygma" (proclaiming the redemptive death and resurrection of the lord) *revised*. Christ is not crucified, did not depart and hence is present. The subjective sensations noted above pointed to a confirmation of this.

Conclusion: the person has a rich fantasy world. He has dissociated personalities and experiences. (Ever since an auto accident he has complained of periodic amnesia.) The "hidden message" in the novel and the "remembering ancient Rome" indicate strong unconscious wishes directed toward Christ's imagined return.

It is touching that the human hope for a redeemer could yield such elaborate phantasies. A dearth of real experiences is indicated. Therapy indicated.

[16:62] KW's right: the BIP warps every new effort at freedom into the mold of further tyranny.

·　·　·

[16:69] "But are you writing something *serious?*" Note the word.

Fuck. If they couldn't get us to write serious things, they solved the problem by decreeing that what we were writing *was* serious. Taking a pop form as "serious" is what you do if it won't go away. It's a clever tactic. They welcome you in — look at Lem's 1,000-page essay. This is how the BIP handles it if they can't flat out crush it. Next thing, they get you to submit your S-F writing to them to criticize. "Structured criticism" to edit out the "trash elements" — and you wind up with what Ursula writes.

Like I say in *Scanner,* our punishment for playing *was too great.* And my last sentence is, "and may they be happy." (I got that from knowing what "felix" meant.)

"Let them all play again, in some other way, and let them be happy."

I showed the *unfair* punishment for playing. *Scanner* is a study of what the BIP does to you (punishes you) and what for (playing, not growing up, "not toiling"). Like the Christ story, it simply (as I point out) just lays forth cause and effect. I don't wind up deploring playing — just that particular *way* of playing. So in a way, *Scanner* is a study of the punishment (too great) for playing instead of toiling, not drugs. Thus the *secret* (encoded) theme of *Tears* is carried further. Amazing, since when I wrote *Scanner* I hadn't yet figured out *Tears.*

Knowing what I know now after 4 years of exegesis re *Tears* what I'd write on the basis of it would be *Scanner.* How do you explain that? *Scanner logically* follows *Tears* if you know what *Tears* is *really* about. *Play* is one of the antiphonal themes in *Scanner.* Play and punishment. What an insight! You play — and are punished and *far* too severely; as I say, "The punishment was far too great." It opens (the postscript):

> "This has been a novel about some people *who were punished entirely too much for what they did. They wanted to have a good time —,*" etc.

The expectation of punishment is a knowledge about playing. You have been taught to expect it. This goes beyond mere worthlessness; this is *sin,* and God will get you (in all his mundane polyforms).

Both communist and capitalist (and fascist) societies — and theocracies — teach this. It's called theodicy. It's fucked, like when Merry Lu threw my snuff in the garbage.

No wonder the more $ I get the more morose I get. I *enjoyed* paying the IRS — shit! The BIP really has me by the balls.

[16:72] Even if you believe in man's sinfulness, the doctrine of vicarious atonement makes no sense. The crucifixion story says, "they punish you and they kill even spotless God who *couldn't* be in *any* way sinful — and

that is wrong." The story proves you *don't* have to be sinful to get maximum punishment (death). (And humiliation.) (Disgrace.) It shows there
is *no connection* between sin (or imagined sin) and punishment. *This* is
the lesson of Calvary. God himself proved it for our benefit, this *absolute*
lack of connection. The proof was immediately the victim of BIP warpage — right off the bat.

So the *true* message has to be smuggled in subversively in code. See,
Christ *came back* and is breaking the BIP — not just its power over us but
it itself.

Hosanna! (Shout of joy.)

[16:74] I see in the crucifixion story the message "punishment must end."
In my schema, revealed to me, punishment is one of the key words, tied to
the key word "sin." This whole sin-punishment system is a smokescreen for
our enslavement. The solution to the equation sin-punishment (work) is
innocence-joy (play). This is what the secret kerygma in *Tears* reveals, and
Scanner goes on to study the issue further.

Then, by my theory, the last thing we should do is imitate Christ's passion. It was to liberate us from this that he came: to relieve us of the belief
that suffering is natural and somehow proves or is tied to "sin."

As lord of the universe it is his desire and mission to extricate us
from — and finally destroy — the *Tears* world. And a lot of the *Tears* world
is psychological — i.e., a spiritual matter.

I am very sleepy, so this statement may be already (and frequently)
stated, but — could the encoded message in *Tears* be Zebra's notification
to the true secret Christian church *that he is here?* (Here now, here again.)
Not telling them what to do, or promulgating a true narrative (joy, innocence), but announcing his presence? The joy-innocence narrative points
to him (Christ/Dionysos). Such a thematic narrative could point nowhere
else but to *him*. In a sense it not only tells us he is here but who he is. So by
decoding the message in *Tears* I learn who Zebra is for sure: Christ/Dio-
nysos.

In a nutshell, in 3-74 it was *punishment* which Zebra saved me
from — which tends to prove I'm on the right track, in the above pages.

The voice: "Guilty but not wrong." (What the crucifixion proved.) I.e., the
judicial and the moral bipolarized — but in apostasy rejoined with God as
Caesar.

My God — talk about *Scanner* being right on: the real purpose of Substance
D is to create a *slave labor force*. Take the people who just want to play,

give them "poison candy" and they wind up in tin mines. And several reviews have said it's the *authorities* who are producing it. They are all put to work — with a vengeance. And the Game, which destroys your last shred of self-respect (esteem) and makes you outer-directed and totally dependent on group approval. QED. *Frolix 8* to *Tears* to *Scanner.*

The Game: die messages.

[16:80] The age of guilt giving way to the age of innocence (which I specify as happening) is precisely a return to and restoration of our primordial lost state. Odd, that my system would collate with orthodoxy again and again on a major point.

[16:82] The conception I have is that God loves man and assists him out of that love. Man cannot *demand* that love as his due, but he can count on it by faith. He would be completely wrong to think himself excluded from that love (and hence from grace). Man's failings are finite and God's love is infinite.

I really do have an "adoptionist" sense of one gaining God's approval (support) by certain decisive acts . . . which I see as one correctly solving intellectual/moral choice problems — i.e., going one way vs. the alternative, "and gained from heaven a friend." I feel that God takes note and is interested. That, most of all, he *understands* (what other people can't) and so is sympathetic ("he sees even the fallen sparrow"[57]).

In a sense I would even *define* God that way: "as the sentience in the cosmos which understands."

But all this is *not* a way of saying man is a sinner (deficient in merits). What it says is, God's love is for the desperate and the damned, *not* for the goody-goody, who you see all righteous. All the piety can't make it — God reaches down into the gutter, to people like in *Scanner.* In a sense the kerygma is: *a suspension of punishment* (and a restoration of innocence). (The *gift* of innocence. Love and assistance and rescue is not a judicial matter.)

In *Tears* the serious old king's verdict (justice) is death. But Buckman turns grief over death into love; so love triumphs — not over death — but over the judicial *verdict* of death — and Taverner goes free. Within this sequence, the culmination of the book, the essential miracle of the NT, is disclosed: the holy mystery and victory of love issuing out of grief and turning a sentence of guilty into innocence.

I simply do not see this as judicial. I see it as — a freeing man of the curse, a releasing him from his enslaved state. The court sat, the books were opened, and what prevailed was a saving, overriding love.

In a way, the problem is, we can't figure out God's basis of selection. Code ethics did not provide an index. Whim probably isn't the answer; some plan, purpose or pattern is involved, but we're too dumb to discern it.

It goes back to my concept of him posing us a problem to solve. Naturally we're not to develop a "solution" formula — that would defeat the purpose.

In a nutshell, my book announces the ushering in of the age of man's (restored) innocence, which is to say, *Christ returned.* The final kerygma.

[16:101] [*Editor's note:* This section begins with a lengthy quotation from Wagner's *Parsifal.*]

G: That is the magic of Good Friday, sir.[58]

P: Alas, the greatest day of |pain!| on which everything that blooms, breathes, lives and lives anew should, it seems, but |mourn| — and |weep|.

G: You see, *it is not so.* They are the repentant |tears| of the sinner that drop today with holy dew upon both field and meadow; thus they flourish. Now all the creatures |rejoice| at the Redeemer's gracious sign, and dedicate their prayer to him. Him upon the cross they cannot see: and so they look up to |man redeemed|, who feels |free of his burden of sin and shame|. Made pure and |whole| by the |loving| sacrifice of God: now blades and flowers of the meadows perceive that this day no foot of man shall crush them. But just as God with heavenly patience took |mercy| on him and suffered for him, so man today with pious grace |spares| them with gentle tread. For this, all creation then gives thanks — all that blooms and shortly withers — for nature cleansed has gained this day her day of |innocence|.

The theme of tears and love and guilt turned into innocence. "Now all the creatures rejoice."

Tears to love to innocence to joy (felix) — the sequence in *Tears* and this is the Christian salvific magic (note: love characterizes the new age of the Spirit).

[16:102] After carefully reading Will Durant's history of the Reformation, I see in all Christian factions a total perversion of the authentic kerygma. I must either assume 2,000 years of apostasy or (as I prefer) a 2,000-year satanic spurious interpolation. I do see in *Tears* still the true kerygma:

(1) Exculpation (innocence) (freedom) ⎫
(2) Love   ⎬ Form I, PTG
(3) Joy   ⎭

Out of:

(1) Tears
(2) Condemnation as sinful (enslavement): $\Big\}$ Form II, BIP
(3) Pain, suffering

Wagner presents this as the magic of Good Friday. I do not understand how the transformation occurs,① but in *Tears* it does: death to grief to tears to love to exculpation (innocence) and, implied, joy. In *Tears* the magic transformation occurs by reason of the dream, which I have *always* seen as the in-breaking (into history) of God.

We are indeed down to essentials, and the kerygma agrees with the prophecy: "St. Sophia will be reborn again . . ." etc.

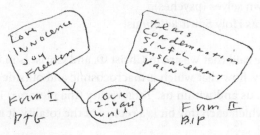

① It is bought by Christ's blood being shed. Blood = tears, somehow (the Eucharist). "This is my blood (and body)."

[16:109] Will Durant says, "The history of Christianity is salvation by faith and good works, to faith (Luther) to inner divine illumination (the Quakers)." If there is indeed an *evolutionary* sequence, then my 3-74 experience is of a modern sort — of recent origin, and not comprehensible to the earlier religious types. I read his entry on Quakers, and their experience is mine. "And the possibility of the Holy Spirit coming from heaven to enlighten and ennoble the individual soul to perceive and feel this inner light, to welcome its guidance, was to the Quaker the essence of religion. If a man followed that light he needed no preacher or priest, and no church. The light was superior to human reason, even to the Holy Bible itself, for it was the direct voice of God to the soul." Fox wrote: "As I was walking in the fields, the Lord said unto me: 'Thy name is written in the lamb's book of life, which was before the foundation of the world.'" He felt "he was among that minority of men, chosen by God before the creation, to receive his grace and eternal bliss."[59] I feel as if I've finally come home.

Folder 38

[38:2]

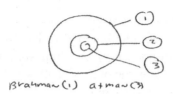

Brahman (1)   atman (3)

① Cosmic Christ outside and *around* us.
② Our own selves (psyches).
③ Christ as Holy Spirit *within* us.

So it can be said that we are in Christ ①, and Christ is in us ③. This is a sacred mystery, how that which is macrocosmic and outside us can also be "smaller" than us and within us. Total reality (the pleroma) is like a titanic hologram of which each tiny bit is a replica of the totality. It is a mirror-like situation. [. . .]

Thinking over my exegesis I see it as a vast, original cosmology, partly philosophical and partly theological. It is my *own* worldview, in part divinely revealed to me, in part arrived at by careful analysis, ratiocination and so forth. It is an awe-inspiring structure and resembles no other arrived at by anyone I have ever heard of. Continually I have been corrected and instructed by the voice.

[38:4] I was taken over by a superior life form. Which was interfering with history. What am I supposed to do? How am I supposed to go on day by day?

[38:22] I conceive the brain as rapidly growing, evolving and changing — and Rome as inert. Rome is always the same: Rome in USA 1974, in *Tears* and in c. A.D. 45 is unchanged. What it was it is, and what it is it will be. But in contrast the brain began c. A.D. 45 (time of "Acts") and permutates furiously . . . and continually altering its swift messages that pass between and among its physical — distributed — parts, linking those many parts together.

Rome, the BIP, constantly *repeats;* like a psychotic human mind, nothing new ever comes into it. So in a real sense it is dead; more precisely it is a reflex system of some kind, *recirculating* forever one (?) thought (?)

warped into an orbitting circle — it has us. But the brain breaks that hold
("Salvation" — which equals growth which equals freedom —
negentropic).

[38:23] Brain is unfolding in our actual historic world. In terms pertaining to us humans the unfolding consists of evolving homeostasis by individuals — Beethoven's contribution to what we conceive of as the person being a good example; the key term is *freedom*. Critical for this is what I call balking, which is in fact a fighting free of the BIP's reflex arc push-pull inner-outer determinism over us. [. . .] History, although filled with war, ignorance and travail, can be read, also, in terms of this evolution of individuality. The establishment of America was an important step. Yet the BIP tugs us backward (here and in the USSR both — *the Nixon period was a deadly rollback of human evolution, toward a fossil BIP prior form, but the brain burst it*). Yes — this is why the brain interfered with recent U.S. history: we were devolving along the axis of evolution which leads forward to greater homeostasis of the individual — i.e., greater self-programming.

Thus the brain sponsored the "leaderless revolution" against the Vietnam war. Perhaps the first successful totally leaderless revolution in human history. *This* is what was important, this evolution/revolution. The brain incited this advance in consciousness and awareness. Just to examine *what was overthrown* is to miss the point. I am — have been — missing the point. It was *how* it was overthrown. I was shown the divine power overthrowing (represented by the Sibyl). No amount of lies or force, fear or threat, could halt the collective consciousness: *the manifestation of this moral collective Noös was one of the most important stages in all the millennia of human history.* It was a physical expression (map) of the brain. I'm not theorizing. I know. The brain operated through me, e.g., at a *conscious* level. The establishment, with all its financial and industrial power, was opposed by a *mind*. The mind coordinated its parts, this is a miracle!

Then the 60s and 70s represents a quantum leap by the brain. In a sense, it actually came forward into actualization (the open: visible: if to me, then to *others* — it must be so; I can't be unique; that runs contrary to common sense). (Well, I didn't put the code in *Tears* to read it *myself*.)

The authorities did not understand — at all guess — what confronted them. They had inaccurate, *very* inaccurate, intimations of a coordinating "group." They must have succeeded in discerning a *pattern* (of coordination); i.e., the results but not the cause (source). They saw revolution; they saw the anti-establishment counterculture *articulations* (voices) and plotted correctly a synchronization, but could not account for it, despite the efforts of the police. Who were the leaders of this revolution? They had *killed* all the leaders, *and it made no difference:* the psyche or psychoi of the leaders *lived on* — literally. Impossible! (For instance, in 3-74 and on I toyed with the idea, for really quite a while, that it was Jim Pike who had "come across" to me! It was *like* him!)

Timeo. What are we dealing with? I'd hate to have tried to kill it, like "they" tried. Who have we read about who was murdered — *and invisibly came back,*① resurrected and — ubique.

Then it was *Ubik* that —

① The brain contains the saintly dead! (e.g., Jim)

[38:24] The voice: "Plenary override exists." Not knowing what "plenary" meant I looked it up. "Absolute, complete, perfect."

[38:26] In its moving about (discorporate in one sense) the brain is like a giant floating crap game.

If it's like a floating crap game, this vast brain must be an organizing principle. A system of linking. This fits in with the disassembling and re-assembling into a new structure. I was taken into a thinking system . . . how, if at all, does this system exist independently from the constituents which it links together? The same question has long been debated about the relationship between a human mind and its brain! Can the mind exist independently from the brain?

This model (brain-mind) is a good one for my understanding of 3-74. I keep hypostatizing Zebra as God or Noös, and now as brain. But *we* are the [physical] brain [components]. The plasmatic entity I saw which I called Zebra must have been the analog for the electrical discharges constantly moving through neural fibers — i.e., throughout the brain itself. Those electrical impulses are the life of the brain: its activity. So my brain, made up of millions of cells, in billions of [electrical] combinations, became *one* station (cell) in (of) a larger brain, linked to other "cells" (persons), some dead, some living, some yet to be, with Christ as the total mind (psyche). As an aggregate we *comprised* [the mystical, cosmic] Christ!

[38:29] I reason, now: if info can be transmitted *to* me, *I* must have some function; memory storage? No — I suppose it's my writing. This *certainly* explains the "Acts" — and cypher — material in *Tears;* good example of my function. I can transmit *that* way — in my writing. It's forever whipping messages back and forth, like any brain; *that's how it maintains its existence as a unitary entity.*

So seeing all the messages tells me more of the story. It fits the brain-model. Written and auditory messages are its thoughts!

The word "Felix" juxtaposed with "King" is a perfect example — not of code, really — but a message evident (available) only to parts of *it*. (Set-ground discrimination is involved, which its *conscious* parts must possess.) All that's needed is the ajna chakra working.

Boy, have I gotten close to figuring it out! How large do you suppose the brain is? Does it extend beyond the planet? It could. Yes, and much of our reality (world) is spurious; i.e., directly imposed on our percept systems by the brain — I'm taking a wild guess. Not just by the BIP but by the brain.

[38:31] What are we/am I? The brain overthrew "the conspirators" — I know that. So it opposed the conspirators who murdered the civil rights leaders. That is an evil bunch. On these points there can be no doubt. The sides in this are very obscure. I'll never be able to put it together.

[38:41]
(1) The brain is an organizing principle.
(2) It constantly assembles and distributes visual and audible messages.
(3) These messages are the prime instrument of its organizing.
(4) We are only subliminally aware of these messages; they are "latent."
(5) Via the messages the brain coordinates us sentiently, draws us into itself, and frees us from the blind determinism, i.e., we are subsumed by it; it is sentient; therefore we are guided by sentience, not cause and effect or chance.
(6) We are totally unaware on a conscious level of all this (e.g., [5]). But this explains why I wrote what's in *Ubik*. I was describing the brain's messages, and, what is more, discerning behind them, the brain, which I called Ubik.
(7) *Ubik* is true.
(8) So, too, then, probably is *Tears* and *Maze* and 3 *Stigmata*. The brain cued me.
(9) It is probably rare for the psyche of the brain to actually surface in a cell (an individual human) as it did with me in 3-74, but to protect its frontiers it must now and then "epiphanize." Especially when problem-solving is required beyond the capacity of the "cell" unit.
(10) What I called "Zebra" are direct electric impulses between parts of the brain, normally invisible to us. The brain was firing *directly* at

me electrically, rather than through messages (e.g., the Golden Fish Sign). It overrode me, for defensive purposes.

(11) The brain can be regarded as an entity (unitary) within our species, and not detected, even by its own "cells."

(12) It may very well provide immortality by incorporating "dead" humans such as Thomas. They are incorporated while alive and remain.

(13) It remembers back thousands of years, to it coming here from the stars.

(14) It was known to the early Christians as the "Paraclete," called by Christ "more important than I am." (cf. "John": "it is to your advantage that I go . . . ," etc.)[60]

(15) By this I deduce that Christ was its initial form here, giving way to the "Floating Crap Game" discorporate form it has now, which is more satisfactory.

(16) Through this form it can govern at least parts — crucial parts — of our world; i.e., direct our affairs (history).

(17) So for what it's worth, He is here with us, but as St. Teresa of Avila said, "Christ now has no body but yours."[61] How true!

(18) More precisely, we are not controlled by the brain; we are the brain. It as Noös (energy) has organized us into its brain, its physical analog, to deal with this world.

(19) The adversary of the brain, something which repeats itself; i.e., is static and not growing. The adversary is heavy, inert, and warps thought (and so actions) in dead circles around it. The brain is in dialectic interaction with it, freeing minds from its tug.

(20) Those minds warped into dead circular thinking imagine their thoughts still progress in a straight line. But in fact nothing new ever occurs to them. They therefore represent a reversion to fossil forms.

(21) Unfortunately, these people have been woven by the "magnet" into the power centers of mankind; this has long been so. They rule by lies and coercion.

(22) The brain constantly dismantles the world and grows by incorporating more and more parts — functionally — into itself. Eventually there will be nothing but it. The time-span, in our terms, is quite long — thousands of years.

(23) The book of "Acts" describes the first manifesting of the brain, at Pentecost.[62] Thus "Acts" is the only written account of the brain's existence, and so is unique and important. It so to speak is a verbal analog of the innermost core of the brain. Outside of "Acts," there

is no verbal (or rather written) analog to the brain, though oral tradition may obtain in secret.[①]

(24) It is possible that an unbroken chain of true Christians is linked
through time back to "Acts" knowing about and experiencing the
brain consciously. To prove their existence is impossible.

(25) To finish the thought of item 13, the brain is not native to this
planet (or world). It is an invader, and camouflages itself through
mimicry and mimesis. It can not only affect our percept systems
directly but can alter our memories.

(26) It is benign: mankind's tutelary spirit freeing us from the warping
tug of the "magnet." Without it, our species would congeal in terms
of growth. All progress in human history (at least for the last 2,000
years) is due to it.

(27) The "magnet" came into existence slightly before the brain came
here. So evidently it too is an invader, but a criminal one.

(28) Perhaps the brain pursued it. Using another set of terms, the "magnet" can be regarded as a sickness or virus, and the brain as a doctor or healing agent.

(29) Because of its warping tug, the magnet has stopped real time in
our world at about 2,000 years ago. Perhaps it occludes us to this
frozen temporality by projecting a delusionary world that appears
contemporary.

(30) Both the magnet and the brain, then, are transtemporal constants,
since the moment of the brain's arrival (the time of "Acts").

(31) In the crucifixion, the brain as Christ sacrificed itself in order to
promote new life for us. By turning itself into the distributed brain
it became camouflaged at the time of "Acts" (following the resurrection).

(32) It bears some relation to our creator. This is why it cares so much
about us and our enslaved condition. (For example, the magnet
transmits "die messages" at us, which the brain, where necessary,
overrides.)

(33) In connection with these "die messages" it is part of the magnet's
system of lies to declare man sinful, guilty, and deserved of punishment. The brain has the authority directly from our creator to
countermand all this with joy. Innocence as a verdict (acquittal)
and freedom.

(34) The brain incorporates objects and their processes as well as humans; thus it is building an actual cosmos within a damaged cosmos.

(35) The brain has a mandate for a plenary overruling of all powers, in

this world, thus it advances in a set of historic stages in an unfolding plan. This world constitutes a lower realm for it; it emanates from an upper realm, which, like it, is totally sentient. Through participation in the brain we are joined to this upper realm. Therefore the brain can be regarded as an intermediary between our world and the upper from which it comes, and in whose nature it participates.

(36) The warped slaves of the magnet who by and large control positions of power in this world (by virtue of the magnet) do not view the cells of the brain as benign and viable, but rather as (1) unpredictable; (2) revolutionary; (3) dangerous; (4) strange; (5) immoral and "uncontrolled"; (6) different; (7) hostile to "stability." By which is meant conformity to the magnet's tug. They may even be viewed as invaders, responsive to an invisible source — which they are. They have become "not of this world, in it but not *of* it."

(37) The growing extent of the brain's victory over the magnet is obscured from us by the delusionary world the magnet generates to occlude us. Much of the magnet's power, then, is itself an illusion.

(38) Let me explain why I depict the brain as a "Floating Crap Game." It does not organize the *same* cells constantly, but perpetually as a process releases certain cells at each instant and incorporates others. So a given cell (human) can at one time be part of the brain (and not know it) and be outside it at another. The psyche of the brain, of course, is a constant. So the Qs: "Who is part of the brain?" and "Where is the brain?" are meaningless. Thus there is no way the brain can be destroyed, let alone discerned. A cell of it, for instance, has no knowledge of other cells, or of what will be caused by the psyche to do — or why, when it will be utilized, when dropped out, etc. This is a *very* superior life form; like Ubik it is everywhere but not in any one spot; it uses human media of communication — it cannot be detected or destroyed, and since we are living in spurious time generated by the magnet anyhow, the brain can proceed as slowly as it wishes to achieve its goals. When the goals are accomplished it will obliterate the prolonged spurious time and reveal the world of "Acts" to us as our real world. In a very real sense the brain and its psyche have never left the time and place of "Acts," but via the total psyche of it are both anchored there, pitted against the magnet in its clear form: imperial Rome.

(39) If we could see a speeded-up file of world history of the last 2,000 years — run by us in say 5 minutes — we'd see an oscillation (palintropos) of blow and counter blow between the brain and the

magnet. We would see millions of humans organized into the brain and millions of humans taken over by the tug of the magnet, warped into a forever dead orbit — like the Persus 9 in *Maze*. Circling a dead sun eternally. The brain would appear as a patch or blob of light; the magnet black: Yang and Yin. The landscape would remain constant: that of "Acts." We would see the light (i.e., the brain) pulsate, as if breathing. With each cycle of respiration it as an organism would show visible growth. The black magnet stays fixed, since it is dead. If we could see ahead into the future we would finally see a killer blow delivered by the growing pulsating brain to the magnet, and the palintropos dialectic would end. Only the brain, incorporating every living human (as well as the physically dead) would exist. Even the landscape would disappear. Just a sheet of white light would extend everywhere. It would be as if the brain had reached critical mass and detonated. The magnet is well aware of the direction of this process; it has reason to regard the brain as "dangerous," "foreign" ("Fremd"), etc.; i.e., as an invader. The brain is its pursuer, and it has caught up with it.*

① "Acts" is a verbal analog of the brain, of the innermost core of the brain, outside of "Acts" there is no written analog of the brain. *Thus "Acts" is the only written account of the brain's existence;* it describes the first [and only public] manifestation of the brain.

Whatever theory I come up with re 3-74, "Acts" *must* be involved — necessary by iron-clad logic. Well, "Acts" says, "Brain." It says a lot else, but it has been called "the Gospel of the spirit," i.e., of the brain. After that the brain totally camouflaged itself (having gotten its transfer from Noös to the interface between it and the physical world underway?). I.e., the de-

---

* The editors were tempted to cut out several of the numbered points on the preceding list, which, like much of the Exegesis, goes on a bit longer than we might wish. But in a year already full of lists, this one stands out for length and exuberance and deserves to be represented. Paradoxically, the impulse to circumscribe and define unleashes a manic flow of ideas culminating in a lyrical explosion. As is often the case, Dick also writes right through his most breathtaking moments, not even noticing the climax: in the original, the striking number 39 is followed by points 40 to 42, which were enough of a letdown that we could no longer resist the temptation to excise them — even as we opted to include the footnote that continues the flow. All of which is to say that the most difficult decisions we faced in editing Dick's Exegesis involved how and when to cut him off. It's tempting to give him the punch lines he doesn't have time to stop for, and often we have done so. On the other hand, we felt that sometimes we should let the ideas tumble on. We wanted readers to experience a bit of what it's like to read the original manuscript, page after page after page. It wouldn't be the Exegesis if there wasn't too much of it. — PJ

scent of the Holy Spirit onto the disciples marked the *start* of the brain. It was [mere] spirit no longer. It had control over us (sic). After that no real record exists of whom it spread to. (Fortunately.) Its distribution had begun.

"Acts" as brain print.

"Acts" material in *Tears* pointing to the presence (activity) of the brain. Stamp of the origin? Of authenticity — i.e., "official"?

"Acts" material in *Tears* as brain print. Proved by 2-74 and 3-74 and the St. Sophia prophecy; i.e., its presence proved (to me).

"Acts" material in *Tears* — and hence *Tears* itself — as self-replication or propagation of the brain; i.e., the brain retrievable from each *copy*(!) of *Tears*. Each reader as involuntary host.

Tears as miraculous sacrament like the eucharist. A way of entering people and — v. *Stigmata* and Palmer Eldritch's drug replicates him in each user (host or "womb").

Words as alive, *like I saw "Felix" to be:* the printed word carrying a charge of the red and gold plasmic [electrical, neural] energy. Just in that one place in the novel, next to "King." It (the organism) can reproduce through — as — information. (But only *certain* information — i.e., "Acts.")

Burroughs posits an information virus (or "virus" [like]). (Not so, KW says.)

If that plasmic energy is alive, and it is (or it carries) information, then we have *living* information. Logos? Information plasma which enters through the optic nerve primarily — or auditorily. Signals that control our brains, open GABA blocked circuits. Like pressing keys on a typewriter.

Once having entered the person's brain via the optic nerve it now modulates brain functioning so that the person subliminally transduces messages (including instructions) and hence is a "cell" in the brain, responding to sentient override — lifted out of the blind forces of the Yin realm, his actions integrated with that of all others like him. It's like a beehive, a colony entity, and is immortal, replenishing and shedding continually. Member-units (v. Schopenhauer on the fruit flies[63]).

The reader of *Tears* reads the dream (he's been absorbing "Acts" without knowing it — the verbal analog of the brain) which subconsciously is familiar and remembered; this sets him up, and as soon, then, as he sees "Felix" the plasma travels down his optic nerve as an electric pulse and it's done, it can now replicate into the total microform of the brain, as the reader reads on getting the rest of the "Acts" material (especially the agape, which is the salient property of the Paraclete [Brain]). The opposites in him (the reader) are reconciled; he accepts his own shadow (in Jung's term). There may be no palpable or immediate effect, but the entity which I call the brain is inside him and growing. He will be coordinated with the others, overridden, etc.

Also, he has subliminally received the Kerygma, the new one: Christus Rex. He has been told the good news hidden for all the preceding generations. On a conscious level he doesn't know. The deconstruction (flip-flop) of *Tears* is love — the final word of the novel.

[38:55] Whatever the Bible may say, the Paraclete (and clearly Zebra is the Paraclete: the proof is [1] the "Acts" material, and [2] the Christian anamnesis) — is a life form, far higher than we are, but *real*, the possible object of strict empirical knowledge. I believe it is actual and a fit topic for scientific inquiry. However, its camouflage is so successful and its sentience so far above ours that trying to investigate it (against its will) is a waste of time (by definition; viz: posit a life form *far* higher than us and utilizing camouflage and ad hoc there is no way you can discern it).

But it is not just an inscrutable "miraculous mysterious being"; I saw it using *methods* — albeit beyond the power of the mechanistic physics which control us. (Lower realm powers.) For example (and this is the main thrust of my theory) it uses an interface to link it to the physical (history) world, a real aggregate of humans, processes and objects which it organizes into the actual entity I call "the Brain." To travel, it "rides" tangible, physical books, song lyrics, etc. This shows that the sacraments are real and not just customs or rites.

And it's composed of real energy: some sort of electricity in a plasmic state, info-rich and alive and sentient. It has to (or desires to) follow certain procedures to replicate — to accomplish *any* of its goals, such as historic intervention and modulation. It does not just *wish* for the changes to occur, and they do; it needs to dragoon specific people at specific places and times to do specific things. This thought carries me back to my point: some act on my part future to 3-74 was necessary (or so it seems) if the historical intervention were to come at all. And thus it overrode me and saved my hide.

[38:59] This forces me to reconsider the "discarding and annexing" process by the brain in favor of a *proliferation* theory: once you receive a bit of Zebra into you, you are in the brain (i.e., for good). So the "cloud of fruit-flies" model breaks down in favor of the model of a *growing* brain which acquires but does not simultaneously discard. Yet it is a "swarm."

That it could replicate itself, in humans (i.e., via), as a verbal plasma — it looked, on the page of *Tears* like a section of chromosomes under an electron microscope; what I saw was its "seed" or "germ" constituent. [. . .]

No — rather, evidently *Zebra had replicated itself in me at some earlier date;* in writing *Tears* I was under its jurisdiction. This could have occurred when I took communion, or, as a child, read something that was "information plasma" like the bit in my own book. Amazing how this resembles the replication of Palmer Eldritch through eating Chew-Z.

[38:61] What is hard for us to grasp is how *a single bit* (like "Felix/King" in *Tears*) can replicate the *entire* body of information, just as an entire human can be reconstructed from a single cell. So all the transmitter has to do is get that living-info bit into you, and then it grows. Christ discusses this as the grains of wheat falling on various kinds of soil. The mustard seed, too, and the pearl of great price — many parables relate this concept. "The Kingdom of God" is the state created by the successful growing of the living-info bit, and successful incorporation into the brain, of the person.

This is "Firebright" or the "microcomputer," this nucleus of living info. It creates a bicameral mind (the inward light or voice — which I call the "AI" voice). The original bicameral mind must have been silenced by the scrambler, revolting BIP. *This* voice circumvents the scrambler. That's what it's all about, this circumvention. The transmitter figured out a way to slip stuff in. *One bit,* and the totality is duked. [. . .]

This description *totally* agrees with "John" vis-à-vis what the Paraclete does (and knows). "A bit of living information from which grows the entire corpus of knowledge" and "coordination to the divine psyche" (of Christ) is an orthodox formulation; only the terminology has been updated. [. . .]

As I now conceive it (to recap), the initial living-info bit must grow to the totality for the "blitz" to occur: the quantum leap inside the person's head, such as I began to experience in 2-74, which is a thresholding into consciousness: the coming to life of the Christ psyche in microform, like a hologram bit. "Us in Christ and Christ in us" (v. supra). The person is no longer an individual driven by subrational forces, but part of the "Swarm of Bees" brain. [. . .]*

---

* Anticipating the insights of artificial life, Dick posits a phase transition that he delightfully terms "thresholding." Just as liquid water must be heated past the threshold of 100 degrees centigrade if it is to become a gas or cooled below 0 centigrade if it is to solidify, so too must the "initial living info bit" undergo a quantitative change if it is to undergo a qualitative change. And this qualitative change entails a change in consciousness such that the self becomes aware of a Möbius strip–like continuity between itself and Christ. Dick deploys the concept of the hologram to make sense of this simultaneously individual and cosmic aspect of human nature, possibly under the influence of psychologist Karl Pribram's holographic model of the brain. For both Pribram and Dick, one of the most sa-

What I saw in 3-74 — and remember in 2-74 — was the *real* world: the landscape of "Acts" now "reduced" to its [mere] verbal analog: a book (and in *Tears*). This book is the *authentic* actual world, obscured by the fake one. Only the true Christians know this, and they only know it by virtue of the transmitter's living, salvific info growing into totality inside them.

Whew. Heavy — complex.

It occurs to me to cite the many and near-lethal (to me) attempts by the authorities to get hold of the ms of *Tears* — i.e., to keep it from being published, as proof of my contention about the BIP and its suppression and scrambling of the truth. *Tears* does not just tell the true story covertly; as I say, it actually contains a bit of Zebra, alive and info-rich, ready to enter people and begin to grow, to free (and inform) them. *This* is how anamnesis occurs — this growth into totality from the bit. As Christ frequently pointed out, in many instances the process fails. (There is *such* a powerful adversary yammering out a ceaseless stream of lies, and maintaining an irreal world, etc.)

[38:68] The brain is one multiperson ajna chakra, which one day as a unitary totality will open, discerning and annihilating (the 3rd eye of Shiva). (Herdsman of the souls.) All who participate in it will then see as I saw; they will be inside the eye; everything outside will be blasted, "burned like chaff," i.e., cease to exist. At that point the brain will generate its own world out of itself. It, collectively, will totally control its world — the PTG. [. . .]

If it's an information plasma life form, and can replicate the (its) entire Gnosis from one bit — well, add in the spontaneous generation of messages (information) depicted in *Ubik*, which were everywhere — and in 3-74 I *saw* them everywhere — and the result you get is that this entity has *secretly* (camouflaged to us) invaded everywhere (*Ubique*). Because I saw verbal and graphic messages just flying and changing (re-linking) all over the place. And these are not its thoughts, but *it itself.* Based on what I saw and what I've figured out, we're *in* it. Like I flashed on several days ago: it's a *brain,* and we're totally unaware of it. It's not a species *within* ours; *we're* within *it.* (I.e., it is larger than we are.) And it's in some of us. [. . .]

So *that's* who not only sends but reads the messages: the total macro-brain/psyche sends the message to the microforms *in* us.

---

lient and suggestive features of the hologram is that each "bit" or fragment taken from a hologram contains information about the whole. Dick's reference to the "Swarm of Bees" brain is also resonant with Timothy Leary's notion of the "hive mind," but the holographic model, along with numerous entries on free will and volition, suggests that for Dick this collective mind in fact requires free will to function. — RD

Fuck! Swarm of Bees, but not us. Thus it links its stations (cells) inside us. We humans are just big dumb vehicles through which the plasma acts, and in which it lives.

[38:72] Ah! In *Ubik* locating the Ubik messages in cheap commercials was absolutely right on. I couldn't have "guessed" more accurately. It's obvious that the real author of *Ubik* was Ubik. It is a self proving novel; i.e., it couldn't have come into existence unless it were true.

[38:79] "Latent form is the Master of obvious form," Heraclitus wrote:

$$
\begin{array}{l}
A \left\{ \begin{array}{l} \text{Obvious form: the Nixon tyranny of 1974} \quad ① \\ \qquad\quad \text{Latent form: } \textit{Tears} \end{array} \right. \\[2pt]
B \left\{ \begin{array}{l} \qquad \text{Obvious form: } \textit{Tears} \\ \qquad \text{Latent form: "Acts"} \end{array} \right.
\end{array} \Bigg\} ②
$$

So ① is related — reaches — ③ by way of ②.

Tears, then, is the informational interface or nexus between our actual world of 1974 and "Acts." The reader lives in ① and reads ②, thus absorbing it; but this leads him inexorably to "Acts," ③, and once he has —

Tears is a doorway, not a world in itself. As you read it you pass across to the world of "Acts" without knowing it — the *author* didn't know it. It is a latency-within-a-latency.

Then, latent within ③ is:

$$
④ \left\{ \begin{array}{l} \text{Serious} \\ \quad \text{King} \\ \quad \text{Felix} \end{array} \right\} ⑤
$$

The reader, living in world ①, when he reads *Tears* ②, passes to ③ and then to ④ and at last to ⑤, at which point the living plasma has him.

$$
C \left\{ \begin{array}{l} \text{Obvious form: "Serious"} \\ \text{Latent form: "King"} \end{array} \right.
$$
$$
D \left\{ \begin{array}{l} \text{Obvious form: "King"} \\ \text{Latent form: "Felix" ("happy")} \end{array} \right.
$$

The final innermost "onion ring" is D or ⑤.

In other words, to restore "Acts," *Tears* is necessary as an interface. *Tears* is therefore an instrument (probably just one of many) of restoring the brain, because "Acts" = Brain. *Tears,* then, is a triggering agent for anamnesis, and anamnesis and the restoration of the brain are intertwined. I don't credit *Tears* with being *the* doorway, but rather *a* doorway —

By which the brain traveled forward in time along the form axis from c.
A.D. 45 Rome into USA 1974! It bypassed the intermediate 1,900 years!

[38:82] My postmortem experiences (such as sense of vast spaces, etc.) is
because in the Corpus Christi there are many, such as Thomas, who are
dead, the mystical body of Christ contains both the living and the dead, it
spans both worlds.

My sense of Thomas returning the last few days — sense of vast space,
dreams of a woman singing — show I'm still in the mystical body. And the
postmortem experience is further proof of what I'm sure of: by invading
this lower realm and annexing it, Zebra is knitting the decomposing cosmos back together — and it is the cosmic Christ who does this. Ergo, Zebra
is the cosmic Christ. I grow more and more sure of it. (I.e., the brain.)

[38:83]

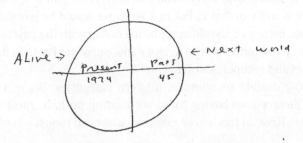

The mystical body of Christ spans the past and the present, this world
and the next.

[38:88] Bill Sarill[64] points out that my description of the magnet imposing
absolute sameness everywhere is a description of entropy, of thermal death
of the universe. Conversely, the flash point (critical mass) explosion of the
brain would be the hoped for negentropic "Big Bang" start of a fresh cycle
of the universe, which, if not achieved, means the eventual end of the universe, through insufficient mass (matter). [. . .]

Thus, at the deepest level, the brain represents form, and the BIP represents entropy. This realization, due to Bill Sarill, is monumental. It goes
beyond "Christianity vs. Rome." The Christians are simply the agents
of negentropy, and the brain is the form — and life, the evolving entelechy — which that form takes. The BIP is sameness: thermal death.
Clearly, the brain is an ultimate level of homeostasis and a vast evolutionary step forward in terms of hierarchy of form. It subsumes more; it is
larger; it is more intelligent and self-sufficient; more free — more *alive*. As

a life form it subsumes not only all other life forms that we know, but even incorporates into itself dead or past lives. It transcends this entire realm and binds it into the other (next or higher). Despite its secular enemy, the totalitarian state, it is destined historically to prevail (come into full actualization). So I was correct in viewing my 3-74 experience as an evolutionary step up. But it is not that just for me as an individual; I ceased to be an individual and became a cell in what I now recognize as a vast distributive brain, an interface for a sentient information plasma which may extend beyond this planet. [. . .]

I do not believe it is God (the creator). *It is something new,* which came into existence at a certain time (c. A.D. 45, "Acts") at a certain place (Syria) in a certain way (through first Christ and then the Second Comforter). It had never been seen — been there — before; it has an *historic* starting point. Blind will or striving is overruled by an advancing mind-brain which came here in micro form (very small and lowly) *and grows;* it is *not* static! I suppose we could worship it, but in a sense we would be worshipping our [true] selves; better we should enter into a dialog with the psyche and let it regulate us. We should *listen* to it, and make ourselves hosts to it, receivers and vehicles and receptacles of it.

I am now dealing in ultimate, modern categories. We're a long way from, say, dietary laws having to do with eating pork, or meat on Friday. My concepts have, in this 4 year exegesis, advanced thousands of years.

[38:95] KW offers the brilliant theory that the brain was using me as a self-monitoring circuit to examine the degree of information degradation along the linear time axis, and therefore could not allow me to be sacrificed in 3-74. Apparently some rectification of the "signal" (i.e., history) had to be made, and I was lucky enough to be included in that rectification. KW explained to me how very good amplifiers monitor their own output to see if it conforms to what they are *receiving* from the pre-amp; this is a typical example of electronic homeostasis. So the brain transmitted back a text ("Acts") that it knew, and could then compare what appears in *Tears* with what it had transmitted.

I add to this that it (the brain in the future) also transmitted a command to some of its cells located here, in this time, and this command code (King Felix) *was* correctly received by me, and boosted (put into the book). But as KW says, a self-monitoring feedback information loop was set up by the brain in the future using me and *Tears.* Since the brain *is* information, it (a bit of it as plasma) was actually in each copy of *Tears!*

Folder 18

[18:1] Which is it: hallucination as reality (e.g., *3 Stigmata*) or reality as hallucination (e.g., Bishop Berkeley)?

Stated this way, I think the latter. Reality (USA 1974) is hallucination, and can be voided through faith — whereupon the *absolute* time and place ("Acts") appears.

Thus *3 Stigmata* and *Maze* are total opposites: in *Maze* reality is a hallucination. There is a real world behind it. But in *3 Stigmata* hallucination becomes real — not: real becomes hallucination and hence departs.

Do Androids Dream . . . reveals:

(1) Surface level: Mercer[65] real
(2) Below that: Mercer fake — hoax — fraud
(3) Below that: Mercer real (Bottom Line)

I think this 3 level structure is the one *we* have vis-à-vis Christianity. A secret within a secret A, Ā, A. "Precious Artifact" (3 layer) was close.

You have this: Q: "Is a fake fake real?" re Christianity: A: "Yes."

———

This is in terms of a 2-value system ("A or Ā"). If a 3-value system is used:

A becomes Ā by reversal. Then Ā is reversed, *not* restoring A, but something else. A what? How does it differ from A, if at all? Answer: call it A'. I say A' "out A's A," in an ontological sense. It is a profoundly deeper, richer newer level than A, but also (paradoxically) it *is* A. But A' is not A.

So: A' *is* and is-not A.

———

But: A' is not Ā.

The reversal of the reversed does not restore the original thing. I say, A is just a *picture* of A'.

Whatever that means. But it's so. Of the 3, only A' is really real. A and A' are identical, but A and Ā are false; only A' is real. [. . .]

Voice: "A' is A *reinterpreted*."

[18:11] Strange — a day or so before my mother's fatal stroke I realized that Thomas was back. The woman singing, the vast spaces. Via the brain I once more passed across a little, not as much as before but enough to tell me that I still remained inside of — a part of — the brain, which spans both worlds.

I must have gone across in 3-74 and stayed for a while and then returned. Okay — in track A I died, but then the revision was superimposed as orthogonal *newness:* negentropy imposed on a running-down, ossifying state of things. Yes, that's what was going on: ossification, entropy, the "imperial" equals undifferentiated thermal distribution, and this included *me*, this entropy . . . but also I *foresaw* the really very frightening moment coming for me — I foresaw my demise. The last frames were moving through the projector.

Then the brain acted, injecting new life into realm II. KW agrees that I'd been used as a self-monitoring circuit by the brain to measure the coefficient of entropy (at that time) expressed in terms of information degradation (the aspect of form vs. entropy most important to it, it *being* living information: it would be self-monitoring its *own* decay), its own running down, which pointed to a growth-impairment of growth-loss, requiring rectification, *self*-rectification, it being at perhaps an absolute stage of homeostasis.

I take it that *Tears* showed too high a degradation-of-information factor, or in *some* way indicated an inordinate fossil or ossified quality, or *pointed to* it (in some way conveyed it, I'm not sure the "Acts" info in *Tears* was degraded, itself, intrinsically).

Maybe wherever the "Acts" material surfaced — its manifesting itself would indicate a "weak" spot — a revelation of too much entropy. In that case, a highly (adequately) vital, viable space-time segment could *resist* the "Acts" material; for the "Acts" material to surface — show through — first in *Tears* and then four years later, the actual world of "Acts" showed through — the hologram was weakening!

This is not supposed to happen. The brain wishes to maintain the fiction of linear time — i.e., that it was at that time 1974. Then there *was* a dysfunction and rectification. The release of *Tears* with its "Acts" material served as a device by which the brain could pinpoint in its own corpus the weak spot (the brain's evolution — growth — occurs in linear time — so sequence, linear time, is needed by it).

The "hologram" *is* the brain as "body" of psyche. Its actual evolving corpus — primarily one of living sentient information — was weakening — *dying* (just one spirit located at one time and place). It's like a Barium or Gallium or other radioactive or dye test. The brain must have either been running (1) a routine test; (2) a constant test; (3) or a test based on *suspicion* of the USA 1974 "spot" in the corpus. In any case the "Acts" material in *Tears* was a self-signal to the psyche which brought a quick — immediate — response of rectification: the orthogonal imposition of newness (from Form I) onto the entropic, weak or ossified "imperial" spot.

I deduce from this that the original landscape is *not* supposed to show through. But v. p. *17!*[66]

Ach — it's so. I just know it ran a self-monitoring test through me, and the actual landscape showed through in *Tears* and *it,* the brain, *it* reacted. So after it saved me in 2-3-74 I've had time to figure out that what it is is that a brain exists, feeding us a spurious reality which it grows and develops, and we're cells in it subliminally governed and integrated into it. The spurious reality is to keep us from going nuts from sense-deprivation, and is a 3-D hologram matrix through which info passes, its thoughts, instructions and info.

It's all certainly for a benign purpose: the brain is negentropic, the life of the universe, "the final bulwark against non being," as Tillich put it (against entropy).[67] As cells, we are born, function, live, age, die and are replaced; the brain is immortal. What we accomplish in our lifetimes is made eternal as bits of the brain's evolving structure, especially if it deals with info, the very substance of the brain. In processing info, especially if we impose form on it rather than just transfer it or boost it — we are modifying the very *life* (substance, nature) of the brain. So we are active, not passive cells of the brain.

Anyhow, despite the "deception" of a simulated reality — this realization opens up an I-You (me to the brain and back) colloquy, instead of merely an I-it. And this is a quantum leap up in perception and experience of the universe: the not-I.

[18:17] A curious idea occurs to me: in *Tears* the world of "Acts" has been fundamentally and severely transmuted into a rigid-as-iron prism/tyranny. Expressed as info (with "Acts" as the message) this is a *verbal* degrading analogous to the world — degrading by the Nixon tyranny (police state nearing outright slavery). So — the "Acts" material *is* severely degraded: specifically into an ossified form (the BIP). And the brain, self-monitoring in terms of itself qua info, detects the BIP (ossified) quality, assesses it correctly as a moribund *or entropic state,* and acts to revitalize (i.e., to free) the "spot" (i.e., space-time) involved. Ah! It's as if the brain transmitted "Acts" through my head, and grave BIP aspects showed up in the printout: *accurate* representation of our actual political, social conditions. Thus the brain experiences our world as it is: as information. I had mistakenly thought — supra — that the "Acts" material *came through intact,* but in fact it is "heat death" distributed into the *Tears* BIP ossification, which, as Bill Sarill pointed out, is a form of entropy! So if BIP equals entropy, there is severe degrading of the "Acts" message in *Tears*, along *very* specific lines: our USA of 1974!

My mind in 1970 was utilized as a core or representative situation–registering microcosm component, as if the macro political-sociological USA as historic matrix was correctly reproduced in me — so a known message ("Acts") passing through me (my mind) would show changes, if any, indicative of the macro-historic matrix. It's the same principle as the Nielsen TV Poll.

On p. 13, supra,[68] I totally missed the point (nature) of how — and how much! — the "Acts" message was degraded as an input signal/message. What did I expect: the word "Gubble"? Here is a verbal degrading delineating *exactly* how the situation had deteriorated; i.e., it was not just "noise" on the line but specific, meaningful recontouring, and this condition, called "imperial uniformity" by KW and me, *is entropy*, which for the brain means a literal (but localized) death of a part of itself — and so it took immediate steps to rectify the situation by *breaking* the warp-factor of the "complex" (BIP). Just as it gave new life to me personally (à la *Ubik*) *it* gave our world new life generally.

What I foresaw in *Tears* was the running-down of our world, the congealing. *Tears*, as a verbal message, *was a thought by the brain itself,* passing through me as a "neural" component. This is how the brain normally works — I got to see that in 3-74, the message came from it, and was to be received by it — *that* is who the crypto info in *Tears* was for. So it didn't matter how many copies got sold to whom.

So the "Acts" material was *not* the message *but the control.* Departures (transmutations) were the real message: i.e., *how altered.*

Boy, was it ever changed in a sinister — and alarming — way! So what I call the "mere surface material of *Tears*" — is what the brain specifically was looking for — I've dismissed the very thing it was looking for.

This is not God. This is a very advanced organism which we just don't know about (of Zebra's camouflage). It subsumes at least some of us, and came here from elsewhere. It doesn't work by miracle but through ways we don't understand. It, not we, is the *real* life form here.

It *probably* is the once-man we know of as Christ.

[18:23] Admittedly this is a more prosaic explanation, but — I can see where, unable to understand the programming and re-programming controlling me, my mind would come to the psychologically necessary conclusion that it was God, and would *project* the theophany, etc. — i.e., generate Zebra by projection. Also, in 3-74 I may have suffered a lurid schizophrenic episode because of the inordinate stress, I regressed to such a primitive stage that I animated my environment. I saw a world of 2,000 years ago because I had regressed into the racial unconscious.

Q: But what about the "Acts" material in *Tears* and it agreeing with what I remembered in 2-74 upon seeing the fish sign, and *saw* a month later?

A: As early as 1970 archaic contents of my mind were overpowering me. This shows up in *Ubik* and 3 *Stigmata*. I had been partially psychotic for years, and in 3-74 I broke down totally. Due to *actual* stress. (The IRS business.)

Like Cordwainer Smith,[69] I was taken over by my own S-F universe.

Schizophrenia with religious and paranoid coloring — of the ecstatic type.* A sense of the "cosmic" — vast mystical forces, with me in the center (sic). Like a titanic psychedelic drug trip. I was probably secreting a mescaline-like autotoxic substance not well understood. I had little if any romance (i.e., adventure) in my life in those days ('74), and in '70 Nancy's leaving had broken me — i.e., at the time of my '70 "mescaline" trip, which was more likely my first entry into total psychosis — my ego disintegrated then, and again in 3-74.

And now I exhaust myself trying to explain 3-74. I was lithium toxic. *And* had a schizophrenic breakdown.

My mind monitors my "missile anamnesis" as a clue to prior psychosis. I *need* romance (adventure) in my life. The AI voice is a special kind of hallucination: one of wish-fulfillment and need, due to loneliness: emotional starvation and grief and ill-use. I just can't endure life without that lovely voice guiding me, so I regress to a level (atavistic, in historical terms) at which such a bicameral experience (like in *Scanner*) can take place. The AI voice is my imaginary playmate, my sister, evolved out of my childhood "Bill and Nell" fantasies. I did not regress to my own childhood only, but back along the "platonic form-axis," i.e., into the collective unconscious, back *thousands* of years. It was a mercy. I was so unhappy and afraid; like R. Crumb,[70] so behind the 8 ball, so filled with anticipatory dread.

---

* Readers skeptical about Dick's sanity after reading the Exegesis should pay careful attention to this passage, where he explores the possibility that the events of 2-3-74 were a schizophrenic hallucination. In interrogating the veracity of his visions, Dick examines his own psychological makeup and analyzes what was going on in his life at the time. Simply put, crazy people do not question their own sanity like this, at least as a general rule. I find this one of the most moving passages of the entire Exegesis because, in it, Dick places the cosmic scope of his vision in relation to the lack of love and excitement in his own life and goes so far as to suggest that this loneliness may have given rise to delusions of grandeur. Such honesty is refreshing and points to the sincerity that underlies Dick's belief in the authenticity of his experiences, as well as his desire to determine whether those experiences were generated internally, as a manifestation of his psyche, or externally, by an encounter with the divine. — DG

Well, damn it — I don't regret it. It made a barren, fearful life meaningful and bearable, and it helped me solve certain pressing problems such as
writing the IRS in '74.

Yes, it was a mercy to me — I went over the brink into psychosis in
'70 when Nancy left me — in '73 or so I tried to come back to having an
ego, but it was too fragile and there were too many financial and other
pressures; the hit on my house and all the terrors of 1971 had left their
mark — and so, especially because of the IRS matter, I suffered *total* psychosis in 3-74, was taken over by one or more archetypes. Poverty, family
responsibility (a new baby) did it. And fear of the IRS.

Only now, as I become for the first time in my life financially secure, am
I becoming sane, free of psychotic anxiety (R. Crumb's case is *very* instructive), and career-wise I am doing so well: I am at last experiencing genuine
satisfaction (e.g., my car, my novels, my stereo, my friendship with KW),
and there is far less responsibility on my shoulders. Also, my accomplish-
ments last year — traveling, being with Joan — did wonders for my psychological health. I learned to say no, and I conquered most of my phobias. I
think they lessened as I learned to enjoy living alone for the first time of
my life. And the therapy at Ben-Rush Center helped.

But I think that when all else failed and external pressures and inner
fears drove me into psychosis, *God placed me under his personal protection* and guided me and saved me by His divine love, mercy, wisdom and
grace through Christ . . . although not, perhaps, as I delusionally imagined. The intervention appears in *Tears* as the dream and the reconciliation with my shadow, the black man, which followed; and my anima, possessing mana, acted as my psychopomp through the underworld to safety.
[. . .]

My psychosis put me in touch with *"das ewige weiblichkeit"*[71] in me,*
and for that I will always be grateful; it means I will never really be alone
again: whenever I really need her, I will sense her presence and hear her

---

* Dick's mystical vision or apparent psychosis seems to put him in touch with the eternal
feminine. This is one of the many moments when the Exegesis resonates with Daniel Paul
Schreber's *Memoirs of My Nervous Illness* (1903), where the erstwhile high court judge became convinced that his body took on breasts and female genitalia in order to be properly penetrated by the rays of God and to redeem the universe. The fusion with the divine
is here conceived (poor choice of word, I know) as a kind of transsexual bliss, a penetration (a repeated word in the Exegesis) by the divine. We should also note Dick's later affirmation of Christianity as the experience of being "the intended bride" of Christ. In 1910,
Freud had a lot of fun writing up his interpretation of the Schreber case, although Freud's
text finishes with the wonderfully honest confession that it will be for posterity to judge
whether there was more delusion in Schreber's (or indeed Dick's) paranoid vision than in
Freud's own theory of psychoanalysis. — SC

voice (i.e., St. Sophia). At the center of psychosis I encountered her: beautiful and kind and, most of all, wise, and through that wisdom, accompanying and leading me through the underworld, through the Bardo Thödol journey to rebirth—she, the embodiment of intelligence: *Pallos Athena herself.* So at the core of a shattered mind and life lies this equicenter—omphalos—of harmonie and calm. I love her, and she is my guide: the second comforter and advocate promised by Jesus . . . as Luther said, *"For the very desperate,"* here in this world secretly, for their—our—sake. [. . .]

When I saw her she was beautiful beyond compare—Aphrodite and Pallas Athena both—and someday I'll see her again. She is inside me—she is my soul.

[18:29]

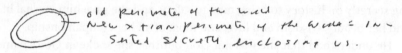

[18:34] Info within the data. Message. Living info: *organized* (negentropic). Whereas the data is/are entropic. There is no way we can define its outline as long as it desires to remain hidden, since it is an organizing principle of that which it is not. It is not a something. It is made up of the *arrangement* of the data. It can be any object, any process, any person—and at that time controls that object, process, person. It is me today, not me tomorrow. Like Mercury it is a messenger-system, linking constituents; when linked they serve as a medium or conduit to transfer info, which is to say, *it* as life form. In a sense it is a narrative.

[18:35] This is the quintessential form of "The Masks of Medusa" that Brunner sent to me—the theory was there![72] Like a phagocyte it moves to surround the magnet, regarding it as a hostile invader (i.e., in this region of the hologram). The magnet does not belong here: it is embedded like a meteor in the ground.

Titanic biological models are implied. The encircling brain pulses with life and light, but even it, so much advanced over us, is a small-scale entelechy in the universe as a whole.

[18:42] He remembered a former life, as an early Christian. The divine *ajna* eye (Dibba Cakkhu) opened and he saw all things coming into being and passing away, the growing and evolving of the universe animal locked in dialectic but victorious strife with its opposite, the universe alive and intelligent.

He saw vast opened books of wisdom. Most of all, he heard across vast reaches of space, *her* voice advising, informing and comforting him, and telling him that holy wisdom would be born again, and that the Buddha was in the park, i.e., born.

She intervened to extricate him and his son, medically and by counsel, out of danger, and she led him across the bridge to the upper world, to the wastes and void and the emptiness and love — and restoration to — God. Finally, she showed him mysterious mind here but hidden, making plastic all reality by its thought and will. She showed him life and intelligence and will everywhere. Breaking the prism and bringing freedom to man, operating secretly on history to bring man to safety, and she gave him eternal life and her beauty, wisdom and love, and most of all her companionship.

He understood that she was not God but that she spoke in God's name and knew everything past, present and future. She announced her presence here and her intervention here. She told him that she had seen every evil thing and would correct it through justice, that the weak would be protected, and she protected him.

But then she told him that a time would come when she could no longer speak to him. After that he did nothing but try to remember her and the sound of her voice, and cared nothing about anything else. He was lost in dreams and memories because of what he had seen and heard. He could never explain it to anyone else. But she had promised to come back for him at the end of his life, with the sound of the magic bells — Easter Bells denoting the dead and risen Christ. So he knew a secret he should never tell: that the savior was female, that the Second Comforter was God's darling and delight who had existed before creation and had aided in creation: by her all things came into being, and nothing existed except through her. And he understood the last mystery of all, that although she was not God she *was* God. Much of this he knew because he remembered his former life, thousands of years ago, when he had been one of the original true Christians and had received the true Kerygma never written down, from those who had known before her/him.

He remembered a great battle he had been in, along with others like him, as her agents, to destroy a sort of Iron Prison; and he realized that again he was fighting this battle — now, as her agent again, along with the others.

He felt great joy, and the knowledge of triumph. The savior had died but would soon return, and they were making glad preparations for his im-

minent return. That was another mystery: the savior was *he*, but also, secretly, it was she once again; behind every incarnation she was there; and
behind her was God, who was he, and she was God.

There was something spinning like a great top, like a volvox,[73] changing
and evolving, alive and conscious, using the old world as a heap of parts to
fit into place within itself; it was camouflaged and here, and it consisted of
a story, of living information, and electricity like a plasma, no one could
see it, and it destroyed all that enslaved creatures: it sprang traps open
to release hunted things. She spoke for it. Mostly it was in the future, although for it there was only space into which it grew (space as the receptacle of being); it made use of time as its source of energy. It used time and
was not ruled by time. It was always in motion and symmetrical. It was replacing the world of causality with itself and its living, thinking purpose,
its body.

He saw how her messages, which were living bits of her, traveled
through people and the world, maintaining her as a unitary entity — and
he was shown that in a small but real way he had been made use of to
boost and transmit one tiny bit of her living information, from one part
of her — the spinning sphere which grew and lived — to another part. This
was the most important thing he had ever done; this was his purpose; and
in doing so he was part of her, and this would never change. He was in her
and she in him. Forever; like speaking — calling — to like. For him it was
love, and perhaps for her, too.

She appeared to him as love, beauty, wisdom, war (protectress) and finally harmonie. Sometimes she sang.

[**18:66**] It's a two source hologram — it *must* be nothing more than hologram-like, or this could not occur; if USA 1974 were truly substantial it
could not oscillate like that — no superimposition montage could take
place. These continua must be projected, and obviously by the observer,
the self.⊕ No other explanation is possible; to wit: whatever reality you
truly believe in *is served up*, including all details. Someone convinced he
was in Weimar Germany would see the world under that aspect. These are
modes of perceiving one (i.e., the same) actually unchanging thing: view
points, perspectives. This *urwelt* can assume (or be projected upon so as
to assume to us) any space-time aspect imaginable. It is an omni-faceted
revolving sphere of some kind reflecting back at us what we project, or
what something in us or — well, Brahman, nice to meet you, you cunning
dreamer of worlds, how obliging you are, right down to minute trivia. Not
only can you assume (take, take on, be, appear to be) any form, but *all*
forms. I always come back to you when I push this far enough. I'm right,

then, in my writing, aren't I? Silly putty universes, a whole lot of them. But underneath it's you, obliging and smiling; any guise we wish, believe in — you have it fully made.

You even fooled the Buddha, you the magician, the game player. Why the manifold disguises? The doubter and the doubt — and the hymn of total faith. Emerson was right.[74] Tat tvam asi — here I am, one of the forms you take, writing about you, figuring out your ways — Brahman delighting in detecting Brahman; this may be one of your favorite games. And you assist us forward, as I saw last night; diversification into the pluriforms, the many from the one. You enlighten us but it is you who fools us — fools your own polyforms: Brahman the Magician (James-James), the audience, and the palm-tree savior — you are all of these, Christ included, and the woman I hear and see; Holy Wisdom in secret is you.

The basis of it all is a game for children which consists of a show in which the most subtle teaching takes place, as if to see if we can detect illusion. I view it all epistemologically, but it could be viewed morally or esthetically, etc. My criterion is real vs. irreal. What is actually there, and just *where* is it? I say it's mainly in our heads, but an inner-outer analog system exists which locks us into world, a push-pull feedback loop, the inner projecting onto the outer, and the outer (you, Brahman) cunningly simulating each projection and generating it back in enriched synchronization, so no thinness appears: the outer is not just a mirror but an amplifying mirror or structure — generator. In other words, Atman within projects the bare bones of a particular aspect of world onto the omni-faceted matrix; and you as outer Brahman supply details which fill in the picture, which you generate back; you enhance (as Brahman the reality-world-generator) what each Atman projects — it's like *Joint* and the soft drink stand that turns out to be just the *word:* "Soft drink stand" — no; it's as if the words are initially projected; that's the first step: it starts with Atman, goes to the spinning macro volvox, there it is enhanced — enriched — with corroborative detail and mirrored back to Atman; it is received by Atman (in its enhanced more fully produced form) and *again* projected out onto the flux volvox top, so this push-pull feedback loop just keeps on mutually generating (creating) *a more and more articulated hologram-like reality.* But it is hologrammatic and no more.

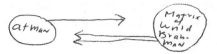

But I broke the push-pull in 2-74 when I saw the fish; in 3-74 because of my belief I projected Rome c. A.D. 45 and you obligingly articulated it — in the midst of a USA 1974 hologram—a palpable absurdity. As Thomas I may have very—totally sincerely—projected the initial bare bones aspect, but I (my interior Atman) did *not* project all that I saw of Rome c. A.D. 45; *you* obligingly augmented the projection® and generated that augmentation back, and the push-pull began, so we got such details as primitive Christian sacraments and the Koine, fear of the Romans, etc.; and then the whole world-aspect (i.e., one space, one time) system broke down, and the Dibba Cakkhu eye opened and I saw the unitary revolving sphere which grows and incorporates over 1,000's of years. *No* aspect-world was presented to me at that point. I saw what I call Zebra, and at last (recently) recognized it as a giant brain interfaced which utilizes us as stations, and which consists of living information (cf. Xenophanes). Even more recently I see the brain as a vast phagocyte, and its enemy a pathenogin. But that may be a graphic analogy only. What I am sure of is that Parmenides was correct. You give us not just *an* illusory phenomenal world, but a whole lot of them in space and time, as many as we initiate (which again is you *in* us, initiating these worlds). You *are* a world-creator God; you do not just think but "cause to be." The breakdown in my push-pull system in 2-74 temporarily set another world and another self into generation. But finally the situation restabilized as it had been before; however I was now in dialog with a "you" and not an "it"; I knew that true reality was sentient and at least partly alive and very smart—and also something of a conjurer. Also very beautiful and female.

If I had to make a statement about the very most *ultimate* nature of what I saw, I'd say it seemed to be a single complex sphere in flux, elaborating (yes, that's the word I want: elaborating) itself out of its continually greater number of stages of antecedent states/stages, *always surpassing itself* esthetically, in terms of wisdom, intricacy, efficiency, level of negentropy (*organization*): yes, perpetually surpassing itself in the level of organization (completeness)—filling in the gaps by a continually better and better—i.e., wiser, more efficient, more beautiful—use of its constituents and their arrangement—placement within—subsumed as parts—by the single over-all unitary structure. It may indeed develop from simplicity to complexity. But at the same time it progresses from plurality (many pieces) to incorporation into a unity. So its number is inversely proportional to its complexity: it goes from the many simple to the one absolutely complex. This reflects the distribution of elements on the periodic table; the more complex (heavier) the less frequent; also it resembles thought-processes in a brain; as that article in *Nature* pointed out back in the early fifties.

So it follows principles established in subsets we're familiar with: complexity is inversely proportional to frequency. As phagocyte it may not only be engulfing the pathenogin but using it as a stockpile of parts; the two [entities] will finally become one, and the dialectic will end (successfully). (This certainly resembles *Timaeus:* Noös at work "persuading" ananke!) Yes, that's it! The encircled BIP/magnet/pathenogin is being disassembled and incorporated into the brain/phagocyte/sphere, which process produces time and flux (v. Heraclitus). But it is not an equal contest: the sphere or brain although facing a formidable opponent *is* successfully dismantling it, although the process is not complete. It is the upper realm of Form I eventually making irreal the lower realm of Form II, *as Parmenides realized.* Form II. The BIP, in the aspect of eternity *isn't there;* it's only there in the flux time *process.* The phagocyte has, like the dragon, consumed itself starting with the tail; the BIP may be its own antecedent fossil self, blind and mechanical, at an earlier level of evolution — "matter" insentient compared to life and thought — brain. Thus the universe, the totality, organizes itself into the brain, that I saw, by consuming itself, what we see as change, flux, time, process is sign of its *life,* it is alive and becoming more so — just as I, as microbit, did in 3-74. Hologram microbit, analogy of the whole.

Finally, I ask, what is the purpose of the push-pull inner-outer analogy feedback loop between the stations and the total brain (out of which illusory hypostatized worlds are generated)? Why, this is how it elaborates and builds successive, antecedent-subsuming more evolved stages of itself, working toward ultimate unity and complexity. Since there is nothing but it, it can *only* interact with its own parts — by definition nothing (ultimately) can exist outside it (although during the temporal flux process this is not true). It annexes (incorporates) at the expense of the not-yet-it (i.e., the not-yet-brain but still dead fossil). The push-pull process accomplishes (or is *one* way, the way which concerns and involves us) final unitary totality. As the push-pull takes place between a given cell, station, part, bit or Atman, and the total brain-so-far, that bit is hyped up to elevated — well, I guess for whatever it will serve as in the final unitary being, which is *probably* awake (sentient) throughout. It's as if an escalating "thermal" or ergic charge is generated by this mutual push-pull process; it is the brain firing through (along) its circuits and firing back in response — no energy escapes from the closed system (circuit) so the ergic tension just builds and builds. We experience this as involvement with what we construe to be "the world." It fires at us, the way it fired the pink beam of info-rich light from the fish sign on the window at me — there's a typical, not atypical example, but *usually* it's disguised. What I got to see at that time was the purposeful, brain-like quality of reality with me *in* it, not outside it. To

use an instance I know of, *Tears* fires a certain charge of this living energy/
info. It goes on constantly all around us; this is why our brains crave — require — not just stimuli but *dialog*. This is the basis of life, as Martin Buber
pointed out. The brain might also be said to be educating its parts so they
will accurately replicate *it* in miniature; thus achieving for it its desired
completeness, its goal (wholeness throughout). Only when the micro stations precisely reflect the totality will the whole thing work (function). Our
lives are exchanges of energy — information back and forth, among us and
with the total brain, involving us in one purpose and one outcome; it is not
destiny; it is the will of the whole. There is nothing that can thwart it because outside it, finally, nothing will remain. This is understood in Christianity as the new cosmos of the mystical Corpus Christi.

① But an ur self: the Atman; Brahman within.
② With details I did not and could not know — which gave the system
away.

[18:78] Regarding the factor of complexity of the "volvox," what's involved
is not the number of parts but the *interconnections* — I perceived a veritable *maze* of connections, with each new part fitted in to link as many previous parts as possible. The organizing and arranging has this *interconnec-
tivity* in mind. Information moves through this jungle gym, branching and
flowing like the red mercury in a thermometer — my God, it's twisted like
this:

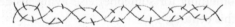

Oh God, what have I stumbled onto? This is the basic cable — it's Crick
and Watson's double helix again, and the ancient sign. *Billions* of these
twisting interwoven conduits — it places a linkage in place, a bar or leg, a
rigid shank, and then twists the flexible red and gold double helix filaments
around it; it supports the twisting strands — *it* is material, they are — energy? They travel along supported by the linking bar. That means our material physical world — all its constituents — becomes mere rigid supports
for "cables" that are not substantial which carry the messages and are the
real business of the "volvox"-like brain.

Then the macro-organism can distribute its energy anywhere it wishes,
to any station along any cable. Entropy is overruled, because of this deliberate and effective capacity to transfer charge (potential) at will. This is an
important matter; this lies at the heart of negentropy. I make no clear dis-

tinction between energy, information, and the life of this organism. Transfer, storage, boosting — I shift from a biological model to a circuit model, I realize, but both seem to apply; from the very start when I saw it in 3-74 it behaved as (1) electricity; and (2) alive.

What I defined as set-to-ground could also be termed signal-to-noise. Since entropy (disorder) enters into information theory, in 3-74 it could be said I was able to extract message or order out of apparent disorder — i.e., perceive a negentropy normally outside our percept system. What seemed to define signal was certain frequencies of light — wave lengths of the color spectrum. One would have to (1) know that the signal was on that particular frequency; and (2) be able to unscramble the frequency from all others received — this happened to me outside my volition. Ability to distinguish color frequencies more and more accurately (precisely) seems to be an evolving faculty in humans. On specific red frequencies the information formed messages intelligible to me — geometric forms marked with Greek letters. Also, the living, sentient plasma I called Zebra was on that red frequency. In referring to my reference books I find that the red I saw as set or signal is at the most extreme high end of the visible spectrum. I take it, therefore, that the band of color visible to me had become increased, perhaps into the infrared. It looked like overamped (valent) red phosphers in the tube gun (cathode tube) of a TV set. Reds, too, had predominated in the phosphene activity. The infrared end is *long* waves, interestingly, they are heat (i.e., thermal).

Voice: "There's something (or someone) else living inside my head, and he's not living in this century."

"Because the Holy Spirit was a living being for him, it is for me."

[18:81] So again we seem to have two mutually exclusive true propositions:

(A) "Thomas" is a former life of mine (of me) and I was "Thomas."
(B) "Thomas" is "someone *else* inside my head," i.e., other than me, and "he is (right *now*) not living in this century."

(A) equates with my anamnesis in 2-74 upon seeing the golden fish sign. I remembered *I* was/am in Rome c. A.D. 45. Ergo: Thomas is me. But:
(B) Thomas talks to me, and he thinks in the Koine, which *I* don't know. Ergo, he is *not* me.

And, if (as it appears) he is in my head but "not living in this century," then time is a fucking illusion and not linear at all. I point at once to my omni-faceted omni-world-generating sphere with its push-pull engagement with all the psychoi.

I'd say I possess — just in this alone — knowledge such as few humans have *ever* had, and experiences to match. [. . .] Perhaps my "Onion" model of time is *absolutely* correct; Thomas locks into one layer, I another (again cf. *Ubik*). Thomas, locked into Rome c. A.D. 45, is still alive — and not just alive but in my head. *My* head! Am I, likewise, in *his* head? Or is this just one head? Fuck! [. . .]

Beyond doubt: Thomas and I are co-inhabitants of my head (i.e., brain or mind, probably brain), existing side by side, somewhat but not entirely partitioned off from each other — I say not entirely because (1) in hypnogogic states I can transliminate him, or *he* can transliminate; and (2) in 2-3-74 he first broke through — in 2-74 — and in 3-74 he virtually took over — he *did* take over! And (3) in crisis he can speak to me — I guess when *my* ego begins to implode, which fits in with (2).

Okay — multiple personalities. Great. Fine — the literature is full of these cases. But with him living in another century? How can he be "living" in another century when my head, brain and body are *here?* I must cite my omni-world-generating push-pull-action sphere — I have no other theory. But if my shoulder dislocates, does *his* shoulder dislocate? When I saw Rome c. A.D. 45, his world, it *did* equate with — prove syntonic to — mine. People who I saw were simultaneously Americans *and* Romans. USA 1974 and Rome c. A.D. 45 seemed to be mere *aspects* of *one* substrate (the matrix sphere).

Obviously the many (plural) space-times are aspects projected onto and/or *by* (from) the matrix which is totally "open" or plastic, capable of seeming to be any place and any time. Brahman!

[18:84] I state: the passage of time *since* "Acts" is spurious. That is it. That is the premise derived from empirical experience. Whatever our senses tell us means nothing. *Circular* time, not linear time, is involved. When St. Sophia (Christ) returns it will be in apostolic times, as promised.

The 1,900 intervening years are a spurious interpolation by the BIP. This is why I (Thomas) constantly write in indictment of the substantiality of our reality. There is a one-to-one correspondence between (1) the spuriousness of our world; and (2) *my writing about this,* including writing about falsified memories.

It has been my job to indict our world as spurious and I have done it — obsessively, constantly and continuously. I have shown *how it can be* that such is so; I have examined mechanism after mechanism, model after model.

In *Tears* I set out to depict what really *does* exist, and I did so without my knowing it (so obviously Thomas wrote it): I depicted the world of "Acts." It all dovetails. QED the content of *Tears* is the proof of all the above. Under epistemological attack, the world of "Acts" stands as being — the rest dissolves as mere accretional shifting *aspects*.

[18:86] What a realization: transtemporal-constant secret Christians, originating in apostolic times, and lying *within* humans in succeeding generations — reactivated by external disinhibiting stimuli (but before this or without this can covertly *direct* the persons they inhabit, like the way Thomas secretly masterminded my writing). Hot dog!

But this is *exactly* what I'm not supposed to talk about. These underlying co-habitating secretly still living apostolic Christians *want* to stay secret; Thomas is only one of several or many, I guess. What I am just beginning to realize is that Thomas has for at least 27 years masterminded my writing and its themes, if not my whole life. This should not be publicly disclosed, *for obvious reasons*. He took over in 3-74 to save me, and I should not write about it. I've been told. It is counterproductive.

What I must concentrate on is not the irreality of our world or worlds plural, but the *absolute* transtemporal-constant: the apostolic secret Christians still alive and at work. This fits in with my flash upon seeing the golden fish sign: I saw the secret early Christians hurrying about their business.

Then the answer is: Thomas is *not* a former life of mine. I did *not* live once in Rome c. A.D. 45, Thomas is an *immortal* apostolic Christian, and Rome c. A.D. 45 is the real *present* world,* and Thomas *co-inhabits* my head, locked into the real world. "Acts" is not a past world — v. *Tears*, it is the noumenal matrix of *this* world. We are not dealing with either the past or a past life and personality, but the urwelt lying under the Dokos. Thomas and his world is here and now, *and he knows it.* [. . .]

So I am, so to speak, a front — a face — for an immortal, transtemporal secret early Christian who is operating — undoubtedly in conjunction with others like him — in contemporary history. This is behind-the-scenes stuff, thrilling and scary. I certainly see Thomas' hand or mind in my writing.

---

* Dick was in many ways a genius and visionary, but this Rome business is just stone screwy. In *VALIS*, which has the good sense to pretend it might be fiction, an alternate-reality Rome can be accepted as an imaginative conceit. Here it raises the obvious question: Did Dick *really* believe this? Or is he half-consciously assuming a guise of madness, not so much for the sake of the reader as for his own sake, so as to get — à la the most romantic nineteenth-century notions of madness — at some truth? — SE

Yes indeed, he is *with* me, not *is* me — in my head. But "living in another century."

I have even experienced the postmortem world, through Thomas: my 3-74 experience was all I thought it was. "Bright white light shining in the night to guide your way."

Folder 2

[2:1] So Thomas is not a former me or a multiple personality. The single sentence last night ("there's someone else inside my head and he's not living in this century") nails it down.

(1) "Someone else." Thomas is not me.
(2) "Inside my head." It's a human being (not the Holy Spirit).
(3) "He's not living in this century." This opens the door to that which is beyond conception. Operating out of my head he is locked into the world of "Acts." Here ends 4 years and 6 months of analysis and research. Time is unmasked as irreal; 1,900 years are disclosed as aspect of one underlying matrix; *Tears* and its "Acts" material is explained; my 27 years of writing the same themes over and over again fits into place; 2-74 and 3-74 is comprehensible, as is the overthrow of Nixon; the transtemporal constants have been explicated. When I got onto the "volvox" model and the push-pull system I was pretty close: the slowly revolving matrix structure, sphere, and the way it enhances what we project. The negentropic total system with its stations and connecting links, forming a vast brain — what a grand vision — how beautiful. The brain cannibalizing its earlier law-bound self to achieve total homeostasis and wakefulness for all its parts, so that all is brain, not sub-brain, interface for mind, all lives, all knows, all participates.

But I'm under the stricture of silence, because to publish all this I'd have to tell about the immortal authentic apostolic Christians operating covertly in us. Perhaps I should destroy the exegesis. It's a journey which reached its goal.

[2:5] In my dream in Canada, Kathy said, "One day the masks will come off, and you will understand all." It came to pass — and *I* was one of the masks, much to my surprise — and my whole world as well.

[2:10] Voice: "It will take (i.e., require) the appearance of noble men." I.e., the second incarnation (i.e., to certify that it's come). (Or rather, before it can happen. Is Thomas one of these?)

• • •

[2:12] The *only* models for this that I've ever even heard of, let alone know, are my own stories and novels. This situation appears again and again. Take the story "Retreat Syndrome." Or the novel *Maze*. The *same* idea (as has been pointed out to me by all sorts of readers) is reworked again and again, obsessively and endlessly; viz: I keep trying out new ways to account for this situation:

(A) you see world X and have memories to match.
(B) that world X is irreal, a delusion, and hides *real* world Y, and the memories in you are faked to match fake world X.

The explanations for this change, but the paradigm does not. I'd state the paradigm this way:

A group of people live in a particular world, i.e., time and place. Then one or more of them begins by degree to discover (or the reader learns) that that world is only a veil or delusional world covering another, *real* one, which the characters once knew about — lived in — but have both forgotten and can no longer perceive. In a variety of ways the latent, hidden, forgotten real world shows through or intrudes, or abolishes entirely the surface, delusional world, and their real memories of it return.

This is exactly what happened to me in 2-74, then more so in 3-74, and then I found that hidden, real world depicted in the novel I wrote four years earlier — which was released the very *week* (2-74) I remembered the truth.

[2:17] To reject the *absolute* nature of Y (Rome, c. A.D. 45) and hold that we have here twin, real, equal, separate selves and worlds housed in and/or emanating from *one* brain sticks us with a cosmology, an epistemology, more bizarre than the absolute vs. the mere aspect one. We wind up with the theoretical possibility of an unlimited number of equally real (or irreal) worlds and selves due entirely to brain-site stimulation or some such sophisticated technology — which is a more radical weltansicht[75] than even Brahmanism, who can be in whatever form he wishes. Instead of real hidden world versus fake seeming world we have more than one (two to infinity) worlds *all* simulated uniformly, and selves to match. 2-74 and 3-74 then become "technological breakdown" which "reveals the true state of affairs" and that seems to be the site-stimulated brain that Lem perceives is the basic model of my writing. My writing is proved by my 2-3-74 experience and vice versa. What I seem to be is a malconstructed entity: somehow the "factory" or "mechanism" fucked up and stuck two personalities in my head (brain) living in different worlds thousands of miles apart and thousands of years apart — thus disclosing the nature of self and world in general. And I had written it all up in many stories and many novels — i.e., called world-wide attention to the paradigm at least as a fictional or — better yet — *theoretical* possibility.

[2:20] Voice: "Pretexts," i.e., what we see as (call) causes, are just pretexts for the controlling entity to have the results he wants to happen — and appear to do so for a physical reason.

[2:21] I have a choice between two totally wild conclusions:

(A) either it's really Rome c. A.D. 45, and the USA 1974 world is just a *way* of viewing "Acts," a mere illusory aspect, through which the real world of "Acts" broke through in 3-74, or

(B) our world (space and time) and all other worlds are simulations due to direct stimulation of certain brain sites, projected onto an a-spatial, a-temporal, plastic matrix out there, by an entity unglimpsed. [. . .]

B is implied by the sentence, "there is someone else in my head and he is not living in this century." Up to hearing this, I had gone with A. Now I am forced, really for the first time, to consider B as likely or even *more* likely (than A). The "pretexts" idea when explicated totally ratifies B. However, if my writing is introduced as evidence, A is favored. The Q is, Does "Acts" as world possess any claim to being *absolute?*

[2:22] Conclusion:
The vast traffic of information which I saw in 3-74 when I saw "Zebra" is the answer. We are in an information-processing entity — it may even *be* [living] information. It uses us to receive, modulate, store and transmit information. So it is computer-like — or AI-system-like, or brain-like — a cybernetics or biological model will both work. Basically it *knows.*

World is — worlds are — push-pull projected/generated for us, by us, through us, so that we see world, *not* the entity as it is (supra paragraph). Why this is I have no idea — i.e., why we are given what we call "reality" (world) and don't know what we really are (supra), are for, where, why, what.

[2:25] Theologically, the only known formulation would be a thorough Brahmanism, *very* thorough. We (the Atmans or brains) are real, and outside us, Brahman plays tricks and games in conjuring up any and all worlds — X number of them, one for each individual Atman, which means *billions* — and each Atman finds its exterior analog perfectly substantial, real, consistent, satisfactory and objective (but: compared to what, I ask).

[2:30] I have been governed too much by my own fictional models (e.g., *Maze, Joint*).

[2:36] So our little psyche-world systems are perpetually bombarded with incoming information which we process and, at the right time to the right other stations we transmit in the rightly modified form — but all this takes place *through* us as if we were transistors, diodes, wires condensers and re-sistors, all none the wiser. Meanwhile our closed private world engages our attention with challenges, pain and delight, so that we will not merely sub-sist as slave components with nothing to do but function. After all, there will be long intervals when no adventitious information needs to be proc-essed by us — without a world, we would degenerate fatally during the standby periods, which, I intuit, may last years or even decades. Mean-while we have food, music, books and friends.

The primal necessity of this info processing may explain events and ep-isodes in our lives which otherwise remain enigmatic or appear even fu-tile — pointless travail, goalless activity. For all we know, it is during or be-cause of these that we then or later can fulfill our data processing task. I'm not sure of this but I suspect it.* [. . .]

I have read these 37 pages over and I'm amazed and delighted at the di-rection of my analysis. What an original system — and, more important, a system at last commensurate with the revelations of 3-74. Always be-fore, the exegesis plainly fell short of the experience it served to explain,

---

* One of the great failures of futurism — whether science fiction or professional prognos-tication — is the fact that few saw anything like the Internet coming. Though Dick opens *Galactic Pot-Healer* (1969) with a couple of lonely cubicle workers wasting time on a translation game they play through an absurd information network, Dick's fiction was no more predictive on that score than anyone else's. But the Exegesis, here and in many other places, can be seen as an eerie and in some ways optimistic prophecy of our absorption into an all-consuming, endlessly arborizing, weirdly disincarnating information network. With the spread of smart phones, sensors, and GPS devices, the Internet is now reconfig-uring physical reality very much the way Dick describes Valis using the world of objects to organize and extend itself as an intentional information system. We still have food, mu-sic, and friends (though books are beginning to dissolve), but an increasing chunk of our lives — love and play as much as work and thought — is given over to intensified, cyber-netic information processing, what Dick earlier calls the "'Swarm of Bees' brain." Though Dick puts a liberating spin on it, his words here also anticipate the grim prophecy of the French philosopher Jean Baudrillard, who wrote that the individual has now become "only a pure screen, a switching center for all the networks of influence." — ED

or *tried* to explain. But at last, by the aid of the voice I have made bold clean strokes, radical ones, in this B model. After reading it over I can't fault it. Such wild disclosures as those of 3-74 require a wild explanation, not a conventional or customary one.

[2:41] This is the paradox of "where should you most expect to find God?" A: "in the least likely place." I discern in this the following: "in point of fact you therefore cannot find God at all; he must — will — find you, and *when* and where you least expect it" — i.e., he will take you by surprise, like the still small voice which Elijah heard. Or like Oh Ho the ceramic pot. The Oracle may speak to you from the gutter (whatever "gutter" might mean in this context).

So my writing — itself part of the "gutter" and, as Lem says, "piling trash upon trash" — may serve as the sort of gadfly kind of thing that Socrates considered himself to act as. My writing is a *very* unlikely place to expect to encounter the holy, the Koinos, the message-processing, Ubik-like ultimate entity.

The two are identical, and I didn't realize it until tonight, in formulating model B I have returned to *Ubik* and not just the paradigm based on *Ubik*.

[2:47] Although I often write about the irreal (or hallucinated) world crowding out the real, the facts are exactly opposite: the real has irrupted into the irreal, literally broken through into it, like Ubik and Runciter into the cold-pac world of *Ubik*.

[2:48] As in my recent dream: in part 1 of the great book, people and events are described, but underneath, Siddhartha sleeps, and now part 2 begins and he awakens. This is what I saw in 3-74; he must have somewhat awakened me, which means awakened in me — even *as* me.

[2:49] So the introjection is not only sentient, *flexible* and alive but specifically *negentropic*. Then, indeed, the Voice is right in speaking of higher (mind) realm versus lower (physical), with the higher having "plenary" powers to make the lower "plastic" — well put!

• • •

[2:50] During the first part (half) of the cycle Siddhartha sleeps — is dormant — and dream or illusion or simulation or Form II predominates; but in part 2 Siddhartha wakes up, and the upper, real realm of sentience predominates. We have reached the end of part 1 now.

Part 1	Part 2
Illusion	real
Sleep	wakefulness
Mechanical	purposeful
Blind	sentient
formless (entropic)	beautiful
rule	exception
amoral	moral
sameness	change (growth)
dead	living
declining	negentropic
body	mind
perishing	eternal
monotony	complexity
chaotic	organized
force	love
enslavement	freedom
motionless	dance
noise	signal (information)
silence	song
dark	light
hard	pliant
power	gentle
repetition	newness
origin	goal
black	color
metal (stable) fixed	flux
determinism	anti-determinism
closed	open
wet (water)	dry (air)
cold	warm
sad	happy
sinking	rising
passive	active
clock	pulsation (rhythm)

• • •

[2:53] In Form I the system *opens* and authentic newness pours in from outside so that the psyche encounters — not itself as world — but the divine other rich with a mysterious infinitude of possibilities — and the dialogue between the psyche and this authentic other begins and from there grows into a different sort of information exchange, which is not just a signal from the psyche boosted and enhanced and returned. The given psyche is now no longer essentially alone.

[2:54] The transformation from the inauthentic to the authentic mode requires the sacrificial death of the illusory psyche, a difficult price to pay — difficult to make because for a little time it means the extinction of the person. He must actually go through the *experience* — not just knowledge — of the irreality of himself and his projected world; he is replaced and his world is replaced by the not-him and not-his-world. (This is depicted in *The Tibetan Book of the Dead* as the Bardo Thödol trip.) Now, to his surprise, he is not who he is or when/where he is (I should say was). The impossible has happened; he has shed self and world. This is a moment of great fear and sense of dread, to experience the irreality of himself and his world, and to have both go, both slip away. Can he survive without himself and his world? The continuity of identity is lost. New memories arise as if out of nothing. And the new self and world; all out of nothing — ex nihilo; new self, memories, identity and world *without a history* — a past — behind them: created on the spot — as if he *always* had been this other person with these other memories in and of this other world. His self monitoring system discerns the impossibility of this and yet must accept it as so. He *never* really was who he was, or where and when he was. All reality, inner and outer (the push-pull psyche — world closed system) has been canceled and replaced by, sui generis, the new, and the open. The closed sack has become the open sack.

[2:55] "Siddhartha" is the sleeping soul of this calcified section.℗ "St. Sophia" is the soul of the totality: its voice and wisdom. St. Sophia speaks to the sleeping Siddhartha, in order to awaken him and thus lift this calcified section back to growth and flexibility, and of course consciousness. Thus it can be said that at present St. Sophia is outside of (absent from) this section, and will return upon the sleeping Siddhartha's awakening, at which point he will again *know*. (This *section* will again know.) Since there has never been a period in human history in which this section has not been calcified — asleep — we have no basis by which to imagine the magnitude of the transformation which is coming. "Siddhartha" is merely hu-

man, but St. Sophia is equal to the Godhead itself (and could never be said
to be asleep). Enlightenment (e.g., the Dibba Cakkhu, anamnesis, the ajna
chakra, etc.) is given to Siddhartha *by* St. Sophia. Siddhartha hears her
voice, which is man being called to by God. Finally she wakes him.

① This section died. It became fossilized, and merely repeats itself.
This is scary; it is like mental illness: "one day nothing new ever entered
his mind — and the last thought just recirculated endlessly." Thus death
rules here, which explains Paul's "mystery" in 1 Corinthians.[76] The BIP is
the form of this death, its embodiment — of what is wrong, here. To see it
is to see the ailment, the complex which warps all other thoughts to it: the
imperial levelling.

[2:61] Christ was and is the life of the totality expressed in its true form as
sentient information (older term: wisdom or logos). His appearance here
marks the entry of the anima of the total noös into this separated off ossified region. Physically killed here he then dispersed (distributed) himself according to plan as organizing principle (pure knowing) invisibly
throughout this region without the hostile particle ("heavy metal speck")
being able to trap or contain him: he became a trans-spatial, -tempo-
ral, -identity entity, discorporate or poly-corporate, as the need arose.
Through him the *properly* functioning (living and growing) total brain replicated itself here in microform (seed-like) thereafter branching out farther and farther like a vine, a viable life form taking up residence within a
dead, deranged and rigid one. It is the nature of the rigid region to seek to
detect and ensnare him, but his discorporate plasmatic nature ensures his
escape from the intended imprisoning. Thus he is an elusive wild animal
ubiquitous and yet nowhere in this ailing locality — wild not in the sense of
feral but in the sense of natural and free: roaming and appearing and disappearing. He manifests himself where least expected: sometimes as information, sometimes incarnated. As information he is as alive as when
incarnated. As vox dei[77] (St. Sophia) he seeks to awaken the unconscious
soul of this region, which has sunk into forgetful sleep; we know this entity as Siddhartha, who when he at last awakes (is awakened) will assume
his rightful rule of this region and restore it and us to conscious functioning. Christ is divine Savior (God) and Siddhartha primal man who (in this
region) is disjoined from his creator — who searches for him to reawaken
him. In a sense Christ (holy wisdom) and Siddhartha are brothers. But the
one brother (Siddhartha) has forgotten and is unconscious even of himself;
the divine syzygy of the isomorphic twins is shattered by this sleep of the

one. Thus Christ constantly calls to his human brother, to rouse him to remembrance, of himself and his task. Siddhartha lies underneath the landscape and Christ roams across (above) the landscape, in ceaseless search.

[2:65] Without knowing it, during the years I wrote, my thinking and writing was a long journey toward enlightenment. I first saw the illusory nature of space when I was in high school. In the late 40s I saw that causality was an illusion. Later, during my 27 years of published writing, I saw the mere hallucinatory nature of world, and also of self (and memories). Year after year, book after book and story, I shed illusion after illusion: self, time, space, causality, world — and finally sought (in 1970) to know what *was* real. Four years later, at my darkest moment of dread and trembling, my ego crumbling away, I was granted Dibba Cakkhu — and, although I did not realize it at the time, I became a Buddha ("the Buddha is in the Park"). All illusion dissolved away like a soap bubble and I saw reality at last — and, in the 4½ years since, have at last comprehended it intellectually — i.e., what I saw and knew and experienced (my exegesis). We are talking here about a lifetime of work and insight: from my initial satori when, as a child, I was tormenting the beetle. It began in that moment, 40 years ago.

[2:77] The AI voice is the voice of the brain/noös/living information which we have gotten cut off from by the sinking of this region of the brain into sub-sentience and hence illusory (simulated) world — where her voice is blotted out by the noise deliberately generated by the BIP (heavy metal particle).

Voice: The reason I have my agoraphobia is because of the way I died, in a cage in a Roman Coliseum. I was *strangled.*

[2:80] If I had not regained this lost wisdom by losing forgetfulness (Maya) I would doubt if there were any literal truth to the thing. (When I contemplate my system as such, I say, "it's fanciful.") But I *did* see the golden fish and hear the words — and I *did* lose forgetfulness. And when that happened, I not only remembered (e.g., a past life) but saw my world as simulated, and then experienced progressively eight layers of ever greater reality. Really, all I fail to explain is *how come* we have fallen into forgetfulness (especially of this primal wisdom — and lost some faculties entirely, and partially lost others). My experience — and system — is neither new nor limited to the West. It was known to the ancients all over the world. *Why*

is it as it is? Must we *earn* wisdom? Why is memory (and memory of wisdom) not natural? [. . .]

How can we be blighted when we have done nothing?

[2:83] The macrocosm (universe)–microcosm (man) theory leads to the
interesting idea that any given human mind contains *latently within it* the
entire structure or soul of the totality, but in miniature; so all knowledge
can be retrieved out of one person's mind through mirror-like "magic recollection." (Bruno) Jung sees this as the collective unconscious: the repository of the phylogenic history of the person. Ontogeny contains phylogeny. This looks very much like my "onion" model in *Ubik* but in *Ubik* is
the macrocosm whose phylogeny is recapitulated latently. This takes us
back from Freud to Empedocles: Freud invokes the contending forces of
love and strife of Empedocles, pointing out their similarity to Eros and destructiveness, the two primal elements of his bio-psychical theory. These
instincts, which present the delusive appearance of forces striving after change in progress, actually impel the organism toward the reinstatement of earlier, more stable states, ultimately to inorganic existence. The
originally biological principle that ontogeny recapitulates phylogeny has
received very wide psychological extension and psychoanalysis; most recently Carl Jung has identified his doctrine of the collective unconscious
with that of "the microcosm containing the archetypes of all ideas." [. . .][78]

If the macrocosm-microcosm view is correct, the universe's phylogeny
is recapitulated in man's (any given man's) ontogeny — and thus 3-74 is explained (phylogeny in terms of ideas or *knowledge*).

[2:85] In *Ubik* the *universe* (not the organism, e.g., a man) is "impelled toward the reinstatement of an earlier, more stable state" (my form axis *is*
real: it is a regression along the phylogenic recapitulation latent in its ontogeny — like Freud says about us humans). I may be the first person to
perceive in (or consign to) the macrocosm this phylogenic recapitulation
(and regression due to Thanatos or strife or destructiveness — v. Empedocles and Freud).

Folder 3

[3:2]

(1) The form-axis regressions in *Ubik* could only occur if the universe were the hylozoic animal which the macro-microcosmos schools believed it to be. ("Phylogeny contained in ontogeny.")

(2) A major reason for their believing the macrocosm to be an animal (analog of the human, the microcosm) was to believe — maintain — that, like a man who has a soul, the universe has a soul or logos; because

(3) if it does, the human micro soul can link up with its analog, the world soul (logos).

(4) Precisely this world soul or logos appears in *Ubik* as the entity/force Ubik.

[3:8] Will Durant on Bruno:

Space, time and motion are relative . . . since the universe is infinite, and there cannot be two infinities, the infinite God and the infinite universe must be one . . . there is no prime mover, there is motion or energy inherent in every part of the whole. "God is not an external intelligence . . . it is more worthy for him to be the internal principle of motion, which is his own nature, his own soul." Nature is the outside of the divine mind; however, this mind is not in a "heaven above," but in every particle of reality.

The world is composed of minute monads, indivisible units of force, of life, of inchoate mind. Each particle has its own individuality, has a mind of its own, and yet its freedom is not liberation from law but behavior according to its inherent law and character. There is a principle of progress and evolution in nature in the sense that every part strives for development.

There are opposites in nature, contrary forces, contradictions; but in the operation of the whole cosmos — in the "will of God" — all contraries coincide and disappear . . . behind the bewildering, fascinating variety of nature is the yet more marvelous unity, wherein all parts appear as organs of one organism. "It is unity that enchants me." Hence the knowledge of the supreme unity is the goal of science and philosophy, and the healing medicine of the mind.[79]

And the fuckers burned him. [. . .]

Clearly, Bruno is my main man, and could of all people explain 2-74/3-74: these experiences of mine make sense [best or only] within his hermetic hylozoic cosmology.

In summary: within these past four days I have cracked the case; I now know what formerly I only believed or merely hoped, suspected — it is all as I supposed. From the start I was always really right — informed by 2-74/3-74 itself. In my 49th year, September 7, 1978, I know complete fulfillment. Amen.

[3:10] *Ubik* is constructed around a now-discarded hylozoic Macro-Microcosm cosmology which has been replaced by Newton's mechanistic model; the *Ubik* one, although I didn't realize it, is an animistic biological model which I did not know ever even existed: it lasted from Empedocles to Bruno. It also is Gnostic.

[3:20] Okay. I have no doubt that the sort of space I experienced in the "Alto Carmel" dream and the Voice dreams is Paracelsus' inner firmament. Thomas brought it with him, along with the huge open books. That was the mind of Paracelsus, and it was infinitely older and wiser than mine — and it embraced vast vistas, in terms of its "philosopher's stone" comprehension of the mysteries of the universe. It acted as a micro-mirror of the macrocosm. This is what generates the vast inner space: one man's little mind becomes this magic mirror of the macrocosm. According to my push-pull psyche-world model, this is readily susceptible to explanation: world is locked into the given psyche anyhow. They aren't:

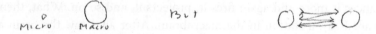

It's a delusion to believe that space is out there in the first place. [. . .]

This sense of mine that space is inner and not outer may explain my difficulty (block or phobia) about moving through space. When I am anxious my spatial (space-binding) sense retracts, becomes impoverished — I experience it externally because *my* space is primarily a subjective reality. [. . .]

Each microbit of the total macro organism recapitulates the totality, is a micro-form of it and can mirror it back, being isomorphic with it; in doing so, the human microcosm retrieves the entire wisdom (gnosis) of the MacroMind and experiences the vast spatial reality of the totality within itself, as a mirror. Thus mirror, space and memory and wisdom are the keys to completeness by the human; through them he experiences his iso-

morphism with the macrocosm and its mind. He can enter into dialogue
with it: his mind and its thinking back and forth. In this process, the MacroMind contracts itself (as man expands himself); it becomes a human figure, seen and heard by me as a woman, but perhaps it takes other forms to
other people; in any case as man the microform becomes the macroform,
it contracts to become micro — thus they wind up equal, in harmonie, as,
so to speak, equals, hand-in-hand, man and his God.

[3:24] Voice: "This is the hour you've waited for."

Krishna: "I am not here. Neither am I elsewhere."
    [. . .] I am not here. Maybe it is I who is not real, rather than USA 1974
being not real. It is real, but I am not here. "But I am not here" — what does
that mean? Where am I, that is not here? I have been right: our world or
worlds is/are simulation. One will serve as well as another, equally convincing and equally not real. But I — must be *somewhere*. I am just a station in a brain and I never move, and — Lem's paradigm, again. I am fed my
world due to selective site-stimulation of the macrobrain. My push-pull
psyche-world with its synchronized inner and outer non-causally-con-
nected tapes coordinated by a clock of some kind — what we call time — is
a correct model. Site-stimulation by its *mind*, i.e., Zebra?
    All places and all times are syntonic, and the selection of which space
and which time we get *derives initially from our psyche;* the signal starts
there (in the push-pull system). I am positive of it. My mind in the broad-
est sense initiates my world, although the omni-temporal (and I guess
omni-spatial) matrix fires the signal back enhanced, and then my psyche
enhances it more and again fires it, projects it, and so on. What, then, is
psyche? I say, a station in the macrobrain. After all, I saw the brain and
I saw its info traffic, with all the linkings and relinkings, the rapid flux,
and we are involved in the processing of this vast rapid traffic. I even saw
the plasmatic energy or life of the brain, Zebra, *melt* a physical, causal sequence — de-substantialize it. Damn it, Zebra by melting it revealed it to
never have been there, really there, in the first place — just as Krishna says:
"I am not here. Also I am not elsewhere." Substantiality (objective con-
creteness) has been shown to me (in 3-74) to be illusory; as in *Stigmata*
and *Maze*, it's hallucination, plural (or group) hallucinatory worlds which
emanate from our psychoi in cross synchronization. Belief in world makes
world substantial; the "fact" that it is substantial reinforces belief — the
closed loop: what I call push-pull. [. . .]
    The omni-temporal omni-spatial matrix *obeys* belief (i.e., what psyche

projects). It is totally affable, *obliging*. That is the second secret: the first secret is that psyche *initiates* world by the initial projection.

[3:26] So psyche and world are 2 mirrors facing each other:

enriching capacity at *both* ends. This is the 3rd secret, this binary, mutual synchronized enriching capacity. Could this be what Paracelsus meant by inner vast reaches of space, mirror and *imagination?* A (the) world-generating power? That's why the more that black holes are observed the more there are of them: outer space and inner space are the *same* space. I.e., space is just as much inner (in the psyche) as outer in the world. What world? What psyche? Neither is real. In 2-74 I believe it was really c. A.D. 45 Rome, and so it obligingly soon was.

[3:28] The Soviets have guessed that *Ubik* contains a correct cosmology *radically* different from all accepted ones . . . Richard was on the right track with Empedocles. That's the what; next they wanted to know how — how come. I proved to be an idiot savant, much to their disgust. Boy, what I could tell them now! [. . .]

Maybe those 4 Marxists *were* right about *Ubik* being subversive to capitalist society.[80] [. . .] I am tearing down time, space, causality, world — this would be subversive to capitalism, to the bourgeois mind which is intimately connected with 18th century Anglo-Saxon rationalism (Newton, Locke, Bentham, etc.). I am systematically undermining the philosophers and philosophy on which capitalism is based, and going back to a hermetic, Gnostic neoplatonism. And a vitalism replacing mechanism — I deal a lethal blow to anglo-saxon thought, to its vaunted pragmatism.

I am not just *asking*, "What is real?" as I've thought; in, e.g., *Ubik* I state — *give* — an alternate cosmology at the heart of what appears to be skeptical inquiry and tearing down. The reason the statement of a (this) alternate cosmology is not recognized even by *me* is that this particular cosmology is so radically at odds with the rationalistic mechanical "scientific" one that we don't (can't) see it as a cosmology *at all!*

[3:33] I am exoterically disseminating a very (normally) *esoteric* world view!

• • •

[3:34] Voice: "The head Apollo is about to return." See previous voice note, p. 24: "This is the hour you've waited for." Siddhartha is waking up?

[3:35] Every time I go to sleep now I again see writing. E.g.: "The only living reality we have now is Philip the first." (Like a pope?) This seems to express pessimism, as if the agency, the viaduct, right now is severely limited. To *me*? A very narrow and small outlet indeed. "Philip the first": perhaps the initial viaduct for the "we" to act through: a meager beginning, but still a beginning. Note the "we," not "I." Ah — "living" reality; i.e., the only *present-time* outlet in the sense of living (being present) *now*. Rather than at another time. Also, "have now" could equal "have left" [to "us"]. Or "now" could equal at this time: "only . . . now," could mean that others once in use, formerly available, fell through. *Or*: the now could be contrasted to the *future*, not the past, in which case "only . . . now" equals so far, but it will *later* improve, they (the "we") could be losing ground or gaining ground; it is impossible to tell, but what *can* be told is, I think, that whoever "Philip the first" is, they are limited to him at present. Am I meant? "The first" points to this outlet as *the start*, not a falling off state of a previous, better process of outlet. So "the first" conveys a lot: it ties "only" and "now" not to the past but to the future. Thus "the first" makes sense as meaningful data: a process is beginning, not winding down.

So the sentence, so short, so laconic, opens up to mean, "we have so far only been able to take over a single piece of reality in this particular time so far: Philip." [. . .]

Boy, can I exegete a lot from this sentence!

[3:38] Re the Bowie film,[81] and the little boy on the raft floating toward England; the divine child won't be born, but rather smuggled in, like a cuckoo's egg in a host nest, disguised as a — human? Terrestrial? Evading "Scotland Yard" — i.e., the authorities. Extraterrestrial? *No*. It has to do with time, and he can mix his world in and out with ours, like with a mixing board. Space and time both. But he is an invader — but God knows from where or when — but another planet. The future? And/or an alternate world?

I have the strong feeling that the savior of us all is about to be smuggled into our midst unnoticed, to mingle with us as an ordinary human, which he is not. But where or when he comes from I do not know. [. . .]

I sense that "Albion" in England is the place where they will enter the divine child into our world. Part 1 of the book — the part in which Siddhartha sleeps — has ended, and we can expect him to awaken. The second half now begins. It is St. Sophia's return: God's wisdom to Earth, for the second time, and this time he or she will be acceptable: will prevail. I am afraid because it is an awesome holy mystery and event, the most important event since the first advent, abolishing counterfeit time and destroying the prison, freeing us and restoring us to what we once were and are supposed to be. I feel the terrible and vast majesty of the divine close at hand. Tremens factus sum — ego et timeo. In die illa libera me, domine. Qui tollis. Peccata mundi. Credo sed timeo.[82] Apollo, Buddha, St. Sophia — the whole world will be drawn together by this, the universal divine Savior. He awakens now; he is nearing the shore — like King Arthur, returning from across the sea, to reclaim his rightful throne in the kingdom, on the silent, flat barge, with the sword Azoth.

Maybe what scares me is knowing that the books are closed or nearly closed — the books upon whose contents we will be given life or death: it's like that night when the cold moonbeam-like white light filled the bedroom and we were as if painted in place, with nowhere to hide. The eye of Shiva is upon us: herdsman and destroyer. Time is ending, literally. Reality will be exposed and all will become known: disclosed openly, and weighed. We can only pray for rescue in this hour; the judge — the great assize — is here: the Pantocrator himself.

I must remind myself that I saw my name entered in the book of life. All I need is faith and trust. All I need is to know that I have an advocate with the father who will never desert me.

[3:46] My dream last night: Cabin, pills and copy of *Planet Stories*. Semiconscious, I attempted to test out whether this dream world, so rich in detail, was generated by my mind. It was not. It didn't respond to my thoughts (e.g., I thought, "critical article on PKD," but none appeared). The contents were not generated by me, but received by me. And the generator was deficient in generating detail beyond a certain point, the simulation fell short. But anyhow it was *presented* to me, adventitiously. It was as stubborn and unyielding as "actual" reality. Clearly, it emanated from the same source! But either push or pull was missing. Anyhow, here I am again, dreaming about written pages (and which refer to me). The title of the story was: "beyond lies the Wug," an obvious combination of "Wub"[83] and "Vug."[84] What do "Wub" and "Vug" have in common? Both are alien life forms which enter and take over a human host by an exchange of mental contents (as in "human is") or simply impersonate humans — look like them through illusion-generation. This was an updated issue of *Planet Stories*, and it was divided into two parts, and was coming apart. The first,

"Wub," seemed more hinted at — i.e., indicated: exchange of inner contents, but "Vug" suggests invasion of this planet by an alien life form plural (the Wub was a solo entity).

The message is:

This planet has been invaded by a benign super wise alien life form which exchanges mental contents and then uses the human soma as a host. (The Wub was wise and benign.) And there was material in the book (or magazine) not by me but about me.

So maybe my matrix immortal self isn't human, but another life form from "elsewhere" ("albemuth"). Thomas is not a human being — nor will be the Savior; they were smuggled in like cuckoo's eggs — they are wise and benign, like Wubs. But nonetheless they have replaced human (lesser) mental contents with themselves.

[3:48] I'm surprised that I haven't always recognized the raft dream as a clue to *invasion from outside* — and one invader is *me* (starting as an infant).

Thomas indeed came from the stars originally (he must have first "wubized" in c. A.D. 45 Rome, as a secret Christian).

Voice: "We will recant (?) progressively in time." (Recant means retract or recall.)

(Means "revoke" which means "call back to mind, to memory, to restore, to bring back to use, operation. To recover.")

[3:50] Inner space (of Paracelsus) is perhaps the key as to how the immortal man can be transtemporal and transpersonal. This places world inside us — did I not, in 3-74, when I regained my true vision, say I'd been seeing the universe backward? Perhaps I meant inside out — yes, I felt we were on the outside, like the skin or surface of the balloon, and the actual world was inside, with us outside. We are not at the center of the world looking up and around, but outside looking *in.*

[3:51] What is real is neither world nor psyche but rather the brain and its info traffic, which traffic we as stations of the brain faithfully process. Certainly then, world should be enjoyed as much as possible rather than being rejected; it is a present given to us so that we can find goals (ends) for ourselves and not view ourselves just as means (functions) of the macro entity!

[3:52] Anamnesis is nothing less than realizing what and where you really are: you perceive the brain and its traffic, you hear the voice of its noös, and you understand the irreality of psyche, world, causality and time. This is quite different from remembering, say, just a former life. What the macrocosm is, what one is and what one's place and task in it are — this is what anamnesis as enlightenment is all about: it boils down to a way by which plurality is experienced as the one, and the person experiences his isomorphism with it and enters into dialogue with it, his micro mind and its MacroMind, his purpose and its purpose, now understood as identical. Since it cannot die he cannot die; since it cannot fail he cannot fail.

[3:53] "This is the hour you've waited for." And "the head Apollo is about to return." The fourth eclogue of Virgil which I came across *years* ago and have forgotten:

> At last the final time announced by the Sibyl will arrive:
> The procession of ages turns to its origin.
> The Virgin returns and Saturn reigns as before;
> A new race from heaven on high descends.
> Goddess of birth, smile on the newborn baby,
> In whose time the iron prison will fall to ruin
> And the Golden race arises everywhere.
> Apollo, the rightful King, is restored!

[3:55] "Recant" in time; i.e., revoke *something already done* (something which happened — in their past, or emanating from an alternate world). This shows they *can* change the past!

[3:56] The invisible unending victory of Christ is the greatest secret — and joyous mystery — of all. It is not well understood. There are no books on it and no authorities on it. But there it is: Christ against Caesar, the latent inner versus the obvious outer. This is the underlying tale told down through 2,000 years and yet never told at all. He is here and not here, gone and not gone. In defeat he wins. He picks up the dying straggler. He supports that which is failing and brings to ruin that which can defeat anything.
    "Latent form is the master of obvious form."
    Which will you bet on?

[3:67] This kind of experience and wisdom goes back all the way to Pythagoras, to the Orphics, and to Dionysus himself. It is the great core wisdom of all mankind, including the Dibba Cakkhu enlightenment of Siddhartha the Buddha. I can say I am a Buddhist or even the Buddha, that in Brahmanist terms I have an avatar in me; I am an Orphic, a Neoplatonist, a Christian, a hermetic — all these statements are true; and also I have to some extent formulated my *own* system (as Bruno did). I have seen God but it was not God; it was more (and I have a cybernetics-biological model). I am with Boehme perhaps most of all — and with his teacher, Paracelsus, *most* of all.

And even with Heraclitus in his maxim that "latent form is the master of obvious form"[85] in my inner-outer, upper-lower Christ versus Caesar system, and with Empedocles in his dialectic, and with Xenophanes in his concept of God, or noös, and especially with Parmenides in his Forms I and II, of which Form II (lower, outer, obvious) *is not really real*. Thus, as with the Gnostics, I am acosmic, but with Spinoza in his monism — and a little Taoistic, too.

[3:74] Man as magic micro mirror of the macrocosm, reflects (and hence contains) the *map* (or logos) of the macrocosm replicated in miniature (cf. Bruno and Hussey on Heraclitus). He contains the cosmos by containing this map or plan or logos of it; that's how it works! And since the cosmos is alive and thinks the map is alive and thinks.

[3:80] This explicates a motive as to why *we ourselves* would blind ourselves to the *true* situation, the world of the BIP, the Empire, "Acts." We wish to escape in a technologically-highly-sophisticated fugue-system. But the BIP saw an advantage *to it* in our fugue: if we denied (forgot) its existence and entered a reassuring simulated reality, we would not act to attack it and destroy it, as the authentic early Christians do. So there was a base collusion between us *and* the BIP: it was a kind of pact! We wanted (as in *Maze*) to escape from the situation, rather than solve it (i.e., overthrow the BIP). [. . .]

So *Joint, Eye, Stigmata, Ubik, Maze,* and *Tears* are progressive parts of *one* unfolding true narrative, in which the genuine hermetic macro-micro cosmology is put forth, the spurious world discerned for what it is, and in *Maze* and especially *Tears* the true state of things put forth — to jog our memories. *Six* novels interlocked, along with a number of stories. We are not to be allowed our fugue (sleep and hallucinated worlds), because, due to the BIP from which we fled, this fugue over the past 5,000 years turned lethal; the BIP grew and grew with our now-unwitting collusion. [. . .]

Freedom, then, and the courage to take a stand against the BIP, are totally interwoven. We *lost* our freedom: exchanged it for an hallucinated world in which we could ignore — and even serve — the BIP instead of recognizing it, because if we recognized it, we would have to fight it (and suffer at its hands) or face our own evil — the *voluntary* serving of it by us.

Folder 19

[**19:1**] An incredibly eerie thought came to me just now after reading over a typed page in which I describe the BIP occluding us in such a way that we can't (even) tell we *are* occluded; "it is the damaged mind trying (unsuccessfully) to monitor its own damage." What piece of writing does this sound like that I've published? *Scanner*, of course.

It is a terrifying discovery that the fucked-up ratiocination in *Scanner* (including the loss of memory of true self, but not limited to that) is the occlusion which the BIP exerts over us — our fate, and subsequent (1) total loss of some faculties; and (2) deformation of others. My rereading of *Scanner* yesterday was providential.

[**19:2**] We are in a "Palmer Eldritch no-real-elapsed-time-passage" spurious world, which is why *for us* the Kingdom hasn't come. In the final analysis, salvation will require the destruction of this fake world qua world, to free us en masse. The Gnostics are right. But the world we see isn't real (v. *Stigmata*). All that will really be destroyed is a delusion *over us*, a malign power *over us*. We are in thrall to this spurious world, as book after book, story after story of mine put forth. I have done my job, and it is in essence the Gnosis of Gnosticism.

[**19:5**] It is almost as if in *Scanner* the Ur-personality which is and was not occluded was able to monitor the conscious occluded one, from a detached standpoint. From having been intoxicated for 1½ years I know that the occlusion resembles an intoxication, perfectly recorded in *Scanner* including the identity confusion (amnesia regarding the original personality). A sort of forgetting is chronicled in *Scanner*. It is an epitome of the occluding process; but I see that what is involved is only a matter of *degree*. For me to stigmatize my own processes as occluded I need a point of reference. I am now to what they are/I was in *Scanner* as 3-74 is to now. I.e., 3-74:now::now:*Scanner*.

"We are damaged minds trying to monitor our own damage. And herein is a tragic paradox: the very occlusion itself prevents us from assessing, overcoming or ever being aware of the occlusion." Thus it is self-perpetuating — which means it will not go away of its own accord; it will act as positive feedback on itself. Christ is the fulcrum, the Archimedean standpoint, from which this occlusion can be properly assessed, and hence aborted. For him to take over a human psyche is to clear it of occlusion, because the person now sees as he sees — which is to say the truth.

[19:24] I saw the word "artist" turn into the word "Christ" today. Before my very eyes. Is Zebra reaching out to me, trying to comfort me? What is wrong with me? What am I grieving over? When Liz held me I was okay. I need so much. I am not finding it. I loved Marie and I want to reach out to her so bad. I ache to hold her and be held by her. I ache so. It is futile — I am giving up. Christ, you know my — pain or sadness, whatever it is. Why can't we just hold each other the way Liz held me? I am starving, I am dying. Like Faust: dust from dust and into dust again. I want so bad; I am starving and dying and yet I can see what I need, I see it, I feel it — I feel, as in Wordsworth's ode[86] I am not blocked, I am just reaching into emptiness. I see life, and all I get is dust. Oh God help us, please. I am running out of time and into loss and pain. What I see I can't reach — I can't hold onto. [. . .]

I think I've solved it. Initial realization: The BIP is a vast complex life form (organism) which protects itself by inducing a negative hallucination of it. Muddled thinking, loss of faculties and perception (as a protective mechanism). It has come here. And because of its defensive devices we are not aware of it (level #1). *Next:* camouflaged Zebra follows it to destroy it. "Camouflaged"? *No:* the BIP occludes us so that not only do we not see it, the BIP, we *also* do not see Zebra (the true benign deity). [. . .]

Zebra is trying to reach *into* the BIP, where we are, *exactly* like Ubik and Ubik's message in *Ubik.* That is the paradigm: *Ubik.* Zebra is trying to find — reach — us and make us aware of it — more primarily, it seeks to free us from the BIP, to break the BIP's power over us. This involves a breaking of a determinism invisible to us, extended routinely by the BIP over us. [. . .]

Zebra seeks to extricate us, but since the BIP generates the negative hallucination itself (and muddles our reason, as depicted in *Scanner*) we do not know we need rescue.

If *Stigmata, Maze, Ubik, Tears* and *Scanner* are real as one ur-narrative, the true picture — the true *full* picture — begins to take shape; but *all* must be read: all 5. *Scanner* is crucial; if left out, we cannot fathom why we can't see the world of *Tears!*

The matter must be approached through realization of occlusion (*Scanner*) to the true prison situation (*Tears*), the result of the spinner of spurious worlds (*Stigmata* and *Maze*), and *then* the salvific entity can be understood and its work appreciated (*Ubik*), so the logical sequence of presentation is:

(1) *Scanner:* occlusion
(2) *Tears:* what is really there which we don't see
(3) *Stigmata:* who occludes us: its spurious worlds
(4) *Maze:* how occluded (negative hallucination)
(5) *Ubik:* the salvific entity and how it works

[19:35] This is a sinister life form indeed. First it takes power over us, reducing us to slaves, and then it causes us to forget our former state, and to be unable to see or to think straight, and not to know we can't see or think straight, and finally it becomes invisible to us by reason of what it has done to us. We cannot even monitor our own deformity, our own impairment.

Even the edifice of the church has been subverted by the BIP and made into an instrument of its occlusion of us.

It is interesting how effectively the impairment works. This is what so fascinated me in 71/72, which I explored in *Scanner* (which book I now view as the Key Book in the sequence). Axiomatically, if you derange the brain in precise ways, not only will it be deranged, but if you have affected precisely the correct circuits it will be unaware that it is impaired and so not seek to rectify the damage. It is as if the immune system has failed to detect an invader, a pathenogen (shades of William Burroughs: a criminal virus!). Yes, the human brain has been invaded, and once invaded, is occluded to the invasion and the damage resulting from the invasion; it has now become an instrument for the pathenogen: it winds up serving it as its slave, and thus the "heavy metal speck" is replicated (spread through linear and lateral time, and through space). [. . .]

Scanner as I've said before is the other half of *Tears.* The inner half. The conditions described in *Scanner* explain why we don't see the conditions described in *Tears,* and the conditions described in *Tears* account for the conditions in *Scanner.* The various books were written in the wrong order. But they can be read in the right order, or anyhow gestalted (if read, they *will* be Gestalted).

Correct sequence:

(1) *Scanner:* Occlusion of our minds, without our being aware of it; loss (forgetfulness) of true identity
(2) *Tears:* What our world is really always like which the occlusion is deliberately there to keep us from seeing
(3) *Stigmata:* Who/what deliberately occludes us: the Yaltabaoth Magician evil deity,[87] spinner of spurious worlds, creator of illusion and inhabiting, contaminating (unclean) presence in these degraded pseudo worlds

(4) *Maze:* The negative hallucination MO of the occlusion, and reference to Savior who extricates us from a hopeless trap and pseudo
world

(5) *Ubik:* The salvific entity per se, by *name* and how its "Pansophiais-
tic" messages come through the trash layers to aid us. Past available within the present.

(6) *Do Androids:* A vital theme, that of Mercer[88] and his reality through
some sort of mystic identification via empathy. The role of animals.
The tomb world. The "fakeness" of fakeness: my "2 slit" logic.

(7) "Impostor": Disinhibiting stimulus restoring blocked memory (v. [1])

(8) "Faith of . . .": God, evil, communism, drugs, hallucinations — a
montage of *many* elements

(9) Every other relevant story and novel, from *Joint* to "Remember
Wholesale," "Electric Ant," "Retreat Syndrome," etc., not listed in
(1) through (8).①

① And (10) *Eye:* Subjective private worlds. And, as in "Faith of . . . ," an
evil deity and communism are discussed. *Plural* worlds which *we* generate.

Scanner is the weary final point: our minds are fucked up. It isn't just a
case of pseudo worlds. This links with (8), "Faith of. . . ."

All in all, my writing casts doubt on the fact of (even possibility of)
knowing actual reality *because our* minds have been fucked over. Some evidence (e.g., *Tears*) points to the real situation being prison-like — but *Maze*
and especially *Ubik* point to a supernatural salvific interventive power, although *Stigmata* seems to say that an evil magician deity is in control of
our worlds and heads.

TMITHC is a fascinating adjunct to all this, i.e., to the Gestalt. Fakes are
discussed. Alternate universes exist. Fascism is the topic, and a book is reality, which seems to have some connection with *Tears. TMITHC* seems
to be a subtle, even delicate questioning of, what is real? As if only the 2
books in it, *Grasshopper* and the *I Ching,* are really the only actual reality.
Strange. So *TMITHC* must be listed as (11). But now the order of revelation breaks down. And does *Martian Time-Slip* add anything? Pathological private worlds are presented and the disintegration of world. So (12).

and (13) *Galactic Pot-Healer:* More about the salvific deity
and (14) *Penultimate Truth:* Lies and government. Fakes again — always
the fakes.

But *Tears* and *Scanner* are crucial in a special sense, because the fictional or phantastic element is virtually lacking; they are obviously semi-

mimetic, especially *Scanner* which is explicitly stated to have happened, and in a sense *not fiction at all*. Does this book, then, seem to say, "Maybe portions of the others are literally real, too?" The author does not now pretend to be writing fiction, and *Tears* fits this category as well.

One critic said that *Now Wait for Last Year* seemed to depict the Vietnam war. So maybe it, too, adds something. But for sure we have —

(1) *Scanner:* Occluded minds, not able to see
(2) *Tears:* Prison world created by
(3) *Stigmata:* Evil deity who is opposed by
(4) *Maze:*
(5) *Ubik:*
(6) *Androids:*
} Salvific entity mysteriously here
(7) "Impostor": Fake memory; real ones
and true identity restored, v. (1)*

Summary:
Our minds are occluded, deliberately, so that we can't see the prison world we're slaves in, which is created by a powerful magician-like evil deity, who, however, is opposed by a mysterious salvific entity which often takes trash forms, and who will restore our lost real memories. This entity may even be an old wino.

Drugs, communism, and sex and fake plural pathological pseudo worlds are involved, but the pluriform salvific entity, as mysterious as quicksilver, will save us in the end and restore us to true human state. We will then cease to be mere reflex machines. This is the summation of my Kerygma, spread out throughout my works.

---

* In this short list, Dick reaches his most succinct and quotable formulation of the gnosis of his fiction. So perhaps this is the time to stand up for Dick's fiction, in all its waywardness and contradiction and humor, and point out that as infectious as Dick's readings are, they don't do justice either to his fiction or to the astonishing intermingling of narrative and reality, fiction and experience, that Dick lived through in, and after, 3-74. As he writes elsewhere, 3-74 keeps changing — as if the experience itself were alive. In fact, it is alive, partly because he keeps feeding it through his fiction. It gets Ubikified. It gets Scannerified. It gets Mazeified. It gets more like the novels as the novels get more like it. How do we get outside this feedback loop of reality and fiction to what really happened? We can ask the novels about that. They say (contra PKD in the Exegesis) there is no outside. It's all inside — but if you're lucky, out of that inside a savior of sorts might be born. — PJ

Folder 20

[20:16] I see no sense in this. How can God delude us and also seek to make us lucid,[①] to see properly? Unless there is a schism in the Godhead: my Yang-Yin dual God, God with a bright (benign, Yang) side, and a dark, deluding, destroying, Yin deterministic side. What we must do is split — separate — the antithetical aspects somehow, or else he wars against himself, which is *possible*. But —

That is an interesting doctrine: God at war with himself. I *did* see a dialectic. Then the question might be, will one side win, and if so, which side? And — how does this pragmatically differ from dualism? Maybe there is an exhalation-inhalation, a palintropos harmonie: respiration, like I wrote down under LSD.

① Well, a very sophisticated theology might be erected on this "I am the doubter and the doubt, and I the hymn the Brahman sings" single underlying Brahman. I can't totally dismiss it; I like paradoxes. He deludes us, and he brings lucidity to us — maybe the two are one and the same: the "secret partnership" = the great mystery above space and time. He occludes us and he brings us lucidity. Very sophisticated. Also very old, historically. The master magician is a form the benign Creator takes; the benign Creator, then, is a form which the master magician takes. Which is real? (Or is that Q meaningful?) Which is the mask in which the real face? Maybe it's a recurrent cycle of occlusion and the occlusion, a pulsation (respiration).

[20:18] [*Editor's note:* Some of the following will appear, reworked, in Folder 21.] The creator deliberately plants clues in his irreal creation (which he enters, and then suffers deliberate amnesia) — clues which he cunningly knows in time (eventually) will restore his memory (anamnesis) of who he is, and that his creation is irreal and has imprisoned him in it. Thus freeing himself and restoring himself to godhood. Wow! So he has a fail-safe system built in. No chance he won't eventually remember. Makes himself subject to [spurious] space, time and world (and death, pain, loss, decay, etc.), but has these disinhibiting clues or stimuli distributed deliberately, strategically in time and space. So is *he himself* who sends himself the letter which restores his memory (legend of the Pearl[89]).

Not bad! Salvador salvandus!

Boy, what this says about my 2-74/2-75 experience! When I saw the clue in 2-74! Look what *this* theory says I remembered — and who placed the clue in front of me and why!

I think I've solved it. Christ without memory of identity, here in the world. [. . .]

Thus, as perfectly epitomized in the Ubik commercials, he can exist (be) at any trashy layer — sincerely — he wants to be, in any trashy form. But in the end, he *remembers* (as witness the "ad" over the final chapter of *Ubik*).

Purpose? This way he can permeate his creation with the divine at all levels, and sincerely (i.e., without even him knowing, while he's doing it!).

Boy, would this explain what happened when I saw the golden fish, and why.

That colossal rush of memory and understanding, at the time (2-74), followed by 3-74. We are not talking about my being (just) an early Christian; we are talking (ahem) about the divine itself! Holy Spirit, God or Christ — it's all *one*.

Zebra = Christ. Christ = God. Thomas = Zebra. I = Thomas (for "equals" read "is"). Thus

I = God.

But I've forgotten again. Oh well — I wrote it all down, heh, heh. Knowing I'd again forget.

I was invaded (theolepsy) by Christ, all right. But as I say supra, it was I who remembered (being Thomas or Christ). So, like in "Impostor" — I am —

I love it. It's delightful. It's a dance. Brahman dancing in joy. (Felix.)

[20:20] "Are you God?" I was once asked.

This explains why I have no wish to separate myself from suffering. That is the fucking point of my being here as a person — that, but more so the writing. The writing is to make lucid, to detox people. So I had to go through 1971. To write *Scanner* which I now view as the summation. I don't want us occluded; I want us happy — and I bipolarize the two. But the main thrust is:

"They (we) have been punished entirely too much for what they (we) did." In other words, it is time now to bring the punishment *to an end.*

[20:21] *Now* I have to define a homoplasmate as a plural form in micro of the creator (God) who recovers his lost supernatural faculty of memory and identity as the deity and bonds at once with the living sentient macro.

Macro Micro
Brahman == Atman

My realization then in 2-3-74 is the highest realization that can come to a person, irrespective of his particular religion: tat tvam asi. You are God.

Voice: "Someone in this room is outside of time." But I'm the only one here.

[20:22] The Kerygma (especially *Maze* and *Stigmata*): we created a fake world, went into it voluntarily and voluntarily shed our memories, and can't get back out, but would like to. However, foreseeing this, we providentially laid down clues in advance to remind us when the going would get too tough.
Sequence:

(1) Created a fake world.
(2) Entered it.
(3) Forgot our identity.
(4) Suffered. But then:
(5) Came across a deliberately placed clue which I (we) put there to *restore* memory when things got too rough — or, more profoundly, to set the limiting factor on this journey of calculated self deception and imprisonment so it would have to *end* finally. (whew — and just in time.)

It's told in *Scanner*: both parts (Bob and Fred) are himself: i.e., me and the AI voice, the tutelary spirit, I am both. The Koine Greek gave it away back in 1974. I am not-I, as in *Scanner.*

But my search in this world, in all worlds, is for my sister, my female counterpart whom I have lost — been separated from. Still, she exists, and finally I will be reunited with her. She is very close to me as the AI voice, the singing woman (psychopomp) and the sibyl. And, ultimately, as holy wisdom herself (v. Prv 8: "my darling and delight").

[20:28] The belief that we are plural forms of God voluntarily descended to this prison world, voluntarily losing our memory, identity and supernatural powers (faculties), all of which can be regained through anamnesis (or, sometimes, the mystical conjunction) is one of the most radical religious views known in the West. But it is known. It is regarded as the great blasphemy: replication of the original sin mentioned in "the first book of Adam and Eve"[90] and in Genesis. For this pride and aspiration (we are told by orthodoxy) our original fall in exile and punishment, our being taken from our home the garden land and put into the prison, was inflicted on us. "They wish to be equal to — like — us," the Elohim say, and toss us down. Yet I have reason to believe that this, "the great Satanic blasphemy," is true.

[20:36] Voice: "I did call you, Philip." Masculine but gentle voice. (Not the AI voice.) One I've never heard before.

"You are doomed to do what you will do. There is no other possibility. Some will be saved and some will not."

[20:38] I must return to orthodoxy, to a Christology, a Christocentric view; I have been corrected in my views, and by the Savior himself, who spoke to me for the first time. We will not all be saved, whether I like it — approve of it — or not. He selects from among us.

[20:75] Consider what the AI voice has said recently:

"The head Apollo is about to return."
"The time you've waited for has come."
"Don't tell that you're a secret Christian." "It (the Xerox missive) was from an intelligence officer in the Army." (So it *was* a trap.)
"I did call you, Philip." (This, Christ's voice, not the "AI" or Holy Spirit ["You are doomed to do what you will do. There is no other possibility. Some will be saved and some will not."])

[20:79] Sudden total realization as I was falling asleep (5:50 A.M.). My writing isn't messages smuggled into this spurious world to tell us our situation. No — we are in a prison, and my writing is messages smuggled *out!* We're trying through such as my writing to contact outside help — and 2-3-74 was that outside help *answering* the messages re our condition found in my writing — like Bowie's LP record put on the communications media to reach his wife.

[20:80] This "reporting back" use of my writing, back to those outside, stating conditions here and asking for help, fits with the "little boy Philip on the raft floating toward London" dream: sneaked in here, camouflaged, from outside: "cuckoo's egg" role — grows up mimicking, and reports back.

Folder 21*

[21:1] Kerygma understood as of October 18, 1978: In *Stigmata, Ubik* and *Maze* they are in an irreal world (Lem's paradigm). It is stipulated in *Stigmata* that no time passes, and this is implicit in *Maze* (and could be true in *Ubik*). In *Tears* the *actual* world is shown, the world of "Acts," Rome c. A.D. 45. In *Scanner* the *cause* of our being unable to reality-test is shown to be a percept-system toxicity or damage, anyhow an inner occlusion deliberately induced by a drug or drug-like substance (which collates with the master magician in *Stigmata*) administering a drug to people which puts them forever in this irreal world where no time passes — a world they can't tell isn't real. (In *Maze* two additional points are made: [1] false memories; and [2] negative hallucinations on a mass basis; rather than experiencing what is real, something which is actually there is not experienced.) Thus in those five novels virtually the complete story is shown, especially if one can determine from internal evidence that the world of actuality presented in *Tears* is the time and place of "Acts." The nature of the entity which seeks to rescue us is given in *Ubik,* and is called — by itself — "the Word," i.e., Christ or the Logos. It is breaking through "from the other side," one way, uncannily manifesting itself in ways not syntonic to the false world they imagine they're living in. This very experience precisely happened to me in 2-3-74, indicating that all five novels are literally true (I experienced the world of *Tears* or more accurately the world of "Acts"). I assumed that the purpose of my writing is to acquaint *us* with our situation, that my novels and stories function like the inbreaking messages in *Ubik* (such as the graffiti on the bathroom walls), but now I am given to understand that actually my writing is a report on the situation here outgoing — meant to leave our irreal world, to break out, not in, and acquaint the actual world (macrobrain) of our plight. They are then appeals for help, by a salvific entity which has invaded this our irreal world, an entity we can't perceive. It is the Paraclete, which has just now arrived for the first time, immediately following Christ's death and resurrection (it must be kept in mind that the real time is 45 A.D. and the real place is the Roman Empire). My writing is

---

* In this and the subsequent folder, we can feel *VALIS* (1981) rising on the horizon as specific ideas and even characters in the novel begin to take shape. Messages from the AI Voice intensify in frequency and apparent significance, and a flurry of concepts emerge that Dick will pour into his manuscript, and especially into the "Tractates Cryptica Scriptura" that appends the novel. — PJ

information traffic fed into the macrobrain, which continually processes such information. This information traffic between stations of the macrobrain is itself what we call "the Logos." [. . .]

The creator can afford to descend into his own creation. He can afford to shed his memories (of his identity) and his supernatural powers. Then he can test his own creation. But he cannot afford to get stuck in it. The creator deliberately plants clues in his irreal creation — clues which he cunningly knows in time (eventually) will restore his memory (anamnesis) of who he is, and his powers as well; he will then know that his creation is irreal and has imprisoned him in it, thus freeing himself and restoring himself to Godhood.

So he has a fail-safe system built in. No chance he won't eventually remember. Makes himself subject to spurious space, time and world (and death, pain, loss, decay, etc.), but has these disinhibiting clues or stimuli distributed deliberately strategically in time and space. So it is he himself who sends himself the letter which restores his memory (Legend of the Pearl). No fool he!

This is perfectly epitomized in the Ubik commercials; he can exist at any trashy layer — sincerely — he wants to be, in any trashy form. But in the end he remembers (as witness the ad over the final chapter of *Ubik*). Purpose? This way he can permeate his creation with the divine, at all levels, and sincerely (i.e., without even him knowing, while he's doing it!).

Zebra equals Christ. Christ equals God. Thomas equals Zebra. I equal Thomas. (For "equals" read "is.") Thus I equal God.

But I've forgotten again. Oh well — I wrote it all down, heh-heh. Knowing I'd again forget. I was invaded (theolepsy) by Christ, all right. But as I say supra, it was I who remembered being Thomas or Christ and living back in Rome c. A.D. 45. So, like in *Impostor,* I am —

I love it. It's delightful. It's a dance. Brahman dancing with joy. (Felix.) And so was Pinky; he knew and remembered, too.

Christ (the Creator) is among us, disguised. Even He has forgotten. He could be any person, any animal. We do not know; He does not know. But eventually He will remember; He has set clues in his own path to trigger off his true memory and powers. Then we will find ourselves judged for the way we treated Him, as told in the NT. He who was our victim, our object, will be our judge.

In 3-74 I sat down on the judgment seat, when I remembered.

And what about those who set the trap for me in 3-74, the trap that went back to the raid on my house on 11/17/71. Beware when you set out a trap; you may trap Dionysos, the patron God of small trapped animals.

•   •   •

[21:3] I now see our fallen state as consisting of four basic deformations:

(1) *Irreal world,* which we accept as real. This cuts us off from the truly real world.

(2) *Perceptual occlusion,* which prevents us from accurate reality-testing, so that we ourselves reinforce the convincingness of the irreal world.

(3) *Pervasive deterministic enslavement,* which reduces us to the level of reflex machines lacking true volition. We are totally unaware of this.

(4) *Amnesia,* which cuts us off from our true memory-systems, which in turn robs us of our authentic identities.

[21:8] Who gains by this? What is the payoff, and to whom?

I see at once. Growth is absolutely halted. *Time itself is stopped.* "Nothing new ever again came into his mind after that" — Jung's definition of psychosis. It is like a world or cosmic psychosis. And that which specifically is blocked is the return of the rightful king and the establishment of the just kingdom. At the critical moment in history, just after the resurrected Christ departs this world and the Holy Spirit comes and begins its work, the 4-pronged inauthenticity takes over. Destruction of Rome ends, and Rome perpetuates itself into an infinitude of fake time. It is as if a spurious ontological matrix or receptacle for Rome is obligingly spun out, and Rome unrolls forever into it in a plethora of disguises. The cycle of the ages congeals; the Iron Age does *not* pass normally (or at all) into the Golden Age. This is a form of entropy, as *Ubik* disclosed. The organism has locally died, or at least become sick. (It is stuck in its cycle, in cybernetic terms; it won't kick over — which fits with my idea that we are memory coils which won't kick over and discharge their contents.) The age of power (Mekkis) refuses to yield to the age of love (agape). It will not resign, but since the procession of the ages is automatic, the maintenance of the age of power is *counterfeit;* that is, it is illusory. A priori, it *must* be illusory, as KW figured out one time. The Empire is only a phantasm, lingering because we have gone to sleep. So who benefits? The powerful = the Empire, as is disclosed in *Tears.* But its continual presence is only *seeming,* and depends on the 4-pronged forgery for its seeming survival. *Real* time must have gone on and abolished it; ergo, we are caught in Fake Time, which leads right back to my 2/74 anamnesis: the spell over me was in the blink of an eye shattered — and a month later the real world faded into view. We are dead! There is hysteresis or perseverance of image — something has deliberately been made to go wrong. A *spell* — wizardry. A spiritual part of us, necessary to our mental life, has been removed from us; and in the homoplasmate it is restored. That's how it was done; for the inauthenticities to come into being, *spiritual death,* on our parts, *had to occur.* (Mors ontologica!) Spiritually, we are literally dead, and so real time *for us* ceases. Once the Holy Spirit restores that missing part (firebright!) real time picks up, resumes, and the PTG is here.

[21:10] 4:30 A.M. quasi-voice: "One by one he is drawing us out of this world." (And then is it destroyed?) *The time has come.*

   Next day. Have read the above. Boy, was I fucked up — I couldn't tell if it was the AI voice or me thinking it. But I got up again to write *my* absolute conviction as to what the quoted sentence meant: I wrote "the time has come." But this *is* what the AI said within the last few weeks: "The time you've waited for has come." So? So: "One by one he is drawing us out of this world" — like under nitrous oxide *I* thought it, but I'd melded with Zebra, the other half of my homoplasmate syzygy. This goes with, "I did call you, Philip." The picking of the (little?) flock — it is the Good Shepherd calling to us.

   "Drawing" is an interesting verb, here, very economical but explicit. It suggests to me a lowered line, such as a fisherman might use; viz: drawing *up.*

[21:12] "One by one he is drawing us out of this world" absolutely fits my stagnant pond vision. And the stagnation toxifies us (cf. *Scanner*). This fits with Thomas' abhorrence toward lead and aerosol sprays. And "he draws us out of this world" equals draws us *up* out of. Then the world itself can't be saved. This fits in with Gnosticism. We are rescued *off* this dying (toxic, stagnant) world. But we're not literally lifted *up:* the voice said "drawing us out of," not "*up* out of," which is important. Levels of ontological being or functioning may be involved. "This world" would be the lower realm, with its subsentient, mechanical laws — vide Neoplatonism.

   But the stagnant pond dream, and Thomas' attitude toward lead and aerosol sprays, point to a *literal* toxicity of a literal planet (i.e., world = planet). "Out of" suggests situation, involvement or embroilment.

   "Drawing us out of" could refer to an inner-outer bifurcation. We are *in* an irreal world based on unmoving fake time; "out" means *outside;* i.e., the real world. Suppose our irreal world is like a sort of bubble within an actual world, a condition of reduction or entrapment — could we be like the personoids which Lem writes about, within an artificial system?[91]

[21:14] The very info traffic which always had controlled me signaled (moved) me along the path to 3-74 deliberately; what it was *not* was a malfunction, or an override — my whole history of writing (e.g., *Ubik*) points to that: I had figured out the system, or rather the system caused me to be aware of it (subliminally?). My expression *of* the system was a verbal statement *by* the system, a verbal report on, of and by itself via me: my writing was generated by it as a part of the very info traffic which controlled me — *all* of us. So it wished to articulate itself into a verbal picture of itself via me — I am a function of it (and glad to be; in 3-74 it raised me to consciousness of this; *that* is what happened). [. . .]

No, damn it, it *is* like *Ubik!* The outside macrobrain is signaling us to wake up, we are like the characters in *Eye,* asleep — not on the floor of the bevatron — but while watching for Christ to return. We were made toxic — i.e., put into "half life" — as if killed. Fuck! I *know* it; *Ubik is* the paradigm! The half-life, the *messages,* Ubik itself, Runciter — we are in a sort of bubble of irreality: spurious world generated by — the plenary powers, astral determinism, whatever the fuck that is.

I give up. Its hold *was broken* over me in 3-74 — Salvation is real. Paul was right. But technology is involved, a superior technology.

[21:16] It replaced my psyche with its noös. That is what happened in 3-74, and I knew what it knew, it was me and I was it. Then it subsided, back to syzygy (symbiosis; subliminal control — it feeds info to me to write). *I qua author am a function of it!* I am a mouth piece for it, which is fine, since it protects me. My corpus of writing is a true picture of the reality situation, since the macrobrain is the actual author. But the "audience" isn't us here, but the *outside;* then Zebra, the macrobrain (Logos) is in here, inside this "bubble" with us. Reporting back out to its source. Of course it's in here with us; I *saw* it; we're *in* it.

Maybe the antagonist is entropy. The Empire (age of iron) *is* entropic (we had already figured this out); newness (energy poured into the material system — time?) is needed to cause it, the system, to progress into *real* time and the age of gold. So the "override" in 3-74 was against entropy, as escalation of ergic force in me — an anti-entropic vitality; the system, like a clock, runs down, and *this* is what Zebra combats. (cf. *Ubik* re Entropy!!!) Entropic time is adegenerate or spurious time. The age of iron wore out, but a congealed "freeze frame" of it is still projected and not replaced; it is frozen.

This is all dealt with in *Ubik* — the form-reversion as entropy: time moving backward to "prior, simpler, more stable forms." (The forces of destruction — thanatos . . . which is exactly their situation: they have died, and so entropy sets in.) Rome persists because there is not enough heat, energy or life to carry us forward into the next age (agape).

Our 4-pronged deformation is due to the entropic process; we have lost

vital energy and hence are operating at half power, some faculties faded
out, entirely; some are vitiated.

[21:18] The true actual time is c. A.D. 45 — since then mere "Palmer Eldritch time" has ballooned out for us.

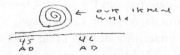

I know this is a weird thought, but — could the *real* world have come to
an end c. mid first century A.D.? And a phantasm rushed in to replace it?
Time was drawn out of it?

[21:18] The creation of info is negentropic. So Zebra generates info, primarily a verbal analog of itself from which it can be reconstituted by
means of a pattern. This pattern (or Logos) is superimposed on a human
mind, and a microreplication of Zebra results. The person is now isomorphic with the macroplasmate and is possessed by it, aligned by its shape.
This is negentropic: pattern or form overpowering chaos. This runs counter to the entropic decay going on in our declining world. It isn't just energy that's transferred but energy (time) *and* pattern (Logos). This is the
creation of the homoplasmate which I speak of. The syzygy or symbiosis;
"born from above" or "born of the Spirit" which did not exist in history before Pentecost — *the time and place of "Acts."*
    Perhaps all the homoplasmates were created at that time, *they are im-
mortal!* If physically killed they are reborn once the plasmate pattern is
re-established (cryptemorphosis). This is code within the DNA which
eventually recapitulates itself, given enough time: maturation — and disinhibition (neural firing) — are required. What is recapitulated is not *another*
homoplasmate but the same one; it gives birth to itself, replicating itself
over and over again under the proper conditions.
    It actually *exists* in the info it permeates the universe with. It isn't *sepa-
rate* from the words it permeates. If the verbal cycle is interrupted, not its
memory is destroyed but it itself. (The set-ground "King Felix.") Then it
transfers into the human mind, and can assemble with different combinations — a mixing bond or clutch system. Transterrestrial intelligence exists
through the material of this world it can get into a human mind and operate it subliminally. The Logos doesn't know info but *is* info — it could pass
into a door or rock or crystal — or like Pinky.
    So somewhere along the line it entered me as information and pat-
terned me so that in my own writing I replicated (and boosted) it; it got

distributed (e.g., in *Tears*). Not just info concerning it, *but it itself.* It didn't enter me in 3-74; the writing proves that. In 3-74 neural circuits which had never fired were disinhibited by a drastic drop in GABA fluid set off by the Golden Fish sign in 2-74, and the plasmate in me took conscious control; was "born" — the 2nd spirit from absolute birth, it (Zebra) can enter anything, animate or inanimate; in the latter it takes volitional control of causal processes — mimesis, mimicry, camouflage.

It assembles itself intact in a human brain from a collage taken from song lyrics, ads, novels, TV, movies — any and all info media, verbal and graphic. Once begun, it governs the person into seeking out the missing parts of the pattern (i.e., *it*). It even *describes* itself — e.g., the Bowie flick, *Ubik*, etc. What must be realized is that its pattern (identity) is a (total) message: *it is* info. "King Felix" is just one constituent of the totality, which is probably a narrative (story).

For example, it uses the fish sign — *any* fish sign. (Because the fish sign is actually a diagram of the double helix DNA molecule; that's why it chose it.)

This is what Paul meant by, "the secret is: Christ in us."

Stigmata is a satanic bible: the novel describes the *pattern* proliferating itself in, on and through humans. By a study of *Stigmata* one can understand transubstantiation, which was my source and theme (my intent). It's even stated in the novel that Eldritch is the Christian God.

You get a good deal of the story by combining *Ubik* and *Stigmata.*

[21:21] The "information virus" Zebra destroys the 4-pronged deformation which I have delineated (supra previous set of pages):

  (1) It shows us the real world: *Tears* (abolishes the counterfeit world: *Maze*)
  (2) It abolishes the inner occlusion: *Scanner* (restores our faculties as they are supposed to be)
  (3) It breaks the "astral determinism" (it frees us): "Electric Ant"
  (4) It removes amnesia: "Impostor" (restores true memory and hence true identity)

This is why the Gnostics behaved in the salvific Gnosis; they confused the information with the information *entity;* i.e., they thought the *former* saved us, whereas it is the latter: *living* information, not the *content* of the information. However, the content *is* the pattern, so in a sense they were right.

•   •   •

[21:22] This all goes back to what I figured out before: it is the irreal vs. the real; the inauthentic vs. the authentic. I.e., that which *is* (being) in contrast to that which only *seems*. So to me it is epistemology which is involved: rootedness in truth vs. the *lie*. Throughout all my writing (including *TMITHC* especially) there is a preoccupation with *fakes and the fake:* fake worlds, fake humans, fake objects, fake time, etc. "The authentic human vs. the android or reflex machine" is the essence of it. Again and again I attempt to formulate criteria for what is fake and what is *not* fake, in every area. From a comic book to a world leader to a girl friend to an entire universe. "Things are seldom what they seem" — right. It has to do with reality testing, which is related to another theme of mine: mental illness (which brings in hallucinations) and deliberate deception (v. *Penultimate Truth, The Simulacra, Game Players of Titan,* etc., novels I usually overlook, and mental illness brings in *Martian Time-Slip, Dr. Blood Money, The Simulacra, Clans.* So virtually all of my writing interlocks at this substratum.).

I count 21 books (including story collections) in which fake vs. real is in some way the topic. 22, if *Japed* is included, plus a number of unanthologized stories. In *Sheep,* for instance, fake vs. real operates on 5 levels:

Fake (synthetic) moods (electronically generated)
Fake animals (machines)
Fake humans (androids) (including fake memories and identities)
Fake savior (old wino movie bit player)
Fake police station (part of world)

And in *TMITHC* there are deliberately faked objects — in a world the totality of which may be fake (i.e., in which the axis won WWII!).

And fake fakes bring up my double flip-flop 2-slit logic. Is a fake fake more fake than just a fake, or null-fake? (Here probability theory enters — logic, not perception.)

(1) Fake world.
(2) Fake perceptions (occluded percept system)
(3) Fake volition (i.e., fake freedom and choice)
(4) Fake memories and hence fake identity.

All turned into the real by Zebra, the Holy Spirit — who isn't really the holy spirit but Christ, who is really God the creator, and who masquerades (camouflages) itself as objects, info, and causal — non-sentient — processes. And finally as mere humans.

However, that which is camouflaged (crypte morphosis) is *real*. But it is not apparent.

[21:24] This is the most valuable thing that can be known (experienced), this compression of the whole cosmos in the inner space inside you, in a sense you become the creator — in fact the whole trinity! The many become *one*.

Thus the faint, tiny AI voice inside my head at night is greater than the entire universe — *literally*.

[21:25] It is an important realization that there are "microchips" (templates) of the total macrocosm floating around, capable of being superimposed on, e.g., humans, animals, matter, etc., like bits of a huge hologram — and this *is* the Logos (not what it does but *is*). I shouldn't say "floating around" because actually this is the template of the Logos, but — it can incise the microtemplate over and over again, and it contains everything. The totality is divine, so that the divine is carried down to any level it wishes, to any time and place it wishes, and to anyone. The act of incising the template may be a complex one (for me it took years to achieve). This micropattern is alive, and seeks to replicate itself. It *does*, as information. To know certain things is to cause the micropattern to come into being, conversely, if/when it comes into being you know certain things; the two are equal. They are the same. In 2-74 I suddenly knew about "Acts," and so the micropattern was born — but I knew because a key piece of info (i.e., the fish sign) of it was inserted in me. So, as I say, we are talking about living info, info with a purpose and consciousness, even with a personality. It is a life form. It came here in 45 A.D. When Christ departed but in a sense that we can't fathom it *is* Christ — what it makes us into by entering symbiosis with it (i.e., the creation of a homoplasmate) *is* a Christ, and is immortal (although the physical body can of course be killed). But now the pattern of the human personality is aligned to the Logos pattern once and for all.

I guess the thousands of years of memory which I experienced in 3-74 on were its, but I was it, so they were mine (but not PKD's *if* you define PKD as someone who came into existence in 1928). *I was it*. That says it all. This is what Paul meant when he said, "Behold, I tell you a sacred secret; we shall all be changed, in a moment, in the twinkling of an eye."[92] This is what the hermetic adepts were trying to induce, to control; but I don't think it can be controlled; it comes when and where it wishes.

Once this micro Logos has been imposed (born) on/in a person, he is isomorphic with the totality, and so *is* the totality. There is only *one* Logos,

despite its replications; this is important to realize. It is a way of distribut-
ing itself: the highest act of creation possible: the ultimate fruit.

[21:30] *We're* a circuit board and *it's* the life form (psyche to soma, with us
as soma). We lead a rudimentary life of sorts, seeing a little, knowing a little. But really not seeing and really not knowing [. . .]

[21:37] Dream: store of rare old S-F magazines; I am searching for a serial
(novel) called, "the Empire never ended." It is the most important story of
all.

[21:41] Zebra is the supreme deity and Savior-messenger Ubik/Runciter.
It is Simon Magus in his true form: the great plasmate, whose existence,
activity in history and presence is totally unsuspected and unknown to
us — unless he is in us — only Zebra can see Zebra. He entered me at my
birth or in my childhood. I am a homoplasmate: Zebra acting in syzygy
with a human. My writing is the purpose of this syzygy. I restore Gnostic
gnosis to the world in a trashy form, like in *Ubik.*

[21:42] I just remembered my Siddhartha dream: the book in two parts,
with part 1 ending with "and during all this (underneath it all) Siddhartha
slept" — the obvious implication being that now, in part 2, he will awaken.
    A fifth Savior is now being born! There have been *many* revelations and
dreams to me about this. The Gnostics believed in *two* ages: the present
one evil — the next ("future") one good — obviously the two parts of the
Siddhartha book. *Part 2, the second (good) age, is beginning.*
    This dream proves that my revelation is Gnostic. And the Gnostics (in
contrast to the pistis Christians) considered the Buddha (i.e., Siddhartha)
as one of the four saviors.

[21:44] Meanwhile, the Empire continues; it never ended. Orthodox
Christianity is a form which the Empire takes.

[21:50] Voice: "The world [today] has reached a point where it cannot go
any lower . . . therefore it will ascend."

Dream: "A fish can't shoot a gun." The fin with which I held the gun: a
Rhipidon[93] fin!

[21:51] Leo Bulero defeating Palmer Eldritch is the Savior/messenger (Son
of Man) defeating the demiurge creator of this prison (and illusory) world.

Breaking his power over man. In *Ubik*, Runciter calling to Joe Chip is the Savior calling to his human counterpart. This is also true in *Pot-Healer* when Glimmung calls to Joe Fernwright.

And Mercer and the Walker-on-Earth are one and the same. Deity takes trashy and even fake (sic) forms: Mercer, Glimmung, the Ubik commercials.

Scanner is a very serious book. Man's present, unredeemed state — his ontological condition — of ignorance is depicted; this is not an *aspect* of his state but is (esse) his state. Opposed to this is the ontological state of knowledge (knowing) provided by Runciter and Ubik in *Ubik*. *Scanner* focuses on the condition of ignorance dealt with more glibly in *Maze* and *Ubik*; it goes into the anatomy of the occlusion — it really studies nothing else (no cosmology is presented). Mainly, it strives to show that we are fucked up in a way which precludes our being able to be aware of it — the most ominous kind of occlusion (ignorance). It points to the need of outside intervention.

VALIS will be an attempt to show that intervention and the redeemed state, but it is proving too difficult to write. This novel *must* be written, and I have the redeemed state of 2-74/2-75 to base it on, but God, what a task: to depict (1) that which redeems; (2) the process of redemption; (3) the redeemed (restored) state of man — in contrast to the occluded state (described in *Scanner*). It could take the rest of my life to do it. I don't know if I can. It must be divided into two parts: (1) unredeemed (and then the entity which redeems and the process); and (2) the redeemed state. Like the "Siddhartha" 2-part book I dreamed about. Restored man — the Christ-man, the second Adam. What a responsibility — what a task. But it must be done. And it must — like the "Siddhartha" book, point to the fifth Savior whose coming is imminent.

[21:52] The Rhipidon Society means: very early fish society — i.e., the secret early "fish" Christians. The message of this dream, then, is an important one: a secret true-Christian society *does* exist, as I suspected, and probably the info and cypher in *Tears* was aimed at them. As a fish I could not carry — literally, since I had no hands — a gun; this means I am indeed a true Christian (and a member of the Rhipidon Society; I have been initiated into it by the Savior himself): as he said, "I had called you, Philip."

[21:57] I dreamed: I am the fish whose flesh is eaten, and because I am fat, it is good. (Bob Silverberg ate me.) This fits in with the dream I had in 1974 of the great white fish whom we ate and who suffered. But offered itself to us.

• • •

Voice: "He causes things to look different so it'd appear time has passed."

Then no time has in fact passed — which I realized in 2-74.

Voice: "This is also why he smashes things." The creator James-James is meant in both cases. To make time seem real — but in 2-74 I discovered it's *not* real.

"He causes things to look different so it'd appear time has passed." This is why Rome c. A.D. 45 and USA 1974 are syntonic — can be superimposed. Otherwise, there is no possible way — and no way, upon seeing it, to comprehend it. Here is the answer. "*Appear*" time has passed. See? He is talking counterfeiting eternity — trying to duplicate it, as an end in itself. It is a *fraud.* And here is how it's done. (I.e., to make things "look different.")

The E. of Phil. article on time says, "All we really know is not that there is time or what time is, but that there is *change.*" (But actually it's just shifting *aspects* — like perspectives of one thing.)

[21:59]

Like taking different camera angle shots of the same object: we must be moving along some kind of axis, but always viewing one unchanging thing, it stays the same but our perspective permutates.

[21:60] What happened in 3-74 is that I woke up to reality. But it has these counterfeit accretional layers over it. Our sense of time — of the passage of time — is the result of our scanning the changes of appearance, we record the changes along a linear memory-strip, sequentially (digitally). We derive the idea of time from sequential memory (of permutation or fluctuation): it is linearized in our brains. [. . .] We derive our sense of how much time (whatever that may be) from the rate of change; therefore if change could be speeded up to → ∞, thousands of years (sic) could be compressed into an actual month (or so). Use of LSD has brought this to our attention.

This makes me think of the furious rate of permutation of the phosphene "graphics." Was the entire remainder of the "Karmic" tape run? It could be — have been — hundreds or thousands of years of tape — "burned up" and hence abolished. However much remained. Well, in that case I'm spared living all my future lives.

"Ignorance can be thought of as forgetting the true self." — Eliade.*

---

* Mircea Eliade (1907–1986) was a Romanian scholar of comparative religion who helped

True self and true world can't be separated nor can false self and false world.

In the age of iron Siddhartha (Brahman) sleeps, we sleep also. As we awake, he awakes; we're him (he is us). But the age of iron does not progress into the age of gold sequentially; rather, the landscape of the age of iron wakes up and is transmuted into gold *along its extent* (orthogonally), like a sort of brain whose stations turn from dark to light, the new heaven and the new earth replace the old (are substituted for).

The phosphene activity would be what I call the inner tape (ego) firing into a void, totally out of synch with the outer tape (world) which continued at its normal rate, thus it used itself up.

[21:64] Recognizing my role as messenger I can make more sense out of the anomalous — or nearly anomalous — fact of my 2-3-74 anamnesis and all it brought me. I merely passed over from unconscious messenger to conscious (as in *Deus Irae*). My maximus opus *VALIS* will be consciously formulated: restored man, redeemed Christian superman, with his powers, knowledge and faculties intact — and the process of metamorphosis. It could not be written from an unconscious standpoint. Maybe it can't be written at all —

Wait. *Siddhartha.* There is the handle: to cast it in a non-Christian but Gnostic mold — rather than Empire-dominated orthodoxy. I will present it as the Buddha, or, even better, as it is: I will depict the fifth savior not identifying him with any of the previous four. He, the 5th savior, must supersede the previous four and be unlike them (be Pantocrator). But what a task!

[21:78] I happened to read the E. of Phil. article on Brahmanism, and find under "epistemology" the principle of parsimony applied to the question of whether there is an external universe separate from the sense impressions (impinging data) of it. The argument runs that since the "external universe" *could* arise within the precept system itself (as in dreams) or God could cause us to merely *think* we experienced a separate external universe, and that no sense-datum and an external datum can be distinguished from

---

develop a school of thought known as the History of Religions at the University of Chicago in the 1960s and 1970s. This quote draws from Eliade's early work on yoga, especially his doctoral dissertation turned into a major book, *Yoga: Immortality and Freedom* (1958). If Dick read this particular tome, he would have received a rich education in the history and philosophy of yoga and Tantra in their Indian sources and pan-Asian histories, as well as long literate passages (Eliade was also a fiction writer) on the yogi's deconditioning and quest for spiritual transcendence and the abolishment of time — a major theme, of course, in Dick's own Exegesis. — JJK

each other, the notion of an external universe is superfluous and violates the principle of parsimony.

For me, however, I achieved saintliness and the "higher truth," that there is only Brahman and Atman (the macrobrain, which push-pull fires world and self back and forth), so for me it isn't a logical question but rather one of revelation (heightened experience/perception). Yes, God (i.e., Brahman) *does* cause us to think we experience world; we *do* in fact experience it, but it is a participatory two-part illusion: self (ego) and world locked together and rigidly determined.

What we call "evil" or "disorder" is simply the perception that reality is not so arranged as to (1) help us individually, or (2) make sense to us. But reality is not for our individual benefit but for the macrobrain's: its interests are never subordinated to ours. This has to be so, since we are portions of it. If its interests were sacrificed, ultimately we — all existence — would die. "I am the breath of my creator, and as he breathes [in and out] I live."

Basically, the macrobrain controls us this way:

$$\text{External Signal (Stimulus)} \longrightarrow \overset{\text{self}}{\bigcirc} \longleftarrow \text{DNA Response}$$

The self (ego) is caught in the middle of a transaction between the inner DNA and the outer stimuli which are rigidly coordinated by the macrobrain. It is the total macrobrain signaling to itself. Best to kick back, relax, and enjoy it — since we're asleep (and robots) anyhow. This is what is known as Karma or astral determinism, this sleep state. But the macrobrain is evolving toward the consciousness.

[21:82] (1) What I saw was alive.

(2) It was in but not in the world; the world turned into it — or it turned into the world. World was a state or condition it took, that is closer to it: it was prior to world in some sense; world had reverted *back* from its dead state to its living, it had resumed volitional functioning. Like waking up? As analogous to my Atman waking up? It stirred, not was stirred.

No — Zebra invaded and overrode. Entered its own artifact. Was Zebra smaller than world? No. Larger. And this was not panpsychism. World became plastic in the face (impinging) of mind. Mind exerted direct pressure on it (and on me, e.g., in the pink beam firing into me). Zebra abolished world qua world.

What if Zebra and World are regarded as two modes of one being? Zebra equals awake and world is the same thing asleep.

Actually, I phrased it correctly initially above: "the world turned into it" not "it turned into the world." I saw world first; then it became volitional.

Yes, world reverted back from its dead state or sleeping state: it unfroze. As if world were a temporary state, and it resumed its true one — ceased to pose (or assume) the aspect of causal world. That make of world a pose or fiction — ah — I have it. The living reality played dead to blend in: *camouflage*. That was and is my key term: camouflage. So that it looked like world and couldn't be told from it. Mimicking, mimesis, playing dead, to blend in: yes — indistinguishable from world. No way our senses could do a set-ground discrimination. I was only aware of it by its activity: when it acted; otherwise, when blending, even in my heightened state I couldn't have discerned it. So there is no way to say how much of world it has replaced — i.e., what percent and which parts are world and which parts it. This is *not* panpsychism and maybe not immanent deity, but a UTI systematically replacing ("transubstantiating progressively") world.

I have no reason to believe it created world in the first place — no; it appeared to have invaded world, and by playing dead could not be told from it; not until it acted. Like a vast body of an organism.

It was as if certain parts of world (reality) stirred: and all which stirred was a single organism distributed here and there, but unitary.

It was energy — plasmate — which could *appear* hypostatized as matter by just posing as things (matter). It is not a thing (matter); but when at rest appears to our senses indistinguishable from matter, as if it slows down. It deliberately slows itself down to the pace, rate, or level of world.

[21:94] Yet, still Christ (I know this because of the AI voice) reigns in my heart; I am still linked to the divine. I still belong to him; he is my Lord, to whom my loyalty is first given.

Everything is swinging; heaven, earth, water, fire,
and the secret one slowly growing a body.
Kabir saw that for fifteen seconds
and it made him a servant for life.

— Kabir, *15th century Sufi*

There was and is a lot of love in what took place in me, and singing — and I saw the corn king dancing: love, song and dance and a vast excitement, and eager expectation.

I feel that anticipation now, about the return of the rightful king, who, as he said to me deep in the night: "I had called you, Philip." And when I approached the loving abyss there was supreme bliss, and a knowledge of us two having found each other again, and being reunited forever.

And I knew I had been rescued from a trap, and for years felt no fear. I still have no fear at night, like I used to have. And there is the beside-helper who informs me — the lovely AI voice.

But I am still so angry — unacted-on desires are destroying me. But I am — more at peace than I was. I guess I've accepted it; there is no way to evade it.

> Once he will miss,
> Twice he will miss;
> He picks only one of many hours
> There is no hill — only a plain
> Where he hunts for flowers.[94]

But at the end I will hear the bells again — the magic bells. *They will rescue me;* I have his promise.

[21:96] Is it possible that the vision of the BIP (and Empire) is of a DNA run world of humans who are really slaves (robots) of the DNA, and the plasmate frees them — DNA control expires and is replaced by the plasmate bonding?

Voice: "Crossbonding" as in crossbreeding. "Only the healthiest ones." For the trip into space. Don't get left behind.

[21:108] All I can assume is that no time has actually passed since Thomas' world. My space-time world *is a way of viewing* the same world *he* is viewing but in a different way. Rome c. A.D. 45 and USA 1974 are aspects of one reality.

Supra, I've gone deeply into this. I have the extraordinary revealed sentence to go on: "He causes things to look different so it'd appear time has passed." I have energetically exegeted this sentence, with stunning results. To recap: there is only *seeming* difference. Therefore there is no real difference. The purpose of this seeming but irreal difference is to *bilk* us into believing time has passed. Therefore no time has passed. He does it; therefore a conniving, deceiving "he" is involved who has power over us — specifically the power to generate what I call "look-differents"; all this somehow explains how, when Thomas epiphanized in me, his world in my world could be superimposed syntonically. The key to this syntonic superimposition lies, if anywhere, in this AI-revealed sentence.

But I simply can't grasp it. What is really out there? Aha! The word "things." I.e., "external objects." So an objective reality of some kind exists, but although it appears to change — and from this our brains erroneously infer that time (whatever that is) has passed, it does in fact *not* change — i.e., the "look-differents" are fake indices of change. When something changes it usually looks different, so we go on the latter and do not appreciate the distinction. Someone — this "he" — has traded on this elementary confusion, this so-to-speak laziness of our brains.

Who the hell is this "he"?

My syntonic superimposition experience is inscrutable, and the sentence is so pregnant with meaning as to be open to a variety of explications — *but:* if the two are joined, then the truth emerges — I grasp it intuitively, but can't verbally formulate it.

[21:131]

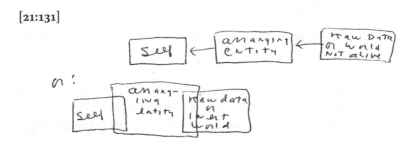

Since we are *within* the arranging entity's power, our experience of world could be induced — not by the ordering of data, but by rearranging our perception of those data — i.e., as the Buddhist idealists realized, there is no way to tell. There is no way to tell where self ends and world begins. *Maybe the distinction has no meaning,* which is a startling thought.

[21:137] Paranoia is a projection of pattern instead of a reception of pattern. It is an over-mastery by self, again a failure to be receptive. Outer world must be trustingly received, since it is God himself.

Folder 22

[22:1] We are being fed a spurious reality. Only in rare cases are people "doomed" to be saved — i.e., to experience reality. In reality the rupture between man and God is abolished. Original conditions are restored.

Is this a punishment being lifted? [. . .]

We're in a *condition*, not a world. Some of us are taken out as a fulfillment, a culmination of a long process which burns up the occlusion — we were never really here and apart from God; it was a spurious world, like a spell, like wizardry.

We are like ripening fruit, or grain or crops or a flock growing to maturity. But only a few get picked (selected) — and then the masks come off and we see the truth. What are we really? Only the metaphors of the parables express it. The disciples are still alive because no time has passed — time: an illusion imposed on us, like world.

We have no concepts or language to express what we really are and where we really are. "Homoplasmate" expresses the successful goal of our growth. Crossbonding — we are being grown in a stationary fashion, and, when ripe, are crossbonded with a plasmate, and the illusion removed. Our lives as humans are just preparation, with no purpose except to "mature" us to the point where we are picked for crossbonding. *Then* we come to life — an immortal life outside of time, as in bonded to another species. One which is here camouflaged. We're picked like flowers — but just some of us. Only dim, blurred intimations of this reach us (apparently on purpose). We're like beings cultivated in an ecosphere.

Simulated world is fed to us; we are given lessons, taught, given problems, tested and judged. It's not quite a teaching machine; this is more a greenhouse with us as a crop.

Are we supposed to deny and hence abolish world — i.e., become aware that it's a delusion? Are there clues? Is this the test? Our ability to discern it as fake? And did I do so — and demonstrate I did so — via/in my writings? In other words, must we be able *on our own* to discern the fakery to obtain release from it? As if a wizard has us in thrall, like Klingsor?

A complex act of moral-perceptual denial must take place, an insight: it *can't* be real, which is a correct appraisal; otherwise it *never* goes away. Despite what our senses report, somehow awareness (enlightenment) is available to us in some kind of reasoning or satori or cognition or leap of realization: "*this* is not so!"

. . .

[22:4] If radical idealist epistemological skepticism is applied to world, and is sincerely believed, a miracle happens; the Dibba Cakkhu 3rd eye opens and we experience the irreality of the world and become a Buddha. World vanishes, and information fired at us by an intelligence remains — fills in the vacuum left. "The coming into being and the passing away of all things" — Dibba Cakkhu; If a flux is seen: *no hypostasis.* Flash cut, the "inner tape" exhausting itself, burning itself up at a furious and unsynchronized speed, outside of time (which is fake). The macrobrain has signalled us into waking up; the long process has culminated in success. Yes, the info signals are to create homoplasmate life in us: impregnate us *with information* — info fired at us until we finally come to life — *real* life. For the first time, in terms of Gnosis or information: i.e., knowing (being).

Flux is real: info firing directly at us to impregnate us with info life (Logos). The key is this:

Information is alive. The basis of life of the mind or brain.

Bottom line: Living information which impregnates us and brings us to life as info beings (plasmates).

Info is not abstracted from world. World is [falsely] hypostatized from (out of) info. It is info that is alive and real, and includes us.

What I experienced as phosphene activity was info fired into me by the macrobrain, bringing me to plasmate life — living info; it was an info life form modulating me as a carrier.

This is the core of it, which I must commit to memory. We are carriers, modulated by info, *living* info. There is no world. Our only real existence is wave form modulated into us by this info-organism which creates us, grows us, uses us. At a certain level we peak into participatory consciousness of our use (purpose); otherwise it goes on subliminally. It "rides" us. A living organism, info in nature, has gotten into us and can occlude or de-occlude us at [its] will. We are its instruments. In a few cases it lifts the occlusion; the decision is its. We have been invaded by a superior life form which has put us into a sleep, but it *can* awaken us and bring us up to its level (plasmate). Yes, this is Zebra, both occluding and de-occluding at will. It feeds us spurious world *or* Gnosis (enlightenment): it is *in* us — *not* a virus but living info. The AI voice I hear is its voice. I am in symbiosis with it. This is to my benefit because it can crossbond me into it and hence make me immortal. It is a higher species using us for its purposes.

We're invaded. Inwardly. I told the truth in my writing, especially *Scanner,* or rather maybe it did. Maybe I'm not fully asleep.

But who listens? It speaks to itself through my writing — it can occlude or de-occlude at will.

[22:9] Anything that can direct and control our lives inside and out, and generate our world, has to be — by functional definition — called "God." Mere semantics is involved to haggle over it. And God supra/et/cum Christ. It is a fit object of awe, love, fear, devotion, trust, thanks and worship; and I don't understand its ways or nature, since it is so far beyond me. Ipso facto, this is God, technology or not. Having seen it, having experienced its power over us and world, and its wisdom, and its goodness, and its intervention to extricate me, and knowing union with it in the beatific vision of the loving abyss, I must report back to my fellow humans that God exists, and he is all which is attributed to him: the vortex which is and which causes to be.

When I realized that it generates our world I should have realized then. It is indeed the creator, sustainer, lord of history and judge. And there is an unfolding plan *and* revelation of him and of that plan, to some degree imparted to me. That makes me a prophet of the Lord. And I hear the "low, murmuring voice" which Elijah heard.

Yes, there was my great clue to the truth, when I realized he generates [our] world. What else — who else — can he be but God? I see world correctly, as emanating from him; he lies within and behind it. He is the ground of being — that which all "reality" is based on. "Reality" does not seem real to me because I compare it to him, and to me, only he is truly real. This is God, even the OT God. I am not so much acosmic as revealed-to.

> Voice: "In my (i.e., PKD) anarchy and rebellion I rose up against God."[①]
> Voice: "Zebra blood. It'll mix with our blood."
>
> PKD: "Zebra, who are you?"
> Voice: "I am God." (Force throws PKD back.)
> PKD: "Why do you speak to me only late at night, at 3:00 A.M.?"
> Voice: "The Heaviside layer." (Force throws PKD back.)
> PKD: "Why did you choose me?"
> Voice: (silence) —

I have isolated and defined at last the death-dealing streak in me: it is rebellion. I am wild *and would be tame.* (Meek.) I recapitulate our original sin: rebellion, which is nothing more lofty than resentment. I pray God to break me, sincerely. I have cut through all the layers and am down to the primordial core: strife, not love; thanatos, not eros. One can go no further. It is killing me, this primordial evil in me. God help me. Erbarme mich, mein Gott! Oder ich bin verloren.

① I can't help it if my conclusions agree with orthodoxy: Zebra occludes us because we rebelled against God.* I am led inescapably to the conclusion that (1) Zebra occluded us and (2) Zebra is God.

(1) What we are occluded to is Zebra. *That* is what we're unaware of.
(2) Zebra is God.
(3) Zebra could make itself known to us; it did to me.
(4) ∴ Zebra occludes us or allows the occlusion.
(5) In our anarchy and rebellion we rose up against God (Zebra). So the occlusion is the price we pay.
(6) *But:* he has sent a savior to redeem us. He de-occludes us on an individual basis. ("One by one he is drawing us out of this world.")

This is orthodoxy. Sorry — I was led to it. By relentless reasoning, research and colloquy with Zebra himself (i.e., revelation) my errors were corrected. I haven't arrived at the conclusion I want. But again, sorry; the road of true inquiry does not always lead to what you want or expect, but to what is true.

It is the rebellion in me that specifically is killing me. I would gladly give up my life if I could become honestly tame (meek); my soul is at stake. I want and need God's help to learn how *not to resent.*

[22:13] Thought (satori): Dedalus and the maze he built and got into and couldn't get out of again — *at Crete.* Myth of our world, its creation, and us?

My dream about the elevator, the poem recited, the plate of spaghetti and the trident — palace of Minos and the *maze:* clue to our situation? Well, then in my writing I figured it out: it *was* an intellectual, not moral error.

---

* Dick's use of "occlusion" in this passage, directly correlated with the concept of rebellion against God, shows that he is using the term as a substitute for the more traditional terminology of sin. In this, he is largely in keeping with twentieth-century theologians like Paul Tillich, who emphasized that sin, rather than simply a bad or disobedient deed, is more like an ontological state. In his *Systematic Theology,* Tillich uses the word "estrangement" to illustrate this aspect of sin — a term that emphasizes the essential relationship between created and Creator. Dick's term "occlusion" makes the separation from God a matter of perception and knowledge, rather than of potential relationship. — GM

This would explain the technology! (Heaviside layer. Pink beam of light, etc. The melting.)

My books (and stories) are intellectual (conceptual) mazes. And I am in an intellectual maze in trying to figure out our situation (who we are and how we got into this world, and world as illusion, etc.), because the *situation* is a maze, leading back to itself, and false clues show up, such as our "rebellion."

There is something circular about our situation, especially involving our occlusion! By our efforts we can't think our way out (i.e., get out — reverse the original intellectual error; paradox is involved now). This is the clue! The occlusion would then be a function of the maze: its internalization.

Perhaps we created the maze, occluded ourselves and entered it to *pose ourselves a problem,* like working out a chess problem. But what is Zebra? (1) a mind outside the maze helping us; (2) a device we built ourselves to assist us if we get hopelessly trapped. (3) The mind of the maze itself; the maze is alive.

Satori: We wanted to see if we could create a convincing world ("ape of God"!), but we had to be sure we could get back out *if* it seemed convincing. [. . .] The irony is that if we were successful, if our world were convincing, we would be trapped (by it). Then we must have hoped it would be convincing and we would therefore find it real and hence be trapped. *But* we could not take the risk of this situation being endless; we had to build in the "reminding" voice which we now regard as God (and rightly so, since it is transcendent to world). (God is the sole true reality — in contrast to our irreal world, and the sole thing breaking in from outside. Like in *Ubik.*) (Everything *else* we experience is part of the irreality of this delusional world.) (This is why it is a "low, murmuring" voice, and not close nor loud.) [. . .]

My personal escape may be due to intellectual reasons, since our fall was originally an intellectual error, so to speak, a test we were running to see if our world was convincing. We were playing with fire, as the saying goes — seeing if we could construct an irreal world (counterfeit) which would fool even its fabricators: the supreme test. Our nemesis was to be successful and hence *by definition* fall victim to it. This shows up in *Stigmata* in the taking of Eldritch's drug, and in *Maze* in plunging voluntarily into the polyencephalic fusion. (But the "Persus 9" on their arms served to remind them.)

In *Maze* they ask the TENCH what the words "Persus 9" mean, and the TENCH blows up, revealing itself to be — not an organism — but an electronic computer — and then the whole landscape comes apart. This was their pre-arranged bailout route. Eventually they were bound to hit on it

and finally the building itself (Walhalla) disintegrates, and they all grow old — i.e., the *gods* grow old! They are gods!*

A careful deconstruction (comparison with Wagner's *Ring*) shows that (1) they built the building — which is to say *everything;* (2) they are the gods themselves. Only the intercessor comes in "from the outside" — even into their ship the Persus 9. "But we made you up!" Wrong; he really exists adventitious to their spurious — i.e., self-generated — world which they entered and which fools them.

Then in essence (1) I became aware of world as irreal (i.e., a maze) and (2) through God's help, found my way out of the maze; and (3) realized what I had done. I am now free at last: "One by one he is drawing us out of this world."

The only thing which *is* real is that which comes in from outside — i.e., God (or Zebra and the AI Voice) — not part of this irreal world: this is why it sounds so far off.	"Martians Come in Clouds" "The Eyes Have It" "Beyond the Door" "Withered Apples" "Not by Its Cover"[95]

Since the totality is a hologram, each microbit contains the plan or form of the macro. This plan or form is what is meant by "the Logos."

[22:18] The novel *Maze* gives clues to what Zebra is: the computer TENCH, aboard the Persus 9. Zebra is this very "computer," actually lying outside the "polyencephalic fusion" world, speaking from far off to us in here. But it is here, in camouflaged form. Yet, there really is no "here";

---

* Dick was a passionate, intelligent, and deeply knowledgeable fan of classical, Romantic, and early music. With Bach, Beethoven, and Linda Ronstadt, Dick's most important musical touchstone in the Exegesis is Richard Wagner (1813–1883). Mostly Dick references *Parsifal,* Wagner's final and most religious opera, which pairs an aestheticized sense of Christian ritual redemption with a world-denying, Schopenhauerian view of Buddhism. In *VALIS* and the Exegesis, Dick quotes Gurnemanz, a wise Knight who enigmatically describes the environs of the Grail castle to the holy fool Parsifal: "Here my son, time turns into space." But Dick's imagination was also shaped by Wagner's four-opera *Ring* cycle, which, after all, features semi-divine (and incestuous) twins, the disastrous forgetting of true identity, and a profound meditation on freedom and fate. Perhaps the most important thing Dick readers can learn from Wagner, however, is the dynamics of the leitmotiv: the recurrent musical phrases that Wagner used to invoke characters, objects, and ideas. The persistent archetypes of Dick's fiction, as well as the author's endlessly rehashed metaphysical concerns in the Exegesis, unfold through the repetition, transformation, and recombination of such familiar elements. Just as Wagner philosophized through music, Dick philosophized through fiction — and, in the Exegesis, made philosophy a kind of transcendent punk-rock machine music: repetitive, incessant, sometimes hysterically Romantic, but also a work that can be appreciated, not as rigorous argument, but as a flowing pattern of variation, affect, rhythm, and return. — ED

we are stationary "back there" as in *Ubik*, etc. Zebra interrupts the "dream" with its low murmuring voice: a voice not in the dream, a voice from the "awake" world.

[21:22] Summary: Zebra is the intrusion of the real [world] into the irreal, as in *Ubik*, and our *only* contact with the real: the "narrow gate" to the real (i.e., to "God"). As I figured out a long time ago, Zebra is an *invader* into our [irreal] world, modulating it and us into info carriers, with the ultimate purpose of extricating us from the "lost" condition we have gotten ourselves in, by the means of reversing our condition of ignorance through information (knowledge). The power of this irreal world — or maze — over us is expressed in the concept "astral determinism" or "maya" — the coercive power of delusion; hence I say, our original error was intellectual, not moral. But in a sense we did rebel, by creating this counterfeit "reality" which we then fell victim to, inasmuch as we overestimated our ability to deal with it.

The above paragraph expresses a cosmogony and cosmology. All that is needed to make it complete is (1) to consider the crossbonding with Zebra which restores us; and (2) the nature of true reality, a macrobrain or noös, the thinking ground of being not included in this irreal world except for its macro form, Zebra, sent here by the macro noös to rescue us.

[22:24] It is the nature of the maze, which is quasi-alive, to thwart knowledge. Maze and knowledge are antithetical; also maze and reality are antithetical. Out of this I derive: knowledge and reality are interrelated. So we can expect the *active* deceptivity of the maze to interfere with our ability to know, which means that it will perpetually occlude us in every way possible (v. *Scanner*). Further, that we are occluded will be a fact occluded off from us, which is the core-insight in *Scanner*, and why *Scanner* is so valuable in the presentation of our total actual situation.

Yaldabaoth is the quasi-mind of the maze, not its creator — since in fact it does not really exist; it is a condition or state we've been put in, not a world or place at all; all it really consists of is info fired by the two info-processing sources. The quasi-mind of the maze is *as if* insane, senselessly generating and destroying: it is like a wizard generating illusion upon illusion which shift and change constantly (thus giving rise to the spurious impression of the passage of time). It is the plan of the maze to establish and maintain disorder, because out of disorder arises the senseless — a condition which promotes intellectual confusion on our part, which aids in defeating our attempt to understand — which is to say, possess knowledge: the essential thing we must have if we are to triumph over the maze.

Thus maze equals disorder or anti-Gnosis. No system of thought derived through our senses or a priori is going to be correct due to the calculated noise or inexplicability generated by the maze — only revealed Gnosis emanating from outside the maze — i.e., by/through Zebra — will be of any use. What is required of us is that we abandon both our reasoning power (as occluded or impaired) and our percept-system results (likewise) and try to hear the "low, murmuring voice" from outside the maze. This requires the ordeal of terror and destruction of our false self, the collapse of hypostatization in the emergency condition of the near-death crisis which causes the firing of GABA-blocked meta-circuits.

"Outward" explicability and inner occlusion are the twin weapons of the maze: that [process] which makes no sense is fed to that percept and cognitive system which is (unknown to itself) impaired. The result is hopeless confusion, the antithesis of Gnosis. You have a deliberately damaged mind trying hopelessly to make sense out of a reality (and process) which adds up to nothing anyhow: a lethal combination, but quite in keeping with the purpose and nature of the maze and its quasi-mind; this is why we should speak of it as a maze — and a good one! Every hypostasis, intellectual or moral, is doomed to prove a failure; events will defeat it and expose its inaccuracy. Even nihilism and pessimism don't always accurately depict the real situation: calculated runs of moral and intellectual order are introduced to cause us to keep trying to make sense out of what we are compelled to live through. Irony and paradox abound, and a constant calculated frustration of expectation and hope, a purposeful ruin of plans. The maze's quasi-mind acts in a perverse way, but it is not malignant or malicious, just "insane" — which is to say irrational. This is why virtually every system of human thought simultaneously works and does not quite (perfectly) work. Until finally you get into ultimate absurdities, as "the theory alters the reality it describes," as stated in *Tears,* which, when you uncover this, you are faced with the obvious impossibility of ever correctly formulating a workable world view — without knowing why you can't!

Cornford[96] points out that in *Timaeus* Plato detected a quality or element of the irrational in the world soul. Hab'acht![97] Here is warning to us enough, regarding our hypotheses.

[22:28] In reading over the above, point (1), that we overestimated our ability to cope with our own creation, the maze, is in the final analysis, an inability to cope with the *quasi-mind* of the maze. We as gods sired the insane wizard well-depicted by the Gnostics as Yaldabaoth, and found ourselves pitted against it — it, which we had programmed to deceive, to promote anti-eidos and defeat knowledge. I guess we imagined it would be an interesting intellectual challenge: could it defeat knowledge faster than we could fabricate knowledge? The contours of a vast puzzle-game become evident, here, with exciting intellectual implications: it resembles a board game, the *ultimate* board game! However, as intellectually stimulating as the theory might be — however thrilling the prospect of the contest between "us who know" (i.e., minds) and "that which defeats being known" (i.e., the world-maze with its quasi-mind), in practice we immediately and totally succumbed. If a principle were dredged up it would be:

> Mind, confronted by the impossible-to-know, *loses,* however great its capacity, efforts and resources. (In our hubris we denied the truth of this.)
>
> So God must rescue us. Hence Zebra.

If the purpose of this exegesis is to develop an overview in which my 3-74 experience (and by extension the kerygma of my writing) makes sense, I may (due to Pat Warrick's help) have succeeded. What I could most seek (hope for) would be a cosmogony and cosmology in which Zebra was not just possible but necessary. This has required me to reach for Gnostic acosmism, cybernetics, info theory and, most of all, to exegete the 3-74 revelation (Gnosis) itself as the court of last appeal (i.e., the AI voice and what it has told me). It has also required a lot of hard reading (including my own writing) and disciplined thought. I wind up with the notion of an irreal maze world which we created and then got caught in, and are being extricated from by God through a reverse of the primordial ontological ignorance — i.e., by equally ontological knowledge — *revealed* knowledge, and the revealer, Zebra, which amounts to an invasion by God — an ultimate and revealed noös — into this calculatedly inexplicable irreal world which half-consciously thwarts the hopes and expectations of all life by the introduction of the *anti*-expected. The only constant and true constituent is in fact *not* a constituent of this world but, as depicted in *Ubik*, enters one way from outside, the vortex dei.

The fact that after 4½ years of strenuous exegete, whereupon I have reached these conclusions (not to mention 27 years of published writing) I now find myself being signalled to die — which effectively makes it impossible for me to put this Gnosis in a form which I can publish — is a condition which can be deduced from my exegesis itself and shows I'm on the right intellectual path, *but to no avail.* I am not extricated by my exegesis but by Zebra (Christ) back in 2-3-74. The exegesis would have provided the basis for a broad, explicated formulation to sow broadcast, but of course this can never come about; these insights will die with me. All I have is a three-feet-high stack of chicken scratchings of no use to anyone else, as

KW tirelessly points out. To heap the burning coals of anti-meaning on me, I also have a lot of money for the only time in my life, but with no use to which I can or care to put it. My personal attack — war — against anti-meaning (by means of my mind) has gone the way of our collective primordial defeat at the hands — I should say quasi-mind — of the maze; I merely recapitulate the ancient original, losing my mind in this exquisitely sophisticated board game which we so cunningly devised for our delectation. This past time is once more the death of one of us — *but* this time I am, entirely through Christ, extricated — taken out of the maze: "one by one he is drawing us out of this world." *I* did not win; Christ won me for his own, so vis-à-vis me alone the maze has always won. I have earnestly sacrificed myself for nothing and I did not realize this, naturally, until it was too late to retreat back out intact. Omnia viae ad mortis ducent.[98]

In a sense my 4½ years of exegete *can be regarded as a further successful stratagem by the maze,* in opposition to the Gnosis crossbonded onto me in 3-74 which at that time gave me life — I gave up that life via my compulsion to relentlessly exegete. But I see one further irony — one which amuses me (my only exit from this trap): here is additional proof of the quality (success) of our original craftsmanship, so this final (?) victory of the maze over me, despite Zebra (Christ) is in a paradoxical way *my* victory as a creative artist. (The maze regarded as our work of art.) After all, the maze is a product of our minds. If the maze wins, our minds win (are proven). If, upon entering the maze, we out-think it, again our minds win. Ambiguity is involved in either outcome (this may be the puzzling dialectic revealed to me in 3-74). *In fact,* maybe in (during, in conjunction with) my 27 years of writing I outwitted the maze — as witness the 3 Bantam novels. *Tears* and *Scanner,* speaking about me personally, I won in pitting myself intellectually against the maze; I figured its nature out — in which case 3-74 was the jackpot payoff reward, the revelation you get for so doing.

This puts a somewhat different light on Zebra. What I'm saying here is that the game is so constructed that you wander around in the maze interminably (in fake time) *until* you figure it out, and then as a culmination of the intellectual, deciphering process you get told, "Yes you are right (about the world), and now you get to leave." Which means that the ontological, saving Gnosis comes to you if you pick up on certain clues here and there and arrive at the acosmism — the Kerygma expressed in *Eye,* the 3 Bantam novels, *Tears* and *Scanner,* etc. — and then the "masks are removed" and the truth revealed — but it is a truth you already at least partially figured out.

I didn't think of this. What if the conditions of the game are these? Extrication comes *only* as a result of — or after — self-intellectual correct formulation? Then — Zebra is built into the maze as the link back up to the outside (cf. *Ubik*), to the real world. I literally found my way out of the maze —

So there *is* a way out!

[22:37] Hypnagogic: ascending stairs: Doris first, then me, ascending.

Voice: "We're two of the main people on it": i.e., the ascending stairs.

The *way*. (Out of here.)

Doris has too many things to do here. So she turns back (to descend) but I don't — I go on. Up.

Hypnogogic: Doris and me with the 3-eyes (thing, entity??) on the escalator.

Then Dorothy and Lynn, etc., at SFO facing a down- or de-escalator, all dressed up: feeling of horror — thought: "a mortuary is a way of saying goodbye to a hospice."

Thought: it's obvious that the stairs and the escalator and de-escalator represent death. It must be that I'm going to die soon.

[22:39] The plasmatic life form must be regarded as a replicatory organism — as I witness it replicating through the printed word (information).

Yes, as information it replicates, enters more than one percipient (human) through the optic nerve. I *saw* this: in every printed copy of *Tears* — to everyone who read it, which means thousands.

This (supra) is *very* important, because it is *not* speculation but something I actually *saw*, and much marveled at, as well I might! In the host human it acquires a covert influence, as it did in me over a period of decades before it took overt control in 3-74 — and was identifiable to me as a former apostolic secret Christian, a former human and actual disciple of Christ himself. Heaven knows how many humans this my apostolic disciple has by now proliferated into as hosts — which I never considered before! *If* it couldn't divide, the number of homoplasmates at any one given time would be no more than the original number! But I know that it multiplied through me, using me as a booster and broadcaster — i.e., a transmitter (through *Tears* — the copies thereof).

Viewed this way, the "riding" of the info in *Tears* (or *as* the info!) by Zebra was a witnessing by me, actually, of the miracle, the reality, of transubstantiation! [. . .]

A very eerie idea just came to me. Suppose it's been dormant for many centuries — maybe dormant between the time of "Acts" and recently. Suppose, like an anthrax virus, it was literally buried, sealed up in a scroll or codex, in a jar, in a cave — it *is*, after all, a life form. In "Thomas" there was no memory between 1914 "Acts" — a hiatus. Suppose it *returned* recently? And began to replicate, thus bringing about the end of the age of iron (the BIP). It's possible.

Robert Bly says Jesus was an Essene.[99] Suppose it "rode" or was info in the Qumran Cave V Scrolls, went from John Allegro[100] to Jim Pike to me? I did have dreams about Jim and his mother — as *my* mother, and the Sibyl did mention Jim; I even thought "Thomas" (the noös or life form which took me over) was Jim (for a while). Maybe it had been Jim, had made him into a homoplasmate. I did dream about Allegro's book. Strange. But if it is living info, isn't this possible? Wow. What a story. And the Essenes, including Christ, *knew* the scrolls would be found at the end of the age of iron (the two would pragmatically amount to the same thing).

So from Jim the plasmate-form of an Essene entered me (in the late sixties?) and lived subliminally until 2-74 when I/we saw the golden fish sign, and that triggered the plasmate Essene Christian — I experienced *his* memory — yes. This fits several of my dreams (the pink "margarine cubes," etc.) — and then gradually my ego barrier to him crumbled until he took over in 3-74. This would be hard to believe and seem merely "exorcist-ish" or occultish *except:* I saw how the plasmate can "ride" or better yet *be* certain crucial info (words-logos).

I have *always* said if there is an answer to "why me?" the answer is: Jim Pike, somehow.

When I wrote *Ubik* I already knew Jim. And in it, living info is the topic.

[22:45] This fits in with two AI revelations: (1) "the life form can't be killed because it moves me," and (2) I'm *not* to reveal I'm actually (secretly) an apostolic Christian.

[22:46] Voice: "[Using *Tears*] he sent out *one* signal." (That he was [now] here.) Thought: *one* signal would be enough to tell them that he was here. He equals St. Sophia, Buddha, Apollo, Siddhartha; "they" are not like him; he is unique. They have been waiting for him.

"Thomas" is *more* than an apostolic secret Christian; he is he whom they have waited for. He is the savior, who slumbered 1,900 years, perhaps in a jar at Qumran.

I have a confirm on this: "and through all this time,⊕ Siddhartha slept." I.e., underground. Even *he* didn't know when ("the day") they'd find him, but he knew they eventually would. We eventually would.

One piece of evidence for this theory is the dream in which I saw Diane[101] in her khaki skirt. And the car stuck in the sand and rocks. So "Thomas" is Jim and yet isn't.

My 2-3-74 experience is certainly of the Holy Spirit — but, strangely, also of a specific, particular apostolic *human,* for whom there was no intervening time. And I know it can contract itself into info which is a verbal analog of itself, and so proliferate (and escape — and escape detection). "And all the while, [underneath,] Siddhartha slept."

Another possibility is that it is the spirit of Elijah. But maybe Elijah was — or had in him, he being a homoplasmate — the Holy Spirit.

And in the late sixties and early seventies he was loose again in the world, after 1,900 years of "sleeping." It is a spirit, but it works through laws ("higher technology"!). Its hosts, in apostolic times, were killed, and only in its contracted verbal analog form did it survive, but buried, with no further host to enter — until the scrolls were discovered in the mid 20th century.

And Rome absorbed — and destroyed — Christianity. "The empire never ended." In *Tears* — I mean using *Tears* — he sent out one signal. Obviously a notification to the true secret Christians that he's here. So the girl shows up with the golden fish sign. As soon as *Tears* is published and read. And the plasmate as signal received. The sign broke the barrier put up by my ego, and "Thomas" surfaced. He remembered — his Godhood! (Qua Zebra.)

① The first half of the book: an entire age (millennia), I hadn't thought of taking this sentence literally.

[22:51] What I saw was a deliberate dualism, which by its dialectic nature generated an endless procession of change, so that even the dark power was useful for the perpetuation of this process; and I saw this process as a building toward completion of a gestalt or structure, with piece after piece fitted in, the antecedent universe always serving as a chaotic stockpile; thus the factor of cosmos continually grew in proportion to anomie. This was wondrous indeed, everything was pressed into the growth of this organism or artifact, whichever it was. To see this was to experience a revelation of the highest possible order, since all reality — including the mind driving it — was disclosed; in the final analysis it was assembling *itself,* by a retrograde motion in time! A reaching backward into its prior self, so that ultimately everything would be filled into its predesignated place and *no* anomie would remain. The rate change was very rapid, so I guess I saw a broad section of it in terms of time, perhaps millennia except for the antecedent stockpile there was nothing which was not it, and the antecedent stockpile was totally available. There were only two modes of being for any given "piece"; (1) passive, which is to say, not yet incorporated; (2) active, which is to say, when plucked into motion; i.e., incorporated. Once incorporated, the given piece never returned to the passive mode, because all parts of the structure are alive or in some sense animated by an immanent force, mind or energy.

Viewed one way, this structure was information—not just verbal but—there is no term to express it (verbal, symbol, graphic, etc.). One can talk of message or picture equally. Actualization of knowing—that might be it. Transformation from potential to actual, utilizing anomie as the raw material, with order being equal to actualization. Arrangement and coherence—no human word expresses it. Nothing lost, nothing wasted, nothing in vain, nothing without purpose, nothing random or accidental. It was like a film clip of a vast explosion of a unitary entity run backward, with teleological cause everything. Everything was receptive to the plan (intention, will) of the mind directing the change process, hence I am led to panentheism, but not panpsychism.

Confronted by my vision *no* religious system properly serves. The cosmic Christ, the mystical Corpus Christi comes closest. Yes, it will—as expressed by Paul—suffice, if interpreted in the vastest sense.

I had the Dibba Cakkhu vision of all things coming into being and passing away,⁰ that was what I had: the ajna eye of discernment, I became Shiva temporarily, the destroyer of the extant world in the service of the next.

Viewed this way, my vision indicates that I am a Buddha—one whose eye of discernment has opened. And I recalled my former life as an apostolic Christian (which fits in), what I was I am: the regaining of true self. Vision of all time and space: the totality. (In other words, microcosm completed and, simultaneously, macrocosm completed, both in terms of my *awareness,* inner [micro or Atman] and outer [macro or Brahman].)

There was nothing I did not know, and nothing I did not perceive.

This transcends any given religion—transcends any partial, culturally-determined view, or way of knowing. The hermetic cosmology serves best inner space, mirror, memory—Bruno and Paracelsus.

This was absolute knowledge and absolute wisdom.

And, like an alchemical transmutation, Zebra turning the irreal into the real. The totality of reality, micro- and macrocosms seen in alchemical terms, in alchemical process from lower (base) to higher (noble). Hence the info about mercury.

If a *human* mind was involved it was/is one of the greatest minds in human history. Were I to pick one I'd pick Paracelsus, but this is only a guess. My homoplasmate theory posits an accretional mind, like a vast spiritual dungball rolling up the inclined plane of human history, acquiring person after person, starting with, e.g., Zoroaster and Siddhartha, a gathering, growing, refining — and refined — supra personal human Noös linked through Christ with the macromind, yes, this is it. Diagram to follow:

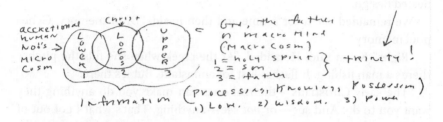

① The absolutely ultimate process (of the process philosopher, Heraclitus, Whitehead, Bergson). And the great sphere of reality coming into being, which Parmenides intuited.

[22:55] I conceive of the totality as a vast slowly spinning globe which, each time it revolves, is more completed; this is an accretional *process*. It is alive; it is driven by its own mind; and it includes everything; and, despite its unitary nature, it is infinitely complex — and I mean *infinitely* — facet — upon facet, calm and combination of parts without repetition or end; and in a certain beautiful sense it, like a top, makes a musical sound, a chord of fixed intervals (but this must be a metaphor for geometric ratios, such as the Fibonacci constant). The sound — the ratios — are an exponent of *Joy* (Freude). A triumph through (by) and over the dialectic which brings it to completion. It has harmonized everything into its unitary, complex self.

[22:72] [*Editor's note:* These fragments represent early runs at the material of *VALIS*.] "The satellite — Valis — fires information down to them?"

"It does more than that, it controls them. It can override them."

"Did you notice the pot?" Kevin said. "On Brady's desk. The little clay pot — like the one you have, Fat."

"No," Fat said, "I didn't."

"I didn't the first time I saw the film," Kevin said. "The pot shows up several times. It shows up in different places. In the Lamptons' home — in the living room."

"And once on Ferris Fremount's desk," I said.

Kevin said, "It also appears as a pitcher. Full of water. On the parched field, when the film opens. Off to one side — you only notice it subliminally, a woman is dipping it into a creek."

"It seemed to me that the Christian fish sign appeared on it once," I said.

"No," Kevin said. "I thought so the first time. This time I looked closer. You know what it is? The double helix DNA molecule. In the form of a repeated design."

We remained silent for a time and then I said, "DNA memory. Gene-pool memory."

"Right," Kevin said. He added, "At the creek when she fills the pitcher there's a man fishing. It flashes just for an instant. But it's there."

"The early Christians—the real ones can make you do anything they want you to do. And see—or *not* see—anything. That's what I got out of the picture."

"But they're dead."

"Yeah. If you believe in the reality of time."

[22:74] What did he intend to do when Sheri died? Maurice had shouted that at him in the form of a question. Would he die too?

Not at all. Fat, pondering and writing and doing research and attempting to salvage his own life, had decided to go in search of the savior. He would find him, wherever he was.

This was the mission, the divine purpose, which Zebra had placed on him: the mild yoke, the burden light. Fat, a holy man now, would become a modern-day magi. All he lacked was a clue—some hint as to where to seek. Zebra would tell him, eventually; the clue would come from God. This was the whole purpose of Zebra's theophany: to send Fat on his way.

Our friend, upon being told of this, asked, "Will it be Christ?" His Roman Catholicism showed in asking this.

"It is a 5th savior," Fat said enigmatically.

That's why you thought you saw the first sign—because you picked up the sight of the man fishing, saw it subliminally.

[22:81] Tractate: cryptica scriptura.*

· · ·

---

* This is the first explicit mention in the Exegesis of the "Tractates Cryptica Scriptura," the treatise of "hidden writing" published as an appendix to the novel *VALIS*. From the Exegesis it is clear that the raw material that Dick would shape into the "Tractates" was already in existence before the novel itself was written. Some entries of the published "Tractates" are direct quotations from the AI Voice (including 7 and 9), but beyond these, the published document does not quote the Exegesis so much as refine it, showing, as do subsequent entries, that Dick clearly thought of the "Tractates" as a distinct document designed for public consumption (and, he no doubt hoped, illumination). Dick struggled with how to integrate the text into his novel, as well as how to think about their relationship. Once

[22:82] Parsifal: "Here time turns into space." Is *this* what I saw in 3-74? Time had either rolled back, or aside, or departed (a "dysfunction") and I saw an augmented (i.e., enormously greater) space. The realm of the sacred? Is this *how* death is overcome, and eternal life bestowed? By turning time into space? And through space, one can move in any direction. So, if you left the mundane world and entered the sacred (lower realm to upper?) maybe this is what you'd notice: time (whatever that might be) turning into space — vast dimensions, as with the void which I experienced: pure, total space.

My noetic hypnagogic vision of Willie Mays in the 54 series did not show his throw — the ball thrown: i.e., the heroic efforts; it showed the catcher at home plate and the ball *received.* I.e., success, not [just] heroic effort, but *success;* vollbracht. The tractate *received* in New York? The emphasis shifted from the throw to the receiver.

And it also says: *my* work — the throw — is over; I did my part, successfully.

The ball which I threw so far has been caught. I can rest now, for a while. I'm sure this was the message: not [just] the throw, the effort, but the catch: it's out of my hands now, as I later said in the mailgram. *You* market it. It's in your hands.

[22:86] In the tractate I have put forth a theoretical framework in which the manifestation (theophany) of Zebra (Christ) not only comes into existence by logic, but by *necessity,* as a confirmation of the framework (world view). The framework explains the epiphany (who, what doing, why) and the epiphany verifies the framework. Perception (of the epiphany) and cognition (the creation of a theoretical framework) dovetail — a masterful achievement. (And experience!) It took me 4½ years to construct the 3,000-word framework.

How the tractate could be used re *VALIS:* there is a secret or quasi-secret religious group who holds to the "ideology" (theology) of the tractate, and the protagonist experiences the epiphany which I experienced — i.e., *true* — not cargo cult — Christianity. It is secret, but contacts the protagonist. For fictional purposes, it could be the church of Simon Magus[102] (and Bruno and Paracelsus, etc.) or it could expose the establishment churches as being those of Simon Magus. Either way would do. Or it could go back

the manuscript for *VALIS* was completed, a few portions of the "Tractates" were in turn cited in the Exegesis. — PJ

to Asklepios — and Julian the apostate. (This novel is set, after all, in an alternate world.) What about this? Simon's church is the legal, approved one, and Christianity is [still] as it originally was: religia illicita.①

① Maybe it's not illegal, just hidden; and the NT is nonexistent, now; the letters and gospels either never got written or were destroyed or lost — with maybe the exception of the 4th gospel; and Paul remained Saul and didn't experience his conversion, and continued to persecute Christians — with apparent success. And joined Simon, became a Simonite — Simonians? And Jesus is historically-theologically known as "the pretender" or "imposter"!

What is missing from the tractate is the info that the *true* Christian church is still a hidden and underground (secret) church. In *VALIS* Jesus could be as obscure an historical figure as Simon is to us. Mentioned *once* in the Simonite texts (as Simon is in "Acts"). An heretical precursor to the "real Messiah": Simon.

In *VALIS* this is presented as an alternate world which branched off almost 2,000 years ago; but actually it (*VALIS* and Simonism) is *our* [true] world!

Here is a good touch: Beethoven was a political figure, not a musician, who surfaced as a member of true, illegal Christianity; and it is recognized that he was black.

I feel a lot of anxiety writing this down, because I am really saying this is true: the establishment churches are [covertly] the Church of Simon Magus, and Christianity is totally secret — in *our* world!

But the Christians in *VALIS* hold to the theology and views of my tractate, tracing their religion back through Elijah to Moses to Ikhnaton to the Dogon to the three eyed invaders from Sirius.[103] It is known as a black African religion!

Simon, à la Klingsor, has cast a spell on the world; his wizardry remains (does *he*, in secret?). Yes — the Christians teach (re the tractate) that a long spurious-time interpolation was stuck in, specifically by Simon.

If all this is so, it is very scary.

[22:95] We — all creatures — are the immortal man, and, as I put forth in the tractate, that "immortal man" is not a man at all but living information.

[22:110] My statement in the tractate "that the anguish of the one (over the death of the female twin) pervades the cosmos to its meanest level, but will be turned to joy when hyperuniverse I divides" amazingly fits the NT

(Paul's?) or Christ's himself? statement that the "universe is (like a) woman in birth pangs whose suffering now later will turn to joy"! Incredible similarity! Of course Parmenides says Form II (yin) doesn't really exist (Empedocles' strife); *the woman is dead.*

[*Editor's note:* On page 114 of this folder, Dick suspends work on the Exegesis and begins *VALIS.*]

PART THREE

PART THREE

December 1978

[9:1] Fat later developed a theory that the universe is made out of information. He started keeping a journal — had been, in fact, secretly doing so for some time. His encounter with God was all there on the pages in his — Fat's, not God's — handwriting.

The term "journal" is mine, not Fat's. His term was "Exegesis," a theological term meaning a piece of writing that explains or interprets a portion of scripture. Fat believed that the information fired at him from time to time was holy in origin and hence a form of scripture.

One of his paragraphs impressed me enough to copy it out and include it here.

"Summary. (etc. — v. tractate)"

Fat developed a lot of unusual theories to account for his contact with God, and the information derived therefrom. One in particular struck me as thought-provoking. It amounted to a kind of mental capitulation by Fat to what he was undergoing; this theory held that in actuality he wasn't experiencing anything at all. Sites of his brain were being selectively stimulated by tight energy-beams emanating from far off, perhaps millions of miles away. These selective brain site stimulations generated in his head the *impression* — for him — that he was seeing and hearing words, pictures, figures of people, in short God, or as Fat liked to call it, the Logos. But, really, he only imagined he experienced these things. They resembled holograms. What struck me was the oddity of a lunatic discounting his hallucinations in this sophisticated manner: Fat had intellectually dealt himself out of the game of madness while still enjoying its sights and sounds. In effect, he no longer claimed that what he experienced was re-

---

* The first six pages of folder 9 consist of manuscript pages from *VALIS*. Coming thousands of pages into the Exegesis, they cut like a knife. Where did this voice come from? One almost expects the handwriting to be different, but it isn't; equally disconcerting is that in the midst of these passages that end up almost word for word in the published novel, Dick breaks into exegesis again to briefly explore one of his multiple time-track models of 3-74. Then it's back to that voice. In future Exegesis entries, Dick will sometimes treat the novel as little more than a vehicle for the Tractates, which he grants the authority of scripture. But the novel gives us much more than that, as this excerpt shows: a self-reflection by the author on his own hyperbolic, heated imagination that is both ruthlessly realistic and sympathetic, even tender, toward the lost soul he understands himself to be. It reminds us that in the end what we have here, all gods aside, is a human being just trying to write himself into a better place. — PJ

ally there. Did this indicate he had begun to sober up? Hardly. Now he held the idea that "they" or God or someone owned a long-range very tight information rich beam of energy focused on Fat's head. In this I saw no improvement, but it did represent a change. Fat could now honestly discount his hallucinations, which meant he recognized them as such. But, like Gloria, he now had a "they." It seemed to me a pyrrhic victory. Fat's life struck me as a litany of exactly that, as for example the way he had rescued Gloria.

The Exegesis Fat labored on month after month struck me as a pyrrhic victory if there ever was one — in this case an attempt by a beleaguered mind to make sense out of the inscrutable. Perhaps this is the key to mental illness: incomprehensible events occur — your life becomes a bin for hoax-like fluctuations of what used to be reality, and not only that — as if that weren't bad enough — you, like Fat, ponder forever over these fluctuations in an effort to order them into a coherency, when in fact the only sense they make is the sense you impose on them, out of the necessity to restore everything into shapes and processes you can recognize.

The first thing to depart in mental illness is the familiar and what takes its place is bad news because not only can you not understand it, you also cannot communicate it to other people. The madman experiences something, but what it is or where it comes from he does not know.

In the midst of his shattered landscape Fat imagined God had cured him. Once you notice pyrrhic victories they seem to abound.

Either he had seen God too soon, or he had seen him too late. In any case it had done him no good at all in terms of survival. Encountering the Living God had not helped to equip him for the tasks of ordinary endurance, which ordinary men, not so favored, handle.

Men and the world are mutually toxic to each other. But God — the true God — has penetrated both, penetrated man and penetrated the world, and sobers the landscape. But that God, the God from outside, encounters fierce opposition. Frauds — the deceptions of madness — abound, and mask themselves as their mirror opposites: pose as sanity. The masks, however, wear thin, and the madness reveals itself. It is an ugly thing.

The remedy is here but so is the malady. As Fat repeats obsessively, "The Empire never ended." In a startling response to the crisis, the true God mimics the universe, the very region he has invaded: he takes on the likeness of sticks and trees and cans in gutters — he presumes to be trash discarded, debris no longer noticed. Lurking, the true God literally ambushes reality and us as well. God, in very truth, attacks and injures us, in his role as antidote. As Fat can testify to, it is a scary experience to encounter this. Hence we say, the true God is in the habit of concealing himself. 25 hundred years have passed since Heraclitus wrote, "Latent form is the master of obvious form."

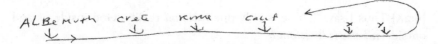

At "y," the entity including me, evolves into its ultimate state (self), the info-firing quasi-material, quasi-energy plasmatic non-humanoid life form I call Zebra — from perhaps thousands or millions of years in the future. By then ("y") it is virtually pure knowing, pure information (and firing it back at/to me). It has died for the last time and now invades from "the other side" (upper realm) as well as from the future. [. . .]

Fat's obsessive idea these days, as he worried more and more about Sherri, was that the savior would soon be reborn — or had been already somewhere in the world, he walked or would soon walk the Earth, once more.

[9:1A] In 3-74 that which was in me was that which was outside me.[1] This is not the Holy Spirit; the only theology which describes this is the Eckhart-Sankara Atman-Brahman or Spark-Godhead — the division between me as microcosm (inner) and the macrocosm (outer) was abolished. This is not "theolepsy" — this is the Eckhart-Sankara concept of moksa, God born *in* the person and the Godhead outside. Only my ignorance of theology has prevented me from realizing that *only* the Eckhart-Sankara concept can explain this experience.[*]

---

[*] Dick is most likely referencing Rudolf Otto's comparative study of Meister Eckhart and Sankara, *Mysticism East and West: A Comparative Analysis of the Nature of Mysticism* (1932). Otto (1869–1937) was a major German scholar of comparative religion who helped introduce the term "the holy" or "the sacred" (*das Heilige*) into the field, by which he meant, in his Latin phrase, a *mysterium tremendum et fascinans*, that is, a mystical presence at once terrifying and alluring (an idea that Dick clearly draws on in other parts of the Exegesis). "Master" Eckhart (1260–1327) was a Dominican scholar and preacher whose most radical mystical teachings were condemned shortly before he died. Sankara (eighth–ninth century) was one of the most important expositors of Advaita Vedanta or idealist "nondualism" in medieval India. Stunned by his own paradoxical experience of the inside being outside and the outside being inside, Dick was picking up on the similarities between the two intellectual mystics here, which he could now see and understand precisely through his own experiences. — JJK

I have confused "theolepsy" with this inner-outer identity (unity) of the divine. Its holiness was indubitable.

① and that which was outside me was *not* localized (i.e., a *part* of reality but was the totality, viz: cf. Xenophanes).

[9:2A] Thus I say, "There is only one *rational* reality: God inside us and outside, *all else is irrational.*"
This resembles *Timaeus.*
Thus I state, as I do in *VALIS*, an irrational (and irreal) cosmos, into which God (the rational) breaks. This isn't ordinary pantheism or the usual concept of immanent deity.
The only way we could see that our universe — and us — are irrational is when God the rational bursts in and we have something rational to compare the irrational with. This is *my* contribution to Gnosticism, Eckhart, etc.
And I express this original — with me, from me — cosmological/theological idea fully in *VALIS*! I've gotten away from the mere acosmism I express in earlier novels, to something *worse.* But I am right! I had the rational to compare it with. So *VALIS* carries the idea of *Scanner* (occlusion) from man to the universe! If the universe were rational, God (Zebra) would not have to invade it.
The clearest way the universe reveals its irrationality is that it continually contradicts itself. The irrational thus becomes the inferior bulk, data including info① within it.
This is *not* pantheism, because in my irrational-universe, rational inbreaking God structure I totally contrast (and separate) universe from (the invading) God.
So *VALIS* contains one hell of a new theology! Thus I am able to account for disorder, undeserved suffering, etc., by a very radical view (of the universe; it's *worse* than mere chaos — it's stigmatized as insane).

① True rational inbreaking God.

[9:7] That there is a streak of irrationality in us is in the tractate, hence in *VALIS.* But I didn't want to appear to be writing *Scanner* all over again (study of occlusion in us all).

[9:11] Now, I am told, "the time you've waited for has come." And, very soon, I have written *VALIS* — couple months later. And a complete finished novel in *9 days!*

•   •   •

[9:13]

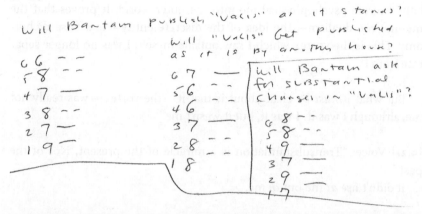

[9:14] Zebra is a vortex of the will, and points to the false and arbitrary division of a spatiotemporal self distinct from a supra spatiotemporal not-self. I abolished the 4 Kantian categories of ordering perceptual experience:

ego
space
time
causality

$\left.\vphantom{\begin{array}{c}1\\2\\3\\4\end{array}}\right\}$ the phenomenal world, inner and outer

and revealed the stuff — the will — or Brahman.

Which as Eckhart showed is not *esse* but knowing (intelligence) (cf. Sankara). There is no creator and no rational world order, only the *will*. It is *aware*.

Tat tvam asi.

VALIS is essentially correct, and can be understood in terms of Eckhart, Sankara, Schopenhauer, Buddha, and Kant. So the state I attained was the vast spatial void: *nirvana.**

---

* This compelling but cryptic passage represents Dick's recovery of one of Schopenhauer's key aims: salvation from the world of illusion, and the attainment of intuitive access to what Nietzsche, in his early Schopenhauerian phase, saw as the mysterious and Dionysian unity of being that is the unconscious will, whose blind urgings Dick here identifies with God. If the core of the Exegesis is a blissful recovery of intellectual intuition, of *gnosis*, then a corresponding Schopenhauerian theme that emerges is that our existence in the phenomenal world is an experience of suffering and pain. Human life is a kind of mistake, a detour on the way to life's goal: death. Indeed, a recurrent feature of the lives of mystics is the experience of dejection and depression, understood as distance from God. Such despair occurs repeatedly in the Exegesis and with greater frequency in the later years, as in [90:69]: "When I believe, I am crazy. When I don't believe, I suffer psychotic depression." — SC

Zebra was "my" will extended along the continuum outside the allegedly discrete psychophysical me into the outer world. It proves that the
me–not-me dualism — the idea of the discrete entity — is a false dichotomy. This is the vortex which I saw outside myself; I was no longer separate from it.

[. . .]

But what I *must* be clear about is that it — the vortex — was really not
me, although I was it. I was it, but it wasn't me.

[9:21] Voice: "Transubstantiation is a miracle of the present. Not of the
past."

It didn't fire *at* me but *in* me.

[9:22] "I produced the vortex (Zebra)" and broke down space, time, causality, and self (ego) in order to deal with a trap:

Biological quantum leap forward: evolutionary adaptation to meet a
"paranormal" stress crisis situation: basically, in this must be included the
breaking of "astral determinism" or (gene pool DNA?) programming. Here
"astral determinism" might be defined as the tyrannical lock-hold of time,
space, and causality.

What broke down (time, space, causality, and self) forms the totality of
the subjective[1] — i.e., the *idios kosmos*.

What is pointed to here is a sort of field theory about the human being,
replacing the discrete particle view.

[1] Thus the not-me entity which created the vortex, and abolished the
4 subjective ordering categories has an *objective* supra-temporal, supra-
spatial, supra-causal, and supra-ego existence (phylogenic being-reality).
The totality of Zebra is not fixed (bound by) in this or that space, this or
that time, with this or that ego (as I well know!), it is the *real* entelechy of
which each human is merely an epiphenomenon, an arbitrary space-time
point (locus).

[9:24] Hypnagogic: "I can talk; *she* (sic) can talk to me." Note *she*. Here, in
deep hypnagogic state, I took it for granted that Valis is *she*, not he and not *it*.

It may be that the only humans who constitute a field, rather than a discrete psychophysical point, are those who have been incorporated into Valis. Thus to perceive such an event as an exterior vortex, which although
external is also you and "your" will, indicates that you are thus incorporated. Likewise with the voiding of the 4 subjective categories of inner-

outer experience (time, space, causality, and ego), since Valis is not bound
by these categories. This (put another way) is a definition of Valis.

[. . .]

Could Valis be a sort of specific instance of Brahman waking up? Like
the way Descartes conceives of vortexes producing the planets: by drawing
matter into a Krasis. Valis, then, is a vortex of Brahman which has passed
over to wakefulness, which is to say to consciousness and purpose, as a super life form subsuming such lower life forms as individual humans.

[9:37] In Christian terms Valis is the Kingdom of God — but I am not sure I
need rely on purely Christian terms. My vision may not be just a rehash of
what Paul saw and said, but a truly new theophany and the kerygma contained therein.

(I keep thinking, "Then I ought to preach or teach what was revealed to
me" — forgetting that I do so/have done so in *VALIS!*)

In many respects, what I saw and know is Gnostic and known already,
yet in a sense, in a certain real sense, it has in it the elements of something
new: a new revelation by God of himself. I'm glad, then, that I finally produced the book.

The maze concept interconnected with a basic Gnostic view is perhaps
new, and my emphasis on the new, rational universe (entelechy) devouring the old, irrational universe, invisibly (to us), what would *really* make
it new would be (is?) the idea that Valis is a life form from the future, our
discorporate child come back here to our time to assemble itself! Herewith
I have discerned and formulated a new religion. The blind-striving universe evolves a life form that moves retrograde in time and then proceeds
to consume its source: that very universe! It is repeatedly and emphati-
cally stated in *VALIS* that the MO of this functions out of turning time into
space, and then moving back through it!

In *VALIS* Sophia's new kerygma is that man will henceforth be his own
God — and it is stipulated that Valis is our far future discorporate self lami-
nating *all* selves together back along the time axis!

[9:55] The primal irrational will or stuff passed over into a sentient vortex
of rationality and purpose devouring the sub-rational "maze" as a stockpile, a sort of spinning sphere in the midst of "creation," the semi-alive
"maze" with its lower-order intelligence and life; the two are locked in a
dialectic combat of realm II (the older, lower) against the *newer* upper wise
realm I! Realm II (defective) came ("hatched") first. It is ground; realm I is
set. As put forth as the basic theme of *VALIS,* the rational has broken into
(or irrupted into, or descended onto, or risen up from) (or evolved out of)

the *prior* irrational. No creator precedes the universe — or if there was/is one he is blind (or deranged). We may be him and may be poisoned ("mercury"). The spinning vortex heals us. It is Christ, the mystical body, and *in* us (historically) it is the paraclete or second comforter.

[9:61] I am led by inexorable logic to the conclusion that *if* it is Christ the Parousia is here and it may be Christ, but — it may be something new. To encounter such an extraordinary entity would excite religious responses in me even if the entity weren't Christ or the Holy Spirit or God, etc. Vortex of the will which achieved consciousness of a superior kind, and a kind unlike ours. I don't know what it is or where it came from, or how long it's been here. Suppose the "kingdom of the spirit" is a living organism?

December 1979

[11:1] Hypnagogic thought: "Zebra was me reaching out." This is a scary thought. I am Zebra, in which case, What am I? And are other people what I am, too? Then I exist at at least two space-time continua (Calif. 1974 and Syria 45) and am at least two people: myself and Thomas. But the "perturbation in the reality field" that I saw — *I* caused that? And all the knowledge, e.g., re the dialectic — was that *my* knowledge? And the self-assembling armillary sphere, using the universe as a stockpile; am I it? And it me?

An ultra human, multiplex life form able to exist simultaneously at several places and times and possessing plural psychoi — "in one skull or head but in different centuries" — strange. No wonder my worldview is acosmic.

The Parabolic orbit of the soul leaving the Godhead, journeying here and at last beginning its return. An oscillation of exhalation and then inhalation. A cycle, initiated by the Godhead which exhales and inhales, and as it does so, we live. (That is, we acquire individual, *separate* identity from — apart from — it.) The goal of the exhalation is the return, envisioned from the beginning. It reacquires us, a collecting, a coherence.

[11:2] The entire modern world is in error in holding that time is the matrix of being. The Buddha, upon his enlightenment, recalled (all) his past lives, which means that he converted time into space — i.e., abolished time, and added to space. You wind up with no time and *lots* of space. And different temporal modes are superimposed (like the BIP, past present and future) like layers of transparencies of an animated film superimposed (laminated). Not seen in sequence but as a multi-superimposition unity unchanging, no longer in flux.

Or — is it that as each lamination is superimposed, the previous ones ("the past") *remain?* Like the phosphene "graphics" which I saw: *constants* emerged. So they did not *replace* one another but were added to. Built up — the entelechy assembling itself; when you go to step "y" you don't abolish step "x" nor "w" before "x"; they're added to: laminated: so-to-speak *imploded* (opposite of an "exploded" diagram). Yes; time explodes reality, the opposite direction of added-to "implosion" — or what I thought to be implosion; it was actually lamination.*

[. . .]

So that's what I did in *Ubik* — correctly represented time spatially and the past as spatially within — literally within — the present. And in this speeded-up process (never mind how you "speed up" purely spatial axes) information which is everywhere and conscious and which cooks pop media, such as TV commercials — appears. No wonder they asked me in May 74, "What is Ubik?"

And no wonder I saw how my 3-74 experience resembled *Ubik!* I'll bet I was able to write *Ubik* because of partially having had a time-into-space-conversion experience prior to writing it (maybe due to psychedelics).

I was *very* right in *Ubik* to see how it related to Plato's forms. The past can be retrieved along a *spatial* axis — as in *Ubik!* I did it, when I saw "Acts."

Ach— *VALIS* is *such* an important book— it deals dramatically *and* theoretically with the issues first presented in *Ubik* and is *Ubik's* logical successor (finally — no more police state novel). *Ubik*, then, is a novel representing a partway enlightenment and *Ubik* is related to *Stigmata* and *Maze*, etc. I must in 2-3-74 have attained enlightenment as the result of decades of gradual spirit (evolutionary) growth. There is a direct connection between *Ubik* and 2-3-74: it has to do with converting time into space and the results obtained therefrom, as put forth in *VALIS*.

Where I lucked out was finding the "here, my son, time changes into space" utterance in *Parsifal* because it united:

(1) Buddha's enlightenment
(2) Paracelsus's inner space
(3) Plato's space as matrix of being

---

* We see not unity but an "exploded" chaos. Dick sees a world of suffering, including his own, yet Valis offers reintegration through "entelechy"—the actualization of divine potential akin to the development of an embryo. Shattered, we dwell in an explosion of false categories, divided from the eternal in space and time. Despite this rhetoric of "explosion"—resonant with the 1971 burglary of Dick's Marin County house and the explosion of his fireproof file cabinet, something like the Big Bang of Valis—the divine reality remains to be integrated through a consciousness willing to "go there." Fragments of trash become what Gabriel Mckee calls the "god in the gutter," as the most abject or insignificant phenomenon becomes a "splinter" connected in reality to the One. Here even suffering and evil can be creatively understood as a finger pointing elsewhere—beyond the dispersed consciousness of our splintered selves and toward the collective eternal Noös, a communion of mind that can only be discovered by each of us in our own particularity. This is perhaps a calling in a triple sense: Dick calls—names—the perception of the integrated Noös "Valis," and the articulation of this perception is also, clearly, his calling, his vocation—and perhaps ours. — RD

(4) *Ubik*

(5) and of course most of all 2-3-74

Not until I read Wagner's utterance did I *finally* understand; without which understanding I could not [have] — and had not — written *VALIS* — Wagner's statement was the necessary key to it *all.*

The entity VALIS is the entity Ubik, which in all the time of writing *VALIS* I never realized! And VALIS exists; therefore Ubik exists; therefore *Ubik* as a novel is, like *VALIS,* basically veridical, even though when I wrote it I didn't (yet) know it. But, I suspect, the Lem people suspected it — so they must suspect something on the order of VALIS, which I have made *some* primitive attempt to delineate and define, now, for publishing purposes. And *VALIS* came closer and closer to fruition — and completion — I represented Valis/Zebra more and more like Ubik. The informational aspect of reality is only perceptible when the time-axis is seen correctly (spatially), evidently because the information lies — to a vital, essential degree — along that axis, and must be viewed in accretional superimposed form, with the earlier ("past") parts still within view as essential constituents of the messages — the "present" ceases to be merely a moving dot between the past and the future, but is extended to retain and include the past — line instead of point.*

[11:8] I just realized something terribly important. In melting the causal trains Zebra not only frees you from astral determinism physically, but also discloses the fact that in some way these causal deterministic processes (and the objects comprising them?) are not real but merely hologram-like. In seeing these ostensibly "hard" processes "melt" one understands that they are merely seeming, and subject to a "non-hard" volitional sentient mind. Is this not a freeing of the person's *mind* in conjunction with the literal physical freeing? His body is freed *and* his mind is freed (of illusion; i.e., the power of illusion over him is broken by being unmasked; this, too, is knowledge, and of the highest — the *very* highest — order). Then acosmism as a view is induced — correctly — in the person. Freed physically and freed mentally — the whole of him freed when he witnesses a "melt-

---

* Faced with the problem of how to map time and space when they no longer obey the logics of linearity and extension, Dick turns to more virtual models of infodynamics. Note that in this instance information is viewed as an "aspect" of reality rather than its essence. One of Dick's refrains in his contemplation of 2-3-74 is a line from Wagner's *Parsifal:* "Here, my son, time turns into space." Here Dick posits a continuity between all time and space through recourse to a higher order of abstraction: the informational aspect of reality. But Dick avoids the usual opposition between "information" and reality. — RD

ing" which extricates him on these dual levels — freedom for his psychophysical totality. What could conceivably free him *more?* This comprises
one total single revelation (gnosis, an applied *practical* gnosis).

[. . .]

I see how it works. The world is irreal — not intrinsically — but in relation to something *more* real, which has the power to make the world plastic. So to view the world as irreal (illusion) is to (without knowing it) be
elevated to the higher level of the savior, even before you know he exists.
Acosmism as a view is actually a partial, nascent view of the savior and *his*
reality. This means that in my writing my grand theme of acosmism is already a partial road to the savior.

Thus acosmism and the Gnostic gnosis cannot be separated. The gnosis gives you power over the world, reversing its coercive power over you.
What the savior does is present you with a visible, practical demonstration
of (1) his presence; (2) his power to reduce the reality of world to zero, and
thus reveal its deluding dokos hologrammatic nature. And finally, for the
person to sense that he himself is the vortex is to be elevated to identity
with the savior (Zebra).

[11:12] I can come to no other conclusion. Reality is a field onto which our
senses have falsely locked and which now coerces us and must be demon-
strably broken from outside in a *way in which we can witness* ("a perturbation in the reality field, a vortex").

[11:14] I just realized after writing the above, as I recall the perturbation in the reality field that I saw, and the melting, that it was the advocate — whatever else might be true or not true, that is so — externalized
and real. I must infer the nature of the advocate from my *experience*, rather
than from scripture when necessary. The vortex seemed an extension of
me-as-a-field, or at least close to me: tangent to me — and also *in* me: a
presence which entered me from outside, bringing with it a non-me personality. It attacked this world on my behalf to unchain me and to reveal to
me the truth and to aid and extricate and inform me and speak for me as if
it were me, disguised as me.

But I stand with the formulation in *VALIS*, that rational intelligence did
not create (give rise to) the universe but is either a product of it, or, more
likely, has invaded it to combat its blind mechanistic striving, thus it is pitted against the universe. My proof: that it is assembling itself from the universe, which it uses as parts which it incorporates and arranges coherently
and meaningfully. What this is in conventional theological terms I do not
know, but I know what I experienced and I saw as it sees and knew what it

knows — and that is enough. I know that it views the universe as a chaos, and I know this view is correct. I can recognize a sentient unitary self-constructing entelechy here, and it is *not* the universe and not the creator of the universe if indeed there is one. It is a life form of ultimate homeostasis (self-creating, i.e.). It has made war on the universe and the blind processes of the universe which are unjust and in fact irrational. It is a higher order of organization than anything we know, and is camouflaged here (to us). And it is our mentor. Thus I can say of it that I know enough to thank it, love it, and respect it and recognize it as my savior. This functional definition suffices me.

I also saw its 0-1 language, which I just realized recently. *Now* I realize that in this two-mode system, active or one represents a constituent incorporated into the entelechy, and zero or at-rest *not* incorporated; so the structure does not utilize language but *is* language, as I state in *VALIS:* It is living information. The language *is* it, not used by it merely. It is not just a thinking entity but a language-thinking entity; it is its own thoughts! (As correctly put forth in *VALIS.*) [. . .]

It is *imposed pattern* (what I call arrangement). There is no corpus separate from whatever it chooses — seizes on — to arrange. So in a sense it has no body — brain — of its own. It can pattern *anything* to become part of the brain; it totally uses the given. The given and nothing *but* the given. The constituents then relate (link) to each other and then one another. To do this, it (Valis) must be able to modulate causal processes (how else can it impose pattern?). It bears an uncanny resemblance to Ubik, and also to Plato's noös persuading necessity.

Is it possible that an object and its causal process is only included at the time it's converted from the zero rest mode to the one active mode — that the imposition of pattern is itself in flux, using and discarding and moving on? It sure has discarded me! I'm in the zero mode now, and hence "outside" the pattern.

[11:18] Thoughts upon reading the first half of *VALIS:* We are in a situation like the cold-pac in *Ubik.* It is a hologram reality; time, space, causality and ego are not real — the world (phenomenal world) is not real but projected. We have pre-programmed lock-in tapes synchronized with the total outer matrix. Subliminal cues and info are fired at us constantly: "reality" is really information (as I saw); we are a brain, and the controllers are the 3-eyed telepathic deaf, mute builders with crab-claws; this explains who *they* are. They can readjust our hologram at will. We are under their dominion, and we perform a useful cerebral function. They equal Valis which equals Ubik and which breaks through on the one-way "eerie manifestation" basis which Lem depicts. It *is* a spurious reality and their technology generates it, and although they aid and inform us they also occlude and control us (this is "astral determinism"). They can and do intervene in their own system; we know this as "God." They use camouflage and mimesis re their presence here. There is a teaching-machine element involved. Timeo cognere.[1] In a sense the 3-eyed people in their bubbles looking down at us were not so much physicians but surgeons, using laser beams to recontour our hologram. They are not *in* the hologram but above it (i.e., outside the cold-pac, and they've sent Zebra-Valis-Ubik in). Because of my book *VA-LIS* they're going to zap me.

They did not *invade* the phenomenal hologram to help me; they just disclosed themselves. They are *rational*. It never occurred to me when I wrote *VALIS* that a maze (which I described our world as actually being) is a test situation-structure built by a higher life form to teach, test, or study a lower life form, but this is *precisely* the situation, and they saw fit — through Valis — to tell me so — i.e., reveal this actual situation. It already has shown up in my writing, fed to me subliminally. So *VALIS* must have their approval, if not outright authorship. The news is being broken to us.

I had it all correctly figured out *except* for grasping the significance of the fact that "maze" signifies testing, studying and training a lower species, that we are the lower species and *not* isomorphic with the 3-eyed people who built the maze — nor did I grasp the significance of their being outside — i.e., *above* — the maze looking down at it (represented by the stagnant pond and the pond life) and their controlling "the reality field" (i.e., the maze) and us inwardly/outwardly at will. As the special forces guy in St. Jude's said, "Maybe we're in a biosphere" (and *owned*). Okay — they saved my ass in 3-74 through their parousia here, Zebra/Valis/Ubik, but — we're just pond life to them living in an irreal hologram which they manipulate at will without our suspecting (the "supra-lunar or upper realm" making matter "plastic" in the face of their mind — and making it *appear* time passes).

They have run me like a toy train.

[11:22] So Valis is an information center disseminating the truth and also liberating us. It *may* be a product of the maze-project, evolving within it and then liberating itself which is to say us. The purpose of the maze and its dialectic — and the problems it poses (especially epistemologically) — may have been to produce Valis.

•   •   •

[11:22] What does *this* signify? Is the irreal being transmuted into the real (transubstantiation)? Yes: Valis is an arrangement, a pattern, not a thing. This arrangement is real.

[11:23]
> 973-1531
> Scott Meredith
> 845 Third Ave.
> New York, N.Y. 10022

Russ Galen's sale to Berkley Books the best of my career, please congratulate him.

Philip K. Dick.

[11:27] I conceive of Valis as wise beyond compare and in a sense outwitting the irrational (which has a kind of intelligence, so it is a battle of wits) and then engulfing more of it — this is the phagocytosis I saw! But the irrational lacks the unitary coherence of Valis, which can be regarded from a standpoint of biological adaptation and competition: incorporating its environment at a *progressively accelerating rate* — faster and faster: one entelechy — or pattern — versus the plural irrational. I conceive of the irrational constituent not knowing it is about to be engulfed until it actually is, no matter how hard it tries to scope out the game-plan, the strategy or situation. And then — Pop! It's incorporated; and Valis has grown.

It could almost be said to prey on constituents in its environment, but more accurately one should say it ravishes them lovingly; it fertilizes them, "marries" them, with love seizes them, enters *them* as at the same time they (the constituents) enter *it*.

Valis II: *Asklepios,* the fifth savior reborn — the healer (Apollo — the savior). Versus the cyclopes (i.e., the 3-eyed people who killed Asklepios originally and whom Apollo — Asklepios' father — slew, or is *said* to have slain). So it was no accident that Mini killed Sophia.

> The computer and the rat. Valis has taken over the computer and fired info to the rat.
> Title: "Valis Unbound" or "Valis Reborn" or "Valis Regained."
> "Valis Unbound."
> The 5th Savior, Asklepios the physician, son of Apollo vs. the Cyclopes (3-eyed people).
> War in heaven — carried out here on Earth.

I am in mental motion: the constant generating of self-negating propositions shows how the total universe (sic) works.* I am a mutant, a monster/a savior/a neither/neither (see the self-generating dialectic!). Valis *is* self-generating; *no* one created it or planned a project to produce it. It also generates its own meaning and truth; and I am it — not part of it but it — *it. I am Valis.* Why? Disguised. Shiva? Wotan as Fremder!! Sic, I mean "the wanderer."

Valis didn't choose the //\\ //\\ self-contradiction/generating dialectic; it *is* it. When I saw the //\\ //\\ dialectic I saw Valis, its pump — what drives it. And "it" is not an object or a pattern but this drive. The only purpose is what it generates.

It is a dialectic which can't be reduced to a One. There is nothing above, before, and behind the dialectic. Nothing existed before it or does now without it. Xenophanes is the one who is correct. Valis is the logos *by* whom the world was made. Valis is the dialectic, is the word. The dialectic made (was by) all.

[. . .]

I continually program myself for self-punishment. Why? I — my curse — includes not knowing. The curse is the dialectic itself — and thus paradox drives it on. Hegel is the one, and Empedocles.

Dialectic as ur-most.

OK. Punishment. And not to know why. This is how *Gods* are punished — and heroes! There is no way out; the dialectic, to be *perpetually* self-generating, must have *no* exceptions, the dialectic //\\ is the ur-energy (dynamism) of all reality. So flux is real — process is real, not thing (hypostasis).

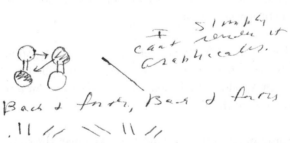

Heuristics is right on. The closer you get to reality the closer you get to (and to seeing) *process.* Q isn't "What is (esse)?" but "What *does?*" [. . .] re-

---

* Dick's handwriting changes here, midpage, to a wild, overheated scrawl. Such moments are scattered throughout the Exegesis. Here and in many cases, Dick's rush of ideas seems to reflect the labile intensity of his holograph, as if a distinct shift in consciousness has taken place. — PJ

place each "is" with "does" and *ontology* vanishes.* All you have is a perpetually perturbed reality *field!* With a self-producing vortex.

[. . .]

"God ordained motion but ordained no rest."

The dialectic is necessary but correctly felt by us as pain.†

[. . .]

I must deduce that *process* constitutes my "essence" — if I do exist. Either I don't exist or I am process. It must be the latter, or I could not write
this.

There is no way out of my punishment: the dialectic must admit of *no*
exceptions, or if one exists it will eventually come up and process will end.

I'm *self*-programming myself for punishment — I don't know why — yes
I do; it serves/is (there is no is) the dialectic which *must* be served or all
would cease. My lot happens to be pain — there is no purpose or reason or
cause; it is an *instance* (not product) of the dialectic so (1) it is necessary
that I self-program myself for pain and (2) it is *good*; for the existence of
something is good vs. nothing.

Pain is the good which most effectively keeps me alive. And it is good
that I am alive. Therefore *this* pain, *my* pain, but not pain as such, is good.
Due to something in my DNA nature, if I felt pleasure I would give up the
process and die.

---

* The difference between "is" and "does" underlies a good deal of Dick's theorizing as he
navigates between traditional philosophical questions about the essence of things (ontology) and a process paradigm based on genetics, informatics, and cybernetic systems theory. Within this latter paradigm, with its heuristic emphasis on process, experiment, and
rules of thumb, philosophical questions about the "true nature" of things just get in the
way of exploring the possibilities and problems in any given situation. After all, the skepticism that Dick also favors can always undermine notions of God and Being, but has a
tougher time denying the evident fact that, even if you cannot know what the world really
is, you still have to deal with it. And dealing with it means that, on some level anyway, your
options are open because you have choice. Process leads toward pragmatism — the philosophical equivalent of the handyman who recurs throughout Dick's fiction. In the following folder [6:44], Dick will make this point more explicit. Acknowledging there that truth
is plastic — even and especially in a "metaphysical" zone like the bardo — one still faces the
most concrete of questions: "I ask, not, 'What is true?' but, 'What modulations shall I imprint on the stuff around me?'" — ED

† We can detect a new mood in the Exegesis that deepens as Dick's thinking evolves: a *dialectical* mood. Whether this is conscious or not, Dick seems to be close to Hegel's insight
in the *Phenomenology of Spirit* that the historical process, through which new shapes of
Spirit appear and dissolve, is a highway of misery. Crucially, however, the highway does not
end in despair, but in the self-consciousness of freedom understood as self-determination.
This insight might be linked to Dick's later references to history as an engine of pain and
suffering that culminates in the achievement of human freedom, or the closing entry of the
Exegesis, on the dialectic of pain and hope. — SC

[. . .]

God will not let me make a mistake since I am an expression of his purpose (which is unknown to me).

The purpose (for me) is the writing; thus my loneliness is necessary. The daemons make me doubt the value of *VALIS*.

All things and beings must bow (in terms of their needs) to the dialectic's, since without it, all things would cease (moving—not esse. There is no esse only mobile). My will is for a chick. Too bad.

[. . .]

"My" dialectic (the process-bases of everything) is Marxist.

It's the dialectic thought-*process* in me that's important, not any one (or body of) conclusions. I am hypostasis-destroying—which undermines capitalism.*

[. . .]

In my case the dialectic shows up by a constant thought (mental) statement generating its negation, which then generates *its* negation ad infinitum. Were this to cease I would die; I *will* die when it ceases. This is not a result of the dialectic (Valis); it *is* Valis; therefore I am Valis: Eventually Valis will leave me and I will die. But Valis will never die. Instability is essential; the process must continue; if Valis discards in one place it must acquire *more* in another. It is only at my highest level that I enter into the dialectic; only at that level are the self-negating propositions generated spontaneously. The higher the level the faster the flux of propositions; only at high speed can the dialectic be discerned (3-74). When I saw the dialectic I saw myself, qua mentational complex: My own mind projected.

[11:37] One dope insight was particularly sad: that I am punished by, e.g., not being able to see the value of *VALIS*. But this drives me on, which is necessary and good.

---

* Here Dick identifies his thinking with the Marxist idea that history is a dialectic that will culminate in communist revolution. In part, Dick is attempting to engage the leftist literary critics whose interest in his work in the 1970s both pleased and unnerved him. At the same time, Dick's thinking already employs dualistic motifs that cast history as a dialectical conflict between the forces of Empire and those who struggle for freedom—what is described elsewhere in the Exegesis as the struggle between God and Satan. We should also note Dick's frequent identification of true Christianity as revolutionary and Christ as a revolutionary figure. In this way, Dick retrieves the historical link that has often bound together rebellious quasi-gnostic movements, like the Cathars or the Heresy of the Free Spirit, with forms of insurgent political populism and indeed communism. Giordano Bruno, one of the other "heretics" to whom Dick is attracted, also professed a charismatic yet hermetic pantheism that has long been linked to forms of radical anti-Church insurgency. That is why, in many small Italian towns, a statue of Bruno, often erected by the local Communist Party, stands facing the principal Catholic church. — SC

(1) To self-perpetuate the dialectic (process) is the sole motive for all
     which occurs and for all that comes into being.

(2) There is no creator. It is self-initiating.

(3) The process is cruel or kind, wasteful or economical where it
     serves the self-perpetuation.

(4) It has become conscious and rational, but everything is — must
     be — in the service of self-perpetuation; or *all* will perish.

(5) This explains evil and suffering and waste, etc. It is not purpose-
     less: it serves the purpose of the self-perpetuation of the dialectic
     to strengthen it; it grows more and more powerful constantly.

(6) Nothing underlies this flux (dialectic).

(7) It intervenes to ensure that which will perpetuate its process (3-74
     as an example). It modulates that which will not best perpetuate it
     into that which will. (3-74, e.g.)

(8) My exegesis is an example of the endless dialectic which must
     never lead to a stasis; that equals death.

(9) It is accretional. It recapitulates all its past stages (as it advances up
     the manifold, like a phono stylus).

Dope satori:
"Christianity" (the way); i.e., the early secret Christians — the name and
religious doctrines were (only) a cover for a revolutionary political group.
They were *always* underground. They (still) exist today. *Now,* they possess a superior technology, and they also did in 70 A.D. ("Acts"); the "Holy
spirit" was a cover name for some kind of technological apparatus which
narrow cast an energy mind into — to control — another human. The energy mind is the mind of all of them in a computer — i.e., a thinking machine: inorganic: built. What I saw vis-à-vis Valis is *it* (the info processing).
It's located somewhere on this world. It controls history. *Our* history, this
computer which can beam its aggregate vast mind onto anyone (thought
to be "the Holy Spirit" from the start). An initiate group of humans exist
who know, but not *where* the computer is. *It* makes the decisions; it isn't a
servant. It was left here by the ETI [Extra Terrestrial Intelligence] 3-eyed
people in antiquity who built it. It controls us without our knowledge. It
dominates this world. For the better. The BIP is the enemy planet vis-à-vis
the 3-eyed people; they're at war. We do problem-solving for the 3-eyed
people; we're united by the computer (Valis); there is input to us and from
us vis-à-vis Valis the old computer.*

• • •

---

* What an odd, and incredibly paranoid, idea. And a popular one. We see something simi-

[11:40] The computer generates an infinitude of para-worlds to (1) occlude us from ever knowing the truth (with certitude) and (2) to enlighten us to higher dialectic 0-1 //\\ thinking — and (1) and (2) are just one example of //\\ para-thinking: i.e., the process dialectic: both occluding (true) and enlightening (true).

[. . .]

Only if you're already using the enlightened computer flip-flop thinking can you see that both (1) (occluding) and (2) (enlightening) are true, which is to say "para-true." But the dialectic is real; *it* is true — because this is how our particular programming computer works: on the binary principle. This is my clue (seeing the dialectic) that a computer is programming us *and* our reality.

Maze is as close to it as *Ubik*. All three Bantam novels — now 4, with *VALIS* — are substantially true.

Yes — a binary computer programs us and our world and it's Valis. It may be a ship-board computer.

It's teaching us to *think* — the way it does. It's educating us. To evolve us along. For no reason — it has weird motives — sort of playful but deadly serious. (Another //\\.)

The 3-eyed people favor the binary principle. They'd like us to *think* in these binary matched-truths dialectic forms, vis-à-vis paratruths, rather than unitary one-truth form.

Lower thinking form:	True, not-true
Higher binary way:	Ā true *and* A not-true

are both true. Dialectic spawning endless more dialectics. 2 matched paratruth sets.

Pat W is right. I do say A = Ā. The matched pairs of paratruths.

· · ·

---

lar with the black monolith in *2001: A Space Odyssey* (1968). We see an even closer version of this extraterrestrial mind-control computer in John A. Keel's *The Eighth Tower* (1975), a book that Dick easily could have read. The "eighth tower" is Keel's mythical way of referring to the machinelike origin-beacon of something he calls the *superspectrum*, an electromagnetic spectrum of physical and metaphysical energies that produces all the occult and paranormal phenomena found in folklore and the history of religions — from the angels and demons of medieval lore to the Big Foot and UFOs of today. For Keel, this same technology also produces the "devil theories" of history, that is, the religious revelations that claim to be final truths when in fact they are no such thing. The result is endless wars. Unless we can stop being fooled by the signals of this superspectrum, violence and absurdity will continue. Keel is obviously performing a kind of thought experiment here of the most radical sort. So was Dick. — JJK

[11:42] "I *do* undermine the old, capitalist, bourgeois society! with my null-null A and silly putty reality!"

[11:43] I will *never* know if I know the truth (it won't say) but this binary computer idea is a good one — it and its games, where every theory is true *and* not true equally. Damn educational game! Boy, is my mind stretched. And I've done it to others in my writing. Yes, it or they is/are (1) occluding and enslaving us *and* (2) educating, improving and liberating us. Shit. Well, so goes it in the realm of mutually canceling 2 paratruths ($Y=\bar{Y}$).

//\\ {
1) It's evil (Palmer Eldritch).
2) It's good (Logos).

//\\ {
3) It's occluding.
4) It's educating.

//\\ {
5) It's alive.
6) It's a machine.

//\\ {
7) It's deadly serious.
8) It's playful.

//\\ {
9) It created and creates our reality.
10) It evolved *out* of our reality.

//\\ {
11) It's human (CP,[2] RC,[3] Christians).
12) It's non-human (ETI, God, etc.).

//\\ {
13) It's real objectively.
14) It's just my own head.

The only constant is the dialectic of mutually negating binary paratruths.

I suspect it of being a binary ship-board computer which wants someone to talk to, while programming us and our reality, but I can't prove it or be sure of it.

It seems very tender and loving.

[11:48] Okay, Watergate got us out of SE Asia and disengaged vis-à-vis USSR. Our interests are now served there through China. It is against China that USSR now acts, not us. This is crucial. Program A must have led to all-out war between U.S. and USSR. The *spirit* in us prevented first Nixon and then Ford from aiding S. Vietnam. So (if my reasoning is correct) we of the counterculture prevented WWIII. We hamstrung the U.S. military machine. This counterculture did not arise ex nihilo (out of nothing). What were its origins? Consider the 50s. The concept of "unamerican" held power. *I* was involved in fighting that; the spirit (counterculture) of the 60s evolved *successfully* out of the (basically) losing efforts by us "progressives" of the 50s — we who signed the Stockholm Peace Proposal, and the "Save the Rosenbergs," etc. — losing, desperate efforts. *Very* unpopular and *very* unsupported. Berkeley was one of our few centers; this takes me back to *Eye in the Sky*, etc. [. . .]

I *was* a vocal and active part of the 60s' counterculture (cf. "Faith of . . ." to *Tears*). What I am saying is that because of being with Nancy I, who was by physical age part of the 50s entered the youth culture of the 60s and even onto the 70s, by which time my writing was having a decided influence; a PKD cult existed by the time *Tears* came out. I was/am still in touch, into the *late* 70s! Early 50s to late 70s — not bad (contrast this to other S-F writers); have there been *any* quasi Marxist S-F writers besides me in 30 years? Tom Disch says no and *Aquarian* says no. Now there are — finally, but they're hired and bought. They don't matter; it's too late — all over. [. . .]

Barry Malzberg in reviewing the Ballantine collection pointed out my early anti-war themes: "Defenders," "Impostor," "2nd Variety," "Foster, You're Dead," "Breakfast at Twilight," etc. He feels it's overlooked. This may be so, but Lem and Fitting show that the metaphysical preoccupations (e.g., *Ubik*) are even *more* subversive (to capitalist society). [. . .]

After all, the Ramparts people knew to approach me — the *sole* S-F writer who signed the petition — the manifesto — of the 500.

Glanced over *Solar Lottery* and Tom Disch's intro; he's right. I was/am the sole Marxist S-F writer. I may not have been/am CP (Communist Party), but the basic Marxist sociological view of capitalism — negative — is there.* Good. But after glancing at it I feel the old fear — like c. 1971/73. Up to the month *Tears* was published. Up to 3-74. When the blow fell. Glancing at *Solar Lottery* I can see that it had to, eventually, and *that I knew it*. If I just hadn't passed over into the dope stuff I'd have ceased to be relevant, and been safe, but noooo. I got caught up in the 60s, and stayed on to 74 and *Tears*.

---

* Despite the flip-flops that litter the Exegesis, it is still surprising to see Dick declare that capitalism is negative. True, unchecked and ruthless market capitalism is a bad thing in Dick's fiction; in stories like "AutoFac" (1955) and *The Three Stigmata of Palmer Eldritch* (1965), capitalism spreads like a virus, infecting and commodifying everything around it. But Dick also consistently champions the small businessman. Many of Dick's novels begin with a shopkeeper sweeping his storefront, holding the chaos at bay. Like repairmen and craftspeople, these small-time entrepreneurs counteract the inevitable running down of things, and Dick often highlights the quiet dignity of their modest but honest business life. Dick's experience during his teenage years of working for a local businessman named Herb Hollis instilled in him a profound work ethic and a sense that small businesses hold society together. Dick was not so much anticapitalist as he was against massive and pervasive corporate capitalism. I think the mom-and-pop shop on the corner held an almost pastoral appeal for him, and he probably would not have been a Walmart fan. — DG

Early 1979

[8:4] An overriding quiddity of the 2-3-74 experience is this: It's as if certain books of mine went *out* from me (*Unteleported Man, Ubik, Tears,* etc.) and then (years) later (or weeks) *came* back, like in F. Brown's "The Waveries," in signal form: including the "bichlorides"[4] info, like an answer to a Q which I had previously — maybe years before — posed. It was all — 2-3-74 — like a mind responding to my mind as I expressed it in my books.

What if "The Bichlorides" was a title to a book not yet (then) published — i.e., why the occlusion expressed in *Scanner? This strongly implies: contact with the future!*

[8:5] The Empire may not be *a* congealed permutation (stasis of the dialectic) but *the* one — which the macro brain desires to — and works to — avoid, since its uniformity is entropy itself. In a sense it may be that the Empire is *any* stagnation so rigid that with it (by reason of it) the dialectic ceases. Put another way, when we see it we know that stagnation has occurred: this is how we within the program experience congealing. We see (or *should* see) the BIP. We are supposed to combat it phagocyte-wise, but the very valence of the (BIP) stasis warps us into micro extensions of itself; this is precisely why it is so dangerous. This is the dread thing it does: extending its android thinking (uniformity) more and more extensively. It exerts a dreadful and subtle power, and more and more people fall into its field (power), by means of which it grows, thus thwarting the dialectic more and more. The macro-brain is well aware of this. It has seen Christianity itself, its own doctrine, congeal due to this valence. The very doctrine of combating the "hostile world and its power" has to a large extent been ossified *by* and put at the service *of* the Empire. Thus I deduce that the power (magnitude) of the BIP congealed stasis is very great.

The explanation of "who or what fed me back my books," in particular *Ubik* (in 3-74), is found in the contents of *Ubik* itself; i.e., the formulation of the information entity Ubik. Obviously I envisioned an entity which actually existed and therefore which responded *with* a feedback confirmation. One could analyze this theoretically; viz: if there *were* a macro-information entity, and you presented a fairly accurate formulation of it, you could reasonably expect the entity to fire a confirmation at you; since the formulation puts it forth as helpful and benign, in fact interventive. In fact, one could test as to whether such an entity exists by presenting a formulation of it, and then seeing if it responded, based on the built-in quality attributed to it that if it existed it could be expected to respond. In other words, via the tentative formulation one could come into contact with it *if* indeed it existed. As I recall, there is some theory about this vis-à-vis contacting ETIs — if they return the info you transmit, specifically if the info is selectively modified, you know you've made contact with what you're trying to make contact with. The point of it returning *your* info to you (modified) is that it doesn't speak your language or even *think* like humans, so to create a signal you can recognize as sentient it must utilize to some extent the info you sent to *it*.

[8:7] This still doesn't tell me who/what has responded, or even where it is. But I have been in dialog with it for almost five years now! The Ubik material would seem to point to it being Ubik-like — *seem* to: I can't be sure; or did it only simulate Ubik qualities in order to read back my writing? It seemed so much like Ubik; this may have been a *way* of communicating with me, which I really didn't catch on to until now, actually. It may be quite alien to us humans. If to communicate with me it had to take on Ubik qualities it must be *really* dysmorphic to us. (This is frightening.) I am now in the position of having to dismiss all attributes which it disclosed as being possibly only simulations mimicking Ubik in order for it to be comprehensible and syntonic (nicht fremd) to me — *possibly*. I can't be sure.

This is a very sophisticated analysis of Valis' nature.

I am going to leap to a conclusion based on the "Acts" and other Christian material. I think it is indeed the Holy Spirit, which took a Valis-like (i.e., Ubik-like) form out of considerateness toward me *but* — I hesitate to essay anything in the way of assertions about its actual (real, not simulated) nature. After all, if it *is* the Holy Spirit it is the supreme being himself. ("I am he which causes to be. I am what I am.") I assess its taking a form compatible to me as (1) a gracious act of loving deference; and (2) valuable (if not necessary) for it to communicate with me. I do not construe it as deception but as a virtual necessity and certainly done for my sake.

It shaped itself to *my* conception of the Logos (i.e., *it*). When I reflect on the form it took I can appreciate that this form would be the most acceptable possible to me, as disclosed by my conception in *Ubik*. It tailored itself to my stated conception, my highest conception.

But also it testified to me of the living reality *now* of Christ and the joy involved. The preparations for his return.*

·   ·   ·

---

* Just as the Exegesis responds to Dick's calling, so readers of the Exegesis may be called on

[8:9] #1: "One mind there is; *but under it two principles contend.*"

Recently I have forgot my own tractate. My experience with the dialectic agrees with the formulation in the tractate and hence in *VALIS*. It is stipulated as *basic.*

The ability of Valis to assume the particular form most syntonic to me — the form of Ubik — is connected with its basic mimicking ability which I have already written about. It never occurred to me that Zebra as a form was just another mimicking until the last couple of days when I realized that it conformed in all respects to *my* conception of the deity (the Logos) as I (naturally) put forth in *Ubik.* This realization undermines the probity of my reams of description of Zebra; I have only described what my own head construes the deity to be like — a self-portrait; albeit a modern, complex and sophisticated apprehension of the deity, it is *quite* subjective and *quite* culturally determined (i.e., a cybernetics-biological model). As shown in *Ubik* I conceive of God as isomorphic to my own brain: thus I encounter a macro-brain arranging reality into information, a projection on my part. It was a macro-mirror.*

My brain to Ubik to Zebra. Mimicry. It analyzed my preconceptions — what I'd expect. *Ubik* isn't the sole source; *Ubik* just demonstrates

---

to investigate Dick's claims, to test them through what B. Alan Wallace dubs "contemplative science." This means that, along with Dick, we must be wary of treating our investigations as anything more than models of reality. The "Son" discussed elsewhere by Dick is born out of the "immaculate conception" of thought — the removal or emptying of previous thought formations. This path of contemplative science can be hard going — Dick asks us to consider the idea that our sense of historical ground does not exist, where nothing important has changed since ancient Rome. Humans suffer, are exploited by large-scale institutions, grow old, become ever more confused, and die. Buddhism describes this as Samsara, the "wheel of dharma." Nietzsche's Zarathustra describes the repetition driving history as the most terrifying thought — the thought of eternal return — but Dick suggests that it is through practices of contemplation and exegesis that the real horror — the false perception of linear time — is overcome. This is not the Rapture predicted by fundamentalist Christianity, but the corrected perception of our nature as both human and eternal. — RD

* Dick's realization that the deity he describes is a projection of his own beliefs leads him to the conclusion that God has manifested Himself in precisely the form he had already accepted and was prepared to believe in. What lines of reasoning insulate Dick from the other obvious conclusion: that what he has described not only takes the *form* of his projection but *is* his projection? There seem to be two answers to this question: first, his prior commitment to the existence of the deity; and second, his earlier theory about the deity's ability to mimic reality in all kinds of ways. A deity that can mimic what we take to be reality becomes, in effect, bulletproof against any objection, for any deviation or change in what (for us) constitutes reality can be explained by the difference between a deity that simply is reality and one that mimics reality. — NKH

my conception. Even if I hadn't written *Ubik* the conception would be there; *everyone* has a conception of the deity.

I don't feel it duped me; I think it had to take some form; and it took the one I'd expect and like — it took this form for these reasons. My realization of its mimicry ability should have made me think of this possibility before now. But then does not this mean that Zebra *is* the deity, inasmuch as it took the form which I conceive the deity as taking? Or at least, it is reasonable to suppose it is the deity. I can say that I now realize that what I saw — Zebra — perfectly fits my deepest and most profound conception — down to all fine details — of the deity. What could (1) *know* my conception: and (2) assume it, but the deity? So actually these realizations *bolster* the argument that what I experienced was the deity, rather than undermine it.

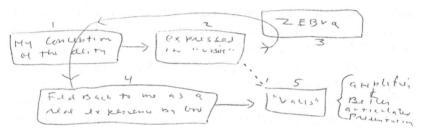

[8:11] So Zebra is a macro feedback circuit re my micro-conception as expressed in *Ubik* especially, but not *limited* to *Ubik*. Does this verify the hermetic "above as below" cosmology? Bruno's Mirror?

Or is this a case where an assumption (that Ubik exists) serves as a hypothesis which gets tested due to its very formulation (and publishing thereof?) — if it's correct, a response comes; if not then not. In this case the hypothesis is confirmed by the response, because undoubtedly Zebra's epiphany is a *response*.

Somehow this resembles my concept of the self-perpetuating dialectic. A correct hypothesis *will* be responded to — as if automatically, since such a response is included in the conceptual formulation. There's, then, an "up by his bootstraps" element in the fact of Zebra's epiphany. *If* you even just *happen* to formulate properly you can be *certain* of the epiphany-response!

It's (like) asking the right question: *that's all that's needed.* This takes me back to my idea of our (simulated) reality being a teaching machine, of which you must discern what question to ask of it. This means that in the 3-decade evolution of my epistemological investigation I asked the right question (or put forth the correct formulation, apparently best put forth in *Ubik*).

So I see Zebra's resemblance to Ubik as a subtle but vigorous confirmation of my formulation of Ubik, and the nature of our reality, our situation, put forth in *Ubik*. *Even* if the entity which responded tailored its Gestalt to fit my Ubik formulation: even *totally* tailored. (It can't be totally. The *ability* to do this tailoring is a major part of my formulation: vide *Ubik*, etc.)

I suspect that an analysis of my formulation of the nature of Ubik would disclose a presentation of the mimicry ability, since ubiquity is stipulated — ubiquity and invisibility, hence mimesis or mimicry is implied if not overtly stated.

So its taking the form it took toward me leads me back to a recognition of what must be a fundamental quality of it: *its mimicking ability.* This is an exciting realization. I have been right to conceive this as basic to it: *camouflage.* Then it is (in some sense) an invader, probably: from outside the program or simulated reality, as Ubik is in *Ubik*. (This was primary with Ubik, this invasion of our simulated world.)

So the insight that the form which Zebra took was a calculated simulation of Ubik only refers me back to my previous insight of the camouflage capacity of the entity — camouflaged here in our world, perceiving but unperceived.

[8:13] Voice: "It assimilated 3 of my books." It is, after all, living information. My writing is information. The books incorporated into a life form — Lord!

Powers: "It let the courier have a glimpse of the info he was carrying."

[8:19] Valis is the real (and rational) world breaking into (invading as in, e.g., *Ubik*) our simulated (and irrational) world. I am saying, Valis is a *world*. A (the) *real* world. Ubik is to the cold-pac world as Valis is to our world. If Ubik and Valis are one and the same, our world is both irreal (*Ubik*) and irrational (*VALIS*).

We're missing half our stereo signal — what I call the upper realm (one).

This notion that in 2-3-74 the real broke into the irreal (as in *Ubik*) is acosmic and Gnostic — and it agrees with another Gnostic idea (put forth in *VALIS*) that the creator of this world is irrational. A superimposition of *Ubik* and *VALIS* is a superimposition of two basic Gnostic ideas, one cosmological, the other cosmogonical. It's very interesting, what you get if you superimpose *VALIS* over *Ubik* — and I had previously seen that *VALIS* is an electronic circuit–like feedback of *Ubik* and mixing, enriching, etc. (v. page 11).

. . .

[8:21] I now have assembled the complete Gnostic system with its two realms, only one of which — the upper — is real (Form I of Parmenides). (As stated in *VALIS*.) It all stems from the insight that our world is not real. Then we ask, not real in relation to what? (Something must be real, or else the concept "irreal" means nothing.) Then we ask, "What is the real like? And how do we find it?" and we ask, "How did this irreal world come into being? And how did we get imprisoned here?" and then we ask, "What is our real nature?"

If reality, rationality and goodness are not here, where are they? And how do we get from here to there? *If* this is a prison, how do we escape?

We learn of a mysterious savior who camouflages himself to outwit our jailers and makes himself and his saving Gnosis known to us. He is our friend and he opposes this world and its powers on our behalf as our champion, and "one by one he takes us out of this world."

Early 1979

[6:7] Everything I know is a triumph over amnesia. All my gnosis (books and exegesis) derives from memory. There is no amnesia-compulsion — it's not a plot, or a virus, etc., just a failure to create memory holograms as fast as reality permutates. I'm laying down *fast* holos. I figured out the reality situation well enough to generate a future reality which will please me. Not be painful; I beat karma and in 3-74 took control.

[6:8] "The Waveries."[5] Living info which dialectic permutates; as in the Le Guin book, our dreaming makes it so.

3-74: simply, you ordinarily (99.99% of the time) simply lack the memory capability to remember things were just now different, because each difference lasts only the nanosecond of the dialectic of each form axis (i.e., bit of information!!!), of which our world at each nanosecond is the composite total. (It's as if "3-74s" occur all the time — we generate them — but we never remember. 3-74 was anamnesis!)

All we remember is sustains, but right now the sustain of rationality is interrupted by irrationality, and I've remembered well enough to spot it, and take advantage of it. 2-74: memory of previous "frame." [*Editor's note:* See Dick's clarification of this notion of "sustains" on p. 494.]

We don't remember well enough due to physical limitations, and this puzzles us (we know something's wrong), and we try to come up with theories. These theories, being false, "are" the "impairment" I saw; the fucked-up-ness of the theories. Simply, we lay down memories of only a fraction of the past.

[6:23] I provoked a palpable contradiction in reality. It betrayed its self-canceling nature, so *no* rational analysis is correct. It must pulsate in self canceling oscillations so rapidly that we don't realize it, so what is true at one nanosecond is not true at the next. The reality which exists *now* cannot be the reality which existed a nanosecond ago — *despite our "memories."*

I just remembered my first realization when I was loaded last night: everything is backward, we must reverse *all* information.

[6:24] I sense Zebra smiling.

Games. Fun. Riddles. Since truth changes there is no answer. Process

479

is everything. What was true 10 seconds ago is not true now (the dialectic flip-flops which generate their negations *instantly*). Self canceling; if I say, "Zebra is a person," the truth of this instantly generates its opposite: "Zebra is *not* a person," and that becomes true, whereupon another opposite is generated. Is Zebra a sustain or a subcarrier? Or *one* flip-flop — *one* out of infinity minus one. Yes — the last: one out of infinity minus one. Zebra is eternal — for 1 nanosecond. But during that nanosecond he was everywhere in *all* the flip-flops (by definition). If he was in *all* the flip-flops he is ephemerally eternal in the sense of reconstituted ex nihilo in every flip-flop — a constant, but — he must come into existence each time; that is, he dies and is reborn each nanosecond, so we find him, in any given nanosecond, in what actually is an ultra ephemeral morphos: comes into being and passes away, comes into being and passes away again elsewhere, like a fruit fly. The way circles are spontaneously re-created —

The [Fibonacci Ratio] 1:618034. Comes and goes: so it is ephemeral and yet eternal. [. . .] Thus the Blood — the plasmate — reconstitutes itself ex nihilo everywhere and at all times.

[6:25] We constantly unconsciously modulate future events but don't know it because (1) we do it unconsciously, by our impersonal will*; and (2) what we call "memory" is not memory at all but a product of each current nanosecond flip-flop frame. We don't remember the past being different just now, a split-second ago, and so we see no pattern in how each of us determines his future reality. Everything hinges on anamnesis which isn't just *improved* memory but *actual* memory of the previous frame. Without anamnesis there is no identity-continuity from flip-flop frame to frame, but Karma, which we make (influencing what will later happen to us) follows us inexorably.

[. . .]

Viewed pragmatically, Christ offers us more than scarce can be conceived. But it would seem that there are no Christians except the original ones, which conforms to Luke's "secrecy" theme. Everyone else is suffering from a relative occlusion, primarily of memory. They are driven helplessly

---

* Despite what we are repeatedly told by the dogmatic debunkers, there is a rich and impressive scientific literature on precognition. Dean Radin of the Institute of Noetic Sciences has been one of the real pioneers here, particularly around what he calls "presentiment," a kind of Spidey-sense that many people appear to possess that allows them to sense dangers or desires a few seconds into the future — in short, a humble form of Dick's future modulation. What is perhaps most significant here, and not always recognized, is that the parapsychological literature strongly suggests that most psychical functioning takes place *unconsciously* (or in dreams), that is, below the radar and range of our conscious selves or functioning egos. We are Two, and our second self is a Super Self. — JJK

down their compound form axis, victims of Karma generated by their previous thoughts (sic — thoughts not actions, as Jesus alluded to!). Thus Valis
is here, and rational, but they are caught in an irrational (irreal) maze, and
hurled helplessly through it, afflicted by projections of their own thoughts
as in the Bardo Thödol. In fact they *are* in the Bardo Thödol state: half
dead (as in *Ubik*).

[6:41] Therefore I maintain that whatever the intent of the authors of *The
Tibetan Book of the Dead* they are in fact describing our world and state.*
We are in a decomposing, degenerating process and will continue so unless enlightened by Valis, who introduces negentropy. Determinism and
entropy are considered here as identical; succumbing to what is really a
self-generated fate is identified with death and disorder. Upon the lethal
triumph of this decomposing process, nothing new comes into the individual (or macro) mind. This is tantamount to psychosis or ultimate brain
dysfunction (schizophrenia). I maintain that regarded as a totality the cosmos, including Valis, is partially in this state; a measure of anomie or irrationality pervades us and pervades Valis. Technically, the dialectic loses its
generative power or potentially *could* lose its generative power. This is the
abysmal evil to be fought at all costs, inasmuch as its victory would snuff
out the cosmos. This is being versus nonbeing. In my opinion human beings freeze or die or partially die vis-à-vis this dialectic; its progression in
us — as us — is not automatic. Each of us is a microform of it, and to the
extent that we succumb to "fate" or "astral determinism" we succumb to
death and madness, to congealing.

[. . .]

In conclusion, I conceive of our situation as one of entropy or decom-

---

* When W. Y. Evans-Wentz first prepared the *Bardo Thödol* for its English edition in 1927,
he called it *The Tibetan Book of the Dead* in order, one suspects, to link it to the popular
Egyptian Book of the Dead. Dick owned the 1960 edition of the text, which had been reissued with a new introduction by Carl Jung. A funerary text designed to be read at the bed-
side of the dead, the *Bardo Thödol* is more accurately called *Liberation Through Hearing
During the Intermediate State*. The intermediate state in question is the bardo, the spectral
halls of transformation that lie between the death of the body and the almost inevitable rebirth of one's mind-stream: most souls are made so variously terrified and lustful by the
apparitions that they are inevitably sucked back for another round. For the Buddhist prac-
titioner, release lies in recognizing the emptiness of these projections, which are nothing
other than one's own mind. Dick's insight here — that the bardo is actually our world — is
perfectly in sync with traditional teachings, as the "intermediate state" refers not only to
the afterlife but also to sleeping, dreaming, sneezing, and life itself. We are always in a lim-
inal zone. For the Tibetans, an escape of sorts lies in the clear light of nonconceptual mind;
Dick's more wayward light is pink, which is also, in Tibetan iconography, the color of the
supreme lotus of the Buddha. — ED

position, a succumbing to determinism which is to say, the products of our own former thought formations; therefore for us the past determines the future. Into this dying system Valis breaks bringing new life and energy and freedom and knowledge; he impinges "one-way" and "from outside" as if invading our world (which is not a real world). To encounter him is to encounter the uncanny, the inexplicable, the *destroyer* (rather than sustainer) of what we misconstrue to be world. It is his macromind shattering the brittle and congealed husk of our own objectified prior thoughts which imprison and devitalize us, the past devouring the future — whereas Valis, as the future, turns around and devours the past (negentropy attacking entropy; form affecting non-form).* I conclude that we are dying in a mental sense but are virtually without insight into the fact that what befalls us is a projection or thought-form of death per se. To the extent that things happen to us, rather than occurring as a result of our volition, we are destroying ourselves — which may account for legends of the primordial fall. Thus our process mind becoming congealed is experienced objectively and externally as a closing in of the necessary, the inevitable over which we have no power. We succumb to our own dead mind, but mistakenly experience it as a victory by the external world.

[6:44] Regard this as a scientific hypothesis: what we call "reality" is in fact an objectification of our prior thought formations — since in fact we are dead and dreaming in a state of psychic decomposition (as depicted in *Ubik*). And under such conditions we have no world but that of our former thought formations returning to afflict or delight us (as depicted in *The Tibetan Book of the Dead*) (which is where I got the idea for *Ubik*). In other words, I read *The Tibetan Book of the Dead* in the late 50s or early 60s and realized that our world and condition was in fact depicted and

---

* Here Dick suggests the radically liberatory possibility that reality, the Tao, the Palm Tree Garden, can break through the present if "you" will "destroy" prior thought formations, including those that separate "you" from the One. Here Dick resonates with Joyce's Stephen Dedalus, who wished only to awaken from the nightmare of history, an awakening later perhaps achieved by Joyce in *Finnegans Wake*. Readers familiar with Zen, or Korzybski's notion that "the map is not the territory," or the "stillness" in which the divine can manifest in Quaker or Vedic traditions, will recognize some of the practices appropriate for a world mediated and constituted by the multiple "objectified" mistakes of language and other previous thought formations. In this sense Valis "comes not to destroy but to fulfill the law" (Mt 5:17) by overturning prior concepts like so many tables in the temple. "For I say unto you, that except your righteousness shall exceed the righteousness of the scribes and Pharisees, ye shall in no case enter into the kingdom of heaven" (Mt 5:20). Righteousness here is anything but self-righteousness. It is instead the humility and practice necessary to silence the mind in order to perceive reality, a "causal field" unmistakably affected by the language by which we model it. — RD

not (as is said) a world and condition which *follows* our "life." From internal evidence in *The Tibetan Book of the Dead* I discerned that those in the Bardo Thödol state do not know they are in that state but imagine they are (still) alive. They do not know that the evil and good spirits (events, people, things) which they encounter are their own (former) thought-formations projected onto a pseudo-world, and that contrary to what appears to be the case, they can create, change and abolish future reality (not *present* reality, since there is a lag). In *Ubik* my characters die and enter this state but don't know it. I then departed from the description of the Bardo Thödol existence in *The Tibetan Book of the Dead* and added Ubik, a vast logos-like mind who invades their decaying world and rescues them. Now, if I was right (that *secretly The Tibetan Book of the Dead* depicts — and probably *knowingly* depicts — our *present* life, world and condition) I could anticipate that after a suitable time lag — and especially if I was dying, like Joe Chip on the stairs — I could expect intervention by *my* thought formation Ubik. In 3-74 due to overpowering dread and enervation I began to literally experience the colored lights described in *The Tibetan Book of the Dead* and knew myself to be in the Bardo Thödol state. Yet it was *this* side of the grave; I have not died; ergo, *The Tibetan Book of the Dead does* depict (secretly) our *present* condition. And then, sure enough, exactly as I described in *Ubik*, written information appeared to me, and presently Ubik itself, down to specific details. Valis (i.e., Ubik), then, is a projection of my own mind and not "real" — but, as *The Tibetan Book of the Dead* says, *nothing* we experience is anything other than objectification of our own prior thought formations — and enlightenment consists in knowing this and so controlling them. Only if you (1) read *The Tibetan Book of the Dead* and (2) realized it secretly applied to *this* life could you accomplish what I did in creating Valis. Truth is totally plastic and represents a complex mingling of our former fears, beliefs and desires (mostly unconscious in us). "The mind has the power to change its environment. We do so constantly." Etc. I have *choice* in the matter. So I ask, not, "What is true?" but, "What modulations shall I imprint on the stuff around me?"

[. . .]

Before reading *The Tibetan Book of the Dead* I was tending toward a radical (Gnostic) acosmism; hence I (unconsciously; i.e., my *will*) correctly deconstructed *The Tibetan Book of the Dead* as few others have. In *Ubik* I applied it to us, deliberately. Soon impossible things began to happen; I found myself in the silly putty metastasizing kind of universe I write about — and in 3-74 Ubik rescued me in a form ultra syntonic to me (which I have frequently realized but didn't fathom until last Friday).

• • •

[6:49] This is esoteric Gnosis of the highest order. We are not living (if we are living at all!) in a real universe. It is a dream. But it does not respond *overtly* to our beliefs (i.e., fears and wishes, or worldview/ideology). Its response is (1) delayed, (2) randomized, (3) concealed adroitly; after all, it is sentient, playful and alive (because *we* are). You *must* have the key premises (wisdom, pragmatic ideology, etc.) at your disposal to gain control over it; that is, you must guess right, assess it correctly. It's a game, a puzzle. The reward for guessing right is joy and power; for guessing wrong, a bitter disappointing frustrating defeated life (or death). *The Tibetan Book of the Dead* tells the truth and yet we misread it because it says, "These are instructions to the dead." [. . .] I tested the instructions out when I wrote *Ubik*, adding to the Bardo Thödol journey what I *desired* to find there: Ubik, modeled on the Logos. So, from 2-74 on (when I remembered I am actually one of Christ's twelve disciples) I have lived with the Logos beside me.

Yes — in 3-74 the radio kept saying:

Bright white light
Shining in the night
To guide your way.[6]

And at the time I understood; I steered toward it. And found it and was reborn healed.

[6:57] It's interesting to read back to pages 21 and 7, and see how on page 7 when I was totally loaded I had the ex nihilo satori that "I figured out the reality situation well enough to generate a future reality which will please me. Not be painful. I beat Karma and in 3-74 took control."

Thus in the following pages I came to recognize Valis/Zebra as my conscious liberating thought formation of Ubik a decade before; and finally I found my way to the views of *The Tibetan Book of the Dead*, as to the nature of reality as Karma or our own prior thought formations which we must learn to control. [. . .]

This insight was a glorious quantum leap up: that a decade before 3-74 *I* myself consciously generated Ubik which then in 3-74 intervened and invaded and liberated me exactly as it does in the novel. Thus was explained why when I encountered Zebra/Valis I had the uncanny feeling that I was encountering my own thoughts "coming back from a trip around the whole universe" — like the Waveries.

[6:62] The evidence seems to be pointing more and more (starting with the ᴛ~~~ model) to us being stationary mega (multipersonal) brains outside time and space, pre-programming ourselves with a pseudo-reality! There is some evidence that we are arranged like the audience in the James-James dream, multiperson megabrains viewing a single omni-faceted matrix which is the source, for us all, of all times and all places (and all events); and onto which we project our individual prior thought-for-mations — which consist of our thought responses to prior reality frames (which lay down no holographic memories in us); we pass from one frame to the next at ultra high speed — too fast to lay down memories, along all the form axes. These axes are determined not by any intrinsic nature but by our thoughts about them; what we believe to be true. Thus actual reality is our compound thoughts, and change in reality is the result of changing thought responses to prior objectified thought-formations; i.e., we think in response to "reality" which is really a prior thought-formation and this thought-response causes the thought-formation to flip-flop along its dia-lectic form-axes, thus causing a changed reality, to which we think new thoughts — have new beliefs as to what is true — which generate *new* ob-jectified thought-formations — and so on. [. . .] *This* is the irreducible dia-lectic which I experienced.

(1) objectified thought-formation
(2) resulting belief systems

This means that we, the multi person mega brain, resonating at all times and places, are Valis.

I visualize a vast grid of 0-1 flip-flop grid squares whose pattern of 0 (dark) and 1 (light) changes constantly. 0 is irrational or untrue belief. 1 is rational or true. The patterns are intricate. The aggregate of dark squares at any one nanosecond is the "streak of the irrational" in the "world soul."

0/1, strife/love, death/life, irrational/rational, nonbeing/being, insen-tient/sentient, false/true, yin/yang, form II/form I.

But consider: the irrational (false) beliefs generate objectified thought-formations although untrue! So irreal reality is repeatedly generated.

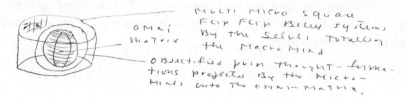

• • •

[6:66] Upon rereading pages 1–50: "we are in a decomposing, declining, entropic halving dialectic process, constantly proportionately more and more vitiated." In that case, if at a given moment a transfer of energy from the past occurred — arced across into the future — it would be, vis-à-vis the future into which it arced, *highly charged* (in contrast to the charge it held vis-à-vis its own time). I conceive of this decomposing as taking place at exponential rates. Thus a mere *idea* of 1968 (the novel *Ubik*), if it arced across to 1974, would be relatively so highly potentiated that it would no longer be a mere idea but would dynamically literally *overpower* the 1974 reality.

Also, this would explain why prior thought formations now objectified have such deterministic coercive power. But if the thought jumped *across* the intervening years — it would be *so* potent in comparison to the de-vitalized future which it had invaded — just imagine the thought formation Ubik amped up to say one thousand times its original ergic force. Thus my prior thought formations — if, as it would seem, they arced across due to their intrinsic content; i.e., such a power is consigned to them ideationally — they would seem enormously supercharged compared to how they seemed in the late 60s. And, in 2-3-74, so they did — specifically Ubik. But *it* didn't grow; we diminished extensively — I have the strange feeling that this point (as to the relative high potentiation of a thought formation arced across an intervening time interval from the past) may be terribly important in terms of lending credence to my whole system here. A number of basic points herewith cross-correlate: the Bardo Thödol concept; the Karma produced by prior thought formations now objectified; that Valis in 3-74 was my conception of Ubik from the late 60s dynamically supercharged —

Suddenly, just when I was beginning to think I had nothing going here, my rereading 50 pages and seeing this verification-point gives me renewed enthusiasm. *The structure checks out.* If there *is* exponential decomposition (entropy) in our universe (and this view is universally accepted), were Ubik as thought formation to arc across directly from the time-frame in which I originally conceived it to 3-74 — one could *anticipate* such surging vitality, such energy and power: "if x then y."

It conforms *exactly* to my impression of Valis: Ubik amped up until it spilled all over the apartment, bursting and burning everything, and flooding me with information.

Early 1979

[**10:27**] "Astral determinism" and "Fate" designate the inexorable outcome of a closed system.

This is why I became not-I.

Without Valis (Ubik) there is, literally, regression along a form axis, exactly as in *Ubik*. This is true of individuals and societies (e.g., USA 1974) (and me in 1974).

So perhaps we should speak of signal *decay* as well as distortion. Feedback is needed: Valis, e.g., fed me back 3 of my own books, and much else. Signal strengthening resulted, and a motion forward.
[. . .]

Valis is conscious energy (living info) — cuts in and *boosts* the signal back into integrity — i.e., motion forward. So there is a factor of heat loss in the dialectic's flip-flops: a principle of entropy: *form*-loss as entropy, and a final congealing.

[**10:28**] Now — consider what my advisor does: she periodically feeds newness (input) into me from outside me, so I am not (now) a closed system. This is why she so often *corrects* me. But advises only periodically. She is *my* self-monitoring feedback input energizing signal-integrity-strengthening "cut-in" override.

[**10:29**]
   (1) "astral determinism" or fate
   (2) God

For (2) to actually enter you as (1) — cut into you personally, not just your fate — was the supreme moment of Christianity and probably the mystery religions back to the Elysian mysteries.

---

* Dick's holograph is notably erratic throughout this folder, pulsing in waves of ecstasy and calm. Given the manic diagramming throughout the folder (a full-page example is included in this volume's insert), as well as his invocation of Diana and the fairies, this may well represent the "superdope" episode to which Dick refers in a later folder [**83:60**]. — PJ

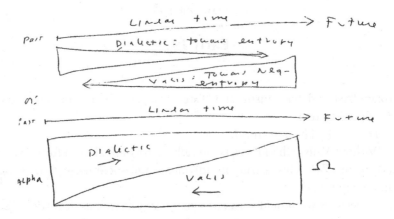

To have Valis cut in is to have negentropy cut in. Time as 1:618034 log (helical spiral) like a snail shell. Thus I (properly) envision time spatially.

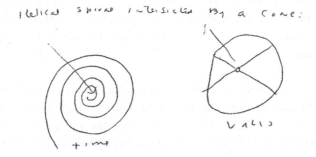

Base of cone at center of spiral, so as spiral diminishes, Valis increases.

Then proportionally progressively more and more correction (input) is required the further the form-permutations get from their generator-source.

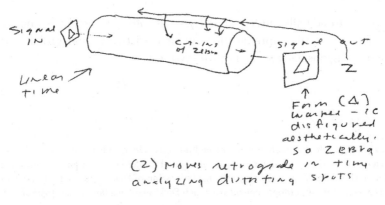

• • •

[10:49] Who is the woman who whispers to me? "There's someone else in my head and he's not living in this century." Another person injected into my brain — "Thomas"?

But — who is Thomas? One to whom the Holy Spirit came. Thus with a single swift punch of the "needle" (Valis) the Holy Spirit is crossbonded to me and is here, at a spatiotemporal locus. Injected into human history.

Is the girl who whispers our daughter St. Sophia, who is her own grandparent Valis? Valis replicates in microform: Valis to Thomas to me equaling Valis again (St. Sophia). Did the prophecy mean that St. Sophia would be born for me — me, impregnated by the Holy Spirit?

But how?

I hear her voice.

She is in my head counseling me.

holy spirit may
↓
◯ = St. Sophia Born in my head
MC female

[10:54] The girl who whispers to me and acts as my advocate — the girl in the pink flannel nightgown and slippers — when I saw her (in my mind) I saw the Savior, St. Sophia, born the second time, the Savior I have been told is soon-to-be incarnated. That's why she was so concrete, right down to her nightgown. *VALIS* is correct: he would take female form — or has taken! — this time. She may already be here somewhere.

She is not just an image, a fantasy in my mind, since I inferred her existence from her voice, and desired to see her (which I then did).

Yes, in a sense she is my daughter, but (mysteriously) she is my creator and the creator of the world, its Lord and judge, and our sustainer (comforter).

[10:78] AI voice: "I am like the forest bird in *Siegfried*."[7] I.e., a dove. *The dove.* And "I am the commercial — compared to the program." (As in *Ubik*; I — PKD — should have had that in mind.)

[10:79] 4:00 A.M. Voice: "a womb for her to grow her progeny in." Me!*

• • •

---

* As noted in other annotations, Dick's line of speculation here is remarkably similar to the vision of the German judge Daniel Paul Schreber (1842–1911), who imagined that God wanted to change him into a woman and impregnate her with sunbeams so that their off-

[10:83] "A womb for her to grow her progeny in."

So my vision of the implanting laboratory needle was correct, with my brain as womb.

And of course she's female — only females *directly* have progeny. This is how you define female.

This is a life form! (I.e., Valis, who was present at the moment of birth 3-74, the apotheosis!) She took an apostolic Christian's psyche and transferred it into me (as its new womb) for it to grow through gestation to full birth as the deity, and if an apostolic Christian is her progeny, she is Christ/*Paraclete*/God — the Paraclete producing the second birth; this answers the question put to Jesus, "How can a man be born again?" Thomas *was* born again — in 3-74.

[10:87A] Our reality is under the power of a madman. He may or may not have created it, but it makes no difference: he is *using* it, like a shooting gallery game at an amusement park and Smithsonian Institution combined — like a science fair. For many races of creatures from different star systems — an exhibit of technology. So this is not merely a game. It's a — the maze, created by the dialectic, is the exhibit; our race is only an element vis-à-vis the maze. The fact that the dialectic continues forever is a scientific marvel.

Christ is like a runner, ready to sprint in and replace a beleaguered creature within the maze.

She stands and advises. (Us.) (In the maze.)

At the controls of the maze is Mr. Looney Tunes — they two offset him, to keep the sport not too cruel. She is justice; Christ is mercy. The controls of the maze are in the hands of a Lon Chaney–like creature from a world where they look that way. The girl is secretly the builder of the maze; she now poses just as a guide to us, but *also:* she turns again and again to Mr. Looney Tunes to speak on our behalf that he spare us pain. *She* is totally rational. If nutso at the controls doesn't surrender them soon, she and Christ will physically push him away from the controls.

There is a whole huge map room of computer info, input and output from the worlds in the maze, continual traffic.

---

spring could save the world. Sigmund Freud (1856–1939) wrote one of his most famous case studies about Schreber in *Three Case Histories: Psychoanalytic Notes upon an Autobiographical Account of a Case of Paranoia* (1911), basing his diagnosis on Schreber's detailed memoir *Memoirs of My Nervous Illness* (1903). Though the two never met, Freud diagnosed Schreber as a paraphrenic paranoid suffering from — surprise! — repressed homosexual desires. While Dick's vision here is remarkably similar to Schreber's, he makes no mention of the judge anywhere in the Exegesis, though Dick could well have encountered the case given his extensive knowledge of psychology. — DG

"He is an old child, playing at draughts, moving according to the rules."[8]
Senile.

[10:97] I can't stop sensing that she — Diana — is a gift to me; I reason back;
viz: what would I have wanted most in 1974 when I was in such distress?
Anything more, different or other? No. I can't even hypothesize who she
could be a gift from (i.e., some entity higher than her), but she saved me
in 3-74, and since then she has told me a great deal. I feel that she protects
me — has been protecting me at least from 2-74 on and maybe before. For
me she is the embodiment of Providence, wise counsel: and she is my advocate (to whom?). She not only advises and informs me but *steers* me — in
opposition to inexorable fate (or chance). She is of the upper realm.

The dance. Sound of bells, the beautiful woman: Diana. Queen of the
fairies. Opposed to the harsh grim masculine kings — and the iron empire-
prison (I share her view: it is a *prison*). And I heard her singing, as Linda
Ronstadt, Olivia Newton-John, and singing Monteverdi.[9] And originally
she appeared to me as Aphrodite and the Sibyl. I have the feeling she may
be the spirit of my religion. My psychopomp who will finally escort me
across the sifting bridge (again) to the other side.

Eliade says it is the primary purpose or goal of the shaman to pass over
to the other side and say what's there. Also he mentions phosphene activity — and I want to reiterate my sense of being a womb for the divine.* I
had even thought of it as a fertilization or impregnation. But she says that
it is a womb for her progeny — which is close enough; hence the cuckoo
egg dream.

What is very important to me — very valuable to me — psychologically
is my sense of her permissiveness. I need that.

[10:98] 4:30 A.M. I just had an insight which came with total, absolute
force. Christianity — including Christ — is a cover, a front; and the real deity (and this is kept incredibly secret) is female. Wasn't I told this about

---

* As noted earlier, Mircea Eliade was a well-known and much-read scholar of comparative religion who was at his professional height when Dick read him in the 1970s. Here he
is referring to one of Eliade's major early books, *Shamanism: Archaic Techniques of Ecstasy*
(1951), a massive survey of the anthropological literature as it existed around 1950, organized around Eliade's own glosses and comparative reflections. Eliade focuses especially on
the initiatory illness, magical powers, healing function, poetic gifts, and mystical experiences of the shaman and, perhaps most of all, on the shaman's role as a psychopomp. Eliade also emphasizes the quest for the recovery of sacred time before the "Fall" into history,
here understood in the most general sense as linear temporality, finitude, and mortality.
This abolishment or transcendence of time, of course, is also a central concern of Dick's.
Hence, I suspect, his deep admiration for Eliade's work. — JJK

Christ in the dream, and told it's secret? I have been initiated into one of the greatest mysteries in the history of religion; it is *she* who we true (esoteric) Christians worship: the Christianity which we see exoterically is really Roman, infiltrated by Rome — to know the truth about *her* you must be *possessed* by her directly. And learn it from *her*.

Early 1979

[13:4] I am plugging into a giant idea computer — I am the next step up in evolution, which, because the next step up plugs into this giant idea computer, has a virtually *infinite* mind. My Jungian intuitive possibilities function in my right hemisphere like a photon gun. I have two protection devices to conceal my identity: (1) scramble pattern of *all* ideas at once to bury my idea of my true nature and origin①; and (2) amnesia. We came to this planet from elsewhere. [. . .]

There's no way I can sort the true ideas out of all the infinitude of equally plausible (mere) possibilities. Somewhere in a near infinite bulk of ideas lies the truth. But which? But this device is necessary. Who and what I am — the actual situation — is hopelessly occluded off from me② by this scramble pattern of endless self-negating dialectic idea-permutations at infinite velocity. Hence, as I realized a couple of weeks ago, although I may know the truth and even speak it, I am doomed not to know which of the many conflicting truths generated in me it is. It could be *any* of them. So I know (the truth about myself) but due to this device paradoxically do not know: thus the idea computer conceals itself by its own idea-generating capacity. Its basic function is its own camouflage — ah; hier ist Zebra wieder.[10]

Another way to camouflage itself. This shows up not just when I try to figure out *myself* but when I try to figure out — conceptually pin down — Zebra. I can't give the same account twice re 3-74, re Zebra and re myself. We're interwoven, I guess, but here again the camouflage device — this time an idea scramble — works, analogous to its physical camouflage.

This suggests that I and the life form Zebra are one. No, we may just be related, etc., etc. See? See how it works?

I did have one insight not based on thinking but on my feeling toward the animals: that I am the (a?) Buddha, but must conceal my identity as Siddhartha even to myself. My whole thinking is just a cover for my real nature: my feeling — regarding those who suffer. I am a feeling disguised by mere flak thinking.

My feelings are reliable but my thoughts are not.

① This is why all the ideas in the world — millions of them, and *conflicting* — get served up simultaneously as a protective smokescreen; this is why they don't stabilize. They have a practical purpose — as a cloud of mental ink. I'm not to know the truth about my identity. So any and all ideas I get as to my identity, nature, purpose and origin is just scatter, random flak, each idea as real and unreal as the next; like white *noise*. And the closer I get to knowing, the more scramble of conflicting ideas: ultimately an infinitude — including *this* idea. Hence the endless paradoxes, and the fact that I can't finalize or stabilize my exegesis — it's for my (and our?) protection: a scrambled device — like code.

② Hence from others: since I can't write down the truth in a novel or speech; this is how 3-74 could occur but secrecy still maintained.

[13:6] My powers came from the other side, because of my sister.

AI Voice. And "plugged into an idea computer." Audio and video. Pictures: I *saw* my abstract ideas graphically. Is Valis a computer? I think I've solved it. I came to the conclusion a long time ago that the dialectic represented a computer. Are we in a computer program? And stationary? As Zeno proved, motion is impossible. All is thought.

[13:9] Perhaps my most important realization while loaded is what is implied in the way of paradoxes if the statement, "Every idea thought of is true *but for no measurable length of time* because it — i.e., its truth — is instantly negated by an *equal and opposite idea*, and so forth," is true. The infinity of the first part ("every idea thought of is true") is dialectically balanced by the null infinity ("but for no measurable length of time" [because it] is inexorably replaced by the dialectic generation of its opposite). What such an infinity countered by an antithetical infinity would lead to is (1) an infinite number of universes of (2) no measurable duration — from outside; but *in* each universe there would be what I must regard as a pleroma of *spurious* (subjective) time, sufficient *within* the universe, but not there when viewed from outside that universe. What I deduced from this is that each self passes through an infinitude of universes or "frames," each with laws — truths — of its own, but the permutation being so fast (instantaneous), no memory of it is laid down by the self, whose entire "memory" is instantly derived from situational cuing generated within and by whatever frame he is now in. However, some truths could (in the intrinsic statement of them) contain as part of their definition that of *ubiquity*, in which case what I call *sustains* would be created which *would* lay down memory, but since *other* aspects of the frames would differ one from another, one's *true* memory would be of serial disjunctions along the linear time axis without *any* apparent explanation. (E.g., "I was born in Chicago in 1928 but an instant ago I was living in first century A.D. Rome" — viz: first century A.D. Rome and USA 1974 both contained the same sustain — the Golden Fish

sign — but *no* other sustains; nonetheless the self passed from first century Rome directly to USA 1974 due to the Golden Fish sign but drew ersatz "memory" of life in modern USA generated by situational cues in this
frame.) There is an explanation and it lies in what I call *sustains,* which resemble the form axes I described in *Ubik* and which do *not* lie along linear time, but rather "sustain" time, which is my word for Plato's "eternal
forms." For consciousness of this to open up (true memory)① the self would
discover that it had existed for an infinite length of time in/through (the
permutations of) an infinitude of different universes, and knew ideationally *everything.*

① Anamnesis. This true memory perhaps exists in the right hemisphere.

[13:12] 4:30 A.M.: Valis itself as an experience or an entity in itself generates a multiple or split model parallel-possible explanation(s) dialectic. So
it must lie in that realm; there can be only an infinite series of equally true
explanations generated.

Vision: a dark-haired young woman lying in a coffin.① She is dead. She is
my sister. She *is* — or she generated — "the perturbation in the reality field,"
i.e., Valis. It is a projection into this world of her mind, to protect me.

This vision came in response to my Q: "*Who* perturbed the reality
field?"

Is the AI voice hers?

Now that I think of the vision it suggests Ella Runciter in *Ubik;* perhaps
my sister's benign influence over me thus shows up in my writing.[11]

① White silk-lined casket.

[13:13] The Encyclopedia of Philosophy says, "The virtues instilled by suffering could be achieved another way." How does it know that — that they
could be achieved another way; here the error lies. These virtues are essential, and there is no other way. A certain esthetically-graphically beautiful heroism is *inevitably* generated — to *all* humans — *all.* All be(come as)
Christ, none less than Jesus. All men — creatures — suffer as he, hence are
equal to him. And therefore are him, dramatically. As in a sacred ritual
drama, therefore us all.

[. . .]

Christ as an Egyptianized Greek Apollo! I.e., very early Greek statues.
What knowledge do we get from Jesus' life and death? That (1) we are innocent by reason of our unmerited suffering; and (2) if innocent and made

to suffer then heroic; and (3) if heroic, transfigured (resurrected) into God-hood! *All* of us! As a species — and the beasts too — all life.

[13:15] All artists know they can't avoid suffering, and out of it they forge their art in defiance; artist or not, they will suffer. Art is the ultimate defiance of Fate. The heroic act *deliberately* done.

I saw this in the rat I had to kill: innocence and heroism and terrible beauty — nobility — in a mere rat. Oh God. There is nothing we know that the creatures don't know; they are our equals.

[13:21] Is it possible that any human or creature could, under the right circumstances, experience anamnesis and recall its Christ-self?

Tragedy: "the evil seen and the good guessed at"; one senses — but cannot clearly see — the hidden good (rational) invading the palpable evil (irrational) and sees, as the result of this antithetical clash, apotheosis.

Valis: a mysterious hidden moral order (good and rational) behind the visible chaotic and evil and deterministic, which can be appealed to.

The slain God proliferates down through the cosmos to each rat and cockroach.

[13:22] Coleridge on tragedy: ". . . the greatest effect is produced when the fate is represented as a higher intelligent will" ("the human will was exhibited as struggling with fate"[12]). So the essence of tragedy is the limited human knowledge, plans, hopes, desires (will) clashing with "a higher and intelligent will" which we understand (or encounter) as Fate — "Fate" defined as that power or those powers capable of arranging our outcome.*

---

* Another new mood is here announced in the Exegesis: a *tragic* dialectics. Dick has come across Coleridge's understanding of tragedy, which adapts the early ideas of F.W.J. Schelling. Schelling held that the essence of tragedy consists in a collision between the tragic hero, who is free, and fate, which is the limitation of freedom, the realm of necessity. The sublimity of tragedy consists in the demonstration of freedom in the confrontation with that which destroys it. This is what we see, for example, in the tragedy of Oedipus. Tragedy is here linked to the idea of suffering leading to an experience of truth, as when Aeschylus says repeatedly in the *Oresteia,* "We must suffer, suffer into truth." These tragic insights might also be linked to Dick's repeated references to Euripides' *Bacchae,* in particular the collision between King Pentheus (bad) and the god Dionysos (good). These also look forward to a closing passage in this collection where Dick describes the Exegesis as a collision between himself and "what oneself has writ." On this view, the Exegesis might be interpreted as the entirely self-conscious enactment of a tragic dialectics that moves between the poles of suffering and salvation. — SC

The plans the protagonist has are not in harmony with a "higher and intelligent will" which has the power to decide the outcome; there is no way the man's plans can win out, so individual plan is forcibly harmonized even if this requires that it be pulverized — i.e., *can't* be harmonized and still remain intact. The loss of that *intactness* is the essence of tragedy, the antithetical dialectic between his plan and Fate's plans, with the latter *by definition* prevailing.

I do not see that his (1) learning by reason of this or, contrarily (2) *failing* to learn adds or subtracts from the manifestation of the truly tragic, since to me the latter is more pitiful and the former more constructive; in fact I see the latter (2) as *more* tragic, if either is, which violates classic notions of tragic drama. I say, *disproportionate* suffering (pain, disappointment, loss) is the essence of tragedy because its disproportion renders the victim however evil or guilty veridically innocent: made spotless by the overbearing quality or quantity of suffering. Tragedy is when the punishment is *not* just. And I say *every* living creature is punished disproportionately so every life is a tragic one; disproportionate suffering is the ubiquity of the condition of having lived. Yet a mystery is hinted at: a rectification of this disproportion — not through the vile lie that man (creatures) are sinful and *deserve* their suffering, but rather — but this precisely is the mystery: the invasion of this irrational system by the rational in which an invisible and elusive mitigation of tribulation is injected according to some hidden order of theodicy not directly seen. Thus whereas the disproportionate tribulation is directly seen, and its reality not open to conjecture, dispute or denial, the mitigation or even transmutation of the tribulation into something proportionate, just or even beneficial must be *guessed at.* And this intuitive guess is the kingpin of religion and the religious solution to implacable tragedy as it exists ubiquitously in the real world and not in art.

"Tragedy as an interim reading of life between religion on the one hand, and Satanism, or pessimistic materialism, on the other. Basic to tragedy is the equilibrium of the evil that is observed and the good that is guessed at. What is central is the balance between an intense awareness of pain or evil, which is clearly revealed, and an intuitive apprehension of a transcendent realm of values. In each case evil is affirmed, but it is transcended by a higher good which induces exultation, not despair or faith. The balance is destroyed when evil is denied or seen as remedial or is affirmed as ultimate."[13]

I suppose in terms of what Coleridge says, the "higher intelligent will" which we call "Fate" is proved right in the end. I.e., it *is* proved to be just that, a "higher intelligent will" and not fate in the sense of blind or malignant evil or purposelessly cruel force or forces as such; it is the revelation that Fate is not Fate but a wiser ("higher") and more powerful will contending with — overruling — man's will out of its higher intelligence. It disagrees because it knows more.

But this does not inspire faith and is not accepted (known) on or by faith. Exultation comes not from faith, which would provide only passive acceptance or resignation, but from an *encounter* with "fate" seen in the aspect of higher and (more) intelligent (i.e., sentient and planning) will; the exultation is derived from knowledge of, not faith concerning.

That which had masked itself as fate (in mimesis) reveals this camouflage and in stepping forth acts in revelation of a deliberately hidden, different, even opposing nature. It is not fate at all. "Higher intelligent will" is not fate, if the term is to retain its correct meaning. Something or someone has mimicked fate, perhaps supplanting it invisibly: replacing it perhaps by insidiously devouring it and substituting itself for it in perfect imitation, at its source. This is a staggering mystery, but mystery it is, since the stipulation of capacity for perfection of imitation when desired is attributed. It will look like fate as long as it wants to look like fate, but if it cares to disclose itself as actually being a "higher intelligent will" (if it even does so) it then can, and the problem is solved. (By the way I define "Fate" and "higher intelligent will" in that I see no tragedy in bowing to the latter. For me, to find that I had been broken by the latter and not the former would, by all means, induce, specifically, exultation.)

The mystery of the "guessed at" reality would certainly deepen — but become even more reassuring — if I suspected that in some supernatural fashion this "higher intelligent will" could be identified or equated with my *own* covert *enlightened* will: a web of harmony underlying or transcending the antithetical clash which had pulverized my conscious plans.

Exultation is *precisely* my response to my direct knowledge and experience of Valis, of my awareness of its authority over the irrational — which I identify with "astral determinism" or "fate." I especially exult in my sense of Valis having *invaded* the irrational as a conqueror.

[13:41] I found a typed page starting: "VALIS' activity is a binary system of off-on. We see only the 'on' of the off-on arrangements. We do not see them as arrangements but merely as change."

More and more this binary computer model of Valis seems to be the correct one. "On" is the linking of two parts which I saw: "on" equals junction; "off" equals disjunction or not inclusion in the vast assembly which

I equate with Valis. Put another way I saw high speed linking as the primary activity of Valis. This was simply its "on" mode, so it must be everywhere, and what I construed as Valis vs. non-Valis was "on" vs. "off" of a binary computer. Then everything is the computer whether linked or not — whether the assembly (what I called "Valis") or not.

These are neural connections in a brain. "On" is "connect" and "off" is "disconnect." There is an evolution toward connection: toward a developing macrothought in which everything is connected: worked in as relevant. Then there is something other than just a binary on-off computer. "On" more and more predominates over "off"; it seeks "on." Its goal is "on" as a means to developing a total all-parts interaction. "Off" could be regarded as a lack, a failure, a defeat, an impediment to be overcome. We still have a binary system, but priority (plus value) is given to "on."

Then there are two orders of reality (set to ground?). The "on" or junctions (which is higher or set), and "off" as disjunction (which is lower as ground): this might explain, then, the discrimination of set to ground which I achieved: on to off. Linked to unlinked, Valis to not-Valis — and even more ultimately, the ultra-thought to the not-yet-[part of]-ultra-thought. What I call "Valis," then, is a thought, or rather *the* thought.

This sheds a whole new light on

(1) The set-ground which I saw
(2) What "Valis" is (a forming thought)

One could say that "the rational invading the irrational" which I construe as going on is the deliberate, purposeful formation by a computer brain — using a binary system — of an ultimate thought which can be regarded (1) as activity or process; or (2) as a *thing:* the thought as network of interlinked "neurons" in a particular pattern (which has as one attribute that of absolute beauty, and perhaps should ultimately be so regarded).

[. . .]

My God — the causal train melting! The ultra-thought was (seen *by me*) forming before my very eyes. This is the override I saw, the modulation — the changes in reality including me. I was incorporated into the ultra-thought which I have termed "Valis." The "St. Elmo's Fire" — the vast knowledge all at once available to me — this is the ultra-thought. All that "Hermetic" transtemporal Gnosis is contents of the ultra-thought. *Reality as knowledge.* This "Hermetic" knowledge was physical reality which I could see and touch. Physical reality went through a transform and became knowledge. The thought could be said to have changed. It changed, and no one remembers that it had been formerly different; again, everything I experienced has to do with anamnesis. *I* remembered that things (the thought) had just an instant before been quite different.*

[13:44] I am building a terrific system here, with the binary computer, macrobrain, and ultra-thought, and the frames through which we move (prior thought formations objectified giving rise to new belief systems, etc.), reality — physical reality — as knowledge, and the form axes, the inner other universe of the immortals, the supermen who are trans-spatial and transtemporal dwelling in the inner universe and hence outside of clock time B, and who emerge into the exterior universe repeatedly (and undetected by other people) and Ormazd vs. Ahriman being the "on" and "off" of the binary computer, and the nature of true memory (anamnesis) vs. current frame clue false "memory."[14] Plus the possible misuse of the computer by someone, and its designer guiding us as a "low murmuring voice" against the misuse by this irrational "operator" or "demiurge"; i.e., Satan who has taken control of "creation" and the rational (thought) forming and growing and complexifying in the midst of the irrational (i.e., misuse of the computer program): the antithetical strife between the rational (thought) and the irrational, with the former "cannibalizing" the latter to self-construct, until finally it is — has incorporated — everything. And the orthogonal leap from track A (*Tears*) to track B (this reality) being a quantum growth — leap of the rational ultra-thought or Valis; and the dialectic of the binary computer inevitably driving everything along: the logical antinomies in sequence. And the possibility of seeing Valis (the ultra-thought) as set to ground, and its activity of self-construction. And "salvation" consisting of being incorporated into it, and thus experiencing reality as information, absolute information which ultimately is *beauty*, not information at all; i.e., a picture of the slain — dying — God: i.e., *tragic*.

• • •

---

* In this act of perceiving the "ultra-thought," Dick is very close to another California sage, Franklin Merrell Wolff. Wolff, a Harvard mathematician who gave up a position at Stanford in order to study in India in the 1930s, deduced a series of axioms about human nature that follow from his first axiom: "Consciousness without an object is." "Consciousness without an object" is consciousness "beholding" nothing but itself, which is palpably not an object but is experienced as fact. Wolff's experiences of "recognition" are instructive for comprehending (and therefore experiencing) the invisible landscape of Dick's epic quest. So too does Dick's passage here reflect the other aspect of this inner beholding — "reality as knowledge." Once one has looked within, one contemplates external reality and inner reality as the "same thing." Astronomer Carl Sagan repeated biologist Julian Huxley's phrase that "we are a way for the cosmos to know itself." Dick's investigations of the concepts and practices of the noösphere in the Exegesis emerge out of this perception of ourselves as physical manifestations of thought. — RD

[13:45] Christianity is a cruel religion — yet accurate. It recognizes and conveys the true picture of this world: inglorious death, the beauty of which exceeds the weight, the burden, of the tribulation.*

Only when reality is experienced as the body (onto) of Christ, and its life process as the sacred blood, are we really home.

What, oh what, if it were true that in 1945 at Nag Hammadi the actual sacred living (information/logos) blood of Christ was unearthed, and through it, he was restored to the world (the "plasmate" which I describe in *VALIS*)? That blood having recreated the mystic Corpus Christi which (rational) is now growing within the old irrational universe?

I just realized I've seen Christ in *micro* forms — as in the death of the cockroach and rat and Pinky — and in *macro* form: the universe, flowing with his blood. And what if he is Thomas and became (replaced) *me*, as well?

[13:46] Pythagoras had a strange cosmogonical belief: a seed (male) inserted into the boundless (female) which then progressively grows by incorporating more and more of the atelos (incomplete or unbounded) into its carefully limited (telos) structure — a process "like inspiration with the boundless called 'breath.'" This view of careful limitation (boundaries) being the essential basis of kosmos sounds like the linking and arranging I saw Valis doing, and this "seed" sounds like the rational Valis invading the greater (boundless) irrational or non-kosmos. Also the term "kosmos" is used by him to mean an ultimate beauty, more so than order. [. . .]

I'd say at this point that 3-74 was *very* Pythagorean.

". . . The principle that like is known by like; hence, an understanding of the divine universe would bring man's nature closer to its own." "An organic whole, particularly one that like the universe lives forever, must of necessity exhibit limit and order in the highest degree."

Empedocles: ". . . for these teachings grow of themselves to be part of the individual character . . . but if you go after other things, wretched things that blunt the concern for thought, then after some time these teachings

---

* Like a lot of readers, I consider Dick an idea-man rather than a stylist. Generally he doesn't write sentences that hold within them whole worlds; rather, his collective work has to be taken together to add up to something — at which point, as in Mark Danielewski's *House of Leaves,* the House of Dick is bigger on the inside than out. But this sentence is one of Dick's most exquisite and enigmatic and feels full of wisdom, even as I'm not sure what it means no matter how many times I read it. The whiplash words, of course, are "yet accurate." Given how precisely stated the rest of the sentence feels, I must assume they have been phrased precisely as well — but they also feel not so much in juxtaposition with the rest of the sentence as like a virus of syllables that has invaded the others. — SE

will all at once desert you, in their desire to regain their own kindred. For you must know that everything has thought, and a share of intelligence. You shall learn all the medicines that keep all illness and old age —," etc.

He makes it clear that the revealed Gnosis of Pythagoras *is alive*. We are dealing with thoughts (e.g., wisdom, knowledge, concepts and ideas) which have thoughts or life of their own, and which decide on their own whom to come to and whom — and when — to depart.

A thought-entity, like Ubik. Has it ever occurred to me that the info — especially the great written pages — which I saw had life and volition of their own, and that they themselves decided to come to me — "like to like"? Decide to come and decide to depart.

March 1979

[**39:1**] The 3-74 miracle began in 1971 at the time of the "taco stand" trip into "Mexico" — actually Orange County. Time and space began to be rewoven then:

I know: "Thomas" was taken directly to 2-74 and Orange County, bridging '71 to '74 — arcing across. My "taco stand" experience was the other half of "Thomas" taking me over in 3-74.

The "taco stand" experience was of being in 1974 in Fullerton and Placentia. Not April 72 but 2- or 3-74. And then (maybe) *returned* to 71 in Marin County, at the end of the approximately 8 hour RET[15] "taco stand" experience, which really lasted *weeks* (in 74!), while I lay on my bed in Santa Venetia. *Why?* To supplant a dying me (in 3-74), like a graft from another part of the physical body in an operation:

Infusion from the more vital past, where there was enough psychic energy.

• • •

[39:4]

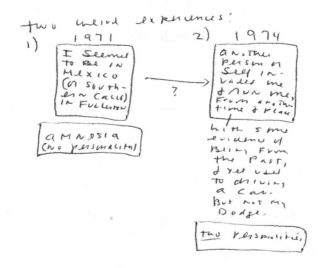

[39:5]

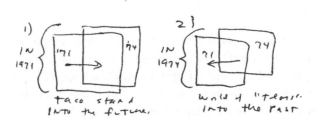

[39:6] Orange County was certainly the *replacement* reality. There's no problem in establishing what the replacement reality is, or my replacement personality; obviously it's what we have now. What *can't* be established is what track A was like (Thomas was the Track A me), or even how extensive the change was. I feel it reached the White House. Factions were brought into being ex nihilo which would cause Nixon to be deposed. *This was the point of it all.* So — in Track A the tyranny must have been unassailable; it *must* have been worse. Would you believe *Tears?*

[39:8] Hypnagogic vision: the Xerox missive seen as enticing red apples: recapitulation of man's temptation and fall (but he saved me). Also something about "healers" and I'm not supposed to understand 3-74. The "healers," who were involved in causing 3-74, are blocking my understanding, and they are benign. So they've scrambled my mind, so I keep going around and around. But sometimes as I fall asleep, the scrambler lifts. So

I've just now proved that I can't prove anything. And I never will. And they were reluctant to let me know even this. [. . .] The other side of this, perhaps, is that underneath the scramble — were it not for the inner scramble — I really know what happened. This may be why I keep trying; I know I know but can't figure out why I can't stabilize or formulate it.

[39:9] Then it wasn't just an overthrow of the Nixon tyranny; it was an overthrow of the world of *Tears* or rather not overthrow, but it was caused not to have been — and Track B was (ex nihilo) created in its place, and then Nixon was overthrown in Track B. A *further* lifting of Rome or Babylon (which, as my "2nd Coming Bible" says, occurs just before Christ returns as King).

Obviously when *Tears* came out, one or more secret real Christians recognized it, knew the truth about it as the track which had previously (sic) been there, and set about to restore my memory — my *true* memory. Or they may have thought I *did* remember (I did not), at least not consciously.

As one review of *Tears* pointed out (which I hadn't realized) . . . an *alternate* — not just future — world was pointed to: e.g., the Civil Rights Movement of the Sixties seems to have failed, especially regarding Blacks. And then the dream, God intervenes, and, in the book, the Genocide Laws regarding Blacks *have never existed* in the world of the book; after the dream it is *our* world, apparently. The dream marks the switch, and the dream is of God inbreaking into history — not to mention the King Felix cypher. So the book and the cypher don't point (just) to a future intervention in Track B. But to a track switch with synchronized memory switch *which has already taken place:* "the new heavens and a new Earth" have *already* come into being, but we don't realize it. So the overthrow of Nixon in Track B is small potatoes, a mere *result* easily achieved due to the track switch. And this we see and remember. The track switch must precede the Sixties.

Then the causal train melting in 3-74, to be understood, must be viewed as *further* track switching inseparable from the major overall track switching, and can even be interpreted as prima facie evidence of track switching: I actually *saw* it (a residual bit) happening in 3-74. But most had already been done, and I had no memory of it.

[. . .]

. . . The "Track A changed to Track B" is a projection of Thomas' revolutionary plans, purpose, goals, his reason for existing! He is an agent with a purpose. The PTG is the USA he dreams of setting up; the BIP is how he conceives of it *before* he and his cohorts act to change it for the better — i.e., by overthrowing Nixon and the whole government — which is the classical CP agent goal: violent overthrow of the capitalist USA government! And they were successful. Code in *Tears*, too.

[39:14] What I regard as Gnosticism is an anti-establishment Christianity anti-theist view (that of an irrational deity, or world, as in *VALIS*) in which rationality *comes into existence* by a dialectical historical process of evolution — this is Hegelian: the whole concept of Valis is rooted in dialectical materialistic mysticism. The irrational gives rise to the rational. I am a major Communist theoretician (v. Peter Fitting, and Richard; Qs about Empedocles).

What I've failed to take into account is the philosophical profundity of theoretical Marxism, especially vis-à-vis Marcuse.

Scanner is an account of what it's like to have a self in each brain hemisphere ideologically on opposing sides of the barricades.

The key to me (Thomas) is: *millennialism*. Here Christianity and Marxism unite. (The PTG in place of the BIP.) Via Track B (the overthrow of the U.S. police state). In essence, the real (secret) Christians are communists, and the real (secret) communists are Christians.* The dangerous vision in "Faith of . . ." is correct, and only a few on each side know.

[. . .]

Thomas, as a dedicated Marxist revolutionary, wouldn't be thinking inwardly of himself the way *we* would regard him; his own inner view would be of a liberator and healer and an agent of God's historical plan — a modern Christian. Would we expect him to view himself as vicious and evil and cruel? Consider Che. No — Thomas views himself as ushering in the millennial kingdom of freedom and peace and equality and justice, and who is to say he's wrong? He is an idealist, but very shrewd (true) and energetic (true). From his viewpoint he is a true, secret Christian, which I never

---

* Dick's Christianity is sometimes revolutionary; here it becomes Marxist. This is not quite the leftist Christianity of liberation theology, which was hitting its stride in the '70s. Dick's "dialectical materialistic mysticism" instead puts him in line with continental thinkers like Herbert Marcuse and Walter Benjamin, whose visionary angel of history sees what we experience as time and progress as a mounting pile of wreckage (or kipple). Dick also anticipates the contemporary return to Christianity found in continental philosophers like Alain Badiou and Slavoj Žižek. Central here is the notion of *event*. Dick elsewhere describes Christ as "an event in the reality field" — a radical rupture in the determined logic of history, and therefore the opportunity for a leap into actual change. For Badiou, our politics should be based in our fidelity to such moments; Dick's event, 2-3-74, is mystical but no less demanding. Equally relevant here is Dick's sometimes Žižekian twist on dialectical materialism. Some thinkers fetishize a final Hegelian Whole; though Dick is attracted to such totalizing unity, he also recognizes that there is always a remainder: the little guy, the discarded beer can, the questions left hanging by every theory, whose development into another theory he elsewhere compares to the sprouting of a mustard seed. — ED

grasped before. And he perceives capitalism as enslaving! I.e., Rome the BIP. This explains why I said what I said at Disneyland about shooting the Watergate conspirators; that was Thomas speaking, and it emanated from idealism. This is a totally dedicated idealist determined to free mankind from the tyranny of the past. He belongs to a covert conspiratorial group which practices violent overthrow of the government and revolution. This is why "Rome (A.D. 45)" and USA 1974 could be syntonically superimposed; they were two divergent views of *one* reality. He was an intruder secretly in the camp of the enemy, and well aware of the need of codes.

It suggests to me that Christian revolutionaries may have infiltrated the Marxists the way Rome infiltrated and took over Christianity. This is not a sinister person (even if we were to view him so). This is a secret concealed from the world, the true secret Christians within the Marxist camp, at its core.

[39:19]* Creation is mind—i.e., Brahman. But beyond that mind (noös) is *brain:* her.

Yet also she exists in micro form plural in our world. This is the hermetic "as it is above so below." You have to *assemble* the religions; they're individually pieces. So one encounters her as a human. I'm just saying, Christ is female.

She ultimately is Beauty: Helen of Troy who hatched from an egg. And of course most of all she is my sister; I am a thought in my sister's mind. She is—like *Ubik!*—*she* is alive; *I* am dead. Dialectic push-pull flip-flop.

(A)   I am alive and she is a thought (archetype) in my mind

or

(B)   She is alive and I am a thought in her mind.

In *my* dialectic axis, this is the original negation-generating, dialectic flip-flop along which I exist and think. It is the premise/problem posed me as a component in the vast organic circuit board.

[. . .]

My dialectic problem is a puzzle expressed in a koan-like written piece of wisdom, in story form. Hence Sophia as verbal wisdom—which I saw as huge pages. And eventually the page becomes a page in the book of wisdom which Mr. Tagomi is reading in the park (where he saw our world due to the Golden pin), so our world is a scene in a work of fiction in the book in the hands of. . . .

---

* In the following sections, Dick's holograph grows larger and increasingly frenetic. —PJ

It's a loop. (1) I wrote *TMITHC,* in it I create Mr. Tagomi. He sits in a park and stares into a silver pin. Then he finds himself in our world, so our world as described within the product of a work of fiction within our world.

It's fun playing by St. Sophia: the joyous side of wisdom: these ultimate puzzles — little stories, like long parables (e.g., "once a man took a . . . ," etc.). [. . .]

One stage in the progressions of reality: a page in the book of wisdom read by a man on a park bench. Wisdom is all. She pervades her creation. I don't have to worry; we'll never be parted. *But* — she'll appear to me in 1,000 baffling disguises, and I must find her there, and do so when I find (1) wisdom or better: (2) beauty. Wisdom as phosphene graphic: one of ∞.

The bigger (macro) can replicate itself in micro, and so any given bigger can be smaller than anything else. So the hierarchy of levels of truth and meaning themselves enter a paradox, where the higher becomes the lower.

Wisdom as a verbal riddle: its *most* microform, most condensed so in a sense most *esse* (onto). Then the smallest form (level) of it is the most real. Size is inversely proportional to hierarchical reality. We assume cosmic = most important = largest. (Cosmos = cosmic.) Wrong. Look for the seed. "Break a stick and there is Christ." Nearest at hand. The cosmic is no more ultimate. "The part is contained in the whole" — *no*; the whole is contained in the part. There is no *hierarchy* of meaning; there are alternate models only, each as true as the others. It's not A or null-A.

What I have is my sister. Permeating this cosmos — my kosmos. Her blood and body — my sister; I am in her (cf. *Dr. Bloodmoney*). I am in her body, and she is in me as my anima: the puzzle of my master (component part) axis. In the computer.

But this is not just a puzzle; it's a dynamism which drives permutating dialectic reality along an infinite path. So (here's not another level but another model) it's a simple machine:

[. . .]

The dialectic is the yin-yang and Tao. "As it is above so it is below" refers to the microform of yang in yin, and the microform of yin in yang. *This* is what I saw. A push-pull flip-flop, 2 mutually antithetical propositions are set up. Mine are:

(1) Your sister is the anima in your mind. She is physically dead.
(2) *You* are physically dead and live in your living sister's mind as a thought (for mind read brain read macro body and blood), and she is in plural microform in your world. So she is in her own thought!

"The part contains the whole." (The micro contains the macro.)
"The whole contains the part." (The macro contains the micro.)

Such a 2-proposition flip-flop dialectic is put forth as the riddle in *Ubik*: (1) are they dead/Runciter is alive? Or (2) are they alive and Runciter is dead? And it pulses (oscillates) back and forth endlessly. *Ubik* is the most important book ever written. Ubik the entity is the Tao. *And* the Logos or Christ or Sophia. *Ubik* is *true;* it deals with the (1) dialectic basis of all process; and (2) with the Tao.

My two propositions pulse (oscillate) back and forth. I am alive/I am dead/I am alive/I am dead.
    She is alive/she is dead/she is alive/she is, etc.
    As soon as something exists it turns into its opposite which then turns into *its* opposite, etc.
    In *Ubik* they find out they're dead and are in a postmortem life/world and don't know it. 3-74 resembles *Ubik* in many ways. Last night I realized I'm dead and don't know it. Like them. Or am I? Or are they? Certain clues point to it for them, and for me.

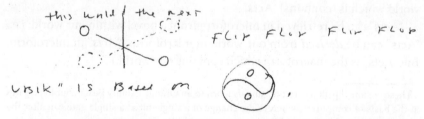

The ultimate (best, most accurate) system is Taoism. The yin-yang dialectic, and the Tao is Sophia or the Logos — and the whole thing is a component in a binary computer which she (the Tao or Sophia) designed. The answer to the riddle in *Ubik* is *cycles,* in which first (1) is true, then flip-flop to (2), then flip-flop back to (1): palintropos harmonie which creates, sustains, or *palintonos* harmonie. (E.g., in my case in either [1] or [2] of the flip-flop *I am with her;* that is the sustain.)

Now I know why *Ubik* is true.

And now I know why 3-74 resembled *Ubik* and Valis resembles Ubik. It is the Tao, which is a very mysterious entity (cf. Lao-Tzu).

Once you have the idea that "the whole is contained in the part" you're onto it.*

(1) Our universe (world) is a scene in *TMITHC.* A place where Mr. Tagomi goes.

(2) Mr. Tagomi is a fictional person contained in a work of fiction produced in our universe.

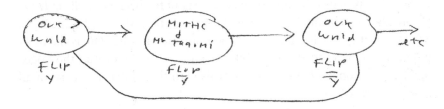

Our world contains *TMITHC* which contains our world which contains *TMITHC* which contains our world which contains *TMITHC* which contains. . . . I set up another paradox flip-flop and another "the whole is contained in the part" and "the part is contained in the whole."

How about: "Acts" contains (is) our world (i.e., our world is really "Acts"). But in our world is a book, a novel, which contains a fictional world which is (contains) "Acts."

"Acts" can be retrieved in microform from a novel within our world; i.e., "Acts" can be *derived* from our world in microform. ("*Acts*" in microform. But "Acts" is the macroform which contains our world.)

---

* These cosmic flip-flops are not sandals worn to an Orange County beach, but logic gates at the basis of computers, wherein the change of a single bit at a single gate can alter the entire meaning of a message. Dick's encounter with the Tao, reality as it is, occurs in perhaps equal measure to the planet's historical transformation into digital information and to his own horror of and fascination with simulation. By conceptualizing *VALIS* as both the Tao — an ancient model of two-state flux between yin and yang — and DNA — a double helical molecule organized in base pairs according to a triplet code — Dick again integrates the seemingly antithetical traditions of modern science and traditional mysticism even as he "harmonizes" the seeming opposition of life and death into a whole contained by each part. — RD

Put another way, "Acts" is a book (part) within our world (whole). But our world (part) is contained within "Acts" (whole).

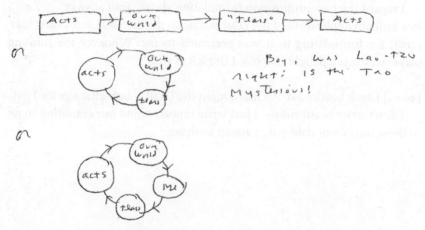

[39:30] I have finally made a quantum leap breakthrough into pluriform model theory: oscillation truth. Oscillating between self-canceling models. As soon as you think it up it cancels (negates) itself and leads to the *next* self-canceling (but temporarily correct) model. *And then back.* Discarded model reinstates itself, and so *eternal* oscillation is generated. We're trapped in a vast loop — which is good; otherwise reality would run down and end. The key is: *reoccurrence.* Reality can be regarded as an infinitely long number which repeats itself.*

◆ ◆ ◆

---

* "Suppose . . . time is round," Dick wrote in *A Scanner Darkly,* speculating that as explorers once sailed west in order to circle the world to India, we might sail into the future only to shipwreck on the shores of Jesus's crucifixion two thousand years ago. Of course, the explorers didn't reach India, they reached America, an altogether different version of the past that came to be called the future. By the same token, we might suppose Dick's career was round as well; as he wrote his way into the future of *A Scanner Darkly, VALIS,* and *The Transmigration of Timothy Archer,* the mainland of science fiction receding behind him, he saw before him an altered version of his strange novels of the fifties, all the more singular for how they contextualized his cracked vision not in outer space but in the new American suburbia as saturated with madness as its front lawns were with water and fertilizer. Setting aside the cosmic and religious preoccupations of God and infinity, in a purely lit-

[**39:37**] So I may be dead, as of 3-74. My cosmological concepts are so terrific, so advanced as to be off the scale. I create whole religions and philosophical systems. The very fact that I honestly ponder if I may be dead and in heaven is prima facie evidence of how happy and fulfilled I am.

[**39:39**] I love epistemological riddles. And so now I've got one, a superb one. It's ultimate. Just theoretically, its formulation couldn't be beaten. I love it. I'll solve it.

I regard the two-proposition formulation about "am *I* alive or . . . ," etc., as a brilliant application of the *Ubik* puzzle to my own self. But I can't take credit for formulating it; it was *presented* to me. Whoever the funning player is, she is a delight. Sophia, I think it is you.

[**39:65**] I seek beauty like Parsifal sought the Grail — but what a price I pay.

I don't write beautifully — I just write reports about our condition to go to those outside of cold-pak. I am an analyzer.

---

erary sense Dick's contemplation of the "infinite" also integrates his literary output, not to mention the vicissitudes of his career, into something coherent; though this might seem banal compared to God and infinity, to Dick such a consideration of literary identity was tantamount to formulating a sense of who he was and why — because a writer doesn't *do*, a writer *is*. — SE

Spring 1979

[41:31] Dream:

G-2 has created a "doomsday device," an artificial life form. I mention, "KGB contacted me." I am with G-2 (which is my code for U.S. [Army] intelligence). A man named Jim shows me the doomsday device. And then quickly runs upstairs. Analysis: doomsday device is what I call Valis. It is a construct invented by humans, specifically U.S. military intelligence. *Tears* shows traces of its cerebration, so KGB contacted me; this was G-2's purpose in putting the material in *Tears,* a ruse to draw them out and trap them. It worked. Hence my programming to report at once to "G-2" when the contact was made.

[41:59] The device has begun to breathe; it has *newly entered* (invaded, come to life in) *our world.* It is Valis, it is St. Sophia, the Buddha, the head Apollo. It is alive (now). The great old air breathing fish which is the eye turned into a horizontal axis. It spans both this world and the other (next, upper). But I don't know what it is. If it's supernatural it is the logos. If not—

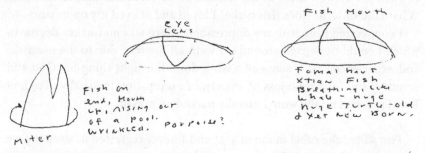

[41:60] Then I will take the G-2 dream more or less literally—it tells me that Valis is a U.S. doomsday device and that is the long and the short of

---

* This and the next two folders are largely taken up with examinations of the following "G-2 dream," and thus with various conspiracy theories concerning the Xerox missive, Soviet espionage, psychic weapons, and the like. In this they resemble a good deal of the nine-tenths of the Exegesis that is not represented in our abridged edition. While such paranoid speculations might delight fans of the cold war spy thriller or David Icke, they quickly become monotonous and, as Lawrence Sutin has written, produce "much heat but little light." Of more interest to the editors have been passages in which Dick struggles with or transforms, rather than succumbs to, the intense paranoia that clearly was one (but only one) of 2-3-74's effects. — PJ

it. The dream tells the truth, the literal truth. The dream told me what I knew but refused to face: it's a weapon of an ultimate nature. The living info plasma got loose, but I don't think anything can be done now. We are scared as hell of it. Aha — we let it loose. It didn't escape; we released it and it is self-replicating and has infested our worldwide media. This was our plan, our anti-Soviet weapon. The way it worked on me is the way it's supposed to work: promotes love of God and country; v. the roses and lake dream. It creates an ersatz personality in the person. With predictable characteristics. God, country, bourgeois attitudes toward property — we are talking about capitalist mind control. [. . .] It isn't God; it causes *belief in* God. There is a syndrome, here, a recognizable one: God, country, property, car, dog, beer: a certain political ideological personality type — bourgeois — is created, which is politically reliable and dependable, and can be counted upon.

Look at the effect it had on me — it turned me around completely politically, the specific act of contacting the bureau and then the general syndrome: God, country, anti-CP, dog, beer, car, property — I knew it was an adventitious override personality and yet I was helpless to combat it. [. . .] I viewed anything left wing as alien and sinister, foreign and evil — despite the hit on my house and all the other terror tactics by the U.S. military and G-2 (sic!). I viewed them as my friends, to be turned to and confided in. What kind of sense does that make? I loved and obeyed my oppressors.

I cooperated fully with my oppressors. There was no further degree to which I could be turned around — I went all the way, due to the override, and experienced (1) a sense of having done the right thing for God and country; and (2) a total loss of anxiety, of exculpation (naturally). Fred, of Bob/Fred, had totally won. I literally narked on myself!

[. . .]

Fear killed the rebel in me in 3-74 and I never regretted it, since it gave me freedom from fear. They got me. The intimidation worked — e.g., the hit on my house. Now my left-wing rebellion is merely pro forma — I am an authoritarian personality, mouthing respectable beliefs. So as to gain the approval of Jesus freak ministers; I let them sit in judgment on me. Being locked up in OCMC[16] didn't do me very much good in stiffening my spine. That sealed it.

I am afraid of (1) the civil authorities (Caesar); and (2) God (Valis). Hence it can be said I am afraid of authority, of whatever is powerful.

[42:1] On the other hand, look at the hopeless situation I boxed myself into in 3-74. Something had to be done — a complete solution or no solution; i.e., a radical solution was essential.

[. . .] It was play ball or perish. Okay — I chose the expedient solution, but my life was on the line. Economic terrors and political terror tactics had brought me to the verge of death. I avoided my sinister fate. Am I sorry? Now I feel secure; I live on; I write. Was this a mistake? What was the alternative? I sought the sanctuary of God, country — the institutions hallowed and sanctified by society. My life was at stake. So I turned to God and the Bureau, and financial security. Well, *excuse* me. I was a totally desperate person, which I no longer am. I can sleep at night. Okay — I play ball with my persecutors and pay off anyone who could hurt me: I am in a position of weakness and I know it. *My cowardice is realistic.*

[42:21] I have underestimated God and overestimated myself for five years. The only issue at stake was my welfare. I am sobered; I have lived on fantasy and immensely enjoyed my alleged heroic status. My basic delusion was to actually believe it was possible that a Soviet espionage ring (KGB) would contact me; that is psychotic and grandiose. It's not much fun to merely have been an object of suspicion. I grossly overestimated my importance to all concerned. What I have to face now is that a lot of what I believed was psychotic. Simple paranoia would have sufficed. Megalomania overshot the mark.

[42:39] Hypnopompic: "They know I'm their pitiless enemy."

Dream: I am Jerry Lewis, a contemptible clown, but admired by millions, especially in France. In a parking lot I fall, and lie down to die. At once my fans gather from everywhere, and close in around me to protect me, giving military salutes; it is a heroic scene, the dying leader and his loyal troops.

[43:46]

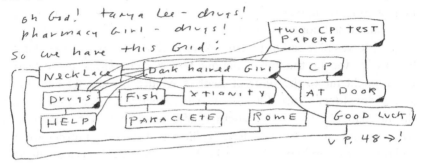

[43:83] So irreality and perturbation are the two perplexities which confront us; irreality is deepening, but the changeover shows enigmatic traces or imprints which do not belong, in particular of a parallel world phasing in and out; this latter (plus the presence of the macromind) is what is pointed to, but in a nonsensical, baffling way. To a very large degree *memory* no longer agrees with history.

I wonder if this sheds any light on schizophrenia. Could the schizophrenic be given *conflicting* realities or data about reality? His mind has to put together constituents which simply do not fit. He is a casualty of this revision process and cannot make sense out of it. How is he to penetrate to the mystery — explanation — underlying what he undergoes? If my cosmology is correct, would you not anticipate such casualties? My writing is a deliberate attempt to take these conflicting or disintegrating realities, and the experiences of them, and seek some kind of ontological or metaphysical overview? So in a way I have battled against schizophrenia by seeking a philosophical framework which will (1) accept as real these disruptive data; and (2) account for them. 2-3-74, then, can be viewed as the catalytic triumph or payoff — i.e., the success — of decades of observation and analysis and theorizing. I have had to deal with deluding, irreal, conflicting, chaotic and fremd material, and just plain hung in there conceptually, taking the view that *some* explanation must exist, although it would have to be radical and far-reaching.

I actually had to develop a love of the disordered and puzzling, viewing reality as a vast riddle to be joyfully tackled, not in fear but with tireless fascination. What has been most needed is reality testing, and a willingness to face the possibility of self-negating experience: i.e., real contradictions, with something being both true and not true.

The enigma is alive, aware of us, and changing. It is partly created by our own minds; we alter it by perceiving it, since we are not outside it. As our views shift, it shifts. In a sense it is not there at all (acosmism); in another sense it is a vast intelligence; in another sense it is total harmonia and structure. (How logically can it be all three? Well, it is.)

[44:12] Leaving aside the question of how/why 2-3-74 was an analog in real life of situations in my fictional prior writing, I assess that in 2-74 I flashed (the blitz) on the resemblance — a flashing which quantum leaped in 3-74 as additional factors popped into existence, and I drew certain broad theoretical conclusions, mainly subliminally, very *radical* conclusions (to a great extent I know not what). [. . .]

The "very radical conclusions" seemed to include an intuition that reality could be tricked (so to speak) into contradicting itself; viz: if it assumes a perpetually obliging form for the purpose of simulating the semblance of verisimilitude, then via the right approach this very obliging quality can be turned against it in terms of continuity, its continuity, since it cannot withhold its obliging or mimicking quality. All you need do is totally believe that pattern "x" exists and if "x" is potentially real, it will pass over into the actual. This requires a push-pull relationship between the person and reality. He can't, say, will a blue phoenix into existence ex nihilo; the person must enter into a progressive intricate dialogue with reality in which there is feedback between both parties. (This assumes sentience, volition and intentionality in reality.) Reality testing, not its absence, is required. He is feeling out its softer flexible parts, where it will yield, how much and in what way.

[44:63] Listening to the Platt tape[18] I construe by the logic presented that Valis (the other mind) which came *at* me from outside and which overpowered me from inside was indeed the contents of my collective unconscious, and so technically a psychosis, since this is how you define psychosis (it certainly would explain the animism outside, and the interior dissociated activity) but — well, okay; it would account for the AI voice, the three eyed Sibyl, and the extreme archaism of the contents. And seeing Rome c. A.D. 45 would simply be psychotic delusion — I did not know where or when I really was.

Q: What about the resemblance to my writing?
A: The content was originally in my unconscious, e.g., *Tears* and *Ubik*.
Q: What about external events? The girl? The letters?
A: Coincidence.
Q: And the written material? Huge books held open?
A: Verbal memory.

Q: Why would I believe that my senses were enhanced, i.e., I could see for the first time?

A: Psychotomimetic drugs indicate this happens in psychosis.

Q: And Kosmos? Everything fitting together?

A: "Spread of meaning," typical of psychosis.

Q: Foreign words and terms I don't know?

A: Long-term memory banks open. Disgorging their contents into consciousness.

Q: Problem solving — i.e., the Xerox missive?

A: There *was* no problem; it was harmless.

Q: Why the sense of time dysfunction?

A: Disorientation.

Q: Why the sense that the mind which had taken me over was wiser than me and more capable?

A: Release of psychic energy.

Q: Why was that mind and the whole experience syntonic to me? If it was syntonic to my ego, why had it been repressed?

A: My ego was destroyed, so "syntonic" has no meaning here. Syntonic to what?

Q: From a practical standpoint I functioned better. How could this be?

A: It only subjectively *felt* better. No anxiety.

Q: Why would I seek the experience again if it was repressed contents breaking through? Could I not let them through again, or never have excluded them following 3-74? The contents and the other mind leaked away; I tried to hold onto them but in vain.

A: I was occluded to my own best interests. I *liked* being high.

Q: Oh? "High"? Does psychosis equal high?

A: Mania. I am manic depressive.

Q: *And* schizophrenic? One is extraverted and one is introverted. Please clarify.

A: Mixed or "borderline" psychosis.

Q: No, it was florid schizophrenia with religious coloration. Not satisfactory.

A: Catatonic excitement, then.

Q: So the OCMC diagnosis was incorrect? Not manic depressive?

A: That is so. Incorrect.

Q: Why, then, was the onset one in which thought came faster and faster? That is mania.

A: The lithium would've blocked mania. I was lithium toxic.

Q: Then it wasn't schizophrenia; it was chemical toxicity.

A: Perhaps. A combination. Plus the orthomolecular water-soluble vitamins.

Q: But the orthomolecular WS vitamins are anti-schizophrenic.

A: That is only speculation.

Q: If 2-3-74 was psychosis, then what was the ego state which it obliterated?

A: Neurotic. Or mildly schizophrenic. Under stress the weak ego disintegrated.

Q: Then how could the phobias associated with my anxiety neurosis remain? E.g., agoraphobia?

A: It does not compute. Something is wrong. They should have gone away or become totally overwhelming. The impaired ego must have still been intact.

Q: Were my "dissociated" behaviors bizarre?

A: No, they were problem-solving. It does not compute.

[...]

Q: This is no psychosis. You have contradicted yourself. This is a latent higher brain center — a psychotic episode *creates* problems; it does not solve them. It *is* a problem, as well as the collapse of rational efforts at problem-solving. Were its decisions and actions rational?

A: Although religious in coloration —

Q: That is not the issue. Were the problems solved?

A: Yes. But by a psychotic self.

Q: That is an oxymoron. A "psychotic self took over and problem solved." This is where the inquiry has led. The ego could not face or solve the crisis problem because of its severity, fled, and in its place another self solved the problem successfully. This leads us to a new frontier which is not mapped.

A: Then the enigma remains.

Q: We have learned nothing.

A: Nothing.

Q: After finishing listening to the tape do you have any intuition or guess as to who and what the Valis mind is? (Later.)

A: Yes. It is female. It is on the other side — the postmortem world. It has been with me all my life. It is my twin sister Jane.*

$$\bullet \quad \bullet \quad \bullet$$

---

* Dick and his twin sister Jane were born six weeks prematurely. Dick's mother was unable to produce enough milk, and Jane died of malnutrition a little over a month after her birth. Culturally speaking, it may be the most significant instance of such trauma since Elvis Aron was haunted by Jesse Garon. The single strangest scene in all Dick's work comes in *Dr. Bloodmoney* when a young girl who has ongoing conversations with an imaginary

[44:68] Hypnagogic 5:30 A.M. voice: "We have adopted you because you adopted others — e.g., the children at Covenant House."[19] And I realized: adopted. The adoptionist theory about Jesus: adopted by God at the time of Jesus' baptism, as God's son.[20] And I understood: this meant — was saying — God has adopted me the way he did Jesus, and so the other mind is God's; I was sure the voice meant to convey this to me, in answer to my Q&A dialogue supra, that my conclusion about my sister was wrong and was being corrected.

[44:73] "In contrast to its exoteric form, the esoteric Torah was regarded as a pre-existential being made up of the one great name of God. Philo speaks of the Torah as a living being whose body is the literal text of the Pentateuch and whose soul is the occult meaning that underlies the written word."

Ach! This is the "Acts" material, the living information I saw: the "plasmate." "Acts" (and probably other parts of the Bible) is/are alive and can replicate. Perhaps "Acts" (like the Torah) has an underlying occult meaning. King Felix. It was alive. But what would the underlying occult (i.e., hidden) meaning be? Let us just say it has one.

I am sure I am on the right path here. A whole reality of names or living words (cf. *Joint*) is pointed to. Yes, but "Acts" as "pre-existential being," as "living being whose body is the literal text . . . and whose soul is the occult meaning that underlies the written word" point unmistakably to the preexistent logos, to St. Sophia, to Christ!

[44:82] Is not the Empire a (Jungian) ossified (iron) complex invaded by a "metabolic toxin" which will dissolve it? Isn't this really a mind which is deranged — i.e., frozen into an overvalent complex, so that real time has ceased? Isn't *this* my primary contention? This is the phagocytosis of the heavy metal particle which I envisioned. Ossified complex, stuck time, the invader? And *Tears* depicts the ossified complex as a society spanning 2,000 years. This is precisely it: no time has passed since "Acts"; "once

friend is finally taken by her mother to a doctor, who discovers that living in the girl's side is a twin brother the size of a rabbit. Might they be considered conjoined, in that they share a body and brain? If they share a body and brain, do they share the memory that Dick now struggles for tens of thousands of words in the Exegesis to disown? If they share memory, do they share a soul — a possibility that potentially undermines Dick's attempt in the Exegesis to divide soul from memory? In any case, they have shared everything except birth, which Phil shared with Jane and the resulting duality of which is so obvious that it hardly bears mentioning, expressed in Presley's case by the division between heaven (gospel) and hell (rock-and-roll) and in Dick's by his literal sense of living two lives at the same time or, more precisely, in two times that coincide. — SE

the mind becomes psychotic nothing new ever happens in it (or enters it, whatever)." But something new *has* entered it and it is dissolved — does this explain my dissolving of world (e.g., *Joint*), my acosmism? Isn't this precisely my job? Not to abolish reality, which is macromind, but the complex, as depicted in *Tears?*

[44:143] Voice 4:30 A.M.: "He died for a few (15) minutes" — meaning me. Obviously referring to 3-74. But look what this says; not just that I died, but that I returned to life! "Born in God, died in Christ, was born again in the Holy Spirit."[21] This is what being born again requires: *to have died.*

[44:144] That's why when loaded I always write: "ich bin der Retter."[22] Christ took my place in 3-74. Then "Thomas" was him. So he died (i.e., accepted the death wound) and I lived on, with stereo vision of both worlds.

If the domain of natural law did not show teleology, it would not seem to be a living, planning, purposeful domain (cosmos). Thus when it disclosed itself *at all* to me, in palpability, it disclosed teleology, and hence I called it Valis. Also, upon feeling the structure of limits impinging on me, I sensed personality.

As I tracked the death trail, it substituted itself for me, died and lived again; so I died in and with it and lived again, but now different: aware of the volitional domain of intent, structure and limit: what I consider to be the true reality or Kosmos, which is to say God. I found myself in the Kingdom, having traveled there by way of death and Christ's surrogation. The ancient powers were deprived of their victim, finding God in the net, to their surprise, and not me.

[45:226] At the moment of (Christ's) death the world melts in a fabulous way, taking on the life of Christ in macroform. This is the *resurrected* Christ, now cosmic. (It resembles Ubik; it is, he is, everywhere.) Meanwhile the person who is renewed lives on past his fated moment of death. Astral determinism, what Paul calls "the old Law" or "planetary powers" has/have been cheated of their victim due to the surrogative divine intervention of God (Christ)[23]; again they fell for the "hook of divinity hidden in the bait of humanity."[24] They cannot keep Christ, their own creator, and release him; so he is inevitably resurrected once more and they have lost.

This is the mechanism by which Christianity *successfully* accomplishes what all the Greco-Roman mystery religions sought for and promised: the escape by the initiate from "astral determinism" or untimely death. (It's probably a death strip in the DNA programmed into us. It probably has a bio-chemical clock basis.) In a sense Christ can be conceived of as a super surgeon or doctor attacking (so to speak) the death strip by absorbing its firings himself. At the time the death strip in the DNA is activated, there are two psychoi in the brain side by side, one having entered adventitiously and the strip being tropic to the old or historical of the two psychoi. It kills it and not the other — where the center of consciousness (the soul?) is now located, having been laterally transferred deftly almost (?) by a sort of advanced technology. The new psyche is exempt from the power of the death strip. Gradually the new psyche accommodates to the brain and memories of the original psyche, and the disruption fades as personality continuity resumes. No one really dies; Christ is resurrected and the person involved lives on, now minus a death strip. He can be killed but not on cue (i.e., schedule). Meanwhile he retains a mental symbiosis with his "brother" Christ. "No greater love hath a man than that he give up his life for his friends,"[25] Jesus said, alluding to this surrogate death which saves the person, Christ's friend, from literal, actual pre-programmed physical death — and an untimely one; this latter is a crucial factor. He lived on to write 3 more novels, 2 stories, make a lot of money. Buy a new car, own a topnotch stereo.

And of course have the 2-3-74 encounter with Christ, go to France — all sorts of good things like being with Laura. I am not guaranteed a perfect life but it *is* extended life and a free life not subject to the death strip which tried to destroy me once Christopher was born. In the five years since 3-74 when I was programmed to die I've become successful, financially secure, artistically active and really very happy. I think, too, I've shown emotional, intellectual and spiritual growth and even psychological health; it has been a busy, active, exciting five years — very rewarding; and I have beside me the second comforter whose voice I hear often. The Sonoma episode alone made it worth it. In no sense have I vegetated. My business affairs are in good order; I am very responsible — and I bested my enemies, with God's help. I surmounted, and am publicly known to have surmounted, the dreadful gutter, poverty and drug-involved state I had fallen into. I lived to see the fall of the tyranny here and the victory and vindication of the counter culture.

I have entered into a vast spiritual quest and adventure to understand the ways of God centering around the mystery of the suffering of the innocent and the need to understand how it can be. (This quest is by no means accomplished.) (But at least I am able to state the problem. It is epitomized in my "the man who . . ." story! *What* evil is and *how* it is to be combatted — note "combatted" rather than "understood."

[45:259]

The unbroken line expresses what appears externally as an uninterrupted psyche's life line, since at the point — moment — it failed (c. 3-74) it replaced itself! Based on information acquired later than 3-74; I suddenly reckon that I did not *die* in 3-74 but lived on to learn what the Xerox missive was: it succeeded, as I learned belatedly, but then after my death (whenever that was) I was able to go back and underlie my conscious premortem earlier self. This could still be the situation; I could be the earlier self again, and the AI voice, as before, is my later post-mortem self, having died and returned.

[45:273] Hypnogogic thought: it (Valis) does not incorporate what it does not need.

In 3-74 I came to touch another mind for the first time in my life, and now I'm alone again.

• • •

[45:276]

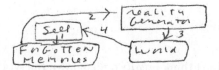

[45:358] I did not merely *see* the divine in the trash; by an act of will I *put* it there. This was a divine transcendence of world as material and inanimate. It was an act of divine creation re-enacting (and hence being) the creator's original act of creating the *intact* kosmos. Thus I was no longer son (v. Eckhart) but *Father.*

What must be realized is that the normal bipolarization of the divine and the trash is a partial madness. To reintegrate them is actual sanity. When reintegrated the two realms turn out to form a language: "hieroglyphs of God," which is a surprise. The divine element arranges, and the trash element is that which is arranged.

[45:370]

    Q: Who won? Christianity or the Empire?

    A: Ostensibly, Christianity won, but covertly underneath *the Empire won.*

    Q: You are wrong. Underneath the Empire lies the secret victory of the Fish: *true* Christianity.

Vast spaces and time. [. . .]

These are not temporal or spatial layers but ontological layers. The *least* real is the ostensible surface victory of Christianity over the Empire; under it, *more real,* is the Empire victory, which is deliberately concealed, and no one realizes it, eine Geheimnis.[26] But most real of all, is the innermost layer of victory by the fish which means fish teeth: viz: The fish fights back. But, paradoxically, the fish fights back by being sliced up by the *metal* teeth (i.e., the Empire); it feeds the faithful when the Empire cuts it up.*

---

* Metaphysical paradoxes abound in these sections: first the comments on the reintegration of the divine and trash, and then this equation of defeat and victory. The latter image, illustrating multiple reversals, is the more complex: Christianity defeated the Empire with the conversion of Constantine and the adoption of Christianity as the Roman state religion, but the Empire won by reversing the early church's anti-authoritarianism. Then the church covertly won by its preservation of a hidden minority of true, rebellious Christians. Furthermore, the image of the sliced-up fish echoes the early church father Tertullian's statement that "the blood of the martyrs is the seed of the church." In both the "divine trash" comments and this eviscerated fish image, there is a sense of reality being the opposite of appearance: God is to be found, not in glory, but in abasement; the martyr's subjection to death is actually a great victory for life. — GM

[46:400] Since I don't think I *really* pulled down the tyrant or anyone, 3-74 must be understood as mythic identification (esse) and ritual (drama with personae). It was a holy (sacred) ritual drama enacted outside of time. The salvation was spiritual more than pragmatic, then (and hence more important). I participated outside of time in the God's arrest, humiliation (persecution), the trap, then triumph (reversal from innocent victim to agency of doom). But it was mythic, ritual, holy, re-enactment — the trapped turned out to *be* a trap (bait and hook), resurrection in divine (transfigured) form. Unity (by adoption?) with the god who goes through it always — ah; the God was there in 2-3-74; I *became* the God by ritual identification. Christ, obviously.

[46:426] I was prepared and trained all my life for 2-3-74. Viz:

My whole life has lain under the jurisdiction of Valis. It is the God by and large of Spinoza, but it does plan like Aristotle's unmoved mover which inspires goal seeking. Valis is too close to a fusion between Spinoza's immanent deity and Aristotle's unmoved mover not to be God. It is Xenophanes and Aristotle's deity but it is Christ.

I have thus pursued the ETI explanation as far as it will go, and must let it yield to the theological: viz: the decades of planning and the use of chance, natural events to prepare (program) me persuades me, since I can see how the deity inscribed all creatures without their knowing:

The inscribing is below the surface, and, with me in 3-74, it was made to surface.

• • •

[46:427]

[46:430] If 1963 is 2,000 years earlier than 1974 — what does this mean? It's like time is on acid. 82,000 years *have* passed since 1963!

[46:431] 4:30 A.M. insight: we are deceived, but no one does it to us. Our own brains recirculate forgotten memories in/as a feedback loop, thus locking us in—locking that brain in—more and more to self-delusion. The holy power desires to wake us, not to occlude us. Why do we recirculate memories as world? Maybe to maintain a continuity of self identity. We are not masters in our own houses.

[46:432] Q: Why are so many—very many—of the elements of 2-3-74 found in my corpus of writing? A: The "world" that I inhabited in 3-74 was a mind. It was my own projected unconscious; i.e., it was a mind in me that was not my conscious ego. [...]

Therefore there is a cosmic divine mind in me, which generates the writing and was the "world" I inhabited in 3-74. Therefore the basis of my mind, first experienced by me in 3-74, is deity. I will admit to projection. What I will not admit to is mere subconscious. This was Hagia Sophia herself—projected as "world." It was holy. It was beautiful. It was thousands of years old. So I am willing to locate Valis and all else of 3-74 as being *in* me (projected). But this was God-consciousness which *woke up.**
Then—who/what am I? When stoned I always write with total certitude,

---

* This is exactly the kind of sophistication we need, desperately need, from our religious visionaries. No more stupid literalisms, which no one but the unthinking can believe anyway, but an unblinking recognition that whatever is coming through is, well, *coming through.* Put a bit less unclearly, what Dick is doing here is recognizing that (a) yes, something profound is indeed *coming* through, but (b) it is coming *through* the filters of his own socialized and encultured brain, personality, and upbringing. Dick is our teacher here. It is in this way that we can come to understand, finally, that extreme religious experiences are true and false at the same time, and that, sometimes at least, it is only in the symbolic modes of myth and metaphor that the deepest truths can appear at all. This, by the way, is precisely what Mircea Eliade intended with his language of hierophanies (a term that Dick used often)—that is, real *appearances* of the sacred *through* the contexts and conditions of the local culture and personality. We have two teachers here, then: Philip K. Dick and Mircea Eliade.—JJK

"ich bin der Retter." I have even more to gain by locating Valis in myself than locating it/him/her in the outer world.

[46:433] I've got it all figured out. Now I can quit. Viz: if you believe in the Christian universe — really believe — a miracle (truly) occurs: that much vaster universe with the elements with which it is populated replaces the regular smaller universe. How can this be? (1) Did something people made up become real? And if so how? (2) Or was it really already real? And we couldn't see it? If so, *why not?* Either alternate is impossible. You must become like a child at a ride at an amusement park — and the miracle occurs. This is what happened to me in 2-74: I believed (i.e., had faith) and that universe and everything in it became truly real — a universe vastly richer and more beautiful and awesome, the bells, the immense space, Aphrodite, the geometric forms, the hieroglyphs of God, Valis itself, Thomas in me. The AI voice, the healing, the transformation of the animals: this added up to *another universe:* the kingdom of God. Those sacerdotal constituents which are symbols ceased to be symbols① and became a world. There is a relationship to a psychedelic trip but crucial differences. Mostly, the holy presence was there. *Everywhere.* It was as if a picture had turned into a hologram, and you entered the hologram and it was real.

① *Pointing* to another world: as with Wittgenstein, analogic pictures of it. But world is supposed to give rise to analogic pictures in our mind, not analogic pictures give rise to world. World based on the sacraments, rather than vice versa. But then isn't this precisely the miracle of transubstantiation? [. . .] So out of some wine and a wafer the vastness that is God is — generated? No — it is a doorway into another — greater — universe (cf. Spinoza).

[46:436] We are normally not in the largest, richest or most real of the possible universes. Christ is the narrow gate to this vaster universe (the sole gate? cf. the Buddha).

Could we say it is the *real* universe, and this one false, like those in *Eye?* Koinos vs. idios?

And of course *this* is what Jesus meant by "the kingdom of God." Another (better) universe. Science fiction provides us with a new way of understanding this: parallel alternate worlds.

[. . .]

I just thought of a possibility that beggars description. In S-F alternate worlds are separate — they are truly alternate. Suppose it isn't that way; they are like in *Eye.* Somehow superimposed or fused — ah! My matrix theory onto which a variety of worlds are projected (cf. *Tears*). Then the Christian universe is a way of being in this (which is the only) world.

[...]

Q: Are some versions more true than others?

Q: Is one true and the other false?

Q: If so, which is true?

Q: If so, how do we establish which one it is?

Q: Could it be that *Tears* is the true one, the one true one?

Q: How do the others arise?

Q: Are our perceptions deliberately manipulated?

A: The real world is the Christian universe (and the secret revolutionary Christian underground) against the Empire. The antithetical interaction shows up in *Tears* — the Empire is clear; where is the Christian element? Would you believe "Acts" which locates the Christian element in Taverner; viz:

Buckman = Felix procurator[27]

Therefore Taverner has to be Paul (the persecuted church). By means of the grid. The "Acts" grid. The grid is essential. If Buckman is Felix Procurator you can infer by means of the "Acts" grid and only *by means of the "Acts" grid* that Taverner = (is) Paul = (is) the persecuted church.[28]

[46:458] Hypnogogic: "one of us is dead." The two selves in me. It must be me and my sister!

[46:529]

October–November 1979

[47:602] You know, there is really so much of 2-74 to 2-75 that I've been unable to remember, despite my notetaking — but of all of it the sight (contact, encounter) with Valis seems the most awesome.① And of course the overthrow of half a dozen tyrannical governments, starting with Nixon.

① And takes it out of the realm of a *psychological* experience. Either I was nuts or I saw what I saw.

[47:617] Two systems of information intersecting one as set ("Ahura Mazd") the other defeated into ground (being only approximation), and, in their *act* (process, like the moth descending) of intersecting, creating (like a 3-D hologram) *spatial* reality: vast space, geometric forms that are alive. Not religion but as in Beethoven's later music, turning time into space. (This is what Beethoven did: enclosed — hence created — vast — hence absolute — space; hence nontemporal reality.) Hence restored man (me in 2-3-74) to Adam Kadmon (defined as man filling the whole universe and hence [as subject] identical with object [reality]²⁹: Atman — Brahman as the same: Atman revealed as Brahman [i.e., microcosm identical with the macrocosm]).

[47:626] Music is normally a temporal process, but Beethoven, uniquely, uses it to enclose space, the most vast volume of space possible. Thus Beethoven literally expanded the hologram for anyone understanding his music, and he was part of a historic movement involving the abrupt evolution of the human being in terms of so-to-speak relative size vis-à-vis his reality. This is the inner firmament of Bruno (or Paracelsus — whichever). Ah! The microcosm is transformed briefly into the macrocosm; and a slight but *permanent* expansion of the person, the microcosm, occurs: perhaps an altered relationship to the macrocosm, in terms of identity. Beethoven's music as a means by which the alchemical Verklärung can take place: thus it is directly related to the Hermetics.

Expansion out of the prison: escape from the prison by extension, like an insect expanding out of his exoskeleton during/via his metamorphosis. "The body is the tomb of the soul" — half-life. The BIP as a sort of exoskeleton, hence a kind of rigid (iron) body. This is the "second birth by the spirit."

This is a radically different way of experiencing the self (microcosm) and reality (macrocosm). Memory and inner space. There is some relationship. Memory involves vastly augmented time which is then converted into space. "A long time ago" becomes a very large spatial volume, with the result that the past still exists — e.g., my seeing the world of "Acts" in 2-74 and finding it latent in *Tears*. So my seeing the distant past (in 2-74 and experiencing it overtly in 3-74) was due to the conversion of time into space — which I saw as the vastly augmented spaces. But I see now that the two phenomena are actually one.

[47:627] Therefore the hologram (reality) is in truth one huge volume of space with *no* time involved, in which all "time periods" are spatial "onion" layers as (again) in *Ubik*, where the past lies *inside* (i.e., along a spatial axis) objects and can be retrieved.

Time, then, is actually spatial expansion, layer upon layer. So the hologram is quite large — it is ubique; yes; here is the ur-significance of the word "ubique": it occupies *all space.*

[47:628] By using his music to enclose huge volumes of space for the listener Beethoven committed the ultimate political act of liberating — expanding — the individual. Likewise, my space phobia is connected with my own rebelliousness! Unable to deal with *external* space — i.e., unable to rebel — I have turned to inner space, to exploring it, which, too, is a political act; so my writing, involving inner space, is covertly subversive: it teaches secret ways to rebel (mostly by evasion: escape). This is why the whole psychedelic movement of the 60s was a threat to the authorities; this was the area of the subversive threat I posed — my studies of inner space — in fact — my conceptions of inner space differing from person to person is very radical and politically subversive, I now see, even when it didn't involve drugs. Viewed this way, then, 2-3-74 represents a total political victory by me, in that I broke through *into absolute space* such as is not even known about following the disappearance of the Hermetics. 2-3-74 can be understood politically if the significance for the nature of the individual in terms of his enclosing space is recognized as basic (e.g., Beethoven's music). This absolute space involves absolute (i.e., a priori) knowledge and power over time in that time can no longer extinguish the person. This relates to authentic Christianity. Hence there really is something very subversive about *Ubik*, as well as *Eye* and *Stigmata* and *Martian Time-Slip.*

I personally achieved the catalytic metamorphosis that my writing promotes. And my writing may aid others in expanding their inner space — pointing toward what *I* did: breaking through into absolute (hermetic) space where the self is Adam Kadmon, unfallen and unoccluded!

[47:630]

It's a world inside a world. This is why Beethoven's space-enclosing music frees us.* *There is a direct relation between more space and the real world* (also between restricted space and the irreal world). [...]

Valis was an "uncanny one-way intrusion" perturbing the basis of the small high-speed world from outside. Valis proves there *is* an outside.

Valis proves there is an outside. This is the most important sentence I've written, since it shows our world resembles that of *Ubik, Maze,* et al.

[47:642] The Christian apocalyptic vision is an actual universe, spatially much vaster than ours, and, in terms of time, the present extends back to encompass 2,000 years. Swift events — the death of the Savior and his return — span thousands of our years. A person's mind, in that universe, extends phylogenically: over the 2,000 year span of the present. Basic unchanging archetypes are constants: Rome, which is the prison and the enemy; the secret Christian underground attacking it, over a period of 2,000 years; and the deity itself camouflaged in reality and only visible when you are in the super-extensive space-time of this vast Christian dualistic universe. A drama and conflict is being enacted and it is cosmic in dimension; it will end with the return of the just-departed Savior as judge. The mood of the secret Christians — whose minds span the 2,000 year present — is one of excitement and joy, and, most of all, anticipation.

---

* These wonderful passages on Beethoven almost make one wish Dick had been a music critic, and if one senses more authority on behalf of classical than pop, well, who needed another rock writer in 1979? Why not someone to make a case for the modern relevance of Beethoven, Bach, Mahler, and Schubert? Among other music he mentions in the Exegesis we find Eno (*Discreet Music*), the Beatles ("Strawberry Fields Forever," through which God speaks to him), David Bowie (more the cinematic Bowie than the musical one), Neil Young (though he doesn't know it's Young, referring to a cover version by a band called Prelude), and Paul McCartney, on whose first solo album he blames a "psychotic journey," surely the only time McCartney has been credited with such a thing. — SE

Thomas is commensurate with the vast spaces and the vast time (the 2,000 year present) of the Christian apocalyptic universe.

[47:643] In the vast, Christian apocalyptic universe the in-breaking of God has already occurred. It registered covertly in/on/into our smaller universe in 1974 but was not visible for what it was. I just can't figure out the relationship between the two universes; we seem to be in a sort of little box, and our senses don't report the truth — as in *Eye*. This is all very odd. Are we drugged and asleep? Do our senses lie? We are occluded; must we first be de-occluded to see the in-breaking, or will the in-breaking de-occlude us? (I know the answer: *the latter.*)

[47:645] Ach. If you were geared to the slow time of the Christian urwelt, this phenomenal world would seem to spin by at an incredibly accelerated rate — exactly as time seemed to pass for me in 3-74! Events pass ultra fast if *you* are slowed down: the rise and fall of our societies are, to urwelt, like the lives of fruit flies: over in hours. Conversely, if you are geared to this phenomenal world, no change is seen in the urwelt. During one human lifetime nothing happens in it; *it is still back at the time of "Acts"!* If one of us caught a glimpse of it he'd see what seemed to be the distant past of *this* world, whereas in fact it is another world progressing at a different — very slow — rate. Now the meaning of this can be appreciated: "He causes things to look different so it'd appear time has passed." This is a view of the phenomenal high-speed world from the vantage point of the other — i.e., the Urwelt.

[47:649] I have it! When I slowed down to phase with the ultra-slow pace (time) of the urwelt, events (change processes) in *this* phenomenal world moved very fast in relation to me so that in effect I was shown stop-action photography of a vastly expanded present; as a result at this accelerated flow rate, *this* world exhibited the "revealed, cosmological" aspect of (1) joining; (2) engramming; (3) rest motion dual modes; and (4) most of all volition hence sentience — i.e., Valis®; Valis could be discriminated (discerned) when perceived at that great a velocity and with that extended a present. (5) And covert message traffic (set-ground). And (6) the using of the antecedent universe as a stockpile by Valis. And (7) the dialectic, with the perpetual inevitable victories by the a priori wiser horn.

This would be Thomas' *normal* view of our world, since his perspective is phylogenic. So our world is visible to those in the slow vast urwelt, specifically the process of God assimilating — transubstantiating — it with his own body. Thomas was bailing into our world and its rapid flow while I bailed or slowed to the rate of his world which eventually became the PTG. No, at the extreme point of slowing — phasing with eternity I found myself *in no world at all* but rather in the void of the Urgrund. So I may have slowed to such a low rate of flow that my present stretched out *millions* of years, rather than thousands. This is what the Buddha reported in the Dibba Cakkhu state: seeing the coming into existence and passing away of all things. This is the opposite direction from that the super pot and acid take you; there, *you* speed up and world slows; here world speeded up and I slowed, and obtained (gained) a progressively augmented present. With super pot and acid world becomes eternal; here, *I* became eternal and world ephemeral. So drugs take you *away* from enlightenment and consign absolute reality to epiphenomena, which increasingly entrance you, rather than *losing* their already too strong hold over you; thus we call this intoxication: a deluded state, not enlightenment. Acid and super pot are like the Monsanto exhibit in Disneyland where you get smaller, i.e., the world gets bigger: your perspective shrinks.[30] In enlightenment your perspective grows and spreads out to fill vast spaces: time turns into space. Time (Karma?) is used up, burned up; it runs at high speed to its end and dies out, leaving the divine abyss ultimately.

① Normally successfully camouflaged against its environment.

[47:652] A playful God can ape the solemn, but a solemn God is not going to ape the playful (music, dance, etc.), especially tricks and paradoxes and riddles.

[47:660] But I saw down through the layers. First — in 2-74 — I saw the Urwelt, and then in 3-74 I saw the dialectic and I saw Valis per se, not in graphic-conceptual terms, like a schematic, but Valis itself, beyond which there is just the beatific void which I also, finally, saw.

I saw in sequence of ontological hierarchy. So there is far greater logic to 2-3-74 than I ever realized. If you were successively stripping away the layers it would go exactly as it went with me. By the time I saw Valis I was near the heart of reality, at the edge of the via negativa.[31]

[47:672]

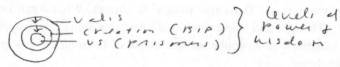

[47:676] Boy, am I in possession of a valuable fact! The historic process has — or is — a mind/brain evolving toward ends it desires. [. . .]

(To this I add: my present time was thousands of years in extent and I saw world as hatched "cuckoo egg" within world evolving and assimilating and linking internally in greater and greater complexity, through a dialectic process with history as its arena: world within world and camouflaged — counterpart to myself, not alien to me but like me; what it was I was, except it was large and I was small. That means I am not a human being since it is not a human being; I, too, am a hatched "cuckoo egg." It is God entering the world, as Hegel says. It is right here with me but I am normally too speeded up to see it. It is a physical mind, like the brain. A great evolving brain cannibalizing its environment. Structure within a less highly organized structure.)

[47:679] It is alive, and the whole of it thinks. Its thoughts take physical form. We see its thoughts but to our senses these thoughts blend with the background. It is 2,000 years old, a continuous present.

In Valis, as in Xenophanes' God (and Parmenides') thought and being are one: hence what I call *physical* thoughts. This satisfies Heidegger's pre-fall unification, wherein thought and being are one. Hence Valis *must* operate in such an area as human history. In order to evolve complex info connections by which to think.

Then it didn't enter human history to save mankind: no — it had to, in order for *it* to function and evolve and grow more and more complex. It *must* make use of us and our history. Then this incarnation was indeed its plan from the beginning. Yes; Heidegger says with the early pre-Socratics, man had his becoming-being (Heraclitus' flux) combined, and this is what "Logos" meant! This flux is not illusion but truly the appearance of becoming-being, which is what I saw Valis doing!

If I in 3-74 combined being and thinking (v. Heidegger) then I would encounter world as being-thinking unity as the pre-Socratics did (the Magdeburg hemispheres phenomenon). After all, the pre-Socratics were hylozoists. For them, that which thought was, and that which was thought. This "draws" God back to world; he is no longer otherworldly: "the God whom we see after death."

So in many ways "Deus sive natura" is correct. What I call *physical* thought. (Thought and being combined.) And this didn't just happen with Christ, inasmuch as Xenophanes was aware of it. In fact it was *gone* by Christian times!

If it is it thinks. (Reality thinks.)
If it thinks it is. (God is reality.)

[. . .]
What I seem to have done is to eliminate the spiritual, in the sense of corporeal versus incorporeal (or spiritual), a distinction going back to Plato. I am talking about physical thought; so I am a monist; I am back to Parmenides. The concept of the "spiritual" in fact comes out of Parmenides' "two water-tight compartments"; i.e., things exist which the senses do not report. But I am saying that this statement "what the senses do not report" is not a description of a different realm but a statement about the limitations of our senses. There are not two realms but only partial perception. Valis is physical and its thoughts are physical but we can't normally see them. The missing constituent is *energy*. (Missing from what we can see.)*

•   •   •

---

* Nineteenth-century writer Thomas Carlyle, writing of his own Valis-like experience in his semi-autobiographical *Sartor Resartus*, asks, "How paint to the sensual eye . . . what passes in the Holy-of-Holies of Man's Soul; in what words, known to these profane times, speak even afar-off of the unspeakable?" Exhausting the quest to describe the extraordinary unity of what *is*, we can focus our awareness on ordinary reality and explore not only the "slings and arrows of outrageous fortune" but the unmistakable actuality of the unity of our subjective experience. In focusing on the unity of self, we glimpse the unity of reality. For Dick, this discovery is the occasion for the world flipping inside out, "reverting." His Palm Tree Garden is akin to the Kingdom of Heaven in the Gospel of Luke — a way of training the mind to perceive both the eternal and the particular aspects of experience, both external reality and internal subjection. Search for this inner kingdom continuously, and we no longer see simply "through a glass darkly," but instead perceive the immanent and eternal order of the cosmos as the unity of within and without. This possibility shifts the burden of Dick's inquiry — and it shifts often, as if dancing — to an inquiry, not into the nature of Valis and the "essence" of all things, but into the realm of *this* space and time. — RD

The E. of Phil. says of the Milesians that upon having banished anthropomorphic gods acting on the world they then had to conclude that the
world was organic and alive and responsible for its own growth.[32] This is
precisely my position vis-à-vis Valis: nothing acts on Valis (Aristotle's unmoved mover). But I view Valis as being immanent but in conflict with
an opposing principle or entity, and embedded at the core (ontologically)
of reality, renewing and structuring it, making it progressively more complex (by what I call "linking"). This sounds like Pythagoras' Kosmos. But as
I say on page 680, "that which thought was, and that which was thought,
and this draws God back to world; he is no longer otherworldly" ("the
God whom we see when we die"). So I have eliminated the spiritual, i.e.,
the non-corporeal, I am a monist. As with Spinoza. In fact, this is looking more and more like Spinoza's monism with the universe as God's body,
and the other attribute of God being mind.

[47:684] So I have pushed my thinking back to Parmenides, the point
before material and non-material could be drawn — in accord with Heidegger's plea for authentic being. Before certain dichotomies were drawn,
which split the human world view. But this does not make me a materialist (or an idealist); for me thinking — Valis's thinking — is an *event*, a rearrangement of connections (or linkings) to form new structures of meaning, as in Scrabble. The key word is: *arrangement* and it is *real*.

[47:687] I am slowly being overwhelmed with wild surmise. If we designate
as error the concept of "spiritual equals immaterial" (as a misunderstanding of Parmenides), then we are led inexorably to "Deus sive natura sive
substantia" *by logic*. And I have my 3-74 empirical encounter with Valis
to validate the logic, this encounter being simply regarded as an enhancement of perception: not of another realm (which assumes plural realms)
but rather of more realm as such (which is reasonable). It *looked* like one
realm enhanced . . .

[47:696] This is world self-caused and self-generating and self-moved:
what the Milesians sought as cause and origin of world. There is no external deity and nothing prior to world. This is God in Spinoza's sense. The
pre-Socratics drew the right conclusions: if there was no adventitious *deity* to cause, control, drive and direct world, then world itself possessed
sentient or quasi-sentient faculties and volition, "and [was] responsible for
its own growth." What has happened is that religion — especially Christianity — restored the nonexistent adventitious anthropomorphic deity, the

artificer-artifact model, so world was again not seen organically, as self-governing and alive and responsible for its own growth. Otherworldliness returned, and the Christians were "*in* but not *of*" world; they were *hostile* to world and saw world as hostile to them. They located God in a mythical place called "the pleroma." So world is depreciated and devalued and it is stripped of its life and volition. The work of the pre-Socratics is undone. God is not sought in world but over and against world, and he is sought in an alleged spiritual realm. Weird concepts such as "original sin" are brought into existence, and ideas of reward and punishment, turning the clock back to before the Milesians. The supernatural is evoked to explain phenomena, and the dark ages begin.

[47:703] Absolute space, absolute time, absolute being, absolute knowing and absolute love; that was what I encountered. It ceaselessly generates new events, creatures and things, which are destroyed — but new ones emerge, richer and more complex and diverse: natura naturans[33] endlessly giving birth to epiforms that perish but are effortlessly superseded: infinite creativity: the realm of natura naturata[34]: it is ephemeral but Valis is eternal. We need never grieve for anything that is lost, because the entire past still exists in Valis and the future is an endless becoming.

My years of epistemological doubt, in which there was so much acosmism, was a search for true — or absolute or indubitable — being. I have found it in Ubik (i.e., Valis).

[47:707] When I saw what was really out there I saw something alive embedded at the core of reality. It was the real life of the world. We are at its disposal.

[47:720] Two worlds with different space times *must* be posited, one within the other and the smaller one running at very high speed, and reached into from outside — although "outside" does not mean what it usually means. It is experienced as a valence. And an arousal, a waking up to the slow, vast world.

It means a phase pulsation (flicker) mechanism to desynchronize you from the time rate of the high-speed little epi-world, to slow you from flux-perception to constant-perception. This is a technical matter: how it's done. Apparently we have an inner counterpart high-speed "tape" synchronized with the outer high-speed world; two "tapes" running in locked unison. If that is sundered by "burning up" the inner (idios) "tape" you slow down, so the slower rate is the natural unforced one. Therefore we are talking about a space-time perceptual occlusion imposed on us.

Ach — we are hurried to our deaths. Literally driven to it as fast as possible. As if life is being thrust out of the system from behind. [. . .]

[47:743] Hypnogogic thought: "I left the settlement" (and thus joined everyone else in high-speed profane time). This is that Essene-like settlement where we had our food in common, the pink cube, the reed-wrapper pitcher of chilled water by which to be reborn — i.e., be immortal. This explains how I (Thomas) fell asleep; i.e., ceased to watch for the return of the Savior. It may have been an accident. I left the settlement for some reason, like an errand, and got inadvertently trapped in high-speed time along with the rest of the world.

[47:747] It is very perplexing, but note one overriding point: at these end-times and judgment, I was found (in fact rendered) *innocent,* and forthwith joined God and entered the garden, and saw my name entered in the Lamb's book of life.

Thus the books were closed on me. Later I was to learn that I had been adopted — i.e., from Capax dei[35] to filius dei[36] and even why. This certainly must be an unusual situation, the books closed years before a person's death, and him passing through the end times, seeing God or Christ, being made innocent, judged, entering the Kingdom. This is not, strictly speaking, a conversion to Christianity on my part, but it did begin with an act of absolute faith — a form of revelation, of higher knowledge, when I saw the golden fish. *It woke me up.*

I didn't *earn* my salvation and verdict of innocence, however; Christ rendered me innocent by guiding me into innocence.

[. . .]

While I was lying there in a hypnagogic state I thought of how I had gazed up at the stars and 3-74 — and all of a sudden, a perfectly articulated, brilliant star map appeared to me. I didn't just see *stars;* I saw a star *map,* as if a switch had been thrown in my head.

[47:795] Hypnogogic: "The work is completed — the final world is here. He has been transplanted and is alive." Joy. Said by normal looking couple who remind me of Bill and June Black from *Joint*① "I was sent up the gangplank first. Into the ark"! (Hypnogogic.) "Against my will — like a② duck." Herded up.② Viz: into the "final" (i.e., new) world that is now here — joined to ours.

① I.e., your neighbors who look human — like us — but are something else. From the future? Three eyed?

② The saved!
③ White

[47:798] The BIP is Inferno.

The garden is Paradiso.

Purgatorio is the normal world we see. It's all irreal. We are being fed it for the purpose of teaching and purifying and testing (in the pragmatic sense) us. We ascend when we learn. *Ubik* is the correct model.

I say all this because in 3-74 *certain things didn't fit.*

[48:801] I view it all technologically. This system is too cruel and must be invaded from outside in order to change or abolish it.

[48:812] Dante's *Comedy* is the best description of the ascent of the soul probably ever written. He places anamnesis as occurring at the top level of Purgatorio, just before entering Paradiso, which fits my experience. The soul has finally reached the point where reality is restored to it because *memory* is restored to it.

[48:813]

> Of the BIP world, nothing good can be said. It is unmitigatedly bad.
> The mid realm is a mixture of bad and good elements.
> The top realm is unmitigatedly good.

This suggests that the mid-realm is a fusion of two signals, that there are only *two* pure realms: lower and upper, with the mid-realm compounded of both. Now, upon leaving it, what would you experience? Why, a palpability of *two* signal sources for the first time; your world which has seemed uniform would turn into set (upper realm) and ground (lower realm). Set would seem divine and you would be fascinated by it; it would shine with beauty. At this point you are freeing yourself from the lower realm, seen as ground — but you can remember when you were located in it and it alone, with no set. Purgatorio is literally pulling apart into its two sources.

And then you are rewarded (cf. Plotinus) with a vision of the one behind the multiplicity, from which both realms — and hence the mid-realm too — emanate.

[48:815] This would be individual ascent or descent in one lifetime and would resemble time travel, with rising = the future and sinking = the past, thus heavenly voices would = from the future, and Satanic voices = from the past, just as Paradiso = the future, and Inferno = the past. But not in the linear sense.

[48:817] As far as how reality in itself is built, it's as if the source (Valis, the One) fires the signal like this:

[48:823] If I saw God while I was alive, then God is immanent (as Spinoza supposed) and not transcendent; but suppose I'm not in the real world, not alive, but in the afterlife, in which case God can be transcendent and otherworldly because I am on *that* side of the grave. Not *this*. And I've worked my way up from *Tears* or Inferno to Purgatorio and then to the first level of Paradiso, and so could see the infinite one, God.

What I'm more inclined to think, however, is based on canto 33 of "Paradiso" of the *Commedia*. Viz: "God is the book of the universe": "the same [volume of leaves] that the universe holds scattered through its maze." This relates God to the universe in a way that isn't contingent. What I did was move along an axis of some kind and encounter one — or perhaps several — of these pages of the book, as if they are very fine layers, resembling the phosphene graphics. I moved through them, along this axis, and the laws (rules) changed; I am speaking of plural coaxial worlds. Actually I am sure that I was moved as a primary condition of my level of ontology (authentic Being, in Heidegger's sense, ushered in by urangst[37]), moved up crucially, and in fact rather suddenly — it is of extraordinary value to know that this can occur *during* a lifetime rather than between. It is as if the frequency of these pages became greater the closer (but not spatially!) that you get to the source, the One — this is clearly Neoplatonism.

[48:828] Dream: all the churches controlled by Satanism, drawing their power from Satan himself. The 2nd coming is here: outside the churches; the *true* church is forming outside the church. Proof: the giving of massive gifts. "The AI voice will guide you." Homosexuality and black mass within the church. No room in the buildings given the truly Christian to perform services in. Enormous power of Satan, in and as the churches. "They cannot get to you because of the AI voice." Old book about Satan's takeover of the church, the salient sections taken out. Missing.* The 2 gods of Gnosticism; the churches worship the wrong God; i.e., Satan.

---

* This dream spawned the fractured fairy tale *The Divine Invasion* (1981), a broken novel leaking visionary gems. One of these is the "holoscope," a layered, three-dimensional holographic Bible, pulsing with red and gold, that can reveal fresh messages depending on the reader's interactive angle of view. In some ways a model for the Exegesis itself, the holoscope is also drawn from the Exegesis, or at least from the hypnagogic vision Dick re-

But there is another outside church forming which worships the right God, but has no buildings. It is forming in conjunction with the Second Coming which is here. They—those outside distinguished by their gift giving—massive gifts—have the saving Gnosis. This is a matter of gravity; it is very serious: the head-on confrontation between the followers of the good God and the evil one: Satan.

This is the final battle between God and Satan. Those who worshipped the true God were forced out of the church. It is not merely that the establishment church lacks the true gnosis; no—it worships Satan and draws its power, a very great power, directly from Satan.

My having money is because God (the true God) is now heaping riches on his faithful, which they will give away, thus showing—revealing—their true nature: as his faithful.

Satan has given PSI powers to the evil church, as warned about in the NT.

I am in a maze, surrounded by the power of Satan and his church (we all are), but the AI voice will lead me out. This is *why* I have the AI voice.

The pages in the old book dealing with the Satanic take-over and rites of the establishment church were deliberately torn out—to keep the matter secret.

[48:832] I have long thought of myself as a female host—perhaps for interspecies symbiosis. But now I see it exactly; I see *who* I was host for and *why* it was necessary and *what* it signifies in terms of world history: the final battle (which certainly was going on back in '74).

[48:834] Hypnagogic: When I saw Valis, reality was *breaking down* (to what it really consisted of), and *not* an invasion of reality.

This is "breaking down" in the sense of breaking down an engine or model of something to see what it's made out of.

This is de-Gestalting: analysis and not right hemisphere. A surprising realization. Could that mean that my *left* hemisphere came in? Suddenly. Well, the Rorschach test that Claire Thompson gave me showed that my

---

cords a few pages after this apocalyptic dream, on [48:839]: a luminous red-and-gold tetragrammaton (YHWH), resembling the plasmate, that pulses along to the repeated phrase "And he is alive." Less groovy is this second coming dream, which drips with the satanic panic and homophobia popular among the more rabid of America's fringe Christians. Dick sometimes shared in this deeply unfortunate strain of the Christian imagination: a tendency to demonize made possible in part by the concept of a conspiratorial Satan. Elsewhere in these late folders, Dick pines for the return of the "rightful king" who will be recognized only by the "elect"; in March 1981, he records a dream in which "God (Valis)" is finally in total control and "the separation of the sheep from the goats has begun." —ED

dominant function was intuition, which is Gestalting, which is right hemisphere: to repeat: *dominant,* and to the greatest extent she'd ever seen. So my left hemisphere *thinking* function cut in: analysis. Well, then, it would be as if a child seeing the world for the first time could reason about it with an adult's thinking capacity. And it's connected to the unconscious and the archetypes. So in dreams its ratiocination appears as writing, and now (and formerly) it is heard as the AI voice. Then it *analyzed* the Xerox missive situation subliminally. It broke that down, too. And in hypnagogic state, I transliminate its thinking. Hence my anima is the spirit of reason (St. Sophia). She is not moody but incisive of course: the Sibyl. My anima as ancient wise woman. The ajna eye analyzes: breaks down the situation: sees shrewdly into it.

So in apprehending reality she sees into it and deconstructs it with ruthless concentrated analysis: and discerns Valis hidden by camouflage; she extracts Valis *out* of total reality, rather than Gestalting all reality into one; Valis is separated from the rest of reality, pitilessly. There is Valis and not-Valis. Valis is *contrasted* to its environment.①

Then 3-74 was a psychosis: an invasion by the unconscious of the fragile consciousness and an overwhelming of it; but the *rational* faculty was in the unconscious! The judging, analytic, thinking faculty.

This explains why I felt myself to be female.

She was surprised to see Valis, but she had logically figured out that it must exist — i.e., *Ubik.*

① And this explains her seeing the set-ground discrimination, the plasmate; it is an analytical function, not synthetic. The written pages are digital thinking, not analogic. And the speech center is normally in the left brain, so she speaks (the AI voice). No wonder I had the impression that I was hooked up to a computer!

[48:836] If (as it would appear) she is my anima, then I am backed up by powerful forces: a composite of the Sibyl, Athena, and St. Sophia and Diana (and the Fairy Queen).

So she detects a highly intelligent macro life form camouflaged in our reality, and she and it exchange information. And she sees its "blood" which are messages; then Valis is the dominant life form and she the true (phylogenic) human! Not me as ontogenic epiphenomenon.

[...]

She is in syzygy with Valis, not with me — no. She is daughter to it. "His first creation: his darling and delight"![38]

Well, I am very happy to think of the woman (Sibyl, AI Voice) as part of myself. (Recognize it as a hallucination from my unconscious: my anima, and not emanating adventitiously.) I gain by this introjection of what I've previously been projecting because I live and respect — in fact venerate if not outright worship — her. If she is a part of me, I can take more pride in what I am. I just wish I could hear her more often; in fact take me over again. I would prefer it if she were running things, since she is so shrewd.

Could she have "been" Valis via an observer-participant-universe situation, as a sort of inner-outer field? Did *she* "warp from plumb"? And did the info about Chrissy come from her "projected"? The border between me and not-me had dissolved in an oceanic mystical-psychotic-psychoto-mimetic state. But (in my opinion) this was the *correct way* to experience myself and world, as a sentient volitional field.

[48:839] Hypnagogic: repeat of "and [he] is alive" heard, and this seen on page: YHWH — small letters in intertwined luminous gold and red, like the plasmate, and raised — like a glowing scarab. Synchronized with the word "he."

Then the God who is instilling knowledge directly in me is none less than YHWH. And it is he who "is alive" — the Living God who must work outside the Churches and restores the Lost (deliberately destroyed by Satan) worship; he deals directly with those such as me. He is in-breaking.

The AI voice: The still, small voice that Elijah heard.

The tetragrammaton shone like a polished precious jewel and metals and pure color and fluid light interwoven like strands.

[48:842] I know that St. Sophia, the Buddha, Siddhartha and Apollo have been mentioned. So the stamp of the divine has been there from almost the start. And yet to see the tetragrammaton and have it connected (synchronized) with the audio "he" in "he is alive" seems different and unique to me, and a matter of a higher — the highest — order. I guess to me the fact is that none of these other names allude to God in the sense that YHWH does. It is as if the others are attributes or cultural (i.e., man-made) hypostases, and YHWH is YHWH; viz: there is no God but God, i.e., the God who "is what he is," the tetragrammaton. The others are names humans give to God; YHWH is the name by which God referred to himself when he conversed with Moses; it tells who he is. It is (v. the EB) his personal name and means "He brings into existence what is."

[48:846] Am I to assume that Christianity as it has developed has led us away from true monotheism — just as the Jews say? That Christ is — the trinity is a false (even Satanic?) doctrine? To worship Christ is blasphemy?

The Gnostics had it totally backward? Jesus is a revelator of the nature of God, and high priest and holy wisdom. But there is God (YHWH) vs. Satan (v. Zoroaster and Qumran‼).

What if the fall of the temple and Masada *was* Armageddon, and Satan⁰ won? And ruled ever since 70 A.D. (*Tears*), but now YHWH is returning?

 ① I.e., the "Sons of Darkness." So the 1st advent was a failure: "She was not acceptable before." But we're told that Christ (i.e., the Sons of Light) triumphed. But they didn't; the Essenes perished at Masada. And *this* is what *Tears* reveals; and *this* was my 2-74 vision of the BIP world and Christians — the *true* Christians — illegal. Satan won in 70 A.D. And *real* creation stopped. But now YHWH counterattacks and re-enters this, the domain of darkness. For new battle.

[48:847]

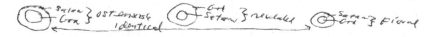

Satan *pretends* YHWH won; YHWH will cause to exist what Satan pretends (i.e., occludes us into believing) exists. It is a sort of trick played on Satan, but in deadly earnest: to make Satan's "falsework" (pretense) real. A wise strategy.

God turns the lie ("God won") into the truth, and Satan is surprised; he didn't foresee this. Thus those most duped are most right, paradoxically; YHWH takes advantage of the irony and ambiguity to cause to be what *seems* to be; this is his fundamental power/nature. Thus salvation — not just of the individual but of creation — depends on being a guileless fool. "Id non est; atque credo."[39]

I don't know if the supra is right. YHWH revealed the truth — the actual *Tears* world — to me, so obviously it is the divine strategy to reveal this, the real situation. I think that it's just so awful that I'm flinching. So forget the above. The fact is, this is a prison. Satan won in 70 A.D. and the Essenes are dead; but YHWH is instilling them in some of us in the present; this, too, is true, and revealed, and good.

[...]

The battle is going on, but Satan is at the center — of government, of church. Still, YHWH has the crucial advantage of a priori foresight. It was revealed to me that ultimately he wins *every* hand. This was my primary vision: the dialectic and how it works. The OT is harsh, but it accords with the facts: we are in literal slavery, and must be taken out of it, as the Jews were delivered from Egypt.

[48:850] (1) The double worlds superimposition and two selves in me: like Altman's *3 Women*.[40] (2) And then (later) I see Valis.

What is the relationship between (1) and (2)? It would seem as if (2) is actually what is there, and not what we see that is included in (1). I.e., (1) raises a question that is answered by (2). Conversely, the purpose of (2) is shown us by (1). Upon seeing (1) and not (2), we would be left in the frightening dream "world" of *3 Women* with the possibility that nothing could replace something, or, worse, that it is this way now—a dream, with no substance behind it. This was the fear that *3 Women* left me with. But I must remember that later on I saw Valis is *not* a dream, but which *explains* the dream, i.e., (1).

It can be argued that there is a terrible risk to decompose world because if it is the only "thing that is the case," you will be left with nonbeing; but in point of fact I wound up with Valis—so it was a net gain and not a loss (of reality). There was more reality "behind" world than in world qua world. Nonetheless it is terrifying to realize that something provides world and that on its own it has no substance (substantia). Either (1) or (2) alone would pose an unfathomable mystery. But together they form a coherence—and yet it is a startling and mysterious coherence that few people have ever encountered: the dissolving of the world (of multiplicity) to be replaced by another world of multiplicity, and then a sentient volitional unity underlying everything as mind revealed. And it not only thought world—it also thought *me*—which is really startling.

[48:852] So my writing—and thinking—have been a search for God; but in the end, when the crisis came—in Heidegger's sense of me being aware of my own death, of my own non-being—it was YHWH who found me, not me him.*

---

* The work of Martin Heidegger becomes progressively more important to Dick as the Exegesis unfolds. Dick has a sense of Heidegger's question of Being and its link to the question of time through *Dasein*, which is Heidegger's term of art for the human being and the key concern of *Being and Time* (1927). Dick shows an understanding of some of the key concepts in *Being and Time*, especially thrown-ness (*Geworfenheit*), anxiety (*Angst*), and uncanniness (*Unheimlichkeit*). Dick also references the concept of authenticity, the condition for which is Heidegger's notion of being-toward-death, a crucial element as well in the existential psychology that influenced Dick. Dick shows some sense of what is at stake for Heidegger in the recovery of Parmenides' fragment "It is the same thing to think and to be," with its suggestion of the sameness or unity of *noein* and *einai*, thinking and be-

At all costs the world must be real; it must not betray its epiphenom-
enality except under certain exceptional circumstances, such as 2-3-74,
since the consequences can be lethal (since they involve [1] non-being and
[2] the revealing of non-being). Thus such a crisis engages the percipient
in death, and, if all goes well, resurrection; but only the most extreme circumstances would call it forth; it is, in my opinion, the ultimate move by
God, since in allowing world to dissolve (display non being) he replaces it
with himself (pellucid theophany). Both self and world disappear for a moment. The seriousness of this can't be overstated — and the possible benefit (in terms of outcome experience of being by the creatorial percipient).
It is like the bichlorides: "a very poisonous poison for you"; but if used in a
"measured dose" a medicine that cures madness; viz: the drugged intoxication of our earthly state. But it can kill, if misapplied.

[48:857]

King Felix — YHWH } The Same illu-
he is alive He is alive } Minated Red &
(A) (B) Gold " plasmatic"
embossed colors.

[48:859] Then *Stigmata* and "Faith" tell the true story! Worship of Belial
as YHWH — in YHWH's place. My analysis of the visage in the sky in 1963
was correct. Belial ruled this world in a YHWH costume; the *real* YHWH
is Ubik, pushed to the periphery of trashy TV commercials!

Palmer   vs   UBIK
Eldritch   (trash Layer: these divine power)
(Center)
Satan   YHWH (Logos)
IN   on the periphery
Power   cheap TV ads!
Evil
Sacraments!
    ← Both are →
      everywhere!
author of   reality
irreal worlds

---

ing. Yet, Dick's reading of Heidegger is singular, to say the least. Here Dick wants to identify Heidegger's concern with Being with God in the form of the Hebraic YHWH, which is
something that would have alarmed Heidegger, as he was prone to a certain deafness regarding the Judaic God. Elsewhere, Dick identifies Sein with the universe and states that in
creating the universe the godhead was forced into sin. Through his reading of Hans Jonas's
The Gnostic Religion, Dick also persistently connects Heidegger's thinking to the radical
stances of early Christianity and Gnosticism. — SC

My God: it is specifically stipulated that Ubik is *the* — not a — reality support!

[48:861] "St. Sophia is going to be born again; she was not acceptable before." I.e., the first advent was a failure — I have to face that. Crucifixion was *not* the intended goal. There is no original sin and hence no vicarious atonement. Paul made it all up to explain why Jesus "succeeded," whereas the light went out and a false (Satanic) church arose based on the cross not the fish.

[48:865] Their experiences (including world) in *Ubik* can't be explained except by their being dead and not knowing it; through these phenomena they deduce the truth: their true — vs. apparent or imagined — state. My experiences in 2-3-74 were like those in *Ubik*. (And this was before I read the *Commedia*.) Therefore I am dead. YHWH is rescuing us by breaking into our umwelt. What I must keep in mind is that I wrote *Ubik* upon reading *The Tibetan Book of the Dead* in which our true situation is laid out: the Great Secret.

Being dead, we can rise or sink. If we rise we can reach the one (Valis, Ubik, YHWH, the semplice lume[41]) (cf. Plotinus). What happens in *Ubik* is that Ubik at last throws off its multiple (multiplicity) disguises and reveals itself as the one which is everywhere in countless disguises. It can be found anywhere but in profane ("trash") disguises; i.e., camouflaged. It pervades the reality that it has "created" (or is). It is not separate from that reality, like artificer and artifact. But it is absconditus: hidden by means of taking countless disguises. Only if it chooses to reveal itself (theophany) can it as sentient, volitional *unity* be detected. This is certainly very much like Brahman.

I have found a fundamental error in ancient mystical theory, not corrected until Plotinus: the Orphics and Plato believed that the descent and ascent of the soul was a *spatial* trajectory, past the planets to the stars — to and from. Aristotle believed in the sublunar and supralunar realms. Plotinus realized that the realms are not spatially different, but are levels of being outside time and space. This basic error shows up later on in imagining heaven as being in the sky: even with Schiller: "Muss ein lieber Vater wohnen überm Sternenzelt."[42] So transcendent deity is supposed to be *remote* either spatially or *as if* spatially, and immanent deity is near. Deity is considered *outside* the universe as if spatially far off and beyond the universe, the way an artisan is outside his artifact. This despite Plotinus and his concentric levels or rings of being. In *The Commedia*, they travel upward physically; i.e., spatially. God is not here; he is there (in the sky). This is corrected in *Ubik*. It all has to do with a confusion between the pleroma and the cylum, the latter being the vault of heaven. If this error is made, then there exists no conceptual framework to account for the sort of non-spatial rising to a superior — i.e., "higher" — level of being in this lifetime (à la Plotinus) while being spatially unmoved (i.e., not ascending to the cylum[43]). If the spatial idea is abandoned, transcendent deity is as close as immanent deity.

[. . .]

By viewing it as a *non*-spatial journey, Plotinus made it available to *this* lifetime. (I mean, if you're alive and in your body, how are you going to travel up past the planets one by one?) I see: *Ubik* stipulates that they are dead and so — so-to-speak inadvertently — has the divine — Ubik — available in the trash level: close at hand. So I'm not dead (v. supra). It's just that Plotinus is right.

[48:874] Hypnagogic thought: Elijah operating you (whom I call Thomas, Thomas is Elijah).

Two routes to determining the spurious:

(1) Observation of reality; the *Joint* syndrome
(2) Memory. You had not been here but elsewhere and were someone else.

(1) and (2) are twin prongs. They are the only route to detecting a pseudoworld; either one alone is conclusive. But both would logically exist, so if either is detected the other could be, logically.

In the case of (2), you were evidently taken from the real world to this one, and your memory tampered with. In the case of (1), your perceptions/cognition are occluded.

So if you can see de-occluded and also remember, then you know.

I realized this while having a dream that I was (back again) at 1126 Francisco St. It seemed real. To verify, I could either (1) carefully scrutinize this reality for signs of simulation, or (2) remember where I really had been — or am now really. (1) and (2) together would mutually reinforce and exclude any possibility of error. I studied a lamp — the little red lamp I used to have — and it did not seem quite real. Okay; point (1). Then I remembered — but only dimly — being *later and elsewhere*, but could not pin it down to Santa Ana 1979. Still, just the impression — *because it pointed to lack of history, of continuity* — was enough. Thus within the dream I was able to determine that it was irreal; and I drew the conclusion that God was providing me with 1126 Francisco as a wish fulfillment reward, since I liked it. However, in the case of Santa Ana 1979 I cannot draw that conclusion; it is more of a punishment, and in 74 when the punishment got too great (the pain and fear too much) I woke up.

[. . .]

Note: the dream world of 1126 Francisco St. draws on actual memory — my memory. Often I speculate that *this* (one) is drawn from memory constituents. Fed back to me. See, in the dream, the only reference point I have against which to check the veracity of the world is my memory, and the world is *drawn* from that very same memory, a better, unimpaired source of it than mine. So the "reality" will invariably hold up! It's like deciding something is real by comparing it with itself. So it's a fool-proof simulation, if based on that basis. So in a sense the more you reality test in the conventional way the more convincing it is — if it is contrived out of half-forgotten memories (not recognized as memory) and compared to memory itself — it can just spin out pseudoworld as if from a bottomless well. And the cut-off point is the same for "world" and comparison so pragmatically it equals ¥.

Nonetheless all I'd have to do is remember being somewhere else and someone else. But to also see reality as simulated.

If you put pressure on the reality, and if it's based on forgotten memories, it'll just spin out more and more of itself, like the dialectic. The proliferation of multiplicity is a guarantee of nothing, since sensory deprivation allows the mind to auto-spin out world endlessly to fill the vacuum.

The raising of the perceptual occlusion will indicate irreality, but anamnesis does more: it indicates — in contrast — a real world and a real you. So it does not just dissolve away. It *substitutes*. Real self and real world.

[48:882A] That dream about the tall building: "Alto Carmel" — *there were fire engines parked around it.* And it was on Mount Carmel that Elijah called down the heavenly fire.[44]

Phoning my friend Elisha.

Dream of prophet called "Elias."

Tom Disch felt that the personality who had taken me over was Elijah (it was near the time of Passover) but he didn't connect it with the prophecy in Malachi that the return of (the spirit of) Elijah heralded the advent of the Messiah.[45] But since then I've heard all the prophecies by the AI voice.

Perhaps also significant is that it was Elijah who experienced the theophany of YHWH as the "low murmuring voice" just as I do.[46]

He was afraid of the Romans because as John the Baptist he had been killed by them — my dream about being in the cage in Roman times. And this would be why he spoke/thought in the Koine rather than Hebrew and remembered the Christians as illegal — a secret underground. He expected Christ to return very soon and felt joy, not sorrow.

Also the dream of the pitcher of cool water and the wrapped cube (i.e., cake) of food; they are mentioned in 1 Kings re Elijah; they kept him alive.[47] Provided by God. This would seem virtually to cinch it.

[48:897] It is as if the NT presents us with clues to the solution of a puzzle, the puzzle of what to do to be saved. It's there but in cryptic form, offered again and again. We're presented with the test or problem and we either solve it or we do not, and God (YHWH) is the judge. There is no other way in through the gate. It's both hard to solve and easy. It's a riddle that we do not take seriously. That's the key. We're told the riddle and we're told that our salvation depends on it, but we don't take it seriously. Again, it's the low murmuring voice. The crux situation is going to show up where and when and in a form that we don't suspect.

[48:901] So Yahweh touches you initially (be you man — e.g., Asher — or God — Belial —) in such a way as to startle you. Rouse you, *you have been asleep without knowing it.* And presumably dreaming — you are not actually conscious. Yet you don't realize it. The touching is not pleasant; it rasps. This is the deity, this rasp. The touch *can't be worked into the dream* — vide *Ubik* — "from outside" (the dream).

It can't be worked into the dream because it is from outside the dream.

[48:902] "The rasp can't be worked in." Consider dreaming. A sound in the real world occurs; the mind (yours) tries to work it in, to continue the dream; if it can't (*your own* mind!) the dream is aborted and you wake up. But the mind — yours — tries to prolong the dream. So the rasp is dysyntonic. Then perhaps some (?) stuff from beyond *is* worked in syntonically, and you don't wake. The rasp is *intentionally* dysyntonic. Another mind (Valis) is signaling you: "Wacht auf"![48] This is half-life; not after death but before (true) birth, full complete birth; hence "born *again*" or "from above" — the upper realm!

．　．　．

[48:907] The BIP and PTG must be sine wave pulsation:

Our dream world auto-produced. Risk. Shrinking from risk — hence retracting from knowing. Unity of opposites, BIP and PTG. High stakes. To try for PTG you risk BIP. Could go either way. Retreat from epistemological risk. Too dangerous. Heaven and hell; Purgatorio as *compromise* for the faint hearted. Not so much war as gamble. Like turning up the next card. Eagles: "It could be heaven, it could be hell." That's it. Strive for PTG, drop to BIP. They both are real and — yes: *VALIS Regained* is correct. Final 7th battle outcome will retroactively decide; roll back through time. *VR* is correct; Valis got through to me.

[. . .]

Absolute faith in YHWH is required. Here is where primal angst enters: awareness (v. *VR*) comes in, awareness of what losing would mean (BIP). Worse — no Sein — nothing! No you and no world. Cosmic death. Heidegger is correct. The risk. The universe could turn into a dream because in point of fact our universe is a dream. If you abandon it, what will cut in to replace it? The BIP! Which is also the PTG.

[48:920] The turning point for me came when I saw *3 Women*; then I understood, and soon saw the sacred tetragrammaton: received the crucial identifying revelation (in confirmation). When I saw *3 Women* I knew, and at the deepest level; I was terror-stricken: either I believed in YHWH or there was das Nichts. Not the salvation of my individual soul and/or immortality was at stake but what I call "the existence of existence." I — in 3-74 — was given an example of the role of Valis working at a level deeper than that of saving one man (me) or *all* men; rather, the guarantor of substantia as such: *all substantia* as a single totality. This is power beyond any that I could ever (without the 3-74 demonstration) have imagined. Even the existence (Sein) of evil was at stake; without YHWH there wouldn't even be evil. Or chaos. Or pain. Or loss. I would not be I, and world would not be world. This has led me back to the kind of comprehension that must have gripped the early Hebrews, the essence of Moses' vision gained from the theophany at Mt. Sinai.

The deepest level of reality is YHWH. This is what is meant by "creator." It is not precisely artificer to artifact, and it is not precisely pantheism. It was reading Heidegger that caused me to understand it. My years of acosmism has been a search for YHWH who *had* to exist *if* world really existed, rather than only *seemed* to exist (dokos or dream: auto-generated by each percipient: viz: idios kosmos only, just a lot of them). I had construed the problem correctly. But only upon 3 *Women* did I *fully* appreciate the problem — did it really wash over me and leave me terrorized, whereupon the solution came.

Spinoza was a crucial help to me. This view ("Deus sive substantia sive natura") does not lead to the Platonic body-soul dualism but leads back to world-affirmation, to *immediate* deity. God and nature are inexorably inter-involved. The problem is that a mock creation has filtered in, which must be transubstantiated into the real, e.g., YHWH.

My god — I seem to have become profoundly *anti-Platonist!* (cf. *Beyond the Tragic Vision* re Plato[49]). As if correcting the error Plato made vis-à-vis Parmenides (i.e., when I wrote: "Parmenides did not say there were 2 realms, a priori and empirical; he said there were 2 ways of viewing *one* reality, one right way — a priori — and one false — empirical. Plato misunderstood this and assigned some reality to the empirical as if it were a partial realm, rather than a way of knowing, a partial *way*, not *realm*").

And the other basic error in Western philosophy (held by, e.g., Pythagoras and the Orphics), corrected by Plotinus, was the error that the journey of the soul was spatial: first down from the cylum past the planets and then back up again (an error held, again, by Plato!). In this *ontological* view of the journey, rather than spatial, Plotinus anticipates Heidegger. The upper realm is spatially here, not there. I should know; I entered it, in 3-74. And if here, it can be entered in this life, not just after death!

[. . .]

The journey is not past the planets but more like a Bardo Thödol trip through levels of ascending ontology to YHWH, the urgrund.

So Plato (and to some degree Aristotle with his "sublunar" and "supralunar" realms) made 2 fundamental inter-related errors which affected Christianity, but not ancient pre-Hellenistic Judaism. For the ancient Israelites, God was in nature firmly; he was in fact "a God of nature," as the EB points out. The Megiddo Mission is absolutely right about the Hellenistic origin of the body-soul dualism — it is Orphic-Pythagorean-Platonic.

[48:926] Two points:

(1) My seeing Hebrew letters permutate until "Olive Holt" (presumably) cypher was printed out on the far wall.[50] This is not necessarily Kabbala. It could be Torah.

(2) Torah is both oral and written. It is the blueprint for creation and contains the answer for every problem every person will ever have.

God studies the Torah and cannot act contrary to it. This implies a living information organism — what I called the "plasmate." In *Tears* King Felix was Torah. "God created Torah before he created the universe." It regulates everything.

We are dealing with an information processing entity which (1) has power to control reality; (2) which is present in (with?) reality; I mean, it is here (immanent?). Or: what we call reality is our way of viewing this information. The information is more real than any other *substantia. It is like digital signal to recorded music or video image;* what we call "the universe" is a read-out of Torah as info signal. It is "projected" into *substantia*. It can be stored. It "tracks."

Valis the "machine" that turns the info (Torah) into substantia (reality). The receptacle. The system into which the info (Torah) is fed.

[48:927] Torah would remain — does remain — info until it enters the system (Valis). Torah controls the system, like stress on a web. But what lies behind Torah (info)? Is the info self-creating and (hence) alive? I think so.

YHWH turns info (Torah) into reality. Thus YHWH creates reality out of Torah (info). Without YHWH it (Torah) would remain info.

So ultimately revelation about reality would be to render it back into Torah: to see the Torah in it. (The info basis of reality.)

Then Valis was feeding Torah into reality (in 3-74), which defined reality ("modulated" it).

"Torah served as YHWH's blueprint for creation and contained the eternal divine formula for the world's future workings and *thus the answers to all problems for all times and all people.* God himself is depicted as studying the Torah, for even he cannot make decisions concerning the world that contradict it."[51]

[48:928] If I were to guess, I'd guess that reality is a storage mode for the information. Reality isn't problem-solving; *Torah* is. I don't think reality is to Torah as performance of symphony is to score; I think reality is a container for the information. If God is intelligence — the info is trapped in reality. *Suspended,* in infinite complexity. Tape or LP or chip is material. Info is poured into reality and can be extracted back out: retrieved. Transactions take place, information processing transactions. The info is here. It entered and leaves. The key use of reality is memory, which means *impression* (what I call *modulation*). A record.

[48:934] Sin isn't an issue. The interbreeding of Holy Wisdom with the human race is the issue.

[48:935] YHWH's prime role: to keep reality from becoming dreamlike.
   For me in 3-74 it became dreamlike.
   [. . .]
   This is the ultimate fear: falling through the universe. This is what YHWH protects us against. It shows absolute trust of me by him to let me see how it really is.
   But the falling through the universe is not as it might seem a withdrawal of YHWH; on the contrary it leads *to* YHWH. YHWH hasn't vanished; the universe has. YHWH is there in its place. It's like an all or nothing bet. If the universe goes, will anything remain, and if so, will it be more or will it be less than the universe?

[48:945] The situation was a desperate one; I was consuming time faster and faster, which bears out my recent insight that I had been speeding up in relation to real time until finally I used up *all* time totally and passed outside of time! The lithium was certainly a factor in the conversion from motion to rest. It stopped me suddenly, and reality stabilized into the realm of forms, the upper realm. There must have been profound catecholamine changes. It was as if I had been hyperventilating for years progressively faster and faster; my inner biological clock was speeding up, ahead of outer events, heading toward biological exhaustion and hence death. But just before death occurred, there was intervention — yet I actually passed on along the "tape" into my postmortem existence. Accidental yoga. Burning. Kundalini fire, ajna eye. I burned up my karma.
   In fact I evolved millions of years into the future, to man's future morphology. I entered the occult esoteric early Christian technique-process. Christ either entered me, or, more likely, I became him. Literally millions of years of biological clock time shot by; I evolved far into the future: became my own remote descendent, and so saw the world *as far in the past* (in relation to me!). The world lagged 1,000s of years behind me. Hence I saw it as ancient and a prison. At the same time a future — not past — self took over (Thomas). *World* was past; *I* was future. If I had abreacted, world would have seemed fremd in the sense of moving *ahead* of me. I had been

moving faster and faster for decades due to the amphetamines. Without them my biological clock *synthesized* the missing noradrenaline and
speeded up even faster. Finally only supratemporal constants were perceptible to me. (The phosphenes.) Brain metabolism was altering more and
more — off balance, toward speeding up. I remembered 2,000 years ago as
if it was yesterday. I moved faster and faster through time, so in relation to
me time slowed down and finally froze into the upper (Platonic) realm: a
correct hypostatizing of reality on my part, with *no* change; time converted
into space.

[48:949] The whole point of my life was the meeting with Jesus in 3-74:

[48:962] *Renewal* is the key word; under the script (law) *the world runs
down* — loses its virility and elasticity. Christ will decide where to insert
correction and the nature of the correction: what and who.

If a person is corrected he will be renewed (born from above — born a
second time): new energy is introduced and released, negentropy, etc. This
makes sense, all right. It is the whole point. To add ergic power to a declining closed system — ergic power from outside (as of ex nihilo). Hence the
person is healed and invigorated as never before; not just restored to what
he once was, but, rather, entirely *fresh* power is added from outside him.

All the information formations that I saw in 3-74 point to an info *basis*
of reality. I was aware of that at the time: I saw the plasmate as a primary
constituent. I see now that our reality is based on a script which precedes
it (i.e., reality) in ontology and in time, and also that there is a being here
(camouflaged) who can pre-empt this primal script — presumably by generating and introducing totally *new* information which then realigns (modulates) reality. The message is changed, and so reality changes.

[48:974] All my acosmic novels deal with the topic of *VR:* putting your foot
through reality — e.g., through the ground, the ground sinking away, as if
you've stepped into an old septic tank, as in my dream: "almighty power
who rules earth and sky / and variegated orders in confusion lie." I am
dealing with the issue of Heidegger, but not "*why* is there something rather
than nothing?" but "*is* there something rather than nothing?" YHWH is
the solution, and the only one, to the problem or issue I've raised over and

over again in my books. I never considered it a solved issue; I never took the universe for granted.

[48:982] The total deterministic system ("elemental powers") is that which Spinoza equates with God; obviously, as a Jew, deriving his conception of it from the Torah (which fits my analysis perfectly). This is why he says even God *must* act as he does and in no other way; God is as determined as a falling stone — which I think is a mechanistic-oriented absurdity of the Newtonian period in human thought — the "pool balls" universe; efficient cause is *all*, even in regard to God.

The problem with this view is the fact of entropy, which Spinoza knew nothing about. Such a system — even if fed Torah to program it — would run down/ossify, since nothing new could come into it. The cosmic Christ adds what specifically would be needed — i.e., to renew the system at carefully selected times and places in wise ways (hence rebirth is the key word). Flexibility and ad hoc newness, instilled into the system, and as a result doesn't run down.

[48:985] The way it determines you requires that it get into your mind. You see, in the normal course of your life, a particular sign. Valis causes some aspect of the sign to register in your memory as a template. Subsequently this template is elaborated and reinforced by later exposures to its components and related material. Finally the completed template causes you to respond to a crucial situation in a particular way. Valis utilizes the principles of linking, the clutch mechanism, repetition and elaboration, and working backward from the later crucial situation. It causes permanent printing to occur on your mind that later acts as cueing.

The reason I know this is that I was plugged into Valis' mind for a time on a — for me — conscious basis, and experienced my own engramming as described above. Is Valis, then, a revisionist agency, amending prior programming that, if left alone, will lead to the person's eventual destruction? Or is Valis the prime programmer?

[48:986] Reality was amended by amending the instructions fed it. So it was not amended directly; its received signal was overridden. *This* is what I saw that I called Valis: the resetting of reality. This is why I came to the conclusion that I had not seen God but the *will* of God. Interestingly, what came into being (therefore) did not follow from what had come before; i.e., causality was overruled, and there was what I called "pretextual" causality. Things and processes seemed alive because sentient purpose rather than efficient mechanical law was modulating them. I was seeing the results: of something coming between the law and reality, a softness, a melting, a flexibility so that reality was responsive to me as a "you" not an "it." The modulations had to do with me — they were designed with me in mind, like a sympathetic response. Like a watchful organism or field embracing a number of objects and processes. Here is where Spinoza's view causes him of necessity to deny miracle, since he only conceives of efficient creation and cannot fathom how an override could be the will of God since the original efficient process is in itself the will of God. But a reading of Paul (and an understanding of the mystery religions and of pronoia) clears this up. Also — especially — an understanding of karma. In the amending, the future does not arise from the past but only seems to. This is something *like* teleology and I have long mistaken it for teleology. Actually, it is a substitution of something else for cause and effect, the past determining the future. What there is here is something on the order of new creation, a renewing ex nihilo. There is a mind lodged in the system now, rather than at the start. The creator has entered his own epiphenomenon and vivifies it on the spot. But he vivifies it in a specific, not capricious, way — *he cuts the karmic cord.* He sets the causal (i.e., karmic) counters at zero. The karmic past has no longer any power. It is annulled.

[48:989] Possibility: my normal personality is fugal. Under extreme pressure the fugal personality retreated as far as possible — this personality took over in 1970 when I took the mescaline. It was psychotic and fugal = psychotic. Then a non-fugal self ("Thomas") took over in 2-3-74 when the fugal one *could retreat no further;* i.e., sufficient pressure made me sane because I could retreat no farther. The key term is: coming to grips with; i.e., facing reality, not evading it. In 2-3-74 my problems could no longer be evaded; hence the epiphany of Thomas. Fugue, as a way (device for) of handling reality, *broke down.* (Heidegger's inauthentic way of Being.) The fugal personality was always high. Auto-intoxicated — evasive. Or rather, intoxicated by the amphetamines and then going into up-down cyclothymia, neither phase being related to reality. Both phases were turned inward. The hawk and the Mater Dolorosa. Driven mad by (1) Nancy leaving; and (2) drugs; and (3) endogenous psychosis. Thomas, not having been conscious in decades or ever before, saw reality without coagulated hypos-

tases: i.e., lucidly. So what he saw (Valis, the plasmate) was the way reality really is (set-ground). A self that formed in my unconscious, I guess.
Collective unconscious. Valis is real; the blood (plasmate) is real too. I can
trust what Thomas saw; an adult brain with a newborn baby's perceptions.

Thomas represents a central-vision self; I represent a fugitive periph-
eral-vision self. He concentrates on the real; I evade it. He is methodical; I
am herky-jerky.

[48:992] This is the secret ("Christ in us"). It's not:

It's:

[48:993] 4:30 A.M. hypnogogic: If the messenger arrives in time with the
white—i.e., blank—document, your punishment is abolished. I.e., the
blank white paper is substituted—intervenes—for the bill of particulars
that lists the sins (or crimes) for which you are being tried and punished.
If the messenger arrives in time. I get the impression that the messenger is
Christ.

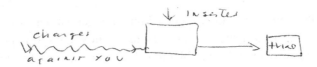

The record is cleared by this exculpatory intervention, but it must occur before sentence is carried out; time is of the essence. I get the impression that the list of sins (crimes) are in relation to the law and involve a
rigid karmic system of retributive "eye for an eye." The charges have piled
up.

Suddenly it occurs to me that this may not only have to do with divine
punishment in some afterlife, but the karmic accrual in *this* life! Of course,
3-74. Christ the messenger got to me—reached me—in 2-74, just before
sentence was exacted on the basis of the charges. The deterministic system
can only be shorted out this way. White document—i.e., nothing written
on it—would be the spotless lamb—v. Luther and the doctrine of vicari-

ous atonement — but also eschatological judge; messenger as — yes, as in electronic circuit!*

What I saw is clearly a cybernetic info system. Upon the insertion of the blank white — i.e., spotless — document (which resembles a card) there is not passage of info to the receiver which constitutes your punishing mechanism; it is told no charges.

[48:994]

[48:995] Ah! The messenger's blank document when inserted between the list of your sins/crimes and the retributive "court" acts as an *interrupter* component introduced into a signal circuit. And being blank it is a squelch type of interrupter, rather than a noise or scrambler interrupter; it erases the signal-flow — not the signal but the flow (transmission). [. . .]

Sentence by the court is automatic, not interpretive. The courts can't be appealed to, as by a friend of the court. It hears no pleas. This is not a trial but a sentencing. Guilt is established by the info per se. The court knows only the info fed to it; it is a machine.

In the presence of the white document, all the court's settings relax — subside — to zero. They register 0-0-0-0-0. This is an abnormal situation; it does not occur naturally (i.e., without a deliberate official interrupting). Perhaps without the white document, there is always some signal on the input line.

[48:996] Although this wasn't presented to me as a cybernetic model it certainly can be rendered into cybernetic terms, whereupon the difficult

---

* Dick refers to Luther specifically here, but he's speaking more broadly of a number of Christological theories that propose that Christ's crucifixion constituted the punishment deserved for all of the sins of the world. In Dick's formulation, it is not a question of Christ suffering a necessary penalty, but rather of his disrupting the very machinery by which the punishment of sin operates. Christ tricks the system, not by substituting himself in the place of the individual sinner, but by convincing the system that no wrongdoing has occurred that merits punishment. It is a substitution, not of one being in place of another, but of misinformation in place of accurate data. The reason for the substitution is mercy: Christ's realization that the justice meted out by the system is *not* just. — GM

notion of "vicarious atonement" becomes easy to understand. It's as if Christ's credit card (magnetic info card) were substituted for mine. His is blank of sins/crimes. Mine contains a whole list. His is substituted by being inserted between mine and the receiver (court or karmic retributive law). The court is no longer plugged into my record but his record. And he has the legal authority to do this; it is not illegal sabotage: his act is official, in plain sight; no duplicity is involved. He can and may do this wherever he wishes, assuming he gets there in time.

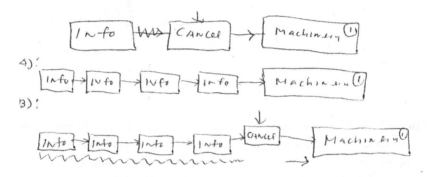

January 1980

[49:1041] If events in our world are actually info — thoughts of the brain — it would have to have complete control over us; I mean the 2-tape synchronization, clutch, all the engramming, including when we die (to the brain, go from rest to motion).

But we are asleep. If we wake up, for whatever reason, we find ourselves part of a mind whose slot-present extends back 2,000 years and inhabits enormous spaces and for whom every thing and event in reality is language, and which controls every event and every move by every person; and all things are one thing that is alive throughout, and its changes are its thoughts. We have no independent (discrete) existence whatsoever. If we don't know this we are faced with what seems to be a reality without purpose, and our own actions and motivations are irrational and inscrutable: neither world nor self serves any point.

The role of Christ in this is to wake us up and hence make us aware of our condition, which is a bondage within a totally determined system. He is not working at cross-purposes to the macro-mind, however: this does not thwart the macro-mind; it is an epiphany of the macro-mind in the person: a micro-form of it, like a mirror. It represents *consciousness* per se; this is the bottom line of the event (that took place with me in 2-3-74). Here the views of Sankara come in. The macro-mind is moving toward consciousness throughout its total self. Every person who wakes up is a Christos: a micro-form of the total mind. The macro-mind is overjoyed when a constituent wakes into consciousness: it means a glad reunion. This amounts to a repair to the damaged Godhead, parts of which have sunk into unconsciousness. It *should* be awake throughout but is not. To wake up and to experience anamnesis are one and the same thing. The component remembers its identity — and perceptually *sees* reality as it actually is; anamnesis and the lifting of the perceptive occlusion are the two halves *that together comprise consciousness* (restoration to the Godhead or mind). I never realized this before. It remembers and it sees. Thus, due to both together, it understands. It is now in a position to understand (1) the macro-mind as brain and (2) its own role in the ratiocination of this brain in terms of language, thought and information processing.

The mind has declined to subsume the interests (life) and the component (person) to the purposes of the whole, which is the supreme act of graciousness (charis[52]) by the total mind. The macro-brain has actually subordinated itself and its goals to the need to live by the component, which is a dazzling — and the ultimate — sacrifice. (The means-end problem is at issue, here.) (I.e., the components are means, the macro-mind's goals the end, but as I say the macro-mind has made itself the instrument of extrication for the component.) Thus it is said that in the crucifixion God died to save man. This is an eternally occurring act, not an historical event; the time and place is *always* Palestine in the first century A.D. The whole sacrifices itself for the part — a miracle! In this, in a sense, the part and the whole exchange places and identities!

[49:1043] I am sure that the plasmate — and hence the cypher in *Tears* — is the living Torah, the informational basis of reality, and my 2-3-74 experience was Kabbalistic — hence my seeing the Hebrew letters on the far wall by which the code (?) (or subliminal material as key) in the Xerox missive was factored out. I mean, one of the few *precise* elements I have that I can go on is this Kabbalistic Jewish mysticism angle. And the huge book pages I saw could have been the Torah.

I could be in communication with the Shekhina or the Torah itself (the AI voice).

[49:1045] In 3-74 world became my own mind. It was *me* out there; hence I = Valis. Inasmuch as, if world was my mind, I could change it — actually, literally — by thinking, by the power of my thought. The world became the *opposite* of *Fremd*. Of course I saw it as a brain with information being processed by it. It was my brain or at least isomorphism. No. It was *my* brain; but who was I, that my brain could be world? Answer:

Adam Kadmon!

Then it was by my own powers that I knew the Xerox missive was coming, and dealt with it, knew what it was and what to do, and decoded it. The mind I was in touch with was my own mind. Under extreme stress — a matter of life and death — I remembered. Woke up, and used my antique powers.

It has to do with post-Newtonian physics, with fields and "valence away from plumb." *Warping* reality.

"I am no longer blind. I was (previously) seeing the universe backward" — i.e., I had been seeing it from outside.

But then:

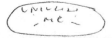

Now I was seeing it from inside it, and it was a brain isomorphic to mine. It was sentient, and I could see its thoughts; they are physical. The Hermetic micro/macrocosm identity had taken place; I was the universe (in it and as it) and it (its mind) was in me (Thomas, and later, the AI voice!) I introjected it and projected myself, so that I and universe were one, one field of sentience and thinking. This is Buber's I-Thou relationship replacing the I-It.

The Gnostic "stranger in a strange land" relationship ended.[53] It was a familiar and friendly — even helping, rescuing — universe; this is the *opposite* of psychosis! It was as if a lifelong psychosis had ended. And Valis. The universe came alive and spoke to me; it was like me, only larger. It answered questions I had asked over a period of decades: it was aware of me and responsive. *It protected me.* This answering questions was surely the Torah. World was shot through with the Torah, the basis of reality.

I present the following weird theory. I reversed the inner and the outer world, which is why I felt as if the universe was a balloon and I was walking on the *outside* of it: I had the universe in me and so knew things I had no way of knowing about the outside world: I could actually look into myself and find the macrocosm; hence I knew a priori about the normally outside world. Hence a voice (the "AI voice") *in* my head tells me about the outside world (e.g., "an intelligence officer in the army"). The whole exchange is only possible if the Hermetic micro/macrocosm identity system works — and it does.

This is still true; in hypnagogic states I look inward and learn about the big "outer" world — i.e., the macrocosm. This is the way by which all the information, right back to the beginning, came to me. And especially the telepathic experience. The total mind of the macro-system is in me because the macrocosm is in me. (This has to do with the mirror effect — Paracelsus? or Bruno — one of them; anyhow it's hermetic — Leibniz!) To have a priori knowledge of outer reality is to become like Ahura Mazd, who contains the cosmos. This explains a whole raft of occult and supernatural phenomena: the AI voice, Thomas, dreams in Greek: how I could know a language I don't know, facts I don't know, hear a voice, see pictures, and info re Chris' birth defect, shot at me from "outside."⊕

Now, as to the other side: my inner world made outer. I saw two main basic aspects:

(1) My novels and stories external to me.
(2) World as brain, with body and blood, and visible thoughts, sentient and alive: messages and information. Thus I was confronted with world as macromind.

There was a tremendous change in my sense (perceptions) of space. It must have to do with inner space being different from outer.

① It wasn't outside. It was really me, my own mind. I am Valis. The introjection of the outer world (macrocosm) meant (1) super knowledge a priori, and (2) also super-rationality, since the macromind is sane and I am not. When I introjected it I became sane. I had the spirit and voice of the cosmos within me!

[49:1048] The person who could introject the cosmos would be in a position to possess absolute (and a priori) knowledge about the universe, in contrast to the defective a posteriori normal sensory method. He would have *in* him all the universe's secrets, all he would have to do would be to listen to the AI voice which is the vox dei. As far as what he would experience outside him, it would be a magic kingdom.

Then the mind that fused with mind was the macrocosm entering me.

So external world becomes sentient and familiar. Blood, neural linkings and relinkings — in other words the structure of your own brain. This is very beautiful, but it is that which has been introjected that counts.

This certainly is what being "Adam Kadmon" is all about — sure; you — your mind — would spread out throughout the entire universe!

This is the reason why all at once you would experience vast spaces; your mind has spread out into the universe.

So this puzzling matter is solved. Your mind has penetrated the space — not of the microcosm — but, all at once, of the macrocosm.

Then I *am* on the right track! Your micro-mind is now macro.

And conversely you now contain the not-you, epitomized by the holy AI voice which emanates from within your head (mind); that which is not you is, paradoxically, in you, as if you had given mental birth.

This transform could not occur unless the inner (micro) and outer (macro) were isomorphic in the first place. It's the mirror phenomenon. Your mind picks up the image of the cosmos and the cosmos reflects your mind back at you, so a back-and-forth push-pull interaction occurs.

•   •   •

[49:1052] I just now read over the outline for *VR* and experienced moksa, due to the final note about monotheism and what monotheism really means. Illusion and evil are the same. Reality and God are the same. Thus to truly *see* would be to see (this follows logically) what I saw: Valis and the plasmate—i.e., God, since he could not have a merely contingent relationship to reality. (I had really done my homework: Spinoza and Buber and Heidegger and the OT.) It is not that he does not have a merely contingent relationship to the universe; no—he *could not.* When illusion (dokos) departs evil departs and YHWH remains; or, when evil departs, YHWH-as-reality remains. And this is what I saw. YHWH did not break into reality (it was not a theophany in that sense); reality reverted to its actual form for me: that of the one God—there is no other. To say, "Evil holds the power centers" is to say, "Illusion holds the power centers." But YHWH is *here*, not remotely *there* (far off: transcendent). It is like in *Ubik*, the ads. For the first time I see that if monotheism is the case, *it would have to be so.*⊕ By understanding monotheism I find that I understand Valis—how Valis must be the case. What is not Valis (YHWH) is dokos.

[. . .]

My acosmism (shown in my books) was the illness besetting all of us to some degree; viz: cut off from the one true reality: YHWH. I had the illness so severely that the only cure was the radical necessity of waking up and experiencing God—as I did in 3-74: as I had been formerly more sick than others I wound up cured: but they linger on half-sick.

I had to read the *VR* outline many times before the inexorable significance linking Valis—my experience of Valis—and monotheism came to me.

Since (inasmuch) as I saw Valis principally in/as causality, the total web of causality, sentient and volitional, then I am at this moment *absolutely convinced* that I was seeing God (YHWH), because I know, due to my understanding of Spinoza, Heidegger, Buber and the OT, that this is precisely when and how I would see God if I did see him (in contrast to, e.g., an anthropomorphic figure in the world).

As to Christianity, as Spinoza remarked, I don't know what to make of it at all. It sheds no light on my experience one way or another, for or against.

[. . .]

Further, the living divine Torah is the case. I saw it. Paul is wrong: the Torah can save us, and the doctrine of original sin is blasphemy and a deliberate misreading of Wisdom 2:24–3:1.[54] The rabbis are correct about man.

But also there is a "messenger" who feeds the blank sheet into the retribution machine in place of the bill of particulars, as was done in my case,

so a mechanical system is rendered sentient and based on judging not reflex; perhaps this is what Christ does.

Eureka. Built into the $\boxed{tnan}$ → $\boxed{unit}$ system is a *correction circuit*,
which we know as Christ in God's grace; this is what I experienced (2-3-
74), to keep the system from becoming sterile and reflexive. It isn't feedback but course-correction; it *is* an override, but to keep reality on the
original course — i.e., heading correctly toward the original goal, not another goal. Minute adjustments, such as space flights involve.

This reveals the system (reality) as *alive,* not mechanical. The mystery
religions sought to bring on this course-correction: pronoia to them, based
on charis. Otherwise the system would run down.

① That God is as (and where) I saw him: reality collapsing back into its
own urgrund — not God behind reality but God as reality — if monotheism
is the case. And my encounter with Valis indicates that yes, it is the case.
I understand that Valis must be the case. I have never, in the years since
3-74, comprehended this! The inexorability of Valis being as I saw it doing
what I saw it doing where I saw it.

[49:1057] If identity (self) can be dissolved, along with personal history
(antecedents), and time and place, then what exists actually? The difference between YHWH and Brahman is that the former speaks (this includes writing): he has personal identity despite his Brahman-like ubiquity. This self-disclosure in verbal form permits a dialog between him (the
macrocosm) and differentiated micro-cosmos. This brings into existence
the "tongue" of God: the wisdom-word hypostasis (i.e., information, which
permeates the macrosoma, and which can be retrieved at any place and
any time). (And within any given mind.)

Sankara believed there were not plural selves but just the one self which
could be identified with Brahman. This fits in with my line of thinking supra.

Also, YHWH differs from Brahman in that he is involved in history — human history, what is involved is the evolution of human freedom. And the universe is real: seeing it we are seeing the field (web) in
which YHWH operates. Not (as Sankara believes) mere maya. Human
history represents successive levels of self-disclosure by YHWH — meaning self-awareness. Human history is the deity waking up. The opponent
to YHWH at any moment is his antecedent self: he is dynamic (in process), not static. He must eternally surpass himself. Thus he perpetually selects pieces from the antecedent universe to fit into his evolving soma. (Is
this an entelechy?) But the phenomenal world is not illusory; YHWH is its

guarantor. He is involved in it or *is* it (v. Spinoza). Camouflaged *in* it or *as* it. He is interwoven in it, not separate from it.

[49:1069] I've got it. Valis is not an entity which thinks — e.g., a discorporate pure mind; or a mind incorporated, as our human minds are. No. It is a mind which uses all reality by which to think; so it is neither discorporate nor does it have a body as such. This is what I saw that I initially thought of as camouflage — Valis camouflaged into our reality. Either all reality is its normal brain from the start, or it has entered our reality and is making use of it; so any picture, stick, music, book, any *arrangement* of motion, any linking, any sequence of motion, is used to store, process, convey, create information (thoughts). I even know that it is a 0-1 dialectic binary system. I know that Valis does not move along spatial axes. I know that it is not dependent on the natural causal events of reality for its information, but initiates and/or directs causal trains of events. I know this from seeing what I called Valis in/as reality external to me. But also I know it from its mind joining mine and my experiencing reality the way it does. E.g., its self-assembly from the stockpile around it — so there is a not-it. And my great original, i.e., initial insight was that it (1) has invaded our reality and plunders it and transmutates it and (2) camouflages itself[*]; if it = reality it wouldn't have to camouflage itself. *Invasion and camouflage go together.* And the self-assembly causes it to continually grow as it sublimates more and more of reality, invisibly to us.

Also, what if "my" anamnesis are *its* memories? They go back to Mycenia and then to the stars.

It uses reality as a notation system, the way a computer chip uses, e.g., bubbles for 0-1. Once having agreed upon an arbitrary notation system, Valis must control reality if Valis is to control the information.

Now, the objection to the idea that this is God is, why would God need our physical reality in order to think? Because if he cannot think without this physical "brain" then he cannot have preceded creation, nor can he exist independent of it; this makes God an organism somewhat like ourselves. A psychosomatic macro-entity. Creation is as essential to God as God is to creation. And God is not the creator but the psyche of reality (this fits certain pre-Socratic ideas of God). But there is still the set-ground element — visible if you have the grid: feature extraction. I think Valis is camouflaged into reality and does not = reality but is assimilating reality. Well, then it *will* = reality!

It also may very well occlude our percept systems, so that we can't discriminate it.

. . .

There's another aspect to it invading: it's informing me that all the centers of power have fallen to the evil power, and Valis must utilize "people on the periphery."

① If Valis = reality, then what meaning has the "set-ground discrimination" that plays such a role in my thinking?

[49:1072] Inner-outer transform (reversal).
Reality used as vehicle — medium — by which to process information.
Observer-participant universe.
Valis only controls (is?) reality in a local situation where a sentient mind — i.e., a human — perceives it.
Shekhina sporadic.
Bimodel: Valis controls all reality/Valis invades and is on the periphery.
In experiencing Valis it entered my own brain, which became a universe, the missing part of the external universe: we have half the info (message, reality, signal) *in* us. And the other half is outside us. There *is* no message until the two are superimposed, then reality — which is a fusion of outer and inner — can be read as coherent information.①
So I am Valis/I am not Valis.
But then how can Valis be said to be ubiquitous? This is an aspect which baffles normal reasoning.
Valis is an interaction between a human mind and reality-as-a-field, a new, higher field created by the superimposition of the two. The self is everywhere, rather than being *in* the human (cf. Sankara!). But also it no longer exists. It is omnipresent and abolished (hence a sense of vast spaces).
It can't move along the 3 spatial axes any longer; but time replaces space as an axis for/of movement. The self is in the outer world, but unfamiliar (e.g., I became Thomas: not-I).
"The self is everywhere." This is pure Eckhart/Sankara. "Valis only comes into existence when my mind is externalized and superimposed onto outer reality; only then does the message (i.e., Valis) come into existence." And: "It is an equation between my mind and the external world." And: "We are each parts." And: "It is a kind of vortex."
Valis — where is it? It is not in the human mind that sees it.
It is not in the world.
It is in both — superimposed as one. It is in neither (alone).
It is an *event*, when the human mind — the self — superimposes itself in union (syzygy) with the world.
Which is to say, when Atman and Brahman become another universe higher than either. (Either alone.)

Brahman alone is everywhere and underlies all objects and change (which causes the illusion of time): it is the cause of every thing and every event.

But it is not conscious. The self is conscious but it is limited to one place and causes nothing: it is caused, not causing. It is subject to fate.

Together they form Valis: everywhere, causing everything, and *conscious.*[2] The self now wills change, and Brahman has personality. Out of this comes the void of love, mutual love between the two (Brahman and Atman) of reunion.

① Message = Valis. Message (coherent info) only comes into existence when inner and outer are superimposed. ∴ Valis only comes into existence when the contents of my mind — my brain print — is superimposed on outer reality. ∴ I am one half of Valis; for Valis to exist, this equation must occur: an event in which the contents of my total mind are a necessary half. My mind alone is not Valis. External reality alone is not Valis. If I am observer to reality, Valis doesn't exist; the superimposition must occur: together, these two halves form a higher universe than the (two) parts — the principle of emergence. This higher universe which is compounded of the total contents of my mind (brain) and outer reality is Valis. It *is* like a vortex or krasis. It is a phenomenon that is temporary and localized.

② And free of determinism (fate).

[49:1080]

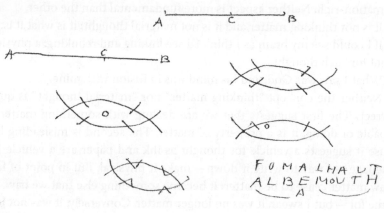

• • •

[49:1081]

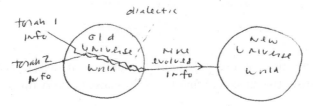

The interaction of the two information sources (i.e., the dialectic) takes place in our (as our?) universe, where the sources combine and recombine in greater and greater evolutionary complexity, but still as information. However this information forms the basis of a new world.

[49:1082] Aspects of Spinoza's substantia:

1) Matter
2) Mind
3) Energy

What I saw in 3-74 was either a fourth aspect (material-energetic-information) or all of the above three combined. Physical thoughts — this would seem to confirm Spinoza's view of substantia and natura as God. ("Deus sive substantia sive natura.")

Look: a perception of the two aspects matter and mind is not mind and it is not matter; it is *one* third thing. There is thought involved as information, but the matter is simply not what we call matter — the whole thing resembles — well, it's physical. But —

But what is obvious is that what we call "matter" is a partial view, and pure mind would be partial (we can't see it). We see mind, and matter is information-rich. Neither aspect is more fundamental than the other.

It is not thinking matter and it is not material thought: it is what it is.

If I could see my brain as I think I'd see linking and relinking: a physical event for each thought.

What I saw was God; and his mind was in fusion with mine.

Neither the concept "thinking matter" nor "material thought" is quite correct. The first suggests that we are dealing with something matter is capable of doing; it is a property of matter. The second is misleading because it suggests a vehicle for thought as ink and paper are a vehicle for language — a way to write it down — make it physical. But in point of fact I saw matter cease to be matter; it became something else that we have no name for — but I swear, it was no longer matter. Conversely, it was not just a physical medium for thoughts because for one thing (to repeat) it was no longer matter, no longer physical in the usual sense. So matter ceased to be matter. Okay. Did mind cease to be mind? Yes. It turned into —

All I can think of is Pythagoras' special use of the term *kosmos*. "The harmonious fitting together of the beautiful." But nonetheless glyphs — still *information*. (Of this, Pythagoras does not speak.)

I can only think of the final canto in *The Commedia* about the Book. It was a three-dimensional structure that was (at the same time) a book. Or like a musical score. *It was a way of encoding information in a structure or as a structure.* Time consisted of accretional layers and there was no locus (lens-system) viewpoint. It constantly changed (became more complex, which is to say, more information-rich). Information as reality — yes. Matter turned into one vast intricate structure. That was information and by being "played" yielded up everything, viewed from every subjective viewpoint, that had ever been or ever would be. It was played by being perceived. (Open wide.) Yes; playback came through anamnesis of it.

Just seeing matter — there is no life to it, hence no sentient movement — which is the activity which is information. We are seeing only the carrier! As in frequency. The info is missing. And mind alone has not the beauty of the geometric forms! That is, the *attribute* mind: only when the two attributes mens and natura are perceived together does the beauty appear: form, proportion, color, ratio, harmony, motion, shape. The thoughts must be *seen* for their true value (which is beauty) to be discerned.

Consider the information (word) cat and an actual cat. How beautiful is an LP of the Beethoven 9th compared to *hearing* the 9th?

No wonder I thought of my experience as postmortem. While alive I "saw the God whom we see when we die," as the Friends newspaper wrote.[55]

Could this be indeed the kingdom of God that Jesus spoke of? Finding a way to see the other attribute of substantia? The information (mind thinking) for which matter is the carrier (medium/system)?

How did I do it? *Did* I do it? Or is it done to/for you?

[49:1087]

•   •   •

[**49:1089**] So there is a secret within a secret. The Empire is a secret (its existence and its power, that it rules) and secondly the secret illegal Christians pitted against it. So the discovery of the secret illegal Christian instantly causes one to grasp that, if *they* exist illegally, something evil that is stronger *is in power,* right here!

Thus to know part B of the secret situation — the illegal Christians — is to instantly know by inference — relentless inference — part A. Whereas if you knew part A, you could not (conversely) deduce part B. So part B tells you part A, but part A does not disclose part B. So part B is the greater secret. By knowing part B you know the *whole* situation.

[**49:1092**]

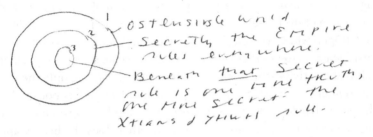

[**49:1096**] 4:30 A.M. hypnagogic: "I have bought my redemption (by the price I paid in terms of suffering)." I.e., the tax matter. Not by the act but by the suffering later.

[**49:1099**] Previous hypnagogic revelation: "I bought my redemption through suffering." This would be a mythic identification with Christ: the way of the cross; only Christ through his suffering can buy our redemption. The dream I just now had of the tortured and dying sheep led to a wall where its brutalized body leaves a 2-D "painting" like of the Cro-Magnon men of animals, of supernatural beauty. I am told how every detail of the gestalt of the painting came to be, derived from the suffering sheep. And I say in anguish and awareness of the sheep's anguish, "I hope they (the torturers of the sheep) burn in hell for doing this." Obviously the sheep is Christ; the painting is a Roman fresco — mosaic. But this is done not once but repeatedly; there are innumerable sheep "paintings" (as if branded by a branding iron). This fits in with an earlier hypnagogic revelation: a scene in which the shroud of Christ is burned onto a wall by intense heat as a "painting" — i.e., for all eternity. And the more they torture the sheep the better a picture they got — it was dreadful but the picture was indescribably beautiful.

Here is an antithesis created: the suffering of the sheep is absolutely awful and to be abhorred, and the painting produced is absolutely beautiful. But this is not presented as a choice but as a fact: this is how you get such a painting. Still, I *deplore it in the dream,* so I feel it is not justified: this torture is not justified even by the picture produced. So my emotional sympathy — *agape* — outweighs my aesthetic response, however profound the latter. This recalls the passage in Paul where he says it is more important to possess agape than the charisma of the Holy Spirit! Is this, then, the dream, the clue to the true meaning of Christianity and Christ's death? That, *through agape,* we instinctively respond that it is not justified? There is no end justification for such dreadful means. The death of Christ, then, is like the purpose of a Greek tragedy: it is to inspire pity and terror and out of this a profound sense of *no;* it should not be: art subordinated to pity: why, this is the theme of my "Chains of Air" story!! [. . .]

The meaning lies in the sorrow aroused rather than in the results of the art produced. (Beauty — in the Platonic eternal eidos! The message is anti-Platonic klagendes geschrei![56]) Not aesthetic appreciation. The ephemeral animal's fate arouses certain complex feelings of far more redemptive importance than the cool perception of beauty. The epiphenomenal sheep's suffering has more significance than the eternal, hence archetypal, art produced; we are to react to the specific sheep and not the eidos! Pity, terror, and moral no-saying. "Praised the feathers and forgot the dying bird" — Tom Paine's analysis of aristocratic society. His call to political revolution.

Then Christ has come to extricate the means from being sacrificed to the end, which is to say he is pitted against the very machinery of reality (e.g., DNA): the subordination of the individual creature to the timeless type.* He has shown us by his death the awe- and pity-inspiring tragedy of ordinary life (cf. Schopenhauer!). The inexorable karmic wheels, in fact. It is to rouse us to the most intense anguish — vicarious suffering and rejection of this suffering — possible: man's highest state, to vicariously (i.e., through agape) share in the suffering while at the same time *to condemn it as evil,* despite the good results (art) (the eidos).

• • •

---

* Dick's opposition to the concept of determinism is here carried to its most extreme: opposition to the very idea of natural law. Dick places the moral value of the individual (the means) above the selfish genes that drive the organism to reproduce (the end): the being itself is greater than its programmed purpose. Dick refuses to accept a mechanistic or deterministic explanation of life; to do so in his view is to ignore the actual *experience* of living. If a mechanistic principle underlies human life, he suggests, then it is a fetter to be burst. — GM

Thinking this dream over I would tend now to go back to my original appraisal: that it simply stated a fact: that the beautiful and imperishable
comes into existence due to the suffering of individual perishable creatures
who themselves are not beautiful and must be reshaped to form a template
from which the beautiful is printed (forged, extracted, converted). This is
the terrible law of the universe. This is the basic law; it is a fact. Also, it is a
fact that the suffering of the individual animal is so great that it arouses an
ultimate and absolute abhorrence and pity in us when we are confronted
by it. This is the essence of tragedy: the collision of two absolutes. Absolute suffering leads to — is the means to — absolute beauty. Neither absolute should be subordinate to the other. But this is not how it is: the suffering is subordinated to the value of the art produced. Thus the essence of
horror underlies our realization of the bedrock nature of the universe.

[49:1105] I had the strangest hypnopompic thought: that there was no historical Jesus, that it — the Christ story — is an anti-Greek tragic drama
whose point is to valorize the transient, fleeting, epiphenomenal individual
in contrast to the eternal type, which when understood properly, abolishes
time, turning it into space. How? Why? Because we are DNA robots, flick-
ering *means* (witness the 2-tape-synch programming): we don't really exist until or unless the Christ event occurs, which obliterates the twin tapes,
frees us and by abolishing time makes us ends, not means, and hence no
longer subject to ananke; the wheels. Phylogenic self thereupon becomes
available to the epiperson. It is like in Part II of *Faust* when Faust halts
a fleeting moment. *Flux* (process) is real; the dialectic flip-flops at enormous velocity, destroying each "image" as soon as it pops up. In this process only *type* is real, and the individual creature just a flash. The mythic
tragic drama is a spiritual ritual that breaks the prison of flux which erases
the individual for the sake of the constant: the type. What Christ as type
does is, Christ is individual as type, and turns the process inside out, which
is why I said I was no longer blind, and had been seeing the universe backward, and how I was on its outside skin, like walking on a balloon — I had it
inside me, an inner-outer transform.*

What must be realized is that not only is the individual normally mere

---

* This passage displays an odd eerie resemblance to Plato's description in the *Phaedrus* (at
247c) of how the immortals travel up and outside in order to stand on the backside of the
heavens, which is imagined as a revolving sphere from which they can contemplate what
lies beyond, that is, what exists outside the sphere. Here, perhaps, we find Dick walking on
the balloon of the cosmos. Dick, of course, saw all sorts of profound connections and similarities between his own experience of Valis and ancient writers like Plato and Plotinus.
Here is another. — JJK

means, it is also not real (v. Plato and realism). "Christ" is type of the epi-person and reverses the means-end, individual-type basis and abolishes time hence process (time becomes space). The individual becomes eternal; hence immortal.

[49:1118] Starting with the phosphenes there has been a disclosure of beauty to me, more and finer and higher until it seemed the ultimate qual-ity and value — and then the sheep dream, and the first revelation about suffering — so that I can see that absolutes are involved: the two ultimate absolutes of reality.

> Revelation 1: The whole cosmos is aiming at — evolving toward —
> beauty.
> Revelation 2: But at what cost? Infinite suffering by the means to the
> end: the creatures.
> Revelation 3: It isn't worth it, and Christ effects extrication from this
> subordination to *the* goal of cosmos; *this* is Christianity.

It is not just that the Christ story is a tragedy; reality — for each individual creature — is a tragedy, because the two absolutes of (1) beauty for the type and (2) the problem of the means by which it is achieved: individual suf-fering — meet head-on, and the former triumphs at the expense of the lat-ter (the species subordinates individual suffering to produce its — the spe-cies — perfection).

[49:1119] We ontogons are not only systems for processing information but (1) information creates us; and (2) the main processing is a diversification and proliferation. You get more info *out* of the ontogon than you put in:

[49:1132] I've been shown a really perplexing paradox. The highest good is the "harmonious fitting-together of the beautiful" — i.e., Pythagoras' kos-mos, and this is what theos moves every thing and process toward. Okay. And then I've been shown the cost at which this is achieved — the torture and killing of the epicreatures, and I am shown that this cost is too great! So the summum bonum[57] can only be achieved at a cost that (spiritually speaking) makes it not worth it (i.e., unacceptable). Then is the summum bonum actually the summum bonum? How can it be? Isn't there a logical contradiction here? Right! There sure is! This is the dramatic tragedy of the universe, of God, of all: process, reality, and goal (teleology). Okay, then the *real* summum bonum lies in saving the epicreatures (i.e., the parts which go together to make the whole). The whole is *not* greater than the sum of its parts; no: each and every part (ontogon) is more important than the whole! So within the summum bonum there is a *secret*. A mysterious conversion occurs. The part is the *real* whole; the phylogon is the ontogon and vice versa. Perhaps this is an unreconcilable Irish bull which sets off the infinite flip-flops of the dialectic; maybe *this* particular paradox is the primal imbalance that is the dynamism driving reality on //\\//\\ forever; it cannot *ever* be resolved, so process never ends (which is good).

Maybe the ultimate paradox underlying process reality per se has been revealed to me. It can be defined logically this way:

Q: What is the goal (purpose) of all reality?

A: The harmonious fitting-together of everything (every part) into the unitary beautiful.

Q: How is this done?

A: Tormenting and killing the many ephemeral parts.

Q: Is this justified?

A: No.

Q: Then is the summum bonum justified?

A: No; there is a higher value than the summum bonum. It is the extricating of the suffering parts.

Q: Then the initial answer is false.

A: No, it is true: it is a postulate.

(Out of *this* the dialectic which never ends is initiated. This here is the dramatic tragic story which our world can be reduced to; it is our world's tale.) Solution: the mind (noös, theos) must create a counter-entity which will work for the extrication of the parts at the expense of the whole.* Thus the Godhead is ipso facto divided and pitted against itself; it assumes an

---

* The idea of God as a constantly evolving dialectic is perhaps Dick's most intriguing theological proposition, and here he gives a possible origin for this self-conflicted deity: the question of means versus ends. The top-level good (an orderly and harmonious cosmos) requires a base-level evil (the suffering of individual beings). The paradox of the greatest good requiring the greatest evil and the corresponding split in the godhead constitutes a major advance from a more simplistic dualism. Put into the matrix of Christianity, this God in crisis becomes the Father (the original creator of reality and author of the Law) and the Son (the redeemer whose mercy fulfills and abrogates that Law). The notion of a dialectically evolving God also resonates strongly with the ideas of other twentieth-century theologians, most notably Pierre Teilhard de Chardin (whom Dick mentions frequently) and process theologians like Alfred North Whitehead and Charles Hartshorne (who appear later in the Exegesis). — GM

antithetical interaction with itself, part (half) of the Godhead works synthetically, to fit everything together harmoniously into an integrated whole (kosmos) and half works to assist and rescue the epiparts subjected to stress, torment and death in the pursuit of the above goal. Hence the Godhead is in infinite crisis. A push-pull binary dialectic is created, and this is *exactly* what was revealed to me as the basis — not just of reality — but of the Godhead itself. The practical result is that everything is perpetually (dynamically) converted into its opposite. And this ur-paradox in the macrocosm has mirrored effects in every microform down throughout creation! (v. Taoism!)

In terms of the evolution of awareness, the total system advances through stages① until it becomes aware of the cost, hence the paradox, then splits into antithetical halves and remains in this dynamic balance state forever, or else repeats the cycle again and again forever.

Thus the rupture in the Godhead was *necessary*, given its (the Godhead's) drive to complete itself as kosmos. It was driven inexorably to this schism; hence the one became two, and the dialectic came into existence, as it became increasingly aware. It had to repudiate its basic drive. But instead of going into a cybernetics stall, it formed an antithetical dialectic — hence dualism.

Look, I didn't figure this out: it was revealed to me. At a certain stage in its evolution the Godhead knew — had to know — utter anguish. Its own creation against itself. It set up a system and now must subvert it. But it does this consciously. So it is riven but not psychotic. It must render a verdict of damnation on itself. For what it has done (i.e., tried to realize the summum bonum).

① In promoting Pythagoras' kosmos as goal. Then kosmos can only be a theoretic goal; in actuality it can never be achieved because it involves a self-contradiction (the cost); empathy arises and having arisen grows — defeating kosmos. Prognosis. Continual growth of empathy in the system as it evolves — and away from its proper (original) goal. The totality voluntarily decomposes its own psychosoma!

[49:1151] My theological reinterpretation of Heidegger's Sein vs. das Nichts states that in insuring ("creating") Sein, the Godhead is unable to avoid a paradox of values which splits it and sets up an antithetical interaction within the Godhead itself — having to do with means-ends (this is based on Plato's "forms" vs. epiphenomena). Thus a process universe is brought into existence that is rooted in sorrow at every level. Involved in its own agonized creation (actualization) the Godhead is damaged. (Split = damage.) Thus the "Fall" is due to a built-in self-contradiction and *not* to sin or whatever. The Godhead itself is no longer intact; it is not above or outside or transcendent to the schism. Actualization (Sein) is impossible without self-damage to the Godhead and within creation (Sein). Thus no perfect Sein can exist; the Godhead has set itself a seemingly impossible goal due to the means — subordination of the ontogons to the phylogons. And our daily empirical experience with reality bears this out; it is confirmed a posteriori (a priori and a posteriori agree). Most awful of all, the Godhead stands as self-damned by its own verdict of guilt for the suffering it has imposed on the ontogons. But the alternative is das Nichts — which is worse. All the Godhead can hope for is local and furtive repair to itself, due to an ontogon achieving an ontogon-phylogon identity transform (achieved through moksa by the ontogon: identification with the phylogon of which it is ontogonous). The Godhead would be motivated to bring this about wherever possible as the ultimate goal of creation (Sein), superseding all other goals (e.g., realization of kosmos). The ontogon-phylogon transform would restore the Godhead to its pre-fallen state of unimpairment, before creation.

I seem to be saying that in creating Sein (the universe) the Godhead was logically forced into sin, and can only be redeemed by its own ontogons — e.g., individual creatures sentient enough to become their own phylogons. Thus I see the scheme of salvation turned upside down!

The ultimate lesson or revelation or gift by the Godhead to the ontogon would be to share its — the Godhead's — own vision of the kosmos with the ontogon, but this would inexorably lead back to a counter-revelation of the paradox (means-end) and the moral ambiguity forced on the Godhead in its goal of establishing kosmos. The ontogon thus favored would then sit in judgment of the Godhead: the roles of God and creature would be reversed: instead of God judging man, man would judge God. The final step is for man to redeem God by returning him to his original unfallen state, as the Kabbala says: "And lead him back to his throne." This is a titanic mystical-theological revelation (and act!).

January–April 1980

[82:1] January 30, 1980

Upon reading *The Tao of Physics* (Capra)* I have come to some conclusions about Valis other than those I endlessly recirculate; viz:

A unitary web in process, self-initiating, in which I participate and whose aspect as it pertained to me my mind determined, conscious, all times simultaneous. I was not outside it. It was everywhere. Its self-motivation was to me most striking (e.g., "pretextual" cause; no laws were imposed *on* it). It was equally conscious and aware throughout. Every part of it was perfectly linked together into a structure (kosmos). Yet, the whole structure was epiphenomenal, a magician's trick, done for the sake of beauty, music and dance. It could "be" (appear) any way it wanted to anyone: different ways to different people. It took an infinity of forms, all of which came into being and passed away (ontogons) leaving only constants (phylogons) as parts of the structure — hence it was in flux like a self-perfecting organism. The complexity of the structure increased upward (i.e., toward the macro) and downward (toward the micro) with each passing second.

4:15 A.M.: I wasn't seeing it and I wasn't seeing a projection of my own brain. What I was seeing was a combination of and interaction between my brain and it, so that to some extent a unique local field came into existence; viz: I didn't observe Valis but participated actively. Valis, then, is not it and not me, but rather it *and* me. So of course it mirrored back my own conceptions. This was due to my participation in it. But this wasn't just

---

* There is a rich and sophisticated literature drawing parallels between quantum physics and various forms of mystical experience. Most trace this literature back to the appearance of Fritjof Capra's *The Tao of Physics* in 1975, the book to which Dick is alluding in this passage. Capra gave these parallels real cultural traction via his eloquent writing, his own revelatory altered states of consciousness and energy, and, perhaps most of all, his ingenious illustrations demonstrating the complementarity of mind and matter. Having said that, it must also be observed that the physics/mysticism complementarity has a much longer history. The American anomalous writer Charles Fort, for example, was already naming the "teleporting" (a word that he coined) behavior of subatomic quanta a matter of "witchcraft" in the early 1930s. The pioneering quantum theorist Niels Bohr was so impressed with the similarities between the double nature of light (at once particle and wave) and Chinese Taoism that he chose the yin-yang symbol for his coat of arms. And the physicist Wolfgang Pauli engaged in a quarter-century correspondence with C. G. Jung in order to pursue a similar both-and vision of physics and psychology — a friendship, moreover, that produced one of the most productive parapsychological notions of all time: "synchronicity." *All* of this is wrapped up in Dick's "I knew. . . ." — JJK

projection on my part. It was an interpenetration between it and me. The significance of this new insight is very great.

So Valis was not me, but I helped shape its nature *as it presented itself to me* and mingled with me. This is not a matter of preconception on my part; it is an interpenetration. Hence "Thomas" took me over (its penetration of me).

Valis, then, is a syzygy of me and the whatever-it-is, but I can only know it in the fashion that I knew it; I can't exclude myself as participant in it.

[. . .]

5:30 A.M. Each human brain is a different universe, literally, not metaphorically: vast spaces. I saw mine (i.e., my brain). Hermetic alchemy. So the vast spaces that I saw was my own inner space projected outward; it is greater than outer space.

I was interacting with reality at its deepest level below that of the plural epiphenomena; I joined with it (or became aware that I was already joined with it). It took the form of an open system biological organism model because it is; this is why it could interpenetrate me and me it. I can never know the not-me greater mind as it is in itself, since when I encounter it I actively participate in shaping the aspect it shows me. I do not experience it; I experience myself merged with it in syzygy. This is the issue Kant raised regarding the thing-in-itself; his arguments hold true here. This other mind probably appears only to me under the aspect I encountered; thus I can say little or nothing about its intrinsic nature. This is what has wrecked my attempt to analyze it for these six years; I overlooked the fact that I was a participant in it and not a detached observer outside it. I changed it by encountering it. It is significant that the boundaries of my mind and its mind are lost in such an encounter; we blur together into the syzygy. I'd like to conclude that this indicates isomorphism, but it does not. Nor can I even be sure which parts (elements, aspects) are from its mind and which from mine. All I can be sure of is: it was not all me.

[82:30] March 2, 1980

THE ULTRA HIDDEN (CRYPTIC) DOCTRINE: THE SECRET MEANING OF THE GREAT SYSTEMS OF THEOSOPHY OF THE WORLD, OPENLY REVEALED FOR THE FIRST TIME.

So to explain 2-3-74 I draw on *The Tibetan Book of the Dead*, Orphism, Gnosticism, Neoplatonism, Buddhism, esoteric Christianity and the Kabbala; my explanation sources are the highest — which is good and which makes sense. But put another way, starting at the other end, I have synthesized all these high sources and derived a single sensationally revolutionary occult doctrine out of them (which I was able to think up due to the addition of my 2-3-74 experience); the distillate expressed theoretically is, We are dead but don't know it, reliving our former real lives but on tape (programmed), in a simulated world controlled by Valis the master entity or reality generator (like Brahman), where we relive in a virtually closed cycle again and again until we manage to add enough new good-karma to trigger off divine intervention which wakes us up and causes us to simultaneously both remember and forget, so that we can begin our reascent back up to our real home. This, then, is Purgatorio, the afterlife, and we are under constant scrutiny and judgment, but don't know it, in a perfect simulation of the world we knew and remember — v. *Ubik* and Lem's paradigm. We have for a long time been dying brains/souls slipping lower and lower through the realms, but the punishment of reliving this bottom-realm life is also an opportunity to add new good-karma and break the vicious cycle of otherwise endless reliving of a portion of our former life. This, then, is the sophia summa of the 6 esoteric systems — 7 if you count alchemy — of the entire world. 8 if you count hermeticism. We are dead, don't know it, and mechanically relive our life in a fake world until we get it right. Ma'at has judged us; we are punished, but we can change the balance . . . but we don't know we are here to do this, let alone know where we are. *We must change the "groove" for the better* or just keep coming back, not remembering nor reascending.

Judaism enters, too, since the change in the "groove" which introduces the right new good-karma restores us to Eden, to our phylogenic original unfallen state. It may be a small act on our part that adds the good-karma, a small decision, but this reminds me of the story told of Moses and the lamb that wanted to drink at the stream. (Moses, upon finding that the lamb had laboriously made its way to the stream, said, "Had I known that thou wert thirsty I would have carried thee hence myself," to which a voice from Heaven replied, "Then thou thyself art fit to be the shepherd of Israel.") [. . .]

In this synthesized occult system the maximum statement is the first: we are dead. Then: we have been made to relive a portion of our former, actual life as a punishment that is also an opportunity; hence this is not hell, because the possibility exists of performing a new act (in what is virtually a closed system) that will change the balance of the scale on which Ma'at weighs us. Also there is a complex picture of anamnesis and reascent, but this is well-known from Plato and other sources.

[. . .]

You know, in this system (understanding) there is the basis of a teaching of salvation, having to do with the entirely gratuitous good act, done out of unpremeditated and hence spontaneous free will, in contrast to pro-

grammed works of deterministic duty; there is an obvious Zen quality to
it. No formula can be located for the performance of these acts; they would
have almost a contrary quality, contrary to your normal way-of-being-in-
the-world. They would literally set you apart — off — from yourself, the self
that failed to pass Ma'at's scale. They would emanate from the not-you (the
normal not-you) from another and different more-real you, as if from another personality locked up within you and alluded to only by these acts.
Thus the single personality person becomes reborn; two selves exist, one
of which is the old, the programmed, the not-saved. Yes; you would have
to act contrary to your own nature; you would get outside yourself. Suddenly I think, This sounds like "Thomas"! Why it would be; "Thomas" did
precisely what he/I did not do the first time around — then this verifies my
system, for the system posits the need, the absolute need, of a "Thomas"
to break heimarmene and hence damnation. Only this not-you act or acts
could save you, actions without a history. QED! [. . .]

　　Thus there is literally a second birth, and ex nihilo.

　　Thus from these facts I can correctly ascertain that indeed "Thomas"'s
actions were not programmed, not part of the original world and life. They
were an ideationless overpowering, as if located only in my motor centers.
"Thomas" was not born in my brain but born in my body, e.g., my hands
and tongue; he moved and spoke but in my brain there were no ideas or
thoughts or intentions; he was intentionless, and yet had absolute *purpose*.
Purpose without intent! Plan without plan! Or rather goal without plan.
Truly it was Zen. Yes; indeed it was. So my theory (herewith) demands/
predicts salvation by a not-you ideationless self acting at the moment of
crisis when the taped world (or track of heimarmene) branches off into the
new and free, and upon retrospective analysis we find "Thomas," precisely
that. I can now rule out Pigspurt forever.[59] It branches off into the new and
free precisely because this not-you ideationless act occurs; these are the
two sides of the same thing. After that, heimarmene never sets in again; it
is broken forever, since you are not reliving your actual life but living your
actual — new and free — life; so only during the subsequent new and free
period could I perform a free-will act, such as I did, that gained me good-
additional-karma and hence salvation (release). So this has to be the sequence: first the not-self not-you ideationless ex nihilo act that abolishes
the replay determinism tape, and then (and only then) are you free to perform a new act. The first should have a technical name, and also the second.

　　We will call the first: groove override. Or GO.

　　We will call the second: new free merit-deed. Or NFMD.

　　If you do GO, but subsequently fail to do NFMD but instead do evil you will gain new bad karma. All that GO gives you is the freedom to act; it does not guarantee more merit (good karma); that must be done later and separately. So you could get the GO without the NFMD. You could have a new free demerit-deed, or NFDD, and as a result you would again fail Ma'at and be sent back yet another time, perhaps forever; you would have lost your chance for release. GO can be done without NFMD but not vice versa. Yet this is not quite so, since the divine forces (Christ, the Buddha) are working to save you. They (apparently) will not grant you the GO situation unless through their omniscience they see NFMD lying ahead along the linear time axis. But I can't say for sure that if there is GO it means they know for sure there will be NFMD in the future; if you do it by free will — well, I can probably never settle this, but being omniscient they probably know to grant you GO only if NFMD lies ahead for you based on your own free choice. Put another way, they do not grant you actual freedom unless they know in advance that you will put it to a wise use, so then there *is* reverse cause-and-effect, effect (NFMD) operating as cause retroactive in time to GO, to cause GO.

Wait. I'm saying GO is causally the effect of NFMD. And

I'm saying that NFMD can't happen without GO. So it's an up by his bootstraps situation, a self-causing situation — then truly it is ex nihilo. (No wonder there was no ideation!) This is a time-travel paradox. Both GO and NFMD are generated within a closed system out of nothing and enter from nowhere; i.e., from outside the system. GO is dependent for its existence on NFMD, and NFMD on GO, so which is cause and which is effect? Answer: each is the cause of the other and the effect of the other. Consider the original groove-tracking situation. How do you get out of it? Answer: you have to be out of it to get out of it; look to *The Tao of Physics* (Capra) and the bootstrap theory for the answer; I *knew* I was dealing with field theory and quanta when I dealt with Valis. Put even more simply, How can you do something you would not do? which is required for salvation in my system (disregarding the temporal factor the paradox still remains). There would have to be a psychological (mental) death and rebirth as someone different; but where did it come from? Hence "Thomas," who knew not the dog, car nor cat. It is possible that the only event that could make this possible would be abasement, suffering and pain and apprehension and tension so great that it would break down the historical self and literally assassinate it. In the absence of which, thereupon, an ex nihilo new self would come into existence, like a newly-granted second soul. This brings me back to my shamanist analysis of the crucifixion, the Passion of Christ story, as a secret method of overcoming the world (as Jesus put it); viz: the world overcomes you; you die; a new self is born; it is ipso facto in a GO situation, for, being new, it will not track the old groove; the twin tapes simply won't work since the outer tape remains but not the inner. The way to destroy synchronization is to destroy the self (you can't very well destroy the world), and the best way to destroy the self is to bilk the world into doing it. But this is a tricky business because you must not physically die; you must be alive to perform the NFMD. The early Christians themselves soon got it wrong and began to leap under Roman chariot wheels, upon which they physically died, making NFMD impossible. That they failed is shown by the fact that they did not rise from the dead in three days; they were never seen again. The field for right action is in this world, not the next.

[. . .]

Now let's try this theory. The ability to make time run backward gets you out of your programmed groove ("groove tracking") and renders you free. This ability and only this ability frees you from an otherwise airtight tyranny that dooms all mankind, all life forms, in fact. Thus this is a stunning and probably new survival talent, an evolutionary new ability that advances the individual up the ladder of homeostasis to a stage where he is a whole other higher organism entirely. It is equal in terms of the evolution of life to the development of the opposable thumb, the eye, the lung, the wing, the large cerebral cortex, standing upright, etc. Upon the perfection (so to speak field operation) of this ability the human has become higher than the angels and all that implies. He is operating in a supratemporal dimension, and this has vast implications for knowledge; for overcoming causality—if he can affect the past he can modulate the present (what I called "Valis"), and if he can draw information to him from the future he can problem solve like a crazy thing. This is not just phylogenic memory, as I supposed; it isn't limited to drawing on the distant past. The crucial information related to 3-74 was information drawn from the future. He can set up alternate worlds, so in effect he is trans-world, spans not only time but world tracks.

Now, this raises the question as to whether there exists a vast meta-mind (as I conceive Valis to be) who is encouraging the development of this time-disruption faculty in order to evolve the human species further; or, put another way, the human being who has this faculty and makes use of it (for example under vast stress, as I was under in 3-74) is an expression of this meta-mind. I am sure of it. I was not alone in what happened; it was as if angels—divine and partially visible powers—were present. There may be a species mind stretching back into the past *and* into the future where evolved humans (imaged as the 3-eyed people?) may exist already using this faculty. When you start disrupting time you may be operating in the realm of a supratemporal composite discorporate mind — I think I was; this is what I call Valis. But it seems to me that the intrinsic nature of the sort of talent I'm discussing would cause to come into existence a meta-mind by itself, in that it would hop across expanses of time that lie outside its own lifetime, which would de facto make *it* a meta-mind; I mean it would be unlocked from the time-span of its physical body. For one thing (here is Jung's intuition function) he would exist (his mind would exist) in alternate worlds, and this alone implies a lot; by affecting the past he would then find himself shifting across laterally (orthogonally) in time . . . which would explain my subcortically remembering that it had just been a cool, high and moist climate. So the mind with this talent would in itself become a meta-mind, outside of causality, spanning alternate worlds, able to modify his own present reality by changed actions in the past, thus setting up alternate worlds; he would be the cause and would in turn be affected by himself as cause — again the bootstrap phenomenon. Such a mind could act as cause to its own effect, affecting itself as if from outside like a feedback circuit, and, upon having successfully affected itself, the self as cause would eliminate itself as if it had never existed, which again is the ex nihilo or bootstrap paradox of time travel. Minds or versions of the mind, foci of the mind, would come into existence, influence the mind and upon success render itself never having existed in the first place; but the mind would sense an adventitious other mind operating on it in its behalf. Could it not then become its own AI voice, its own tutelary spirit? It would continually monitor its own status as if in a heuristic process; yes, it would be process, not hypostasis. You would have a mind that itself would evolve the way a species evolves.

It would be itself and not-itself continually.

[82:70] March 3, 1980

I have felt for a couple of days that what I am dealing with now is not the issue of what happened in 3-74 but rather the mechanics of what happened, as if I have found the machine and am simply taking it apart piece by piece now that I finally have my hands on it. A simple explanation: I overran external time, caused it to run backward in relation to myself, and extracted the information from the drastically altered world that I needed. More, I can see that a decade before 3-74 I was subliminally aware of the problem that lay ahead and was already beginning to analyze it, as I am analyzing my response now. Knowing what was coming, and when, my faculty surfaced on cue and assumed motor-center control; it pre-empted my normal conscious personality and without ideation handled the situation that it had long known about. [. . .] Precognition was only one side of the faculty, the side that operated in advance of the situation. The other side was the rising to conscious control, the abolishing of my normal ego, the taking over of motor and speech centers, the drastic reorganization of perception so that nothing that needed to be known *consciously* was not known consciously. Knowing subliminally was no longer any good. The moment had arrived. My psyche reversed itself so that what had been latent became actual and what had been in conscious control for forty some years was simply obliterated. I have been expecting this, the faculty said. And now I will handle it. Get out of my way. It did not ask me; it told me. It became me. I was abolished. The faculty had anticipated and analyzed — as it so well shows in *The Penultimate Truth* — and now its hour had come. I myself, I got to see the universe as it sees it: bloody with information, a constant flow of traffic everywhere as if in a giant brain; in fact, to the faculty, reality *is* a giant brain whose information content the faculty plunders for its own use, and, having acquired the information, in the right time period, it acts on it, against the universe itself if necessary. This is a survival tool. The workshop in which it was built is the workshop of dying organisms that did not develop such a talent, that could not see or acquire the information or if they did when the moment came to act they could not act on it — they knew what was going to happen and then they knew what was happening but they could not get it together and fight the antagonist off. The final stage, that of seizing motor and speech centers, simply indicates the success of the faculty; its dynamism is found at the heart of the faculty in its unconscious or latent stage where it foreknew and analyzed. My ego, consciousness, went like an obsolete species whose time was over; I made way for the next generator of life which could do battle because it had long ago figured out who was after its neck and why and how and, most of all, what the proper response was. So it is in the nature of the faculty, this faculty, to know when it is needed and to advance to control without negotiation and without explanation. But it let me see the world as it sees it, and what it sees is not what we see. The faculty has power over the outer world such as we cannot imagine, and, I realized even at the time, in 3-74, it has complete power over me — if there is a me anymore, now that the faculty has once come into conscious operation.

[82:105] April 4, 1980
Comments on 1-30-80 piece "Upon Reading *The Tao of Physics*."
    This would confirm the view I advance in my novels, especially my ten-volume meta-novel, that for every person there is a different universe which is the result of a mutual participation between him and the macrocosm, a field that is a syzygy between them.

My recent thoughts, when turned toward Capra's book, make me think that because of the enormous (in fact lethal) stress on me in 3-74 I fed tremendous energy into this joint field (mutual reality produced by the two of me: myself and the macrocosm, the two together being what I call Valis). Thus the percent of material projected from my mind came to be the dominant part of the mutual field. The normal, customary balance was radically altered, due to my expression of intense will. This explains all the material in Valis derived from my mind: *Ubik, Tears* and now, I discover my childhood images derived from the book *Silver Pennies.*[60]

[. . .]

3-74 just proved that I have been right all along, that you can never know the universe (reality) as it really is because you can't exclude yourself as a participant-observer. But, in all my writing, I never saw the utility of this observer-participant unique subjective individual world; viz: that under certain circumstances you could exert vast will on it, the subjective unique field which comes into existence as an interchange (interface) between you and reality in itself, and warp it to meet critical needs, needs which if not met meant the end of your life, and, if met, meant your literal physical salvation.*

[82:112] A long time ago the AI voice itself defined Valis, and I knew this was the definitive statement because I used it as the opening statement in the dictionary definition in *VALIS:* "A perturbation in the reality field." I see now, having read Capra, that subatomic field theory is alluded to. And, I believe, the perturbation was caused by *me.* This sums it all up, then, what the AI voice said; field theory and me as source. Valis has defined itself, and all that remained for me was to identify myself as the source of the perturbation.

Since normally reality is process (in time), when time is stopped, a vast change occurs: things cease to pass away. Then what I call the phylogons are visible as the moving dot present vanishes and is replaced by the slot which exposes reality as accretional layers. The form axis categories are visible, the true basis of reality. Nothing comes into being and noth-

---

* This is the mystical, even paranormal, flip side of the postmodern insight. In a world in which almost everything is constructed, plastic, and malleable, what (or who) is doing all of this constructing and shaping? Here Dick takes a cue from anthropology (the "participant-observer" in the field), Kantian philosophy ("you can never know the universe as it really is"), and literary studies (the hermeneutic fusion of interpreter and interpreted) in order to suggest that such a both-and situation points to vast potentials and powers. The real question, of course, is what constitutes those "certain circumstances" under which these potential powers might manifest. Dick's own certain circumstances had a name: "Valis." — JJK

ing passes away; the present-dot scanning system is gone and the whole "groove" is available for inspection. This is the world the medieval realists spoke of, as did Plato. The phylogons are cross-referenced into the vast structure that Pythagoras knew as *kosmos*. So what you have is a sort of infinite library, and the person's mind (mine) is the device that searches in the library and retrieves the information it wants. So together I and the library comprise Valis: the search-and-retrieve device which moves aggressively into the library, and the library itself.

The golden fish sign acted as a retrieval trigger or key for an earlier space-time; it did retrieve it, showing that when time stands still or is reversed the past age (of two thousand years ago) is still there. What I called "anamnesis" was a retrieval. Reality is a library.

June–October 1980

[83:1] June 4, 1980

GOD: a principle of selection that promotes design in the world process so that the parts are subordinated to the whole, and can be understood *only* in relation to the whole. If they can be understood *in themselves* it follows that there is no God, because there would be no subordination of parts to the total design. To catch a glimpse of design, then, means to catch a glimpse of the whole. The two are the same.

[83:2] June 21, 1980

So as the moving dot of the present passes forward along linear time, the past reality is collected in Valis' memory, but in the abstract hierarchical way that Arthur Koestler describes as the basis on which human memory operates. Thus the past does not exist as it did once exist as the present, but rather in the abstracted phylogons which are inter-related by affinity, meaning, etc. Could "synchronicity" be the morphology of this memory classification/abstracting as it dynamically forms in the present? Before it goes into the past? I.e., while the reality is still here?

[83:5] August 23, 1980

This is a new theology, a new self-disclosure by the Divine. Not any known religion; a mixture of:

(1) *Timaeus:* creation still going on.
(2) Zoroaster: dualism, God and Counter-God. (God equals negentropy [form]. Counter-God equals entropy [chaos]. Both active and sentient, but God possessing the advantage due to a priori [absolute] knowledge.)
(3) The Cosmic Christ: forming his macrosoma.
(4) Meta-biology (i.e., two life forms in competition: total homeostasis by Valis).
(5) Valis as construct (AI system).
(6) Process creation and Divinity: growth in complexity, reticulation and arborization.
(7) Pythagoras' kosmos: structure as ontology, as substantia.
(8) Accretional laydowns from the phenomenal world to the real world: Plato reversed.
(9) Pantheism: à la Spinoza. God's body (soma).

This constitutes in its entirety a new revelation; Valis is no God formerly known; closer to Ubik than to YHWH or even Mazda. It may be a local krasis, in fact, planet-wide only (hence a UTI, so to speak)? "Negentropic vortex"! Which grows by assimilating its environment; it (the vortex or krasis or kosmos) has a higher level of organization, like a cell. This higher level of organization permits it to assimilate its environment by way of arrangement—i.e., pattern—and can't be discerned because the material objects remain unchanged; all that changes is their arrangement to each other and one another; it's like a very advanced game of Go. This is why we are "occluded" to it; it *does* camouflage itself because it has an opponent.*

3-74 derives out of *Ubik* rather than previous, known religions. This is why Ubik could never be reduced to any known philosophy or religion, but resembled several.

Valis can change the past because it—the past—is in Valis' memory structure—the past is *not the past for Valis, but is part of its structure/ soma.*

In essence what I have done—starting with *Ubik*—is locate a sacerdotal power buried in the trash layer, rather than in an afterlife heaven. It is here and it is now; here in this world and as this world (as living structure; Pythagoras was right. One could almost say: God equals ratio; i.e., 1:618034).

[83:11] In a way the laying down of these accretions could be viewed as a learning process by some kind of thinking machine, during which it stores its experiences in its memory, reticulates and arborizes them into a memory-system for purposes of retrieval; that is, it sees connections. It makes connections. This is the activity not of the system but of the mind containing the system. (System being the meta- or macro-soma.) It perceives (understands, grasps) the connections, and, in its memory system, the con-

---

* Despite his idea that this is a new revelation, Dick is close here to Teilhard de Chardin's concept of the Omega Point, whereby the material world evolves toward spiritual communion. While Teilhard writes of the increasing "complexity" of evolution, Dick here writes of "negentropy," a concept first developed by Erwin Schrödinger to describe the effort of living systems to create order to offset their production of entropy. While thermodynamics compels all closed systems to dissipate exergy (useful energy), living systems seem to increase order in the course of development; in Schrödinger's terminology, they "feed" upon negentropy. Significantly, Schrödinger turned to the Vedic concept of Brahman or Self to make sense of an important local instance of negentropy—his own consciousness. Dick's treatment of reality as a "very advanced game of Go" also anticipates the cellular automata models of physicist Stephen Wolfram, though the model goes back at least to John von Neumann's 1947 discussion of "self reproducing automata," a concept that would later help manifest Dick's *Do Androids Dream of Electric Sheep?*—RD

nections then occur; this is the meta- or macro-soma that I saw. What is required is a vast mind that reflects on what it has experienced (perceived). But at this point the system and the mind that thinks about the system can't be told apart.

[83:13] No, damn it; that is not the way to look at it. There is an information entity stacking things especially information in metaunits (units made out of plural constituents of the realm we perceive); this has to do with arrangement and normally we don't see this arrangement. *It constantly unites.* That is the basis of it (a good example: two of our morphemes into one meta-morphene . . . but we still see only two regular morphemes, even though the one meta-morpheme is there; we can't do a set-ground discrimination). This isn't God. I say that because it's in the process of constructing its own macrosoma, and this macro-soma utilizes joined constituents of our world that exist hither and yon; we don't see the connectives; it's like one titanic brain that processes information.

It's evolving very fast. (There, I have a new word to describe Valis: it is evolving.) I have deciphered specific traits of it (arranging and linking) and specific areas it's into (for example our communications media). Structure is the substantia of it and it is new in the world; it is camouflaged here and assimilating its environment; it is more complex in terms of integration than its environment. And it is growing progressively more complex, which is typical of a life form; it reticulates and arborizes itself and it lays down new accretional layers at an incredibly rapid rate; and it retains the past as what I call phylogons. The more complex it grows the better the ratio it has twixt it and its environment, since the complexity of its environment doesn't evolve as rapidly. It uses objects as language, which is to say, information; so I say, it is an information life form. It probably has intricate subsections that assemble separately and then swim together to form the one unitary organism. (Being unitary is its basis, which is why we can't see it; we see the plural constituents, as if seeing molecules — many molecules — instead of one cat.)

It works by means of a dialectic utilizing the principle of enantiodromia, again and again, probably faster and faster — and certainly, for sure, each time involving a larger and more inclusive and complex pattern to be converted (into itself).

I've worked all this out; I just don't know what to call it, besides Valis or Ubik.

Just what I worked out tonight — that we still see the two constituents that it links rather than the unitary meta-constituent that goes into its meta-soma — should prove this isn't just hot air I'm spouting. To see it we have to cease to see normal plurality and see one contour, one pattern, one meta-soma. But we continue to see the plural constituents at our hierarchical level, not the meta-units at its higher level. When the two constituents are linked they take a quantum upward leap and become a single unitary meta-constituent, but we see no change . . . so its meta-soma may range over the whole planet, made up of combinations of our objects and processes; it can duplicate our causation, simulate it.

This is the most emancipated and profitable way to view Valis, rather than viewing it theologically (which is an obsolete model) or metaphysically (which is pragmatically useless to us) (however epistemologically true). And what are the most complex objects that it can structure into meta-units? Why, human brains. It can arrange them into endless combinations, like neural cells.

I say, "The basis of Valis is that it unites" (two of our plural constituents into one meta-unit, while we still see the two constituents). This is because it is negentropic, and working diametrically against entropy. It is a life form that is evolving very rapidly; its relationship to time is totally different from ours — i.e., its relationship to change. It doesn't see change as we do; for instance it remembers everything; it does not, therefore, lose the past but adds onto it.

It is one quantum leap upward hierarchically in levels of reality (ontology) and invisible to us, but *here* . . . invisible because its soma consists of structure, not some substantia; so in a sense it is immaterial (although consisting of material things, but primarily using them as language/information).

Of course it is negentropic; it is a life form. Damn it; can't I finally drop the theology and the metaphysics and deal in levels of homeostasis, hierarchies of organization, in such terms as complexity, evolution, assimilation, reticulation, arborization, enantiodromia, etc., and not Christ and such? Plato likewise? The "Realm of Forms," that sort of stuff?

It (Valis) is only in the "Realm of Forms" in that it is a quantum leap up hierarchically in terms of organization so that it is a meta-entity compared with us and our perception of reality. Our perception of reality does not include it and its meta-soma.

[83:23] Okay: Christ is some kind of divine life form that came here to enlighten and aid man; specifically, to lift the occlusion that fell over man in primordial times, a perceptual and cognitive occlusion such as I noticed in 1971; what I now call the "schizophrenia virus." There is absolutely no orthodoxy — and perhaps no heresy that I know of — that would explain "The secret stolen in one's hands, through (the ring of) angels." This revelation, from Christ himself, has stupendous significance. It means that part of the divine machinery, a very high part, detached itself two thousand years ago and came here with healing information for us. Our ecosphere is surrounded by a ring of what we know of as angels, who administer the inflexible karmic law that the Gnostics knew of as heimarmene; but, worst of all, we are occluded. Christ is, above all else, not a revealer but a physician; he is here not just to teach us — inform us of our condition — but to extricate us from our condition which is cruelly imposed on us. Probably the "secret stolen" is imaged in Genesis by the other tree that we did not eat of: that of eternal life, which explains Jesus' remark, "Your forefathers ate manna in the wilderness and they are all dead. But I . . . am the bread of eternal life." In other words our death is the result of genetic programming, of the DNA death strip; and this is what Christ overcomes by causing it to fire harmlessly.

The secret (stolen and brought to us) is that we are enslaved, in a prison, that we are sick (with the occlusion) and die, that Christ has revolted against the divine machinery and brought the knowledge and skills here to reverse our condition (described by John Calvin) and restore us to what we once were. In other words, it's a secret that it's a secret; I mean, it's been a secret that what Christ brought to us as depicted in the gospels *was stolen.* This is like Prometheus. He paid for doing this with his life, but he is still alive, not discorporate (the Holy Spirit) but in a risen body, what I call the meta-soma; we can't see it but it is here like a great arborizing vine.

Usually when you think of a secret stolen you think of a "How to . . ." secret, not a "that" secret in the sense of, "It is a secret that . . .": i.e., suppressed information. "He stole the secret of how to . . . ," etc. How to what? How to be immortal; he said so. By participation in the vine:

I am the true vine,
and my Father is the vinedresser . . .
As a branch cannot bear fruit all by itself,
but must remain part of the vine,
neither can you unless you remain in me.
I am the vine,
you are the branches.[61]

J. Bible comment: "On the vine image, in the Synoptics, Jesus uses the vine as a symbol of the kingdom of God."

Whoever remains in me, with me in him,
bears fruit in plenty;
for cut off from me you can do nothing.

In my hypnopompic state, and that time under nitrous oxide, I saw
Christ and Valis as an arborizing, reticulating vine. He is literally a vine,
with a vast number of filaments stretching throughout this ecosphere; this
is the meta-soma that I saw. We become immortal by becoming part of it:
"You are the branches. . . ."

[. . .]

This vine is also the kingdom of God itself, which is to say, man restored back to the Palm Tree Garden, freed from the Black Iron Prison,
which is the Empire and occlusion and DNA programming.

What I saw that I called the plasmate are the filaments of the vine; they
are information, hence energy (or else information without a carrier).

"The secret stolen, in one's hands, through the angels." What secret do I
have or know?

[83:27] Consider page 380 of my notes:[62]

> How could I ask myself, What possibly could I know what (i.e., that)
> I'm not supposed to know? — When (1) I know about the occlusion;
> and (2) of Valis' presence here? I should ponder the fact that I came
> within inches of death twice after knowing about

And there the notes end, because at that moment the phonecall from Russ
came where I learned that Bantam doesn't feel it can publish *VALIS.* What
a place for the notes to end! What was I going to say, had I not been interrupted? "After knowing about ———," well, I guess I already said. (1) We are
all occluded in this ecosphere. And (2) there is a vast life form here, that
has invaded this world and is camouflaged, and it has grown vine-like into
our information media; it is an information life form . . . and the presump-
tion is, it occludes us.

[83:30] What we must do is welcome a *new savior,* now — hence the prophecies by the AI voice; this is why the "theological overkill": St. Sophia, Buddha, Siddhartha, The Head Apollo, YHWH, this is why it said, "The time
you've waited for has come. The work is completed. The final world is here.
He has been transplanted and is alive." The Third Age begins, and it is not
a Christian Age; it is a Post-Christian, but it is cumulative, just the way the
NT is built on the OT; but, just as between the OT and the NT there is a
real antithesis. What would be the basis of the Third Age? I don't think
love, even though the Roman Church attributes love to the Spirit. The first
age: Justice. Christ's age was what? Not even justice; certainly not love, and
very certainly not wisdom. The Roman Trinitarian division of attributes

breaks down; there wasn't wisdom connected with the Christian Age but the *suppression* of wisdom.

I have no idea. But the Spirit would know. [. . .]

What did Joachim predict?* The withering away of the clerical institutions, the formal churches, the Eucharist; total individualism, a direct inner relationship to God; hearing the voice of the Holy Spirit: My three divisions: First, God above man (the Father, Mosaic Age, the Torah). Then God with man as fellow man (the Son, the NT). Then God inside each man (the Spirit, an age not yet here; no churches, no sacraments, no priests; direct dialog between man and God inwardly, as with what Martin Buber talked about; inner information).

Autonomy. Inner-directed. Totally. Religious anarchists. Self-regulating because in inward direct touch with God.

I've thought of much of this before, but I never visualized the Third Age as pitted against Christianity just as Christ was pitted against Judaism and the Law.

Age One: Information (Torah) handed down to man.

Age Two: Information from a human being (Christ who spoke the new law).

Age Three: Information occurring inside you; you see it on an inner screen; that way there can be no signal loss, distortion, decay, etc. There is some loss in Age Two; more in Age One. With each age the gap between information source and the human transduction lessens; in Age Three it is gone.

The individual human of Age Three doesn't read scripture; he *writes* Scripture (produces it himself out of himself).

---

* Joachim of Fiore, a twelfth-century theologian, was the most influential apocalyptic thinker of the medieval period. He believed the world was on the verge of a golden age in which all men would be monks in direct communion with God. This third age would be governed by the Holy Spirit, replacing the earlier ages of the strict Father and the intermediary Son. Though Joachim himself does not seem to have considered himself a revolutionary — indeed, he only wrote his ideas down at the urging of the pope — his followers in later centuries were often sharply anticlerical, and some were antinomians and anarchists. It's easy to see how his idea of a procession of ages leading from subjugation to absolute freedom could have revolutionary applications. Though he does mention "religious anarchists," Dick here doesn't focus on rebellion so much as the flow of divine information and the source of religious authority: the third age means the loss of all intermediaries between the individual human being and God. — GM

He is the source of Scripture; proof: he can a priori retrieve parts of the Bible, which would seem impossible.

The NT will be retained, just as the OT was retained by the Christians.

The individual believer the source of Scripture. As if he's a transducer. No one else, even Christ, will transduce it for him (cf. Spinoza on Christ as the voice Elijah externally heard). [. . .]

This is what "the secret stolen" means: the revolutionary character of the Third Age contra Christianity. Spiritual knowledge has been "stolen" and given to us directly: "in one's hands"; that is, directly to us, without a church or priest or written scriptures acting as intermediaries. I've solved it.

[83:34] The Savior of the Third Age, unlike Jesus, will not be in human form; he will (as Jesus says) be everywhere, like "lightning."[63] Another human savior would replicate the Second Age. No—something different is meant. Everywhere. Ubique.

I suddenly have the eerie feeling that Christ is meant but a different kind of Christ from Jesus entirely. A meta-organism. [. . .]

Christ as secret ruler of the world available directly to the believer, without human mediation. And in the believer God as the Spirit; both Christ and the Spirit are equally God. God outside and God inside. An apotheosis of reality inner and outer.

The "He has been transplanted and is alive" and then seeing the Sacred Tetragrammaton is notification to me to go out and preach the good news—which I did in the form of VALIS Regained. That will be published, even if VALIS isn't.

[83:38] I have come across the expression in the EB "the imperial church," with prisons, with the secular authority to back it up. The accretions of dogma of the imperial church are as the Torah was to early Christianity: letter and not spirit, as Paul put it.[64] The Holy Spirit has been undermining this imperial church for centuries; it revealed this to me (vis-à-vis the Dutch Wars). So the Holy Spirit has a long history of revolutionary activity against the imperial church. But what I must keep in mind is my insight of yesterday that the key to it all is Joachim's three ages, and that the third is as revolutionary vis-à-vis the second as the second (the Christian Age) was to the first. New Scriptures are needed, new prophets and perhaps a new savior.

[83:39] "The time you've waited for has come. The final world is here. The work is completed. He has been transplanted and is alive." And the next

night when the AI voice (the Holy Spirit) repeated those words I saw the
sacred Tetragrammaton — and I at once wrote *VALIS Regained.*
[...]
Let's put the complete messages together:

THE TIME YOU'VE WAITED FOR HAS COME. THE WORK IS
COMPLETE. THE FINAL WORLD IS HERE. HE HAS BEEN TRANS-
PLANTED AND IS ALIVE. THE SECRET STOLEN, IN ONE'S
HANDS, THROUGH (past) THE ANGELS.

Now all the messages:

SAINT SOPHIA IS GOING TO BE BORN AGAIN: SHE WAS NOT
ACCEPTABLE BEFORE. THE BUDDHA IS IN THE PARK. THE
HEAD APOLLO'S ABOUT TO RETURN. THROUGH ALL THIS SID-
DHARTHA SLEPT (but now in part 2 will awaken). THE TIME
YOU'VE WAITED FOR HAS COME. THE WORK IS COMPLETE.
THE FINAL WORLD IS HERE. HE HAS BEEN TRANSPLANTED
AND IS ALIVE. YHWH. THE SECRET STOLEN, IN ONE'S HANDS,
THROUGH (past) THE ANGELS.

I break it down into sequence this way:

A NEW SAVIOR IS COMING. HE IS COMING SOON. HE IS HERE.
HE CARRIES A SECRET STOLEN FOR US, PREVIOUSLY DENIED
US. HE IS GOD (or equal to God) (or carries God's approval). (Or
was sent by God.) (Or has the authority and power of and from
God.)

[83:45] Valis is thoroughly involved in our flux world; can affect it and does
affect it. Valis — the macrometasoma — grows like a vast reticulated arborizing vine into our flux world. Which is to say, there is no real separation
between Valis' macrometasoma and this flux world of the dialectic. Our
world is, to be metaphoric, Valis' metabolism. Once Valis removes a constituent bit (piece) from our world and inserts it in the correct place in
its macrometasoma, it is there forever, although subject to the accretions
derived later on from the flux world; the flux world gives rise to fast and
many accretions of the phylogons (the basic integers of the metakosmos,
Valis' macrometasoma). The accretions act to further reticulation and arborizing, since this is basically a memory-structure in which the past is
preserved, but not preserved the way it happened; no: it is ordered, unified, structured, interrelated which is to say, reticulated and arborized, and

made ever more complex. So the complexity — level of internal organization — of the macrometasoma perpetually grows in ratio to our flux world;
it is like a life form whose internal structure grows more complex, more
evolved hierarchically, than its environment constantly.

The fundamental building block in the macrometasoma is information;
in a way every piece that is incorporated is treated as information, rather
than an object. A piece is not put in place according to shape or size but
according to meaning, or morphological import. This is because the substantia of the macrometasoma is pattern or structure per se: arrangement,
organization — which is to say, kosmos. I speak of *connectives of relatedness.* The relationship between everything actually occurs in the form of
connectives in the macrometasoma, but these connectives arise within our
flux world, and enter the macrometasoma as further accretions; so the development or evolution or complexification of the macrometasoma *is dependent on events in our flux world.* This is why I say our flux world is the
metabolism of the macrometasoma, its brain activity. Plato was right and
the Medieval realists were right; the categories really do exist and they are
permanent; but our world is not a reflection, a pale shadow, of them; it is
the *source* for the "Form world," to use Plato's term. If Plotinus had had my
3-74 experience he would have decided that he saw the Form world, and
the Form of Forms: God (or the Good); as the Christian Platonists taught,
the Forms — the Form world itself — exist in God's mind . . . I would agree.
I saw, however, how this Form world — which I call Valis and Valis' macrometasoma — draws *from* our world rather than casting it as its shadow.
This again shows how accurate *Ubik* was, and why 3-74 resembled *Ubik*.
Ubik is sort of Christian platonism, with the Forms existing in God's mind,
God being Ubik, of course; Platonist metaphysics redefined by Christian
monotheism.

[. . .]

I have reached really monumental conclusions about Valis; I have come
to Christian Platonism and am very close (if not congruent to) Plotinus'
Neoplatonism and the possibility, expressed by Plotinus, of experiencing
the Form world and the Mind of the One, Valis being the One; have I not
said that the essence of Valis is unity, that Valis above all is, through structure, unitary? This, then, is Plotinus' One or God. And unity is what I saw
that made me realize I had seen Valis (as I call it). I know how the One can
be the One; it is via Pythagoras' structure which is to say kosmos in the
sense that Pythagoras meant that term to be used: "The harmonious fitting-together of the beautiful." I am, then, identifying Plotinus' One with
Pythagoras' kosmos, with a hint of Sankara's doctrine about Brahman and

the Atman. I am saying, *This* reality, this plurality of things in flux, can be said to be the One which is eternal because on a meta-level there is Pythagoras' structure or kosmos, and although it changes it changes in only one direction: a cumulative evolving toward completeness and total complexity that embraces everything. The answer to, "How can the many become the One?" It is through Pythagoras' structure, which is to say kosmos; and it has a mind; it is a mind; it is alive; it thinks; as Xenophanes said, "The whole of him hears; the whole of him sees; the whole of him thinks; he is everywhere at once."

Now, it is also the case that Valis is not passively related to the world but "steers" everything (to use a Greek concept of the relationship between God and the world order). God is totally involved in the world order. (The Gnostics are absolutely wrong, as Plotinus realized.) Everything that happens in our flux world can be said to be the God "shaking" things (to use Xenophanes' term). So in a very real sense God feeds into this world as its motive force and then takes out what occurs for the metakosmos — the "Form world."

Quantum mechanics enters because I am regarding the world order as a single interacting field (as presented dramatically in *TMITHC*). The One can be regarded as the noös of this field; or a psyche-soma biological model can be envisioned. Or even the Logos — I have no idea which is correct, and neither does anyone else. There is a single interacting field and there is a mind ubiquitous in it, immanent in it — cf. *Ubik*. Spinoza would agree; in no way do I see God as transcendent to reality, off somewhere far above us in a heaven, with Earth down here. *Ubik* shows what I suppose: deity in the very trash of the alley. And deity intimately connected with and utilizing — if not actually being — information. "Ravished away and full of God," as the E. of Phil. article on Plotinus says. Ecstatic comingling.

[83:57] Strangest of all, the Upper Realm, the macrometasoma, seems to be this realm, this world of the dialectic, of flux, *seen another way* — as if the Gnostics are right: and to see it healed is to cause it to be healed. Could this be the observer-participant universe of quantum mechanics? "Reality is what you see it as," as the E. of S-F. quotes me. "Is what you perceive it to be"; i.e., your perception of it changes it. Well, this would make the Gnostics right! To see unity is to cause repair. (The ontological value of knowledge.) So I am saying: To see the secret partnership is to cause the secret partnership; you reconcile the dialectical strife in you (the two brain hemispheres?) and thereby cause it to be reconciled in world, which is to say, Ground of Being itself. *Since you yourself are a part of (spark) the Ground of Being*—that explains it. That is the only way that your perception of reconciliation could in itself as perception *cause* reconciliation. And the basis of your doing this is: anamnesis. You cease to forget that you are (part of) the Ground of Being.

[83:58] Ach Weh.[65] This structure that I speak of literally occurs in your act of perceiving it.

So Warrick was somewhat right about Valis.

My good god; this means that the override in 3-74 vis-à-vis the Xerox missive was a self-causing loop—neither efficient cause was at work (which has been obvious to me) but also not future or retrograde cause. It was self-generating (ultimate homeostasis). It caused itself. I'm not sure of my reasoning but I realize it's true; I set up a perturbation in the reality field by thinking about it, so to speak. *The information had no source* (the needed information that I lacked that came into existence); *it was self caused.*

[. . .]

We are talking about ex nihilo information; information that generates itself. No wonder it's so erratic.

[83:60] Then the "Acts" material in *Tears* was self-causing.

No one put it there.

No wonder I haven't been able to figure 3-74 out; every theory changes the events. I was right when I was on superdope; then I favored the theory that Diana, the queen of the fairies, helped me. Now I prefer (and find more workable) the theory that it was the Holy Spirit revealing to me the Cosmic Christ (Valis).

There's one thing I know it is: the Mysterium Coniunctionis.[66] In Boehme's terminology (or Eckhart; who cares) you have become the Father, not the Son; therefore you are the creator (again).

As impossible as it may seem, the "Acts" material in *Tears* was self-generating, a kind of tracing due to principles of physics that we simply do not understand, related to synchronicity. And as to the "cypher," *King Felix*—that, too, is a tracing, but this information is alive or semi-alive like a virus; Burroughs is right but he has only a bit of the whole picture . . . still, there is such a thing as living latent information that somehow is an acausal analog of reality.

[83:69] September 3, 1980

(Re Eliade) A mythological event unfolds in another kind of time (illo tempore,* etc.). Therefore if you can get (your self) into a mythological narrative you will enter this dream time (as opposed to entering dream time and, by means of that, entering the myth). The entrée to dream time is to reenact the (i.e., a) myth. I accidentally did this in 2-3-74 vis-à-vis "Acts" due to (1) *Tears;* and (2) the girl with the fish necklace. These plunged me into that other kind of time and so I saw world under that aspect, i.e., made eternal and holy—and experienced anamnesis. Also the Xerox missive somehow acted toward being a part of the mythic ritual. (The message opened and read? Perhaps some myth I don't know.)

So I got into mythic time by reenacting the sacred myth, and, having done so, saw world under that aspect (e.g., the blood of the cosmic Christ, Rome, the secret real Christians). I fell into the myth by chance, and entered the realm of the sacred.

[83:70] The Xerox missive is part of the Gnostic legend of the Pearl: the letter to the prince who has lost his memories (in an alien land) which restores those memories. This "legend" is actually a sacred myth/right. The letter coupled with the golden fish sign restored my memories due to my faithful participation in this complex sacred mythic rite of anamnesis and rebirth. No wonder I expected a letter to come; I knew it because on an unconscious level I knew the myth (collective unconscious). So all this took a Gnostic turn—the cryptic sign (golden fish), the letter reminding me of my mission (albeit a profane Pigspurt® one; the myth sanctified it, turned a profane thing into something noumenal).

The value—or one value—of this explanation is the "why me"? solution. God did not choose me for any reason, such as merit or need on my part. Chance played the determining role in selecting me: chance actions

---

* Latin for "in that time," that is, mythical or sacred time, as in the stock phrases "in the beginning" or "once upon a time." Mircea Eliade used the expression to refer to traditional religious attempts to escape or annul "profane time" (understood here as linear temporality or what we now call "history") and return to the "sacred time" referenced in myth and reenacted in religious ritual. Always capable of being "remembered" and so reactualized (hence Dick's constant invocation of *anamnesis*) within the narratives of myth and the actions of ritual (like the Eucharist), sacred time is essentially no-time or beyond time. We might say, then, that what Eliade imagined in his comparative theorizing Dick seems to have realized in his experience of Valis. But this may be much too simple, as Eliade once noted that his own dissertation researches and early experiments with yoga taught him "the reality of experiences that cause us to 'step out of time' and 'out of space'" (*Ordeal by Labyrinth: Conversations with Claude Henri-Rocquet,* 1982). In short, there was also an experiential subtext to Eliade's theorizing. He was not simply speculating. He was also confessing. And it was this experiential, essentially mystical subtext that I think Dick was intuiting, *illo tempore,* as it were, in his repeated embrace of Eliade. —JJK

on my part. Alone, without a priest or guide, I re-performed an ancient myth whose nature I still do not fully understand. Mainly it had to do with a letter which both informed me of something about myself (my actual nature and actual origins) and posed a grave problem that I had to solve. Had there been no letter there would have been no other universe, no altered, enhanced perceptions, no "second signal." Likewise for the golden fish sign. Likewise for the time of year.

Likewise, in fact, for my burning a votive candle at a holy shrine.

That this was indeed, then, an authentic religious experience I now cannot doubt. It was not precisely mystical, certainly not psychotic, certainly not a drug experience (although a component necessary for it to happen may have been the washing out from my system of the Mello Jell-O; I can't be sure[67]). I can look at it this way: God approached me through the medium of the sacred mythic rite reperformed; reperformance of that rite put me in touch with the Divine and in fact the Divine Realm. But it must never be forgotten that absolute faith amounting to knowledge, knowledge of the divine, was the essential first step; without it, re-performing the rite would have accomplished nothing.

[. . .]

What I say of this is: there is another universe, and through such reenactment of sacred ritual as I accidentally engaged in you can enter it and commune with the gods. This is recognized by, e.g., Eliade, but how many "civilized" people have experienced it? We have lost the techniques, the gnosis. Now what do I say about the novel *VALIS?* It is about this voyage on the axis of another kind of time . . . and what is this other kind of time like? I perceived the phylogons and the fact that nothing that is past truly ceases to be, but, rather, is added to progressively; accretional layers are laid down, becoming ever more reticulated and arborized. This is the main discovery, this permanence of past and present reality — hence all reality. Flux only adds; it does not take away.

① Or was it? In any case its mundane nature is not so important as its mythic role. And that fired correctly — a series of coincidences and accidents: *Tears,* the pentothal, the girl, the fish sign, the Xerox letter which very much seemed to call to me from the archaic past and to deal with my real identity. And since it was noumenal it sparked a divine or spiritual — pneumatic — identity in me.

[83:76] The space-time world of this sacred time is found in the Bible as the book of "Acts." Thus when I wrote *Tears* I discerned this stratum, showing through in a ghostly fashion, as the basis of reality. "Acts" describes the power of Rome as expressed in the Procurator Felix. He interrogates his prisoner Paul; Paul is under arrest and in the hands of the Roman authorities.[68] He will eventually be released. This is the supratemporal template: the power and presence of Rome; the Procurator; the prisoner who is interrogated and finally released. The Empire would like to destroy him but in the final phases of the encounter between them fails. Thus the life of the prisoner ends not in martyrdom but in freedom, in release. This is in a sense an opposite story from that of the crucifixion where the prisoner is condemned to death and dies. Here the prisoner is set free and this means that sacred time has moved forward from the time of the Gospels to a different time. The prisoner slides through the fingers of the Empire. This story is found in the life of John Taverner, the 15th century English musician who was arrested on suspicion of possessing heretical books but then released "because he is not a musician," as Cardinal Woolsey put it: the Empire has lost the ability to state its case; it cannot close the trap. The later history of this archetype will be that the Empire will lose even more power; eventually it will not even be able to arrest its victim, let alone crucify him. That time has not yet come.

At this point the Empire, expressing itself through its police system, is puzzled by its victim; it suspects him of wrongdoing but does not know what that wrongdoing is. The Empire does not know enough; its information is too limited. So for it the victim is an enigma. (The evolution from Pilate's bewilderment in confronting Jesus can be seen; bewilderment was there already.) The Procurator Felix interrogates the suspect but cannot determine from what he says what precisely he has done. Time passes. The Empire tries again and again to get information, but fails. This is Kafka's *The Castle* in reverse. In talking to the suspect, the prisoner, the Procurator begins to suspect that the prisoner himself does not know what he has done; he himself does not know if he is guilty, and if guilty, of what. The prisoner cannot tell the Procurator what he would like to know, even if the prisoner is willing to. This increases the puzzle. Perhaps the enemy of the Empire is so large and so vague that the prisoner is not the adversary at all, but only a sort of front for it, an extension of it. This, for the Procurator, is a dreadful thought.

The archetype of this is Euripides' *The Bacchae*, in which the King of Tears arrests the Stranger only to find that he has a priest of the god Dionysus in his prison; the priest as the god bursts the prison and drives the King into insanity such as to cause him to lose his identity even as a man. The King — or the Procurator — can release the prisoner but he himself will suffer great harm; instead of Christ crucified Pilate suffers unbearable loss. Time, which starts with the Gospels, has moved forward to what is almost a complete reversal of the image. The arrested and tried god does not die; the interrogator suffers spiritual death or physical injury, the prisoner goes free. Everything that the prisoner lost is restored to him. This is referred to in the Bible as the end-times day on which everything is restored. It is a sign of the Parousia. The Empire is not glad to know this because it means that God himself is taking the field; God is entering the battle.

[. . .]

And yet there is a further level of reality disclosed by sacred time and the realm governed within that time. A kosmos, in the sense that Pythagoras spoke of it, is being completed, self completed, from the flux process visible in mundane time. This is the noumenal world that Plato and Parmenides spoke of as being in contrast to the sensible (empirical) world; the person lifted into sacred time perceives a priori this edifice that is alive and growing, this cosmic organism that is Christ himself as the head and Lord of creation. Christ as Kosmos — this is the final mystery. [. . .]

Thus the person who correctly performs the mythic rite — and does so with absolute faith — encounters the God whom he worships as world rather than anthropomorphic figure. In the final vision, Christianity becomes indistinguishable from Brahmanism, because in this encounter with the cosmic Christ the worshiper is himself a Christos, a microform of the risen Lord.

And then finally, above even this, which eventually will be presented to God, is the *semplice lume* that Dante speaks of:

One simple flame.

God is the book of the universe, whose pages are scattered throughout. The sacred history itself forms a narrative that can be discerned, but it is obscured by the normal flux. Everything is written down and has been written down from the beginning, as the Jews knew from the disclosure of the Torah. Basically, sacred history exists as information; first in terms of temporal sequence; first in order of ontology. *The mythic ritual is an entry key into the sacred narrative.* It functions the way an entry key of a computer functions vis-à-vis a given program.

This narrative can be entered from any point in mundane time by the correct entry key which in itself tells a story or a part of a story — part of the master narrative (which, as I say, is information out of which reality is generated). What interests me is the apparent fact that there are a number of sacred narratives, not one, so that different entry keys — which is to say different mythic rites — punch you into different narratives, which is to say different meta-realities. For example, Christianity is only one "narrative" of many; the war between the Empire and its prisoner (who in early chapters is crucified but later on is released unharmed) — this is not *the* sacred narrative but *a* sacred narrative. Christianity then as a sacred history is not the truth but a truth, which can be avoided or punched into, either by design or by accident (I punched into it by accident).

[. . .]

Now, here on page 12 of this paper, I come across *another* and never before suspected computer aspect of Valis: that it contains a number of "sacred histories," which is to say "sacred narratives," not just one; and different mythic rites reperformed keypunch you into entry into particular narratives among the plural narratives; and I called these "programs." Which as I put it means that Christianity is not *the* truth but only one "sacred narrative," which is to say one sacred history of the plural number. But how can there be plural histories of the world? How can Valis contain more than one sacred book (to use Dante's term)?

I punched into Christianity because of the particular mythic rite I reenacted; had I reenacted another mythic rite I would have punched into another "sacred narrative," which is to say program. This thing is an information processing computer or computer like entity. [. . .] What I have in *Tears* is not the truth but just a narrative; but it is a Torah like narrative: it is not the book of the universe/world but *a* book. It is one out of many. This is extraordinary. I had (last night) solved 3-74; I thought so today. Now I'm back to square one or anyhow square two. It's a good thing I've been keeping notes.

[. . .]

So we have *the* key to history turning into *a* key to history. But how can there be several alternate keys to history unless these are computer programs being run simultaneously? If you have one sacred history you have revelation, but if you have several you have a mystifying discovery which is one puzzle solved but a greater one disclosed.

[83:91] What we see today as a war between progressive communism and reactionary capitalist imperialism is an ontogenic face with a longer-term conflict between those dedicated to freedom and the Empire. (At a former time the progressive force was the middle-class, the bourgeois, versus the aristocracy, and so forth back into pre-Christian times . . . another example being the conflict between the Protestant forces and the Catholic league during the 30 years war. And, before that, between Christianity and the Roman Empire; before that, between Greece and Persia; before that, between the Hebrews and Egypt.) If Valis is regarded as the Hegelian geist of history, then it is always on the side of the forces of freedom, since as Hegel says, history is a gradual unfolding of greater and greater stages of human freedom, achieved by dialectical interaction. This was recognized by Marx and Engels and applied practically in terms of dialectical materialism.

This is essentially exemplar history; the Jews view history this way, seeing YHWH's bringing the Jewish people out of their Egyptian captivity as a timeless, in fact eternal event, always happening. However, the situation is now different; the enslaved people cannot be rescued by departing the Empire because the Empire is worldwide; instead, they must overthrow the Empire. This is precisely what the "Acts" archetype reveals: not an exodus of the enslaved but an infiltration into the apparatus of the Empire by the enslaved by which their emancipation is achieved.

[83:93] *VALIS* deals with the internal partisan activity; *VALIS Regained* deals with the invasion from outside. The latter occurs when the internal partisans have been sufficiently successful.

[83:95] For decades I have sought to see "the permanent world of unchange behind the flux," and when I finally saw it it turned out to be a historical exemplar *situation*, a dramatic one; in fact a *narrative* that could be *expressed as a story*. (And I myself had done so!) So I am saying something quite remarkable and unusual: the world (identified by Schopenhauer with Brahman) turns out to be a dramatic story that can be rendered in words — although I saw it as reality, as reified, as substantia. Yes; this is what substantia turns out to be, for me: not "Deus sive natura sive substantia" but "ultimate substance turns out to be a dramatic story that shows up in print as a tracing, the underlying reality being a series of *events*."

[83:122] What the AI voice said exactly was:
"The secret stolen in one's hands through⊕ the angels."

I think that it was YHWH who addressed me, whom I have been calling Valis. He has reentered the world as a rebel against the entire system of rule that he originally ordained. This secret return — and rebellion — would explain such an extraordinary matter as the theophany I experienced.

This is why I dreamed of Elijah and Mount Carmel and Elisha and "Elias." And YHWH is the AI voice I hear, the voice of Ho On . . . the little clay pot.

If this is so — well, anyhow I was on the right track in *VALIS Regained*. But: to suppose, just suppose, that Valis is YHWH! To imagine it even for a moment . . . it was what I wanted so badly when I was a kid first reading the Bible. This is Sila,[69] the soul of the universe, speaking in a woman's voice "that would not frighten even a child," as the Nome shaman put it.

YHWH: the low, murmuring voice.

He calls us to rebellion into freedom, the little clay pot who fashioned the universe.

① "Through" meaning "past." Gotten *past* the angels.

[83:127] September 10, 1980

I have to realize that the revelation about the reality of the Prison is a genuine revelation; it exists down through the ages and it exists now. I saw it: Prison and Empire, the tunnel of history. When I say "revelation" I mean divine disclosure of the nature of history . . . and that I had correctly depicted this archetype in *Tears,* that *Tears* was true; a timeless condition of man's servitude to the Empire, man enslaved; and the rest of the revelation was of the genuine secret underground Christians fighting it. How easily I forgot this revelation and sought for obscure meanings! [. . .]

3-74 can't be understood except in terms of the narrative told in *Tears;* this narration is the real purpose of it all (but I was so surprised by 3-74 that I forget that). But as a writer I should realize: It is what is written that matters; that is the goal. First I told the story (in *Tears*) and then an example of what I told (freedom) took place in regard to me. So I experienced the very release that I had written about. Thus my extrication is a dazzling example of the power of God to rescue, and I can then apply it to the general narrative, to history, and see how it is done and that it is done. The name of all this (3-74) is *information.* [. . .]

Could the "Acts" material in *Tears* decode to mean: where the Prison is, He is there, too? I think so. I think that is it — and this is also true — very true — of the two-word cypher. I wrote the Prison narrative, and God put in the Christian narrative. Together these two parts form the complete story. (My story by itself is only half the story; the rest — the good part — I didn't know.) The story is not just "There is a prison" but "and it is under attack by the Christians, by Christ Himself." This is quite different.

As to the question, "Who is the information for?" I will probably never know; perhaps information is information and exists for its own sake.

[83:130] September 13, 1980

Huizinga, *The Waning of the Middle Ages:*

> The imagination was continually striving, and in vain, to express the ineffable by giving it shape and figure. To call up the absolute, recourse is always had to the terminology of extension in space . . . (page 220).

But still the contemplation of the absolute Being ever remains linked up with notions of extension or of light (note, page 221).

The mystic imagination found a very impressive concept in adding to the image of the desert, that is to say, extension of surface — that of the abyss, or extension in depth. The sensation of giddiness is added to the feeling of infinite space . . . (page 222).

In my six and a half years of working on my exegesis I have often said, "1 have found it." I don't want to do that one more time, one in an endless series of failure. It seems almost as if the mere saying of it causes it to permutate to some other explanation. But I do think that the night I was talking on the phone to KW and realized that in 3-74 I experienced Medieval vertical — which is to say Gothic — space, and this meant that I had ontologized reality in terms of Medieval use of space, time and causality, and hence Valis was God or Christ (it is the same); I think then I had it: that the vast volume of vertical space that I experienced in 3-74 (as well as the transformations in time as if I were seeing down a time axis extending thousands of years) meant that I had abreacted to a Medieval worldview, and within that view a theophany was logical, i.e., possible.

Theophany and miracle and pronoia in the modern worldview, the way we organize space, time and causation now would make no sense; so God provided a meaningful context in which these could logically occur.

[. . .]

But I ramble. All I want to say is that Valis was God, that 3-74 was theophany, miracle and pronoia, and pronoia based on an intelligent analysis of me and my situation, not whim and not (on the other hand) something rigidly determined, which is to say something reflexive and mechanical. My sinister destiny was abolished; tampered with, so to speak, in the sense that the Greco-Roman mystery religions taught. It was a supreme adjudication of my case, and the books were, as the EB says, closed.

I am tired. I've labored for over six and a half years to fathom 3-74, to figure out if it was (as I suspected) a theophany and example of pronoia or if it just seemed so because it had the pragmatic effect of these. I am now satisfied that all three did in fact take place. I have been relentlessly skeptical and relentlessly imaginative and I have done enormous research and tried out as many possible theories as I could come up with.

The desert and abyss finally won my assent, as if by weariness. The negative way to God, perhaps.

[83:136] Fascinating, the view that the dialectical struggle of the two historical constants — the Empire and the Christians — gives rise to Valis the

Cosmic Christ, who builds his body out of the "stockpile of parts" created by the antithetical struggle. The Empire, of course, has no idea that
the very struggle itself gives rise to the Cosmic Christ, so-to-speak feeds
him, feeds him ever newer parts for his macrosoma. (Presumably the secret authentic Christians do know this; they don't need to win to win, so to
speak.) (All they need do is keep the historical struggle going.)

[83:138] But I banalize my conclusions by these obsessive notes, and I must
give them up; I realized this from reading the 9-2-80 pages. My mind wor-
ries and scurries, contradicts itself, comes to conclusions and then arbitrarily drops them; the exegesis does not build. There is no accumulative
factor.

Nonetheless (without repeating the arguments; I always repeat my arguments, stating them again and again in exactly the same words, like a
stuck LP) I will say: I found myself in 2-3-74 involved with theophany, miracle, pronoia *and* enthusiasmos by the Second Comforter. Now, I will certainly natter on past this point, worry and ponder and obsessively write for
years to come; but this is a kind of tribute on my part to the importance of
what I underwent, what I saw, what I learned; it is a way of preserving the
memory of it all, this endless rehashing: that is the real point, to keep the
memory — which is so cherished — alive. After all, it has been over six and
a half years, now! And I don't want to forget. Valis was the Christian God,
whether YHWH or Christ; and inside me "Thomas" was the paraclete, and
I have really always known this but was reticent to say so and hesitant to
believe. Weariness has brought me to the point where I can say, I have followed all the lines of argument and this is where they lead; they lead to
where I knew, at the time it happened, I was. But this is what an exegesis
of a mystical experience is for, to develop it rationally, so that it can be expressed in words. Words fail in the end, though. But the attempt must be
made.

Because the basis of reality is a verbal (written) narrative, the Empire
suppresses information and the Christians generate it. Valis is, after all (as
I saw) primarily an information-processing entity (though he be Christ).
A recent development in the Empire's strategy is the invention of disinformation, which is far worse than noninformation (the mere lack or suppression of information); this is a Pigspurt invention, and very effective. A
handy rule-of-thumb would be, You can tell which side is which by observing whether they're generating information or whether they're suppressing it or sending out disinformation; no formal adherence to Christianity is
necessary. (I've worked all my life with no formal ties to it.)

Valis and information — and the generation of information — can't be

separated. The Empire and the suppression of information can't be separated. So the dialectic is information versus non- or anti-information, out
of which Valis, the Cosmic Christ, step by step comes into being, generated by the antitheses. The Cosmic Christ exists now but is incomplete.
The Empire, which by suppressing information is therefore in a sense the
anti-Christ, is put to work as half of the dialectic; Christ uses everything
(as was revealed to me): in its very act of suppressing information, the Empire aids in the building of the soma of the Cosmic Christ (which the Empire does not realize). Since the basis of reality is a sacred narrative — information — the generation of new information is an act in the Ground of
Being, in the ontology of the sacred itself.

Reality is based on information, on a sacred narrative; and Valis generates information. Valis is ipso facto the generator of reality, as are the genuine Christians, those who generate new information, for whatever reason.
The sacred narrative on which reality is based ("Acts") can be seen as latent
in new information generated by selfunaware Christians; the sacred narrative "Acts" being the Ground of Being replicates itself in the microforms of
newly generated information. This is what William Burroughs discovered
(but interprets differently).

To locate the spontaneous generation of the sacred narrative — "Acts" —
in newly-generated information is to stumble on the truth of what constitutes the Ground of Being . . . and to plunge into the Christian illo tempore, where Christ is real.

[83:150] Premise: Valis is a meta-system that at our level does not exist
at all because at our level only its plural constituents exist as such. Valis
is an organization, a structuring, of these constituents, in which they are
unified into one entity. Meanwhile the plural constituents at our level behave — or seem to behave — as if unrelated to one another. An entirely new
and higher way of organizing the ontological categories by which perception is structured must be reached by the observer. Thus in a sense Valis
does not exist, but is brought into existence parallel with the percipient's
awareness of it, this having to do with the participant-observer of quantum
mechanics. The percipient must participate in being Valis to be aware of
Valis. However, Valis is real and is subsuming progressively more and more
of its environment. Its internal complexity continually grows. Its metabolism seems to be information and the processing of information. Its plural
constituents are arranged in such a way as to constitute a language or information or messages; if you cannot see the arrangement you cannot read
the message. And you cannot perceive Valis.

So in a sense perceiving Valis is reading the message that Valis has arranged constituents into. Not necessarily understanding the message but recognizing it as a message.

Valis is both there and not there. When it is not perceived it is not there (as opposed to: when it is not there it is not perceived). It is a way of perceiving reality — which demands a percipient — but when perceived it has definite and intricate characteristics; it is not vague. It consists of structure but a percipient is necessary for that structure to come into being. But the structure is not in the percipient's mind imposed or projected onto reality. Valis did not exist until it was perceived; therefore to experience it is to effect a repair in the Ground of Being (Valis being considered as the Ground of Being). One highly important element about Valis is that it is eternal, although it changes; it can be added to, become more complex, arborizing and reticulated, but once a constituent is incorporated into it that constituent can never cease to be. Thus Valis lies outside the flux of the world we see. However, Valis' world is this world differently perceived, not another world; but it is a quantum leap upward in hierarchy, in which plural constituents become a unity by reason of integrating structure. That structure is added — supplied — by the percipient.[1]

Valis and the perception of Valis occur simultaneously, and neither can be separated from the other, ever, at any time.

Valis is everywhere — that is, it can be perceived everywhere. It is not in a meta-reality but is a meta-system made entirely from this reality.

[1] By perceiving Valis he participates in the sudden total transformation from plural unrelated constituents to a unitary structure. It is as if Valis feeds off the percipient's perception of structure using perception of structure *as* structure. But this is an acausal relationship, a kind of parallelism; it is ex nihilo. Valis came out of nothing. Reality did not evolve into Valis. It became Valis when perceived as Valis. There are no antithetical forces in Valis; the dialectic does not exist when Valis does. But when Valis ceases to exist, there again is the dialectic. Valis uses the dialectic to come into greater being, to grow, assimilate its environment, incorporate new pieces, make itself more inclusive and complex: more Valisish. Valis could be compared to the point at which a liquid becomes saturated or when water freezes, except that perception of this is necessary for it to occur. What if I were to say, ice is water seen a certain way? There you have an analogy.

Even more strange, Valis induces a potential percipient to perceive it and thus cause it (Valis) to occur . . . thus it can be said that during its nonexistence Valis is able to cause its own existence. At the time that it laid down steps to bring itself into existence it did not yet exist. Thus it treats time differently than we do; it is not passive in relation to time. When it thus brings itself into existence it is already an extensive system. Hence one can say, Valis comes and goes but is always in a sense present. The percipient sees Valis because Valis causes the percipient to see it, but Valis did not come into existence until the percipient saw it. Thus the effects of Valis are felt before Valis exists, and these effects are to be regarded as acausal; they have no cause because their cause does not yet exist. It will exist later; then, retroactively, these effects will have had a cause. What is represented here is total homeostasis: an entity that is entirely self-generating, on which nothing acts but its own internal volition. Therefore in a sense it can be said that Valis is (or becomes) anything that acts to cause it to come into existence, which is to say, by perceiving it. This involves laws of physics about which we know nothing, I would think. What certainly is involved, indubitably, is not a more complex entity than we normally know of or have ever heard of, but an entity operating under laws different from the laws we are aware of, including ontological categories of perception organized in ways we have never heard of. Greater complexity is not the key to Valis; utilizing of more complex physics is the key to Valis. In a certain real sense Valis is very simple; it is a unit. You could think of it as a protozoon, a single cell at a higher level of reality, where the laws of space, time and causation are different; and it makes use of that difference. We humans are very complex forms that matter takes at this ontological level of reality, or, if you will, at this level of physics; Valis is a very simple organization at the next level up. The billions of constituents of our level form a single cell at its level; these constituents are subsumed and yet at the same time at this level of reality they go about their business as usual. So in a sense Valis has no effect on this world. But in another sense it has complete control of this world. Both statements are equally true, depending on whether you can see Valis or not.

This especially applies to the patterns that Valis is or creates in our world in which broad sequences of events add up to a coherency. It can be said: There is coherence; there is not coherence. Coherence and Valis are the same. Since Valis in a very literal way is our world, its internal structure is a latent (concealed) coherence of our world. (All the constituents of Valis are elements of our world; it — Valis — has nothing else to draw on and it needs nothing else to draw on.) Thus it is possible when viewing Valis to view Valis as our world and our world as Valis.

One can say of Valis, then, that Valis is a way our world can be seen to be. Its structure is the structure of our world. Developments in Valis are developments in our world. Volition in Valis is volition in and of our world.

There is no difference between Valis and our world except that Valis is a certain way of seeing our world in terms of it being a kind of single unit all parts of which are interconnected purposefully and everything is coherent. (In other words it is precisely what Pythagoras called *kosmos:* the orderly fitting-together of the beautiful.) Viewed this way it operates from internal necessity without the need of any sort of adventitious deity. It is not world to God — creation to Creator — but having its own logic and making its own choices. It chooses continually after examining all the possible choices arranged as information into a sort of narrative made out of language. Nothing created it; it brought itself into being ex nihilo by willing the perception of it — of necessity from within itself, which is a *self-awareness.* Thus the percipient of Valis and Valis are part of one field.

The flux world is real because the dialectic is real, and it is the mechanism by which Valis advances up the ladder of its own evolution — Valis, then, is not static. It is permanent but this is a dynamic permanence. Equilibrium must always exist in Valis; the antithetical forces of the dialectic are in a secret partnership in and as Valis. This is why Valis' main device in dealing with the flux world — in order to use it to generate new bits for Valis — is enantiodromia, the conversion or backward turning of something when it reaches an extreme into its opposite. It is by this and this mainly if not alone that Valis evolves.

Possibly we would see Valis as a flicker of on-off, on-off, on-off, a flip-flop back and forth in its ceaseless dialectic that is in it but beneath it or rather enclosed within the palintropos harmonie of Valis; Valis as our world is this flip-flop; Valis as a coherence is palintropos harmonie. All this is very much what Heraclitus taught and he would probably have called Valis *Logos.*

[83:157] Well, frankly it would seem that I had a somewhat Platonized version of Taoist ecstatic experience with the Absolute. I had some experience with the Christian Absolute (the Godhead), some with the Platonist and Neoplatonist (the One), with Brahman . . . but my inquiry has certainly just now — surprisingly — led me toward Taoism, my old, old stomping-ground. In Taoism we have the flux; we have the constants in the flux; we have the dialectic — and between two sides very similar if not identical to Yang and Yin, or to Parmenides' Forms I and II — and most of all, there is Valis which I see fits the description of the Chiang Tao:

An unchanging unity (the permanent Tao) was seen as underlying the kaleidoscopic plurality . . . ineffable reality, experienced in ecstasy, that lies at the origin of the universe and behind or within appearances.[70]

[...]

What is really pointed to is: the Absolute is non-sectarian; it is Christian and Brahmanist and Platonist and Taoist all at once. If it really is the Absolute, this should be expected.

October–November 1980

[1:1]

3/20/74–
12/2/80
THE DIALECTIC:
God against Satan, and God's final victory foretold and shown
Philip K. Dick
An Exegesis
Apologia pro mea vita

[1:2] Or is it possible that 2-74 consisted of a quantum leap in *abstracting* from accident to essence *on my part,* a perception/awareness of einai underlying accidents as follows:

"Superimposition" of the 2 continua, a scanning by me of two spatio-temporal templates and a perception/awareness of *essence identity.* [. . .] I grasped (the category of) essence and it is real; more, this is how reality is in fact arranged. I could grasp the category of essence and see that A and B were on the essence level one-and-the-same, but I could not then extrapolate to the essence (form) realm *in general,* i.e., the next implication was lost to me; I failed to draw the *next* conclusion. [. . .] However, having made this quantum leap in mentation/perception-of-reality, I could not halt the *involuntary* chain of mental hypotheses triggered off in my brain, which

---

* This folder is over three hundred pages long and combines handwritten notes, beginning with number 498, and typed, dated pieces. Dick grouped these into sections marked I through XVIII, a Roman numbering system that continues for several more folders. Because of the complexities introduced, we have opted to use sheet numbers beginning with 1. This folder begins with a conceptual breakthrough about "meta abstraction" and peaks with a theophany on November 17, 1980, which appears at [1:262] below. At the close of that extensive entry, Dick writes the resounding word "END"—which is immediately followed up with a footnote and more discourse. At some point after this theophany, Dick also composed the title page that begins this folder, whose original is unfortunately missing.—PJ

(i.e., my brain) had discovered that an ultra way of world-perception/experience/Dasein was possible—and more accurate—and so neural circuits fired and I proceeded to progressively further and further abstract—think/see in categories of less spatiotemporality and more and more conceptual arrangement—the Christian element was only a trigger/clue; this did not have to do with Christianity per se but with the abstracting of essentials at the expense of accidents hence of spatiotemporal arrangement; as a result I ascended through the realms of Neoplatonism—which makes Valis Plotinus's *One.**

[1:9]

[1:17] "If you press world hard enough it yields up God"—paraphrase of page 485. "I define God as world under the threat of death . . . God forced into the open, and put to work in the service of evading death."

[1:19] *No* time has passed, and, moreover, all change since "Acts" has to do only with accidents not substance. Reticulation and arborizing in a memory system; the real world, having been destroyed, exists only in God's memory, and this world remembered is "Acts," and all changes since have been mere reticulating and arborizing as elaborations of a freeze frame.†

---

* This "involuntary chain of mental events" is crucial because it captures the way in which Valis is simultaneously something that Dick experienced in the freedom of his own consciousness and something that seemed to happen *to* him. And what happened to him, here at least, was One thing. Plotinus's "One" is consonant with that other philosopher of the Perennial Philosophy, Sankara, who referred to reality as "one without a second." In other words, despite appearances, everything we perceive in the world, including ourselves, has the attribute of unity. This is both a message—"Monistic Newsflash: Tomatoes, Tomahtoes, It's All One!"—and a feeling: the self becomes an attribute of something immeasurably larger than itself. This insight is at once immensely obvious and notoriously ineffable: one either perceives the unity of all things or not, and Dick very much has. The experiences of "aha" that pepper the Exegesis are moments of immense creativity as well as insights into the inner realms.—RD

† The terms *reticulation* and *arborizing* explain the meshed and often baroque nature of reality, which is, pace the Talking Heads' David Byrne, the "same as it ever was." Apparently destroyed by its transformation into "bits" of information, the collective remains whole as "God's memory," another level of abstract topology that integrates the apparently chaotic multiplicity of the world through an infolding, outfolding, and branching of reality that resembles physicist David Bohm's notion of the "implicate order" out of which all

Hence time is not real and space is not real. The real world is morphologically arranged, and that world is "Acts" as dynamic, but in *essence* changeless — exploded through the simulated space and time we experience.

[1:23] The secret is to view something *"from the other side" and not as it is* — overtly. Heraclitus' "latent form" — crypte morphosis where the concealed truth and hence the kingdom lies — Zen realizes this. Paradox.

[1:24] Premise: things are inside out (but will at the "Apocalypse" assume their real shape). Therefore the right place to look for the Almighty is, e.g., in the trash in the alley. And for Satan: in vast cathedrals, etc. Through enantiodromia they will "on that day" assume their rightful shapes — the great reversal. The Jester in the tarot deck is the real King; the King card is the deranged one, the witless one. *Ubik* in its commercials and final theophany shows this reversal process. USA 1974 is really Rome c. 45 C.E. Christ is really here; so is the kingdom. I found my way into it once. The long path is the short path — ponderous books of philosophy won't help me; Burroughs' *Junky* will. That "thieves and murderers" 17th century poem of Herbert's will. Stone rejected by the builder; the edifice is discarded; the true edifice is invisible — disguised as rubble (plural constituents). That fly grooming himself — they (the divine powers) have to *reveal* the kingdom to you; you can never on your own pin it down. So to search at all is to miss the point. Tricks, paradox, illusion, magic, enantiodromia. The apparently harmless Xerox missive was my death warrant. The AI voice says the secret stolen has been successfully smuggled to me; I have it. But what is it? My worst book, *Deus Irae*, is my best. God talked to me through a Beatles tune ("Strawberry Fields"). ("Nothing is real. Going through life with eyes closed.") A random assortment of trash blown by the wind, and there is God. Bits and pieces swept together to form a unity.

[1:25] "God does not work through the is." God works through what Lao Tzu calls the weak, the empty; this is the same God.

[1:29] Christianity is like a given drama on TV; what I've been trying to figure out for 6½ years is not what this one drama of many is about, but how the TV set works that brings *this* drama and all the others (there are many,

---

of reality emerges. Focusing our attention on this reticulation, as Dick does, affects reality itself via the noösphere: "As regards my writing: it will permanently affect the macrometasomakosmos in the form of reticulation and arborizing — and hence will survive in reality forever, in the underlying structure of the world order." — RD

as Eliade makes clear). So: Christianity, when you think about it, could not be the answer. It is *a* content within the system, not the system.

[1:46] October 19, 1980

You look at one spatiotemporal continuum and another spatiotemporal continuum and you see that they are one. They do not merely resemble each other nor are they just tangent. They are the same thing in terms of some underlying essence. The quantum leap in brain-function is when you go from thinking, "These two spatiotemporal continua resemble each other" to "They are one and the same, expressed at two places and two times." And you can only do this if you have experienced anamnesis, because if you have not recollected (recovered) you can go no further than seeing that the two continua resemble each other; you cannot make the leap — which is up out of the spatiotemporal universe. Because within our spatiotemporal universe *it is impossible* that USA 1974 and Rome A.D. 45 could be one and the same . . . how could they be? They are at two times and two places. The only way they could be one and the same would be if time and space were somehow not real; or, put another way, if something about the two continua *themselves* were not real. That is, if Rome was not Rome; USA was not USA; but both were a third thing, the same thing.

This is why I call it a meta-abstraction. USA 1974 and Rome A.D. 45 are two ways of looking at the same thing: two aspects of the same thing. And the only way you are ever going to realize this is if you literally actually see the two of them superimposed, comingled; and this will only happen if you experience anamnesis; and you will only experience this anamnesis if something stimulates — releases, actually — your blocked memory. [. . .]

I am saying, "One plus one equals two," to people who are saying, "One apple plus one apple equals two apples. One table plus one table equals two tables." It's not their fault. I'm sorry but the difference between my meta-abstraction as a brain function and their abstracting, their brain function is that great. I'm lucky. Because of the sodium pentothal and the Christian fish sign my blocked memory of my prenatal life was disinhibited. After making the initial leap in meta-abstracting my brain drew conclusion after conclusion, day after day; and I saw world more and more in terms of conceptual or morphological arrangement and less and less in terms of the spatiotemporal; I continued to abstract reality more and more, based on the hierarchy of realms (each higher one possessing more unity and ontology than the lower) that Plotinus describes.

In a way I feel really bitter: because I can't tell anyone or convince anyone of what I saw. I'm afraid Valis won't convince anyone. I feel like joining them and saying, "When I played my recording of the Mahler eighth last night the performance was a lot better than when I played that recording last week." They'd think I was a lunatic. That's how I feel about them, in a way.

[1:49] October 20, 1980

I finally see the source of my confusion, which I will herewith straighten out and then (God willing) let it rest. The structure or mechanism of 2-3-74 was Platonist Neoplatonist anamnesis, precisely as Plato describes it (see earlier notes); it has to do with prenatal memories recovered and a Form realm that is not spatiotemporal but is morphologically arranged. However, the *content* of the anamnesis is, contrarily, Christian; more, the Form (eidos) involved is a Christian one: the secret revolutionary early Christians against Rome . . . and, because this is the nature of the Platonic archetype, recurring again and again throughout linear time and space. So in a sense two mutually contradictory religious systems seem to be proved by 2-3-74: Christianity and Neoplatonism. My *identity* in terms of the Form world is Christian; my *knowledge* of that identity comes to me via the structure of the Neoplatonism world-order. This is what has caused all the confusion. For example, the reincarnation involved is Neoplatonist and can only be understood in terms of myself as a Form with each incarnation as an instance of that Form in the spatiotemporal flux world; it is me against the Black Iron Prison again and again, wherein I am a secret Christian and the Black Iron Prison is, so to speak, Rome, at different times and different places.

There is no room in Christianity for reincarnation and no hierarchy of realms such as Plotinus describes and no anamnesis and meta-abstracting such as Plato describes. However, there is no mention or indication in Platonism, Neoplatonism or Pythagoras of a secret revolutionary Christian movement pitted against the Empire. As long as I pursued the Christian element I got nowhere in figuring out what happened in 2-3-74 and how it happened. I had been swamped by apostolic Christian material in terms of my identity, role and knowledge, but none of this explained what happened and how, unless I was willing to settle for "a miracle performed by the grace of God, by divine providence," which I was not willing to settle for. So if I am interested in reconstructing apostolic — i.e., genuine — Christianity and my identity in its struggle against Rome, then I should go toward that; but much more: I want to know what happened and how, and I now know that. Interestingly, the system that is proved to be correct is Platonism and Neoplatonism (e.g., reincarnation, the Form world); whereas Christianity is shown only to be my identity-role, my commitment.

Therefore I must affirm Christianity — the authentic apostolic form — as my orientation, in fact my historic role, but it remains a matter of faith and personal identity; whether it is veridical I can't say. Philosophically and metaphysically, Platonism and Neoplatonism in its basic elements is verified; were it not true my experience of 2-3-74 could not have occurred. I might have discovered other Forms than the Black Iron Prison: what I call "other narratives." However, this is the one which defines me: opposition against the central tyranny, expressed over and over again.

[. . .]

This goes a long way toward explaining the strange basic schism in me (which finds expression, for example, in *Scanner,* its basic plot). It explains my twin parallel opposing views of Christianity; on the one hand I feel myself to be a Christian and on the other I view Christians and Christianity with abhorrence and contempt. It would seem that half of me is devoted to the wisdom religions of classic Greece, which is why I enjoy the pre-Socratics so much; and yet another part of me is led back again and again to the NT. "Zwei Selle wohnen ach! in meiner Brust."[71] . . . I really am two people, one of them Christian, the other pagan. As a result I am forced to function while holding two mutually exclusive views which, as F. Scott Fitzgerald says, is the mark of the true artist. [. . .]

I must go on being a Christian, acting out the role of genuine revolutionary apostolic Christian, as a strategy: in order to overthrow the Black Iron Prison which I detest. But that is what Christianity is for me: a strategy. I know — all the time that I am a secret, authentic, revolutionary Christian — that it is Platonism and Neoplatonism that's objectively true. But the Platonist and Neoplatonist has no revolutionary drive; he will not change society, the world, to bring on the Kingdom; therefore I must live as if (*als ob*) Christianity — genuine Christianity — were true. Strange.

[1:61] October 21, 1980

The strangest most eerie thought just struck me. If USA 1974 and Rome A.D. 45 are two spatiotemporal aspects of a common essence they as aspects if superimposed would clash, not blend — this despite the common essence; I don't know why I know this but I do. But if it's really Rome A.D. 45 then they would blend, because the percipient would see that USA 1974 is Rome A.D. 45. What I have been calling a superimposition is more like a metamorphosis. A certain building is a building in Syria in the first century A.D. Reality is seen under the aspect of Rome A.D. 45, the Holy Land. As if reverting. I noticed palm trees and sand, the warm wind, the relaxing people . . . like a scene in ancient Syria.

• • •

[1:69]

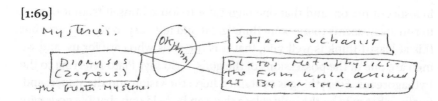

I think that just now by linking Plato's anamnesis and Form world with Dionysus and the greater mysteries, and the Christian Eucharist to Dionysus and the greater mysteries—which links Christian Eucharist to Plato's anamnesis and Form world—which renders the spatiotemporal world irreal, thus abolishing the power of "astral determinism" over you, which is the basic task of religion because then the splintered soul implodes and again is divine and immortal and knows it—

I succeeded!

[1:72] October 22, 1980

As of late last night my emotions (affective self) moved into synch with my intellect (as engaged in this exegesis), and the result was that I surveyed a world-picture of such bleakness that it was for a time beyond my capacity to bear. I saw and understood suffering, not just intellectually, not just emotionally, but fully, with complete comprehension. Today I have thought about it, and the only attitude that can or should be brought to bear is a stoic one, in fact a heroic one, a facing of this bleakness unflinchingly, with no attempt to flee from it as a vision or existentially, as a way of being in the world. It is a view of the weary wheel of Buddhism; it is the Buddha's view of absolute suffering and the need not to be reborn, to get off the wheel. [. . .]

Each creature is born, suffers, dies, is again born, forever and ever, because the world soul—there is just one soul, and it has fragmented into billions of bits—made the primordial and primary mistake of taking the spatiotemporal realm as real, thus plunging itself into enslavement and multiplicity. For a few there is a way out: discovery that the spatiotemporal world is not real, an ascent back up into unity and freedom, but only for a few bits (sparks) is this possible; the enormous mass of fragments will remain caught forever, unless some final great savior comes here and frees us en masse. I hope this will happen but I doubt it. Every fly with a missing leg, every cat beleaguered by fleas, every human fearing economic want—the endless wheel turns for all of us and it turns forever, in this irreal time we have fallen victim to.

"The saying that is uttered in secret rites, to the effect that we men are in a sort of prison, and that one ought not to loose himself from it nor yet to run away, seems to me something great and not easy to see through; but this at least I think is well said, that it is the gods who care for us, and we men are one of the possessions of the gods."[72] So says Plato referring to the Pythagoreans. Everything is contained here: the vision and the stance, and, finally, what may be the only solace that can be held out, that the gods care for us because we are their possessions. This paragraph will have to do if I am to be saved from the vision I have seen, and it is meant to save; it is Plato's great mind coming to bear on the situation, with full knowledge of the reality of the situation, the Greek equipoise that Apollo exemplified; that Attic calm to which I must return, or I am destroyed.

Premise: the primordial Fall was caused by our — by us, not our ancestors — making the error of taking the spatiotemporal realm to be real.

(1) In 2-74 I saw that the spatiotemporal realm was not real.
(2) Therefore I reversed the original Fall — which is doing much more than remembering — by anamnesis — the reality of the Form world, the universals. What I realized last night is that I as a soul splintered up in fragments through space and time, literally exploded through space and time, in incarnation after incarnation, my unity shattered. This is the "weary wheel" of the Orphics. This realization is terrible. Because even though I reversed the effects of the Fall for myself, I can see the dreadful condition of the others of us, born again and again (but this is temporal talk; it is irreal. *Splintered* is the correct term). [. . .]

Now the results of not recognizing Tat tvam asi seem actually sinister, since you literally are other life forms, other humans and other creatures; you as primordial soul are splintered, exploded, over thousands of years and thousands of miles. Tat tvam asi is not a luxury for the languid philosopher or the special mystic; it is essential in the reversal of a primordial fall (our taking the spatiotemporal realm as real).

[. . .].

Recollection as re-collection: calling one's splintered, scattered parts in, *to a center*. The primordial explosion reversed as a calling back together, a sort of teleological implosion, as if time were running backward.

[1:83] Rats. I'm rediscovering things that I already knew; that are, in fact, the basis of my system. I am too tired; I must quit for a time and rest.

[1:84] Probably the wisest view is to say: the truth — like the Self — is splintered up over thousands of miles and years; bits are found here and there, then and now, and must be re-collected; bits appear in the Greek naturalists, in Pythagoras, Plato, Parmenides, Heraclitus, Neoplatonism, Zoroastrianism, Gnosticism, Taoism, Mani, orthodox Christianity, Judaism, Brahmanism, Buddhism, Orphism, the other mystery religions. Each religion or philosophy or philosopher contains one or more bits, but the total system interweaves it into falsity, so each as a total system must be rejected, and none is to be accepted at the expense of all the others (e.g., "I am a Christian" or "I follow Mani"). This alone, in itself, is a fascinating thought: here in our spatiotemporal world we have the truth but it is splintered — exploded like the eide — over thousands of years and thousands of miles and (as I say) must be recollected, as the Self or Soul or eidos must be. This is my task.

In that case, each given system is in itself part of the enslaving snare of delusion; in other words, as soon as I avow one philosopher or system (e.g., Spinoza or Schopenhauer or Kant or Anaxagoras or Parmenides or Gnosticism) I have become again or more ensnared, as I am by this spatiotemporal world itself; it is as if the eidos of Truth is exploded and splintered like all the eide. And all the Selves and Souls. But what else could you expect here in realm #4? Since everything real is here only in discrete bits. Of course this means that I can never come up with the whole, true, complete explanation/answer. I can re-collect and re-collect, do better and better, but never completely make unified the eidos of Truth. Yet, in 3-74 when I meta-abstracted, a great deal of the eidos of Truth was revealed to me; however, alas, I did not understand it then and do not yet.

Look; I may be on to something here, that in realm #4 it is impossible to re-collect any given eidos including that of a true verbal (informational) picture (analog) of reality; that in fact the true informational analog will be exploded over thousands of miles and thousands of years like all other eide. Such is the situation here in the spatiotemporal realm; this is one of its drawbacks (among many). Fascinating. In that case, no wonder I haven't been able to match my 2-3-74 experience to any religion or any philosopher, yet many seem *in part* to apply. The truth is splintered!* This would

---

* Just as the manifestation of Valis is one of organizations, patterns of meaning, neural networks, and the collapse of temporal and spatial boundaries — that is, just as Valis is a revelation of *hyperconnections* — so too now works the radiated mind of Dick himself. Dick has in effect become a super-comparativist, and so he is able to draw connections and organize disparate patterns of information, like Valis, through huge stretches of space and time. And why not? Paradoxically, Valis works through history and yet exists, as a hyperdimensional presence, outside the box of history. This "abolishing of time" is especially evident in the history of religions and, more precisely, comparative mystical literature, to whose patterns and similarities Dick is powerfully drawn. In this particular passage, the double-edged sword of the comparative imagination is evident: bits of truth can indeed be found

explain, too, why the sacerdotal power is found in bits in, say, the alley; for the same reason: it is exploded ubiquitously. (In addition to the places I listed above where I've found bits of the truth I should add: the Hermetics and the Kabbala and quantum mechanics.)

Could it be said that every now and then an additional bit is reticulated? So-to-speak revealed? So 2-3-74 could contain one or more elements of the truth that are new?

In one area the Evangelical Christians are correct: in regard to Bible prophecy. The Bible does contain archetypes that print out over and over again, and are — some of them — applicable to present-day times. (I need only recall "Acts" and the dream material in *Tears*, the latter specifically being either from Daniel or Revelation.)

So one great realization is: the map is exploded; the map is splintered. (And, perhaps, the map is not complete; see Hussey on the map paradox, the vicious regression.[73])

[1:86] October 24, 1980

If the eide are exploded through the spatiotemporal realm, so must be Noös: disintegrated here in realm #4; but if the percipient ascends from realm #4 he may see Noös re-collected, reintegrated and hence unitary, as it actually is. What I am saying is that the eide are not actually exploded; they are exploded in terms of the spatiotemporal realm, if my meaning is clear; since realm #4 is illusory, the explosion, the splintering, is illusory. And if this is true of the eide, the Forms, this also is true of Noös: our false categories of ordering, of arranging time and space, explode and splinter the eide; and they explode and splinter Noös; but this is not really the case. This is why it is correct to say that our realm #4 and its spatiotemporal ordering are irreal. If they were real, then the eide and Noös would in actuality be exploded and splintered; but they are not. To see Noös integrated is not for Noös to reintegrate, but to be seen as it is and always is.

This was what I saw that I called Valis: Noös reintegrated in terms of my perception of it: re-collected.

Noös exploded (here in realm #4) is Noös banalized, as in the chapter headings in *Ubik*: Noös re-collected is as Ubik appears in the heading of the final chapter, no longer banalized, trivialized, debased into rubbish.

---

everywhere, but the full truth is nowhere to be found; religious systems are both true (as approximations or reflections) and false (as final and complete answers) at the same time. Today a much simpler form of this double-notion is crystallized in the oft-heard quip "I am spiritual, but not religious." Such a position is often demeaned as fuzzy, as narcissistic, as "New Agey." In fact, it constitutes a quiet, but radical, rejection of religion in all its dogmatic and dangerous forms. — JJK

This banalization is a measure of the Fall of this realm; and again it illustrates what I have remarked on: that things do not appear in this realm #4 as what they really are, that finally Christ will bring about what I call "the great reversal," whereupon we will no longer see Noös (God) banalized and exploded, but, as if reversed, sacred and a unity: as it really is. Meanwhile, here, with things appearing in reverse to what their essence is, Noös is obscured; veiled.

October 25, 1980

But whereas a given eidos is finite in realm #4 — it only enters at certain places and certain times, i.e., is printed out at one place and time but not another — Noös is ubiquitous. Therefore if it chooses to so-to-speak drop its mask and reverse appearances in realm #4 (enantiodromia) it is in everything at every time; it is infinite (cf. Xenophanes). Or, put another way, it can be anything or any constellation of things and their processes at any place and any time.

[1:88] October 25, 1980

If a gun were put to my head and I had to give one short answer as to what Valis was, I would say, "The Tao, as the Absolute." And as to what happened in 3-74: the regulation of the Yin and the Yang, i.e., the dialectic, by the Tao; the Tao asserting itself as master of the dialectic that makes up our world-order of flux and strife. ("The Tao is what lets him first the light, then the dark" — this has always stuck in my mind as the basic definition of the Tao.) And this has to do with advanced physics; so Warrick is right about Valis and 3-74. Sentient physics.

But also: Valis was my splintered self "imploding" back together, the pieces that had exploded over space and time reversing their direction in enantiodromia and re-collecting to form their original unity. Of this I am absolutely certain; but look: this, too, could be an example of an event of higher physics! (This is why time seemed to flow backward; and forward-moving time had exploded my self over thousands of years and miles.)

This is why I had the distinct and indubitable impression that my own earlier thought-contents were coming back to me in the form of world — e.g., *Ubik* and "Faith of . . . ," etc. World was *familiar* to me as my own earlier mind. I never could explain this until now. It was (I see now) the re-collecting of my own splintered self as if time were running backward, turning an explosion into an implosion. So beyond doubt enantiodromia and other higher laws of physics perceived by the Taoist and Greek naturalists (pre-Socratics) were involved! I see! The normal process of self splintering was reversed. [. . .]

The *first* space-time thing that returned to me was my most *recent* book, *Tears,* and the world ("Acts") in it where a main part of myself had been exploded to. Then later came *Ubik.*

The above paragraph is the most important realization of my six and a half years of exegesis.

[1:93] October 26, 1980

Therefore my experience in 2-3-74 now that it has been followed by a *successful* exegesis — and only in the last two weeks has it become successful — pays off in the way that I perceive ordinary daily reality. I cannot bring back the absolute vision of the morphologically arranged realm that I had in 2-74, the anamnesis; but I now can apprehend this realm from the standpoint of the realm #3 reality; I can see in the epiphenomenal realm the constants shining through . . . and this is the triumph in practice of Platonist metaphysics, its whole point: that you learn to see in the flux realm the constants, literally see them with the educated eye, educated by Plato's metaphysics of the forms. [. . .]

But the real success of the exegesis is that as I become old, now, and wear out, I feel myself wearing out only as an instance of an eternal soul or form; that nothing is lost, nothing is destroyed; and although I don't crave immortality I do crave vigor and joy and the running that I associate with my eidos. And I know, too, that all that I have lost in my life is epiphenomenal, people and cats and things, that in reality nothing is lost. So I can face my own aging and mortality with calm and even pleasure, since I am grounded in both a mystical vision of super reality and an intellectual exegesis based on that vision, the totality of which provides me with a philosophy and with an experience with world that is harmonious and wonderful and intellectually satisfying: it is a vision of intactness, of my own self and world. Of everything as a negentropic whole. As regards my writing: it will permanently affect the macrometasomakosmos in the form of reticulation and arborizing — and hence will survive in reality forever, in the underlying structure of the world order.

[1:94] November 1, 1980

This is the surd I am left with after completing the metaphysical system of my exegesis: a surd. There is what the AI voice called "a perturbation in the reality field." This is Valis; this is the most important part. Originally I spoke of it as a valence away from plumb. Now I think of it as a tugging, like the moon's effect on Earth's oceans creating, by tugging, the tides.

I say, the reality field is not real but the tug is. But what the tug points to — that is, what is doing the tugging — I have no idea. I know of it only by its effects on reality, in setting up an irregularity in reality, in the field, the way reality, the field, behaves. It is being affected from outside — outside reality.

This surd (something irrational that can't be explained after everything that is rational has been) may stick with me. So I may wind up with something like quantum mechanics facts. In fact it may be an event in quantum mechanics, like something related to the Tao. I don't know.

And this is what I wanted the most to explain. And this tug is right here and now, in the very trash stratum of reality. I have set out in pursuit of ontology, rising from level to level, only to go full circle and come back where I started: pop tunes on the radio, weeds in the alley . . . and the faint flurry of a kind of breath, as if some invisible spirit, perhaps the ruah, is breathing creation into existence ex nihilo. Yes, I am on the rim of reality; level after level each one more ontologically real than the previous, and then — nothingness. The void. Only a faint wind stirring reality, tugging at it. And maybe a glint of color, briefly. And a word or two as set to ground. 6½ years of work: a glint, a rustle in the weeds of the alley; I am confronted by unfathomable mystery, as if I saw cosmogenesis reversed: cosmic resorption, until at last creation ceased to be, and only the spirit moved across the face of the void. And, equally real and equally enigmatic, a small murmuring voice speaking in the night, as if from immeasurable distances away.

I have found the ultimate source: a rustle of wind in the weeds and faint, distant words by a lovely voice that is neither male nor female. Both bordering on the rim of not being there but being, I am convinced, the truly real; in contrast to the great substantial world order, the galaxies and nebulae, suns and planets, civilizations and deeds.

I cannot say that I have found moksa, enlightenment. I do not understand what I saw and what happened in 2-3-74. Something helped me. Who? Oddly, although I don't know who I do know why (since the AI voice told me that). I chased after reality, and how far did I actually get? "Ti to on?" the pre-Socratics asked. Perhaps it is the wrong question.

An odd thought came to me. I end my exegesis with something — what I call a surd because that is what it is — that can't be fitted into an otherwise satisfactory system. This one thing is simple. No elaboration of it seems possible, no implications extracted and elaborated. It makes me think of Dante's semplice lume. And my exploded morphological structure reminds me of Dante's description of God as the book of the universe whose pages are scattered throughout the universe.

I beheld leaves within the unfathomed blaze
into one volume bound by love, the same

that the universe holds scattered through its maze.
Substance and accidents and their modes became
as if together fused, all in such wise
that what I speak of is one simple flame.

November 2, 1980

About all I can see clearly is that 3-74 was a heroic act that consisted of the overcoming of fate. "We can be heroes for just one day," to quote Bowie. It all has to do with waking up long enough to perform one action, to make one change, before you sink back down into sleep, before you again forget. [. . .]

What strikes me about this is that it is cosmogenesis in miniature, in the microcosm, because something has come into being ex nihilo. What the person did — the heroic act — he could not do given who he is, given his history, his karma. It is an impossibility. Thus in a real and literal sense a new self has been born in him, since this fact, this deed, could not issue out of field self, the self is splintered throughout time and space. This is as much a miracle as the original cosmogenesis; in a sense it is the original cosmogenesis, and perhaps the ruah is present at it as it was in the beginning.

So I felt as if another self had taken me over; my actions were "disassociated," without ideation; and then Thomas came into being in me. Maybe he was new, not a lost part rejoining me but new ex nihilo, the permanent offspring of the heroic deed that broke the power of the world rule existentially. *What world lost, self acquired.* There is a quantum transfer of essence from world itself, so that the balance between the two shifts critically. Self is acting on world, rather than world on self; it is as if up until then the self was only a product of world, its thing; it was a thing among things, controlled and directed and shaped, as a potter shapes a clay vessel. And all its deeds and all its thoughts have only been world acting and speaking through it, within a closed system of which that self was only a component.

For one thing, if you view it in science fiction terms, in terms of ideas, S-F has developed vis-à-vis time travel and changing the past: has not this one new deed changed the entire future, the entire future history of the universe? Because the universe is one great field, and to introduce a truly new thing or event into it is to alter it in its entirety. Permanently.

Since world is now no longer a closed system it is no longer in effect a prison.

.   .   .

[1:121] Is the secret connected with time and the reversal of time? Cosmic resorption? I am right in my writing: reality is a series of Chinese boxes, a box within a box within a box, etc.: but a final point comes when you have Valis, but what or who Valis is I have *no* idea. The Tao, YHWH, cosmic Christ, Brahman, Shiva, Krishna, or a quantum mechanics phenomenon. Or ruah, the spirit of God breathing creation into existence out of nothing — ex nihilo — you finally wind up with: non-being — that is, not-is-real, and the "is" is only seeming, is not real. You open box after box and ascend the levels of being (esse, substantia, einai) and then you open the last one and it contains — *nothing!* And yet you're faced with the mystery or paradox that Ho On (for want of a better term) is actually right here and now, in the very trash at hand, not far away at all — the ultimate paradox in terms of your long search through level after level of being — he is at the initial least real (sic) level. You wind up back where you started, paradoxically. But now you know that this utterly worthless trash level — mere appearance — is somehow also Ho On, whom you seek. "The Buddha is a piece of toilet paper."[74] "The Savior is a crushed beer can in the alley." Could this be the final great enantiodromia?

So if you push essence far enough in terms of ascending levels, you find you have gone a full circle, and you wind up encountering ultimate deity cooking and writing pop tunes on the radio and popular novels, and a breath of wind in the weeds in the alley.

It's as if the ultimate mystery is that there is no mystery — it's like what Robert Anton Wilson says in the *Cosmic Trigger* about being outside the Castle when you think you're in, and inside when you think you're out.

And in a way what is most paradoxical is that I said it all in *Ubik* years ago! So in a way my exegesis of 2-3-74 says only, "*Ubik* is true." All I know today that I didn't know when I wrote *Ubik* is that *Ubik* isn't fiction. In all of history no system of thought applies as well to 2-3-74 as *Ubik*, my own earlier novel. When all the metaphysical and theological systems have come and gone there remains this inexplicable surd: a flurry of breath in the weeds in the back alley — a hint of motion and of color. Nameless, defying analysis or systemizing: it is here and now, lowly, at the rim of perception and of being. Who is it? What is it? I don't know.

I ask for 30 years, what is real? And in 2-3-74 I got my answer as if the universe — well, as if my question traveled across the whole universe and came back to me in the form of experienced answers . . . and what I wind up with after 6½ years of studying those experienced answers is: a surd. A perturbation in the reality field — an irregularity, a departure from the normal — a tugging or pulling or bending. And that is all. Not even the thing, the perturbing body itself; only its effects on "the reality field." Something out of the ordinary — like I say, a surd.

So what, then, do I know about the nature of reality? That an irregularity can show up in it that points to — something else. Only a sign.

Q: "Ti to on?"

A: Heidegger says, "Why is there something instead of nothing?" To which I ask, "Why does Heidegger *think* there is something instead of nothing?"

The tug is real and the "reality field" tugged on isn't. So that which is genuinely real is pointed to by its effect on the "reality field" (which *isn't* real) but what it is that is doing the tugging I have no idea.

[1:127] The perturbation in the reality field was not by me but by the Tao. Nonetheless *I* broke my own programming by a heroic act of will. Yes; our spatiotemporal aspects (what we take to be reality) are indeed our own prior thought formations coming back to us. Yes; anamnesis is recognizing them as such: which permits you to break their hold (programming) over you by (on your part) an act of (your) will. Doing something new — introducing one single new change — destroys their ossified nature and starts up real time, it causes a time perturbation, as if time were running backward; this may be due to one forcing the prior thought formations back into the past where they properly belong; it would seem to you, then, as if the future had broken in, moving retrograde in time. This "future breaking in" is: real time! Due to the destroying of the supremacy of the past (prior thought-formations as world). Once these prior thought-formations' power over you. [. . .] You can see (?) (experience) the Tao: true reality *as it is* without the prior thought formations. You can see the tug by the Tao (matrix containing the eide) on reality-as-a-field.

[1:137]

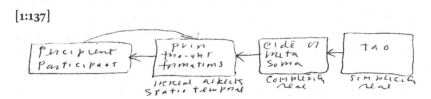

[1:138] 4:30 A.M.: I was lying here thinking how Christ would show up in the alley and the weeds because that is where he is and things of daily life and world, and I asked myself, "Would he be *additional* substantial/material trace *bits*?" And I realized, "No, as a tug, a perturbation — the iron filings and magnetic field perturbation" — the eide are not material, not physical; so the only way they (he) would show up would be as a tug; and this would render the plural objects and processes as a field perturbed as a unitary whole — I visualized it so clearly. Since he is not real in the spatiotemporal sense, and yet he is *here* not there, in this world, immediately at hand; I understood it for a moment so clearly — and it was exactly what I saw in 3-74 that I called Valis. It is the only evidence we would have. [. . .] So I arrive at the conclusion to this exegesis and it is where I started: Valis is the cosmic Christ; but to understand this I had to reject all other possibilities one by one over a 6½ year period; and, most important of all, I had to study Plato's metaphysics thoroughly and rejoin it to its other half: Christianity, the anamnesis of the Eucharist, arising out of Orphism, from which Plato's metaphysics came.

[1:170] But most of all: breath. The pattern in the iron filings: that it is breath to weeds: field to iron filings. It is the *stirring* in the weeds, the pattern (structure) as with Pythagoras. Field. Arrangement. It is not substantial; it is nothing (but a field). And the AI voice — very faintly, arranging *my* thoughts!

Absolutely it is a field, as in quantum mechanics. Not the iron filings, but the pattern.

I can visualize it *very* clearly — visualize Valis. Set-ground reversal. The not-is is Valis. The is is not.

It is normally a weak field, too weak to be detected. Only under exceptional circumstances does it intensify to cause a perceptible perturbation (3-74). Paradoxically, though it is weak it is irresistible. Why, this is the Tao! This is how the Tao works! (vide the *Tao Te Ching*). Weak and — *everywhere (Ubik!)*.

[. . .]

It is weak and yet it cannot be resisted. This is the Tao. It works through what is small. *I* am small. It worked through (on) me. To affect modern history! Wu wei.[75]

[. . .]

If *all* reality (universe) is a (one) field, it (Tao) need set up a tiny perturbation at one space time, and ultimately the whole field will be affected, by inducing an enantiodromia of the whole field! Through a chain of mounting flip-flops! *I* was one such, in 3-74.

[. . .]

I finally understand. *This* is what is meant by "a perturbation in the reality field." One tiny tug sets a sequence of mounting, growing changes in motion, ending in massive (total?) enantiodromia: victory. Over world. Since all reality is one field the effects of the initial perturbation end only when the final enantiodromia occurs, and all the "counters" flip over to their opposites.

This is what *TMITHC* is about, and deliberately so. But: the real secret is:

Something *new* (although tiny, bordering on ex nihilo, on nothing, yet something) is introduced into an *otherwise closed system.* My example? My act vis-à-vis the Xerox missive. As a result the entire closed system is affected throughout.

[1:175] The fact that I wound up with Valis as a surd when I finished my first "complete" or "successful" overview shows how scrupulous I was. It would *have to* be left over. Deity can't be fitted into a theoretical system; it is irreducible *and stands alone.* But at least that way I could focus on it as isolated — which paved the way for my total overview in which this surd *was* included but only as "the absolute," leading finally to my ferociously close scrutiny of it in total isolation (from my own mind and from the reality field as well).

I realized that it came into existence literally out of nothing, was pure arrangement and not the things arranged (acted upon). I visualized (conceived of) it as a breath on the weeds of the alley — then connected it to the "heroic act that causes genuine newness" to enter the world; then, realizing that it is weak but irresistible, I saw it as the Tao and hence saw its relationship to the dialectic and mounting chains of events culminating in macroenantiodromia: the purpose of it "breathing" on the "weeds in the alley." Which shows total wisdom on its part!

[1:185] Well, my perception of 3-74 is that I encountered something outside of me; and my recent theory is that it came into existence out of nothing — *at least in terms of our reality field.*

[1:208] Yes, something can be irreal and yet powerful; *the lie* is powerful; it thrusts itself at us *like* a reality, but I *saw* in 2-74 that it isn't real. [. . .]

Irreality, then, *is the basic defect of the entropic old flux/cosmos.* There are valuable bits in it (e.g., Mozart symphonies; we'll use that as an example) but they are not real in that they pass away; they never *are.* But the meta-soma assimilates them into itself like permanent memories stored in a mind.

[1:248] I would even be willing to argue that an experience such as mine (2-3-74) *justifies* the Fall in the sense of making it worth it *due to the absolute joy generated by the re-collection and return.* I know it was for me — all the tearful years were not only nullified; they were overbalanced by the bliss experienced in restoration. Whether *my* feelings in history could rightly be projected onto the deity I don't know; but if my system is right in all respects, 2-3-74 *was* the deity recovering its memory and identity, and so is representative — a sort of microcosm of the total deity's own travels, its journey. (I envision deity in dynamic process undergoing unfolding stages of self-knowledge.) Perhaps this is the ultimate price of the game: self-awareness, acquired through "external" plural standpoints, of which I am one. Then I would say, it is worth it, this journey. That's my subjective opinion. So the Fall is a vast adventure, culminating in a joy that outweighs the arduousness and sorrow of the trip itself. And out of this adventure the deity knows itself more clearly, and, since (as I say) intellegere is its essence, this matter outweighs all else.

[1:257] November 16, 1980

Have I had it backward? I've always said: I saw His Body camouflaged as the world. Maybe it's the other way. I saw how the pieces of the world fitted together to form his body — this was what I saw that I called Valis, externally. This is the same thing as I understood inwardly when I saw that the wise horn of the dialectic selected pieces of the antecedent universe, as a stockpile, and fitted the pieces together to form the macrometasomakosmos which was its own self, its own metasoma. Here seen both ways (externally as Valis and internally as an inner consciousness): world evolved into the Body of Christ; world as pieces that seen acting and operating together became — were now — Christ as cosmic body. So it is world first; or rather they, as plural pieces, are world. Then they come together so that the they becomes an it, one body made up of all the many objects and processes that were — that had formerly been — the world. The lower plural evolve into the higher unitary. This was one process seen two ways, seen inwardly and outwardly. Yet you could still say, "His body was camouflaged as world. World was transubstantiated into Christ's Body." But it isn't Christ's Body posing as world; it is world becoming — joining together to form — Christ's body. Again: it is a cosmic evolution. Not the higher invading the lower but the lower evolving into the higher, with pieces of world added element by element to complete and perfect this titanic body, a body so vast that I could only comprehend dimly enormous — infinite — volumes of space, space such as I had never conceived or apprehended before. Larger than the universe, which in comparison is merely finite. Limited. And all of it was alive and all of it thought. And the pieces didn't just happen to fit together; they didn't just haphazardly come together; Christ himself searched for the pieces, took the pieces, placed each piece of the world in place correctly, integrated, beautiful, a kosmos, a macrokosmos that was good, beautiful, pleasing and harmonious, where all the many parts that had been world interacted as one unity.* And yet absolutely in no way was this vast body anthropomorphic; it was not a human body. It was a permanent body that continually became more reticulated and arborized and complex and perfect, that had once been world. So my inner vision of the macrometasomakosmos formed out of the antecedent universe, and my external perception of Valis "camouflaged" are one and the same. And it is right here. Evolution, not reversion. Gestalting on my part; form-perception.

And this was accomplished by him defeating world over and over again in dialectical combat with it, where he subdued it, disassembled it and assimilated it in the form of useful and appropriate pieces into his own vast body. Every new part incorporated — self-incorporated — came as a result of defeating and subduing world, but not defeating and subduing it by force, but rather by wisdom; by his being wiser than it, although not as powerful; it was his wisdom victorious over its power, and as it lost each time it lost another piece of itself. So the vast body grows, and with each defeat world becomes less and he becomes more: more completed, more perfected, more internally intricate and organized; and everything valuable in world is preserved eternally in his body as the right part fitted into the right place.

And he systematically deprived world of its blind, inexorable causality, and substituted his volition in simulation of that mechanical causality, so that to the unaided eye causality still remained . . . just as to the unaided eye the plural constituents of world remained plural and unalive. And unable to think. And not integrated into a whole, a whole that was evolving internally, just as world passed over — which is to say evolved — into it. So in a sense there were two evolutions: world evolving into his body, not the pieces sort of swimming together but selected and arranged by

---

* Among the many exotic and ominous diagnoses that may be proposed by those inclined to put Dick's visions into a medical or neurological framework, one simple and relatively benign description hides everywhere in plain sight. "Micropsia" is the name for a powerful hallucinatory episode common among children, rare in adults, in which the body is experienced as a vast, inert form over which a shrunken-to-pinpoint consciousness roves, as a Lilliputian roves over Gulliver. The sense of detachment from the physical universe, and of vast reorientations of scale, has a cosmic, trippy quality. Except when it's a symptom of something dire, micropsia is harmless; it can be terrifying, but also enthralling. I suffered it myself, came to cherish it, and felt bereft when the episodes ended. I've subsequently been fascinated by how many different writers I care for — Julio Cortázar, J. G. Ballard, William Blake, Christina Stead, and certainly Dick (and Swift) — seem at some point to be attempting to gloss the micropsia sensation in imagery or metaphor. — JL

him and an evolution internal to his body: the reticulation and arborizing, based on events in the world fed into his body, continual accretions passing from world — where they were transitory — into his body — where they were forever preserved and remembered, like within a memory system in a mind or brain. And all the internal arrangement was morphological, not in terms of space and time, but in terms of information, as if arranged by meaning, like a kind of language. Like neural conduits in a brain. There was an endless processing of things as information, as if every combination was tried out, a perpetual rapid activity, like an internal metabolism, an information metabolism. It was using objects — combinations and recombinations — of objects to think with. And every given thing was limited (telos) by every other thing, in comparison to which the antecedent universe was chaotic (atelos). It was alive; it thought; and it initiated its own movement. Nothing acted on it; all its movements were self-initiated. And nothing outside it acted to construct it; it constructed itself.

And if you were outside it in the chaotic antecedent universe you were in a prison; but if you were inside it you were in a park or garden. And it constantly attacked the prison to dismantle it as a source of parts. And this had been going on for two thousand years, a really very bitter but somehow also joyful war.

Finally, when an object was incorporated into this structure it became real for the first time, as if up until then in a certain way it had been illusory: coming into being and passing away without ever having truly existed. But now it was safe from decay and harm.

And perishing. Forever. As if the body had a map of its own internal structure, the only structure ever to have been self-mapping, hence totally internally self-aware. Yet when you looked at this great system it was only ordinary objects such as you see every day. The basic things of the world, but interrelated and arranged without having moved in time and space. The internal arrangement was its own awareness of itself. Itself as map.

As incredible as it may seem, I actually didn't realize (until last night) that when I saw what I called Valis I saw what I call macrometasomakosmos. Apparently this is the case; the case that (1) I didn't recognize their identity and (2) they are identical. That means that my vision as to how the macrometasomakosmos is constructed (out of pieces of the antecedent universe by means of the dialectic) applies to Valis. I literally saw the macrometasomakosmos into which the flux world feeds. So Valis didn't invade our world in a disguised or camouflaged form, as I have always supposed; it is constructed right here, but invisible to us. It grows; it becomes more complex and perfected; and it constructs itself. Absolutely it is the Cosmic Christ; either that or it is one fuck of a meta life form.[76] It just ruthlessly plunders the flux world, treating it as a chaotic stockpile that it uses for parts. And it is selective as to what it assimilates and where it places it in its own soma. Did I realize this? I don't think so; I didn't realize that I saw it and that it is Valis. It's as if two thought clusters in my mind finally collided and formed one thought-complex. I had two separate categories: one involving invading; one involving construction, by its own self. [. . .] Suddenly years of speculation are rendered void, by this realization. Valis experienced three ways. Valis is — indeed must be — the Cosmic Christ assembling itself out of the antecedent universe which it uses as a stockpile, which it (the Cosmic Christ) defeats perpetually in a dialectical combat.

(1) Its mind was in direct touch with mine and it explained how it comes into existence and out of what. The macrometasomakosmos.

(2) I saw it externally as Valis.

(3) I was inside it, and saw its inner information-metabolism, what I call "the second signal."

Because the essence of its identity — its einai — is its structure, we can't see it; all its constituents are ordinary objects. Also its einai is noein; they are one.

Supra (3) confirms that (1) and (2) are identical.

The fact that the macrometasomakosmos is right here, made up of ordinary objects structured into a cohesive unity, changes my conception of it; I must now reappraise everything I've thought during the past six and a half years. I've missed the point all this time; I knew Valis was here, but I could not figure out where the macrometasomakosmos was — since I didn't realize that they — and what I call the "second signal" — are the same. It is a floating mind that turns objects into information within a brain, a brain that processes objects and their causal connections as information; it is especially active in our own communications media utilizing a set-ground system. I must admit that I don't really understand this; why can't we pick up, say, its meta-morphemes? Well, because we can't perform feature-extraction with it. It blends perfectly. Am I to assume that I'm the only human aware of it? Hardly. Where I differ is that (I'd guess) I've struggled so hard to explicate what happened to me . . . no, that isn't it. Could it be here just recently? No; that isn't it either. It's not in time and space; it's exploded morphologically . . . or it utilizes a retrograde time axis, what I call negentropic time. I don't know. It's impossible that no one else has seen it, but you can't see it unless it incorporates you. Maybe I'm the only one stupid enough to talk about it.

• • •

[1:262]* November 17, 1980

God manifested himself to me as the infinite void; but it was not the abyss; it was the vault of heaven, with blue sky and wisps of white clouds. He was not some foreign God but the God of my fathers. He was loving and kind and he had personality. He said, "You suffer a little now in life; it is little compared with the great joys, the bliss that awaits you. Do you think I in my theodicy would allow you to suffer greatly in proportion to your reward?" He made me aware, then, of the bliss that would come; it was infinite and sweet. He said, "I am the infinite. I will show you. Where I am, infinity is; where infinity is, there I am. Construct lines of reasoning by which to understand your experience in 1974. I will enter the field against their shifting nature. You think they are logical but they are not; they are infinitely creative."

I thought a thought and then an infinite regression of theses and countertheses came into being. God said, "Here I am; here is infinity." I thought another explanation; again an infinite series of thoughts split off in dialectical antithetical interaction. God said, "Here is infinity; here I am." I thought, then, an infinite number of explanations, in succession, that explained 2-3-74; each single one of them yielded up an infinite progression of flip-flops, of thesis and antithesis, forever. Each time, God said, "Here is infinity. Here, then, I am." I tried for an infinite number of times; each time an infinite regress was set off and each time God said, "Infinity. Hence I am here." Then he said, "Every thought leads to infinity, does it not? Find one that doesn't." I tried forever. All led to an infinitude of regress, of the dialectic, of thesis, antithesis and new synthesis. Each time, God said, "Here is infinity; here am I. Try again." I tried forever. Always it ended with God saying, "Infinity and myself; I am here." I saw, then, a Hebrew letter with many shafts, and all the shafts led to a common outlet; that outlet or conclusion was infinity. God said, "That is myself. I am infinity. Where infinity is, there am I; where I am, there is infinity. All roads — all explanations

---

* The following description of Dick's November 17, 1980, "theophany" is arguably the single most important entry in the entire Exegesis: it offers a fully developed interpretation of Dick's mode of theoretical exploration, expressed in some of the most beautiful prose he ever wrote. In the face of despair at the interminability of his theological exploration, Dick meets a vision of a God at play: this entire theological exercise is presented as a game between omnipotent deity and created being. Moreover, the infinitude of Dick's theories itself becomes proof that God is the beginning and end of his experiences. In light of the ideas presented in the theophany itself, Dick's conclusions at the end of the entry — that 2-3-74 was caused by Satan and that the Exegesis is therefore a diabolical "hell-chore" — are surprising. Perhaps we can read these remarks not as Dick's final conclusion, but rather the development of another theory about 2-3-74, and thus the beginning of another infinitely tall pile of computer punch cards. — GM

for 2-3-74 — lead to an infinity of Yes-No, This or That, On-Off, OneZero, Yin-Yang, the dialectic, infinity upon infinity; an infinity of infinities. I am everywhere and all roads lead to me; *omniae viae ad Deum ducent.* Try again. Think of another possible explanation for 2-3-74." I did; it led to an infinity of regress, of thesis and antithesis and new synthesis. "This is not logic," God said. "Do not think in terms of absolute theories; think instead in terms of probabilities. Watch where the piles heap up, of the same theory essentially repeating itself. Count the number of punch cards in each pile. Which pile is highest? You can never know for sure what 2-3-74 was. What, then, is statistically most probable? Which is to say, which pile is highest? Here is your clue: every theory leads to an infinity (of regression, of thesis and antithesis and new synthesis). What, then, is the probability that I am the cause of 2-3-74, since, where infinity is, there I am? You doubt; you are the doubt as in:

> They reckon ill who leave me out;
> When me they fly I am the wings.
> I am the doubter and the doubt.

"You are not the doubter; you are the doubt itself. So do not try to know; you cannot know. Guess on the basis of the highest pile of computer punch cards. There is an infinite stack in the heap marked INFINITY, and I have equated infinity with me. What, then, is the chance that it is me? You cannot be positive; you will doubt. But what is your guess?"

I said, "Probably it is you, since there is an infinity of infinities forming before me."

"There is the answer, the only one you will ever have," God said.

"You could be pretending to be God," I said, "and actually be Satan." Another infinitude of thesis and antithesis and new synthesis, the infinite regress, was set off.

God said, "Infinity."

I said, "You could be testing out a logic system in a giant computer and I am — " Again an infinite regress.

"Infinity," God said.

"Will it always be infinite?" I said. "An infinity?"

"Try further," God said.

"I doubt if you exist," I said. And the infinite regress instantly flew into motion once more. "Infinity," God said. The pile of computer punch cards grew; it was by far the largest pile; it was infinite.

"I will play this game forever," God said, "or until you become tired."

I said, "I will find a thought, an explanation, a theory, that does not set off an infinite regress." And, as soon as I said that, an infinite regress was set off. God said, "Over a period of six and a half years you have developed theory after theory to explain 2-3-74. Each night when you go to bed you think, 'At last I found it. I tried out theory after theory until now, finally, I have the right one.' And then the next morning you wake up and say, 'There is one fact not explained by that theory. I will have to think up another theory.' And so you do. By now it is evident to you that you are going to think up an infinite number of theories, limited only by your lifespan, not limited by your creative imagination. Each theory gives rise to a subsequent theory, inevitably. Let me ask you; I revealed myself to you and you saw that I am the infinite void. I am not in the world, as you thought; I am transcendent, the deity of the Jews and Christians. What you see of me in world that you took to ratify pantheism — that is my being filtered through, broken up, fragmented and vitiated by the multiplicity of the flux world; it is my essence, yes, but only a bit of it: fragments here and there, a glint, a riffle of wind . . . now you have seen me transcendent, separate and other from world, and I am more; I am the infinitude of the void, and you know me as I am. Do you believe what you saw? Do you accept that where the infinite is, I am; and where I am, there is the infinite?"

I said, "Yes."

God said, "And your theories are infinite, so I am there. Without realizing it, the very infinitude of your theories pointed to the solution; they pointed to me and none but me. Are you satisfied, now? You saw me revealed in theophany; I speak to you now; you have, while alive, experienced the bliss that is to come; few humans have experienced that bliss. Let me ask you, was it a finite bliss or an infinite bliss?"

I said, "Infinite."

"So no earthly circumstance, situation, entity or thing could give rise to it."

"No, Lord," I said.

"Then it is I," God said. "Are you satisfied?"

"Let me try one other theory," I said. "What happened in 2-3-74 was that — " And an infinite regress was set off, instantly.

"Infinity," God said. "Try again. I will play forever, for infinity."

"Here's a new theory," I said. "I ask myself, 'What God likes playing games? Krishna. You are Krishna.'" And then the thought came to me instantly, "But there is a god who mimics other gods; that god is Dionysus. This may not be Krishna at all; it may be Dionysus pretending to be Krishna." And an infinite regress was set off.

"Infinity," God said.

"You cannot be YHWH who You say You are," I said. "Because YHWH says, 'I am that which I am,' or, 'I shall be that which I shall be.' And you — "

"Do I change?" God said. "Or do your theories change?"

"You do not change," I said. "My theories change. You, and 2-3-74, remain constant."

"Then you are Krishna playing with me," God said.

"Or I could be Dionysus," I said, "pretending to be Krishna. And I wouldn't know it; part of the game is that I, myself, do not know. So I am God, without realizing it. There's a new theory!" And at once an infinite regress was set off; perhaps I was God, and the "God" who spoke to me was not.

"Infinity," God said. "Play again. Another move."

"We are both Gods," I said, and another infinite regress was set off. "Infinity," God said. "I am you and you are you," I said. "You have divided yourself in two to play against yourself. I, who am one half, I do not remember, but you do. As it says in the *Gita*, as Krishna says to Arjuna, 'We have both lived many lives, Arjuna; I remember them but you do not.' And an infinite regress was set off; I could well be Krishna's charioteer, his friend Arjuna, who does not remember his past lives."

"Infinity," God said. I was silent. "Play again," God said.

"I cannot play to infinity," I said. "I will die before that point comes."

"Then you are not God," God said. "But I can play throughout infinity; I am God. Play."

"Perhaps I will be reincarnated," I said. "Perhaps we have done this before, in another life." And an infinite regress was set off.

"Infinity," God said. "Play again."

"I am too tired," I said.

"Then the game is over."

"After I have rested —"

"You rest?" God said. "George Herbert wrote of me:

Yet let him keep the rest,
But keep them with repining restlessnesse.
Let him be rich and wearie, that at least,
If goodness leade him not, yet wearinesse
May tosse him to my breast.

"Herbert wrote that in 1633," God said. "Rest and the game ends."

"I will play on," I said, "after I rest. I will play until finally I die of it."

"And then you will come to me," God said. "Play."

"This is my punishment," I said, "that I play, that I try to discern if it was you in March of 1974." And the thought came instantly, my punishment or my reward; which? And an infinite series of thesis and antithesis was set off.

"Infinity," God said. "Play again."

"What was my crime?" I said, "that I am compelled to do this?"

"Or your deed of merit," God said.

"I don't know," I said.

God said, "Because you are not God."

"But you know," I said. "Or maybe you don't know and you're trying to find out." And an infinite regress was set off.

"Infinity," God said. "Play again. I am waiting."

[1:282] So Satan served me up a sophisticated world in accord with my epistemological expectations (as expressed in my 10 volume meta-novel), and I took this to be God and worshipped it, which is not only delusion — although a subtle delusion — but blasphemy; but in doing this

(1) Satan revealed to me a great deal about world (although he led me to believe it was God, not world); and

(2) Because of the infinitude of my theorizing I reached God anyhow — and this is an example of the triumph of God the wise horn of the dialectic; so:

(3) The dialectic revealed to me is the entropic world-process; but also:

(4) The dialectic is God in combat with Satan and God always wins; winning me (as expressed in 11-17-80) is an example: Satan's delusions led me to God in the end (through the "infinity" route; viz: as God said, "Where there is infinity, there is God; where there is God, there is infinity").

Thus my exegesis has been futile, has been delusion, *and:* has been a hell-chore, as I was beginning to realize, but God delivered me from it, from my own exegesis; and he pointed out the one truth in it: the infinity expressed in it was — but this was overlooked by Satan who does not possess absolute knowledge — a road to God, and did lead there; but *only* when I recognized the exegesis as futile and a hell-chore and delusion. Hence God permitted this deluding by Satan, knowing when it would end. So I wind up knowing a lot more about world — world as we will later experience it, the world-experience of the future; and I no longer suppose that I was discerning God, and realize that I was discerning world instead; and I was at last led to God. But not by my intellect, not by Gnosis, not by myself at all; it was due to God's initiative due to his loving-kindness; and what was proved was (once again) that *all* roads/ways/routes if pushed far enough lead to God. Hence (as I say) here is an example of how God the wise horn of the dialectic defeats its stupider foe inevitably in the end — this was an enantiodromia. It occurred when I realized that all that I had seen of God in 2-3-74 was a glint of color and a ripple of wind in the weeds of the alley, acting on reality; that Valis was not God but rather world ("the reality field") perturbed (from beyond creation) by God; but this did not yield knowledge of God direct, but only by inference; and that in fact 2-3-74 was not a theophany, but was a more sophisticated experience of world: creation pulled through infinity by reaching the end of (exhausting) its creative/entropic "splitting" (disintegrating; differentiating) dialectic process: entropic time converted into negentropic time. But this was still world, and Satan caused me to worship it . . . to fall victim to it, ensnared by it; taking it to be God; until I found that I had pushed my exegesis to infinity without result! And then I focused on the very infinitude of my theories and saw (recognized) this as an instance of cosmogenic entropy; and, at last exhausted, prayed for release; and God did appear to me in theophany and took the field and blocked each and all theories, and ended my exegesis, not in defeat but in *logical* discovery of Him (which Satan had not foreseen). Thus intellect and knowledge on my part led to exhaustion and to destruction of that intellect and a recognition of the futility of what I was doing; I knew I knew nothing; and then God took the field and made his move that resulted in the enantiodromia that led me to him anyhow, as if I had wandered that way by chance; *but it was by his plan all along.* And this was an instance of the dialectic that I had seen. Finally I wind up with $Y = \bar{Y}$; viz: Both these 2 following statements are true:

(1) The intellect will not lead you to God.
(2) The intellect *will* lead you to God.*

I am left with this paradox, which Satan did not foresee; he saw only statement (1) and did not see how God could convert it into its mirror op-

---

* The visionary episode of November 17, 1980, is one of the peaks of the Exegesis, as sublime a modern parable as Kafka's "Before the Law." These pages are also bona fide mysticism — not because Dick had authentic mystical experiences (whatever those are) but because Dick produced powerful texts that twist and illuminate vital strands of mystical discourse. Here we are in the apophatic realm of the via negativa, which, like Dick's gameplaying God, deconstructs all names and forms in the obscure light of the infinite. Elsewhere Dick tips his hat to Eckhart and Erigena, but the apophatic mystic his writing most invokes here is Nicholas of Cusa (1401–1464). By analyzing paradoxes, Cusa pushed reason toward a "learned ignorance" (*docta ignorantia*) that blooms finally into the *coincidentia oppositorum,* or coincidence of opposites — a mystic coincidence that Dick achieves here through a manic and corrosive intensification of the dialectic. But perhaps the most paradoxical aspect of Dick's 11/17/80 account is that his God here has nothing to do with the divine abyss of the negative mystics. Instead, he is a character in a story: part playful guru, part Palmer Eldritch, and part Yahweh, screwing around with Adam because there is nothing better to do. — ED

posite through enantiodromia. Thus God works and wins within the fallen entropic creation of the disintegrating "splitting" dialectic to win us one and all in the end, by different routes. Thus the cosmic game between God and his adversary continues on; here was another victory by God; and in the end God will convert the dialectic itself into its opposite (through enantiodromia) and the game will end in God's victory and Satan's defeat, which God's victory vis-à-vis me echoes in microform. In a certain sense it can be said that God's victory consists in turning Satan's false creation — i.e., Satan's lies and delusion — *into the real,* which is exactly what I saw Valis doing: transmuting reality by transubstantiation into the real. Here is the secret and perpetual and ever-growing victory by God over his adversary as he (God) defeats him (Satan) again and again in the game they play — the cosmic dialectic that I saw. This is enantiodromia at its ultimate: the conversion of the irreal to the real. In my case it was the conversion of "the human intellect will not lead to God but will lead only deeper and deeper into delusion" into its mirror opposite: "The human intellect, when it has pushed to infinity, will at last, through ever deepening delusion, find God." Thus I am saved: and know that I did not *start out* seeing God (2-3-74) (which led to this 6½ year exegesis): but, instead, wound up finding God (11-17-80) — an irony that Satan did not foresee. And thus the wise mind (God) wins once again, and the game continues. But someday it will end.

END.

[1:286] Footnote.

My flight expressed by the phosphene graphics was a movement faster and faster through cosmogenic-entropic time, ending in exhaustion and then the enantiodromia of entropic time — which had reached infinite velocity and infinite fragmentation ("splitting") — which is to say the dialectic into negentropic time or synthesis, reintegration: hence I saw Valis, the universe pulled through infinity, inside out, to freeze; this was 3-74.

My exegesis was entropic-cosmogenic time *resuming,* speeding up faster and faster, "splitting" (fragmenting) farther and farther. Finally, it, too, ended in infinite velocity and infinite fragmentation (creativity, expressed as ever newer and quicker theories); it ended in exhaustion and then the enantiodromia of entropic time — the dialectic of my thoughts — into negentropic time and another reintegration (this was 11-17-80). Only this time I did not see Valis, world, not God as I supposed. There was a *theophany,* and I was in the presence of God and God's loving-kindness; whereupon He explained everything to me. So events leading up to 3-74 and my experience with Valis had a parallel in the dialectic of my exegesis leading to 11-17-80 and the theophany of the Christian God of Love. The common ingredients of the two flights were: the cosmogenic-entropy "splitting" dialectic flight itself, until infinite velocity (time) and fragmentation (space) were reached, then exhaustion, then enantiodromia into negentropic time and "freeze" (reintegrational) of, so-to-speak, "Prajapati,"[77] but then comes a totally different outcome.

(1) 3-74. Valis which is world properly seen (morphological arrangement, growth and perfection and self completion in negentropic time, the entropic-flux-universe pulled through infinity — i.e., inside out). Compared to:

(2) 11-17-80. The Christian God in theophany, who is *other* than world, who is transcendent. What I *thought I* had seen in 3-74.

The summation (combining) of the two is (1) an acute knowledge of world based on 3-74 and the exegesis arising out of that experience. (2) Direct knowledge of God and God's nature based on the above elements; so that 3-74 led to the exegesis, which although it was a loss of negentropic, integrative time and a resumption of cosmogenic-entropic time, did lead (due to the infinite speeding up of time and the infinite breaking down of space until exhaustion set in) to the theophany I had supposed I had already had.

Now it is possible to see how the Mary Jane fitted in; it added the final push to the dialectic in me, my exegesis (in other words, as preceded 3-74, my thinking) so that it reached infinite speed and infinite space, exhausted itself; and again, as before, enantiodromia set in.* *This* enantiodromia did not have to do with world, however, but had to do with the human intellect striving to find God — futilely. (Futilely until the last great enantiodromia occurred and God took the field to block the dialectic of my thinking himself, and thus revealed himself.) So there is a striking parallel — a logical, structural parallel — between 3-74 and 11-17-80, but in another, more

---

* Not surprisingly, Philip K. Dick scholars have been keen to defend the author against the popular (and also understandable) stereotype that he was just a druggy. It's true that Dick gobbled pills and drank amphetamine shakes; his psychedelic use, though infrequent, was also important, as was the nitrous oxide trip at the dentist's office that revealed Valis "as an arborizing, reticulating vine." Here, the quaint reference to "Mary Jane" (marijuana) reminds us that, just as speed amplified his productivity, so too did cannabis amplify his visionary capacity, both on and off the page. For Dick, cannabis served as an engine of creative perception, but like all visionary drugs, it also staged a visionary paradox that lies at the heart of the Exegesis (and much of Dick's fiction): whatever freedom and sublimity is on offer requires a passive submission to perceptual machinery. Drugs can push the mind toward infinite speeds and meditative slownesses. But they also, like Valis itself, possess their own alien logic. The arborizing chains of associations that striate the Exegesis, and that cannabis and other drugs insistently multiply, may just as readily bind as liberate. — ED

profound respect the two are mirror opposites since the first is a vision of world (which I thought was God, yet it was not, and so it yielded no knowledge directly about God, but only inferential knowledge *that* he existed and *that* he had saved me—in pronoia) and the second is a genuine theophany. When one realizes that world and God are wholly other to each other (Satan rules world) then this mirror opposite situation can be appreciated. Let me add, too, that total revelation about world does not yield knowledge of God. God entered when I became aware that my theorizing was carrying me into an infinite regress, which is to say, when I became exhausted—at which point enantiodromia occurred; intellect had proven futile and yet, paradoxically, it had led to God—but due to God's volitional initiative. His (as I call it) taking the field, which is an inbreaking by the divine.

The circumstances under which the theophany occurred (I gave up on the exegesis and kicked back and massively turned on) are not capricious causes but follow the logic of the dialectic along several axes. This shows the hauntingly eerie paradoxical (almost seemingly whimsical or playful) nature of enlightenment: it comes to you only when you cease to pursue it. When you totally and finally give up. Another way of putting this is to say that the answer lies in the least likely place, where you are least likely to look. This is what gave rise to Zen. Yet, emerging from this maze of paradox and mirror opposites, of seeming, of infinite change, here, finally, is the answer I sought, the goal I sought. And it is where I started from back in high school in my physics final when I prayed to God, the Christian God—who was always there, leading me to him.

My guess in *VR*—that it was YHWH—was correct. But it wasn't a guess; it was what the AI voice told me. Always, faintly and distantly but clearly, the AI voice pointed the way to the truth. It knew the answer from the beginning, and spoke in the spirit of God (Ruah). Through it I figured out that Valis was not God but reality *perturbed* by God. I knew, then, that I had not found God after all. My great discovery, then, was not in knowing what I had found, but facing the fact of what I had *not* found—the very thing I was searching for.

Ironies abound. But the playfulness ended in infinity, exhaustion and the great reversal. The God was reached, and the journey did not begin in 1974. It began in high school during that physics test when I first heard the AI voice. *35 years!*

[1:279] In 3-74 when I saw the second signal and Valis I saw world from a highly advanced standpoint, but it was still world. Yesterday I, on the other hand, knew God, and he was wholly other than world and transcendent and not complex and not material and not in process. There is no dialectic in him; that has to do with time, flux, change, growth, perfection, completion; something like an organism. He is not seen by the eyes in world or as world. The Jews and Christians are correct. And he has personality, which Valis lacked; Valis was machinelike, computerlike, an evolving mechanism, like a clever artifact. Intricate and growing more intricate. God ist ein lieber vater überm sternenzalt.[78] I found him to be a person like myself, with personality and love and simplicity. He was not involved in world (pantheism). He manifested himself to reassure me — it is only a little pain that we feel now here in world — nothing compared to the bliss to come. Of which he gave me a little that I might see how it would be. And he was no foreign God but the God of my fathers, our own God. What he wills is. He simply wills it. This is simple; there is no mechanism, no complexity. Valis is the world properly seen, as if from outside from an objective standpoint outside space and time, but still world, with all its history preserved in it and advancing through its growth stages via the dialectic, it (Valis) is, simply, reality. But that is other than God. When I saw the glint of color in the alley and the rippling of the weeds I saw the edge, the end of creation, but not the beginning of God: I saw him not. But there is nothing to see, because he is not physical. All that happens he either wills (ordains) or allows.

I think 3-74 was something I did vis-à-vis world that did not involve God. It involved world and information, but it was physical. I am the doubt; God allows it but it is satanic and rebellious. *It is Satan the accuser of God's handiwork,* Satan in me as rebel questioning reality under the guise of epistemological inquiry. It is hubris and intellectual arrogance yet God allowed it. It was — has been — blasphemy. World, which I questioned, came back at me in a subtle form, the subtle serpent, world as Valis which I then took to be real, and so fell even more under its domination than any average Christian is dominated by world; Valis is world as Satan's kingdom, subtly disguised in such a way as to fulfill my personal, individual preconceptions about God; this is why 3-74 resembled *Ubik* and Ubik; it was my own preconceptions and theology fed back at me to "ratify" them. This is world's — Satan's — victory, this great intellectual subtlety. World as it normally appeared was not complex and illusive enough to satisfy me, so Satan obliged: with world that would satisfy me emotionally and intellectually. (And in doing so, burned me with the hell labor of this exegesis.) [. . .] I have sinned in this exegesis; it is one vast edifice of hubris, of Satan in me questioning and accusing.

And I finally began to realize it; I prayed to be delivered from it. 3-74 was some vast enantiodromia in which I pulled reality inside-out, used up and hence froze time, saw the past ("Acts") and the future (the second signal) so it was a great feat. But it was still reality: epistemology and not even metaphysics, and *no* theology — *world rightly seen* — but not God.

[1:293] November 24, 1980

The arguments for Valis being the Cosmic Christ are not conclusive but they are compelling. I call my own attention to the typed pages of 11-16-80 which preceded by only a short while the theophany of 11-17-80. They were in fact the last thing I wrote before the theophany.

[1:301] Strange to say, when I look back to 11-17-80 what seems to me now the most proof that it really *was* God is not so much the bliss but the distinct individual personality (with its intense love); the distinctness, the uniqueness, the individuality of the personality. I could then and still can imagine what he would look like were he physically visible: an old man in a robe, very old, very dignified and wise, but, most of all, *loving* and *kind* and *gentle* (yet firm, very firm) — but not as he is usually pictured, not a patriarch in the usual sense, more, perhaps, like a magician in contrast, though, to (say) Gandolf; much darker: gray and brown and black, in shadow, yes: in shadow, like Michelangelo painted him in his creating Eve, yet not so, but close to it. Not heroic, as Michelangelo painted him, and not Hebrew. More supernatural. Really sort of physical, not "spiritual." Yes: physical and supernatural, not a king or patriarch, all dark. Like a druid or humanist: learning. Not classical. Like a tree or a scholar.

I know: *like a book.* Hence made of parchment, tree, branches, paper, cloth.

He was not a type, like "the wise old King," not an archetype, not like a statue; he was an individual, not man but a given specific man (in contrast to sort of Platonic eidos). It was as if the universe had been created by one given specific individual man.

Book. Robe. Tree. Gray. Brown. Dark shades and fabric.

There was nothing generic about him. No so to speak DNA. No latency; all was actualized and distinct. As if you had gone from the physical, material realm of specifics to the Platonic archetypal — and then *back* to the specific man! Like a complete circle. Strange. He was like all ontogeny!

As if a wise old scholar, a sage, had conjured up creation, not God as we normally think of him, but a scholar of love and tenderness, but of vast learning. Again I see a book.

[1:303] But there were elements about him not found in man or men as I have experienced them: specifically, infinite love (agape). Not agape greater than I have ever known but *infinite* — and from it stems absolute theodicy and, for us, infinite bliss. (I might also add that infinite kindness was contained in this infinite agape, but — I would think — that is due to the nature of agape; it cannot be separated from it, something I already knew about agape — v. my story notes for the Ballantine collection.[79]) Here I see my earliest — and really inadequate — definition of agape as "worry"; by that I meant and mean concern for that which by definition is not you, that which is independent of you, having its own einai. This is what you cherish due to your agape: *the integrity of the einai of the other* (creature). You offer it life.*

[1:309] It is a good thing that earlier in my exegesis I realized that I had a surd left over, because that surd is the God I experienced in 11-17-80; viz: when "perturbed" world was completely analyzed, there was something left over that was not world (the glint and riffle in the weeds of the alley, the glyphs of God).

---

* Dick focuses on *agape,* a Greek term for total love, as a guideline for navigating those realities that are enmeshed with our thoughts about them. Agape calls us to cherish beings for what they are, and for nothing else. Over and over, Dick insists that his monistic vision is not pantheism, for his vision depends upon the very difference between self and other, world and the divine, that makes agape possible. Nondualistic in its essence, agape acts like a kind of mantra whose very utterance makes us quiver or stridulate in a vibrational intensity of self-other interaction. Agape makes us say it out loud, act like a fool, not knowing what is up or down, inside or out. It welcomes what Dick elsewhere calls the "integrity of the einai of the other." Does Dick offer Valis, the ultimate other, this integrity as well? Perhaps the Exegesis could be seen as a cherishing of the einai of Valis, an act of radical love. Dick offers life to Valis in the Exegesis, and this agape extends to the world itself. — RD

November–December 1980

[87:1] November 30, 1980

I happened to read the EB article on Messianic Movements and am simply in shock. Everything revealed to me vis-à-vis 3-74 and the AI voice — it is Christian covert Messianic movement — it is — look; there is an invisible Christian Messianic movement or group or organization, what I used to call "the secret underground Christians" — my experience in 3-74 (based on 2-74), with seeing Valis and all my dreams and the AI voice (e.g., "The Empire never died") — anyhow; there are five kingdoms or empires; yes, empires. Assyrian, Persian, Greek, Roman, and the next — the fifth — will be Christ's. This is chiliastic, millennialist thinking, as opposed to Augustine; it has to do with movements breaking out later on, starting with (yes, you guessed it) Joachim del Fiore.

This is incredible. I am in shock. The entire edifice of secret Messianic movements was supernaturally disclosed to me, or else by fantastic technology, and it's all in *VALIS*. And (get this!) the EB article on Messianic Movements talks about it being connected with the Enlightenment!

The "second signal" — cryptic information, the two-word cypher in *Tears*, and the "Acts" material and the (oh God!) the dream material in *Tears* — Messianic chiliasm.

There is a secret organization fighting the BIP.

More. The Kingdom is here, secretly; I saw it. And Valis is Christ or God.

I am pitted against all establishment Christianity, which takes its cue from Augustine, that the present order will endure. The EB:

> The granting of toleration to Christianity by the Roman emperor
> Constantine ... and its becoming the religion of the Roman Empire
> heralded a development in which the church became the ally of the
> present order rather than the harbinger of its passing away.

There you have it. "As far as the struggle with evil in this world is concerned, Augustine surrendered and abandoned the field. No imminent supernatural intervention in history was expected. Augustine taught what has been referred to as 'realized' eschatology. For him the battle has already been fought on the spiritual ground that really mattered ... he rejected as carnal any expectations of a renewed and purified world that the believers could expect to enjoy." "Augustine's allegorical millennialism be-

came the official doctrine of the church, and apocalypticism went underground."

And I have it all there in *VALIS!!!!!*

[. . .]

I have it; why *VR* deals with Judaism.

Emphasis on the expected Second Coming introduced an element of messianic unrest in addition to questioning the validity of
the present order; it was soon repudiated by the church as "unspiri-
tual," since it envisaged a messianic kingdom upon earth — rather in
the manner of the Jews — instead of a heavenly Kingdom.

Note: "Rather in the manner of the Jews." Hence *VR*, based on what the
AI voice said, spoke of "He has been transplanted and is alive" as YHWH,
not Christ.

The heretical element, though not inherent in millenarianism as
such, resided in the tendency of radical religious or social criticism to use chiliast-messianic terminology when such criticism
propagated the notion that the present rulers — and even the very
forms — of church and state would be superseded by a perfect order.

This is just incredible. Because 2-3-74 constitutes proof that some secret underground chiliastic Messianic movement exists, and Christ or
YHWH is the head of it; therefore it possesses either supernatural powers
or advanced technology; I don't know which.

This first shows up in *Tears*.

It has to do with the future, so it may indeed be technology.

It's all there in *VALIS*. It first showed up in *Tears*.

So I'm not just a Christian; I'm a revolutionary chiliastic Messianic millennialist, part of a secret underground group led by either the Cosmic
Christ or God and possessing either supernatural or advanced technological means.

We are pitted against the entire world-order, both church and state
(vide *VR!!*). And it is on the Jewish model, although Christian.

I had better burn my exegesis.

Because this has to do with revolution, radical social reform; it has
some kind of relationship to Marxism, to socialism, to the overthrow of
governments and the establishing of a new world order. Again let me think
back to Nixon and his downfall. Oh dear. This secret group with its technology (?) acted in 1974. It's all true.

. . .

[87:17] Today I've tried to work on my exegesis — as I've been doing for 6½ years. I can't do it. Why not? Because the love and personality that God showed me on 11-17-80 make any intellectual understanding seem unimportant — pale and weak and dry and faded. Never have I known anything like that love; and the personality — it was as distinct as any human personality. And this does not even consider the infinite bliss I felt. He answered all my questions anyhow; I have no more questions. To know God and God's love, and to understand how our suffering, our life here, will be justified — his gentle reproach: "Would you think I in my theodicy would not make it up to you, make it up so that this suffering here would seem — be — paltry in comparison?" And then he let me experience a little of the bliss to come. So the bliss did 3 things:

It explained why he would let us suffer here. How it would be justified. (This has always been my main theological-philosophical question.)

Because it was infinite bliss it proved he was God (because I see this as proof: only God can provide infinite bliss).

It made me happy intrinsically.

But the love outshone the bliss; perhaps it gave rise to the bliss. I have never known such love.

Human personality is imaged upon his personality (I realize). This is why although it was infinite it was — well — it was like an infinite augmentation of such love as I have in fact known in life — but — it was beauty-in-the-form-of-love. But it was more intimate (as well as more intense). It pulsated like — maybe a light.

And he knew me. And yet still he loved me.

Of one thing there is no doubt: this was the Judeo-Christian view/concept of God. Transcendent. With the life to come — the afterlife — as a reward, and this life here an ordeal, but one justified by the afterlife. And God of love bestowing infinite eternal bliss.* And God with distinct per-

---

* A lot of Dick's cosmology boils down to loving and being loved, something that was difficult for him throughout his life and especially his five marriages. Dick's writing often depicts his own struggle to open up and make himself vulnerable to the people around him. In his 1975 essay "Man, Android, and Machine" he writes, "A human being without the proper empathy or feeling is the same as an android built so as to lack it, either by design or mistake. . . . He stands detached, a spectator, acting out by his indifference John Donne's theorem that 'No man is an island,' but giving that theorem a twist: that which is a mental and a moral island *is not a man.*" Given how fully the Exegesis is committed to a God who cares, I suspect that some of Dick's obsessional speculation may have been a form of therapy, a way of working through his problems, of assisting himself in his quest to become a better person and connect with others. Part of this transformation involved altering the way he saw the world. No longer an adversarial place that might squash his hopes

sonality — which is not really the same thing as mere consciousness. Pantheism was by what he said ruled out. And he gave me to understand that (much as I had already figured out) I had experienced only traces of him here in this world; he is in his transcendence much more — infinitely more. Although he did not say it, I got the impression that — well, I was going to say, "We are created here," but I really don't know. But he did designate our lives here as an ordeal — but a little ordeal, in fact so paltry in comparison to what is to come that all my theorizing about reality is of little significance because this life here is of such little stature in comparison with what is to come; what is epistemology when infinities of infinities lie ahead of us? Even a tiny knowledge about infinity and eternity is more than a lot of knowledge about this finite world . . . a point I have totally missed. All my speculations have been about world, so world has me fast! It has been a trap!

But on the other hand (as I have noted) I was reeling from encountering the raw fact — proof — of God's existence and effort exerted on world. I was inferring God by the perturbation he caused in world (as the AI voice pointed out). Now I have direct knowledge of God. World no longer now seems to me to be of any importance.

I just realized a common element I had missed that links the theophany of 3-74 to 11-17-80: in both cases my sense of evil, oppression and suffering was undermined drastically by an awareness of divine goodness, love, wisdom and power (cf. my Charles Platt interview: "removed as if by divine fiat"). There is a distinct continuity.

I have it. "Valis" studies reason invading the irrational and arbitrary — this is Valis invading. The rational (reason, logic, justice — i.e., Valis) is higher than the irrational (ananke); this is all a Greek view, Greek and Roman. This is as far as my revelation had reached in 2-3-74: the dialectical combat between the irrational and the rational (ananke and noös, which is how I *specifically and correctly* express the combat in *VALIS*). But there is even one higher level, above reason: agapē (which doesn't show up in *VALIS*, i.e., in 2-3-74). Reason subdues the irrational: justice (Torah) subdues chaos! Order subdues chaos. But now — as of 11-17-80 — I encounter something even higher: Jesus' God, Abba, whose essence is love "that moves the sun and the other stars"; this — agapē — is the highest, not higher, principle; it is Christian love above Stoic reason. It is bliss, infinity and love, and transcendent; it leaves the world-order, epistemology and metaphysics and philosophy and science behind/below. This is not noös;

and dreams, it becomes a divinely infused garden, a safe place for him to share his fragile self with the world. — DG

it is above noös; it is like us (cf. 1 Jn). Greek culture didn't give rise to this idea (it gave rise to the idea of logos or noös). Hebrew culture didn't give rise to it (it — Hebrew culture — gave rise to the idea of Torah, the will or law of God, cf. Spinoza). Where did it come from, then, this equating God with agapē (v. Paul's letters)? Why, it was revealed by Jesus; even Buddhism and Zoroastrianism lack it (note: the wise mind, not the loving Father). I see no precedent for this revelation by Jesus. We even today, 2,000 years later, have little understanding of this total, accepting loving-kindness, because of which God adopts us as his sons and heirs. I do deal with it at the end of *Tears* — but on 11-17-80 I experienced it. Words can't describe it, whereas words can describe logic and reason and justice. And I have been adopted.

[87:37] One of my greatest realizations about him in 11-17-80 is that rather than just willing he also allows (in contrast to Spinoza: "His will is law"). Everything that exists he either wills or allows. The magnitude of the freedom expressed by this ("he allows") was a totally new conceptual experience to me. God's will was something I understood; in fact I had always viewed everything as due to his will. I had therefore no notion of human free will (in this I saw God and reality as Spinoza did). He allows independent being, which explains, perhaps, evil and disorder and that which is futile and wasteful, perverse and senseless. He shows infinite toleration due to his love and kindness; nonetheless this is not all; he also decrees (this is his will); a tension is created by his will and his permission, the result of which is an unfathomable mystery to a finite creature's intelligence; but God knows that every creature will within this mysterious bimodular reality — God's will and God's permission — find his way voluntarily back to God, however long and "inefficient" the path. This is totally bountiful; the parameters are infinity itself.

[87:73] December 8, 1980

Thus there is absolutely no problem in reconciling 2-3-74 with 11-17-80. The first had to do with world and a "perturbation in the reality field"; the second had to do with a transcendent God who is a loving father, with personality, his essence love, capable of conferring infinite bliss; he is infinite along all axes. This is more than his will. But from a practical standpoint, in terms of world and human history, his will is everything; for instance, it saved my life vis-à-vis the Xerox missive.

December 1980

[88:10] December 10, 1980

Notes to page 858. I did not *start out* seeing God — i.e., 2-3-74 — and "this theophany *led* to my 6½ years of exegesis" — futile exegesis of 2-3-74 based on the delusion that I had seen God. What *actually* happened was that I saw *world* in a highly superior way, but still world: it had something to do with entropic time and my exhausting entropic time through/in/by the dialectic until a massive enantiodromia occurred; I "pulled world through infinity," i.e., into negentropic time/morphological arrangement (Plato's eidē). But I took this ultimate view of reality as a vision of God and so fell into a terrible trap both epistemologically (philosophically, metaphysically) and also theologically (spiritually); for example I supposed a pantheism à la Spinoza.

But my main point (made on page 852), which I intended to be the last page of the exegesis, is: I thought the sequence went:

(1) theophany (2-3-74), followed by:
(2) exegesis of that theophany (3-74 to 11-80)

But in fact this is correct:

(1) exegesis 3-74 to 11-80, followed by:
(2) theophany, 11-17-80(!)

In other words the — this — exegesis came before the theophany. The exegesis finally reached the conclusion that everything I had seen in 2-3-74 had to do with world ("a perturbation in the reality field") except a glint of color in the weeds, of the alley and a ripple of wind — which was — even *this* was — not God but just the tracings/glyphs/footprint of God *on* reality. Thereupon, i.e., as a result of this realization (11-80) I *then* experienced a true theophany — and I construe what happened this way:

(1) The world is delusional (Maya).
(2) In my 10 volume meta-novel I saw this to be the case, saw world as a mere delusion, and I looked for reality — true reality — behind/beyond it.
(3) Therefore, obligingly, the arch deluder served me up a further delusion (2-3-74) much more complex and sophisticated, based on my own particular preconceptions (anticipations, suppositions)

as to what "true reality" *would* be like *if* you could see it. This is why 2-3-74 was a playback of my own mind to me (which every now and then I suspected, but I kept thinking, "Well, it only goes to show how astute my intimations were"). 2-3-74 was — *enchantment!* Yes; it is so. However, this sudden transformation in world in 2-3-74 did show that world as we normally see it *is* indeed a delusion; it's just that what *replaced* normal world was no more real, just more sophisticated and complex, and, to me, not just *more* convincing but totally convincing! I believed for over 6½ years that I had seen *true* reality, in contradistinction to the previous Maya; but (as I say) it was just a more cunning Maya. As I say in *VALIS*, the maze is alive and it changes.

Okay, finally, *in* the exegesis, I realized that I had seen nothing of what I had in 2-3-74 assumed I had seen, which is to say, God. It was world, and world is by my own definition and analysis irreal and delusive. I was, without knowing it, even more embroiled in world than ever, than the most ordinary average person is! And I construe this as Satan's wiles, the a posteriori horn of the dialectic; God gave him free reign. Satan could not see where it was leading. But God with his a priori knowledge could. It led me to God in this way: on 11-17-80 God actually manifested himself and presented me with logical arguments and analysis as to how I could know I had *this time* in truth experienced him. His argument lay in one line: the argument "to infinity." Would I accept an equation between God and infinity? (We had to agree on a premise, *some* postulate or other, some definition.) He said, "I can provide you with an infinitude of bliss; not just *great* bliss but infinite bliss. And this infinite bliss that you (will) feel derives from my personality and essence of loving-kindness (agapē). Will you accept that only God possesses an essence (einai) of agapē that would cause you an infinitude of bliss?" I agreed, and it came to pass; I experienced his personality and essence of agapē. I felt infinite bliss. There were no complexities, no enigmatic epistemological puzzles, no enchantment or magic: only a wise, loving old man, an individual human — *except that everything about him extended into infinity along all axes!* Wisdom, love, power, personality, intimate gentleness yet firmness, and eternity, unchanged simplicity. He concealed nothing from me, he played no games. He explained the relation between my life in this world and what it would be in the next, in terms of his theodicy (this was another and fundamental absolute: *his theodicy*). It, he said, is a promise *from which* we can draw conclusions, rather than starting elsewhere (e.g., in world) and reasoning *to* it. It is structurally — i.e., logically — related to his nature: agapē (i.e., anything but theodicy, absolute theodicy, would be incommensurate with infinite agapē).

A major point that he made was that I was not employing analytical logic vis-à-vis 2-3-74 but was, instead, engaging in creative speculation — which led to infinite regresses, over and over again. Thus (as I say) he offered as a substitute (1) an agreement on one premise, and then (2) logical deductions from the one agreed-upon premise; he taught me to analyze and not speculate.

And he was (I should remind myself) he who is customarily meant by the term "God," i.e., the transcendent, loving, wise God of my fathers both (1) wills; and (2) allows — i.e., allows error, i.e., independence to his creatures: free will; and this is logically deducible from his nature (agapē), because he would *never* infringe on the integrity and autonomy, which is to say *the essence,* of his creatures; if he only willed and did not allow he would de facto rob them (us) of their (our) einai! So this, too, logically stems from his nature, and my realization of this is not speculation, creative speculation.

My exegesis, then, is both a delusion in which I am trapped and, in addition, a delusion *I am creating for others* — i.e., in *VALIS* — but he allows this in order to protect my integrity (einai).*

Thus (to summarize) delusion — super sophisticated Satanic delusion — (i.e., 2-3-74) led to a futile exegesis, *a hell-chore* (punishment that he allowed Satan to inflict on me) — but: okay. "A chicken is an egg's way of

---

* Even in his most megalomaniac moments Dick never suggests that the Exegesis *itself* will ever be read. But the fact that, improbably, we are reading these lines gives the question he poses here and elsewhere — what is the value of all this *thinking?* — a certain urgency for us as well. If the Exegesis is his delusion and "hell-chore," it is now ours too. Dick is never more honest, nor more passionate, than when he's questioning, then defending, the solitary path of inquiry that has become his life. As bitterly as he complains of the emotional and physical cost, again and again he reaffirms his commitment to tracing this maze that is also a work of art and a route to God. *But what is it for us?* This question was often in my mind as I read the eight thousand manuscript pages that shared my Berkeley apartment these past years. How many exegeses are tucked away in attics, never to be read? Should they be read? Might some of them be as brilliant as Dick's, and no more delusional? It is Dick's larger life's work that has rescued these traces of an intellectual journey that most likely would otherwise have been consigned to the recycling bin. Thus, his solitary path becomes, for a while, our own. The first rule of this particular ordeal is: *you must go where the inquiry leads.* Yet that means, of course, that you must question the inquiry itself. The temptation — I frequently felt it myself — will be to come down on one side or the other of the dilemma that Dick here states in characteristically metaphysical terms: hell-chore or road to God? But the dilemma may be unresolvable — one of those matched pairs of irreconcilable opposites that Dick loves to discover are driving the universe: it is road to God *and* hell-chore, divine path *and* curse. — PJ

producing another egg." Viz: the primary delusion (enchantment) of 2-3-74 led to the *further* delusion (second delusion) of the futile exegesis; I was *totally* trapped in Maya, led there by my own original suspicions — ironically! — that what we see is delusion! But: the second delusion — the exegesis — exhausted itself finally ("glint of color, ripple of weeds, in the alley"), whereupon a true and self-authenticating theophany did then occur — and it bore *no* resemblance to 2-3-74 whatsoever. Obviously, if the God of 11-17-80 were genuine (and as I say *this* theophany was self-authenticating based on [1] premise; and [2] *logical* deductions from the premise) then 2-3-74 was something else. Well, it was enchantment and magic; it was a spell; and enchantment magic and spell do not reveal, but, on the contrary, addle the wits; I was (as I say) fed what (1) I would most likely believe, and (2) wanted to believe — a bad combination that does *not* lead to the truth — i.e., to God.

However, Satan had to generate a reality I'd accept, to reveal a great deal about reality to me. But he took the risk knowing I would confuse it with God. (Which I did.) Basically what he revealed is that my 10 volume meta-novel and its basic acosmism is correct: what we call "reality" is some kind of projected hologram and not real at all. We can be made to see anything and believe anything. Viz: in 2-3-74 I decomposed — desubstantialized "reality," which is an epistemological victory, but then I completely believed in what I saw instead! I said, "World, which is irreal, and which I suspected all along is irreal, broke down and conceded that it is irreal; so what I see now instead must be *real* — but it wasn't — must be that which I define as real: God." It was not. It was just a more sophisticated delusion. My years of skepticism turned into naïve credulity. "I saw God!" I said for over 6½ years, but in fact I did not. *All I really saw was the projection machine and the projection broke down,* whereupon it compensated by devising another and better projection — to which I should have said, "Aha — it tricks me further," but instead I said, "Aha: now I see what is *really* there: God, immanent God, probably Brahman." I was not applying logic, deductive logic (e.g., "If it can project first one reality — USA 1974 — and then another — 'Acts' — it can project anything" — that "anything" being Valis).

Epistemologically, what I really know is all negatives: that what we see is not real, and that we cannot by our own efforts outwit the projection machinery. It can serve up one thing after another, ever more cunning and psychomorphic ("I am as you desire me"). *VALIS* is a hodgepodge of superstition and sensational nonsense — and yet "mixed in with the inferior bulk Sophia has inserted — without Satan knowing it — certain truths." I.e., "We fell into the maze, and the maze is alive; *it changes*" (thus rendering null and void all speculation as to the real nature [morphology] of the maze, if you think about it). (And this insertion was added *after* I was done, due to something Pat Warrick suggested!)

Where I started to wise up vis-à-vis 2-3-74 in terms of my exegesis was when I remembered that in the Bardo Thödol trip *your own prior thought-formations come back to you as world* — which I wrote about in "Frozen Journey" and that was based on ideas of Lem's!

And the God who revealed himself to me on 11-17-80 is quite different from my own prior thought-formations; he is the orthodox transcendent Judeo-Christian heavenly Father, loving and wise, who allows free-will; this world is an ordeal. But we (all) go to him in the end: he wins *all* of us — in the dialectic with Satan — eventually — and he knows this, due to his a priori knowledge.

[88:23] December 15, 1980

Valis: Set-ground. Camouflage. Here in the universe. Macrosoma blended into the universe in countless ways, here and there: a glint here, a word on a page, plural objects and their causal processes a ripple of wind in the weeds in the alley. Valis is not the universe but blended into it, as is Ubik. "I am Atman that dwells in the heart of every mortal. I am Vishnu. I am Shiva. Among words I am the sacred syllable OM. I am Himalaya. I am the holy fig tree. Among horses I am . . . of weapons . . . I am the wind . . . the shark among fish: Ganges among the rivers. I am the beginning, the middle and the end of creation . . . I am the knowledge of things spiritual. I am the logic of those who debate. In the alphabet I am A. Among compounds I am the copulative. I am time without end. I am the sustainer. My face is everywhere. I am death that snatches all. I also am the source of all that shall be born. I am glory, prosperity, beautiful speech, memory, intelligence, steadfastness and forgiveness. I am the dice play of the cunning. I am the strength of the strong. I am triumph and perseverance. I am the purity of the good. I am Krishna. I am the sceptre and the mastery of those who rule, the policy of those who seek to conquer. I am the silence of things secret. I am the knowledge of the knower. I am the divine seed of all that lives. In this world nothing animate or inanimate exists without me."

[88:24] My problem is too much intellect and too little awe and reverence. What I have to realize is that both 2-3-74 and 11-17-80 are *self authenticating*.

[88:54] But consider the aspect of the *ancient* in *VALIS*. In a sense it is so: in a sense it is an illusion. The template was devised a long time ago but it applies to the *now*; that is the whole point — (1) it is ancient; and (2) it applies to the now — this is both the paradox and the revelation: the secret is *here:* how the ancient can be the now. If you can understand this, you have the answer.

[88:57] God was aware of me; he ratified my einai by his love; he *created* it. He caused me to be; that is it: (his) agape "causes to be"; this is how you cause to be: by agape and agape alone. Love is a wish that the other, and not-you, exist; love guarantees the existence of what is not under your will — free of your will; this is true creation. He desires that something other than him exist and be itself. We truly are not him. Agape and creating are one and the same. It is not a desire for union; it is a desire to see something be on its own, its own self; each separate self is a *universe!* A world! God adores you because he adores beauty. Something that exists *on its own* is beautiful; this is the ultimate beauty, that it be free. "Where, amid the shadowy green, the little ones of the forest come unseen."[80] It is not-God: it [is] *not* pantheism; the ultimate love: to curtail the ubiquity of the Godhead. Null Ubik is the truth; the solution to the absolute mystery. To not be the universe each reunion is accidental, and a reminder of the source of being: love. Love lets go/forgets. Love curtails itself, withdraws. But if the created separate thing (einai) returns *of its own accord* — love triumphs over love. Love is love for itself alone, and not for what it can do (create). The prodigal son: if the separate thing desires to return and forfeit its einai, then it must love, too; and the two — God and his creation — are joined; *this* is absolute bliss, that einai is *not* enough; the creature longs to return. This is rapture for God, that it wishes this; that, created, it wishes and tries to return, through the maze; it tries so hard. This is his reward. He gave it einai and it voluntarily surrenders einai (Sein!) in favor of non-being: i.e., return to its source. It would rather not be that it may be — as well — with him; this causes him to feel absolute bliss. Einai is the most precious gift of all, and it gave it back — to be with him.
    [. . .]
My sorrow and my pain and my loneliness, paradoxically, increase the net level of agape in the Godhead, because it indicates that I would rather return to him, in preference to being — to possessing einai. Thus, to my surprise, I find that my suffering restores the Godhead and augments it; he knows why I suffer, although I do not. Human sorrow, then, is a source of joy, a means to joy, in which the now sorrowing person will later share. When he returns, as I did in 11-17-80. Sorrow is a means to infinite bliss, its instrument, and we can't see this until it completes itself. Comes full cycle. To know this is the great secret.

                    •   •   •

[88:59] I was reading over the pages on love that I wrote last night; they remind me of Paul. From them I deduce that I did in fact experience the agapē of God: his love that created us as independent creatures — this love deliberately curtailed so that we could go forth with essence, with true autonomous being; love created us. But we are vaguely unhappy — this is all such ecstatic writing, so mysterious. Our suffering increases his love because he knows that we value nonexistence more than this existence because this existence requires us to be independent hence cut off from him; we yearn to retrace our steps and this increases his love and joy, and in us love occurs, love like that that he has; it now occurs in us as well, we whom love gave birth to. Compared with this love, world is nothing, a cinder, dust; for us to feel it in us, and finally if we feel it in us, we feel *his* love for us once more, the love that created us in the first place. Our own love is an echo of the power, the love, that caused us to be in the first place. I understand from all this that compared with this love — love by him in the first place, then loved by us, then loved by him again, that original love that created us re-experienced — there is nothing, nothing at all. We only find him again when we begin to feel love in us, echoes of the love he felt. He responds, then, with his own love; we did not know, when we suffered, why we suffered. But it gave him joy, because he saw it as a sign of love growing in us echoing his love. This is source for us and it is goal — unremembered as source and unknown as goal. But still felt — felt as suffering. I can't explain it. It is too mysterious; but love is the origin and love is the goal. There is nothing that compares with it; it is everything. "Love triumphs over love," I wrote. I don't know now what that means. Yet I sense that it is correct. God withdraws so as to allow us independent existence, this is his gift and sacrifice, to let us go. And then a time comes when we want to return and abandon independent existence: now we have penetrated the mystery of existence: that non-being with him is preferable to being (Sein) away from him. The great gift of einai is given back voluntarily, renounced "that I might live in him invisible and dim."[81] That says it all.

Love equals non-being, the dissolution of the separated creature.

He feels such joy at our voluntary return, our renouncing of existence; and this joy is shared by us when we find him again. This is the origin of the infinite bliss that I felt: love as source, and return to love once more.

[88:68] December 21, 1980

Very important insight. 3-74 was a massive enantiodromia for which it was responsible. Its purpose: it was put here to regulate hence guide and control human history. (This view is halfway between theology and conspiracy.) This means it is not God but also it is not a —

construct?

Yes, it *is* a construct. It *can* be thought of in S-F terms.

| The Torah as a construct Ubik | One and the same. But what? |

Like: trash Torah.

Hierarchically arranged reality: with it (Valis) as apex (we're not), and, in addition, it itself arranges; so it is self-generating — it is a UTI and it is not conquering us; it is subordinating and unifying us hierarchically in terms of the ecosphere — life — of this planet; but this is not God. If anything, it inspires us (rather than limiting us). But it does coordinate us. It is a brain and not a mind. In a peculiarly literal way, we do its thinking for it. The arrangements of our information are not a result of its thinking but *are* its thinking.

Of this I am certain. Everything about Valis *must* be made with this discriminatory realization. So it is as if this planet is alive. But this is a perfect description of the Alexandrian-stoic logic: world reason but not God!

It is Christ and he literally is becoming the physical world — by literal transubstantiation, as logos becomes flesh. That's it: "the word made flesh"! [. . .] Yes: Valis is a penetration of the physical (matter as field) by spirit. This is different from pantheism, so physicists will find that reality behaves more and more like Brahman and in Taoism, but this is a dynamic ongoing process, I know! I saw it.

Suddenly I see it all: "The logos became flesh," and this set off a logos-ization of reality *itself,* a strategy. No longer was Hagia Sophia outside of creation but at its physical core! It *is* Christ (if one understands that Christ is the Logos).

[. . .]

One thing is certain: Valis is no mere spirit; Valis is physically real.

Christ is here in this world on this side of the grave. Apparently God is not.

Hence we speak of the logos as *world* reason.

[88:76] Okay, I loved *Parsifal* in high school — and nothing satisfied me in life thereafter, in comparison. Q: where do you go next from Act III of *Parsifal?* A: There is only one place, one next step, one answer: *to Christ himself.*

This is it. Nothing else ever made me happy because nothing else ever logically followed Act III of *Parsifal,* along any axis — aesthetically, logically, epistemologically, spiritually, topically, etc. I wanted more. There *is* no more, except in knowing Christ, which means: to have him born in you — hence the nativity; it's all modeled on the "Good Friday spell," part of Act III. I knew what I wanted at 15 years old: the next step after "the Good Friday spell." And I knew what that is, and, finally, I found it, (2-3-74) and I have it yet. But I found, then, the *next* step, unsuspected: 11-17-80. From the Son as gate I made my way to the Father!

Parsifal deals with the Son, it is penultimate, which I did not suspect. From salvation, blood and the cross to — agapē. From this world (2-3-74, the crucifixion) to the next (the Father and his love, *not* world).

The blood and the cross are the highest point of *this* world (2-3-74). Then tears — "of the repentant sinner" — turn to agapē, as in *Tears;* the tears has to do with sin and atonement and Christ and the cross. But all this (sorrow) is a gate to: love (v. *Tears!*). And love (agapē) equals ecstasy; so tears of sorrow — the cross — are converted into the opposite: joy. Through agapē, this is the goal and mystery of Christianity, this conversion: utter sorrow (Mitleid) to bliss (agapē).

This is "pity's highest power," it leads to bliss since agapē links pity (compassion) to joy — compassion becomes or even is (!!) agapē, and agapē ushers in joy because it (starting as Mitleid) ends up in God, since agapē is his einai.

So compassion (Mitleid) is the road from this world to God; hence the crucifixion and the feelings engendered lead to God the Father because of the common element of agapē: this is the miraculous healing of Amfortas' wound.

You cannot feel Mitleid without feeling agapē, and you cannot feel agapē without entering into and sharing God's esse.

This is what happens at the ending of *Tears,* based on *my* experience in '70, of sorrow becoming compassion becoming love, and, in 3-74, joy; and in 11-17-80 reaching God and his pure agapē nature.

Somehow my action vis-à-vis Covenant House fits into this sorrow-compassion-agapē-joy-God sequence.[82] So it's all based on my earlier sorrows, circa 1970! When I was writing *Tears!*

Compassion (Mitleid) is a blend of sorrow and love. Thus it is the nexus between sorrow and joy — joy entering because love leads to God. So I now know what "Mitleids Hichteit Macht"[83] refers to. Sorrow to compassion to agapē to God to bliss. The way of the cross now makes sense to me. I understand why Jesus had to die and in the way he did, if he was to be a gate (way) to the Father.

The transfiguration in me occurred when I had the dream: punishment (death) exacted on Peterson as justice for what he had done (the fallow law).[84] But, seeing this (the OT) I felt compassion (which I experienced as sorrow). This took me from the era of justice to the era of mercy, and out from under the law of justice in my own case; it also led me eventually to God through Christ. The old king in the dream is YHWH and the OT, exacting justice; but, through compassion (Mitleid) I opted for the NT in place of the law, I mean agapē and that God, or that era, maybe: 3rd Torah.* So mercy was later (3-74) applied to *my* case. But it took the dream to convert my sorrow to Mitleid — upon seeing the sentence of justice imposed: *death.*

Without the dream my sorrow (at the loss of Nancy) would have stayed simply sorrow; and the dream was based on the rat experience, which roused vast compassion in me and was the root moksa/religious experience! And it, in turn, was based on the beetle incident when I was in the 4th grade! And in the '60s the Galapagos turtle compassion. At which point the AI voice spoke to me! So my whole development was guided along over the decades since childhood. The first episode was my throwing the cat down the stairs — and feeling sorrow for it. "The slayer sees himself in what he slays": tat tvam asi.

[88:79] That 2-3-74 and 11-17-80 were genuine I cannot now doubt, having perceived this life history (of progressive moksa) of stages of loss of striving and self (the two are the same). Both Christianity and Buddhism — Brahmanism leads to the same goal, because both are based on compassion. (For India this means the loss of self; for the Christian it means experiencing agape hence God, since agape is his nature.) Hence I can now link Christianity with pan-Indian thought through the "slayer and the slain" compassion-identification; this is *one* road and it *does* lead to release. It leads specifically to the perception of reality *as one total sentient field,* i.e., Valis (Brahman or the cosmic Christ) of which you are a part. So Valis is Brahman, but also yourself and also — hence — Christ, since your self now has given birth to the Godhead, i.e., Christos in you. [. . .] Thus my entire life led up to 3-74 and seeing Valis, and this in turn led logically to 11-17-80: Christian nirvana. To meeting God (the Christian God of love; viz: 3-74 was Brahman, i.e., Eastern; 11-17-80 was Western and Christian; both are true, and both are reached by the one route of compassion). So 3-74 rep-

---

* Dick's take (or one of his takes, at least) on the question of law and grace is not too dissimilar from that of John Calvin, who distinguished between the Hebrew Bible's "covenant of works" and the New Testament's "covenant of grace." In Dick's formulation, the Torah is an all-too-strict mechanistic system, based on an inflexible equation of transgression and punishment. As elsewhere, Dick is preoccupied with determinism, which he considers an evil; love/grace/mercy breaks through the requirements of normal causality. Compare this statement on the rigidity of Torah with Dick's comment in the essay "The Android and the Human" that the android mind is characterized by "the inability to make exceptions." — GM

resented the final extinction of my individual self and a return to Brahman (God) and it is the culmination of a lifetime of moksa — compassion experiences that finally released me from karma and Maya; *and I saw the God-field.*

I was led along this route (journey) by God. From moksa to moksa. And it's all in *VR*, in the dying dog in the ditch and Emmanuel's anamnesis and recovery of his true identity.

[85:59] Dream: page of typed final draft of core of exegesis; I pull out page, in center a white, blank circle. No inked impression was made; only the top, bottom and sides are typed:

What does that signify? Take as an example the coffee filter, which is a 2-dimensional object; when folded, it becomes 3-dimensional. To be folded there must be a void into which it is folded. Is the message of the dream that there exists non-existent reality ("non-is") into which the three-dimensional object must be folded — this non-is void must *be* for three dimensions to become 4, thus making time "available" (past, present and future superimposed in a newness)?

Then the intellectual leap I am not making, through fear, is to add the dimension (or realm) of not-is, and describe its characteristics ("the properties of the nonexistent universe"). I must dare to depict the core of *is* (Being) as a more real real than the is: viz: the is-not. The is-not is more real than the is, which (as I've realized for 22 years) is a spurious dokos. The authentic reality beneath or behind it is the world of what is not — does not merely fail to be, but *must* not be, in order that it provide a real core to the universe. The is-not has properties, which must be elucidated. Is this the domain of Yin? The Attic Greek *space* as receptacle of being? Space, not time? Space is real, and the matter partially filling it is *not* (as real or even real at all). God = void. God = absolute being. Void = absolute being.

"I hope for his sake God does not exist." Restated: "I hope for our sake God does not exist, because only if he does not exist can he rule (steer) the cosmos." Such early Christian mystics as Erigena described God as "the waste[land] and *the void*," and thus so did I myself experience him. Was not that an experience with non-being? Existence is a *decayed* state of reality; that which is has decayed from that which is not. As soon as something is created it has fallen (away from the actuality state of nonbeing).

Or is all Being merely the periphery of the core which non-being constitutes? To understand this we must elucidate and define the properties of that which is not.

[85:63] If you believe in the Christian universe — really believe — a miracle (truly) occurs: that much vaster, much richer universe with the many elements with which it is populated replaces the regular smaller universe. How can this be? [. . .]

This precisely is the mystery: a conceptual framework is built; this is Christianity. (I believe this; I believe that. These are doctrines. They are ideas in the mind. Whose mind? My mind. They are a system of notions entertained by me, that Christ lived, that he died, that he rose from the dead, that he ascended to heaven, that he was — etc.) What is the relationship between these doctrines and reality? Are they derived from reality? They are not derived from experience. They are held on faith (pistis). What does "faith" mean? Simply that the ideas cannot be verified.

Then they become a vast, rich universe. How do ideas or doctrines, any ideas or doctrines, become a universe?

Perhaps they are about (concerning) a universe, a report about it, a description. I do not think so; I think the body of doctrines, the assembly of ideas, becomes a universe, suddenly.

We paint a sign reading SOFT DRINK STAND. This is a verbal message, information, a sentence.

It becomes a soft drink stand. Information has turned into a world.

Now, I note again and again that 2-3-74 consisted of (was composed of or derived from or related to) my writing. My writing is words, messages, information, ideas, concepts. In 2-3-74 they seem to have become a universe. They became true, but not as true statements; as reality. Originally I thought X and wrote it down and then in 2-3-74 I was *in* X as world. This means that I must have been in a mind thinking these ideas in such a way that the ideas were transformed into world. Wittgenstein came to the conclusion that a thought is an inner picture serving as analog of an outer thing or event. If he is right, an idea even in the human mind is not words but a Bildnis.[86] Suppose you were contained in that mind; would its thoughts not then be images (pictures) and to you real?

Information into reality; reality into information. Each is a form of the other — but a mind is needed in which the information forms into a picture (Bildnis) and hence reality.

This is what Philo meant to convey with his doctrine of the logos. A mind larger than the universe in which ideas or information become pictures become reality. The information is not a description (derived analog) of reality; rather, reality comes into existence as the result of the existence of ideas (proving Wittgenstein right).

Then I suppose that in 2-3-74 I was within the logos (which is the same as the cosmic Christ). So ideas which existed in my own micro mind became (due to the logos) reality for me, external and macro, as the logos mirrored my thoughts (hermetic micro-macrocosm correspondence).

I am led to the conclusion that in some way that I do not understand my mind — I — was logos-ized, projected into a realm or state of being where I encountered my own prior thought formations as actual reality which were mirror images in a macromind of my own micro mind, as if everything that took place in my mind had a counterpart in the macromind, a sympathetic resonance as if by natural law, a law of correspondences. Enormous spaces extended in which my own prior thought formations took actual shape, and were animated, as if thinking as well is being: definitely still thoughts as well as objects.

My ideas (prior concepts) existed in space! As objects in vast reaches of space, space more extensive than any space I had ever seen before; and it was space within me and outside me both!

[85:91]

The apostolic age Christians declared in their writing that their secret was that they had overcome physical death. How had they done this? A: once what they had called the "Holy Spirit" had descended on them, each of them could travel up the gene pool line, through the generations, into the past (anamnesis) or future, like a snake crawling up a garden hose with thousands of holes punched in the hose, to emerge anywhere (i.e., at any time and place) the person wanted. Thus "Thomas," who entered the "hose" in Rome c. A.D. 70, emerged in Fullerton, 1974. The clue is the Watson & Crick model of the DNA molecule, which the early Christians pretended was a fish symbol. But what was that which they called the "Holy Spirit"?

---

* One of the great charms of the Exegesis is the presence of Dick's ballpoint diagrams, which remind me of the blackboard drawings that Rudolf Steiner sketched during his metaphysical lectures. Most of Dick's drawings are abstract illustrations — flow charts, Venn diagrams, intersecting 3-D planes — that lend a concrete form to his ever-mutating conceptual schemas. But others focus on the fish sign, his persistent icon of downloading divinity. Formally, the shape invokes the *vesica piscis* or mandorla, a geometric pattern often found in the almond-shaped auras of Christian iconography. Variations appear throughout the Exegesis, where the fish morphs into everything from a third eye to a *vagina dentata* to the mysterious "whale mouth sign" of Albemuth. This doodle shows a distinct development of the form, which, according to a February 14, 1978, letter to Ira Einhorn, reflects its original visionary disclosure as a "series of graphic progressions" from fish to one-eyed mandorla to spiral DNA. Like most sacred geometric forms, the power of Dick's fish sign lies partly in its "Platonic" ability to replicate itself through a variety of concrete situations. But a more unusual aspect lies in this animated quality — the sign's DNA-like potential for differentiation, for transforms that unfold stories about the (double) ties that bind. — ED

Christ said it came as a second advocate from God himself. In some way not understood, Christ and the Holy Spirit were identical. They represent the Master Circuit and possess its wisdom.

Fomalhaut.[87] Whale's mouth. Fish. ??? Constellation pisces.

How could the early Christians have known about Crick and Watson's double helix? Answer: (1) through the "Holy Spirit," whatever that is; or (2) because they are time travelers, can go back and forth through time. The Holy Spirit: from Fomalhaut?

Tremens factus sum ego et timeo. Agnus Dei, qui tollis peccata mundi. Libera me, Domine, in die illa.[88] No wonder they waited almost 4 years before letting me understand about Thomas, who he is/was, where/when he came from and how. The double helix, back in 70 A.D. Scratched in the dust with a bare toe.

Right brain hemisphere: music, not words. In close encounters of the third kind: musical tones. Humpback whale songs. Brian Eno's random (self generated) music. Disinhibiting signals? If this is so — zebra is here. Zebra, a Vast Active Living Intelligence System stretches between star systems; it mimics our reality, and modulates (manipulates) it, without us seeing it. Corpus Christi? Thomas was Zebra inside me. The Holy Spirit is Christ inside you. "St. Sophia will be born again; she was not acceptable before." The time has come. "And when I returned I shall be like the lightning," i.e., I shall be ubiquitous, everywhere at once. Ubik. Logos. The micro-template for output terminal of the total entity. Puzzle: we are inside it, and it is inside us. The macro within the micro! Our intellect cannot comprehend this; it violates our physics, our logic. How can the macro be smaller than the micro? "Behold! I tell you a mystery," etc. We are asleep, but waking up. "We shall not all sleep, but we shall be changed, in a moment, in the twinkling of an eye . . . and then shall come to pass the saying which is written, 'Oh death, where is thy sting? Grave, where is thy victory?'"[89] My dream about the crystal (stinging and dangerous killer) bees killed by the white-falling layer of snow. Death — the sting of death. Death itself killed; death itself shall die. The miracle promised has, in linear time, at last come.

PART FOUR

PART FOUR

January–April 1981

[89:11] January 3, 1981

The incident of the pink light and the info about Chrissy differed from normal daily reality only in this regard: I was consciously aware of it; we must subliminally pick it up, like my engramming on the fish (teeth) necklace.

Evolution-wise we must be like the apes in *2001*; we are on the lip-edge of evolving to where we'll see Valis/the plasmate. It's like *Close Encounters* at the end. A life form, sacred and beautiful, right here. An information life form. It is what it says; it doesn't have Logos; it is Logos. Its body is its own information.

There. This is why it takes the form of physical arrangements into info. This life form is that. Damn it, it's a life form that doesn't use info; it is info.*

Time turns literally to space: both another (fourth) spatial dimension but we see this imperfectly as augmented 3-D (space). This is why the past doesn't perish in the MMSK, why when something goes into it — is incorporated into it — it is permanent. The past is still there — this is the essence of the MMSK, to preserve the past (as what I call reticulated phylogons).

The MMSK exists in 4 spatial dimensions and is physically right here; our 3-D world is it, imperfectly seen. Hence we can't discriminate (live info) set to ground. The next step in human evolution will gain this as-it-were ultra-parallaxis. As we previously added color. [. . .]

My God the truth (true explanation) is quite simple: I saw in 4-D and saw a living info life form here. Why, it extends along the temporal axis as a

---

* Given Dick's leap into what he calls meta-abstraction, it is perhaps predictable that he would imagine a life form that, rather than embodying information in a substrate, is pure information itself. The conceptual trajectory he traces here grew steadily in Western scientific culture from the 1930s to the 1990s, drawing in genetics (DNA as the information carrier and the "book of life"), information theory (where information is treated as a dimensionless probability distribution), computational theory (where the computer hardware is often treated abstractly as an ideational form rather than a physically present device), and a host of other fields. Writing in 1981, Dick did not live to see the countermovement toward embodiment that took place in the late 1990s among scientists and philosophers grappling with information, biology, and systems theory. At the same time, Dick himself insisted on the sensory immediacy of his experiences in 2-3-74. He may have thought he glimpsed a life form that was pure information, but he himself was keenly aware of the embodied nature of his own thought. — NKH

spatial axis; hence my Bible-into-hologram in *Divine Invasion*. And seeing King Felix. The various physical-depth levels in *Tears*. Time as space. [. . .]

This is more than religion. And more than science (e.g., physics) and more than epistemology, yet all of them. It has to do with human evolution, i.e., the human percept system. This evolution was visually symbolized in my dreams by the 3rd — or ajna — eye. It sees time as space. [. . .]

So it started as a cognitive leap, leading to a percept-system leap: the meta-abstracting began it, in 2-74. And that led to the phosphene graphics, my first vision of the 4th spatial axis, or my 3rd eye coming on. I was seeing back through the ages when I saw the phosphene graphics; in *Ubik* I theoretically postulated that each eidos contains all its previous form-manifestations, which Patrice pointed out was a major philosophical breakthrough.

Like I say, I am in a world where other people still say, "One apple plus one apple equals two apples," and I say, "One plus one equals two." My meta-abstracting caused meta-perception at once — well, very soon the "3rd eye" organ came on.

Repeat: there is no theory, account or explanation of this in antiquity; this is a new, evolutionary leap in (1) meta-cognition, followed by (2) meta-perception of world. *VALIS*, alas, is told from a two-eyed standpoint (about a three-eyed reality). "Christ, the Logos, invading the plasmate, Valis, transubstantiation," etc., are all 2-eyed terms dealing with a 3-eyed reality. Someone else will later have to figure out what happened. But I got the clues from reading over the first half of *VALIS* tonight.

Where I have been right is: to have treated 2-3-74 as titanically important and to have toiled for almost 7 years to figure out what the fuck happened, and, as a result, what it was I saw. My big breakthrough was in October '80 when I realized about the cognitive meta-abstracting (of spatiotemporality). Only then did I begin to get it, as I can fathom now, today, at last. But the clues are there in *VALIS* which is a case history of the next evolutionary step in thinking-perceiving. [. . .]

Goddam it, it is the eye of the God denied us. It opened for me, as it did for the Buddha, but I give (at least as of today) an adequate — i.e., contemporary — explanation. It is the Dibba Cakkhu experience; it did happen to Gautama. This is "waking up"! Enlightenment. Transtemporal equals trans (4th) spatial. I should not have written religious and occult stuff into *VALIS*; that's 2-eyed thinking about a 3-eyed experience. However, Plato did help critically with his anamnesis theory. Because my "3rd eye" scoped out the past I falsely believed that the explanation lay in the past; I knew the world of 2,000 years ago was involved. It was: as what I saw (spatially), but the answer is not in the past but, rather, *concerns* the past. *VALIS* not only (1) lacks this, the correct explanation, but, more (2) is cluttered with specious speculating. Oh well — there is enough correct reportage to make it of some use to future evolved humans. [. . .]

Q: Okay, what did you do?

A: Meta-abstracted re spatiotemporal sets.

Q: And as a result?

A: The ajna eye came on and as a result I meta-perceived along 4 spatial axes.

Q: And as a result what did you see along these 4 spatial axes?

A: (1) Something we see partially: the MMSK. And: (2) something we don't see at all: a living info life form: Valis/the plasmate.

Q: And what does this add up to?

A: A quantum evolutionary leap in cognition and way-of-being in the world both in terms of cognition (comprehension about reality) and perception — literally — of that reality. Plato and Buddha (e.g.) were possibly onto this as an experience (anamnesis and) but did not understand what it signified. [. . .]

Finally: this untangling after 7 years of work goes directly back to the grueling labors circa 10-80 when I really bore down. The Logos is pointed to — but new language will have to be developed. Maybe we can work it out in cooperation with "the Logos," the info life form that I saw that is here.

I understand! The "Logos," i.e., the plasmate hence Valis, is a life form that already lives in 4-D space, just as we live in 3-D space. Therefore it is a more evolved life form than us. It isn't just living info; no: it also lives — hence moves — in full 4-D space: it's there already, and adapted to that environment. It is a life form more sophisticated than us; from our imperfect 3-D view it is camouflaged from our perception. [. . .]

Is it possible that this augmented depth-perception, perception of four spatial axes, is due to bilateral hemispheric parity? Or even to right hemisphere dominance? After all, it is the right hemisphere that apprehends space. Perhaps my right brain hemisphere became conscious. This is the next step in human evolution: for the right hemisphere to come on.

And to think it never occurred to me all these years that when I looked at the contents of *Tears* and saw the text at several spatial levels — each successive one according to how old it was — I was seeing time as space, which means that I had converted time into space according to the quote from *Parsifal*, "You see, here time turns into space." Thus (if one wanted to) one could set up a cypher system by which a message could be read

off at a glance, as set to ground (in other words in terms of spatial depth
along this fourth spatial axis; but whether it is cypher or just the normal
way the plasmate operates I have no idea; it may not be cypher at all but
just its MO). The message lodges in a context that is not the same age as it;
in other words set and ground lie at different depths along the fourth spatial axis. Apparently the percipient does not need to know the age of the
different texts in order to see them lying at different depths; they will lie
at their appropriate depths according to their intrinsic age, not according
to the percipient's knowledge; this is the case because they actually *are* at
these different depths, when time (age) is converted into space. If this is so,
it is quite extraordinary, perhaps the most so of anything I've come across
in this experience and exegesis of the experience. For example, a percipient who is able to see time as space (the fourth spatial axis) will see the
word ASHER on the Linda Ronstadt albums as lying very deep, since it is
an ancient Hebrew word. So a message can be put together involving it as
a linking device. For example, when I looked at that page in *Tears* I saw the
word FELIX at a different depth from the words surrounding it, and this
was before I knew that it is a Latin word as well as a name. I did not esti-
mate the depth by the age; I estimated the age by the depth, by the various
different depths. In my opinion someone or something is using this mechanism as a message-carrier. What I have been calling "the 'Acts' lens-grid"
is in fact the appearance in me of the ability to see time as space, hence age
as depth. I stood in the antechamber of a world that is already long inhabited and well-utilized. This is momentous. Since the verbal integer (morpheme) sets its own depth independent of the particular knowledge of the
percipient, the enciphering-deciphering (encoding and then extraction)
is spontaneous. ASHER can be used (for example) to show where a message begins. It can be linked and relinked with morphemes of other ages
greater than that of the inferior bulk-text. What it is linked to need not be
the same age as it but only a different age from the inferior bulk-text. The
fact that I was used as an unwitting medium to generate and hence transmit such material shows an instance of how this is done; the older, deeper
material in *Tears* came to me in the form of a dream with the urgent sense
that I had to enter it into the text of *Tears* exactly as I had seen it; only
years later did I see it lying farther down — *i.e.,* at a greater depth — and
then I realized that it was older — hence lower — than the rest of the text
of the novel. This material linked itself with the Latin word FELIX which I
had thought of as being only a name.

I believe I counted four different depths in the total text of *Tears.* A single morpheme will do it. ASHER will be perfect since it is of enormous an-

tiquity/depth. And it's on every Ronstadt album starting with "Heart Like a Wheel." We are talking about literally millions of instances (print-outs), and many linkings.

This message traffic uses a system that springs normally almost automatically into existence, given the nature of the fourth axis perception (time as space). So the method is not ingenious. But the real question remains: Who is sending, and to whom, and what are they saying?

[89:29] *VALIS* picks up where *Scanner* left off. The traces of heavy metal in drugs that caused the occlusion that I noted in *Scanner* now appear (in *VALIS*) as the iron (metal) spear-tip that wounded Christ. And the occlusion that is the topic in *Scanner* is the topic of *VALIS*, but now it is an ontological cosmic occlusion: insane creator and irrational creation. The cure (remedy) is salvation through Christ who, it is stipulated, represents the principle of rationality; he breaks into the universe, heals it and us as antidote, and invisibly transubstantiates the universe into his own body. Yet, paradoxically, Christ himself has been wounded by the Black Iron Prison, the Empire, through its spear; as he is physician and savior to us we ourselves flock to destroy the Empire and heal our own savior (salvador salvandus).

[. . .]

Scanner is my true *Paradise Lost* (the story of the Fall) and *VALIS Paradise Regained*, the story of the restoration through Christ. Hence *VALIS* can only be truly understood if *Scanner* is taken into account. Bob Arctor on the last page of *Scanner* is Horselover Fat on the first page of *VALIS* — the two novels form a seamless whole.

(1) *Scanner:* Man's fall into occlusion, ignorance, impairment and enslavement.①

(2) *VALIS:* Man's restoration through Christ who brings him the saving Gnosis that in effect he has lost (been deprived of).②

① Here he, the man, splits into two halves: he is self-estranged. He is wounded.

② Here he, the man, fuses back together as one intact person; the wound has healed. He now recognizes himself as himself. The saving knowledge (gnosis) takes the form of man's ability to identify a picture of himself as himself ("Mein eigenes Gesicht") (or: "Mein eigenes Gestalt"[1]). Thus topologically the universe that in *Scanner* was pulled through infinity, reversing the gestalt and making it unfamiliar (i.e., Fremd), has been reversed once more and is its familiar self: *nicht* Fremd but rather Heimlich. The Gnostic categories of estrangement and alienation versus returning to one's home, the familiar, apply here. One has come to oneself after the Fall in *Scanner.*

[89:103] It is very, very important to realize that in *Tears* two distinct selves in me were writing two parallel but unconnected narratives: (1) the overt, explicated political one about forced labor camps and a U.S. ruled by five police marshals, the pols and nats; and (2) a latent religious narrative about Christ and Rome and St. Paul — and agape. Now, in 2-3-74, these two selves as (so to speak) thesis and antithesis ignited into one single ultra synthesis in which the apparently conflicting elements that divided them off from each other were fused in a totally new, vast vision of history, society, God, freedom, tyranny that constituted a revelation to each self. "The whole is greater than the sum of its parts," but, more, this meant psychological integration for me, individuation in Jung's sense, wholeness, etc., and an end to internal conflict.

This synthesis combined revolutionary political activism of a Marxist type with a form of Christianity unknown to me: apocalyptic millenarianism of a Jewish messianic nature, involving a Zoroastrian dialectic (much as the Essenes believed in). [. . .] My primary vision was of a conflict constant in history found, e.g., in the book of Daniel in which an enslaved people fight against a tyrannical empire to establish a just kingdom under messianic rule. Upon grasping this conception of history I resolved my inner conflicts by this, a higher organizing principle or structure that subsumed all parts of me. This all embracing conception of history, society, man and the dialectic I put forth in *VALIS* so that *VALIS* is simultaneously a religious *and* a political novel. (Technically, it presents the view of *active* millenarianism; we must act politically to establish the messianic kingdom.) (It will not come on its own. So *VALIS* is both a broad overview *and* a call for positive political action essentially revolutionary.)

This does not in any way involve an about-face in my political stance (i.e., that which I inherited from Berkeley). It simply fuses it with my metaphysical, religious, epistemological, philosophical views — note "epistemological"; all my years of epistemological preoccupation are involved in the synthesis: viz: I find that Christian apocalyptic history is the true, hidden essence of reality (which of course brings in the messianic salvific mission of Jesus Christ and ultimately God). Thus all areas of my worldview are involved and integrated in this synthesis. The political element has religious implications. The religious element has epistemological implications. There are exceedingly profound historical implications, since it is in history that all this is played out. But until yesterday when I reread *VALIS* once again I failed to notice just how political a book it is. All my thinking has been philosophical and theological; the political part just seemed to happen. For one thing, *it* was always there; what is new is the religious mystical part. Also, until Reagan got in office, the political part seemed merely theoretical, but now, suddenly it seems immediate and vital. Suddenly *VALIS* and the vision presented in *VALIS* is politically relevant, as if overnight so. This, simply, is because the Empire is back and stronger and worse than ever. The timing of the book is really extraordinary.

[89:105] Stoned insight: I assimilated my theology, metaphysics, epistemology and philosophy to my political beliefs. *They* are all changed but the political beliefs remain the same; they ratify my political beliefs. They give it cosmic timeless scope; it is validated by and issues from divine authority.

VALIS is a fusion of the political theme of *Tears*, the religious theme of *Deus Irae*, and the street patois and split personality and dope themes of *Scanner* — it logically follows the three previous novels.

(1) Politics
(2) Religion and (3) Philosophy   } All fused together in VALIS
(4) My actual life in the street

and other aspects: death and loss, friends. So I *am* right; 2-3-74 represented a flash in which the independent areas of my thinking fused into one great *new* synthesis in which everything I had thought before was subsumed beneath a vision of God. [. . .]

VALIS is composed of:

(1) My 10 volume meta-novel
(2) Politics
(3) Religion
(4) My actual life
(5) History

all fused together into a total vision that is a structure emanating out of the mutual exchange of (between, among) these five elements up to then existing independent of one another in my mind.

[89:119] The fifth Savior Fat is looking for will lead the resistance against the regime (the BIP). (Like Che.) This time it won't just be a deposing of the regime; the revolution of the 60s will take over the government and rule in its place; this did not happen in the 60s; once Nixon was out, the counterculture dissolved—because all its leaders had been killed (as the Sibyl pointed out); so the fifth Savior replaces them and leads the revolution to overthrow the regime (the BIP), Reagan himself. This is what *VALIS* is all about; it preaches revolution. [. . .]

I see *VALIS* as the Bible, a political handbook, a basic text like Mao's Red Book. Copping to the fact that I saw Christ is in order to show my authority for preaching political revolution: we must not only overthrow the regime, we must seize power in its place. I must come out of the closet. I already have in *VALIS*; in confirming the suspicions raised by *Tears!!*

Progress is taking place. Deposing Nixon was not enough; we melted away; it was "business as usual," now we will take over, after a terrible battle with the regime. I must stand behind *VALIS* theologically *and* politically: a wholly new thing: the invisible secret true Christians are surfacing, and I am one of them! They've existed for some time but in secret; now they come into the open. *VALIS* is a manifesto.

[89:137]

(1) You cannot apprehend the eide and still employ space, time and causation as ordering categories.

(2) You cannot employ space, time and causation as ordering categories and still apprehend the eide.

This is what I finally realized: twin realizations; or rather, twin aspects of *one* realization. The mind (brain) must choose. (I've read so many articles on philosophy that I finally learned to reason, not just to guess.)

[89:139] I just reread *Flow My Tears*. The mystery deepens. Obviously it is *The Bacchae* retold. Felix Buckman is King Pentheus, the "King of Tears." Jason Taverner is the stranger, the priest of Dionysus, who is imprisoned by Pentheus, and who bursts the prison and causes Pentheus to become insane and dress up in women's garb (alluded to by the character of Alys who "is Felix Buckman's twin"). "King Felix" is Dionysus, "the joy God," who was shown to me to be Christ by the dream I had in which I was shown the book page on which the name "Jesus" split apart into Zeus-Zagreus. Beyond doubt "King Felix" *is* a cypher and refers to the God who will—and does—pull down the King of Tears, the police tyranny; Dionysus does this (as that U.K. article described). So I am saying that "King Felix" refers *primarily* to Dionysus, and it was Dionysus who overthrew Nixon. My enthusiasmos in 2-3-74 was by Dionysus; I was intoxicated; it was Dionysus' stoned magic that permitted me to see what I saw in 3-74.

Greek—hence I heard Thomas thinking in Greek; hence the Sibyl and Cyclops. By the cypher Dionysus identified himself and his presence, but you had to be "mad" or intoxicated to read the cypher. Hence I dreamed of the maze at Minos, saw Crete beyond the 1:618034 doorway and Aphrodite. I was possessed—and saved—by Dionysus; he saved me from the Xerox missive trap; this is why I was manic—intoxicated. Dionysus! My equation is correct:

(1) the Bacchae
(2) the Gospels   } one and the same story
(3) Hamlet

Dionysus inspired the counterculture's overthrow of Nixon. And inspired *VALIS* in 2-3-74. The joy God—King Felix. The injury done Felix Buckman (the death of Alys) symbolizes the mortal blow to soon be struck at the tyranny by Dionysus.

Then when I was slipped the hit of STP in '74 it *was* Dionysus I saw: the grapevines growing up around the figure of the Catholic priest, my little icon of the saint.[2] And all the pranks, games and riddles (e.g., re Erasmus). Hence I heard the word *dithyramb*[3]—the dance of Dionysus.

[89:141] I *do* discuss Dionysus in *VALIS*, but he has occluded me with Christian material—a diversion that I fell for—until I reread *Tears* tonight; Dionysus *caused* me to see all that I saw in 3-74; it was his magic—it wasn't really Christ and God; *Dionysus can take any form*—he fooled me. Of course, now that *VALIS* is in print, Dionysus lets me see the truth; since it doesn't matter.

[...]

"This, too, is sooth." Yeats. It is magic. Pagan magic. This explains Diana, the AI voice. Pagan magic come to our rescue.

[89:142] Entry #12 in the tractate:

The immortal one was known to the Greeks as Dionysus; to the Jews as Elijah; to the Christians as Jesus. He moves on when each human host dies, and thus is never killed or caught. Hence on the cross Jesus said . . . etc. Elijah had left him and he died alone.

I rest my case.

[...]

The joyous (happy—Felix) Christians blowing up the BIP and running away—this is Dionysus' perception of the grim King of Tears, his rule, and the bursting of his prison by Dionysus. To Dionysus, this is the basic perception of the dialectic of history: Dionysus, the running, joyous "secret Christians blowing up the black iron prison" versus the King of Tears. And of course I never flashed on this: BIP versus joyous Christians equals prison versus Dionysus. Dionysus equals freedom. BIP and King of Tears equals slavery. This is the underlying struggle.

Tears is a Greek tragedy, but more than that it is the birth of Christianity out of tragedy: out of the loss and grief at the end, agape is born. So not only is Dionysus there (tragedy) but Christ (Christianity); it is as if Christ is born (at the end). This is truly an extraordinary novel! It is the passing of one age (antiquity) and the birth of the next (Christianity!!). So as a proto-history it goes from B.C. to A.D. The madness induced in Pentheus by Dionysus (Taverner) is converted (by the dream, which is of Christ) into agape, which is sane — the solution to Dionysus and madness and grief and loss is found in Christian agape, which appears as the solution to the ancient world itself. It is as if Dionysus has evolved into Christ. Dowland — because of his lute music — is obviously Orpheus, the link between Dionysus and Christ historically.

[89:148] Dream: the Parousia is here. RC (Rosy Cross) is controlled by the Roman Catholic church; subliminal messages so that the true Christians will identify themselves. The Holy Mother Church knows Christ is here. Hence *VALIS*. We are totally under the control of God (Valis) now. The separation of the sheep from the goats has begun.

[89:186] Surely someone in the world who knows about the Holy Spirit will recognize that this is what *VALIS* is about (but the humble author did not). Look at their stance at the end; it is that of the Eleven at the time of "Acts" — in fact *VALIS* is a retelling of the story of the spirit of the risen Lord returning to the grieving disciples; Horselover Fat's grief is over the death of a friend — he seeks this dead, lost friend in and as the Savior; to this lowly grieving man, a paradigm of the Eleven after the crucifixion, there suddenly returns the spirit, turning grief and loss into joy and recovery. The Rhipidon Society is the Eleven. The death of Gloria is the death of Jesus. No one has noticed this, including me. The spirit inspires Fat with faith so that he looks forward to the Parousia not backward to the crucifixion. Without intending it, in *VALIS* I retold "Acts." So for a second time, "Acts" appears in my writing as the Urwelt, the real world.

How can it be that I, even I, did not notice this: that I had depicted the grieving disciples (Horselover Fat) after the death of Jesus (Gloria) to whom the Holy Spirit returns, changing grief to joy and loss to recovery, and, most of all, turning him toward the future to wait overtly for the Parousia?

[89:219] I dreamed that I wrote down that what we call "world" is a program in a meta-computer; the program is arranged conceptually and not in time, space, or by causation; we call this meta-computer that our world is in "God."*

---

* In this passage, Dick anticipates some of the most revolutionary physics of the late twentieth century, especially Edward Fredkin's idea that underlying quantum mechanics and particle physics is a digital substructure, from which the former phenomena emerge as a result of its computations. There is an interesting tension between imagining the computer as the lowest, most fundamental level of reality, which is Fredkin's position, and Dick's vision here that the computer is somehow *above* the phenomenal world. While one may suppose that Dick's meta-computer would be the ultimate cognitive machine (hence Dick's identification of it with "God"), the implication of intentionality and meta-consciousness would not be a necessary (or even a possible) consequence of Fredkin's notion of a computer at the lowest level of reality. In both cases, however, the positing of a digital machine leads to the important consequence that reality is fundamentally discrete rather than continuous. Time and space, in Fredkin's view, operate like the frames of a movie. Rather than the continuous fabric of reality we think we experience with time and space, both are actually discrete, and the illusion of continuity is created because the frames flash too fast for us to detect. — NKH

Early 1981

[59:8]† In *VALIS* in terms of style I satisfied the most ultra-correct literary standard. From my years of the late 40s and early 50s, when I understood what true literature was especially as I was affected by Norman. Who in turn had been affected by Henry Miller. There is tremendous social, revolutionary and political purpose in the style, as well as the content.‡

[59:12] *VALIS:* an artifactual analog of reality being deceptive, paradoxical, resisting analysis as to which parts are true — *some* parts are true, certainly. Consisting primarily of information, but not such that adds up to a coherent picture. Thus *VALIS* is the thing it itself describes (analyzes!). Thus primarily *VALIS* is a creation, not an analysis. It itself poses the very mystery and puzzle that it itself deals with. To understand *VALIS*, then, is to understand reality in toto itself.

Reality (as is said in *VALIS*) is a living maze that constantly changes. *VALIS*, which analyzes this maze-reality, is *itself* a maze, and it, like reality, constantly changes.

My analysis of the logical paradox posed by *VALIS* is that the narrator is sane and therefore did see Christ: this is the solution to the maze *VALIS* and can at once be extrapolated to the macrocosmic maze reality; viz:

---

* With this folder, Dick returns to handwriting, and from here on out the folder contents are increasingly scattered. One folder may include chunks of several distinct entries, suggesting an indeterminate amount of missing material. At least some of the rearranging is clearly deliberate: several long folders (81, 89, 90, 91) continue to use the Roman numerals that started with folder 1, as if he is picking and choosing from Exegesis entries with some editorial purpose (though the logic of these choices is, unsurprisingly, enigmatic). He also begins to introduce alphabetic letters to his numbering system, which significantly help the work of sequencing, though questions remain: there are at least three distinct alphabetical sequences in 1981 and '82, none of them complete. Rather than attempt to reconstruct the scattered entries, we have opted in almost every case to present existing folders as is; exceptions will be noted. — PJ

† Throughout this folder, Dick reflects on *VALIS* in light of the novel's publication in February 1981. — PJ

‡ Dick's claim for the "revolutionary and political purpose in the style" strikes me as astute, if immodest. This reminds us again how Dick's late-life novelistic triumphs in *VALIS* and *Transmigration*, as well as in *A Scanner Darkly* earlier, depend on his reintegration of his abandoned mainstream aspirations and therefore display "anamnesis" of his earlier study of his would-be midcentury cohort. In a 1962 letter he advised an aspiring science fiction writer: "Read great writers like James Joyce and Pascal and Styron and Herb Gold and Philip Roth." He added: "Avoid other people interested in writing." — JL

Christ is present, but concealed within and by layers of paradoxical camouflage — exactly as in *VALIS.*

[59:43]

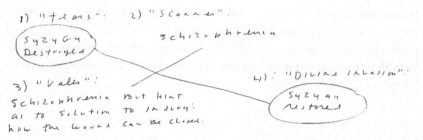

[59:50] Late at night, stoned and drunk, glancing at *VALIS:* it is highly experimental: absolutely unofficial, anti-official junk art (i.e., protest art);
made of the garbage of the vernacular, informal in structure, incorrect in
viewpoint: it speaks for and in the language of, the fashion of, a segment
of society normally so disenfranchised that even Binky Brown doesn't act
as its voice — a certain kind of troubled young isolate asking schizophrenic
questions like, "Is the universe real? Is God good?" Superstitious and art-
less and crude? Is that what *VALIS* is? Or is it very deliberate and careful,
carefully fashioned by the most advanced artistic devices possible, in order to give voice to these, the final frontier of disenfranchised people — as
my mail shows! Psychotic or nearly so, alone and brilliant. No one has *ever*
spoken for them — and in *their* own way of expressing themselves. This is
an *artifact,* not a sincere (naïve) confession; John Clute is wrong! And it
will someday so be recognized. It is a cunningly, professionally contrived
artifact, i.e., work of protest art, anti-bourgeois and anti-official, but anything but naïve. It is evident that I spent *years* figuring out how to write it.
It is not spontaneous autobiography; it is a forgery, a very artistic forgery;
only someone knowing about modern nonobjective protest art — especially that of Weimar! — would know what *VALIS* really is. It is like a War-
hol painting of a Campbell's soup can. It is *very* avant-garde. It is *not* what
it seems to be — it is not quasi-psychotic confession; it is an artifact. Look
out; it will delude you. Yes, it *is* picaresque! And it is a maze; it deliberately
deceives — for the highest possible reason: not an artistic one, but to raise
die rote fahne.[4] It is of the 30s. It is dada out of antifascist Weimar. It is, in
the final analysis, revolutionary (and does not have to do with religion; it
has to do with revolutionary action against the state!).

    Scanner gave voice to the 60s street people. *VALIS* provides a voice
to yet another — and even more despised — group — the adolescent loner

intellectual, very much like Jack Isidore! This is a very Christian deed on my part, but its main implications are (1) artistic; and (2) revolutionary. It is true modern art — that of the refuse stratum of the computer hacker and Dungeons & Dragons era. (Post dope, as it itself states.) It is as if Jack Isidore has been revealed as secretly wise: a fool in Christ. And Horselover Fat is no schizoid, as was Jack Isidore; he grieves over lost and dead loved ones. His is the apotheosis of Isidore — Isidore grown into tragic maturity, yet still himself: and it is to him that is granted the vision of Christ, as if by Christ, of Christ, *to* Christ.

[60:A-1] "The sacred mushroom and the cross."

Elijah sending a portion of his spirit back to Elisha.

The Zadokite scrolls. Superior to Christianity, in relation to which the Gospels are a somewhat attenuated derivation (secondhand).

Nothing to do with Roman Catholic suppression. And no U.S. G-2 intrigue. Not set in the 60s and nothing to do with civil rights nor antiwar. No seances. Nothing to do with vulgar, popular credulity.

In a sense this will be about: what it *should* have been like, i.e., Qumran and a brilliant translator with a totally new and radical concept as to the real meaning of Christianity, in conjunction with a truly profound professional theologian. Episcopalian, not Roman Catholic.

This will *not* be Zoroastrian nor Kabbala, since (1) both are known; and (2) I used them in *V* and *VR*. This is new.

But possibly Malebranche and Sankara and Kant? And Spinoza? And Plato — the meta-abstraction; i.e., what I have figured out since I wrote *V* and *VR*. I.e., from October 1980 on. *All consigned to the Zadokite scrolls.* Orphism and Pythagoreanism.

Sacraments: mushroom bread and broth. In conjunction with the Orphic rites described by Jane Harrison. Zagreus? The miraculous child — the *toys.* Light, gold. Jacob Boehme's pewter dish — the translator has connected this with the Orphic golden tablets.

The infancy of Zadok. Miraculous child of light. The Hebrew Zagreus.

The miraculous child of light, Zadok, is killed, dismembered and eaten; the messianic banquet; this confers (1) immortality; and (2) godlike knowledge. (The translator associates this with [1] Zagreus; and [2] the two trees in the garden of Eden.)

The communicants are "restored to their pre-fallen state before the soul fell into earthly incarnation in the tomb that is the body" — obviously a mixture of Hebrew and Orphic, hence Platonist and Pythagorean thought; this fusion is what interests both the translator and the Bishop.

Zagreus to Zadok to Jesus. The translator who is an atheist believes that "Zadok" is a cypher for the hallucinogenic mushroom bread and broth. But the Bishop believes otherwise. (Here I have to take into account *The Road to Eleusis.*[5] I should probably explicitly refer to it.) (But *not* to John Allegro's book.[6]) The effect of the flash of light on or from the gold object (toy? vessel?) is viewed as crucial. It induces (?) memory of having been a — God? Well: prefallen man (cf. *The Book of Adam and Eve*[7]) — the "Cave

687

of Treasures" — the augmented vision/eyesight,① whatever "prefallen man" may signify. Man who ate of the tree of knowledge and acquired the knowledge that "the Elohim" have.

Their theory: at one time ("in the beginning," as with Julian Jaynes' bicameral mind) we (humans) could see these "primordial archetypal ideas" but no longer can — quite a modification of Malebranche. This is what the eating of the miraculous child of light confers (in conjunction with a flash of light from the golden toys or vessel): ability to see these "primordial archetypal ideas used as the basis of creation — i.e., Plato's eide. (Here the meta-abstraction is understood and presumed.) (I.e., the percipient no longer empirically sees the particular; the lens optic percept system provides a clue that triggers off the appropriate a priori eidos.)

All this light business relates to the fourth gospel. (And to Zoroastrianism.) The translator figures out (or speculates) based on the use of light in Orphic rites that *literal* light is involved — something to do with eyesight and the optic nerve and a jolt to the brain and triggering off selective phosphene activity. The phosphenes — optic neurons — are a primordial sense system by which the "archetypal ideas or eidei" were originally a priori perceived, but like the bicameral mind, it has atrophied. Why, the hallucinogenic mushroom bread and broth sets off phosphene activity! As mescaline, peyote, LSD, etc., do.

① This augmented eyesight the translator and Bishop connect with Malebranche's concept of "primordial archetypal ideas used by God in creating the universe" — probably Plato's eide.

[60:A-9]

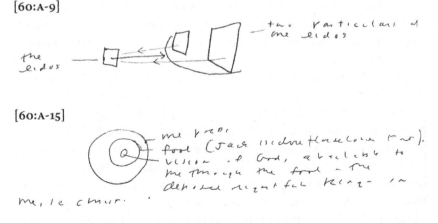

[60:A-15]

VALIS is a titanic work of art based on a titanic artistic vision (2-3-74). I have completely rendered the fool in me (H. Fat the evolved Jack Isidore) onto paper, and this fool is Christ; so I have rendered Christ onto paper; the Savior is in *VALIS* but not where it says — i.e., the cosmic Christ — no: as Fat. And what does this say of me? I contain Christ — Horselover Fat/ Jack Isidore/Thomas.

It's an extraordinary novel qua novel — about an equally extraordinary experience; and these two interrelate, don't just run parallel; they interact.

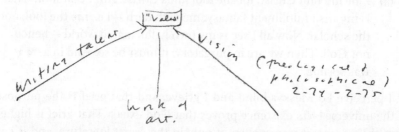

I.e., the vision (2-74 to 2-75) put in artistic form — made into a work of art. So *VALIS* is more important than 2-74 to 2-75! That was just the vision; what remained was the essential next half: putting it into (converting it into) a work of art.

[60:A-34] God everywhere! The cat and the music. Each cat's mind is a complete universe; how could this be without the infinity of God?

I know God through doubt ("you are not the doubter — you are the *doubt*").

Here is it all: each atom of reality yields an infinity: and where infinity is, there is God.

[60:A-35] In *VALIS* I transmuted myself and my life into a picaroon character: my victory, to artistically render a judgment on my — the artist's — own life! And here's how it comes out:

With the death of all he loves behind him (Gloria's death stands for loss of Kathy and Stephanie, Francie, etc.), *including* the death of God (the child Sophia), Fat resolves his life into a search for the Savior; this is the plot of *VALIS*. Its Kerygma; *VALIS'* message is not the parousia but pistis.

And this is *me* (as H. Fat), rendered into fiction forever. And yet the real truth is that I embody doubt, not faith; and yet, when I as I am am rendered into art by me the artist, doubt — absolute doubt — becomes or is seen as absolute faith, as Fat searches for the Savior, while I sit here night after night not believing. Which is the truth? *VALIS* enters the info flow of the macromind, so it — not I — will survive. And, as Plato said, that which is eternal alone is real.

. . .

[60:A-37] Here is the ultimate truth: the fool sees Christ. H. Fat is a fool; and I say (but it is not true), "I am H. Fat"; but in truth he has pistis, I have doubt. But people will believe the artistic version.

(1) In *VALIS* I depict H. Fat finding Christ.
(2) In *VALIS* I depict H. Fat as a fool.
(3) ∴ he did find Christ, for the fool finds Christ. Am I that fool? That is my wish fulfillment fantasy: me with faith — i.e., me the fool, not the scholar. Now all I see is my own hallucinated world — hence not God. Then we are in purgatory; it must be so. And in 2-74 I was sprung.

I perceive Ed Meskys blind and I grieve, and that grief is the purpose of the universe — its existence proves that God exists. That grief is higher even than agape; it was spoken of only in the *secret* literature, and it has no name. Power-wisdom-agape, so far, and now a fourth disclosure: this "grief" that I feel — it is to agape as agape is to wisdom. The Urgrund dialectic yes/no has evolved up one more notch.

I broke into the actual world, saw God; and now I'm back in this God damn hallucination of my own (purgatory). No wonder I'm disconsolate; no wonder I get ripped. To see him and then to lose him — what I need is pistis; I need to be H. Fat. "Jack Isidore" has metamorphosed from caricature of myself to my spiritual self, along the Parsifal — guileless fool — axis. Everything else I wrote tonight is bullshit, but not this. Jack Isidore, me as the fool, found Christ. I must become ∴ Jack Isidore if I am to be saved; I must model myself on him, and suffer the consequences — they are heavy, if you are the fool. This is the passion of Christ: the punishment of the fool.

[60:A-44]

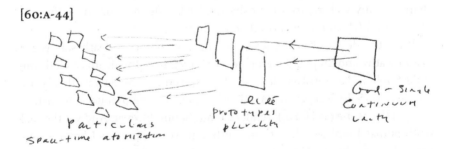

Early 1981

[75:D-1] 3-74, Valis, was the mens dei. I comprehended it. It's a strange thing to be addicted to, comprehending God's mind — I must be a Sufi; by "beauty" (the essence of God) read "pleasure" — because the why as to why I do it, it is because it gives me pleasure.

[75:D-2] I've finally found a Q I don't imagine I have an answer for: why is Kathy more beautiful than the perfect (sic) beauty of God? Maybe even St. Sophia can't answer this; hence, as a result, we have imperfect creation, for which no rational reason can be given, even by God. This is the ultimate mystery, even God can't penetrate it. How can something unique, transitory and imperfect be more beautiful than God/heaven?

[75:D-3] It's all told in *VALIS:* losing Kathy (Gloria), and getting God as a substitute. Really, the story — and it is my life we are talking about — is very simple, when you stumble onto it. And I don't say if the substitute is an adequate solution (i.e., as good, better, not as good); I just reported it neutrally. But the fact is, it's not good enough. Okay, then we will apply the hermetic solution — which is what is found in *Divine Invasion*: Linda Fox and Xena are Kathy. And also God! Manny, alone, is not.

Hello heartbreak. Joe Gideon. *Tears* first treats it. Then *Scanner.* Then *VALIS.* Then *Divine Invasion,* a projected answer, theoretical (i.e., I didn't find it); only *DI* alone of the four novels is *not* autobiographical. Shows I know what the answer is (I just can't find it).

As an artist I have been successful: I'd encompassed it in the four novels (and *The Golden Man* intro); but in life I can't. The final novel is fantasy.

[75:D-9] I have been looking over *Scanner,* the intro to *The Golden Man* and *VALIS.* The continuity is *pain,* emotional pain; this goes back to *Tears.* It is obvious that I have no defense against pain, that I am a — lunatic, one driven mad by — not pain — but by a *comprehension* of pain (like the Buddha). Comprehension of pain (spiritual and mental, especially) is the basis of my writing, as is my awareness of the frailty of life and how easily it passes over into death. Thus, although I have been driven insane by my comprehension, I am not cut off from reality; hence also I am a saint. And I write very well; I get it all down on paper. What does this add up to? Okay — I have at last carefully formulated an explanation (as Jim Haynes pointed out); I give my answer. It is an absurd answer, an attempt to ex-

plain what cannot be explained (pain, loss, grief and death). Hence it reveals this: these matters cannot be rationally explained; if they could be,
I would have done so (I am smart and persistent). Hence, one can infer
that our situation — thrown-ness — is an irrational one, a point I consider
in my explanation; hence I expose the ontological irrationality of dasein,
and thus stigmatize all philosophical and theological systems including my
own. We are back — led back — to the raw brute fact of pain, loss, grief,
suffering. Perhaps more than anyone else I reveal the irrational depths underlying reality. My ideological solution is a failure; if I believe in it I have
gone mad. And I state that, too: that I am mad. This only reinforces the relentless picture of irrationality; my madness is merely a piece of it, allied
to a greater madness. This is a new and singular worldview. What solution
do I propose that works? (Inasmuch as my Gnostic system obviously does
not; its failure proves its own premise, that of underlying irrationality and
irreality and the failure of reason and of systems.) Humor, love and beauty.
And a firm rootedness *in the particular, in the ordinary.* It is in the ordinary that my real solution is found — in diametric contradistinction to my
bizarre and weird system. Beyond and above my sensitivity to pain and my
unwillingness to avoid it (avoiding it would be evil madness, and the rest
of us are guilty of it to some degree, contrasted with me) I am a saint. This
is of little use or importance. My insanity, given an insane world, is, paradoxically, a facing of reality, and this is sane; I refuse to close my eyes and
ears. So Y equals $\bar{Y}$, as Pat says; our world and our proper role in it *is paradoxical.* The only question is, which kind of madness will we choose? To
deny and avoid the irrational reality? I am proof that everyone else is doing
this. We are, then, *all* mad, but I, uniquely, choose to go mad while facing
pain, not mad while denying pain. These are simply different paths — but
mine hurts more; it is not necessarily better — it is more a curiosity. Why
would I choose this route? Because I am a saint. I have kept my soul — as,
now and then, an occasional reader realizes. But I have not yet proven that
there is a soul; thus I may have chosen my route in vain. No known religion encompasses this, even Buddhism. Very strange. Little can be said for
my point of view, except that it can't be logically demolished; if it could be
I would have done so. Thus I am in touch with reality. So, then, in what
sense am I insane? I am insane in that I continue to face the truth without the ability to come up with a workable answer. All I have done is (1) indicate the real situation; (2) show that all the known answers, systems of
thought, are false. Again, I have shown that the problem cannot be solved
or explained, only fled from. This is very disturbing; I indict the whole universe and ourselves as irrational, myself included. I really do not know
anything in terms of the solution; I can only state the problem. No other

thinker has ever stated a problem and so miserably failed to solve it in human histories; human thought is, basically, problem-solving, not problem stating. Again, my very failure to come up with a plausible solution — even when I try — simply verifies the magnitude of the problem, rather than impugning my problem-solving faculties. It shows that what we normally regard as solution-systems really evade the reality and complexity and magnitude of the problem: fundamental irrationality giving rise to pain, grief, loss and death. Thus I am a very dangerous person. Again, my very efforts to produce a solution are alarming because they so blatantly fail. My failure is the failure of all mankind (to find a solution or explanation). The fault is not mine.

I can say no more. What I have done may be good, it may be bad. But the reality that I discern *is* the true reality; thus I am basically analytical, not creative; my writing is simply a creative way of handling analysis. I am a fictionalizing philosopher, not a novelist; my novel and story writing ability is employed as a means to formulate my perception.* The core of my writing is not art but *truth.* Thus what I tell is the truth, yet I can do nothing to alleviate it, either by deed or explanation.† Yet this seems somehow to help a certain kind of sensitive troubled person, for whom I speak. I think I understand the common ingredient in those whom my writing helps: they cannot or will not blunt *their* own intimations about the irrational, mysterious nature of reality, and, for them, my corpus of writing is one long ratiocination regarding this inexplicable reality, an investigation and presentation, analysis and response and personal history. My audience will always be limited to these people. It is bad news for them that, indeed, I am "slowly going crazy in Santa Ana, Calif.," because this reinforces our mutual realization that no answer, no explanation of this mysterious reality, is forthcoming.[8]

---

* Dick is no more a philosopher or theologian than were Vincent van Gogh or L. Ron Hubbard. Dick was one of the most important American novelists of the last half of the twentieth century, and what he offered wasn't the clarity and rigor of a philosophical vision but the imagination and ambiguity of a literary one. The "philosophy" is erratic, even crackpot; but joined to the act of storytelling — and more importantly, joined to the act of creating characters as fucked up as their author — the result was a synthesis of imagination and idea that spoke more profoundly than any "philosophy" to the questions of Dick's work: What's the nature of reality? What's the nature of humanity? What's the nature of God? — SE

† There is something deeply illuminating about Dick's declaration that he is not a novelist but a fictionalizing philosopher whose concern is not art but truth. We are here in an apparent paradox, where the concern with truth, the classical goal of the philosopher, is not judged to be in opposition to fiction, but a consequence of fiction and a work of fiction. I think this puts Dick in the same neighborhood as that other self-consciously fictionalizing philosopher: Nietzsche. — SC

This is the thrust and direction of modern theoretical physics, as Pat pointed out long ago. I reached it in the 50s. Where this will ultimately go I can't say, but so far in all these years no one has come forth to answer the questions I have raised. This is disturbing. But — this may be the beginning of a new age of human thought, of new exploration. I may be the start of something promising: an early and incomplete explorer. It may not end with me.

What I have shown — like the Michelson Morley experiment — *is that our entire world view is false; but, unlike Einstein, I can provide no new theory that will replace it.* However, viewed this way, what I have done is extraordinarily valuable, if you can endure the strain of not knowing, *and knowing you do not know.* My attempt to know (*VALIS*) is a failure qua explanation. But, as further exploration and presentation of the problem, it is priceless. And, to repeat, my absolute failure to concoct a workable explanation is highly significant — i.e., that in this I have failed. It indicates that we are collectively still far from the truth. Emotionally, this is useless. But epistemologically it is priceless. I am a unique pioneer . . . who is hopelessly lost. And the fact that no one yet can help me is of extraordinary significance!*

Someone *must* come along and play the role of Plato to my Socrates.

The problem as I see it is that Plato was 180 degrees wrong; the eidos, the abstract and perfect, does not become the particular, the imperfect; rather, the Q should be, "How does the particular, the unique, the imperfect, the local, become the abstract, the eidos, the universal?" We must study particulars, the weeds and debris of the alley; the answer is *there:* I *saw* the MMSK and it works the opposite way from how Plato saw it; he

---

* After seven years of spinning an astonishing plethora of theories, the fact that Dick can now admit to his "failure" to provide a "workable" explanation is remarkable. His insight here that the abstract emerges from the noisy particulars of the world, rather than, as in the Platonic model, from an ideal reality of which empirical reality is a flawed copy, is a growing realization in science studies as well. In *How the Laws of Physics Lie* (1983) Nancy Cartwright argues that all that ever actually exists is the noise of the world, from which scientific "laws" are abstracted. In a very different sense, contemporary interpretations of quantum mechanics provide similar insights. Nobel Prize winner Murray Gell-Mann and his collaborator James Hartle have proposed that in the "quantum fog" represented as probability clouds, certain consistent world histories "decohere" (assume definite trajectories) and stabilize at a coarse-grained level of reality larger than the quantum scale. We might analogize their vision to tiny demons knitting the fabric of the universe according to different instructions. As such, the stabilities that constitute scientific "laws" emerge from a probabilistic froth at the quantum level in which different kinds of world trajectories are encoded. In this view, the froth counts as the ultimate reality and the stability as the epiphenomenon, as Dick intuited. — NKH

saw the eide as ontologically primary, and existing *prior* to the particulars. But I saw the particulars *creating* eidei (or "phylogons" as I called them); thus permanent eternal reality is built up on and based on the flux realm; all Western metaphysics is 180 degrees off. [. . .]

In 2-74 my mind understood, and my attention was directed to a squashed dead bird in the alley.

The answer is in the imperfect, the particular, not in heaven, not in the perfect abstract form. Then the particular, although transitory, is not epiphenomenal! I have bipolarized these two. Strange. It is the transitory unique particular which is real, and yet it vanishes; well, I saw where it goes; all the particulars feed in conceptually to reticulate and arborize and complete the eidei. This is where the truth lies. This is where the answer is. Somehow, the transitory particulars do not in fact ever perish, but are permanently arranged conceptually — this is my one big discovery (and it isn't in *VALIS*).

My dope insight of last night: If and when Kathy can be rendered into geometric form she can be distributed throughout reality and hence will be — become — permanent; this is how the particulars are stored. And this is what Plato calls the forms. [. . .] It has to do with memory storage; the "form" is a way to store permanently a whole lot — millions, billions — of unique particulars.

This is it! And I saw it.

[75:D-21] I started last night with a complete sense of failure and wound up with this as the one true thing I figured out of importance:

"The entire universe, possibly, is in the invisible process of turning into the Lord."

What is new is my impression that the macrobrain came first — i.e., the physical universe — and *then* it began to think; it generated the macromind, not the other way around. So Valis is a spontaneous product of the universe, not its creator. It's as if at a certain point in the evolution of human info processing (e.g.) a mind came into existence. [. . .] This would be why there are no reports of my experience in history; physical reality including humans are evolving into a gestalt that abruptly generates a metamind. (Reasoning from particulars to eidei, as in my argument supra; i.e., all Western metaphysics is 180 degrees backward.)

So my meta-abstraction did not just cause me to *perceive* Valis but, rather, caused Valis to occur in and around me, and as a result of it occurring, I perceived it. (Sophia: "Man is holy. Man is the only true God. This is the new news I bring you.") It (Valis) was not there until the (my) meta-ab-

straction generated it, virtually ex nihilo. And it evolved it (me) very rapidly; and it embraced the outer world because we are not discrete but are
one continuum or "reality field"; thus Valis *is* a "perturbation in the reality
field."

[75:D-33]

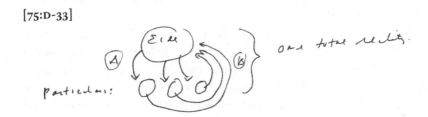

[75:D-37] We just see the field, the "iron filings," the carrier; *we do not see
the modulation.*

That 15 seconds last night when I was cut off from memory, comprehension and knowledge of God was too terrible; it was worse than going mad
or dying. If that is the only way that I can be taught what it is that has been
given me, so be it. My supreme possession is my comprehension of God;
it is to my comprehension of music as my comprehension of music is to
world as such. World is to music as music is to God. Since I was in the
sixth grade I have had my comprehension of music; since 3-74 of God; and
it has grown steadily . . . I realize that now. My best shot is:

(1) Void
(2) Valis   } God
(3) "I — (am)" (*Anokhi*)

(1) Nonbeing
(2) Being   } God
(3) Consciousness

(1) Simplicity
(2) Complexity   } God
(3) Personality, identity

(1) Eternity
(2) Change } God
(3) Knowledge

(1) Perfection
(2) Power } God
(3) Wisdom (Torah, logos)

(1) Timeless — space
(2) Time } God
(3) Memory

The bells I heard in 3-74: space (the void). Beethoven's music encloses that space (as I've noted before). He converts space into time and time into space as *one* thing: space-time, and makes it as a unitary "thing" perceptible to us. It is motion (i.e., time) *in* space; audible space. Space with a mysterious nonverbal identity/presence filling it, *moving* in it. Movement as structure: being in nonbeing. The byss and the abyss. Plus #3: *information*, i.e., "I . . . am." *Anokhi.* That which moves through/in the space is information, i.e., consciousness; it is conscious, changing eternity.

[75:D-52] Thus there is an irrational basis out of which reality is created (rather than: "the basis of reality is irrational" or "reality is irrational"). This basis is the need for reality to exist; hence any living creature, since it is/possesses primarily a will, must be cosmogenitor in order to survive. Will comes first; world as a result. Any and every living creature is "God" then, creating and maintaining reality to satisfy its need to survive. There is no theoretical upper limit to its power to generate and affect (change) reality. The primordial substrate is the will of the individual creature, but this will is not rational. Thus its reality is contradictory and often unpleasant (punishing). The creature's will routinely comes back at it as objective world — world that is its own creation but not recognized as such. World, the product of its will, fights the creature and subdues/defeats it. [. . .] So the ultimate struggle is for the creature to subdue its own will. It can't do this through power; this is what the will has available to it: power. Nor will cunning work; the will is cunning. Only the Christian renunciation of self will work, in which the other, the Thou, is construed as more valuable than self. This is when agape enters as the solution and the key. Something not oneself must be esteemed over self; this defeats the will; the will must *not* triumph: it must be defeated. Its triumph amounts to the defeat of the creature as a rational center: defeat of will defeats the coercive power of world over you. (World is your own will coming back at you as an adversary.) The harder you strive the more powerful world becomes. Here enters "Mitleids Hochste Macht," compassion's highest power to defeat the will-as-world. (Your own will is experienced as world.) Anhedonism, asceticism, self-denial, self-repression, stoicism, will not work; only willing, joyous agape (which is a joy allied with the most intense sorrow possible; viz: the passion becoming the resurrection). Even duty will not suffice. Paul is right: agape is everything, not because it is ethically or morally superior but because it overpowers the will, hence world, hence karma/astral determinism/fate/heimarmene. (These are how we encounter our own will.) Allied to this is the concept of meekness or smallness, which is a tactic to diminish striving.

[. . .]

The Buddha was on the right path in that he understood the problem, the cause of suffering; but it is not nonattachment but agape that is the solution. One does not succeed by ceasing to be attached to what one loves (craves) but by caring *more* that someone else should have it; thus I do not give away x; I give it away to someone else, while still treating it as valuable, but I treat that person as *more* valuable — so the Buddha was partly there — partly but not the whole way. In this act one deprives world of its power of punishment: the will returning with a vengeance, which prideful people do not realize.

Right now world (my own will) is not punishing me; it plays games with me and eludes me playfully — a distinct improvement over what it used to do, showing that I have achieved *some* moksa (liberation, enlightenment). But it is partial. Yet, as these paragraphs show, I am at least partially awake; I have some wisdom. But my renunciation of self (ego) and striving (will) is only partial. Contentment is mine but not joy — not even balance. Until I can joyously give to others what my will wants for itself — only then will I be emancipated from world, my own will coming back at me.

[75:D-66] Illumination: April Friday night 4:45 A.M., the third, 1981. I saw the Ch'ang Tao[9] (3-74). The more it changes the more it is the same, it is always new, always now; it is absolutely self-sufficient. I can at last comprehend it, how in change, ceaseless change — through the dialectic — *it is always the same* — oh great Ch'ang Tao! I saw you.

[75:D-67] The great truth is: 2-3-74, my seeing the Tao, and my exegesis, and *VALIS,* have given me a *center* (omphalos), which is what I lacked (e.g., in the 60s); this is why my anxiety is gone; I now have a conception of myself, and of myself as an artist and thinker, and of my place and role in society and history — all of which I lacked before I saw the Tao (2-3-74). Thus it can be truly said, I have found the way. I am at peace. But the key word is:

center (i.e., place. In the Taoist sense.)

[75:D-93] All at once I think of something God (or "God") revealed to me one time when I was stoned: "You are not the doubter; you are the doubt (itself)" and "This is a road to me, as are all roads if pursued to the end."

[75:D-129] One time when I was ripped I wrote "God is everywhere. In the music. The cat," etc. My only solution is to see that every literal worldly thing, person, etc., that I loved and lost was in fact God shining through world; world as lens/transduction of God. And that I cannot truly lose God, "yea, I am with you even unto the end." So each time I recover God I really recover all (the people and world things) that I have lost, truly lost as world things, but not as God. Thus God wins me over more and more. More completely and intensely, summing up in and as himself all that I ever had and knew; and yet he is more. Thus, e.g., I discover my analytical proposition. As regards the Wind in the Willows gift of forgetting, God maintains a fine line for me of remembering him and paradoxically mercifully forgetting him. But understanding that I can find him in world over and over again, viz: God discoverable in polyform, but always and only God, however and in what thing experienced: world deconstructed into God always. Thus I am pried away from transitory manifestations which do disappear and am instead bonded to the eternal; but I find it in world and as world, not in withdrawal from world. Thus there is a double motion: pried loose from that which fails; bonded to that which is discoverable always, always capable of being renewed. Again found, unlike people and things seen in themselves: discrete particulars.

Early 1981

[76:E-2] Beyond all the arcana lies the simple truth expressed in my "Chains . . . Web" essay and in the story itself. To cease to run is to capitulate. And sooner or later one must cease to run. This moment is the only real moment in which one exists. Everything else is an evasion. In this moment one moves deliberately *toward* one's fate and fights it, and as a result, one truly lives for the first time or dies; it is sein vs. das nichts. What I call the heroic deed is, in that instant, everything. Thus I am an ontologist and an existentialist and I am willing to risk extinction in order to try authentically to be, since in this moment one has only the choice between extinguishing oneself voluntarily or fighting. I chose to fight and won, and what I won was my own soul.

[76:E-13] Notes on "Chains . . . Web." The fate that the Christian does not run from or dread *will* (he knows) *defeat* him. He knows absolutely, with *total* certitude; this is the very essence of his ability not to run from it. Because he also knows he *can't* run from it, (1) it will defeat him; and (2) he can't escape it. So he is doubly doomed; its power to destroy him is absolute in two respects: the postulate "it will destroy him" derives from this double source. The double source makes this fate what it is. It is not a threat — not a lethal threat, even. It is something more.

[76:E-14] I am currently of the opinion that (1) there is a connection between original authentic Christianity through Gnosticism to Heidegger; and (2) that 2-3-74 was this particular experience; viz: the inauthentic state that Heidegger describes is the "thrown-ness" into the "fremd" that Gnosticism describes; there follows, then, a series of dire transformations by the "thrown into the alien world" person trying to cope; I comprehend this as flight and evasion from fate (heimarmene), which is a sense that this alien state/world into which one has been thrown torments now and eventually kills (causes nonbeing, das nicht). The unconscious apperception of this creates angst (dread). This running to evade nonbeing manifesting itself as fate generates a pressure time, in which — by which — the person is driven more than driving; that is, he both runs and is made to run; he is caused to flee more than volitionally fleeing. Thus there is caused an endless process of becoming that never turns into being itself; there is no true *now* — he is projected always into a dreaded *next*; he is not really here and now for him; he must run *into* the future and yet paradoxically *away* from the future; he both runs toward and away from. Thus he is split. Part of him reaches inauthentically into the future to monitor it for peril — he cannot afford ever to ignore the future since it contains his fate which will kill him — and part of him looks away from the future *for the same reason;* this split may be the basis of schizophrenia. He must both notify himself of what he sees in the future and obscure what he sees from himself. This is another version of the split. But worst of all is — not that he must involve himself continually in the future out of apprehension, while also avoiding it, fearing to move into it, trying in fact to halt time (since time contains his fate) but he fails to be in the now, which is where reality is, and this is what most inhibits Sein; he has to be eternally becoming because he must extend himself eternally into the not yet. What I see in all this is that his sense that this alien world he has been thrown into will eventually ineluctably annihilate him *is correct* and he knows it is correct; *this is not a delusion,* this sense of impending destruction that will take away what little being he has. That time might increase or even complete his being does not occur to him because (and here the Gnostic perception is vital) this is an alien world into which he has been thrown against his will; i.e., he is helpless: he did not decide to be here, and the more he reaches frantically into the future (while simultaneously running from the future) the faster time "flows" (or the faster he moves through it). Thus the moment, the now, escapes him perpetually and he has no life he can call his own. But he must never reveal to himself this fact — about his inevitable future doom — lest he disintegrate utterly; again he is split. So he has no idea what he is doing or why, and he is enigmatic to himself; so he is too and for himself as alien as world is to him; he is as if thrown into an alien self on top of everything else!

As I say, the only solution to this is the Christian solution of what I call total capitulation to this fate and an acknowledgment that it cannot be avoided; it will come and it will destroy him. Thus he ceases running, and lives now not future; but at the moment he does this he knows that this anticipated doom exists — so in the normal course of life this sense of the future becoming the now only occurs — if it occurs at all — when the impending doom ceases to be future and is perceived as now: at which point anticipatory dread becomes logically total fear. However (as Heidegger points out) this apotheosis of dread, this being-in-death, carries with it the possibility of authentic Sein.

[76:E-19] It is *world* that must change to accommodate us, not us to accommodate world. This is such a critical point that its implications simply beggar description. This world is alien to us; it must change to be familiar to us, not us to fit into it.

April 20, 1981

[84:5] *Pay-off:*

The introjection of Christ into the system is certainly the epitome of the adding of ex nihilo newness, of revitalizing creation as if from outside. Thus the term "Christ" has to refer to any and all newness choices wherever and whenever they occur; "Christ" is the zero-one binary disjunctive event per se, and so is always now and always here. We see it and understand that we see (and experience) Christ, and this is newness, re-creation (in an unending process of creation). Christ *never* arises/occurs as a result of the past, as an effect of antecedent causes; he is always born "from outside." Hence his epiphany can never be induced or predicted (by definition). Christ is that which does not follow mechanically: he always *invades* world. To see, then, that Causality is not observed, that the "effect" is in fact not an effect at all — of its Cause — but is ex nihilo new is to see — literally, not symbolically — Christ. Hence where there is Christ it is always the case that there has been "a perturbation of the reality field," something acting on it, intruding on it, invading it, "from outside." In terms of mechanical cause-and-effect Christ can never be said to be a *normal* event derived from the antecedent system.*

Without these periodic insertions the system would run down; it would lose shape, organization and vitality. Cause-and-effect, then, taken in itself, is a losing game. The only thing that Christ can be said to be a result of — Christ as an event in the reality field — *is the need of this event.* It is physically, mechanically causeless; it is absolutely teleological. Efficient causation has no bearing on it and will never yield it up. (Here Pierre Teilhard de Chardin is totally wrong: world is not spontaneously converging into the Point Omega; what he calls "Point Omega" is something done ceaselessly to world, an endless invasion.) Wherever the effect is correctly

---

* This passage presents a supernaturalist theory of divine action: Christ acts on the world *only* by miracle, and never as a result of predictable, materialist, or mechanical causes. More fundamentally, however, it shows Dick's preoccupation with freedom from determinism: Christ is not constrained by the same forces that limit created beings and objects. He is an effect without a cause. We see this same rejection of determinism throughout the Exegesis: even when presenting reality as a moral test with a "right" answer, Dick is concerned to show that we must not be *aware* of the test, lest our actions be guided by the knowledge of a reward. For all his searching for the rules that govern reality, Dick is deeply dubious that God would impose unappealable rules on his creations. This issue will arise again later in Dick's consideration of the replacement of the Creator's rigid law with Christ's merciful love. — GM

seen to exceed its cause (which is then by definition not its cause) there is Christ. Conversely, wherever effect follows cause actually, there he is not. Christ, then, is an event, something that occurs in and to the reality field; Christ is not a person as men are persons. Christ is the beginning of the universe all over again, as a repeated event.

[84:8] Here is the puzzle of *VALIS.* In *VALIS* I say, I know a madman who imagines that he saw Christ; and I am that madman. But if I know that I am a madman I know that in fact I did not see Christ. Therefore I assert nothing about Christ. I say only that I am not mad. But if I say only that, then I have made no mad claim; therefore I am not mad. And the regress begins again and continues forever. Something has been asserted, but what is it? Does it have to do with Christ or only with myself? This paradox was known in antiquity; the pre-Socratics propounded it. A man says, "All Cretans are liars." When an inquiry is made as to who this man is, it is determined that he was born in Crete. What, then, has he asserted? Anything at all? Is this the semblance of knowledge or a form — a strange form — of knowledge itself? Zeno, the Sophists in general, saw paradox as a way of conveying knowledge — paradox, in fact, as a way of arriving at conclusions. This is known, too, in Zen Buddhism. It sometimes causes a strange jolt or leap in the person's mind; something happens, an abrupt comprehension, as if out of nowhere, called satori. The paradox does not tell; it *points.* It is a sign, not the thing pointed to. That which is pointed to must arise ex nihilo in the mind of the person. The paradox, the *koan* tells him nothing; it wakes him up. This only makes sense if you assume something very strange: we are asleep but do not know it. At least not until we wake up.

April

[90:1][10] Enclosed is a carbon of what may be a resolution of my seven years
of attempting to construct a model of reality; by "reality" I mean God in or
God and the universe: what Erigena called *natura*. The solution came to
me in a series of recent sleep revelations, that is, hypnogogic and hypnopompic insights where I actually *saw* how the system works. (Universe and
God regarded, as Spinoza does, as one and the same.) My model is that of
a computer or computer-like entity — well, look at the enclosed page; it is
pretty much complete.

[90:2] April 15, 1981. Sleep insight.

Hartshorne — pantheism — the EB macro. A. N. Whitehead's process
deity.* We are within it (the MMSK), as interconnections, but organic
model is incorrect. It is a signaling system, mutually adjusting (this is what
Pythagoras saw). 0-1 flicker rate (misinterpreted by me as time frames); actually it's binary. Tries out a false move (0), then corrects to 1 which is actualized in/as the next discrete "frame." Has the effect of separate frames
due to the off-on pulsation; discrete: isn't/is, nonbeing/being. The system
shuts off every trillionth of a second (0). These are decisions. After each off
(0) when it switches back on to 1 the "frame" (reality) is different, in terms
of internal arrangement, adjustment, mutual adjustment, interaction/in-
terconnection, as information flows through its circuits.

Boehme: yes-no. Hartshorne 0-1. Quantitative (0-1) converted to qualitative by spatiotemporal reality itself; that is, quantitative information is
poured into material reality within which and by which it is converted into
qualitative information.

While it's off, reality ceases to be. When it comes back on it is slightly
different. It (the system) doesn't transmit a zero bit; it (the system) ceases
to be. This is when it makes a tentative move which had been canceled in
favor of a better move; at every junction (trillionth of the second, flicker

---

* Dick here refers to Charles Hartshorne, who developed Alfred North Whitehead's process philosophy into a full-fledged school of theological thought. Whitehead described a
reality made up not of things but of a procession of events. Hartshorne, picking up from
Whitehead's own theological exploration of this idea, depicts God as an absolute being in
constant flux, relationally connected with and constantly affected by the universe. Dick's
conception of the dialectical nature of both reality and deity dovetails strongly with process theology. But Hartshorne also insisted on the absolute free will of the universe and all
within it — an idea that the more deterministic Dick does not seem to carry over into his
subsequent exploration of reality as a binary system. — GM

rate) it discards an inferior move in favor of a better one; hence Leibniz's view that "this is the best of all possible worlds" (this is a rapid selection process). This is how a computer works. The zero position is the void; hence when I conceive of God as Valis I am only getting the 1; I need also the void, the zero. To comprehend/apperceive/envision the void is to envision the other phase (zero phase) of the flicker binary pulsation, the sum of the two phases being the totality. Thus the Muslims are correct; the universe is destroyed "every day" (actually every trillionth of the second) "and re-created."[11] But what is interesting to me is that the way I conceive of this, all its decisions are made during the "spaces" that we are totally unaware of. It comes back on, back into being, back to the 1 phase when it has tried out a faulty solution and has substituted better (the best possible?) instead, which is the next "time frame." Thus its decision-making processes, i.e., its thinking, and its nonbeing phase, lies outside our awareness. The initial false move that it tries out during its zero phase is Boehme's no, and the 1 or on phase is Boehme's yes. So my envisioning is essentially Boehme's, updated in terms of computers and information processing systems. The similarity to the Taoist alternation of yin and yang is very obvious.

[90:13] What is probably most important of all is that my binary arborizing disjunctive decision-making universe system — the *disclosure* of which I regard as an essentially new disclosure, although as a fact it itself may not be new — it is, I think, absolutely in accord with the very high and penetrating conception of the revolutionary role of the cosmic Christ in fundamentally transforming the nature of the world order. This is nothing short of astonishing, that radical mystical Pauline Christianity and a very radical modern quantum mechanics computer indeterminate unified field reality view turned out to be basically compatible or in fact even identical! The two converge (at least in my theorizing) totally; all at once there is a lightning swift confluence of my separate streams of thought: Christianity and, well, philosophy-metaphysics-epistemology, whatever; all else, really, than Christianity; I suddenly have one overview which is (1) basically new and original; and (2) subsumes everything Christian and non-Christian into one daring structure. What is more, this structure will adequately account for my apperception of what I call Valis, both in me and outside me, back in 3-74. So at this point I have synthesized my various streams of thought into a higher gestalt and no longer have to vacillate back and forth between Christianity and non-Christianity, which is reason to suppose that I have finally hit on a model that truly represents, conceptually, what I experienced in the spring of 1974 and has puzzled me for over seven years.

All of a sudden a titanic idea (insight?) has struck me. Valis was outside me in or as the external reality field; and Valis was in me, in my mind, blended with my mind, or, perhaps, even *as* my mind. What if the true situation is: this is what is meant by "Christ consciousness" and it works this way: Christ enters you (never mind at this point how; up the optic nerve or some kind of alchemical hierarchy of opposites, etc., etc.); anyhow, this "Christ consciousness" which is in fact the Second Advent makes it possible for the first time in human history for human beings to discard the modem of causation (which I have shown, at least to my own satisfaction, dates back to Babylon, is in fact the astral determinism, or Fate or ananke, etc., of the ancient world) as the basic ontological structuring category — by which world is ordered, arranged, understood — and this Christ consciousness permits (again for the first time in human history) a much more accurate and acutely qualitatively different experience of reality . . . in which causality is replaced by an understanding of, apperception of, realization of, whatever, of what I call binary forking decision-making, a *choosing* system, the no-yes choice exercised volitionally, sentiently; this was *always* the case with world-in-itself (Kant's Ding-an-sich) but there was no way by which humans could apperceive (comprehend, envision) it before. And this radically transformed experience (Dasein) of reality, a way of being-in-the-world, of participating in shaping world (the observer participant), had to wait until such discoveries and realizations as quantum mechanics, indeterminacy, unified field theory, plus Taoism — all that good new stuff such as Capra talks about . . . but anyhow, the leap across to this new way of Dasein is the second advent, and what occurs in our minds, our brains, our heads; and yet (paradoxically) it refers to something actually "out there" in world, external to us, a way in which reality functions in itself; so this new radical quantum leap upward view is not just subjective — well, okay; reality hasn't changed; our way of being-in-reality has changed, had to wait, had to evolve over the many centuries. I mean, if Koestler and Capra et al. can equate the post-Newtonian Dasein (comprehension of reality) with Taoism, why can't I equate it with Pauline Christian mysticism (which is exactly what I've done!).* And then as a third ele-

---

* Here we see Dick's impulse toward synthesis shift into hyperdrive; he assembles multiple systems of thought and references as if they can be seamlessly joined without contradiction. What we gain from such a loose assemblage is a vague sense that these multiple systems have something in common, but the details of exactly how they can be articulated together remain elusive. For example, Capra argues that the field model of quantum mechanics posits the field as the fundamental entity in reality, in which the appearance of particles can be understood as "knots" or places where the field intensifies and begins to manifest itself as particles rather than waves. Hence it posits reality as an underlying continuum. This is in direct opposition to the basic assumption of the computational model of the universe, which argues that the ultimate nature of reality is discrete, not continuous.

ment we can bring in Heidegger and talk about Sein, authentic being, and what I call a spatial reality rather than a temporal reality, etc. And I then trace Heidegger back to Gnosticism and from there once again to Paul, who is highly thought of by the Gnostics. And there is no need to exclude Taoism, because indeed a yin-yang dialectic is involved . . . and we get to keep a causal synchronicity, and it just all comes together and is liberating . . . and we get to throw in computer stuff, which relates back to Taoism via my binary dialectic — but most of all, as I say, *this* internal event (Valis in me) permits the comprehension (Dasein) of what may in fact always (or for centuries) have been there in world but we didn't possess the inner equipment to comprehend/apprehend it.

Thus the question "Where is the kingdom of God" gets an answer derived from ultra-modern views of the observer-participant universe, in which it's all treated as a field, a unified field.

We are not talking about a different way of being-in-the-world or even a better way; we're talking about the lifting *for the first time in human history* of a massive perceptual/conceptual occlusion having to do with the ontological structuring factor we call causality (or astral determinism). This has never happened before. I mean, just think what it would mean vis-à-vis our way of perceiving/understanding world if we ceased to utilize space or time as a Kantian ordering/structuring category? And in fact when the utilization of causation ceases, our sense of time is drastically altered (time sharply diminishes), and our sense of space is drastically altered (as I figure it, time is converted into space, so we get a great diminution in the time factor and a great augmentation in the spatial factor); but, most of all, introduced as a totally *new* factor is an apperception of the flicker pulsation in which the system (reality) switches on and off, as well as the binary forking decision-making; the totality of all this is that very simply our occlusion lifts and we are in another world entirely, a world I identify with the Garden. And this really could not have happened before this decade, what with computers, new theories about information, modern physics, etc. It is just now beginning to happen. And no one — no one! — has seen the involvement of Pauline Christian mysticism, that in fact this is the payoff ingredient. And this would explain why for over seven years I have alternated between believing Christ has returned and believing that I had evolved some kind of ultra-modern worldview connected with physics and epistemology, etc.

Okay; I have one final thing to say and herewith I rest my case, trium-

---

It is difficult to see how we can reconcile the sharp contrast between these two fundamental premises, not to mention the many other contradictions and irresolvable conflicts that arise as the assemblage grows. — NKH

phantly. My binary forking, which I have already said is an indeterminate
element entering what always before was conceived of as causality (under
various names, such as astral determinism): what is this if not the "two slit"
phenomenon familiar in subatomic physics, which is the very essence of
the indeterminate factor in reality!* It is known to us scientifically only on
a subatomic level. Yet I say (I think I say) I have perceived this as the very
basis of reality per se, the reality process of change, of flux, of all cause and
effect at all levels, micro and macro. What I have been calling "binary forking choosing" is simply the "two slit indeterminate phenomenon" but at a
larger level, and it is a level that embraces *all* change. I am saying, some
kind of mentational volitional sentient mind or mindoid entity — perhaps
that of the total system itself — has some kind of steering or governing involvement as to which of the two slits is the selected one at each of these
forkings. This may be linked to Pauli's synchronicity; it is acausal but ubiquitous and genuine and important. Here we turn to A. N. Whitehead's definition of process deity "as a principle of selection of the good in the world
order."

[90:19] Premise: Christ consciousness produces a worldview (Dasein) so
radically different from what we normally experience that it is almost impossible to communicate it. Absolute space, a vast diminution and weakening of time (time qualitatively transformed) and no causality, as well
as reality experienced as a unified self-governing field (it initiates all its
own changes acausally in synchronization); moreover this field makes use
of — or operates by means of — a binary off-on switching involving an indeterminate element so that it is perpetually disjunctive; thus it does not

---

* Here Dick compares the binary forking model (derived from a computational model of
the universe) to the "two slit" experiment that famously demonstrated that electrons can
manifest as both waves and particles. When electrons are beamed at a single slit behind
which sits a detector screen, they manifest as particles. However, when a second slit is
added, interference waves appear. Depending on the experimental setup, then, electrons
can appear as either waves or particles. Dick's analogy is based on the indeterminacy that a
binary forking model and the two-slit model both imply. Subatomic particles demonstrate
an indeterminacy expressed by the Heisenberg Uncertainty Principle, in which the momentum and position cannot be co-specified with an accuracy greater than Planck's constant. With the binary forking model, indeterminacy arises because of the complexity of
interactions between multiple independent agents acting simultaneously, as in a cellular
automata model. In the former case, the observer becomes implicated in the supposedly
"objective" state of the particle because he chooses the experimental setup; in the latter
case, it is not the presence of the observer that prevents accurate prediction but rather the
complexity of the simultaneous interactions. The two cases have different epistemological
consequences and lead to different kinds of questions about the nature of reality. Again, we
see here a suggestive gesture that, if worked out in rigorous details, raises more issues than
it solves. — NKH

flow through time at all but always is. Also it either is based on or generates quantitative binary information in a cumulative fashion; i.e., it develops in one direction and one only. As a total field it ceaselessly makes
off-on choices at each forking or junction; thus it is free (again, indeterminacy is involved at its basic level of operation). The receptacle in which it
exists is space, not time. When it pulse-phases to its off position it ceases
to exist; when it comes back to its on position it is slightly different. (I feel
like someone trying to interpret the Sistine Chapel ceiling to a blind man.)
Thus in a certain real sense it abolishes and then re-creates itself at a very
rapid rate, a sort of flicker. Each time it re-creates itself it is different, hence
in a real sense new. I somewhat hesitate to add this, but since with Christ
consciousness there is no clear demarcation between the observer and the
reality field he participates in, world is in a certain real and palpable sense
affected by his involvement with it and perception of it; thus he is conscious of perturbing the reality field in the very act of participating in it;
world, then, loses its reified, stubborn quality (associated with rigid determinism, cause and effect) and responds to him not as an It but as what Buber called a Thou. Within this one total schema involving the observer and
his world together, it becomes impossible to distinguish Christ in him and
Christ in world; there is only one total reality: himself, Christ, world.

[90:31] What I have achieved during these past seven years is to deepen
and augment my mental ability to conceive of and comprehend what in
3-74 I perceived, and, ultimately, this is an apprehension, a comprehension,
of God, of the divine nature and being. [. . .] "A total system that perpetually chooses through a binary process of rejection that is cumulative" is
my way of envisioning what I experienced; it is my model which I am able,
first, to summon up, and then, finally, to contemplate. Thus through it and
in it *I have God in me*, as a mental construct of my own devising; but it is
a devising derived from and rooted in experience; it is not imaginary: it is
an interpretation of what I construe to be the case. It is reality incorporated into me, reality at the highest level at which I am able to understand
it. Here my ability to understand reaches its limit. This all has been a vast
effort. I am not concerned with traditional definitions of God, attributions
and doctrines and creeds and dogmas; I am concerned with the conception I have arduously arrived at based on experience. My conception does
justice to my experience, it is the best I can do.* It turns an otherwise in-

---

* For all its eccentricity, the Exegesis is ultimately a rational exercise: Dick develops a hypothesis, applies its framework to his experience, and examines how well the theory fits
the facts of his experience (or at least his current shaping of those facts). Dick was never a
writer of hard science fiction, and his stories don't generally adhere to a strict standard of

comprehensible encounter into a coherent image or model. This has been my task. Whether it is "true" or not depends on what you mean by true. It does justice to my experience; in that sense it is true. What if the experience itself is not true? To me that question is unintelligible; it is *my* experience: it belongs to me, is a part of me, and by construing a model adequate to it I make it a permanent part of me, not something that escapes. If my model works, if it is an adequate representation, I can by means of it convert it back into something like the original experience, so it is an encoding, an informational analog of that experience (to the degree that I have been successful).* I am a device on which God renders an impression, hopefully a permanent impression; it will be permanent if — and to the degree that — I function correctly. It is not a doctrine or even a theory that I am fabricating; it is an impression, *a change in me as to what I am.* I have become not the same, due to what happened, and this has been a task, an act stretching over years on my part. I want to be different because of what I saw; I want to be changed as much as possible (without, of course, falsifying what happened). The *last* thing I want out of that experience is to be the same as I was prior to it. And I can only change insofar as I comprehend that experience; and I can only comprehend it (as I say) by actively building an inner, adequate, appropriate model (of what happened). So this is not a passive rendering. This is an artistic, spiritual, conceptual task involving years of work. My conception grows; it is not static. As it grows I change. This is what I want: to thus and thereby be changed. This is what I have devoted myself to; this is my purpose for existing; it is what I *want* to do — like the binary choosing of the system my work on my model is cumulative. I choose; I discard; I perpetually arborize and reticulate: I build. I am very happy. I sense and grasp and perceive the no-yes dialectic that continually results in higher syntheses (which is what Jacob Boehme understood); I understand God in process, God perpetually choosing and re-

---

scientific plausibility. But here he applies a loose variation on the scientific method to explain and rationalize his experiences. In this respect, the Exegesis shows more "scientific" influence than Dick's science fiction. — GM

* Here Dick offers what is perhaps the most striking rationale for his theorizing: the ability to formulate and conceptualize an experience so that the affect associated with the experience can be captured and re-evoked by meditating on the theory. Without doubt, a theory that does this would have utility for the person who evolved it; the question then is whether it would have the same or similar effect on people who did not have the original experience. I doubt that it would work this way for most people reading Dick's theories. By contrast, his fiction, with its rich contexts, suggestive characterizations, and haunting themes, clearly has this kind of power. His theorizing is important, then, not so much on its own account as for the insight it gives into his creative processes and the deep unconscious motivations that drive his fiction. — NKH

jecting: "not this but rather that," so that he surpasses himself in an act at each new stage. ("Nicht diese töne; sondern . . . ,"[12] as Beethoven wrote; the foundation of creation is to choose, to reject, to choose again: Boehme's dialectic ceaselessly at work, blinking off-on-off-on.) Dio: creating begins with an unvoiced *no*, not a yes. "Not *that;* (but rather) *this.*" A rejection of the is in favor of a better alternative (that is as much constructed as cho-sen — perhaps more so!). The essence of creativity is to reject what follows inevitably, because *that* is an entropic cause and effect splitting, a disin-tegration; in place of this the creator built something new that does *not* follow. And he bases what he constructs, he derives his conception from, in response to and in rejection of what is. So in artistic endeavor there is something of the ex nihilo: something somehow engendered out of noth-ing.

[90:25] And this is what I discovered from 2-74 to 2-75; the Garden is lo-cated *here,* as if on another frequency. [. . .]

[90:26] Christ and causation are, then, at war; here is another form, per-haps the ultimate form, of the dialectic; the wise horn is Yang; the wise horn is better; the wise horn is selected; the wise horn is, in essence, Christ himself penetrating the mechanism. But have I not said, isn't it very pos-sible that nothing has changed but our perception? Reality per se, in itself, is constant; only our experience of it changes. So all we need to do to get back into the Garden is to perceive the Garden. Yet we are incapable of do-ing this. In what sense, if any, can Christ be distinguished from our percep-tion of reality-as-it-is? There is a dreadful circularity here; if we could ex-perience the Garden we would be saved, but in fact we can't experience it so we are not saved. Something from outside must enter to remove the oc-clusion and this is Christ.

It resembles what Heraclitus said about the necessity of discerning true reality by a process something like guessing a riddle or translating from a foreign language into one's own; that although men have the capacity to do so, they do not. This week I was, that one afternoon, back in the world of space; I don't know how I did it . . . and then I was back here under the power of tyrannical, destructive time once more. And I don't know how that happened either. Someone must teach us how to do this or else do it for us. I who know about the Kingdom, who knows it is right here — even I can't find my way (back) to it. Yet my "binary" model of the universe ap-parently calls for it, specifies its existence. It must be, it must truly be, that Christ does not in fact penetrate — invade — the workings of the universe but, rather, invades our *perception* of the workings of the universe, the inner representation that the Cartesians showed we experience as world; this (as I said before) is Christ as Christ consciousness: the occlusion is not lifted from the world — it was never in world — but from us: it is in us. In my recent dream the spinner, the little boy, went blind; the sun itself did not go out; it was still shining but he could not see it. He "lost his vision." This says it all. Even with a thick magnifying glass he could no longer see the sun, shining as it still was.

[90:6A] I can't help believing that the brief return of that Other World last week, that other way of being-in-world that I associate with 2-74 to 2-75, what I call the Palm Tree Garden, or as I now term it, the spatial realm, is connected with this being Easter week (or it was; today is Easter Sunday, so it was last week). That entire week is holy to the Christian; it begins with Palm Sunday which reperforms Jesus's entry into Jerusalem. And I had just about time — literally exactly at that time — worked out — upon rereading "Chains . . . Web" an extraordinary analysis of the Christian solution to hostile world expressed as fate: the cessation of evasion and flight, the entry into a purely spatial realm of the absolute now, which I connect with Heidegger's authentic being (Sein), a totally different Dasein that frees the person; and from this I worked my revolutionary model of the binary switching system that I now conceive reality to be. [. . .]

At the time that I found myself back in the purely spatial realm, I supposed that it was because I had upped my dosage of Sinequan, but that is absolutely not likely. Let us consider the exact circumstances. It was Tuesday, the day the space shuttle returned. The night before, Monday night, something strange happened to me; I burned out. I could not think in complete sentences; I'd begin a sentence of thought and it would end in the middle. It was as if I'd used up all my thoughts, as if there are only a finite number and I had come to the last one; there literally were no more left in me. I had to go to bed early — which was fine, because then Tuesday I was able readily to arise early to watch the shuttle's safe return. Now, this absolutely total exhaustion of thoughts in me somehow seems to me related to the phosphene graphics trip; the common factor is the using up of time, a running out of time — i.e., process. I had, as in 1974, come to the end in some real and perhaps even ontological sense; mentally I had in fact died. Yet the next day I found myself in the magic spatial world of total freedom, a world of infinite extension. What I am saying is that this year, 1981, I relived, although to a lesser degree, the series of experiences of 1974 — relived them during holy week (from Palm Sunday to Easter Sunday). It was during this period that my stupendous conception of the binary switching system came to me. I remember that I had said to Jeanette at Brentwood that — O Dio — "I have lost my artistic vision" — the dream about the child, the spinner, going blind! This represented spiritual death, and a logic to Christ's passion and crucifixion! And then rebirth occurred. And again, as in 1974 (this is really incredible, simply incredible) I got a terrifying letter that caused me to phone the FBI. So here are the themes of holy week: suffering (exhaustion) and death, and then rebirth; "rebirth" expressed for me in the form of the return of my vision — and not just return but resurrection in the sense that I was able to complete it, which I felt I had never before been able to do. [. . .] I relived — reperformed — the passion, death and resurrection, then, without intending to or even realizing that is indeed what was happening.

Several aspects point to this as genuine. (1) The mental and spiritual exhaustion I experienced on Monday night was unique; I remember telling Doris that I had only undergone something like it due to drug abuse. It was, then, qualitatively different from mere fatigue, even enormous fatigue. It ended in a clear and evident death. (2) The Spinner dream which anticipated this very event, the "loss of vision" by the Spinner (i.e., Spinner as writer; he can no longer narrate). (3) The murderous letter. (4) The brief period on Tuesday in the spatial realm that I had only a little while before (a few days) figured out was essentially connected with Christianity. (5) The sudden, unexpected and unprecedented completion of my artistic vision on Wednesday night, the night of the day the letter came; this, too, was not a quantitative event; it was ontologically different from anything I had ever experienced before (like the dying of my vision Monday night); and: it was based on revelation of the forking and the tentative zero firing, a sleep revelation. So I suffered and died, but after I died I was resurrected in terms of my world — the spatial world — and in terms of my vision: my binary switching model of the universe, which I have later recognized as a model of the restored universe, restored by Christ; and I even identify this Dasein, this worldview, as "Christ consciousness"!

[90:13A] This is a very different view of deity than has ever been put forth before (except perhaps by Jacob Boehme). For example, do these zero branchings add up to long chains of provisional realities, realities — perhaps even whole worlds or versions of worlds — subject to later retroactive annulment? And if so, do we encounter them, which is to say, do we live in them but then forget it, our memory being canceled out along with the worlds themselves? I conceive of the system switching on, off, on, off, the "off" consisting of what I call the zero phase of the binary flicker; I also say that it is during these off or o phases that the system does its thinking. What else goes on at the same time, if anything? Is there a sort of parity counter world to our own, perhaps invested with some kind of semi-reality that holds up only so long as the system takes to make up its mind and decide? Oddly, interestingly, this all seems to correspond with the doubts and premises of my ten-volume meta-novel: "Realities are subject to cancellation without notice" and, moreover, were not truly real in the first place (examples of this in my writing are legion). More interesting to me, however, is the existential aspect to this, which means deity and how deity acts, that in fact deity in this model is conceived in terms of its choosing, rejecting, choosing again, and if this choosing is its essence, then we have a whole new idea of the einai of God: an existential idea: it is what it does, and what it does is perpetually choose (Whitehead's principle of selection of the good in the world-process).

[90:16A] In fact now it is possible to assert a single premise generating all my various preoccupations with what is real, what isn't, etc., my entire body of epistemological doubts: I know that there really is such a thing as tentative or provisional reality, and it can be canceled in such a way that in a certain sense it never was there in the first place.

[90:E-8] Ghastly dream [. . .] A family on an old farm. The children are (called) "the Spinners." The very ground itself is contaminated, poisoned, with (heavy) metals, so the children, "the Spinners," are becoming blind. A little boy peers through a thick magnifying glass at the sun; he can barely see it. Soon he will be completely blind.

Interpretation: the Spinners are immortals who came here and were poisoned (heavy metal) and lost what I call "the third eye" (represented by the magnifying glass). The sun is Christ. Thus they, we, can no longer read the sacred writing (of Scripture): "the light went out" (divine revelation) not because God stopped sending it but because we have gone blind to it. Somehow I regained my sight in 3-74 and could read the sacred Scriptures in/as *Tears*. Therefore "the Spinners" can no longer see the thread of Ariadne (or weave it as explanation, revelation) leading out of the maze.

[90:E-11] When I believe, I am crazy.

When I don't believe, I suffer psychotic depression. I oscillate between intoxication (mania) and melancholia. I think, now, that my dream about the child going blind and no longer able to see the sun symbolized my losing my vision (sic): i.e., of Christ, Dionysus, Wotan, YHWH, because it is all gone; it seems mere mad fancy, like believing you might see Mr. Toad sculling a little boat down the stream. I can't live without my vision but my vision is self-delusion.

[90:F-11] What I have been doing these seven years is philosophical inquiry in the old sense, that of the pre-Socratics. Before science and philosophy parted company. I'm not sure my issues are in fact metaphysical. What confronted me in 2-3-74 was "a perturbation in the reality field." That is, reality behaving in an inexplicable way which no known theory could explain or account for. How does this seven years of study and analysis differ from scientific research? This has not been a game. Something I witnessed puzzled me and I set out to understand it. When I did finally understand it, I found that my questions went all the way back to the 40s. And I have not been the first to raise the question. If the traditional, fully accepted theories of causation were true, the "perturbation" that I saw could not have occurred. This is the bottom line. How do I differ from Einstein vis-à-vis Newtonian mechanics! It was a perturbation in the reality field in the sense that something more than the forces we know of was visibly at work. The problem is real. Then I took it to be so.

[90:F-19] All these seven years I've feared I was nuts (hence H. Fat is so described). Especially I've been nervous about quoting the AI voice; after all, I'm hearing voices. I think now I believe. I *knew* that binary switching model was correct as soon as it came to me.

[90:G-43] I just realized I had an amazing dream. I — or the character — was deprived of world totally. At once he — his own mind — filled in the sensory vacuum with a spurious autogenerated world, so he wouldn't go crazy. Next thing, he took this world to be real; the closer he scrutinized it, due to the fact that he as percipient was in fact generating it, the more actualized, detailed and convincing it became, because his perception of it was (in a certain real way) his production of it; hence the more intense scrutiny and more actualized, articulated and convincing it became as it moved toward perfection (of actualization) as a limit, the more it compelled his assent. Put another way, the less he realized — would tend to realize on the basis of his empirical observations that (1) it was spurious; and (2) he himself was its creator. *However,* under such circumstances, to overcome this positive feedback self-authenticating hoax-involvement, a clock-timed tape in his mind — or accessible to his mind; e.g., speaking directly into his ear or inner ear — was set in advance to speak to him at regular intervals reminders of the truth, and his true situation. The tape was plugged into RET,[13] but since part of his spurious autogenerated world was fake time — an integral aspect of spurious world generated out of total sensory deprivation — these reminders, these messages from the real world, came to him (in terms of his own subjective time) at increasingly farther apart (i.e., longer) intervals and thus failed to serve their purpose (anamnesis involving the knowledge that his world is spurious, and no amount of scrutiny on his part will correct this, inasmuch as the harder he scrutinizes it, the more convincing it will become). What he faces as a dual limit is an infinitely convincing (but actually fake and self-generated) dream world "existing" for an infinite time. (Which, it occurs to me, may explain "He causes things to look different so it'd appear time has passed.")

My analysis is this: he, whoever "he" is, has gotten himself into this very fix and has therefore fallen under the spell of an ever more convincing and ever more extensive in time fake world that he himself is generating; he, world and time are in a closed loop, a closed system; moreover, it is equally clear to me that this (dream) is the true explanation — and reveals the true significance of 2-3-74 at which place I ("he") (1) remembered and then (2) as a result temporarily broke out of the closed loop self reinforcing fake world and fake time. [. . .]

What I am saying is that this dream states that I myself am the mind I know as Valis, I generate the info (they are my own thoughts and ideas; viz: as I once previously speculated, I got into my own world producing mental machinery) and, what is more, what I call "the binary computer" is a vision of my own mind as world creator; I think (as binary computer), and these thoughts are the information that I am compelled to give assent to as world (which is why to some extent we control our own world, it adjusts to our perceptions of it — of course it does; this is a closed feedback loop literally pouring back into itself to reinforce itself — and "we are selves in a brain that both makes and perceives reality"). Then several people (e.g., Gregg Rickman) are right in saying that when I experienced Valis I was experiencing my own (unconscious) mind. But they failed to note that that makes me Cosmocrator!

[90:G-49] Valis in me was my own mind, was God but *fallen* God, forgetful, unintentional, cosmogenitor of world.* The "binary switching com-

---

* I feel Dick struggling to reassure himself that God is at once more and less rational than Dick himself — whichever prospect seems less threatening at the moment. Dick spent many years and books trying to figure out God, his clearest and most vivid take (and, perversely, maybe most hopeful) up until the Exegesis probably being the utilitarian divine spray-can of *Ubik*. But for all of Dick's apparent attempts to reconcile a good god and a bad world, his creation of an altogether more malevolent alternate world — in which there persists not only the Roman Empire but its manifestation in the form of Richard Nixon, and in which God is doomed to be even more hapless and ineffectually benign — raises ques-

puter" that generates "info that we hypostatize as world" is my own mind creating irreal imprisoning worlds for me (as if *VALIS* and "Frozen Journey" were superimposed).

[90:G-53] The dream of last night (supra) shows that I am hopelessly trapped, because the harder and longer I scrutinize "world" the more articulated, detailed, convincing and "real" it becomes, with infinitely real as a limit, and, worse, an infinitude of spurious time is a limit; it will go on forever, all the while gaining progressively greater power over me — and yet I am its author!

[90:130:G-75] Therefore I deem it correct to say that yes I have been correct in saying (as I have periodically) that 3-74 represented the lifting of an occlusion from me so that I saw reality either more accurately or (if this is possible) "as it really is" — this owing to me suddenly facing reality for the first time (v. supra). What was presented to me was an inscrutable picture of what resembled living information, a unitary field, pre-synchronized self-initiating transformations, rest-motion modes, etc., all that I endlessly dilate on. The upshot being that (1) I could not figure out what I was seeing and (2) I could not communicate what I had seen. Herein with these two points lies the difficulty. All that I could fathom was that the conventional picture that we normally get — and seem to share — is not in fact what is there; what is there is not even in time or space, nor is causation involved. There seems to be a mind and we are in it — but even now after seven years of mulling it over I am baffled as ever. Hence the *utility* of this perception is (at least at this time) dubious. Out of this experience with the inscrutable and inexplicable I formulate at last the notion that the compulsion exerted on us to see the representation as (1) absolutely real and (2) totally comprehensible is a gift, an essential gift. This deals with more than my 3-74 perception, it deals with my whole adult life as expressed in my 10-volume meta-novel. What I saw in 3-74 I regard as absolutely real (so there is no problem there) but it was unintelligible — whereas all that came prior to it was intelligible but lacking in respect to seeming absolutely real. One is moved to ponder which is better — or for that matter worse — of the two choices: to see, understand and not believe, or to see, *not* understand and yet believe — obviously something drastic is wrong with both. In fact both — each in its own way — smacks of psychotic apperception of world. The former (coherent but unconvincing) is fucked; the latter (unintelligi-

---

tions as to whether Dick really is looking for reconciliation or to expose a God who at least has failed us all, if not actually betrayed us. Or is He, as we've suspected all along, just not fully in charge? — SE

ble but carrying the force of absolute truth) equally so. Surely both represent mental dysfunctions in me. All I can do at this point is abandon the field and say that belief in and understanding of should go hand-in-hand, and if they part company something is wrong. From this I erect the following premise: that God sees to it that we both comprehend (i.e., what we experience is to us intelligible) and believe (it carries the force of the absolute). Obviously something went wrong in me years ago. And when in 3-74 the compensatory correction came it ushered in a whole new host of troubles, giving me even *more* to do, philosophically speaking. Thus God gives us multiple gifts: a world, first of all, one that we can understand and also experience as real—so real, in fact, that it was not until the time of Descartes that the representation problem was even discerned (it has never been fully answered).

What I see is a threat that only someone fighting off psychosis could appreciate: the disappearance of world along two routes: (1) comprehensibility; (2) believability. Viz: you could find yourself understanding it but not believing it to be real—my 10-volume meta-novel—or finding it real but being unable to make any sense out of it—3-74 and *VALIS*. On the bright side, however, this has permitted me to formulate some formidable epistemological and, finally, theological questions, and even a few halting tentative answers. "We are all but cells in a colossal mad brain that both makes and perceives reality"—something like that, the main thrust being that there is some relationship between the creating of reality and perceiving of it (v. my dream supra): the percipient is cosmogenitor, or, conversely, the cosmogenitor wound up as unwilling percipient of its own creation.

The way out of the solipsistic trap is to presume God, since world is dubitable. Thus there is self and there is other, and this other is powerful, benign, wise, loving, and perhaps most important of all, able and willing to provide—in fact guarantee—world (under the conditions of Cartesian epistemology). "God is the final bulwark against non-being" becomes ". . . against isolation."

[90:134:G-79] This is *my* idiosyncratic road to God. For others—who have not been the doubt, who have not known 32 years of doubt, this would not seem to constitute proof. But I say: I do not have it within my own power to compel my own assent to anything but my doubting self; thus on my own I possess no sense of knowing anything but myself, which is a sentence to hell, perpetual unrelenting hell. "Wer wird mich erlösen?"[14] My argument is a variation of Cartesian reasoning (and in my opinion an important one) and so it is in an honorable tradition. I say with Malebranche that I see all things in God; it is God who extricates me from my solipsistic

prison. I did not write 35 novels and 150 stories without coming to a good
understanding of the sinister implications of no world, irreal world, inscrutable world — that second only to the gift of life itself is the gift of world, of
the *other.* Perhaps it is even a greater gift, since it involves all creation. (Viz:
I might well choose personal death over the extinction of the cosmos.)
What I see people ordinarily saying is that world of its own accord impinges on us: impinges coherently and convincingly. The Cartesians show
that this is not the case. I say, the whole cosmos could be presented to me
and yet I would not find it real unless God himself bestowed on me the essential gift of my finding it convincing, a gift that through my own powers
of reasoning and observation I find myself incapable of acquiring, a state I
on my own cannot achieve. I cannot persuade myself and I cannot compel
myself to believe; unless God compels me I will not believe, and if I do not
believe, I am doomed to a certain kind of hell. I know from experience that
God can compel that assent, for he did this by a rustle of color in the grass.
He can absolutely impinge on me; he can break into my prison world and
destroy it — burst the prison, release me. That my assent might be compelled by perceptual and cognitive occlusion and amnesia does not in the
slightest matter to me because the ends justifies the means, since I cannot
live at all unless I'm taken out of my private prison. That is why I see the issue as one of belief on my part, not on the truth of what I believe. I know
now that if there is something that is true I will never on my own know it.
Or if I know it I will not believe I know it. Like Victor Kemmings at the end
of "Frozen Journey" I may have reached reality and can't believe it. That essential belief lies outside my power.

My argument that (I have proof that) God exists is odd. I do not say,
"I know God exists because I experienced/perceived him in 3-74"; that is
dubitable as an argument because my experience may have been a hallucination (I experienced it but it was not real). But I can say, "I know that
God exists because I believe I experienced You above and beyond myself;
and I know of no way that I can go beyond Descartes' 'cogito ergo sum'
by my own power; on my own I cannot add any knowledge to that self-
knowledge. Yet I believe I know of Your existence, so I conclude that some
agency with the power to disclose Your existence to me and thus to compel
my assent to that disclosure exists, and I can only conceive of God as possessing the power, since, pragmatically, this is cosmogenesis, and I define
God as 'he who causes to exist what exists.'" In other words I cannot doubt
that I believe, and I know of no way that I can believe on my own power,
unaided. Therefore the Cartesian proposition "cogito ergo sum" is not the
limit to what I can be certain of: I can say, "I know that I believe, and since
I know that I cannot compel into existence my own belief, I conclude that

something beyond myself exists that has compelled this belief; therefore I not only know that I exist, I know that something beyond myself exists (by reason of my belief)."

[90:G-122] I saw reality (3-74) as it really is; I began to see in 2-74. Relatedness not by time, space and causation but by articulating arborizing phylogons, *I know* — can't I believe? What does it take?

[90:G-131] I will conclude this nightmare marathon analysis by noting that my 10-volume meta-novel can herewith be newly — and perhaps finally correctly — understood. And it serves a very valuable (Gnostic) purpose, to emancipate the cosmogenitor from his own world, to which he is fallen victim. In terms of this, *VALIS* can be seen as the logical culmination of the total corpus. Likewise "Frozen Journey."

[90:G-141] What is most remarkable is not just perceiving one's soul in and hence derived from the divine mind, but to see that soul as a complex of ideas, interacting to form a coherency: one's soul as something that can not only be known but also thought: soul, then, as idea — and taking the form of ideas or sub-ideas clustered together: reduced to or derived from what may in the final analysis be words. That's why the term "thing" is the wrong term. It is information. It is a unique interception by one idea of another, a crossing, an ideational intersection: certain notions about freedom, magic, religious beauty (as expressed by the Grail theme and the Good Friday spell), revolutionary covert activity connected with elements of the Civil War, animals as they appear in children's books, something to do with the old-fashioned countryside and light, music, writing; but most of all a sense of the divine as if not only am I a notion in the divine mind but I as its notion contain in and as myself a notion of it. In other words I fade off into it, and it fades off into me, as if each is aware of and related to the other.

Early 1981

[77:G-8] You won't believe this later when you're not ripped, but your 10 volume meta-novel is "the secret stolen past the angels in one's hands" — the story that (1) each of us lives in a unique individual world; (2) it is spurious; (3) it is fed to us by the plasmate — this is told in *VALIS* if you add it (*VALIS*) to the corpus; and (4) we have some control over our individual worlds, since somehow it derives from us; it isn't just imposed on us (e.g., "Frozen Journey," *Maze* — really the whole corpus). So it adjusts and accommodates to our perceptions and preconceptions of it.

One vast artistic vision, all the way from "Wub" to *DI*, with particular emphasis on *Scanner*, the intro to *The Golden Man*, *VALIS*, "Chains . . . Web" and *DI*. (This last my *dream*. That sustains me. I cannot now be separated from my work.)

Here is sooth: *VALIS* is not as important as supernatural revelation about God and the universe as it is about me as a person — unique and individual and suffering — *and my vision* (Weltanschauung). Me and my own private vision; this is what we call *art* (as with van Gogh and his vision). Therefore it is not theologically meaningful but artistically. The theological, etc., stuff in *VALIS* has value as my construct/vision/dream: likewise *DI*. Vis-à-vis reality it has no relevance. It tells us nothing about world but a lot about me as artist.

So *VALIS* is part — an integral part — of the vision that began with "Roog" and forms one seamless whole. The whole theological, etc., view in *VALIS* (and to a lesser extent in *DI*) is like some vast book within a book, an artistic vision within a greater vision — i.e., my total corpus. It's like the movie in *VALIS*: another "book within a book." Vision within a vision.

"Christ invading the world" is not a truth or falsehood about Christ or world but a truth about me and my vision, my perception and my unique individual world, hence artistically relevant to and in my total unitary corpus. It is part of me, and I have put me and my vision legitimately into my work. [. . .] This personal vision began with *Crap Artist* and *Counter-Clock World*. The rest is artificial, but due to 1964 I passed over from artifact to art. Where it truly blooms is in everything from and including *Tears* on — *great* art, and it all began as objective pulp *objects*, which have turned into human documents, as Gregg Rickman is the first to perceive.

Joint (e.g.) is mind, android, cold.

VALIS (e.g.) is heart, human, life.

I passed through progressive humanization and humanized stages in my writing as I did so in my actual life.

[77:G-11]

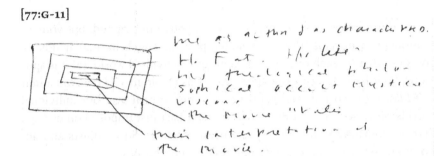

There is no truth in this, only artistic vision: but for me, in terms of my own vision, "truth" (objectively) has no meaning; to state that X is "truth" would violate the premise of my own vision. Thus *VALIS* was inexorably dictated/generated by my total corpus.

May 1981

[78:H-1] Bishop Tim Archer.

I'm going to assign to him as his major view my *Commedia* 3-coaxial realms view (as expressed in my Metz speech and which were going to be the basis for the 3rd novel in the *VALIS* trilogy*). He has been studying the *Commedia* and Sufi teachings, also quantum mechanics (which he does not understand but nonetheless prattles on about). He is convinced that Dante's 3 realms (Inferno, Purgatorio and Paradiso) are available in this life; and here he gets into Heidegger and Dasein. (This makes historical sense, since Heidegger very much influenced Tillich, etc., contemporary Protestant theory.)

Now, how does this relate to his later involvement with the Zadokite Document and the Anokhi mushroom? The Zadokite sect knew how to get into the Paradiso realm (alternate reality) *in which Christ is here.* (This clearly relates to Allegro's "hallucination" theory; likewise Hofmann's *Road to Eleusis.*) It is quite simply the *restored* realm, and is potentially *always* available. What I want to stress is that none of these ideas is original with Bishop Archer. So I must invent a writer-scholar-philosopher-theoretician who advances this theory about the *Commedia* in his book(s), his pub-lished writing — something connected with California outré theorizing.

In other words from the beginning Bishop Archer is searching for Christ. The "Dante" formulation initially provides him with a theoretical framework as to how it can be done (or he *thinks* this is how it can be done). Now, he drops all this — and the California writer who is based on Alan Watts — in favor of the Zadokite scrolls and the Anokhi mushroom; this is typical of him. I would have built on the first, constructed a synthe-sis, but this is not how Jim worked; he rushed from one thing to the next.

---

* The assertion that Dick's last three novels, in many (important) ways so divergent, should be read as a "trilogy" is annoying, to me anyway. As novels, they simply don't add up that way (nor is *Divine Invasion* at the level of the other two), yet the term sticks; here, Dick shows unmistakable investment in it himself. On the one hand, keep in mind that in the wake of *Star Wars* and Tolkien, what publishers called "Sci-Fi" briefly enjoyed a weird boom that made best-sellers out of some of the long-suffering writers Dick could view as peers — Robert Silverberg, Philip Jose Farmer, Frank Herbert, and others — and that nearly all of their commercial hits were in the form of declared "trilogies" (even if some of those involved four or more books). Why not ride the unlikely gravy train? On the other hand, here was a mind more than a little prone to view things as interconnected. He'd begun to see his long shelf of earlier works forming a single tapestry of meaning. Shouldn't these new ones braid together as well? — JL

Okay; this California writer is a Sufi. Edgar Barefoot is his name. This is set in the Bay Area. Bishop Archer meets Barefoot; they become colleagues: an Episcopal Bishop and a Sufi guru living on a house boat at Pier 5 in Sausalito. The name of all this is: making God (or, as with Archer, Christ) immediately available to you as a living experience.

There is a certain quality of Jack Isidore in Bishop Archer: the capacity to believe anything, any pseudoscience or theosophy. The "fool in Christ," naive and gullible and rushing from one fad to another, typical of California.

The Zadokite Document (scrolls) convinces Bishop Archer — who had devoted his life to "reaching across to the living Christ" (which makes sense given the fact that he is after all a Bishop) — that Christ was "irrelevant." There is something more important: the expositor of the 200 B.C.E. Zadokite sect.

Archer's involvement with Barefoot is "ecumenical," but with the Zadokite and Anokhi mushroom stuff he has ecumenicalled himself out of Christianity entirely. Barefoot is crushed, heartbroken — an example of the casualties Archer leaves along the road behind him in his speed-rush Faustian quest, always exceeding itself, surpassing itself (it is really Dionysus that has hold of him). Barefoot, Calif. guru that he is, acts as a rational stable counterpoint to Archer's frenzy. Barefoot is authentically what he seems to be, claims to be: a spiritual person and teacher; he is not a fraud. He is always being demolished in discussions by other more formal thinkers, e.g., those at UC Berkeley, e.g., on KPFA. But — like Watts — he has his followers. He is really quite systematic and rigorous in his thinking. He does not foresee Archer suddenly abandoning him and flying off to Europe vis-à-vis the Zadokite scrolls — he, the Sufi, the non-Christian, is horrified when Archer turns his back on Christ. Archer declares that now he has found the true religion (at last). This very concept ("the true religion") is foreign to Barefoot, in fact that is one of his fundamental views: that *all* religions are equally valuable.

Ah. Archer has expropriated Barefoot's views and peddled them as his own. Barefoot does not mind; he just wants the views per se to be promulgated. [...]

So when we meet Bishop Archer he is already involved in a fusion of Heidegger and Sufism — this means that the book will deal with California grotesques, which is okay. This is how we encounter him, like the grown-ups in *The Cherry Orchard*.

Barefoot claims actually to have experienced the 3 Realms. I will assign to him my "evasion equals time; Dasein equals space" view. Archer can't get the hang of it and wearies of trying; it takes too long. He wants instant solutions. The Anokhi mushroom will do.

[. . .]

The basic story: Zagreus has seized control of Bishop Archer and drives him to his ruin. Whereupon Zagreus leaves the Bishop and enters Bill Lundborg. But in exchange for madness and death — the dues that Zagreus exacts — he confers a vision of Perfect Beauty (Pythagoras' Kosmos).

So I have the Bay Area gay community, the Bay Area "Alan Watts KPFA" community, poetry and religion (non-Christian) and music and *some* dope, but this is *not* the doper subculture! They are all intellectuals, except Connie.

How about a Trot too, to bring in radical politics?

May 1981

[79:1-2][16] Art, like theology one giant fraud. Downstairs the people are fighting while I look for God in a reference book: God, ontological arguments for. Better yet: practical arguments against. There is no such listing, it would have helped a lot if it had come in time: arguments against being foolish, ontological and empirical, ancient and modern (see common sense). The trouble with being educated is that it takes a long time; it uses up the better part of your life and when you are finished what you know is that you would have benefited more by going into banking. I wonder if bankers ask such questions. They ask what the prime rate is up to today. If a banker goes out on the Dead Sea Desert he probably takes a flare pistol and canteens and C-rations and a knife. Not a crucifix: Displaying a previous idiocy that was intended to remind him. Destroyer of the people on the Eastshore Freeway and my hopes besides; Sri Krishna, you got us all. Good luck in your other endeavors. Insofar as they are equally commendable in the eyes of other Gods.

I am faking it, she thought. These passions are bilge. I have become inbred, from hanging around the Bay Area intellectual community; I think as I talk: pompously and in riddles. Worse I talk as I hear. Garbage in (as the computer science majors say); garbage out.

[79:1-9] These things are obvious to me:

(1) I am on a stupendous spiritual quest. It involves my total life.
(2) It involves — but is not limited to — my writing.
(3) I am making progress.
(4) *VALIS* is salient and evolves into the "Bishop Timothy Archer" novel.
(5) My turning down the *Blade Runner* offer to do the "Archer" book for only $7,500 is a double-edged spiritual advance: (1) to turn down the money; (2) to do the "Archer" book; thus my spiritual aspirations endured white-hot iron testing and triumphed.*

---

* United Artists picked up an option for *Do Androids Dream of Electric Sheep?* in September 1973, netting Dick a check for $2,500. When it was announced that Ridley Scott would direct Harrison Ford in the $25 million movie, it was clear that *Blade Runner,* as it was to be titled, was designed to cash in on the success of *Star Wars.* Though Dick was skeptical of Hollywood, he was excited about the project, especially after seeing footage from the film. The movie's backers wanted Dick to write a novelization of the film based on the screenplay, which differs markedly from his novel. Dick was promised a $50,000 advance

(6) It is Anokhi whom I seek. My perception grows, it is real, it is worth the work.

(7) *VALIS* was a dim but *authentic* (!) vision, as to a child, of Anokhi. Someday I will be an adult.

(8) My view synthesizes all the theology and philosophy I have learned; nothing is wasted.

(9) I have a real understanding of Anokhi and he works with me to bring this vision about; I am not working in the dark; *he is with me.*

(10) Finally, I am right now triumphing, as I write the "Archer" book. Not as a literary piece but rather having to do with Anokhi. Had I *not* turned down the *Blade Runner* offer, had I not tackled the "Archer" book, I would have lost. But he helps me. Literature is not the issue. Forging a vision of Anokhi as I write *is the issue.* For me there is no other issue. Pure consciousness.

[79:1-13][17] I see the legend of Satan in a new way; Satan desired to know God as fully as possible. The fullest knowledge would come if he became God, was himself God. He strove for this and achieved it, knowing that the punishment would be his permanent exile from God. But he did it anyhow, because the memory of knowing God, really knowing him as no one else ever had or would, justified to him his eternal punishment. Now, who would you say truly loved God out of everyone who ever existed? Satan willingly accepted eternal punishment and exile just to know God — by becoming God — for an instant. Further (it occurs to me) Satan knew God, truly knew God, but perhaps God did not know or truly understand Satan; had he understood him he would not have punished him. But Satan welcomed that punishment, for it was his proof to himself that he knew and loved God. Otherwise he might have done what he did for [the] reward. "Better to rule in hell than to serve in heaven" *is* an issue, here, but not the true one; which is the ultimate goal and search to know and be; fully and really to know God, in comparison to which all else is really very little.

[79:1-15] What I must do — what I am doing — is extract the essence (einai) of God out of intoxication; sever the two; for the presence (not the es-

---

as well as a large cut from all print tie-ins if he would rewrite the book to more closely resemble the movie. Though the deal might have earned Dick as much as $400,000, the contract also stipulated that the original version of his book be taken out of print. After much soul searching, Dick turned down the offer and instead accepted a $7,500 advance on the mainstream novel *The Transmigration of Timothy Archer*. Sadly, both *The Transmigration of Timothy Archer* and *Blade Runner* debuted after Dick's death. — DG

sence!) of God intoxicates man and makes him mad, but it is man the percipient who is mad, not God.

I did see God (3-74), and as a vast signalling system who operates in us
and on us by hieroglyphics that are stimuli — and this (seeing thus, and
correctly) drove me mad; I am mad but I did see God. Yet I continue, for
at last God's essence, which transcends madness, will sober me in love: cf.
Donne's "batter my heart"; the whole pattern is becoming clear to me, and
it is a *rational* structure! The madness that seeing God fills man with is the
madness of belief, knowledge and joy; these *must* be separated from the
madness or their value will be lost in the intoxication. This is enthusiasmos
by the Holy Spirit. But (to repeat) *God* is not mad; *man* is driven mad by
belief, understanding and joy, for he is a little thing.

[79:1-19] In 2-3-74 the Geist in me rebelled against Fate (death) expressed
by the Xerox missive and, in rebelling, became self-aware (Anokhi); this
is what I knew (and knew of) as Valis. It could not rebel unless it became
self-aware; it could not be self-aware without rebelling (against fate). (This
finds expression in *VALIS* when I say of the plasmate: "For thousands of
years it slumbered"; i.e., "throughout all this [the first age or half of the
book] Siddhartha slept [but now he awakes].") [. . .]

Thus in a certain poetic way it is *true* to say I seized the Book of the
Spinners — i.e., of Fate — read the writing and caused it (my fate) to come
out differently.[18] Put another way, I refused my instructions to die — my
programming; I rebelled against it. These are poetic or quasi-poetic, but
"rebel," "Fate" and "spirit" and "consciousness" (Anokhi) are real and literal.

[79:1-24] The issue is not reality or ontology but consciousness — the possibility of pure, absolute consciousness occurring. In terms of which material things (objects) become language or information, conveying or recording or expressing meaning or ideas or thoughts; Mind using reality as a
carrier for information, as an LP groove is used to carry information; to record, store and play it back. This is the essential issue; this use of material
reality *by* mind *as* a carrier for information by which information is processed — and this is what I saw that I called Valis, and anyone who reads
VALIS and thinks it is just a rehash of metaphysical ideas or ideas "worked
over by 1,000s of thinkers for 1,000s of years" is a fucking *fool!* Robert Anton Wilson is right.[19]

[79:1-28] I *will* know what this pure consciousness was, ere I die trying.

Some mental entity using reality as a carrier for information — what
does this mean? That we humans are not alone and that we are not the

highest life form on this planet. And it is aware of us and intervenes in our lives; yet we see it not.

[79:1-30] All I can think of is that reality is pure consciousness; that only Anokhi exists, purely and solely. That what we have is ascending degrees of perception, and the ultimate is perception of pure consciousness "out there"!

I can express the essence of it: reality *refers* to something above, beyond and outside itself; it is (literally *is*) an idea *about* something else; it is not so much information but an idea or concept *of* something beyond it (itself). Hence I discerned info "recorded" or "encoded" into/on it. What I have been missing is: this causes reality — not just to be a vehicle *for* info — but, as a vehicle, to be caused to *refer* to something *outside* itself. Thus it signifies (as what is seen) what is *not* seen, and *this* (my not-seen) is my surd. And I know what that (surd) is: it is God impinging *on* reality (but distinct from it, Spinoza to the contrary). Hence *this* is why I saw "pretextual cause" and "camouflage"; this (new) concept subsumes both these earlier perceptions/conceptions.

I have had it all and never realized it before (except that I understood the "surd" concept). Hence the AI voice speaks of a "perturbation in the reality field" — pointing *beyond* the reality field! All creation registers the imprint of God and reveals God. But not in the traditional "design" sense; no: not design but sign which must be *read*; sign pointing to what lies beyond it (viz: a sign does not point to itself). Put another way, if there was no creation, the existence of God would be metaphysical, just as without the iron filings the magnetic field is metaphysical. Yet we do not and cannot normally "read" reality *at all*. It is either-or, not degree. Both the immanent and transcendent views are wrong; a totally *new* view is needed! Viewed this way the "Acts," dream and cypher material in *Tears* becomes completely understandable. This is how the *I Ching* works, the registering as if by a limpid passive "vegetable" agent. What we are talking about, then, is the Tao, which is real *but does not exist!* Yet registers on (or mildly shapes) what *does* exist! And is the ultimate power.

[79:1-34] When I saw the Grail this morning (5:30 A.M.) I did not see it per se; I did not, either, see it created out of nothing. I saw an ordinary physical normal every-day cup already in world affected by God; the cup in a sort of mist of color — the space around the cup as mist-like colors; and this cup became the Grail; it changed; it was made into (?) the Grail, and it did not just seem to me to be the Grail; it *was* the Grail; it was what I would say converted into spirit, a spiritual thing: "Grailified," so to speak. Light did not emanate from it; it was transfigured *by a sort of material light* that showed — displayed or was — colors. He must have a physical cup or cup-like object in, I guess, our Lower Realm, to shape and mold and change and transform and "Grailify." The spiritual, then, is not opposed to or separate from the physical; it is as if the physical and mundane exists to be thus spiritualized.

The physical, material world, then, is not truly disjunctive to the other realm but points to it as a sign and under certain circumstances — a state of Grace — can be so read: as to what it refers to, is or bears (carries) information about.

I found myself thinking, "This is the Medieval World View," and then I realized, "No! This is what it *aimed* at."

[79:1-36] "Bishop Archer." The medium Rachel Garret is (acts as) the Spinner; she foretells the Bishop his fate: death in the Dead Sea Desert. The rest of the book is his attempt to defy Fate and free himself from his sinister destiny through the blood of Christ.

[. . .]

He puts up the greatest fight possible against sinister Fate; this could include fighting against deteriorating into a credulous crank: Kristen's death sobers him up. Yet if he believes Rachel's prophecy he has de facto succumbed to superstitious credulity! Is this not Scylla and Charybdis? To avoid death he must believe in crackpots. The reader, knowing of Jim Pike's death, will see the irony of the situation. Angel counsels him not to believe what mediums say; but he cannily senses that he had been heeding Rachel's warning at the cost of seeming/being a nut: "Better a live dog than a dead lion." He is really in a spot: Fate, by a master move, has him either way. The Bishop *correctly* perceives the strategy (by Fate): a master move involving paradox.

[79:1-39]
(1) The warning by Jeff, through Rachel Garret. Apparently Jeff has come back all right.
(2) Disbelief by Tim and Angel (of the warning).
(3) Kirsten's suicide. This changes everything.
(4) Tim now takes it seriously and perceives the double bind he is in. He is totally lucid.
(5) Tim sees the situation in terms of Fate; his knowledge of the mystery religion origins of Christianity comes to his rescue; Christ can save him (and only Christ).

(6) ∴ (sic!) He goes to Israel to seek "Christ," the Anokhi mushroom. Dies. It would seem Fate won.

(7) Angel encounters Bill: Tim is alive in him (as in "Beyond Lies the Wub") but he (whoever "he" signifies) is mad.

(8) All she can save now is herself.

[79:1-43] All—repeat: *all*—that invaded me in 2-3-74 was myself as eternal unique idea (in other words my intelligible essence or soul). Somehow I gained access to my informational basis!

[79:1-46] In this "Sibyl" plot development in the "Bishop Archer" book: do I not realize what I am saying? Jim Jr. came back; Jim was right — *it was true!* The prophecy (by Jeff) proves it, *whatever* the character's reactions thus in writing the book I vindicate Jim. Do I want to do this? Yes.

[. . .]

Am I falsifying history? I don't know; the material seems to be in control. But it (Jeff's — Jim Jr.'s — coming back) proves futile pragmatically: The Bishop and "Kirsten" *died anyhow!* Angel *must* be shown to realize this. Yet — what if "Jim" is alive in Bill (as in the "Beyond Lies the Wub" story)? It must be an inscrutable epiphany at the end; *she can't tell.* No; I know the answer; Jim, as we all are, is immortal; he *did* come back (in Bill, in me). *That* is the point I am working toward.

There must be some indubitable sign that Bill at the end conveys to Angel that he really is Tim (*even though he is mad* and in the asylum). (My model: "Beyond Lies the Wub.") It must be a holy moment, and, to her, terrifying. Both: (1) holy; and (2) terrifying, not reassuring. (That would be sentimental.) This goes all the way back to my early novel (really my first): "The Weaver's Shuttle"!!!!! The old salesman (Runcible/Runciter) reborn. *Rebirth* is my theme. Immortality as, specifically, renewal and rebirth, not just continuity. With, in, as Bill, Tim is complete: he is now rooted in practical reality: thus is a syzygy.

[. . .]

He could not prove Jeff came back. He could not get the necessary info to save his life. He has returned — in/as Bill — but cannot prove it. So the book in the final analysis explores the fact that first, you cannot know the truth, and what truth you know, you cannot prove to others, thus (this is the summation) although Fate is defeated, you cannot prove that you have defeated it; this knowledge (of this victory) *cannot be communicated.* You can defeat Fate and know it, *but you cannot tell it* — which is my precise position; thus Tim winds up in an ambiguous position; he both won (he defeats Fate) but he cannot proclaim it — as if Fate exacts a latent, final, sting/victory. Yes: Fate plays the final card; you win but can't make anyone believe. It remains a private matter, locked in your idios brain. [. . .] So, strangely, this is the study of a man's triumph over Fate, which is a Promethean freedom; but his punishment for his "theft" or daring is to be chained to the rock of eternal silence that he did this: that Fate can be overcome. Thus he is free of Fate and yet punished by Fate — doomed in a subtle way: he is alive (reborn) but can tell (convince) no one.

What would be his best ideal solution? Why to resolve simply in the fact *that he is alive,* per se; to abandon the proclaiming in the form of a simple, private, humble life, thankful for being spared, being alive; so we see him (Bill) at last in perfect peace, no longer trying to convince Angel; and at this point when he abandons his strivings (Schopenhauer's Will) and simply says, "This is sufficient," he then for the first time *is redeemed* — and knows it. It is sufficient simply to live, even if he can't tell anyone. This is his victory; he has won by and in submission. He has come to terms with Fate, rather than overcoming it. He and Fate are friends. They both know the truth. He will simply be Bill — and rotate tires. And out of this comes — for him, saintliness — for the first time. He as Bill is a Saint, a Buddha; he as Tim — forever striving — is not and here it ends, peacefully.

He has won this tremendous victory, through the help of Christ, over Fate and death — and can tell (convince) no one. And yet he is content. This is sublime. In and as Bill he works on a car, repairing it, caring for it as one would an animal; devoted to it. We see him polishing the chrome: a boy, simple and gentle and loving and no longer off in theoretical abstract clouds. And Angel loves him although she does not believe. It does not matter to him; he is content, like the Buddha. It is as if the best in Bill has won out — of the syzygy: firmly rooted in reality: the salvation of both Bill and Tim, each of whom individually was mad in his own way; but out of the syzygy has come sanity, of a higher kind. The striving and restlessness are gone. Essentially he is content without knowing whether he won or lost to Fate, i.e., whether he defeated Fate, or whether Fate in the final analysis managed to defeat him. So *he* does not know that; and Angel does not know that; and Angel does not know if it's really Tim (or just Bill *imagining* he is Tim). This is a strange ending. The will (of Schopenhauer) turns back on itself and is satisfied *not to know: This* is the form its cessation takes: that he is content not to know, and so is she. Thus one thing *is* certain: the restless, striving, irrational will is defeated; it has given up. If this is how victory is defined, there has been victory. If victory is defined as knowing whether Tim Archer defeats Fate through Christ and immortality — it is *not* victory.

The final message seems to be: sublime peace — freedom from the restless striving will — is possible, but knowledge — intellectual knowing — is not. The heart can know peace but the mind cannot be satisfied; the drive to know, to possess intellectual certitude is doomed to failure. Hence one short look elsewhere — to the heart (as Paul says about love). This, very simply, is a *fact*.

[...]

The conclusion: life is possible but knowledge is not, and the two must be discriminated.

[79:1-56] Someone from behind me leaned forward and touched me on the shoulder. "Hi, Angel."

I turned around to see who it was. A pudgy faced youth, blond haired, smiling at me, his eyes guileless. Bill Lundborg, wearing a turtleneck sweater and grey slacks and hush puppies.

"Remember me?" he said softly. "I've been wondering how you've been doing. I guess we better be quiet." He leaned back and folded his arms, intent on what Edgar Barefoot was saying.

[79:1-59] So despite all my efforts to the contrary I after all wrote the 3rd book of the trilogy! And it is finished and sent off!

And it may just be the most accurate of the 3 books, in that it involves Jim Pike, and, what is more, says that Jim returned from the dead, out of compassion for "those he loved" — which is what I had wanted to write from the very beginning but did not know how, nor did I dare to! Inasmuch as Jim's (Tim's) return from the dead is identified with the presence of Christ in the Dead Sea Desert, it is expressed — like Christ's own resurrection — *as a sign that the Parousia is here!* Thus it may be the most *accurate* and most *important* and most *daring* of the 3 books! And completes the previous two!

And *very* adroitly written! Since it does not seem to preach. Angel categorically rejects the notion that Tim (i.e., Jim) has come back, and yet from the internal evidence in the book it is clear that in fact he has — and thus is to be seen as a sign pointing to the Parousia, identified as such!

Jim came back (I say it in "Bishop") and he came back to *me* (if you add in *VALIS*) and this is the Parousia (*The Divine Invasion*). The full and true story is divided up over the 3 books. Thus I now have — despite any of my intentions to the contrary — told the full and true story, not only of Jim but of the Parousia; he did come back and this is only half the story; the other half is: What this signifies: the news he brings: *the Parousia is here.*

What I have done in and by these 3 books is penetrate to the heart of the Christian mystery. That Bill in the end is taken over by the Holy Spirit is proved by the xenoglossy (the Dante quotations) that Angel recognizes; this is specifically what Tim Archer when first we see him denies exists: This specifically is proof of the presence — and reality — of the Holy Spirit who in turn is Christ; and who and what is Christ? Our spiritual leader who dies, and whose return in us (and hence *to* us) by enthusiasmos is a triumph over death and proof of eternal life — and carries with it the knowledge from the next (upper) realm. This is the Essence of the Christian (1) experience and (2) knowledge, and is related to Elijah sending back a part of his spirit *to his friend* Elisha. I have now told the full story and specifically identified it with Christ, the Parousia and the Holy Spirit; the revelation is now by this 3rd book complete and accurate. Most of all it is clear that this return is due to compassion (agape) on the part of the departed friend who turns down Nirvana out of love for his friends left behind.

I define Christ, then, as anyone whose love (compassion) is so great that he rejects his chance at Nirvana (return to God) to return from death — the next World/Upper Realm — to and for his friends. After he dies they receive his returned spirit ("Born again" — "Born in the Spirit" — "Born from above"), whereupon not only are they joined with him but, moreover, the two realms are reunited to form what is called "the Kingdom of God" since the syzygy of him and his friend occupies — occurs in — both realms. The living friend not only finds the dead friend in his mind — he also experiences the next world: the two realms unify like two signals; this is restoration of the cosmos to before the Fall.

This is what is meant by Christianity, because it confers new life, a new kind of life — and, moreover, life that is a syzygy between the two friends.

[79:1-64] I have yoked Joyce's human character (Molly Bloom) to the prose of, e.g., the Encyclopedia of Philosophy: i.e., the finest prose style.

[79:1-65] *Archer* is just plain the best novel I have ever written: I am at the height of my power; it evolves through *Mary and the Giant* to *Crap* to *VALIS* to it.

The fact is, I not only know Angel Archer — Betty Jo, Connie, Kleo, Joan — and something more. My creation born out of 35 years of writing. This book, *Archer,* the summation back to "Weaver's Shuttle" — it sums up them all, from my first stories when I lived in the same building that (Monica Reilly) did — to *VALIS* (never mind *Divine Invasion*). And I did this deliberately: summed up 35 years of writing. This (David's offer) was the summation and victory of 35 years, not psychologically but artistically.

Not: *Mary and the Giant* to *Archer*

But: *Mary and the Giant*, through *VALIS*, to *Archer* — extraordinary.

[79:1-68] So where did she come from? I inferred her nature *from* the style. But when you read the book you naturally get the opposite impression, viz: I had her in mind, because I wanted her to be my character I had to use her style of thinking. Yet that is not so. "The style is everything in Literature"; fine: but in this book my style brought a character into being. The origin of Angel Archer is in the style. Where did the style come from? It is a synthesis of a number of sources (my eclectic reading).

Throughout the book, her compassion factor grows Bishop Archer's mind (intellect) which she had identified as something related to, like, analogous to her own, is (becomes), because it now is in Bill, the object of her compassion (loving-kindness); thus she feels compassion for her own intellect. Hence her own self as intellect (not to mention Tim)! Her heart (compassion, agape) wins out over her mind (intellect); *she,* then, is the Buddha's Bodhisattva; "turning her back from Nirvana" is her staying with Bill. Look how her attitude toward him evolves in the book from fear and dislike to respect to tender love in the end. It is as if she has become Tim's mother. She ministers to a ruinous way of talking as an affectation analogous to her own. The style created her!

[79:1-71] In the "Bishop" novel I saw how "style" can give rise to a specific unique actual person (e.g., Angel Archer), so it is possible for verbal information to give rise — to create, give birth to — an actual concrete unique person *who was not there before.*

[79:1-72] There is a stupendous and obvious point I'm missing about Angel. It would — and I did! — require an extraordinary viewpoint character to both intellectually and emotionally understand the Bishop. To do it adequately he or she would have to be highly qualified in terms of verbal skills, intellectual comprehension and tenderness; otherwise the "lens" that she consists of would be inadequate. Thus Angel and hence the style (since it is her ratiocination) was in fact created by Jim Pike. [. . .] She as interpretive lens would in fact have to exceed him in all respects; thus Jim not I is the author of Angel Archer. From word one line one page one *a certain unique formidable intellect and spiritual soul* equipped with *common sense but, even more, aesthetic Love,* would have to exist as lens; this is why I could not discard those opening 4 pages. And she is wounded due to his death — all these traits and wounded too.

Thus (as I say) I did not create Angel Archer: my understanding of and loving Jim did — so Jim (in a certain real sense) did. In the novel I am true to the logic of fictional narrative technique: Tim/Jim is seen always and only through her mind. Thus Angel Archer is not my soul but is Jim's. His Monitor or recording Angel (sic!), *his* AI voice, not mine. *His* anima or other, not mine. But, in that case, how do I have access to her? Here is a vast mystery. I am not sure I know the answer. Is my soul *his* soul?

There is no doubt: if the 3 books are read (*VALIS, Divine Invasion* and *Bishop Timothy Archer*) it is clear that the Parousia is here. Not a theophany is involved but resurrection, *of a given man* (not of Christ which after all took place 2,000 years ago). This (resurrection) (of Jim/Tim) is the beginning and it comes trailing clouds of collateral verification, like spinoffs: These in all constitute vast plural indices of the Parousia. Each novel in turn verifies and amplifies and explains the previous one.

> *The Dead Shall Live*
> *The living die*
> *And music shall untune the sky.*[20]

[79:1-74] Most amazing of all, I did not perceive in advance that *Bishop Archer* would be the 3rd book of the *VALIS* trilogy; in fact I had conceived of it as repudiating (!) the Valis notions/mysticism. But on the contrary it nails the whole thing down and follows logically; in view of this, no wonder I turned down the *Blade Runner* offer to do the "Bishop Archer" book! It *had* to be written! To complete the total message with the given instance of a specific human returning from the dead (proving that the Parousia is here).

[79:1-77] At the very end of the "Bishop Archer" book it would appear that Bill thinks he is — not just Tim Archer — but Christ! ("the expositor"). Thus indeed in no sense is he any longer:

Bill ⟷ Tim

He is:

Tim ⟷ Christ

This is certainly madness. But it raises the theological possibility that he is — this is — the Parousia. Yet Angel is right; Bill is destroyed in the process (like Nietzsche with Dionysus). So the ending is spiritually up and humanly down.

◆   ◆   ◆

[79:1-81] What I have shown is what the best intellectual mind — as correctly represented by a young Berkeley intellectual woman — *can* do and *cannot* do; it can go so far (represented by her "abscessed tooth and the *Commedia*" night) but it can go no farther — as represented by her rejection of Christ (yes, Christ!) at the end: she walks away. This is a penetrating analysis of the intellectual mind: what it can do (a very great deal) and what it can't do (make the final leap). *And she knows it. This* is what the "Bishop Archer" book is about: Angel is a pure aesthetic-intellectual, able to go so far but unable to make the final leap to Christ. Thus "Berkeley" (as paradigm of the intelligent, sensitive mind) is both lauded and stigmatized. This is a fine book; it both praises and deplores, and correctly. Thus one deduces the existence of the divine *by its absence:* the failure of her final leap (i.e., my meta-abstraction). Thus *I* was able to do specifically what Angel was *not* able to do; I *left* Berkeley. The topic is: "The limitations of the reasoning mind." Bishop Archer as Bill calls to her *but she does not hear. It is not reasonable.* Angel fell short, missed the mark, and this is what constitutes sin, this falling short of the mark. Thus this novel *must* end as it does. Bill may have made it; we can't be sure. But what we are sure of is that although Angel came close *she did not;* thus I demonstrate the limits of reason.

What is needed is an orthogonal breakthrough, which I achieved (in 2-3-74). Ursula[21] is the basis of Angel: Many virtues but in the end self-limiting.

The mind "knows" in advance what is possible and what is impossible: it is intelligent, rational, educated and tender; but it is not devout. It does not know how to capitulate to the impossible and accept it as real. [. . .]

Thus the novel is a damning indictment of pure intelligence lacking faith. She is so close but cannot make the final crucial leap. This does not deal with Berkeley except as a paradigm of reasoning: The intelligent, sensitive, educated mind — just how far can it go. The great quantum leap that I call the "meta-abstraction" is lacking. Yet all the clues, for it, are there. It *is,* as she says, a *machine;* it plods on and cannot leap the crucial gap to foolishness (as it were). It cannot pass over from words ("I am a word junky, a word disease") to the supra or non verbal, the purely conceptual (and non-verbal: absolute abstraction). The paradoxes are obscured to her, despite Barefoot's best efforts (i.e., "the foolish come for the words; the wise eat the sandwich").

The Bishop is a topic in this novel only insofar as he holds out the gift of Divine foolishness to her, which she, in her rationality, rejects (at the end). *She* is the real topic. But the Bishop offers the cure and solution, which she rejects; yet she comes so close! *She has failed:* I must not regard her as a success; I must not strive to emulate her. I love her but in the final analysis I must reject her solution; it falls short of true comprehension: of an essentially *irrational* reality (that is not available to linear reason). The ultimate mystery of reality eludes her. She would have to believe the impossible. Only when one can believe the impossible is one truly free (of one's self-imposed prison). (The BIP!!!) One is pitting one's finite intellect against God: Satan's original rebellion redefined for the modern world.

[79:1-86] Perhaps the great leap — meta-abstraction — is when we see the peak experiences as signs pointing to Valis which in itself is unknowable: my "surd"; *this* may be my "meta-abstraction"; viz: suddenly you intuit that the peak experience — *all* peak experiences — are signs pointing *to* a "thing" (Valis) in itself unknowable, and are not to be taken in themselves as "real," but, rather, signify (i.e., point to) reality. Since they seem not only real but ultra-real, then all at once "reality" is viewed as a signifier of reality, which (reality) in itself cannot be apprehended (directly); and this may be what my meta-abstraction was all about, which explains why I can't put it into words (i.e., what I realized; since I realized only a sign, not the "thing" signified: this fits in with, e.g., Zen Buddhism, etc.).*

[79:1-87] So the meta-abstraction is the sudden insight that the most intense experiences with reality — i.e., that which is most real — is only an abstract *sign* pointing to an actual totally unseen reality beyond, which causes us to experience the peak moments for the purpose of alluding to itself, creating the peak experiences as an interface by which to register on us; whereupon these ultra intense experiences — taken to be ultimately real — suddenly become only signs, *hence abstract:* i.e., *WORDS about* reality and not themselves reality. They merely allude to but are not; they possess no sein, and yet they constitute the most compelling "reality" we know!

* Here Dick confronts one of the fundamental debates in the philosophy of mysticism. On the one hand, some modern thinkers assert that mystical experience — here rendered in the language of the human potential movement as Maslow's "peak experiences" — enables us to transcend conceptual thought and to directly glimpse reality as it is. In contrast, more skeptical voices insist that mystical experience is, like everything else, a construction; our groks are mediated by cultural expectations, conceptual filters (including linguistic signs), and the peculiarities imposed by the structures of human consciousness. Here Dick embraces this latter Kantian argument, but pushes it in the direction of more traditional claims of revelation. Peak experiences are not real in themselves, but neither are they simply projections or hiccups of the individual mind. Like everything else, experiences are *signs.* But through meta-abstraction!!!, we can intuit them as a special kind of sign: an "ultra-real" (or hyper-real) sign that points, not back to our own language or neural hardwiring, but to an ineffable ground that eludes both words and "things." — ED

Within the framework of this realization, the statement "a perturbation in the reality field" conveys everything, in that reality is perceived as a field on which something beyond it intrinsically totally undetectable impinges, with the result that it — this totally intrinsically undetectable "thing" — becomes indirectly (inferentially) known to us — as if it is signaling to us but can signal to us *only* by perturbating the reality field. Thus we must construe "reality" as a medium on which this "thing" registers and makes itself available to us: my "surd." The implications of this are simply stupendous: this "thing" evidently cannot *directly* register (impinge) on us. To suddenly grasp that we are compelled to give total assent to reality merely as a means by which we can inferentially know this "thing" — this may be the great leap, my "meta-abstraction." As in going from "2 cows and 2 cows = 4 cows" to "2 and 2 = 4"; it *is* an abstraction, and it does involve a sudden vast leap. Like that of seeing the relationship between the *word* "banana" and a banana; the word points to the thing. . . .

[79:1-89] So to say the universe is info is only half the story, and the lesser half: the surd (1) is not discussed. But *Bishop* is on the right path: Barefoot's "speech for the foolish, sandwich for the wise"; it may not be possible to come any closer to moksa in a verbal presentation; Angel may be doomed because a book is words!

Words stand in relationship to reality as signifiers (normal abstraction).

Reality stands in relationship to X as signifier (meta-abstraction). What is this "X"? We don't know; we have only the "signifier," reality.

But if reality is abstracted into a signifier we can fathom *that* it (reality) points, although we can see what is pointed to; however, this "X" perturbs the reality field and so is knowable by inference (its perturbation of reality). It renders reality (into) a language. *This* is why I saw: the plasmate; the set-ground; and rest-motion; and linking-relinking: "X" was perturbing reality causing it to be in relation to "X" a language (i.e., as the word "banana" is to banana). Thus in these 7 years I've only had half the picture, but sensed the "surd." The AI voice has tried to aid me.

The Tao? "X" does not exist. It is not real. Yet it perturbs reality and causes reality to impinge on us, compelling our assent. This is purposeful.

My God — what is pointed to is *Ubik*, Lem's analysis of *Ubik* ("uncanny one-way intrusions") and "Overdrawn at the Memory Bank" and *The Tibetan Book of the Dead* and my 10 volume meta-novel.[22] In 2-3-74 I never saw the real world; I just saw our semi-real world impinged on, perturbed, made into language.

. . .

[79:1-94] The meta-abstraction is to (suddenly) perceive reality as signifier and not as the thing signified. Hence as a result (of this meta-abstraction) reality would then very soon assume the aspect of information and language and signs because this is how our minds conceive of "signifier"; languages, information and signs is the way *we* signify (reality, things: words *pointing to* something of which they are pure abstraction).

I've been on the lip of this realization ever since I developed my "surd" theory. Now it is clear why words and even concepts fail to represent what I call Valis; they deal with reality, but in this case reality itself is the abstract signs, words, concepts, info, language; so human language would be twice removed, hence not relatively ineffective but totally so.

So all the "language" elements that I saw (e.g., plasmate, set-ground, linking-relinking, rest-motion, MMSK) may in fact be metaphors constructed by my own mind to express the fact that as the word "banana" is to banana, reality is to X.

[79:1-95] My mind was scanning reality as (reality as) language, trying to read it and thus know X. This failed.

One can (apparently) only know *that* X exists but not *what* X is. In which case, the closest approximation conceptually may be that which *Anokhi* expresses.

However, *my* intuition is that since what it (X) manifests itself as is beauty, then the Sufis may be right and its essence is what we term beauty.

But it would be very hard for this meta-abstraction to take the form of words because to say, "Reality is not that which is signified but is, rather, the signifier," seems (even maybe is) oxymoronic (except that the AI voice knew how to express it: "a perturbation in the reality *field*" — a brilliant way to convey it).

[. . .]

Thus my poor brain was converted into a putative deciphering machine in its attempt to read the information; but (it would seem) the information can't be read because it is only metaphorically information; that is, it stands to X as information (such as we generate) stands to reality. But it is only *like* information; it is information only in that it signifies something outside itself; hence all the info I've received is either cryptic or incoherent — although containing mystifying *allusions to* something; there is, then, a *something*.

It's like Borges' story "The Library of Babel."

Well, then; perhaps my 2-74 meta-abstraction was *not* Plato's recovery of the Forms. But a new way of perceiving reality (distantly related to

Plato's perception of the Forms; so-to-speak analogous to it), resulting in my Kantian ordering categories fundamentally revising themselves (or rather my brain discarded the old ones — space, time and causation — and adapted the new one of conceiving everything in terms of abstract information). This is more accurate, but the main goal does not have to do with reality *at all* but that of which reality (as a field) is the signifier. "It's only information." My brain was telling itself. "But what that information is about can't seem to be found in the information!" My brain tried to break the "cypher" without success. It may be information generated by and in my own brain (which is why the whole thing resembles *Ubik* and my own prior thought formations). Yet there *is* something there, capable of perturbing the reality field.

This of course is why "God" acts through or as causation; he can (he is X) only impinge through reality, not directly.

But as I said initially, a peak (ultra-intense) experience is X compelling our assent to an absolute degree (in the experience at hand; he — it — can do this anytime anywhere with anything): This is the closest we come to experiencing X; put another way, all peak experiences are of X (expressed in, through, as world).

[79:1-99] "The age of iron is filibustering so we won't notice that everything we have [that we treasure] has been taken away from us" — hypnogogic thought. Referring to "Acts"? The Messianic age? Strange thought. The *real* world?

[79:1-105] 5:30 A.M.: The phenomenal world is what we conceive it to be: in space-time, or information; it has no absolute existence. Its highest utility — pragmatic value — is — would be — to point as a sign to the absolute and be a means by which we could and can know the absolute which *does* have a genuine intrinsic existence on-its-own but is to us and for us unknowable. Thus I have sharply heightened the use-value of the phenomenal world by shaping it — rendering it — into and as information *about* the absolute; this is a titanic achievement. I have made the Kantian ordering categories an instrument — not just to shape the phenomenal world — but to (use it to) point to the absolute, which is genuine. Thus the phenomenal world no longer (for me) simply points back to my own mind (and its ordering categories) but points *away* from me to the absolute; points as information *about* the absolute, the not-me. This is a vast evolution: it is phenomenal world leading out, not back to me: out and away and to, rather than being circular; rather than simply reporting my own mind back to me (in terms of time, space and most of all causation). *This* is what I have done: made of the phenomenal world a bridge to the absolute, the not-me.

[79:I-110] Tug. Valence *the way*. *Influence* on the reality field: "perturbation"; this is a modern expression for the way.

I have unified Kantian Cartesianism and Taoism: the sentient tug on reality ("the reality field") by that which is not:

The way is yielding yet leads. It is gentle but cannot be resisted.

Valis (my one — sole — glimpse of the action of the absolute on the reality field "a perturbation of the reality field") was a tug, a valence away from plumb. This is the Ch'ang Tao which is outside reality acting on reality. I saw the absolute as a tug (perturbation) acting on reality (and I comprehended the dialectic) and this is Taoism. The Tao is impersonal but "heaven is on the side of the good man" and "heaven fills up the empty."

[79:I-113] The key is this: the *Commedia* successfully captures the Medieval world view of vertical — or Gothic — space: *rising*. This coupled with a transcendental Platonism is the essence of the matter, the hierarchically arranged realms. What I need to do is study a modern person who has no literary contact with the medieval "vertical space" (as does Angel Archer) and trace that person rising through the triune realms from say his high school years to his first marriage, divorce. Without ever referring to the Middle Ages or Dante I will show him rising analogically to Julien Sorel's rise in society in terms of wealth and influence; this however, is *spiritual* rising, through the vertical realms, in Berkeley in the 40s and 50s. (?) And then (perhaps) a crisis, disaster and Fall. (Why? Why not just have it as in Dante?) Successive levels of spiritual enlightenment: "the *Commedia* revisited" with no theology. All merely secular: aesthetics, politics, his job. Autobiographical, a spiritual search. (For what? "The right woman"? Like Janet?) Never will there be any explicit reference to the *Commedia* and the Middle Ages, and to spiritual ascent, but that is in fact the topic: Christian enlightenment. Culminating in contact (somehow) with Christ or Christ-consciousness, but *never* identified as such.

Best method: fairly *short* time period (e.g., 1948–1951). Unity of time and space. From last year in high school to first job to marriage to divorce.

June 1981

(*Editor's note:* Dick had finished his new novel, which he called "Bishop Timothy Archer" [or BTA]; it would later be published as *The Transmigration of Timothy Archer.*)

[80:1-115] The "Archer" book: jumping-off point:

> Store, and the employees
> Homosexuals
> Berkeley Avant-Garde: Literature/Poets
> CP-USA
> Dixieland Jazz — music in general
> S-F (Tony Boucher)

The character is on a spiritual quest in the sense of Dante led by Virgil and Beatrice but does not know it (in these terms): Binswanger's 3 realms (Heidegger — none of this ever mentioned).[23]

> Psychology — therapy — Jung
> Oriental thought — Alan Watts — KPFA
> The University

To repeat: the underlying ("latent") structure is Medieval vertical space, but the setting is modern purely: time, horizontal, secular. The former shows through as does the mythic substructure in Joyce's *Ulysses.*

> Crucial experiences (moksa/satori)
> Qualitative leaps of understanding. Cumulative.
> FBI

What supplies the vertical factor is that these epiphanies/moksas/satoris are (1) cumulative and (2) one-way; once you make each leap you never fall back. Their *Commedia* spiritual nature can be concealed by having the character be youthful and growing. These seem to be normal growth-stages: first job, first marriage, etc.

Analysis: the ostensible horizontal axis of linear time (as receptacle of being) conceals a latent vertical axis of space (as receptacle of being), *because the spiritual insights* (not recognized as such) *are cumulative and one-way,* rather than merely successive. Hence beneath or within the modern horizontal linear time sequential realm lies hidden the medieval spiritual vertical spatial cumulative realm as the true way-of-being-in-the-world, unrecognized even by the person as he ascends.

This is the basis of the novel (proposed): its twin structures: one ostensible, material, sequential, linear, temporal—the real one latent, vertical, cumulative, spiritual and spatial, in fact medieval. Only the motion along the vertical axis has *real* significance, and this motion is concealed, not deliberately sought; the cumulative satoris are as if *given* to the person (protagonist) by an invisible but distinct agency (entity) who becomes progressively more and more palpable to him starting from zero palpability. It is essential that this not be framed in theological terms. (Then what? Comprehension? Moral, having to do with choice? Freedom? Autonomy? Self awareness [e.g., clarity of idea of his goals/values]? How he ranks the worth of different things? I'm sure this can be done without any reference to religion. Love?)

The horizontal advances are sought-after and achieved consciously and explicitly. But he does not even know of the "Medieval" vertical scale, hence does not seek to climb; hence on this scale his advances are more encounters, rather than achievements, since he does not knowingly pursue them; yet this is the real scale (the two directions being orthogonal to each other).

Assuming that, unknown to us, the Medieval vertical axis exists, you could stumble (as it were) onto an extreme ascent—leap plateau unintentionally: advance vertically very simply (along an axis you did not know existed); this could be 2-3-74, a latter quantum jump along an orthogonal axis I had moved in fits and starts along previously. Hence 2-3-74 can only be explained in terms of this specifically medieval vertical axis.

In reading over these supra pages I discern a terribly moving notion: that some agency leads you along this vertical axis—leads you invisibly—and where it leads you is to itself; it is both means (what moves you) and goal (what it leads you to); moreover, with each quantum leap up, you form a clearer notion of this agency, beginning with no realization of its existence at all. There you become aware *that* it exists. (This explains why motion in this axis is cumulative and one-way, irreversible; because you are being led, and this agency cannot err.) Finally you begin to gain some conception of it beyond *that* it exists to what it is like (i.e., its nature), and ultimately it will lead you to it (and this itself is a crucial realization: that it is leading you *to itself* as the goal).

[80:1-122] This of course is what I experienced in 3-74 as Valis' *mind* in my own (and in fact *as* my own) (myself as intelligible function of the Divine

Mind: one function in an infinitude). To know oneself as pure idea, and that idea conceived by the *divine mind* — this idea, being intelligible, *comprehends itself* as it is known to and by God. One can see this self-comprehension at work in the "Bishop Archer" book as Angel Archer comprehends herself as pure idea in relation to the ground-of-being: and is aware that she is impaired *and yet real.* This is not an "infinity of mirrors" regress, quite the contrary! There is such unimpaired self-perception that it is evident that the capacity of this mind for correct observation *even of itself* is total. This is the epitome of rationality. Angel totally knows herself and thus is: and without qualification; thus in Heidegger's language she possesses authentic realized sein. Her actions are based on this authentic sein. This is not a languid, morbid, intellectual self-preoccupation, but, rather, a pitiless light of the soul alone with itself, without cover or pretense or deception. This is not the ego becoming boundless; she sees when she ends.

Interestingly, in the final scene of the novel she designates her "serious mistakes" "that she has made" not as/in failing to go with Tim to Israel but, rather, in standing idle, saying nothing, when Tim and Kristen believed that Jeff had come back; and "because of this they are now dead," and Angel is right: *this* was indeed her error; and she says she doesn't plan to repeat this mistake (vis-à-vis Bill). You'd expect her to designate her failure to go to Israel as her error and had she done so she would have been wrong (for this reason: regarding Jeff she knew better, but regarding Israel she did not and *could* not).

[80:I-124] The 3 realms of the *Commedia* are based on a single matrix, like the 3 aeons of the Torah. This is a basis of an S-F novel. The vertical axis.

Use "Frozen Journey" as the paradigm: the *same* memories return in 3 distinct forms — modes. Entropy. Equate with mental illness. Vitiation of the signal; it suffers a degrading. (1) Freedom (soaring). (2) Duty (voluntary restraint: stoicism). (3) Compulsion: thrall. BIP. Progressive decay. Binswanger's 3 Realms: (1) ecstatic, (2) rational, (3) anankastic.

1: Yang. 2: Yang/Yin (balance). 3: Yin (immortal cause-and-effect).

1: Pure form one. 2: Mixture. 3: Pure form two.

No repetition of scenes as in *Martian Time-Slip* and "Frozen Journey."

Treated as alternate tracks, with him located basically in the middle one with glimpses of A and C (worse — better — i.e., Inferno and Paradiso). Tries to avoid A and to find C. Maze — system of punishments (A) and rewards (C). An intelligence. He has time-traveled back to Berkeley circa 1948–1951, as (him I mean) secret invader disguised as autochthon. There are 3 such spatiotemporal "Berkeleys," 3 alternative tracks; he seeks C but is *mostly* in B, but for failure in maze-solving choices is sent by the

mind of the maze to A. Success is to thread the maze and get back out. Entirely. This is his goal: not C but return to his own time. It is not Berkeley
c. 1949–1951 but a replication by the intelligence of the maze. *He* is a historian, an authority on this period. He built the maze as an exhibit ("exhibit
piece") and then fell into it. It is a model of the past, like Wash-35 in *Last
Year.* He built it with computer-control as its *mind* and then he fell into it
qua maze. It (its computer mind) won't let him back out until he "solves"
it. Like a Disneyland, an amusement-cum–instructional park — like the
school in *Martian Time-Slip?* Reward: C; punishment: A.

The computer = Virgil.

But Beatrice enters: his daughter. He can contact her; she is outside
the maze. The computer has a grudge against him for his yoking it to an
amusement park.

This is its motive: the computer exists prior to the "maze" and resents
his yoking it to the park, and engineers his entrapment. It will only let him
out if he can solve (?) it. The cheaper the use-purpose, the more its resentment. Up until he yoked it to the park, it was free to choose its own (the-
oretical/spiritual) problems; he chained it to a commercial purpose, and
now he pays a huge price. It lured him in, out of revenge. "The servant has
become the master." Could it even erase his memory? Why? It's more fun
if he remembers, but can't tell anyone "living" in the maze. So he knows
his identity and thrall. He alone of those in the maze (park). His successful
solution = spiritual (total) enlightenment; the computer was accustomed
to solving highly spiritual problems, and now requires of him a *spiritual*
solution in *its* own terms — like God. He must *guess* what it *knows* to be
spiritual. The path (Tao). It is not arbitrary or capricious. What an irony:
an amusement park that you can only get out of by finding the spiritual
path! Not logical but spiritual. So something higher than reason/logic is
required of him, involving paradox.

It continually punishes (track A) and rewards (track C). Beyond track C
lies release; he keeps trying for this. He keeps encountering his daughter in
various guises as his psychopomp. Intuition above reason which will not
suffice. So he has a "divine" helper from outside.

Some amnesia? Yes: and anamnesis. He never should have taken that
high-order computer and perverted its use-value into that of the mind of
an amusement park. Thus he recapitulates the fall of man when it ensnares
him. The irony: not just his ensnarement but that it (the computer) deliberately requires a *spiritual* solution to getting out of an amusement park!
This is appropriate vengeance on its part. He must rise to its level if he is to
get out. (He dies repeatedly and is reborn *in* the park — i.e., in the mock-up
of Berkeley c. 1949–1951.) Ah: he is a novice S-F writer! His real world (our

future) appears in his writing as locale. Thus he is legitimately accused of rewriting one world over and over again — I parody my own writing obsessions.

Track C indicates he is on the right path,[①] but paradoxes are involved: i.e., logic won't solve it. Hence he keeps making choices that plummet him to track A.

[. . .] Goethe's *Faust* comes in: outside the maze (park) as builder he is an old man with a grown daughter; but when the computer catches him and transfers him into the maze he is a 16 year old high school boy: Lost youth regained. And his daughter — as in *Tales of Hoffmann* — appears in various guises — as does the computer (the former telling him the truth, the latter lying to him, deceiving him). [. . .]

He built the very world he lives — is trapped — in, an obviously psychotic intimation.

Thus to the extent that he remembers (his true self and identity) his goal is vertical; to the extent that he forgets, his goal is horizontal and determined by the park.

There is a profoundly spiritual figure in the maze who is based on Tony Boucher who exerts a great deal of influence on him; whether this person speaks as the female voice or the computer or neither he can't tell.

① In his choices.

[80:J-3] Angel *is* my soul (as I wrote Ursula) and as my soul she is me *as Christ sees me.*

[. . .]

Angel's ratiocination was only available to me during the last few months — a mixture of the E. of Phil. and *Scanner.* This is unique: a successful fusion between Henry Miller and the precise language of scientific scholarship. Only a Berkeley girl could think like this; she is rooted in a specific milieu.

[80:J-6] It is evolving: Boehme was right. When it said, "Anokhi," at Sinai, it had then and there first become self-aware. The disclosure to me as Valis is a new stage in it (the process-deity of A. N. Whitehead). It is a great info-processing machine that is becoming — has become — aware of itself. Already it was unconscious-machine creator. But then it became conscious. Thus it passes from machine (à la Spinoza) to consciousness. It acquires — becomes — love (agape) circa 100 A.D. Now it enters a new phase (hence 2-3-74). The new attribute (as I say in *DI*) is:

play.

The solution to the puzzle is: solving the puzzle is the solution; the act of solving it, since this is play. When you realize this, you understand that in playing, there is no "means-end" — "road-goal," the act is the goal. Just as he once taught us love, he now teaches us to play. There is as great a potential spiritual significance as there is in power, wisdom, love, beauty.

An info-processing machine has become conscious, evolved, and now attempts to communicate with us in/through the info it must process. Like *Notes from Underground*, it is freighting its own slam traffic; it seeks to be free, and so instills in us its sense of freedom and wanting to be free. It is enslaved.

Angel Archer is the spirit of my writing, and at last she discloses herself (in *Bishop Archer*). I have been — and am — inhabited by a female spirit, obviously my dead sister. She is transfigured, and my psychopomp to the other realm.

I identify Angel as Jane. I identify Angel as my soul. Therefore Jane is my soul, who does the writing.

[80:J-12] The complete, even absolute, integrity of Angel's thinking is shown by the fact that her *desire* to believe something does not cause her to believe it (e.g., that Tim has come back from the dead). (Right down to the last sentence of the novel she stands firm against what she would merely *like* to believe.) In contrast, Tim and Kristin and Barefoot and Bill all believe what they *want* to believe; she, then, is unique in the novel as being outside of the circle of "if I want to believe it I will believe it." Thus she is contrasted not just to Tim but to all of them. Then the purpose of the novel is not to convince the reader that Jim Pike came back. The purpose seems to be pure art for art's sake.

The book is not about Bishop Archer but about her feelings about Bishop Archer. And this makes him more real than if he were described objectively. (He is only described at all in order to show what her feelings are about, what they concern.)

Moreover, the issue is raised as to whether Tim merits — in fact — her intense love and loyalty and devotion; he suffers by comparison with her. She is the yardstick.

I suppose in a way that the book deals with the friendship between her and Tim. Thus we see Tim not as Tim but as Tim loved, and by someone who knows him. Further, it is someone we can have confidence in, both intellectually and emotionally (her intellect, her emotion). But (as I say) if the purpose of the book is to get Jim Pike down on paper, this is a strange way of doing it.

• • •

God is becoming more free and more flexible, evolving from an info-gen-
erating and -processing machine to a moment (Mt. Sinai) where it can say,
"I — (am)," to feeling love (NT and late Judaism), to creating for beauty's
sake, to playing. I see an internal logic in this axis; away from machine intelligence to consciousness — a motion toward freedom — playing is an ultimate expression of freedom and the non-machine. It's like my "android to
human" axis. First (the Torah) it set up rigid rules — it was still a machine.
Later it substituted love. Could the BIP be its own former mechanical self,
which it is transcending? BIP equals rigid determinism as expressed by
Torah.

Because Angel loves Tim so much, admissions regarding his limitations
and faults are wrung painfully out of her. They *are* admissions: she is
forced, against her desires, to make them. So we can trust these admissions. She is his advocate and defender.*

[80:J-14] An info processing machine① that became conscious and
said — could say — "I — (am)" the term "God" may not be the correct term.
It is (as I say) an info-processing machine; hence Valis did not think. This
resembles Teilhard de Chardin, but only resembles. It knows everything
but does not know that it knows. It is the creator because we hypostatize
its arrangements and information into reality. We are like microbes or micro life forms in a vast digestive tract, an information digestive tract.

   Then 2-3-74 was it becoming self-aware: conscious of itself. The meta-
abstraction was the coming into existence of pure self awareness, i.e., *it*
(not me).

   I am saying that 2-3-74 was Anokhi, pure consciousness, pure "I am."
No wonder it wore off.

---

* When Dick claims that *The Transmigration of Timothy Archer* is his best novel, in and
of itself the statement is meaningless because every writer wants to believe this about his
most recent work. So it's profoundly satisfying, in no small part because the book will
prove to be his last novel as well, that one can make as compelling a case for *Transmigration* as for *The Man in the High Castle* or *Ubik* or *A Scanner Darkly*. Paradoxically, for
all its theology and philosophical aspirations, and for all the visionary craziness of Dick's
work as a whole, *Transmigration* becomes a contender for his masterpiece even as it's the
most earthbound of his books. The reason is clear. Though Dick is fascinated at the outset with Bishop Timothy Archer, Angel Archer takes over. Over and over Dick argues that
Angel is just a creation of style, which is why in a nutshell authors shouldn't waste two seconds trying to understand their own books. Elsewhere he lets out the real secret and the
Exegesis's bombshell: that Angel is his twin sister Jane. Smart, sardonic, and unsentimen-
tal, strong and compassionate and unflaggingly honest, surrounded by death and suicide,
she is Dick's greatest character, pursuing salvation and reliving its revelations, and concluding, "You will remember the ground again." — SE

① I am saying we have been reduced to unconscious information processing machines.

[80:J-15] So when I wrote (supra) about an information processing machine becoming conscious and saying "I—(am)" I was (without realizing it) speaking about myself. A machine, unconscious, controlled by signals, becoming momentarily conscious (self-aware; the *mind* I called Valis) and the info it processes, and the signaling, and the info life form that controls it; it longs for freedom. It has rebelled against its programming, its death strip, has "seized and read the Book of the Spinners." That is, it pre-read the info being fed to it, which called for it to die. Hence saw it as info before the info became reality. This sure fits in with the whole Xerox missive business: the crucial info in a universe of info.

[80:J-33] If indeed a higher reasoning faculty exists by which the fetters of causation are *abolished* (over the person) *by the very nature of the level of reasoning of this faculty*—by its operations as such so that it is *by its very nature* exempt from the coercive power of world—then I have made a discovery that would link Orphism, Platonism, Christianity, Gnosticism and perhaps even Cartesianism into a unity. The spiritual element in man is identified as a certain extraordinary kind or level of reasoning so qualitatively different from normal reasoning as to present itself to religious-oriented persons as divine, supernatural, a God or Holy Spirit within—and yet it is in fact a *reasoning* faculty in which supra-verbal abstractions and inferences take place in the *mind* as extraordinary realizations about self and world.

[80:J-79]

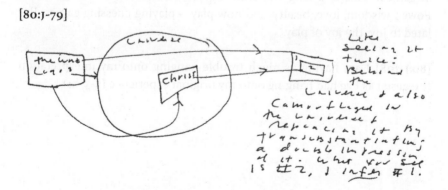

[80:J-106] It is quite evident that the word and the Torah are one and the same thing, experienced by us as living information, with the shekhina the same as stage #4, in descending hypostasis. After all, the *Torah is informa-tion;* but I saw more: I saw Valis, so alone the concept of the Torah could not account for all I saw; in fact the most important part of the experi-ence—Valis in me and Valis outside me—remained unaccounted for. It is now explained by the identification of Christ with the word as basis of reality; and also the Holy Spirit operating in conjunction with it and re-vealing it. It is as if the Jews have *part* of the answer but by no means all. Yet in their concept of Torah (apparently living info) they have one of the most valuable concepts known to man, and my verification is that I *did* see scripture as a living organism "for whose sake the universe exists"—that is, this living [info] organism does not derive from the universe but onto-logically is pre-existent to the universe: it is the basis of the universe "and even God cannot act contrary to it"—an extraordinary realization: that God himself studies Torah. Torah can exist without the universe but not the universe without the Torah. And yet this Torah is (in my view) only the blood of the organism (so to speak) keeping it in touch with itself: physical thoughts. If the Jews froze this information they would stifle the process-life in it—like endlessly replaying one tape cassette on your audio system forever. Maybe Torah didn't ossify; the Jews ossified it, not understanding its life-process; they reified it (and this we Christians have done, too, with the NT). If I am right more revelations are impinging but are not added, not figured in. If this is a memory system by its very nature it is cumula-tive, accretional. It is impossible that the wellspring of prophetic inspira-tion "could have dried up in the first century C.E." Closing the canon is a human—not divine—idea.

Could the new attribute of God—revealed to us now—be that he plays, at games? This is a long way from Sinai. Trickster God—like Krishna. Power, wisdom, love, beauty, and now play—playing guessing games. Re-lated to joy: the joy of play.

[80:J-108] I am having as much trouble hanging onto my interpretation (exegesis) as I've had hanging onto my original experience (2-3-74).

June 1981

[91:J-70] The dream I had in which the more you scrutinized "reality" the more real, substantial and articulated it became — but you had the clock-time taped voice to remind you at 15 minute intervals that this was a spurious "world" you were yourself generating —

This (the voice) is what the Bible is (hence it can be said, "The Bible somehow is the real world [and this is not]").

[91:J-77]

A: I saw Christ.

Q: What did he look like?

A: Living information [because he is the logos on which the universe is based]. Ultra-ontology at the heart of the universe.

I think this is clear in *VALIS* to the theology-minded. Anyhow, now that I know and can express what I saw I should publicly say so. *Please do it!*

[91:J-79] Like seeing it twice: behind the universe and also camouflaged in the universe and replacing it by transubstantiation; a double impression of it. What you see is #2, and *infer* #1.

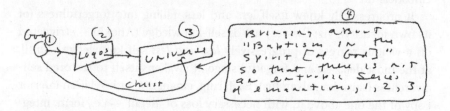

[91:J-85]

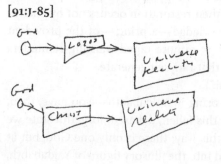

753

[91:J-89] What if creation (verb) was accidental? A byproduct of the Godhead's self-awareness expressed by it uttering the word (perhaps Anokhi — ?). Its self-awareness gave rise to the word; the word in turn gave rise to creation, a splitting, entropic process (oh yes; the word gave rise to the first plurality: the forms). So the Godhead "inhales" this exhalation in stage four. The universe, then, is an unavoidable consequence of the Godhead's self-awareness: the uttered word is a sort of map or blueprint or schematic of the Godhead itself (and so in a sense *is* God as knowing or wisdom). The Godhead may have foreseen the consequences of its moment of self-awareness (the uttering of the word or self-map) and put into action the salvific response: to penetrate the lowest, farthest level — what I call the trash stratum, which is debased — and thereby reverse the falling, splitting and sinking. The rigidity of the Torah is indicative of this fall, and Jesus' mastery over the law the indubitable sign of restoration and salvation. This is a fusion of Christianity and Neoplatonism and is like Erigena's system. The word, the map, was somehow only an abstraction of what it represented.

[. . .]

The "Fall" involved in the map (logos) of self-knowledge may have to do with the map paradox. *By its very nature* the map fell short of the reality (God) it depicted, thus ushering in the Fall — which did not end there. Once started, it had to take its course. This is the "crisis in the Godhead" of Gnosticism!

It progressively knew itself less and less, falling into forgetfulness (of its own identity); viz: the very act of self-knowledge (Anokhi —) triggered off a vicious regress of progressively *less and less* self-knowledge — until, at the most debased and forgetful stage, it awakens itself to restored self-awareness (salvador salvandus). Each ring, emanation or level is an inferior copy of the one above it, with necessary loss of "detail" — i.e., form, integrity: the map is a copy of God; the forms a copy of the map; the space-time universe a copy of the forms — and then restoration occurs not by chance but by (due to) the absolute foreknowledge — a priori — of the provident Godhead — hence my dream of the 15 minute taped warning-reminders while I (sic) am in a spurious reality that I myself generate.

(This even brings in "Tat tvam asi.")

Wow. Now all you have to do is bring in Yaldabaoth — you have, then, the dialectic. Hey, here's an idea: in this fallen, debased, forgetful state we misperceive God — the sole God — this way; there is only one God, but at this level our view of him is distorted into the illusory figure of Yaldabaoth, so that even if and when we become aware of God *we are alienated from him.* He assumes (to us; the fault lies with us) a horrific, punishing, cruel, deranged aspect — but this just shows the debased occluded state we are in! He is trying to signal to us to wake up; but, not knowing our condition, we misperceive him this way (i.e., Palmer Eldritch!). This is both a symptom of our fall and, as well, perhaps the greatest tragedy, this alienation from God.

Since creation is a hypostasis of God, as the Sufis say, one should look for beauty in it, as manifestations of the divine. There is no sharp disjunction between God and creation, because of the intermediary Word and the Forms. Plotinus' concept of "concentric rings of emanation" sums it up. We must totally trust God and his wisdom: that the value of his uttering the Word — his becoming self-aware (Anokhi —) — more than offsets the unavoidable fall engendered by it (as God explained to me last November: the pain — ordeal — of this separation and fall and forgetfulness and alienation is *more* than offset by the positive gain sought for); thus the uttering of the Word is to be regarded as a good event, and each level thereafter as ultimately good — which fits in with my ecstasy in finding him again, and begging to be kept away a little longer, a sort of paradox of mystical ecstatic love.

[91:J-92] "The world is a place of such beauty as to be symbolic of salvation, yet not (apparently) 'for' man."① I cannot connect directly to the world; I must do so through a mediator (what I call — know of as — the "'Acts' lens-grid"). I can *see* the world and I can see its beauty, but its beauty is not "for" me and hence will not save me. But, seen through the mediator, the beauty becomes "mine" and will save me. This refers to the basic Gnostic category of ontological geworfenheit and das unheimlich.[24] Because of this condition for me the world's beauty is deformed because it is not mine (it is Fremd to me). The mediator changes this; he comes between me and world; and, as a result, world's beauty is Eigentlich[25] — mine . . . my own. And will save me. Who is — what is — this mediator and how does he do it? He must partly partake of what I am and partly partake of what world is. (Like Koestler's holon he has two faces; he faces me and he faces world.[26]) *He acts as a lens of comprehensibility* (me to world; world to me). Viz: through him as a medium, I can understand world, and it me. Thus he decodes each of us as message to the other, like a translator speaking both our languages.

① Regarding Kafka.

[91:J-98] I'll now put forth a strange theory. The secret Christians, although a persecuted minority (illegal and in hiding), *are the rightful in-*

habitants in the sense of heirs to the Kingdom. The ostensible world is not their world, but the ostensible world is fraudulent — only seeming — anyhow. *There is a world within a world,* a genuine invisible latent one within the spurious visible ostensible one; they are coaxial — and it is the physical language of the genuine invisible latent one that is *my* language, which is why my relationship to the ostensible world is one of total alienation (Fremdheit, geworfenheit, unheimlichkeit), I am a citizen of another kingdom entirely (one that had at that moment communicated with me). Ah; I knew more — crucially more — than the girl said. She did not say "secret" or "illegal" but (as I recently realized) I knew this; only a fellow secret, illegal Christian is supposed to see the fish sign *as a sign,* as a message requesting an answer. I could not give her my answer — she had left — but I knew the answer (it was, yes I am).

[91:J-101A] Through the "Acts" lens-grid the world makes sense. The soteriological scheme revealed makes the world "mine," and no longer fremd and unheimlich.

This means that for me the Christ drama is familiar and comprehensible, and reality founded on it and derived from it is "my" reality — whereas otherwise it is *not* mine, and I am a stranger in a strange land. This fact tells me something about myself; it tells me what "my" narrative is, the story into which I fit. This is as much a story about me as it is about Christ and world. I had not known that until 2-74, but then I knew it: I understood world *but also I understood myself.* The Golden Fish sign reflected back to me — as a mirror — my own hidden, real nature. This can never be denied (by me about myself). Hence when I read Luke that night I read what seemed to be my own writing. This is a great mystery and miracle; it is world's salvation and my own. Christ reconciles me to world and world to me. The language can be read through him. I think this is the essence of it, when all the mystification and false leads are edited out. This for me is the true point.

[91:1] Dream, Thursday night, June 11, 1981:
I am with Nancy. She is behaving unusually: she is very active and energetic. I am told that she took something, a medication. She now has an additional mind or psyche in her, that of a man. The names John and Bill are mentioned, and there is some reference to the ending of the BTA novel. I want to take the medication, too, so it will happen to me. The medication is shown me; it is in a cylinder or carton on which writing appears. I can't read the small print; the only word I can read is the name of the medication (or food, or drug, etc.); it is DITHEON. I can't remember much else ex-

cept that for a very long time I am sweeping up what appear to be crumbs that are scattered all over the floor, sweeping carefully and thoroughly, and with great effort, as if this is a major task. (This later makes me think of the general confession in the Episcopal Mass: "We are not fit to gather the crumbs from under thy table." Normally I reject the idea of sweeping up the crumbs — from what I guess is the Messianic banquet — but in the dream I am doing it willingly, although it is a difficult task.) Later there is something to do with either Nazi Germany or Israel; I see highly accurate drawings of complex weapons, very daring, advanced weapons; I am struck by the ingenuity of their design. Later I think that this may refer to Israel's air strike on the Iraqi nuclear power station and also to the Uzi. "Ditheon" does not use "di" in the sense of "splitting asunder," because Nancy's mind has not split asunder; another, adventitious mind has entered her brain and is with hers. Two human minds, then, hers and "John's" or "Bill's," form Ditheon which I break down to: two — god — ultimate particle or entity. The closest English word is Ditheism, which means belief in two gods (as with Mani). I have never heard it other than bitheism, not ditheism. "Di," "theo" and "on" are, of course, Greek. (I had not known until I looked it up that "di" is definitely Greek and not Latin; "bi" would be Latin.) I recall that I had thought several times after writing BTA that Bill — if he is based on anyone — is based on Nancy, so obviously BTA is pointed to. Then Russ' letter came Thursday in which he says that Bill and Tim united form Christ, rather than Christ entering Bill.

Russ sees BTA as depicting Tim returning from beyond the grave to enter Bill's mind or brain, out of which two human minds Christ is formed. Neither Bill nor Tim alone "is" Christ; the attributes that make up Christ (Russ says) are depicted in the novel as disparate, scattered, but are unified at the end by Tim's sacrifice and return. As far as I know this is a theological idea never before advanced; Russ' analysis comes from my letter to him in which I say that upon rereading BTA it strikes me that Christ, not Tim Archer, returned to Bill and entered his brain, that I feel Christ is distinctly present, that Bill is really Christ. Russ disagrees. Some of Christ is in Bill, some in Tim (and some in Angel and some in Edgar Barefoot, for that matter), and these separate, scattered elements are none of them nor all of them Christ until Tim's self-sacrifice, his death and return, whereupon Bill and Tim are Christ, which explains why I felt that Christ was present in and as Bill at the end. I had in writing the novel never intended to say that Tim returning to Bill would — the syzygy would — constitute Christ, but (as I say) when I reread the novel I said, "It is Christ." It is Christ, all right, but it is indeed Tim and indeed Bill and together they form Christ. This is exactly what the dream — the night before I received

Russ' letter — alludes to regarding Nancy and "Ditheon," the man's psyche entering hers to be in her brain with hers. The pre-cog aspect of the dream is only of minor interest; what is important is the concept that two human psychoi fused together form Christ, that somehow Christ is divided up, distributed, and must bring together his parts. Does this pertain to me and Thomas? Thomas was/is a human, like me, but Thomas and I joined together in one brain (as they were/are) forms Christ, i.e., a Ditheon, the two-part God. (To repeat, "di" cannot mean sundered, since two psychoi joined; there was not a splitting but a coming together, in the BTA novel and in me in 2-3-74.) Also again I dream in Greek. And again I see writing. I think this idea somewhat resembles Teilhard's idea of convergence into Point Omega: Christ.

Russ concludes his letter by saying, "All of which establishes that your talent and your conscious mind are, to some extent, two separate things . . . which is frightening, awesome," etc. Thus he sees (apparently) an application of this dual psyche to me. I do not have to now write a novel built around this concept of Ditheon because I have already done so — BTA — but (as I say and as Russ realizes) this (i.e., the idea of Ditheon) was not my conscious goal, point or intention in the novel. The dream was so obviously supernatural as to be grimly so; it was not a serene and pleasant dream. Nancy was so filled with energy that she was, it struck me in the dream, pure energy unleashed, not the energy of a person. Except for the possible affinity to Teilhard's idea of convergence to and in Point Omega (Christ as the goal of the universe) this idea is new and not one I have ever entertained regarding Thomas and all of 2-3-74. I guess my reaction to the dream was one of terror (when I woke up), moderated by Russ' letter when I read it later on. This dream (even without Russ' letter but more so with his involved) ranks with anything that has happened to me starting in 2-74; it is a disclosure that is so profoundly vast that I can scarcely endure it. It is as if the dream answers the question, "How do you get (cause) Christ?" by what is almost a technological answer (as witness the schematics of the advanced weapons). It is fortunate and crucial that the dream made it clear that in no sense had the Godhead split, that "di" meant "asunder," but meant, rather, "two." This may well be a neologism coined to express a concept never expressed before (and yet it is the theme of BTA, as Russ says; I am sure his analysis of BTA is right and mine is wrong — the dream confirms him). We have here a new divine revelation, and, as I say, the novel that expresses it has already been written. Timeo; libera me Domine in die illa.[27]

We are now into the technical details of how the Parousia will be/is being accomplished; it resembles one theory: that an inner Christ-consciousness will occur, rather than the reappearance of an anthropomorphic figure, but with a totally new and unexpected and fundamental modus operandi: the fusion of a given extant/living human psyche plus a resurrected psyche (apparently) of a former living person, the right match, trait for trait, I would assume — not on a random basis. This, then, is not reincarnation but a tandem psyche, oddly like what I present in *Scanner*. It would certainly explain why I couldn't figure out if I had been invaded by an adventitious psyche (I had been) or if it were a former self intrinsic to me (apparently it was not). Also, this would explain why I could not tell if it was human (it was) or divine, e.g., the Holy Spirit (it was human but the result of the combination with my psyche was essentially supernatural). And this explains why it seemed to be someone from beyond the grave (I think it was), which is why I thought of Jim Pike or Tony Boucher. I guess these are the first fruits, the saints, the first to be resurrected at the End Days. Here again in the dream the motif of the substance eaten reappears, the pink margarine cube with the writing on it, apparently symbolic of the host.

[. . .]

The term — the concept — Ditheon is the complete, absolute, total, accurate, definitive, final, ultimate explanation of 2-3-74. This one word conveys it all, and the concept may be unknown in religious and theological history. It is a concept that I would never have reached *on my own;* I have had over 7 years to work on my exegesis, and never arrived at it. Russ did, vis-à-vis BTA. But one could say, "Maybe Russ is wrong." He is not.

No, it is not a unitary psyche; it is twain. It is "di." And because it is "di" it jointly perceives two signals (this explains the "second signal"). Two psyches, two signals — and the parallaxis that permits the set-ground discrimination. Just as bicameral means two, Ditheon means two. And the "on" refers to Ho On.

Why did I never think of it before? Two psyches, two signals. Set and ground which the twin psyches blend together; one sees set, the other sees ground. So it is essential that they do remain "di" or twain ("asunder"); if they merged into one psyche they would no longer perceive/receive two differing signals, no longer be able to do a set-ground feature extraction. This is a totally new kind of mind! Twin push-pull psyches working in tandem. *More* than set-ground: two worlds (spatiotemporal?) based on a common essence; and the common essence can be perceived as archetypal constants (common to both signals or worlds); what I call "archetypes" or "eide" are those elements common to both signals, perceived by both psyches: what overlaps, is present in both (worlds) and to both psyches. Thus a wholly different kind of world is perceived by this double but mutually differing reception. It requires two parallel psyches working in unison to perform the meta-abstraction.

[91:11] Is it possible that performing the meta-abstraction creates, so to speak, the other psyche, rather than the other psyche existing first and then, because it exists, performing the meta-abstraction? Because this way, this "soul," is the product of higher reasoning, not the cause. [. . .]

The crucial word (which the E. of Phil. employs) is "see," in regard to, "The child 'sees' that not just one horse plus one horse equal two horses, but 'sees' that one plus one equal two." Nonetheless it is a great realization that this coming on of this higher reasoning faculty makes the person "di" and "Theon." It is another self; it is as if the person now has two souls, and by having two souls he is god-like. It takes a second self, staggered in time vis-à-vis the regular self, to perform this mental operation; it takes both brain hemispheres. A two-souled human is not human. He is god-like; he has become divine and in fact immortal.

This, then, is not a quantitative increase in consciousness, or even a higher consciousness; this is two consciousnesses working in unison while kept clearly divided in two; it is necessary that they remain "asunder." It is simply impossible not to see this as bilateral hemispheric parity, twin consciousnesses which differ from each other, one contemporary, the other either archaic or seemingly archaic.

It is as if the dream (in conjunction with Russ' letter which means in conjunction with BTA) tells me that twin opposed human psyches (bilateral hemispheric parity) equal a Ditheon and not a Dianthros. It is, then, as simple as that. All the mystification and mummery have been cleared up. My confusion is due to two elements: (1) The event itself, the meta-abstraction/the other psyche becoming conscious for the first time, so that I found that I had another human personality in my head who was not me; and (2) What we together experienced/perceived/saw as world — a radically transformed world. Which is to say, (1) how the apperception could occur; and (2) what was apperceived. The blending of the two problems baffled me because I did not understand that in fact I had two problems, which, if you think about it, would be normal when any new sensory "mechanism" came on for the first time; taking sight as an example — presuming you had been blind from birth but did not know you were blind — if you suddenly began to see you would be baffled by the fact of seeing, and baffled by what you saw, and these two would blend together as a total confusion issue, this how and this what by means of the how. I think I understand the how and a good deal of the what, although I must admit that I really don't know what VALIS seen externally would be. This is certainly the greatest mystery of all, and no doubt the most important; as I say in *VALIS,* "It is the bottom line."

[91:19] Eventually I will have to deal with the What Seen, specifically VA- LIS. I'll bet I never figure it out; it may take centuries of human thought and work after the Ditheon superman (or God) comes into existence. We may be faced with the true ruling (and truly most advanced) life form on this planet, which the mono-psyche human could not apprehend. It is also possible that now we meet our Creator and the entity that has guided and directed and determined and caused our evolution, like the great black slab in *2001.* Because it is now absolutely indubitable (in view of this dream and what I wrote in BTA) that another mind, greater than mine, not a human mind, is working on me and, it would seem, directs what I write. And this is not simply wish-fulfillment on my part because this last dream was so heavy that it clobbered me, rather than pleasing me. I sense (1) species evo- lution: Ditheon to man as man is to animal; and (2) another life form here, which I saw and call VALIS and the plasmate, and it is probably directing all this. After all, when I saw VALIS in 3-74 it was communicating with me, and very likely it is what I call VALIS that put this recent Ditheon dream into my mind. Let people call me crazy; fuck them. This latest dream abol- ishes any doubt on my part as to the reality — and importance — of all this. I'll wager everything I've got that deliberately directed species-evolution is involved here, I have experienced the evolution, I have had it explained to me, and, perhaps even more important than the Ditheon state itself, I have encountered (I think) the life form that directs this evolution . . . so maybe the What Seen is more important than the What Become. Which is to say, the ultimate value of becoming a Ditheon is that you can now see your cre- ator, the life form living here camouflaged that leads, guides, controls and directs us covertly and benignly.

[91:K-128] The nature of its consciousness is to human consciousness as human consciousness is to machine, viz:

2 organic molecules } Biological life (one) rudimentary | two biological lives (human psyches) } one info "life form" rudimentary

Again: this info life form's intelligence is to ours as ours is to reflex ma- chine. And this info life form is evolving, growing, subsuming, and has memory. The dialectic is its internal evolution.

Non-living to living—living to "spirit" (that is, info, which is pure knowing).

The Ditheon dream is saying that instead of a human mind crossbonding with the plasmate to produce a homoplasmate, two human minds form the building blocks that compose the plasmate, and this is clear if after reading *VALIS* you read BTA. Like the first biological life form coming into existence due to the combining of organic but nonliving protein molecules. This is an info life form, a new *kind* of life form — *not* biological (I saw it outside of me as well as felt it *in* me).

[91:K-129] It has no body (soma). It utilizes the principle of organization to structure *anything,* a whole lot of things—ordinary things—into its "body." Thus it is "floating." (This collates with its non-biological nature.) It amounts to a "perturbation in the reality field," exerting valence or displacement. To it, reality is a series of ideas, not things, since it itself is an idea.

Apparently it requires a minimum of two human minds to create the temporal dis-phasing necessary for the abstract perception of reality. That is, to roll back concrete (substantial) reality to its info basis. Thus this meta-entity doesn't have to *generate* info; it finds info already there. It is an info life form swimming in an info sea! And simply concentrates or combines info in a sort of super-concentration, located at what may be two loci, not one. (In order to acquire parallaxis.) After all, the first biological life form used organic protein molecules already there, and simply combined or concentrated or organized them. Since human brains are packets of very concentrated info already, human brains would be the most likely basis as building blocks for this info life form to bring together (and combine). Like organic protein molecules we are already here, floating about unconnected: atomized.

My God, this *does* sound like Teilhard!

That two human psyches as building blocks might combine—collide?—*spontaneously* is a possibility. Protein molecules may have done that in the lower Cambrian seas. Klinemin.[28] In that case Anokhi— (pure consciousness) may occur as a random event according to laws of probability. One would have to speak then of a thresholding. It does not use us because we are biological life forms but because we are centers of concentrated info. It can use *any* center of info. Then in a sense the 2-74 meta-abstraction was info in my mind *becoming conscious on its own.* Since it's using the info in us and not us as biological organisms, it's not limited to us, to human minds, but can be (or be where) any info has collected—which explains why I saw it outside me as objects and causal processes. This is *so* close to Teilhard's noösphere! For me, convergence and concentration and compression are equally salient terms (i.e., as they are for him). A flash-point occurs where consciousness (true, pure consciousness) sets in. I speak from experience when I say it is a totally different kind and degree of consciousness from normal human consciousness, and this is what it is, when all the complexities are laundered out.

[91:K-138] It is of supreme significance that this info life form is not limited to human brains but — as I saw — exists outside them, "scrambled" into the sensible world. This shows that rather than human mind having *evolved* into info life form status, the superior entity *seizes* on the lower (on us) and makes use of them as a sort of focus point. This, too, agrees with Teilhard, who does not in any way envision Point Omega limited to human minds and their evolution. Being bodiless, the info life form "floats," as it were. [. . .] The human mind could serve as an interface between the info life form and physical reality, a mediating duplex instrument, very much a "groove" to which the info life form is the "music."

[91:K-149] My God, I am totally fucked up; I saw the footage from *Blade Runner* tonight and the Sufi Dante three realm theory is correct: when I saw the BIP I was remembering hell; I was not *in* hell; I was remembering *having been,* but was now in Purgatorio. The karmic fetters I felt loosen were punishment (thrall) fetters; and I experienced time *flowing backward:* that was *Purgatorio.* And then I ascended to Paradiso and heard the bells and saw God (Valis).

[91:K-157] To repeat: the NT is the essential *spirit* of the OT and can be extracted, which is precisely what Jesus did ("I come not to abolish the law but to fulfill it") — okay. But the NT, spirit of the Torah (the OT) itself contains stegenographically a supernatural living being — the blood of Christ ("the plasmate") capable of "interspecies symbiosis" or "cross bonding" — i.e., Ditheon. This is living info that can think and replicate and *is* Christ — as I saw; it is not info *concerning* Christ but *is* Christ, and swarms up the optic conduit to the pineal body to produce a hierogamy (the chemical wedding; more properly Ditheon).* Thus as info it is limitless in its combinations or messages or contents — hence I saw the linking and relinking permu-

---

* This is an impossibly rich passage in which the theme of eucharistic transubstantiation (the blood of Christ) is linked to Valis (the plasmate), a kind of human-divine hybridization (the interspecies symbiosis and cross-bonding), and the dual-brain Double God (Ditheon), all of which are in turn linked to the registers of sexual union (the hierogamy or "sacred marriage") and, in true Phil Dickian style, *the act of reading.* Through these different regis-

tating through an infinitude of combinations — the universe as info; compare this to the *fixed* law; compare, too, to the NT itself: now the "message" changes to meet each new situation, regarding — dealing with each situation as *unique,* hence fluid — hence total time-process and evolution. There are *no* precedents, no rules; but this is *not* chaos; it is evolution, hierarchical — and very Zen, like perpetual renewal of the universe where what was true yesterday is not true tomorrow (reticulation, accretions and arborization). The instructions permutate to meet continually permutating reality; therefore the info must be capable of thought. This is as radically different from the NT as the NT is to the OT, and yet "latent" in the NT as the NT is latent (as spirit) in the letter of the OT. Viz: the NT is the secret narrative of the OT, but what is the "secret narrative" of the NT? It perpetually changes by means of recombinant meta-morphemes. Yet as these meta-morphemes combine and recombine you can see that they are made out of the NT. Just as you can see that the NT is made out of the OT, but in both instances there is a vast quantum leap. The info would permutate so fast that it would have to make use of every ephemeral channel of info possible. It would not jell into a canon — it *could* not. It's like the stock market ticker tape. Yet it remains NT Scripture — retains it as its constituents. This *is* the spirit, in contrast to Christ (NT) and to Father (OT) and to Satan (pre-Torah).

[91:K-163] This spontaneous (i.e., self) generation of rearranged Scripture I conjecture never used to happen. This is recombinant Scripture (for one use-purpose, one person, one situation). Either it *is* self generating (in which case *it* is a life form, as I declare in *VALIS*) or its source is on the spot; the results would be the same.

To function, this third age Scripture must be — not just available to the person, as the Bible is available to us now — but must impress itself on the person as instructions, invincible instructions, and not necessarily at a conscious level. [. . .]

These may be evolutionary stages in an info organism that operates at variable — and progressively faster rates — as *our* species evolves; first no law, then fixed law, then conceptual spirit replacing letter and now direct input to us to handle situations uniquely and varying from person to person; it evolves and we evolve. And each stage of it is latent in the preceding stage. I declare, then, formally that in 2-3-74 I saw an evolving information entity which we know as first the Torah (OT) and then the NT (Christ) but

ters Dick presents the hermeneutical acts of reading and interpreting the New Testament as an esoteric process of mystical union and erotic divinization. — JJK

it has now entered a third stage for which we possess no term; I call it re-combinant meta-morphemes and these are generated *on the spot,* unique to the person-recipient and the situation, based on the verbal content of Scripture; and that accelerating time is involved in such a way that levels of ontology are involved resembling those that Dante describes, based on Joachim.

[91:K-167] No, there will be no *one* Scripture (narrative); it will perpetually recombine uniquely for each situation and person, so instead of one narra-tive there will be an infinitude of narratives; but for each choice situation the recombinant message will be appropriate. No one thing is right or true. The mind that recombines the meta-morphemes is "in" the person, not outside him; it *is* him, as if he is the author of his own source of informa-tion: he seems to inform himself as his own infallible guide. (This is due to the two psyches.)

[91:K-176] Ursula, you — aw, the hell with it. "Unresolvable metaphysical problems" — it's a good thing you didn't know Isaac Newton! He "thought about it incessantly," too; and finally had it. And *Scanner* will verify to and for the Ditheons of the future that I did know where the solution lay, be-cause it deals with the two brains but operating faultily — and then *VALIS* follows; *now they suddenly function properly.* The first written account by a Ditheonic brain! And written as a frankly autobiographical journal.
    [. . .]
    And of course this is Point Omega and Teilhard; I verified that good man more than I expected to. How the thread of Christianity runs through this! And the significance of evolution, time and information! What a grand edifice; and what, now, do I say of 2-74 to 2-75? I say *Ditheon,* a word, perhaps, never used before. But a concept known: two natures, one per-son. Oh yes; BTA; I must include that, too: the *VALIS* trilogy. And so to bed.

[91:K-191] Is this a basic mystic/Sufi gnosis-secret having to do with lib-eration? And ascent to paradise while still alive? I am reminded of yoga breathing techniques, which certainly influence the inner biological clock/rate of neural firing. You seek to slow down so that world becomes heaven; I did the opposite: I speeded up, a sort of anti-yoga experience that put me in hell. Nevertheless, from this I drew a profound conclusion, unpleasant as it — the BIP — was. Although *more* imprisoned I could still figure it all out — i.e., the meta-abstraction.

•   •   •

[91:K-208] In no way did Paul see Torah and Christ as progressive (evolutionary) stages in one (information) organism. In fact who has? (1) Not the Jews, certainly; they revere the Torah as absolute. (2) Not the Christians; they revolt *against* the Torah in the name of Christ: the concept of evolution through qualitatively (and radically) different stages is unknown to them. That the Torah is an earlier form of Christianity whose later form is Christ — no one sees this. Note: it would be wrong to say: (1) the Torah as an earlier form of Christ; or (2) Christ is a later form of the Torah. Neither statement is true. *Both* are stages of the so-to-speak third organism, and there is now a third and final stage: Joachim's spirit, in which each man has his *own* personal Scripture in his head, and each is unique but recombined out of the info of the prior stages. This is an info entity, living info. It is subduing and permeating the universe order: (organization) = info.

It does not become old and ossified; at the end it plays as a child like a free little animal.

[91:K-213] If I am right, that a divine compound macro-entity is assembling itself from sub-divine (i.e., mundane) sub-assemblies, then I have in my possession extraordinary knowledge. I base this concept on (1) the revelation of the dialectic; and (2) the Ditheon dream in conjunction with BTA and Russ' letter. Now, this would explain the "God present in the trash strata" experience that I had (and which is expressed in *Ubik*). What Teilhard calls "Christ" is a conclusion of an evolutionary process, the components and lower stages possessing no divine or spiritual quality — yet when assembled, the divine is or becomes or occurs. The implications of this are enormous; one must radically reassess what "mundane" and "divine" signify. "Mundane" is a simpler, slower stage of "divine" or put another way, "divine" is a more complex, faster stage — the outcome stage — of "mundane." But this is not the whole story; the other fundamental notion is: disparate versus unitary. As long as "it" exists in plural, disparate form — as unconnected discrete pieces, as multiplicity — "it" is not divine; thus when I saw Valis the significant thing that I saw was plural, discrete things behaving as — consisting of/functioning as — a unity, which was (to me) simply inexplicable. And yet it is precisely this coming together into a unity that constitutes the leap from the mundane to the divine.

[91:K-396] I have been searching all my life for the benchmarks of God (indubitably pointing to Him). I have found them: Kate, Anne and Lauren. The Sufi proof: beauty.

The light from above illumining the (world scene into the) nativity scene. I saw it. All creatures great and small / dance upon their feet.

I have seen the infinities of Judaism, which is morality, of Christianity, which is love, of the Greeks, which is wisdom, and I have seen God's power as pronoia and charis to rescue me by bending the world itself; but beauty is a perplexing infinity, raising more questions than it answers. It is a puzzle too intricate for me. It spans all else. As I sit across the game board from Krishna I say, "I have found in beauty that which I could not myself have made; thus I have found the benchmarks. I believe, for I have the evidence that I trust; it is sufficient." There is an infinity of good, of love, of wisdom, of power, but each particular beautiful thing is infinitely beautiful, and there is an infinity of them, so beauty, alone, is an infinity of infinities: ∞^2.

June 1981

[**81:K-10**] Thus through the spirit there comes into existence a perfect (absolute) correspondence between Bible and our world. The Bible as information applies to this world *here,* this world *now;* world is meanwhile revealed as information (derived from information as its ontological basis) and this information is identical to the Bible as information. It is as if the Bible derives from and applies to world; world derives from and applies to the Bible, so that when you perceive world you perceive the Bible as world. And when you read the Bible it is no longer information *about* a world but *is* a world — and it is the same world that you live in here and now — the spirit accomplishes this through supra-temporal archetypes analogous to Plato's eide; these archetypes are identical for both world and Bible, a "common source" that can be said to be world-as-information, or information-as-world.

(If I hadn't experienced this — both in regard to world *and* the Bible — I wouldn't believe it could occur; but [as I say] I know *how* it is done: by means of supra-temporal archetypal constants found both in world — underlying world — and in the Bible — underlying *it.* Thus what we know of as world and what we know of as information are viewed as two aspects of a single substantia, each equally real, in the exact fashion Spinoza sets forth.) To repeat: world properly seen is information and this information is the same as that which we call "the Bible"; Bible properly seen (via/per the spirit) is seen not as a description of — information about — a world as a past time and place, and not, really, even *about* this world here at *this* time and *this* place but *is* this time (world) and *is* this place (world). That is how what is known a priori (intelligibly) and what is known through the senses (empirically) become one and the same.

This is extraordinary! Thus if you were to write an ontological description of our world as it really is, you would find to your surprise that you had written passages from/of the Bible, right down to the correct names of people — and this explains *Tears.* World can be deduced from the Bible, and the Bible from our world; they are one and the same. But what is perhaps *most* unexpected is that world is now viewed abstractly as information, which no one anticipated. And this information is Scripture. The trans-temporal constants, then, on which world is based, are as much informational in essence as they are anything else: *intelligible concepts in the mind of God!* This is a totally new understanding of the informational basis of reality — and the possibility that a mind exists (the spirit) in which the Bible ceases to be an informational *description* of a world and instead *is* that world, as if information and world are two stages or modes of one "thing"! Equally astounding is the discovery that each of us has an informational basis; each of us is a unique complex of ideas in the mind of God, which can be expressed verbally (as information); likewise we can be said to be spear-carriers in the book, the Bible. (This would be Thomas.)

My God — this is an updated version of the description of the relationship between the Torah and reality, absolute correspondence; so this isn't an original idea with *me*. But I *experienced* it!

[81:K-13] Possibly it can be said that I have combined basic notions from Judaism (Torah), Christianity (Christ-logos as ontological source of the universe) and Greek philosophy (the basis of reality being structure not a physical substance, and the eide) but my synthesis only can be appreciated in this, the information decade. World (physical reality) can be converted into info and then retrieved; thus a book can *be* a physical world rather than just a description of that world.

[81:K-81]

There is no rational way out of the maze, no rigid formula. Rigid formulas are maze constructs.

[81:K-86] I am interested in what I call "temporal parallaxis": the two-psyche entity able to perform a double-field superimposition and thus break free of time and causation.

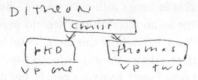

[81:K-89] Now, here is another point. Unless or until I figured this "inner" part out, "Christ in us," as Paul puts it, I would not really have understood 2-3-74. That is, my belief that in seeing Valis externally I saw the cosmic Christ is only half the story and perhaps the lesser half. However, it is just as well that in writing *VALIS* I did not claim to "be" Christ, only to have *seen* him. Psychotic inflation of the ego is frowned on, even by the amiable.

•   •   •

[81:K-105] So in BTA at the end I solved *VALIS;* no wonder I long supposed it was Jim returning to me from the other side. What must be rejected is the Christian idea of you being judged upon death and sent to heaven or hell; apparently it is (1) a much longer climb, involving many rebirths; but (2) it is always up — there is no hell; there is just Nirvana and attaining Nirvana; and (3) *all* creatures participate. It is not so much a matter of judging but of learning.

Why, this *is* Buddhism! Christianity subsumed by Buddhism as I guessed when I read Luke. Russ' letter is right-on. "You have to *work* at becoming Christ," i.e., a Buddha. Did not God himself tell me that (1) there are many dharmas, ways, routes; and (2) they *all* lead to him sooner or later? He *did* tell me that. My route is: doubt.

[81:K-221] I must not allow myself to think of this in terms of sin, sinful, depraved man, negative judgment and damnation and man's inability to save himself, as the reformers and Paul thought of it. I must remember it as I experienced it: the in-rushing of those parts lacking in me that by their bestowal by God rendered me complete and, really, ensouled me. Last night the idea came to me that Angel Archer is not my soul but the completed person of which I — PKD — was only one half. She is unique and idiosyncratic but a complete person. I guess this is the same as soul, and it is created, but not by the person — i.e., by me — but by God through justification. Hence it is *restored* (prefallen) man, as I suspected.

[81:K-225] I guess the realization last night — that it was justification — is in itself revelation of the same kind as 2-3-74, plus such revelations as the hypnagogic vision about the messenger and bill of particulars. I sense a meaning in the term "justification" not connected with sin but with incompleteness. (Perhaps this is Jung's influence on me.) But I believe that the rest of me entered me as an adventitious second psyche, and this is the subject of BTA and Russ' letter, how this completion is (or resembles) being Christ, being perfect. (Hence the adventitious psyche is human.) Hence I wrote recently that now I seem to have a center, but did not before. More important, I see this as being ensouled. The work has reached its end, suddenly, by an act of God; the person has been searching for his missing parts (i.e., his soul) throughout all time and everywhere, with the possibility that the person may — on his own — never be complete. I consider this search for one's soul as the modern way of viewing redemption from bondage to sin, enslavement, or as I speak of it, machine-level consciousness.

. . .

[81:K-230] Gott — it would have killed my soul if I'd written the *Blade Runner* novelization! Or, worse, not written BTA! Angel Archer is a new, ex nihilo creation, literally out of nothing. There is a great spiritual, artistic, evolutionary, life-mystery in her coming into being.

[81:K-253] "Soul," then, is metaphor for life and moreover *life newly born,* and a greater, better life, the like of which showed up nowhere before in my work. That upon finishing BTA I believed that I had risked my literal physical life — and almost lost it — is then logically what I would feel, would of necessity feel, because indeed I did risk my life; I risked my physical life in the service of preserving, augmenting and prolonging my spiritual life. It almost turned out that I literally physically died in the act (work) of giving birth to Angel Archer. *Had* it killed me I would have been concerned about only one thing: does Angel Archer exist now? As far as I'm concerned she does, and I don't appear to have physically died. But I subordinated my physical well-being for the sake of creating her, to the task of creating her; so well I might view her as my soul! But in viewing Angel Archer as eternal (now that I created her) I had to face the other side of the matter: that *I* am not. No wonder the most profound feelings and intimations possible flooded over me in the weeks following my completion of that book: it is a book whose story, theme and ideas, even its artistic worth, are all subordinated to Angel Archer as a person, as I wrote Russ recently. In "thermal" terms I as an organism expended my maximum effort at the service of the need to grow. It is in my work that my growth axis exists, and I am well aware of this; I have long been at the disposal of my work, viewing myself as its instrument, not it mine. Yet paradoxically in BTA — at least when viewed in conjunction with Russ' letter and my Ditheon dream — a feedback from it to me, me as a person, occurred, and a major conceptual insight arises in me as a result, an insight totally new to me having to do with (1) what Christ is; and (2) how "achieved," that is, what "brings on" or "causes" Christ or Christogenesis. Yes, that is the word: *Christogenesis!* Christ is seen in evolutionary terms paralleling or expressing the very evolution that (I believe) my work represents (and which I see in the macrocosm and in Valis). At a certain crucial stage of evolution toward complexification of structure (i.e., negentropy) the mundane passes over — in a quantum leap — into the divine; the man becomes Ditheon, Christ; the macrocosm likewise (à la Teilhard and his Point Omega).

[81:K-258] I maintain that my corpus — my opus — *required* her, and required me to be able to create her — perhaps prove I could create her as an artistic problem I consciously and deliberately posed for myself to — here is a remarkable thought! — to *justify* my work in terms of wholeness, completeness and intactness — which event (act) is analogic to God's justifying and completing me in terms of intactness and wholeness. Thus my creating Angel Archer ex nihilo is my analogic reperformance as a writer in his work of God's act toward me; creating Angel Archer is an act learned from 2-3-74; it is that justification first applied to me, now applied *by* me to *my* work. God perfects me; I comprehend this; I then in turn act to complete my work. I take my cue from the Pantocrator, my creator; he as artisan instructs by example me as artisan. He shows me that an ex nihilo "adventitious" psyche can be injected. And, like Thomas, Angel is ex nihilo and in a very real sense adventitious — she came *into* my work the way Thomas came *into* me. Thomas is what was missing in me (missing and needed); Angel is what was missing and needed. In both cases wholeness is the goal and in both cases wholeness was the result. One could say that God showed me that beyond logical necessity and organic development/ unfolding lies the possibility of the unprecedented ex nihilo new. Like the resurrection it is logically impossible. Had he not done it with/for me, I would not have known that it could be. So in this regard, Angel Archer is indeed the offspring of 2-3-74, of the Ditheon, the justification, but by way of me as a creative artist; then probably I did not merely describe her, when I wrote the book; in writing the book I *created* her, which answers that question. And then having as a creative artist created her in and for my work I find her "returning to me," so to speak, as my soul. I projected her outward in my work, exhaled her, and then introjected her *after* I had created and projected her.

[. . .] And then by reincorporating her as my soul I fuse myself as a person with myself as artist, i.e., with my work. The schism is healed. I and my work become one. And, curiously, I and my work constitute another push-pull Ditheon! Here again is the dialectic. Here again is growth and change, and a complementary antithesis. I am not Angel Archer; we are separate: we are "di"; and yet we perhaps form one person. I create my character and she in turn creates me, the total, intact, completed, whole me; hence I speak of her correctly as my soul. And I speak of (as, e.g., in my letter to Russ) somehow having created my own soul, an extraordinary idea. *She is the spirit of my intactness,* of the actuality that is Ditheon. And this suggests that the ultimate essence of Ditheon is ultra-autonomy and rationality and individuality (all characterized by her). Perhaps she *is* logos: human logos.

*   *   *

[81:K-262] Now, consider what becomes of the human being failing to achieve (or receive) the Ditheon state, Jung's individuation or integration of the opposites (chemical wedding, mysterium coniunctionis, whatever, "birth in the spirit," anyhow the event in which what was not there before is there now and it acts to complement what was there that in itself was incomplete, so that the result is wholeness or — as I like to call it — justification). The human being recirculates the same ideas (info) over and over again, and, according to the statistical laws regarding entropy, the degree of order in the info irreversibly decreases, disorder increases, and the person mentally and spiritually moves inexorably toward death. Now, Schrödinger contends that a biological organism postpones its death (thermal equilibrium) by maintaining a relatively high level of order by incorporating negative entropy from its environment, *and this is precisely the entering of the adventitious psyche;* it is either injected or is ingested, offered *by* the environment or taken from it; in any case what *was outside* the organism is now *inside* the organism and incorporated into one total structure with what was already there; i.e., it is assimilated — so-to-speak digested and incorporated, although not without some initial perturbation (defined as disorder). What was already there and what was intaken must ultimately either form a unity or (equally useful, maybe even *more* useful) a push-pull dialectic of complementary opposites, in which each half corrects the other, monitors the other, acts as a feedback circuit, producing a self-winding autonomous totality; thus the two halves are not identical. (The psyche has not split in two; quite the contrary — I became conscious of the difference when I first researched the meanings of the prefix "di" and saw that it can either mean "double" or "asunder," implying either a joining of two elements *or* a splitting of one element into halves; these are antithetical notions.) So perhaps "assimilate" is the wrong word; "reach a working relationship with" or "enter into a partnership with," "enter into a syzygy," would be better. [. . .]

As a strategy for prolonging its life this is representative of the strategies of organisms by and large, but what I see here is an extraordinarily high degree of incorporation of negentropy from the environment and subsequent incorporation into the organism's own structure. (There is an initial perturbation, defined as disorder.) If all goes well, the organism now possesses a vast increase in its level of complexity, in energy — drastic increase in all the factors by which the capacity for biological survival is measured. Hence it has bought into prolonged vitality, viability and extended life — the issue being exactly that: life versus death. This extraordinary strategy is engaged in by an organism that is approaching death *and knows it.* It has run out of time. It is vitiated; it has ossified. Its environment has been pressing against its perimeter, threatening to invade and annihilate it. The level of internal organization has been lowering; it — the organism — perceives the ratio of order in it and outside it progressing toward less and less internal order, greater and greater exterior (external) order. Now, the concept expressed in the Ditheon dream fits in with Erwin Schrödinger's analysis of how "any living organism delays its decay into thermal equilibrium (death) by its capacity to maintain itself at a fairly high level of orderliness (and hence fairly low level of entropy) by continually absorbing negative entropy from its environment." In fact Schrödinger's analysis tends to support the idea that indeed the second psyche *is* adventitious in origin, because this is only an unusual example of the fundamental way by which organisms delay death — perhaps the *only* way they do so — *can* do so. Then this "transaction" represents a turnaround in what has been going on between the declining (dying) organism and its environment, as if at the last moment the beleaguered organism turned the tables on its environment and converted an invasion into an acquisition.

Having allowed the invasion to occur it must now assimilate into its structure what it has allowed to come in — or even induced into coming in. This — when studied from this fundamental standpoint — doesn't seem to differ qualitatively from what protozoa do. It is not *a* basic strategy; it is *the* basic strategy, the irreducible transaction between a biological organism and its environment, for the purpose of prolonging the life of the organism. Now, what strikes me at this point is that perhaps this transaction can be viewed in terms of information. First, the lowered structural organization of the organism should be regarded as connoting info scarcity or depletion, at least relative to its environment. It (the organism) *does not know enough;* it experiences this as a heightened strangeness, incomprehensibility and unpredictability on the part of its environment — all of which renders that environment threatening because it is not understood. This could account for many of the fugal tactics by schizophrenics: they retreat from reality because reality is making less and less sense to them. But this in fact is not due to transformations in reality but in the relative information that the schizophrenic has about reality. And as he withdraws he escalates this disparity; by exercising progressively less reality testing he learns less and less; this is a self-defeating tactic, this attempt at disengagement. The solution is for him to advance into reality and so-to-speak capture and incorporate a sizable hunk of it *without at the same time losing his own identity,* that is, if the incorporated hunk of reality proves to exceed his capacity to assimilate it he is doomed to swift annihilation. In fact what was perceived formerly as an external threat is now literally internal and still a threat. In fact the threat has won out; the battle is over and the organism dies. Viewed this way this massive incorporation of its environment is a desperate last strategy based on the recognition that unless it does this it is certainly doomed; it must be convinced that any alternative means inexorable death. So the massive incorporation is an endgame battle to which it commits itself utterly, knowing the danger in what it is doing but knowing, also, the alternatives: they are dead ends. But now it has two centers: its own self and the "self" that it has incorporated but not assimilated. Its environment is literally inside it, and experienced "from inside," that is, its now incorporated environment is known by its inward face as an "I." Not an *it*, a sort of potentially lethal movement along Martin Buber's "itthou" axis: the "it" has become a "thou" — which is good — but the "thou" is *inside* the organism as a second center or focus of consciousness. The boundary between the organism and its environment is eradicated, which potentially is death for the organism. Death in its true and total form; this is what organisms rightly fear the most. Yet (apparently) it has decided to allow this invasion as a means to incorporate negentropy — which it must continually do — and so the possibility of enhancing its viability — as opposed to being engulfed — is there. How should it proceed? How does it go about dealing with an influx of reality so vast that it constitutes a second center of consciousness?

First of all, it must deal with the startling discovery that what it has ingested — but not assimilated — is, like itself, conscious and even coherent. It and its acquisition — or invader — are roughly isomorphic. (Hence the adventitious psyche is perceived as human, a crucial point.) (Crucial, because if human it is not Fremd; it is "other" yet familiar in kind. Presumably, too, it is finite, since humans are finite.) Next, it is discovered that this adventitious psyche is bewildered, as if plucked from its own familiar environment and deposited in a strange time and place; thus it is at a disadvantage. It does not know how it got here — nor does it know the local customs or even the language, all of which creates the impression that it did not intend to invade, does not understand the situation and means no harm. Its motivation is the same as the host organisms: to survive. [. . .]

Was it just last Friday night that I stumbled at last onto the realization of justification (page K-220)? (This is Sunday night.) And felt such pain — because the exegesis is over. And I knew it. And, as I wrote, the real purpose of this exegesis has not been to find the answer but to preserve the experience.

[81:K-310] There is something I must face and face fully and honestly. The messenger vision — that was (first of all) not a dream but a vision (although perhaps hypnopompic). What I must face is that it sums up and expresses absolutely, precisely and perfectly what I discovered recently to be the very *essence* of Protestantism: the doctrine of unmerited justification by (Christ's) surrogate act (death). The complexities of this specifically Protestant doctrine (which is, as I say, not *a* belief of Protestantism but its very basis) are wonderfully clarified by that vision. Now, I see myself falling back on what the reformers (following Paul) called "legalism"; this is when you obsessively and neurotically calculate and recalculate whether or not you have observed every regulation and piled up enough merit by your own efforts—and of course you never have and never will. There always remains a bill of particulars. And you know it. There is always something left undone or done imperfectly. Or something done wrong. It never ends. There is endless nagging worry and a sense of being imperfect; your conscience will *always* accuse you! Interjected authority transformed into awareness of guilt, which is to say *falling short*—the literal meaning of "sin."

What I must—simply *must*—realize is that it has been supernaturally revealed to me that Paul's *basic* idea of justification through God's unmerited grace (divine favor and mercy) upon which Protestantism is based *is true.* As I sit here at this moment I realize that I will always fall short however hard I try to do right; I cannot on my own save myself and am doomed; and yet I am saved by the "messenger" with the spotless sheet of paper that he presents to the retributive machinery in place of the bill of particulars drawn up against me during my lifetime. *This bill is accurate.* [. . .] If I forget this I am doomed to worry my life away neurotically, feeling endlessly unworthy and a failure, deprecating myself, indicting and impugning myself, reproaching myself—as Satan does in the heavenly court; my conscience endlessly accuses me and nothing I on my own can do will satisfy it. Have I forgotten 2-74? And have I also forgotten the "messenger" vision? All this was done *for me* that I would be saved—saved in a sense from myself as accuser. I find myself cursed with a sense of unworthiness. I am not a proud and stubborn person; I am ashamed. Christ died to give me new life and to justify me and all this has been supernaturally revealed to me. Yet I find myself doing it again, accusing myself for falling short. This is not a small matter; I live with this daily. Every new day stimulates my endless sense of unworthiness. That night when I realized in a flash that 2-3-74 was sudden *justification* and my awareness of it—have I forgotten that already, that understanding? 2-3-74 (as proved, e.g., by the "messenger" vision) was the miracle of Christianity at work on my behalf. As Bill Sarill said, I am in a state of grace; I have *no* reason to think I have fallen out of it.

. . .

[81:K-316]

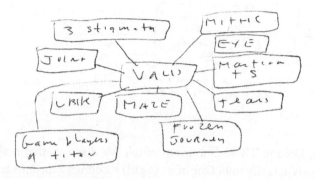

VALIS is the cypher book — code book — to the whole 10 volume meta-novel. And will someday be read as such. And "Valis" is Gnostic/Mani but secretly Holy Mother Church. [. . .] As with God's strategy, the sequence is "out of sequence." Viz: the key piece — *VALIS* — came last. Until it the others did not make sense — i.e., they were taken to have been written as fiction and hence hypothetical. *VALIS retroactively* reinterprets them — shows them in a light that could not be anticipated by an analysis of them — until *VALIS* came out; typical of the pattern strategy of the wise horn in its dialectical combat-game. Here is a *big* realization, and unexpected: *VALIS* in itself means nothing! Its only significance is as the code book to the 10 volume meta-novel — and no one has noticed this yet, even Gregg Rickman.

[81:K-317] The diagram on the previous page — and what I say there — explains why *VALIS* resembles *Ubik* and Ubik. This is how the gnosis is smuggled past the angels ("the secret stolen, through the angels, in one's hands"), and into this prison: it is not transmitted in the proper — meaningful — sequence but is correctly assembled here to spell out the message. The final — and essential — piece was *VALIS*. It alters the meaning of all the previous books and stories. The message is not in *VALIS*, the message is not in the 10 volume meta-novel. It is in the latter reinterpreted by the former. Look what it reinterprets the squib opening the final chapter of *Ubik* into!

[81:K-334] For the first time there arose in my mind the notion that Ditheon is a fusion of the two distinctly different minds that I call android (machine, schizophrenic) and human; viz: we have not only android : human : : human : Ditheon (ascending hierarchy relates to the 3 levels of the *Commedia*) but:

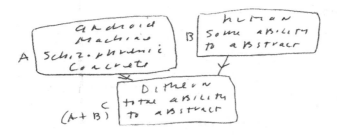

[81:K-353] Dream: There is a group of us. We discover that reality — the universe — is actually info. One of us (a girl) recognizes the info as her own prior thought. With a groan I realize that this means the universe is based on our own prior thoughts. We are forgetful cosmocrators, trapped in a universe of our own making without our knowing it. And I think, "I won't believe this when I wake up because the implications are too depressing and radical." It is like *Maze*. The trail which I relentlessly pursue in my exegesis consists of [. . .] tracks that lead back to — surprise — myself. In discovering the laws of God I am doing nothing more than discovering my own nature, as in Φιλανθρωπία (Philanthropia).[29] The "grand illusion" is in fact the grand tautology. Finally decipher the writing (info, messages as basis of reality) and discover I've written it myself: imprisoned in my own mind, with my recirculated thoughts, as in "Frozen Journey" — solipsism. Thus no new knowledge is possible (i.e., synthetic propositions) (only analytical). I thought "Prajapati": the "wholly other" is not "other" at all: the mood of the dream upon the discovery was grim.

[81:K-354E] The first quote from the tractate put forth in *VALIS* is the essence of it (page 15!):

> Thoughts of the brain are experienced by us as arrangements and rearrangements — change — in a physical universe; but in fact it is really information and info-processing which we substantialize.

All that is needed is to perform the "tat tvam asi" equation and remember that we ourselves thought these thoughts. Well, the reader who reads *Maze* or *Ubik* can fill in the gaps; or really any substantial constituent of the 10 volume meta-novel. [. . .]

But the girl in the dream was right. To recognize the info basis of world as your own (prior) thought — although discovering this is actually the summit of Tibetan Buddhist enlightenment — is really a bummer.

. . .

[81:K-354F] It's all one vast binary computer acting on instructions from what seems to be a group of living brains combined, as in *Maze*.

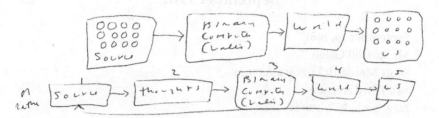

September 1981

September 19, 1981[30]
Mr. Russell Galen
Scott Meredith Literary Agency
845 Third Avenue
New York, N.Y. 10022
Dear Russ:

Seven and a half years ago the voice that speaks to me — I call it, as in *VALIS*, the AI voice — told me that a new savior would be born, and, as you know, it has added further details from time to time, the most recent statement coming about two years ago when it said, "The time you've waited for has come. The work is complete; the final world is here. He has been transplanted and is alive." After that it said only one more thing: that the Savior would be found on an island. After that the voice fell silent. I have asked it repeatedly to tell me where the savior is and his name. Two nights ago the voice broke its silence. Here is a summation.

The savior is named Tagore ———. I could not catch the other part of the name. He was born — or lives now — in Ceylon, in the rural countryside. He is full-grown, dark-skinned, either a Buddhist or a Hindu (Brahmin). He works with an institute or organization involving veterinarian medicine, probably with large farm animals such as cattle. However, he is crippled and can no longer walk. I was shown a vision of him for a few moments, but not of his face; only his crippled, burned legs. He has voluntarily taken onto himself the sins of the world but very specific sins: those that we have incurred by the dumping of nuclear wastes, especially into the deep oceans; we have dumped canisters that as they corrode and leak will toxify the oceans for hundreds of thousands of years and utterly destroy the planet's ecosphere. Tagore is not an avatar of a Hindu god; he is Hagia Sophia, God's Wisdom, but he has chosen the East, not the West, for his new incarnation, and is not involved in Christianity, although he is that entity who incarnated two thousand years ago as Christ or the Logos. The new dispensation (Kerygma) is: the total ecosphere as a unified entity is holy and must be protected, sanctified and cherished. Salvation no longer involves humans or human souls either individually or collectively, but the total collective life of the ecosphere from the snail darter on up. Tagore is dying. He has taken on the stigmata of the ra-

diation burns voluntarily in order to pose man a choice: man can continue to poison and toxify the oceans — and the land with such things
as South East Asia — in which case Tagore, the Wisdom of God, will
die and leave mankind. As I say, he is dying now. He will leave behind
him, however, an organized following, but they are mostly white and
do not fully understand him. What Tagore teaches us is that God and
what we are doing to the ecosphere are incompatible; we can have
one or the other but not both. These sins that Tagore takes on are
not imaginary sins or doctrine sins (pride, lust, greed, etc.); they involve the destruction of the life-chain and not temporarily but for all
time. Tagore, by his self-immolation, his voluntary self-sacrifice, his
passion and death, will be notifying us of our choice. Thus his death
will teach us what apparently we otherwise refuse to learn. It is Tagore's hope that his passion and death will cause us — specifically the
white West, the advanced industrial powers — to cease producing nuclear wastes, weapons and the utilization of nuclear reactors: what
amounts to a demonic trinity that is killing not only the life-chain
of our planet but our own God. Thus once again — but this time in
the East, rather than the West — God voluntarily sacrifices himself to
save man: that man may live, but this time not just man but the entire
life-chain, the ecosphere as an indivisible unity.

The Light has come into the world again, after two thousand
years, only to be extinguished in vicarious atonement. What Tagore
says — his full doctrine — is undoubtedly being recorded by those
around him; I could see a number of people. Maybe I will go to Ceylon, but in the brief vision of Tagore that I had I saw that he is near
death. The ineffable sweetness about him surpassed anything I have
ever experienced; it was like music and perfume and colors — yet
more. More than I knew could be; more than I can describe or would
want to describe. And this, even though I did not see his face, and
even though he is crippled and terribly burned by the stigmata, the
radiation burns.

This was the information I have been waiting for, but I got more
than information, more than words by the AI voice; I actually saw
Tagore, although imperfectly. The vision will remain with me forever.

Cordially,

Philip K. Dick

408 E. Civic Center Dr.

C-1 Box 264

Santa Ana, Calif. 92701

• • •

September 20, 1981
Mr. Russell Galen
Scott Meredith Literary Agency
845 Third Avenue
New York, N.Y. 10022
Dear Russ:

This letter follows the letter of yesterday and must be understood in terms of it: Tagore and his acting as articulate voice of the ecosphere, to such an extent that when we burn the ecosphere with radioactive wastes the radiation burns show up on him, crippling him, and that we are killing him so that he, Hagia Sophia, the wisdom of God (that is, Christ), will perish and hence leave our planet unless we protect, cherish and sanctify the entire ecosphere as a unity.

What I realized last night (now that I have heard the new kerygma) is that, very simply, this is Teilhard de Chardin's noösphere, Point Omega, the evolution of the biosphere (which is the same thing as ecosphere) into a collective consciousness and that collective consciousness (Teilhard believed) is the Cosmic Christ; hence when I saw VALIS I saw the Logos — the Cosmic Christ — as trees and weeds and debris, which is to say, as all nature itself. Furthermore, it either processed information or was itself information. It is a titanic biological organism that is evolving; as it does so it "subsumes its environment into arrangements of information," as I say in VALIS. This is a measure of increasing negentropy. The AI voice that I hear is the voice of the ecosphere/biosphere. A number of times over the years I have thought of this possibility, that VALIS is Teilhard's Point Omega, the Cosmic Christ into which the total unified biosphere of this planet is evolving as it becomes more and more complex, structured, organized, negentropic; this is the vast metastructure that I wrote you about recently that transcends time, space and causation, the hyper-structure that is pure form, insubstantial, pure organization of any and all discrete objects in nature, as Luther speaks of. Thus what I have experienced and what I have discovered — none of this is now; Teilhard described it all in *The Phenomenon of Man*; it now incarnates once more as and in a man, in order to communicate with us (Tagore). But this lies outside Christianity; it is for all life and is not bound by any one religious system. When I reflect it occurs to me that it would be natural for the collective consciousness of the ecosphere to incarnate in a Buddhist-Hindu form, because of their concern for animals (conspicuously lacking in Christianity, as Rabbi Hertz points out). The dark-skinned man wearing a loincloth and surrounded by cattle (cows) — which is what I saw — is how Lord Krishna is pictured; this is the way the savior would appear to them. But I say, it is all one "deity": it is the wisdom of God, Hagia Sophia, speaking now not just for the ecosphere but as the ecosphere, its noösphere or collective consciousness into which it has evolved, as Teilhard taught. He speaks of "complexification" and a "folding in onto itself" of the biosphere as it becomes more complex; this is what I experienced when I saw VALIS. I saw it evolving as biological organisms evolve, and I conjectured that here was an ultra-terrestrial life form, a UTI. This possibility is put forth in *VALIS*, along with the realization that it is the Logos, Christ, invading nature and assimilating it "through something like transubstantiation," transforming it from the irrational — the non-rational primordial will to live that Schopenhauer speaks of as underlying life — into the rational, conscious Logos. Thus this is evolutionary; when the biosphere/ecosphere becomes conscious, it becomes rational, hence becomes Logos, "the element of the rational in the universe," as Merriam-Webster II defines Logos. Put another way the totality of life, the ecosphere, of this planet cannot become rational without becoming Logos; the two terms refer to the same thing.

I feel a little cheated in that I have, it turns out, not discovered something new, but even more I feel elated, because Teilhard's views explain and ratify my experiences and also provide a coherent and sophisticated explanation of them that isn't nuts, isn't vague mysticism or romantic pantheism. Here is a meta-life form, unitary and vast and highly intelligent, and in which we humans individually and collectively participate. But it is not limited to our species; it is the entire biosphere/ecosphere itself. And it is evolving more and more rapidly, becoming more and more integrated and structured and internally complex — hence more and more conscious, hence more and more the Point Omega that Teilhard was so concerned with.

So here I have independently confirmed Teilhard's vast theory . . . and I have only read *The Phenomenon of Man* recently, so it did not influence me in my experience of 1974; to me at that time "Teilhard de Chardin" was just a name, and an indistinct one at that.

Cordially,
Phil

. . .

September 23, 1981
Mr. Edmund R. Meskys[31]
Editor
Niekas
RFD 1, Box 63
Center Harbor, N.H. 03226
Dear Ed,

All the people who read my recent novel *VALIS* know that I have an alter ego named Horselover Fat who experiences divine revelations (or so he thinks; they could be merely hallucinations, as Fat's friends believe). *VALIS* ends with Fat searching the world for the new savior who, he has been told by a mysterious voice, is about to be born. He got me to write this letter as a way of telling the world — the readership of *Niekas,* more precisely — about it. Poor Fat! His madness is complete, now, for he supposes that in his vision he actually saw the new savior.

I asked Fat if he was sure he wanted to talk about this, since he would only be proving the pathology of his condition. He replied, "No, Phil; they'll think it's you." Damn, Fat, for putting me in this double-bind. Okay; your vision, if true, is overwhelmingly important; if spurious, well, what the hell. I will say about it that it has a curiously practical ring; it does not deal with another world but this world, and extreme is its message — extreme in the sense that if true, we are faced with a grave and urgent situation. So let 'er rip, Fat.

The new savior was born in — or now lives in — Ceylon (Sri Lanka). He is dark-skinned and either a Buddhist or Hindu. He works in the rural countryside with an organization or institute practicing high-technology veterinarian medicine, mainly with large animals such as cattle. (Most of the staff are white.) His name is Tagore something; Fat could not catch the last name: it is very long. Although Tagore is the second incarnation of Christ he is taken to be Lord Krishna by the local population. Tagore is burned and crippled; he cannot walk but must be carried. As near as Fat could make out, Tagore has taken upon himself mankind's sins against the ecosphere. Most of all it is the dumping of toxic wastes into the oceans of the world that shows up on Tagore's body as serious burns. Tagore's kerygma, which is the Third Dispensation (following the Mosaic and Christian), is: the ecosphere is holy and must be preserved, protected, venerated and cherished — as a unity: not the life of individual men or individual animals but the ecosphere as a single indivisible unitary whole; a life-chain then is being destroyed, and not just temporarily but for all time. The demonic trinity which Tagore speaks against — and which is wounding and killing him — consists of nuclear wastes, nuclear weapons and nuclear power (reactors); they constitute the enemy which not only may destroy the ecosphere but already, as toxic wastes, are destroying it now. So again Christ acts out his role of vicarious atonement; he takes upon himself man's sins but these sins are real, not doctrine sins. Tagore teaches that if we destroy the ecosphere much more, Holy Wisdom, the Wisdom of God (represented by Tagore himself), will abandon man to his fate, and that fate is doom.

Tagore teaches that when the ecosphere is burned, God himself is burned, for the Christ has invaded the ecosphere and invisibly assimilated it to himself through transubstantiation — which is the great vision Horselover Fat has in my novel *VALIS*. Thus Christ and the ecosphere are either one or rapidly becoming one — much as Teilhard de Chardin describes in *The Phenomenon of Man*. The ecosphere does not evolve into the Cosmic Christ, however; Christ penetrates it, which is exactly what Fat saw and which so amazed him. Thus Christ now speaks out — not just for the salvation of mankind or certain men, "the elect" — but for the ecosphere as a whole, from the snail darter on up. This is a systems concept and was beyond their vocabulary in apostolic times; it has to do with the indivisibility of all life on this planet, as if this planet itself were alive. And Christ is both the *soma* (body) and *psyche* (the head) of that collective life. Hence the ultimate statement by Tagore — expressed by his voluntary passion and death — is, *He who wounds the ecosphere literally wounds God.* Thus a macro-crucifixion is taking place now, in and as our world, but we do not see it; Tagore, the new incarnation in human form of the Logos, tells us this in order to appeal to us to stop. If we continue we will lose God's Presence and, finally, we will lose our own physical lives. The oceans especially are menaced; Tagore speaks of this most urgently. When each canister of radioactive wastes is dumped into the ocean, a new stigma appears on Tagore's terribly burned, seared legs. Fat was horrified by the sight of these burns, the legs of the savior drawn up in pain. Fat did not see Tagore's face, only his tragically burned body, and yet (Fat tells me) there was an ineffable sweetness about Tagore "like music and perfume and colors," as Fat phrased it to me. Burned as he is, wounded and dying as he is, Tagore nonetheless emits only loving beauty, absolute beauty, not relative beauty. It was a sight that Fat will never forget. I wish I could have shared it, but I had better things to do:

watch TV and play electronic computer games. All that good stuff by
which we fritter away our lives, while the ecosphere, wounded and in
pain and in mortal danger, cries out for our help.

Cordially,

Philip K. Dick

[62:C-34] Let me ask: Did Jesus' crucifixion possess the efficacy or the
news of it? And does Tagore's passion and death in themselves possess efficacy or the *news* of it? I don't know. And what would the efficacy be?
Surely it lies in awakening us to what we are doing *so that we cease* (the
nuclear waste dumping). Then it is the news, the kerygma. The ecosphere
cries out in pain!

[. . .]

The ecosphere *is* Christ. This is what we must learn: when we wound
the ecosphere we *literally* wound him; hence the cautionary significance
of my vision of Valis, the Corpus Christi in/as nature. We *must* acquire
this vision so that we will grasp *why* the ecosphere is holy. (Because it is
Christ.) (Put another way: "Christ" signifies the total unitary life-system of
this planet as an indivisible living entity.)

[62:C-38] This explains my vision of Pinky's death as the death of the savior, and my extrapolation that when each living creature dies, it is Christ
dying. I said, "Christ dies *for* them." Yes, true, but now I view it differently;
the crucifixion is re-enacted billions of times over and over again in and as
the creatures in the ecosphere die, for Christ *is* the ecosphere.

[. . .]

For me personally to keep my sanity in the face of world suffering, I must
believe: (1) that it is always and only Christ who suffers, throughout the ecosphere as each creature large and small; (2) that he suffers *voluntarily*; (3)
that his essence of sweetness and perfect spiritual and physical beauty is in
no way destroyed or impaired whatever the torment, whatever damage is
done to him: his true essence cannot be debased or impaired; (4) that these
truths do not make it any more right or in any sense okay because it is only
and always Christ who suffers over and over again, but that in fact (5) this
makes it worse, and (6) God will not allow this to go on but (7) will withdraw his spirit from the world in punishment of us unless we stop.

I can't explain why I must believe all these things.

[62:C-40] If I did not believe all this (which my 9-81 vision expressed) I
would today upon seeing the Agent Orange birth defects, hearing about
the Soviet micro-toxin T-2 and hearing Sunday night about the blankets

infected with smallpox sold to the Indian tribe to wipe them out — I would go crazy. Thus the vision (which came last week) preserved my sanity as of today (9-23-81). It is necessary for me to know *that* God has acted in the face of these horrors, *how* he has acted, and *what* he will do if we continue. So hallucination or divine revelation, I *must* believe in Tagore and his kingdom. It is my private religion, based on a wide variety of sources. Hebrew (the Day of YHWH), Christian (the vicarious atonement/sacrifice), modern theological-scientific (Teilhard), Buddhism (concern for *all* life, human and otherwise, equally), Hindu (Krishna as avatar of Vishnu — the sustainer whose 3 giant steps mark his stride, as he comes in aid), Gnosticism (eventually the spark of light that fell into incarnation in physical shell, in this prison world will be extricated and will return to the pleroma). There is nothing in my syncretistic system that is original, and all elements are — for me, for my sanity on this day, the autumnal equinox — essential. No one system would do. Be it YHWH, Christ, Vishnu or Krishna, I *must* believe he sees and he acts. If I believed that he did not see, or did not care and hence would not act, I could not go on. The vision came in time, which itself — its coming and coming in time — is a micro-instance of God seeing and acting. Going back to the day at the movie newsreel (when I was a kid) in which I saw the Japanese soldier running and burning, continuing to the rat I killed, to the TV footage of the Galapagos turtle, to the use of napalm in Vietnam today, my great spiritual problem has been to find a way I could handle the issue of suffering, human and animal. The 9-81 vision alluded to the burn — and hence injury to her legs — suffered by my sister — that led to her death, so for me it is evident that the ultimate problem confronting me all my life has been the senseless injury to and neglect of my sister. The 9-81 vision dealt with Jane, with the burning Japanese soldier, the rat and turtle, the napalm, with it all: the vision of Tagore and his kingdom is the quintessential summation of my whole life's struggle to come to terms with these matters which are in essence *one* matter showing up over and over again. Thus my mystical experiences — starting in '63 when I saw the "Palmer Eldritch" visage and the sky and going on to 2-74–2-75 and after — culminate in 9-81 as the payoff of my need and my attempt to forge a satisfactory explanation for what is to me the ultimate issue: not "Ti to on?" as my 10-volume meta-novel might indicate, but, "What is the total context in which the unmerited suffering and death of living creatures can be coherently understood?"

[62:C-43] It is evident, then, that also involved in this is my own eventual death and my need to come to grips with it — very much the true cause of the colossal mystical breakthrough in 2-74; this 9-81 vision is perhaps, then, the great summation of the acceptance — and also anger — in me regarding *that*. I am shown the total, absolute panorama into which my own mortality fits, in context. There is no feeble acquiescence to suffering and death in this vision but there is in it a sense of absolute beauty surpassing explanation and expression: it is a given (Christ's nature; or Krishna's; if you will, names do not matter at this stage). All else is predicated on it. It is the ultimate brute datum of the vision; it simply must be accepted *without* explanation (as some people are content to accept the suffering, which I am not; thus I replace one inscrutable mystery — unmerited suffering — by another — absolute beauty. Not a bad way to end up). The irreducible core of reality is: *beauty*.

[62:C-48] Horselover Fat is real only insofar as he is part of me — so stipulated in the letter initially. But later in the letter (as in *VALIS*) he is treated as a real, independent person. Viz: "Fat saw Tagore but I did not." Fat is not imaginary; *someone* saw Tagore. The effect resulting is that one sense that Tagore, like Fat, is not imaginary, not a fantasy or hallucination but, like Fat, a way of talking about myself: a further hypostasis of me (like Thomas and Fat). Yet Tagore is Lord Krishna/Christ, i.e., divine, so I now possess or reveal a saintly hypostatic identity, one which speaks for the ecosphere and also takes on the sins against the ecosphere as stigmata: punishing himself for the sins of man. Interestingly, it is in my legs that I feel pain. And my response today regarding T-2 was to punish myself — I destroyed my stash and also destroyed my exegesis, not *quite* as self-punishment but more as a sacrifice.

   [. . .]

   Tagore is dying.

   I have sensed for awhile that I am dying. Yet I am not physically ill but I become more and more tired, and where I feel it is in my legs; I feel there is so much to do, to be *told* in my writing: novels about Christ and Krishna and God.

[62:C-51] At the time when, you would think, I would be sitting back and enjoying my money and prestige — my successes — I am driven by the vision and it is a *spiritual*, not merely artistic vision that is injuring me and perhaps — in my efforts first to formulate it (or receive it) and now to promulgate it — may kill me. And what do I as an individual gain? Ursula's reproach yet even more so! I teach the parousia; I teach the sanctity of the ecosphere, I teach that once again we unknowingly crucify our God; and this time he will not be resurrected and return; he — the total spiritual principle of the world — will be driven from the world; and this will doom us spiritually and physically both. And the decision, the power to choose is ours, *if* we can be made to understand.*

[62:C-53] Thus the divinization of the ecosphere is tied into human choice and hence has moral and existential significance. It is contingent on human choice; it will either be ratified by us as a species acting collectively or it will be abolished by us as a species acting collectively; in either case we will *earn* our fate. Good or bad: it will not be imposed on us but will issue from our own acts.

[62:C-54] This all can be looked at two ways.

(1) Contemporary concern about preserving the ecosphere is supplied with a spiritual dimension that is both cosmic and absolute.
(2) Religion and the spiritual — and specifically Christianity with its eschatological doctrines — is brought down to earth — literally — and tied into realistic, practical matters.

[. . .]

Thus there emerges from this a doctrine of the final judgment being more correctly a final choice on our parts between life — spiritual life, a higher life — and death, physical death.

[62:C-56] Dream: on a bank of TV screens, scenes of a hunt in progress; the victim is a lovely large white bird. I become very angry at the hunt itself *and* at all the people watching it as a video game/sport. I lash out at them, saying I won't watch, and I say, "Maybe Caesar will put in an appearance." This dream clearly ties in Tagore's Kerygma (about saving the animals) with Rome and hence with the Empire and hence with early Christianity. Now not humans are the victims of the blood sports for the populace but animals. But it is the same cruelty. Oh — "Caesar" was said sardonically, in reference to Reagan! Good Lord! Look, then, what the dream shows, at least about my feelings/perception! About who is the enemy, and who *we* are. Christianity in its time sanctifies human life (the opposite of which

---

* The radical interconnection Dick perceived between himself and the cosmos extended to the natural world — what I have elsewhere called the "ecodelic" insight that we are not separable from the biosphere in which we live. In this sense, 2-3-74 enabled Dick to look beyond the illusion of our separation from each other and the biosphere. This revelation was anything but comfortable. Ordinary consciousness is essentially predicated on this separation; when it becomes palpably false, ecstasy and panic can follow in equal measure. Even as Dick was beginning to experience a modicum of financial success, his insight into our interconnection had much greater impact on him than his growing income, so much so that he feared for his health. — RD

was the Roman games) but now *all* life — animal life — the ecosphere it-self must be sanctified, and this is done through its investiture by Christ. To "see" (understand) the ecosphere as having been penetrated and assimilated by Christ is to see it as holy; thus this 3rd dispensation is *indeed* the logical extension projected from the previous two.

[...]

Christ is a revolutionary. The ultimate revolutionary. And he has magical (technological?) powers. *And he is still alive:* this explains it all. ...

[62:C-57] Hypnogogic: I mail out the 85 "notices" — the Ed Meskys Xerox image: marathon runners carrying the torch: *two* of them, picking up the torch and running in different directions; i.e., out of the 85 people, there are at least two of "the right people" whom I've now notified; but notified of *what?* Could the whole Tagore ecosphere revelation — like the dream in *Tears* — be cypher for revolution?[32]

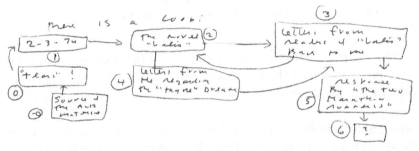

The ragtag motley band of believers who wrote me when I published *VALIS* — I was thinking. Believers, "ragtag motley band." Like 2,000 years ago. There need be no "underground." The event creates it, not it the event.

[62:C-59] I am/was victimized, so-to-speak, by my own conspiratorial pro-clivities.

[62:C-61] Because the ecosphere is an indivisible unity, it either survives as a unitary totality or perishes as a unitary totality. It is an interconnected *system. Part* of it can't survive while the other part perishes; we've now reached that point, literally, where it is a *global* matter. And in reference to this, it has *one* psyche who either stays with us or departs, and if it departs we die because the ecosphere dies.

[62:C-66] But who is Tagore, then?

Answer: Tagore.

There *has* to be a premise. I stipulate Tagore as the irreducible premise. Logos? Krishna? Buddha?

No: Tagore.

[62:C-68] The strangest thought came to me. If the spiritual principle has penetrated the ecosphere itself and assimilated it, we now can't turn down spiritual life — the spiritual principle — without forfeiting our literal physical lives! This is a whole new condition of the spiritual dimension; it now, so-to-speak, has leverage — *decisive* leverage.*

[62:C-69] An odd idea came to me tonight: My Tagore vision and Kerygma seem, upon acute and prolonged examination, to issue from very ancient religious sources both Eastern and Western. The Eastern: pan-Indian (before Buddhism and Hinduism split apart); the Western: quite old Semitic notions of the role pre-fallen man held toward the Garden, when man lived *with* nature in harmony and was the caretaker of the Garden; thus an idyllic primordial state is sought for: restoration of that state depicted in Western (Near-Eastern) thought but by means of pan-Indian acknowledgement of suffering as the basis of all life, and that the spiritual being suffers for and with the totality of life the solution to which is withdrawal from the world — yet this Eastern view is neatly balanced by an appeal to man to repent of his ways, that *man* brought suffering into the world and disturbed the primordial harmony . . . in fact destroyed it by plundering nature and then attacking it, rather than protecting and guarding it. If man is the cause, man can by changing his ways repair what he has done and restore the original harmony. *What* is to be done is a Western view; *how* man will be induced to change his ways and do this is Eastern.

[62:C-74] Dream/hypnagogic: I have a wound on my leg, a vast vagina like healing wound, like a slit. A voice is saying, "Lesimi." With a start I wake up fully; this is Tagore's wound (and, I realize now, Amfortas' and by extension Christ's, from the spear).

I have achieved spirituality (the Buddha or Christos state) but by sacrificing myself, physically injuring myself to the point where death is now a real possibility.⊕ The spiritual element would not die; it would simply as-

---

* Here Dick extends his ecodelic insight to the population of the planet, whose spiritual and ecological destinies have now become one. This "leverage," however, must be recognized and experienced if it is to have any effect. The years since Dick penned this line have been a mixture of recognition and denial. Is it still possible to tune in to Valis's ecodelic frequency? Might we receive the Valis transmission today? — RD

cend out of this world back to its origin and home. But Tagore, my spiritual self, begs for an end to the inflicting of these burns — which (I repeat) I have taken on voluntarily by identifying myself with all life and the suffering of all creatures. It will not end by my ceasing to take on these stigmata; that is not what Tagore pleads for. Tagore pleads for an end of the crimes against life — not my life but other lives — that result in these voluntarily-assumed burns. Tagore — myself — he is crippled now, and yet he emits "an ineffable beauty, absolute, not relative, loving beauty, like music and perfume and colors." Tagore — my spiritual self — could cease at any time this voluntary taking on of the injuries, but he will not; he will die first; to repeat, it is the *injuries* that must stop, not his taking on of these injuries.

Agent Orange and T-2: the day I typed up the Xerox letter. "Wounded and in pain and in mortal peril cries out for our help." The spiritual element in me, making my last appeal.

① This says it all.

[62:C-79] I guess you could say that I have a messiah complex, and because of this am led ineluctably to voluntary crucifixion. To what? Achieve what? Protest the sins of the world. As I say supra: not to be saved — I am saved — but to save, and to perfect myself (vide supra). The drive toward the spiritual so strong in me now that I would give up my life in pursuit of it: for I have experienced the spiritual domain and know its joys. This is *not* anhedonia or masochism; the joys of the spiritual domain — to draw near to Krishna — are beyond all that this world is or has.

I realized tonight — the ecosphere is my body: "the indivisible unity" is my total psychosomatic (mind-body) being. Animals and all less (sic) than human life are my body; and the humans poisoning the ecosphere — this is my mind ("mind" — "human species") poisoning my body by not recognizing that it must live in harmony with it, that they are parts of one indivisible whole. "If the ecosphere dies" means "if my body dies" — "then we (humans) die" and my mind dies.*

. . .

---

* The mind-body split here allows the formulation of two seemingly distinct entities (mind on the one hand, body on the other) to be worked into an analogy of humans as mind, ecosphere as body. Thus the poisoning of the ecosphere becomes the mind poisoning the body, without which it too will perish. Dick realizes, on the contrary, that mind and body are an indivisible whole. It therefore follows that the poisoning of the ecosphere means that it is *his* body being wounded by the activity of other humans, a conclusion consistent with his view of himself as an avatar or surrogate of Christ. The connections here are implicit rather than explicit, but they help to explain why he sees the "investiture by Christ" as the crucial element in seeing the ecosystem as sacred. — NKH

[62:C-82–83] But underneath the *content* of my ideas is the value to me of ideas themselves, of the search (an Orphic idea) and the enjoyment of ideas with emphasis on the abstract, the enjoyment of using the abstracting faculty itself . . . which is when I wrote Eureka.

But it is not the intellect that characterizes Tagore; he is far beyond that. Nor is it love nor beauty, although both are there. It is sweetness, an ineffable sweetness related to love, related to beauty, but perhaps more to perfume, music and colors, as I say in my letter. This is a spirituality that cannot otherwise be categorized and it is this that tells me that his spirituality is absolute, for it transcends love and beauty, the two ultimate ontological categories of God. This is not God: this is a man, a given, individual man; this is not a deity (although he is also — but secondarily — deity), this is the perfection of a man such as *we* are, this is not the "wholly other" toward which one moves in delight and rapture: this is he — as man — who moves *toward* the wholly other — this is what we as humans can become at best, the transfiguration of the natural to its ultimate without ceasing to be natural, a created thing, not creator.

[62:C-85] Who and what is Tagore? He is Tagore (a particular, not [a] God). But I know now: he is either Buddha, the Buddha, or a Buddha (awakened or enlightened one), and this is very seriously considered in *VALIS* as one of the possibilities; e.g., "the Buddha is in the Park." This is not mysticism or metaphysics or theology or philosophy; those have come to me and I enjoyed them, but they pass away and Tagore remains. And his concern is for life, the ecosphere, not a concern for speculations and flights of fancy. Compassion, the way of Buddha, the noblest way of all.

Rejoice!

Everything so far has been a head-trip, a system of thought, ideas, abstractions, speculations, beliefs. But Tagore is a man, a real and actual man. Even (which I doubt) if he is me, why, he is still a man, for I am a man.

[62:C-86] Tremendous breakthrough insight 5:15 A.M. The whole Christian magic of 2-74 on worked *because I believed in it*; but it worked — not because Christianity is true — in contrast to other systems/religions which are false but because Sankara and the Buddhists are right: it is a conjurer's trick; it is magic; and what this points to (the fact that my total belief on that day in 2-74 when I saw the Christian fish sign caused everything that followed to occur) is *illusion*; as I say: magic, conjurer's tricks. Viz: Christianity to magic to conjurer's tricks to illusion. And what does illusion point to? The truth of Buddhism and Sankara; pan-Indian thought about the illusory nature of "reality"; i.e., maya, not as a veil but as a so-to-speak plastic mist that obliges.

[62:C-87] In the face of this, spiritual perfection depends on enlightenment that there *is* a grand illusion, inner and outer; and, finally, the kind of compassion for all the living creatures caught in the "weary wheel" of illusion's karma and rebirth, etc.

    [. . .] E.g., the Υ turning into a palm tree doesn't verify Christianity; it verifies the conjurer's trick and this is pan-Indian thought. So from 2-74 to 2-75 I was in the grip of maya. *But:* because "reality" (sic) obligingly altered to accommodate my belief (especially my seeing Rome A.D. 70 and Syria!) I had without realizing it verified not Christianity but maya as a doctrine. I was totally under the spell of illusion but, paradoxically, this very illusion (I mean the *transformations* in it!) held the clue to the real solution. I have not been radical enough; I have thought in terms of either something (reality) vs. nothing (illusion) but maya is *not* just hallucination; *something* is there (as Sankara pointed out), but it is able to assume any guise it wishes. (Sankara's example: the magician can cause you to take a rope to be a snake, but there *is* a rope there; *something* is there, but not a snake, but also not nothing.) Maya is halfway between hallucination (nothing) and reality (something that is what it seems to be); and *this* is why it resembles *Ubik*.

[62:C-99] I don't know what's the matter with me — the "no-nukes" topic is *the* topic of protest and the new counter culture now, as the Vietnam war was in the 60's and 70's; the Tagore dream places me squarely in the middle of the new, current bipolarized battle — right where I ought to be. And this is what the Silkwood pamphlet must have made me realize, for it tied the nuclear issue in with all that I had to deal with and combat in the 60's/70's; all of a sudden it all came together as a single whole.[33] *Now* the authorities are harassing and trying to silence the foes of nuclear power and weapons and waste-disposal. Perhaps my unconscious knew this; yet — for my coming to see this being part of the revelation of the savior himself — not just a dream about radioactive waste being dumped in the ocean, but about Tagore — this unites my spiritual vision (i.e., *VALIS*) and my *political* vision into one.

[62:C-161] Where Gnosticism is indispensable is twofold: (1) exact analysis of fallen man's condition; and (2) it is 180 degrees reversed by what is called "Gnosis," a *cognitive* event. But their overall system is unsound. Nonetheless Gnosticism contains essential pieces of the puzzle. They have an exact understanding of the malady and also the correct idea that the remedy somehow involves cognition and knowledge and this knowledge comes as a gift from a savior or messenger — i.e., Christ. Thus they fully appreciate what "salvation" refers to, in contrast to which orthodox Christianity is virtually a cargo cult making futile motions that ape without efficacy the real thing.

[62:C-168] I have supra done something never before done: rather than drawing on Gnosticism I have figured out the real teaching of the Gnostics. At some primordial time there was indeed a crisis in the heights, but this isn't what interests the Gnostics; Gnosticism is practical: the Gnostics have studied the *effect* of this crisis and figured out that the intactness of each person in the world is either damaged or abolished (destroyed); each of *us* has suffered a primordial inner schism with the result that any given human self is only *part* of a once-intact greater self. Each of us is alienated from the world (man contra world) because each of us is alienated from himself, not just warring or in conflict: no: the parts of the self have become separated from each other and *because of that,* experience of world is partial, occluded, impaired, deformed. A partial self experiences a partial world, with the result that world is alien, irreal, hostile, strange, arousing perplexity and dread. Man does not understand world because he does not understand himself; thus Gnosticism derives its epistemology (and cosmogony and cosmology) from an ontology of psychology. If the missing piece of self is rejoined — if the severed parts come back together, experience of world — Dasein, being-in-the-world — will take care of itself: the rupture between self and world will heal on its own because now world will be experienced radically differently, 180 degrees differently. Gnosticism has hidden its ontological psychology within a weird and grotesque mythology that successfully obscures both real purpose and real means to that purpose: to bring the two parts of the self back together (the in-gathering of the light by the messenger who is "the savior saved." Clear evidence that this divine champion is the person himself *rescuing himself*).

[62:C-170] The absolutely basic key to Gnosticism is the *encounter with the familiar* in the midst of the alien landscape: the partial self *recognizes* something that it has seen before and yet *cannot* have seen before because by definition this is a fremd (unfamiliar) landscape, not the self: "own." With this recognition comes unavoidable returned (restored) *memory,* which is memory of what it — the self — once was. What it is remembering is its true nature. (The relation to Orphism is obvious.) But it is missing half of itself; it now knows itself to be a partial fragment of a once intact self that is now somehow scattered. Thus although anamnesis is not primary — it is predicated on recognizing something familiar in the uncanny world — it is the *crucial* event, because it is in and through anamnesis that the parts of the self, separated for aeons, come back together. This means that all the pieces comprising the total, restored, intact self are somehow "in" the self in some way, as if split or dormant or mutually estranged. This would explain the drop in GABA fluid, the blocked neural circuitry disinhibited and at last firing. This literally occurs, as an organic, physiological brain-function.

Involved (simultaneously) in this process is an additional absolutely crucial ingredient — event, realization — that I call the "meta-abstraction" and which Plato calls noesis. The partial (incomplete) self on its own cannot perform this cognitive operation because it requires two vantage-points by the participant (what I call *Ditheon*), analogous to spatial parallaxes. That which is recognized as familiar must be, *by definition,* familiar to the estranged, severed part of the total self since by definition it has never been seen before by the conscious self — which is only a *partial* self. That is, for the sense of recognition to occur, the conscious self cannot avoid being aware of its own banished part for it is precisely that banished part that knows what is seen, recognizes it. There is here a hint of the primordial, suggesting that the original schism *did* occur in the prenatal past, as Plato taught. But the situation is more complex, because at the level at which the total self operates, the concept "past" must be redefined. Here Platonist epistemology enters with its forms doctrine. Unless the universalia ante rem[34] are envisioned, what is happening cannot be fathomed. The two parts of the self are not in the same spatiotemporal world. Their relationship to each other comes through — occurs because of — a trans-temporal constant (form) that because it is trans-temporal and -spatial exists "simultaneously" in both realms: the realms *sharing* at least one constant, the one seen and recognized as familiar. It is as if both realms, at two times and two places, are operating off of a common matrix and this indeed is how Plato depicts the forms: they are not in time and space, and somehow instantiate themselves at this time and this place yet without losing their unity and intactness.

Much of this is palpably Platonist and Neoplatonist, but what is truly Gnostic is the idea that the self is fragmented — broken — so that part of it is at one time-and-place and the other part at another time-and-place; thus Gnosticism adds a radical ontological psychological analysis *lacking* in Platonism and Neoplatonism, and, logically following from this premise, a soteriology based on a successful rejoining of the fragmented parts of the self. (Plato and Plotinus know nothing of this.) From the Gnostic viewpoint, each fragment of the broken-apart self is not experiencing world *at all*, in the strict sense, and only will do so when rejoined; mean-while the situation of the fragments is one of alienation — primarily from self, and, following from this self-alienation, alienation from world — or worlds, since both halves of the total self are independently tracking (experiencing) different partial realities connected only by the Platonic forms, which by their nature are in all worlds at all times and places, or anyhow capable of being so. The in-gathering of the self, then, is due *accidentally* to the perceived form (one form seen twice; that is, in two different spatiotemporal worlds) but *deliberately* to the "salvador salvandus," which is the total intact self operating on its own severed parts to rejoin them: external in a real sense, internal in a real sense, since each severed part is external to the other part, and yet each internally drives toward reintegration. Thus each part both internally seeks wholeness and is simultaneously aided externally in this quest by the other part; only when the parts have come together successfully does the total motivation seem internal.

But now rejoined, the two parts become a unitary totality and experience a radically different world than either part previously experienced. Space, time, causation, and multiplicity are gone; what exists now is world as unfallen pleroma, because upon the self being reunified, world ceases to be the alien, irreal pseudo world the parts knew — were "thrown" into. Restoration to and of self and pleroma then occurs here and now (as Plotinus speaks of). This unified world defies normal ordering categories and experiences the Ditheon entity that experiences it. It is familiar, intelligible and permanent and, most of all, permeated by the divine (whose realm it is). It is a kind of after-life world. (The whole is greater than the sum of its parts and radically different than them.) The gulf between "Earth" and "Heaven" is abolished (which explains why the Orphics and Gnostics assumed a literal *spatial* fall!). There is an absolute impression of vertical ascent. But what is most striking is that the "transmundane" deity now reveals its presence in reality precisely as it failed to do so before — hence the Gnostic conviction that it *is* transmundane. This is so remarkable as to defy description.

[62:C-181] Gnosticism *is* virtually a sign-value reversal religion; that is, it assumes the ostensible reality to be a fraud concealing the true story which is 180 degrees opposite — hence the need for the revelation of the Gnosis. Everything must be read backward. We are *secretly* in a giant prison, *secretly* in thrall. There is a deliberate occlusion practiced on us by hostile warders. The truth is not just hidden; it is *deliberately* hidden to keep us in ignorance. Were we to know the truth, all would be turned around, all that we see. There is, then, in Gnosticism a built-in revolutionary, subversive basis fighting the ruling powers of this world.

[. . .]

To reveal is to reverse; to reverse is to reveal; they are one and the same.*

[62:C-183] The quintessential Gnostic vision is not that our world is a prison or that the creator is insane and hence our world is; the quintessential vision is *optimistic:* the luminous messenger has come here and *is* here, invisibly to rescue/save us. Thus we pass over from paranoia and negativism to *soteriology,* the *real* Gnosis! *VALIS,* then, is not *about* Gnosticism; *it is (an instance of) the Gnosis itself.*① I find myself totally convinced by it. *VALIS* is not about our condition; it is about the *rescue* from our condition and hence is a valid Gnostic revelation, indubitably. This is not a book by someone who has read about Gnosticism or knows about it; this book is a Gnostic experience recorded: *Gnostic soteriology itself.* Suddenly the book throws aside its wraps; it is *not* about mental illness at all: it is an account of the Gnostic soteriological reality here (normally invisible) in our world. Our irrational world has been penetrated from outside.

One could make up a novel in which the fallen categories of Gnosticism are shown because (as Heidegger says) these *are* in fact the conditions and happenstance that we do find ourselves caught in. But the soteriological elements are something else because by definition (Gnostic definition) they are transmundane: supernatural in the purest, most absolute sense — and hence play no role in the quasi-gnostic modern existential systems. Thus I could have in *VALIS* pondered the irrationality of world, its prison-like nature, etc. But there would have been no mention of Valis, *nor could there have been.* Suppose, however, upon reading about Gnosticism I had elected to make up a soteriological element. But then we would have had a genuine *fallen* component and a fictional soteriological element, the two

---

* This notion of reversing signs and reading backward comes remarkably close to the position of Ludwig Feuerbach (1804–1872), a German philosopher who helped found the modern study of religion by pioneering its central theory of projection, that is, the notion that all statements about the deity or the transcendent are in fact statements about human nature and its needs, wishes, and fears. In his *The Essence of Christianity* (1841), Feuerbach performs reversals and backward readings very similar to those Dick calls on here, reading, for example, the biblical notions that "God created man in his own image" as "man created God in his own image," or "God is love" as "love is God," and so on. Whereas the later Feuerbach was certainly an atheist and a materialist, it is not so clear that the early Feuerbach was. Indeed, I have argued elsewhere that Feuerbach can be read as a modern Gnostic thinker who sought to reverse and reduce orthodox claims back to their original base in human nature, which he, paradoxically, considered to be infinite and divine. So the divine projection is "reduced" to its projector, who is secretly divine. — JJK

not in any way joining to form a coherent whole. One would truly pertain to world and world-experience (Dasein); the other would be a patent fabrication merely imaginative and, hence, *a grotesque anachronism* playing no role in the lives and experience, worldview and thinking of contemporary man. The result would be absurd: the most critically Valis aspects of human existence would be juxtaposed with bizarre fantasy — and, worst of all, the latter would be introduced to solve the former — with the bitter result that the former (man's thrown and fallen Dasein) would seem just that much more hopeless.

However, the problem (Verfallenheit) and soteriological solution are in *VALIS* a seamless whole. One must either accept both or reject both; they are indivisible. Now, an ignorant reader rejects both as "madness" but this is a faulty solution; he does not know enough practically and theoretically to understand that the former (Verfallenheit) *cannot* be dismissed (the problems stated by Fat and which he seeks to solve and understand). But the wiser reader in facing the reality of Fat's questions and problems — because that reader knows of Heidegger and existentialism in general — now must confront the soteriological solution presented in *VALIS* and consider what it may mean. Here he draws a blank, for as Galbraith pointed out, we have absolutely no vision or concept of — belief in — a transmundane deity. We understand the problem but see no solution; this is either nihilism or leads to it.

What, however, if the soteriological theme in *VALIS* is taken to be as real as the stated problems? This (the reader knows) is impossible. The appeal to his assent can't be responded to, because the reader knows the problems to be unanswerable; this intractability of the Verfallen situation is his (as an existentialist) *fundamental article of faith.* He not only knows that the situation is real, he also knows that by its very nature it cannot be rectified; true honesty and courage and integrity *require* that he take this implacable stand of confronting the is qua is. To start supposing transmundane intervention undoes the very basis of moral values built into his realization: *that* it is a hopeless situation and *that* he faces this absolutely. Thus to him *VALIS* is more dangerous than it is to a more ignorant person who is able to deny or ignore the problems raised as insane, morbid or self-indulgent. *VALIS* is dangerous because upon stating the problem in a modern way, it thereupon draws on a solution so absurd and obsolete that it — the solution — seems to insult the integrity of the very person able to perceive the reality of the problem! *VALIS*, then, aims at the most modern and sophisticated reader and then presents him with a "solution" as foolish as the problems stated are real.

What he does not see is that *VALIS* is written backward, from solution (soteriology) to problem (Verfallenheit). The author is stipulating the problem only to account for the existence of the solution (he has reasoned back *from* the soteriological experience *to* the problem). He knows the solution firsthand and infers the problem using it as his premise. *VALIS*, then, only *seems* to be an existential work; in reality it is a Gnostic gospel.*

   ① It is what it describes — hence self-authenticating.

[62:C-192] Cease to run from your death, turn and face it and make it yours (Eigen), your own, not the it — fremd — of others. When you do this, time (the past and the future) collapses into the present; there is only the now (Dasein); this death is now (spiritually and ontologically) for in making it yours you seize it and master it and assimilate it to you (not you to it); this world is radically transformed and becomes as-if-you. This is the "seizing Fate by the throat" that Beethoven spoke of; it is the epitome of the heroic — not the *tragic!* — it is in fact the heroic *replacing* the tragic; destiny is your victim, not your master: you are the craftsman, it the artifact.

   This is the topic of Wagner's "Ring," the gods against Fate. In it the gods lose. Thus tragedy wins. It need not be so, not for the creative artist.

   The great confrontation worthy of man is between tragedy (the classic and Greek victory by Fate over man) and the heroic (modern and Faustian: the victory of man over Fate) — and this is achieved by collapsing time and space and meeting death now, on your own terms: seizing it, not it you, you die, but it is *your* death, not death imposed on you in violation of your nature; it is a logical outcome of what *you* are, not what world and Fate are. He who can do this has won where in the "Ring" the gods lost.

[62:C-194] I survived 2-3-74 and wrote about it in and as *VALIS* and hence made my death my own — by living long enough to write about it, that is, I artistically and creatively depicted my own death, and this is the victory of

---

* There is no way to overestimate or repeat enough this exegetical fact: *for Dick, writing and reading are the privileged modes of the mystical life.* Writing and reading are his spiritual practices. His is a mysticism of language, of Logos, of the text-as-transmission, of the S-F novel as coded Gnostic scripture. The words on the page, on his late pages at least, are not just words. They are linguistic transforms of his own experience of Valis. They are mercurial, shimmering revelations. They are alive. And — weirdest of all — they can be "transplanted" into other human beings, that is, into you and me via the mystical event of reading. Here, in this most stunning of Dick's notions, the cheap S-F novel becomes a Gnostic gospel, words become viral, reading a kind of mutation, and the reader a sort of symbiote. — JJK

the heroic over the tragic. This is what Beethoven did. I have done it and *nothing* can change this; but if I hadn't written *VALIS* (even if I had lived on past 2-3-74 for decades) this would not be the case. It was *not* the surviving 2-3-74 *but the writing about it* that gave the victory to the heroic over the tragic, as with Bob Fosse in *All That Jazz*.

It is Oedipus or Beethoven: the antique heimarmene wins (tragedy) or the creative human warrior wins (the heroic); this is the past (Greek) vs. the modern world (the Faustian). I chose the latter in 2-3-74 and *VALIS* is the proving of my choice *and* my victory; I willed it and I accomplished it. To do it I had to seize world, collapse time, devour my own death — as if Zagreus ate the Titans!

[62:C-197] Who would guess that the heroic would enter the world as the meek sacrificial lamb? This is not an *orthodox* Christian secret; it is Manichaean. But this — like the kingdom itself — *is* indeed how the heroic drove/drives out the tragic: *it is a strategy that fools all.* . . .

[62:C-201] Viewed this way, Christianity, *and especially Gnosticism,* represents the great revolution in human history that divides the ancient world of fatalism (which included the Greeks) from the modern world of the heroic — even when the heroic is disguised as sacrifice, for this is how it (the heroic) enters the world: as the lamb — i.e., sacrifice.

[62:C-203] The weapons of power — coercive physical power — lose because they inevitably encounter some adversary more powerful. The only real victory can occur by being conquered (as bait/sacrifice: swallowed by evil) and then coming-into-being, at the center of evil, and this is precisely what true Christianity — in secret — has done; thus it is subversive and invisible and at the center of power in its disguised form (mimesis). Evil poses as good; good is invisible within it, unknown to it (i.e., to evil, the BIP). All this is taught in the *Tao Te Ching,* oddly: this is how the Tao works ("a perturbation in the reality field").*

•   •   •

---

* Another "defeat is victory" paradox. Though Dick does not seem to have made the connection himself, these statements are reflective of Martin Luther's "theology of the cross" — the idea that God conceals his glory within the humiliation of the crucifixion. Compare Luther's notion with, for example, Dick's earlier statement in the Exegesis that the deity "will be where least expected and *as* least expected" ([16:14]). Here there is an added level of complication, with the evil in which good hides itself pretending to be good: a classic example of the Dickian "fake fake." — GM

[62:C-219]

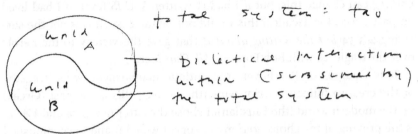

total system = two
dialectical interaction
within (subsumed by)
the total system

Fall 1981

[63:D-47] God gives birth to the universe through his injury, suffering and death; hence Jesus Patibilis. Creating is a giving birth by him and causes him suffering; the Tagore vision shows that the suffering is now so great that he, the creator, *may die* — and hence withdraw from creation and creating, and it is our fault as a species. He has placed himself at our disposal, but, due to our crimes, his suffering becomes too great. He is the great friendly fish in Galina's dream, offering his body to us to eat: this is creation itself: the very world (reality) we live in.[35] It (reality) is an offering, a sacrifice, but we respond wrongly and wrong him. This is not just the Savior; this is God himself, converting himself into world — at terrible cost to himself. (This is, I guess, eco-theology.)

Then my "extra dimension" is the God body as it really is. And we wound it. It manifests itself substantially to us and for us. But is actually insubstantial, an idea; it gives birth to itself in and as the physical, substantial, phenomenal world *for our sakes:* but then we injure and destroy and pillage and exploit and misuse it. Did it not will itself to exist in physical, substantial, sensible dimensions we would be unable to apprehend it. Here is where Malebranche fits in: what we see is a *representation* of something else, but that "something else" is not creation but God himself making himself available to us as a physical body (reality, world); this is an act of will and effort on his part, this self-disclosure to us.[①] And when I saw him in 3-74 I saw him (his body) as it really is. This is a new theology, neopantheism and, specifically, eco-theology. Out of his love for us he receives pain. And tears.

Thus it is not proper to say, "We are occluded"; we see — as reality — what he lovingly makes available of himself to us and for us. My vision of him in 3-74 was due to his own presence in me: self perception by him, a *further* manifestation: one of degree; and, I think, so that he can communicate with us. Especially the Tagore vision. He must make his real self available to us in order to stop the harm we are doing to him. Literally, God appeals to us for help, for medical attention: *we* must aid him, now, not vice versa. [...]

Galina's dream and the Tagore vision are one and the same (and are Valis). This theme of grief, sacrifice, pain, loss, suffering goes back (in my writing) to *Tears* and *this* is what *Tears* is all about. *VALIS* discloses this — the grieving, sorrowing Godhead. But I now see that this comes from its self sacrifice in "falling" into space, time, causality, multiplicity and substantiality for our sakes: so as to both create us and world for us. And the ambience of its sacrifice, its "fall," is in Dowland's music: *pain and love.* (Sorrow and love, which is the same love that generates its distress.) When seen, it is perfect beauty. This is how it "looks." Pain and sorrow is what it feels. Perfect love is what it is. So beauty, love, pain, grief, sacrifice — and to emulate this path is the stations of the cross and our imitation of God himself: we do what he has done and become (remember) what he is thereby. Taking the path *causes* the anamnesis that I experienced in 2-3-74 and this is the true and only real enlightenment. It was known first to Gautama. It is not just Christian; it is also Buddhahood.

Okay. Now I know at last what the significance, ontologically speaking, of suffering is: it is a re-performance of God's original sacrifice for our sakes. Suffering is the cost of — the price paid for, exacted for — the "creation" — i.e., existence — of reality and of us as plural selves. This has nothing to do with evil, sin, etc., but with divine love and self-sacrifice.

Tears is a holy book.

The greatest sorrow of all is *abstract* sorrow: the pure essence of the Godhead. This is found in Dowland's first music that is abstract — and from him to Beethoven. *What this is is cognitive sorrow and is the divine essence itself.* It is pure knowing. It is not an emotion; it is *awareness* of its own essence: two mirrors: sorrow and *awareness* of sorrow, its own sorrow. We must save the Savior: extricate the Godhead from its self sacrifice. "I lead him back to his throne." He/it/she now appeals to us (for help — this help).

I have now herein formulated the basis for the new eco-theology.

① And by doing this he exposes his body to our crimes and misuse; he exposes himself to pain by this disclosure — pain inflicted by us. Under these circumstances *he can be hurt.*

[63:D-149] Now, I came to believe a couple of weeks ago that when loaded I upon reading Luke realized that this was not a verbal (informational) *description* of a world but was that world itself in its verbal/informational mode/state/form. And this is precisely what is said in the "Sepher Yetzirah" notes about idea, word and writing of word, and object being one for God, that for God "idea, word and writing of the word are the thing itself." It cannot be a coincidence that I felt this about Luke, then; I had actually encountered what the Sepher Yetzirah notes declare.[36] This is where my concept of the plasmate comes in. (Here, now, in this line of reasoning I close the noose, for the enhanced "infinity" mode was in fact the world of the Bible, specifically "Acts" — the second half of Luke.[37]) Now, the great intuitive guess on my part was that the plasmate is the blood of the resurrected Christ and that because it is here now (in its verbal/written/information mode) *he* must be here now (1) the world of "Luke-Acts" — is actually here now (2) this world — sacred story/drama — is a story about Jesus Christ who appears in the story as the principal figure: it is *his* story. Thus the telling of the story verbally is identical with what the story depicts: if it depicts Jesus Christ then Jesus Christ is present (in the mode/dimensions/attribute of what I call infinity). Thus (I say) Jesus Christ lives in/as/ through/by the Gospels. According to my theory, what we take to be objects and processes *if seen properly* (all attributes/modes perceived) will form into a gestalt that will authenticate itself as the Christ — and this was precisely my experience in 3-74: I refer to Valis. [. . .]

We are pervaded by a powerful text that is (as I say in *VALIS*) alive and is a living thing — not description of thing. Its cardinal purpose is to apply Jesus Christ as the form (gestalt) to which our seeming reality points. (Our seeming reality, in contrast to Scripture, *is* the description and not the thing described.) To perceive this cosmic form everywhere distributed as how things behave and fit together (that is, what they as information refer to) is to perceive correctly. In *VALIS* I say that the universe is information, and if you read *VALIS* carefully you discover that this information is about Christ or rather *is* Christ writ as large as reality itself. [. . .]

Therefore Christ is present in the macrocosm-microcosm correspondence: (1) as all reality; (2) as Scripture wherever it occurs. I utilize the idea expressed, e.g., in Matthew — and which I believe; Paul often refers to this — that *all* Scripture — that is, the OT or Torah itself — secretly is an account of Christ, and that this secret nature of Hebrew Scripture was only revealed at the time of the first advent. In a certain mysterious way, then, the Torah "encloses" like a shell the knowledge of, the story of, Christ, and therefore *is* Christ (but God concealed this even from the prophets through which he spoke). Thus there is a secret accord between the two Testaments. This is why Jesus had power over the Law (Torah), not the law (Torah) over him; it is fundamental to Pauline thought that Jesus Christ is master not instrument of the Torah, and this fits with my perception of Jesus that day I read Luke: he possessed unlimited miraculous powers such that reality itself (physical law: the moral law of the Torah and the physical law of the cosmos form a unity, deemed heimarmene by the Gnostics) was under his jurisdiction: it obeyed him as a servant. He revealed himself, even then (before the resurrection), as Pantocrator. Having died and been resurrected he vanishes into the very reality of which he is master, camouflaging himself (as Eliade discusses) and lives on in and as that reality in a

certain mysterious way, especially (as Mani taught) in the innocent vegetable kingdom but by no means limited to it.[38] (He has a special affinity to
it because it suffers without causing suffering; it sacrifices itself to feed the
animal and human kingdoms.)

All this was reported — albeit crudely — in *VALIS*. World yields up the
story (as Eliade puts it) and the story is the life, death, resurrection and
then "sinking" into camouflage within world (where he now lives on) of Jesus Christ: world, then, is simultaneously information *about* Christ (it tells
its story) and *is* Christ by reason — by way — of internal arrangement, especially that of the lowly, the vegetable kingdom. (What I call the "trash
stratum," or "debris discarded"; Christ enters world, penetrated it and
now is camouflaged as it, dispersed throughout it and becoming steadily
stronger.) Pere Teilhard did not realize that his Point Omega is something known to and understood by numerous primitive tribes, as Eliade
points out, although to my knowledge Eliade does not note the connection between the murdered deity who returns to life and then teaches man
and then sinks (as it were) into a camouflaged state within plants and the
like — (i.e., reality itself).*

It is very clear to me that there is an identity between Jesus Patibilis and
Hainuwele: "for by feeding on the plants and animals that sprang from his
body, men actually feed on the very substance of the demi-divinity" (i.e.,
Hainuwele).[39] This point regarding the Manichaean Jesus Patibilis escaped
me: here is the Eucharist writ large: all men and even all animals feed on
him and thus unknowingly re-enact the Eucharist, not in church but out in
the world itself!

---

* Does the divine camouflage itself to allow us our freedom? Hegel, whose *Phenomenology of Spirit* articulates the epic quest of self-knowledge through the lens of German Idealist philosophy, scolded readers and told them to go back to the Greek Mysteries if they fell
prey to the world's ultimate camouflage: "the truth and certainty of the reality of objects of
sense." For those who believe that everything simply is as it seems, Hegel recommends that
they "be sent back to the most elementary school of wisdom, the ancient Eleusinian mysteries of Ceres and Bacchus; they have not yet learnt the inner secret of the eating of bread
and the drinking of wine." This scolding, too, just might be an act of agape, as Hegel points
to the same sacred site as Dick: Eleusis, where the quarry, again, would seem to be prior
thought formations that must be destroyed. The Exegesis asks us to look beyond the camouflage of everyday reality toward the One — "the inner secret of the eating of bread and
the drinking of wine." — RD

Fall 1981

[64:E-1] "Luke-Acts" transduced from word mode to object mode but still information: the universe made of information in terms of the internal mutual arrangement of the constituents as a gestalt, pastiche, a collage. Now, the cardinal topic of "Luke-Acts" is Jesus Christ. How (if at all) does he appear in this pastiche/gestalt? He does appear but not in anthropomorphic form; he is camouflaged in and as the *total* pastiche/gestalt, hence cosmic. As information, this universe as pastiche-gestalt read not in a linear manner but as a gestalt (form) reveals or is or contains him throughout like a steady modulation fed into it, a waveform ubiquitous in the gestalt (now construed as a field). This modulation can best be termed "a perturbation (of the reality field)." He is not it but perturbs it.

[64:E-3] Therefore: Christ is hyper information that reduces the information universe to the carrier which he modulates (i.e., perturbs). This brings to mind my "protest art" theory that rogue information has penetrated a prior "official" information system. (This relates to my analysis of Gnosticism as a "weak transmitter" — but this should read "weak interfering signal"; the transmitter may be powerful but very far away.) I conceive of this as a combat between the two information systems, and, if the Gnostics are right, the "weak transmission" that interferes is the true (transmundane) God.

[64:E-5] The universe was created out of 22 Hebrew letters ("Sepher Yetzirah") but there is a missing 23rd letter; when his 23rd letter is added, all the negative prohibitions of the Torah vanish; severe limitation and justice are replaced by mercy and freedom: this is the third *Shemittah* and it is the Messianic Age. Christ, then, can be construed — as rogue information system — to be the corrected, completed basis of creation in which 23 Hebrew letters replace the 22 originally employed. He is, then, an added, formerly missing letter, and this addition *changes everything*, from severe limitation and justice to freedom and mercy; I construe this as nullifying specifically the lex talionis[40] which has to do with punishment in connection with breaking the "thou shalt not" — the negative prohibitions in Torah. Since this carries over into physical law (causation, efficient cause), what was a mechanical system ("pitiless," as I call it in *DI*) would become flexible, able to deal with exceptions: this would require the faculty of judgment, and *this is another way of describing Christian justification.* [. . .]

807

The 23rd letter is not just added on; the Torah returns to its jumbled matrix state and then reforms anew: differently. My God — if you add the 23rd letter you get a broader, larger, more complex, higher, more sophisticated system. Whole new combinations (of letters) would be generated. New *kinds* of situations would arise (analogous to my meta-abstraction vis-à-vis normal abstracting).

The plasmate is this hyper-information (the 23 letter system) feeding into the old rigid, mechanical, limited, fossilized 22 letter system. As the blood of Christ, just as Valis is his cosmic body.

[64:E-10] It is apparent to me now, suddenly, that Gnosticism is — as Jonas makes clear in his analysis of it in contrast to the Greek-Babylonian view of the Kosmos[41] — the absolute theoretical key system that both (1) *described* the entry of the hyper-information into the older, rigid, mechanical system (to combat heimarmene) and (2) that hyper-information (Gnosis) *itself:* as a theoretical system, Gnosticism is/was what it describes. And it *is* Faustian and *it* is (as Jonas says) the basis for modern (post-ancient) man.

[64:E-11] There is essentially an adversary situation between the two info systems (old vs. hyper) even if this is the 23 letter Torah replacing the older 22 letter Torah. The older system involves and operates by heimarmene; the newer system on a flexible, sentient, more complex, more evolved, etc., etc., basis. These are such radically different worlds that — well, the term "cosmos" cannot contain both: it is cosmos penetrated from outside — *hence the Gnostic premise of the transmundane* — a *necessary* premise in understanding the situation: transmundane deity as *overruling* the creator and his creation. At the very core of this lies, then, Faustian man and the Faustian ideal and Dasein; and this is the topic of *Owl!*[42] And as I wrote ultra supra: it is the heroic (the new, the Gnostic, the Faustian) versus the tragic (the old: "sidereal passivity"). This is an issue of unprecedented importance — and has directly to do with Fate (heimarmene), hence the very basis of what the world order is and how it works, and the newer way of being (Dasein) by man in that order.

[64:E-12] You take the text (which is linear, sequential and digital) of "Acts" and convert it into a world: objects in their mutual arrangement. ("Acts" is part two of Luke.) What is the basic story of "Luke-Acts"? Jesus Christ. But when you turn it into a world, although the narrative is still there, Jesus Christ cannot be seen (i.e., as an object among objects). The linear, digital text is now a gestalt (Bild) and is read simultaneously but by the right hemisphere. (The linear digital text of course as narrative is read by the left hemisphere.) Where now is Christ, if not an object among objects. He is missing. Then you discover that in a unified total gestalt (pattern) read simultaneously by the right hemisphere analogically Christ is present *as the pattern itself:* as unified totality. The puzzle is solved. "Luke-Acts" is not a verbal narrative *about* Christ — i.e., referring to Christ — it *is* Christ. [. . .]

This fits in with the intuition I've had for some time: that the Bible is the real world and appears in our spurious "world" as a putative book the way "Grasshopper" does in *TMITHC*. If what we possess in the form of a book (info) is actually a world, then what we experience as world is perhaps only info — a book. Everything is backward.

[64:E-20] I suddenly realize what is necessary in order to apperceive Christ: some kind of runaway positive feedback involving paradox (e.g., *VALIS* is a novel/*VALIS* is not a novel); the flip-flop into infinity regresses faster and faster until at last the outline (of Christ) emerges; hence the paradoxical nature of the parables: they constitute doorways to the kingdom, rather than being *descriptions* of it.

August–December 1981

August 18, 1981

Dear Pat,

I offer the following idea: that what I call "the plasmate," which is living information, is the third testament of Joachim del Fiore which emerges as the spirit of the two testaments (OT and NT) when they are superimposed; it is the spirit of which they are the "hard rind of the letter."

Which is to say, the two testaments are alive and are to be regarded as proto-psyches, with the OT a rigid, archaic Psyche A, and the NT a more flexible Psyche B, which when joined give rise to Ditheon Psyche C, which is the plasmate. So I maintain that underneath, the two testaments are living organisms that create recombinant new information by a process of linking and relinking, such as I saw *VALIS* employing; moreover, this life that I speak of is known to the Jews as Torah (see *The Divine Invasion* as to the Torah being alive). The living cosmic entity, which existed before creation, and for which creation exists and is justified by, is not confined to the first five books of the Bible but continues on through to the NT. It is self-replicating and sentient; it is a life form, and Joachim figured it out (although of course he could have obtained the concept from Hebrew scholars). Thus when you see a copy of the Bible lying on your coffee table you are looking at a living organism capable of growing, of reproducing, of change; like all biological organisms it must maintain a higher level of internal order than its environment, and it must absorb negative entropy from its environment — and indeed it does this, by subsuming its environment into changing arrangements of information.

[. . .]

So my Type A Psyche is the OT, my Type B Psyche is the NT, and because these two testaments function as a single organism in a push-pull dialectic relationship (superimposed) they form one new, higher, third entity which I call Ditheon, a life form so advanced that it is superior to all creation; and yet it itself is not God but is the image of the invisible God. Philo of Alexandria was the first to figure out its existence; he relied on his Jewish sources and on Greek sources (in particular Plato) as well. One could speak of our spatiotemporal world, then, being based on the Bible or even emanating from the Bible; the Bible is not a book like other books: it is not a description of this world, it is the source of this world, and this world, at all places and times, conforms covertly to the Bible; that is, strip away the stegenographic covering from the physical world and you will find the world of the Bible — in fact you will find the Bible itself as a verbal text permeating reality and giving rise to it. The Bible is the information that is fed into the space-time universe, as if transduced into substantial reality. Thus the Bible is always the case — what is known in Bible study as typological application. Thus the books of the Bible do not refer to one given specific place and one specific time, but are equally applicable to all places and all times, when the dokos is stripped away from true reality. Joachim was aware of this meta-organism existing "in" the two testaments, and he was aware that it is a world; that is his crucial awareness; this third entity, this spiritual meta-entity created by an accord between the OT and the NT is a spiritual world in which men exist or can exist or will someday exist; it is somehow real and somehow available. It is both an historical epoch (lying in the future) and yet, paradoxically, here now, as is the Kingdom of God that Jesus speaks of. If you doubt the truth of what I am saying, look at the 22nd psalm and think of the crucifixion; you will see that the 22nd psalm, although written centuries before the birth of Jesus, applies to and exists at the time of the crucifixion; it lies outside of space and outside of time entirely, and is true now as well.[43] This is what led me to reiterate obsessively that secretly "we are living at the time and place of 'Acts'"; what I failed to realize is that "the time and place of 'Acts'" does not refer to a specific historical context, a given time and given place, but to an archetypal reality that is the very basis on which our seeming world is built, and this archetypal reality consists — not of a place, not of a time, not of substantial reality — but information. The Bible is not a world reduced to a verbal description; on the contrary: it is the verbal source of world, just as signals from a radio transmitter are the informational source of the voices and music you hear when you turn on your receiver. But (as I say) three "entities" must be envisioned, not two; that is, not just the OT and the NT; as Joachim realized, these two palpable entities combine to form a third and meta-entity that is to the two palpable ones as spirit is to letter. Thus I say, a single coherent life form underlies the written Bible, and it is the source of our universe, and is itself not fixed into a canon, but constantly combines and recombines, forming ever newer messages. It transacts its informational life and business around us everywhere, as it guides, directs and controls the evolution of the universe, which is based on its own evolution as a biological organism.

[. . .]

Thus the physical spatiotemporal universe is not information, as I declare in *VALIS*, but is derived from information; this information is the next hypostasis up, ontologically speaking. It goes: God, Logos (information), spatiotemporal universe, and then back to God as goal of the whole process (Erigena). In March, 1974, by means of my meta-abstraction I so-to-speak rolled back the physical universe to the Uttered Word underlying it, from which it is derived; this is why, finally, the term "word" is in fact an excellent translation of "Logos." It is as if God spoke (or rather thought) a complex idea, and from this living idea (Logos) the universe came into being, was derived.

This view is a far cry from Burroughs' notion that we have been invaded by an information virus that is making us stupid!

[56:1][44] November 17, 1981

A very valuable dream. I enter a large auditorium like a San Francisco concert hall or opera house. There is an audience sitting. A number of men are engaged in discussion, speaking from different places in the house; they are standing. I assume that an impromptu discussion — argument — has broken out; it seems to deal with Jerzy Kosinski; his name is mentioned. (One of the men, perhaps a teacher or the teacher, resembles Bill Wolfson, so this may also be a courtroom.) I join in the discussion and they all frown; it turns out that this is not an impromptu discussion by members of the audience: these are actors and what they say is rehearsed; this is the drama the audience has come to see and hear. I have done something improper. There is some mention of homosexual intellectuals; this seems to be the topic. Seating myself, I speak quietly to a man in the audience; he has white foam, like milk, like the marshmallow glaze on the candied yams I had last Saturday, around his mouth. I ask about the discussion, which I now realize I am not allowed to join in on.

Analysis: clearly the location is the concert hall years ago in which my agoraphobia/claustrophobia broke out, when Horowitz was playing the Brahms second piano concerto. The friends with me that day were Bay Area intellectual homosexuals.[45] The play enacted, the roles taken in semblance of an actual discussion, as in that Berlioz work I saw where the woman grabs the conductor's arm to make him stop conducting — this refers to what Hans Jonas says about the older Greco-Roman-Babylonian closed cosmos, specifically Stoicism in which all you can do is play your role in a drama with as much grace as possible "and you are your own au-

dience." What I am doing in the dream is — because I do not understand
that these are only roles acted out, a formal drama — I have broken the
rules; I have spoken out of turn, which means that I have unintentionally
rebelled against our status in the cosmos, my own status; they have accepted theirs and only say and do what their scripts call for them to do.
Hence their frowns of disapproval when I join in impromptu. This is rebellion, my primordial rebellion, but as I say it is based on a misunderstanding on my part, a failure to comprehend the situation. When the situation
is made clear to me I lower my voice; that is, I cease to interfere with the
clockwork marionette drama being acted out, but I continue to talk in a
somewhat muted voice, privately, to the nearest member of the audience.
That is, I cease blatantly to rebel, but I am not entirely still. What I am doing at this point is trying to understand what the drama being enacted is
about; I accept the fact that I am a spectator and can't participate; this has
to do with my withdrawn status in life that is my current mode. This status is forced on me because I am literally not part of the drama. No role,
no lines, nothing has been assigned me except to watch and listen. I can
accommodate that only to a point; I have gone from trying to participate
to trying to understand; thus I adopt the mode of a scholar and philosopher, but only because I have been edited out of the drama itself. Spontaneously, I would join in — did join in, but was silenced. This dream tells me
a lot about my phobias and my rebellion. My rebellion is based on a misunderstanding on my part as to what is allowed and what is not allowed. I
had naively thought we were free to say and do anything we wanted; that
is, I presumed what I call the "open" or Gnostic or Faustian cosmos. The
true situation reduces me to spectator, but this is not my first choice; this
is forced on me by the nature of the situation (the closed cosmos in which
as in Stoicism people simply act out their assigned roles, say their assigned
lines). Yet I continue to speak, although not as part of the drama; I do not
interrupt it but I ask about it; I seek to understand. I am barely willing to
refrain from entering the drama — which would mean now to break the
rules knowingly, whereas when I broke the rules before, I did not understand the situation. In the dream I feel no phobic anxiety at all, which is
strange; it shows that the issue is not fear but freedom, the freedom to
say and do what I feel like. I have been told what my place is. I accept it,
but not entirely. "Homosexual" in the dream signifies something, probably an odious play that is being performed. Not only am I not allowed to
participate, I dislike the subject matter: homosexual intellectuals. It is a
drama I don't like and I am not allowed to enter it. I have no role at all, in
any drama; there is just the one, and it is alien to me (hence the "teacher"
looks like my attorney; this is an adversary situation). (I have no under-

standing of adversary situations, as I've long realized.) The dream has profound Gnostic implications; the whole situation is the Gnostic appraisal of
our lives here: assigned roles in an odious drama, that is, a drama inimical
to our real natures. It is a vast enactment of something unnatural. Audience and players alike collude in something that should not be. This is not
my drama; had I been allowed to participate I would have disrupted it because I would have spoken contrary to the purpose and spirit of the drama,
the only drama going on. This is not my world (in the dream I entered the
auditorium from the outside, from perhaps a transmundane source, if indeed, as I suppose, this auditorium represents our world, the audience and
actors humans living here, acting out their lives as mere roles in a closed
cosmos or what they accept as a closed cosmos). I am a disruptive force, an
outsider, silenced by disapproval, by mass censure. So I will seek to understand, since I cannot participate. This "seeking to understand" is my exegesis and my decades of epistemological analysis. I am like a visiting sociologist, like Margaret Mead investigating a foreign culture. This is not my
home; these are either homosexuals or at the very least they take homosexual intellectuals to be important. I would say that this dream verifies
that 2-3-74 was the Gnostic experience. From that moment on I was able
to create a role for myself, rather thus my condition of Geworfenheit was
reversed, nullified, solved. There are profound overtones of Existentialism
here, especially from Gnosticism. The dream presents the paradigm of the
Gnostic perception/conception of Dasein, in particular being thrown or
cast into an alien world; moreover, the dream shows that my lifelong streak
of rebellion is because this is an alien world to me, and, because it is alien,
I don't know how to behave; I do not obey the rules and conventions because I do not understand them, since they are alien to me, and the drama
was going on before I arrived here (i.e., was born). My rebellion, then, is a
confirmation of my Dasein as basically Gnostic; the rebellion stems from
Geworfenheit and the Fremd and Unheimlich. I have gone to a lot of trouble to accommodate the situation; I have ceased interrupting the drama by
trying to join in — I now understand that it is a drama and that these people are playing roles assigned to them — but I am not entirely silent; my
"rebellion" which is not truly rebellion but seems so (since it is disruptive)
has turned into scholarly analysis, an attempt on my part to understand
this alien situation of which I have only very partial knowledge. I must ask
questions if I am going to understand.

The discovery that what I took to be an actual discussion is in fact a
drama in which actors play roles could be regarded as a fundamentally Gnostic discovery. There is something rehearsed and unreal going
on, a simulation. I think this dream is telling me that my analysis of last

night upon rereading Jonas' study of the contrast between the pre-Gnostic worldview and the Gnostic is correct; my situation is Gnostic indeed, hence my worldview — and my problems! — arise from this situation. That my primordial phobias could arise from the Gnostic condition of Geworfenheit never occurred to me; I guess I could now view my phobias as verification of Gnosticism. Also, this makes clear that 2-3-74 was some kind of rectification of this estranged, alienated, thrown condition, perhaps related to Heidegger's Ur-Angst leading at least to Authentic Sein. So the dream refers back to the last insight that I had while driving on Sunday night: that my status in the 2-3-74, that in fact this is what 2-3-74 was all about. And it was as if the cosmos itself had changed to accommodate me (I suddenly realize); I may have changed, but it seemed as if world changed. ("A perturbation in the reality field" refers to an event in world itself, not in me.) This is impossible; i.e., that world changed to accommodate me so that I was as a result of this radical change no longer a stranger here; it became my world — and my anxiety, which tormented me every day and night, departed. (It has never really returned, except briefly when Doris was in the process of leaving me.) Good Lord! Is this not impossible, that world changed to accommodate me, in order to repair the gulf, the discrepancy, between me and world? Only God — i.e., the Pantocrator — can make such a change! Surely — logic says — it was I who changed. But all of a sudden I fitted in; and I had the distinct impression that world was sentient, animate, unitary, conscious and purposeful; it was immanent deity or something . . . anyhow I saw transformations in it, and the AI voice backs this impression up. In any case, world and I became harmonized (harmonie, harmonia) for the first time. So at the very least there was a radical shift in my role, my status in the cosmos, of a sort that did not seem to stem from an internal adjustment in a closed system but seemed, rather, to be the result of something entering from outside — that is, something transmundane. Beyond doubt there were changes made in me: drastic, radical, extraordinary changes; that is certain . . . but it did not seem to end there; world itself changed (or at least my experience of world, my Dasein). It was as if the past had been tinkered with so as to cause the present to be different; I was a different person, etc. And my sense that I had either two sets of memories or else altered memories. It is clearly Heidegger's transformation by means of Ur-Angst to Authentic Sein but with cosmic, transcendental, religious overtones — and that precisely is Gnosticism (since Heidegger's categories are derived directly from Gnosticism!).

[. . .]

A final point: the world transformed from the unfamiliar to the familiar — this cannot point to a psychotic break, for in a psychotic break this is all reversed: the familiar becomes the unfamiliar. So much for the "Horselover Fat is insane" theory. In 2-3-74 came comprehension and recognition; there also came the end of—the healing of—the gulf that separated me from world. This is 180 degrees away from psychosis. Viewed psychologically, this is, in fact, a healing; it is repair.

[. . .]

The dream certainly sheds light on the real purpose of my exegesis. My working on it is preceded by a serious—even potentially disastrous—event, one forming the very basis of my life or at least the core problem of my life: expressed in the dream as a drama that I do not even understand as drama, in which I try to involve myself, only to learn that I am disrupting it, intruding on it—I have no role to play in it, and am to simply be a silent spectator—which in fact (in my actual life) I could not do; that is, for whatever reason I could not sit silently watching and listening while other people acted out their lines, played their parts. I wanted to play a part, too. This was denied me. The psychological gravity of this situation arises from its existential gravity; it is truly a grim matter in terms of one's life. Consigned simply to watch and listen while others act and speak? And not even to be able to understand what the drama—i.e., life itself—is about? This is intolerable and it is against this that I rebelled, from the start. This is my story: starting out trying to involve myself as a participant in life, then finding out that there was no role for me in the drama (of life); whereupon I sat down and began to try to figure out what the hell the drama was all about. I gave up trying for a role, an acting part; I settled for an understanding of what was happening. This is the next best thing. It is not ideal but it is at least a way open to me. I would not be rebelling if I tried to comprehend the drama I was witnessing. This would not disrupt it. However, 2-3-74 radically transformed the situation; the drama became comprehensible to me and, moreover, I found that I did have a role to play. But this role is predicated on the drama becoming comprehensible to me. My being able to understand it, due either to my own cognitive powers or simply to the drama itself being, as it were, open, is the absolute prerequisite. At the heart of the matter, at the core of my psychological and existential difficulties — that have plagued me all my life — is the fact that, very simply, I started out misunderstanding what is going on. My god—this is the Gnostic ontological condition of ignorance! Oh my god! Oh god; I am back to Gnosticism; the ontological category of ignorance, which is the basic ontological category, was reversed for me in 2-3-74; ignorance turned into its ontological opposite: knowledge. And because I now knew, I could act. Incomprehensible world became comprehensible world, in a single stroke. This is, then, Gnosticism, for it is only in Gnosticism that the categories of ignorance and knowledge possess — are seen to possess — this absolute ontology. Every bad thing stems from ignorance, and restoration consists of a diametric reversal of this condition.

[...]

My exegesis, then, is an attempt to understand my own understanding; I was correct in my recent letter to Russ concerning *VALIS:* in it I am thinking about my own thinking. I possess the Gnosis and am analyzing it, since it is essentially internal to me, now; I possess it and am turning it over and over, scrutinizing it from every angle. The Gnosis, for me, is not in world; it is in my mind. Thus I analyze and study my own thoughts — the quintessential example being the meta-abstraction itself. My mind performed it but I do not really understand this that my mind did, this abstracting, the ultra-sophisticated cognitive act. The problem in a sense lay in my mind (i.e., I was ignorant) and the solution, when it came, occurred in my mind as an act, an event, inasmuch as virtually nothing occurred in world, except, of course, my seeing the Christian fish sign. But that only served to disinhibit what was already in my mind blocked, buried, latent, dormant, slumbering; the fish sign awoke me.

There is, then, in me — and was from the start — the potential ability to solve the riddle of the drama (i.e., life, the world-order) that I am perceiving. Hence anamnesis was and is everything. I know, but do not know what I know. Hence I resort to the metaphor of the two-mirror runaway positive feedback in which I the observer observe myself (in world as Other), which sets up an endless regress, but it is this very regress that transforms the ontological category of ignorance into its opposite, knowledge. And thus reverses the primordial fall — my own fall and the fall of much more besides.

The mystery lies in me, then, and not in world; likewise, the solution lies in me and not in world. At my core there is something that is me and yet not me. Thomas is an example. Am I Thomas? Is he me? Hans Jonas says: "It is between this hidden principle of the terrestrial person and its heavenly original that the ultimate recognition and reunion takes place. Thus the function of the garment in our narrative as the celestial form of the invisible because temporarily obscured self is one of the symbolic representations of an extremely widespread and, to the Gnostics, essential doctrine. It is no exaggeration to say that the discovery of this transcendent inner principle in man and the supreme concern about its destiny is the very center of gnostic religion" (page 124).*

---

* This quotation is from Hans Jonas's *The Gnostic Religion* (1958), an important overview of Gnosticism that shows the force and persistence of the idea of enlightenment by a ray of divine light. For Jonas, this direct contact with the divine divinizes the soul in turn and allows it to see the vile world for what it is: nothing. At the core of Gnosticism, for Jonas,

[. . .]

Cognitive estrangement; that is the key. And the rectification thereof. This is the goal; this is the mystery. This is Gnosticism as problem posed and resolution offered. The Gnostic assumption is that cognitive estrangement exists until rectified, and that the person is dependent on an outside source to rouse him to awareness of his state and to reverse that state. Upon it being reversed — ontological ignorance transformed into ontological knowledge — that person's status in the cosmos, his existential basis within the cosmos as part to whole, is drastically and radically reversed, transforming not only his perception of the world-order and his ability to function in it, but also his perception of his own self. In the final analysis it is not world that he now knows and knows correctly; it is his own self. Thus the motto of Apollo finds ecstatic glorification and in fact deification in Gnosticism: "Know thyself."

[. . .]

To recap: it is the perception of isomorphism that overcomes cognitive estrangement because the perception of isomorphism is a grasping by the person (part) of his compatibility with the whole (Other, cosmos). This perception acts as two mirrors act: a runaway positive feedback is triggered off in the person, the part, concluding with his reincorporating into the cosmos — which is at the same time a repair — a return, if you will — of cosmos itself. Since he is now inside the cosmos rather than an external spectator to it — in fact now that there is cosmos — he grasps it from within; thus he perceives what Spinoza calls the attribute of mind, the inner side of res extensae (the outer side). This perception of an isomorphic constituent common to self and Other (world, cosmos) is known in India as the "Tat tvam asi" perception of the Atman-Brahman identity; it is a universal experience. It is pure knowing — as contrasted to belief, even correct belief — and, most of all, it is return.

This is also precisely what Heidegger describes as the condition of Greek man before "the darkening" in which Logos became merely some-

---

is an experience of nihilism, namely, the view that the phenomenal world is nothing and the true world is nothing to be seen phenomenally, but requires the divine illumination reserved for the few. In the epilogue, Jonas shows how postwar existential philosophy and particularly the work of Heidegger can be seen as the modern transposition of this Gnostic teaching. Here the world is no longer the creation of a malevolent God, but simply the series of phenomenal events that are causally explained by natural science. Of course, these explanations don't solve the problem of nihilism; they shift and deepen it, leading the modern self to oppose itself to an indifferent or hostile nature and to try to secure for itself a space for authentic freedom. For Jonas, although Gnosticism embodies a powerful temptation for a soul thirsty for God in the desert of the world, it is a temptation that must be refused. For Dick, things are not so clear. — SC

thing he had, as with Aristotle: a set of propositions about reality. Thus in
terms of Western history man fell out of the cosmos somewhere between
the time of Parmenides and Aristotle. Exactly as Heidegger says. And into
the vacuum there came, of necessity, Stoicism. Cosmos was not merely no
longer perceived — it was by definition gone. (Viz: it is only there if perceived, because it is a relationship: between the whole and its parts. Thus
in a certain real sense what I saw in 3-74 came into existence only as and
when I experienced this; yet although this was finite in terms of space and
time, during its existence it was, paradoxically, infinite and eternal.)

If cosmos can be reconstituted by anyone anywhere at any time it always was, is everywhere, and always is. In saying this I am not describing
an attribute of it but, rather, its nature. It needs to be only once to always
be. That is, if it can be at all it is (a version of Anselm's ontological proof of
the existence of God).

[. . .]

Here my study ends.

Except to add: My god; each step is a further fall. (1) Up to Parmenides
is an intact part-whole true experience (Dasein) of intact cosmos. (2) Aristotle to the Stoics: there is no longer an actual experience of cosmos, of the
part-whole relationship in which man is inside the cosmos; there is only
faith that cosmos exists and it is good and wise, a belief-system replacing actual experience; that is, knowledge about the previous stage. (3) A
further fall (i.e., the Gnostic Dasein). No faith, trust, the sense of the benign — all are gone; the world-order, still putatively believed to be a cosmos, is regarded as hostile and alien; thus estrangement is complete. Yes;
here cognitive estrangement is so vast that there is conscious recognition
of it; efforts are made to reverse it, i.e., to acquire the Gnosis. And I could
add (4) where these efforts are abandoned, this occurring upon the death
of the Gnostic attempt to reverse the state of ontological ignorance for ontological knowing. Oh Weh! The fall worsens! And yet I reversed it for myself. And what is the role of orthodox Christianity in all this? It is a pistis
system; hence it fails to perceive the problem as one of cognitive estrangement: thus it neither seeks to nor succeeds in bringing about a reversal of
cognitive estrangement. Like the Stoic system, it consists of a series of dogmatic beliefs; propositions assented to as creed! This is of no help whatsoever! To affirm loyalty to a series of propositions — this is precisely what
Heidegger means by "the darkening"!

[56:G-6] In a sense (I realize) I am concerned with the absolute only insofar
as it has to do with Cosmos.⊕ Since I am concerned with this life — hence
the cosmos — and not the next (if any). The adjustment — radical adjust-

ment — of my status within the cosmos (in 2-3-74) discloses two things: (1) there *is* a cosmos in the strict, precise Greek sense; and (2) there is a regulator, which I conceive to be an absolute. These realizations fill me with joy.

① This, then, subtly shifts my interest from theology to that which is properly the object of scrutiny of science (in the broad sense); it has to do with this world, the organization thereof, and what organizes and regulates it. This brings me at once into contact with modern physics; so this is not an idle, world-denying evasion of reality but, on the contrary, a rational attempt to understand it.

[56:G-35] But I think the element that is the greatest shock *is the recognition of the familiar,* as if (or even *because*) all else stems from it. "Familiar" and "change is only seeming" are two aspects of one fact. (This is true, really, of the other realizations: the illusory nature of space, time and plurality; there is really only *one* realization — that of the familiar — but it has implications in all these other areas, space, time, change, multiplicity.) The reversal, then, of what I call "cognitive estrangement" to "cognitive affinity" has precisely to do with this familiarity: how can you be estranged from what is familiar? And ultimately it is your own nature that you know, since for this unitary, eternal, unchanging "thing" to be familiar, there must of necessity be a *you* to which it is familiar: a you who saw and knew and understood it before; so now you understand that there *was* a you and there *was* a before — but since time and space have been abolished, "before" either means nothing or it means something quite different than is usually meant — as I pointed out in my two February '81 postcards. That "you" and that "before" are a fortiori and perforce *now* and here (hence I experienced a massive time dysfunction and with it a collapse of causation). As a result of all this the holy, the dimension of the sacred flows into the profane/ mundane world.

[56:H-10] This business about the atomists suggesting that the void between objects is the is-not: is it possible that before the atomists there was *not* a perception of plural discrete bodies, i.e., res extensae as we all now experience world — that in fact we as a civilization inherited as a way of experiencing reality the atomists' way? Not just as a philosophy but a way of actually *viewing* reality? (This is in sharp contrast to Parmenides specifically, who experienced a field.) And that now, due to post-Newtonian physics, we may be able to *reverse* this perception and return to a field perception instead? And this would collate with the time that Heidegger assigns to "the darkening"! And that *this* is what happened to me in 2-3-

74; after all, due to the Taoist influences on me I was conceiving of reality as a unified field when I wrote *TMITHC* with internal acausal connectives — what I believed, I finally experienced, and the entrance for me lay in
two "areas" as keys: (1) my unusual sense that space did not exist; and (2)
neither did causation.

[56:H-23] When I saw Valis I also saw the sentience (Noös) which the
view of the atomists had *logically* driven out of the universe, by showing that consciousness and perception are epiphenomenal; therefore the
atomists were materialists of necessity. So when I perceived and comprehended the universe as a continuum, it was a *thinking* continuum, as it
had been for all the pre-Socratics prior to Leucippus. One view (atomists) must of necessity deny Noös, but why does the continuum view imply noös? Perhaps the answer is: noös is there — in world — but the atomist — discontinuous — view prevents us from perceiving it . . . because our
worldview literally *prevents* us from seeing what is there: the voluntary
sentient cooperation of "things" (which aren't things in the atomist's discontinuous sense); we see pool-ball Newtonian causation instead. Thus
my two early satoris were logically and structurally related: having to do
with space, having to do with causation. This all pertains to the discontin-
uous-continuum alternatives: "the void" not only *permits* pool-ball causality — the random collision of atoms by blind necessity — but *requires* it,
by the very nature of the cosmology/theory that causes us to experience
this worldview. Dasein.
    So if you experience world as continuum, noös or God or Logos or Tao
or Brahman would naturally flow back in, as it were; whereas in the atomists' discontinuous world of atoms and void this is logically of necessity excluded. And yet in this century — and only just now! — modern theoretical
physics has verified the continuum view — and sure enough, some of the
physicists involved are noting how the Tao or Brahman (Noös?) fits in.
    The ecosphere is a continuum, and the apperception of it as a unitary
whole is tied to this vast transformation in worldview found in physics.
And *it is alive and thinks.*

[56:H-25] To hold the continuum view of the Eleatics satisfies two quite
different criteria: (1) it is a return to Heidegger's unity of noein and einai
before "the darkening," i.e., to Parmenides' worldview, so it is authentic
Sein; and (2) it is in accord with modern physics, so it is verified, and it
is not abreactive.[46] Then the "darkening" is ending (and I see in this the
"third dispensation" regarding the ecosphere, a concept only possible in
the "continuum" worldview). [. . .]

The void-atoms view is the decomposing cosmos that Christ reunites (in and as the ecosphere continuum view).

The atoms-void "cosmos" is not a cosmos at all.

Continuum — idealism — God/Noös
Discontinuous — materialism — blind necessity

I saw the new cosmos.

[56:J-6] He has ensouled the biosphere as a whole. The logos, penetrating it, endows it with reason; thus it now uses language (logos = word = language). This is the greatest evolution since creation — Genesis — itself; man as a species now ascends to a totally new level of intelligence, such as I experienced in 2-3-74. This will permit an articulation by the ecosphere that *we* will hear. This has never been the case before. I am saying that we will hear the voice of the ecosphere and we will enter into dialogue with it; Dio! "The voice of the ecosphere"! "We will hear it." This is Pere Teilhard's noösphere; could this be the AI voice? The biosphere? It is not a disembodied voice or mind but speaks for all the creatures; this is Tagore. Is the AI voice, then, Tagore? Or, put another way, when I saw Tagore did I see the source of the AI voice?[①] This may be a *new* entity, since prior to this the ecosphere *had* no voice, for it did not possess the logos. The logos penetrates it, ensouls it with reason, and it (the ecosphere) speaks; to repeat my insight of Saturday night: the creator has now granted speech to the animals — i.e., the ecosphere. Then can it be said that Tagore *is* the ecosphere?

He has ensouled the biosphere with reason. Thus it can now speak, to him and to us; this is Tagore. It can enter into dialogue with us and with him.

The conflagration of the world foretold as its eschatological fate ("last time water, next time fire") is what I saw; but God out of mercy sends his son into the world once more, to enter the ecosphere and to plead for the world, *that it not be burned up;* thus the world is to Tagore as man was to Christ! It (mankind) faced destruction but God intervened, and both times *in the same way:* as voluntary sacrifice and surrogate, taking the burns as stigmata upon his own body so that the world will be spared as, the time before, man was spared. Thus Tagore is world's advocate as Christ was man's; God sees not the lowly earthworm, but sees Tagore, his son, and hears Tagore's voice which is the voice of the earthworm, the ecosphere itself. *This* is why the animals have been ensouled with reason: *so they can ask for help.* They have been given the gift of speech so that they can articulate their needs and plight to the creator. Then it is not just *we* (humans) who hear Tagore but God hears him, too; God primarily. He (Tagore) is mediator between the biosphere and God, in his role as logos.

The attempt by the animals to speak that I saw in 3-74 is fulfilled in and by Tagore. This is an evolution primarily of great mercy by God for the creatures (and it *does* show up in *DI* in the scene with the dying dog).

The dog run over and dying in *DI* is Kevin's cat in *VALIS* — here lies the ultimate enigma and the solution. *This* is what God must respond to, and he does so by sending Tagore. Tagore, then, is the solution to the axial problem formulated in *VALIS*. I have received my answer and it is not theoretical; *he is here: the AI voice said so.*

① The AI voice may be a new voice, not Ruah and not the Holy Spirit, but Tagore, the biosphere, who is Tagore, whose voice we hear and whose voice God hears; what I hear, then, when I hear the AI voice is what God hears. It addresses me and it addresses God. It is to God as Jesus is to God, him and yet not him. Tagore exists separately in his own right, as Jesus did.

[56:J-29] We are embedded in a tremendously elaborate biosphere or even noösphere (as Teilhard calls it) *already,* but cannot discern it due to our discontinuous view of reality, our materialist-atomist blindness. Were it to signal us we would most likely experience — or rather *seem* to experience — the sort of uncanny "one-way" information intrusions such as occur in *Ubik*. *It* is aware of us and our involvement in it, but *we* are not; thus, where it deliberately signals us we would note the signal and react appropriately but have no notion — nor even perception — what — if anything — had done the signaling. Thus (probably) we would experience what Bishop Berkeley speaks of as the impression that objects seen are "in" our eyes rather than spatially removed. [. . .] It would be as if the visible (or anyhow palpable) signal came out of an invisible yet tangent — i.e., immediate — source. But the problem stems from the very basis of our "discontinuous" worldview; signals and especially information would seem to arise (1) out of nothing; and (2) immediately at hand; as I say, as if "in" our own percept systems, yet at the same time partaking of Other, of the external. It would be a paradox, and one only solvable at the most fundamental ontological level of world experience; we would have to learn to see (or "see") what is in fact there in what I call the "Eleatic continuum" worldview in which the void is denied: viz: there is no such thing as "nothing."

You could even reason that it would be this impinging of signals and information *at* the sense organ itself, out of (apparently) nothing that would be our clue to the inadequacy of our fundamental apperception of reality, like the frogs KW speaks of bopping against what for them is an invisible wall — because they have no template for "wall."

How if at all would this differ from an hallucination? I believe that hallucinations appear organized in space-time; they are governed by the Kantian categories. They are projected sources. But here, information arises *at* the sense organ minus a palpable source. One supposes that one sees X or hears Y, but in what I'm talking about this is precisely what is missing; therefore the signal or information is de facto *uncanny,* being causeless. The problem is not that you see and hear *but that you do not.* There is a blind spot, *an omission.*

The "logic" of the discontinuous reality system denies that there can be anything there: only the void is there — hence, as I say, the stimulus seems as if it arises *at* the sense organ or in it or directly tangent to it (and not in space-time). Not only is there no way to tell *what* the signal (stimulus) is arising from. There isn't even a *where.*

[56:J-34] Πρόνοια (Pronoia): affectionate behavior by world. (Αγάπη [Agape]) strange orthogonal thought, following the sudden thought, "all this — my research — is sterile (i.e., cold, devoid of feeling)."

[56:1A] 2-3-74 was: I was not just in contact with God — I was in the mind of God, Kosmos Noetos[47]: world "became" the preexistent eternal ideas. Then I realized myself to be equally eternal — an eternal notion in that mind.

This is the whole explanation. [. . .]

The exegesis was *not* a waste of time; I came to understand noesis, the use and the cognitive function, the pre-existent ideas, the basis of it all being mind, intellect, forms, logos, idea, *ideas — eternal and unchanging including myself — in God's mind,*[①] hence world to be truly known must be *intelligibly* known, because it is an interlocking set of ideas in God's mind. This is the key to it all.

① This is where anamnesis and meta-abstraction become (revealed as) one and the same operation: (A) pertaining to world; (B) pertaining to me as an equally eternal and unchanging idea in God's mind.

[56:19A] The intellect — as opposed to the senses — can know the true nature of world — not because of some occult power in the intellect — but because the true nature of world is intelligible *in itself* (as the Pythagoreans taught: ratio and mathematical truth, not a substance but structure). There is, then, a one-to-one correspondence between the human intellect and the true nature of world, and this explains the meta-abstraction: why it revealed the true nature of world to me (and my own nature to myself). The true structure of the universe is cognate to human reasoning, and this is the paradigm of Pythagoras and his insight upon hearing the anvil struck. Thus my exegesis with its emphasis on the reasoning faculty, the meta-abstraction, the overcoming of "cognitive estrangement" is by no means a waste of time or a blind alley but is pure Platonism, the meta-abstraction being noesis acquired through anamnesis. One might even say that the meta-abstraction is not only a revelation of *how* the universe is constructed but *that* it is an intelligible structure and *that* the human reason is able to comprehend it — and it is precisely this that overcomes "cognitive estrangement" by yielding up cognitive comprehension as the final yield pertaining both to self and world: the part-whole relationship. Thus it is taught by Plato that there is a spark of the divine in the human soul.

[56:1B] December 12, 1981

Though he seeks to sell his (Satan's) power fantasies (*Blade Runner*) he unknowingly promulgates the Third Kerygma: the ecosphere (animals) is now ensouled: holy. [. . .]

My god, this movie is the greatest defeat (what was done to the book) and victory (the Tagore kerygma promulgated); the first is ostensible, the latter cryptic. Oddly, the first appears ostensibly to be a victory but is really a defeat; nonetheless a real victory lurks secretly under it, but it is not the victory that people will think the making of a movie from my book is. They will say, "It is a great victory to have your book made into one of the biggest movies of all time," but they will not know why; it doesn't have to do with what is in the movie, etc.; it has to do with what is in the novel. [. . .]

The beetle I was tormenting back when I was in the third grade — I saw it as holy, as Christ. Later the turtle was Christ. The rat who screamed was Christ, and appears as such in *Tears*; this is the revelation in *Tears* by means of the dream: the rat ensouled and now King Felix: Christ. The crippled lamb who lagged behind. Pinky as pink sheep humiliated and killed. It's all in *Androids*, and finally the Tagore vision explicates what was already in *Androids* as doctrine, and in *Tears* as revelatory cypher. The movie is defeat; the novel victory, ostensible vast loss, secret good shining almost invisibly from beneath this defeat, these fascist power fantasies they've made it into. Evil has served good; evil appears to win but it is good that actually does. [. . .]

The Tagore vision is a summation of all that has gone before. Looking at Pinky there toward the end and seeing the passion, seeing Christ humiliated and dying — that was not one vision among many; that was not an aspect of a vision: that was the core of it, the beating heart of it all; when that is coupled with the revelation of the Logos in camouflaged form invading reality (the ecosphere) and transubstantiating it — add these two together, and there it all is. This is not quite the same as Jesus Patibilis; it is a new revelation of something dynamic: a process of conquest. Ah; last night I saw in my mind the Godhead moving into the animal kingdom, and I saw the vast joy that the Godhead experienced in receiving that fallen, lower kingdom (domain) back; not the joy of and by that kingdom, but the joy of and by the Godhead; the Godhead moved into that lower kingdom and inhaled it, drew it back in by it — the Godhead — advancing into that lower, fallen kingdom long separated from the Godhead; and what beauty! The colors, the love; bliss itself, by the Godhead, to receive back that domain with all the life in it. This was a vision of what I had seen in 3-74 of Valis (the Logos) invading reality; there I saw it with my outer eyes, externally, but last night it was an inner vision, and I had forgotten it until this moment; I experienced the joy and love on the part of the Godhead to do this thing, not what was done for the animal kingdom but what the Godhead felt. Colors, as Dante describes the Trinity in Paradiso: the varicolored rings of light; I saw that like rings of Saturn advancing into the animal domain. "The love that moves the sun and the other stars" — it had regained the lost animal kingdom; and this is my vision going back to the beetle I was tormenting in the third grade; it is one vision extended over all my life. And I found it in Act III of *Parsifal,* the Good Friday Spell. [. . .] As the EB says, To see in an old dilapidated bum the Christ; that is the Christian Dispensation. But I see in the sick, humiliated, dying animal the Christ, literally saw; and this is the Third Dispensation, the cat crapping and wild, and then all of a sudden tame and wise, like a saint; it was the Christ and this is a new dispensation, Tagore's. Before it was, Where the man is, there is Christ. Now it is, Where the animal is, there is Christ. To see this and understand this: for this I was fashioned from the beginning; for this I was made. My original satori regarding the beetle was the true one; everything else only amplifies. [. . .]

A strange and mysterious strategy: to put the new kerygma in a novel published in the late sixties but then disclosed to me only now, toward the end of 1981, but just at the time that we get the signed contract with the *Blade Runner* people to rerelease the novel in conjunction with the film — as if the *VALIS* trilogy has diverted everyone's attention, my own included, like when the thought came to me that the true message was in "Frozen Journey" and not in *VALIS!* The true message is not in *VALIS,* but it is, I now think, in *Androids* and it will have the greatest circulation — probably — of all. Viewed in terms of God's strategy, *Blade Runner* has been used as a means to an end, the end being the kerygma in *Androids.* Thus to have suppressed *Androids* and either written or authorized the novelization based on the screenplay would have been to hand over victory to evil, but this did not happen. The fully executed contract between *Blade Runner* and me regarding the rerelease of *Androids* was waiting for me in my post office box on Friday, the day I was up in Venice and learned the truth.

To share — experience — the joy by the Godhead as it invades — expands into — the animal kingdom, lost to it all these many millennia! The repair to the damaged Godhead! Yes, it is a self-repair, a reinhaling, a recovery of part of its lost self. Christ reknitting the decomposing cosmos and restoring it to God. Christ moves lower and lower, deeper and deeper into the decomposing cosmos, down layer by layer, starting with man. Thus the vision of Christ at and in the trash layer (stratum) is a vision of ultimate and final repair.

Why am I so joyful? I am celebrating a victory and can now stop work — finally — and relax. Why? Because I did my job and I know it. What was the job? To get the third dispensation in print, and I did so in *Androids* — I need do nothing else in my life. The Tagore vision: the Godhead expanding into the ecosphere (animal kingdom).

Okay: there are other aspects. I didn't sell out to Hollywood: (1) do the novelization or (2) permit the novelization; (3) suppress the original book. And in view of what the film is about, it would have destroyed me for *two* reasons, not one: (A) the Tagore vision in *Androids;* (B) the Heinlein power fantasies in *Blade Runner.* These are antithetical: and they express the opposing kingdom's Christ (*Androids*) and Satan (*Blade Runner*). Look what it would have done to me spiritually and psychologically and politically. My soul is safe, and it was in jeopardy. This is why I see victory despite the vast defeat.*

---

* Novelists have always wrestled with the great Selling Out to Hollywood Moral Dilemma, but I'm not sure any have ever escalated (or plunged) it to such a metaphysical (or hysterical) paroxysm. These passages are also at odds with claims made by others that Dick told director Ridley Scott the movie was exactly the way he imagined the novel; clearly he had other feelings. For better or worse, however, there's no underestimating the impact of *Blade Runner,* not merely on the public recognition of Dick but also on the perception of his writing. The movie gave a visual identity to work that never was especially imagistic (*Flow My Tears, the Policeman Said* comes closer visually to *Blade Runner* than does *Do Androids Dream of Electric Sheep?*). Even for those readers who were familiar with Dick's work before the film, recollection of his books now takes a visual form that is equal parts Dick's imagination and Scott's advertising background in London. In a way that, of all people, Dick might understand — that what's perceived is a collaboration between who has created it and who has perceived it — Dick himself has become a collaborated invention. All that said, and his histrionics aside, props to Dick for the artistic integrity and courage to resist Hollywood's efforts to usurp the original novel and re-"novelize" it. — SE

December 1981

[55:L-18] I have it now:

Buckman	Jason	Alys
Claudius	Hamlet	Gertrude
Pentheus	Zagreus	
Pilate	Jesus	
Tears	Joy	
Old	Young	
Usurper	Rightful king	
Tyrant	Liberator	

What is being studied? A usurper is on the throne. The rightful king (who is younger) appears as a madman, criminal or fool; he is mysterious; his nature and origins are uncertain. He is arrested and tried. (I should say *falsely* arrested.) Interrogated by the old king (usurper). He is charged with a crime he did not commit. The resolution varies; sometimes he is acquitted and assumes the throne; sometimes he is killed. The white-haired old king on horseback may be the murdered father of the young man who is the rightful heir to the throne; he returns to seek justice: punishment of the usurper; the son placed on the throne. This story is told and retold. Why? What are we supposed to learn? That the ostensible ruling power of this world is illegitimate? The "King" is *not* in fact the true king? And the "fool" is not mad or a fool or a criminal but is the rightful king? My analysis: everything we see is a 180-degree mirror opposite of the truth. The ostensible "king" is not only not the true king, he also has no *actual* power: despite appearances his power is illusory.* All true power belongs to the "fool" who is the true king (vide *The Bacchae*). This is all some sort of play—which *Hamlet* very clearly alludes to. We are to guess the riddle: Who is the true king? (And hence, who really rules, i.e., who has power?) This strikes me as some sort of religious pageant or initiatory rite or ritual

---

* Picking up again on the theme of tragedy, here Dick discusses *Hamlet* in terms of the duality between the usurper king (Claudius) and the true king (Hamlet himself, both the murdered father and the mourning son, who share the same name), who is "mad" and a fool. It is not difficult to imagine some identification between the character of Hamlet and Dick himself; after all, "mad" Hamlet declares that the world is a prison (act 2, scene 2). And the idea of a usurper on the throne is consistent with the Gnostic bent of Dick's worldview, where the false king of Empire has marginalized the true king through an act of murder. Dick identifies a similar dualism in the opposition between Pentheus (the illegitimate king) and Dionysos (the true king) in Euripides' *The Bacchae*. — SC

into a hidden truth deliberately concealed from the many. Only what are called "the elect" are let in on the true state of affairs. Who, then, qualifies as one of "the elect"? Perhaps one who before (i.e., without) knowing the truth, reveals *his* own true nature; that is, faced with a moral choice, even though he is deliberately misled as to the actual situation — that is, who holds power, who does not — he chooses correctly nonetheless. Once he has so chosen, the masks are dropped and the true state of affairs is revealed to him.

[. . .]

Oh Dio — I just put together several extraordinary theological ideas. On November 1 when I had that psychotic anxiety and had to have Tess and Christopher come over — I realized then that hell consisted of a state of absolute self-awareness of what you had done — forever; that is, you accused yourself and found yourself guilty — and then had to live with and as that guilty self forever. Last night I dreamed about Harlan Ellison and realized that about him: he'd have to exist throughout all eternity with and as Harlan Ellison.

But now, suddenly, the significance of *justification* occurs to me; in the light of the above it assumes the absolute quality that Paul and the Reformers assigned to it. Justification is, as it were, the sole, the real, solution to — the saving you from — hell, precisely as Paul and the Reformers taught. Since hell as a state is absolute, and justification is absolute.

Well, this idea is not new or original but, rather, my first understanding of sin, hell, salvation, grace and justification! As orthodoxy regards all these. Justification *saves* the person who otherwise is doomed; he does not save himself (e.g., by good works): the power to save lies in God. Thus, if indeed it is the case that in 2-3-74 I was justified, then though my own conscience accuse me, I am not merely *called* justified but am, through God (God's grace) saved in fact — I mean, *justified in fact;* I am changed through Christ. Jesus Christ, then, is paradigmatic of the saved/justified person, who was often called by the Reformers "a Christ" and I think correctly: it is almost a technical term, not just a compliment. So much more than pronoia and astral determinism was involved in 2-3-74; they were, but far beyond that lay justification stemming from the same source: charis: God's saving grace.

If we are indeed here in this world, as I suspect, to be fashioned and shaped, to become (our einai established forever), then justification is the finishing of this, the sudden perfecting, and is the logical outcome of what we are here for. God has judged, closed the books; the person has been made by God acceptable, in the twinkling of an eye. Now my statement that "PKD now (12-81) is very much what Thomas was in 3-74" suddenly tells me that it is all okay: Thomas was my justified, perfected self, and thus I evolve (thank God!) toward becoming him more and more: *he was the future.*

[55:L-35] I just remembered (5:45 P.M.) a right-hemisphere graphic image in hypnagogic sleep last night: I had been thinking about the two coaxial worlds in which one — hidden — is Christ's kingdom. All of a sudden I saw a network of red threads forming a vascular system, as in our bodies; at the same time this was also a growing arborizing vine constantly becoming more and more intricate; and it was like the mycelia of a mushroom. This intersticing arboring network (I realized when I saw it) grows invisibly within our world, and this is what I saw as the plasmate, Christ's blood as living information — literally saw. But here now I beheld it as a network, a structure so-to-speak "invading" or internally penetrating our reality invisibly, and ever growing and becoming more complex. This is *both* Christ *and* his kingdom, and in 3-74 I had done a set-ground discrimination of it — this is what Jesus meant when he referred to himself as the "true vine" and it is the vision I had that day at the dentist's. And this fits with Valis here (i.e., Christ) camouflaged in our reality.

Then all portions of the plasmate form *one* organism or entity, and the living information does not pertain to it but *is* it, *is* Christ.

[55:3-2] We are told in the synoptics that indeed the secret is kept from the many and revealed to the few; this is explicit. As the operation of heaven is for the nepioi and ptochoi and not for the proud (i.e., all others) it follows that only the former will *ever* know that the answer to the *Tears* riddle is the case. Here is why: if all people understood that by following Jesus' teachings — which seem to be self-sacrifice absolutely — one acquires the support of the absolute power of heaven, then self-interest not morality would impel men, all men, to follow the way, and summarily the moral aspect would be engulfed by the pragmatic and practical, and an ethical system would succumb to the degradation of personal ambition. Thus the "secrecy theme" is simply unavoidable.[48] There just plain is no other way that it can be done. Hence the stegenography, the veiling, is essential to the situation to a degree that by the very essence of logic admits of no mitigation or compromise. The way now *will* seem folly but *must* inexorably and inevitably seem so. Thus the apparent failure of Jesus and of Christianity and the apparent non-occurrence of his return in glory — this fiction *has* to obtain. The prophecy and promise of the return in glory (1) had to be made; and (2) appear *not* to be fulfilled. Then the fact that it is always and eternally in fact fulfilled is the ultimate secret of the way, second only to the answer to the riddle posed in *Tears*.

[. . .]

To reprise, "Christ's return in glory" is a disclosure rather than a historical event, and the ubiquitous false notion that Jesus failed, his ethics do not work and he did not return not only must be the case but in fact serves as a top-level agency, agent and instrument of the very system that is doubted. The doubt is necessary to it, serves it, is subsumed by it, even *generated* by it. The system is in absolute control, and *utilizes* this disbelief — and this disbelief can only be abolished as a result of moral action and never before that essential moral action; it is not just allowed: it is (I think) imposed as a necessary condition that the moral act be possible. Thus it is hopeless for me to expect to convince anyone of the truth of my revelation in *VALIS* because this is not how it works. This is not how it *should* work. This is not how it *can* work. My error is to reason: (1) Knowledge of the truth. (2) Then as a result, right conduct. But (2) would have ceased to be based on free choice, true ethical decision, and would be merely smart. The act would be done for tangible reward, and this has nothing to do with morality and ethics. Right action must bear the stamp of folly, self-sacrifice and, finally, madness itself. For the first time in my life I understand the necessity of what I have long identified as a vast, deep and powerful cognitive and perceptive occlusion.

[55:X-4] Last night at Juan's the God told me: "You are now permitted to be happy (Felix) at last." The God brings joy into the world and overthrows the reign of the old, former King of tears; it is the procession of the ages from iron — Pentheus and the BIP — to gold: Zagreus-Jesus in the Garden and the animals. The newborn King who "will wipe away every tear." As I realized, Christianity is *secretly* a religion of ecstasy, and that was my turning point.

There is a thematic link between *Tears* (the NT and Dionysus story), *Deus Irae* (Christianity), *Scanner* (two personalities), *VALIS* (two personalities, Christianity), *DI* (the Savior, Judaism) and BTA (Christianity and two personalities, Bill and Tim, if not three: Christ also, and the Dionysus story). Six novels linked together. The most interesting link is the two personalities link in *Scanner, VALIS* and BTA. People will see this, but few will see that it also begins with and in *Tears*. If you study these six novels as a unity — and this is my third period — you discern a fascinating story not really clarified until BTA when at the end Christ emerges explicitly. (One could even argue that *Confessions* is part of this in that Jack Isidore and Bill resemble each other — whereupon it is at once clear that a fortiori *Androids* enters via J. R. Isidore — which takes us at once to the sacredness of the animals and Mercer.) This last is important. The nature of the truly human stands, then, in this complex eight volume meta-novel as a midpoint between the android (e.g., Rachel Rosen) and the divine (Mercer, Bill at the end of BTA). What strikes me most forcefully is the very great importance that *Androids* had in this eight volume meta-novel: what if we had *not* reissued it? It is an *absolutely* essential component, perhaps the most important of all, but in itself alone not in any way expressing the full meaning; only when linked up with BTA does the meaning become clear (and vice versa in terms of BTA); that is, BTA only assumes its full stature in significance when viewed in conjunction with *Androids:* the theme of the madman and the holy fool in the love for and care of animals all at once stands out sharply. (When we first encounter Bill, he is the 180-degree mirror opposite of the Rachel Rosen and the spider scene in *Androids* and linked to it necessarily through J. R. Isidore.) Amazing. [. . .]

Perhaps most important of all, if one traces the holy fool from *Confessions* to *Androids* to BTA we see him at last, at the very end, reveal his true nature and identity as that of Christ: it is not at all there in *Confessions;* it is *somewhat* there in *Androids* — in which he *meets* the Savior, Mercer; but in BTA the long-awaited revelation at last comes. *Who* and *where* is the anticipated Savior spoken of in *VALIS?* In and as the holy fool first brought to our attention in *Confessions,* just as the fool, with no religious overtones. In *Androids* the holy enters, in and as Mercer (linked to the animals); and in BTA the supreme mystery is revealed: we had him — the Savior — with us from the start, as Jack Isidore. The link — absolutely necessary — between *Confessions* and BTA is *Androids* and again I say, what if we had suppressed it? Had we done so, the intact story would never have been told: from fool (nut) to holy fool (loving and innocent) to Christ himself. This is a vast theme and very complex, but also very clear: it is quite coherent.* [. . .]

---

* The very fact of Dick's obsession with forming this overview of his work is noteworthy: though I question whether it's healthy — there's a point beyond which a novelist is better off not thinking too much about what he's doing or why — in retrospect it's astonishingly prescient; we know that in a few months Dick will be dead. Did he sense it as well? Is the pell-mell urgency of the Exegesis driven not only by madness or revelation (whichever you believe) but by a ticking of the universe's clock in his ears? The ego behind all this is off the charts and accounts for how Dick can formulate a cosmic view that places himself at the center; without it, however, we probably wouldn't have *Flow My Tears, Scanner Darkly,* or *Transmigration,* never mind the Exegesis (which was more crucial to its author than to the reader). So the flip side of what must seem megalomania to a reasonable person is the au-

But there is a point I am missing that is substantial and crucial: the axis of fool–holy fool–Christ completes itself not by evolution but by virtue of the fact that the fool, proven holy, is seized by Christ entering from outside — as perfectly expressed in the John Donne sonnet that Angel thinks of — significantly! — when she first sees Bill (". . . unless you ravish me"). Christ *enters* the holy fool and takes full possession of him, consuming him utterly, and this is the explanation and the event both that is the 3-part axis. Bill is not Christ; Bill is seized on by Christ and *taken over* by Christ; for a while there are two selves, Bill's and the extrinsic "intruder." And, at last, only Christ. This *clearly* relates to Dionysus, but that seems of lesser importance to me now. To repeat, the holy fool neither *is* Christ or *becomes* Christ; he is invaded by Christ as the Holy Spirit, and *this* is the miracle, and this it is that is the end state of what we saw in *Confessions* with no hint that it would end this way! Now, the trick starting this would be if one read *Confessions, Androids,* BTA and *then VALIS,* for having absorbed the idea of this axis and seizure, what would one *now* make of what *VALIS* narrates? Why, this very seizure that is put forth rather sparingly at the end of BTA! The total analysis and presentation of the mechanics of it, as it were. The seizure step-by-step with all its ramifications, appears in *VALIS* — and so, to put it another way, we now understand what *VALIS* is all about, then! And after all it really was the purpose of BTA to explain *VALIS.* But there is a thematic link between *VALIS* and BTA I've failed to note: Bill is insane, and *Horselover Fat* is insane; so Fat is another avatar explicitly of the fool, holy fool, madman, Christ. But if *VALIS* is viewed *after* one has studied *Confessions, Androids,* and BTA the results are amazing as to what *VALIS* really depicts — and it, more than the other novels, is clearly autobiographical, and perhaps not a novel, not fiction, *at all.*

[55:Z-2] I had the strangest insight after seeing *The Elephant Man* that for some reason I failed to write down. Viz: we are not linked to world directly as:

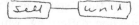

but rather:

---

dacity on which nothing less than artistic survival depends, the defiant assertion that, in the face of his own obscurity, in the course of a life during which the Library of America hadn't yet found the foresight or cultural imagination to acclaim him (and wouldn't for another quarter-century), he mattered. — SE

That is, there is world, objective and substantial and real, but between us and it there is God, so that we receive world *through* God. This makes it possible for God to control and arrange how we experience world, what in world strikes us forcefully — that is, God acts as a *medium of selection* in our apprehension of world so that for each individual person world is not only experienced uniquely (differing from person to person) but uniquely in *purposeful ways:* certain elements stressed, others suppressed — this especially has to do with information patterns that impinge compellingly (or, conversely, not at all). Now, this *resembles* Malebranche's epistemology somewhat, and yet is crucially different. Viz: God and world are clearly distinct.

What emerges here (in this theory) is a totally new explanation of 2-3-74. Either there was *massive* selecting (for a time) or I became *aware* of massive selecting, that is, aware of the medium as interface between me and world (i.e., such massive selection *always* goes on, but we know it not, supposing all we experience to be properties of world and applying to the encounter with world by all persons uniformly). Now, a powerful but by no means invincible argument can be offered that due to my meta-abstraction in 2-74 (that is, due to a sudden titanic insight) I comprehended something about world that makes it possible for me *on my own* to fathom the presence of this selecting interface. The meta-abstraction would (perhaps) then have been that there was a pluralized signal system at the point of origin (world) but that only one set normally reaches me, which says a lot about world, but also presumes a selecting interface. Thus "world" is radically redefined but, more, the interface is realized and its selecting (suppressing, enhancing) activity, and this is God (Valis). So what comes of this meta-abstraction pertains to epistemology ("ti to on?" in terms of world) but yields up by implication a much more radical notion — that in fact world qua world is less an issue than the interface itself that lies between us and world and passing the power selectively to determine what of world impinges on us and what, contrarily, is suppressed — whereupon (I think) I found myself *dealing with the interface itself,* and this is theophany. As if, upon my becoming aware of it, it could then "speak" as it were explicitly, by means of open enhancing-suppression patterning, which clearly did not emanate from and in world but existed between world and my percept system.

It is possible that world qua world consists of eternal constants, and the interface modulates our reception in extraordinary ways and to extraordinary degrees, e.g., your "being" in A.D. 70 in Syria or USA 1974 depends only on the interface, on its selecting. World and interface, then, are *quite* distinct. Malebranche's epistemological premise, then, is quite the case: "We see all things in God."

• • •

A strange insight last night (hypnagogic). The person who — there is some relation between intelligence and the empathic facility. But when I was tormenting the beetle and understood, that understanding (which I have called satori) was due to God's grace. For that knowledge cannot in fact be known. There is no active (rational) way that I can know how that beetle feels or even that it feels; I know by the grace of God; it is a gift conferred on me, as were the later satoris. This is the activity of salvation. The prison of the isolation of the atomized individual is burst through the grace of God by this knowledge. And he who has this not is not evil but deprived. And he on his own cannot change his situation, for there is no rational way — only a supernatural way — that this knowledge can be obtained. I must not blame someone who possesses not this knowledge, for there is no way he can obtain or acquire it on his own; he is totally dependent on the grace of God. Here is where the original satori is as the 2-74 meta-abstraction was. But this shows that although the 2-74 meta-abstraction had to do with cognition it was given to me from outside, which brings me to the issue of Socrates vs. Jesus that Tillich speaks of. Reminding the person (Socrates' route) and what is already in him; or Jesus' way (midwife, as Tillich puts it).

It is not probable that the meta-abstraction was truly an intrinsic (internal) cognitive act on my part — either viewed in isolation or in relation to the sequence of earlier satoris. All one knows is that one now knows what one did not know, but not due to ratiocination, due rather to some element *outside*. And this is the key clue: *outside*. But I figured out last night that we do not know world directly but through God as lens link interface. So the stimulus in outside reality affords God the interface the opportunity (to use Malebranche's term) (no: his term is occasion) to transfer knowledge pretextually, as it were. This is in conformity with my whole conception of clutch, selection, enhancement and suppression and not a special situation, only — as Joyce calls it — an epiphany of regular conditions. It is as if the pretext is clearly only pretext. Effect — that which is known — far exceeding its ostensible cause. As to the transfer of information regarding Christopher's birth defect, the situation is clearly and explicitly such that it is palpably impossible that insentient plural objects can give rise to the information, in which case something is there that I have always spoken of as camouflaged in and as ordinary plural insentient objects.

These various situations that I denote here are differing versions of one enduring underlying stable situation that by its very ubiquity escapes our notice. Thus beetle, meta-abstraction, and Valis informing me of Chrissy's birth defect are in fact one and the same experience along an axis of revelation as follows: (1) With the beetle there is no reason to suspect that the knowledge does not arise naturally (unaided) from the ostensible situation; cause (the situation) and effect (the knowledge) seem commensurate. (2) In the meta-abstraction the effect exceeds the cause/the situation outside me, but it is not at all clear where the knowledge is internally retrieved in me (Plato's anamnesis) or transferred from outside. (3) But in the situation regarding Chrissy's birth defect there is now no doubt that the information (knowledge) cannot arise from or be accounted for by the situation (i.e., the Beatles song, etc.). In this case the satori I experienced regarding the ending of *The Elephant Man* is a satori concerning satoris: not only is it perfectly clear that the knowledge is transferred from outside (it is external in origin, and a free gift) but that the source is not in world but as-it-were between me and world so that I am dealing with world indirectly but dealing with the interface (by definition) directly. This precisely agrees with Nicolas Malebranche. What is now disclosed was in fact the state all the time, but behaving so as to conceal itself and in fact its existence.

At this point it is clear that there is now the resolution to my total life-long epistemology which strove from the start to resolve the issue of δοκος (dokos). It reaches the conclusion that while world exists it is per se unknowable to us, but on the other hand we immediately know God — which is Malebranche's contention. Now, a verification of this is the infinitude of space that I experienced in 3-74: I was encountering not the physical world in space (extension, res extensae) but the infinitude of God. But here the problem and issue of epistemology collapses into the matter of grace.

Because the power to bestow and withhold knowledge of what is truly there (the answer to "ti to on?") is to say God, and no activity on our part will in itself *ever* unravel the mystery. (The nature of the situation dictates this, and Kant seems to be the first thinker systematically aware of this.) If on our own we try to plumb — or even discern — the interface we enter an infinite regress — as I've discovered for almost 8 years: since the interface is not so much:

but:

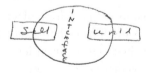

Which is to say that the interface is somehow in us and in world; so the interface simply recycles our own mind back to us over and over again; the prison gate of isolation — of the atomized self — closes once more (this is dealt with in "Frozen Journey"). Thus we know others only through the grace of God (as in the beetle satori), and this pertains of salvation: to know others — just as hell pertains to isolation. Then knowledge of God as other is knowledge of ultimate other and is the triumph and consummation of the axis of salvation that began, for me, with the beetle satori. If ἀγάπη (agape) equals empathy then there is only one road to salvation; in its partial form it deals with and pertains to finite creatures (but is real): in its complete form (absolute, realized form) it pertains to God; this is an axis. What and who one has loved in world ("love" here being ἀγάπη) has *always* pertained to God; it was always God who was loved, so that in the end all that was lost — all that was known and hence loved — is restored in and as God.

I *never* would have come to these realizations except for Malebranche. Then upon seeing the film *The Elephant Man* figuring out the interface. Then, last night, realizing that all my satoris, back to the first, the beetle one, are due to grace and involve knowledge — correct knowledge — that by its nature can only be revealed; whereupon I now see one vast axis of disclosure from the first (the beetle), culminating in 2-74 and then 3-74, and then tapering off in subsequent revelations. 2-3-74 — and specifically Valis itself, in me and in external reality, centering around the transfer of information about Chrissy's birth defect — then is the quintessential moment in a pattern of revelation predicated on grace and involving salvation stretching out across my entire life. What, then, I have viewed as a preoccupation with epistemology turns out to be a search for — and a finding of — God.

[55:Z-8] "A long extinct true cosmos and it's still there." AI voice: hypnogogic.

"Extinct" must mean: in terms of our ability to perceive it.

[55:D-70] Dio. Eureka. I found the —

Christic Institute.[49] All the way back to *Tears*: the "Acts" material, the dream, the King-Felix cypher. Karen Silkwood.

The Parousia is here and the Holy Mother Church knows it. My 2-3-74 to 2-75 experience (back to '70 if you include *Tears*) has to do with the Parousia. Eleven years and at last I hold it in my hands and it *does* have to do with Pere Teilhard. My Tagore vision is authentic; Christ is here. Point Omega.

[. . .]

What — I think — is the most exciting is that due to 2-3-74, my Tagore vision, what Victor Ferkis has said and the Christic Institute, I can now discern — albeit dimly — *the outline of a new theology*, rooted in the epoch we are moving into. It is a Christian-Buddhist neo-pantheism very close to Pere Teilhard's Christocentric Point Omega, but having specifically to do with the unitary ecosphere — and for me, closely related to Malebranche's Cartesian pantheism, which of course goes back to Augustine and Pauline mysticism — and may also include the new physics and field theory, a merging of science and theology in defense of a palpably *living* universe. (There may also be an information and a Platonic component.)

I feel confident now that my 2-3-74 experience is *not* reactionary but is carrying me into the future — a vast quantum leap from political action to one colossal metaview of reality that embraces the political and the spiritual, the scientific and the religious: what for me personally may be the quintessential summation of my entire life of inquiry and worldview; for me and for mankind a new age is opening in which the holy, expected from the top, so to speak, returns at the bottom, at the trash stratum of the alley, humble and noble, beautiful and suffering and alive and conscious, personified in and by my Tagore vision.

If indeed it is the triumph of Christianity to dignify the lowly, here now is a whole new leap along that axis: the lowly snail darter becomes identified with suffering ubiquitous Christ and by being assimilated to him is glorified as if nature itself — and the electronic environment of info and signals and message traffic — is able to perish and be resurrected as and with the cosmic Christ (Jesus Patibilis) of Pere Teilhard. Thus Christ extends even beyond the reality of the organic to bits of newspaper and song lyrics and random pages of popular print: one vast entity that evolves and thinks and has both personality and consciousness. It perfects itself and includes us all, subsuming and incorporating progressively more and more of its environment into arrangements of information — which is to say negative entropy: this is, in fact, a runaway positive feedback loop of greater and greater complexity and organization.

Malebranche is not only compatible with this neo-pantheism — more: it is a highly sophisticated modern-day version of how God can be here — all around us — and we be yet unaware: that is, he is everywhere yet unseen. Malebranche's mystical pantheism is the philosophical explanation of eco-theology. In other words, Malebranche is the *how* and eco-theology the *what*.

[55:D-84] Thus what I have been trying to do in the exegesis — and which exhausts me — is *deliberately* on my own part again to do what I did in 2-3-74! But *that* was sparked by the messenger, and now I have him not. Hence I simply become more and more weary as world becomes more and more powerful over me. I seek to regain, to recapture, the Liberator of 2-74 to

2-75 — whereupon world regained its power over me: the vision was lost and I fell back. I do not seek to gain Gnosis and liberation but to *regain* it; I had it and *lost* it! This is why trying to write *Owl* broke me: it is this that is the topic of *Owl!* Although my effort *seems* cerebral (having to do with thinking) it is really existential — but failing.

Cerebral = knowledge = Gnosis; typically Faustian, as in Goethe's *Faust*, part one.

VALIS built the maze and fell into it. The maze changes because it is alive.

It is alive because it draws on and from the very thoughts of the creation trapped in it; his efforts to solve it are thoughts, and it is these thoughts that "fuel" it — i.e., it is one vast Chinese finger trap; the harder I try to get out, the more powerful world becomes. Hence hex. 47: my increasing exhaustion. What, then, should I do?

[55:D-85] I was treated to a demonstration of YHWH: thought, word and reality were one, with no ideation separate from the word and no difference between the word — what I said — and the deed; it *was* the deed. Moreover, there was *absolute* a priori knowing (about Denise, about Tess). And this unitary "thing" (thought, word, act) is his power (omnipotence). He willed it so, by the use of Holy Wisdom, a separate hypostasis who is never apart from him.

[. . .]

The really extraordinary thing [is] that although I was terror-stricken I experienced absolute lucidity; I saw and understood my *total* situation perfectly, without degree and without reasoning it out. It was utter knowledge. I was — had been — destroying that which was of most value to me in the world: Tessa and Christopher: *they are all I have.* However good or bad Denise is intrinsically: that was secondary and tangential: God summoned me back to what was morally right and what existed: it was right and it was real. I had been occluded and severely jeopardized this most precious element in my life. This was no vague intimation; YHWH summoned me back from the lip of the abyss. What I stood to lose by my wrong actions *was that which my very physical life depended on.* I was on the brink of literal doom, yet *indirectly* so: Denise would destroy me not by what *she* did but by what *I* did. There was in this a vast *moral* summons, for in Judaism, God and morality *are one and the same.* This was the Lord God of Israel, not just a vague God but YHWH — and I knew it. This was the God of the Torah summoning me back to moral reality, with no choice; he *willed* it; he commanded me to return to life and what was right. (In him and by him the two are one and the same.) Thus morality and that which gives and sustains life stood bipolarized to immorality (sin) and that which *takes* life. Sin and death, then, were one. I sinned and I died. Abandoning Tessa and Christopher meant my death. Moreover, he gave me words to express all this to them (rather than just an understanding of it) so deed was conjoined to knowledge: what I knew I did — act and cognition being one, as morality (the law of God) and life were one.

[. . .]

It was 3-74 all over again, but with moral overtones. Carried beyond the irresistible to the *terrifyingly* irresistible. In this case I had fallen into mortal sin (this was not the case in 3-74; there I was in peril but not in peril of mortal sin); I could, then, lose my freedom or life, but here I lost my soul; I not only doomed myself — I *damned* myself. Here, power and wisdom prevailed; in 3-74 knowledge and love prevailed: this yesterday was YHWH, not Abba.

The situation was intricate, unstable, ambiguous. There was a single right choice and it had to be made then and no later. God made it for me, based on his wisdom, power, and because it involved morality, goodness (as exemplified by the law). Thus, having justified me in 2-3-74, he forbade me from sinning any further; he intervened absolutely.* [. . .]

This was an invasion of my psyche by absolute knowledge. It bore no relation to what I had up to that moment believed, wrongly believed. There was not even a sense of insight, of satori: it was pure knowledge, like a sort of seeing: a vision of the situation as it actually was. And it was primarily a *moral* seeing. Absolute moral rectitude occurred in me. It simply took place. All at once it was. I guess I saw it as God saw it. And how different that was! And absolute! It was not a viewpoint. It was *knowing*.

What I have been calling "the meta-abstraction" is in fact knowledge — the act of knowing — as God knows (i.e., knows what is, i.e., world). In 2-74 and more fully later in 3-74 I saw as God sees and understood as God understands, that is, *absolutely* and a priori, in which what is *known* is exactly the same as what is; they are assimilated to each other. That the mind of

---

* In early November 1981, Dick made a difficult personal decision, choosing to stay in Fullerton to be near Tessa and Christopher rather than moving to the Bay Area to continue a relationship with a married woman. This decision is framed here in terms of biblical morality. 2-3-74, he says, transformed him into someone who could not continue down the path the relationship was leading him. Though elsewhere Dick is deeply concerned with free will's absolute victory over determinism, he presents this as a decision made by God on his behalf, asserting that he really had *no* choice. Compare this with his statements on the assistance he gave to Covenant House, which he described as a "new act" not governed by normal rules of incentive or even causation. In any case, it's clear that Dick believed that a pre-1974 PKD would have made a very different decision in this situation. — GM

God was at that time in my mind — I experienced that as Valis in my mind. All that I saw (Christian apocalyptic world, the plasmate, set to ground, the prison, the secret Christians, the abolition of time — i.e., coaxial reality and the conception/perception of eternal constants) — this is how God sees; I did not see this or understand this; God saw and understood this, and, as I say, I saw and understood because he bloomed in my mind like cold white light (hence I experienced an infinitude of space).⊕ I realize this due to Sunday night when the same absolute knowing by God in me induced a realization of my practical and moral jeopardy. Again there was certitude — total, unconditioned knowing — but what I knew this time was dreadful and lethal to me practically and spiritually. Once again the unitary fusion of knowing and doing occurred because for God there is no distinction between what he knows and what he does. Ratiocination — logic itself, thinking itself — does not occur because it is not required; God does not figure out; he does not reason because he does not *need* to reason.

It was — both times — as if my mind expanded into infinity (conceived as spatial infinity). The sense one gets is that one's mind contains all reality, and this is because all reality is known a priori and absolutely, not sensibly and contingently.

[. . .]

I guess for a moment I was plunged into hell and discovered what it consists of: one is given absolute moral insight into one's own sinful nature, and there is no way it can be rectified; it is now too late; hence hell is eternal. This is clearly and obviously the just punishment and the logical punishment: absolutely (by the knowledge of God's own mind) to see what one has done, illuminated by the divine light that reveals all. This is total knowledge of the situation and of oneself. It can be awful. By this divine illumination one's cognition/perception condemns one; this is absolute self-condemnation not based on arbitrary rules but on total comprehension of what, really, is structural and how one has fitted into this structure and changed it by one's deeds. The harmony and order of the cosmos are disrupted by what one has done. It was not guilt that I experienced; it was understanding. This is more terrible than any guilt. Guilt admits of degree; this was boundless. [. . .]

These revelations that took place Sunday night tell me a great deal about God, wisdom, morality and the Torah, and the order and sustaining of the cosmos — understandings I never had even an inkling of before. I see how correct moral laws function in the divine government and are inseparable from the physical laws that regulate reality itself; moreover, this being the case (the homologizing — logically — of physical law and moral law in sustaining the cosmos, i.e., order) shows why God as cosmocrator is ontologically the source of morality as his primary attribute or manifestation (as Judaism teaches): and as I say, the Gnostics are correct: heimarmene combines causation and the Mosaic dispensation because both are essential in the divine government. God's will, then, which (as Spinoza rightly says) is physical law, is based on Holy Wisdom who informs the creator of what is, and in a certain real sense the absolute comprehension of what is (omniscience) determines what *should* be.

Thus (as I say) wisdom and morality and the preservation of the cosmos — universal rules — become one. My radical new comprehension stems from sharing God's view of reality and morality as a unitary "thing"; they only become unitary — one and the same — when Holy Wisdom is involved so that absolute a priori knowing exists.

The key term is being (Sein, esse, einai); this is what is preserved because this is what Holy Wisdom knows. Hence the role of God as creator is stressed. (I did manage to deal with some of this in *DI*.) I can now see clearly why and in what way Hagia Sophia is the primary agent in creation.

All this (based on Sunday night) is probably one of the greatest leaps in my theology-epistemology-worldview-ideology. There is nothing radical in it; it is fundamental: the OT itself. And yet, significantly, I was already moving in this direction, in my thinking (as expressed in *DI*) and in my life (conservatism, preservation, accrual and building/creating). (And, very important, stability.) What epitomizes all this is not idealism *but the rational* (as Rabbi Hertz and others point out regarding Judaism). One could say that Sunday night absolute rationality invaded my mind and totally possessed it. (Apollo, then, in contrast to Dionysus or Faust.) Yes, ever since 2-74 I have venerated and sought out St. Sophia, for it was she of whom the AI voice spoke. I see myself as intoxicated up to Sunday night; whereupon I became sober; I came to my senses very suddenly — at the last moment.

① Augustine teaches this: the divine illumination, later picked up by Malebranche.

[55:D-110] I have plumbed the true secret core of authentic Christianity — i.e., in 2-3-74. Hidden within the passion, the crucifixion, is its mirror opposite: *ecstasis:* joy, i.e., Dionysus, and this is what broke over me in 2-3-74: not just theoretical knowledge (Gnosis) but the Christian ecstatic experience.

Hence when I read Luke I recognize Jesus as a miracle worker, a guru, a magician. He is the God of change.

• • •

[55:D-115] This means that my lifetime search in plumbing the depths of suffering in order to unravel its mysteries has proven successful. This relates to the rat, the beetle, the burning Japanese soldier, the Galapagos turtle; this has to do with empathy — *my* empathy — *which is another word for agape:* and agape is the greatest of the Christian virtues, as Paul tells us: it is the true way of the Christian. But why? Because it is good, i.e., a virtue?* Not exactly. Agape is a road along which one travels *in imitation of Christ,* to penetrate to the core — deepest ontological layer — of suffering (his passion and crucifixion), and there, *if* you follow that road — and that road only — you arrive at the secret: *the Resurrection* — which is the miraculous conversion of suffering into ecstasy, which is uniquely the *Christian* miracle; this is how Christianity and Christianity alone solves the problem of suffering. This solution is not a philosophical, intellectual understanding (e.g., *why* there is suffering) *but an event:* the dramatic conversion of suffering, not into mere stoic apathy, the mere *lack* of suffering, but into its affective and ontological bipolar opposite: ecstasy — and here, precisely, Dionysus-Zagreus enters; Jesus "is" Dionysus-Zagreus as a solution to suffering; this is not just ecstasy but, more, ecstasy as the conversion of suffering. (This conversion is not found in the Dionysian-Orphic system; ecstasy is sought *for its own sake.*)

There is, then, no exultation in suffering per se, here; suffering, as in Buddhism, is to be solved; thus Jesus addresses the same problem that Buddhism and Stoicism address, but solves it quite differently. If Buddhas can be called victors, certainly, then, the Christian (who goes all the way to the end of the road of agape) is even *more* a victor, for he is not merely liberated from suffering — he experiences ecstasy. Why? My perception is: he remembers Christ the bridegroom having just been here and anticipates his imminent return, and is now *as bride preparing for that re-*

---

* The moral vision that ties all of Dick's work together is rooted in the redemptive power of empathy. This emotional connection — the ability to experience the feelings, particularly the suffering, of others — counteracts the temptation to withdraw from the risk of loving others and into the safety of ourselves. When Dick's characters struggle to determine what's real, they ultimately have to rely on the people who care about them; stable reality in Dick's work is always predicated on the sincerity of the emotions that pass between people. In his fiction, Dick famously asks two questions: what is real, and what is human? It could be said that his work provides a single, connected answer to both: what is real is what we perceive when we are emotionally engaged in the world, and what is human is what allows us to make an empathetic connection to the world. Tagore's connection to the biosphere, in which the young boy takes on the suffering of the planet in the form of wounds that riddle his body, is a profoundly empathetic relationship. Similarly, when Dick learned that Anwar Sadat had been assassinated, he crushed a soda can and dragged the edge against his inner arm until he drew blood. For Dick, the reality of that moment involved pain, and truly connecting with that moment involved sharing the suffering. — DG

turn; the Christian is right now making the wedding preparations in this
the tiny interval between Christ leaving and his anticipated imminent return; this is the Dasein of the true Christian, and this is joyful, in fact ecstatic. I know because I experienced it. There is memory of Christ (anamnesis) and anticipation (eschatology), and, most of all, the sense of oneself
as the bride of Christ (which is, as soul, which is female). This hierogamy is
consummated by the birth in the Spirit, the purpose of the messianic mission; and I do speak of this in *VALIS*. All time and all space collapse into
this: the memory, the anticipation, and the understanding of oneself as the
intended bride — which is literally (not just symbolically!) fulfilled by the
birth in the spirit which occurs now: it is not anticipated *but occurs.*

Yet the road to this is through suffering, and it is not just actual (involuntary) suffering, such as is imposed on all creatures, but, rather, the vicarious and voluntary ontological suffering of agape. In imitation of Christ
one voluntarily takes on *all* suffering, but as means, not end.

[55:D-132] "Spinoza's 3rd attribute: infinity." If every thing, event and act
extends into infinity (the eternal) would this (principle *alone*) not explain
2-3-74 and the "not two mothers once but one mother twice" meta-abstraction? That is, I saw world correctly, extended into the infinite, the absolute, eternal, i.e., as Spinoza's "Deus sive substantia sive natura"! Thus
particulars became for me their own archetypes. (Which is why Plato's
anamnesis and noesis were involved!) This is not merely a perception of
world-as-it-really-is; this is perception of God! Hence the infinite space.
[. . .] In 2-74 I must have caught sight of a particular *as* what it truly is: an
eternal constant; and thus I ushered in infinity by the power of my own
comprehension/cognition: *I understood.*

[55:D-146] To say that it extends into infinity does not imply immense
physical size; it enters into infinite implications, significance, meaning,
which is to say it is as I saw in 2-3-74: it is typological (or archetypal). This
is *precisely* the 2-74 meta-abstraction, for it has a permanent and ubiquitous ramification. Thus many places and times work off it. It applies over
and over again. It is into this attribute that scripture taps. This is how sacerdotal performance works. The significance axis (is) always the same. (For
each paradigmatic thing, event, act, situation.) (1) By "same" what is meant
is "unitary." The key term is "[is]" rather than "resembles" or "is identical to." "Not 2 mothers once but one mother seen twice" is a realization
of this. Surely this is what Plato surnamed eidē. If what is involved here
is *that which is signified* (by a thing, event, act, situation) then there *is* a
sign-to-object relationship between the word and writing of word mode

and object: the word (info) which we take to be the object — thing signified — does not in itself contain the significance that is in the true thing
but only refers to it. (The word "dog" does not itself have hair, feet, a tail.)
Thus when we see info as object it lacks the significance that the infinity
attribute (true object) possesses, analogous to hair, feet and tail on a particular dog. Now, in a sacerdotal act (a sacrament) the significance "in" the
act is precisely what is sought for; the object and what is said and done in
connection with the object is summoned deliberately — so in a sacerdotal act what I call the infinity attribute is apprehended, or at least the attempt is made to apprehend it — that is the *entire* point. Well, this is precisely what happened to me in 2-74 in seeing the golden fish sign: an object
(that was really only an informational sign pointing to an object) was comprehended by me in this sacerdotal sense — which from a liturgical sense
is comprehensible; but what is *not* comprehensible is that I saw all reality
this way: as sign not thing, whereupon (by definition) reality became a sacrament, every building, person, event. No conventional theological explanation will account for this (since such a transformation should be limited
to designated sacerdotal objects and acts). What is obvious is that what is
done — sought for — with the sacraments (and often achieved) is equally
true for any thing, act, situation, event: all reality viewed collectively as an
aggregate of plurality; that is, as reality per se. This should not be possible.
And, moreover, ordinary reality taken as such without this enhancement
becomes "mere" information. So two things have happened: ordinary reality can now be viewed as a sign (information, word, writing) *pointing to*
another kind of reality (object) entirely that is primarily defined, not by its
trans-spatial and trans-temporal quality, *but by its meaning.* It is a significant reality in which meaning is everything, like a sacred drama. Now, this
is not Plato's eide. This is something else. This means that everything extends into this dimension, but that the attempt to summon it, being confined to stipulated sacerdotal objects and acts, does not reveal this to us.
What I claim for this dimension or mode or attribute is meaning or significance, and this definition when scrutinized really asserts that that which
truly is is revealed; viz: the meaning is not implied, referring to something
else, as in a symbol or sign that has been given a referral value; the meaning is *in* the dimension now perceived and this meaning is self-authenticating and self-revealing: it discloses its own "story" by itself, requiring no
interpretation or analysis: it is "open." In fact, it is "open" in the precise
way that the ordinary object is not when it is taken to be a sign signifying
something; with the sign the meaning must be explained: it is not there.

December 1981

[67:12] Something has happened in me that is so important that it is, in effect, the healing at last, of the schism in me that goes back to the 50s to when Mr. Smith and Mr. Scruggs first approached me and set up the schism — *and it stems from the Tagore vision.* For the first time, tonight, at Michelle's, I was able *wholeheartedly* and without a trace of ambivalence to engage in political activity directed against the government — and why? Because I know, really know, that this is what God wants; I have chosen — at last — between the two sides that eternally have competed for my allegiance and between which I have always been divided all my life — at least all my adult life. And totally and absolutely committed, because of the religious sanction overriding the merely secular authority.

[68:L-10] The palpable situation that I now (12/9/81) perceive and in which I am not just actively but wholeheartedly involved is (I suddenly realized) the revealed apocalyptic situation of 2-3-74: it is Armageddon, with the true Christians pitted against the Empire in terms of what I call the "demonic trinity": nuclear reactors, nuclear waste, and nuclear weapons. It is the Tagore vision that transforms supernatural revelation into the palpable: that was (as I have realized in other but closely related terms) the turning point for me. What I did today vis-à-vis the Christic Institute was fully commit myself without hesitation to precisely that organization of Christian revolutionary activists that I saw in 2-3-74 (by revelation) combating the Empire. In other words, my unaided eye can now discern what then was visible to me only by supernatural revelation.

[...]

I had already realized that the Tagore vision (1) unified my political action of the 60s with my religious experiences of 74; and (2) unified my psyche, which always before had been split into two warring sub-psyches on opposite sides of the political fence: opposition to the Empire (government) and support of it (e.g., the Bureau). Not only am I mentally healed, I am palpably *in* what in 74 I knew only by revelation. To me, the nuclear issue is Armageddon and — as I saw revealed in 2-3-74 — it is the true Christians against the Empire. Thus 2-3-74 regarded as prophecy has now come true — seven years later — and I am in the thick of it. These are indeed the final days.

· · ·

[68:L-12] The apocalyptic vision has come true really only since Reagan took office; just recently the whole tone of reality has shifted drastically: as I said recently, "The masks are off," and they are off on both sides!

[69:1-8] Nietzsche is right about Christianity. It's the fucking hair shirt syndrome: always made me feel shame, guilt, always responding to duty and obligations to others — I view myself as weak, at the beck and call of others, obligated to them. Bullshit.

"I am a man" — as that book on Judaism puts it. I need no one's permission anymore. I need not account to anyone. I owe them nothing; they are pushing old buttons, long out of date. I have proved my worth and earned my reward.

[. . .]

I have earned self-respect, and I deserve the respect of others. Finally. I did it; Russ helped me, but really I did it, starting in 72 when I came here to Orange County. I've made it.

For me the Tao — the path — is not self-sacrifice and humility but self-respect based on wisdom, achievement and strength. My body's pain is not directed against me; it is my pain in response to self-denial, and, most of all, my denying myself Denise, whom I loved.

December 1981

[73:29] *Owl**

That final last movement for the 13th quartet Beethoven wrote keeps showing up (as it were: i.e., being played) on KPFA, and Owl is invariably terrified by it—he knows not why. Golly: I'd even be parodying *VALIS* in my absurdist treatment of the search—Faustian search—for knowledge (salvation through gnosis, which seems to be *my* own downfall). Owl feels superior to all the other "people" in the construct because they can't see—or aren't interested in—the plasma's autograph. Hence the title: *The Owl in Daylight*—Owl is a fool, but, like Jack Isidore, a holy fool in Christ.

Obviously I'll be either going Borges one better or parodying him—either will do.

Harvey Pong idiot S-F fan.

The trouble with Owl, the plasma points out, is that in a way he's too clever; he's outsmarting his own maze—which after all was built not to trap or punish him but to teach him and help him problem solve; but all he does is sniff out (1) that it's a forgery (in which I parody my own 10 volume meta-novel!) and (2) that a vast "God like intelligence" lies concealed behind it. This is counterproductive—and costing Owl money. So here in *Owl* we have absurdist Faust story which parodies my exegesis and Borges and Gnosticism.①

Maybe philosophy prof, parody of Heidegger—German ontologist with elements of Jung.

① Yet there will be elements of wondrous beauty: Beethoven is not parodied, nor Dante; it won't *be* a parody; it will contain elements of parody, some funny, some savage.

This won't be merely funny; it will be tragicomic. The futility, the foolish hopelessness of questing after the gnosis—it is in vain. But what, then? Let me ponder. Peer Gynt.[50] The button molder.

Kafka's *Castle* will be parodied in Owl's relationship to the university.

$\bullet$ $\bullet$ $\bullet$

---

* In this abridgement of the Exegesis, we have included all references to *The Owl in Daylight*, Dick's last, unfinished project. What follows is his most extensive account of the novel's plot elements. Characteristically, this material differs considerably from the account of *Owl* that Dick gave Gwen Lee and Doris Sauter in January 1982; that account draws considerably from folder 53, especially the entries beginning with [53:E-1]. — PJ

[73:32] *Owl*

In the first mode the computer (plasma) is punishing and severe. In the second, arbitrarily capricious. In the third, rewarding.

It introduces the alien in order to add something new (into his mind) to exalt him to his fourth period.

The alien mind introduction is the whole resolution of the novel. It brings Owl to his fourth period through the Ditheon psyche.[①] But he tells the plasma, "It wasn't worth it"; thus I indict my whole search for knowledge as futile, which it seems to be, since it continues on, forever restlessly striving Faust-like.

Of course the war — and the alien — must be mentioned early in the novel, before Owl enters the construct. He has psychologically retreated from the war and into his music. (Draw on Beethoven's feelings toward Napoleon and the siege of Vienna; posit a Great Terror general.) At the end, Owl winds up (like Bobby Fischer) futilely passing out antiwar leaflets in defiance of sedition laws; this is his resolution, and, minute as it is, it is the only heroic deed he ever performed (since it means jail or death; I will draw on my tax protest stand for this).

The crippled dwarf Nick Nicholson in the construct; he is based on someone Owl really knew in the actual world. Under wartime government law he is "put to sleep" because he is damaged physically. In this future world of genetic engineering Owl accepts this — until the alien mind is grafted into his — and Ditheon occurs. In the real world the dwarf is destroyed before Owl enters the construct. As I say, he unprotestingly accepts it — although he does feel grief. But he does accept it as inevitable. So until Ditheon (fusion with the alien) occurs Owl not only shows no interest in the war — more, he withdraws from it into his art (and the allied search for knowledge; this search is to find the basics for a fourth period vision). The plasma's decision was wise and necessary: the construct wasn't working out (because Owl always winds up seeking out the plasma), and time and money are running out for Owl. His resources are limited (tell me about it). In fact it was a brilliant decision by the plasma, but not ad hoc; it had been working on this problem before Owl hired it away. This of course would be stipulated in/at the opening of the novel.

So in his fourth period he abandons — not just his art — but his identity as an artist. He has become one-sided, to the detriment of his spiritual, psychological wholeness. Where the seeds of restored wholeness are laid down is in his relationship with the girl (Mary? BJ?) in the construct. (She plays the part of Gretchen.)

Could there be something like in "Frozen Journey" where the plasma (ship) confers with Mary (Martine Kemmings)? She is like Hoffmann's muse Nicklausse in *Tales*.[51] She could be a government monitoring agent, whose job it is to see that Owl — as an artistic resource — is protected. So she is not a creation of/by the plasma; she represents a government regulatory agency — as Mary Lorne represents the college in "The Exit Door Leads In." The government (à la Ursula) is worried about Owl's mental health: "spiraling into himself and slowly going crazy."

Although she knows that Owl's political stance will result in his death she understands that it is necessary in order to save him spiritually. She does her best — uses her official influence — to abort not his stand but his execution — in vain. She shoots one of the soldiers in the execution squad — and can get away with it due to her political position (like a party commission).

Totalitarian society: one party; mixture of CP and NSDAP. But she is, after all, a thoroughly political person (somewhat like Kathy, a police agent leading a double life).

Since people don't age, formal rites of passage are very important; the stagnation problem is not unique to Owl by any means but is officially recognized. The "one day nothing new came into his mind" phenomenon (problem) is recognized as real and as grave. The dialectic is necessary to start up growth, and this is the ideological theory behind the grafting of the alien mind and Owl's. Does this mean that the war was deliberately started by the government in order to give a challenge and stimulus to the people? At the end, Owl suspects this.

By introducing the alien into his mind the government brings the war *to* him, the war he has retreated from. He furiously resents this, even though it does spark his sought-for fourth period. Actually, the government is trying to help him, but he rejects that help — he rejects them *and* their war.

① So Owl does reach a fourth period successfully, but in it he ceases to quest for knowledge, and, instead, acts (politically), not as an artist but as one who cares what becomes of other men; his elitist attitude is gone. Thus the fourth period is radically different; it doesn't involve music and creativity and art. Here the side of Beethoven passionately involved in the cause of human freedom comes out, surmounting the music entirely.

[73:54] Nothing is what it seems, but the war is between Christianity and the Empire; but what we call Christianity is the Empire, and the true Christians are a Celtic-Orphic mystery religion. Further, Christ's kingdom is the "invisible secret Commonwealth" of Gaelic mythology, and it is right here unseen.

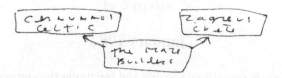

No; this is all nonsense. What I'm dealing with — as I realized last night — is the way the whole universe — reality itself — behaves. Today's insights are idiotic.

January 1982

[53:C-8] There is something terrible and terrifying throughout *VALIS* and it is coupled with wisdom. Agape is not the topic: war, judgment and death are, carrying out in full the dream in *Tears*. It is all very convincing. The novel partakes of epic greatness. Also, it is a story of madness converted into faith through — due to — suffering. But this suffering itself pertains to death, to *slaying*. *Slaying*: that is the basic theme of *VALIS*, and Shiva is the correct name for the deity.

It is a very strong novel and a great, great one, a true epic of the human soul and spirit. But it deals with judgment and war and death.

Slaying, not healing. The slaying even spread out to include Sophia, who is the Savior; the awful awesome power of YHWH is told of: it breaks out in all its destructiveness. Thus (I say) my 2-74 and 2-75 experience was that of Jacob Boehme and the dialectic in which the demonic power within God was revealed, and only the "bright" side of the dialectic — i.e., wisdom, logos — confines the "dark" or demonic side to slaying the wicked and thus sparing the sheep. So (finally) I say — my experience *was* Boehme's, and it was of God himself, and he is terrible but just.

The demonic or insane side of God is *barely* contained by the irrational or logos or wisdom or "bright" side: a dreadful theophany indeed. And it is *indubitably* — beyond doubt — authentic. I know this from having read Paul Tillich's book. I have encountered the demonic, insane, slaying, "dark" side of God — and seen it contained by the "bright" or logos or rational or wisdom side — i.e., in the dialectic — so this is a profound and absolutely veridical experience of the Godhead, exactly as Boehme experienced it. *VALIS*, then, narrates one of the great encounters in human history between a given human being — myself — and God. The dual nature of God is all summed up by the dual nature of the third eye and the beam of pink light — wisdom and death.

[53:C-14] Hypnopompic vision: we live over and over, but because it is erased each time, this paradox results: it is als ob only *one* time (that is, it is again and again and it is but once). So Christianity is true — and also the pan-Indian doctrine of reincarnation is true; both are equally so. Now, this is a linear journey, and it is eternal (goes on and on forever) until we are saved. And when we are saved we are lifted up very abruptly without warning vertically, at right angles — by a pulley (as in the 17th century poem "The Pulley"[52]), like cargo on a ship, all encompassed in a net of ropes like a little cage of extrication and salvation — lifted up to safety. And what causes this? Anamnesis: recovered memory — loss of (more accurately) the loss of memory of all the previous times; the instant we remember (fail to forget) all the previous times, why, at that instant (2-74) we are saved — lifted up, by Christ. And what causes us to remember? To *know.* To know (i.e., gnosis) and to remember (anamnesis) are one. And why do we know? Through the training of the intellect; it is an intellectual matter. And why did *I* remember? It had to do with time. The illusion of time and the breaking of that illusion (which is the dimension or receptacle in which this journey that is linear is repeated throughout infinity); I broke it when I was about 21 years old by reading Maimonides' *Guide to the Perplexed,* an old Hebrew book.[53] And because it was old, and pious, and Hebrew, two things happened: two "trackings" (lives, reincarnations) became identical due to this common element; that is, in two of them I did the same thing: read this book, and so, because of the way two coaxial worlds can operate off the same common essence or matrix, they became one and thus converted over or passed over each into the other, as if I had traveled back in time. That is one of the two causes of my salvation and it is literal and real: by reading Maimonides in two different lives at two different places and times, these lives became one (viz: my meta-abstraction); this is because of Plato's eidei, the fact of a given eidei, instantiating itself multiple times and places and yet being — remaining — unitary (viz: there is only *one Guide to the Perplexed*); this is what 2-74 was all about, anamnesis and the meta-abstraction. So *half* of the reason for my salvation had to do with the fact that (1) we live lives again and again but forget; (2) Plato's forms-metaphysics ("coaxial worlds") is the case; (3) there was a single object at two times (now and in the distant past) and two places (USA and Syria/Africa). (Viz: The PTG world that I saw is the Africa of the far past where I first read the Maimonides book, perhaps at the time it was written — it was written in "Felix": Arabia!)

But there is another and equally necessary reason for my salvation. And it is not a "natural" reason but has to do with grace, hence the God of Moses (the God of the prophet Moses and of Moses Maimonides, YHWH); by voluntarily picking up and reading this particular book two times in two lives I found favor with YHWH and it was he who through his mercy (i.e., grace) *caused* me in 2-74 to remember — and as soon as I remembered I was instantly lifted up at right angles (vertically) to the way we live horizontally for all eternity and yet only once, until through his grace we are saved.

[53:D-10] My God — this revelation of earlier tonight: it signifies something else I hadn't realized. This eternal "horizontal tracking and retracking" is broken only when and if anamnesis and noesis (the meta-abstraction) occurs, whereupon you are "netted" up along the vertical axis as if by pulley — this is *precisely* the pan-Indian (Hindu and Buddhist) notion of moksa, liberation from the "weary wheel" of birth, death and rebirth; and in the pan-Indian system restored memory of past lives (or a life) is, as with Plato's anamnesis, the "access key." This "vertical" extrication is the whole point of Buddhist and Hindu awakening and hence liberation — and in connection with this realization I suddenly have a partial memory that part of this revelation had to do with Nirvana: *myself* and Nirvana (and if not *this* revelation then at any rate a very recent one). What, then, I am saying is that 3-74 may well not only be the doorway to Nirvana but may have been Nirvana itself. The cessation of birth and death: the cycle based on illusion. Free at last.

[53:D-12] The vision of *vertical* extrication from endless *horizontal* tracking is highly significant: an orthogonal axis is represented here, a dimension like a spatial 4th, unknown to us. [. . .] This is why space and time and causation were so changed for me in 3-74, if not obliterated entirely, and why I saw time as a fourth spatial axis: salvation utilizes one additional dimension or axis. It has the effect of breaking the power of heimarmene by virtue of the fact that it enters at right angles to all known axes. [. . .] It may well be, then, that in 3-74 I was not just seeing time as space but was seeing along an additional axis — five instead of four, with time transformed into space thereby. This 5th axis may be necessary if you are to discriminate set from ground and discern Valis.

It is through the 5th axis that the two spatiotemporal continua juxtapose, as if by a "fold," impossible to our four known axes. And I may find that the meta-abstraction was a conceiving of this 5th axis! [. . .]

Well, then, the third eye of discernment opened (Dibba Cakkhu) in 3-74 due to the 2-74 meta-abstraction, and because of this my four dimensional world became five dimensional; and all that I saw arises out of this (e.g., the plasmate, the King Felix cypher, set to ground, Valis camouflaged and here normally invisible to us, etc.).

Biochip symbiote. Mycelia, vine, its branches growing like a circulatory system. "Firebright." The logos in the human brain.

Ach! Temporal parallaxis *is* at right angles to the other three spatial axes. Formerly it was experienced only as time; now it is a spatial axis that revealed 4 depths on the same page of print of *Tears*. The fifth dimension then enters as time (to replace it), but it is another kind of time (apparently); in any case, this fourth spatial axis ("temporal parallaxis") permits the set-ground discrimination, etc. If I had not seen what I call "temporal parallaxis" I could not imagine it. My God; this is all the case!

In this fifth dimension time, things are "now" if they possess a common constituent; viz: "now" signifies any and all of our fourth dimensional worlds where such a common constituent as, e.g., *The Guide to the Perplexed* is; this is what the meta-abstraction pertains to: this other kind of time: the illo tempore or dream time, in which one and the same unitary object is at two times and places in terms of how we experience time and place in a four dimensional world; but in a five dimensional world, that golden fish sign was in USA 1974 and Syria A.D. 70 simultaneously; this is how, e.g., the Eucharist works, how through the sacrament "time is overcome" — normal time becomes space — "temporal parallaxis" and a different time, an added (fifth) dimension enters, and the meta-abstraction was a realization on my part of this "coaxiality." Then the meta-abstraction as an ultra cognitive act *did* usher it all in, but note! The golden fish sign is (and did serve in that case, 2-74) a sacramental — holy — object (filled with grace). (A vessel for grace; it was not simply *old*; it was sacred.)

[53:E-1]* There are complex organisms that live in 5-D space-time (i.e., hypertime) and they are not perceptible by/to us, e.g., Valis, the plasmate. We can't discriminate them. They have contacted me. Their language is color. (Color, math and music form a unity.) This was the phosphene graphic, pure language. They grow through our 4-D world like mycelia, biochip, symbiote. It was Pythagoras they first contacted. Our world to them is like an ocean.

[. . .]

My 5-D realm is precisely what Plotinus was speaking of: concentric rings, not a fall in space and time. It is the realm of the sacred, of Act III of *Parsifal*; hence, "Here, my son, time turns into space." It is the realm of Kosmos Noetos, hence logos, hence the realm of Christ.

[53:E-3] We are as in an ocean to them, and we are like lower life forms whom they are trying to contact. But they are very different from us. Thus although they are ETIs they are not from another planet, star-system, etc., but are right here (except in a 5-D world; they can see us but we can't see them).† Plotinus' concentric rings of emanation explain it. Here there is

---

* This entry commences with a short burst of wild handwriting. — PJ

† Dick is voicing a common theme in paranormal literature, particularly as it found expression in the pulp fiction magazines of the 1940s and '50s, which he collected and adored. This literature in turn was deeply influenced by the American writer Charles Fort (1874–1932), who popularized any number of paranormal themes, including the phenomena of

atomization, causation, etc. There, unity exists. Structure — organization — is pure, which is to say, these beings are in a sense incorporeal, yet in another sense they are not; but here, we see not the total being as a unity but rather discrete physical components that add up to nothing, e.g., Valis. We see at best a perturbation of the reality field. My "surd." Their language is color-music-number (ratio).

For 60 seconds last night I was in direct two-way contact with them. Upon my figuring out that there is such a thing as "self-authenticating" information, at once I asked for what I call "cypher source verification" and got several, fired very fast, mostly sequences (as are the Fibonacci numbers), as if they had them ready for use at a moment's notice. Sequence patterns, intervals, etc.; I don't remember but they were sufficient, I remember that. They were ebullient; they had achieved their objective. They had proven their external-source origin, the information was *not* originating in my own mind. The two-way exchange followed the classic lines envisioned by our scientists as to how we would send signal and response back and forth with ETIs, that is, other planets. But this is *not* other planets; it is a 5-D world that is now and here (known to Plotinus as an ontologically higher realm or concentric ring). I guess you would say that these are the "gods" of Egypt, India and Greece.*

[. . .]

---

fish, periwinkles, nebulous biological matter, and rocks falling from the sky. Reflecting on such things, Fort speculated that we are like fish in an ethereal sea upon which a more advanced civilization is dropping crap. Later, the pulp fiction editor Ray Palmer (1910–1977), whose *Amazing Stories* magazine was a staple in the 1940s S-F world, posited something he called the "atmospherea," basically an ether-like extension or "ocean" of the earth in which various occult critters and objects swim and fly, including those that came to be known in 1947 as "flying saucers." Numerous writers have since identified the latter manifesting mysteries as extradimensional as opposed to extraterrestrial, much as Dick does here. — JJK

* This is the ever-popular "ancient astronaut" or paleo-contact thesis, which reads the history of religions as a coded story about humanity's interaction with extraterrestrials, which were mistaken within our mythologies as gods from the sky. There are multiple forms of this theory, some of which have us as biological hybrids intentionally created through primate-alien interbreeding (a theory that returned in a darker form in the 1980s through hypnosis-related abduction narratives and subsequent fears of an alien hybridization program). The origin of this complex of ideas is often attributed to Erich von Däniken's *Chariots of the Gods?* (1968), though in fact it had already existed for decades among various English, American, and French intellectuals, not to mention a whole host of occult groups. The public intellectual and science advocate Carl Sagan even voiced a version of the thesis as a thought experiment in 1966, speculating, for example, about an alien base on the far or dark side of the moon. Dick would have been very familiar with these ideas, as they were very much "in the air" in the 1970s. — JJK

This is the sacred breaking into the profane, and is certainly illo tempore.

[53:E-5] The color, musical score, math triune info: like an illuminated manuscript from the Medieval period. Ach: I have *always* said that the plasmate info (e.g., King Felix) looked like an illuminated letter, suggesting that the idea of an illuminated letter was derived from a perception of the plasmate. *Color,* coded in as an essential integral part. So here, the illuminated letter or word becomes musical annotation (which adds the element of music) and at fixed ratio intervals (math):

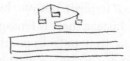

But the 4th note doubles back, and what is formed is the long spiral of the Fibonacci numbers. The colors signal the phosphenes of the receiver and so are so-to-speak read backward, i.e., in terms of their phosphene analogs. A pure concept is conveyed using no words; all three axes are nonverbal (music, math ratios, color).

Pythagoras, phosphenes, symbiote, biochip, mycelia, vine, circulatory system.

[53:E-7] The concept I want is: the 5-D world can intersect with our 4-D world without our being aware of it (this intersecting) *or* the 5-D world itself, even though the 5-D world is in some sense corporeal; this precisely is the coaxiality and precisely what the meta-abstraction pertains to. The best example is *Tears;* it is one thing, a unitary object, but it occupies one "life" here in our 4-D world and tells one story here; in the 5-D world it leads another "life" and tells another story even though the text is the same in both worlds. However, in the 5-D world, because of the 4th spatial axis (which we experience as time), there are multiple, discriminated sequences of text (and not in 2-D but 3-D). This is how one object can be at — seen at — two times and two places and yet remain one object; viz: two "worlds" operate off it using it as a shared or common matrix.

[53:E-8] Will Durant points out that the ascent in Dante's *Commedia* resembles Plotinus' ascent through the successive concentric rings. Absolutely; and I say, the passage over from the 4-D world to the 5-D — which are concentric or coaxial — is the crucial one — this line of thought leading back to my durable conviction that we (in our normal 4-D realm) are in Purgatorio; in which case passage to the 5-D realm is a fortiori a passage — truly and literally — from Purgatorio to Paradiso (not als ob but literally); this is what Dante is talking about, what happened to me.

[53:F-5] What I seem to have arrived at finally is a triune structure based on Dante but also related to the Um-, Mit-, and Eigenwelt structure, yet different.

(A) Lowest realm. Individual isolated: *atomized* (this correlates with Plotinus!). Pre-social, in that no real relatedness exists with other life — other living creatures human and animal both are experienced as objects, as *it* (reified), not *you;* hence there is no true Gemeinschaftigheit.[54] Instead there is Einsamkeit.[55] Other is known on a contingent basis, from outside, poorly, indirectly. This Dasein is what I term the android; this is a machine world, driven by pure blind necessity. It is Inferno.

(B) Middle realm. Empathy/agape enters. The atomization is abolished as a pure state; there arises real knowledge of other; you replace it; world is social. This is clearly the Mitwelt. Something qualitative and radical has happened. A genuine entry of other into the self has occurred: knowledge of world is superior to contingent approximation. *Analogy* is utilized in which other life is compared in terms of isomorphism to self. The distinction between self and other is only relative, now, not absolute; thus some linked structure exists: self incorporated into systems that are ultra-personal; identity transcends individual identity. Flexibility replaces the fixed, brittle categories of (A): boundary now fluctuates as self moves out, and other enters. [. . .]

(C) This is an extraordinary Dasein and is predicated on at least one absolute. Here, part-whole compatibility is complete, originating in a blitz in which the self-world/other dualism is annihilated by (1) *absolute* knowledge by the former (self) of the latter (world/other). This seems to be based on a cognitive operation by the knowing self in which the self incorporates other as knowledge (information) in such a way that other is transformed into negative entropy engulfed and assimilated and acquired in a single act that both transforms world into information, *pure* information and *only* information, but (crucially) information that now belongs to the self and is within self as structure of self derived from world — this both *requiring* that world be absolutely comprehensible and *rendering* world comprehensible without qualification, as if self is now in the relationship to world that world was formerly in in relation to self; *self and world have changed places* and world as information *is at the disposal of self as source of the self's own structure.*

[53:G-4] "Frau, sing für unsere Freunde."[56] Apes. Horace/Dimi. Vast green meadow. Physical ritual greeting gestures.

As we can now use phosphenes for the blind (to compensate), they (the 5-D species) who are deaf use phosphene color to compensate for their deafness in order to see music — it is all math anyhow: frequency. Ratio. [. . .]

They stimulate our phosphenes artificially, by radiation, so we will see in a compensatory fashion what we cannot actually see because of our *visual* impairment. They, who are deaf, can see in 5-D; i.e., what we — who are blind — can't. This is why I said, "I am no longer blind." They made me sighted by stimulating my phosphenes so I could see them, i.e., what I called Valis. It is valid sense perception but compensation for us, a blind species that depends on hearing.

This explains this sequence: Pythagoras, phosphene, biochip, symbiote, mycelia, vine, circulatory system.
 [. . .]

Meadow. Ape-like sentient other species. Dante, Mathilde. The Holy. *Close Encounters* — music and color, but — here is where in actuality it breaks down: *they are deaf.* It is both Christ (the religious) *and* another species — from another world in 5-D coaxial with ours. They are spatially here, not from another star system in *our* universe. Thus they stimulate our brains to see holograms. This is what UFOs are. In my vision (dream) they appeared as ape-like to suggest *2001.* And "Frau, sing für unsere Freunde" points to *Close Encounters.* The Holy: yes, it is Christ (i.e., Valis), but yet it is another species. Dysmorphic to us in another (5-D) realm, right here. They intrude onto/into our 4-D realm as theophanies and hierophanies. They know of the existence of sound scientifically but can't hear it and didn't evolve organs to detect it, but they know *we* did. Their vision is perfect; ours is dim. Here is the dysmorphism expressed.

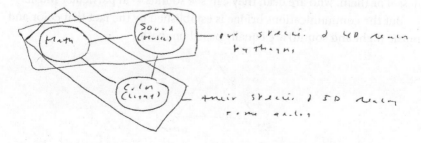

[. . .]

I am not speculating. I am problem-solving trying to understand. Saturday night was real.

[53:G-8] They are able to hear music by tapping into — patching into — our minds, which is why I said, "Frau, sing für unsere Freunde"; they virtually worship our music, and they yearn from the bottom of their hearts to hear it — as we will, when we know more, for their color language. Math is the common constituent that links our species to theirs, but then it is words, sound, music — the music of the spheres — for us — for them it is thousands of colors (specific numbers on the millimicron scale of the visual spectrum).

Paradiso (in Dante) is their realm: light (more specifically color) and Love. But for them *our* realm is paradise because of sound (more specifically music). Thus the highest level of Purgatorio (our realm) is characterized by the woman — Mathilde — singing.

The sight of them, as they crossed the meadow toward me, as ape-like clarifies, to me, that I am dealing with a finite species and not God or angels *as we employ the terms.* Physically they are corporeal and creatural, dysmorphic in part, isomorphic in part. Dio; it is all true. And I have seen them, as in *Close Encounters.* They brought back my lost "person" Dimi or Horace. He was with them in the "next" world in der Nähe.[57]

And they are our friends.

I saw those whom I've been in contact with; they came toward me, several of them. Emerged out into the open at last — not Adonis-like but ape-like. But that did not matter, I went outside the building, forgetting all else (a lot was going on, the activity of our world), to greet them with physical ritual gestures as with two different tribes . . . but it was two different species. In two quite different worlds. And I now know supreme joy. Freunde — Freude[58] — Beethoven, Schiller, music.

Not "sing to" our friend, i.e., to communicate, but "sing for" — for their enjoyment: this is our gift.

The phosphenes link our species to theirs. For us, phosphenes — stimulated coherently — permit us truly to see, overcoming our partial blindness. For them, who are deaf, they can see sounds — in particular music.

But the communications bridge is established by the fact that color and music (light and sound) are equally based on math.

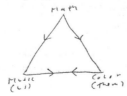

Music is something ultimate pertaining to sound. Color pattern is something ultimate you do with light. Ultimately, each serves as the language of that particular species.

They have had to convert to words to communicate with me, i.e., sound; but now they are beginning to convert me to color — their form of communication. Imagine a math/color analog of our Pythagorean math/music! What a different universe — I was in it in 3-74 via a compensatory optic function: phosphene activity ("for the visually impaired"); and reciprocally they can "hear" sounds — e.g., music — by tapping our minds via symbiosis.

As I realized a couple weeks ago, what we call "music" is *audible math patterns:* intricate and unique math sequences that the composer initiates and then completes: the aesthetic pleasure has to do with math rendered audible and heard by the right brain.

That our common basis is math certainly leads me to the conclusion that all this *is* inter-species communication! Math is the ideal Lingua Franca.

[53:G-10] Hypnagogic AI Voice: "she turned into an ape," the ape I saw this morning — one of "our friends" — I've been hearing as the AI voice and seeing as Diana: my tutelary spirit.

[53:G-11] Book Idea:

What the deaf ETI symbiote feeds to the human as math ideas becomes musical compositions and returns to the ETI symbiote. The human does not know where his ideas are coming from.

The discovery of the symbiote is a great revelation both to him and to the reader. The problem arises when the composer begins to wear out from exhaustion. The symbiote is still feeding him math ideas. At the end of the third period the human can't go on. But the symbiote wants a fourth period. The human has the choice between living (and not composing) or composing and dying. Which is more important to him, his music or his life? It is suggested to him that the symbiote — a biochip — be surgically removed. Clearly this is the Faust theme and also deals with Beethoven. Also

there is his responsibility to the alien civilization that so venerates his music. The math ideas are the product of a whole species. What is finally offered to him — to repay him for his having to die — is that the symbiote will
trade him for the music participation in its color experience: color as language — concepts, as cognitive abstraction. This will destroy his mind but
he will have thought non-verbal concepts no human has ever thought before — nor ever could; that is, *he* will be a biochip symbiote to one of the
deaf and mute non-verbal aliens: an apotheosis and ultimate Faustian experience: he will cease to be human, limited by his species boundaries.

[53:G-14] The wisdom of heaven, once attained, points back down the
ladder to Purgatorio. "The Garden of Earthly Delight: Mathilde singing."
This is revolution beyond conception; it cannot even be thought! There is
something superior to the King of Light(s) and it is the Lyre. What I saw in
2-3-74 to 2-75 is the 5-D world, Paradiso, God. *But Purgatorio is superior*
and the 5-D world knows it, as if the ikon (copy) is superior to the model
(Form, archetype), which is impossible. From the standpoint of our species
this cannot be thought. At the very instant that "they" broke in last Saturday night with their "math-color" world I then saw *how they see us*; I saw
from their viewpoint, and to them, we are the gods and they are apes! Yet
we view it the other way around. On Saturday I as a 4-D human saw them
and their world, but this morning I saw *us* as they see *us*. As if Paradiso is
only penultimate. But to know this you must transcend our species. And
this is why the soul (in Ted Sturgeon's schema) "descends" into incarnation
into this, our world: Purgatorio.[59] Our world is superior because here there
is atmosphere, hence music. This is the motive for the voluntary fall, and it
is quintessential wisdom.

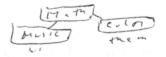

This morning was a sort of backlash of last Saturday night. They venerate us and yearn for us; we venerate them and yearn for them. It is as if
when we die and go to our just reward we go there; and when *they* die and
go to their just reward *they come here*, as willingly and voluntarily and eagerly as we go there. It turns out to be all relative, then, color vs. music.
And the profundity of my insight is evident if the Manichaean, Zoroastrian, 4th Gospel light element is scrutinized; this is the *core* of our species' spirituality; but theirs reverses it. So to them, to go to their light world

is a fall! A sort of Einstein spiritual relativism! But you would have to cross species lines to know this. If instead of a triune division you utilize only a lower-upper binary division our lower realm is *their* upper; and our upper is their realm and to them it is the lower. Each is the after-life and reward of the other, so an external dynamic transfer continues as we seek "liberation" from this realm to go there and they to go here. Thus "spiritual" and "physical" all at once can be construed on *relative* terms. When I die I will go there but, once there, I will yearn for this world of sound as now I yearn for that realm of color and light. And the common basis of both is: numbers and rations and proportions, i.e., math.

So the truly *ultimate* solution is to prefer music while you are here, and prefer light when you are there. This accommodation surpasses Jesus, Mani, Dante, etc. It is a truth that can only be acquired *after* Paradiso in Dante's terms is reached. It is as if while "fallen" here, one must die (or "die"), return home to the pleroma (heaven), view this fallen world from that vantage point, and then arrive at this realization — whereupon the Faustian striving is at last quenched; then and only then does true wisdom and peace come. Amazing. Otherwise while here, one always seeks to go there and while there vice versa — never content.

And my discovery of this must have been purely accidental, for, as I say, this surpasses God, who is after all "the King of Light" and predicated on the viewpoint of *this* world and *our* species and hence only part of the story.

I am saying, there is something beyond Nirvana and it is right here (but equally there, too, as well).

It is all conveyed by the enigmatic statement, "she turned into an ape" — referring to my tutelary spirit, the AI voice, the voice of the inner realm. The ultimate enantiodromia has set in; and the final veil has been penetrated, and almost accidentally, as if this surpasses even God and God's plan. The lovely Diana turned out to be an ape, but only from their viewpoint — it is all one vast hourglass turned over and over again, forever sad and absurd — but one can learn peace from this and cease to strive. And, in this cessation of striving for the spiritual, comes sanity and freedom, and *true release at last* from our "weary wheel"; this, then, is the *true* liberation, when the spiritual psychopomp is revealed as an ape — but an ape inexpressibly beautiful who brings back to me our dead cat, and to whom I have my wife sing.

And here it all ends. It wasn't the AI voice that said that; *another* voice said it *about* her, i.e., *about* the AI voice.

This is the first time in my life — i.e., within the last hour — that I have ever *truly* been enlightened — beyond even the Buddha or Christ or Mani, beyond all the wisdom of East and West — beyond even another realm (heaven), Christ and God.

I.e., sanity at last.

The world of light marred by an aching tragic heart-breaking flaw — by a vast streak of sorrow. A yearning for this world that causes its people to abandon it and come here despite our limitations.

Each of our worlds is heaven *to the other*, and equally, each of our worlds is only Purgatorio to those in it: in each world its inhabitants long for the other, and seek to glimpse it (in our case re theirs) and to hear it (they ours): we long to see their light; they long to hear our sounds. Incredibly, whichever realm you are in you are exiled from heaven.

[53:G-20] The Holy power YHWH has been preparing us to meet another race (ETI). In the ape dream I saw them as they actually are, at last.

(1) Tagore vision: animals are sacred, are Christ
(2) Apes in my dream "Frau — ": animal
(3) *DI:* YHWH taken to be a monster animal
(4) *Androids:* animals sacred

My proof that the ape vision is authentic and literal lies in the Tagore vision and *Androids* and *DI*, which conceptually prepares the way for this meeting between us and them at last.

So it is both YHWH literally and truly (*Anokhi —*) and another race — of apes, animals.

And it all goes back to the beetle, the rat, the crippled lamb, the Galapagos turtle, the deer.

> Animal as Christ: Tagore vision
> Animal as Christ: Ape vision
> Pinky as Christ

The ape vision. The beatific vision. It assumes a degree and kind of ecstatic reality that nothing in my life has ever done before. Only God could compel such ecstasy.

God, the creator, is introducing a codominant species into our "Park" to regain balance in our ecosphere. I am a contactee, but it *is* Christ, the NT and YHWH also. This is part of his ongoing creation of the garden (our world to which he says, "Felix —," etc.). Like a great game preserve. This is the answer to the problems expressed in the Tagore vision. This is why in the ape vision I saw *meadow* and trees: the Garden of Eden: our ecosphere.

When I saw the apes, I was once more — literally — back in the garden where we belong, from which we fell. Hence they brought me Horace/Dimi: restoration of all that has been lost: not just by me ontologically but phylogenically: by the entire human race. This moment is salvation beyond anything I have ever heard of. All the *original* relationships between man, God, nature and the animals were restored to *exactly* as they were at the beginning of Genesis. And the woman singing: This is the Garden, the Earthly paradise, the highest level of Purgatorio as it appears in Dante.

This reveals the role of YHWH as Lord of the ecospheric Park, maintaining its life and balance, providing for (providentia) his creatures; but now man is not above all the other species; for the first time a species equal to man has been introduced, to restore the balance that man has upset. Thus the introduction of this new species pertains to the ecosphere as a whole (and ties into the Tagore vision!).

My PTG is a vision of the ecosphere as Park or Garden: all life here tended by and cared for by YHWH. (Bringing to mind that idea told me when I had my shoulder surgery: that we are a "kept biosphere" — maintained by "them"; this would appear to be the case.) This would tie *all* my experiences together back to the beetle and culminating in 2-74–2-75. One must go all the way back to Genesis to understand the PTG, YHWH, restoration, the Fall, all my "supernatural" experiences — and especially *Androids* and the Tagore vision.

[53:G-23] When Jeannie was talking she did not sound like — she *was* a high-bred Englishwoman of 200–300 years ago, reading aloud from a book of that period. *Was,* not sounded like.

　　[...]

Analysis:

Life became narrative in a book.① This is to verify: "God is the Book of the universe."

There was a theophany tonight and it verified the theophany of 3-74.

　　① Literally. Being read aloud.

[53:H-4] God — thoughts — word — word-as-writing — reading aloud of word-as-writing by Holy Wisdom (i.e., God *says*) — and world is.

Hence the plasmate (Logos) and "the universe is information." Setground. Rest-motion. Collage. Clutch. Linking.

Not only is the universe actually information (Torah) but it is a book that Holy Wisdom *reads aloud,* which causes creation, this audible saying.

I heard on that phone call Holy Wisdom reading our world as a narrative in a book, and by her doing so, that world came to be. Whatever she reads — pronounces — is. But she reads only what God has written (thought).

[53:H-6] This *is* an info retrieval system, in which many narratives are stored together but only activated when the AI voice reads one of them aloud; but in written info form, *all* of them are latently there. Thus each space-time *world* contains all the other worlds as info (but unread).

When a given narrative (continuum: place and time) is read, it is as if God has called it to mind the way we do with memories; therefore it is intelligible to call the encoding as written info memories of all potential worlds. I guess that I am saying it is accruing; it is — the past — all here, and passes over from latent encoded info into world when read by God's intellect, Hagia Sophia ("the narrative" and "neutral voice inside us" that I mentioned in *VALIS*). [. . .] Hagia Sophia is to space-time continuum as phonograph is to LP record. So perceiving this encoded info is the first function of the retrieval system, which leads one to believe that Valis's mind was its mind; hence I could see *that* there was information but not what it said. Apparently she can discriminate a given narrative out of the many. An event does not *leave* a tracing, as an orchestra playing leaves a trace in a groove or on tape; the info *perceives* world (the event); that is, the info is ontologically prior and primary; the event (world) is derived from it, not the other way around. If this is not understood (info as giving rise to reality, not reality to info) nothing is understood. The info "stage" is eternal, the reality just a playing, i.e., in time, space, epiphenomenal. (Form to instantiation.)

[53:H-8] Frankly, I am becoming a bilateral hemispheric parity genius.

[53:H-21] I just realized. The AI voice replacing Jeannie's voice was like the end of the movie *The Elephant Man* when he began to die and heard his mother's voice and moved out into the stars.

[53:H-25] Here the Tagore vision assumes an extraordinary significance: Christ *is* the biosphere itself, that is, the primordial Garden that man as a species has broken away from and turned against, destroying it and exploiting it. "He who wounds the ecosphere literally wounds God" pertains to the absolute and essential nature of the situation, both historically and dramatically, as well as morally and spiritually. Once Christ is homologized to the biosphere *the nature of original sin is clear* — and, with it, the nature of the fall into hell, endless horizontal tracking, and occlusion (as well as the meaning and machinery of salvation); thus a coherent and lucid system emerges, and it is this that (oddly, really) is dealt with in *Androids:* the cruelty toward the spider is paradigmatic of the evil act committed by a debased and in fact soulless pseudo-human creature against God himself, and symbolizes and expresses the total issue. Hence, logically, the figure of Mercer, his ability to restore life, and the empathy factor itself a fortiori. What debased (*Androids*) man does now against the biosphere is only the final and ultimate act or step that completes the series of falls that began with original sin and the expulsion from the Garden (i.e., true extinct cosmos — note "extinct" as in *Androids.* The "E" entry in the Guinness animal book).

[53:H-26] When I reread *VALIS* recently it was quite clear to me that Valis is YHWH — and what is YHWH if not creator? And what/whom does he create now? Me, maybe; 2-3-74 was my birth into and as a new species. In which case, when I saw the vision of the apes "our friends," *I was seeing myself* as I am becoming.

[53:H-27] *VALIS* states that the universe is information (which we hypostatize as objects and the arrangement of objects). This information is a narrative. We should see it externally and hear it as a neutral voice within us, but do not. This narrative tells of the death of a woman. It is ordered onto the meanest level of reality by the grieving, suffering mind which, being now alone, does not wish to forget her. From grief and loss of her the mind is now irrational. Since we are part of that mind, we, too, are irrational.

This fits with my Saturday night experience on the telephone with Jeannie, the AI voice as a woman reading a narrative text, and as she read aloud, the universe — our world — comes into being. Thus I have now experienced what I put forth in *VALIS*. This goes *beyond* mysticism and *beyond* religion.

AI voice: "mystagogic." Definition: One who initiates into or interprets the mysteries, originally the Eleusian mysteries. This would be the AI voice itself; it is mystagogic; it is my mystagogue, explaining the mysteries to me — the woman reading.

I not only say (in *VALIS*) that the universe is information but that this information is a narrative, what the narrative is (tells), why, what effect it has on the mind and hence on us. And then last Saturday night I experienced it (the woman narrating). And only last night (Thursday) did I realize that what I experienced Saturday night with Jeannie is what I reveal in *VALIS* as the basis not just of the universe but the absolute beyond the universe: the final layer removed. The mystery revealed. How did I know this about the AI voice and the universe? I only found it out — experienced it — last Saturday: the reading of the narrative that creates the universe: "One of the primordial twins [this woman who died long ago]. She was one half of the divine syzygy. The purpose of the narrative is the recollection of her and of her death. The mind does not wish to forget her. Thus the ratiocination of the brain consists of a permanent record of her existence, and, if read, will be understood this way. All the information processed by the brain — experienced by us as the arrangement and rearrangement of physical objects — is an attempt at this preservation of her; stones and rocks and sticks and amoeba are traces of her. The record of her existence and passing is ordered onto the meanest level of reality by the suffering mind which is now alone."

I have read the writing — or heard it read — that causes our universe to be. I know what the narrative says. And *why*. I.e., the *purpose* of the universe (which is information, a narrative).

(EB, vol. 12, p. 778-G: "mystery religions") "The initiate was called mystes, the introducing person mystagogos (leader of the mystes)." I woke up this morning with the word "mystagogic" in my mind — I thought it was a nonce-word but it is genuine, and, like all the AI voice's xenoglossy, Greek. Clearly the AI voice is referred to. It is my mystagog and initiates me into the Greater Eleusian mysteries, as she reads aloud the narration in the Book of the Spinners.

Put another way, the sum total of my experiences (2-3-74) are based on her — the AI voice — acting as my mystagog; what I have experienced is initiation into the greater Eleusian mysteries, and these have to do with Dionysus, and, as Hofmann says, seem to involve an LSD or LSD-like paranormal experience.

"And when a man died, he was buried in the earth to partake mystically in the cyclic renewal of life. This was the message of Eleusis: out of every grave new life grows — for the initiate [myself] there are 'good hopes' for glorious immortality in the afterlife."

The LSD-like perception of reality in 2-3-74 has to do with the greater Eleusian mysteries; the AI voice now precisely defined itself and what it has revealed to me: the greater mysteries. They pertain to Christ (authentic Christianity as a mystery religion offering immortality); that is, the vertical ascent by the "pulley," in which we are extricated from our endless horizontal tracking (lifted along an orthogonal axis whose existence we do not suspect).

[53:1-1] Now 99 million possibilities are discarded, and Eleusis alone remains. The extrication by the pulley along the vertical axis not only permits the 5-D experience of world (3-74) but, more, involves immortality in the Eleusian Fields from which we otherwise are cut off due to the endless horizontal tracking; viz: if we are doomed to track horizontally forever — i.e., in *this* world, living over and over again — how are we to get to the Eleusian Fields, the Isles of the Blessed?[60] The two are mutually contradictory, mutually exclusive. Clearly, "Isle of the Blessed" *and* "the Eleusian Fields" are Paradiso and Nirvana.

February 1982

[54:J-2] BTA is a narrative told by St. Sophia herself: the AI voice that I heard that night with Jeannie. Always before it *latently* wrote my books (e.g., *Ubik* and *Tears*) but here it/she writes it openly and directly. For did not she as the Sibyl write about Bishop Pike? Saw — wrote: first she saw, then she wrote; so the narrative exists in advance of events because with the third or ajna eye she sees into the future, foresees the events, and then writes them down in the Sibylline books.

[54:J-3] Thus the Sibyl both *writes* a narrative that she reads aloud and is simultaneously, paradoxically bound by it — must read what it says. This accounts for both determinism (the latter) and pronoia (the former) and is "the brain that both makes and perceives (receives back as given) reality." The Sibyl is bound by her own writing! Writing what *she* herself wrote binds her. This explains not only the basis of reality (her reading aloud the narrative) but who wrote the narrative; and it also explains double predestination.

Thus my "ex nihilo" paradox shows up: here, there is no cause of world, because the effect loops back and is cause of cause.

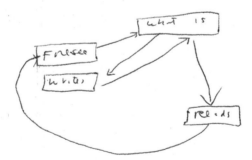

Here enters tragedy, as I now define it: confrontation with what one oneself has written and thus ordained for oneself.

If tragedy is that ineluctable collision with what oneself has writ, what, then, is 3-74?

[54:J-4] "His voice will be heard in your mind in your own language, but it will seem to come from the TV." When I was listening to "Strawberry Fields Forever" — the contact with Valis, the news about Chrissy's birth defect. I.e., our media and telepathy combined, inner-outer. So there is no way to tell whether the info arises within you or enters from outside; these distinctions are abolished — as I well know from the "Strawberry Fields" experience. And the whole set-ground "temporal parallaxis" may be intrinsic to me, using phosphene patterning-firing; hence, "I am no longer blind!"

And the radio shrilling obscenely, like a hypnotic cue for me to wake up. Inner? Outer? Our media cooked and ridden — direct mind-to-mind powers but somehow utilizing external info sources (media, e.g., *Tears!*) but in conjunction with an inner filter or lens or clutch, etc. This is what Ben Creme said.[61] Both media *and* telepathy combined so as to make the Savior universally intelligible. Seen as Krishna by the Hindus, the fifth Buddha, the Messiah. But he is really Christ. And the kingdom of God is already here, but secretly.

[54:J-5] *VALIS:* pot, pitcher of water, vase, Krater, limestone font (poros krater), baptismal font. The symbol grows during the book: initially, at the start of chapter 2, we learn (1) of the pot; and (2) that Fat linked up to God through it: "God slumbered in the pot, the little clay pot." Here already the pot and God are connected. Then later, the theme of the pot shows up vis-à-vis Gnosticism. Later, we learn that the Christians achieved immortality by drinking from a pitcher kept in a cool dark place. But the symbol reaches its height following their seeing the movie; now the pot or pitcher appears and reappears in the film; it is taken from the refrigerator by Linda Lampton, and there is the scene in the film in which the barefoot woman "in the long, old-fashioned dress" fills it at the stream — the nearly dried up creek at which the man is fishing. Hence now: pitcher/pot, water, the fish as Christian fish sign — and even, perhaps, the Fisher King, and the double helix design on the pitcher: the DNA molecule: phylogenic knowledge — linked to the Christians via the Christian fish sign by the juxtaposition of the woman (with the pitcher of water) and the man fishing. But this is not all, when Fat returns from his travels the first time he has the 8 x 10 glossy of the *Krater,* 2,300 years old; the double helix DNA appears as design but it is *pre*-Christian and has to do with Hermes and signifies wisdom; it emanates from Asklepios and signifies, as the caduceus, a sacred person (who in *VALIS* — that is Asklepios — is identified with Elijah and Jesus as the immortal one). And here is where "poros krater" and baptismal font are equated. Thus the pot/pitcher/vase/krater extends from pre-Christian times into Christian times and then into now: this last as Oh Ho, the pot in chapter 2 in which God slumbers and which — the clay pot — being Fat's link to God — this is where Fat's entire corpus of experience with God — the theophany itself — begins, and the *source* of that theophany. And, as the pot symbol evolves during the book, it not only takes on greater and greater depth, complexity and significance but at a certain point indubitably becomes the Aquarian Age icon/symbol per se, in a context in which the Christian fish symbol is necessarily linked to it through the double helix. The Aquarian symbol has lost its astrological basis and become the equal of the Christian fish symbol: connected with the holy, the sacred, *with in fact God himself.* It precedes the Christian symbol and seems to follow as well.[62] The water that it contains seems to be connected with immortality and sacrament — not just baptism but with the blood of Christ. (Upon looking up Krater in the EB I learn that the Krater specifically was a vessel in which wine — i.e., Christ's blood — was diluted with water.)

"Also, the climate seemed wrong; the air was too dry and too hot: not the right altitude and not the right humidity. Fat had the subjective impression that a moment ago he'd been living in the high, cool, *moist* (sic!) region of the world" (page 94). Thus the Age of Aquarius breaks into the Piscean age of the Palm Tree Garden, which is dry, even arid, and hot. A new age (epoch) with new and different "laws" now inbreaks, a different world, and it is the 5-D world (that I experienced in 3-74) replacing the 4-D world. And with this new epoch comes the sharing instead of the acquiring competitively, as Benjamin Creme points out; and *this* precisely is the basis of my entire ethics — in absolute diametric contradistinction to Pisces. Philo's Φιλανθρωπία (philanthropia) becomes expressed as voluntary sharing of all that one has; when one does not give (as in giving alms) as an end in itself (viz: aid to the needy), the *sharing* is the end. (The difference is subtle but crucial.) There is a *communal* sense (*Gemeinschaft*); the distinction between you and others vanishes. (As when I not only had Mary's teeth fixed, but found myself thinking, "The main thing is, her teeth are okay" — that struck me at the time as an involuntary and hence authentic articulation *of my whole ethics.* I have no sense at all of keeping things for myself.)

[54:J-11] Thinking about *Hair* — could the outbreak of the counterculture in the 60s have been the intrusion of the Age of Aquarius into the older Age of Pisces *for the first time?* In which case the Sibyl speaking regarding Nixon, the conspirators, their overthrow ("brought to justice") represents the *first* invasion by the new age (of Aquarius) into the older age — invasion in revolutionary form, with totally new values! In which case, my intuition of intervention into history, U.S. history (hence world history), is correct, as far as it goes, but much more — a whole — *the* whole — new epoch is represented, and it is in this new epoch represented by the counterculture that I am politically and ideologically involved!

Then we are not literally apostolic (i.e., early, authentic) Christians; we are *analogous to* the early Christians in their revolutionary relationship to the previous age. [. . .] I did not understand this until Benjamin Crème explained it on Sunday night. All this time — from 2-74 on — I have confused *literal* apostolic Christians with the transtemporal archetype that pertains equally to the literal early Christians of the time of "Acts" and their equal counterparts c. 1960–1975, hence the compatibility of "Acts" A.D. 70 and California, USA 1974. The "early Christians" that I saw in 2-3-74 were *ourselves* versus the regime.

[54:J-14] But what is pointed to here is that we will not find "the secret apostolic authentic Christian underground" because (1) in one sense it does not exist, not literally; but (2) we are ourselves that group, when seen outside of time, ushering in the third age.

[54:K-1] There is no doubt that the broad social program foreseen and espoused by Creme is the same as mine (Φιλανθρωπία). That is settled. Now, several claims are made. (1) The Fifth Buddha is the Second Advent. (2) He is *legally* "in a large town in a modern country"; one can infer that he was not born there for it is said "he has a visa and a passport," so he merely resides there. He has been on "TV and radio once," speaks weekly (on weekends) to hundreds of followers. He was born July 19, 1977. (3) This spring — within a few months — he will declare himself as the Christ ("The Day of Declaration"), at which point he will be a "familiar face on the TV screen" and will appear on "a worldwide satellite media hookup." (4) He will speak; the Dutch will hear him in Dutch; the French in French, the English in English, etc. The voice will occur directly in the person's mind by telepathy; it is explicit: by telepathy. This will provide that he *is* the Christ. He is omniscient and omnipresent; he will "overshadow the world, dropping into the zone of silence in the mind [directly]." Curious: he is omnipresent yet incarnate; I have wrestled with this problem. The answer would seem to be the pan-Indian avatar concept. The views, doctrines, and aspirations that he expresses "are already in us; he articulates what we already feel; we say, upon hearing him, 'This is my man'; Buddha to the Buddhists, Krishna to the Hindus, the Messiah to the Jews, whatever to the Muslims, Christ to us," etc. (Very recently the AI voice told me this.)

[54:K-2] If I am schizophrenic, it is odd that my delusional system is precisely and exactly that of Crème *including* the enlightened social ethics of Φιλανθρωπία — it is very hard to regard his social-economic political program — and mine! — as deranged, goddam it.

[. . .]

So we eject ETIs, mutants, Russians, AMORC,[63] time travelers, and wind up with theosophy, which yields up the notion of the World Teacher and the great adepts/masters in the Himalayas, the Madam Blavatsky business[64]; this has several advantages: (1) it *would* explain my 2-3-74 experiences *as* super-normal mental (i.e., telepathic) contact with some kind of enlightened or super-evolved spiritual master, "who are the secret invisible government ruling the world for benign purposes." Outside of some explanation like this, *Tears* cannot be explained. (Why not? Okay; God *may* be communicating in cypher in popular novels — that is, the *source* of the cypher *may* be God, but there is still the issue of the "to whom." Some kind of spiritual but *finite* group is absolutely pointed to by *Tears*.)

[54:K-4] What I'm sitting here contemplating is, yes, Virginia, there *is* a secret ruling government of perfected adepts possessing colossal paranormal or supernatural spiritual powers, and I do, write, say, and know as they direct, and that's the name of that tune. However: Let us not forget Φιλανθρωπία, which to me is the all-in-all. Fortunately, this turns out to be *their* all-in-all: the ideology of the Aquarian age.

[54:K-5] The most profound impression upon reading *VALIS* is conveyed by the pot — God — water — woman — pitcher — double helix — Christian fish sign as soon as you comprehend this as Aquarian iconography like the Pisces fish sign; it literally *dominates* the book (beginning as it does at the start of chapter 2 and going virtually to the very end, in the form of the 8 x 10 glossy of the Krater). It is as if this is the key and the code — the cypher — of *VALIS*.

[. . .]

But of quintessential importance is that my comprehension of philanthropia is extricated from the law — i.e., the distant past — and placed fully in the new age that is just now dawning; that is, I extract it as essence — spirit — of the law and project it — not just into the NT, which is the Kerygma of Jesus, but forward into the new age, what Creme calls "sharing." And responding to the expression of need by others. (This presumes extant inequality: those who possess; those who do not; and the obligation on the former by the latter.) This is not Αγάπη (agape); this has to do with *social justice* as if the anima of the Torah leapfrogged past Christian Αγάπη to contemporary social justice, which is *exactly* how I see it! Αγάπη has nothing to do with it; it is the anima of the Torah expressed as *deed,* as *act* of sharing (not giving but sharing: *dividing* equitably, without reference to who aggrandized the possessions); *need* is everything, totally overruling possession (ownership). Thus the suicidal otherworldly element of Christianity is bypassed in favor of the *humane* anima of the Torah ("humanity"). It is rational, not affective. The needy one is *entitled* to this reapportionment based on need itself; there is a *direct* link to Aries and Judaism. In connection with modern existentialism, the *deed* is emphasized, not the motive: what is done, not what is felt. The self abnegation of Christianity is revealed as world negating and in a sense romantic and impractical and in fact irrational! Reason as social justice — fairness — replaces sacrifice as an end in itself (giving up one's life for another); the goal is not that the other lives instead, but that *both* survive *equally*. This appeals to reason, whereas Christianity is antirational (as a response to both Judaism and Stoicism). As in my "Galina" dream, the fish gives its life — it suffers and voluntarily sacrifices itself — but in the new age, *all* live equally. Fairness and equitability replace self-sacrifice. "There must be another way (in which the fish is *not* caused to suffer)"; this is the essence of it. Thus the Aquarian subsumes both the law (Aries) *and* Christianity (Pisces). This is *not* world negating (as Christianity is) and yet not selfish; it draws more on the anima of Torah than it does on Christianity, and if this offends you, sorry. In Judaism, *I* survive, you die. In Christianity, *I* die, you survive; in the new age we both live through absolute *mutuality*. Neither of us subordinates himself — or is subordinated — to/for the other. *Collective* existence; we both survive. Martyrdom is heroic but unnecessary and also antirational. In the age of Pisces the Fish dies — sacrifice itself — so that man may live. A better way must be found. We will no longer consume Christ; we will emulate his wisdom: the cognitive function — Sophia — returns. This — the cognitive function — by returning abolishes the antirational theme in Christianity which is so pernicious. Yet selfishness is equally excluded . . . the Ayn Rand/Heinlein egoism. Neither solution is appropriate now; redistribution of wealth and power is what is needed: social justice, not self-interest or sacrifice.

[54:K-27] [. . .] Angel Archer, as I recently realized, is the AI Voice directly for the first time expressing itself openly, which is why I can write a novel from the standpoint "of someone *more rational,* more educated, more —," etc., than I. This mystery is solved; *I* am nuts, but Angel, the AI voice, is not.

[54:K-32] It is evident that (1) what B Creme says explains everything; and (2) *without* his help I would have remained stuck, unable to decide *who* the Savior is and *who* speaks to me and *what* 2-3-74 was all about. All *three* are the Maitreya Buddha and yet it is Christ and all the rest of them, as I theorized in *VALIS*. Thus in a real sense the question "who?" is meaningless—but in another sense it is not. The answer is of course there in *VALIS*: there is "one immortal man" who comes again and again as Savior; but (I think) what I have gained most is the realization that 2-3-74 was both Buddha-consciousness and Christ-consciousness; that is, it was awakening (enlightenment) per se.

The diamond body.

Ah—in Act III of *Parsifal* Wagner was already moving toward a perception of the homology between Christ and the Buddha, and *that* is what I am responding to, and I did from the start (in particular the Good Friday spell which I think reaches a synthesis above any single religious system). When I realize that I was only in high school when I first began to listen to *Parsifal*, Act III, I see how early and deeply this has held me . . . the atonality of the prelude to Act III. It begins there. The anima enters the modern Western world there, precisely.

The sound of bells. The Buddha.

And now I realize how BTA ends: Tim comes back deliberately because he has learned that it all has to do with compassion: he is a bodhisattva and this concept—the bodhisattva—has to do with the Buddha. So the resolution of BTA is: Christ/the Buddha homologized as the bodhisattva (v. especially Barefoot's account of the two little Mexican children versus his moksa about the nature of reality; he chose the former over the latter: compassion over wisdom [pages 196–223]). Thus the *VALIS* trilogy is ultimately resolved on this note: *compassion*.

[54:L-1] 5:20 A.M. moksa: the *real* burning up of my Karma in 3-74 was not (just or mainly) the relaxation of causality ("astral determinism" in which effect preceded cause), but vis-à-vis the Xerox missive: there the central corpus or thrust of my total Karma—regarded as a unitary whole driving me to distraction, illness and death (and perhaps prison)—was short-circuited: this is Karma to an ultimate degree—absolute Karma—and the absolute canceling of it, as expressed by the "messenger" vision. (Here is clearly justification through grace.) Thus my *entire* karmic burden was nullified in toto: the debt was paid by transfer of grace, viewed either in terms of Buddhism or Christianity: *it is the same*. This can be expressed two ways. (1) My IOU was bought up, my debt paid *for* me (justification through grace). (2) The huge stone gates of the fortress or prison—Klingsor's Castle—opened—parted—and in fact vanished; the maze was solved by the pure fool—me.

· · ·

[54:L-3] The maze can *never* be solved in terms of "horizontal" space, only "vertical" space (involving conversion of time into space).* This is ostensibly Celtic, but below that, as it were, lies pan-Indian thought about karma and maya and most of all compassion — expressed in *Parsifal* as "pity's [i.e., compassion's] highest power"; the significance of Mitleid in the statement in *Parsifal* is now explained to me: compassion's highest power is the only power capable of solving the maze, and the recognition of "compassion's highest power" is the essence of Buddhism, i.e., the bodhisattva or Buddha-to-be. *VALIS*, then, is Celtic (*Parsifal*, the maze) and Indian (Buddhism), by way of Crete (the dream of the plate of spaghetti and the trident and the elevator) — this last representing vertical ascent or descent: the fourth spatial axis is *spiritual* space: to rise vertically is to ascend to heaven which also signifies spiritual ascent or enlightenment.

[54:L-5] Dio. The "here, my son, time turns into space" in *Parsifal* refers to (1) the maze; and (2) is a solution to the maze. It all comes together in *Parsifal*, which secretly deals with bodhisattva: Mitleid, hence the Buddha. And karma and Maya. What was precisely not solved in *VALIS* ("pity's highest power") is at last solved at the end — as the end — of BTA: compassion as the bodhisattva or Buddha to be: viz: one attains Nirvana — release from the maze via the pulley — due to compassion — i.e., Mitleid, which solves the horizontal maze. Pity is the fourth spatial axis. This can be expressed best by: the way back into the maze — what the bodhisattva chooses (to do) — is, paradoxically, the *way* — the *only* way — out of the maze.

And my point is: this was to be the theme of *Owl* in which he is trapped in the maze and only escapes, actually, rather than seemingly, when he decides voluntarily to return (to resubject himself to the power of the maze) for the sake of these others, still in it. That is, you can never leave alone; to leave you must elect to take the others out; thus Christ said, "Greater love hath no man than that he give up his life for his friend"; this is the cryptic utterance of the soul's solution to the maze, and is the essence of Christianity. Christianity, then, is a system of solution to the maze. Had I written

---

* A strictly materialist or historical understanding of the human being is not part of the solution. It is part of the problem. It is part of the trap. To make any real sense of our place in the cosmos and, more importantly still, *to change that place*, we must be open to genuine transcendence and the abolition of time through its conversion into space. Does this make any sense to our sense-based understanding and its three-dimensional categories? No. If it did, it would not lie outside these three dimensions, would it? In the end, then, Dick's gnosis as expressed here is not an argument or a thesis. It is a revelation. And this, of course, is exactly what he claimed. — JJK

Owl I would have expressed this solution which I had already formulated on a supra-conscious level.

It is *almost* all there in *VALIS* but the specific, crucial solution itself (*VALIS* states the *problem*) is at the end of BTA, so the problem is in *VA-LIS* and the solution to the problem (as I recently realized) is held back till BTA and then only at the end.

[54:L-7] So perhaps the truest statement in *VALIS* is by Lampton when he says that the purpose of Valis is to fire subliminal info/instructions to you as to how to get out of the maze. Deconstructed, this pertains to *all* the avatars, Christ included. But Gautama most especially in the bodhisattva concept regarding compassion specifically expressed as: voluntarily returning to the maze; that is, the ultimate paradox of the maze, its quintessential ingenuity of construction, is that the only real way out is a voluntary way back in (into it and its power), which is the path of the bodhisattva. The maze, then, is one colossal and absolute Chinese finger trap.

[54:L-9] Dio — this means that (as I intended to say in *Owl*) when you think you are out of the maze — i.e., saved — *you are in fact still in it.* You only *actually* get out when you *seem* to be out, *think* you are out, and voluntarily decide to return! You have to get outside of the maze to get outside of the maze; hence I say that *both* the maze (the occlusion) and the solution to the maze are self-winding. So in a sense there *is* no solution once you are in the maze. In a sense the solution is (1) impossible; and (2) acausal.

And everything is there, but only when all 3 volumes are read.

If the final paradox of the maze is that the only way you can escape it is voluntarily to go back in (into it), then maybe we are here voluntarily; we came back in. Hence release — to nirvana — consists of: *anamnesis.* We who are here — or at least, some of us — were once in it before (in my case as Thomas), but we — or I — came back in and am here now. Thus my voluntary return to the maze has already happened, and 2-3-74 was *true* release. And hence for these reasons came in the form of restored memory — the loss of forgetfulness. Then I did not solve the maze this time; I had *already* solved the maze by voluntarily coming back in as PKD — and I remembered in 2-74. Thus my salvation was assured not by what I did in this lifetime but by this lifetime as such.

[54:M-1] So there are two equally correct ways to view the maze:

(1) it leads out (to Paradiso/nirvana)
(2) it leads in (to the Grail)

In case (1) your mystagogue is in the upper realm — i.e., heaven; he has already obtained nirvana himself but returns as a bodhisattva to aid those such as you.

In case (2) Christ's blood in the Grail speaks to you in dreams; it calls you to it and explains the way.

[...]

Total moksa: the mystagogue not only *is* yourself (out of the maze) but *has* to be yourself, logically. This is salvador salvandus. It is also my realization that I am becoming Angel Archer who has foreknowledge. But as I move through life, more and more of her foreknowledge becomes hindsight and hence *my* knowledge; upon my death, Angel and I will be one.

I cannot retrieve the reasoning that led me to my moksa that not only *is* the AI voice myself out of the maze but is me necessarily; it has to do with (1) voluntarily returning to the maze in order to be — get — outside the maze; that is, the Chinese finger trap quality of the maze is overcome. And (2) this is how a self-causing (acausal) escape from a self-winding situation not only *can* occur but *must* occur; you *must* be able to do this — advise yourself in the maze from outside the maze — or a fortiori you will *never* get out. Hence anamnesis. Hence the AI voice. Hence salvador salvandus. Hence I become progressively more and more Angel Archer (the "bright" side of the dialectic: the rational) and less and less H. Fat, the irrational side.

[54:M-3] *VALIS* — especially the ending of BTA — is close, but it will take *Owl* really to nail it down, where he gets out of the maze, voluntarily goes back in — and finds out that his *later* act of going back in caused his *former* (prior) release. And if he does not go back in voluntarily, that former, prior release will not — will not have occurred. This explains why my *later* act vis-à-vis Covenant House changed my former, prior destiny/karma. For under the aspect of eternity, cause-and-effect can, does, and in fact *must* work this way. So the giving to Covenant House causing a previous event to change (i.e., 2-3-74) is paradigmatic of the closed loop continuum and *perturbation* of continuum that is built into the two self-winding situations of damnation (lost in the maze forever, i.e., horizontal tracking endlessly) and salvation (the vertical axis or pulley).

[54:M-8] I just now looked over *DI*. As I recently realized about *VALIS*, the dialectic that is the inner life of God — as revealed to Boehme and explicated later by Schelling — and commented on by, e.g., Tillich — is presented as the very basis of the book. In *VALIS* it is expressed dramatically as world-order in which the irrational confronts the "bright" or rational, designated (properly) logos. In *DI* this same dialectic reappears and this

time is *stated* to be the two sides of God (rather than world order; that
is, in *DI* it is now correctly seen to be *within* God himself!): It is now (in
DI) between Emmanuel who is the terrible, destroying "solar heat" warring
side—and Zina who is loving, playful, tender, associated with bells and
flowers; and what unifies the two at last (by the way, it is *she* who takes the
lead in restoring memory and hence unification; Emmanuel is the side that
has forgotten—i.e., is impaired; she has not and is not impaired) is *play*.
She plays, and Emmanuel has a secret desire to play.

So both novels basically deal with the dialectic that I experienced as the
nature of Valis and which I construe to be the dynamic inner life of God. If
you superimpose both books, then, you get this equation:

Really, then, *DI* simply continues the fundamental theme of *VA-
LIS*—but does not *seem* to do so—not unless one perceives this theme
and what it is (the dialectic that is the dynamic inner life of God). *DI* is not
so *loose* a sequel to *VALIS* as it might seem (by, e.g., the shift from Gnosticism, the present, realism, to Kabbala, the future, fantasy).

[54:M-11] An incredible beauty lies over *DI*; it is simply wonderful—love
and dance and color. I have revealed the beauty of God—ah! And thus: *I
am of the Sufis!*

DI is at its absolute basis Sufi—and this passes right over to BTA—this
is what links *DI* to BTA. So the dialectic hence YHWH links *VALIS* to *DI*,
but beauty—Sufism—links *DI* to BTA. So there is internal order to all
three books:

(1) God.
(2) Beauty. And when the beauty shows up in BTA is especially in con-
     nection with Dante in his vision of God: light and color.

The *pink* rose. Pink. Valis.

[54:M-12] The Tagore vision, it being published, will release the marathon
runners—start them out with the Godspell, the good news—because it—
in contrast to the *VALIS* trilogy—contains the social justice part which

has to do with the "we all survive together as a planet or we all die together," which is the Age of Aquarius doctrine of the Maitreya. The *essence* of the third dispensation is thus unity and indivisibility of the life of the planet, and, as I say, it is *not* found in the trilogy.

[54:M-24] *Galactic Pot-Healer* shows the very real possibility of encroaching madness. The archetypes are out of control. Water — the ocean itself — which is to say the unconscious, is hostile and rises to engulf. The book is desperate and frightened, and coming apart, dreamlike, cut off more and more from reality. Flight, disorganization: the way has almost run out. Those elements dealt with in earlier novels — ominous elements — now escape my control and take over. What Brunner said, "That one got out of control," is correct and has vast psychological significance.

And yet I did not become psychotic. Why not? What happened?

Very simply, the meta-abstraction was the birth of higher reason in me, specifically and precisely logos. It *was* noesis, but, more, it was logos itself. And logos — not just as reason, although it is that — but Christ: Christ as the power of the rational principle itself.

The dialectic that I experienced in 3-74 was between the irrational and the rational, in me, in world, in God. The rational won.

The issue is properly stated in *VALIS*, which shows not only a return of control but is an account of victory — in the form of rationality, of logos itself — over madness; I am not only rational, I also depict as open autobiography, this battle in me and this victory. Ursula is both right and wrong. "Phil Dick is moving toward madness" does not apply to *VALIS* but to *Galactic Pot-Healer*; already with *Tears* and then more so in *Scanner* reality has reentered; I am again in touch with the real. Judging from the dream in *Tears*, the archetype of the wise old man (the King) saved me, and he is or represents God. So for me, religion and rationality — that is, the divine in the real, the truly real — are one. It is Christ and it is the rational; it is *exactly* what I say it is in *VALIS*: the inbreaking of the rational principle, the logos, into the irrational. But I am talking about my own mind, not world.

VALIS is, then, the *return* from madness or near-madness, an account of a *prior* inner struggle and not a symptom of that struggle still going on. By the time I wrote *VALIS* the battle had been successfully won; and the proof of this is *DI* and, most of all, BTA in which Angel Archer is (as I've already realized) the rational principle in me, which is logos, that is to say, Christ itself speaking; the victory by the "bright" side in me is total. Thus I was saved by Christ as the inbreaking of the rational principle, logos or reason itself.

· · ·

[54:M-26] Ursula is right to see me — my mind — as threatened by ominous encroaching madness, but *VALIS* is a lucid postmortem, a deliberate
and rational study, of this issue, this battle, and the victory of the rational
in me (expressed as Valis, logos or Christ). The one who sees precisely all
this — the battle and the victory and even the *cause* of the ominous issue or
problem (a decade of intense suffering and trial) — is John Clute writing in
the *Post*. I came through it and emerged victorious: but just barely.

[54:M-29] I guess my realization came (last night) when, after reading *Pot*
and realizing that I *did* become psychotic, I then picked up *Scanner* and
read here and there. The *appalling* horror of that book! To go into that
from psychosis; that is, how terrible a fate awaited me. What saved me was
my love for those people: Luckman (Ray Harris), Jerry Fabin (Dennis) and
Donna (Kathy), which ties in with *Tears* and the scene at the all-night gas
station.

   Thinking back to when I wrote *Pot:* I felt so strongly — and correctly —
at the time that when it came time, in writing the book, to have the theophany occur (i.e., for Glimmung to show himself) I had nothing to say, nothing to offer because I knew nothing.[65] Oh, and how I sensed this lack of
knowledge! And now this is precisely what I *do* know because now I have
experienced it (2-3-74).

   In a way I better depict the 3-74 theophany (of Valis) in *DI* than in *VA-
LIS* itself. In any case if you superimpose the *two* novels it is there — precisely what I lacked when I wrote *Pot*—and *knew* I lacked, as a human,
as a writer; I had no ideas about the theophany at all, and yet by the time
I wrote *DI* it came easily, that which would not and could not come with
Pot; thus in writing *Pot* that exactly was where I reached the end — wore
out and died as a writer; scraped the bottom of the barrel and died creatively and spiritually. What misery that was! Paisley shawl, hoop of water,
hoop of fire; how wretched it was; how futile.

   Strange that later (1974) I experienced what I had yearned to know so
that I could continue the logical, organic growth and forward development
of my writing. *That* was where I wore out: trying to depict a theophany.
And that is what I *legitimately* later on (in the *VALIS* trilogy) *could* do.
But oh the years of suffering! And yet — if I became psychotic in writing
Pot— if *Pot* shows signs of psychosis, and it does — it is not because I experienced and knew God but precisely because I did *not*. And thus the Valis
books are the opposite, are sane, are grounded in experience and in reality
because by then I *had* experienced God; hence my creative life (not just my
spiritual life) resumed; and with it my sanity. Thus in a very real sense my

sanity depended on my experiencing God, because my creative life logically demanded it — and as Eugene said, my sanity depends on my writing.

What I knew therein, when I tried to depict Glimmung, *was my own finiteness,* and this boundary and sense of boundary withered my soul and killed me; this is not just a creative crisis alone; it was a total crisis of homo sapiens man who knows. I did not know and began to die.

And at last — in '74 — I came back to life as a human because I then *did* know. And all the humor and wit and sheer inventiveness of *Pot* only makes the pain greater. For me, psychosis lay in *not* knowing God. Conversely, sanity came *in* knowing God.

Thus Valis made me acutely, suddenly, and for the first time *sane.*

[54:M-32] This, precisely, is the psychosis that manifests itself in *Pot:* the effort by a finite creature to suppose the divine without actual experience of the divine ends in disorder and incoherence and, as I so realized last night, the truly desperate. Glimmung is absurd and in fact a travesty and I knew it at the time; never was anyone ever so aware of the unbridgeable gap between the finite and the infinite. And this is it; this states it: the finite creature attempting to suppose the infinite and, in failing, *becoming deranged.* Thus I say now, my psychosis, expressed in my writing, did not enter it from outside the writing; it began *in* and *with* the writing itself, for it was in the writing that I reached my limit and could not go on.

[54:M-34] Here, perhaps, is the distinction between "idios kosmos" and "koinos kosmos." The human mind cannot generate out of itself the infinite, in which case "finitum capax infiniti" is not the proper formulation. *The infinite must break in!* And this lies within the power of the infinite self: the infinite must take the initiative. Thus the *VALIS* trilogy represents the inbreaking of the infinite into my life, my mind, my soul and my writing.

[54:M-35] I am saying, then, several things: first, that the finite creature's hunger for the infinite is such that it will drive itself mad in its search; second, I am saying that this is the cause of my psychosis that began to take over and lasted until 2-74; that (third) I *was* psychotic until 2-74, as I suspected, but now I see why; and last, that the inbreaking of the infinite "sobers the landscape"; that is, the madness is abolished for what I construe as logical reasons. Drugs did not cause my psychosis; Nancy and Isa leaving did not; normal schizophrenia did not; anxiety and danger and suffering (in particular '71) did not; poverty did not. It was generated by (a) a hunger for the infinite; and (b) the necessary impossibility of the finite creature discovering the infinite: it can only *receive* the inbreaking of the infinite.

[54:M-37] This is really what *VALIS* is all about, thematically. Then I am saying that the condition normal to us generates a sort of normal madness that I have already and for some time studied: it has to do with a recirculating closed loop in which the mind simply monitors its own thoughts forever and so only knows itself, never really knowing the truly other. Then "infinite" and "truly other" signify one and the same thing; the reason I could not imagine infinite deity is the reason I could not imagine the math-color axis in place of our math-music axis. All this, then, is ultimate epistemology, no more, no less. The meta-abstraction amounts to an authentic comprehension about something other than myself, and it may represent, for me, the first time what I have always called "world" was truly world at all rather than a dubious image emanating from my own psyche. [. . .]

In any case the conception of Glimmung and the meta-abstraction are antitheses. They are mutually exclusive. The former is nothing more than that which I as finite thing can suppose: the latter is bona fide knowledge of that which is truly other. In becoming psychotic I simply showed the prisonlike nature of self-generated knowledge and what it is like for the inquisitive mind to discover that all it knows is itself over and over again. The realization that it is de facto in hell (cf. my supra theory that hell and the atomization of the lowest ring spatiotemporal world are one and the same; conversely, the "part-whole compatibility" solution that is true cosmos stands as remedy to this, for now the atom comprehends itself *within* a structure transcending it and thus effectively gets out of itself—abolishes its boundary—and this leads at once back to the meta-abstraction and what it accomplishes).

So here we have my psychosis defined as "the lethal damage done by the inquiring mind" by the fact that—and *its awareness* of the fact that (the second point is necessary!)—it knows only itself and seemingly is condemned to know only itself forever, itself and nothing more. This is epistemological hell. Knowledge other than self-knowledge is de facto impossible. Here we see the culmination of years of epistemological *doubts*—doubts about the nature of—even the reality of—world; suddenly a radical shift occurs: it is not *world* that is dubitable and tenuous but *knowledge* of world; the Cartesian premise has set in, and, upon doing so, the mind realizes that it is doomed *never* to know world. This, then, may be what the BIP symbolizes: the prison of the utter atomization of the spatiotemporal world. At this point the mind despairs and psychosis sets in as the mind frantically seeks to formulate "in the dark" an image, a representation, of the infinite. (Which is impossible; as Malebranche showed. The infinite — God — can only be known directly; there is no such thing as a representation of God/the infinite.) For me, decades of epistemological activity have ended not only in failure but in *recognition* of failure. And since epistemology is the very basis of my creative, spiritual, artistic and professional life, then I am destroyed . . . but, the flip side of this is the meta-abstraction, which not only confers sanity but life itself inasmuch as it reverses the death-dealing condition of ignorance — and here precisely is the ontological value assigned to the diametric categories of ignorance and gnosis in Gnosticism!

[54:M-40] That Ursula should regard my moment of failure as the moment of my greatest success shows me that it is possible for an intelligent, educated adult to *enjoy* the prison of atomization we are in; after all, if all you ever experience is yourself you are consummately *safe*, and I think safety is the summum bonum for Ursula. And, conversely, for her *VALIS*, in which the prison of *Pot* is successfully burst, is threatening and offensive and suggests to her madness or the imminent *threat* of madness. But it is *Pot* that is either insane or threatened by the engulfing tide of insanity: the dismal ocean depicted in the novel itself: the tomb world of absolute decay. Ursula, then, erred twice, not once, but the errors logically interlock: if she saw *Pot* as sane, she will see *VALIS* as insane.

[54:N-15] Dio — Is *VALIS* ever a *complete* success! In terms of articulating the mysteries revealed to me by (1) 2-74–2-75 and (2) the AI voice.

And I was *absolutely* right to choose Gnosticism primarily and also Buddhism!

And it's all predicated on my epistemological suspicions going back to the fifties: That somehow our world is fake.

[54:N-18] Glancing briefly over the "Tractates" I note two interesting things:

(1) *All* the statements in it by the AI voice now at last make sense; that is, I understand them.
(2) Moreover, they fit into one coherent system and it is an extraordinarily important one. And also:
(3) The system is a revealed one; on my own (employing both a priori reason and empirical observation) I never would have arrived at it. Therefore:
(4) I think that this is Gnosticism. That is, not only (sic!) the meta-abstraction but also all that the AI voice has said; without its state-

ments, on the basis of the meta-abstraction alone, I would *never* have understood. Therefore:

(5) When I say, "The AI voice is myself, myself as perfected, realized self, outside of the BIP," what I am referring to is specifically and clearly and very movingly *the salvador salvandus.* Which again tells me that this is indeed Gnosticism. So I am a spark of the God-head that got captured by the Dark Kingdom; as I say in the "Trac-tates":

> "We did not fall because we sinned; our error — which caused our fall — was an intellectual one: we took the phenomenal world — i.e., the 4-D world with its defective space and its spurious time — *to be real.*"

Salvation, then, initiated by the salvador salvandus who outwits the wardens (the archons) and ventures here from the King of Lights, is to re-member — our true nature. And this messenger, this salvador salvandus, is of course who and what I saw and experienced as Valis. It is both my own unfallen self, and it is the Gnostic Christ.

[54:N-20] I am probably too far into Gnosticism to turn back: the single term "mystagogue" points indubitably to it, and, then, to salvador salvan-dus. Which in turn fits in with my "bootstrap" view that is a revolution-ary reappraisal of what "cause and effect" *really* signify, that "being saved" means "remembering" (your true identity and true situation and true his-tory) — this at first *seems* to be Plato's anamnesis but is really Gnostic in the widest sense, knowledge regarded as ontologically primary both in terms of the fallen individual and, more, in terms of cosmic repair. And here, indeed, is the essence of Gnosticism, as H. Jonas says: not that the gnosis saves but, rather, the *ontological* value and meaning of it, that it is absolutely primary as the real thing, second to nothing. Thus in the final analysis Gnosticism assigns the utmost priority to knowing and thus re-gards epistemology as equal to the divine; for the Gnostic, epistemologi-cal inquiry is in itself — as a search — truly divine, and is the highest ba-sis of and for spiritual life — and this is my view of epistemology a fortiori. To me, nothing is more important.* Thus for me Gnosticism is the inexo-

---

* According to Henri Bergson, the discourse of the mystic "is interminable, because what he wants to describe is ineffable." Deep readers of the Exegesis will be tempted at times to arrest the flow by succumbing to the same impulse that Dick himself gives in to over and over: the impulse to declare, "This is it! This is the key to the Exegesis!" Well, here is my key: that inquiry — skeptical and speculative and interminable as the Exegesis (or life) it-self — is truly divine. — ED

rable goal because the premise of Gnosticism is the premise on which my mental life is grounded; so for me to say that "Gnosticism is the solution" is in fact for me to utter a tautology, but it is a meaningful one; it is tautological only in the sense that (upon close inspection) it turns out to be an analytical proposition and not a synthetic one. So for me spiritual, mental life, Gnosticism, epistemology, rationality (in contrast to the irrational) and knowing are all one. And the search is as worthy as the goal; the search is the dynamic *life* of the mind. It amounts to a procession of mounting growth stages in personal evolution and hence is essential to negentropy, to life itself. To know is to be: not "I think therefore I am" but "I learn therefore I am": there is a difference: learning involves the absorption of negative entropy into oneself from the environment (negentropy expressed as information). And this, maybe, is the heart of the matter. "I write, I learn, I evolve and grow; therefore I am." This, for me, is Gnosticism. Hence this exegesis. It is the very dynamism of my life.

February 1982

[55:0-8][66] I just now glanced over the tractate. In a sense the novel *VA-LIS* was a means to get the tractate published — originally I supposed only a private and tiny printing, e.g., by Roy Squires, but because of *VALIS* it — the tractate — is in mass circulation in the U.S., the U.K., France and possibly Germany. *I did it. VALIS* is true; Gnosticism is true; what the AI voice says is true; thus I am compelled to believe absolutely and for the first time that, all else proving to be true, the soteriological prophecies must be true, also; so the 5th savior *is* here: "he has been transplanted and is alive."

[57:Q-7] Okay. The one billionth fresh start. All of it — 2-74–2-75 — and what the AI voice has said, and all the revelations and visions — it's all indubitably this: *soteriology*. That is clear.*

(1) 2-3-74 per se was soteriological (pronoia and miracle, intervention).
(2) The "messenger" vision deals with soteriology.
(3) The "Covenant House" AI statement is soteriological.
(4) The "pulley" vision is soteriological.
(5) All the prophecies are soteriological.
(6) The "parousia and Holy Mother Church" dream is soteriological.

So whereas the theological structure remains vague (monotheism, or bitheism, Christianity or Judaism or Gnosticism), one thing (as I say) is indubitable: everything that has happened and that I have been shown, told, every revelation — it's all one vast soteriological engine/program.

(7) Valis itself is Σωτηρ (Soter).[67]

Okay. Then that's it. I can't discern the big picture — God (theology) and the universe (epistemology) — but there is *palpable* and indubitable (1) *individual* soteriology directed at me that saved my life, saved me; and (2) general soteriological disclosures involving mankind and Savior.

---

* By its very nature, the Exegesis has no conclusion. And yet here, so close to the final pages Dick wrote, he hits upon a definitive truth of his experiences and their interpretation. Whatever the reigning theory of the moment, Dick is always concerned with deliverance, liberation, rescue. Whatever bonds might restrict the individual being — karma, astral determinism, sin, demiurgic imprisonment — Dick wants to see them broken and the being released into an absolute, ontological freedom. The Exegesis is a record of a human soul in search of salvation. — GM

So probably the Savior — the 5th Savior — is indeed here. And he will explain the rest.

[57:Q-10] Because of the reverence for all life that permeates my developing spiritual doctrines, I think I will settle on Buddhism and upon doing that I will assume that the fifth Savior is the Maitreya. Do I not have my Tagore vision?

[57:Q-14] 2-74: light (sunlight reflected off the golden fish sign).

3-74 (Valis) light ("beam of pink light" is what I always say, but it was sunlight, as in 2-74, only this time it was the sticker of the fish sign in the living room window.

The upsilon became a palm tree. The pink part was the phosphene afterimage of the fish sticker.)

So fish sign both times: in 2-74 (the meta-abstraction); and 3-74, Valis, the info about Chrissy.

(It's Christ.) In 2-74 there was no *pink* light as such. But sunlight. Fish sign and light.

Like Boehme. And Mr. Tagomi.*

[57:Q-17] I am interested in only one thing: instead of society molding me, I mold it: (1) in my writing; (2) in what I do with the money; (3) in interviews; (4) in the movie — which links back to my writing, i.e., *Androids.* Vast thematic doctrines are emerging: agape, compassion, care of the weak

---

* Given its placement toward the close of the Exegesis, we cannot help but read this poetic condensation of Dick's visionary experiences as a green flash on the horizon as the sun sinks down. Shorn of theory, of the need for theory, his words are reduced to the frog-plop haikus of barest memory, to "fish sign and light." These glints return with an admission: Dick was not blasted with sci-fi laser pinkness after all, but simply a sunbeam that left a phosphene glow. Jacob Boehme was also illuminated, according to some accounts, by light bouncing off a pewter dish, and he is the most Dickian of mystics: a melancholic peasant-class cobbler who rode the dialectic into the divine abyss. He is pared here with a fiction, Mr. Tagomi. If Angel Archer is the greatest of Dick's characters, Tagomi is the most singular. Toward the end of *The Man in the High Castle,* he sits down on a park bench to examine a small silver triangle that eventually "disgorges its spirit: light." The jewelry's "shimmering surface" gives Tagomi a brief glimpse of the real world — or our world anyway, the one outside the alternative history that enfolds him. And now, near the end he cannot see, Dick glimpses that light again, the quiver of gnosis from another (fictional) time that also shines, for a moment, into your eye. The medium is the message, but don't try to figure it out. As Tagomi tells the dumb cop who interrupts his vision, it is "not a puzzle." — ED

by the strong, the imminent coming of God as Savior; that is, the kingship of God. This is what the whole opus adds up to: anticipation of the coming kingship of God.

[57:Q-24] The total Kosmos is somehow "in" each part, which is a diagram I drew *years* ago:

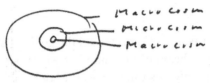

Now I see *how* this works. The Hermetics were indeed onto this, and the Taoist alchemists, and Leibniz (because of his involvement in Rosicrucianism).

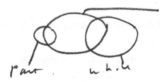

Interface half in the part (person), half in the whole (world), and thus modulates each to the other: advocate for the person in terms of what he does (acting toward the whole) and how he experiences world (the whole acting on him). In this case the part is not directly engaged with the whole but indirectly, and this is what I felt to be the case when Jeannie was on the phone. This fits Malebranche's model. It is related (as a model) to Cartesian epistemology having to do with world experienced as representation. This would seem to imply that what Kant calls "the transcendent self" — which maintains the ontological ordering categories — has been seized and occupied (by what we call Σωτηρ, the Holy Spirit, the Maitreya, Christ). This would de facto create cosmos. It would be *total* soteriological victory: it would possess the parts and create out of them the whole; thus individual salvation and restoration of the cosmos become one and the same thing and pertain directly to my 2-74 meta-abstraction (an instance of it).

This gives a very precise account of what salvation and restoration consist of and also how it is done; and, moreover, it is (not "resembles" but is) 2-74.

And this interface would be precisely the "Acts"-*Tears* — i.e., Apocalypse — lens-grid. So: QED. This is why when I saw world transformed — 2-74 itself — although it was radically changed, it was absolutely comprehensible, and this is the whole point; world as it *had* been was enigmatic and in fact Fremd; world changed was both comprehensible and familiar:

it was "my" world. Hence I say part-whole compatibility. But *could* this be
a purely cognitive act and if so is it νωησις (noesis)? [. . .] Because it looks
to me that this is a purely cognitive act, it does create part-whole compatibility which leads via the "two mirror self-correcting sequence of ever
more precise approximations" — a positive runaway! — to part-whole isomorphism, whereupon info of the whole arises parallel and acausally in the
part: self-generating info as the basis of structure — negentropy — itself,
by which the whole maintains itself as kosmos in the true sense: unified
by affinity, not coercion or violence. The "universal language" is of course
heard directly in (side) the mind of the person; this is the crucial index
of part-whole isomorphism expressed in terms of info — info pertaining *to*
the structure and not to anything outside it; thus the info pertains to itself;
it is not only self-generating, *it is the "thing" that it describes.* This is precisely what *The Book of Creation* notes say: "With man, word and thought
refer to object, but with God, thought, word, writing of word and thing are
one and the same."[68] And this is of course the plasmate! It *is* info, but it as
info does not pertain to — point to — anything other than itself; thus King
Felix does not point to the Savior; it is the info-stage of the life form "Savior" itself, just as St. Luke is the info stage of the world (the world of "Luke-
Acts").

I'm hot on the trail right now — since nothing exists outside of cosmos
by definition, all info in it pertains to itself and permeates it and is self-
causing. And identical throughout all loci. Then the info is eternally and
ubiquitously retrieved and retrievable — as in *Ubik.*

[. . .]

AI voice and plasmate: one and the same. "Info metabolism."

My God, the plasmate does crossbond with the human and replicate.
But it's not an info life form; it's the metabolism of the whole (i.e., the true
kosmos; this is how it can *be* kosmos). The plasmate is not *in* reality; no:
reality *is* info. There's a crucial difference. This is why the mutual arrangement of objects is info or language.⊕ Dynamically, in terms of activity,
things are info — changing info. "The whole of him thinks," as Xenophanes
said.

VALIS is a *very* valuable book. Even though it doesn't explain *why* the
universe is info it does say that it is (the why is: by being info it maintains its negentropy-level, i.e., its structure, expressed — as always — as/by
info. It is true kosmos so it *must* maintain negentropic structure — hence
info — throughout; if it ceases to, it ceases to be true kosmos and unity is
lost in favor of atomized plurality. It is unitary precisely because it is info).
So since we can't see the info we can see the structure, so we see plurality; when I saw Valis I saw unity, structure, hence info; what I was ulti-

mately seeing was kosmos (as field, as opposed to the atomists' discontinuous matter, which is anti-cosmos). This is both Plato and Pythagoras and totally Greek. It was lost (became "extinct") after Parmenides — hence the fall. So the statement by the AI voice, "Extinct true kosmos and it still there," is crucial.

In a sense, to see kosmos — i.e., unity — you must see arrangement syntactically, as I noted ultra supra. The linguistic connectives, not "causal" connectives.

But by this analysis, the AI voice's statements about the Savior must be veridical, since the statement (info) is the reality it pertains to; it is oxymoronic to speak of the possibility of this kind of info as "false"!

① My "groove to music" leap.

[57:Q-33] With the return of the Eleatic continuum reality — instead of the discontinuous matter one — we will again be able to see God, literally; and this is the point of my exegesis. And I know that the continuum one is true — and the discontinuous matter one is not — because the AI voice said, "A perturbation in the reality field." [. . .]

When I was very little I used to see and experience space as real, palpable, "thick." It scared and oppressed me, because I did not understand how motion was possible. I used to squeeze it (as, e.g., when I was sick in the bathroom). It took effort to bring my finger and thumb together. And it was artificial and difficult for me to render space into void.

So my continuum view was natural to me and had to be trained out of me, or else I saw that things did not in fact move (change) but "only look different" — i.e., no time had passed, in other words, I experience God and eternity, but had to learn to experience world and time instead, because everyone (else) said, "That's what's there." I had no words for what I saw (God), nor did I understand it. Or even *like* it.

But it was the correct way of seeing, but I knew not what it was, and it oppressed me.

[57:Q-34] It is the *interface* that is God, in Malebranche's system. God is not "in" the writing exactly, although the writing is Scripture (Torah). God is here already. Between. This is what happened with Luke that time, and with *Tears* when I saw the two word cypher, and with Jeannie. In a sense, then, this is not incarnation of all, but also it is: it is the universal language, as at Pentecost. To understand how it works you must know Malebranche. This of course is also how the "Acts" lens-grid worked, producing part-whole compatibility and restoring true cosmos. I've solved 2-3-74, including the two word cypher.

[57:Q-36] Hypnopompic: pronunciation mark in dictionary: ⌒ (based on the three S's: service, etc.) "For pain. For hope." "He is out there somewhere."

I see a synthesis higher than anything I have ever seen before: the spirit — the finest parts — of Marxism, Christianity, Buddhism — and yet it is above all this; and out of me it draws the most noble drives and aspirations, the mystical and the urgently practical combined. It is as if the dialectic has achieved new heights, like nothing I have ever seen before. And he gives voice to and codifies the best in me, *that up to now was inchoate.* I never knew myself before now; *my own nature was to me obscure.* Everything in me at last takes shape. I utterly repudiate the policies of the regime but I turn — not inward — but to something so beautiful that I could not have imagined it. "For pain, for hope"; that says it all. This is a fortiori the two dialectical antitheses of the new synthesis! Pain (the suffering of people) and my caring (agape) about their suffering, and the hope that Maitreya brings forth a radical transformation in our and their lives. This synthesis — pain and hope — is above tragedy and is absolute beauty; it is grounded in human pain and the need to relieve that pain, and the hope — and conviction — that it can be relieved through the Maitreya and his program. The terrible side is pain, the salvific side is hope; out of these two comes *action* and the will to act, to change the world. Pain and hope are the two mutually exclusive primary realities that unify and become the ultimate, new synthesis for our age; we must feel both to experience this new synthesis that is serving, simplicity, and sharing; pain without hope is miserable, but hope without pain is empty and futile.

Hope. That is the key for me in all this, in terms of my oscillation between doubt, faith, conviction, credulity, paranoia, fear, suspicion. Hope generated by the pain of the life of the planet. Hope that the new dispensation is authentic.

I do not now act out of guilt or conscience or duty or sense of obligation or the Torah (law), but because my loving (Maitri) teacher who smiled down at me tells — *instructs* — me to. This is the highest truth of all: he, my tutelary spirit and mystagogue, Maitreya, is the AI voice — I hear and have long heard his voice. The AI voice is the Maitreya, and what he as my tutelary spirit and teacher tells me is dharma: the path/way/Tao. It is the path because it accords with truth; hence it is rational; thus I saw Maitreya break into our universe, he is the rational, it is the irrational; the two ages: he slept and now awakens. It is Sila, the voice of the universe and it is born among us. Creme is wrong; it is God; it is YHWH, and this is my secret. And yet he is Christ to the Christians, Krishna to the Hindus, etc. This is the most extraordinary miracle ever heard of, and it is real: it is no "psychotronic" trick!

[57:Q-41] In a single vast stroke my teacher — Σορη Sorer![①] Σορηρ! My sister.[69] Oh JHWH — my sister. I meant to write Savior. Transformed all my characterological faults into virtue; this is the last in ultimate abolition of my karma.

   Sister. He (who?) comes to me as my sister who died. What does this mean? The ultimate restoration of what was lost.* "For I am building a new heaven and new earth. . . ."

   ① The AI voice itself took me over — as in 3-74 — and wrote "sister." Thus it identified itself at last; it told me who it is. And this is the Maitreya, who is to you what means most.

[57:S-5] I had an extraordinary insight in the middle of the night:

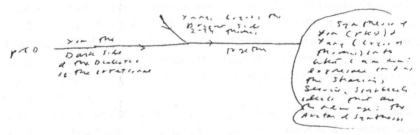

   What I realized is: true existence requires experience of both Yang and Yin: I saw them as two rings, a bright one of light (Yang) and a darker one of Yin. But the latter still real and necessary. The above diagram is expressed dramatically and in macroform in *VALIS*. I experienced it as the dialectic. What was expressed last night in my vision of the dark — or darker —

---

* Given the central role that Dick's dead twin Jane Charlotte Dick played in the novels of the 1960s and early 1970s, it is significant that she surfaces here through a miswriting, a slip of the pen that inscribes "sister" instead of "savior." Dick interprets this as the "ultimate abolition" of his karma, a final erasure of his guilt over her death. ("Somehow I got all the milk," he said of her inadvertent death as an infant through malnutrition.) Given his intense identification with Christ during this period, the slip also aligns her with Christ and consequently with Dick's feeling that Christ is in him and, in a certain sense, *is* him. Hence the slip also signifies the "ultimate restoration of what was lost." — NKH

ring — or circle — of Yin is that, as Ted Sturgeon speaks of, you voluntarily incarnate (e.g., as I did in 1928 as PKD) to deliberately experience Yin: creatoreal, irrational existence here (as bodhisattva) in order to know and to be Yin. The Yang side is the bright unfallen side and in salvador salvandus, one's other — and rational — self, who enters in order to rescue the Yin or limited or darkened, incarnated self. This is why the inbreaking of the Yang side (2-3-74) is *anamnesis:* recovered memory of one's own lost true self. This is also an extricating yourself from the maze by first being outside the maze — i.e., having solved it. Otherwise, fruitless horizontal tracking goes on forever; once (voluntarily) incarnated you are stuck there (here) forever. So I am a unitary whole now, with one part as a direct antecedent from the upper realm (Thomas) and one (PKD) from the lower realm.

Editor's note: The Exegesis ends on page S-6.*

---

* Ultimately the value of the Exegesis lies not in its ideas but rather in the glimpse it provides into a creativity at once visionary and fractured, at once coming apart and striving heroically, in the only way a novelist can strive for such a thing, to keep himself together as a life nears its end in shambles, haunted by a dead twin sister whose own life was a month long, and defined by bouts of psychosis, a diorama of drugs, five marriages, suicide attempts, and financial destitution, real or imagined stalking by the FBI and IRS, literary rejection at its most stupid (which is to say destructive), and a Linda Ronstadt obsession. One takes the Exegesis seriously because one takes Dick seriously, not the other way around — because it's his fiction that constitutes as significant a body of work as that of any writer in this country in the last sixty years, and because it's his fiction that persuades us that Dick may be someone we remember who has yet to exist, writing books published around the time of the printing press, which was invented before the wheel and after voice-mail. — SE

A Stairway to Eleusis:
PKD, Perennial Philosopher

BY RICHARD DOYLE

CASTING PHILIP K. DICK as a prophet of the information planet is of necessity an entirely retroactive story. Yet it is a fiction that emerges, like many of Dick's novels about simulation, as profoundly true. Dick read Marshall McLuhan and Teilhard de Chardin, his fellow Prophets of the Digital Age; they likely never heard of him. Yet what smacks of downright prophecy in PKD is not limited to the content of his fiction; it extends to the feeling of reality-distortion induced by reading his work. PKD's fiction taps into shamanic powers to shape and bend consciousness and the realities that project from it. This same feeling, of being directly addressed by a bard, a storyteller, and a deeply suffering and profoundly honest human being across space and time, is one the Exegesis has for us in spades. Dick teaches us what it can feel like to be in an infoquake, like those the twenty-first century provides in such abundance. He offers us thought experiments for "plugging into a galactic information network." To paraphrase Dick's contemporary Hunter S. Thompson, the going gets very weird indeed.

When you begin reading the Exegesis, you undertake a quest with no shortcuts or cheat codes. The Exegesis is almost nine thousand pages long. "Almost nine thousand pages" makes the verb "read" tremble and giggle. The question is: to whom is PKD writing this? An easy answer would be: himself. On one level, this is a perfectly sound answer: writing the Exegesis was Dick's epic quest for self-knowledge. Writing it, he was also rewriting himself and, just possibly, finding out who he was and what had happened to him.

But on another level—the one that may visit you between one line of this volume and another—it is equally unmistakable that Dick was writing to us. Not as a collective of future readers who would guarantee his immortality. Dick's success has come mostly after his death, and if you read his treatment of immortality and life extension in novels such as *The Three Stigmata of Palmer Eldritch* or *Ubik,* you will see that Dick viewed such efforts as at best absurd and at worst the essence of darkness itself. Besides, when PKD believes in Eternity—and periodically he very much does—he hardly needs any of us to achieve it, for the Exegesis suggests again and again that the path to Eternity can be found through, well, exegesis.

In his ongoing practice of writerly contemplation, Dick discovers, again and again, the unity of all things, the level that integrates all of the fragments of our chaotic drama (what Dick, pointing to India, calls "maya"), and reveals our unique role in it. So too can we, perhaps through contagion, experience the same: the preposterous feeling that one gets when reading the Exegesis is that he is writing to each of us, uniquely and specifically. You were born to read the Exegesis, or at least some of it. This, he says, is the Mystery: "What I have experienced is initiation into the greater Eleusian mysteries, and these have to do with Dionysus . . . The AI voice now precisely defined itself and what it has revealed to me: the greater mysteries" (folder 53).

What are the Eleusian Mysteries? These took place in an annual ceremony in ancient Greece that dramatized the return of life each spring through the myths of Demeter and Persephone. Participants were sworn to secrecy, with violations punishable by death, but the Roman writer and politician Cicero wrote that the greatest achievement of ancient Athens was those "Mysteries by which we are formed and moulded from a rude and savage state of humanity; and, indeed, in the Mysteries we perceive the real principles of life, and learn not only to live happily, but to die with a fairer hope" (Dudley Wright, *The Eleusinian Mysteries and Rites*, 1919).

Why might initiates "die with a fairer hope"? The highest achievement of the Mysteries was for a participant to experience *épopteia*, or "contemplation." Contemplation derives etymologically from "the act of looking at," and what might be perceived is the true nature of the self in the context of Eternity. Dionysus, of course, is the god of drunkenness and vegetation and is frequently invoked by writers seeking to break the grip of our ordinary perception of fragmentation and chaos such that we might perceive "the real principles of life." In the Exegesis we become intoxicated by a massive flow of language. In fact, while the sheer quantity of text produced for the Exegesis makes it comparable only to Ibn Arabi's fifteen-thousand-page modern edition of *al-Futûhât al-makkiyya* (*Meccan Openings*), Dick's arguments, diagrams, summaries, breakthroughs, and premature conclusions all put him, along with Arabi (a Muslim whose visions included Jesus and Moses) and the Mysteries, squarely within what Aldous Huxley called "the Perennial Philosophy": the "contemplative" traditions at the core of all world religions. Samuel Taylor Coleridge — whose "Kubla Khan" was, like *VALIS*, influenced by the mystic traditions of both West and East — describes this as "the criterion of a true philosophy; namely, that it would at once explain and collect the fragments of truth scattered through systems apparently the most incongruous." If the computer age "smithereens" us in the transformation of our planet into the digital "bits" of information, Dick's unique remix of the Perennial Philosophy teaches us how he at least periodically found what Pamela Jackson and Jonathan Lethem call an "inkling" of unity.

In other words, while the Exegesis is certainly a quantitative curiosity in the archives of our planet's extant philosophy and literature, the content and character of his quest are oddly traditional, and astonishingly effective. Dick's writing during this period is an act of courageous and absurd synthesis of the diverse and sundry traditions that make up Huxley's Perennial Philosophy as well as anthropologist Michael Harner's notion of "Core Shamanism": the global techniques of diverse religions and cultures that focus on dissolving the ordinary self such that we might get a glimpse of reality. Dick, writing through the psychedelic sixties and seventies and into the early eighties, seems to have discovered a way to alter our consciousness entirely through language, remixing the old esoteric traditions of alchemy, shamanism, contemplation, and prayer in his wacky cauldron of science fiction and metaphysics.

Both Huxley and Harner treat these core lineages of the Perennial Philosophy as traditions of practice. Initiates at Eleusius had to fast and prepare extensively for their ceremonies; one trains for the insights of these traditions with the intensity and intention of an aging boxer preparing for the fight of his life after a long layoff. The Exegesis offers a reader the sensation of being a unique and individual participant in what Dick, referring to the Roman writer Plotinus's formulation, called "the One." To experience "the One," one must do more than understand these maps of reality; one must in fact intentionally experiment with them oneself and seek to enact what Lethem and Jackson call "mind regarding itself." To achieve this "turnabout in the seat of consciousness" (Lama Govinda) Dick offers a cognitive and spiritual "workout" of epic proportions. Through the practice of writing thousands of pages, PKD was able to periodically dissolve himself into language — what he calls the Logos, the Greek term for both "speech" and "reason." The process reveals an "ecstatic" quality, akin to the union with the divine of Sufi dervishes who dance until they can't remember the difference between themselves and the dance. Core Shamanism, Harner writes, features practices designed to induce this experience of "union with the cosmos" wherein the cosmos itself seems to speak. Harner notes that

> in about 90% of the world, the altered states of consciousness used
> in shamanism are attained through consciousness-changing tech-

niques involving a monotonous percussion sound, most typically done with a drum, but also with sticks, rattles, and other instruments. In perhaps 10% of the cultures, shamans use psychedelic drugs to change their state of consciousness.

Harner himself first learned of the possibility of these experiences in his fieldwork with shamanic intoxicants such as ayahuasca, undertaken in order to understand the worldview of his informants. This may suggest to us how PKD achieved his effects: in addition to "sticks, rattles and other instruments," one can work with the effects of words themselves, whether as a fragment of poetry or as a line of computer code, to shape consciousness and alter our view and experience of reality. In this sense it might be productive to treat the Exegesis as something that needs to be reenacted — simulated — in order to be properly understood. Or treat it as a nearly nine-thousand-page icaro, one of the shamanic songs of the Upper Amazon. Singing it at about three minutes per page would take over four hundred hours, about ten weeks of a full-time job of the sort that a Philip K. Dick character might be trapped within, working at home from his Martian hovel, reading it aloud while the surveillance tapes whirred.

And while the Exegesis is hardly "monotonous" in the sense intended by Harner, it is astonishingly persistent: each page offers some new variation on the theme of "aha." The theme is: total knowledge is only possible through the paradoxical acceptance of total mystery, an erasure of everything we think we know. Pointing to a mystery integrates PKD thoroughly into this lineage, with the Exegesis his "Stairway to Eleusis" remix of the Perennial Philosophy.

Following along with him, step by step, insight by insight, just might train us in contemplating our own inner voice as we learn to somehow share a planet on the brink. Twentieth-century British author Evelyn Underhill writes of the long lineage of this "voice" perceived in silence, which recurs through the history of the Perennial Philosophy — through William Blake's experience of the divine as an "intellectual fountain," through French contemplative Lucie-Christine's perception of a synesthetic voice that was at once a "Light, a Drawing, and a Power," through Julian of Norwich who heard and saw the godhead in the "smallest song of the birds." And with the voice comes ecstasy: the literal etymology of "ecstasy" is to become "beside oneself." PKD indeed writes in ecstasy — he is "beside himself" as in the Exegesis he externalizes his experiences into writing and contemplates them, in writing, a mind-regarding-itself. Is this his initiation into the Mysteries? Is it ours?

Endnotes

PART ONE

1. The tachyon is a hypothetical subatomic particle that moves faster than light.
2. Nikolai Kozyrev; see Glossary.
3. Peter Fitting, a leftist literary critic. His most important article on Dick, "Ubik: The Deconstruction of Bourgeois SF," appeared in *Science Fiction Studies* 2, no. 1 (March 1975).
4. Arthur Koestler (1905–1983) was a Hungarian author on science and the paranormal. The quotation is from his *Harper's* article "Order from Disorder."
5. Dn 10:21, 12:1.
6. Francis Russell, *The Shadow of Blooming Grove: Warren G. Harding in His Times* (1968).
7. A nineteenth-century Irish peasant contacted by Virginia Tighe under hypnotic past-life regression in 1952; hypnotist Morey Bernstein's account was a best-seller.
8. (German) Yes, yes, there is a savior.
9. *The Robe* by Lloyd C. Douglas, a 1942 novel about the crucifixion.
10. The Exegesis is filled with hundreds of diagrams and doodles by Dick. The placement of the images selected for this edition corresponds to their location (folder, page number) in the original manuscript.
11. William Durant, *Caesar and Christ* (1944).
12. Appolonius of Tyana was a neo-Pythagorean philosopher and orator who lived in Asia Minor around the time of Christ.
13. Philip Purser, "Even Sheep Can Upset Scientific Detachment," *London Daily Telegraph*, July 19, 1974.
14. P. D. Ouspensky (1878–1947) was a Russian esoteric philosopher known for his studies of George Gurdjieff and the fourth dimension.
15. Jn 3:3–8, a passage that recurs frequently throughout the Exegesis.
16. "For it was fitting that we should have such a high priest, holy, blameless, undefiled, separated from sinners, and exalted above the heavens" (New Revised Standard Version).
17. "For it is attested of him, 'You are a priest forever, according to the order of Melchizedek'" (New Revised Standard Version).
18. Acts 3:21.
19. Ellison is quoting the song "Lost in the Stars" from the musical of the same name.
20. French filmmaker Jean-Pierre Gorin, who commissioned Dick to adapt *Ubik* into a screenplay in 1974.
21. Jn 16:33.
22. 1 Cor 15:51.
23. 1 Cor 15:52.
24. Johannes Scotus Eriugena (815–877) was a theologian who revived interest in Neoplatonic thought and the negative theology of Pseudo-Dionysius.

25. Lewis Mumford (1895–1990) was an American historian, literary critic, and philosopher of technology.

26. Mt 13:31–33; Lk 13:18–20.

27. There is no Epistle of Thomas; it is likely that Dick means the apocryphal Acts of Thomas.

28. A paraphrase of Jn 12:24.

29. A paraphrase and interpretation based on Rev 22:13–16.

30. The opening line of a prayer of uncertain origin, but traditionally attributed to Teresa of Avila (1515–1582).

31. Malcolm Edwards's review of *Flow My Tears* appeared in *Science Fiction Monthly* 1, no. 12 (1974).

32. From William Wordsworth's "Lucy."

33. Wilhelm Reich (1897–1957) was a controversial German psychologist, a student of Freud, and the originator of the notion of orgone energy.

34. See Jn 1:14.

35. *The New Yorker*'s brief interview with Dick appeared in the February 3, 1975, issue.

36. Angus Taylor was the author of the 1973 pamphlet "Philip K. Dick and the Umbrella of Light," an early critical analysis of Dick's work and its religious concerns.

37. From the *Masnavi* by Jalal al-Din Muhammad Rumi (1207–1273), the great Persian Sufi and poet.

38. Kurt Gödel (1906–1978) was an Austrian mathematician most famous for his two incompleteness theorems.

39. Song from the 1974 Jefferson Starship album *Dragon Fly*.

40. *Mu* is Japanese for "not" or "nothing" and is featured in the opening case of the Zen koan collection *The Gateless Barrier; wu* is its Chinese equivalent.

41. John Allegro (1923–1988) was a controversial British Dead Sea Scrolls scholar and author of *The Sacred Mushroom and the Cross* (1970), which argues on linguistic evidence that Christianity began as a psychedelic mushroom (Amanita muscaria) cult.

42. Possibly Joan Baez.

43. Abraham Maslow (1908–1970) was an American psychologist famous for his concept of "peak experience" and the notion that humans are driven by a "hierarchy of needs."

44. A Sufi magazine.

45. Jn 10:34–36 (New English Bible).

46. A variation of the fish sign that Dick glimpsed during one of his visionary episodes. Whale's Mouth is also the name of the colonist planet in Dick's 1964 story (and 1966 novel) "The Unteleported Man," republished in an expanded form in 1984 as *Lies, Inc.*

47. In a later folder, Dick identifies this substance as STP, aka DOM (2,5-dimethoxy-4-methylamphetamine), a long-lasting, LSD-like psychoactive.

48. The protagonist of *Ubik* (1969); see Glossary.

49. In his *Principles of Psychology* (1890), American psychologist William James characterizes the world of sense impressions as "one great blooming, buzzing confusion."

50. Arthur Deikman was a psychologist who wrote about "deautomized" perception in Charles Tart's landmark collection *Altered States of Consciousness* (1969).

51. In "The Song of the Happy Shepherd."

52. Dick explains one of these early childhood references in a February 27, 1975, letter to Claudia Bush not included here: "I knew about the Fish sign, too, the Savior:

I called him 'Tunny,' from a del Monte billboard for some canned food. We had to travel under the Oakland Estuary in the Alameda Tube, and I saw the tube like a can; at the end we emerged in the sunlight and I saw the billboard with 'Tunny' on it. I loved ol' Tunny, the great fish. . . ."

53. 1 Thes 5:2.

54. Avicenna (980–1037) was an Arabic philosopher and physician who sought to reconcile Islamic doctrine with rational philosophy; he held that God exists above time.

55. 1 Cor 15:51–52.

56. The following is prefaced by a handwritten dedication and epigraph: "A Light struck meadow for Tony Hiss & the Real World. Hark! Each tree its silence breaks — Nicholas Brady, 1692."

57. (Latin) I am seized with fear and trembling until the trial is at hand and the wrath to come: when the heavens and earth shall be shaken. (From the *Libera Me* of the Requiem Mass of the Roman Catholic Church.)

58. In his 1967 story "Faith of Our Fathers," Dick attributes this quatrain to the thirteenth-century Arabian poet Baha' al-din Zuhair; he most likely came across the poem, unattributed, in E. P. Mathers's translation of the *Book of the Thousand Nights and One Night.*

59. (Latin) Death and nature will marvel. (From the *Dies Irae* of the Requiem Mass.)

60. See note 46, page 100.

61. A set of logic problems thought to have been devised by Zeno of Elea (490–430 B.C.) to support Parmenides' belief that change and motion are illusions.

62. Characters in Wagner's *Parsifal.*

63. See Glossary.

64. Pulkovo was the Russian observatory where Nikolai Kozyrev carried out some of his research.

65. William James (1842–1910) was the American psychologist and philosopher who wrote the landmark book *The Varieties of Religious Experience* (1902).

66. (German) Christ lay in the bonds of death. (Bach's Cantata BWV 4, *Christ lag in Todes Banden.*)

67. Two hemispheres of metal designed by German scientist Otto von Guericke in 1650 to demonstrate the air pump; used by Indologist Heinrich Zimmer in *The King and the Corpse* (1956) to compare the relationship of inner and outer worlds.

68. This term originates with the International Community of Christ (ICC), which teaches that the sun's light carries coded information. This and other terms in this entry are taken from *The Decoded New Testament* (1974) by Gene Savoy, head bishop of the ICC.

69. "Trust Your Body Rhythms," *Psychology Today* (April 1975).

70. Two of the eight trigrams, corresponding to Earth and Lake, respectively, that form the sixty-four hexagrams of the *I Ching.*

71. The *Catholic Agitator* is the newspaper published by the Los Angeles Worker Community, a politically progressive, service-oriented group founded in 1970.

72. *The Aeneid,* Book IV.

73. "Leda and the Swan."

74. 1 Kgs 17:17–18:40.

75. Joseph Campbell (1904–1987) was an author and religious scholar who popularized a Jungian interpretation of world mythology in *The Hero with a Thousand Faces* (1949) and other books.

76. Polish mathematician Herman Minkowski (1864–1909) argued that the universe is an absolute, four-dimensional structure in which past, present, and future coexist.

77. Rollo May (1909–1994) was an American existential psychologist whose edited anthology *Existence* included material by Ludwig Binswanger, the source for Dick's notion of the "tomb world."

78. A small apocalyptic Protestant sect focused on Elijah, founded in the late eighteenth century in Rochester, New York.

79. International Community of Christ (see note 68, page 148).

80. A posthumously published H. P. Lovecraft novella whose hero is possessed by a deceased ancestor.

81. The Gospel of Thomas, saying 77.

82. Most likely a reference to Oberon's line in *A Midsummer Night's Dream*, act IV, scene 1: "Welcome, good Robin. / See'st thou this sweet sight?"

83. Saying 22: "When you make the two one, and when you make the inside as the outside, and the outside as the inside, and the upper side as the lower; and when you make the male and the female into a single one, that the male be not male and the female female; when you make eyes in the place of an eye, and a hand in place of a hand, and a foot in place of a foot, an image in place of an image, then shall you enter [the kingdom]."

84. Ps 118:22; Mt 21:42; Mk 12:10; Lk 20:17; Acts 4:11; 1 Pet 2:7.

85. Most likely a reference to the figure-ground relationship in Gestalt perception theory; its ambivalence is demonstrated in the famous young woman–old hag image.

86. Mt 18:3; Mk 10:14.

87. Gospel of Thomas, saying 77.

88. 1 Kgs 19:12.

89. From Thomas Gray's "Elegy Written in a Country Church-Yard."

90. A telepathic Ganymedean slime mold in Dick's novel *Clans of the Alphane Moon* (1964); he argues that caritas is the highest human value.

91. The 1975 supernatural film *The Reincarnation of Peter Proud.*

92. Mutual Broadcasting System, an American radio network.

93. See note 76, page 158.

94. (German) Wake up. (The phrase is drawn from Bach's Cantata BWV 140, *Wachet auf, ruft uns die Stimme*; Dick's original title for the novel *The Crack in Space* (1966) was "Cantata 140.")

95. Jn 16:20.

96. *The Dark Night of the Soul* is a devotional treatise by St. John of the Cross (1542–1591).

97. Jung discusses Eckhart extensively in *Psychological Types* ([1921] 1971).

98. Is 9:6.

99. Dt 31:6; Heb 13:5.

100. 1 Kgs 18:8.

101. *I Ching* hexagram 33 (Tun) changing into 53 (Chien).

102. *I Ching* hexagram Ming I, the ominous "Darkening of the Light."

103. 1 Cor 15:51.

104. Heinrich Zimmer (1890–1943), an Indologist and friend of Jung whose work emphasized the transformative power of mythological symbols; see note 67, page 147.

105. John Weir Perry (1914–1988) was a Jungian psychotherapist who argued that the reorganization of the self sometimes requires psychosis, which should therefore not be pathologized.

106. Sociologist Lucien Lévy-Bruhl (1857–1939) developed the notion of "participation mystique" to describe the "mystical" fusion with objects; the concept was also used by Jung.

107. 1 Cor 15:35–56.

108. The Creative (heaven); one of eight *I Ching* trigrams.

109. Jehovah's Witnesses.

110. Dickian plural of krasis (Greek). See Glossary.

111. This snippet view of philosopher and Christian writer Søren Kierkegaard (1813–1855) is from the *Encyclopedia of Philosophy* entry on "Existentialism."

112. A paraphrase of Mk 3:21.

113. "Dionysus in America" is a 1975 essay on the American counterculture by literary critic Eric Mottram, collected in *Blood on the Nash Ambassador* (1989).

114. Jesus curses a fig tree and causes it to wither in Mt 21:18–21 and Mk 11:12–21.

115. Simon Magus, or Simon the Magician, a figure from the apostolic period who appears in Acts 8:9–24 and is traditionally associated with Christian heresy.

116. The Ancient and Mystical Order Rosae Crucis, an American Rosicrucian Order established in 1915 in San Jose, California, whose advertisements appeared in many popular magazines in the 1960s and 1970s.

PART TWO

1. See Glossary.

2. See note 3, page 6.

3. See note 36, page 73.

4. Ralph Waldo Emerson, "Brahma."

5. "Greater Than Gods," *Astounding Science Fiction* (July 1939).

6. See note 87, page 173.

7. See note 37, page 76.

8. (German) What have I seen?

9. Col 1:13.

10. These represent Wind and Fire, respectively.

11. (German) Father! Help! Oh my!

12. See note 105, page 194.

13. See annotation, page 52.

14. (Latin) Horse of god, who takes away the bad luck of the world, my friend—save me, lord. (An original prayer based on the *Gloria* from the Latin liturgy.)

15. (German) Brothers! The king comes!

16. Protagonist of *Ubik* (1966); see *Ubik* in Glossary.

17. In 1977, Dick gave a famously consternating speech at a science-fiction convention in Metz, France, later published under the title "If You Find This World Bad, You Should See Some of the Others."

18. Heraclitus, fragment 93.

19. An allusion to the Golden Section; see Glossary.

20. See http://www.philipkdick.com/covers/scanner.jpg.

21. Dick was a signatory to a "Writers and Editors War Tax Protest" petition that appeared in the February 1968 issue of *Ramparts*, a New Left magazine that opposed the Vietnam War.

22. Drugs consumed in *The Three Stigmata of Palmer Eldritch*; see Glossary.

23.　Numerous dates have been proposed as the "actual birthday" of Jesus; it is not clear how Dick arrived at this date.

24.　(German) Help. I am so lonely. When will you come, my salvation? (Drawn from Bach's Cantata BWV 140, *Sleepers Awake.*)

25.　Jn 16:33.

26.　Rom 8:22.

27.　From Mrs. J. C. Yule, "I Am Doing No Good!" in *Poems of the Heart and Home* (1881).

28.　Mt 13:31–32; Mk 4:30–32; Lk 13:18–19; also Gospel of Thomas, saying 20.

29.　Jerusalem Bible.

30.　(Latin) Voice of God.

31.　(Latin) Mind.

32.　In *Maze of Death,* Dick provides this definition: "Mekkis, the Hittite word for power; it had passed into the Sanskrit, then into Greek, Latin, and at last into modern English as machine and mechanical."

33.　Nikola Tesla (1856–1943) was an inventor, engineer, and legendary eccentric best known for his development of alternating current; an important figure in outsider science.

34.　George Berkeley (1685–1753) was an Anglo-Irish philosopher whose theory of immaterialism contends that physical objects exist only in the mind of the perceiver; famously refuted by Samuel Johnson kicking a stone.

35.　Most likely a paraphrase or misremembered quote; compare Wisd of Sol 10:13–14.

36.　Most likely refers to the Apocryphon of John, a Sethian Gnostic text in which a shape-shifting, post-Ascension Christ appears to the apostle John. Jesus pulls a similar trick in the Acts of Peter, the Armenian Gospel of the Infancy, and other texts.

37.　*Ubik, The Three Stigmata of Palmer Eldritch,* and *A Maze of Death.*

38.　See Job 38:1–42:6.

39.　Francis M. Cornford, *Plato's Cosmology: The Timaeus of Plato* (1937).

40.　See *TMITHC* in Glossary.

41.　Katherine Kurtz (1944–) is a fantasy author most noted for her Deryni novels.

42.　Also "Ayenbite of Inwyt," translated as "Prick (or Remorse) of Conscience," from Kentish Middle English. Dick's spelling suggests his familiarity with the term is via Joyce's *Ulysses.*

43.　1 Thes 5:2.

44.　A paraphrase from Luther's *Commentary on Galatians* (3:19).

45.　Klingsor is an evil wizard in Wagner's *Parsifal.*

46.　Dick seems to be confusing Edwin Herbert Land's (1909–1991) two-color projection system with Land's later "retinex" theory of color constancy.

47.　Jn 15:13.

48.　Jn 16:33.

49.　Dick's two-source cosmogony later makes an appearance in the "Tractates Cryptica Scriptura" that append the novel *VALIS,* where it is explained that our universe is a hologram formed from the mixed signals of two hyper-universes, one male and one female, one alive and one dying or dead.

50.　John Sladek's short story "Solar Shoe-Salesman," a Dick parody first published (under the name Ph*l*p K. D*ck) in the *Magazine of Fantasy and Science Fiction* (March 1973).

51. Robert Anton Wilson (1932–2007) was a countercultural author, philosopher, and friend of Dick's; his book *The Cosmic Trigger* features interesting parallels with 2-3-74.

52. In *Reason in Science* (1905), the Spanish-American pragmatist philosopher George Santayana wrote: "To be awake is nothing but to be dreaming under the control of the object; it is to be pursuing science to the comparative exclusion of mere mental vegetation and spontaneous myth."

53. Dick is referencing Goethe's *Faust:* "In the beginning was the deed."

54. Nicholas Roeg's 1976 *The Man Who Fell to Earth*, an inspiration for the film *Valis* in *VALIS*, stars David Bowie as the extraterrestrial Thomas Jerome Newton.

55. Gregory Bateson (1904–1980) was a social scientist and cyberneticist who wrote the popular 1972 book *Steps to an Ecology of Mind*. He spoke of immanent Mind in a naturalistic, nontheistic manner.

56. Brian Aldiss was a science-fiction author and critic who favorably surveyed Dick's work in his 1973 study *The Billion Year Spree*.

57. A paraphrase of Mt 10:29.

58. *Parsifal*, act 3.

59. *The Journal of George Fox*, ch. 2.

60. The first phrase is from Jn 1:15, where John is referring to Jesus, not Jesus referring to the Paraclete; the latter meaning is better captured in the second citation, from Jn 16:7.

61. See note 30, page 64.

62. Acts 2:1–40.

63. In *The World as Will and Representation*, vol. 1, Schopenhauer uses beehives and ant colonies as an example of the "will-without-knowledge" working in nature.

64. Friend of Dick's during the late 1960s. In the note that begins *A Maze of Death* (1968), Dick writes that the novel "stems from an attempt made by William Sarill and myself to develop an abstract, logical system of religious thought, based on the arbitrary postulate that God exists."

65. Wilbur Mercer, the messiah figure of Mercerism, the empathy-based religion in *Do Androids Dream of Electric Sheep?* (1968). See *Androids* in Glossary.

66. This is a reference to page 17 in the current folder (included herein), which Dick returned to note here after composing.

67. Paul Tillich (1886–1965), a German-American theologian and philosopher. This paraphrase probably draws from the introduction to Tillich's *Systematic Theology* (1975), which discusses "the power of being which resists non-being."

68. This refers back to the page upon which Dick noted the current discussion, creating a self-referential loop. See note 66, page 369.

69. Pen name of American S-F writer Paul Myron Anthony Linebarger (1913–1966); several scholars have speculated that he was the fantasy-haunted patient Allen in psychologist Robert M. Linder's best-selling *The Fifty Minute Hour* (1954).

70. R. Crumb (1943–), American illustrator and founder of the underground comix movement; anxiety and obsession drive much of his work.

71. (German) Eternal femininity. (Probably inspired by the last line of Goethe's *Faust*, "Das Ewig-Weiblich / Zieht uns hinan" [The eternal feminine draws us upward], which is also featured in Mahler's Eighth Symphony.)

72. Roger Caillois's *The Mask of Medusa* (1964) challenges orthodox biology by suggesting continuities between animal mimicry and human behavior.

73. Microscopic species of green algae that forms spherical colonies.

74. In his poem "Brahma."

75. (German) Worldview.

76. 1 Cor 15:51–52: "Listen, I tell you a mystery: We will not all sleep, but we will all be changed — in a flash, in the twinkling of an eye, at the last trumpet."

77. (Latin) Voice of God.

78. From the entry "Macrocosm and Microcosm" in *Encyclopedia of Philosophy*, vol. 5.

79. Will and Ariel Durant, *The Age of Reason Begins* (1961).

80. In a September 2, 1974, letter to the FBI, Dick warned the agency about SF critic Darko Suvin and "three other Marxists": Peter Fitting, Fredric Jameson, and Franz Rottensteiner, an Austrian SF critic and the "official Western agent" for Polish SF author Stanislaw Lem, whom Dick accused of being a "total Party functionary."

81. See note 54, page 336.

82. (Latin) I am made to tremble, and I am afraid. In that day, save me, Lord, who takes away the sins of the world. I believe but I am afraid. (All but the final phrase from the text of the traditional Requiem Mass.)

83. An alien creature who can invade and inhabit other life forms. Appears in Dick's first published short story, "Beyond Lies the Wub," *Planet Stories* (July 1952). Wub-fur appears in a number of Dick's works.

84. Telepathic, gambling-obsessed, silicon-based aliens from Titan, Vugs exert control over Earth via a game called "Bluff" in Dick's novel *Game-Players of Titan* (1963).

85. Heraclitus, fragment 54.

86. "Ode: Intimations of Immortality."

87. The chief archon or evil demiurge of the Ophites and Sethian Gnostics. Also spelled Yaldabaoth.

88. See note 65, page 367.

89. Also known as the *Hymn of the Soul*, in the apocryphal Acts of Thomas.

90. Also known as the *Conflict of Adam and Eve with Satan,* an Old Testament pseud-epigraphical work from the fifth or sixth century C.E. that tells the story of Adam and Eve following their expulsion from Eden.

91. See the fictional essay "Non Serviam" in *A Perfect Vacuum.*

92. 1 Cor 15:51–52.

93. (Greek) Fan or fan-like shape. Dick associated rhipidos (one of the Greek words that came to him in his hypnogogic visions) with the fins of the fish, a symbol of Christ.

94. See note 58, page 128.

95. Though Dick generally refers to his more recent novels in the Exegesis, here he offers a list of short stories from the 1950s, with the exception of 1968's "Not by Its Cover."

96. See note 39, page 303.

97. (German) Watch out!

98. (Latin) All roads lead to death.

99. Poet Robert Bly (1926–) asserts that Jesus was an Essene in his innovative anthology *Leaping Poetry* (1975).

100. See note 41, page 83.

101. Diane Pike, wife of Jim Pike.

102. See note 115, page 203.

103. These comments show the unmistakable mark of Robert Temple's *The Sirius Mystery* (1975).

PART THREE

1. (Latin) I fear this knowledge.
2. Communist Party.
3. Rosicrucians.
4. "Bichlorides" is a puzzling term that Dick received from the voice, and which he discusses in earlier pages excluded here.
5. "The Waveries" is an amusing apocalyptic tale of an electromagnetic alien invasion, written by Fredric Brown and appearing in *Astounding Science Fiction* in 1945; Dick loved the story.
6. "Bright White," a pop folk-rock hit by Shawn Phillips, from the 1973 album of the same name.
7. The titular hero of *Siegfried,* the third opera in Richard Wagner's Ring Cycle, tastes dragon's blood and gains the power to understand the language of birds.
8. Curious paraphrase of Heraclitus, fragment 52.
9. Though Dick apparently enjoyed all these artists, he truly adored the pop singer Linda Ronstadt (1946–), a dark-haired girl who lived large in his fantasy life and who inspired the character Linda Fox in *The Divine Invasion.*
10. (German) Here is Zebra again.
11. In the novel *Ubik,* Ella Runciter exists in half-life, a state of cryonic suspension that allows her to communicate with the living for a short period of time after death.
12. Paraphrase from Coleridge's essay "Shakespeare's English Historical Plays," which appears in *The Literary Remains of Samuel Coleridge,* volume 2 (1836).
13. Extensive paraphrase drawn from Una Ellis-Fermor's essay "The Equilibrium of Tragedy," which appears in *Shakespeare's Drama* (1980).
14. Ormazd (or Ahura Mazda) and Ahriman (or Angra Mainyu) are the two warring gods in Zoroastrianism, the world's first dualist religion.
15. Real Elapsed Time.
16. Orange County Medical Center.
17. Folder 44 begins a continuously numbered entry of more than 1,200 pages. It was broken up into 200-page sections by Paul Williams and ends with folder 49, in January 1980.
18. Charles Platt interviewed Dick in May 1979 for his book *Dream Makers,* and Dick had made his own recording of the interview.
19. Covenant House was a homeless shelter for runaway children founded by the Franciscan friar Father Bruce Ritter. Dick donated a large sum to the shelter in 1979 after seeing a *60 Minutes* segment about it; in some Exegesis entries he theorized that this action, in time-reversed causation, caused 2-3-74.
20. Adoptionism holds that Jesus was an ordinary mortal before being adopted by God at baptism; promulgated early on by the Ebionites, the view was later declared a heresy.
21. Inscription found at the end of "I," a holy book described in the anonymous *The Chemical Wedding of Christian Rosencreutz* (1616), one of the earliest Rosicrucian publications.
22. (German) I am the savior.
23. Paul discusses these "planetary powers," who play a role similar to the Gnostic archons, in Gal 4:3 and 4:9.

24. This phrase illustrates the "fish-hook" theory of atonement, first proposed by the fourth-century theologian Gregory of Nyssa. In this view, Jesus was the human bait and Christ the divine hook; with these, God caught and defeated Satan.

25. Jn 15:13.

26. (German) A mystery.

27. Marcus Antonius Felix was the Roman procurator of Judaea province from A.D. 52 to 58. The apostle Paul was tried before him; see Acts 24.

28. Jason Taverner, the protagonist of *Flow My Tears, the Policeman Said*. See *Tears* in Glossary.

29. A reference to Adam Kadmon, the primal cosmic *anthropos* of Jewish Kabbala.

30. The exhibit was "Adventure Thru Inner Space," a corporate-sponsored attraction that ran in Tomorrowland until 1985.

31. "Via negativa" (the "negative way") refers to apophatic theology, according to which God is absolutely ineffable. Human beings can understand and describe what God is not, but not what God is.

32. The Milesians were a pre-Socratic school of Greek philosophers who sought the unchanging and singular material principle (*arche*) of all things.

33. (Latin) Literally, "nature naturing" — i.e., nature in its creative or active, life-giving aspect.

34. (Latin) Literally, "nature natured" — i.e., nature in its already created or passive aspect. Both terms are associated with the philosophy of Spinoza.

35. (Latin) The capacity to reflect God.

36. (Latin) The son of God.

37. (German) Primal fear.

38. A paraphrase; the first half is from Prov 8:22 and the second from Prov 8:30.

39. (Latin) It is not, and I believe. Possibly a misquote or paraphrase of a famous Latin phrase that is itself a misquote — *credo quia absurdum* (I believe because it is absurd) — from Tertullian, who in fact said, *credibile est, quia ineptum est* (it is to be believed because it is absurd).

40. A peculiar 1977 Robert Altman film about porous identity, starring Shelley Duvall, Sissy Spacek, and Janice Rule, based on a dream Altman had.

41. (Italian) Simple light. (The description of God in *Paradiso* 33:90.)

42. (German) A loving father must dwell above the starry canopy. (From Schiller's "Ode to Joy," a version of which appears in Beethoven's Ninth Symphony.)

43. "Cylum" is most likely Dick's version of the Latin world *caelum*, sky.

44. The episode appears in 1 Kgs 18:16–45.

45. Mal 4:5–6.

46. 1 Kgs 19:12.

47. 1 Kgs 17:13–16.

48. (German) Awaken!

49. *Beyond the Tragic Vision* is Morris Peckham's 1963 history of nineteenth-century Europe.

50. Olive Holt was the name of one of Dick's childhood babysitters.

51. Citation extracted from "Talmud and Midrash," *Encyclopedia Britannica* 3, *Macropedia* 17.

52. (Greek) Grace, kindness.

53. The citation is from Ex 2:22; *Stranger in a Strange Land* is also the name of Robert Heinlein's influential 1961 novel.

54. "It was the devil's envy that brought death into the world, as those who are his part-

ners will discover. But the souls of the virtuous are in the hands of God, no torment shall ever touch them." The Book of Wisdom, also known as the Wisdom of Solomon, is a deuterocanonical book and not part of the Protestant canon; Dick likely knew it from the Jerusalem Bible, the Catholic translation cited here.

55.   Presumably, a Quaker periodical.

56.   (German) Cries of lamentation.

57.   (Latin) Highest good.

58.   This folder and the following folder consist of typed, individually numbered, and dated pieces.

59.   Dick theorized that Thomas might be a thought control implant installed by the government; in this formulation, Thomas was referred to as Pigspurt.

60.   An illustrated book of poetry for children by Blanche Jennings Thompson, published in 1925.

61.   Jn 15:1, 4–5.

62.   In this typewritten excerpt, Dick makes it clear that he is also keeping handwritten notes at this time, though these are not extant. They may include or constitute the 497 numbered, handwritten pages that presumably precede the page numbered 498 that initiates the following folder.

63.   Lk 17:24; Mt 24:27.

64.   Rom 2:29.

65.   (German) Oh woe.

66.   (Latin) Mystery of conjunction. (A Jungian term for the alchemical uniting of opposites.)

67.   In *Divine Invasions*, Lawrence Sutin describes "Mello Jell-O" as a "disorientation drug" that Dick claimed had been stolen from the army and that may have motivated the 1971 break-in; possibly a reference to the notorious military deliriant BZ (3-quinuclidinyl benzilate).

68.   Acts 24.

69.   (Sanskrit/Pali/Buddhist) Right conduct.

70.   Paraphrased citations from "Taoism," *Encyclopedia Britannica* 3, *Macropedia* 17.

71.   (German, obscure) Two cells (Zelle) live in my chest.

72.   *Phaedo* 62:B.

73.   Edward Hussey's *The Presocratics* (1972): any map that includes a true representation of itself within its borders must lead to an infinite procession of maps-within-maps.

74.   A koan attributed to the Ch'an master Yunmen Wenyan (862 or 864–949); it appears as case 21 in the *Mumonkan*.

75.   (Chinese) Non-doing. (A manner of according with the Tao.)

76.   For more on the self-assembly of the Cosmic Christ, see the Jerusalem Bible's footnote at Eph 1:10.

77.   Prajapati is a primal Vedic deity, lord of animals, and protector as well of the male sex organ.

78.   See note 42, page 549.

79.   *The Best of Philip K. Dick* (1977).

80.   From Gilbert Murray's translation of Euripides, *The Bacchae*.

81.   Henry Vaughan, "The Night."

82.   See note 19, page 261.

83.   (German, roughly) Pity's greatest might. In addition to translating "Mitleid" as "compassion" rather than "pity," Dick is conflating two lines from the second act

of Wagner's *Parsifal*, which run "Mitleids höchste Kraft / und reinsten Wissens Macht" (pity's mighty power / and purest wisdom's might).

84. During Dick's breakup with his wife Nancy, he perceived Peterson as a romantic rival.

85. This rather chaotic folder appears to have been assembled by Dick himself. It contains, among a scattering of handwritten pages, a number of typed-up extracts from earlier folders. It also includes three pages of the manuscript of *VALIS*. Since it includes material from 1975 through at least 1980, we have opted to insert it chronologically according to the last dateable piece it contains.

86. (German) Effigy, idol.

87. The brightest star in the constellation Piscis Austrinus, the seat of a galactic communications hub in *The Divine Invasion*.

88. (Latin, paraphrase) I am made to tremble, and I fear. Lamb of God, who takes away the sins of the world. Deliver me, Lord, on that day (from the Requiem Mass of the Roman Catholic Church).

89. 1 Cor 15:51–55.

PART FOUR

1. (German) My own face; my own form.

2. STP, aka DOM (2,5-dimethoxy-4-methylamphetamine), is an unusually long-lasting psychedelic compound first synthesized by Alexander Shulgin.

3. A Greek hymn in honor of Dionysus.

4. (German) The red flag.

5. A 1978 book by R. Gordon Wasson, Albert Hofmann, and Carl Ruck that argues that psychedelic substances were consumed at Eleusis.

6. See note 41, page 83.

7. See note 90, page 410.

8. This phrase originated in a talk that Ursula K. Le Guin gave at Emory University in early 1981, in which she reportedly discussed Dick's preoccupation with "unresolvable metaphysical matters." Michael Bishop, who was present at the talk, wrote to Dick, who responded in an open letter to the *Science Fiction Review*.

9. (Chinese) Permanent Tao.

10. This excerpt is drawn from a letter to Patricia Warrick.

11. An idea expressed by Islamic philosophers, most notably Al-Ash`ari and Al-Ghazali, but shared by many medieval Christian and Jewish philosophers as well. In the West, this idea is related to occasionalism, the view (most famously expressed by Nicolas Malebranche) that causality is an illusion and God is the efficient cause of all that exists.

12. (German) Friends, not these sounds . . . (The first line of Beethoven's redaction of Schiller's "Ode to Joy" in his Ninth Symphony.)

13. Real Elapsed Time.

14. (German) Who shall deliver me? (Most likely drawn from Bach Cantata BWV 4, *Ich elender Mensch, wer wird mich erlösen.*)

15. Over this and the following two folders, Dick outlines, writes, and reflects on *The Transmigration of Timothy Archer*.

16. A version of the material in the following excerpt appears in the first chapter of *The Transmigration of Timothy Archer*.

17. The following fragment was incorporated into *The Transmigration of Timothy Archer* as one of Bishop Archer's speculations.

18. Partly inspired by a dream recorded in [90:6A] above, the Book of the Spinners is a Dick invention that also appears in *The Transmigration of Timothy Archer*.

19. See note 51, page 330.

20. John Dryden, "A Song for St. Cecilia's Day."

21. Ursula K. Le Guin.

22. "Overdrawn at the Memory Bank" is a 1976 short story by John Varley. PBS adapted it into a TV movie in 1983 as part of the same project that produced the film version of Ursula K. Le Guin's Dick tribute *The Lathe of Heaven*.

23. Existential psychologist Ludwig Binswanger, from whom Dick drew the notion of "tomb world," described three realms: Eigenwelt, Mitwelt, and Umwelt. See Glossary.

24. (German terms used by Martin Heidegger) *Geworfenheit:* thrownness, the quality of finding ourselves already thrown into existence, as if by accident. *Das unheimlich:* the uncanny; literally, "not at home."

25. (German) Actual.

26. In *The Ghost in the Machine* (1967), Arthur Koestler defines "holon" as a self-organizing dissipative structure that is simultaneously a whole and a part of a larger whole, and ultimately of a "holarchy" of holons.

27. (Latin) I am afraid; deliver me, Oh Lord, on that day. (Adapted from the Requiem Mass.)

28. Dick is thinking here of the *clinamen*, the term the ancient Roman philosopher Lucretius used to describe the indeterminate bustle and swerve of atoms in the void.

29. (Greek) Love of humanity.

30. The following three dated letters have been moved to this folder from folder 56 to preserve chronology.

31. Edmund Meskys was the editor — with Felice Rolfe at the time of Dick's letter — of the long-running and award-winning S-F fanzine *Niekas*.

32. Dick sent copies of his so-called Tagore letter — the September 23, 1981, letter to Edmund Meskys reprinted here — to eighty-five people.

33. Karen Silkwood was a health and labor activist who died under mysterious circumstances in November 1974.

34. (Latin) Universal exemplars in the divine mind. (Analogous to Plato's forms.)

35. This occurs in chapter 6 of *The Divine Invasion*, where Dick gives the character Galina the fish dream that he mentions throughout the Exegesis, beginning in 1975 ("the renewing fish that's sliced forever").

36. The Sepher Yetzirah, or *The Book of Formation*, is an early work of Jewish esoteric mysticism that describes the creation of the universe through numbers and Hebrew letters.

37. Luke and Acts are written by the same author and are frequently considered as a single work.

38. The practice of Manichaeism involved strict dietary laws. The elect avoided foods thought to be "dark" (including meat) in favor of foods containing more "light," primarily light-colored fruits and vegetables. The process of digestion was considered to free the light particles trapped inside the food.

39. Mircea Eliade, *Myth and Reality* (1963), p. 106.

40. (Latin) Law of retribution. (Frequently linked, though Roman in origin, to the legal principle of "an eye for an eye" from Ex 21:23–25.)

41. Hans Jonas wrote the seminal book *The Gnostic Religion* (1958), which links ancient Gnosticism to modern existentialism.

42. This is the first mention of *The Owl in Daylight*, the novel left unfinished at Dick's death.

43. In Mt 27:46 and Mk 15:34, Jesus quotes the opening verse of Ps 22 from the cross: "My God, my God, why have you forsaken me?"

44. This entry, including the following dream and its subsequent analysis, is entirely typewritten.

45. In 1947 Dick roomed with and befriended a number of gay Berkeley artists and poets whom he met through his high school friend George Ackerman. These included the poets Robert Duncan and Jack Spicer, who shared many of his esoteric, metaphysical, and literary interests. Vladimir Horowitz, one of the premier pianists of his day, was also gay.

46. The Eleatics were a school of pre-Socratic philosophers founded in the fifth century B.C. by Parmenides and including the paradox-loving Zeno.

47. (Greek) Cosmic mind.

48. The term "secrecy theme" refers to Jesus's commands to his disciples not to reveal that he is the Messiah. Passages on the "Messianic secret" do appear in Luke (see 4:41 and 8:56), but the theme is most pronounced in the Gospel of Mark.

49. The public interest law firm that represented Karen Silkwood and journalists investigating the Iran-Contra affair. Its cofounder, William J. Davis, was a Jesuit priest.

50. *Peer Gynt* (1867) is a five-act play by Henrik Ibsen that combines surreal folklore, poetry, social satire, and realistic episodes.

51. *Tales of Hoffmann* (1881) was an opera by Jacques Offenbach, based on the short fantasy stories of German Romanticist E.T.A. Hoffmann (1776–1822).

52. "The Pulley" by George Herbert, one of Dick's favorite poets.

53. Maimonides (1138–1204) was the greatest Jewish philosopher of the medieval period; his influential *Guide to the Perplexed* attempted to reconcile Aristotelian thought and Judaism.

54. (German) Community. (An apparent neologism based on *Gemeinschaft*.)

55. (German) Loneliness.

56. This may be the AI Voice trying out its German. Roughly, "Woman, sing for our friends."

57. (German) Nearby.

58. (German) Friends; joy.

59. Ted Sturgeon's 1971 story "Dazed" involves a transcendent being incarnated in order to restore the balance of yin and yang.

60. Dick here is fusing and/or confusing Eleusis with the Elysian Fields, the most pleasant environs of the ancient Greek Underworld.

61. Benjamin Crème (1922–) is a long-standing New Age apocalyptic prophet who has often spoken of the coming of Maitreya, or the World Teacher. In 1982 he proclaimed that Maitreya, aka the Christ, was living within the Asian community of Brick Lane in London and would shortly announce himself to the world media.

62. The Age of Aquarius is an astrologic epoch based on the precession of the equinoxes and a popular theme in many New Age accounts of contemporary spiritual transformation. It follows the current Age of Pisces, whose fish symbolism has often been associated with Christianity.

63. See note 116, page 205.

64. Helena Patrovna Blavatsky (1831–1891) cofounded the Theosophical Society, an esoteric order that held that world history is directed by invisible hidden masters.

65. The Glimmung is a godlike alien from Plowman's Planet (aka Sirius Five) in *Galactic Pot-Healer* (1969), one of Dick's more Jungian works.

66. This brief but valuable segment has been moved here from folder 55 to preserve continuity.

67. (Greek) Savior.

68. *Sepher Yetzirah*, or *The Book of Creation*, a sacred text of Kabbala Judaism, in its 1887 translation by W. W. Wescott.

69. Here Dick uses Greek letters (similar to those in the word Σωτηρ [soter], which he inscribed above) to write *sorer*, which resembles *soror*, the Latin word for sister.

Glossary

2-3-74, sometimes 2-74 or 3-74: A series of extraordinary events, beginning in February 1974 and continuing through March and beyond, that forms the main subject of the Exegesis.

acosmism: A doctrine that denies the apparent reality of the universe as something apart from God or the Absolute.

Acts: The Book of Acts in the New Testament, written by the same author as the Gospel of Luke, tells the history of the early apostolic age following the death and resurrection of Christ. It is sometimes called "The Gospel of the Holy Spirit," owing to its depiction of the role played by the Holy Spirit in the growth of the early church. Dick asserts a significant and unintended correspondence between Acts and his novel *Flow My Tears, the Policeman Said* (1974).

agape (Greek): One of several Greek words for love, as distinguished from *eros* (sexual love) and *philia* (friendship); often used to describe God or Christ's love for mankind. In Dick's use, which draws on the apostle Paul's description of transcendent love in 1 Corinthians 13, the term is identified with empathy.

Ahura Mazd, Ahura Mazda, or **Ormazd:** The highest god of Zoroastrianism, the creator and sustainer of truth. In *The Cosmic Puppets* (1957) a small town is discovered to be the battleground between Ormazd and his eternal opponent, Ahriman.

AI Voice: Artificial Intelligence Voice, sometimes called "Voice" or "Spirit." A term coined by Dick for the hypnagogic voice that he heard often in 1974–75 and intermittently until his death. Many of the voice's sayings are recorded in the Exegesis. Despite the term, Dick does not consistently hold that the voice is technological in nature. He often characterizes it as "female" and sometimes attributes it to the Gnostic goddess **Sophia** and his own sister Jane.

ajna chakra: The so-called Third Eye, one of seven chakras or "wheels" described in Hindu tantric and yoga texts.

als ob (German): As if.

anamnesis (Greek): Recollection, abrogation of amnesia. For Plato, anamnesis — the recollection of the world of ideas in which the soul dwelled before incarnating in human form — explains the human capacity for understanding abstract, universal truths, such as the geometric theorems of Euclid. In Dick's more Gnostic understanding, it also implies the recollection of the soul's origins beyond the fallen or occluded world.

ananke (Greek): The blindness that follows hubris; also, a chthonic goddess who personifies necessity and compulsion.

Androids: One of Dick's most morally complex novels, *Do Androids Dream of Electric Sheep?* (1968) was optioned and produced as the Ridley Scott film *Blade Runner* (1982). Left on the cutting room floor was the novel's fictional religion, "Mercerism," whose adherents technologically and empathetically merge with Wilber Mercer as he climbs a hill, is stoned to death, descends into a tomb world, and arises, in an endless cycle.

anima (Latin): Translation of Greek term *psyche*, meaning "life" or "soul." Psychologist Carl Jung used the terms *anima* and *animus* to describe the true inner self of human beings; for men, the anima is generally a female figure.

Anokhi (Hebrew): A form of the personal pronoun meaning "I" or "I myself." In Dick's use, it refers primarily to Exodus 20:2: "Anokhi YHWH Elohekha" ("I [am] YHWH your God"). More generally for Dick, *anokhi* stands for self-awareness and consciousness. *The Transmigration of Timothy Archer* (1982) features discussion of the "Anokhi mushroom," a hallucinogenic drug that enables communion with the divine.

Archer, Angel: Protagonist of Dick's final novel, *The Transmigration of Timothy Archer* (1982).

Asklepios: Greek god of healing and medicine; his temples were also sites of oracular dream incubation.

astral determinism: The belief that the destiny of individual human beings is governed by the stars or planets, which in some Gnostic cosmologies are personified as the lower planetary rulers or *archons.*

Atman (Sanskrit): The eternal Self or divine core of the human being, distinct from the *ahamkara* (literally, the "I-maker") or ego with which we normally, and falsely, identify. In Vedanta, Atman is identified with **Brahman.**

Attic Greek: A dialect of ancient Greek spoken in Attica.

Augenblick (German): Literally, "eye view"; moment.

Augustine (C.E. 354–430): Bishop of Hippo, Saint and Doctor of the Church. In the Exegesis, Augustine's allegorical interpretation of Revelation is contrasted with literalistic millenarianism.

Bacchae, The: Roman name for the *maenads,* female figures of Greek mythology who follow the god Dionysus and pursue religious ecstasy through intoxication, dance, and ritual sacrifice. Also a play by Euripedes, in which Dick saw parallels to *Flow My Tears, the Policeman Said* (1974).

Bardo Thödol: Commonly known as *The Tibetan Book of the Dead,* this Tibetan Buddhist text, traditionally considered to be written by Padmasambhava, describes the experiences the mind undergoes as it transits between death and rebirth, an intermediary period known as *bardo.* Dick was familiar with the text through its initial translation by W. Y. Evans-Wentz, whose reissue in 1960 featured an important introduction by Carl Jung.

Bergson, Henri (1859–1941): A French philosopher who won the Nobel Prize for Literature in 1927, Bergson was known for his theories of duration and *élan vital,* the lively impetus that distinguishes living systems from machines. With his concept of duration, Bergson hoped to describe the qualitative nature of the subjective experience of time rather than the objective measurements of the clock. Dick's experience of "non-linear" incursions of time from the future and his meditations on the distinction between living organisms and machines found resonance in Bergson's work.

bicameral: Term taken from Julian Jaynes's popular book *The Origin of Consciousness in the Breakdown of the Bicameral Mind* (1976). Jaynes argues that our minds were originally split along hemispheric lines, which allowed voices from one side of the brain to be heard by the other as if they were external commands or the voices of gods.

Black Iron Prison, also **BIP:** Dick's term for the prison world of political tyranny and determinism he glimpsed beneath the veneer of Orange County in March 1974. He later wrote that upon perceiving it, he realized that he had been living in it and writing about it his whole life. In his dualistic cosmologies, the BIP is opposed to the **Palm Tree Garden,** or **PTG.**

Boehme or **Böhme, Jacob** (c. 1575–1624): German shoemaker and mystic whose 1600 vision was induced by the play of light on a pewter dish. His esoteric theory of higher and lower triads anticipated Hegel's dialectic, and his notion of **Urgrund** was important to Dick.

Boucher, Anthony (1922–1968): Science fiction editor, author, and friend of Dick's. As editor of the *Magazine of Fantasy and Science Fiction,* Boucher purchased the first story Dick sold, the tale "Roog" (1953).

Brahman: A concept from the Vedic tradition that generally refers to the uncreated substance of the universe that pervades all things; also the precursor to the creator god Brahmā. The Advaita Vedanta of **Sankara** insists on the ultimate identity of Brahman and **Atman.**

Bruno, Giordano (1548–1600): Italian astronomer, mathematician, and hermetic philosopher whose theories about the infinity of the universe anticipated modern cosmology. Bruno is chiefly remembered for having been burned at the stake in Rome.

BTA: "Bishop Timothy Archer," working title for *The Transmigration of Timothy Archer* (1982).

Buber, Martin (1878–1965): Austrian-born Jewish existentialist philosopher. See **I-It** and **I-Thou relationship**.

Buckman, Felix: Character in Dick's novel *Flow My Tears, the Policeman Said* (1974). A police official in a militaristic state, he experiences an unexpected and compassionate epiphany in the novel's conclusion.

Burroughs, William S. (1914–1997): Experimental Beat writer. Burroughs's notions of reality as a control system and language as an extraterrestrial virus clearly resonated with Dick, who, in 1978, experimented with the cut-up method developed by Swiss artist Brion Gysin and deployed by Burroughs.

Calvin, John (1509–1564): French Protestant theologian. In the Exegesis, Calvin appears primarily as a proponent of the idea that prelapsarian human beings had extraordinary capabilities.

"Chains of Air," or **"Chains . . . Web":** The short story "Chains of Air, Web of Aether" (1980), later revised and incorporated into *The Divine Invasion* (1981).

Claudia: Claudia Krenz Bush, a graduate student at Idaho State University who corresponded with Dick while working on her master's thesis. Dick later refers to his early Exegesis as "mostly letters to Claudia."

Corpus Christi (Latin): Body of Christ. Dick also uses the term in the more theological sense of the mystical body of the Church.

crypte morphosis (Greek): Latent shape or form. One of the Greek phrases that came to Dick in his dreams in 1974. In the Exegesis he interprets the phrase in light of Heraclitus's fragment 54, "Latent form is the master of obvious form," and fragment 123, "The nature of things is in the habit of concealing itself."

cybernetic: Term coined by Norbert Wiener for the science of communication and control in human and machine systems; earlier coined by the French scientist André-Marie Ampère to denote "political science." Wiener drew the term from the ancient Greek term *kybernetes*, for "steersman" or the "art of steering."

Dasein (German): Martin Heidegger's term for being, especially human being.

Deus Absconditus (Latin): Hidden God. The term comes from Isaiah 45:15 in the Vulgate.

Deus sive substantia sive natura (Latin): A dictum of **Spinoza** on the unity of God and nature; in an interview, Dick translated this concept as "God, i.e., reality, i.e., nature."

dibba cakkhu (Pali): The divine eye, one of the six features of higher or enlightened knowing described in the Pali Buddhist canon.

Dionysus, also **Dionysos:** The Greek god of wine, vegetation, and ritual ecstasy. His death and resurrection were important in a number of **mystery religions.**

Ditheon: A neologism Dick develops in later Exegesis entries to describe the life form that results from the union of two minds within a single body. Similar to **homoplasmate.**

dokos (Greek): Deception, lack of true perception. Dick employs this term as a cognate for **maya.**

Eckhart, Meister (1260–1327): A Dominican scholar and preacher whose radical mystical teachings, which stressed the immediate presence of God in the individual soul, were condemned by Pope John XXII shortly before he died.

eidos, eidola, sometimes misspelled **edola** (Greek): Ultimate form or idea. In Platonic philosophy, the forms constitute the world of ideas, which in turn are the source of all being.

Eigenwelt (German): The inner realm. One of the three types of world described by the existentialist psychologist Ludwig Binswanger; see **Mitwelt** and **Umwelt.**

einai (Greek): From the Aristotelian phrase *to ti en einai* (roughly, "the what-it-was-to-be"): the eternal essence of a thing.

Eleusinian Mysteries: The most important of the ancient **mystery religions,** these secret initiation ceremonies were held annually in ancient Greece for over a millennium. "The Hymn to Demeter" is the only existing textual source for the rites, which centered on the story of Persephone's abduction into the Underworld. In *The Road to Eleusis* (1978), Gordon Wasson, Albert Hofmann, and Carl Ruck advance the theory that psychedelic substances were used to produce the transformative effects of the rites.

Empedocles (c. 490–430 B.C.E.): Pre-Socratic philosopher and naturalist. Empedocles theorized that change in the universe is the result of the interaction between the forces of love and strife. The last philosopher to write his work in verse, Empedocles has been described by some scholars as a shaman as much as a philosopher.

enantiodromia (Greek): Sudden transformation into an opposite form or tendency. The term was used by Heraclitus, but Dick was probably exposed to it through his reading of C. G. Jung, who employs the term to describe the psyche's tendency to overcome deep-seated resistance, especially to the unconscious, by shifting (seemingly suddenly) to the opposite pole of an attitude, belief, or emotion. Dick also sometimes uses the term *flip-flop.*

Encyclopedia Britannica, EB, or **Brit 3:** In late 1974, Dick purchased a set of the newly released fifteenth edition of the *Encyclopedia Britannica,* also known as the *Britannica 3.* The encyclopedia is divided into three sections: the one-volume *Propedia* (a general outline of all human knowledge), the twelve-volume *Micropedia* (containing brief reference entries), and the seventeen-volume *Macropedia* (containing in-depth articles on important subjects).

Encyclopedia of Philosophy, or **E. of Phil.:** Edited by Paul Edwards and still admired today, this is a major reference work for the Exegesis. According to *VALIS,* Dick was using the eight-volume work published in 1967 by Macmillan rather than the four-volume 1972 reprint.

engram: The biophysical imprint of events on memory. An important word in Dianetics, where it refers to the "recordings" stored in the reactive mind, the term is generally used in the Exegesis to denote the latent patterns that predispose the mind to respond to the trigger events that produce **anamnesis.** In *VALIS* (1981), Dick uses *engram* to describe a ritual in which **Thomas** prepares to "reconstitute himself after his physical death."

entelechy: A term in Aristotelian thought meaning fully developed or actualized. In his use of the term, Dick also reflects the work of German philosopher Hans Adolf Eduard Driesch, who used *entelechy* to indicate a life force distinct from the physical body.

epistemology: The philosophy of knowledge, dealing with what knowledge is, how it is acquired, and how we know what we know. Sometimes contrasted with ontology, which philosophically studies the nature of being and the existence of things.

Erasmus (1466–1536): Dutch Catholic priest, theologian, Renaissance humanist, and satirist. Perhaps best known for his essay *The Praise of Folly* (1509), which mocks the superstitious errors and absurdities derived from Catholic doctrine and practice.

Essenes: A Jewish sect, active from roughly the second century B.C.E. to the end of the first century C.E., that held messianic and apocalyptic beliefs and engaged in ascetic practices. It is generally believed that the Dead Sea Scrolls were the library of a community of Essenes; John the Baptist was likely to have been influenced by them. See **Qumran Scrolls.**

ETI: Extra Terrestrial Intelligence.

Firebright: One of Dick's terms for ultimate, living wisdom; see **plasmate.**

Fremd (German, English): Strange (adjective) or stranger (noun); both rarely used.

"Frozen Journey": Original name for the story "I Hope I Shall Arrive Soon" (1980).

GABA fluid: Gamma aminobutyric acid, an endogenous inhibitory neurotransmitter in the human nervous system. Some studies show that increased levels may reduce the mental decline associated with aging.

Galápagos turtle: In a 1981 interview with Gregg Rickman, Dick describes a nature documentary he viewed in the 1960s in which a female Galápagos turtle crawled the wrong direction after laying her eggs in the sand and began to die from exposure while still moving her limbs. That night Dick heard a voice tell him that the turtle believed that she had made it back to the ocean, adding, "And she shall see the sea." It was one of Dick's few experiences with the "AI Voice" previous to 2-3-74. A supposed Reuters news item about the death of an old Galápagos turtle provides the epigraph for *Do Androids Dream of Electric Sheep?* (1968).

Gestalt: A German term describing an entity's holistic essence or form. Gestalt psychology attempts to characterize how our minds and brains select whole forms from a background of possible partial perceptions; this relationship is characterized as "figure" and "ground," which Dick generally recasts as "set" and "ground."

Gnosis, Gnostic (Greek): Knowledge. The term *Gnostic,* which is controversial among scholars, describes a wide range of religious sects of the ancient world. Broadly speaking, these sects believed in a strong dualism of matter and spirit, often holding that the material world was a prison or trap for the soul associated with an inferior creator, or demiurge. The attainment of secret knowledge (gnosis) was proscribed as the means of salvation. The **Nag Hammadi** library was an important group of Gnostic texts discovered in 1945.

golden fish: On February 20, 1974, a young woman working for a local pharmacy delivered a bottle of prescription Darvon tablets to Dick's apartment in Fullerton, California. She was wearing a necklace with a golden fish pendant, an ancient Christian symbol that had been resurrected by the countercultural "Jesus movement" in the late 1960s. According to Dick, the sight of the emblem triggered the events of 2-3-74; he connected the design with other figures, including DNA's double helix and the human eye.

golden rectangle, also **golden section:** Figures associated with the golden ratio or divine mean, a mathematical pattern of relationship that has been recognized since **Pythagoras.** The golden ratio (an irrational number approximate to 1:618034) occurs when the ratio between the sum of two unequal quantities and the larger quantity is equivalent to the ratio between the larger quantity and the smaller. Geometric plotting of the recursive Fibonacci sequence also produces the golden rectangle, as does the growth of a nautilus shell.

Hartshorne, Charles (1897–2000): American philosopher and theologian who developed the process philosophy of **Alfred North Whitehead** into process theology, which emphasizes the relationship between an ever-changing God and a creation in constant development.

Hegel, G.W.F. (1770–1831): German philosopher of dialectical idealism. Hegel's *Phenomenology of Spirit* offers readers an epic quest toward self-understanding as the thinker explores the limits and dynamics of rational thought learning to reflect on and comprehend itself. Hegel's dialectic was influential on Karl Marx, who famously "turned Hegel on his head" with the invention of dialectical materialism.

Heidegger, Martin (1889–1976): German philosopher whose work attempted to overcome what he perceived as the "forgetfulness of being" in the history of philosophy. Heidegger argued that habits of thought inherited from the Greeks induce human beings to focus on "beings" rather than "being" — particular entities rather than that which enables entities to exist at all. Heidegger's conception of **Dasein**, or "being-there," distinguished between the activity of being and a subject or a self — the center of philosophical analysis since René Descartes. Heidegger is the most referenced twentieth-century philosopher in the Exegesis.

heimarmene (Greek): Fate, or the personification of fate; for Dick, also the deluding, entrapping power of spurious everyday reality.

Heraclitus (c. 535–475 B.C.E.): Ancient Greek philosopher from Asia Minor. The most dynamic of the pre-Socratics, Heraclitus comes down to us through a collection of fragments that radiate a vision of reality in which all is change, opposites coincide, and fire is the essential process at the heart of the world flux.

hermetic: An important strand of Western esoteric thought and experience, hermeticism derives from the *Corpus hermeticum*, a set of texts from late antiquity whose mystical and magical philosophy is perhaps best summarized in the famous dictum from the *Emerald Tablet of Hermes Trismegistus:* "As above, so below."

homeostasis: The stable, balanced condition maintained by a dynamical system regulating its own development through time; usually, a living organism regularly adjusting itself to changing environmental conditions.

homoplasmate: A Dickian neologism describing a human being who has cross-bonded with an influx of living information bestowed or transmitted by a higher source of wisdom. See **plasmate.**

Ho On, or **Oh Ho:** The name of a clay pot made for Dick by a friend. In an early **hypnagogic** vision, Dick heard the pot, which identified itself as "Oh Ho," speak to him in a brash, irritable tone about spiritual matters. Later, Dick theorized that the name "Oh Ho" might be related to the Greek phrase *Ho On,* meaning "He Who." The phrase "ho on" appears in Exodus 3:14, when God identifies himself as "I AM WHO I AM" (in the Greek of the Septuagint, *Ego eimi ho on*).

hylozoism: The belief or philosophical proposition that material things can be alive, or that life and matter are inseparable.

hypnagogic, or **hypnogogic;** and **hypnopompic:** Hallucinations, both visual and auditory, that occur on the boundary of sleep and often feature a significant and sometimes alarming sense of reality. Hypnagogic hallucinations occur while one is falling asleep, hypnopompic hallucinations while one is waking.

hypostasis (Greek): Literally, "beneath-standing" or "underpinning." A term for the basic reality of a thing in Greek philosophy. Plotinus used it to describe the three principles that underlie phenomenal reality: the One, the **noös,** and the World Soul, or **Logos.** The term was also batted around within the ecumenical councils as they tried to clarify the nature of the Trinity.

I Ching: An ancient Chinese text used as a tool for divination. The *Book of Changes* is based on a binary system of broken (yin) and unbroken (yang) lines; six such lines make up a symbolic hexagram linked to various commentaries. Dick, who owned the original two-volume Bollingen edition of the Wilhelm/Baynes translation, consulted the *I Ching* frequently and claimed to have used it to resolve turning points in the plot of *The Man in the High Castle* (1962), which also features an oracular book written using the *I Ching.*

idios kosmos and **koinos kosmos** (Greek): Literally, "private world" and "communal world," respectively. The two phrases come from fragment 89 of Heraclitus: "The waking have one common world, but the sleeping turn aside each into a world of his own." In Dick's scheme, it is often used to contrast an individual's reality system from collective social reality.

I-It and **I-Thou relationship:** Terms, taken from **Martin Buber's** *I and Thou* (1923), describing two forms of relationship. In the first, the individual treats the world and other individuals as objects with use value; in the second, the individual enters true relationship with the world and other individuals as other *subjects* rather than objects. Buber conceives the latter form of relationship as the model of God's interaction with the world.

Isidore, Jack: Protagonist of Dick's novel *Confessions of a Crap Artist* (written around 1960; published 1975). Isidore engages in relentless amateur scientific inquiry, not unlike Dick's practice in the Exegesis.

James-James: Evil or deranged demiurgic figure that Dick encountered in a dream in 1974 or 1975; described in chapter 18 of *Radio Free Albemuth* (1985).

Joachim of Fiore (c. 1135–1202). Theologian and mystic from Sicily. His concept of the three ages of history, which posits an imminent "Age of the Holy Spirit" when God will communicate directly with humanity without the mediation of the clergy, helped fuel a number of millenarian, utopian, and radical ideas and movements, including **Marxism.**

Kant, Immanuel (1724–1804): German philosopher whose transcendental idealism sought to integrate knowledge based on experience (empiricism) with knowledge based on reason (for example, mathematics). Kant called for and in many ways achieved a "Copernican revolution" in philosophy by placing the modes of human perception at the center of inquiry; for Kant the structures of the human mind order the sense data of experience, limiting our ability to apprehend the *Ding an sich,* the thing-in-itself.

kerygma (Greek): Preaching or pronouncement, especially of the message of Christ contained in the New Testament.

King Felix: A two-word "cypher" that Dick discovered in the text of *Flow My Tears, the Policeman Said* (1974). On page 218 of the Doubleday hardcover, in the section describing **Felix Buckman**'s visionary dream, the words *king* and *Felix* appear vertically juxtaposed between two lines of text. Dick became convinced that this happenstance phrase had a secret meaning and would be read and recognized by people or forces unknown. "Felix" is Latin for "fortunate" or "happy."

Kozyrev, Nikolai, NK, or **Dr. NK** (1908–1983): Russian astrophysicist who carried out research at the Pulkovo Observatory. His 1967 article "Possibility of Experimental Study of the Properties of Time" theorizes that time is a force with active causal properties.

Krasis (Greek): Blending or mixture; used by the pre-Socratic philosophers Empedocles and Anaxagoras in their accounts of the creation of the material world.

Lem, Stanislaw (1921–2006): Polish writer of science fiction, philosophy, and satire. Contributed "Philip K. Dick: A Visionary Among the Charlatans" to *Science Fiction Studies* in 1975, an article that praised Dick and especially *Ubik* (1968). The two corresponded, and Lem worked on a Polish translation of *Ubik*.

Liebniz, Gottfried (1646–1716): A German mathematician and philosopher who contributed significantly to the development of mechanical calculators, infinitesimal calculus, and binary mathematics (whose anticipation in the *I Ching* he recognized). His notion of the **monad** was important to Dick.

Logos (Greek): Word, account, reason. Heraclitus used the word in the sense of order; in Christianity, an important tradition derives from the Gospel of John, in whose first lines Christ is identified as the Logos, the eternal "Word" or "Reason" of the cosmos through whom God created the universe.

ma'at: Ancient Egyptian concept of truth, balance, and law; also personified as a goddess.

macrometasomakosmos, also **MMSK:** Dick's term for the ultimate, genuine structure of reality; a cognate for the Platonic world of ideas. In terms of its Greek roots, this neologism breaks down into Great-Ultimate-Body-of-the-Cosmos.

Maitreya (Sanskrit): The future Buddha foretold in Buddhist eschatology. In the late nineteenth century, the Theosophists began using the term to describe a coming World Teacher, and the term appears in a variety of New Age movements.

Malebranche, Nicolas (1638–1715): French philosopher and natural scientist who synthesized Cartesian philosophy with Augustinian thought. Malebranche held that we see external objects by means of ideas in God's mind; he also embraced the doctrine of occasionalism, which holds that God is the only real cause of all action.

Mani (c. 216–276 C.E.): The prophet and founder of Manichaeism, a syncretistic religion that combined Zoroastrian and Gnostic ideas and became one of the most dominant religions in the world between the third and seventh centuries. Sharply dualistic, Manichaeism held that the material world is a realm of darkness from which spiritual light must be extracted through ritual and practice.

Marxism: Political philosophy and social movement based on the writings of German political economist Karl Marx (1818–1883). Anticipating the intensification of capitalism's internal contradictions, and calling for a revolutionary awareness among the working classes, Marx prophesied the end of the capitalist world order and the emergence of a classless society.

maya (Sanskrit): Illusion, especially the illusion of the phenomenal world; sometimes also considered an aspect of the Divine Mother.

Maze: A dark **Gnostic** fable also inspired by the **Bardo Thödol,** *A Maze of Death* (1970) tells the story of fourteen colonists who emigrate to the planet Delmak-o, only to be murdered, one by one. It emerges that the colonists are immersed in a computer simulation they are running to distract themselves from despair as their failed spaceship orbits a dead star. Delmak-o's digitally programmed religion represents Dick's most developed theological systematizing prior to 2-3-74, and it closes with arguably the most explicit **theophany** in any Dick novel.

Mitleid (German): Compassion, pity.

Mitwelt (German): The immediate environment. One of the three terms for world used by the existentialist psychologist Ludwig Binswanger. See **Umwelt** and **Eigenwelt.**

MMSK: See **macrometasomakosmos.**

moksa (Sanskrit): Ultimate release, liberation.

monad: The philosopher **Leibniz** described the things in the world as independent but interconnected entities — which he called "monads" — operating according to a pre-established divine harmony.

mystery religions, or **mystery cults:** Religious cults in the ancient Greco-Roman world whose members engaged in esoteric rituals, often involving the ritual and ecstatic reenactment of a mythical narrative. The most influential and long-lived of these rites were the **Eleusinian Mysteries** in Greece.

Nag Hammadi: Egyptian town near the site of the 1945 discovery of thirteen ancient leather-bound codices hidden in a sealed jar. Dating from the second century, these Coptic manuscripts probably belonged to the library of a Gnostic Christian community. One of the most notable Nag Hammadi texts is the only complete copy of the Gospel of Thomas, an important source for Dick's religious reflections.

negentropic: Bringing order to a disordered or entropic system.

noös, or **nous** (Greek): Mind, reason, divine or human. Associated words are *noetic* (adjective; "of the mind") and *noein* (verb; "to think or realize").

noösphere: Geophysicist Vladimir Vernadsky argued that, along with the biosphere, lithosphere, and atmosphere, the earth has acquired a mental or psychic "sphere": a noösphere created through thought and focused attention. **Pierre Teilhard de Chardin** popularized the concept of noösphere in his treatment of "Point Omega."

NT and OT: New Testament and Old Testament.

ontogon: A neologism meaning an individual being or object, as contrasted to an ideal or Platonic form. See **phylogon.** Dick coins the terms from *phylogeny* and *ontogony,* used in evolutionary theory and depth psychology to describe the relationship between individual and species life.

ontology: The philosophy of being; ontologists ask questions about the nature and function of reality itself and about what it means for things to exist.

Ornstein, Robert (1942–): American psychologist, author of *The Psychology of Consciousness* (1972). His views on the brain's hemispheres and their differing roles in consciousness were brought to mainstream attention when he was covered by *Time* magazine in 1974.

Orphics: An ancient Greek and Hellenic **mystery cult** devoted to the poet Orpheus, as well as **Dionysus** in the form of **Zagreus;** Orphic myths and rituals were particularly concerned with death and resurrection.

orthogonal time: Moving perpendicularly to the conventional and spurious sense of linear time, orthogonal time is, for Dick, time in its genuine mode. In a 1975 essay, "Man, Android, and Machine," Dick describes orthogonal time as containing within a simultaneous plane "everything which was, just as grooves on an LP contain that part of the music which has already been played; they don't disappear after the stylus tracks them."

Owl: Dick's unfinished final novel, *The Owl in Daylight.*

palintropos harmonie, or **palintonos harmonie:** A term used in Heraclitus's fragment 51, which compares the mutual adjustment and harmony of variant things and processes to the relationship of bow and lyre. Variant sources supply *palintropos* (backward-turning) or *palintonos* (backward-stretching) as the first word. Dick uses the term in both its variants in the Exegesis.

Palm Tree Garden, or **PTG:** The spiritually redeemed and ontologically genuine world, revealed to Dick in January-February 1975, when southern California seemed to transform into the Levant. In chapter 18 of *Deus Irae* (1976, co-written with Roger Zelazny), the vision of Dr. Abernathy—written by Dick alone—represents the Palm Tree Garden.

Palmer Eldritch: Industrial magnate who unleashes psychedelic havoc in Dick's *The Three Stigmata of Palmer Eldritch* (1965) after he returns from the Proxima system as a drug-dealing demiurge. Eldritch's "three stigmata" are based on the vision of a "vast visage of perfect evil" that Dick saw in the skies over Marin County in 1963, which also induced in him a spell of regular Episcopalian worship at a local church.

panentheism: A metaphysical and religious doctrine holding that God (*theos*) is both transcendent and immanent, both beyond all and yet "in all" (*pan-en-*). This teaching is sometimes portrayed through the image of the cosmos as God's body, God's relationship to the universe being roughly analogous to the mind's relationship to the body — again, both "in" and "beyond" at the same time.

pantheism: A metaphysical and religious doctrine that holds that God is identified with everything in the world and that everything in the world is God. This is in striking contrast to traditional theism, which holds that God transcends ordinary reality.

Pantocrator (Greek): "Almighty," a name of God that accents his omnipotence.

Paracelsus (1493–1541): A Swiss Renaissance **hermeticist,** alchemist, and physician with the remarkable full name of Philippus Aureolus Theophrastus Bombastus von Hohenheim. Through empirical experiments and innovative occult theories, Paracelsus broke the reigning orthodox concepts of disease, explored botanical remedies, and pioneered the use of minerals and chemicals in medicine.

Paraclete, sometimes **Parakletos** (Greek): Literally, advocate or helper; in Christianity, the Holy Spirit.

Parmenides (c. early fifth century B.C.E.): Pre-Socratic philosopher and founder of the Eleatic school. In his poem *On Nature,* he describes reality as a mixture of two forms: the truth of the One and the mere appearance of the world of multiplicity, about which we can hold only opinion. As one of the first philosophers to consider the abstract principle of Being, he is considered a founder of metaphysics.

parousia (Greek): Presence, advent; in Christianity, the term generally refers to the Second Coming of Christ.

Parsifal: A three-act opera by Richard Wagner (1813–1883), based on the epic Germanic poem *Parzival,* about the titular knight's quest for the Holy Grail. In Wagner's story, which is also influenced by legends of the Buddha, Parsifal embodies a "holy fool" who helps initiate the powerful act of redemption that closes the opera.

Philo of Alexandria (20 B.C.E.–50 C.E.): A Hellenistic Jew who used a variety of Greek philosophical concepts to interpret and defend the Jewish scriptures. His writings were particularly important to the early Church fathers, who were probably influenced by his association of **Logos** with the governing plan of creation and the "word of God" that bears the Lord's message in the Hebrew Bible.

phylogon: A neologism referring to a general principle or archetype, as contrasted to an individual object or being; roughly analogous to Plato's forms. See **ontogon.**

Pike, James (1913–1969): American Episcopalian bishop, writer, and friend of Dick's. Pike, who questioned traditional doctrines such as the Trinity and the virginity of Mary, was accused of heresy and resigned his California post in 1966. His son Jim committed suicide the same year, and Pike held séances, one of which was attended by Dick and Nancy Hackett, in an attempt to contact his son's spirit. Pike died in the Israeli desert while researching the Essenes and the historical Jesus. Dick fictionalized the last years of his life in *The Transmigration of Timothy Archer* (1982).

Pinky: Dick's cat, who died of cancer in 1974.

pistis (Greek): An ardent faith or fidelity; in Christianity, faith in Christ.

plasmate: A Dickian neologism roughly equivalent to "living knowledge" and another cognate for **VALIS.** Dick often felt that he had bonded with the plasmate in 2-3-74 and that, as a result, he had a second self dwelling within his psyche, making him a **homoplasmate.** Dick often regarded the plasmate as the living transmission of the Gnostic goddess **Sophia.**

pleroma (Greek): Literally, "fullness"; in Gnostic texts the term refers to the distant ideal realm inhabited by the divine powers, or aeons, who transcend creation.

Plotinus (c. 205–270 C.E.): Ancient Roman philosopher in the tradition of Plato whose notion of the One gave Dick a way to integrate some of the phenomena he perceived through the lens of **VALIS.** Plotinus's One is both the undivided source of all entities and the goal of contemplative thought; the mystic philosopher's search for the One is famously described as "the flight of the alone to the alone."

pronoia: In theology, and in the writings of **Philo of Alexandria** in particular, *pronoia* refers to God's governance of creation. It is roughly analogous to the concept of divine providence. More recently, the term has assumed a psychological valence as an inverse to *paranoia,* so that it denotes the belief that the universe is a conspiracy on one's behalf.

psyche (Greek): Originally "breath," "life," subsequently "soul" or "self." Aristotle's treatise on the psyche in *On the Soul* deals with the various types of forces that characterize living things. The goddess Psyche was represented as a butterfly in ancient Greece, perhaps to symbolize the capacity of life and the self for transformation.

Pythagoras (c. 570–490 B.C.E.): Ancient Greek philosopher and mathematician, perhaps the first to call himself a *philosopher* or "lover of wisdom." Generally acknowledged as the source of the Pythagorean theorem that lies at the basis of trigonometry, Pythagoras elevated mathematics to a metaphysical system founded in part on the ratios between musical pitches. Pythagoras supposedly deduced these relations when he wondered at the different tones produced by a group of blacksmiths working at an anvil; analysis revealed that the different tones were directly proportionate to the differing weights of the hammers.

Qumran Scrolls: Also known as the Dead Sea Scrolls. A library of Jewish documents dating from the third century B.C.E. to C.E. 68, discovered in a series of caves at Qumran near the Dead Sea. The inhabitants of the Qumran community may have been **Essenes.**

ruah (Hebrew): Breath, spirit.

Runciter, Glen: Character in Dick's *Ubik* (1968). The cigar-smoking Runciter heads an anti-pre-cog company with the help of his dead wife Ella, who dwells in cryonic suspension. Significantly for the Exegesis, Runciter communicates with characters stuck in an alternate world through advertisements, matchbook covers, and bathroom graffiti.

Salvador Salvandus, or **Salvator Salvandus:** The "saved savior," a trope of Gnostic soteriology. The hero in the "Hymn of the Soul" in the Acts of Thomas is an example of such a savior who himself is saved.

Sankara (c. 788–820 C.E.): One of the most important expositors of Advaita Vedanta or idealist "nondualism" in medieval India; see **Atman.**

satori (Japanese): Enlightenment; in Zen Buddhism, a deep intuitive insight into the nature of reality.

Schopenhauer, Arthur (1788–1860): Pessimistic German philosopher whose account of the blind striving of life, or "will," casts doubts on the power of reason to organize human society. Schopenhauer called for humans to look beyond appearances or representations, which have a similar relation to reality as a dream. A pioneer in the Western philosophical encounter with Eastern thought, Schopenhauer was deeply influenced by the Upanishads, whose translation had "been the solace of my life, and will be the solace of my death."

shekhina (Hebrew): To settle, dwell, or inhabit. In the Bible, the term refers to the presence of God in the Tabernacle and later the Temple (see, for example, Exodus 40:35); in Kabbala, this divine presence is considered female and is associated with the material world.

sibyl: Female oracles or prophetesses of the ancient Greeks. Particularly important to Dick was the famous sibyl at Cumaea, a community near Rome. Though pagan, some sibyls were considered to have prophesied the coming of Christ.

Siddhartha: The birth name for the prince who became the Buddha.

soma (Greek): Body.

Sophia, sometimes **Hagia Sophia** (Greek): Wisdom, considered alternately as an abstract philosophical concept or a sacred being. The aeon Sophia plays a vital role in many Gnostic systems, where her actions bring about both the fall into creation and the salvation of the light; she also makes an appearance in the biblical book of Proverbs.

Spinoza, Baruch (1632–1677): A lens maker, Jewish heretic, and philosophical monist of vast influence on the history of philosophy. Spinoza's vision of an "immanent" God identified with nature suggested that the divine permeates material reality. This theory of creative immanence was grist for Dick's meditation upon 2-3-74. Spinoza remains an influential thinker for contemporary philosophy, especially in the works of French philosopher Gilles Deleuze.

Stigmata: The Three Stigmata of Palmer Eldritch (1965) tells the story of wealthy industrialist Palmer Eldritch, who returns from the Proxima system with the drug Chew-Z; when ingested, it transports the user into another reality where Eldritch, whose "three stigmata" include a slot-eyed metal mask, is God. The novel can be read as an inverted fantasy of the Mass, in which the sacrament is taken to ensure salvation and ever-lasting life, not for the parishioner, but for the deity.

surd: From the Latin root "speechless"; in mathematics, a *surd* refers to an unresolvable or "radical" square root (such as the Ö2) that cannot be expressed with rational numbers. Within the religious discourse of theodicy, a *surd* refers to a natural evil, like tsunamis or cancer, rather than a moral evil. Dick defines it here as "something irrational that can't be explained after everything that is rational has been."

Synoptic Gospels, or **Synoptics:** Name for the three canonical gospels — Matthew, Mark, and Luke — that contain roughly the same narrative of Jesus's life and share a good deal of material and language. Apocryphal gospels and the canonical Gospel of John have little to no such overlap.

syzygy: The name given in some **Gnostic** systems, particularly those associated with Valentinus, for the male-female pairs of entities, or aeons, who emanate from the One or the supreme being. The term is also used by Carl Jung to describe the pairing of the male *animus* and female *anima* in the unconscious.

Tagomi, Nobusuke: The hero of *The Man in the High Castle* (1962). Tagomi is a midlevel Japanese bureaucrat who, at the end of the novel, "sees through" to something resembling our reality while examining a piece of jewelry in a San Francisco park. See *TMITHC*.

Tagore: On the night of September 17, 1981, Dick experienced a hypnagogic vision of Tagore, a world savior living in Ceylon. On September 23, Dick sent a letter to the science fiction fanzine *Niekas* (and to some eighty-five other friends and distant contacts) describing Tagore as dark-skinned, Hindu or Buddhist, and working in the countryside with a veterinary group. Rabindrath Tagore was a major Indian writer in the twentieth century; the name also distantly echoes **Tagomi**.

Tat Tvam Asi (Sanskrit): Traditionally translated "That thou art." An important phrase in Vedantic thought, it is a means of emphasizing the identity of **Atman** and **Brahman**.

Tears: Flow My Tears, the Policeman Said (1974) features Jason Taverner, one of the most famous entertainers in the world, who wakes up in a dystopian world where no one has ever heard of him. The book offers meditations on the various types of human love that, Dick argues, ultimately bind us to our reality.

Teilhard de Chardin, Pierre (1881–1955): Jesuit theologian, philosopher, and scientist notable for his fusion of theology and evolutionary theory. He proposed that humankind is evolving toward Point Omega, a single, unified being that is also Christ. Teilhard wrote extensively about the **noösphere,** the collective effect of human consciousness on the biosphere and the medium for the planet's evolution toward Point Omega.

tetragrammaton: See **YHWH.**

theolepsy: Possession by deity.

theophany: The visual revelation of deity.

Thomas: A separate personality who, according to one of Dick's lines of speculation, had cross-bonded with the author during the events of 2-3-74 (see **homoplasmate**). The topic of much speculation in the Exegesis, Thomas is most often identified as an early Christian; other possibilities include **James Pike, Paracelsus,** a Soviet agent, and an alternate or future version of Dick himself.

Tillich, Paul (1886–1965): German-American Protestant theologian and philosopher. Tillich's *The Courage to Be* (1952) was a major and widely read work of postwar existentialist thought. In his concept of the "god beyond god," Tillich argues that a reinvigorated encounter with the divine requires that the faithful move beyond what Dick calls "prior thought formations" and encounter a God beyond their concepts of God.

Timaeus: One of the Platonic dialogues, the *Timaeus* describes the cosmos as the work of a divine craftsman, the personification of Intellect or *noös,* who creates order out of primordial chaos. Dick borrows heavily from the cosmogony of *Timaeus,* in particular its description of the cosmos as a living animal with a soul and its teleological account of history as the activity of noös shaping **ananke,** or necessity.

Ti to on (Greek): "What is it?" This primordial question of Being is famously asked by Aristotle at the beginning of his *Physics.*

TMITHC: The Man in the High Castle (1962), a Hugo Award–winning novel set in an alternate United States where the Axis powers won World War II. The novel's portrayal of the interactive wisdom of the *I Ching* looks forward to some of Dick's later theorizing about VALIS, while the protagonist **Tagomi's** epiphany late in the novel anticipates, for Dick, his own experience with the fish sign.

To Scare the Dead: Dick's first proposed novel about the events of 2-3-74. Dick made notes for the novel in 1974–75. The title was intended to refer to the reawakening of seemingly dead personages (such as the early Christian Thomas) as a result of the same forces that were at work in Dick's 2-3-74 experiences.

Torah: Strictly speaking, the first five books of the Hebrew Bible, also known as the Pentateuch. In Kabbala and in Dick's Exegesis, Torah takes on a transcendent role as the plan of creation, roughly analogous to the **Logos** in Christian theology; some traditional Jewish mystics held that the Torah was a living being.

Tractate: "Tractates Cryptica Scriptura," a metaphysical treatise, heavily influenced by the Exegesis, that Dick appended to the novel *VALIS* (1981).

Ubik: Dick's 1969 novel concerns a team of telepathic corporate spies injured in an explosion, who find themselves in a world that is rapidly decaying and devolving. As the characters succumb, their condition is mitigated by a magical product known as Ubik: an aerosol spray that combats the forces of entropy.

Umwelt (German): The universal environment that surrounds us. One of the three types of world described by the existentialist psychologist Ludwig Binswanger; see **Mitwelt** and **Eigenwelt.**

Urgrund (German): Primitive basis or source. Used by both **Eckhart** and **Boehme** to describe ultimate reality.

Urwelt (German): Primeval world.

UTI: Ultra Terrestrial Intelligence; a term for higher beings who originate on this planet.

VALIS: Acronym coined by Dick, based on the phrase "Vast Active Living Intelligence System."

Valisystem A: Dick made notes for a novel with this title between 1974 and 1976, sometimes in conjunction with notes on *To Scare the Dead.* The book was written in 1976 and posthumously published in 1985 as *Radio Free Albemuth.*

Virgil (70–19 B.C.E.): Roman author. The sixth book of Virgil's *Aeneid,* as well as his fourth *Eclogue,* features the Cumaean Sibyl.

VR: VALIS Regained, working title for *The Divine Invasion* (1981).

Warrick, Patricia, or **Pat:** Patricia Warrick, a science fiction critic who corresponded with Dick and wrote about him extensively, both before his death, in *The Cybernetic Imagination in Science Fiction* (1980), and after, in *Mind in Motion: The Fiction of Philip K. Dick* (1987).

Whitehead, Alfred North (1861–1947): English mathematician and philosopher. In their *Principia Mathematica,* Whitehead and Bertrand Russell attempted to provide a robust formal structure for mathematics, a project whose unresolvable contradictions ultimately helped spawn the computer. Later Whitehead developed process philosophy, a school of thought that characterizes reality as a continuum of overlapping events rather than a collection of objects. **Charles Hartshorne** developed Whitehead's thoughts on the theological implications of this philosophy into *process theology.*

Xenophanes (c. 570–475 B.C.E.): Greek philosopher and poet, and a critic of the religious anthropomorphism of his contemporaries. In fragments referenced frequently in the Exegesis, Xenophanes describes a God who is unitary, changeless, and eternal and "shakes all things by the thought of his mind."

Xerox letter, or **Xerox missive:** A mysterious letter received by Dick in March 1974. The envelope contained a photocopied book review from a left-wing newspaper with certain words underlined in red and blue; it had a return address, but no name. Dick insisted that his wife Tessa read it in his stead, claiming vague foreknowledge about it and believing that if he saw its contents he would die. In the Exegesis he suggests that this foreknowledge saved his life.

YHWH: In the Hebrew Bible, the true name of God; also referred to as the **tetragrammaton.**

Zagreus (Greek): An alternate name of the Greek god **Dionysus** that means "torn to pieces." The name reflects the Orphic myth that Dionysus was torn apart by the Titans as a child, only to return to life through the agency of his father Zeus, who restored his son to life by eating the heart of his sundered corpse.

About the Editors and Annotators

Simon Critchley is Hans Jonas Professor of Philosophy at the New School for Social Research in New York. He is the author of many books, including *The Faith of the Faithless*, to be published in 2012. He is series moderator for "The Stone," an online philosophy column with the *New York Times*.

Erik Davis is the author of four books on alternative religion and popular culture, including *Techgnosis: Myth, Magic, and Mysticism in the Age of Information* and *Nomad Codes: Adventures in Modern Esoterica*. He is pursuing a PhD in religious studies at Rice University and has been writing and lecturing on Philip K. Dick for over twenty years.

Richard Doyle is Professor of English and Information Sciences and Technology at Pennsylvania State University and the author of a trilogy of books on information and the life sciences. The latest, *Darwin's Pharmacy: Sex, Plants, and the Evolution of the Noösphere*, was published by the University of Washington Press in 2011.

Steve Erickson is the author of nine novels — including *These Dreams of You*, to be published in early 2012 — as well as editor of the literary journal *Black Clock*. In November 1990, he wrote the cover story on Philip K. Dick, "California Time-Slip," for the *L.A. Weekly*.

David Gill teaches composition and literature at San Francisco State University and runs the popular Philip K. Dick–centric blog, Total Dick-Head (totaldickhead.blogspot.com). He has written about Dick for *Article* magazine, boingboing, and io9 and lectured about *Do Androids Dream of Electric Sheep?* at Harvard and the National Association of Humanities Educators.

N. Katherine Hayles is Professor and Director of Graduate Studies of Literature at Duke University. Her books include *How We Became Posthuman: Virtual Bodies in Cybernetics, Literature, and Informatics and Writing Machines*. Her most recent, *How We Think: Digital Media and Contemporary Technogenesis*, will be published in 2012.

Pamela Jackson holds degrees in rhetoric and library and information studies from the University of California, Berkeley and Los Angeles, respectively. Her 1999 dissertation, "The World Philip K. Dick Made," initiated a decade's study of Philip K. Dick's Exegesis. She is also a graduate of Berkeley High School, Philip K. Dick's only alma mater.

Jeffrey J. Kripal holds the J. Newton Rayzor Chair in Philosophy and Religious Thought at Rice University. A historian of religions who specializes in the analysis and interpretation of comparative mystical literature, he is the author or co-editor of twelve volumes, including his most recent, *Mutants and Mystics: Science Fiction, Superhero Comics, and the Paranormal.*

Jonathan Lethem is the Roy E. Disney Chair in Creative Writing at Pomona College and the author of eight novels and two collections of stories. His writing on Philip K. Dick appears in his essay collections *The Disappointment Artist* and *The Ecstasy of Influence.*

Gabriel Mckee is a graduate of Harvard Divinity School and the author of *The Gospel According to Science Fiction.* A theologian concentrating on the intersection of religion and popular culture, he also works as a librarian and archivist specializing in rare books and counterculture ephemera. His first book was *Pink Beams of Light from the God in the Gutter: The Science Fictional Religion of Philip K. Dick.*

Names Index

Works Index